ISBN 978-1-332-51915-6
PIBN 10289830

THE

HISTORY

AND

ANTIQUITIES

OF THE

CITY of BRISTOL;

COMPILED FROM

Original RECORDS and authentic MANUSCRIPTS,

In public Offices or private Hands;

Illuſtrated with COPPER-PLATE PRINTS.

By WILLIAM BARRETT, SURGEON, F.S.A.

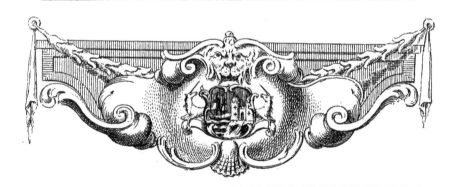

BRISTOL:

Printed by WILLIAM PINE, in Wine-Street;

And ſold by G. ROBINSON and Co. *London*; E. PALMER, J. B. BECKET, T. MILLS, J. NORTON, W. BROWNE,
W. BULGIN, and J. LLOYD, Bookſellers in *Briſtol*; and by BULL and MEYLER, in *Bath*.

TO THE RIGHT WORSHIPFUL

LEVI AMES, Efq; Mayor;

The Worſhipful the ALDERMEN, and COMMON
COUNCIL of the City of *B R I S T O L.*

GENTLEMEN,

TO you is the HISTORY OF BRISTOL with propriety
inſcribed, to which you have a natural and peculiar
Claim. By public Spirit, Virtue and Loyalty, your
predeceſſors procuring Liberties and ample Privileges by
Charters from our Kings and Queens raiſed this City to
an high rank in the nation, and by the ſame their
ſucceſſors have exalted it to the dignity of being the
Second City in the kingdom.

Reformed as it is in its POLICE, enlarged in the
number and extent of its Buildings, and increaſed in its
Trade and Opulence, may it long flouriſh by your
vigilant and active Care, by the great Credit and
Reputation of its Merchants, and the VIRTUE AND
INDUSTRY of the Citizens; and by uſing the natural local
advantages of improving its Port and Harbour to the
utmoſt, may the Honour be yours of compleating its
Grandeur, that Ships may reſort hither more and more
from every Quarter of the Globe, and the Commerce
and Proſperity of the City continue to advance to lateſt
poſterity.

I have the honour to be,

Worſhipful S I R S,

Your moſt obliged and obedient

Humble Servant,

WRAXAL,
APRIL 15, 1789.

WILLIAM BARRETT.

P R E F A C E.

HOW the Hiſtory of Briſtol, ſo long expeſted, is at length offered to the public the reader may be curious to know. Twenty years have elapſed ſince collections for the deſign were fought for with great affiduity and no ſmall expence, and ſome progreſs made in compiling it, and even the copper‑plates were engraved for the work in folio ; but the author, engaged in a buſineſs that commanded all his time and attention, receiving no encourage‑ment to proceed, and finding there was more likelihood for him, " oleum et operam perdere," ſat down contented with his firſt loſs and wholly deſiſted from the undertaking, locking up his papers for ſeveral years, intending to leave them to one of more leiſure and to a time more auſpicious and favour‑able to the undertaking. Retiring from buſineſs into the country and often confined by the gout, he thought he ſhould find ſome amuſement in this lite‑rary employ, and reſumed the long intermitted taſk, that he might leave it in a leſs unfiniſhed ſtate to be compleated and publiſhed hereafter. At this time a worthy Doctor of one of our univerſities, deſervedly eſteemed by all for his ſingular humanity and friendly diſpoſition, viſited him and warmly ſolicited him to proceed with the work and publiſh it himſelf in his life‑time ; for poſthumous works were often neglected, ſeldom executed to the author's mind, and not unfrequently loſt. In a letter afterwards he urged the matter with great earneſtneſs, and moſt generous tender of his friendſhip, concluding with the following ſpirited expreſſions, which he applied to this occaſion. " Hominem te durum et penè crudelem, qui tam inſignes libros tam diu teneas. Sine per ora hominum ferantur, &c. Quoſque tibi et nobis invi‑debis? Tibi laudem, nobis maximam voluptatem. Magna etiam longaque expectatio eſt quam fruſtrari adhuc et differre non debes. — HABE ANTE OCULOS MORTALITATEM ! Define ſtudia tua infinitâ iſtâ cunctatione frau‑dare, quæ cum modum excedat, verendum eſt, ne inertiæ et deſidiæ vel etiam timiditatis nomen accipiat." This added a ſpur to irreſolution, and the " habe ante oculos mortalitatem" made an impreſſion irreſiſtable; applied to one in a declining ſtate of health and years. In a word, the work was imme‑diately reſumed and proſecuted without intermiſſion, and then offered to the public, who have liberally patronized it, as the liſt of ſubſcribers will ſhew,

which

which would do honour to any work, and cannot but excite in the author a due fenfe of gratitude.

Some readers may perhaps be furprized at the length of this Hiftory, whilft others may exprefs their wonder at its being comprized in one volume : the former may think it unneceffary to defcend to minute particulars, whilft the latter will judge every thing not fully related and every authority not quoted in the original words an omiffion. — The author has endeavoured to fteer a middle courfe, and will readily give his reafons. Had he been more brief, he could not have given fo much information about the religious houfes, the caftle, and their governors, their antiquities, nor of the manners of thofe times; nor indeed of their prefent ftate. The reader muft have contented himfelf with a fuperficial view of things, fuch as his own eyes and obferva_tion might have prefented him with, in which cafe he would have turned away difpleafed at not being informed more than he knew before. On the contrary, if he had been more prolix, and tranfcribed at length the feveral Latin deeds of endowment, original authorities, and charters, he muft have filled a large folio or two quarto volumes. The learned antiquarian would receive much fatisfaction doubtlefs in perufing the antient deeds and authentic documents in the original; but as all fuch are long and tedious, if the prin-cipal matters contained therein be noticed, the reft would unneceffarily fwell the volume, and ferve only a certain clafs of readers: and therefore though the beginning of the original deed is often given, the tranflation follows in Englifh for the eafe and information of the lefs learned reader; but fometimes where the deed is very important and curious, and not too long, the whole is given. The number of Latin deeds, that might with propriety have found a place here, is fuch as alone would have filled a volume. They were col-lected at different times, the greateft number by the late Mr. Alexander Morgan, (whofe indefatigable pains and induftry in this way for many years, as well as Mr. Haines's, fhould have their due praife) befides others tranfcribed from Dugdale, Stevens, and Rymer; but to refer to them and to abridge others was judged to be in general fufficient, though to avoid deforming the page few marginal references are fet down, but the great ftorehoufe of TANNER is conftantly referred to. The original deeds and copies collected for this Hiftory have been procured with fo much labour, it would be a great lofs to have them difperfed, after the extracts for this work have been made from them; it is intended therefore to lodge them in fome public repofitory, pro-bably the Briftol Library. Whoever confiders well the time and trouble employed in making fuch a collection, will readily agree to the propriety of fuch a meafure.   As

As to thofe manufcripts of Rowley, now firft publifhed; whatever judgment be formed about them, they are here faithfully tranfcribed, that by producing all the evidence the judicious reader may be enabled the better to form his opinion concerning that controverfy.

Before I conclude I muft add, that by a manufcript in Corpus Chrifti college library, Cambridge, CCCCV. p. 26. entituled " Conftitutiones Villæ Briftolliæ," (which I did not receive till the laft fheet of this work was printed off) it appears, among other curious particulars, how they were enabled to build the old bridge, which I have faid " no where appears," fee p. 79. " Petunt burgenfes fibi reftitui pontem Avenæ, &c." i. e. " The burgeffes alfo defire that the bridge of Avon be reftored to them and the rents upon the bridge, which bridge they and their anceftors built new from the brink or ftream (filo) of the water at their own charges together with the alms of the faithful, and have fupported until this day, and are ready perpetually to fupport it ; and in aid of fupporting it they have erected certain rents upon the fame bridge; and for the Indulgence of thofe who help, and prohibition of thofe who would deduct from it, they have a bull of Pope Innocent 3d. the predeceffor of Honorius and Gregory. They alfo defire to be reftored to them the rents of a certain houfe and ground, which they bought at the head of the bridge on the fouth fide, for which they have the charter of the abbot and convent of Keynfham, of whom they hold the faid ground; and alfo have the confirmation of King John concerning the faid ground, upon which great part of the faid bridge is founded and fupported."—They fay alfo, " that out of the profits of the guild merchants and of the town they fupport eight bridges, the pavement or pitching, five conduits of water, the Key (Kayam) before the fhips, and the public officers; and that the murage is expended only in inclofing and fortifying the town and fuburb, for which it was granted; and that no waggon, no packhorfe, no man, fhall unload his burden, without firft paying the cuftom to the prepofitor, (nifi cuftumetur ad prepofitum,) &c."

Though there is no date to this curious manufcript, it muft be about the year 1314, for they defire therein " to choofe a mayor and bailiffs whom they know will be more ufeful and faithful to their Lord the King," who were chofen in that year.

The author having thus endeavoured to fulfil his engagements to the public muft now take his leave, requefting the candid reader's favour to excufe all omiffions and errors;

Quos aut incuria fudit
Aut humana parum caveat natura.

E R R A T A.

Directions to the Binder where to place the Plates.

SUBSCRIBERS.

His Royal Highness PRINCE WILLIAM.

A

THE Right Rev. the Lord Bifhop of St. Afaph.
John Acland, Efq;
Mr. Acraman.
Mr. Gawin Alanfon, Briftol.
Rev. Edw. Aldridge, Vicar of North Petherton.
Mr. Richard Aldridge, Briftol.
Mrs. Aldridge, ditto.
Mr. Samuel Allen, ditto.
Mr. James Allen, architect, ditto.
Mr. John Allen, organift, ditto.
Levi Ames, Efq; Mayor of Briftol, 2 copies.
Mr. M. Ancrum, Briftol.
Mr. J. P. Anderdon.
John Anderfon, Efq; Alderman, Briftol.
Mr. Thomas Andrews, ditto.
John Archer, Efq; Welford, Berks.
Mifs Archer.
Mr. Edward Afh.
John Audry, Efq; Notton, Wilts.
Mr. Aaron Auftin, Briftol.

B

Earl of Berkeley, 2 copies.
The Right Rev. the Lord Bifhop of Briftol, 2 copies.
The Right Rev. the Lord Bifhop of Bath and Wells.
Lord Belgrave.
The Hon. George Berkeley, 2 copies.
Mr. A. B. Briftol.
Rev. Mr. Backhoufe, Fellow of Bennet College, Cambridge.
Dr. Bain, Phyfician, Hotwells, Briftol.
Rev. Slade Baker, Briftol.
Jeremy Baker, Efq; ditto.
John Baker, Efq; ditto.
Samuel Baker, Efq; Dundry.
Rev. Sackville Spencer Bale.
Mr. Balme, F. C. Magdalen Col. Cambridge.
C. W. Bampfylde, Efq; Heftercomb, Somerfetfhire.
Rev. Dr. Barford, Fellow of Eton College.
Rev. Dr. Barker, Mafter of Chrift College, Cambridge,
Dr. Barnes, Mafter of Peter Houfe, Cambridge.
William Barnes, Efq; Redland.
Mr. Anthony Barrett, Notton, Wilts.
Rev. W. T. Barrett, Rector of High Ham, Somerfetfhire.
Mr. Samuel Barry, Briftol.
John Barry, Efq;

Sir Francis Baffet, Bart. M. P.
Mr. Thomas Batchelor, Briftol.
Thomas Bathurft, Efq; Lidney Park.
William Batterfby, Efq;
Mr. Benjamin Baugh, Briftol.
Mr. Robert Bayley, Clifton.
Mr. William Baylis, Briftol.
Mr. John Bayly, attorney at law, ditto.
Zachary Bayly, Efq; Widcomb, Bath.
Mr. Thomas Baynton, Briftol.
Meffrs. Bazleys, ditto.
Dr. Beadon, Mafter of Jefus Col. Cambridge.
James Becket, Efq; Collector of Salt Duties, Briftol.
Mr. J. B. Becket, bookfeller, ditto, 3 copies.
Jofeph Beck, Efq; ditto, 2 copies.
Mr. Thomas Bedoe, ditto.
Mr. James Bence.
Mr. H. Bengough, ditto,
Mr. John Bennett, ditto.
Bennet College Cambridge Library.
—— Benyon, Efq; F. C. St. John's College, Cambridge.
Mr. John Pain Berjew, apothecary, Briftol.
Rev. Mr. Berjew, Vicar of All Saints, ditto.
James Bernard, Efq;
Dr. Bidle, Phyfician, Windfor.
Mr. Matthew Biggs, Briftol.
Mr. Edward Bird, ditto.
Mr. John Birtill, ditto.
Rev. Wiliam Blake, Vicar of Stockland.
Mr. Richard Blake, Briftol.
William Blake, Efq;
Mr. Thomas Blagdon, ditto.
Mrs. Bliffet, Clifton.
Mr. Bond, Caius College, Cambridge.
Rev. Mr. Borlafe, Regiftrar to the Univerfity of Cambridge.
Rev. Jonathan Boucher, Epfom.
Mr. Bowden, wine-merchant, Briftol.
Rev. Mr. Boycott, Caius College, Cambridge.
Mr. Bradford, Fellow of Bennet College, Cambridge.
Mr. Nehemiah Bradford.
Edward Brice, Efq; Briftol.
Nathaniel Brice, Efq; ditto.
Matthew Brickdale, Efq; M. P. for Briftol.
Richard Bright, Efq; Briftol.
Lowbridge Bright, Efq; 2 copies.
Briftol Library Society.
Briftol Education Society.

Mr. Broderip,

Mr. Brodrip, apothecary, Briſtol.
Mr. Robert Brodrip, ditto.
Rev. Mr. Broughton, Rector of St. Peter's, ditto.
Mr. James Brown, ditto.
Mr. Henry Brown, ditto.
Mr. F. Brown, Surgeon, ditto.
Mr. Wm. Browne, bookſeller, ditto, 3 copies.
Jacob Bryant, Eſq; Cypenham, Bucks.
Mrs. Ann Bryan, Briſtol.
Rev. John Bull, ditto.
Daniel Bull, Eſq; Calne, Wilts.
Rev. Mr. Bull, Briſtol.
Mr. Francis Bull, ditto.
Mr. Thomas E. Bull, ditto.
Mr. William Bulgin, ditto.
Hon. Mrs. Bulteel.
Mr. Daniel Burges, attorney at law, Briſtol.
John Berkley Burland, Eſq;
Miſs Townly Bury.
Robert Buſh, Eſq; Briſtol.
Mr. George Buſh, merchant, ditto.
Mr. William Buſh, ditto.
Dr. Buſick, Harwood Profeſſor of Anatomy, Cambridge.
Rev. Mr. Bywater, Magdalen Col. Cambridge.

C

Earl of Clarendon.
Earl Camden.
Mr. Thomas Cadell, Briſtol.
Rev. Dr. Camplin, ditto.
Rev. William Camplin, ditto.
Rev. John Camplin, ditto.
Rev. Dr. Caſberd, ditto.
Mr. John Caſtelman, Surgeon, ditto.
Mr. Robert Caſtle, ditto.
Mr. G. Cattcot, ditto.
John Cave, Eſq; ditto, 2 copies.
Stephen Cave, Eſq; ditto.
Mr. William Cave, junr. ditto.
Mr. Thomas Cave, ditto.
Dr. Samuel Cave, Phyſician, at Liſbon.
Mr. John Chandler, Briſtol.
Rev. Mr. Chamberlayne, Vic. Provoſt of Eton College.
Mr. Thomas Chamber, Briſtol.
Mr. Edward Pye Chamberlain, ditto.
Robert Claxton, Eſq; ditto.
Mr. John Chivers, ditto.
Mr. John Clark, ditto.
Rev. Thomas Clark, Henbury.
Mr. Peter Cliſſold, ditto.
Mrs. Clayfield, ditto.
Mr. Edward Rolle Clayfield, ditto.
Mr. Charles Morgan Clayfield, Oxford.
William Coates, Eſq; ditto.
Rev. Dr. Coleman, Maſter of Bennet College, Cambridge.
James Coles, Eſq;
Robert Coleman, Eſq; Briſtol.
B. F. Coleman, Eſq; ditto.

Mr. Collier, Profeſſor of Hebrew, Trinity College, Cambridge.
Mr. Robert Collins, Briſtol.
Thomas Collinſon, Eſq; London.
Rev. Alexander Colſton, Vicar of Henbury, Gloceſterſhire.
Mrs. Colſton, Filkins, Oxfordſhire.
Rev. John Collinſon, Long Aſhton, 4 copies.
Mr. Collins, Briſtol,
Rev. Thomas Cockayne, Stapleton.
Rev. Dr. Cooke, Provoſt of King's College, Cambridge.
Mr. John Court, Briſtol.
Mr. William Court, ditto.
Mr. Charles Court, ditto.
Mr. John Cox, ditto.
Samuel Cox, Eſq; ditto.
H. Hippiſley Cox, Eſq; Stone Eaſton.
Rev. Mr. Cranke, Fellow of Trinity College, Cambridge.
Mr. John Crocker, Briſtol.
Rev. Dr. Croſſman, Rector of Monkton, Somerſetſhire.
Mr. Richard Cruttwell, Bath.
F. C. Cuſt, Eſq; Lincoln's Inn,

D

Rev. James Dallaway, Trinity College, Oxford.
Rev. Dr. Dampier, Dean of Rocheſter.
Henry Dampier, Eſq; Middle Temple.
Mr. Thomas Danſon, Briſtol.
Mr. William Daniel, ditto.
John Daniel, Eſq; ditto.
Thomas Daniel, Eſq; ditto, 2 copies.
Mr. Edward Daniel, ditto.
Thomas Darch, Eſq;
George Daubeny, Eſq; Alderman, ditto.
John Daubeny, Eſq; ditto.
Rev. Dr. Davies, Head Maſter of Eton School.
Mr. John Davies, Briſtol.
Rev. Edward Davis, Prebendary of Llandaff.
Mr. Davis, Fellow of Trinity Coll. Cambridge.
Francis Dawes, Eſq; St. Peter's Coll. Camb.
John Deverell, Eſq; Clifton.
Mr. William Dibdin, Briſtol.
Mrs. Mary Dimſdale.
William Dinwoody, Eſq; Twidee.
Mr. John Dowell, Briſtol.
Mr. William Dowell, ditto.
Lieut. Col. Robert Donkin.
Lieut. Rufane Shawe Donkin.
Mr. Henry Durbin, Briſtol.
Mr. William Dyer, apothecary, ditto.
Mr. W. Dyer, ditto.
Mr. William Dymock.
Dr. Duck, ditto.
Mr. Dykes, F. Com. Magdalen College, Camb.
Dr. Archibald Drummond, Ridgeway, Gloceſterſhire.
Dr. Colen Drummond, Briſtol.
Rev. Dr. Drury, Head Maſter of Harrow School.   Right

E

Right Rev. Lord Bishop of Exeter.
Hon. John Elliott, Pembroke Hall, Cambridge.
Hon. Edward James Elliott, ditto.
Right Rev. Bishop of Elphin, at Cambridge.
Mr. T. Eagles, Bristol.
Rev. Mr. Easterbrook, ditto.
Goodenough Earl, Esq; Pitminster, Somerset.
Mr. George Eaton, Bristol.
Edinburgh University Library.
Alexander Edgar, Esq; Alderman, Bristol.
Rev. Mr. Edwards, ditto.
Samuel Edwards, Esq; ditto.
Mr. J. Edye, ditto.
Isaac Elton, Esq; Stapleton.
Rev. Abraham Elton, Clevedon Court.
Abraham Elton, Esq;
Mr. William Elton, Bristol.
Mr. Philip Elliott, ditto.
Mr. J. K. Escott, ditto.
Rev. J. Prior Estlin, ditto.
Mr. William Evans, ditto.
Mr. H. F. Evans, ditto.

F

Dr. Farr, Physician, Taunton.
Dr. Farmer, Master of Emanuel Col. Camb.
Mr. Thomas Farley, merchant, Worcester.
Mr. Samuel Fear, Bristol.
William Fellows, Esq; F. Com. St. John's College, Cambridge.
Rev. Mr. Fisher, Caius College, Cambridge.
Mr. George Fisher, Bristol.
Mr. Thomas Flower, ditto.
Rev. Thomas Ford, L. L. D. Rector of Melton Mowbray, Leicestershire.
Mr. Patrick Foreham, Bristol.
Rev. Mr. Foster, at Eton.
Samuel Franklyn, Esq; Barrister at Law.
John Freeman, Esq; Letton, Herefordshire.
Mr. William Fripp, Bristol.
Mr. William Fry, ditto.
Mrs. Anna Fry, ditto.
Mr. Edmund Fry, London.
Mr. Joseph Storr Fry, Bristol.
Mr. Samuel Fry, ditto.
Mr. Joseph Fussel, ditto.

G

Samuel Galton, Esq; Birmingham.
Rev. Edmund Gapper, Charlton Adam, Somersetshire.
Mr. James George, Bristol.
Mr. Hugh George, ditto.
Sir Philip Gibbes, Bart. Hilton Park, near Woolverhampton.
Mr. William Gibbons, Bristol.
Nathaniel Gifford, Esq; ditto.
Mr. H. Gillam, ditto.
Dr. Glynn, Clobery Physician, Cambridge.
Dr. Glynn's Friend, anonymous.

Mrs. Ann Goldney, Clifton, 3 copies.
Mr. Samuel Gomond, Bristol.
Henry Goodwin, Esq; Clifton, 2 copies.
Peter Goodwin, Esq; Charlton, 2 copies.
Rev. Thomas Goodwyn, Vicar of Pitminster.
Rev. Thomas Goddard, Vicar of South Petherton and Clevedon, Somersetshire.
Rev. Mr. Goodall, of Eton.
Mr. Jos. Goodale, Bristol.
Milner Gossip, Esq; Thorp Arch, Yorkshire.
Rev. Dr. Gooch, Prebendary of Ely.
Rev. Dr. Gordon, Prebendary of Lincoln.
John Gordon, Esq; Bristol.
William Gordon Esq; ditto.
John Gore, Esq; Barrow Court, Somersetshire.
Edward Gore, Esq; Kiddington, Oxfordshire.
Mr. Thomas Griffiths, Bristol.
Rev. Mr. Gregory, F. C. of Trinity Hall, Cambridge.
Rev. Mr. Gresly, Rector of Aller, Somerset.
Mrs. Graves, relict of the late Admiral Graves.
Mr. Kingsmill Grove, Thornbury.

H

Lord Howard, of Walden, Essex.
John B. Hale, Esq; Alderly, Glocestershire.
Mr. J. Williams Harding, Bristol.
Mr. Richard Hale, ditto.
Mr. Joseph Hall, ditto.
Mr. G. W. Hall, ditto.
Rev. Dr. Hallam, Dean of Bristol.
Edmund Trowbridge Halliday, Esq;
Mr. Thomas Hanmer, Bristol.
Dr. Hardwick, Sodbury.
Rev. James Hardwick, L. L. B. Vicar or Tytherington, Glocestershire.
Rev. Mr. Hart, St. George's, Kingswood.
Edward Harford, Esq; Bristol.
Joseph Harford, Esq; ditto.
Charles Joseph Harford, Esq; ditto.
Charles Harford, Esq; ditto.
Mark Harford, Esq; ditto.
Samuel Loyd Harford, Esq; ditto.
Mr. Richard Swymmer Harford, ditto.
J. Scandret Harford, Esq; ditto.
John Harmer, Esq; Penpark.
Thomas Harris, Esq; Alderman, 5 copies.
John Harris, Esq; Sheriff of Bristol.
Mr. W. Harris, Deputy Chamberlain of ditto.
Mr. James Harris, Bristol.
James Harvey, Esq; ditto.
Mr. Joseph Haskins, ditto.
Mr. Joseph Haythorn, ditto.
Mr. Rich. Hawkeswell, Chamberlain of ditto.
Richard Haynes, Esq; Wick, Glocestershire.
Capt. Thomas Haines, Bristol.
Jos. Haynes, Esq; Clone, Ireland.
Rev. Dr. Head, Master of Rugby School.
Rev. Mr. Heath, of Eton.
Rev. Dr. Heath, Fellow of Eton College.
Sir Isaac Heard, Garter King of Arms.

Dr.

Dr. William Heberden, Phyfician, London.
Mr. T. Hellicar, Briftol.
Mr. Jofeph Hellier, Dundry.
Anthony Henderfon, Efq; Briftol.
Mr. William Henley, ditto.
Mr. C. Heineman, ditto.
Mr. Thomas Hetling, ditto.
William Hicks, Efq; Bitton.
Mr. Jer. Hill, junr. Briftol.
Mr. William Hill, ditto.
Mr. Richard Hill, ditto.
Mr. Benjamin Hill, ditto.
Rev. Mr. Hill, Refident at the Englifh Factory at Lifbon.
T. C. Hippifley, Efq; Briftol.
Henry Hobhoufe, Efq; Hatfpen, Somerfet.
Thomas Hobhoufe, Efq; at the Temple.
Mr. Robert Hodgfon, Briftol.
Mr. William Hooper, ditto.
Rev. D. Horndon, ditto.
Mifs Howard, Levenham, Lincolnfhire.
Mr. Matthew Howell.
Mr. James Hughes, attorney, Briftol.
Mr. John Humphries, ditto.
Mr. Hughes, ditto.
Mr. James Hunt, Liverpool.
Mr. Hunter, Fellow of Sydney Col. Cambridge.

I

Mr. Walter Jacks, Briftol.
Dr. John Jacob, Phyfician, Salifbury.
Mr. Jacob, Fellow of King's Col. Cambridge.
Jefus College Library, Cambridge.
Mr. Jof. James, Briftol.
St. John's College Library, Cambridge.
Rev. Mr. Johnes, Briftol, 2 copies.
Mr. William Jones, ditto.
Mr. James Jones, ditto.
Mr. Johnfton, Vice Provoft of King's College, Cambridge.
Dr. Jowell, King's Profeffor of Civil Law, Trinity College, Cambridge.
James Ireland, Efq; Briflington.
Rev. Dr. Ireland, Rector of Chrift Church, Briftol.

K

Mr. Keene, Briftol.
Mr. Kelfon, ditto.
Rev. Mr. Kerrich, Prefident of Magdalen College, Cambridge.
Rev. Dr. Keys, Dean of Lincoln.
Mifs King, Nafh Houfe, Wraxal.
Mr. Henry King, Alvefton, Glocefterfhire.
Mr. H. King, junr. Briftol.
King's College Library, Cambridge.
Mr. Jacob Kirby, Briftol.
Samuel Knight, Efq; Cambridge.

L

Right Rev. Lord Bifhop of Landaff.
Right Rev. Lord Bifhop of Lincoln.

Mr. Lambert, Trinity College, Cambridge.
William Gore Langton, Efq; Newton Park, Somerfetfhire.
Mr. William Lane, of Cork.
Rev. Dr. Langford, Under Mafter of Eton School.
Rev. Charles Lee, Mafter of Briftol Grammar School.
Mr. John Ledyard, Melkfham, Wilts.
Mr. John Lewfly, Briftol.
Mr. John Lewellin, ditto.
Mr. William Lewis, ditto.
Mr. John Lewis, ditto.
Mr. H. Link, ditto.
Lady Lippincott, Stoke Bifhop, Glocefterfhire.
Mr. Lockier, Briftol.
Mr. Jofeph Lloyd, Briftol, 3 copies.
Mr. Jofeph Lock, Briftol.
—— Lombe, Efq; Cambridge, 2 copies.
Mrs. Lonfdale Linton, Cambridge.
Mr. Low, Surgeon, Briftol.
Mr. John Robert Lucas, ditto.
Dr. Abraham Ludlow, Phyfician, Briftol.
W. P. Lunell, Efq; ditto.
James Fownes Luttrell, Efq; Somerfetfhire.

M

Mr. John Maddick, Briftol.
Dr. Mahony, Hotwells, ditto.
Rev. Mr. Manfel, Public Orator of Cambridge Univerfity.
Mr. John Marks, Tetbury.
Mr. Martin, Profeffor of Botany, Sidney College, Cambridge.
Rev. Mr. Mafters, Rector of Landleach.
T. J. Matthias, Efq; Scotland Yard, London.
The Hon. T. Maude, F. Com. of St. John's College, Cambridge.
Mr. Jofeph Maurice, Briftol.
Mr. John Maxfe, ditto.
Mr. Andrew Maxfe, ditto.
Mr. Matthew Mcafe, ditto.
Mr. Thomas Mcafe, ditto.
Mr. Merrick, attorney, Briftol.
Mr. Merril, bookfeller, Cambridge.
Mr. William Meyler, Bath.
Mr. Diederick Meyeroff, Briftol.
William Miles, Efq; Alderman, ditto.
Jeremiah Mills, Efq; Harley-ftreet, London, 2 copies.
Mr. Thomas Mills, Briftol.
Mifs Virtue Mills, ditto.
Dr. Milner, Mafter of Queen's College, Cambridge.
Rev. John Milton, Briftol.
Dr. Moncrieff, Phyfician, Briftol.
Mr. Thomas Morgan, attorney, ditto.
Mr. John Morgan, ditto.
James Morgan, Efq; ditto.

John

John Morgan, Efq; Briftol.
Mr. John Morgan, ditto.
Mr. Peter Morris, junr. ditto.
Mr. John Mortimore, ditto.
James Morris, Efq; Cambridge.
Lady Moftyn, Kiddington, Oxfordfhire.
Mr. James Mofs, Briftol.
Mr. James Mountfher, ditto.
Samuel Munckley, Efq; ditto.

N

Mr. John Nailor, Briftol.
Mr. Thomas Nafh, ditto.
Sir Stephen Nafh, Knight, ditto.
Rev. Dr. Nafh, Bevere, Worcefterfhire.
Rev. Mr. Nafmith, Bennet Col. Cambridge.
Richard Nelmes, Efq; Briftol.
Rev. James New, Rector of St. Philip's, ditto.
Mr. Newton, Fellow of Jefus Col. Cambridge.
Mr. Edward Nichols, Briftol.
Mr. John Padmore Noble, Surgeon, ditto.
Rev. Dr. Norbury, Fellow of Eton College.
Mr. North, Caius College, Cambridge.
Mr. Norcrofs, Pembroke Hall, ditto.
Mr. Norton, bookfeller, Briftol, 6 copies.
Mr. Onefiphorus Norman, ditto.
Mr. Norris, Trinity College, Cambridge.

O

Mr. Okes, Surgeon, Cambridge.
Rev. Mr. Olderfhaw, Emanuel Col. Cambridge.
Mr. William Oldham, Briftol.
Mr. Jer. Ofborne, attorney, ditto.

P

The Right Hon. William Pitt, Chancellor of the Exchequer, M. P. for Cambridge, &c.
Right Rev. Lord Bifhop of Peterborough.
Hon. Mr. Percival, Lincoln's Inn.
Mr. John Page, Briftol.
Mr. Arthur Palmer, ditto.
Mr. James Palmer, ditto.
Mr. Henry Palmer, ditto.
Mifs Palmer, ditto.
Thomas Partridge, Efq; Cotham, ditto.
Mr. William Parfons, ditto.
Rev. Mr. Parkinfon, Fellow of Chrift College, Cambridge.
Mr. Henry Pater, Briftol.
Mr. Thomas Patty, ditto.
Rev. Samuel Peach, Eaft Sheen, in Surry.
Mr. Richard Pearfon, Briftol.
Pembroke Hall Library, Cambridge.
St. Peter's College Library, ditto.
Mr. John Peters, Briftol.
Rev. Mr. Peckard, Mafter of Magdalen College, Cambridge.
Dr. Pennington, Phyfician, ditto.
Edward Phillips, junr. Efq; M. P. for the county of Somerfet.
Mr. Thomas Pierce, Briftol.

Mr. William Pine, Briftol, 12 copies.
Mr. Edmund Pitts, Burcomb, Wilts.
Richard Plaifter, Efq; Briftol.
Dr. James Plomer, Phyfician, ditto.
Mr. Nicholas Pococke, ditto.
Rev. Mr. Porter, Cambridge.
Mrs. Porter, ditto.
Rev. Mr. Powis, Prebendary of Briftol.
Onefiphorus Power, Efq; Briftol.
Richard Pottinger, Efq; Burlington-ftreet, London.
John Powell, Efq; Briftol.
Mr. Proffer, ditto.
Mr. John Purnel, junr.

R

Mr. William Rackfter, Briftol.
Mr. G. Rackfter, ditto.
Mr. Raine, Fellow of Trinity Col. Cambridge.
Mr. William Randolph, Briftol.
Rev. F. Randolph.
Mr. John Rawlins, Briftol.
Rev. Robert Ready, Rector of Bufcot, Berks.
Rev. T. Renell, Prebendary of Winchefter.
Mr. Thomas Reynolds, Briftol.
Mr. Richard Reynolds, ditto.
Hon. Richard Rider, Lincoln's Inn.
Dr. Thomas Rigge, Phyfician, Briftol.
Rev. Mr. Rimbron, ditto.
Mr. Archibald Robe, ditto.
Mr. Thomas Roberts, ditto,
Mr. Samuel Rogers, ditto.
Mr. James Rogers, ditto.
Mr. G. Rogers, ditto.
Rev. Dr. Robbins, ditto.
Mr. Jofeph Rogers, ditto.
Rev. Dr. Roberts, Provoft of Eton.
William Roberts, Efq; Wandfworth.
Sir James La Roche, Bart. Briftol.
Mr. John Roach, ditto.
Mr. James Room, ditto.
G. Rofe, Efq; M. P. Weftminfter.
Mr. Edward Roffer, Briftol.
Mr. John Rudhall, ditto.
Mr. John Ruffel, Wraxal.
Mr. Thomas Rutter, Briftol.

S

James Sadler, Efq; Briftol.
Mr. George Salway, ditto.
Edward Sampfon, Efq; Henbury, Glocefterfhire, 2 copies.
Mr. Thomas Saunders, Briftol.
Mr. Sandiver, Surgeon, Newmarket.
Rev. Mr. Savage, Eton.
James Scarlet, Efq; F. Com. of Trinity College, Cambridge.
Rowles Scudamore, Efq; Briftol.
Mr. Seager, attorney, ditto.
Mr. Seward, ditto.

Rev.

Rev. Samuel Seyer, Redland.
Mr. Seymour, Briftol.
Mr. T. Shapland, ditto.
Mr. Joseph Shapland, ditto.
Mr. Alexander Shedden.
Rev. Mr. Shipton, ditto.
Mr. Shepherd, Provoft of King's College, Cambridge.
Mifs Wall Shelford, Cambridgeshire.
Mr. Robert Simpfon, Briftol.
Rev. Richard Symes, Rector of St. Werburgh, ditto.
Mr. Samuel Simmons, Newland, Glocesterfh.
Denham Skeat, L. L. D. Henbury.
Henry Skirme, Efq; Lincoln's Inn.
Rev. Dr. Jofeph Atwell Small, Minifter of St. James's, Briftol, 2 copies.
Sir John Smith, Sydling, Dorfet.
J. Wildboar Smith, Trinity Col. Cambridge.
Mr. Smith, Fellow of John's Col. Cambridge.
Robert Smith, Efq; Clifton.
Jofeph Smith, Efq; Briftol.
Rev. Dr. Smith, Mafter of Caius College, Cambridge.
Mrs. Smith, of ditto.
Rev. Mr. Smith, Biddeford, Devonfhire.
Partridge Smith, Efq; Weftholme.
Mr. Smith, Surgeon, Briftol.
Sir John Hugh Smyth, Bart. Afhton Court, Somerfetfhire.
Lady Smyth, ditto.
Thomas Smyth, Efq; Stapleton.
Hugh Smyth, Efq; ditto.
Mr Robert Southey, Briftol.
Mr. Thomas Southey, ditto.
Samuel Span, Efq; ditto.
Francis Spilfbury, Efq; London.
Rev. Mr. Spry, Vicar of Bedminfter, &c. cum Redcliff, Briftol.
William Stephens, Efq; Broad-ftreet, London.
G. Stevens, Efq; Hampftead.
Mr. James Stevens, Briftol.
Mr. William Stephens, ditto.
Rev. Lewis Stephens, Rector of Semly, Wilts.
Mr. Edward Stephens.
Rev. Mr. Stevenfon, Eton.
Robert Steward, Efq; F. Com. of St. John's College, Cambridge.
Rev. Edw. Stillingfleet, of Kellfield, Yorkfhire.
Mr. T. Stock, Briftol.
Thomas Stratton, Efq; ditto.
Thomas Strong, Efq; F. S. A.
Mr. William Studley, Briftol.
Rev. Dr. Sumner, Eton.
Mr. James Sutton, Briftol.
Mr. Walter Swayne, ditto.
J. Symmonds, Efq; Profeffor of Modern Hiftory, Cambridge.
Mr. John Symmons, Surgeon, Bath.

T

Rev. Mr. W. Tandey, Briftol.
Mr. J. Mayo Tandey, ditto.
Mr. Tew, Fellow of Eton College.
Mr. Thackeray, Surgeon, Cambridge.
Mr. Thomas Thomfon.
Mr. George Thynne, F. Com. of St. John's College, Cambridge.
F. Thrufton, Efq; Wefton, Norfolk.
James Tobin, Efq; Briftol.
Mr. Richard Tombs, ditto.
Mr. John Townfend, Surgeon, ditto.
Richard Greaves Townly, Fulborn, Cambridgefhire.
Sir John Trevillian, Bart. Member for Somerfetfhire.
Trinity College Library, Cambridge.
Sir Thomas Trollop, Bart. F. Com. of St. John's College, Cambridge.
Mrs. Margaret Tucker, Briftol.
Mr. Philip Debell Tucket, ditto.
Martin Tunftall, Efq;
Rev. Dr. Turner, Mafter of Pembroke Hall, Cambridge.
William Turner, Efq; Belmont, Wraxal, 3 copies.
Rev. John Turner, Archdeacon of Taunton.
Edmund Turner, junr. Efq; F. R. and A. S. Panton Place, Lincolnfhire.
John Tyler, Efq; Redland.
Thomas Tyndall, Efq; Briftol.
Richard Tyndall, Efq; ditto.
John Tindale, Efq; ditto.

V

Hon. John Villers, Efq; F. Com. of St. John's College, Cambridge.
Richard Vaughan, Efq; Briftol.

W

Mr. John Wadham, junr. Briftol.
Mr. Daniel Wait, ditto.
Sir William Wake, Bart.
Mr. Walefbry, F. Com. Trinity Col. Camb.
Mr. Walford, Caius College, ditto.
Mr. John Waring, Briftol.
Mr. F. Ward, attorney, ditto.
Walter Waftfield, Efq; Chippenham.
Mr. Edward Watkins, Stoke Bifhop.
William Weare, Efq; Briftol.
J. F. Weare, Efq; ditto.
Mr. Francis Weaver, ditto.
Mr. William Webb, ditto.
Mr. John Weeks, ditto.
Mr. Walter Wellick, ditto.
Mr. Jofeph Were, ditto.
Mr. Henry Whatley, ditto.
Rev. Mr. John Wheeler, Upper Grofvenor-ftreet, London.

Thomas

Thomas Whithead, Efq; Hambrook.
Mr. Thomas Whitehead, Briftol.
Mr. James Whitaker, ditto.
Mr. Whitchurch, Surgeon, at Backwell, So-
merfetfhire.
Mr. Whitmore, Fellow of St. John's College,
Cambridge.
H. Whitmarfh, Efq; Bats Place, near Taunton.
Rev. Mr. Wylde, Yatton, Somerfetfhire.
Mr. Jofeph Whittuck, Briftol.
Rev. George Wilkins, Rector of St. Michael's,
ditto.
Mr. William Williams, ditto.
Mr. Luke Wilmot, ditto.
Mr. Thomas Willis, ditto.
Mr. T. Wiltfhire, ditto.
Wm. Wilberforce, Efq; Member for Yorkfhire.
Mr. James Windey, attorney, Briftol.
Sir William Winne, Doctor's Commons.
Mr. John Winpenny, Briftol.
Mr. Jofeph Winpenny, ditto.

Mr. John Winwood, Briftol.
Rev. Mr. Woolafton, Fellow of Trinity Col-
lege, Cambridge.
Leighton Wood, Efq; Briftol.
Mr. Abel Wood, ditto.
Thomas Woodall, Efq; ditto.
George Woodroofe, Efq; Lincoln's Inn.
Mr. John Woodward, Briftol.
Mr. Matthew Worgan, ditto.
Samuel Worrall, Efq; Clifton.
Samuel Worrall, junr. Efq; Town Clerk of
Briftol.
Mr. Matthew Wright, Briftol.
Rev. Mr. Wyatt, Fellow of Pembroke Col-
lege, Cambridge.

Y

Mr. Yeatman, Surgeon, Briftol.
Ch. Ifaac Yorke, Efq; F. Com. of Queen's
College, Cambridge.

ADDITIONAL SUBSCRIBERS.

LORD Eufton, Trinity College, Cambridge.
Lord Henry Fitzroy, ditto.
Hon. Dudley Ryder, M. P. ⎱ Cambridgefhire.
Hon. Philip Yorke, M. P. ⎰
Dr. John Hey, Norrifian Profeffor of Divinity,
Sidney College, Cambridge.
Mr. Edwards, of Norfolk.
Mr. Wilkinfon, ditto.
Mr. Johnfon, ditto.
Rev. Dr. Grape, ditto.
Lord Ongley, Trinity College, Cambridge.
William Hall, Efq; ditto.
H. F. Mills, ditto.

C. L. Dundafs, Efq; ditto.
R. N. Ogle, Efq; ditto.
T. Clapham, Efq; ditto.
H. J. R. Soame, Efq; ditto.
Auguftus Cavendifh, Efq; ditto.
Rev. Mr. Hutchinfon, ditto.
Rev. Dr. Lort, F. R. and A. S.
Francis Fownes Luttrel, Efq; London.
Mr. William Hare, jun. Briftol.
Mrs. Mary Were, Wellington.
Mr. Jofeph Atlay, Briftol.
Mr. David Lewis, ditto.
Mr. Hyatt, Attorney at Law, Shepton-Mallet.

CONTENTS.

C O N T E N T S.

CHAP.

Chap.

THE

OF BRISTOL IN GENERAL.

CHAP. I.

Of its ORIGIN, NAMES, *and* ANTIQUITY.

THE GREAT JEHOVAH, " who hath made of one blood all nations to dwell upon the earth, and determined the bounds of their habitation," affigned to man at firft this one employ, with labour to till the ground in which he was placed. — Thus we find patriarchs and people engaged in agriculture only and the paftoral life, till increafing they went off in tribes to feek more diftant habitations; and mutual wants requiring mutual affiftance, various occupations became neceffary; new countries producing new commodities were inhabited, and a commercial intercourfe by barter and exchange was foon eftablifhed betwixt them.

The borderers on the great rivers and fea coafts employed themfelves in fifhing, which naturally produced a race of feamen; and probably laid the foundation of fea voyages, to which the iflands when peopled feem by fituation to have been neceffarily addicted.

The ifland of BRITAIN received its firft colony from GAUL; and Cæfar upon his invading it found it full of inhabitants, who made a bold refiftance: but as he did not penetrate far into the country, his account muft be very imperfect — though the Roman conqueft of it afterwards laid the foundation of its civilization. The rough manners of the natives became more polifhed; their wandering courfe of life more fixed and fettled; camps were laid out and fortreffes erected with greater fkill; arts and arms began to flourifh; their paftoral employment to be neglected for more ufeful occupations and traffic; which brought together into focieties the difperfed inhabitants, and towns arofe and cities were built for them to live together united under a civil government.

A   The

The firſt riſe of ancient places and the early period in which they became diſtinguiſhed as Vills, Towns, Burghs, or Cities, it is always difficult with exactneſs to aſcertain : and the greater the antiquity of the place, the more intricate and perplexed muſt our reſearches into its original neceſſarily be. I ſhall endeavour to trace this city back through the obſcurity of remote times, to remove the vague conjectures of ſome, and adopt the cleareſt account of it that can be derived from the beſt authorities and rational inveſtigation.

BRISTOL, though ſome writers will not allow us to boaſt of its antiquity, through prejudice or too ſuperficial enquiry, may yet juſtly lay claim to a very early origin : its natural advantages of ſituation, its two rivers, its eaſy communication with the main ocean by its channel, and with the inland parts of England and with Wales by the rivers Avon and Severn, its convenience and ſecurity for defence, invited our Britiſh anceſtors to fix their ſeat here in the earlieſt times under the name of *Caër Brito,* or *Briton,* i. e. the *Britiſh City,* nigh to and juſt under the *Roman city,* or ſtation *Abone,* at Clifton and Rownham Hill, at the time of the Romans governing this iſland, and during their reſidence in this neighbourhood at their camps there, which appear venerable in their ruins at this day.

Gildas, about the year 580, gives us a very particular account of 28 cities that adorned this nation ; and Nennius, about the year 620, gives us the catalogue of them, and mentions *Caër Brito* as one of the 28, famous in ancient times. Bede, who died 734, aged 59, ſays in like manner, " *Britannia erat,* &c." i. e. " *Britain* was famous in ancient times for 28 moſt noble cities, beſides " caſtles, both furniſhed with gates and ſtrong bolts, walls, and towers." Henry of Huntingdon, in 1148, copying from Nennius, gives us *Caër Briſtow* for *Caër Brito.* — But Mr. Cambden, though he acknowledges its Britiſh name *Caër Brito,* yet very contradictorily ſays, " It roſe in the declenſion of the " Saxon government, ſince it is not any where taken notice of before the " year of our Lord 1063, when Harold, as Florence of Worceſter has it, ſet " ſail from Briſtow to invade Wales." That this excellent antiquary was deceived in his opinion, and that Briſtol was a very ancient and renowned place contrary to what he has intimated, will be made appear in the progreſs of this Hiſtory. The ſilence of the monkiſh writers can at beſt be no proof of its late riſe ; for according to the confined miſtaken notions that then prevailed, thoſe places alone which could boaſt the moſt early eſtabliſhment of monaſteries, the moſt rich and ſplendid endowment of religious houſes are chiefly celebrated in their writings, and claim particular notice or attention from them ; while places of trade and commerce were little noted or mentioned.

The

The authority of Mr. Cambden has unhappily so influenced succeeding antiquaries, that they seem all to have copied his error and rested in his authority. But his allowing *Caër Brito* in the ancient catalogue of British cities to be *Briſtow*, and yet immediately afterwards giving it so late an origin as the very decline of the Saxon government here, ſhews ſuch overſight and inaccuracy as can ſeldom be imputed to this great author, whoſe indefatigable induſtry and extenſive knowledge enabled him to produce ſuch a work as the BRITANNIA. The eaſieſt ſolution to be given of this ſeeming contradiction in Mr. Cambden is, that he meant it made no very conſpicuous figure in the annals of hiſtory, roſe to no great pitch of honour-as a feat of war or port of commerce, (*emerſiſſe,*) emerged not out of a kind of obſcurity in thoſe reſpects till towards that period; being probably induced to think ſo by a paſſage he might have ſeen in Leland's manuſcript, though ſeldom quoted by him, who (in *Cygn. Cant.*) ſays, " *Venta Belgarum* (meaning Briſtol) was not a " large city, it was increaſed by the SAXONS."

Though the chroniclers make no very early mention of it, being ſituated out of the road of moſt of the military operations of thoſe days; yet that it was altogether an unnoticed place both as to Religious and Secular matters cannot be conceived, ſince Mr. Cambden himſelf, in his Somerſetſhire, takes notice, that " Jordan, the companion of St. Auguſtin, had his oratory and burial " place here, and his pulpit of ſtone, ſaid to be in the old hoſpital of Bartbo- " lomew:" But Leland better deſcribes it, " at St. Auguſtine's Black " Channons; extra mœnia, ibique in magna areâ ſacellum, in quo ſepultus " eſt S. Jordanus, unus ex diſcipulis Auguſtini Anglorum Apoſtoli;" the monaſtery itſelf afterwards erected here being called after the name and dedi- cated to St. Auguſtin, probably in commemoration of that event.

Neither can it be ſuppoſed with the leaſt ſhadow of reaſon, that Harold and Swain were the firſt of note that ever took ſhipping here, though none may be mentioned before them in our chronicles, as its port muſt have been ever ſo convenient for voyages into Ireland and paſſage into Wales.—Anderſon in- deed ſays, in his Hiſtory of Commerce, printed 1764, vol. 1. p. 19 and 86, " Briſtow is reckoned by Gildas among the fortified and eminent cities of " Britain ſo early as the year 430;" (though he has not mentioned the page in Gildas;) " and that it exiſted as a town or fort in the fifth century, notwith- " ſtanding the aſſertion of Mr. Cambden to the contrary; and again that it " was a place of account in the fifth century when the Romans left Britain."

It will be ſhewn hereafter, that upon the retreat of the Romans, and the ſubverſion of their great cities at Caërleon and Caërwent, the Britons in great

numbers

numbers paffing the Severn back again to Briftol, occupied the town here in the room of thofe deftroyed; as this was by nature a fecurer ftation, and out of the road of thofe invafions and tempefts that have fallen heavy on other ground, nor fubjeĉt to fudden furprifes, furrounded as it is by the Avon' and Froom. — And when afterwards the Saxons came and difpoffeffed them, thefe enlarged it, and foon rendered it a moft flourifhing place and port of trade, to the great decay of Chepftow and other places, which never fince have recovered their trade.

But there is an ancient Britifh name which they feem to agree it had at firft, *Caër Oder Nante Badon*: Leland fays, " Briftol in early ages was probably " called the city Odera, and that Nante Badon, i. e. in the vale of Bath, was " added to it, becaufe Bath was but eleven miles diftant from it;" and then he makes this remark, that " Nante fignifies a valley in which a river flows, " I fhould therefore read it Nante Avon from that river, which may be con- " jeĉtured from a place in Antonines Itinerary, called Abone, or Avone, the " name of a city."

The original authority, befides Leland, for Caër Oder, is not known : Humphry Lhuyd is cited by Ortelius for it, who fays in Thefaur. Geograph. 1587, (under *Venta Belgarum*,) " Ptolomæo & Antonino Britanniæ Infulæ " Oppidum, quod Humphridus (fcil. Lhuuydus) fcribit Britannice Caer Oder " yn Nante Badon & Anglice Briftou vocari: Briftollium hoc nominant " Juniores Latini. Cambdenus dicit hanc Belgarum Ventam hodiè Winchefter " vocari : idem Ventam Icenorum Cäifter interpretatur. Ventam habet Beda " quoque, quam Saxonicè Wintancefter nominatam fcribit. Venta Silurum " Antonino Britanniæ urbs eft, quam Cambdenus & Humphridus Caërwent " appellari aiunt."

The city " Caër Brito, Britodunum, Briftol or Briftold," fays Baxter, p. 187, " was by the Britons called Caër Oder, Civitas Limitis, a frontier city;" and *Stol* and *Stow* he makes to be p. 220, " a place, a feat or city." This agrees very well with its fituation as a frontier town of defence for the Britons before they were driven into Wales their laft refuge, and for the Mercians or Weft Saxons afterwards.

We need not wonder at our want of an explicit account of the Britifh cities, (which though called Britifh, yet if not Roman, were certainly built by their means, and under their proteĉtion ;) for Gildas himfelf acknowledges, " Libri " Britanni combufti fuerunt, &c." i. e. the books of the Britons were burnt, " and it came to that pafs, through the Roman Governors and Proprætors left " here, that whatever Britain had of copper, filver or gold, was marked with
the

" the image of Cæfar:" Leland's remark upon which is, *hoc verum videtur,*
" this feems to be true."—But whatever credit is given to the names of the
Britifh cities mentioned by thefe early writers, or whether rightly afcribed to
certain cities, now flourifhing or arifing from them or not, yet that their firft
original was from the Roman ftations near to them feems fcarce queftionable:
and moft of the Britifh cities of note, if not founded by the Romans, yet afterwards through them foon increafed in number and elegance. Some indeed
contend that the Britons towns and ftrongholds at firft were nothing but fpots
of ground furrounded with trees, felled down and fecured with a ditch and
rampire, according to Cæfar's and Strabo's account, and their temples were
groves confecrated by the Druids.

Dr. Stillingfleet obferves with great probability indeed, that the twenty-eight
Britifh cities mentioned in Nennius and Gildas, are to be underftood of the
Roman times, and were certainly Roman-Britifh, arifing out of their ftations
or camps in the neighbourhood of fuch. — And Dr. Stukely in his account of
Richard of Cirencefter, fays, " that Nennius and Gildas name twenty-eight
" moft famous cities in Britain, which the excellent Archbifhop Ufher has
" commented upon; and though the catalogue is different from Richard's, yet
" he is confirmed in calling *Verulam* a municipium, which in Nennius is called
" *Caër Municip.*" But it is very clear that the Romans had many cities that might
lie out of their general road or tract, unnoticed either by Antonine, Nennius,
Gildas or Richard: the laft indeed plainly confeffes it in cap. 7. de Situ
Britanniæ.

" *At præter allatas modo Urbes,* &c. i. e. Befides the cities here produced, let
" no one haftily believe that the Romans had not more in Britain; for I have
" only mentioned the more famous cities: for who can doubt but that thefe
" Lords of the whole earth chofe at their will, and claimed to themfelves many
" other places which they knew convenient for their purpofes," adding this
remarkable expreffion, " plerumque aliàs in caftris quæ confiderant ipfi,
" degebant;" that " for the moft part they otherwife lived in the camps which
" they had founded."

It might indeed be juftly obferved, that out of twenty-eight flourifhing cities,
which were famous in this ifland in the times of the Britons and Romans, it is
highly probable that Briftol fo happy in its fituation by nature, fo capable of
being made the moft defenfible place by art, was one of the number.*

It

* Lel. Coll. v. 3. p. 250. " Civitatum nomina funt hic obfcure & confufe pofita; *multa vetera
pretermiffa,* recentiora aliquot adfcripta:"—" The names of many old cities are omitted, and fome
" new ones fet down in the catalogue of cities."— It is no wonder then that Briftol fhould not
be more plainly noticed in that confufed lift.

It may be further urged, that Briſtow is but an eaſy alteration of the name Brito, and that it ſeems to have ſuffered this change at the Saxon conqueſt, as has been the fate of moſt places when conquered, the name being Saxonized, and afterwards variouſly modified according to the different manner of ſpelling and fancy of the chroniclers of early ages; ſome times preſerving ſomewhat of the original name, at other times transferring it into their language wholly. Caër-Brito ſignified the painted or embelliſhed city. The Saxons ſeemed to have regard to the conſtruction of the word as well as the found of the letters in naming it Bright-Stow, the illuſtrious city; and received it with little variation of found of the original word in their own ſenſe to expreſs a town, whoſe agreeable ſituation and circumſtances, like the Callipolis of the Greeks, and Clarence of the French, give a propriety to the name. Or it may have received the name *Caër-Brito*, the Britiſh city, ſeparated as it was from, and ſo called in diſtinction to, the Roman city or ſtation Abone near it: *Brit* in the old Britiſh ſignifying alfo *ſeparated*, and *Britain* the ſeparated place or iſle, according to ſome.—Thus the orthography of the word *Brito* might paſs into Bryſto, Bryſtoe, T. Ed. Conf. Bryghſto, * Briſtou, Brightſtoe, Bricgſtowe, and Brigeſtow, early in the Saxon times: in 1106 Brigſton; † in 1140 Briſtowe.— By Florence of Worceſter, in 1114, it is called Bricſtow. By Henry of Huntingdon, 1148, Brigeſtou. In 1190, in King John's Charter, when Earl of Morton, now extant in Latin in the Chamber of Briſtol, it is throughout wrote Briſtallum: the Normans wrote it Briſtoit—ſo in the old French deeds: ſince, by Leland and moſt of the old manuſcripts, Bryghtſtowe: but the Saxons, who ſeem to have impoſed this name of Brycghſtowe, i. e. a bright, illuſtrious place, we may reaſonably preſume found it in that flouriſhing con-dition, or the name could have been applied with no ſort of propriety, unleſs we ſuppoſe it to be a caſual variation of Caër Brito, its old original name. It might indeed have the name of Brigſton from the Saxon Brieg, a Bridge, i. e. a town with bridges, ‡ as Biſhop Gibſon has derived it, which ſeems well enough calculated for the peninſular ſituation of the old town, ſurrounded almoſt with water, which had great need of, and ſtill hath, of bridges to preſerve a com-munication

* Saxon Chron. p. 193. 230. 241. and in H. 2. time called Briſton in Mag. Rotul. 31. H. 2. Rot. 10. 1191. 7s. 5d. de exitu Briſtou molendinorum & Nundinarum.

† In Atkyns's Gloceſterſhire, p. 738, where we find the church of St. Peter of Brigſton, and the tithe of the rent of Brigſton granted to the monaſtery of Tewkeſbury in 1106, in a charter of H. 1. to that houſe.

‡ That the etymology of the name of Briſtol ſhould be a little uncertain, is not to be wondered at, being the caſe of all cities of antiquity, even of London itſelf, which is ſaid to be derived from the Britiſh Lhong-dinas, i, e. a city of ſhips.

munication with different places about it; though the great bridge over the Avon till a later date was not in being: *Bricgſton quaſi locus pontis*, Bridge-Town: in Doomſday-book, and in the ancient charters of H. 2. and H. 3. and in other public acts, where we might expect to find the orthography beſt pre-ſerved, it is moſt uſually ſtyled Briſtold, Briſtou or Briſtol, though the latter ſeems to have been moſt commonly uſed, and is now adopted, the reſt among the moderns being deemed quite obſolete.

In a manuſcript charter *penes me*, from King Edw. Conf. a. r. 9°. I find it wrote Bryſtoe : this with the other charters will be inſerted hereafter, in the annals for the reſpective year.

Having thus ſhewn its ſeveral names, and how the original name Caër Brito might probably have been altered at different times, yet has preſerved never-thelefs the ſound of the original in ſome reſpects, we muſt not omit the Roman name *Venta Belgarum*, with which it has been thought by ſome to have been diſtinguiſhed by that military people. This name is aſcribed to it by Leland, Lambard, and ſome others; and it ſeems to agree well with Ptolomy's deſcription of ſuch a city lying next under the Dobuni or Gloceſterſhire: but Mr. Cambden is certainly right in giving to Wincheſter this name, as the Itinerary of Antonine, confirmed by Richard of Cirenceſter, plainly and indubitably points out. And in this opinion all at preſent ſeem to concur, how widely ſoever they have differed about placing the Abone of Antonine. But now at length this may with equal truth be aſcertained. It was here in the neighbourhood of Briſtol the Romans fixed this their ſtation Abone, calling it after the name of the river, on the banks of which they erected it; and it certainly became the parent of the city of Briſtol : whether it ever extended its borders after-wards, and took in all the heights adjoining even to Briſtol itſelf, and ſo included the whole under one name Abone, is difficult now to determine : the city was certainly dependent on, if not immediately connected in one with, the Roman ſtation. But that Abone, the Britiſh name of the river, gave name to a city on its banks, is highly probable and very common; the cities often took their names from rivers, and aroſe as often out of the ruins of ancient encampments and ſtations of the Romans in their vicinity, or flou-riſhed under their protection.

Whether

---

* *Bricg-ſtowe*—either Bright-ſtow or Bridges-ſtow, ſo wrote in the Saxon Chronicle, which ſeems to be a derivation more plauſible, and a name it at ſome time or other more likely had obtained than Burg-ſtowe, or Borough Town, as ſome have inſinuated.

Whether the city Caër Brito, Caër Oder Nante Badon, or rather Nante Avon, afterwards by the Saxons called Brightſtowe, did not thus take its origin, deſerves a particular enquiry.

There certainly was a Roman ſtation a little way down the river from Briſtol, and the Roman coins dug up at Clifton and in making the Sea-mill dock, and in plowing the adjacent fields, point out their ſtation here, and are proofs not to be doubted; and it is very extraordinary that neither Cambden, Horſeley, Stukely, nor any antiquary has ſo much as even thought of this ſtraight and and neareſt paſſage between Bath and Caerwent; but their attachment to Oldbury, as the only Trajeƈtus mentioned in the Itinerary in theſe parts, certainly diverted their attention from it. And beſides the communication of of Roman poſts and ſtrong holds acroſs the Severn here, particularly to be deſcribed hereafter, hiſtory will afford us ſomething for confirmation. *Tac. Annal. lib.* 12, ſays, " Oſtorius detrahere arma ſuſpeƈtis, cinƈtoſque caſtris " Sabrinam & Antonam fluvios cohibere parat:" i. e. " Oſtorius took away " their arms from thoſe who were ſuſpeƈted, and reſtrained thoſe on the rivers Avon and Severn, by ſurrounding them with camps." Hence it appears, that Oſtorius, the better to curb the Britons, poſted his forces on the banks of the Antona and Severn; * and having before defeated the Iceni, who not brooking ſome indignity had taken up arms for the liberties of their country, he afterwards fell upon the Cangi, † and ravaged almoſt as far as the Iriſh ſea, which could be no other than the ſea that beats on the Weſt Country coaſt. From hence he was called back to repreſs a ſedition of the Brigantes, and then paſſed into the country of the Silures, where he defeated Caraƈtacus, who had politicly tranſlated the war thither, as a country of difficult acceſs: by this ſeries of aƈtion and deſcription of countries which Tacitus gives, it appears that the Cangi bordered near the Severn; that to reſtrain them Oſtorius placed garriſons near the Severn and Antona, which was a river emptying itſelf into the Severn, and lay equally advantageous for placing his ſoldiers as the Severn did; which cannot be more truly affirmed of any river than the Briſtol Avon: at leaſt the Avon oppoſite to Caerwent of the Silures acroſs the Severn (where they had ſuch ſtrong camps) could not have been negleƈted by him in this important ſervice. — There are other Avons indeed, one partienlarly in Warwickſhire, to which ſome would attribute the name Antona, and ſome

* Horſely, p. 36, ſays " Sabrina doubtleſs is the Severn. And Antona muſt alſo be the " Avon. Some write the ancient name Aufona, and the anonymous Ravennas writes it Abona."

† There is much advanced concerning the Cangi, but nothing ſatisfaƈtory. It is clear from the ſtory, however, that Oſtorius paſſed through the country of the Cangi, which he had waſted, and after this came near the weſtern coaſt.

fome to the river Nen. And though Mr. Cambden would feem to retract and perfuade himfelf and us, that Oftorius blocked up the Britons betwixt the Warwickfhire Avon and the Sabrina; yet it is not probable that he fixt his ftations and encampments there, fince this river falls into a higher part of the Severn, nor could the Cangi, if of Somerfetfhire, be affected by them. — But the alliance of the Briftol Avon with the Severn and Irifh fea is apparent; and Pliny, (*Nat. Hif. lib.* iv. *c.* 16.) fpeaking of Ireland, makes it thirty miles from the Silures, which though a miftake in the calculation does evidence, that the country where the Silures inhabited, on the other fide of the Severn, to the Weft of the Oftium where the Avon difcharges, was efteemed in the Roman account as bordering on or defcending towards the Irifh fea: the little liland and village called Scilly in the Briftol Channel points out the feat of the Silures, though others place the Cangi in different parts.

But the name of Cangi feems ftill to exift in the names of fome places in the weftern parts; Cainfham, Wincaunton, and the Cannington or Canningham marfhes, in the Saxon chronicle, which were the marfhes of Somerfetfhire. — Befides thofe places mentioned by Cambden as preferving in their name the found of Cangi in Somerfetfhire, to which the Roman army was led, (*Tacit. l.* iv. *Ann. Ductus eft ad Cangos*) there were many others as Congerfbury, Cangfield, Canford, Caundell, &c. And thefe traces of the Cangi, in the names of towns of Somerfetfhire and its confines, are more demonftrative of the Cangi's habitation, on confidering that there is no town nor parifh in Glocefterfhire, Devonfhire, &c. that hath the fyllable Can, or Caun, or Cang, (or Quan, as in Quantock) in it: fo that it is highly probable the antient inhabitants of thefe weftern parts were called the Cangi, and coins of the Roman Emperors have often been found here, at Conqueft, Brent-Knoll, &c. Baxter, Gloffar. p. 38, fays, *Ceangi vel Somerfetæ, &c.* " the " Ceangi or thofe of Somerfet were of the Belgæ in the time of Ptolemy, for " he makes Ilchefter and Bath belong to them," and p. 71, " the Ceangi were " not lefs apt for war than the paftoral life they followed:" we fee that the Danmonian Cangi or of Somerfet, " fortem operam in Oftorium Scapulam navaviffe," performed great exploits againft Oftorius Scapulæ, and p. 74, " thefe Cangi were of that country called, from the Summer-feats of fhepherds, " Somerfet, of which Somerton or Summer Town was very old and the chief."

Thefe military works and difpofitions of fome great General fo nigh Briftol then feem very probably to have been made here by Oftorius, viz. at Clifton; on Leigh down feveral, efpecially on the banks of the Avon and Severn; at Cadbury camp, and near Naifh; and at Henbury, Almondfbury, Oldbury,

B   Elberton,

Elberton, and Old Abby, on the Glocefterfhire fide; and lower down in Somerfetfhire, at Dolbery, where coins have been dug by Mr. Swimmer; at Worle-hill and Eaft Brent, where on Brent-knoll coins of Severus and Trajan and others in an urn have been found. On both fides the river, befides the encampments hereafter defcribed at Rownham-hill and Clifton, in the vicinage of Briftol, many others are to be noted at the lower part of the Avon, parti-cularly at St. George's and Portbury, which in Leland's Itinerary is called Portchefter, where on a rifing ground are evident traces of a camp; alfo near Shirehampton, on the other fide of the Avon, are aggera ftill to be feen as you defcend the hilly ground, and coins have lately been found in making the the new road in Lord Clifford's park, as you go down to Shirehampton, many of which are in my poffeffion. Add to this, fuch a regular chain of camps and entrenched pofts for fo many miles in view of the Severn and near to it, are no where elfe to be met with in the courfe of that river; which fhews the fkill and attention of the Roman General to fecure thefe parts, agreeable to what Gildas fays, p. 12, f. 16, " Quia Barbarorum irruptio timebatur, Turres (Caftra) per intervalla ad profpectum maris collocant." At Snead-park, and at Sea-mills and its neighbourhood, might be the place of their great refort and principal winter ftation, and in the river Trim the Roman gallies and boats were fecured. It is very remarkable, that, allowing Abone of the Itinerary to be fituated at or near Briftol, the diftances will nearly agree, and the Trajectus between Caerwent and Bath at length more eafily be found. And to this may be added, that fome rofe-up ground, like an old Roman road, croffes Durdham-down, (where a coin of Conftantine was lately dug up) looking towards the ftation here and in a direct line with it, and pointing towards Han-ham in the high road to Briftol (near which road an urn of coins was found lately, not a mile and a half from Briftol) and Bath, (*Aquæ Solis* of the Romans).

An inconteftable proof of this being a Roman camp nigh Briftol on Clifton hill, * may be brought as well from the ditches and aggera ftill to be feen, as from Roman coins of Nero, Domitian, Trajan and other Roman Emperors being dug up there, alfo from a curious Roman urn with two handles, tiles, bricks and broken potfherds being found there, when Sir Wm. Draper levelled the ground near the camp, which is moft advantageoufly fituated for the purpofe: " All Roman encampments, forts or ftations were generally fet upon hills," as is well obferved by Burton in his Comment on the Itinerary. This camp with others at no great diftance and in view was placed on fuch an high afcent to defcry an approaching enemy, as the Romans were in an

enemy's

---

* Coins were found in digging the foundations of the new houfes near it, in 1783.

enemy's country ever upon the watch, and at the fame time to guard the river, as the river was a guard and fecure defence to them.

A particular defcription of thefe ftrong camps near Briftol may be neceffary to give the reader fome idea of them. And we find they were not unnoticed fo early as the year 1480. In a manufcript of Wm. Bottoner in Bennet college library, Cambridge, (lately printed and publifhed by the ingenious Dr. Nafmith 1778,) there is the following defcription of Clifton rocks, on the fummit of which the Roman camp was fituated: Thus in Englifh, " At the " high rock of Clifton cliff, which begins near the village of Rownham, unto " the hermitage and camp on the other fide of the waters of Avon and Frome, " which high rock begins one mile's fpace from the town of Briftol; and the " faid rock continues in its height for a mile long and farther towards Rown- " ham road for laying up fhips. And the faid rock contains in height from " the water of the Avon and Frome 60 brachia (fathom) viz. from the firm " land to a certain hermitage whofe church is founded and dedicated to the " honour of St. Vincent, is in height 20 brachia, and from the faid hermitage " to the bottom of the faid river are 40 brachia; and underftand, that a bra- " chium contains fix feet in length.

" The fortified camp upon the height of the ground not diftant a quarter of " a mile from Clifton cliff is faid by vulgar people to be there founded before " the time of William the Conqueror by Saracens or Jews by one Ghyft · " a giant in the land. And that fuch a fortrefs was in all likelihood founded " there in ancient times, there remains to this day in a great circle a heap of " ftones, great and fmall fcattered and fpread abroad. It is very wonderful " to behold thefe ftones globularly lying in fuch order and in a great circle, " for there feems to have been a very ftrong caftrum, which is faid to have " been for fome hundred years paft, and is now levelled with the ground. " And it therefore is an ornament and honour to my native country Briftol, " and to the county of Gloucefter, to have or to hear of the foundation of " fuch noble fortreffes and camps. I write this among other things for the· " fake of commemorating this camp or fortrefs."

By the above extract, incorrect and vague as it may appear to be, however we learn; that the camp or fortrefs on Clifton rocks did not efcape the notice of our anceftors, and though it might be the vulgar opinion, that it was erected before the conqueft by jews or Saracens, yet doubtlefs the learned of thofe days certainly knew better, later difcoveries have proved it; and as to the height of the rock he feems to have been pretty exact; and it is remarkable, that the place of the hermitage is at this day called Giant's hole, and is about

the

the diftance here fet down from the fummit of the rock or firm ground. There are ftill extant the like Roman camps on the oppofite fide of the river to Clifton, at Rownham-hill, on Leigh down in two places, called Stokeleigh and Bowre-walls now a wood, a deep comb or valley there called Stokeleigh-Slade only feparating the two, which have both the advantage of the like lofty fituation ferving for fpecula or watch towers, as well as defence and fecurity againft the fudden attack of an enemy. The aggera and double ditches are there ftill to be feen, and they appear magnificent and venerable in their ruins, and a ftronger and more defenfible fituation could no where be chofen. The height of the rocks, the deep intermediate comb, the river below, the deep fofs, and the high banks, fhew it to be an advantageous, fecure and well chofen ftation, capable of a good defence, and highly worthy their care and attention. A ford or vadum there over the Avon communicated with both camps on each fide of the river. A little lower down the river feems to have been placed the Caftra Hyberna, being the Roman winter ftation, abundance of coins having been dug up there in making Sea mill dock in the year 1712. They alfo met with a fine arched gate way under ground in digging out the dock at its upper part, which feems to have led to fome principal part, and the rudera of buildings deftroyed, and remains of old foundations have been traced up the adjoining hilly ground next the river fide, and were remarked by the ingenious mechanic Mr. Padmore, who conducted the undertaking: and in a field called three acres Roman coins are found at this day, and are turned up there in plowing the fields called Portburies or Polburies. It is remarkable, that under Kingwefton hill, in Laurence-wefton near the river was a common field called Abone town as mentioned in the rental of Sir Ralph Sadlier, dated 36 Hen. 8. one acre in Campo Abone town. There have been found a Vefpafian of a large fize; alfo coins of Conftantine, Conftance, Galienus; one of Nero thus incribed, *Nero Claud. Cæfar. Aug. Germ. p. m. T R. p. Imp. p. p.* a fine head with a radiated crown; on the reverfe *S. C.* a *Victoria Gradiva*, with a fhield in the right hand, infcribed with *S. P. Q. R.* this was picked up by me in a garden adjoining to the dock in 1768, and in a field called the three acres next the Avon I found one of Conftance in the year 1775: and in Abel Wantner's manufcript in the Bodleian library it is faid " At Pollbury where Trim goeth into the Avon, much coin has " been found, conjectured to be the ancient ftation of the Romans " between Bath and Avington, mentioned by Antoninus the Emperor in his " journal book." About two miles diftant from thefe and in view of them was another Roman camp, on Blaze-hill near Henhury late the

feat

feat of T. Farr, Efq; who there dug up great quantities of coins in laying the foundation of a caftle-like building he erected on its fummit, which commands a moft enchanting profpect of the country around, of the Severn and the fhips at anchor in Kingroad, and of the veffels paffing up the river to Briftol. I cannot but acknowledge his great civility and readinefs in fending me the collection he had faved out of the whole.

This camp at Henbury, a manor formerly belonging to the Bifhop of Worcefter, who had a park here, and which was taken from the Bifhoprick and granted to Sir Ralph Sadleir 1 Edw. 6, was of large extent, with a high vallum and double fofs, and is about two miles diftant from Clifton camp and Sea-mills. Another at Knoll-hill, Almondfbury, and Over, about two miles farther: and at Old Abby a few miles farther was another, where a curious teffelated pavement, in the year 1787, was found in a farmer's yard.

The following coins were found at Henbury, in the year 1708, by Sir Simon Harcourt, from an autograph.

FACE or OBVERSE.	REVERSE.
Conftantinus Magnus.	*Romulus & Remus.*
Trajan: a very fair medal in copper, of a large fize.	A female figure fitting, in her left hand a cornucopia, in the right the rudder of a fhip, fubfcribed S. C.
Marcus Aurelius Antoninus.	A female figure facrificing on an altar, *Salut. Aug.* S. C.
Vefpafian: feveral in middle fize copper.	A large altar, fubfcribed *Reverentia.*
Conftantius: very fair in fmall copper.	A Mars marching, circumfcribed *Confervatio.*
Ditto, fmall copper.	*Felix Temporum reparatio.*
Ditto.	A caftle, and circumfcribed *Provident. Aug.*
Licinius.	*Genio populi Romani.*
Geta: fmall filver.	*Invictus.*
Marcus Aurelius Antoninus.	A funeral pile, S. C.
Adrian: large copper.	A fhip with feveral figures.
Trajan. Fauftina.	
Antoninus Pius.	A female figure captive, *Britan.*
A Britifh gold coin, coined at Malden or Colchefter, in Effex; an ear of corn on one fide.	A horfe, C. A. M. O.
Caligula: large copper.	
Nero: ditto.	*Julian,*

FACE or OBVERSE.	REVERSE.
Julian, the Apoſtate.	*Votis* x. *Multis* xx.
Domitian: middle ſize copper.	
Nerva.	Two hands joined, *Exercituum Concordia.*
Ditto.	*Fortuna redux.*
Galienus; a radiated crown.	A deer, *Cos.* Aug.
Probus.	*Lætitia Aug.*
D. N. Conſtans P. f. Aug.	Drawing a captive out of a den.

The following coins were dug up at Sea-mills, 1712.

Imp. Cæſ. Veſpaſianus, P. f. Aug.	*Concordia Militum.*
Ditto.	A temple, in the *Exergue, Providentia.*
Imp. Dioclefianus, P. f. Aug.	A fitting figure.
Imp. Cæſ. Domitianus Aug.	A figure holding a flower in her hand.
Imp. Cæſ. Antoninus, P. f. Aug.	A figure holding a cornucopia.
D. N. Conſtantinus, P. f. Aug. p. p.	A Man transfixing a ſuppliant captive with a dart.

The following were dug at St. Baze-hill, Henbury, 1768.

Imp. Cæſar Domiti. Aug. Germ. Coſ. xiii. *Cenſ. Perp. p. p.* within a laurel crown.	*Virtuti Auguſti.* S. C. a ſoldier holding in his right hand a dart, in his left a parazonium.
Imp. Cæſ. Domit. Aug. Germ. Coſ. xi. *Cenſ. Perp. p. p.*	A winged female figure, or Victory, holding in her right hand a ſhield, S. C.
Imp. Cæſ. Nerva Trajan Aug. Germ. P. M. a radiated head.	*T. R. Pot. Coſ.* iii. *p. p.* S. C. a figure fitting with a ſtaff, between two cornucopias.
D. N. Gratianus P. f. Aug. bright ſilver.	*Virtus Romanorum.*
Imp. Cæſ. Carauſius P. M.	*Pax Aug.* a female figure with an olive branch.
Criſpina Auguſta.	A fitting figure, in her right hand ſhe holds a patera to a ſerpent aſcending from an altar.
Imp. Cæſ. Alectus P. f. Aug. a radiated head.	*Virtus Auguſt.* Q. C. *Navis.*
D. N. Magnentius P. f. Aug. a naked head.	*Salus D. N. Aug. & Cæſ.* a monogram of the name of Chriſt, I. M. B. in a croſs with Alpha and Omega.
Imp. C. M. Poſthumus P. f. Aug.	*Victor. Aug.*
Imp. Cæſ. Poſthumus P. f. Aug.	A figure of Æſculapius with a ſerpent.

Imp.

FACE or OBVERSE.	REVERSE.
Imp. Cæf. Vefpafian. Aug. Cof. viii. *p. p.*	S. C. an eagle with his wings expanded fitting on a globe.
Imp. Antonin. Aug. Pius, p. p. Tr. p. p. Cof. iiii. head crowned with laurel.	A ftanding figure, holds out a patera to a ferpent rifing from an altar.
Magnentius Nob. Cæf. a naked head.	*Victor.* D. D. N. N. *Aug. & Cæf.* two Victories fuftaining a globe, on which is *Vot.* v. *Mult* x.
Conftantius, Caraufius: feveral of them with their infcriptions worn out.	
Valentinianus: feveral of them.	*Securitas Reipublicæ.*
Imp. Nerva Cæf. Aug. P. M. T R. P. *Cof.* iii. *p. p.*	*Fortuna Augufti:*
Imp. Claud. Auguft.	
Urbs Roma, a head with a helmet: feveral of them.	A wolf fuckling two infants.
Marcus Aurel. Antonin. Aug.	
Antoninus Aug. Pius, p. p.	
T. R. *Pot. Cof.* iii. S. C.	A Mars marching.

Conftantinus, Gratianus, Conftantius, and many other coins of various fizes.

The following were dug up at Clifton near the camp, in digging the foundation of the houfes then built there, in the year 1784.

Dom. Nofter Conftantius Aug.	*Felicitas Reipublicæ,* a ftanding figure holding in her right hand a fmall figure of Victory, in the left a dart.
D. *N. Valentinianus Aug.*	
Conftantius Aug. fmall.	*Victoria Aug.* two winged figures.
Conftantius Nobis Cæfar	*Gloria Exercitus:* two foldiers with fpears and fhields; in the middle, two military ftandards, with a type M. R. B. T.
Dom. Nofter Conftantius Aug.	An armed figure : —*fides Exercitus.*
Conftantinus Pius Aug.	The Emperor in a chariot drawn with four horfes, with infcription, *Soli invicto Comiti.*

Befides thefe, a great many more were found by the workmen, and embezzled and fold to private gentlemen. A few Saxon coins, filver, were alfo difcovered, of Æthelred, with *Rex Angl.*; and thefe with the others are now in my poffeffion.

Thefe

Thefe camps at Henbury, or Blaze-hill, and Almondfbury, look directly towards the greater works of Abone at Rownham and Clifton-hill, and form one grand chain of fortification, with the Severn in its front; and fignals of an approaching enemy might be communicated to either from a great diftance. Blaze-hill, feparated as if by art from the down adjacent called Kingfwefton-hill, commands a full profpect of the Avon and Severn, and a diftant view of Venta Silurum, Ifca or Caerleon, as well as of all the Roman ftations nearer at hand, and was the moft defenfible poft next to that at Clifton and Rownham-hills, in the neighbourhood of Briftol, that Oftorius and the Romans had.

Bifhop Stillingflect fays, p. 510, that it was the Roman cuftom to place their garrifons on rivers, as a fecurity of their frontiers againft the enemy, which was the occafion of towns being built there, called by them Burgi, i. e. limitum caftella, as Veignier obferves, " caftles on the borders:" fo that Briftol feems to have been a burgus on the borders, called by its moft ancient name Caer Oder Nante Badon, or Avon ; a name that has puzzled all anti-quaries to account for; and the authority for which is Leland and Lhuyd, though the reafon for the name is not mentioned by Cambden or them. Amidft this uncertainty, if one might be allowed to guefs, the city Oder in the vale of Bath, or on the Avon (the vale river), might not improbably have been written at firft the city Ofter, and by dropping the Sibilant letter f, not unufual among the Britons after the French, the name Oder (from Ofter) was by them formed ; and fo Oftorius, the Roman Propraetor under Claudius, may have dignified our city with his name : and Auft-paffage over the Severn is in Doomfday-book called Auftre Clive, retaining ftill the name of Oftorius in its found without the Latin termination; a proof of that General's having acted much in thefe parts.

The town, as well as the camps near it, could not but come under the Pro-praetor's government, as it fell thus within his circuit and view, and might with them be included in their ftation Abone, though affuming afterwards another name : the new modelling it fince and the frefh foundations and enlargements have left us few marks of its ancient ftate, which was fo much altered, as was its name afterwards by the Saxons.

But to be a little more particular on thefe veftiges the Romans have left nigh Briftol, their camps here deferve a defcription at large.

The Britons no doubt on the firft invafion of the Romans did at their leifure and on preffing occafions prepare many ftrong places of retreat for their wives, children, flocks and herds, &c. making every vigorous ftruggle for their defence, and fortifying at intervals all the heights for places of refuge. Thefe

afterwards

afterwards being feized by the Romans, were occupied and enlarged, and greatly improved by them; the Britons having fcarce ingenuity enough to erect fuch camps at the time, the grand remains of which are now to be feen. Hence however they ftill retained the Britifh name Abone, hence we fee Britifh coins and fome Saxon (as they afterwards occupied them) found together with the Roman on fome odd fhaped camps on hills, which before moft probably were Britifh; (as it is well obferved by the ingenious Dr. Nafh, in the hiftory of Worcefterfhire) : but the politic Romans more fkilled in the military arts left no advantageous poft unoccupied or unimproved.

As they profecuted their conquefts through the ifland, they eftablifhed forts at the moft convenient places for their greater fecurity; fome for the immediate occafion only, whilft others were erected into ftationary camps, efpecially on the banks of rivers, with a view of better maintaining their conquefts and fettlements, and of uniting and readily communicating by fuch a chain of forts with their countrymen. No fooner were the Britifh towns fubject to their arms, but they furrounded them with forts and with camps: *Civitates-Præfidiis et Caftellis circumdatæ,* fays Tacitus, c. xx. Oftorius about the year of Chrift 50, extended his victorious arms upon the banks of the Severn: and fecured that river and the Avon: but Julius Frontinus conquerd the Silures and gave name to the *via Julia* or *Julia Strata* of *Necham,* between Bath and Caerwent. And as our camps at Clifton, Rownham, and Henbury lay in the direct road to the country of the Silures and Caerwent on the other fide of the Severn, there is reafon to believe this ftation was formed or greatly enlarged under Oftorius's government here. The commanding fpot on Leighdown and Clifton-hill, on the very fummit of the rock on each fide the river being chofen; they marked out the compafs of the intended camps, allotted a convenient area in each, dug out the four foffes, rofe the three ramparts or valla, and with the ftones here ready at hand, conftructed the high ftrong walls, heaping the ftones together in a very irregular manner, and floping it gradually to the top, from eighteen or twenty feet at the bafe to two or three at the creft, pouring their boiling mortar among the loofely piled ftones; which being thin and fluid, infinuated itfelf into the many openings and hollows of the work, and by its ftrength bound together all the irregular pieces of ftone into a compact wall, as appears evidently at this day. The fhape of the hills confined them to a conftruction and form nearly circular. *
A deep and hollow valley or comb (D) alone feparated the two camps on the

C   Leigh

* Vegetius fays, *Interdum Romanorum Caftra &c.* i. e. fometimes the Roman camps were fquare, fometimes triangular, fometimes half round, as the nature and neceffity of the ground required.

Leigh-fide, and ferved as a paffage down to the river, for each to get water for their ufe, where was a vadum (E) or communication over a fhallow ford with their companions at Clifton camp (A); by which they had the command of both fides of the Avon. There are two entrances into this camp at Rounham hill called in old writings * Bowre or Bower-walls, (B) perhaps Burgh or Borough-walls i. e. of .the fort or burgus, one in front, the *porta prætoria*, the other at the fide the *porta finiftra*, the back part and right fide of it joining the very edge of the precipice next the Avon, the *porta decumana* and the *dextra* had no place here. At .Stokeleigh-camp (C) on the other fide the deep comb may be traced two openings or gate ways; and on the right fide appear the ruins of the *prætorium* (F) at this day; the northern extremity of the area and rudera of the building fhewing it to have been round, encircled with a trench, and fituated at the very angle of the two concurrent precipices, a proper and fecure place for the citadel of the garrifon : if it were not the *prætorium*, which is fometimes placed on one fide on the lofty margin of rivers, it might be a *facellum* or facred armoury for laying up the *vexilla* or enfigns of the feveral cohorts which had the *Aquilæ fimulacra deorum & Imagines principum* upon them, and were accounted facred by the Roman foldiers; the place being dedicated it is likely to *Mars fignifer* or *Mars ultor*, not unlikely *Arthur's oven* in Gordon's *itinerarium feptentrionale*. ·

The tremendous height on the rocks on which thefe camps were formed gave the Romans a vaft advantage of defcrying any enemy at a diftance by land, or any invafion by fea, the whole country around and the Severn being here open to their view. And a fire from this lofty fite ferved as a beacon to alarm all at their diftant camps, at Henbury, Amefbury and parts adjacent.

The importance of their ftation here is fufficiently proved by the high and ftrong walls, treble ditches and fences with which they are fecured. Art and nature joined to render it a moft impregnable fortrefs, fecured on one fide by the lofty rock and precipice, a deep comb, the river below with a fort on the other fide oppofite the comb, and on the other by lofty ftrong walls, three deep ditches one within the other. Their fituation anfwered every purpofe and advantage for a defence-poft, for here they enjoyed the privilege of ufing their baliftæ and catapultæ, their only miffive weapons for throwing huge ftones with the greateft force from thefe heights, which muft fall with the greater weight and effect; here the land itfelf was more defenfible and tenible; here they

* In *Bower latere videtur Burgus Iter. Tho. Gale p.* 61. The vale under and in view of this camp is called Borough-Afhton to this day. The word chefter or burgh, fays Horfely, gives us fome help in fixing a Roman ftation.

Roman Camps on the River Avon above the Bristol Hotwells.

they had a full view of their enemy and an army, veffels or fleets at a diftance, when meditating an attack; here by being on the narrow arm of a large navigable river, and its loweft pofition towards the Severn and fea, they could cut off all navigation by an enemy and keep open a free and effectual communication with their friends acrofs Kingroad to Caerwent, their next ftation, and by the camps being double and on oppofite fides and facing each other, they commanded two fides of a fine country, and could from at leaft one of them annoy any veffels or boats paffing under them or near the banks of the river, and if in the middle of the ftream at full tide they could eafily reach them by a double attack, and difcharge of their miffives from each fide of the river; here laftly they had a free ufe of water to drink &c. and at Sea-mills a good and fufficient ftrand for buildings, &c.

From thefe two camps Bower-walls (B) and Stokeleigh (C) on Leigh down, a *prætentura* or fence againft any inroad or attack upon their lines is to be traced, the ranges of ftone appearing ftill for fome miles, joining in one from each camp at the top of the comb, then proceeding in a nearly ftreight direction toward Fayland. At every opening towards the vales and at every eminence where a diftant profpect of the country around and of the river afforded an opportunity of defcrying an approaching enemy, there circular watch-towers were raifed, there the ruins of walls croffing the fence and outworks for garrifons, &c. ftill appear; the ftones ranging in that manner loofe above ground at this day. This fence may be traced all the way weftward by the broad high ftony bank for many miles fkirting the hill, fronting the fouth and extending towards Clevedon and Walton, * where are now traces of camps marked out near the Severn, which feems to have been its bounds; there is a large camp now compleat called Cadbury, which is circular with a double fofs and high aggera, and under it near Tickenham, Roman coins have been dug, many of which were in poffeffion of the late Sir Abraham Elton of Clevedon, Bart. alfo three urns of Roman coins, fome of Conftantine and others of different ages were dug up in Nailfea and Ken-moor not far from the camp,† at a place called Nailfea-wall, which divides Ken-moor

and

* Gual is a rampart, from thence is formed Wall, Bal. Val. in the name of towns, as Walton, a rampart town or place.

† Thefe coins are many of them now in the poffeffion of Mrs. Hinkes of Nailfea, and a far greater quantity to the amount of feveral hundred were given to the late Sir J. Smith of Afhton-Court, by Mr. Chatterton, father of that Thomas Chatterton, who has occafioned fuch difputes relative to fome ancient poems publifhed under the name of T. Rowley, faid by him to be copied from fome manufcript originals once in his father's poffeffion. - Sir John Hugh Smith Bart.

and Nailfea-moor. There are veftiges alfo of a circular caftrum on the brow of a hill oppofite Nafh-houfe, and near Fayland Inn, about feventy feet diameter a caftellet, and about three quarters of a mile farther eaftward is a fquare fort or exploratory turret about feventy feet fquare. Thefe were fortreffes or chefters all garrifoned, attendant on the principal ftation of Clifton and Abone, and the old roads from the camps on Leigh-down may be ftill traced through an orchard at the village of Leigh, and through Leigh-wood down to the river Avon at Sea-mills; on the Banks of which was the Roman fummer ftation, occupying the heights on both fides the Avon down to Sea-mills, from whence the whole with great propriety was called Abone: —a ftation which for fecurity, by having a view and command of the country and of the rivers Avon and Severn, could no where be chofen more properly by this military and politic people. And by erecting other camps at Henbury, Almonfbury, &c. they completely fortified the Severn and Avon, agreeable to Tacitus's defcription; who, lib. xii. Ann. fays, " the General Oftorius prepares to difarm the " fufpected Britons, and to keep or comprehend the rivers Avon * and Severn " fenced with camps." Baxter fays, in Gloff. " Antona Tacitor dicitur flumen Abona quod aquas calidas feu Badixam præterfluit etiamfi plurima fuerunt per univerfam Britanniam etfi minoris notæ."

Thus fituated, the Romans lived in garrifon here in fummer, and in winter chiefly under the hills, for a great extent of country. They were fecured from any invafion from the Britons on the South fide by their camps and fences on the hills, with the river Severn in the front, the banks of the Avon on both fides, and a fruitful vale in their poffeffion, guarded by little agrarian camps. Here they had a ready fupply of water, food for their cattle, and corn for themfelves. A ftone with a hole in the middle, a little handmill-ftone with which they ufed to grind their corn is ftill preferved, found at Stokeleigh camp; and the hilt of an old fword was found there. As this was the direct road to Caerwent from the Aquæ Solis or Bath, fo doubtlefs there muft have been a great and frequent communication acrofs the river Severn at this place with the ftation at Caerwent, after the conqueft of the Silures, &c. by Oftorius. It appears, that

the

hath many of thefe coins at prefent, and has been fo obliging as to communicate feveral to the Author of this Hiftory, and is a living witnefs of Chatterton the father's fpeaking about them, and faying that they were found near Ken-moor; a proof of his having fome tafte for antiquities.

* *Aufonem Authore Camdeno.* —In Britifh language Avon is frequently contracted into *Aun*, *An*, or *Un*, as is obferved by the Rev. Mr. Whitaker, in his elegant Hiftory of Manchefter: fo that it is not improbable that the Romans formed Antonam from Avon. Horfely calls Antonam the Avon; and p. 33, fays, " Oftorius we find with his army upon the rivers Severn and Avon, and hereabouts the body of his army, for the moft part, feems to have lain."

the Britifh towns were all connected with, or fituated nigh, the Roman ftations, as before obferved, and antiquaries have been critically nice in pointing
out their connection and fituation; except thofe towns which were formed into
colonies from the beginning, and therefore no camps attendant on them.

Under the hill of Clifton, nigh to their ftation Abone, lay Caer Oder nant
Avon, (Caer Brito,) or Briftol, not a mile Eaft from and juft under the Roman
camps. And Horfely obferves, p. 464, " a Roman ftation may be at a mile
or two diftance, and yet the town may have arifen out of its ruins." Lipfius,
in his Commentary on Polibius, lib. v. p. 9, where he is treating of the Roman
camps, fays, " the winter camps were more accurately, and with greater
works conftructed than the fummer; the former being calculated for longer
ftay, and more neceffaries therefore required. Thefe were ftationary, and
had more apartments and places belonging to them, as a place of arms,
workfhop, hofpital, and the like: indeed they were often built more like
towns, efpecially in the lower times of the empire, and where there were continual ftations and prætenturæ or outworks againft an enemy; fuch are on the
banks of rivers, of the Danube, Rhine, and Euphrates:" and then he adds,
" this is the origin and birth of many noble towns at this day,"—" hæc ea origo
& genitura nobilium aliquot hodie oppidorum." And an excellent obfervation it is, which leaves but little doubt of the city of Briftol, as well as many
other cities, deriving their origin from the camps of this polifhed military
people in their neighbourhood.

It is alfo well obferved by Horfely, in his Effay on Antonine's Itinerary,
in the Britannia Romana, p. 393, " how careful the Romans were to have
their ftations placed near a river, and there was no fituation they feemed fo
fond of as a lingula, near the confluence of a larger and fmaller river. If we
run along a military way, we are almoft fure to meet with a ftation whenever
we meet with a river, at any reafonable diftance from a preceding ftation."—
" The places alfo mentioned in the Itinerary feem generally to be caftra ftativa,
and there are generally rubbifh, lime, and remains of buildings, in fuch ftations as thefe. For befides the fort or citadel, garrifoned by Roman foldiers
or auxiliaries, there was ufually a town adjacent, which in all likelihood was
moftly inhabited by the Britons."

How well thefe obfervations of Mr. Horfely agree with the camps at Clifton
and the city of Briftol in the neighbourhood, is very obvious to any one; nor
is it an improbable conjecture, that the very name Caër Brito, (the Britifh city,)
might at firft be given to it for diftinction, as inhabited by the Britons, under
the protection and government of the Romans in their ftation near it.

Although

Although thefe curious remains of antiquity are within a mile of Briftol, yet little or no attention has ever been paid to them hitherto by a bufy and commercial people, wholly engaged in other purfuits; and what is more to be admired, they have been paffed by unnoticed by Cambden, Gale, and other writers. If the more obvious antiquities fhould be fo carelefsly overlooked, it is no wonder the fecret whifpers of tradition fhould be difregarded; though fuch traditions, however mixt with fable, do often lead to the difcovery of truth. Of this kind is the following ftory, recorded by Sir Robert Atkins in his Hiftory of Glocefterfhire.

" Before the port of Briftol was fettled in Frome river, there feems to have
" been a difpute, whether a place called Sea-mills was not as convenient a port
" as the other, feveral large and fmall fhips having been built there. This
" occafioned the extravagant fabulous ftory concerning St. Vincent and Goram,
" whom the ftory makes to be mighty giants, and that they contended which way
" the rivers Avon and Froom fhould vent themfelves into the Severn: if the port
" of Sea-mills had been judged more convenient, then Goram had prevailed,
" becaufe his hermitage was at Weftbury, on the fide of the brook Trim, which
" runs to Sea-mills. But the port of Froom being thought more advantage-
" ous, therefore the miracle relates, that St. Vincent clave the rocks afunder,
" and fo gave paffage to the rivers, becaufe thofe rocks derive their name
" from a chapel there, dedicated to that faint."

This feems to take its rife from fome reality, and may have truth for its foundation, though obfcured by fable and fuperftition. The Roman coins, old foundations of walls, bricks, tiles, &c. dug up here, efpecially in making the great dock at Sea-mills, fhew it to have been a place inhabited by that military people; having feveral camps (caftra æftiva) or entrenched pofts on the high hills of St. Vincent and the oppofite rocks, at Henbury, and other places in the neighbourhood. The Romans in time having deferted their ftation of Abone, on the banks of the river Avon, and the port and harbour here in the river Trim, where their gallies for paffing over by water to Caër-went their next ftation lay; the port of Briftol, Caër Nante Avon, (the city in the vale of Avon river) flourifhed, and became a great city in its ftead: Goram, the ftrong champion of the river Trim, (or the ftrong warlike Romans there) no longer keeping that ftation; and St. Vincent (or the civilized, religious, converted Britons under his patronage) fettling the port of Briftol at the more convenient conflux of the two rivers, the Avon and the Froom; which, in thofe times, could not but be attributed to the interpofition of a faint, who had a chapel and hermitage on the fummit of Clifton rock, (of

which

which fee before William of Worcefter, p. 13.) But it would add greatly to our fuppofition of the Abone of the Romans being at this place, if it fhould appear upon examination that the Roman road, betwixt Aquæ Solis (Bath) and their next ftation Venta Silurum (Caerwent), lay in this direction: and that the diftances of the miles betwixt the two ftations fhould exactly anfwer, both in Antonine's Itinerary and in Richard of Cirencefter. This would be a great confirmation of the truth, worthy of the nicest enquiry, efpecially as that Iter xiv. of Antonine has been fo much difputed: — *& adhuc fub judice Lis eft.*

Dr. Stukely, in his Itin. Curios. p. 144, v. 1, gives the fourteenth Iter of Antonine thus: Ab Ifca ad Callevam M. P. c. iii. fic.

Ifca Leg. 11 *Aug.* - - -	Caerleon.	
Venta Silurum, - - - -	Caerwent, -	ix M. P.
Trajectus, - - - - -	Oldbury, -	ix M. P.
Abone, - - - - - -	Henbury, -	ix.
Aquæ Solis, - - - - -	Bath, - -	vi.
Verlucio, - - - - -	Hedington,	xx.
Cunetio, - - - - - -	Marlborough,	x.
Spinas, - - - - - -	Newbury,	xv.
Vindomia, - - - - -	Silchefter, -	x.
Calleva Attrebatum, - - -	Farnham, -	xv.

and is of opinion with Dr. Gale, that Trajectus and Abone are tranfpofed. It is very remarkable he makes Abone to be Henbury, which indeed was one of the camps dependent on their ftation of Abone. — Where in the Itinerary of Antonine and Richard of Cirencefter, the rivers ad Abone, ad Sabrinam, are mentioned; the Romans might have only ftrong camps by thofe rivers, and before the towns and cities were fully built; which were afterwards raifed by the Britons near thofe camps, which ferved as inns and defenfible pofts to the Romans in their journies acrofs the rivers to their other cities or ftations, as obferved by the judicious Doctor, in his obfervations on Richard of Cirencefter. It is mentioned in Somner on forts and pofts (p. 38.) in Kent, that the numerals in Antonine are often wrong, and not to be relied on: " there is not " much heed (fays he) to be given to the diftances there, being (as fome have obferved) often miftaken;" therefore if the beginning and end of the Iter be well known and fet right, the intermediate places may be eafily made out by camps, coins found, or Roman remains, as well as by rivers, roads, and fituation. But the Doctor, in his account of Richard of Cirencefter, makes fome alterations in the names, and interprets the eleventh Iter of

Richard

Richard thus. — From Aquæ Solis, Bath, by the Julian-ſtreet to Menapia: thus in Richard, Iter xi. Ab aquis per viam Julian Menapiam uſque Sic.

Ad Abonam M. P. vi. Sabrinam vi. unde Trajectu intras in Britanniam ſecundam et ſtationem Trajectus M. P. iii. Venta Silurum ix. ubi fuit Aaron Martyr; Iſca Silurum ix. Tibiæ Amni M. P. vii. Bovio xx. Nido xv. Leucario xv. ad Vigeſſimum xx. ad Menapiam xix. ab hac urbe per triginta M. P. Navigas in Hyberniam. To which Dr. Stukely aſſigns the following names.

Aq. Solis, - - - - -		Bath.
Ad Alone for *Abone,*	vi. -	Olland, near Kainſham, Gloceſterſhire.
Ad Sabrinam, - -	vi. -	Auſt upon Severn.
Statio Trajectus, -	iii. -	Tydenham or Chepſtow.
Venta Silurum, } *Stipendiaria,* }	- ix. -	Caerwent, Monmouthſhire.
Iſca Silurum, } *Colon. leg Aug.* }	- ix. -	Caerleon.
Tibia Amnis, - -	vii. -	Caerdiff.
Bovium, - - -	xx. -	Cowbridge, Glamorganſhire.
Nidum, - - -	xv. -	Neath.
Leucarium, - -	xv. -	Loghor.
Ad Vigeſſimum } *Lapidem,* }	- xx. -	Narboth caſtle.
Menapa, - - -	xix. -	St. David's.

To make this agree with Antonine's Iter and it proves Abone in that is tranſpoſed and ſhould be placed before Trajectus, I would interpret it thus

Aq. Solis, - - - -		Bath.
Ad Abone, - -	vi. -	To the ſtation at Clifton on the river Avon.
Ad Sabrinam, -	vi. -	The Severn.
Trajectus, - -	iii. -	Portiſhead camp on the point.
Statio Trajectus,	- -	Sudbrook ſquare camp the place of landing on the other ſide in going to
Venta Silurum -	ix. -	Caerwent.

Here the ſix miles at Abone is demonſtrably a wrong numeral; it ſhould be xi. which exactly make the miles the ſame as in Antonine.

The diſtance from Bath through Hanham to the ſtation at Clifton, may be reckoned about eleven or twelve computed miles: and the other intermediate diſtances agreeing with each other, we need not be too curious about the names of the ſtations in Richard's time, as they might alter; but both the

diſtances

diſtances and ſtations agree in bringing the road through or near to Briſtol, in fixing one at Abone next to it, and proceeding to one common Tra‑jeſtus and ſo to Caerwent: whether any likelier places proved to be Roman by ſo many camps coins and other antiquities can be found, muſt now be ſub‑mitted to the judgment of every candid enquirer. Cale, Horſely and Stukely take us to Oldbury on the Severn as the only Trajeſtus, quite a circuitous road in no reſpeſt anſwering to the order of the places, ſtill leſs to the diſtances, nor to the courſe of the country, to which the road tends. There may be errors in the numerals, which appear too clearly, neither is ex‑aſtneſs pretended ; but we cannot err as to the right road pointed out in both Itineraries, and as to the beginning and end of the Iter, which are plain enough. Leland indeed ſays in Colleſt. Tam corruptum eſt &c. " This Itinerary of Antonine or whoſe ever it be, is ſo corrupt, as to require ſome Apollo to decypher it, for many names are miſpelt, the order of the places and numbers inverted and vary in different copies, being ſet out of their places." This granted, it muſt breed ſtrange confuſion ; but if we are certain as to the beginning and end of an Iter, whatever differences there may be in the number of miles or order of the places, we cannot err much in purſuing the direſt road, open and uninterrupted as it is with hills ; and this line of road can no where be ſo proper and ‑eligible as through the Roman camp at Briſtol and their ſtation there in their paſſage over to Caerwent. To ſuppoſe with Cambden and others, that Trajeſtus meant Oldbury, or Newenham with Baxter, and Abone to be Alvington or Avington, can have little ſhew of probability. It contradiſts the order of places ſo much, it does not in any degree coincide with the diſtances ſet againſt each, and makes ſuch unrea‑ſonable allowances in the computation as leaves us in the wildeſt uncertainty : abſolute certainty and demonſtration muſt not be inſiſted on ; but it may be left to every impartial enquirer, whether in general thoſe are not moſt probably the real places deſigned in the Itineraries above, where the diſtances are in the neareſt conformity with thoſe ſet down ; where Roman ſtations can be proved to have exiſted, even now to be traced by old encampments and coins found therein, and where the ſtraiteſt road to the place lies. But to go from Bath to Oldbury in Gloceſterſhire, or from Abone at Clifton ‑thither and then over the Severn to Beachly as the Trajeſtus, and ſo over the Wye to Caer‑went, would be ſuch a diverſion of the road as is ſcarce credible.

The fourteenth Iter of Antonine may be explained thus, Iter alio Itinere ab Iſca callevam uſque m. p. C. iii.

D

Ab. Iſca,

Ab Ifca, - - - - - - - - - Carleon.

Venta Silurum, M. P. ix. - - - - Caerwent.

Trajectus, tranfpofed for Abone, M. P. ix. The paffage over the water, or
to Portifhead.

Abone M. P. ix. - - - - - - - The ftation and camps at Clifton.

Aq. Solis, M. P. vi. - - - - - - Bath xi.

Verlucione, M. P. xv. - - - - - Lacock, where and at Leckham,
Naifh Hill and Notton, coins
have often been found.

Cunetione, M. P. xx. - - - - - Marlborough on the Kennet.

Spinis, M. P. xv. - - - - - - Speen.

Calleva, M. P. xv. - - - - - - Silchefter or Wallingford.

The fum total prefixed is one hundred and three miles, but the particulars
amount to but ninety eight, which proves the numbers to be erroneous. If
eleven be the numeral at Aq. Solis, it would make up the one hundred and three
miles of the Iter, and it would come very near to the true diftance betwixt
Bath and Abone at the Clifton camp, and the nine miles over the Severn from
Caerwent would be as near the truth as can be expected.

Roger Gale, who communicated to Mr. Hearn an account of the four
Roman Ways, has in addition to that letter publifhed in Leland's Collectanea,
p. 275, v. 6. 2 ed. fome obfervations concerning the Weftern Avon—and
fays there, " that beneath Gloccfter we have but one ftation, Trajectus, at
" Oldbury;"—but quære's, " whether the old names, or fituation of their
" ftations on the Weftern Avon are yet retrieved by us, which I fufpect muft
" be left to time, and the obfervations of thofe, who are better acquainted with
" that country than I am, to determine."—This is no lefs candidly than judicioufly remarked; for Trajectus at Oldbury has been ever looked upon as the
only Roman ftation here by Cambden, &c. yet it now comes out, that the Romans in their journies into Wales or Caerwent, might and did fix other ftations,
particularly this at Abone and Clifton, on the banks of the Avon, near which
was the Trajectus in a ftrait road from Bath or Aquæ Solis, to Caerwent,
anfwering nearly as we fee to the m. p. or miles fet againft each in Antonine's
Itinerary, which no other Trajectus does.—Oland, or Oldland, near Hanham, though no traces there afcertain it, has been conjectured by fome to be
one, about nine miles from Bath; but from Abone, Sea-Mills or Portifhead, the
Trajectus acrofs the Severn about nine miles, is direct to Caerwent:—The
other Roman way from Bath to Oldbury, being over the hilly ground of Landf-
down pailing near Wick, (*Vicus,*) where Roman relicks were found juft under
the

the hill by R. Haynes, Efq; — fo by Pucklechurch to Bury-hill, on the Froom; whence the road was to Almonfbury, and to Auft or Oldbury, and over the Severn to Lydney, where is a great camp, (delineated in Archœol. v. 5.) near the borders of that river; and fo into Herefordfhire, &c.

It appears hence the Romans had more than one Trajectus acrofs the Severn; but to Caerwent they could have none fo convenient and direct as this at Abone near Briftol: — if they croffed at Auft for that ftation ftrait to the other fide to Beachly, or to Tidenham on the fame fhore, they muft have had a fecond trouble to ferry over another dangerous and rapid river the Wye, where Chepftow Bridge now ftands, or muft have failed down the Severn from Auft fome way till they came on a line with Caerwent, many miles out of their direct courfe.

Horfely, p. 469, fays, " the military way running Eaftward from Caerwent is large and remarkable: I obferved it to leave the high way to Chepftow, and inclining to the South to bend its courfe towards the Severn, but I had not opportunity to trace it to the fide of the river. — The name Old Paffage may not have fo diftant a retrofpect as the Roman Trajectus, but yet I conclude from the courfe of the military way which I obferved myfelf, that the Roman paffage has been below the mouth of the Wye, and I fcarce think the landing place on the South fide can be near fo high as Oldbury, though this is generally fuppofed; and for this reafon, Oldbury has got the name of Trajectus, a tranfpofition of names being now more generally admitted." — Had Mr. Horfely continued his rout on the military way to the bank of the Severn, he would then have found the grand camp of Sudbrook to be the ftation, where they croffed the Severn to Abone the other fide near Briftol.

It is worthy of obfervation, that the little river Throggy, on the bank of which lies the great fquare camp Sudbrook, opens here into the Severn, in a direction almoft oppofite to the Briftol Avon on the other fide, as appears on viewing it acrofs Kingroad, Penpoll near Shirehampton rifing to the view very diftinct; the mouth of the Throggy forms ftill a kind of pill for veffels, and the river itfelf, though now fmall and filled up, was evidently once navigable up to the city of Caerwent; the bed of the river ftill appearing open, broad, and deep in many places, fo that the communication with the Aquæ Solis or Bath and the Abone near Briftol and Caerwent, was direct, free and well guarded; and doubtlefs fuch a well peopled city as Caerwent evidently was, the feat of Roman arts and arms, grandeur and luxury, held great correfpondence acrofs the Severn with the other ftations and commercial intercourfe with all the country they poffeffed. — In the year 1777, a teffelated pavement

was

was difcovered in an orchard at Caerwent, about 21 feet long by 18 broad, made by fmall fquare pieces of ftone about half an inch or more fquare, inlaid in an elegant form in waving lines and twifted chainlike fhapes, with a very large rofe in the center of the floor, furrounded with a circle charged with ten fmaller rofes, painted with four colours, red, yellow, white, and blue; the fide-wall was plaiftered fmooth and painted red. It feems to have been the ftate room or tent of the Prefeƌ of the *Legio fecunda Aug.* an infcription on a ftone dug up here was, " *Julia Effeunda vixit annos* xxxv.

Upon the Romans leaving their ftation here and at Caerwent and Caerleon, and upon their departure from the ifland of Britain, the cities and manfions on both fides the Severn, which grew up and flourifhed in peace under their ftriƌ difcipline and government, became in a ftate of confufion, being terribly harraffed by the inteftine divifions of the Britons themfelves, and afterwards by foreigners called in to their aid. Caerwent and Caerleon encompaffed with brick-walls, and celebrated for their lofty palaces and temples, Roman baths, teffelated pavements, hypocaufta and theaters, as well as a vaft concourfe of merchants and learned men, fell under the general calamity : the firft dwindling into a place of no note but for the coins and Roman bricks and infcriptions ftill dug up there, the latter lying buried in its ruins, and *ipfæ periere ruinæ* ; — now it cannot be fuppofed the petty towns in their neighbourhood, Newport and Chepftow, which rofe on their ruins, (being alfo as much, if not more expofed,) fhould receive and afford a fecure retreat and afylum to the numerous inhabitants, as well merchants as others, of thefe populous cities, which muft have had then the greateft commerce and free trade of any in the Weft of England, to fupply the conveniences and luxuries of fuch a multitude of polifhed citizens; — no; they would naturally apply to places and ftations of greater fafety and well adapted to trade ; and where they could enjoy, uninterrupted, a free navigation and fecurity of commerce. It may therefore be believed, and with the greateft probability if not certainty, that they immediately fled from their difturbed condition at Caerleon and Caerwent, and tranfported themfelves direƌly acrofs the Severn at Kingroad, to Briftol, then a city alfo under the proteƌion of the Romans at Clifton and Leigh in its neighbourhood; and the well-known ftation of the Romans here, and ufual intercourfe acrofs the Severn, pointed out to them the propriety of their choice, and the fecurity they fhould enjoy here unmolefted.

After they had once feated themfelves here, and the Romans had left their fortified ftation at Clifton, the Britons confining on the Severn and in its neighbourhood foon flocked hither and increafed the eftablifhment of the city : —

The

The colonies the Romans had at the camps of Henbury, Almondſbury, Old Abby, Sodbury, Hinton-Durham, and other adjacent places, ſupplied many inhabitants that did not follow the Romans, but contributed to the ſpeedy advance and population of the city. Briſtol is juſtly reputed to be a ſecure place in times of tumult and popular commotions, which we know from hiſtory to have been the caſe of Britain when the Romans left it, as appears from their complaints ſent to Rome afterwards, of which Gildas gives a moſt pathetic and lamentable account.

Where then could the merchant, the tradeſman, the rich or the poor mechanie, find a place of greater ſafety in ſuch times than Briſtol, not liable to be ſuddenly ſurpriſed and attacked, the Avon being its guard on the Somerſet ſide, and the Froom winding round it formed it into an iſland, a very natural and moſt effeƐtual defence; and the Severn in ſome reſpeƐts, with its ſeveral fortreſſes and entrenehed poſts, formed a diſtant defence and barrier on the North and Weſt ſide; and at the ſame time by its free communication by water with other places and the ſea, was the beſt adapted for a convenient habitation and enjoying all the advantages of commerce, and thereby a quick ſupply of every neceſſary of life.

Beſides what has been advanced of the Roman camps and ſtations here, under which the city of Briſtol roſe and flouriſhed, it muſt be added, that it is highly probable that military people occupied the very hills within the precinƐts of the city ;— as experienced Generals they would poſſeſs themſelves of all the heights near their principal ſtations — accordingly we find Roman coins have been dug out of the earth on St. Michael's-hill, within the city, by Thomas Tyndale, Eſq; at the Fort, when he formed and walled in a large garden there. The coins were of Conſtantine, Conſtantius Gordian, and Tetricus ;— and in the field behind the Montague Inn on Kingſdown, in 1780, was found four feet deep, a coin of Conſtantine, with the following inſcription, *Imp. C. Conſtantinus p. F Aug.* a laüreated head:— on the reverſe, a figure of the ſun, with *Soli InviƐto Comiti.*

But both St. Michael's-hill and Brandon-hill have undergone ſuch alterations by time, large fortifications and entrenched poſts having been made there in later days, eſpecially in the great rebellion 1641, that their ſurfaces have often taken a new form, and the appearance of the ancient entrenchments is loſt; and every veſtige of Roman antiquity muſt neceſſarily be deſtroyed and effaced, the coins found being now the only proofs of their having once occupied theſe hills.

As

As it was then from the Roman camps in its neighbourhood, and the road betwixt Bath and Caerwent paffing this way, Briftol may be faid to have dedu_ced its firft origin,* the Britons living there under their protection and govern_ment. So from the downfal of thofe populous cities of Caerwent and Caerleon, upon the retreat of the Romans from Britain, it flourifhed and increafed in a moft rapid manner by a great acceffion of new inhabitants from acrofs the Severn ; who foon enlarged its commerce, and fupplied thofe conveniences and luxuries, with which the numerous and polite inhabitants of thofe cities in Wales ufed to be fupplied; and upon the coming of the Saxons, who afterwards occupied the ftrong camps and pofts deferted by the Romans, (as Saxon coins dug up there alfo fhew,)—Briftol we fhall find foon became the grand feaport and mart of the Weft Saxon kingdom, agreeable to what Leland has faid of it, " Aucta eft a Saxonibus,"—it was increafed by the Saxons—who ufually built on Roman foundations, and occupied places deferted by them.

If it fhould be farther afked, at what particular period of time it was founded? To anfwer this queftion with precifion may not perhaps be in any one's power, involved as it is in fo much obfcurity, and difficult from the remotenefs of the time, it can only be faid to have taken its rife, beyond doubt, from the Roman ftation Abone; growing up by degrees from it, and at laft being blended with it, while the Romans ufed to pafs the Severn to Caerwent;—rifing within the century after the birth of Chrift, and advancing in population, trade and grandeur from that time, keeping pace with the Romans, while here, and after their leaving the ifland, increafing by a vaft acceffion of inhabitants from every quarter.

C H A P.

---

* Though I fuppofe this to have been the firft origin of the city of Briftol, it is not to be omitted, that there is a traditionary account mentioned alfo by Rofs, Leland, and in William of Worcefter's manufcripts ; and a manufcript by Ricaut, in the Chamber of Briftol, that Brennus founded Briftol ;—but as the ftory of Brennus and Bellinus is not well authenticated, and there is little hiftorical evidence for it, like the accounts of Jeffery of Monmouth, of Brute and his Trojans coming hither, deemed all equally fabulous, it will be needlefs to purfue the enquiry.

C H A P.   II.

Of B R I S T O L *in the* S A X O N *and* N O R M A N *Times.*

HAVING inveftigated the origin and firft rife of the city at the Roman-Britifh period, I proceed next with the Saxon and Norman accounts.

A manufcript difcourfe on Briftol, which has the marks of great antiquity, faid to be wrote by Turgot, a Saxon, in *Saxonnes Latyn*, muft be acknowledged to be of great weight; and as the writer lived to give the following account of Briftol not long after the very time, in which Cambden afferts Briftol to have firft rifen, it will be a full confutation of that eminent antiquarian. I fhall add the fame Turgot's " account of auncient coynes found at and near Briftowe, with the hyftorie of the fyrft coynynge by the Saxonnes, alfo an account of monumental incriptions, faid to be done from the Saxon ynto Englyfhe by T. Rowlie." This Turgot is faid to be a Briftol man, was prior of Durham, afterwards Bifhop of St. Andrews in Scotland; he writ a hiftory of Scotland, alfo chronicles of Durham; annals of his own time, and the life of K. Malcolm. It is faid he wrote alfo a Saxon poem called, the Bloody Battle of Haftynges.

All the works of Turgot have never been publifhed; efpecially the following curious account of Briftol, faid in a very old manufcript to be tranflated by T. Rowlie out of Saxon into Englifh, now in my poffeffion. Turgot * it appears was prior of Durham in 1088, having fucceeded his preceptor Aldwin who died 1087 in that priory, and was confecrated Bifhop of St. Andrews in 1108, and was buried at Durham feven years after 1115.

" Sect. II. of Turgoteus. — Strange as it maie feem that there were Walles to Radclefte, yet fulle true ytte is beynge the Walles of Brightrycus pallace, & in owre daies remainethe there a fmall piece neie Efelwynnes Towre. I conceive not it coulde be fquare, tho Tradytyon fo faieth: the Inhabiters wythyn the Walle had ryghte of Tolle on the Ryvers Severne & a part of Avon. Thus much of Radclefte Walles. On whych paffage of Turgot, T. Rowlie

fubjoins

* Leland in Collectan V. ii. 512, 538, gives an account of Turgot *(quodam Clerico Turgeto)* taken out of a manufcript book, of the Bifhops of Lindisfarm.

fubjoins the following Emendal or Note:—Hence myghte be the reafonne whie the Indabiters of Radclefte callyd much of the River Avon, Severne; becaufe formerlie reckoned in theyre Tollege with the Severne, as Inhabiter of Radclefte have I ufed Severne for Abona or Avon, & accounted Severne to reeche over anent Radclefte Strete.

" Sect. III. of Turgotus. — Nowe to fpeake of Bryghtftowe, yttes Walles & Caftelle beynge the fayreft buyldinge, of ytte I fhalle fpeake fyrfte. The pryncipale Streets meete in forme of a Crofs, & is a goode patterne for the Cityes of Chryftyannes. Brightrycus fyrft ybuylden the Walles in fafhyon allmofte Square wythe four Gates — Ellè Gate, Baldwynnes or Leonardes Gate, Froome or the Water Gate and Nycholas or Wareburgha's, fo cleped from Wareburga of the Houfe of Wulverus Konynge of Mercia (& here be ytte noted that Brightftowe was fometymes inne the hondes of the Mereyes fome_ tyme of the Weft Saxonnes, tyll Bryghtricus walled ytte, ande fyxede ytte for ever to hys). Thys Wareburga was baptyzed bye Saynte Warburgus, & had a Chyrche ybuilte to her by the Bryftowans — Almoft arounde the Walles was Watere & fowre Brydges or fordes. Elle forde, Santforde or Halleforde beynge where Tradition fayes Saynte Warburgus paffyd; Frome Forde & Bald_ wynnes's Forde, beynge where Tradytyonne faies Sayente Baldwynne fleen the Danes that fled from Bultyngeatune. The Walles have fuffred alteratyon fynce Edward Sonne of Alfrydus Magnus A. D. DIVG-XV.* ybuylden the the Walles & newly ybuylden the Caftle — beeynge the goodlycfte of the five ybuilden on Abone Bankes & a greete checke to the Danes: he caufed the Gate neare Baldwynnes forde to be callyde Baldwynes before Leonardes. The Caftle thus ybuilden ytte was yeven in fure keepynge to Ella a Mercyan fynce hee routted the Danes at Watchette wythe hys Bryftowans: and at Wykewarre with hys owne Menne and thofe of Wykewarre, at Canyngan & Alluncengan† with his Bryftowans. At the lafte place he conquered: but Eng_ lande payde dearlie for the Battle, he dyed in Bryftowe Caftle of hys Woundes. He was the ftaye of the Wefte and the Guardyan of Glouceftre, whyche after hys Dethe was pyteoufllie facked—hee gave Name to Ellingham ande Eleceftre. Coernicus fucceeds in the Caftle, but was not fo fortunate as hys predeceffoure, affordyinge ne Helpe to others, havyng Employmente enowe to keepe hys owne. In his days were Bathe & Glouceftre brente: the pagannes affayled Briftow ande fome entrynge Coerne commandynge alle the fordes to be cutte, whereby all the Dacyans whyche entered were forflayne or drowned. Inne his daies and the reygu of Kynnge Aedelftan was twayne of Coiners in Bryghtftowe. From hym faie fome came Corne-Street‡—he builden anew

Wareburgas

---

* 915.   † So in the original.   ‡ Called old Corn-ftreet in antient writings I have feen.

Wareburgas Chyrche and added thereunto Houfen for preeftes. He was brave and dyd his beft agaynft the paganes. After hym was Harwarde, who was fleyn in Redcleft fyde fyghteynge againfte the paganes, Whoe gotte ne honoure in fighte lofynge three Capytaynes Magnus Hurra & Ofbraye & fleying the feeld — Then Smallaricus, Vincent & Adelwyn — then Egwyn, from whome the Street Egwynne Streete was ybuildenne. Likewyfe in his tyme was the greate Earthquake; manye houfen in Bryftowe fallene downe & the Fyre levyne enfyrede Radclef Strete — Shortely after on the vyolente enfeefynge of the Crowne bie Ethelrede, an Infurrectyon happened in Bryght_ ftowe whych Egwyuno appeafed. After him Aylwardus, Adelbryghte, Am_ ftuarde, Algarre, And thenne Leofwynne Sonne of Godwynne Erle of Kente. Upon the afcendynge of Edwarde Confeffour the Natyon was all turnyd French; ynne the nynthe Yeere of the reigne of Edwarde beeynge m. o. xxxxxx. Leofwynne bye thys Charter badde Bryftowe.

Iche Edwarde Konynge, Yeven Bryftoe Caftellynge
Unto the keepynge, Off Leofwynne de Godwynne
Of Clytoe Kyndlynge ; Of Ballarde and Battell
Le Bartlowe * for Cattayle
Alle that on the watters flote, To take Brugbote ?
Eke at ye Stowe of Wickwarre breme, And yttes Sylver Streeme
Toe take Havenyche, As Eldermanne of Iche
To hys owne Ufe, At his goode Thewes
Wytnefs owre Marke before Ralph Dunftan & Egwyn
Of owre reygne and Eafter Month Yeere & Daie uyno:

Thus had hee the Caftel; & hys fadre Broders, & the Cityfens of Bryghtftowe ande Nobilytye of Kente entered ynto a folemne League agaynfte the Lon- doners, Who were almofte alle frenchmenne, makynge the fayde League at Bryghtftowe. Inne M. L. 1. the menne of Dover & Kente beynge murdred by the Bullonyans, Godwynne & his Kentifhmen Harolde & the Weftfaxons came to Bryftoe to Leofwynne, Who receevd them kyndly ynto hys Caftelle & fet forwarde wyth them to Gloucefter & after the appoyntment came agayne to Briftowe but throughe treacheree the expedytyone myffede: Whereupon Kynge Harolde & Leofwyne came wyth Swayne, Toftye, Wolnothus & Gyrthe to Bryghftowe & Shypped for Hybernia: ande nowe bee ytte noted that When Gryffithe Kynge of South wales & the Irifh pyrates attack'd them Leofwynne ftroke Galfride Kurke Capytaine to the grounde ande toke hym pryfoner leavyng his armie Where by the South wallians retyrd to the Coun-

E   try

* Q. If Berklaw or Bartalaw — vid. Spelman.

try withe greete loffe, Leofwyne entreated Kurke kyndlie & let hym departe to Hibernie Where upon he invited hym to Hybernie, Whither he went with 280 Bryflowans."

Such is the account of our city faid to be given by Turgotus. Whatever may be objected to the authenticity of this manufcript, the author can only fay, it has the marks of being genuine, and is faithfully tranfcribed from the original parchment, not without great difficulty to decypher it, on account of the palenefs of the ink and peculiarity of the character.

It is very certain, the Saxons, after the retreat of the Romans and confe-quent divifions and wars of the Britons, greatly increafed the city both in extent of buildings and in population, and made it a place of greater commerce and refort of fhipping than it had ever had in the Roman-Britifh times. It lay more fecure from Danifh invafions by its inland fituation, not to be ap-proached but by a long and difficult navigation up the Briftol Channel; and this accounts for the little mention made of it by our hiftorians, as not diftin-guifhed in the Danifh wars: though they tell us, the Danes came as far as the Holmes, where they fuffered a defeat and famine. Though fome manufcripts infinuate, that this city did not efcape their piracy and ravage.

The Saxons diftinguifhed Briftol fo early with their notice, that Edward, the fon of Alfred, built a caftle here for its defence; and Alfred, in the fifth year of his reign, is faid, in Hollingfhead, to have driven the Danes from Exeter to Dartmouth, where they took fhipping, and difperfed others, " fome of whom fled to Chippenham and fome to Briftol." And in the *Chronologia vitæ Alfredi*, and in the Saxon Chronicle, we find the Danes fpoiling all the country on the Severn, and making irruptions into various parts upon it; and there is no reafon to believe Briftol to have wholly efcaped.

An account at the end of Langtoff's Chronicle by Hearn, vol. ii. p. 465. fays, " the Danes landed near Brent in Somerfetfhire, but were put to flight, a great number drowned and flain by King Alfred, and others efcaped and fled to Woorle-hill, where they fortified themfelves, &c." There is to be feen at this day on the faid hill, a camp of wonderful ftrength, with many ag-gera; whether Danifh, or not, deferves the attention of the curious.

There are many accounts of the Danes infefting Somerfetfhire, which about the year 900 was much expofed to their ravages, and greatly haraffed by fre-quent invafions of them; their fhips came up the Briftol Channel, and making defcents on the open and defencelefs towns, fpread terror and defolation wherever they came. In the year 878 they landed near Biddeford with thirty-three fail of fhips, and wafted the country with fire and fword; but they were

overcome

overcome by the victorious Alfred, their captain Hubba and 1200 men flain, whom they buried on the fhore near their fhips, and the place is fince called Hubbaftone. " In the 915, (fays Stow) a great navy of Danes failed about " the Weft Country, and landed in divers places, taking great preys, and " went to their fhips again. The King Edward fenior, (the fon of Alfred) " for ftrengthening the country, made a caftle at the mouth of the Avon."— That they certainly infefted this country as far as Briftol Avon, appears from the Saxon Chronicle. " And the Cyninge hæfde funden wyth him mon fat " with on futh-healfe Sæfrenn-muthan weftan from Wealum Eaft oth Afæne- " muthan, &c." i. e. " In the year 918 King Edward thought fit to difpofe " his army at the South part of the mouth of the Severn, from the Weft of " Wales towards the Eaft to the mouth of the Avon, that they might not dare " to infeft any where that part of his land: neverthelefs they withdrew them- " felves privily by night at two times, once in the eaftern part and at Watchet, " and another time at Porlock. But they were conquered both times, that " few remained but thofe only who fwam to their fhips. Then they fet down " at the ifle of Bradanrelic, (i. e. the Flat Holmes,) till they were in great " want of provifions, and many perifhed with hunger." *Henry of Huntingdon,* *l.* v. 11° *Edwardi fenioris.* " The King caufed the fhores of the Severn, on " the South part from Wales to the Avon, to be guarded, &c." and " that " it was at the ifland of Stepen, or Steep Holmes, they fuffered." Both are not far diftant from each other in the Briftol Channel below Kingroad, where the Briftol fhips lie at anchor.

The Anglo-Saxon kings and earls of Glocefter, the then lords or thanes of this country, long held this city under their protection and government, and received great advantages from the rents and profits of the town. Aylward Maew, or Sneaw, was lord of it before the Conqueft, mentioned in Leland's Itinerary. He was a Saxon nobleman of the greateft rank and fortune, defcended from Edward fenior, (the builder of the caftle, from whom he feems to have held Briftol by gift or inheritance.) About the year 900 he is faid to be *vir in armis ftrenuus,* (Lel. vol. vi. p. 82.) a man of great prowefs, and " Lorde of Brighteftowe, and founder of the monaftery of Cranbourne." His fon Algar, with his wife Algiva, fuceeeded to the honour of Glocefter and lordfhip of Briftol by right of inheritance; and Brictricus, the fon of Algar, after them. He, being a very rich man, refided much at Briftol, and diftin- guifhed it greatly.

Brictric, or Brightick, had great poffeffions, is called in Leland *viro prædi-* *viti;* he tranflated the body of King Æthelbert, buried privately on the banks

of

of the river Lugg, to Hereford. There is an Earl Brictrick mentioned in Leland's Collect. vol. i. p. 349, the brother of Edward Streona Duke of Mercia. I have in a manuscript a note of the genealogy of Earl Brictric, from Brictric King of the West Saxons. Little Froma and Cranbourn three hides was held (with other great estates,*) by our Earl Brictric, T. E. C. worth 12 l. per ann. : the name in Doomsday-book is sometimes wrote Brihtricus.

That Brictric was a great repairer, founder, or improver of Bristol, appears from some Latin verses taken from a chronicle of Tewksbury, quoted by Dugdale in Monasticon, vol. i. p. 161.

" Atque ego Brictanus ultimus ante conquestum Dominus
Hoc Templum fundo ; mihimet vere corde jucundo
Bristow construxi, *Honor fiat ut Crucifixi.*"

That Brictanus, or Bictanus, means Brictrict, or Bithric, is very certain from the order of the founders here recited. Brictric, or Bightric, was a name, *quod versu dicere nequis,* unfit for Latin verse. Brictric being a founder of the church of Tewksbury and at Bristow at the same time† proves, that it was he probably that first annexed a cell at Bristol, dedicated to St. James, to Tewksbury abbey, afterwards attributed to Robert Fitzhaymo, a Norman knight. — Aylward above-mentioned, in the time of King Athelstan, is said in Mr. Lant's manuscript to have been a principal founder at Bristol, which indeed received great improvement afterwards from most of the Anglo-Saxon earls of Glocester, who from him continued lords of it: it became afterwards a part of the honour of Glocester, and the castle here the *caput honoris Glocestriæ,* in the later Saxon times.

Thus the Saxons having driven away the Danes, and expelled the ancient British inhabitants of this city from their native seat here acrofs the Severn into Wales, the Caer Brito, or Bristol, of the Britons became Saxonised, and the place wholly in their possession ; and the West Saxons brought into subjection all these parts. And as they could not subdue the British spirit of our Romanised ancestors, they contented themselves with fixing their station here, possessing themselves of the city and strong Roman camps in its neighbourhood, (some Saxon coins in my possession having been found together with the Roman coins dug there.) They strengthened the Saxon government here by every politic step ; and by walling the town to a larger extent than before, and increasing its trade and shipping, it soon became more and more flourishing, whilst

* Of his great possessions, vid. Annals below.
† In an old grant to the abby of Tewksbury the rents (exitus) and tythes of Brigeston is mentioned to be paid to that abby. Vid. Sir Robert Atkins's History of Glocestershire.

whilſt Caerleon and Caerwent, ancient ſeaports, loſt their former gran_
deur, trade and importance, and from famous cities dwindled away into
obſcure towns, and Newport and Chepſtow roſe up in their ſtead.

In the time of Edward the Confeſſor, in the year 1051, (1043 ſay ſome)
* Harold and Leofwine the ſons of Earl Godwin, are mentioned by our
hiſtorians to have been proſcribed, and that coming to Briſtol, " They went
" aboard a ſhip that their brother Swayne had prepared for them and were
" carried into Ireland :" this confirms the account in the manuſcript hiſtory
of Turgot afore mentioned page 33, where the matter is more particularly
deſcribed. In 1063, Harold then Duke of Suſſex and Kent embarked with
his forces aboard a fleet at Briſtowe to invade Wales, to take revenge on
Griffyth King of Wales, between whom and Harold there was a great
enmity. †   .

Coins have been ever looked upon, as a proof of the dignity and antiquity
of the place where they are found. The Roman have been mentioned
before ; and the Saxons have alſo left here traces of themſelves by their coins.

Here I ſhall have recourſe to a curious colleſtion of coins and monumental
ſtones mentioned by Turgot, preſerved afterwards in the cabinet of Mr.
Canynge; and although the coins themſelves cannot be produced, yet an
account of them ſaid to be " drawen from the cabinet itſelf" by Thomas
Rowlie about 1460, in his own writing is ſtill extant. And as I would give the
real and genuine account of theſe coins in the Tranſlator's own words from
Turgot, I ſhall confine myſelf to a faithful and exaſt copy from the original
parchment manuſcript as follows, in which the ink and letters by time were
almoſt defaced, and leave the reader to judge of its authenticity.

" Of the auntiaunte forme of Monies carefullie gotten for Mayſter William
Canynge by mee Thomas Rowleie."

" Greete was the wyſdome of him who ſayde the whole worlde is to
ne one Creature, whereof every Man and Beaſte is a Member ; Ne Manne
lyveth therefore for hymſelf but for . hys fellow creature. Excellent and
Pythey was the ſayeing of Mr. Canynge that Trade is the ſoule of the
worlde, but Monie the ſoule of Trade, ande alaſſe Monie is nowe the
ſoule of Manie. The age when Metalles fyrſte paſſed for monie is unnoticed:
As Oxen and ſheepe is thoughten to have beene the moſte earlie Monie or
Change.

* Pono Haroldus & Leofwinus filii (Godwini) Briſtowam adeuntes Navem quam frater
Illorum Suanus ſibi pacaverat, conſcenderunt & in Hiberniam tranſveſti fuerunt — Sim. Dun.
p. 185. Haroldus & Leofwinus in Hiberniam transfretarunt Chron. Brompt p. 943 apud x
Script. Stows Annals by Horves. p. 95. 96.

† Florent. Wygorn. Alſo Turgot before p. 33.

Change. Butte ytte is ftylle more difficyle to fyx the fyrft tyme of ftampeying
ytte. Abrahame is fayde to have yeven Shekylls bie wayght: An Ebrewe
Writer faithe that in the Daies of Jofhua the Ebrewes enftamped theyre
Monies wythe the Symboles of the Tabernacle Veffylles, butte I thynke
the fyrfte enftampeyng came from Heathenne Ammuletts, whyche were
markyd wythe the Image of theyre Idolle, & preefts dyd carrie from Houfe
to Houfe begginge or rather demaundynge offeryngs for theyr Idolle — The
Ebrewes who fcorn'd not to learne Inyquytye frome theyr Captyves, &
vaynlie thynkynge as in other thyngs to copy other Natyons myghte take uppe
thys enfample Ande enftamepynge theyre Monie in the oulde tyme of Jofue
beyne maie happe one of the Idolatries mentyon'd in holie wrete. Examyne
into antiquytie & you wylie fynde the folk of Athens ftampyd an Owelette
the Byrde of Athene, the Sycylyans fyre the Symbole of theyre Godde Vul-
canne, theie of Ægypt a couchaunt Creeture wythe a Lyonnes Boddie & a
Hawkes heade Symbole of theyre Godde Ofyris: Butte to come to owre
owne Countrie: Oure fyrfte fathers the Bryttons ufyde yron & Braffe ryngs
fome round, fome fhapyd like an Egge: Eleven of thefe were founde in the
Gardenne of Galfrydus Coombe on Sainfte Mychaels Hylle, bie theyre dyf-
pofitionne in the grounde feemed to have been ftrunge onne a ftrynge, &
were alle marquede on Infyde thus *M* Lykewyfe is in Mayftre Canynges
Cabynet an Amulett of Brytifhe Charafters peerced at the Toppe. Julyus
Cæfarres Coynes were the fyrfte enftamped Monies yfede in Englande: after
whomme the Bryttonnes coyned as followes. Tenantius at Caer Britoe,
Cunobelyne at fundarie places, butte notte at Caer Brytoe. Arvyragus at
Caer Brytoe, Maryus at Caer Brytoe, Baffianus at Caer Brytoe, Syke was
the multitude of monies bie them coyned upon Vyftoryes & fykelyke that
neyther anie Kynge tyll Arthurres tyme coyned quantity of Metalles for
anie ufe nor dyd Arthuree make monie but a peece of Sylverie toe bé worne
rounde of thofe who han wonne Honnour in Batelles. * Edelbarte Kynge of
Kente

* Cambden fays Athelbred firft coined money in England, the penny weighed 3d. five
pennies made a fcilling, 48 fcillings their pound, 400 lib. a legacy for a King's daughter. 30
pennies a macus, mancufa a mark of filver, manca a fquare piece of gold value 30 pennies.

But the Saxon coins, names, weights and value, are the following according to Mr. Clarke's
Connexion of Roman, Saxon and Englifh coins.

Saxon Gold Coins.

Mancus - - - - -	wt. 54 gr.	6s.	of their money, —	9s.	od.	of ours.
Half Mancus - - - -	27	3s.	- - - - - -	4s.	6d.	
Later Mancus, ora						
and Anglo Saxon Shilling	22	1s.	- - - - - -	3s.		

Kente was the fyrſte Chryſtenned Kynge & coyner in Kent, Chaulyn or Ceaulynne of the Weſte Saxonnes, Arpenwaltus of the Eaſte Angles, Ætheldfryde of the north Humbres, And Wulferus of the Mercians. The Piece coynd by the Saxonnes was clepen pennyes thryce the Value of our pennyes. In Adelſtanes reygn were two Coyners in Bryghſtowe & one at Wyckewarre at which two places was made a peece yclepen twain penny.

Golde was not coyned tyll the tyme of Edwardus but Byzantes of Conſtantinople was in ure, ſome whereof contayned fower Markas or Mankas ſome two, ſome one & ſome leſs and more. . Robert Rouſe Erle of Glouceſter had hys mynte at Bryſtowe & coyned the beſt monie of anie of the Baronnes. Henrie Secundus graunted to the Lord of Briſtowe Caſtle the ryghte of Coynynge, & the coynynge of the Lord wente curraunte unto the Regne of Henricus the thyrde: the Coyns was onne one ſyde a Rampaunte Lyonne with ynne a Strooke or bende Sinyſter & on the other the arms of Brightſtowe.

Eke had the Maioure lybertie of coyneyng & did coyne ſeveral coynes, manie of whyche are in mie ſeconde rolle of monies — Kynge Henricus ſext, offred Mayſtre Canynge the ryghte of coynynge whiyche hee refuſed, whereupon Galfridus Ocamlus who was wyth Mayſter Canynge and mieſelf concerning the ſaide ryghte, ſaieth, " Naie bie St. Pauls Croſſe badde I ſuch an offre, I would coyne Lead & make ne Law, hyndrynge Hyndes takyng it." No Doubte (ſayde Mayſter Canynge) but you'd dyſpend Heaven to gette goulde, but I dyſpende Goulde to get Heaven.

This curious account is an exact tranſcript from the writing on vellum, which, having all the external marks of antiquity to give it the credit of an original, could not be paſſed by, however readers may differ in their opinions. If genuine and authentic, it proves,

1ſt. That beſides the authorities above recited for the Caer Brito of Nennius being the city Briſtow, Britiſh money was coined here with that name inſcribed, though hitherto unnoticed.

2dly.

Silver Saxon Coins.

Shilling at 5d.	-	-	112 gr.	5d.	of their money,	1s.	2d. ¼ of ours.
Ditto at 4d.	-	-	90	4d.	- - -		11d. ¼
Thrimſa	-	-	67	3d.	- - -		8d. ¼
Penny or Sceata	-	-	22 ½		- - -	above	2d. ¼
Helſling	-	-	11 ¼				

Copper.

Styca two to a farthing.

2dly. That coins of Baffianus and others " have been dolven wythynn its walles," befides the quantities of coins of other Roman Emperors, which have been found fo frequently very near it.

3dly. That many coins of Saxon Kings have been thrown up, on opening the ground, in the very ftreets of Briftol.

From all this the antiquity of the city of Briftol is fully demonftrated.

Befides the coins before-mentioned, faid to be coined here in this old vellum manufcript, there were others certainly dug up in and about Briftol, mentioned before, fome Roman, fome Saxon: and in another manufcript, *penes me*, written in 1708, it is afferted, that " there were many old Britifh coins dug up at Briftol." In the days of King Athelftan, fays Roger Hoveden, it was decreed, there fhould be at Canterbury feven monetaries, viz. four of the kings, two of the bifhop, one of the abbot; at London eight, &c.; and at Briftow, and other boroughs, one.

In Camden's lift of coins we find one of Harold, table 7, of Saxon coins, No. 37; the reverfe is, " Leofwine on Brightftoll;" and in Sir Andrew Fountain's lift, a penny of Harold, coined at Briftow by one Leof, a monetary: and in the lift given by Snelling, wherein are the coins of the two firft Williams, I find thofe of Briftol thus defigned:

B R I C.
B R I C S T O W.
B R I G E T S T O W.
B R I G S T O W.

And the filver penny of William the Conqueror, in Dr. Ducarel's cabinet, reprefents that king full-faced, with two fceptres,

Villem Rex Anglorum. Reverfe, *Leofwine on Brici.*

It is in the higheft prefervation, as Dr. Ducarel himfelf affured by letter the Author of this Hiftory. On a coin of Henry 1ft. it is called Briflo, and on one of Edw. 1ft. *Villa de Briflo.* In the manufcript of Rowley above, it is faid, " Robert Roufe Erle of Gloceftre coyned the beft money of any of the barons;" and in another manufcript is mentioned a " Briftow tway-penny." The late learned Prefident of the Society of Antiquaries, London, Dr. Milles, has communicated to the Author the following obfervations on the coin of this Earl Robert. " The coin of Robert, in which he is reprefented on horfeback, was fuppofed by former writers to belong to Robert Duke of Normandy, the Conqueror's fon, but by later critics adjudged to Robert Earl of Glocefter: it has the following infcription; X RODBERTUS IV. The crofs, which generally precedes thefe nummulary legends, is placed directly before the firft

letter,

letter, but in this coin there is a confiderable diftance, owing to the cap of Robert being pointed and breaking into the circle of the legend, feparates from the R, and makes it feem to follow the V; which made Mr. Colebroke, in Archæol. vol. iv. read it " Rodbertus Dux :" but this would rather give it to Robert Duke of Normandy than to the other. The circumftances that feem to weigh in favour of its being a coin of Robert Earl of Glocefter are, that all the great barons then coined money,* that Robert (as Rowley fays) coined the beft money of any of the barons; that the reverfe, which repre-fented a crofs, and fome fquare and fome round forms in the place of the letters, much refembles thofe of Euftace and Henry 2d. ; and that this coin was actually found, with fome coins of thofe princes, at or near Whitby, as Thorefby fays, p. 350. Antiquities of Leeds." Thus Dean Milles; and though Dr. Ducarel in a letter to me afferts, that " there are none of the old barons' coins that have yet reached our time," there is great reafon to believe this coin of Robert Earl of Glocefter to be rightly appropriated to him.

In the days of Edward 1ft. 1272, there were twelve furnaces at York, and twelve at Briftol, and more in other great boroughs, for melting filver, in order for hammering and ftamping perfect monies; which continued through all the reigns, till about 1663. His coin is circumfcribed with the name of the place of coinage, as *Villa Briftolliæ,* which is not rare. In Henry the fixth's time, there was a mint in Briftol for coining filver; the place in Peter-ftreet, near the Caftle, (now the Hofpital for the city poor) ftill re-taining the name of the Mint; which coining in Henry the fixth's time is alluded to in Rowley's manufcripts, when Mr. Canynge had the offer of the right of coining.

In 42 Henry 8th. were coined in Briftol teftoons, groats, half groats, and pennies, with *Civitas Briftolliæ* on the reverfe: and 1 Edw. 6th. there was a mint at Briftol

The following coins of feveral other kings bear the name of Briftol upon them. — The names of 150 coiners appear on the pennies of William the 1ft and 2d, ftruck at London, York, Winchefter, Norwich, Exon, Briftow, &c.
Henry 1ft or 2d. Penny — a full face crowned, in the right hand a fceptre
fleury, in the left a mullet of five points. — Rev. *Geraud on Briftow.*

F   Edw.

* As proofs, I quote the following from Roger Hoveden, A. 1149. Hen. Dux Normanno-rum fecit novam monetam quam vocabant monetam Ducis, & non tantum ipfe fed omnes poten-tes tam epifcopi quam comites & barones fuam faciebant monetam. — And I find the following in William Newbrigenfis, b. i. ch. 22. " Domini caftellorum in Anglia habebant finguli per-cuffuram proprii numifmatis & poteftatem regio more fubditis dicendi juris."

Edw. 1ft.   Penny — Rev. *Villa Briftolie* 22 gr. $\frac{1}{2}$.

    Halfpenny — Rev. *Villa Briftollie* 11.

Edw. 4th.   Gold Angel — *Ed. Di. Gr.* &c. The king in a fhip with a fquare flag at the ftern, on which is the initial E. on the other fide a full blown rofe, under which is the letter B. for Briftol, the place of coinage; weight 79 gr.

Edw. 4th.   Groat — *Di Gra. Rex Angl. et Franc.* on the breaft B. marked on both fides with a coronet. Rev. *Villa Briftoll.*

Edw. 4th.   Two-pence — *Di Grat.* &c. Rev. *Villa Briflow.*

Hen. 8th, 1545.   Teftoons, Groats, Half Groats, and Pennies — with *Civitas Briftolliæ.*

Edw. 6th.   Penny — *D. G. Rofa fine fpina.* Rev. *Civitas Briftoliæ.*

Gul. 3d.   Half Crown — *Magn Britt.* &c. 1696, under the infcription a B. ftruck at Briftol in the mint there.   There were now five country mints erected for coining bafe money and filver into current milled money. There was brought into Briftol of hammered money and wrought plate as much as made in weight 146,977 oz. in order to be coined there.

There has been dug up when the bridge was taken down and rebuilt, a brafs coin with a pope's head on one fide, and on the other a bridge with four arches, as big as half a crown — *Sixtus* IIII. *pont. Max. facri cultor;* on the reverfe juft over a figure of a four arch bridge, *Cura rerum publicarum.* —— And another of the fize of a large fhilling, with a Queen crowned, perhaps for the Virgin Mary, fitting on a throne with a fcepter in the right hand, with *Ave Maria Gratia plena* round; and on the reverfe, a crofs fleury with a quaterfoil in its center within a border, with a double line in fhape of a quaterfoil, infcribed on the outfide edge alfo with *Ave Maria Gratia plena.*

Whether thefe had any reference to the building of Briftol Bridge of four arches, or to any other, is left to farther enquiry.   It feems to confirm the opinion, of the abbots and religious coining money, called Abby-money in the manufcripts of Rowley.

While upon this fubject of coinage, it may not be improper to add, that it appears the mayor and aldermen of Briftol were authorifed, by the privy council, to ftrike farthing tokens, in 1594: but the ftriking of thefe tokens was an abufe, not a releafe from the royal authority.   And in Queen Elizabeth's days the magiftrates of the cities of Briftol, Oxford, and many fhopkeepers, made tokens of lead and brafs without any authority, which they often refufed to exchange: an order was fent, dated May 12, 1594, to the mayor and aldermen of Briftol, from the lords of the council, to call in all tokens ftruck in

that

that city, and that no private trader fhould make any without licence from the mayor. In 1653, there was a copper coinage of halfpence and farthings by private perfons till 1672, when the king's copper coin took place. One fide of the coin expreffed the name of the place or city, and value of the piece: and the other, the arms of the city; if of private perfons or merchants, their name and trade. Briftol farthings are ftill common to be met with, neatly executed. On one fide, the arms of the city; on the other, *a Briftol farthing* infcribed, and dated 1562, 1594.

As coins dug out of the ground have been ever regarded as proofs of the anti-quity of a place, fo have monumental ftones with infcriptions. If any credit is to be given to old parchments with drawings of fuch monumental ftones, with the account of the infcriptions thereon preferved, fuch can be produced with the name of Rowlie affixed to them, as copied from Turgot. Some are faid " to be dolven in Bryftowe, or wythynne fhort compafs of its walles: one had " this infcribed, *Cynwellinus & Wulferus Merciæ*, & was dolven in the houfe of the " Whyte Friars, ii on St. Mychael's-hylle, iii on Baldwynne's-hyll, iv in " Hie-lane, and the refte in feveral hy'lles & lanes, but fome wythyn the " walls of Baldwyn and Radcleve. One has thys: *Hic jacet Coenred Epifcop.* " *Selfeya*, A. D. DCCCCX.: another, *Tellius Sanctus Epifcop. Brighftow mort.* " xxvii *Maii*, DCXXXII. This was the Coffynne of Saint Tellius, preefte of " Romannus, yclepen- the learned Byfhop of Roiachefter, who dyed at " Brightftowe. Several other ftones wyth infcriptions and moft auntiaunte " Monuments were preferved in the Abbie of Weftburie by Mr. Canynge.— " One fheweth Caër Brito fulle playne, and was dolven on St. Michael's-hyll. " Another more curyoufe, where Caër Brito may be fene, was dolven on St. " Marie's-hyll. There were drawings of other ftones dug up at Brigftowe " formerly; fome with Saxon fwords or feaxes, and Danifh battle axes, but " much worn out."

To this account of coins and coinage, it may not be improper to add the follow-ing account, copied from an old manufcript in my poffeffion, of thofe fcarce coins, monuments, and other valuable pieces of antiquity, faid once to have adorned the cabinet of a very wealthy and ingenious merchant of Briftol, the worthy Mr. Canynge; and to have been chiefly collected by Thomas Rowley, prieft, of the fifteenth century, which he calls his *Yellow Roll*, and entitules it,

" England's

" England's Glorye revyved in Mayſtre Canynge, beynge ſome Accounte
" of hys Cabynet of Auntyaunte Monumentes."

" To prayſe thys Auntyaunte Repoſytorie maie not bee ſo ſyttynge yn me,
Seeynge I gotten itte moſte; but I amme almoſte the onlie Manne acquainted
wyth alle of ytte: ande almoſte ytte is the moſt precyouſe performaunce in
Englande. The fyrſt thynge at youre Entrance is a Stonen Bedde,* whyche
was manie yeers kepte in Towre Errys, and belonged to Erle Bythryck.
Rounde the Cabinette are Coynes on greete Shelfes ſetyvelie paynĉted. The
Coynes are of Greece, Venyce, Rome, Fraunce, ande Englande, from the
Daies of Julyus Gæſar to thys preſent, conſyſtynge of Denarii, Penys, Ores,
Mancas, Byzantynes, Holly Land Moneie, of whych Penys, Denarii ande
Twapenyes there are coyned ynne Bryſtoe fourtie & nyne of dyffarante
Sortes; Barons' Moneie, Citie Monie, Abbye Monie to beſyde the coynes
and moneie would ſylle a redde Rolle.† Goe wee thenne to the oder
thynges.

The Greete Ledger‡ is a Gemme wordie the Crowne of a Kynge: itte
contayneth the Workes of Turgotte, a Saxonne Monke, as followes. Battle
of Haſtynge, yune Anglo-Saxonne, donne moe playne bie mee for Mayſtre
Canynge.§ Hyſtorie of Bryghſtowe,‖ inne Saxonnes Latynne, tranſlated for
Mr. C. bie mee. Auntyaunte Coynes, with the Hyſtorie of the firſt Coynynge bie the Saxonnes, done from Saxonne into Englyſhe. Hyſtorie of St.
—:— Churche of Durham. Alle theſe ynne Latynne. Lyfe of Byghtry-
cus, Kynge of the Weſt Saxonnes, and Annales from hym to Byghthrycus the
Erle. Alle thye ynne Englyſhe. — Neere is mie unworthie Rolles, beeynge
a ſynyſhinge of Turgotte** to the Reygne of K. Edwarde the —. My Volume
of

* That ſuch a bed, or rather bedſtead, was in being for years at the houſe, in Redclift-
ſtreet, where Mr. Canynge dwelt, has been affirmed by an old inhabitant of that houſe.

† From this repoſitory then were derived the coins, mentioned in p. 38. in the little eſſay on
coining.

‡ This ſeems to be a different book from thoſe Ledger-Books named in the will of Mr.
Canynge, which the late Dean Milles juſtly ſuppoſed to be Service-Books for the uſe of the
chaplains. — This was a Family-record Book, in which they entered any thing curious or uſeful
to be preſerved, and in which they read for their entertainment: moſt families formerly had ſuch
for their amuſement.

§ A poem has been publiſhed under this name. See Rowley's Poems, by Dean Milles,
p. 40, 97. Whether the whole was faithfully tranſcribed by Chatterton, or altered by him,
may admit of a doubt. We ſee here there was ſuch a poem extant.

‖ This is the ſubjeĉt of the purple roll, and may be ſeen faithfully copied, page 32 of this
Hiſtory.

** This is wanting. It is remarkable, he writes King Edward the —, without mentioning

of Verſes, * wyth Letters to and from John Lydgate. My owne Hyſtorye of Moneies, Collectyon of Monymentes, † &c. Lykewyſe the verie Lettre ſente bie the Lordes Rychard of Yorke, Warwyck, & Saryſburye, to Kynge Henrie. ‡ Onne one Corner yn the Cabynet is a Syghte moſt terryble, bee-ynge Inſtrumentes of Warre, raunged in ſuche Arraie that in the Lyghte of the Sunne, or the comeynge of a candle, ytte ſhynethe moſte marvelloufe to be-houlde. Ytte ys of Bryttyſh Swordes and Sheeldes, whych prove the Aunti-quitye of Armoureye, beeynge marqued ſome wyth an Ivie Leefe, ſome wyth an Oke Leefe, ſome wyth a Hare or Hounde, and ſuch lyke. Roman Speeres and Bucklers, lykewyſe Blazonede, but all of the ſame Charge. Saxonne Swordes or Seaxes ande Sheeldes, blazoned wyth a Croſſe patee. Danyſh Battle Axes and Sheeldes, blazoned wyth a Raſen. The Armour and laſte Teſtamente of Roberte Roufe, Conful of Gloucefter. § The Gawntlette of Roberte, Sonne of Wyllyam the Conquerour, whych hee lefte behynde hym in Bryſtowe Caſtle. Syrre Charles Bawdwynne a Fulforde, commonlie cleped Baudynne Fullforde, his Bonde toe the Kynge Henrye to take the Erle of Warwyke's Lyfe or lofe hys hede, whych he dyd not perfourme, butte loſte his heede to Kynge Edwarde. ‖ Thus muche for the Cabynette."

Various will be the opinions held of theſe manuſcript accounts, reſpecting their authenticity; they may probably be called in queſtion as much as the poems have been, publiſhed under the name of Rowley. It might however be deemed unfair in an Hiſtorian to have concealed what the public have a right to canvas, approve or reject as they may judge right. — They are here faithfully tranſcribed and communicated; and are ſubmitted to the judge-ment of the candid and ingenuous reader, either to receive or reject them. The Author takes it not upon himſelf to determine; but pays that deference to the judgement of every reader of abilities and candour, as to leave him to form an opinion of it without interpoſing his own. Whatever that be, the external evidence of the genuinefs of theſe manuſcripts was ſuch, as fully to

authorize

him as King Edward the 4th, being a zealous Lancaſtrian, as appears from other paſſages in his Letters, and ſo not acknowledging Edw. 4th. as king.

* This is the poem on Ella, and others not particularly noted.

† Some of thefe are probably thoſe mentioned before, p. 38, 43.

‡ That ſuch a letter was ſent, our chronicles bear witnefs.

§ What a value would be now ſet on thefe Britiſh ſhields and ſwords, and Roman ſpears and bucklers? What an addition even to the Britiſh Muſeum, eſpecially the armour of Robert Roufe, the valiant champion of his day? And what would be the price now of the gauntlet and laſt teſtament of Robert, the Conqueror's ſon?

‖ See this mentioned in Stowe's Chronicle, under the year 1461.

authorize him to give them to the public, whatever fhall be infer'd from the internal evidence. The late learned Dean Milles has already laid before the public in his elegant edition of Rowley's poems with notes, every thing that tends to illuftrate his fubjeĉt and develop this intricate and obfcure affair, and place it before the reader in a proper light, and ftriking point of view, to all which I refer; and if the reader adds to the evidence produced by him, what is here advanced from the yellow and purple roll, and from other original parchment manufcripts under the name of Rowley to be now publifhed in this work, he will then be able to form a juft opinion and judgement of this long contefted fubjeĉt, and have the whole evidence before him to direĉt him in his deter-mination: but " adhuc fub Judice Lis eft." Some fay, the truth may be found not to be with one but betwixt the two contending parties; but as every one will form an opinion of his own in all fuch difputes, who fhall be judge? Each muft after weighing all the evidence judge for himfelf, which he will now be the better enabled to do, from what has been advanced and will yet occur in the courfe of this work.

But whatever credit thefe old manufcripts, and ancient accounts of coins and monumental ftones relating to Briftol, demand from the judicious and candid reader; yet not only in the Saxon but alfo in the Norman times, and later writings we fhall find Briftol making a ftill more confpicuous figure in the hiftory and indubitable records of thofe days.

In the time of W. 1, it appears from records that in that reign the inhabitants of Briftol were ftiled burgeffes, when the furvey of the kingdom called * Dooms-Day was made and the place itfelf confequently a Borough; by which is meant a town with limited boundaries, walled or not, claiming by pre-fcription or by grant the privilege of choofing its own magiftrates or gover-nors, for the better regulation of trade or morals under proteĉtion of the Lord of the fee, from the Saxon *Beorghan* to fence, keep in fafety &c. And it is granted the ancient burgh and city differed little or nothing in fignification. And the honourable ftation it then filled in this kingdom, appears from its being rated in Doomfday-book higher than any city, or town in England, except London, York and Winchefter. Robert the rhyming Monk of Glo-cefter reckons Briftoe among the firft and chief towns in this land:

" The furfte lordes and maiftres that yn yis londe wer,
" And the chyffe tounes furfte they lete arer,
" London & Everwyk, Lyncolne & Leycefire
" Cochefire & Canterbyre, Briftoe & Worcefire."

About

* " Bertune and Briftow paid to the King 110 marks of filver and the burgeffes returned that Bifhop G. had 33 marks and one mark of gold."

About the conqueſt ſay ſome, were built divers towns to guard the frontiers of Wales, Briſtol, Glouceſter, Worceſter, Shrewſbury and Cheſter;
theſe were garriſon towns of the Marches of Wales: Or rather were ap_
pointed ſuch from their ſituation, though built long before. The Lords
Marches were created to watch and ward that country, and were to be
always ready to march againſt the Welſh.

When Briſtol was exempt from the Marches of Wales, which was a great
trouble and expence to the town, will appear in the annals.

In 1ſt year of W. 2, it is certain, that Godfrey the Biſhop of Conſtance
and his nephew the Earl of Northumberland, held the caſtle of Briſtol then
an ancient moſt ſtrong and impregnable fortreſs. * The names of many who
were governors of Briſtol and its caſtle in the Saxon times have been trauſ-
mitted down to us, ſo as to put its antiquity quite out of queſtion.

The firſt chief magiſtrate or governor of Briſtol was called † *prepoſitus de
Briſtou,* under the cuſtos or conſtable of the caſtle who held it under the
Saxon Earls of Gloſter; and in Edward the Confeſſor's time.

In the charter of King John, the chief officer indeed is mentioned in the
tranſlation under the name of a *provoſt* which anſwers to *prepoſitor.*

It thus appears that Briſtol had its magiſtrates and officers or governors of
its own long before it was erected into a mayor town or corporate body. In
the year 1066, Harding ‡ (whoſe name now is in the inſcription over the gate
way in College Green) the anceſtor of the Berkeley family, being a magiſtrate
and rich merchant of Briſtol, held Wheatenhurſt in the hundred of Whitſton
Glouceſterſhire in morgage of Earl Britrick. He is called mayor and governor of Briſtol, and Leland ſays " he removed the fraternity of Calendaries,
(a ſociety in Briſtol exiſting before the conqueſt) to the church of All-
Hallows, which before were at Chriſt Church, and " that the ſchools then
ordained by theſe Calendaries, for the converſion of the Jews in Briſtowe

was

* See chapt. of the caſtle below, and annals for that year.

† Vid. Doomſday-book 75, in Gloceſter, " In Sineſhovede hund. Rogerius fil. Rad. ten.
" manerium quod tenuit Seruuinus p'poſitus de Briſtou de Rege E. &c." Terra Rogerii filii
Rad. Noie Cliſtone In Sineſhovede Hund. Rogerius fi. Rad. ten. unum Marenuim q'd telnuit
Seruuinus p'poſitus de Briſtou de rege E. & poterat ire cum hac tea quo volebat nec aliquam
firmam inde dabat — Ibi iii hidæ. In d'nio s't iii Car. & vi Vill. & vi bord. cum ii Car. Ibi
iii Servi & viii ac. p'ti. Valet. c Solid. Modo Lx ſolid. Suppoſed to relate to the tithings of
Almondſbury — Rudder's Gloceſt. p. 223.

This Serwin being prepoſitor of Briſtou in the time of K. Edward the Confeſſor, ſhews
the chief officer there to have that title, which name continued in Henry 3ds. time, when
there were a mayor and two prepoſitors.

‡ Atkins Gloceſterſhire, p. 261.

was put into the order of the Calendaries and the Mayor;" * which fhews a governor then prefided here even under the name and office of a Mayor long before any lifts of mayors we have at prefent do begin.

About the time of the conqueft Robert Fitzhaymon held the honor of Glocefter of which Briftol was a part, and he then received the rents or tythes, (Decimas de Exitibus Briftolliæ) as paid to the Lord of Glocefter then and before, and he gave it to the Abby of Tewkfbury which he founded. Henry 2, in 1144 was educated four years in learning at Briftol, as will appear below in the chapters on the cathedral and caftle. In the reign of King John one Englard de Cygoin held the ferm (firmam) of Brifto for the account (compotum) or fine of 1451. which Richard the burgefs paid for him.

In † 1177, 23 Henry 2, the burgeffes of Briftou render an account of eighty marks for Sturmis the ufurer: he freed it in the treafury and was quit. Jordan the dapifer of the Earl of Glocefter owed fifty marks for default. Mag. Rotul 3 Gloft.

In the 30 year of Henry 2, the men of Briftou paid a fine of 50l. to have refpite and not to be impleaded without the walls of their town, till the King's return into England.

In 1196, 7 Richard 1, a tallage or tax was laid by William Bifhop of Hereford, Hugh Bardolph and others the King's Juftices upon the King's manors and burghs. The burgeffes of Briftol paid 200 marks (133l. 6s. 8d.) and for the fair of Briftol 10 marks (6l. 13. 4.)

And in 1225, 9 Henry 3, the burgeffes of Briftol accounted to the King for 245l. the ferm of their town, the King having demifed the town to them at that ferm, fo that they were to anfwer for two parts of that ferm at the feaft of St. Michael, and for the reft at the feaft of St. Hillary, faving to the King for ufe of the Conftable of the caftle and his family refiding therein the prizage of beer, as much as they fhall have need of; fo that the burgeffes have the remainder: and faving to the King the Bailiwick (Baillia) of the Berton of Briftol (Barton Regis) and the Chace of Brul of Keinfham and of the Wood of Furches, which the King kept in his own hand.

In 1201, 12 of King John there was a treafury at Briftol, mentioned in Maddox hiftory of the Exchequer, p. 421 c. 2. x. and about that time the towns paid an aid for the King's paffage into Ireland: ‡ "the burgeffes of Gloucefter

* Leland, V. vii. 2 Ed. p. 88 — vid. Little red book of Briftol, manufcript in Chamber of Briftol, p. 88. and in All Saints parifh. the chap. below.

† Vid. Maddox hiftory of Exchequer, 143. 228. 486. & alibi.

‡ Auxilium Villarum ad paffagium Hyberniæ, Burgenfes Gloceftriæ reddunt compotum de 500 marcis de eodem : Homines de Briftou reddunt compotum de 1000 marcis de eodem : Homines de redclive reddunt compotum de 1000 marcis de eodem &c. Maddox.

" eefter render an account (compotum) of 500 marks for the fame, the men of
" Briftow 1000 marks for the fame, the men of Redeclive 1000 marks for the
" fame. In the treafury were 237 l. 6 s. 8 d. and England de Cigoni had 225
" marks to put into the treafury of the king at Briftow. The men of the
" templars of Redeclive render account of 500 marks for the fame."

King John, when Earl of Moreton only, by marriage with a daughter of
William Earl of Glocefter, held the town of Briftol as part of that earldom;
and after he came to be king, Briftol became vefted in the crown, and the
kings of England ever after received a certain annual fum for the ferm of the
town, as the earls of Glocefter did before; Briftol, as mentioned before, being part of that earldom, and a demefne of it.

Thus Hugh Bardolph (Magn. Rot. 31ft Henry 2d.) renders an account
(among other things belonging to the Earl of Glocefter's lands,) of 119 l. 7 s. 5 d.
of the rent of Briftow, and of the mills, and of the fairs, and for having a
houfe at Briftow, 3 l. 0 s. 10 d. where the king's rents are received, and for
mending the tower of Briftow, and for hiring carpenters, and for ftones for
the mills, and for repairing the houfes in the manors, 13 l. 0 s. 6 d.

So populous, flourifhing, and rich was Briftol in Henry 2d's. time, that he
greatly favoured it with his bounty and royal grants, and gave it charters, and
alfo a grant* of the city of Dublin (then called Devlin) in Ireland to inhabit,
poffefs, and enjoy; and a colony from Briftol was fent thither for that purpofe,
who were to have the fame privileges and free cuftoms they held in Briftol.

In 1305, King Edward 1ft. taking a taillage of all towns and cities corporate in England, Briftol gave him 400 l. for a fine.

And in the 45th year of Edward 3d. Rot. 40. by a patent letter of his great
feal he demifed the town of Briftol to Walter de Derby and Henry Derneford
for one year, they rendring and paying the fums of money referved in the
demife. The profits of the town confifted in houfes, fhops, cottages, fheds,
gardens, mills, pools, tyne of the caftle, rents landgable, tolls, pleas of court,
cuftoms of the fair and market, and other rights belonging to them; they
held it in the fame manner as the mayor and commonalty of Briftol held the
fame of the grant of late Queen Philippa, the garden below the caftle and the
garden towards the Berton only being excepted; referving all royal liberties
in the faid town, and others of old belonging to the caftle of Briftol; referving

G

alfo

---

* A copy of it is extant in Dr. Leland's Hiftory of Ireland. Alfo in Camden is the following
note: " An Englifh colony was tranfplanted from Briftol hither (Dublin) by King Henry the
" fecond, giving them this city (which perhaps at that time was drained of inhabitants,) in thefe
" words, " with all the liberties and free cuftoms which thofe of Briftol enjoyed." From that
" time it flourifhed more and more, &c."

alfo (multura bladi) a fine of corn to the conftable of the caftle, for his own table and his family's: and (Garneftura in caftro predicto ad molendina ejufdem Villæ quieta de Theolonio inde præftando)&c. They were to pay befides for that year 100 l. They were to have liberty to dig the king's ground; to mend the mill-ponds, when out of repair; and to pay the conftable of the caftle 20 l. for that year for his wages for keeping the caftle, and every day 2 d. for the wages of the porter, and 3 d. a day for two watchmen, and an halfpenny every night for their wages, and to pay their vail week after week, or every quarter, as the conftable would have it: and to pay for the year to the abbot of Tewkfbury 14 l. 10 s. for the tenths of the town; and to the prior of St. James 60 s. of annual rent for the mill; and to the cuftos maritimus (or water-bailiff) 1 l. 6 s. 8 d. (pro robâ fuâ) and to the keeper of the foreft of Kingfwood every day 7½ d. and to bear for the king all other burdens, expences, dues of charity and cuftoms, fo that a whole 100 l. remain to the king: and to keep up and repair all houfes, gardens, mills, &c. above-mentioned, belonging to the faid town in the fame good order they receive them.

When the fame King Edward 3d. ann. r. 47, made Briftol a county of itfelf, and granted the city feveral franchifes, it was " provided they do " anfwer to the king yearly for his ferms and other dues."

In the 5th year of Edward 4th. John Cogan, fheriff of Briftol, paid 102 l. 15 s. 6 d. charged on the mayor and commonalty of Briftol, for the fee farm of the king's town, to Elizabeth confort of King Edward 4th. fettled on the queen for her life.

In the great roll, 29th Henry 6th. Hugh Withiford, mayor of Briftol, and commonalty of the fame, and their fucceffors, ftood charged to the king with 102 l. 15 s. 6 d. per annum, for the town of Briftol and the fuburbs thereof, the ditches, gates, flefh fhambles, &c. demifed to them for twenty years, which were fettled on Queen Margaret by the king for the term of her life.

But the city was releafed and exonerated from payment of thefe and other fee farm rents charged thereon, by the corporation purchafing them of the crown, in the times of Charles 1ft. and 2d. as will hereafter be made appear.

The annals of the city will alfo hereafter contain more explicit accounts, early records, and charters of Briftol, from which may be deduced a full relation of its ancient ftate and public tranfactions.

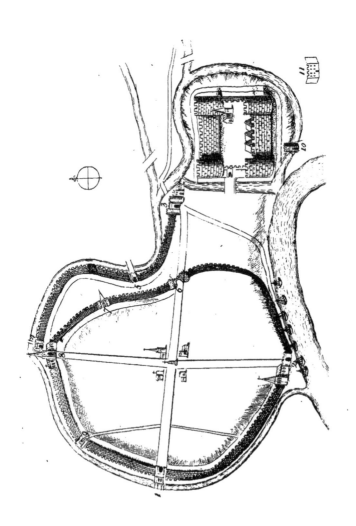

CHAP. III.

A PLAN *and* DESCRIPTION *of* BRISTOL, *in its Early and Middle State.*

IN tracing back the antiquity of the city many things have neceſſarily occured already in the courſe of that inquiry, deſcribing the firſt and early ſtate of it, which ſhall now be farther delineated as well as can be collected from authentic records and manuſcripts, from old plans, and from conſidering the firſt feite and ground plot of the town, and comparing it with any veſtiges and marks that ſtill remain.

About a mile from the Roman camp at Clifton or ſtation Abone, under the hills and within its view was the Britiſh town (Caer Brito) firſt laid out at the conflux of the two rivers Avon and Froom, with which it had the advantage of being ſurrounded except on the northern part, where the caſtle was afterwards erected. The ground on which the city was built riſes each way to the center, forming a pleaſant hill. Having pitched upon this commodious ſtation they divided it into four ſtreets, walling it round after the banks of the rivers for its greater ſecurity and defence, placing a gate at the end of each ſtreet; and being converted to the Chriſtian faith, erecting churches there, and a croſs in the center where the ſtreets interſected each other, and formed a croſs an emblem of their Chriſtian profeſſion. Thus a gate, and a church or chapple terminated each of the four ſtreets, and four churches ſurrounded the croſs at the center. No. 1, Baldwin's afterwards Leonard's gate. No. 2, St. Nicholas gate. No. 3, Elle gate, or that next the caſtle ſince rebuilt and called New gate. No. 4, Froom gate, or the Water gate. No. 5, Pithay, or Aylward's gate. No. 6, Defence gate. No. 7, Tower gate. No. 8, St. John's gate. No. 9, St. Giles's gate. No. 10, Sally-port of the caſtle. No. 11, Godfrey's lodge.

A wall embattled on the top, joined and incloſed the whole, though as related in Turgott's manuſcript account, " the walls and gates ſuffered alteration," yet the ſhape and feite of the city in general muſt have remained the ſame and ſtill continues ſo to this day.

The

The gradual declivity from the center on all fides, contributes greatly to its being neat and cleanly, every fhower wafhing down the dirt into the fub-jacent rivers, befides affording afterwards the advantage of making thofe large gouts fo convenient to this day; through which, by means of the returning tide, the filth of the city is difembogued and daily ebbed away into the Severn fea twice in twenty-four hours. The river Froom, with which it is chiefly moted, arifes at Dodington and Rangeworthy not far from Tet-bury in Glocefterfhire, and running through Aƈton there called Loden, and Hambrook to Stoke, where it meets a fpring from Lord Bottetourt's park and takes the name of Froom, and fo to Stapleton and clofe under the north walls of the city, paffes Froom-bridge; and, before the prefent quay was dug, held on its courfe * through the fifh market and Baldwin-ftreet, built on its banks, to St. Nicholas port, along under the walls of the town, and there it emptied itfelf into the Avon in full current; where was the conflu-ence of the two rivers: it drove a mill ereƈted for the ufe of the town called Baldwin's crofs-mill, juft before its difcharge into the Avon. At Blind-fteps there feems to have been of old a flip or paffage leading to this mill, of which there are fome traces remaining ftill in a cellar at the corner of Baldwin-ftreet; where are three old ftrong arches on each fide of it now to be feen, being the thoroughs through which the water of the Froom then flowed, that drove the wheels, the mill-houfe being ereƈted over them. This courfe of the Froom is not only proved by manufcript and authentic records, but by a whole boat having been of late years found in digging the foundation for a houfe in Baldwin-ftreet, and by other remains of fhipping and naval ftores dug up there formerly. Nicholas-ftreet being the bounds of the old city on this fide, the thick old city-wall may be feen there in many places at this day, as it may alfo in Leonard's-lane, embattled ftill at the top next Giles's-gate; — where being continued on to St. John's-gate along Bell-lane, in which once was a church dedicated to St. Lawrence, it joined the Tower-wall in Tower-lane, which with a ftrong gate in its middle and another at its upper end at the top of the Pithay, extended into Wine-ftreet, called alfo Wynch-ftreet; where at Defence-lane it joined the city-wall on the banks of the Avon, which was fortified with a wall round to St. Nicholas gate; — it was called Defence-lane, or Defence-ftreet, in all old deeds, (and fince

* See Annals for the year 1247. — alfo the plate. — There is in a manufcript in the Chamber of Briftol called Rycaut's Calendar, a coloured drawing or view of the city about 1470 as def-cribed above, the ftreets and houfes laid out in form of a crofs with a gate and church at each end, the High-crofs in the center, and four churches, and the river running round it.

fiuce Dolphin-lane, from the Dolphin-inn once there) as a place of defence or barrier for the city on that fide, and fecuring it againft any attempts or infurrection of the foldiers of the caftle, as defcribed by William Worcefter, p. 236. This was the internal wall of the city, added for the greater ftrength and fecurity ; the external on this fide being conftructed on the very bank of the Froom, from Froom-gate to Pithay-gate and Newgate, there joining the caftle.

On the north-caft fide it was moted with a little arm of the Froom by a channel made by hand quite round till it met the Avon,. which fkirted the city on the fouth fide, where the wall was continued quite round the caftle; thus completing the fortification of the city. The double wall that was built at Tower-lane, and on the banks of the Froom river, is a proof of the antiquity of the place, and of its being augmented from time to time. The old city is faid to have been fortified with that inner wall, by Geoffry Bifhop of Con-ftance ; or it was by him repaired and enlarged, when he, raifing a rebellion againft William Rufus, chofe it for the feat of war, as will hereafter be more particularly mentioned in the chapter on the caftle.

Under the wall above defcribed on the fouth fide ran the river Avon, (fo called from Abone, the antient Britifh word for a river,) which parts Somerfetfhire* from Glocefterfhire ; and during the Saxon heptarchy, Briftol was reckoned in thefe two counties or kingdoms : in the former were the Mercians feated; in the latter, or Redcliff fide, the Weft Saxons : and it was by late writers placed by fome in one, by fome in the other county. This river Avon runs through Wilt-fhire, rifing near Tetbury in Glocefterfhire, at Kemble and Luckington in two ftreams, which join at Malmfbury in one, and pafs through Chippenham, La-cock,+ Melkfham, Bradford, down to Bath and Briftol ; and receiving a branch of the Froom at the Caftle, and the whole river Froom itfelf formerly near Nicholas-port but now at the Quay, glides on in a winding courfe by Redcliff till it paffes the city and the rocks of St. Vincent below it, which feem as if cleft in

---

* Briftol is ever mentioned in the old Parliament rolls to be in Somerfetfhire, as Redcliff really was, and in the Weft Saxon kingdom ; — a proof that Redcliff was part of the antient Caer Brito, and not of late rife : though fome manufcripts fay, William Earl of Glocefter annexed Redcliff to Briftol.

+ A nunnery there, built by Ela Countefs of Salifbury, in Snailmead, now the feat of John Talbot, Efq. Leland fays, " filver money was dug up there in a field called Silver-feld." It was on the Roman road, called by Antonine Verlucio, and by Richard of Cirencefter. There are now the remains of a nunnery, moft compleat of any in England. Ela was buried 1300, in the church of Ofeney ; fhe founded a chapel at Rewly, nigh Oxford, where the foundation ftone, in 1705, was dug up with the name of Ela upon it, and is preferved by Hearn, in the Bodleian Library. Vid. Leland, Itin. p. 94, v. 2.

in a ſtupendous manner to let it through, and about ſeven miles below falls
into Kingroad, or the Severn ſea. Boats of burden uſed of old to carry
goods from Briſtol to Bath, until the river was obſtructed by wears, mills, &c.
as appears by Claus. 4 Edw. 1. p. 1, m. 4, who ordered the removal of them;
but it was again made navigable in the year 1727: ſee annals for that year.—
And might alſo, in the opinion of many, be let into the Iſis at Cricklade by
cutting a new channel for a few miles, and thereby a navigation be effected
betwixt the firſt and ſecond city in the kingdom, London and Briſtol, which
was oppoſed in 1656 by the corporation, as to the prejudice of the city.—
Some ſteps have of late been taken, by the merchants of Briſtol, towards this
great work, by a ſcheme for extending the navigation from Bath to Chippenham; of which ſee annals for the year 1767. The tide in the river Avon
flows up as high almoſt as to Cainſham, or near four miles; but after that the
barges go againſt the ſtream, and are drawn along by men, which renders the
paſſage ſomewhat tedious. Bath is by this means ſupplied with timber, deals,
&c. for building, wine, cyder, iron, and all bulky goods, from Briſtol at a
ſmall expence. Leland well deſcribes the riſe and courſe of the Avon, Itin.
vol. ii. f. 26, and f. 31, and " enumerates the bridges it paſſes through from
" Malmſbury, viz. Chriſtine-Malford-bridge, five miles lower; Caiſway-bridge,
" two miles lower; Chippenham, a right fair bridge, about a mile lower; the
" town on the right ripe towards London, Rhe-bridge, (in the pariſh of La-
" cock,) one mile and a half lower; Lacock-bridge, one mile and a half
" lower; Staverton-bridge, four miles lower; Bradford-bridge, two miles
" lower; Bath-bridge, of five fair arches, five miles lower; Briſtow-bridge,
" ten miles lower. At two miles above Briſtow-bridge was a Commune Tra-
" jectus by bote, where was a chapel of St. Ann, and here was great pilgrim-
" age to St. Ann."—It is in the pariſh of Briſlington, and ſome old arches
remain of the chapel ſtill to be ſeen.

Briſtol, being ſo commodiouſly ſituated at the confluence of two ſuch rivers
as the Avon and the Froom, could not fail of being ſupplied with water, that
neceſſary of human life; but had alſo the advantage of being moted round,
for its greater ſecurity by their united ſtreams, which with the embattled
walls and caſtle muſt have rendered it a very defenſible city againſt the enemy
in thoſe early times, eſpecially as the whole ground plot was on a hill.

In theſe walls, when " they ſuffered alteration," were, beſides the four
gates, others added. The old gates had a groove in the ſides from the top to
the bottom, in which a portcullis (i. e. a falling door, or wooden frame, ſhod
with iron, ſhaped like a harrow,) was let down for the better defence of the
city.

city. Thefe gates are all enumerated and defcribed by Leland. " Newgate
" (as methynkyethe) is in the utar waulle by the caftle, and a chapelle over
" itte: itte is the pryfon of the city. St. John's-gate, a churche on eche
" fyde of it; St. John's churche, it is harde on the north fide of it, and there
" be Cryptæ. St. Giles's-gate be the fouth-weft of the Key, where Frome
" rennithe. St. Leonarde's-gate, and a paroche church over it. St. Nicolas-
" gate, where is a churche cum cryptis. Thefe be the inner gates of the
" oulde towne cis Sabrinam, as the towne ftandithe in dextra ripa defluentis
" Avonæ."

Befides thefe walls and gates, there were others called by Leland the externa or fecunda mænia urbis. The outward wall of the city feems to have
run in a line from Froom-gate, after the river Froom was turned into the Key,
ftraight along the Key, where was a tower oppofite the Drawbridge, to Marfh-
gate, fo round by King-ftreet to the Back-gate in Back-ftreet, the wall there
joining the Avon. In making the new ftrect 1771 from Corn-ftreet to the
Key, by a fubfcription of 8000l. of which the corporation gave 2000l. they
found in digging the ground a gout, the old arched gout, once the bed of the river
Froom, next St. Leonard's church; and at the bottom of Clare-ftreet, a wall
five feet and a half thick next the Key, once the city wall here. Thefe walls
were built when the city enlarged its boundaries, ranging beyond its former
limits. Thus Leland: " In the uttar (outer) walles Marfch-gate e regione
" Avonæ." Back-gate is alfo intended, but through a flaw in Leland's manufcript is not named there. On the Redcliff fide he fays accurately enough,
" In the waulle ultra pontem & Avonam be two gates, Raddeclyffe-gate and
" Temple-gate, and a greate tower called Tower-Harrys, at the very ende of
" the waulle in ipfa ripâ Avonæ." But the prefent Temple-gate is of a beau_
tiful and neat modern ftruĉture; as was Redcliff, now taken down. Leland
fays of the wall, " that certain Bochers made a fayre peace of this waull, and it
" is the higheft and ftrongeft of all the towne waulles."

This infular fituation of the city obliged them to erect feveral bridges to the
gates that led out of it. Froom-gate of old was a grand and noble ftruĉture,
confifting of two arched ways, adorned with the heads of Brightrick and
Robert Earl of Gloceſter; and the bridge ſtill remains, conftruĉted of two
folid Gothic arches, with ſtrong and thick piers, as the cuſtom then was. —
Through Elle-gate, now Newgate, was the common high road into Gloceſterſhire; this gate, though of one opening or paffage only, ſeems to confiſt of
four arches, turned one within the other at different times, which fhews its
antiquity: and had a figure in ftone on each fide; one, holding in his hand a
kind

kind of model of a caftle-like building, reprefents Robert Earl of Glocefter, the repairer and enlarger of the caftle; the other, having a cup with a cover or chalice in his hand, was for Godfry Bifhop of Conftance, who built fome of the walls, and fortified the caftle, in the fecond year of K. W. 2d. — Below this gate was alfo a bridge, ftill remaining, by which we pafs over a branch of the Froom; and another juft below it, over the river Froom itfelf: through the firft the Caftle-mills are fupplied with water, and the laft leads us into the parifh of St. James or Merchant-ftreet. Farther on the Wear is another, called by the name of Ell-bridge* or of Wear-bridge, (mentioned by Leland,) " harde by the northe-eaft parte of the caftle of Briftowe;" he adds, " there brekythe an arme out of Frome, a but-fhot above Werebrydge, and " renithe thrwghe a ftone bridge of one greate arche; and there at Newgate " the other parte of Frome, reninge from Werebridge, cummithe undar ano- " ther ftone, and fervinge the mille hard withote Newgate, metithe with the " other arme."

There muft alfo have been a bridge at Baldwin's (or Leonard's) gate over the Froom, when it ran through Baldwin's-ftreet its ancient courfe, though it is long fince deftroyed and the river itfelf there filled up fince the turning of the courfe of the Froom into the Quay.

At Nicholas-gate, of old called Warburghs, there was firft a ferry to St. Thomas flip on the oppofite fhore or Avon's bank, till a bridge was afterwards conftructed there, of which hereafter in the annals: at †Pithay-gate, Needlefs-gate, and at Bridewell, once called Monks bridge, (formerly a place of great ftrength, fortified with bulwarks and a tower, which give name to Tower-lane in its neighbourhood) there were afterwards and ftill remain bridges for the better communication with other places.

From the defcription already given it appears how well the old town was fituated and fecured on all fides, with every kind of defence by nature as well as Art. By the neighbouring hilly ground of St. Auftin, St. Brandon-hill, ‡ St. Michael's and Kingfdown hills, with the river Froom running in

a

---

* Or Ellebridge, fo called in old writings from Elle, lord of the caftle; now the ftreet next it is corruptly called Ellbroad-ftreet, for Ellebridge-ftreet.

† Pithay was formerly called the Putte, or pit, from its low fite; and the gate of old had the name of pons Aylwardi, Aylward's-gate, from Aylward, the Saxon governor of Briftol; of whom fee the chapter on the caftle.

‡ In the county of Kerry, in Ireland, there is a very high mount, called Brandon-hill, with the remains of a fmall oratory on its fummit, dedicated to St. Brandon, who founded a monaftery, (Clonfert,) in the year 558.

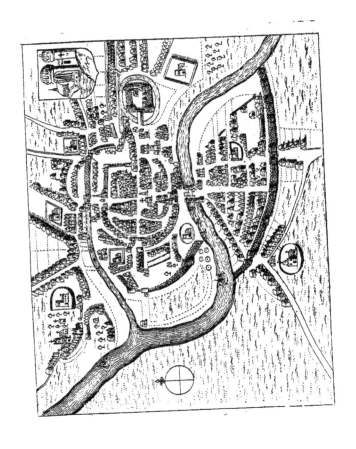

a winding channel underneath was it environed on the north fide; by Redcliff, Pyle Hill and the river Avon on the fouth, by the Caftle very defenfible on the eaft; being feated on a hill, in a valley betwixt thefe hills, it has
given occafion to its being compared to ancient Rome on its feven hills,
its ground plot like that being nearly circular, with a fomewhat greater diameter one way then another, enough to make it oval, the river cutting off
one part about a fixth from the reft; like it indeed a great part of the city
in its improved ftate is fituated on feveral hills.

A place fo happily feated as Briftol foon began to extend its ancient boun-
daries beyond the firft erected walls, and how far, appears by the plan annexed.
Redcliff fide becoming large and populous was foon added to the city, which
very early became a borough town, defended by a caftle. Andrew De
Chefne (Cefta Steph.) thus defcribes it as in the time of King Stephen:
" Eft Brifloa civitas omnium fere regionis civitatum opulentiffima, &c." i. e.
" Briftow is the richeft city almoft of all the cities of this country, receiving
merchandize from neighbouring and foreign places with the fhips under fail,
fixt in a very fertile part of England, and by fituation the moft defenfible of
any city in England; for as we read of Brundufium, a certain part of the
county of Glocefter is. here confined in form of a tongue, and ftretched out
into length; two rivers wafhing its two banks, one on each fide, and in its
lower parts where the ground finks, joining together into one flow of water,
form the city: a quick and ftrong fea tide, flowing up night and day, occafions
the rivers from both parts of the city to ebb into the broad and deep fea,
making a moft fafe and convenient port for a thoufand fhips; and fo ftrictly
inclofed is its circuit, that the whole city feems to fwim in the waters, and
wholly to be fet on the river banks."

This admirably defcribes the city every high tide, when the rivers being full
give it this appearance. William of Malmfbury, in the time of Henry 2d.
(de Geftis Pontif. p. 283 fol.) thus defcribes it: " In eadem valle eft vicus cele-
berimus Briflow nomine in qua navium portus ab Hibernia & Norwegia et cæteris
tranfmarinis terris venientium receptaculum, ne fcilicet genitalibus divitiis tam
fortunata regio (Glouceftrienfis) perigrinarum opum fraudaretur commercio."

Lord Lyttelton, (in his excellent work, the Life of Henry 2d. vol. ii.
p. 177.) quotes Malmfbury's authority, " that Briftol was then full of fhips
" from Ireland, Norway, and every part of Europe, which brought hither
" great commerce and much foreign wealth." And if a place of fuch trade
fo early, we may be well affured, that the buildings of the city muft be very

H   numerous

numerous and flourishing, and have been improving long before, as trade always brings together a conflux of inhabitants.

The uniting of Redcliff with the city, by means of a bridge, feems to have been one grand ftep towards this great improvement, or rather the effect of the population and continual refort of fettlers; who, impatient of the narrow confines of their firft erected town walls, attempted to enlarge their boundaries and erect buildings beyond them, and to join by a bridge their neighbours of Redcliff, by a free, uninterrupted communication; having no other at one time but by means of a ferry at St. Thomas-flip, and perhaps fome other part of the river.

Thefe buildings were conftructed chiefly on the north and weft fide of the town. A monaftery, dedicated to St. Auguftin in 1148, a priory to St. James, and other religious houfes, began to be eftablifhed through the favour and opulence of great men, and the charitable difpofition of the people. And where thefe houfes devoted to religion rofe, there the inhabitants flocked; as if defirous of dwelling near thofe confecrated buildings, and under the protection of thofe faints and martyrs, to whom the facred enclofures were dedicated, and which they were inftructed the Deity honoured with his more immediate prefence.

Leland has enumerated the feveral religious horfes in Briftow in his time, vol. vii. fol. 70, fecond edit. of his Itinerary.

" Howfys fumtyme of religion in Brightftowe. — Fanum Auguftini, nunc S. Trinitatis: Infcriptio in porta. There be three tombes of the Barkeleys in the fouth ifle agayne the quiere. Fanum St. Jacobi; it ftandithe by Brode Meade by northe from the caftle, on an hilly grounde, and the ruines of it ftandithe hard buttynge to the efte ende of the paroche churche, non longe a dextra ripa Frai, (i. e. not far from the right bank of Froom.) St. Magdalene's; a howfe of Nunes* fuppreffyd, on the north fyde of the towne. The Gauntes: one Henry Cannte, a knight, fometyme dwellinge not farre from Brandon-hyil by Brightftow, erectyd a college of priftes with a mafter, on the green of St. Auguftine. Hofpitales in ruin. Fanum [1] Barptolomei. Fanum [2] trium regum juxta Barptolemeos extra Froome-gate. Aliud [3] non procul, &c. i. e. Another not far off, on the right bank of Froom as you go to the priory of St.

---

* On St. Michael's-hill, now the fite of an inn, the King David.

[1] The hofpital of St. Bartholomew, once the city-fchool, now Queen Elizabeth's Boys' hofpital.

[2] The houfe and chapel of the Three Kings of Cologn, an almfhoufe at the upper end of Steep-ftreet, in St. Michael's parifh.

[3] Now Spencer's almfhoufe on the banks of Froom in Lewin's-mead, 1460.

St. James, in Lionsmede-ftreet. One 4 in Temple-ftrete. Another 5 by St. Thomas-ftrete. St. John's, 6 by Radeclef. An hofpitalle 7 S. Trinitatis hard within Lafforde's-gate. The Tukker's hofpitall in Temple : the Weevers' hofpitall in Temple-ftrete. 8 There was an hofpital of old tyme where of late a nunrye was, caullyd S. Margaret's.

" The Grey Friers' howfe 9 was on the right ripe of From Watar, not far from St. Barptoleme's hofpital. `The Blake Friers 10 ftode a little highar than the Gray, on Frome in the right ripe of it : Ser Maurice Gaunt, elder brother to Ser Henry Gaunt, foundar of the Gaunts, was foundar of this. The White Fryers 11 ftode on the righte rype of Frome agayn the Key. The Auguftyne Friers' howfe 12 was hard bye Temple-gate wytheine it northe wefte."

In another place, vol. v. f. 64. or p. 60. 2d edit. he mentions, " St. Auguftine's Blake Chanons 13 extra mænia (without the walls) ibique in magni area facellum, in quo fepultus eft S. Jordanus, unus ex difcipulis Auguftini Anglorum apoftoli. A houfe without the waulles, as I remembre, cawllyd the Gauntes, 14 otherwyfe Bon Hommes. [iiii] howfes 15 of Freres, of the which the White Fryers place ys very fair."

Befides thefe hofpitals mentioned by Leland, there were others mentioned in the will of John Gaywode, 1471, thus :

" Pauperes fraternitatis St. Joannis Baptiftæ in ecclefia St. Audæni ; domus Elemofynar. de Long Row Burtoni : domus Elemofynaria Richardi Fofter juxta Redcliff-gate ; pauperes de lazarehoufe de Brightbowe ; pauperes domus

H 2 Wil.

---

4 Spicer's hofpital, on the weft fide within Temple-gate.

5 Burton's almfhoufe, founded 1292.

6 St. John's, in Redcliff-pit, near St. John's-lane there.

7 Trinity hofpital, on both fides the way juft within Lawford's-gate, the upper end of the Old Market.

8 Still in being there with fome endowment ; fee chap. on Temple parifh.

9 Oppofite Spencer's almfhoufe in Lewin's-mead, now a fugar-houfe, founded in 1274.

10 On the Wear, now the fite of the Quaker's Meeting-houfe, 1229.

11 On Frier's-hill, next Pipe-lane, in the parifh of St. Auguftine, now the fite of Mr. Colfton's hofpital and other buildings. It extended back to the Red Lodge.

12 On the eaft fide juft within Temple-gate, oppofite Temple pipe conduit, now the fite of the Great Garden, called alfo Spring Gardens.

13 The cathedral of the Holy Trinity in College-green.

14 The Mayor's chapel.

15 The White, the Grey, the Black, and Auguftinian.

To thefe add St. Sepulchre's in Bell-lane, near St. Laurence church, now warehoufes, where was a nunnery.

Wil. Canynges fuper montem de Redcliff, 1442 : domus Elemofynaria Johannis Spicer juxta portam Templi; pauperes Fraternitatis Sanctæ Catherinæ; pauperes & egeni apud Aulam Fullonum ; domus Elemofynaria prope ecclefiam omnium fanctorum; pauperes St. Joannis de la Redclive-pytt; carcerati egentes de Monkebrigge (or Bridewell) ; pauperes domus Elemofynariæ fanctæ Trinitatis juxta Laford's-gate." — To all thefe he was a benefactor.

Others alfo have arifen fince, or fucceeded fome gone to ruin ; as St. John's and All Saints' almfhoufe, new built ; the Merchant Taylors' almfhoufe, in Merchant-ftreet ; Colfton's almfhoufe for old men and widows, on St. Michael's-hill ; the Merchants' almfhoufe, in King-ftreet ; St. Nicholas almfhoufe, in the fame ftreet ; all which are well built, and have excellent accommodations for the poor, fome are alfo amply endowed. Add to thefe that fpacious and general afylum for the poor, the old, the infirm, the difeafed, and the helplefs, St. Peter's hofpital, the public poor-houfe of the city, near St. Peter's church, the Orphan fchool for poor boys, called Queen Elizabeth's hofpital, formerly next College-green, now removed into Chriftmas-ftreet ; as alfo the great fchool for poor boys, called Colfton's hofpital, on St. Auguftine's-back, in which one hundred boys are clothed, fed, and educated, from feven years of age till fourteen, when each has 15 l. given him at his going out to an apprenticefhip.

The chapels, religious boufes, churches, hofpitals, and almfhoufes, are particularly noticed and the meafurements of them as they ftood in 1480, in William Botoner's book, extracts of which will be given in the particular defcription of each as it occurs.

In the regifter of William of Wickham, Bifhop of Winchefter, is the following particular of the chapel of St. Brendan : " Ibidem 14 die Augufti, 1403 dominus conceffit, &c." i. e. " he granted to all benefactors to the chapel of St. Brendan nigh Briftol and to Reginald Taillor the poor hermit of it, forty days of indulgence by his letters for one year only to continue;" by which it appears there was an hermitage of religious here with a chaple dedicated to St. Brandon an Irifh Saint. And in an old Latin deed relating to the Gaunts, I find a piece of ground or croft juxta pafturam fancti Brendani, near the field of St. Brendan held by a female reclufe or hermit — quam reclufa tenuit. In the year 1351, Lucy de Newchirche repeatedly offered to the Bifhop of Worcefter and defired leave to be fhut up in the hermitage of St. Brendan of Briftol, and to quit the world, which after due inquiry into her conduct and purity of life and neceffary virtues for it, was

granted

granted her: as we find by this deed, E. Regiſtris Wygorniæ, Thoreſby f. 21 a

Commiſſio ad includendam Luciam de New Chirche Anchoritam.

Johannes miſeratione divina Epiſcopus &c Salutem; dileſto filio magiſtro Johanni d' Severley Archidiacono noſtro Wygornienſi gratiam & benediſtionem: accedens ad nos Lucia de New Chirche ſe Anchoritam in Heremitorio St. Brendani de Briſtol noſtræ diocefeos cum inſtante et humili devotione, prout nobis per fui geſtus habitum apparebat, includi repetitis vicibus poſtulavit. Noſque de vita & converſatione prediſtæ Luciæ notitiam non habentes vobis, de veſtra fidelitate & induſtria & circumſpeſtione plenius in domino confidimus, ad inquirendum per viros & mulieres fide dignos de converſatione illins Luciæ; &·fi eam vitæ laudabilis eſſe et mundæ & alia virtutum infignia quæ in hunc mundum relinquentibus vigere deberunt, in ea pollere perpenderitis: ac diebus & temporibus, prout expediens fuerit ac juri conſonum & rationi eidem pro fui examinatione veſtro arbitrio aſſignandis, ipſam in mundo propoſito perſeverantem inveneritis & conſtantem, ſuper quo veſtram coram Deo conſcientiam oneramus, eam in diſto Heremitorio Anachoritam includendi per vos vel alium vobis quantum cum Deo poſſumus inoffenſo jure, committimus vices noſtras. Dat. London: 7 die Maii Anno Dom. milleſſimo CCCmo LIo & tranſlationis noſtræ 2do.

Beſides theſe Chapels noted by Leland, there was alfo the chapel of St. Giles annexed however to St. Leonard's in 1301, and there were others of a much earlier foundation, and ſo old as not even to be ſeen in their ruins in his time. — The following I met with in an old manuſcript *penes me* in Chatterton's hand writing from Rowleie.

" St. Baldwyns Chapelle in Baldwyns-ſtreet: Brightike haveing made it " ynto a houſe, Kynge Harrie ſecundus in hys yinge daies was there taughte: " yn the wall of it was an Ymagerie of a Saxonne Abthane crabattelie " ywroghtenne with a mantille of Eſtate which yonge Harrie enthoughten to " be moke fyner dreſſe thenne hys, cauſeynge the fame to be quaintiſſen yn " elenge ſelke & broderie; thus came Courte dreſſe from a Briſtoe Ymagerie.

" St. Mary Magdelens Chapelle: founded by Elle Ld. Warden of the " Caſtle near Elle-gate, ſythence ycleped New-gate. Yn thys Chapelle of " the Caſtele was yſworne a Treatye between Goodwyne Earle of Kent, " Harold eſtſoons Kynge of Englande, Leofwinus, hys Broders, & other " Nobles of the Londe.

" St.

" St. Matthyas is Chapelle — Thys Chapelle was fyrſt ybelden bye
" Alwarde a Saxonne ynne 867 & ys now (about the year 1460) made of the
" old walles of the fame a Free Maconnes Logge, of wyche fame amme I
" unwordie & Maſtre Canyge Brendren; ytte ys cleped Canynges place,
" Canynges Logge & Lyon Logge.

" Seynĉte Auſtins Chapple : Thys freemied pyle ytte is uncouth to faie,
" whom the fame dyd ybuyld. But it mote nedes' be eld : fythence it was
" yn ruyn in the days of Wm. le Baſtarde, The dribblette remaines wyll
" ſhewe yts aunciauntrie and nice Carvellynge — An aunciaunte Bochord
" faieth, Geoffrie a norman Carveller dyd newe adorne the fame in Edward
" Confeſſors daies." This chapel ſtood next the fine gate leading to the
lower Green. ——— In another manuſcript by the fame alfo is thus defcribed " Seynĉte Baudwins Chappele : yt ſtooden ynn Baudwynne Street :
" the preeſte thereof toke Churfotte of alle boates paſſeyng the brydge of
" woode there ſtandeynge. Brighticke Erle made ytte ynto a dwellynge
" houſe for wych faĉt Codds Ire dyd hym overtake & he deceafyd yn pry-
" ſon : fome faie hys Corſe was forewyned as ſtryken wythe a Levyn Brond —
" After his putting it to lay ufe K. Harolde lodged there, Robertus Fitz-
" Harding lyved there. To this daie ſtandeth the Croſs yn the Glebe whi-
" lom the Glebe or Church-yard nempt Baldwyns Croſſe." This houſe is
now called the Back-hall in the fame ſtreet, for weighing and houſing goods
on the Back. There was hereabouts one called in fome mannſcripts St. John's
chapel.

The churches in the city of Briſtol being formerly eighteen befides the Cathedral with the chapels and churches now confolidated with others, had of old
feveral chauntries belonging to each, as will appear more particularly in the
enfuing hiſtory of each parochial church ; but the following table will give
a general account of them in the year 1547 when " the worſhipful John
Cottrel, Dr. of Laws, Vicar General to Paul Buſh, the. ·firſt Biſhop of
Briſtol, fequeſtred to the King's ufe all fruits, profits, emoluments whatfoever
&c. for non-payment of fubfidies and tenths then due, on the firſt May and
at Chriſtmas laſt paſt, and made John Rumney keeper of them fo fequeſtred"
1ſt Apr. A. D. 1547. 1. Edw. vi.

	l.	*s.*	*d.*
The monaſtry of St. Auguſtin near Briſtol, — —	67	16	0¾
The hofpital or houfe of Gaunts or St. Mark, — —	11	4	11¾
The hofpital or Domus Calendar, — — — — —	1	1	10½
A chantry by Wm. Dean there — — — — —	0	16	0
Another by Sir Thomas Merryfield — — — —	0	16	0

The

					l.	s.	d.
The rectory of the Holy Trinity, [the yearly tenths]					1	2	0
A chantry by Richard Erle in the fame church,					0	13	4
A chantry by Catharine Jonys there, - - - -					0	12	8
A chantry by Rob. Alef and Roger Cantock, -					0	8	0
Another by Thomas Ball, - - - - - -							
The rectory of the church of St. John the Baptist,					0	14	$5\frac{1}{2}$
Chantries founded by Walter Frampton, - - -					1	1	$10\frac{1}{2}$
A chantry there by Thomas Rowley, - - -					0	14	0
The vicarage of St. Leonard, [the yearly tenths]					1	4	0

l.	s.	d.			l.	s.	d.
			The rectory of St. Stephen, - - - - - - -		1	2	0
7	13	4	A chantry there founded by Richard White, -		0	15	4
3	0	0	Another there by the fame, - - - - - -		0	6	0
6	0	0	Another there by Thomas Belcher, - - - -		0	12	0
6	0	0	Another there by Edward Blanket, - - - -		0	12	0
			The rectory of the church of St. Audoen, - -		0	6	8
			The vicarage of All-Saints [the yearly tenths] -		0	8	4
			A chantry by Thomas Holway, - - - - -		0	13	4
			The rectory of St. Lawrence [the yearly tenths] -		0	8	$9\frac{3}{4}$
			A chantry there by Cecily Pollard, - - - -		0	12	0
			The rectory of St. Werburge, - - - - - -		1	0	0
			A chantry there by John Fofter, - - - - -		0	14	0
			The rectory of St. Mychael, - - - - - -		0	12	0
			The vicarage of St. Auguftine, - - - - -		0	12	0
			The rectory of St. Peter, - - - - - - -		0	12	9
			The rectory of St. Mary in foro, [tenths] - - -		0	14	0
			The vicarage of the church of St. Phillip, - - -		1	10	0
			A chantry there by John Kemys, - - - -		0	12	0
			Another by Robert Forthey, - - - - - -		0	12	0
			The vicarage of the church of St. Nicholas, - -		2	2	$0\frac{1}{2}$
12	7	11	A chantry there by Richard Spycer, - - -		1	4	$9\frac{1}{2}$
26	3	9	Four chantries there by Everard le French, - -		2	12	$4\frac{1}{4}$
5	0	0	Another by William Spencer, - - - - -		0	10	0
13	6	8	Two chantries by Thomas Knapp, - - - -		1	6	8
			St. Mary's chapel on the bridge, a chantry there				
6	13	4	by Edward le French, - - - - - - -		0	13	4
			The church of St. James, a chantry there by				
			William Ponam, - - - - - - - -		0	12	0

Another

	l.	*s.*	*d.*
Another by John Spycer, – – – – – –	0	10	8
A chantry of the Holy Crofs in All-Saints church,	0	16	0
Another chantry there, – – – – – –	0	16	0
The hofpital of St. John the Baptift in Briftol, –	5	3	0½
The houfe of St. Mary Magdalen, – – – – –	2	3	9¼
The rectory of St. Mary port, – – – – –	0	10	7
The vicarage of the church of St. Mary de			
Redcliff, [tenths] – – – – – – –	1	4	7½
A chantry by William Canyngs there, – – –	1	6	8
A chantry there by Richard Mede, – – – –	0	14	0
In the church of St. Thomas, two chantries there			
by John Stokes, – – – – – – – –	1	0	0
A chantry by John Burton, – – – – – –	0	13	4
Two chantries by Robert Chepe and others, –	0	13	4
The vicarage of Holy Crofs, alias le Temple, – –	0	6	5
A chantry there by John Frances, – – – –	0	10	3¾

Thefe were the churches chapels and chauntries therein celebrated, fequeftred to the King's ufe ; — of which chauntries more particular notice will be taken in the account of each parifh church.

In a manufcript entituled Liber Taxationum Beneficiorum in Anglia, now in the Bodleian Library at Oxford, taken 19th year of Edward 1ft. 1291, is the following account, — In the Archdeaconry of Gloucefter and Deanry of Briftol.

Ecclefia St. Stephani, – – – – – – – – 7 Marc. dimid.

Portio abbatis Glaftoniæ in eadem, – – – – – 10 Sol.

Portio abbatis de Keynfham in Ecclefia St. Laurentii, 2 Sol.

Portio prioris, St. Jacobi in Eccles. St. Joannis, – 10 Sol.

Ecclefia St. Michaelis, – – – – – – – 6 Marc. dimid.

Portio St Jacobi. – – – – – – – – – – 4 Sol.

Ecclefia St. Warebrigge, – – – – – – – – 6 Marc. dimid.

Portio abbatis de Keynfham in ecclefiâ Beat. Mariæ, 20 Sol.

Portio abbatis St. Auguftini in ecclefiâ omnium

   fanctorum, – – – – – – – – – 30 Sol.

Portio ejufdem abbatis in ecclefia St. Auguftini

   minoris, – – – – – – – – – – – 1 Marc.

Ecclefia St. Nicolai, – – – – – – – – 6 Marc.

Portio vicarii in eadem, – – – – – – – 7 Marc. dimid.

Portio prioris St. Jacobi in ecclefia St. Petri, – – 11 Sol.

Ecclefia

Ecclefia St. Trinitatis, - - - - - - - - 7 Marc. dimid.

Ecclefia St. Jacobi, - - - - - - - - 23 Marc.

Ex exactiffimo facrarum ædium catalogo cum annuo valore e Dugdal. Mon. Anglic. v. 1. p. 1039.

	Gloceft.	l.	s.	d.
Can. St. Aug. Briftol ab. St. Aug. - - - - - -	670	13	11 ob.
Can. St. Aug. St. Marc. hofp. alias Gaunt's, (alias Bilyfwyke,)	112	9	9 o.
St. Laurence hofpital, - - - - - - -	51	10	4 o.
Kalendar. domus, - - - - - - - -	10	18	8 o.
B. M. Magd. domus, - - - - - - -	21	11	3 o.
Weftbury colleg. - - - - - - - -	232	14	0 o.
St. Catherin. hofpital, - - - - - - -	21	15	8 o.
Bendict. Tewkfbury abb. cum cella Jacobi, - - -	1598	1	3 o.

Somerfet.

		l.	s.	d.
Keynfham abb. - - - - - - - - - - - -	419	14	3 o.
Mynchinbarrow, - - - - - - - - -. - -	23	14	3 o.
Temple Comb comandria, - - - - - - - - -	107	16,	11 o.
Bridgwater priory, - - - - - - - - - - -	120	19	1 ob.

The nineteen churches have been thus enumerated in Latin verfe.

De ædibus facris urbe fpectabilibus.

Sunt ædes, quarum furgentia culmina cælo
Formofam reddunt fpectanti turribus urbem:
Redclivia, & Thomas, Templum, Phillippus & omnes
Sancti, Auguftinus, Nicolafque, Maria, Johannes,
Audænus, Petrus, Micael, ecclefia Chrifti,
Werburgæ et Stephani, nova Pauli, itemque Jacobi,
Gauntes, pontificis tandem fpeciofa Cathedra,
In quibus æternæ tractantur verba falutis:
Hæc jactant variis fefe præcellere rebus,
Una fuam jactat ftructuram, atque altera tectum,
Altera fublimem, qua tendit ad æthera turrim:
Concamerata fibi jactant fundamina quædam,
Atque fepulchretum quædam; funt tumque feneftras
Suntque pavimentum jactantes, funt quoque multæ
Quæ fibi campanas guadent jactare fonoras,
Altera prægrandes, atque altera jactat amænas,
Altera fe numero reliquas fuperare triumphat.
Sed quibus ulla putat claram fefe effe feorfim,
Omnibus his junctis jactat tranfcendere Redcliff.

I

Of thefe places of religious inftitution, and of the hofpitals or almfhoufes, a more particular defcription and account will be given in the parochial hiftory hereafter.

The city, by the virtue * and induftry of our anceftors, and by the unwearied application of its merchants and inhabitants to trade (not to be taught to undergo poverty †) became daily more and more populous, and increafed not only in extending its buildings on every fide but alfo in its credit, opulence, and rank, in this commercial nation. A work was now fet on foot, which, for its boldnefs, grandeur, and defign in benefiting pofterity, would do honour even to the the prefent age : it was no lefs than turning the courfe of the river Froom, filling up its old channel, and digging a new one, to make the Key or Quay for the fafe birthing of the fhips, by which they at low water grounded on a fafe bed of mud, with lefs danger to their bottoms : which is excellently defcribed by Leland, vol. vii. 2d edit. fol. 70. or p. 87.

" The haven by Avon flowithe about a two miles above Brightftowe-bridge.
" The fhips of olde tyme cam only up by Avon to a place caullyd the Bek,
" where was and is depthe enowghe of watar, but the bottom is very ftony
" and rughe ; fens by polecye they trenched fomewhat alofe by northe-wefte
" of the old Key on Avon anno 1247, and in continuance bringing the courfe
" of From-ryver that way hath mad a fofte and whofy (oozy) harborow for
" grete fhippes."

·This

* *Virtute et Induftriá,* is the motto of the Briftol arms ; a due regard to it will ever preferve its honour and renown to lateft pofterity. — The old arms of the city of Briftol are, gules, a caftle upon an hill by the fea-fide, and the helm of a fhip paffing by, all proper; to which were afterwards added, fupporters, &c. See the prints.

† *Indocilis pauperiem pati,* the motto of the arms of the Merchant Venturers here. The arms of the Merchants' Society are, barry undé of eight pieces argent and azure on a bend or, a dragon volant vert, on a chief g. a lion paffant gardant or, between two bezants,

This enterprize of making a new key, and of conftructing a ftone bridge acrofs the Avon, and joining to Briftol Redcliff fide, (which though before a part of the city yet belonging to the honour of Glocefter, was under a feparate government till the charter of Henry 3d. (which fee in the annals for the year,) was undertaken about the fame time, and formed together one grand complete fcheme, which made fuch amazing alterations, was attended with fuch beneficial confequences to the community, that it ought juftly to be fig-nalized apart as a particular æra, from whence to date the rife of thofe great improvements that followed; advancing, with a rapid progrefs, the honour, riches, and commercial interefts of this city: which, by the virtue and induftry of its citizens, has rofe to its prefent grandeur and dignity in the nation; and that alone reflects greater honour on Briftol than any thing that we have faid or can fay in its praife for its antiquity, the only thing many places, more extolled in chronicles or old hiftories, have now left to boaft of; whilft this, like a well cultivated fpot, has been continually flourifhing with renewed vigour, extending its commerce to the moft diftant regions, enlarg-ing its antient bounds by additional buildings and magnificent public ftructures, and has thus merited its antient Saxon name Brightftowe, i. e. an illuftrious city, by becoming yearly more and more illuftrious.

Previous to conftructing the ftone bridge and making the new key, in the year 1239 our prudent forefathers purchafed of the then abbot of St. Auguftin, William de Bradeftone and the convent, ground in the marfh of St. Auguftin fufficient for their purpofe of making the new trench, haven, or quay: a copy of the original covenant between them follows.

" Conventio facta inter abbatem & conventum St. Auguftini, Briftolliæ, & maiorem & communiam Briftolliæ, de terra in marifco St. Auguftini verfus aquam de Frome.

" Hæc eft conventio facta inter dominum Willielmum de Bradeftone, tunc abbatem fancti Auguftini Briftolliæ & ejufdem loci conventum ex unâ parte, & Ricardum Aillard, tunc maiorem Briftol & totam communiam Briftolliæ ex altera parte: fcilicet quod dictus abbas & conventus concefferunt pro fe & fuccefforibus fuis in perpetuum maiori & communiæ Briftolliæ, et corum here-dibus totam terram illam in marifco St. Auguftini Briftolliæ quæ jacet extra foffatum, quod circuit terram arabilem dictorum canonicorum directè verfus orientem ufque ad marginem portûs Frome: quod quidem faffatum extenditur a grangia dictorum canonicorum verfus Abonam; falvis abbati & conventui predicto terrâ proximâ dicto foffato verfus grangiam predictam, ubi dicta com-munià incipit foffare feptics viginti & quatuor pedibus terræ in latitudine et in

medio

medio dicti marisci quater viginti & duodecim pedibus terræ in latitudine; & in exteriori parte dicti marisci versus Abonam sexaginta pedibus terræ in latitudine, super quam terram sic mensuratum communia Bristolliæ & eorum hæredes habere debent liberum iter suum, introitum & exitum & transitum ad naves suas & ad spatiandum pro voluntate eorum de die & nocte, longe & proxime, pacifice & sinc contradictione in perpetuum, sicut semper hæredes consueverunt: debent autem prædicta communia & eorum hæredes salvare abbati & conventui prédicto et successoribus suis eandem terram mensuratam ita scilicet quod in cursus aquæ terram deterioraverit, dicta communia illam debet emendare: residuam vero terram dicti marisci Sancti Augustini Bristolliæ ex orientali parte & australi prædicti fossati debent predicta communia & eorum hæredes integre habere et possidere ad faciendam inde unam trenchiam, portum & quicquid dictæ communiæ melius servierit absque omni impedimento & contradictione in perpetuum: pro hac concessione siquidem & pro bono pacis dederunt prædicti maior & communia Bristolliæ prædicto abbati et conventui novem marcas argenti: undi ut hæc concessio rata et stabilis permaneat, tam sigillum prædicti conventus quam sigillum communitatis Bristolliæ mutua appenda sunt huic chirographo: hiis testibus Domino Johanne filio Galfridi, Thoma de Berkleia, Rob. de Gourney, W. de Pycott, Ignatio de Clyfton, Rogero de Warre de Knolle, Johanne le Warre de Brixtulton & aliis; facta autem conventio vigiliâ annunciationis beatæ Mariæ, anno regni Domini regis H. filii J. vicessimo quarto." — A. D. 1239, 24th Hen. 3d.

By this the abbot grants to the mayor, Richard Aillard and the commonalty of Bristol, all the land lying without a certain ditch of their's, that surrounded their arable land, directly towards the east unto the brink of the haven of Froom, which ditch extended from the Grange of the Cannons towards the Avon. The ground next the said ditch towards the Grange, where the commonalty began to dig, being reserved to the abbot and convent, seven score and four feet broad; in the middle, four score and twelve feet broad; and in the outer part of the said marsh towards the Avon, sixty feet broad. Upon the ground so measured out, the commonalty of Bristol and their heirs were to have free passage, ingress and egress, to their ships in the new trench or quay, and to walk as they pleased, by night or by day, without let or molestation for ever: but the city was obliged to amend and repair the lands so measured out, if by the current of water it should be damaged. The remaining ground of the said marsh of St. Augustin, from the east and south part of the ditch, the mayor and commonalty of Bristol were to have wholly and possess, in order to make from thence one trench, haven, or whatever should best

ferve

ferve their purpofe, without hindrance, for ever, paying nine marks of filver.

This grant being obtained, it was not long before they put the work in execution. Some difpute has arifen betwixt the Corporation of Briftol and the Dean and Chapter, who are now in the ftead of the Abbot and Convent aforementioned, concerning the limits of this ground on St. Auguftine's back, granted unto the city by this deed, and it is yet undecided in the year 1788. It appears that fome years after the above grant the Abbot fued the city for trefpaffing upon the privileges of his monaftry, where he held a court of view of frank pledge and a fanĉtuary except for treafon, and complains, " quod non faciunt reparationes circa littora aquæ vocatæ Frome devaftantis terram diĉti abbatis ficut tenentur," meaning doubtlefs the land fecured to the Abbot by the above grant;—by which it is clear that a large portion of ground was given to the commonalty of Briftol, then called Avon marfh, lying on the eaft fide of the fame river, by the abbot and convent, on con_ dition that the faid Mayor and commonalty fhould defend from the water Frome a certain parcel of ground belonging to the monaftery and adjoining the fame, which in the time of Abbot John Newland was by them negleĉted, to the great damage of the ground called Cannons marfh; which was one great caufe of difpute in Henry 7th's. time betwixt them. (Great white Book p. 18, 6.) In 1496, 11th Henry 7th the conteft was compromifed by the Lord Chief Juftice and Lord Chancellor—(p. 36 G. white Book) during the difpute the Mayor forbade the burgeffes to fell any provifions to the con- vent, grinding corn at their mill called then Trenel now Trin-mill, hindred the courfe of juftice and performed many other ill offices.

The following was the petition of the Abbot by which the caufe of the difpute will appear.

Supplicatio Abbatis.

1. Pro denariis levatis & diftriĉtionibus captis de tenentibus infra privilegi- um Monafterii Sanĉti Auguftini juxta Briftol eifdem reddendis & fub injunĉtione pecuniaria ne iterum facere prefumpferit.

2. Pro viĉtualibus & aliis neceffariis emendis vel vendendis nullum pof- tea fiat impedimentum.

3. Quod inhabitantes Briftoliam volentes grana fua molere ad molendina diĉti Abbatis non impediantur.

4. Quod fiat exccutio Juftitiæ in caufis diĉti Abbatis fine dilatione vel cavillatione.

5. Quod reddant Terras & redditus detentos prædiĉto Abbati.

6. Quod

6. Quod faciant reparationes circe littora aquæ vocatæ Frome devaſtantis terram diɛti Abbatis

To exaɛtly aſcertain the ground ſpecified in the deed would now be very difficult, the limits being deſtroyed and the places ſo much altered by time; but in general we may aſſert, that ſo much ground as is parted from St. Auguſtin's ſide and now makes the channel of the river Frome and the Quay, was fully aſſured to the city by this grant; and a privilege alſo allowed the citizens of ſo much more ground as is there mentioned to be meaſured out next the Grange and towards the Avon for their uſe of going to their ſhipping, &c: and this indeed was all that was wanting to compleat the work. They began digging and forming the new channel from the Key conduit towards the Gib, unto the place beyond the Grange of the Monaſtery, which I ſuppoſe to be below Toms's dock, the ditch incloſing Cannon's marſh beginning there about: by which neither the water of the Avon or the Froom interrupted the work. — The trench thus dug towards the Avon and then towards the Froom ſeparated the marſh of Briſtol (now built into a ſquare) whence the name of Marſh-ſtreet from the marſh of St. Auguſtine (now called Cannons marſh) partly built on and converted to the uſe of a dock, timber yard, rope walk and dwelling houſes, the privilege of paſſing to and fro there, being retained to this day. — As they were obliged by the covenant to keep on the outſide of this ditch, they were confined to that direɛtion and could not make it quite ſtraight, eſpecially oppoſite the marſh of St. Auguſtin, where it is a little winding, till it opens into the Avon. From whence having dug quite to the preſent head of the quay or quay-conduit, (as ſome manuſcripts have it) where the river Froom in a winding courſe followed the walls of the city in its natural current to Baldwin-ſtreet; this new communication with the Avon was effeɛted, that through Baldwin-ſtreet being ſtopped up, the Froom changed its courſe and ever after paſſed through this new channel, which being enlarged and walled, makes a ſafe and convenient quay, equal if not ſuperior to any in the kingdom, being a mile and a quarter round from the head of the quay to Briſtol bridge; and the ſhips are admitted by it into the midſt of the city.

In ſeveral manuſcripts *penes me* the digging the quay is variouſly expreſſed; one by Adams in 1626 has it, " Anno 1245, (Richard Alayne mayor, William Concord and John Northfolk prepoſitors) a trench was made and caſt at Gibtaylor up to the brazen ſtock of the key by the Mayor and commonalty of the town." Another thus, " Anno 1240, 24 Henry 3d. as Ricaut's Kalendar ſays, ſome ſay in 1245, 1246, 1247, the trench or key

was

was made from Gybb Tailleur * to the key conduit as well thofe of Redcliff-
ward and of Temple fee as of the town of Briftol taking their turns in the labour and charge: the Froom running before along Baldwin-ftreet where it
drove a mill called Baldwin's crofs-mill, and fell into the Avon near a place
where now ftands the Back hall, then was the old channel dammed up and
formed into a ftreet, to which there was an eafy back paffage and communication from St. Leonard's church as far as St. Nicholas church, though in two
places in St. Nicholas-ftreet there was a defcent by a flight of fteps for foot
paffengers. Before this time Cannons marfh took in all thofe places where
are now the Key, Gibb Tailleur and Princes-ftreet, and the ground next
Marfh-ftreet, the feite of part of which formed what was called Chanters clofe
and was exchanged by the Corporation with Sir William a Bradftone the
abbot for the Treen-mills with refervation of the privilege of hunting the
duck there for the difport of the magiftrates, as one manufcript declares, but
another fays it was granted upon a refervation of a yearly rent, but the kalendar fays in general it was purchafed for a certain fum payed down at exe-
euting the grant:" which appears to be the truth, though it looks from fuch
various relations of the facts that the bargain proceeded upon all thefe confi-
derations. Leland gives a very juft and particular relation of this whole
tranfaction wherever he picked it up. " The year of our Lord 1247 was
the trenche made and caft of the river from the Gibb Taylor to the Key by
the Comonalty as well as Redcliff fyde as of the towne of Briftoll; and the
fame tyme the inhabitants of Redcliffe were combined and incorporated to the
aforefaide towne. And as for the grounde of Saynt Auguftins fyde of the
river it was geven and granted to the comonalty of the fayed towne by Sir
William Bradftone, then being Abbot of the fame Monaftery for certayne
money therefore payed to him by the comonaltye, as it apperithe by writynge
thereof made betwinge the Mayor and comonalty and the Abbote and his
brethren." In another place he thus defcribes the river Avon as (when the
tide is in) filling the river and bringing in the fhipping. " Avon ryver about
a quarter of a mile beneath the towne in a † meadow cafteth up a great arm
or gut by which the greater veffels as mayne toppe fhippes cum up to the
towne. So that Avon doth peninfulate the town and veffels may cum of both
fides of it. I marked not well whither there cam any frefh water from the
lande

* Whence this name is derived is no where faid — I find a man named Gilbert le Tailor,
who might give rife to it.

† (Meadow, i. e. Cannons marfh) and the marfh of Briftol now Queen's-Square, betwixt
which is the quay, dividing both.

ſlande to bete that arme.''' By this he ſaw it, I ſuppoſe, when it was high
tide, when the little river Froom is loſt in that of the Avon.

That the Key of Briſtol was made at the joint expence of the men of Redcliff, as well as of thoſe of the town of Briſtol, appears evidently from a writ
of mandamus ſent to them by Henry 3d. dated 27th April, the 24th year of
his reign, which I have tranſlated from the Latin original. — " Henry, by the
grace of God, King of England, Lord of Ireland, Duke of Normandy, Aquitain, and Earl of Anjou, to all my honeſt men dwelling in la Redclive, in the
ſuburb of Briſtol, wiſbeth health.   Since our beloved burgeſſes of Briſtol, for
the common profit of the town of Briſtol as well as of your ſuburb, have begun
a certain trench in the marſh of St. Auguſtin, that ſhips coming to our port of
Briſtol may more freely and without hindrance come in and go out, which
trench indeed they cannot perfeƈt without great charges; we therefore
command you, that ſince from the bettering the ſaid port no ſmall advantage
will accrue, not only to thoſe burgeſſes, but alſo to you, who are partakers of
the ſame liberties which our ſaid burgeſſes have in the ſaid town, and are
joined with them both in ſcot and lot, that you lend the ſame aſſiſtance as they
do ; as it will be alſo very profitable and uſeful to you to have the work of the
trench happily compleated, according to what ſhall fall to your ſbare, together
with our burgeſſes; and ſo effeƈtually, that the aforeſaid work, which we
regard as our own, receive no delay, through any defeƈt in you.   Witneſs
myſelf, at Wyndleſhore, 29th April, 24th year of our reign." — Before this
was made, the uſual place, as Leland ſays, for landing goods out of the ſhips
was at the Back,* where was the old Cuſtom-houſe, ſtill remaining, having the
arms of England in its front ; and at St. Nicholas-port, above the bridge before that was built, where on taking down the ſhambles large Gothic arched
cellars, running back almoſt into Maryport churchyard, were diſcovered,
uſed formerly for reception of merchants' goods there landed : and an old
mooring poſt was diſcovered in the ground on entering the north door of
Maryport church itſelf, which poſt was removed about 1750.   It appears, by
a note in the great White Book in the Chamber of Briſtol, that the cutting
of this trench, for the courſe of the Froom through the Key, coſt the commonalty of the city the ſum of 5000l. a vaſt ſum of money in thoſe days. —
Such a convenience to a trading city as this Quay, which admitted the ſhips
laden up to the merchants' warehouſes built near its banks, could not but be
attended with the good cenſequence of promoting the commerce of the city.
The Quay being compleated, and the marſh of Briſtol thereby effeƈtually

divided

---

* Back, or Bek, a Saxon word for a river.

divided from that of St. Augustin, houses and streets began to be built there; Marsh-street terminated with a chapel, dedicated to St. Clement, and a gate; and Back-street with a gate also, and a chapel near it, dedicated to St. John, and belonging to St. Nicholas; the church of St. Stephen and its dependent parish, and the buildings between the Back and the Quay, seem to have taken their rise at this period, and were all inclosed with a strong embattled wall, *externa* or *secunda mœnia urbis*, extending from the Key to the Back, where King-street has since been built. Vid. second plan of the city.

The inhabitants, now impelled thereto by a noble spirit of improving their city, not depressed by the consideration of expence attending the work, applied themselves to the business of erecting a permanent stone bridge across the Avon. That there was a wooden bridge there before the year 1247, the year in which all the manuscripts I have seen agree the stone bridge was erected, there is no sort of doubt. It is very unreasonable to suppose the contrary, as the city had been flourishing and very populous, and would certainly not labour under the great inconvenience of passing by boat a rapid river in the winter, as the only commuication with their brethren of Redcliff. The river indeed was a proper separation of the kingdom of Mercia from that of the West Saxons, but as soon as the latter were possessed of Bristol, and Brightrick walled it, a better intercourse with the Redclivians, and between Somersetshire and Glocestershire, than by an uncertain ferry, soon became necessary. Accordingly we find that there really was a wooden bridge there for some years, which, falling to decay and being unfit for the service required, was at this time pulled down and re-edified, in a more commodious and lasting manner, with thick stone piers and arches. London, in like manner, had no more than a wooden bridge till the year 1209, and Bristol seems to have copied it in that as well as in erecting a chapel and houses on the stone bridge after they had built one. It has been said indeed, that there was no bridge at Bristol over the Avon till 1247, the 31st of Henry 3d. but a charter of Henry 2d. without date, and the following grant from Robert Fitzharding quite disproves that matter. " Robert, the son of Harding, to " all his friends and to all men present and future health. Know ye, that I " have granted and confirmed that my men, who dwell in my fee in the marsh " near the bridge of Bristol, have their customs and liberties, &c. which the " men of Bristol have, as our Lord the King has granted unto them; and I " will that they remain to them whole and full during my time, and that of " my heirs. Witness, Richard Abbot of St. Augustin, William Prior, and " others." Maurice de Berkly, son of the above Robert, confirmed to his

K   men

men of Redcliff, by his grant, the customs and liberties which they had in the time of his Father, and which were confirmed to them by his said father.

Now it appears, that it was in the time of Henry 2d's. reign that Robert Fitzharding made the above grant; in which it appears, that the *men dwelling in the marsh* near the *bridge of Bristol* are the fame men that afterwards are called by Maurice, in H. 3d.'s time, his *men of Redclive*: from whence it may be inferred, that Redcliff being low ground, liable to be flooded by the high tides, was firft called the *marsh near the bridge,* and that a bridge was built there long before the trench was cut in the marsh by the Gibb, whether of wood or ftone does not appear; though I am moft inclined to believe it was the former, the old ftone bridge certainly not being built till 1247, the very time when the new trench or key was dug out, and Froom river diverted from its ufual courfe through the Fish-market and Baldwin-ftreet into it. This firft bridge, which might probably be of wood, was faid by William of Worcefter to be made in 1215 by King John, and to contain 140 greffus, or 72 virgas, p. 366. (vid. annal. for that year below, in Henry 2d's. reign.)

William of Worcefter, who wrote about the year 1480, meant doubtlefs the ftone bridge then meafured of the length he fets down, and fuppofed it to be the fame built by King John; but that was his miftake, as well as that King John founded any bridge here. We fee by King Henry 2d's. charter that great prince,* who feems to have fignalized Briftol, the place of his education, with his favour, could alone be faid to be the founder of a bridge here, as one is mentioned in his writ of mandamus, in the reign indeed a little before that of King John, which might have deceived William of Worcefter, the Briftol antiquary. In a manufcript of one Mr. Lant, *penes me,* it is faid, William Earl of Glocefter founded and annexed Redcliff to Briftol, fuppofing that the time of the foundation of a bridge. Leland alfo gives it to him in thefe words, in Cygn. Cant. Poftea, ponte facto; i. e. " afterwards a bridge being made, Redclive, on the left bank of the Avon, was added to Briftol, and defended with a ftrong wall, at the time when William Earl of Gloucefter governed this county and efpecially Briftol."

How this ftone bridge was conftructed, I fhall fet down fimply the account as it occurs in antient manufcripts, which generally agree all in the manner of relating this fact; though fome are more explicit than others. One, wrote in a very old hand in my poffeffion, has it thus:

" 1247.

---

* In the nich over Nicholas-gate, at the entrance of the Bridge, was a ftone figure of a young prince (Henry 2d.) with a crown and fceptre, taken down and deftroyed when that gate was removed, in 1760.

" 1247. This year the mayor and commonalty concluded to build a bridge over the river Avon, with the confent of Redclifft and the governors of Temple fee, thereby minding to incorporate them with the towne of Brighteſtowe, and ſo make of both but one corporate towne : for they paſſed by bote from St. Thomas ſtepp, unto St. Mary le Port to come to Brighte-ſtowe : for at that time the port was, where now St. Nicholas ſhambles is and there the ſhippinge did ride : for which cauſe the church is called the church of our Lady her Affumption, and the port St. Maryport : at that time noe water did run downe the key, but with one courrant did runne to the caſtle : for the maſh of St. Auſtines ſyde was one mayne cloſe called Chanters cloſe, belonging to the Abby of St. Auſtines, and for the conveyinge the river from the poynte called the gibb, unto the key, the Mayor and commo-nalty as well of Temple ſyde as of the towne of Brigheſtowe boughte ſo much ground as is parted from St. Auſtins ſide of Sir William a Bradſtone the abbot, for a certeine ſome of monie to him payd, as apeerethe by an old writeinge made betwene him and the mayor with the convent : and then the trench was digged for to bringe the river unto the key; for at that time a freſh river from behind the caſtle mills did run down under Froome gate bridge, and ſo throghe Baldwynne-ſtrete now ſo called and it drived a mill called Baldwin's eroſſe-mill : and when the trench to the key was finiſhed the water was ſlopped at the poynt againſt Redcliff; and all the while the foun-datyon of the arches was layinge and the maſons buildynge, the water did run under the bridges of Redcliff and Temple gates, being made for the fame purpoſe : and at Tower Harris, or Harrats, the water was there bayed up, that it could not come down to hinder the building but it keept its current that way, and ſo the bridge being builded the beyes were broken down, and the current dothe ebb and flowe as it did formerlie. Then the freſh river that did run by Baldwins-croſs was dampned up, and made a ſtreete. Thus theſe two townes were incorporated into one, both on Somerſetſhire ſide and Gloceſterſhire ſide, that whereas they had uſually on every Munday a great market at Stallenge eroſſe and in Brigheſtow every Wedneſday and Friday at the High croſſe * and it was much trouble for people to paſs from one ſide to the other, the bridge being built the market was kept in the High-ſtreet, at the High-croſſe."

Such is the account given of this tranſaction ; in which the mayor's Calen-dar by Ricaut, preſerved in the Chamber of Briſtol, and all the private ma-

K 2

nuſcripts

---

* Some manuſcripts ſay the market in Brighteſtowe was held in the Old Market now ſo called, and at this time was removed to the High-croſs which was there erected and adorned with figures.

nufcripts generally agree. Some indeed fay, " it was done at the charge of the Mayor and Aldermen and with the confent and charges of Redclift and of Temple fee;" and that " befide the large cut made from Tower Harris to Redclift for the ebbing and flowing of the tide, the river Avon was damed up on each fide the foundation :" — but this feems to be owing to the variety of tranfcripts, and different expreffions of the copiers.

They pitched upon the fame fpot for this work where the ancient ferry was of old, and near the place where the wooden bridge (then perhaps ruinous) ftood; — it was oppofite St. Nicholas port which led to the center of the city, and fronting St. Thomas-ftreet, the center parifh on the Redcliff fide : they could not have chofen a better fituation though it is rather in the bend of the river; and the buildings on both fides of the water feem afterwards to have been laid out in a direction agreeable to this fite of the bridge or paffage over the Avon.

That the river was then turned into the new channel above defcribed, evidently appears from the marks of it to this day. At Tower Harrits we fee even now a deep wide trench, which the high bank on one fide of it fhews to have been made by art, and fuch a quantity of earth thrown out proves its having been very large and much deeper then at prefent, — it runs in a direct line to Temple gate, and were the tide not fhut out by a hatch it would ftill flow as far as Temple gate through it; there the channel is now covered by building, though open with a bridge over it formerly; but appears again at the back part of Pile-ftreet, (which took its name from its being once a pill or paffage for water) and fo paffing by Redcliff gate goes into the river Avon again, where it is now converted into a very large gout or common fewer for that part of the city. The city being walled on this fide, it ran juft under the wall and doubtlefs afterwards ferved as a very good additional fence either as a dry or wet ditch.

Another proof of the river being thus diverted into a new channel, while they were laying the foundations is the immenfe fize of the piers, of folid mafonry, which as they could build without any interruption, they made as big and as firm as they pleafed, to fecure the bridge for ever effectually a-gainft any injury from bodies of ice floating down, from the violence and rapidity of the current, from frefhes after rain, and accidents from veffels breaking from their moorings or the like.

But what puts it beyond a doubt, is the account of a boat, and materials belonging to fhipping having been dug up here in the gardens behind Pile-
ftreet.

ſtreet. The cut neceſſary for it was not very long, and the great advantage derived from it of building without being hindered by the water coming down upon them, points it out as the moſt eligible method they could have put in practice on ſuch an occaſion. That part of the river has been ever ſince called Back-Avon, which ſeems to infinuate that the Avon was once made to run on that back-ſide of the city.

That the bridge was not erected on a foundation made with piles has been proved ; and the old piers were perforated to examine their ſtructure if they would ſupport the new bridge erected on them in the year 1767, and found firm and ſolid, when to the great ſurprize of the workmen they found in the middle of Redcliff pier a fell of oak about one foot ſquare and forty foot long with two uprights near each end about nine inches ſquare and eight or nine foot high morticed into the fell, ſuppoſed by the workmen who had been down and examined it, to be the remains of the old wooden bridge firſt built on this ſpot, which decaying, a ſtone one was erected in its place, when theſe pieces of timber were not removed, but as they built ſuch large piers at leiſure, undiſturbed by the current, they walled them into the middle of the pier without the trouble of taking them up, but thinking perhaps it might give ſome ſtability to the work.

The whole breadth of the river being about two hundred feet, they divi-ded it into four arches and three ſolids or piers ; but theſe laſt were made ſo very thick and large, that the water way left was hot more than one hundred feet, rather inſufficient eſpecially in high tides and freſhes, as the water being kept back and confined, thereby it made a fall at the arches dangerous to the navigation; which has occaſioned their judgment being greatly called in queſtion by our modern builders. But whatever might be their reaſon for making the arches ſo narrow and the piers ſo large, the projectors of this bridge and the key ought ever to be remembered with the utmoſt honour gratitude and regard to their memory : a work that one ſhould ſuppoſe, they would not have been equal to and through diffidence never have attempted ; but their public ſpirit which ſeems to have animated them to ſuch a noble undertaking, ought to be extolled to lateſt poſterity. — The idea of duration and ſtability ſeems to have influenced their judgment too much in conſtruct-ing ſuch thick large piers, but as they built in a manner on dry land, they thought they could not poſſibly make them too ſtrong, having ſuch an oppor-tunity of doing it with caſe ; — however the ſuperſtructure might decay, they rightly judged, that might eaſily be repaired, but the piers or pillars they were for building for eternity.

To

To turn the river another way was no trifling matter, therefore while it was done they rightly confidered, that the firmeſt foundations they could build were the beſt, either for the preſent or any future uſe they might be applied to.

But there has been another objection made, that has more weight, and deſerves ſome confideration, viz. how they made the Bridge ſo narrow at firſt, being only nineteen feet broad, and afterwards turned other ſecondary arches from the ſpaundrels of the firſt, and parallel with them ; and laying large timbers, or rather trees, from the bridge to theſe ſecondary arches, not four feet thick, erected houſes thereon; which was, in fact, building a bridge for a ſafe and open paſſage, and afterwards ſtraitening or incommoding it with buildings, ſo as to render it difficult for two carriages in aftertimes to paſs abreaſt or by one another, without endangering the lives of foot paſſengers or driving them into thoſe very houſes for their ſecurity. As to the firſt, it is very unfair for us, at this time, to cenſure our anceſtors for not making the bridge wider ; for doubtleſs at that time, it was amply ſufficient for all the carriages they then uſed, and fully calculated for a free paſſage of the people over it, and the boats under it. The increaſed number of carriages ſince, and vaſt concourſe of inhabitants, could not then have been an object of any human foreſight.

The houſes built on the ſecondary arches were not a part of the firſt plan. The bridge ſeems to have been built for ſome time before this ſcheme took place, or was allowed. A chapel, dedicated to St. Mary, I think, was the firſt building erected there. William of Worceſter deſcribes this chapel, as thirty-ſix ſteppys long and twelve wide; in another place, twenty-five yards long and ſeven yards wide ; and p. 234. gives the following deſcription of it : ſ 1361, dedicatio capellæ pontis, &c." i. e. the chapel of the bridge of Briſtol was dedicated Feb. 4, 1361 ; its length is twenty-five yards, breadth ſeven yards, its height fifty ſtairs ; and there is a vault or arched room in its lower part, for the aldermen of the town, as long as the church with the nave, and it has four great windows on each ſide, and each window three lights, and an high window at the caſt part of the altar, and another little altar, with a ſmall chapel on the caſt of the principal altar, of the length of three yards. And the chapel contains a vault, a chapel, and an hall with offices, and a lofty chamber of ſtone." This chapel was erected and founded by Edward 3d. and his Queen Philippa, and called the chapel of the Aſſumption of the Bleſ-ſed Virgin Mary, as appears p. 185. of the great Red Book of Briſtol : and John Hakſton and John Hanker gave two meſſuages and three ſhops on the

Bak

Bak Avon to John Gweyn, chaplain there, for a perpetual chantry in this chapel to pray for the king's health, 49th Edward 3d.

In a letter from Pope Sixtus 4th. dated April 10, eleventh year of his con_secration, this chapel is faid " to be built and well endowed by certain bur_geſſes and commons of the town," (in honore & ſub vocabulo beatæ Mariæ Virginis) which might be the cafe, though the king and queen above had the credit aſſigned them, by granting the charter for it, as was uſual. The pope grants leave for ringing the bells and performing all divine offices therein, do_ing no prejudice to the rights of the pariſh church of St. Nicholas, in which pariſh it was ſituated. In the will of Nicholas Chapman, 1382, I find a be_queſt to the chapel of the Aſſumption of the Bleſſed Virgin, on the bridge of Briſtol. Great Book of Wills, p. 6.

This chapel probably took its rife as much from a view of profit as devo_tion; and it is not improbable but they collected in it money for defraying the expence they had incurred, and for the ſupport of the bridge afterwards, from the devotees, who came there to worſhip. They imitated the London_ers alfo in this, who in 1209 built a chapel to St. Thomas, ſixty feet long and twenty-five broad, on the great pier of London bridge : and Leland ſays of it, vol. v. f. 22. " a maſon being maſtre of the Bridge-houſe buildyd a funda_mentis, a chapel propriis expenſis." This on Briſtol bridge was but a ſmall room, having three Gothic windows on each fide, and was ſupported on an arch, turned from the pier of the Bridge to a pillar breaking out up the ſtream in the middle of the river, and over the chapel were the prieſts' cham_bers. It ſtood for many years, and was not deſtroyed till the year 1644; and in 1649 the two ſtone arches, on which the prieſt tenements formerly ſtood, belonging to the chapel, which had been burnt, were granted to Walter Stevens and fon to be built upon, from Sir William Birch of Weſtminſter, and a chief rent of 4l. per annum for a houſe, that went acroſs the bridge at top, called afterwards the chapel houſe.

In imitation of London, or partly to defray the great charges of the bridge, (for it no where appears how it was defrayed) houſes were afterwards ſuf_fered to be erected on each fide of it, that it had the appearance of a dark, narrow ſtreet. Theſe, which were let at very high and advantageous rents, in reality did not confine the paſſage, or make the bridge any narrower than it was at firſt; for the whole breadth of the bridge was in the road, and as foon as you ſtept into any of the houſes that hung, as it were, between the bridge and the fecondary arches, you were immediately on a floor of timbers and over the water, their ends reſting on the bridge and fecondary arches, which

were

were Gothic, very flender, and not fo compact nor fo well turned as the real, primary, femicircular arches of the bridge itfelf, and hardly fufficient to bear fuch a weight of lofty buildings, preffing unequally upon them. But no words can give the reader fo juft an idea of Briftol bridge as a view of the following draught of it, which was made in 1760, at the time it was about to be taken down, which being courfe reprefents to the eye more truly the appearance of it.

This bridge, when naked and unincumbered with houfes, (which were afterwards erected thereon by turning fecondary Gothic arches oppofite the old ones, for a foundation for one end of the buildings to reft upon,) confifted of four neat, ftrong, femicircular arches, the paffage over it being only nineteen feet wide, which muft have had a parapet wall at the fides before the houfes were erected, to fecure people from falling over into the river.

There was great folemnity ufed and public joy difplayed * on the firft opening of Briftol bridge: all joined in celebrating this great event, being well apprized of its extenfive utility. Their care in preferving it afterwards was equal to their diligence and eagernefs in erecting it. † Wheel carriages
laden

* The ceremony and joy faid to be difplayed on this occafion, with the fongs to St. Baldwin and St. Warburgh, are defcribed already and publifhed, p. 433. of Rowley's Poems by Dean Milles, to which I refer the reader.

† Donations were made from time to time by well-difpofed people for its repairs, by Mr. Thorn and others. Even fo early as Henry 3d. it appears he granted letters patent to the mayor and

laden * very heavy were but a century ago, not fuffered to pafs over it for fear of injuring it, and were halled on a kind of fledge for that purpofe firft and fo brought over. — And after it was crouded with houfes, to fhew how little they provided then (by its firft-intended width) for wheel carriages, they alfo had bulks before their houfes there, which were not removed till the year 1698, by an act or bye law of the corporation for that purpofe ; and fo late as the 5th Jac. ii. Oct. — " The chain at the bridge was ordered to be locked every Wednefday, Friday and Saturday, and every market day in High-ftreet from eight in the morning till two in the afternoon, and no hallier, brewer or other great carriages with drays fuffered to pafs over to the dif-turbance of the people going that way." But the greateft damage the bridge ever fuftained was from fire, about the year 1646, as the date on the large chimney piece of the houfes rebuilt afterwards plainly declare; when near one half of it from the chapel almoft to St. Nicholas gate on both fides was confumed. But the great advantage derived from the conftruction of this ftone bridge foon began to appear ;—parifhes enlarged, churches and reli-gions houfes built, and a new charter † to the Redclivians, new markets, fairs, increafe of people, trade, and manufactures were the confequent good effects : fome time after the pomerium or bounds of the city were enlarged and fixed by public charter of King Edward the 3d. and from this and making the new Quay moft of thefe great events feem to have taken their rife, and every im-provement we can now boaft of, in regular and fpeedy fteps followed the execution of thefe grand and nobly projected works of thofe days.

The fhips indeed were now ftopped from going up to unlade at the port of St. Mary, where the old well-turned gothic arches now pulled down extend-ing fome from the banks of the Avon (where the late Shambles were ‡) almoft back into St. Mary le port churchyard, fufficiently demonftrated what a place of bufinefs that formerly was. The back of Briftol begun now alfo to yeild

L

as

corporation in regard of their great charges in repairing the keys, walls, pitching and the bridge of the town which received great damage from floods, carts and carriages, by which they were empowered to purchafe and fettle lands to the value of 100l. per ann. notwithftanding the ftatute of Mortmain to repair the fame. — Little Red Book, page 93.

* So late as the year 1615 there was an act of common council that no cart with iron-bound wheels fhould even enter the city further than St. Peter's pump ; which gave occafion to what . Cambden afferted, that (in his time) they ufed no wheel carriages, for fear of injuring the gouts (cloacæ) or finks arched under ground, but drays in their ftead : but now all wheel carriages are ufed as well as drays.

† Of this charter of Henry the 3d. to the burgeffes of Redcliff, and public tranfactions af-terwards, and of the other fubfequent charters, fee annals for the year 1248, and after.

‡ Vid. Wm. of Worcefter, p. 170. 237.

as a place of wharfage to the new Quay, where the fhips lay ftill and undif-
turbed by the current on a foft bed of mud, the fmall craft only coming to
the Back.

The edifices erected afterwards to the honour of God, and the munificent
endowment of hofpitals and religious houfes, by the natives and inhabitants,
fufficiently prove their increafe in trade and opulence. And it may be faid of
the merchants here in general in thofe days, they refunded great part of the
wealth they acquired here to the city again, either in their life time or at their
death ; of which many illuftrious examples will be given, when I come to
enumerate and fpecify the benefactors' names, and record their good deeds,
whofe charity and humanity do fuch honour to our city, that not to endeavour
to do them juftice, or to conceal or flightly to pafs them over, in the future
pages of this work, might with reafon merit the fevereft cenfure.

The great improvements of the city, that fucceeded faft the erection of the
bridge and making the Quay, come now in courfe to be particularly noted,
which will bring us to the prefent modern improved ftate of it.

C H A P. IV.

Of BRISTOL in its prefent improved State.

BRISTOL lies in 51 degrees of northern latitude, diftant from London
115 miles, through Bath 123; and the turnpike roads around it, being
kept in repair, render its environs the more pleafing and inviting. The many
agreeable profpects, and walks or rides on the adjacent downs of Durdham
and Leigh, and over the hills at Portifhead, Walton, and Clevedon, in view
of the Briftol Channel ; the delightful villages of Afhton, Leigh, Wraxal, and
Backwell, on one fide; of Kingfwefton, (the feat of Lord Clifford) of Weftbury, Henbury, Almondfbury, Stapleton, and Frenchay, on another ; and
of Briflington, Knowle, and Dundry, on the other, &c.; and the pleafurable
excurfions to the Old and New Paffages; add greatly to the amufement,
health, and happinefs of its inhabitants. The fituation of the city itfelf is
very comfortable, being defended from the cold north winds by the adjoining
hills. Now greatly enlarged by an additional extent of buildings on every
fide, and improved by the liberties and franchifes it enjoys from feveral kings,

it

it continues to flourish in manufactures and commerce; and consequently becomes more and more populous. Even so early as the year 1347 it had weight enough to obtain the charter from Edward 3d. for constituting it a county within itself: that great prince's words are well worth mentioning, viz. " that in consideration of the good services, by their shipping and otherwise, " done to us in times past, we have granted it to be, and be for ever called " the county of Bristol, and to enjoy the liberties and freedoms under- " written, &c."

But the greatest dignity and highest honour from a crowned head it next arrived to, was the being erected into a bishop's fee and constituted a city by the royal letters patent, which in the Latin original are dated June 4, the 34th Henry 8th. though it had enjoyed the title of a city before, it was now legally and by authority so denominated.

An old manuscript before me words it thus : — " Bristol hath been always loyal to the king's majesties progenitors and the next to the crown, not con- senting to the proclaiming Q. Jane, tho' she was so proclaim'd in sundrie places. Bristol has been found willing and serviceable ever to their prince, in Q. Maries time against the French, when they sustained great losses by sea, to the undoing of many, whereof some were taken prisoners; and also in the time of late Q. Elizabeth against the Spaniards and in the wars of Ireland. — Bristol is accounted the queen's chamber, * as London is the king's chamber: it maintaineth the state of government there at their own charges, in most commendable sort. It always has been zealously affected to the advancement of God's word, and maintaineth preachers at their great charges. The maior, being the king's lieutenant, giveth place to no man but unto his majesty. — The Duke of Norfolk, the Earls of Leicester, Warwick, and Pembroke, the Lords President of the Marches, the Justices of Assize, all have and do give place unto the maior; so also the bishops predecessors have ever done the like. Always good service the town did unto the king.

" Bristol, being *villa regalis & libera*, was first made a county of itselfe the 47th Edward 3d. for notable services done to the king; and in the 34th Henry 8th. made a city, in regard of the love the said king did bear to the place, and of the great services done by the said towne, especially in the wars against the French king, who would have landed in the Isle of Wight; at which time this town did set forth eight ships. When King Henry 8th. came

L 2

on

---

* London is called the " king's chamber" by Shakespeare, in Richard 3d. act 3, scene 1, speech of Buckingham, vide Pope's note. " Camera Regia" was anciently the name of London.

on board Briſtowe's fleet on that memorable time, he aſked the names of their ſhips; and they anſwered the king, it is this: The firſt is

The barque Thorne, of	- - - - -	600 tons.
The barque Pratt,	- - - - - - -	600 tons.
The barque Gourney,	- - - - - -	400 tons.
The barque Younge,	- - - - - -	400 tons.
The barque Winter,	- - - - - -	300 tons.
The barque Shipman,	- - - - - -	250 tons.
The Eliphant,	- - - - - - - -	120 tons.
The Dragon,	- - - - - - - -	120 tons.

The king wiſhed he had many ſuch Thornes, Pratts, Gourneys, and the like, in his londe."

In a manuſcript it is ſaid, " in 1543, twelve ſhips ſailed out of Briſtol, in the king's ſervice, to aſſiſt at the ſiege of Bulloign, with Matthew Earl of Lenox, under whom ſerved Sir William Winter and Sir Richard Maunſell, who returned again with the earl."

By theſe charters and other grants of privileges it ſoon became of great repute in the commercial world and of high rank in the nation, and every year almoſt was productive of improvements. New ſtreets and public ſtruc-tures aroſe, more regular buildings were ſet on foot; till at length, embel-liſhed with ſquares, and adorned with a better ſtile of building, it has advanced itſelf to the preſent luſtre and magnificence it may juſtly claim, as appears by the large plan facing the title, and a farther deſcription or delineation of it.

The centre of the city ſtill occupies the hilly ground of an eaſy aſcent, being the whole of the old town or vill of Brightſtow; the plain around it was firſt built on, and converted into ſtreets. St. James's diſtrict ſoon became full of houſes and inhabitants, and enlarged its borders to the very ſummit of Kingſdown (called formerly Prior's-hill); which with the ſteep hill of St. Michael, both covered with elegant houſes, afford the diſtant eye a very agree-able proſpect of pendent houſes and gardens; and a ſpectator is ſtruck with ſurprize at the firſt ſight of a large town, hanging in continued ſlope, as it were, from the very clouds. From hence, and from the Park and Brandon-hill,* may be taken the moſt comprehenſive view of the whole city below: the pleaſantneſs of this ſpot, and delightful proſpect of the adjacent country to a great diſtance, has occaſioned ſuch a train of buildings to be erected there, to grace the brow of this hill and overlook the buſy town. From hence

we

---

* See Buck's views, who publiſhed two views of Briſtol, very fine; one taken from this ſpot, the other from Pile-hill on Redcliff ſide.

we defcry, at a fingle glance, the towers and fteeples of nineteen churches which adorn this city; whofe comely form and ftately elevation, as well as cleannefs and elegance confpicuous in their infides, is juftly admired by ftrangers, and reflects deferved applaufe on the inhabitants.

> A folemn neatnefs fhines on every fide,
> A neatnefs unadorn'd with Romifh pride;
> A comely form the ftately buildings grace,
> The inward worfhip fuits this outward face.
> Refin'd from all extremes, in order clean,
> The Englifh church obferves the golden mean:
> As temperate climes a due proportion hold
> Betwixt the fcorching heat and freezing cold.
>
> Goldwin's Poem on Briftol.

This hill and St. James's parifh beneath it was but thinly inhabited formerly, and, with the priory afterwards erected there by Robert Earl of Glocefter, was reckoned only the fuburbs of Briftol; but now being every where full of buildings, and embellifhed with three regular modern-built fquares, St. James's-fquare, King's-fquare, and Brunfwick-fquare (the laft begun 1769 and now 1788 completed) it is become a very confiderable part of the city;— fo great a part, that in 1787 an act was obtained for dividing this large parifh, and erecting a new church to be called St. Paul's church, already begun; where an elegant new fquare, of two hundred and eighty feet every way, is intended to be formed foon, with regular buildings and uniform fronts, the ground being already purchafed and laid out for this purpofe. On the weftern fide, formerly called the marfh of Briftol or Avon marfh, beyond the fecond or outward wall of the city, great improvements alfo were made by building new ftreets, as King-ftreet, Prince's-ftreet, and above all a fpacious, handfome fquare of houfes, fronted in an uniform manner, called Queen-fquare, in compliment to that good and amiable princefs Queen Anne, began about the year 1708 and completed in 1726; which, for its delightful walks, fhaded with rows of elms, and the crofs walks with lime-trees, (which were taken up in 1776, as making it too fhady) is efteemed an agreeable place of habitation, as well as of refort in fine weather, for the gentlemen and ladies, according to Mr. Goldwin's poetical defcription:

> Here elms and limes in treble order run,
> To fcreen our walking beauties from the fun;
> Natures umbrella here confus'dly meets,
> And fummer breezes fan the cool retreats.

In

In the center of Queen's-fquare in 1736, was fet up an equeftrian ftatue in brafs by hte ingenious Mr. Ryfbrack, fixed on an high pedeftal and in-clofed with iron pallifadoes. It was long difputed at that time, what great perfonage fhould grace this elegant and fpacious quadrangle: many were for Queen Elizabeth, more for Queen Ann, others for any of our Kings who had been benefactors to the city, by granting charters of privileges or immu-nities, but William the 3d. prevailed and had the place affigned to him in preference to all. It was fet up by the corporation of that time at the ex-pence of the chamber, and is efteemed one of the beft equeftrian ftatues in the Kingdom, were the horfe lefs incumbered with trappings, — for which the artift is not to be blamed. It is thus defcribed by H. Jones in a " Poem called Clifton and its environs."

> What grand magnificence on virtue grows,
> What fquares, what palaces of late arofe!
> How wealth, how tafte in every pile appear
> With ftill improving grace from year to year!
> Lo Queen's, — enrich'd by Ryfbrack's Roman hand;
> See William's finifh'd form majeftic ftand:
> His martial form, exprefs'd with attic force,
> Erect, like Antonine's, his warlike horfe:
> With lofty elegance and Grecian air,
> To feaft the well-pleas'd eye and fill the fquare.

This fpacious fquare, which is one hundred and feventy yards each fide and upwards, rofe like the creation out of chaos, to fuch beauty out of a muddy marfh, overflowed often with the tide, and was once the common receptacle of all the afhes and fcavengers' fweepings of the city. Such are the alterations human induftry is capable of effecting! The Grove alfo in this neighbourhood, fronting the river Avon, is very pleafant; but a new mud-dock, for the ufe and fecurity of fhipping, was there built in 1769, at the expence of the Merchants'-hall, amounting to the fum of 10,000l. with proper cranes, which is a very ufeful and neceffary work, the trade of the city requiring more room for the fhipping, which the Quay alone could not commodioufly hold: and as it now continues the Quay wall quite round to the Back it completes that work, and together forms as fine a Quay, of a mile and a quarter round, as any in England, encircling in a manner that fide of the city; and the fhips, like a thick foreft of tall trees, after failing up with the tide into the midft of the city, lie fecurely on a foft bed of mud on the return of the tide by the Quay walls, and are there difcharged, the goods and

merchandize

merchandize weighed off at the king's fcales, and immediately depofited in warehoufes at the merchants' backdoors, conftructed there very conveniently for that purpofe. To land the goods with greater difpatch, ferveral cranes are erected on the wharf of the Quay at proper diftances; that built and contrived by the ingenious Mr. Padmore, by the Mud-dock, near the Gibb, is an excellent piece of mechanifm, fixed on large pillars of wood, and under it the goods are fecured from the weather: fee the view or engraved print of it.

There cannot be a more pleafing walk than round this Quay, when the fpring tide is coming in bringing with it fhips and veffels of all kinds, laden with wares and treafures from different parts of the globe; a fight that cannot fail to gladden the heart that cherifhes any regard for his country, or bears a love to Britain. The tide rifes at Briftol Quay more than twenty-five feet perpendicular; at Rownham, not a mile lower, about thirty-two feet; at Cheptow, fixty feet.

In the year 1765, it was propofed by fome enterprizing, fcheming genius, to keep the veffels conftantly afloat in the Quay, by damming the water up, and erecting double gates or locks, to let the fhips in and out occafionally. — A plan of Briftol Quay, with the projection of the fluices and canal for floating the fhipping and Severn trows, and for enlarging the harbour by making a new canal through Cannon's-marfh, was engraved and publifhed by the ingenious Mr. Smeaton in January 1765, to which I refer, only remarking, that the Froom alone was in this to be dammed up at the lower end of the Quay, and diverted into a new canal and difcharged at the glafshoufe, the lower end of Cannon's-marfh; but the expence of doing this was fo great as to quafh the enterprize, the following being Mr. Smeaton's calculation:

	l.	s.	d.
" To digging, - - - - - - - - - - -	6555	0	0
Key walling, - - - - - - - - - - - -	4887	0	0
The two fluices, - - - - - - - - - -	8000	0	0
The dam and hatches acrofs the prefent mouth of the Froom river, - - - - - - - - -	1000	0	0
The hatches at the new bridge and upon Newgate millpond, - - - - - - - - - -	600	0	0
Contingent expences, - - - - - - - -	3958	0	0

Total - - £ 25000 0 0

Exclufive of purchafe of lands and damages to Bridwell-mill and Tombs's dock, &c."

But

But Mr. Champion propofed in the year 1767 a much more extenfive fcheme, which was, to dam up the river Avon itfelf juft above the Glafs-houfe and ftream of water at the Red clift above the Hot-wells, and making a new cut through that point of land, that runs out into the river there, and forming a chamber in it fecured by two fluices with double gates one above and the other below, to receive the fhips into the chamber betwixt the gates with the tide, and fo pafs them on towards Briftol or down the river, as might be required; and by making a bridge over the dam and draw-bridges over the chambers, to effect a communication there betwixt Afhton and Clifton parifhes or the counties of Somerfet and Glocefter: a plan of this was alfo publifhed to which I refer, but being thought ftill more expenfive to execute than the other, and attended with many obvious difficulties and fome perhaps not to be forefeen or known but on trial, the whole was dropt, * and the merchants are at prefent contented with the new additional large mud-dock in the Grove aforementioned and a new dock for keeping fhips afloat, made at the expence of the Merchant's-hall, in the road to the Hotwells, at the expence of near 15,000 l.

The north fide of the city was not alfo without its improvement as well as the fquare and weftern part: for a better communication with it a Draw-bridge acrofs the Froom or Quay was erected in 1714, at the expence of 1066l. 6s. 1d. And in 1718 a by-law was made that no hallier under the penalty of 20s. for each offence fhould draw any timber on drays or any loaded cart or waggon over this bridge, which being of wood was repaired at a very great expence: and being fince conftructed in an improved method of drawing up the gates by a curious mechanical contrivance of iron wheels with cogs, it is more expenfive to repair it when out of order, and the by-law more neceffary to be obferved and enforced. Another permanent bridge of ftone was alfo built afterwards at the charge of the city Chamber, at the head of the Quay oppofite Small-ftreet, a great convenience as well for carriages as foot-paffengers. Superb houfes were alfo erected on St. Auguftin's-green, now called College-green, the fweeteft and moft delightful fituation in the city in the opinion of moft; indeed it was ever efteemed fo: for in the year 1259, in a difpute between the monks of St. Auftin and the brethren of St. Mark about the right of burial in this green, (then the common cemitery of the former) the Bifhop of Worcefter awarded to the latter the liberty of burying there before their houfe, but on condition of

leaving

---

* But this fcheme, it is thought, will be yet put in execution at fome future time; fo defirous are they ftill of keeping the fhips always afloat.

leaving the ground always level ("in planitiem redigatur terra propter loci amænitatem,") "becaufe of the pleafantnefs of the place." And before the houfes were built and confined the profpeɛt, it muſt have been exceedingly delightful; as indeed it is at prefent, and on Sundays and holidays it is the Mall of Briſtol, a great concourfe of well dreſſed people flocking hither at fuch times for a walk. Trinity-ſtreet, formerly an orchard belonging to the diſſolved monaſtery and then to the Dean and Chapter, and Orchard-ſtreet, belonging in the like manner formerly to the houfe of St. Marks, are all newly ereɛted within thefe late years.

Stoney-hill on this fide is alfo almoſt covered with fine houfes, and the hill of St. Michael, ſteep as it is, has but little void ground upon it.

On this fide alfo are two dry docks for repairing and rebuilding ſhips, and two others very large and convenient acrofs the Avon at Wapping, to which there is a paſſage at two places by a ferry-boat. At both places ſhip-building is carried on with great fpirit and induſtry; at Wapping a large fpacious wet dock with double gates is built lately to receive the ſhipping and keep them conſtantly afloat; a proper method to fecure them from being injured in their bottoms, as is fometimes probably the cafe at the Quay by grounding fo often, viz. at every tide. — But a much larger dock than at either of the above places was made at a very great expence in the year 1768, by Mr. Champion, farther down the river; which in Jan. 1769 received a 64 gun ſhip with eafe through its gates.

But the largeſt dock of all for receiving and difcharging ſhips of great burden and laying them up afloat afterwards, was ſtill lower down at a place called Sea or Say-mills on the little river Trim, where ſhips are admitted with the tide into the dock, capable of containing feveral fcore fail afloat always, through very large gates, particularly contrived for the purpofe; which being ſbut down they ride fafe moored, and by the help of cranes they were unloaden there into large lighters or boats of burden, and by them the goods and wares were brought up to the merchants ſtore-houfes. It was made at the great expence of feveral private gentlemen, whofe families fince have been great lofers by the projeɛt, for the expence attending the keeping the gates and docks in repair, and inconvenience to the merchant of unloading into lighters and having their ſhips at fuch diſtance have made this dock in 1788 little ufed.

Farther down the river is Hung-road, where is a fafe harbour for the large ſhips, and where many unload into lighters as above: Leland fays, " Hunge-road is about three miles lower in the haven than Brightſtow, at this

M   rode

rode be fome howfys *in dextra Avon ripa.* About a myle lower is King's rode, and there be alfo fome howfes *in dextra ripa Avonæ.* There is a place almofte agayne Hungrode caulyd Portcheftar, where Hardynge and Roberte his funne had a fayre howfe, and another in Brightftowe towne. Some thynke a grete peece of the depenes of the haven from St. Vincent to Hunge rode hathe be made by hande: fome fay, that fhipps of very auncient tyme came up to St. Stephanes churche in Brightftowe." As to this laft, there might have been a wet ditch between St. Auftin's fide and the marfh of Briftol, which the tide might flow up, and fo bring boats even to St. Stephen's church, which might put the city upon the projeÆt of making a quay there afterwards; but it is certain, no fhips could come up fo high till that took place, unlefs through the Froom at Baldwin-ftreet, &c. Near Hungroad, on the fouth fide of the river, are two fmall branches, called Crockern Pill and Morgan's Pill, where fhips fometimes lie, and fmail veffels come to an anchor to wait for the tide. On the north fide of the river, oppofite almoft to Crockern Pill, King William 3d. landed, near the village of Shirehampton, Sept. 6, 1690, and went to Sir Robert Southwell's, at Kingfwefton, adjacent to it.

Rowley (in manufcript *penes me*) fays, " Hardinge, fadre of Fytz-Hardynge, han fayre and godelie poffeffyons atte Porteburie eke ycleped Port Ceaftre: Fytz-Hardynge gotte of Hen. 2d. a baileve, a markette, and fayre, on St. Decumbe's day, the fyrfte Mondaie in Whytfon week, the whyche did abyde durynge the whole weeke. Atte thys fayre the bayleve dyd doe hommage to the abbot of Seynt Auftine's yn Briftowe, who dyd dhyther goe wyth hys brederen to amount of twa hundredth botes: the hommage was done by fpreddynge hys fcarlete cloke at the flyppe of Crcocham, wherebie the abbatte dyd londe upon ytte, which hommage dyd entytule the bayleeve to hys rule and an hommage or oar money of fhyppes."

Kingroad is reckoned a good open harbour and fafe anchorage, accidents very feldom happening to fhips that lie there; though to come to it through the Briftol Channel however fafe it be with good pilots, is very dangerous for ftrangers and thofe unacquainted with it, but by firing a gun for a fignal, the pillpilots bred up to the bufinefs and acquainted with every rock or fand bank, &c. from their youth, pufh out immediately to meet the fhip and take charge of conduÆting her fafe into harbour.

In 1635, a decree paffed for demolifhing all houfes and buildings at Crockern Pill, (except one for paffing the boat over) which had been ereÆted there by Mr. Morgan, to the prejudice of the city in harbouring bad people there, and deftroying the pofts for mooring fhips in the river Avon, which

pofts

posts are placed on the banks of the Avon from Kingroad up to the city, and are kept in repair by the corporation; who in consequence of this decree appointed persons to put it in execution. But Mr. Morgan and his tenants again erected houses there, so that in the year 1656, by letters patent of Oliver Cromwell, the city was again impowered to set up mooring posts, and to demolish the buildings there; but though the mooring posts remain, houses. have since been built, and a little town is erected at Pill for the habitation of the pilots and others.

On St. Augustine's side of the city, a mile down the river Avon, is the noted rock of St. Vincent,* which furnishes the naturalist with those beautiful pieces of spar called Bristol stones, and other fossils, corals, and shells, and. the more noted fountain of Hotwell water, issuing from the bottom of the rock, which has given to the place the name of the HOTWELLS. William of Worcester mentions the hot spring at Bristol as of note when he wrote, in 1480, and describes St. Vincent's rock and a chapel there and hermitage. — " Fons ibidem una bow shot apud la black rocke in parte de Ghyston clyff in fundo aquæ, et est ita calidus, sicut lac vel aqua Badonis." p. 185. And in page 223. he again mentions it in the following words : " Fons calidus emanat de profundo aquæ Avyn sicut est Bathoniæ in le rok de Ghyston clyff in eadem parte in le sbole place. Scarlet-welle est directe in parte opposita in alta parte de Hungerode emanante de rupe." And p. 105. " Scarlette welle est fons perclarissimus emanans de alta rupe in parte opposita aquæ in Dominio de Lye, & est in altitudine in altiori parte de le rok de parte villæ de Lye altitudinis 12 pedum." He thus describes Giant's-hole : " Fox-hole est volta mirabiliter feita super in alto de Ghyston clyffe super ripam de la rokk altiorem et valde periculosus locus ad intrandam voltam ne cadat in mare profunditatis 60 brachiorum & ultra." He also describes the chapel of St. Vincent in plain English, more intelligibly than in his bad Latin, p. 184. " The halle of the chapell of Seynt Vincent of Gyston clyff is ix yerdes longe, and the brede 3 yerdys; the length of the ketchyn is ... yerdes (in another place 6 virgæ) the brede of the ketchyn is 3 yardes; and from the chapelle of Seynte Vyncent ys to the lower water 40 vethym, and from the ovyr parte of the mayn grounde londe of the seyd hygh rok downe to the seyde chapelle of Seynt Vincent ben 20 vethym rekened and proved ; and so from the hygh mayne ferme londe of the seyde rok downe to the lowest water ground of the channel of Avyn and Froome is 60 vethym and moch more, proved by a yong man of smythys occupation in Radcleff-strete, that seyde yt to me, hath both des-

cended

* A view of it may be seen in the plate annexed.

cended from the hygheſt of the rok down to the water ſyde." He goes on to deſcribe the chapel of the hermitage as twenty fathom (one hundred and twenty feet) from the firm ground in height, as meaſured by himſelf, Sept. 26, 1480, or one hundred and twenty-four ſteps or thereabout, and ſituated about the middle of the rock as you aſcend to the high ground.

This rock or cliff of St. Vincent is not more remarkable for its amazing height than for its being equally ſo on both ſides of the river, the ſtrata declining to the ſouth and anſwering on each ſide alike ; a proof they were never broken or diſturbed by the violent and irregular motion and diſruption of an earthquake, and that the chaſm betwixt for the paſſage of the tide was formed at the deluge, and the rock left in the ſame ſeparate and divided ſtate it was then ſplit into, when the ſhell of the earth was cracked through, and the fountains of the abyſs were broken up, according to the true Moſaic account of that great event. It is a very hard marble, or limeſtone of a peculiar kind, from a duſky red to a light grey, and when poliſhed is beautifully variegated; in the fiſſures are found thoſe fine cryſtals, ſmoothed and formed into angles by nature * as well as by the moſt ſkilful lapidary can be done : ſometimes they are found incloſed in hollow reddiſh nodules, which are as it were pregnant with theſe gems, and contain them as in a ſafe matrix, which muſt be broke before you can diſcover them ; theſe are turned up often by the plow in the fields near Durdham-down and about Kingſweſton. This rock furniſhes the natural philoſopher with many curious foſſils, the botaniſt † with ſome ſcarce plants,

the

---

* Vid. Braun's deſcription in Theatrum Urbium, lib. iv. " On the top of the rock, where it is plain, are ſo many diamonds, that a ſhip may be laden therewith." Camden ſays, " One may get whole buſhels of them." — This ſure could never be the caſe.

† A catalogue of the rarer plants, &c. found about St. Vincent's rock, by the ingenious phyſician and botaniſt, Dr. Broughton, of Briſtol.

PLANTS. — Veronica ſpicata, ſcabioſa columbaria, rubia peregrina, gallium montanum, glaux maritima, chenopodium maritimum, bupleuſum tenuſſimum, ſmyrnium oluſatrum, pimpinella dioica, ſcilla autumnalis, chlora perfoliata, monotropa hypoſithys, arcuaria rubra, ſedum rupeſtre, potentilla verna, galeopſic ladanum, turritis hirſuta, arabis ſtricta, geranium ſanguineum, ornithoſus perſieſillus, hippocrepis carnoſa, hypericum montanum, erigeron acre, viola livida, orchys ſpiralis, ——— apifera, ——— muſcifera, aſplenium ceterach, polypodium fragile.

FOSSILS found here. — STONES, limeſtone, grey, lead coloured, variegated with ſpar. — STARS, irregularly formed, rhomboid, dog-toothed, ſtalactitic. — FOSSIL CORALS, porous, tubular, lythoſtrotion, mycetitæ, aſtroites, lapides juncei.

EARTHS. — Vegetable mould, ochres, deep red or purple, bright red, yellow, pale yellow.

CRYSTALS. — Diaphanous, red, amethyſtine, yellow.

METALS. — Iron, lead.

MARINE EXUVIÆ. — Anomiæ, dithyperiæ, trochitæ, &c.

the antiquarian with the remains of a Roman camp,* and the lefs curious en_
quirer with a view of the moft aftonifhing and dreadful precipice. It is on
the north fide, at the bottom of the rock within the channel of the Avon on
its bank, the Hotwell fpring rifes up with fome force from beneath, upwards
of ten feet above low water and about twenty_fix feet below high water mark.
The late worthy and ingenious Dr. Randolph, whofe excellent treatife on the
Briftol water will be admired and held in efteem as lafting as the fpring it
celebrates, attributes its firft reputation to its efficacy in the gravel and ftone ;
but above all in the diabetes, in which it was deemed a fpecific. About the
year 1670, one Mr. Gagg, a baker, in Caftle_ftreet, dreaming one night,
as he lay defpaired of in that diforder, that he had drank plentifully of Briftol
water and was wonderfully refrefhed by it he was much inclined next morn_
ing to quench his thirft with it, and found it to anfwer his wifh fo well that
by continuing.its ufe in a few days he came abroad, gathered flefh and ftrength
daily, and recovered to the furprize of every one. Though the fpring was
known in 1480, (vid. William of Worcefter) and in 1632 ufed outwardly for
the itch and in old fores with fuccefs, by letting the water which then ran down
from a wooden pipe upon the pavement fall upon the part, which being thus
well wafhed, they wet a cloth in the water and wrapt it round; yet it was this
cafe of the diabetes that brought it into fuch reputation, that the city began to
think the water worth their care. In 1660, the way was improved and made
paffable by Rownham to the Hotwell, Kal. p. 198: and in 1691 Sir John
Knight, mayor of Briftol, endeavoured to inclofe the fpring in fuch a manner
that the tide fhould not mix with it, by raifing a ftone work round it higher
than the tide ever rofe ; but the weight of the water inclofed endangered the
lofs of the fpring, by altering its courfe. In 1695, the merchants of Briftol
granted a building leafe for ninety years at 5 l. per annum to certain proprie_
tors, J. Jones and — Gallowhill, to fecure the fpring, and contrive if poffible
that the water might be had as well at high as low water; who, finding the
fpring, made proper foundations for pumps, which now carry the water thirty
feet high : the tide water being kept out from it by valves, which open to let the
water out, but fhut againft any that would force itfelf in. Though this is of
great ufe, yet it has almoft fet afide the old ufe of it externally, and prevented
bathing in it immediately warm from the fpring; a matter perhaps of fome
confequence, and as beneficial fometimes as its internal ufe ; the fpring-head
being now fo inclofed as not to be come at, the water is pumped into cifterns
at a diftance, and internally ufed it may not be quite fo efficacious as formerly,

* Vid. p. 18. the plate.

merly, lofing no doubt fome of its heat in being pumped up, and probably fome of its virtue, efpecially if that depends on an impregnated air contained in the water; which, being very fubtle, may foon fly off with the bubbles: the ineffectual analyfis of it by many feems to prove fome fuch latent principle in it, not to be arrefted or difcovered by any art. The celebrated ufes of Briftol Hotwell water are, to temper an hot acrimonious blood, reftrain hæmorrhages and fe_minal weakneffes, to cure the hectic fever and fweats, relieve confumptive people if the difeafe be inveterate, cure them if recent; above all, its virtue in the diabetes has been deemed unqueftionable : it may vie with the Selter waters in efficacy. Patients with thefe complaints in the fummer months flock hither from every part of the kingdom, where and at Clifton, a healthy and delightful fituation, moft elegant lodging-houfes and every convenient accommodation for families that arrive can be had at the fhorteft notice; the pleafant rides on the neighbouring downs, the amufements, the mufic at the Long Rooms, the balls, affemblies, &c. make it alfo the refort of plea_fure as well as the retreat of the fick and valetudinary. And the buildings lately erected there give it more the appearance of a large town than of lodgings, for the fick alone, and have fo increafed of late as to join the Hotwells quite to Briftol, by an uninterrupted chain of houfes; fo that in 1776 on account of the new-erected docks in the Hotwell-road, and additional build-ings and inhabitants there, all the fouth fide houfes of the faid road next the Avon are placed under the civil government of the mayor and corpora-tion of Briftol as far as Rownham-ferry, by an act of parliament for that pur-pofe, and exempted from Glocefterfhire as to civil government.

On the fouth fide of the city Briftol has alfo increafed : Redcliff is now joined by late erected buildings to Bedminfter ; — Guinea-ftreet and its neighbourhood is an addition to the former flate of this part of it, and the new buildings, in the Addercliff garden there fronting the river Avon now called Burton-ftreet, Canning-ftreet, and Redcliff-parade, are pleafantly fituated, and command a moft entertaining and ftriking profpect of the water, of fhips coming up and down the river every tide, of the bufinefs on the Back, of the whole city, and of the diftant country to a great extent on all fides. The erection of feveral glafs-houfes, fugar-houfes, the brewery and diftillery, pottery and other manufactories have made a great acceffion to this fide. The beft part of the old outer wall of the city here is to be feen at this day. By two modern built handfome gates, Temple and Redcliff, one built in the year 1736, the other lately taken down, we enter the city from the county of Somerfet. On the caft fide at this time we are prefented
with

with quite a new face of things. The caftle, once fo confpicuous and defenfible a fortrefs, is now quite demolifhed, and two ftreets, terminated with a
gate erected in 1659, but pulled down in 1767 to widen the road, are laid
out with buildings in its ftead. The caftle orchard is built into a ftreet called
Queen's-ftreet where is a gate and arch over a branch of the Froom, formerly
the Sally-port, and at the bottom of it is a ferry for paffing over the Avon
to Temple fide, which when firft eftablifhed in the year 1651 was rented of
the Chamber at 40s. per ann. and now at 90l. per. ann. a proof among others
how much the inhabitants are increafed fince that time. St. Philip's alfo
in this neighbourhood is become a large town of itfelf full of inhabitants; and
the large diftilleries, plate and bottle glafs works, the iron founderies,
fmelting works and the like, have greatly contributed to its increafe.

Having taken a view of the out-fkirts of the city, let us now fee what improvements of late have taken place in the center. — By purchafing and taking down the old houfes there to make room for the erection of the exchange,
a convenient fpace of ground was gained for that and a new market behind
it, which before ufed to be kept in High-ftreet and Broad-ftreet * to the
great obftruction of paffengers and general inconvenience of the inhabitants;
the city was made alfo thereby much more airy, pleafant and healthful. In
the year 1760, an act of parliament was obtained for taking down and rebuilding the old bridge of Briftol and erecting a new one there and at Temple
backs, if thought neceffary; and opening avenues leading thereto. The
increafe of commerce, and confequently of inhabitants, the number of carriages of all kinds, drays and horfes conftantly paffing over the bridge,
and of boats, lighters, &c. under it, in fuch a trading city rendered a freer
and lefs interrupted paffage here abfolutely neceffary, and a better communication between the two parts of the city now became indifpenfibly requifite,
accidents daily happening there for want of it, befides the delays occafioned
by carriages meeting and obftructing it. So various were the opinions of the
commiffioners appointed by the act for rebuilding the bridge, that a whole
year paffed after obtaining the act in difputes whether it fhould be a one arched
bridge or a three arched one, on new or on the old foundations. Architects
were confulted, and builders of all kinds; warm contefts arofe, and parties
were formed on this occafion not without weekly publications in the public
prints and in pamplets in defence of their notions, by which the neceffary

work

* The moft ancient market-place for the Glocefterfhire fide of the city, and for the ufe of the
Caftle was in St. Philip's parifh; at a place or ftreet ftill called the Old Market, the old vaults
and cellars there, and the Pie-powder Court ftill held there once a year the 29th September
being proofs of it, now remaining.

work was greatly protracted, as procuring the act had been before through disagreement in the methods proposed for raising the money to defray the expence; which was fixed at last by a toll taken at the bridge itself, a tax on the houses of the city of 6d. in the pound, half paid by the landlord and half by the occupier, and by a small tonnage on the shipping, and vessels.

A temporary bridge by the side of the old one above it was at length agreed on, and in the beginning of July 1761 they first began taking down the houses and old buildings on the bridge; being first sold with all their materials to the best bidder. The temporary bridge was now in great forwardness, and was opened for the passing of foot people by the end of September, for horses and carriages Jan. 1st 1762, paying certain tolls. Great sums of money were taken up at interest by virtue of the act, and expended in purchasing the houses on the bridge and in its avenues and in the Shambles, which began all to be taken down apace; which gave this part of the city, before very close and dark, quite a different appearance: yet the plan of the building the new bridge was not agreed upon. But after long debates and great expence incurred to architects for their opinions, plans and models, the first design of constructing a three arched bridge on the old foundations was carried by a majority, 45 being for the old foundation, 18 for the new; — which though the most obvious and best scheme for the span of the river and for every other advantage to be expected in the building was frequently changed, and violently censured in comparison of a one arch, yet at last happily preferred and adopted, the masonry of the old piers being found on boring to be very firm and good and adjudged by the examining masons not to be constructed of a casing only of masonry with rubble in the center, but contrary to the notions of some of the architects to be throughout firm and and fit for the great incumbent weight of the intended superstructure.

A large quantity of stone of proper size was now laid in, but not without frequent interruption by the tide's not serving, being brought by water from Courtfield in Wales, but the balustrade is of Portland stone. The grand objection of making too steep an ascent, which was justly made against the one arch scheme, is removed by keeping the middle arch as low as could be without injuring the beauty of the bridge, by making it only an ellipsis or segment of a circle, while the side arches are both semicircles, but nothing can give the reader a just idea of the elevation of the bridge without a print of it, which is here subjoined and to which I refer. It was the month of September 1768 before it was finished to be opened for foot passengers, and November for horses and carriages; — for the tolls &c. I refer to the act of parliament.

liament. It is not the bridge alone, that adds new beauty to this part of the city, but taking the old ruinous buildings of the fhambles down, * and laying out the ground into a new, fpacious, handfome ftreet, called Bridge-ftreet, in their ftead; erecting new houfes in Thomas-ftreet and Redcliff-ftreet, in the avenues to the bridge; conftructing the new church and fpire of St. Nicholas; filling up the lower part of High-ftreet, and thereby making the afcent, before very great, much cafier and more gradual; opening a free and unconfined profpect over the river and into the city and diftant country, where the eye before was confined to a dark ftreet (for nothing elfe was the old bridge with the houfes on it on both fides); thefe, I fay, all confpire now to render this a moft pleafant fpot, as well as an airy and healthy part of the city.

But the great expences incurred in purchafing fo many houfes at once, with which the old bridge was incumbered, alfo the whole ftreet of houfes on both fides called the Shambles, thofe in Tucker-ftreet and Redcliff-ftreet, &c. to open the avenues, obliged the commiffioners from 1760 to 1769 to take up at intereft fuch large fums of money, amounting to 49,000 l. that, notwithftanding an immenfe toll collected at the bridge, let out at 1505 l. per ann. in 1788, the duty on houfes about 952 l. per ann. and tonnage on fhipping about 730 l. per ann. (much complained of by the merchants) it was feven years before any part of the fum raifed was advertifed by the commiffioners as ready to be paid off, being 13,805 l.; and 1783, a farther fum of 10,045 l. was difcharged; and 1785, a farther fum of 2000 l.; and June 24, 1788, a farther fum of 7916 l. was difcharged, being a third part of the bridge debt then due.

Notwithftanding the immenfe fum expended on the bridge and avenues to it, and the toll ftill continuing to the great injury and unequal burden of thofe on the Somerfetfhire fide, and the other duties fo long paid, which were much complained of; yet in 1787, application was again made to parliament to raife more money to purchafe the houfes on the right fide of Tucker-ftreet and in Temple-ftreet, to open a new road or ftreet to be called Bath-ftreet, which though greatly oppofed by many was yet carried through the houfe, and an act granted for purchafing the houfes in Tucker-ftreet and St. Thomas-ftreet for that purpofe, which is now carrying into execution.

N   Befides

* Shambles, once called Worfhip-ftreet, as it is in old deeds; and William of Worcefter fays, p. 170, 189, 237. " Eo quod vicus honoris, &c." becaufe it was a ftreet of honour or dignity, on account of the merchandize of wool landed there, being a port for loading fhips, and having the king's cellars," which was proved to be true from the large Gothic arched warehoufes difcovered next the river, when the fhambles were pulled down at this time. This was before any bridge was built, or the Quay made.

Befides the additional beauty and great advantage the city was about to receive from the erection of this elegant new bridge, the fpirit of improvement did not ftop here; but in the year 1772, the church of St. Leonard, with the arched gateway there called Blind Gate, at the bottom of Corn-ftreet, joining the old wall of the city, and all the houfes behind it in St. Stephen's-lane, as far back as the Quay, were taken down, an act of parliament being obtained for that purpofe; and a new ftreet laid out on the fite of thefe buildings to make a ftraight, commodious communication with the Quay on St. Auguftin's fide from Corn-ftreet, the Exchange, and the center of the city. — The money to the amount of 8000l. to effect this was rifen by a fubfcription amongft the citizens; 500l. was advanced by the Chamber, and 500l. by the Merchant's-hall, and 1000l. lent by Lord Clare, member for the city, towards this ufeful work: the borrowed fums were to be repaid by a fale of the ground, when cleared for the new buildings; the ground rents of this new ftreet, called afterwards Clare-ftreet were fold in 1775 for above 9000l. This was a very great improvement as it opened a free paffage to the Quay, and a ready intercourfe with St. Auguftin's parifh, and led ftraight to the Draw-bridge. Soon after by the public fpirit of the city a new road and ftreet called Union-ftreet, was laid out to open a better communication with St. James's parifh from Wine-ftreet, by a bridge acrofs the Frome into Broadmead, and a new market called St. James's market was eftablifhed there for the accommodation of that fide of the city, and to leffen in fome degree the vaft concourfe of people market days in the center of the city at the market place behind the Exchange, found very inconvenient and troublefome to all who refort to it. The park, called Bullock's park, having alfo been lately laid out for building two grand new ftreets of houfes called Park-ftreet and Creat-George-ftreet, leading from College-green, a new road was hereby opened into Glocefterfhire, over Durdham-down: and in 1770 the Bifhop's park was alfo agreed for by Mr. Worrall an eminent Attorney, who procured an act of parliament to enable the Bifhop to fell it off for building at a ground rent of 60l. per ann. for 90 years, when the leafe expires; and renewals muft be then made with the Bifhop for the time being: this was called College-ftreet and the buildings began in 1772, and already extend to a great length, though the whole is not yet compleated.

New ground alfo in 1786 is laid out for building a row of houfes or crefcent in the field above Park-ftreet next Brandon-hill; and above College-ftreet on the other fide of that hill a new ftreet of houfes leading up the hill out of

Limekiln-lane

Limekiln-lane called Brandon-ftreet, has been built lately in a high and pleafant fituation.

By fo many additional buildings and whole ftreets being lately erected, it muft be readily allowed to have received a great acceffion of new inhabitants, and how much it has increafed in populoufnefs within thefe thirty years paft is almoft incredible. In the year 1757 it is faid to contain 13,000 houfes in all, and 90,000 fouls. Anderfon in his Cronological Hiftory of Commerce fays " in the year 1758 he perambulated the city for two fucceffive days, and from a near examination of the number of houfes on new foundations and ftreets erected fince 1751, he cannot but think it contains not lefs than 100,000 fouls, and is as big as London within the walls. Dublin appears more populous in the ftreets; but it is the refidence of the chief governors, of all public officers, guards, nobility and gentry with numerous retinues of people in the ftreets without being larger than Briftol, where the inhabitants are private families, manufacturers in employ within doors," &c.

Though the number may not be quite fo high as here rated, yet it is certainly a very populous city, greatly increafed of late years; and though this calculation may be rather too great a number; that made by Mr. J. Browning in the Philofophical Tranfactions is as much too little. The medium reckoned at about 70 or 80,000 fouls may be perhaps nearer the truth.

Houfes in Briftol city, befides what are in the fuburbs and out of the corporation liberties, which are not reckoned and may be computed at 1000 or upwards.

Houfes in Briftol in the feveral parifhes, viz.

Parifhes.			Anno 1712.			Anno 1735.			Increafe.
St. Nicholas,	-	-	380	-	-	418	-	-	38
St. Stephens,	-	-	450	-	-	503	-	-	53
St. Mary Redclift,	-	-	280	-	-	402	-	-	122
St. Thomas,	-	-	302	-	-	320	-	-	18
St. Grofs alias the Temple,	-		240	-	-	380	-	-	140
St. James,	-	-	682	-	-	1407	-	-	725
St. Philips,	-	-	263	-	-	330	-	-	67
The Caftle Precincts,	-		260	-	-	270	-	-	10
St. Peters,	-	-	221	-	-	230	-	-	9
St. Mary Port,	-	-	104	-	-	104	-	-	0
Chrift Church,	-	-	160	-	-	164	-	-	4
All Saints,	-	-	57	-	-	57	-	-	, 0
St. John Baptift,	-	-	155	-	-	160	-	-	5

St. Leonard.

St. Leonard,	-	-	68	-	-	68	-	-	0
St. Werburghs,	-	-	57	-	-	57	-	-	0
St. Owens or St. Ewens,	-	27	-	-	27	-	-	0
St. Auguftin cum St. Marks,	327	-	-	454	-	-	127
St. Michaels,	-	-	278	-	-	350	-	-	72
			4311			5701			1390

Houfes in 1735,	-	-	-	-	-	5701
In fuburbs not reckoned, about	-	-	-	1000
						6701
Additional houfes fince 1735 to 1788, about -		-	2000
						8701

Proportionate increafe of the following parifhes.

		Year.			Number of houfes.			Rental.
St. James's,	-	1744	-	-	1474	-	-	7173
		1783	-	-	1561	-	-	8201
St. Mary Redclift,	1744	-	-	504	-	-	3896
		1783	-	-	571	-	-	4598
St. Auguftin,	-	1744	-	-	462	-	-	3585
		1783	-	-	563	-	-	4628
St. Michael,	-	1744	-	-	357	-	-	2256
		1783	-	-	416	-	-	2359
St. Nicholas,	-	1744	-	-	409	-	-	5466
		1783	-	-	362	-	-	4736

By the lift of houfes as laid before the Houfe of Commons by the tax officers (which muft be of 5l. per ann. or upwards) it appears there are of fuch in Briftol 3947, Liverpool 3974, Manchefter 2519, Oxford 2316. It muft however be obferved that Liverpool being a new-built city, there may be a greater proportion of houfes of the above defcription than in the very ancient city of Briftol, in which the houfes rated under 5l. per ann. muft be a very great number.

The whole city is in general well-built, yet has never been burnt down and rebuilt, or ever fuffered much by fires: its public halls, and other ftructures have many of them a good elevation ; the exchange * is a fine piece of architecture well proportioned, light and elegant and is a great ornament to the center of the city. That it may not be deftitute of places of rational amufement

* The public buildings will be particularly defcribed in the hiftory of the parifh in which they are fituated.

ment, the *lenimen dulce laborum,* a theatre was built in the year 1766 by fubfcription, at the expence of 5000 l. and upwards, and is large, fpacious, and
well contrived for the purpofe, and richly adorned both in the painting of the
fcenes and carving, gilding, and ornaments of the houfe ; and an elegant affembly or mufic room is erected in Prince's-ftreet, bearing this motto on its
front, *Curas Cithara tollit.* At night the city is well lighted with lamps, the
figns being taken down their light is not intercepted ; and it is provided with
a regular watch by acts of parliament paffed for thefe purpofes.

No place can be better fupplied with all the neceffaries of life, and at a
more reafonable price. Water is here to be had always the beft and in the
greateft plenty; public conduits or pumps, fupported at the public expence,
are here in almoft every ftreet. Leland, in his Itinerary, takes notice of
this advantageous circumftance, and has enumerated all the conduits in Briftol
in his time.

" Conducts *cis pontem.* — St. John's, harde by St. John's-gate. * The Key-
pipe, † with a very faire caftellette. All Hallow-pipe, ‡ hard by the Calen-
'daries, without a caftelle. St. Nycholas-pipe, § with a caftellet. — *Ultra pontem.* Redcliffe-pipe, ‖ with a caftellet, hard by Redcliff churche, witheowte
the gate. Another pipe, without Redcliff-gate, haveing no caftelle. Another
by porte waulle, without the waulle."

To thefe I may add St. Thomas-pipe, a feather from Redcliff, for which
the parifh pay 2 s. per annum to Redcliff parifh, and are always by a covenant to pay one third part for the repairs of all the pipes leading to Redcliff.
Temple-pipe, at Temple-gate; the water formerly brought there for the ufe
of the friers of St. Auguftin there. And another pipe at the Neptune in
Temple-ftreet, a feather from the former. There are alfo the following public pumps for the ufe of the citizens : St. Peter's, the Pithay, and one in
Wine-ftreet; for the fupport of all thefe, benefactions have been left at different times by well-difpofed, charitable citizens.

Befides thefe conveniencies for the fupply of water, that no part of the city
fhould be without this ufeful element, it was brought in elm pipes from a large
pond or refervoir, a mile without Lawford's-gate, to the remote parts of the
city

* This fpring-head is at the top of Park-ftreet.
† The fpring that fupplies this rifes at Glafs-mill, a mile and a half diftant, and the water is
brought hither in leaden pipes, at the expence of the chamber.
‡ This is in Prior's Orchard, above Maudlin-lane.
§ This water was brought by a pipe from the Key-conduit to St. Nicholas, but on building the
new bridge in 1764 was taken down.
‖ The fpring rifes above Lower Knowle, and the water is brought in leaden pipes.

city that ftand moft in need of it for their families and their bufineffes that require a great fupply. This refervoir is filled by a large wheel engine, erected
at a place on the bank of the Avon two miles above Briftol bridge. An act of
parliament the 7th and 8th of William 3d. paffed for this purpofe; and in Auguft
1696, Daniel Small, of London, draper, Chriftopher Fowler and Richard Goddard, of London, merchants, and Richard Berry and Samuel Sandford, citizens
of Briftol, on behalf of themfelves and others, contracted with the mayor, burgeffes, and commonalty of the city, for fupplying and furnifhing the inhabitants with frefh water at reafonable rates. Thefe perfons, interefted in the
undertaking, were impowered to dig the ground in order to convey the water
through any perfon's lands, except houfes, gardens, and orchards, from Hanham mills or other place, in aqueducts or pipes, with liberty to repair and
change the fame. The fheriff of the county of Glocefter, by a jury of twelve
indifferent men not interefted therein, upon examining them upon oath, was
to afcertain the damages to be allowed the proprietors of the foil: and every
one obftructing the undertakers afterwards were to pay 5 l. for every offence,
half to the profecutor and half to the poor of the parifh. The undertaking
was perfected at a great expence, (the whole being divided into ninety-five
fhares, at 65 l. a fhare) and water brought thus into the city to its great advantage, efpecially into fuch parts of the town as ftood moft in need of it, at the
eafy rate of 40 s. a year to each family who received it.

But this fcheme, not anfwering the expence of the proprietors, was fet afide
in 1783, and the machine for raifing the water appropriated to the ufe of a
grift-mill there erected: the great fupply of water for the ufe of the citizens
from pumps and other public conduits, rendering it the lefs neceffary; and the
great expence attending the repair of the engine and the pipes, &c. made
it at length of little advantage to the proprietors.

· The advantages arifing to the inhabitants from having coals in plenty fo
near the city are very great, as well from its ufe to families as from the great
confumption of it in glafs-houfes, fugar-houfes, diftilleries, iron-founderies,
and the like. It is brought in by horfes and in waggons but a few miles off
from the city gates, being rifen in great plenty in Kingfwood, Bedminfter,
Afhton, Nailfea, and Briflington. Butter remarkably good and flefh meat,
ox beef, veal and mutton, the beft of every kind, together with all the produce of the kitchen-garden in great abundance, are to be had at the markets,
held every Wednefday and Saturday, behind the Exchange and in Union-
ftreet; and fifh at the Fifh-market twice a week, Wednefday and Friday, in
Union-ftreet, befides the falmon, cod, mackrel, herrings, plaice, flounders,

oyfters,

oyſters, ſprats, &c. brought to the Back by the boats during the ſeaſon. A
market alſo is held on the Back every other Wedneſday, where the Welch
boats, arriving at ſpring tides, diſcharge the produce of their country for ſale;
fine ſalt-butter, poultry of all kinds, roaſting pigs, and geeſe ready for the
ſpit; fruit, as apples, pears, &c. The great brewhouſes and malthouſes, the
bakers and cornfaſtors, are furniſhed with corn and flour by water carriage
from the Weſt Country and the fertile vale of Eveſham, and the counties of
Hereford, Monmouth, and Worceſter, which is landed on St. Auſtin's wharf,
at the head of the Quay, out of the trows; or on the Back, where convenient
market-houſes are built for ſeenring it when landed from the weather, and
there expoſed to ſale every ſpring tide:—here are alſo landed great quantities of cyder. Beſides theſe, there was a corn-market in Wine-ſtreet, where
corn was brought by the neighbouring farmers for ſale, now converted into
a cheeſe-market; and a hay-market was eſtabliſhed in Broadmead in the year
1786, every Tueſday and Friday. The great market for fat and lean cattle,
ſheep, and pigs, (great droves of which come in from Wales) is held in St.
Thomas-ſtreet every Thurſday, and is much frequented alſo by the woollen
manufaſturers at the ſeaſon of the year for the purchaſe of wool, the wool-hall
being in this ſtreet; of which more particulars in the chapter on St. Thomas
pariſh.

Mr. W. Goldwin, A. M. ſometime maſter of the grammar-ſchool here, in
a poetical deſcription of Briſtol printed in 1712, after mentioning the market
on the Back, and the poultry fold there by the Welch women,

> Where cackling geeſe with cackling females try,

ſums up, in the following lines, the plentiful ſupply of neceſſaries at our
markets:

> Here Cornucopia, from her rural ſtores,
> In various ſhapes luxuriant plenty pours;
> Bright Cereal grain and ſweet Pomona's fruit,
> Or herbage cloath'd in Nature's lovely ſuit:
> Or tender fatlings from the herd or flock
> The city's wants with life's refreſhments flock,
> With thouſand dainties of delicious meats,
> Which Catius better knows than verſe repeats;
> The plenteous ſcenes ſuch vaſt profuſion ſhew,
> As if tranſplaned fields in cities grew.

It

It may be juſt mentioned here, that the diſb called elvers, taken notice of by Cambden, though once in great eſteem, is at preſent not much in requeſt at Briſtol. They ſeem to be a kind of very ſmall young eels, ſkimmed up at the proper ſeaſon out of the Avon, betwixt Briſtol and Keynſham, and duly cleanſed, are made up into little cakes or flat bundles, which fried are good and pleaſing to the palate. As the markets, in general, are well ſupplied with all kinds of proviſions, of the beſt kind and in great plenty, the people here may be ſaid very juſtly to eat well, or live on the heſt, of which our city feaſts, turtle feaſts, and all our public entertainments indeed are a ſufficient proof.   -

Briſtol hath the privilege of holding two fairs in the year, each to continue eight days, one on the 25th July, in the ſpacious church-yard of St. James, the other on the 25th January in Temple-ſtreet, the times now changed by aἀ of parliament 1761, to the 1ſt March and 1ſt September: of the grants of theſe more particularly in the account of the reſpeἀive pariſhes where they are held : here is uſually a great ſale then of every thing in the woollen manufaἀure, cloth coarſe and fine, rugs, blankets, ſtockings, &c. for exportation ; as alſo of Birmingham wares &c. from the ſeveral manufaἀories ; alſo leather at the Back-hall, beſides all the pageantry of female ornaments, dreſſes, trinkets, &c. uſually diſplayed on theſe occaſions.

Having thus deſcribed the city in general in its preſent improved ſtate, and curſorily run over its principal parts, referring for particulars to the enſuing chapters, I ſhall now add, that the circumference of the whole within the liberties as appears by the perambulation round it, (which to preſerve its true limits and boundaries, is made annually, at chooſing a new mayor) conſiſts of ſeven miles two quarters and fifty-five pearch, and as it may ſatisfy the curious and inquiſitive, the following account is ſubjoined. *

The

* In King John's charter to the city, the bounds of the city are ſet down thus, — " The metes of the town are between Sandbrook and Bewell, Brightnee-bridge, and the well in the way to Adelbury of Knoll."

Sandbrook ſeems afterwards to be deſcribed in the perambulation as a certain little brook or ſluice called Woodwell's lake, where is a ſtone on the eaſt part of the ſaid brook.

Bewell in the highway to Henbury where was an old croſs called Bewell's croſs near St. Michael's hill.

Brightnee-bridge on Bedminſter cauſeway.

The well at Adelbury, was that at Totterdown in the road to Knoll, where the road turns to Bath and there was once a well now filled up, and a city ſtone is there at preſent.

The Bounds of the City on Glocestershire Side.

Stone.   Per. qr.

1. On the bank of the river of Avon, near a limekiln, on the east and a sluice on the west, called Woodwell's-lake, standeth the first stone, - - - - - -

2. From the said stone, ascending the lane, crossing the said lake, N. westerly, on the west side of the said lake, or rivulet, is a leading stone - - - - - - 10 3

3. From the said stone N. westerly, to a stone on the bank where was a mill to blow lead ore, - - - - - - 16

4. From thence N. W. ascending the lane, in the midst thereof, is a leading stone, - - - - - - 25

5. From thence, N. W. to a stone standing betwixt Jacob's well and the vault of the conduit, which leadeth to the college, - 11 3

6. From thence N. and by W. to a stone in the corner of a wall, where one Baily dwelt, - - - - 23

7. From thence, N. to a stone in the hedge of a croft, called Long-croft, - - - - - - - 32

8. From thence, on the N. side of the lane, ascending the same, to the S. corner of Pucking-grove, and there entring into a ground, called Honey-pan-hill, standeth a great stone, - 30

9. From thence, N. by the hedge and ditch of Pucking-grove, stand-eth a leading stone in the aforesaid ground of Honey-pan, 30

10. From thence, N. N. W. by the hedge and ditch of the same ground, into a ground, called the Welsh-close, near the W. N. W. corner of Pucking-grove, is a stone, - 25 2

11. From the said stone, N. and by E. to a stone in the S. S. W. corner of little Fucking-grove, - - - - 8

12. From the said stone, N. E. and by E. to a stone in the E. and by S. corner of little Pucking-grove, - - - 18

13. From the said stone, N. W. and by N. to a stone in the N. N. W. corner of the said little Fucking-grove - 6

14. From thence, over the hedge, into a ground called the Furlongs, where beginneth Westbury parish, E. N. E. along by the wall, to a leading stone, - - - - - 11

15. From thence, E. N. E. by the said long wall, to another leading stone, - - - - - - - 28

O

Stone.   Per. qr.

16. From thence, along by the fide-wall, E. N. E. to a ftone fixed
    on the N. corner of Cantock's, a long flange of ground, cal-
    led Spencer's acre,   -   -   -   -   -   -   15

17. From thence, E. N. E. to a leading ftone in the faid ground,
    near to the N. corner of a ground belonging to the Maudlin's
    or Bartholomew's of Briftol,   -   -   -   -   -   19

18. From thence, E. N. E. by the faid hedge, is a ftone fixed in the
    E. corner of the fame ground, near the highway, which lead-
    eth from Briftol to Henbury,   -   -   -   -   -   8

19. From thence, into the highway, N. W. and by N. to a ftone on
    the N. W fide of the way,   -   -   -   -   -   20

20. From thence, N. W. and by N. to a ftone in the S. E. corner
    of Bewell's-croft,   -   -   -   -   -   -   15

21. From thence, N. W. and by N. along by the hedge of the fame
    croft, to a ftone pitched near the Green-way-grate, on the
    N. E. fide of Bewell's-well,   -   -   -   -   -   17

22. From thence, along the highway, N. E. to a ftone on the other
    fide of the way,   -   -   -   -   -   -   3

23. From thence, back again, to a ftone on the high bank, over
    againft the crofs,   -   -   -   -   -   -   24

24. From thence, S. E. and by S. along the N. E. fide of the lane,
    to a ftone at the head of Brampton's-clofe,   -   -   45

25. From thence, into Brampton's-clofe, N. E. and by E. to a ftone
    in the midft of the faid clofe,   -   -   -   -   21

26. From the faid ftone, S. E. and by S. to a ftone within the bul-
    warks,   -   -   -   -   -   -   -   8

27. From thence, S. W. and by W. to a ftone pitched on the N.
    corner of a garden wall, formerly in the tenure of John
    Pefter, of the city of Briftol, woollen-draper, belonging to the
    heirs of Alderman Jones, and formerly called Mill-lane, and
    one Pownefham's wall,   -   -   -   -   -   -   14

28. From thence, defcending, S. E. to a ftone on the S. corner of a
    ditch bank in the fame ground, near a certain croft called
    Prior's-croft,   -   -   -   -   -   -   -   10 2

29. From thence, along by a hedge and ditch, to a leading ftone in
    the fame croft,   -   -   -   -   -   -   17

30. From thence, along by the faid hedge and ditch to a ftone in the
    lane, called Maudlin's-lane, leading towards Horfield,   -   16

31. From

Stone.   Per. qr.

31. From thence, along the faid lane, called Maudlin-lane, N. and
by E. over a certain mount, called Colſton, to a ſtone in the
W. ſide of the ſame lane,   - - - - -   10

32. From thence, N. E. to a ſtone in the ditch or trench of the
bulwarks,   - - - - - - - -   20

33. From thence, paſſing over the works, S. E. to a ſtone at the
corner of a hedge of a cloſe, called St. Werburgh's-cloſe,
at the E. corner of the ſame cloſe,   - - - -   6

34. From thence, S. W. and by S. by a ditch in the S. E. part of
St. Werburgh's-cloſe aforeſaid, is a ſtone fixed in a corner
nigh the ditch of a cloſe, called Prior's-cloſe,   - -   19

35. From thence, deſcending the hill, S. E. and by E. to a ſtone in
the midſt of a ground, called the Montagu's,   - -   24

36. From thence, N. E. to a ſtone fixed in the Montagu's,   -   11 3

37. From thence, deſcending the hill, to the corner of a ditch, S.
E. in the faid Montagu's is a ſtone pitched,   - -   8

38. From thence, along by the faid hedge and ditch, N. E. to a
leading ſtone,   - - - - - - -   26

39. From thence, N. E. by the faid hedge and ditch, to a ſtone in
the midſt of a ground, near the head of the faid ground,
called Douce's-croft,   - - - - - -   34

40. From thence, deſcending S. E. and by E. into the lane leading
towards Thornbury, to a ſtone on the W. ſide of the ſame
lane,   - - - - - - - - -   20

41. From thence, by the W. ſide of the ſame way, directly N. to a
ſtone fixed on the corner of a ground going up towards
Prior's-hill, called Barnſley,   • - - - -   46

42. From thence, E. athwart the way, to a little round hillock,
called Apeſherd, is a ſtone on the ſame hillock,   -   4

43. From thence, N. E. and by E. along the lane, to a ſtone fixed
in the N. corner of a ditch, called the upper Stoke's-croft,   23

44. From thence, deſcending S. E. and by S. to a ſtone pitched on
the S. corner of the ſame ditch, in upper Stoke's-croft aforeſaid,   29

45. From thence, N. E. by a ditch of a cloſe, called Meer Furlong
to a ſtone fixed in a corner of the ſame ditch, called Shuter's-
ditch,   - - - - - - - - -   18

46. From thence, deſcending S. E. ſoutherly, to a ſtone fixed on
the W. corner of Long-acre, now called Gooſe-acre,   -   28

O 2

47. From

Stone.   Per. qr.

47. From thence, N. E. by the hedge and ditch, to a leading ſtone,   23

48. From thence, N. E. by the ſaid hedge and ditch, to another
leading ſtone,   -   -   -   -   -   -   -   9

49. From thence, N. E. by the ſaid hedge and ditch, to a ſtone on
the E. corner of the ſaid ground of Long-acre or Gooſe-acre,   13 2

50. From thence, N. W. to a ſtone on the N. corner of the ſaid
Gooſe-acre,   -   -   -   -   -   -   -   -   2 2

51. From thence, N. E. into a ground, called Long-lands, now Red-
furlong, along a bedge and ditch on the S. E. part of the
ſaid ground, near Cook's-croft, ſtandeth a ſtone,   -   45

52 From thence, N. W. and by N. by the ſaid Cook's-croft, into
the lane, is a ſtone in the midſt of the lane,   -   -   13 2

53. From thence, N. E. and by E. into a ground called Open-cloſe,
near the gate of the N. of Cook's-croft corner, is a ſtone
fixed,   -   -   -   -   -   -   -   -   -   24

54. From thence, S. E. by the hedge of Cook's-croft, and on the S.
corner of Open-leaſe, is a ſtone,   -   -   -   -   -   13

55. From thence, N. E. and by N. to a ſtone near the receipt-houſe
of the Key-pipe conduit,   -   -   -   -   -   -   27

56. From thence, round about the conduit, S. E. to a ſtone pitched
on the Ditch-bank of Picked-croft, -   -   -   -   -   8

57. From thence, athwart the way, S. E. and by S. to a ſtone in the
corner of a cloſe, antiently called Wrington's-cloſe, -   -   2

58. From thence, S and by E. to a ſtone fixed, -   -   -   -   29

59. From thence, S. and by E. to another ſtone fixed near the cauſeway, from Briſtol to Lokenbrig,   -   -   -   -   -   11

60. From thence, W. and by S. to a ſtone pitched on the bank of a
certain ground, called Sage's-paddock,   -   -   -   -   8

61. From thence, along the lane, by the S. W. hedge of Old Market-
lane, to a ſtone,   -   -   -   -   -   -   -   -   52

62. From thence, along the lane, to another leading ſtone, -   -   48

63. From thence, ſtill along the lane, to a ſtone pitched on the
N. ditch-bank of Beggar's-well,   -   -   -   -   -   37

64. From thence, S. E. by the N. E. part of Ditche's-orchard, to a
ſtone near the flood-gate, on the N. W. of the river Froom,   32

65. From thence, along the water of Froom, on the N. part of the
ſaid water, to a ſtone pitched over againſt the great ditch,
leading towards Lawford's-gate,   -   -   -   -   -   38

66. From

Stone.   Per. qr.

66. From thence, E. and by S. athwart the river, to a ſtone pitched
    on the outſide of the ſaid town-ditch,   -   -   -   -   4

67. From thence, E. S. E. along the outſide of the ſaid town-ditch,
    to a ſtone in one Townſhend's garden,   -   -   -   -   37   2

68. From thence, S. E. and by S. to a ſtone pitched near the ſign-
    poſt of the Crown without Lawford's-gate,   -   -   -   18   2

69. From thence, athwart the way, S. E. and by S. to the E. corner
    of a barn, built by one Lord,   -   -   -   -   -   11

70. From thence, S. E. and by S. along the lane, to a ſtone pitched
    on the corner of a hedge near Enderby's caſtle,   -   -   10

71. From thence, S. W. weſterly, along the outſide of the town-ditch,
    to a ſtone in the ſaid ditch, near an old ſquare tower, on the
    S. E. part thereof,   -   -   -   -   -   -   -   34

72. From thence, ſtill along by the outſide of the ſaid town-ditch,
    W. S. W. to a ſtone pitched at the W. end of a cloſe, anti-
    ently called Gold's-burges; this ſtone is in the cellar where
    one Harvey dwells, on the Plain,   -   -   -   -   -   35

73. From thence, ſtill along W. S. W. to a ſtone at the corner-houſe,
    where one Baldwin dwells,   -   -   -   -   -   -   21   2

74. From thence, ſtill along W. S. W. to a ſtone on the brink of the
    river Avon,   -   -   -   -   -   -   -   -   14   3

Somersetshire Side.

1. At Tower-Harratz ſtandeth the firſt ſtone.

2. From thence, along by the brink of the river Avon, S. E. ſoutherly to a ſtone fixed at the end of a great ditch, called the
   Hales,   -   -   -   -   -   -   -   -   -   124

3. From thence, lineally W. by the ſaid ditch-bank, to a leading
   ſtone,   -   -   -   -   -   -   -   -   -   26

4. From thence, by the ſaid ditch, W. to the highway which leadeth
   from Temple-gate towards Bath, ſtandeth a ſtone on the E.
   ſide of the ſame way,   -   -   -   -   -   -   -   23   2

5. From thence, aſcending the lane, by the N. E. ſide of Newall's,
   called Pile-hill-bridge; and ſo down the lane to the eaſtward,
   in the way towards Briſlington, is a ſtone fixed on the N. ſide
   of the lane,   -   -   -   -   -   -   -   -   89   2

6. From thence, directly to a little well, in the way towards Pensford,
   over the ſaid well is another ſtone fixed,   -   -   -   10   2

7. From

Stone.   Per. qr.

7. From the faid ftone, to a ftone fixed on the E. part of the hedge
   called Adleburyham, and on the W. fide of Pensford-way,   2   1

8. From thence, along by the hedge, on the W. fide of the lane, to
   a ftone pitched on the N. corner of Ware-mead,   -   -   83   1

9. From thence, over a ditch. S. W. to a ftone pitched on the bank of
   on the W. corner of the fame clofe,   -   -   -   -   10

10. From thence, N. W. by a hedge and ditch, to a ftone on the N.
    corner of the faid mead,   -   -   -   -   -   -   24

11. From thence, S. W. wefterly, to a ftone pitched on the S. E.
    corner of a clofe, which was of the fraternity of Sattinors,   20

12. From thence, N. W. by a hedge and ditch, to a leading ftone,   17

13. From thence, to a ftone N. W. pitched at the head of a lane,
    called Red-lane,   -   -   -   -   -   -   -   22

14. From thence, S. W. to a ftone in Redcliff-field, at the head of
    Ergle's-croft,   -   -   -   -   -   -   -   -   14   2

15. From thence, S. E. to a ftone at the E. corner of Ergle's-croft,   14

16. From thence, S. W. to a lane which leadeth from Knoll to Red-
    cliff church, on the W. fide of the faid lane, is pitched a
    ftone,   -   -   -   -   -   -   -   -   -   13

17. From thence, by the hedge and ditch up the lane, N. W. to a
    ftone pitched on the S. E. corner of Redcliff churchyard,
    near the houfes called Cathay,   -   -   -   -   -   29

18. From thence, defcending Cathay-lane, S. and by W. to a ftone
    pitched on the corner of Long-croft of the mafter of St. John
    Baptift,   -   -   -   -   -   -   -   -   -   49

19. From thence, along the hedge, W. to the N. corner of the
    Mayor's-acre,   -   -   -   -   -   -   -   -   17

20. From thence, S. W. and by S. to a ftone ftanding upon the bank
    of a watering pool, in the midft of a ground called St.
    George's-clofe,   -   -   -   -   -   -   -   14

21. From thence, W. N. W. to the highway which leadeth from
    Redcliff church towards Bedminfter, to a ftone on the S. E.
    part of the fame way,   -   -   -   -   -   -   13

22. From thence, S. W. and by S. by the fame ditch to a ftone
    pitched on the midft of Brightnee-bridge,   -   -   -   31

23. From thence, athwart the way, W. and by S. into Catherine-
    mead, to a ftone pitched on the W. corner of Cardiff-croft,   14   2

24. From

Stone.   Per. qr.

24. From thence, N. E. and by N. to a stone fixed on the E. corner of Catherine-mead, - - - - - - - 53 2

25. From thence, N. W. to a stone on the N. corner of the said Catherine-mead, - - - - - - - - 30

26. From thence, S. W. and by W. by an old ditch, to the head of the pool of Trene-mill, to the brink of the water called Bishop's-Worth-brook, at the W. head of the same ditch, is a stone, - - - - - - - - - 22

27. From thence, N. W. and by N. athwart the water, to a stone pitched in the S. E. corner of Shepherd's-close, which did belong to the abbot of St. Augustine's of Bristol, - - 12

28. From thence, lineally N. E. to a stone pitched on the Mill-bay, 27 2

29. From thence, N. N. W. to a stone pitched on the bank of the river Avon, near the same mill, - - - - - 12

The City is in Circumference

					Miles.	Qrs.	Perches.
Glocestershire side,	-	-	-	-	4	2	37
Somersetshire side,	-	-	-	-	2	2	18
To Rownham, about	-	-	-	-	0	2	0
Total	-	-			7	2	55

To the former perambulation is now added all the ground on the left hand on the bank of Avon, leading from Limekiln-dock towards the Hotwells, as far as a stone fixed at the ferry called Rownham-passage; all the houses on that side for half a mile being within the liberties of the city by act of parliament, and the inhabitants subject to it as to civil goverment, and separated from Glocestershire. Add to this, beyond the city bounds a town has arisen in St. Philip's without Lawford's-gate, consisting of many streets there, and on St. Philip's-plain; and in the out-parish of St. James, on Prior's-hill, &c. out of the bounds of the city, are many streets of houses, all which are in the jurisdiction and government of the justices of peace for Glocestershire.

The following plans of the city, views and engraved prints of many admired and striking parts of it and places near it, have been published at different times; — for the entertainment and satisfaction of the curious in these things a list is here subjoined: a proof that Bristol and its pleasant environs have catched the eye and engaged the attention of the curious, and been thought worthy of being described by drawings and copper-plate prints,

                                              though

though the hiftory and antiquities of it have hitherto been fo little noticed, and a particular defcription of the whole has never before been offered to the public.

1. Briftol, from Lundy ifland to Kingroad, including the river Avon, by by Capt. Collins.

2. Briftol Channel, from the Holmes to Kingroad, including the river Avon, by Charles Price Heath.

3. The river Avon, from the Severn to Briftol, furveyed by G. Collins.

4. Briftol city, a plan printed about the year of our Lord 1570 in a book, called *Civitates Orbis Terrarum*, Hoéfnagel fc.

5. Another plan, taken from the corner of a map of Glocefterfhire, one of Mr. Speed's maps.

6 Another plan, James Millar delineavit et fculp. 1671.

7. Another by the fame, with fome additional buildings reprefented in the margin

8. Another furveyed and drawn by John Rocque, engraved by Pine, 1742.

9. A view of Briftol, by James Millard.

10. Another, very fmall and neat, two inches long and one inch and a quarter wide, by Hollar.

11. A north-welt profpeft of Briftol, large, by S. and N. Buck, 1734.

12. A fouth-caft view, by the fame.

13. A view of the Drawbridge, by Halfpenny, Mynde fculpt.

14. A north-weft view of the High Crofs, with the Cathedral, and St. Auguftine's Church.

15. A view of part of Queen-fquare, by Halfpenny.

16. A north profpeft of the Cathedral, by Smith.

17. Another ditto, by King.

18. Another ditto, by Harris.

19. Plan of the Cathedral, Harris fculpt.

20. A view of the High Grofs by itfelf, Buck del. et fc. 1734.

21. Mr. Colfton's Hofpital on St. Auguftine's-back and Almfhoufe on St. Michael's-hill, (fold by Benj. Rome) with an account of his charities.

22. The Infirmary, plan and elevation, by Halfpenny, 1743.

23. Another fmall one, W. Milton del. et fc.

24. A plan of the country eleven miles round Briftol, from aftual furvey by B. Donn, 1769.

25. A view of the Hotwells nigh Briftol, Milt. fc. impenfis S. Pye Chirutg.

26. Another by Smith, printed by Palmer.

27. A

27. A fmall plan of the City, by Donn, 1773.

28. A fmall plan of the Cathedral, in aqua tinƈta, 1785.

29. A view of Clare-ftreet, the Drawbridge, St. Stephen's Church, and All Saint's Church, in aqua tinƈta, 1785.

I fhall clofe this chapter with the following general defcription of the city in Latin verfe.

> Cingitur urbs muris, muros cingentibus altis
> Foffis, et foffas unda proterva replet.
> Has iterum cingunt viridantes gramine campi
> Et fata, quæ cereris munere preffa patent;
> Rura replent pagi, quæ rupibus horrida nullis
> Vel fylvis, nulla fæda palude, virent.
> In medio duplex fedet urbs celeberrima portus,
> Turrigerum tollens culmen in aftra fuum:
> Extendens binos fuper amnes æmula pontes,
> Fornicibus magnis flumina magna premens:
> Vela hinc dant ventis roftratæ turgida puppes,
> Huc iterùm plaufu caffis onufta redit:
> Hùc oriens merces, merces occafus et omnis
> Per mare, per terras advehit orbis opes:
> Unde fit emporium, cui qui commercia calient
> Empturi properant undique turba virûm;
> In patriafque fuas redientes, omnibus urbis
> Præftantis narrant haud mediocre decus;
> Cunƈtaque mirantes, quibus haud fatiantur ocelli,
> Bristoliæ, dicunt, non reticendus honos:
> Urbs etenim celebris, fpatiofa, fidelis, amæna,
> Dulcis et infignis, prifca, benigna, nitens;
> Jura, Deum, regem, regionem, crimina, pacem,
> Servat, adorat, amat, protegit, odit, habet.

P

CHAP.

C H A P. V.

Of the CIVIL GOVERNMENT *and* OFFICERS *of the* CITY.

BRISTOL is dignified with the honourable title of an Earldom, John Lord Digby * being firſt ſo created by King James 15th September 1622, which the noble family of the Harveys † now enjoy. It has the higheſt marks of honor granted to magiſtracy, ‡ ſcarlet gowns, § ſword, mace, and cap of maintenance ; and the following officers, an high ſteward, recorder, town clerk, ſteward of the ſheriffs court, chamberlain, two coroners, a ſword bearer, water bayliff, clerk of the market, key maſter, eight ſerjeants of the mace, and other inferior officers in daily waiting : they hold a daily ſeſſions in the council houſe (rebuilt in an elegant manner in the year 1705) to hear complaints and ac-commodate differences, make orders, take bail and commit offenders, beſides their more ſtately courts of judicature at the guildhall (a place of great antiquity) for trial of cauſes of all ſorts, both criminal and civil, and twice a year a general goal delivery is held. The town clerk, who muſt be qualified in knowledge of the laws of England and a barriſter three years at leaſl, preſides as judge of the court of quarter ſeſſions four times a year to be held by any three aldermen, whereof the mayor or recorder for the time being moſt be one, or two of the five ſenior aldermen are to be two. A court is alſo held by the ſheriffs ; and the ſteward of the ſheriffs court muſt

* His arms are f. azure a fleur de lis argent with a mullet for difference.

† Arms are G. on a bend argent three trefoils ſlipped vert.

‡ Gown-days, when they appear in ſcarlet robes with the inſignia of office are, the Tueſ-days in the next week after Michaelmas, Epiphany, Eaſter, and after the 1ſt July being ſeſſi-ons, alſo Michaelmas day, and every law-day : alſo when they go to certain churches to hear the gift-ſermons ; alſo on the 5th November and 29th May, when they go to the Cathedral attended by the city companies with their colours and arms diſplayed.

§ There are four ſwords — an old one with embroidered ſheath, on it is wrote —
    John Willis of London Maier,
    Gave to Briſtow this ſwerd faire.
A mourning ſword with theſe mottos, — Statutum eſt hominibus ſemel mori, — Memento mori. Another plain one, and one large maſſy one with a ſheath of ſcarlet and gold, highly embel-liſhed, uſually carried before the mayor on public days and feſtivals by the ſword bearer.

muſt have the fame qualification as the town clerk. By an order 1605 the recorder, town clerk and ſteward were not to be cleſted yearly but continue in their offices as they heretofore have done. By the charters they were all to continue in office for life, but by that of Queen Ann as long as they behaved themſelves well. The mayor, aldermen and common council have the cuſtody of the city feal, on which are cut the city arms; this feal is fixed to all warrants, deeds, &c. A writ direſted by Queen Elizabeth in the follow-ing words, point out the feveral courts held by the corporation of Briſtol; the Staple-court, Tolzey-court and the Pied-powder-court: thus Majori, Aldermannis, & Vice-Comitibus Civitatis feu Villæ Briſtolliæ; ac Majori & Conſtabulariis Stapulæ ejufdem Civitatis; nec non Ballivis Maioris & Com-munitatis ejufdem Civitatis Briſtoliæ Curiæ ſuæ Tolefey, ac Ballivis diſtorum Majoris Civitatis Curiæ ſuæ *pedis pulverizati*, & eorum cuilibet.

HIGH STEWARDS of BRISTOL.

1540. The Duke of Somerfet.
1546. Edward Earl of Hertford.
1549. Sir William Herbert.
1570. Robert Earl of Leiceſter.
1648. Sir Henry Vane, junr. Knt.
1651. Oliver Cromwell, with a falary of 5 l. per ann. and a pipe of Canary and half a ton of Gafcoign wine ordered him, as a prefent.
1708. Duke of Ormond.
1756. Lord Chancellor Hardwicke.
1786. The Duke of Portland.

RECORDERS of BRISTOL.

The name of recorder occurs the firſt time the 18th Edward 3d.

1344. William de Colford. He drew up an account of the cuſtoms of the city, and the oaths to be taken by the feveral offi-cers, mayors, ſheriffs, &c.
1394. Simon Oliver.
1430. Richard Newton.
1439. Sir John Inyn, Knight, chief juſtice of the Common Pleas.
1463. Thomas Young, declined 7th Edward 4th.
1468. Michael Harvey.
1483. John Twynyho.
1500. John Greville.

1505. William Glenvylle.
1517. John Fitz-James.
1541. David Brook, ferjeant at law.
1549. Robert Kelway.
1551. Mr. Hippiſly, died 1570.
1552. John Walſhe, Efq;
1571. John Popham, Efq; refigned.
1585. Thomas Hannam, died 1592.
1592. Sir George Sniggc, Knt. one of the barons of the Exche-quer, died Nov. 11, 1617.
1604. Sir Lawrence Hyde.
1615. Nicholas Hyde, Efq;

P 2

1540. John

1640. John Glanville.

—— Edmund Prideaux, Efq;

1645. Serjeant Whytlocke,

1655. John Doddride, Efq; died 1658.

1658. John Stephens, Efq;

1663. Sir Robert Atkins, refigned.

1682. Sir John Churchill, Knt.

1685. —— Paulet, Efq;

1704. Sir Robert Airs, refigned.

1727. John Scroop, Efq; refigned.

1735. Sir Michael Fofter, Knt. chief juftice of the Common Pleas.

1764. Daines Barrington, Efq; refigned.

1766. John Dunning, Efq; a noted pleader at the bar, *quoquo jure quaquâ injuria*, and for the Americans in the Houfe of Commons: he was created Lord Afhburton, and died foon after.

1783. Richard Burke, Efq; brother to the late member.

TOWN CLERKS or BRISTOL.

This office is very antient here, and requires no explanation. By an order of the 3d and 4th of Philip and Mary, refidence is enjoined him, that he may always affift the mayor and aldermen with his advice, draw up orders of counfel, &c.

1463. Thomas Ofenby.

1479. Robert Ricaut, author of the Mayor's Calendar, now extant in manufcript.

1503. Thomas Harding, Efq; turned out for extortions in his office.

1514. Robert Thorn, Efq; a great benefactor to the city.

1540. —— Fitz-James, Efq;

1554. —— Maudlin, Efq;

1640. James Dyer, Efq;

1653. Robert Oldworth, Efq;

1676. John Rumfey, Efq; difplaced 1687.

1687. Nathaniel Wade, Efq;

1688. John Rumfey, Efq; reftored, died 1720.

1721. Henry Blake, Efq;

1731. Sir William Cann, Bart.

1753. Sir Abraham Elton, Bart. refigned, on account of his ill health, 1786.

1786. James Kirkpatrick, Efq; who died of a fever in London the fame year he was elected.

1787. Samuel Worrall, Efq;

CHAMBERLAINS.

The office of chamberlain was at firft executed here by the prepofitors, fenefchalls, and bailiffs fucceffively, and was neglected, to the damage of the town, by their daily atendance upon other affairs ; but they were difcharged of the care of the public buildings, &c. by ordinances, 33d Hen. 6th. which was committed to the two chamberlains appointed 35th Henry 6th. ; but one only was inftituted to that office by ordinance, 20th Feb. 9th Edward 4th. to whom

whom it belonged by fpecial appointment to receive all rents and other profits of the city chamber, except burgefs money, fifh money, and the profits of the common hall and caftle mills: and he was to have a colleftor under him to account before auditors, and to have eight marks wages. (Great Red Book of Briftol, p. 214.) But the 15th Henry 7th. the office was more fully fettled by charter, by which the mayor and common council were to choofe a burgefs of the town for chamberlain to hold, *durante beneplacito*: he is to take his oath for the faithful difcharge of his office; is to have a perpetual fucceffion, with a feal of office with the fame power as the chamberlains of London; to receive all the revenues of his office, and out of the fame to expend for the ufe of the mayor and commonalty, rendering account one month after the feaft of St. Luke, fully and truly before the mayor and aldermen, or two burgeffes appointed by them, and the like account a month after he fhall be removed from his office. By the increafe of the public lands and ftock of the city by gift and purchafe, the chamberlain's bufinefs is vaftly enlarged, and it demands more than common attention and care to purfue it with propriety; whence a very able and diligent as well as upright man has been judged neceffary for the office, and his ftipend has been enlarged, as a greater variety of bufinefs has devolved on him. And that the intereft of the city may be duly fecured under his management, upon being chofen he fubfcribes a declaration, that he holds the chamberlain's office, determinable the fecond Wednefday in December after his eleftion, and he does not pretend a right to a freehold therein, and alfo figns a bond of 3000l. to perform duly his office and obey the articles made November 1698.

1306. John de Cheddre, camerariús villæ Briftoliæ.

1469. Henry Dale, at eight marks wages, and to have a colleetor under him.

1507. David Leylon.

1551. John Seybright.

1564. Thomas Hickes.

1566. John Willis, Efq; a very rich man, faid to be the beft chamberlain ever known; by his care and partly at his charges caufeys, feven miles round the city, were made: his adminiftration of the city revenue were not only irreproachable, but he impaired his own fortune by his various charities; and being reduced, that he might not be chargeable to the city, he got removed to the wardenfhip of the Back-hall, in which poft he died, much lamented by all good men.

1582. Robert Halton, Efq; died foon.

1584. Nicholas Thorn, a great merchant and charitable benefaftor.

1603. Thomas Pit, Efq; died May 4, 1613,

1614. Nicholas

1639. William Chetwyn, Efq;   —— James Holledge, Efq;
1650. James Powel, Efq; recom-   —— Chriftopher Willoughby, Efq;
    mended by Oliver Cromwell.   died June 4, 1773, and was
1670. William Hafel, Efq; died Aug.   fucceeded by
    30, Charles 2d.   1773. Richard Hawkfwell, Efq; the
1681. John Cooke, Efq;   prefent chamberlain.
1702. Edward Tocknel, Efq;

STEWARDS of the SHERIFFS COURT.

1711. Nathaniel Wade, Efq;
1731. Edward Brown, Efq;
1760. Rowles Scudamore, Efq;

The civil government of this city has been varioufly modelled, and has undergone feveral alterations at different periods of time, as will appear more particularly in the fubfequent annals; in which will be given a correct lift in regular order of all officers whither under the denomination of præpofitus villæ or prepofitor, mayor, fenefchall or fteward, bayliff or fheriff.

Briftol was certainly at firft under the government of the lord of the caftle, or his deputy the cuftos or conftable of it, in the time of the Anglo-Saxon earls of Glocefter to whom Briftol belonged, and who appointed the præpofitus villæ : and for a long time after the conqueft, when by the great increafe of the town it was neceffary for the people and their good government to have its governor or chief officer within itfelf, he always ufed to take his oath and charge of office at the caftle-gate of the conftable there ; a good proof, that at firft the fole government had been in him.

The earlieft title mentioned in an authentic record of any one that bore rule in this city, is to be found in Doomfday-book, T. E. Confefs, — wherein the præpofitus de Briftou is named Sheruuinus, as holding a manor in Glocefterfhire in the time of King Edward the Confeffor ; and doubtlefs the prepofitor was in early times an officer of judicial authority : whence in the charter of King John the officer named therein provoft, is in the original præpofitus. This name of office changed into mayor (at whatever period is uncertain) till Edward 3d's. time he was fworn in before the conftable of the caftle, but by the charter of Edward 3d. (though it does not appear therein when the election of mayor devolved firft on the commonalty of the town) it is ordained that after the burgeffes had chofen their mayor, the new elected mayor fhould at the guildhall take his oath and receive his charge of his predeceffor before the commonalty there affembled, and it fo continues.

The

The following was the order in which the feveral officers by name took place here fucceffively.

1. A prepofitor under the cuftos of the caftle till the year 1215.

2. A mayor and two prepofitors which continued from 1215 to 1266.

3. A mayor and two fenefchalls till 1313.

4. A mayor and two bayliffs till 1372.

5. A mayor, fheriff and two bayliffs till 1500.

6. A mayor and two fheriffs chofen annually, by whom it hath been go‑verned unto this day.

The city was divided into fix wards under the government of fix aldermen (of whom the recorder was always one) by charter of Henry 7: what are now called wards were formerly called quarters, of which there were five within the walls, Quarterium St. Trinitatis, quarterium Beatœ Mariæ in Foro, quarterium omnium Sanctorum, quarterium St. Audœni et quarterium de la Redclive: all which paid 4 l. o s. 5½ d. for the landgable to the King; for landgable without the walls 1 l. 19 s. 7 d. It was 23d. Elizabeth 1581 divided into twelve wards and empowered to choofe twelve aldermen, the recorder being one and the fenior alderman, who is to be well fkilled in the laws of the land, and a bar‑rifter for the fpace of five years at leaft. They are to be fworn before the mayor, and are appointed confervators and juftices of the peace with the fame authority and powers as thofe of London; and any three or more of them, of whom the mayor and recorder are to be two, may hold a court of general goal delivery, &c. and enquire into the damages of the crown. They have alfo power to chufe thirty common council men, out of which are elected annually the 15th September two fheriffs, who are fworn into their office the 29th with the mayor in public before the commons of the city. The whole common council are to confift of forty‑two of the better and more difcreet citizens, befides the mayor for the time being, the recorder being an alderman and included in that number. They are to affemble yearly before the 15th September, and the major part by their fuffrages are to choofe and fill up any vacancy fo that the number forty‑two befides the mayor be always compleat; to make fuch reafonable laws &c. in writing as may be good, profitable, neceffary, and honeft for the good government of the city, to levy fuch fines and penalties as fhall feem expedient and requifite to enforce the due obfervation of fuch laws; to fill up the vacant offices of recorder, fheriff, common council man, common clerk, fteward of the fhe‑riffs court and coroner; fome to continue their refpective offices as long as

they

they behave themfelves well, others during life; to alter the time or places of any markets ever held or to be held within the city, to make by-laws for their proper regulation &c. provided they are not contrary to the ftatutes of the realm, &c. Many other privileges and great immunities have been granted to this city by different Kings from the time of King John to the late Queen Ann, who ratified and confirmed all their franchifes and liberties and hereditaments whatfoever heretofore ufed or enjoyed by reafon of any prefcriptions, charters or letters patent, made and granted by any of her anceftors to the mayor burgeffes and commonalty of her city of Briftol, as from the charters, abftracts of which will hereafter be inferted, will more evidently appear.

Great form is obferved in election of the mayor on the 15th of September annually; for then the whole body corporate is convened at the guildhall on that occafion. The mayor elect is brought home by the old mayor and the council, attended by all the officers; the fword bearer carrying the great fword: thofe that have paffed the chair, dine with the mayor and the reft of the common council divide and dine at the two fheriffs. After dinner on election days the mayor elect invites the company to his houfe, and the fheriffs elect invite the company they dine with to their houfes. Afterwards they meet in one body and vifit the mayor elect, upon whofe coming the old mayor's company withdraw. Saturday after the election the old mayor fhews the mayor elect the market, and Sunday they all attend in proceffion to the mayor's chapel, the mayor wearing his fringed gloves, and in the afternoon the mayor elect waits on the old mayor to his parifh church. If the mayor rides not round the city bounds, as hath been the cuftom, the chamberlain and town clerk or their officers with the city mafon and city carpenter are fent round to fee that the boundary ftones and marks are not removed.

The 29th September is the day on which the mayor and fheriffs elect are fworn; when they appear in fcarlet with the council in guildhall. When the mayor is fworn, the fword bearer delivers the fword firft, then the cap of maintenance into the hands of the old mayor, who prefents them together with the feals of office to the new, both kiffing them, and the fword bearer then receives the fword from him, when the old mayor gives place to the new.

The old mayor ufed formerly to ftand up in the court to take his farewell of his brethren and the commons in a fhort fpeech, the form of which fhews the honefty, uprightnefs and fimplicity of our anceftors; part of it, as it proves how much they acted upon juft principles, muft not be omitted: addreffing

dreffing himfelf to the commons there affembled in Guildhall, he faid: " I
heartily pray you, if there be any of you who by my negligence, uncunning
or wilfulnefs, have been wronged or hurt in any wife, by colour of my late
office, or if I have done to any perfon otherwife than of right, law, or confcience, come to me and fhew your griefs; I am ready to make you amends,
if my goods will thereunto fuffice, or elfe I will afk you forgivenefs, fo that
you fhall be well contented and pleafed." — Thefe are expreffions fo truly
generous, liberal, and honeft, that they deferve to be recorded for future imitation.   This cuftom is difcontinued now, and inftead of it the mayor only
takes leave of his brethren the aldermen and other officers, by thanking them
for their affiftance to him in the difcharge of his duty, in a fhort compliment
addreffed to them.

The mayor has 120 l. paid by four quarterly payments for his kitchen, and out
of every fhip arriving at the Key, being fixty tons and upwards, (which in the year
1708 to 1709 was 70 fail, but in September 1764 all the fhips amounted to 2353
entered inward at the Cuftom-houfe, fo much has the trade increafed) 40 s. ;
for every bill or letter of health on a fhip's account, 2 s. 6 d. ; for his pocket-
feal to every affidavit, certificate, or depofition, 6 d. ; for the fealing of every
leafe, 4 s. ; befides a good gratuity for making fome one perfon a free burgefs
of the city.   And Mrs. Mayorefs has 20 s. to buy her a muff, and 40 s. per annum out of a piece of ground, called the Mayor's Paddock, which formerly ufed
to yield her 10 l.   The mayor's falaries and perquifites are now much advanced ;
from the 40s. alone for every veffel arifes to him a large fum.   But as the income to
the mayor varied fo much at different times, for the better and more regular fupport of his dignity it was agreed 1777, that he fhould be allowed 1000 l. during his mayoralty, and the fheriffs 500 l. each for their expences, whether their
perquifites produced fo much or not. *   The mayor has the cuftody of the city
plate, and a bond ufed to be given to the chamberlain of the city of 250 l. by every
mayor eleft, for fafely redelivering the plate : a filver cup with its cover, weight
thirty ounces, double gilt, given by Mr. William Bird ; one filver cup and
cover, double gilt, weight thirty ounces, given by Mrs. Elizabeth James, wife
of Dr. James ; one bafou and ewer of filver, double gilt, weight eighty-fix
ounces and a half ; one other covered cup and a fkinker, both of filver, double

gilt,

Q

<hr>

* Great difputes have arifen lately concerning the town-dues, which ufed to be paid the fheriff
for the fupport of his office.   Among the records of the term of Michaelmas, 18th Henry 8th.
rot. 18, ex part. rememb. regis, by virtue of ftatute 9th Henry 7th. Anthony Bridgegood, Nov.
12, put in his bill and information before the barons againft Robert Elliot, late fheriff, for dif-
training four packs of canvas and lokerams, &c. imported by A. B. and obliged him to pay 8d.
for keyage of the fame.   Elliot pleaded, that there had been time out of mind and ftill was a

gilt, weight fixty ounces, given by Mrs. Kitchin Searchfield, deceafed, fome-time the wife of Mr. Thomas Green, and late the wife of Mr. John Boutcher, alderman; one other filver cup with its cover, double gilt, weight fixty-fix ounces, given by Mr. George Smith, deceafed, citizen and alderman of London; one filver falt, with its cover double gilt, weighing forty-eight ounces and a quarter, given by Mrs. Mary Burroughs widow, late wife of Mr. William Burroughs merchant deceafed; to be and remain from year to year for ever in the cuftody of the mayor of Briftol for the time being, as a perpetual memory of the givers, and the mayor is to have the ufe thereof only during his mayoralty, all to be delivered to the fucceeding mayor on the 28th of September in St. George's chapel. The mayor gives bond to the chamberlain for the money for his kitchen, lent him intereft free, given by fome benefactor to this city.

The fheriffs muft firft be chofen common council men before they can be elected, and if there be not any vacancy in the body corporate, confifting of forty-three, to admit new common council men, then one of the body, or two if wanted, are chofen to ferve the office of fheriff again. The following is the oath adminifterod to every common council man.

" You fhall be faithful and true to the king's majefty, his heirs and fucceffors, and to the mayor and commonalty of this city, and their fucceffors: you fhall come at the mayor's fummons to the guildhall, common council-houfe, and to all places within the franchifes of the fame, unlefs you fhall have any lawful caufe to the contrary: you fhall give good and wholefome counfel and advice, according to your beft fkill and knowledge, in all matters wherein you fhall be required for the good and common profit of this city; and no partial counfel or advice fhall you give, for any favour or affection, concerning any matter touching the mayor or commonalty or common profit of the fame city: you fhall fecretly keep all fuch matters as fhall be fecretly communed of in the council-houfe, and which ought to be kept fecret: you fhall

common key upon the back of the river Avon, in the liberty of the town; and for the repair thereof the mayor, fheriff, bailiffs, and commonalty have ufually levied and had of all merchants, as well denizens as foreigners, for all merchandize landed, a certain cuftom called keyage, according to the rate of 12 d. for every dolii weight, and diftrained for the fame till they have fatisfied for the faid keyage; that Maurice Bowcher, importing fuch merchandize as before paid 8 d. keyage for the faid goods. The matter being brought before the judge of affize, the jury brought in a verdict for Elliot the fheriff. In the year 1786, thefe dues to the fheriff, called town-dues, have been again litigated, as oppreffive to trade, &c. but after great expence by a trial at Glocefter the merchants were caft, and the fheriffs dues confirmed.

In the little Red Book of Briftol, p. 92. are the letters patent of 17th Henry 3d. dated May 29, ftating what goods fhould pay for keyage, murage, &c. and how much each fhould be charged.

ſhall wholly uphold and ſtand with the benefit, common profit, and liberties of this city to your power; and truly and indifferently, without favour or par_tiality, ſhall give your evidence and counſel concerning the ſame, according to your ſkill and knowledge. So help you, God."

Beſides the oaths of abjuration and ſupremacy, the mayor as well as ſheriffs take the oaths reſpecting the juſt diſcharge of their offices.

It appears by the great White Book, p. 53. that the Sheriff Dale 11th Henry 8th. diſputed with the mayor and aldermen about ſerving that office, as his yearly charges exceeded the revenues of his office. But on the 4th of October, 11th Henry 8th. John Williams being then mayor, the mayor and aldermen aſſembled in guildhall by unanimous conſent, and commandment of the moſt Reverend Father in God my Lord Cardinal Wolſey, Archbiſhop of York, Chancellor of England, in moderation of the charges before this time yearly ſuſtained by the ſheriffs of Briſtol, and ordained and eſtabliſhed by authority of the king's charters to them granted and confirmed the ordinances following.

		l.	s.	d.
1. The ſheriffs ſhall receive the yearly profits of St. James's fair amounting by computation to - - - -		23		0
2. Of the goaler, for the fee-farm of the Goal, - - -		13		8
3. Of divers obiits holden in the town, - - - -		2	8	4
4. The yearly profits and advantages coming of the Key, by eſtimation, - - - - - - -		66	13	4
5. Ditto of the Back, by eſtimation, - - - - -		16	0	0
6. Of Newgate, 27l. of Temple-gate, 20l. Redcliff-gate, 9l. of Froom-gate and Pithay-gate, 1l. 6s. 8d. the whole		57	6	8
7. Of the ſtanding of the market-folks in the Market, - -		3	13	4
8. Of amerciaments, nonſuits, &c. in courts, by eſtimation, -		2	13	4
9. Of the profits of ſeſſions and law days, fines, frauds, blood-ſheds, entris, felons goods, eſcheats, forfeits, and all other caſualties, by eſtimation, - - - - - -		30	0	0
Sum of the profits to be yearly taken by the ſheriffs, - £		215	1	8

The yearly payments to be made by the ſheriffs.

1. They ſhall pay the fee-farm of the town, amounting to
   102l. 15s. 6d. — to the abbot of Tewkſbury, 14l. 10s.
   — to the prior of St. James, 3l. — to the conſtables and
   officers of the Caſtle, 28l. 7s. 3d. — to the foreſters
   of Kingſwood, 11l. 7. 3d. — in the whole - - 160 0 0
2. For the proffers to the Exchequer at Michaelmas and Eaſter,
   with the writing and ſealing thereof, - - - - 5 4 0

3. The

3. The view of the account at Eaſter, the making the ſheriffs account at Michaelmas, and divers other payments, in the Exchequer, - - - - - - -	*l.*	*s.*	*d.*

	l.	*s.*	*d.*
3. The view of the account at Eaſter, the making the ſheriffs account at Michaelmas, and divers other payments, in the Exchequer, - - - - - - -	14	10	6
4. To the ſteward of the town, his penſion, - - -	3	9	4
5. To the underſheriff, for his fee, - - - - -	1	6	8
6. To St. George's prieſt, his penſion, bread and wine, -	5	8	4
7. To the yearly obit of Richard Spicer in St. Nicholas church,	3	13	0
8. To the wages of the clerk of the ſame church, and for keeping the clock there, - - - - - - -	1	6	8
9. To each of the four orders of friers 8 s. each, - - -	1	12	0
10. To be ſpent yearly at St. George's feaſt, - - -	2	0	0
11. At the drinking at Trinity chapel, - - - -	0	13	4
12. To the two ſcabbards for the mayor, - - - -	1	10	0
13. To the coſt of Midſummer watch yearly, - - -	20	0	0
14. For the town liveries in the whole to all manner of officers, for which the ſheriffs have the profits of St. James's fair,	25	0	0
15. For the coſts of ſeſſions and law days, - - - -	2	0	0
16. For the writers for their wages yearly, - - - -	1	9	8
17. For the wages to the keepers of the Key, - - -	1	8	8
18. Ditto to the keeper of the Back, 26 s. 8 d. — to the porter of Newgate, 30 s. — Redcliff-gate, 20 s. — Temple-gate, 26 s. 8 d. — Froom-gate, 13 s. 4 d. — Pithay-gate, 13 s. 4 d.	7	16	8
19. Wages to each of waiting yeomen, 1 l. 6 s. 8 d. - -	5	6	8
20. For the commiſſion of the ſtaple, - - - - -	1	2	6
21. For twenty quires of paper, bags, and ferrells for the town clerk, - - - - - - - - -	0	6	8
22. To the town clerk for two law days, - - - -	0	6	8
23. For writing the proffers yearly, - - - - -	0	4	0
24. For writing the indentures for the goal between the new ſheriffs and the old, - - - - - -	0	2	8
25. For ringing the common bell at Michaelmas, - -	0	4	0
26. For the meſſengers of the Exchequer, - - - -	0	4	0
27. At the drinking at the Tolzey at St. Nicholas day, -	0	2	0
28. To the chamber yearly towards the charges of the burgeſſes of parliament againſt ſuch time as any parliament ſhall be holden, - - - - - - - -	2	0	0

£ 268   8   0

All

All other charges of the town to be always born at the charge of the chamber.

Total of the yearly charges of the fheriffs, - - £268 8 0

So that their charges ftill exceeded their profits befides the cofts

of bringing up the prifoners, - - - - - 53 6 4

This curious account gives us an idea of feveral particulars relative to the fheriffs office and manners and cuftoms of the age; but in modern times new alterations and eftablifhments have taken place.

At p. 124.—10, 11, and 27, is mentioned a charge for drinking and feaft-ing, which fhews they were no ftrangers here to hofpitable living and enter-tainments formerly on public occafions.

20th May, 28 Henry vi. it was ordained by William Cannings mayor, and the common council, that the drinking at St. John's and St. Peter's nights fhould be wholly to perfons of crafts going the nights before the mayor, fheriff and other notable perfons, and that the mayor and fheriff on forfeiture of five marks a piece, the one at St. John's night, the other at St. Peter's, fhould difpenfe wine to be difpofed of to the faid crafts at their halls: viz. to the weavers and tuckers each ten gallons; to the taylors and cornefers each eight gallons; butchers fix gallons; dyers, bakers, brewers, and fher-men each five gallons; fkinners, fmiths, furriers, cutellers, lockyers, barbers, waxmakers, tanners, whitawers, each four gallons; mafons, tylers, carpen-ters, hoopers, wire-drawers and card-makers, three gallons each; bowers and fletchers (arrow makers) each two gallons; in all ninety four gallons.

Mention is alfo made and orders given about the mayor and council going to their Chriftmas drinking to the abbot of St. Auguftin, as hath been ac-cuftomed.

It appears by a note in the city books dated 1626 the following officers of the city were yearly chofen:

A mayor eleft and two fheriffs eleft; mayor and aldermen conftables of the ftaple; mayor eleft and four aldermen cuftodes clavium or clavigers; fix aldermen and common council men auditors of the accounts; four alder-men and council-men furveyors of the city lands; four elder council-men affiftants in the care of orphans; four of the fame affiftants with the mayor for the loan money of Sir Thomas White and others; one treafurer and one affiftant for the hofpital of Queen Elizabeth; two fupervifors of the fame; two aldermen fupervifors of the hofpital of Lafford's gate; four fupervifors of the free fchool at St. Bartholomew's; five fupervifors of the 60l. for the placing out poor children and provifion of coals; four fupervifors of the gift

money

money of Sir Thomas White and others for the repair of the high ways near Briſtol; but it was ordained 15th September 1633 that no perſon ſhould ſtand in any of the offices of ſurveyors, clavigers (and ſo downwards for the reſt) above two years together at one time, the office of auditors only excepted.

Each alderman by an ordinance 12th March 1621, confirmed by another 13th December 1658, was obliged (unleſs prevented by ſickneſs) to viſit his ward once a month for the diſcovery of ſtrangers and undertenants &c. to remedy any diſorders miſbehaviour &c. under the penalty of 5l. to the chamber for his negleſt therein; and the mayor, unleſs employed in the ſervice of the King, was not to remain out of the liberties of the city above the ſpace of three days and three nights in the whole year of mayoralty, under the penalty of 100l. by an order dated 20th Oſtober 1606; and if he refuſed to ſerve the office of mayoralty when choſen he was fined 200l. and disfranchiſed: John Pope was fined 100l. in the year 1663 for the ſame. But the honour and profit attending the office now have been ſuch, that the mayoralty has not been refuſed by any one, eſpecially as the expences incurred by ſerving the office of ſheriff are amply repaid him during the year of mayoralty. The mayor by ancient privilege recorded in the city archives, has the nomination of a ſecond perſon to be put in eleſtion for ſheriff and the houſe the other, one of which is choſen: and in the year 1656, Joſias Clutterbuck being choſen ſheriff and refuſing to ſerve was fined 300l. and Mr. Thomas Stephens was fined 200l. and committed to newgate for refuſal in 1660. But by an order 4th November 1704, any one refuſing to ſerve the office of mayor in his turn if eleſted, incurred a penalty of 400l. and was disfranchiſed, and the ſheriffs 200l. each in like manner, unleſs they will ſwear they are not worth 2000l.

To add a ſplendor to the office of mayor, and for convenience of his domeſtic affairs during the year of mayoralty, a manſion houſe in the year 1784, for the mayor was ſet apart for his annual reſidence with commodious buildings, offices and banqueting room in Queen-ſquare, which being ſo near the trading part of the city, was thought a proper place for the ready accommodation of captains of ſhips and others, who might want to apply to the mayor in their concerns.

This opulent and reſpeſtable corporation are poſſeſſed of very large eſtates both in the city and in the country, in truſt for charitable uſes and the public emolument of the citizens, for ſupporting hoſpitals, ſchools with exhibitions at the univerſity and almſhouſes; for eſtabliſhing leſtures and gift-ſermons at churches for the inſtruſtion of the people in the doſtrines of
Chriſtianity;

Chriftianity; for relieving prifoners and confined debtors; for keeping the poor at work; for the marriage of poor girls children of freemen; for repairing the roads round the city, and for other public ufes. They have alfo a large fund of money depofited in the chamber for the ufe of young tradefmen, thofe efpecially in the clothing bufinefs to be preferred, 100 l. 50 l. 25 l. or lefs to be lent to each of them intereft free for feven or ten years, they getting fecurity for its repayment then. This has fuch a natural tendency to promote a fpirit of induftry in young beginners, and this little ftock to begin with joined to the aid of their friends and their own diligence has been known to produce fuch a good effeft, that they have rofo often in the world, and thus happily fulfilled and even exceeded the good intention of the donors. By eftates and manors vefted in their hands, and by purchafes formerly made with money out of the city ftock, the corporation are patrons of feveral church livings in the city and country : which they generally prefent upon any becoming vacant to their fellow citizens or the fons of fuch, who have been educated at the Briftol Grammar-fchool, and at the univerfity for divines: this is but juft and right, as thefe advowfons or rights of prefentation were purchafed formerly by the money of the burgeffes, for the difpofal of which to the advantage of the citizens the corporation are in truft, though prejudice and partiality have been fometimes known to have mifguided their judgment in this affair; and thefe church-livings have been prefented to ftrangers, in preference to natives and free burgeffes, who though they would be glad or ftand in need of fuch a provifion, and have been educated perhaps with that view, yet have been fo unfortunate as to have folicited in vain; and notwithftanding their natural right and juft claim to them have had the mortification to find ftrangers preferred before them.

The wife old fathers of our city thus gave exhibitions to encourage the citizens to breed up their fons to learning at the univerfity, that fome of them might fill the learned profeffions with credit, and become ornaments of fociety and refleft honour on their native city, as able and learned divines in poffeffion of thefe churches.

In the Diocefe of Briftol.

The following livings are in the gift of the mayor, aldermen, and common council of the city of Briftol.

Deanry of Briftol. — City of Briftol.

Livings difcharged.

Rectories, &c. with their patrons and proprietors.

Clear yearly value. l. s. d.		King's books. l. s. d.
5 18 1	St. John's and St. Lawrence's rectory, computed to be about 120l. per ann. pays a penfion of 13 s. 4 d. to the patrons, - - - -	7 4 7
5 18 11	St. Michael's rectory, about 200l. per ann. pays a penfion of 4 s. - · - - -	6 0 0
0 6 8	St. Owen's, alias St. Ewen's rectory, about 25 l. pays a penfion of 1 lb. of wax,	
12 5 0	St. Peter's rectory, about 150l. pays a penfion of 1 l. - - - - -	6 7 6
43 16 0	St. Philip and St. Jacob's vicarage; mayor, aldermen and burgeffes of Briftol. Abby of Tewkf- bury propr. about 150l. per ann. - -	15 0 0
33 6 8	Temple vicarage, alias St. Crofs, in com. Somerfet. Mayor, aldermen, and burgeffes of Briftol. Knights Templars olim propr. about 200l. per ann. pays a penfion of 5 l. per ann. -	3 4 2

Not in charge.

	St. James cure, olim a priory, 450l. and upwards per ann. pays a penfion of 3 l. 6 s. 8 d. per ann. city of Briftol patrons. *	
8 8 0	Chrift Church or the Holy Trinity, computed at about 150l. per annum. Mayor and aldermen patrons, olim the abby of Tewkfbury, pays a penfion of 10 s. per annum. - -	11 0 0

Diocefe

* Vide Willis's Survey, p. 841. Sixteen of the eighteen churches in Briftol are in no archdeaconry, but in the bifhop's fole vifitation, by his chancellor; though Bedminfter, the mother church to St. Mary Redcliff and Thomas in Briftol city, is ftill in Wells diocefe and Bath archdeaconry; and the feventeen out-lying churches and chapels in Briftol deanry, yet belong to Glocefter archdeaconry, notwithftanding they are in this diocefe.

Diocefe of Bath and Wells. Somerfet.

Deanry of Bridgwater, in the Archdeaconry of Taunton.

Livings difcharged.

Rectories, &c. with their patrons and proprietors.

Clear yearly value.
l. s. d.

King's books,
l. s. d.

38 1 8   Stockland Gaunts alias Briftol, vicarage. Mayor
and burgeffes of Briftol.   Prior or mafter of
Gaunts in Briftol. About 70 l. per annum, -   6 9 4

Deanry of Axbridge, in the Archdeaconry of Wells.

Livings remaining in charge.

Rectories, &c. with their patrons and proprietors.

King's books.

42 1 8

Yearly tenths.

Congrefbury vicarage, [St. Andrew] with Lau-
rencewick chapel, [St. Laurence] capellano vi l.
fynods vii s. Mayor and aldermen of Briftol, as
governors of Queen Elizabeth's hofpital, patrons.
Dean and chapter of Wells, proprietors. About
300 l. per annum.   -   -   -   4 4 2

Livings difcharged.

Clear yearly value.

24 2 0¼

King's books.

Locking vicarage, [St. Auftin] fynods ii s. iii d.
Proxies iiii d. William Plomley, Efq; 1671,
pri. Worfpring propr. The Society of Merchants
in Briftol. It is about 70 l. per ann.   -   5 6 10½

D. Redcliff and Bedminfter, in the Archdeaconry
of Bath.

Livings remaining in charge.

King's books.

5 10 7¼
33 15 7½

Clear yearly value.

Burnet rectory, about 70 l. per ann.   -   31 3 6

Portifhead rectory, fynods v s. viii d. Proxies xvi d.
Abby Keynfham viii s. Mayor and burgeffes of
Briftol. About 120 l. per ann   -   -

Tenths.

3 5 6¾

The Gaunts or Mayor's chapel, in Briftol, 25 l. per
annum for the reader, and 1 l. 1 s. for the fermon
every Sunday to the preacher.

St. George's new created church in Kingfwood.
Mayor and corporation. About 150 l. per annum.

R

They

They not only prefent to the above livings, but alfo to many other lecture-fhips, chaplainfhips, &c. But it muft be obferved, that the value of thefe livings in the city chiefly arifes from the voluntary contributions of the parifhioners reforting to the feveral parifh churches, which have no endowment, fome not even an houfe for the minifter, except Queen Anne's bounty and certain fums given by charitable benefactors for gift-fermons to be preached on certain occafions and days appointed. Therefore the value of each church living here muft vary every year, and however computed at a medium cannot be exact. The tythes of the city were formerly paid to the abby of Tewkfbury from the moft early times, being the fum of 14 l. 10 s. which at the diffolu-tion came to the crown, and were purchafed by the corporation, 24 of C. 2 among other things. But the good citizens of Briftol, though they have op-pofed any attempt of having an eftablifhed fum levied upon their houfes and lands for the fixed fupport of the clergy, have hitherto generoufly contributed to their maintenance ; nor given any caufe for their applying to Government for relief, which they would probably obtain, as in London, their duties in fuch large and populous parifhes being very great, if a fupport due to their labours were meanly afforded or partly withheld.

It was a great character, we fee given to our citizens in early times, (vid. p. 83.) that " they maintained preachers at their own coft in commendable fort," and there is little reafon to apprehend they will be ever backward in generoufly rewarding the labours of a learned clergy, and fupporting the offi-ciating lawfully inftituted miniftry of the church of England eftablifhed by law. There were certainly tythes as well as offerings collected formerly for their maintenance, though long fince difcontinued, as appears from p. 2. of the great Red Book, that 15th kal. Jun. 1301, in feventh year of his confecra-tion, Robert Archbifhop of Canterbury iffued forth his mandate to the Dean of Briftol, ftrictly forbidding fome irregular proceedings, that in proving wills, they cited the inhabitants to remote places out of the borough, and or-daining the confirmation of the orders made by the bifhop of the diocefe, re-lating to the better fecuring and adjufting the tythes of fuch perfons, who, living in one part of the town, fold their wares in another.

A competent maintenance for the minifters of the feveral parifhes, even in the time of the Protector, was thought fo neceffary, that on the 5th of Octo-ber 1657 the mayor and commonalty, by the powers of feveral acts of parlia-ment, ordained that 909 l. fhould be yearly levied by way of tax and affeffment upon each parifh for their fupport, in the following proportions : St. Michael and St. Auftin, 50 l. St. James, 50 l. St. Thomas, 120 l. Temple, 48 l. Redcliff,

Redcliff, 40 l. St. Philip and the Caſtle, 20 l. St. Stephen, 90 l. St. Nicholas, 120 l. St. Werburg and Leonard, 85 l. All Saints and St. Ewen, 70 l. Chriſt Church and St. John, 120 l. Maryport and St. Peter, 96 l. And to raiſe this maintenance by aſſeſſment, (" the want of which, they ſay, is in no place greater") They further ordain : Firſt, that no officiating miniſter ſhould be de-barred from this benefit. Secondly, that the fabric of all the churches ſhould be ſupported, and their revenues be given and applied to ſuch uſes and the ſame purpoſes as formerly. Thirdly, they recommend to the ſeveral veſtries to concert any other proportions that ſhall be neceſſary, and will join them to aſſeſs and compel the payment of them. Fourthly, that when they meet to make the poor rates to have the allowance of the juſtices according to law, they ſhall bring the rate for the miniſters maintenance, to have the like con-firmation according to aɔ of parliament ; all perſons over-rated to appeal at the next quarter ſeſſions. Fifthly, that when a miniſter is to be choſen, it ſhould be in the liberty of each pariſh to chooſe their own miniſter where none is already officiating, provided he be an ordained perſon or choſen out of one of the univerſities, and approved of according to the laws of the land. And it appears, that the corporation enforced the execution of the ſaid aɔs, and the 14th of February 1658, ordered 100 l. per ann. out of the chamber's revenue towards the better maintenance and encouragement of the pariſh miniſters.

Notwithſtanding the great loſſes, by contributions and otherwiſe, this corpor-ation ſuſtained in the time of the grand rebellion ; yet we find ſoon after, in Charles 2d's. time, they had ſo far improved the city revenues, that they diſ-charged ſeveral rents payable to the crown, which had been ſold Feb. 6, 1650, for 577 l. 12 s. 7 d. by Oliver Cromwell and the Commonwealth, but being recovered in the year 1673, 24th Charles 2d. by indenture, dated July 24, the following fee farm rents reſerved paid annually to the crown out of lands, which had been purchaſed at the diſſolution of religious houſes of Henry 8th. by the city, were bought on their behalf by Thomas Lee, of London, Eſq; and conveyed to the ſaid mayor and commonalty of Briſtol by the Right Hon. Francis Lord Hawley, Sir Charles Harboard, his Majeſty's ſurveyor-general, Sir William Howard, Sir John Talbot of Lacock, Wilts, and William Har-board Eſq; truſtees appointed for the ſale of fee farm rents, and by an aɔ for veſting them in the truſtees and by order of the Lords Commiſſioners of the Treaſury to them direɔed. The conſideration money for the whole was 3024 l. 15 s. 1 d. and to raiſe that ſum, by an order in the corporation books dated 1671, ſome fee farm rents payable to the city were ſold by them to divers people, but thoſe payable out of the marſh of Briſtol (now the ſquare)

were

were then not thought proper to be parted with, as not to the advantage of the city. But feeing whence thefe ground rents paid by the city to the crown arofe, we difcover what lands belonged to religious houfes, and what great eftates are now in the poffeffion of the chamber of Briftol from the diffolution.

Parcel of the late hofpital or houfe of St. John the Baptift with-   *l.*   *s.*   *d.*
    out Redcliff-gate, within the city of Briftol.

For lands and tenements within the city of Briftol, with meffuages, tofts, houfes, meadows, paftures, rents, fervices, and other appertenances, lately belonging to the faid hofpital, (except the fite and precinct thereof) a referved rent of   -   2   7 $1\frac{1}{4}$

Parcel of the late monaftery of Tewkfbury.

For the whole houfe and fite of the priory or cell of St. James, near Briftol, lately belonging to the diffolved monaftery of Tewkfbury, and all the meffuages, buildings, barns, dove-houfe, pools, orchards, lands, &c. within the faid precinct as well as without, to the faid cell adjoining. Alfo for all the rectories of Stapleton and Mangotsfield, with their rights, &c. thereto belonging. Alfo for the rectory and church of St. James in Briftol, and for the rectory and church of the bleffed St. Philip and Jacob in the faid city, with their rights, &c. to faid cell or priory of St. James appertaining, with right of patronage : and all manors, granges, mills, lands, &c. in Stapleton, Mangotsfield, Itchington, Tockington, Cadbroke, Saltmarfh, and Barton hundred, in the county of Glocefter, howfoever belonging to the faid priory, granted among other things to Henry Brain, Efq; by letters patent 35th Henry 8th. for 666 l. 7 s. 6 d. with penfions of 20 s. out of the rectory of St. Peter, 10 s. out of Chrift Church, 10 s. 4 d. out of St. John's, 1 l. 6 s. 8 d. out of St. Philip's, 4 s. out of St. Michael's, 6 d. out of St. Ewen's, — at only per annum,   -   -   3   10 $9\frac{1}{2}$

For the referved rent of 2 l. 3 s. 4 d. out of the manor of Olvefton, belonging to the late diffolved monaftery of Bath, granted among other things to Sir Ralph Sadler,   -   -   2   3   4

    N. B. This was afterwards fold off by the corporation to Sir Robert Cann, for 15 l. 15 s. the fame fum the city gave for it.

Parcel

Parcel of Tewkſbury monaſtery.   ı.   d.

For a yearly rent of 14 l. 18 s. 2 d. out of the chantry of St. Michael in Winterborne, and lands, &c. thereto belonging in
Winterborne, Froomſhaw, Churchfield, Hambroke, and Clif-
field, in Gloceſterſhire, paid by the ſheriff or chamberlain of
Briſtol,   -   -   -   -   -   -   14 18   2

Parcel of the poſſeſſions of the late monaſtery of Bath, aſſigned
for life to the Queen Henrietta Maria, for her jointure.

For all that yearly fee-farm rent of 41 l. 3 s. 5 d. reſidue of 95 l.
3 s. 5 d. iſſuing, due, and payable out of the manor of Congerſbury, Somerſet, and for the patronage of the church of
Congerſbury, and its appertenances : alſo the courts leet, &c.
in Congerſbury and Lawrence Wick, paid by the city of
Briſtol,   -   -   -   -   -   -   41   3   5

Parcel of the houſe of St. Mark of Belliſwick.

For all that yearly rent of 20 l. per ann. payable by the city out
of the houſe and ſite of the hoſpital of St. Mark of Belliſwick,
near Briſtol, called les Gaunts, and for the church, belfry,
churchyard there, and for the manors of Erdcot and Lee in
Gloceſterſhire, to it belonging ; and for the manor of Stockland Gaunts, with its rights, members, and appertenances, in
Somerſetſhire, to the late diſſolved hoſpital belonging ; and
the donation, patronage, and free diſpoſition of the vicarages
of the churches of Stockland Gaunts and Overſtowey ; and
alſo for the manor, &c. of Winterbourne Conner, called
Cherburg, in Wilts, with its rights, &c. to the ſaid hoſpital
heretofore belonging ; and out of and for all meadows, granges,
tenements, and hereditaments, &c. to the ſaid manors and
premiſes belonging, in the town of Briſtol, or the pariſhes of
Lee and Almondſbury, in the county of Gloceſter, or in
Stockland Gaunts, Overſtowey, and Brewham, in Somerſet-
ſetſhire, or in Winterborne Gonner, in Wilts, to the late
hoſpital les Gauntes belonging, as parcel of the ſaid houſe or
hoſpital, (except the manor of Pawlet Gaunts, Southam, and
Northam, granted by letters patent of Henry 8th. to Richard
Cupper) and alſo for and out of the manor of Hampe and its
rights and appertenances, in the county of Somerſet ; parcel

of

of the late monaftery of Athelny, and meffuages and lands in   *l.*   *s.*   *d.*
Hampe aforefaid in the tenure of Sir Richard Warre ; and
for the fite of the houfe of Grey Friers, Carmelite Friers
and their appertinences, all purchafed of Henry 8th 33d.
year, for the fum of 1000l. and 20l. per annum rent,   -   20   0   0

Parcel of the antient crown lands.

For the ferm of the caftle of Briftol with its appertinences the
manfion houfe within the caftle in the tenure of Francis
Brewfter, the clofe lying without the ditch of the faid caftle
called the King's orchard ; the inner green and for forty
three feveral tenements within the circuit or walk of the caftle,
and for the wood yard there, and three gardens there, and
barns, ftables and other premifes ; and for the walls, towers
and ditches inclofing the faid caftle referved in purchafe of
the caftle of C. 1ft. an. regni. 6°.   -   -   -   -   -   40   0   0

Parcel of chantry lands lately concealed.

For and out of the fee-farm of the chapel or hofpital of the
holy Trinity in the parifh of St. Phillip and Jacob, and all
the lands &c. belonging thereto at the rent of twenty fhillings,
alfo for the fee-farm of the chapel of the three Kings of Cologn, in the parifh of St. Michael and the lands thereto belonging, an annual rent referved of 13 s. and 4 d. for it, both
granted to Peter Gray by Queen Elizabeth by letters patent
dated 8th day of March, in the 19th year of her reign, paying
yearly per annum,   -   -   -   -   -   -   -   1 13   4

Parcel of lands of the priory of St. Mary Magdalen of Briftol.

For a rent affize of one tenement on the Back of Briftol,   -   0   4   0
For an annual rent or tenth referved for all the tenements, lands
and other premifes within the city of Briftol, paid by the
mayor and burgeffes at per annum,   -   -   -   -   2   7 $1\frac{1}{4}$
For an annual rent iffuing out of the office of water bayliff of
Briftol, granted to the mayor and burgeffes by Henry 7th
18th December, 15th year of his reign, — paying   -   -   0 13   4
For a fee-farm rent iffuing out of the tythes of the city of Briftol, payable by the fheriffs at per annum,   -   -   -   14 10   0

For

l. . d.

For an annual rent iſſuing out of an ancient farm of the city of
Briſtol granted to the mayor and commonalty at per annum
(being paid for the fee of the city and its ſuburbs, gates,
ditches, walls, the rents of the fleſh ſhambles there, ſhops,
mills, waters running to the mills, tolls, courts, fairs &c.
which farm was granted 1 Edward 4th 12th Feb.)   -   142 10 0

The ſale of the afore-mentioned fee-farm rents were contracted for betwixt
the city and the crown 30th Auguſt 1671. viz. 2l. 7s. 1d¼. per annum:
1l. 13s. 4d. per annum: 3l. 10s. 9½d. per annum: 2l. 3s. 4d. per annum:
and the 20l. per annum, at ſixteen years and half purchaſe, and for the
thirty three ſhillings and four pence per annum, the 4s. per annum,
14l. 18s. 2d. per annum, the 14l. 10s. per annum: and the 4ll. 3s. 5d.
per annum, at ſixteen years purchaſe, — and for the reverſion after the Queen
of the rents of 40l. 0s. 0d. per annum: and 142l. 10s per annum, at eight
years purchaſe. The clear money paid was 3024l. 15s. 1d. though the rate
of the particulars aforementioned at the rates expreſſed is   £ 3078 6 2
Deduct intereſt for one moiety for 139 days from the 9th
November 1671, at the rate of ten per Cent, &c. -   -   53 11 1

The clear purchaſe of the whole   -   -   -   -   - 3024 15 1

A purchaſe ſo well judged by the governing members of the city at that
time, that they cannot but be greatly applauded for it by their ſucceſſors at
this day, as by clearing the city lands from the incumbrance of ground rents
payable to the crown, it has rendred theſe eſtates they purchaſed very rea-
ſonable at firſt of the crown in Henry 8th's time much more valuable now;
and has enabled the corporation to found hoſpitals, increaſe almſhouſes, improve their original endowments and render the public charities more extenſive, and employ larger ſums of the public money to public uſes and the
beneficial advantage and emolument of the citizens. Beſides theſe great
eſtates the corporation are poſſeſſed of the manour of Burnet in the county
of Somerſet, by the gift of the good and truly charitable Mr. Alderman
Whitſon, for the perpetual ſupport and education of poor girls, and erecting
a ſchool called the Red Maids School; they have alſo eſtates at Weſton in
Gordano in the county of Somerſet; at Hinton Derham and Winterborne
in the county of Glocester; at Portiſhead in the county of Somerſet; at
Congerſbury the manor; at Overſtowey and Stockland-Briſtol in Somerſetſhire; the manor of Gaunts Ercot and the Lea; lands in Stapleton, Portbury,
Aſhton,

Afhton, Briflington, and at many other places as well diftant from as near to the city; and an infinite number of houfes, lands, &c. within the city itfelf and in the fuburbs, the market, the whole of Queen-fquare, Prince's-ftreet, part of College-green, all Orchard-ftreet, &c. all which are leafed out on lives, paying ground rents, &c. befides feveral eftates in hand, ground rents, and rents from all the ftandings in the feveral markets, &c. As thefe were given in truft for charitable ufes and common profit of the city, they will be noted more particularly, and each endowment given, in the parifh where thofe charities are eftablifhed; or in the annals, under the year when they were beftowed on the city.

The following is a fhort fcheme only of the general charities that have been eftablifhed, and agreed on as payable yearly by the chamberlain, befides the larger foundations for the fupport of fchools, hofpitals, and others, hereafter to be particularized.

In 1737, on the 14th of December, an order of common council was made for a committee to infpect and examine into the feveral charities given to the chamber, and payable by them, and for which they ftand in truft.

The firft fitting, December 16, 1737, Nathaniel Day, mayor.

The laft fitting was Auguft 17, 1739, William Jefferies, ditto.

		l.	s.	d.
1566. Sir Thomas White's gift, in the year 1738 produced, to be lent to burgeffes, 50l. each, for ten years, intereft free, on fecurity; clothiers and cloth-workers to be preferred, - - - - -		1400	0	0
1579. John Heydon, 100l. to two merchants for four years, paying 1l. 13s. 4d. each for intereft, to be given the prifoners in Newgate. - - - -		100	0	0
1532. Robert Thorn, 500l. to clothiers and others, who fet the the poor at work, 50l. each, for ten years, intereft free. - - - - - -		500	0	0
1634. Alderman Robert Aldworth, 1000l. to thofe who fet the poor at work, 50l. each, for ten years, intereft free.		1000	0	0
1634. George White, 200l. 20l. each to ten men, for ten years; clothiers to be preferred. - -		200	0	0
1627. Alderman John Whitfon, 500l. 250l. to five young men, being meer merchants, for feven years, 10s. a year intereft to the poor of St. Nicholas parifh in Briftol; and 250l. to handicraft tradefmen, inhabitants and freemen of Briftol, for feven years, intereft free. -		500	0	0

Alder-

		l.	*s.*	*d.*
Alderman Robert Rogers, 100l. to ten burgeffes, for five years, intereft free; foap-boilers to be preferred.		100	o	o
1627. John Dunfter, 100l. to ten handicraftfmen, free burgeffes, for five years, intereft free. - - -		100	o	o
1623. Thomas Jones's executors paid 380 l. 20l. a piece to freemen, for fix years. - - - -		380	o	o
1594. Alderman Robert Kitchen, 125l. to five merchants, 25l. each, for five years, intereft free; and 250l. to freemen, by 5l. and 10l. each, for five years, intereft free.		375	o	o
1651. Robert Redwood's executors paid 250l. 10l. to burgeffes, for five years. - - - -		250	(	
1616. Dr. James, 50l. to five burgeffes, for two years, intereft free. - - - - - -		50	o	o
1629. Alderman Doughty, 100l. to ten handicraftfmen, for five years, intereft free, - - - -		100	o	o
Margaret Brown, ten pounds. - - -		10	o	o
	£	4965	o	o

Thefe are the benefactions of the loan money, * and the meetings to receive petitions from the burgeffes for it are, the fecond Tuefday in October, fecond Tuefday in January, fecond Tuefday in April, and the fecond Tuefday in July.

In a manufcript wrote in 1746, and copied from the Council-books, the following are the yearly payments to be made by the chamber of Briftol, viz.

		l.	*s.*	*d*
Sir Thomas White, to twenty-four corporations, to each yearly in rotation, - - - - -		104	o	o
Humphrey Brown, to Weftbury parifh, - - -		2	10	o
To Iron Acton, - - -		2	10	
To St. Werburgh's, for four fermons, -		2	o	o
To St. Nicholas, for a lecture, -		20	o	o
Abel Kitchen, for apprenticing poor boys, - -		14	o	o
To All Saints' church, - - -		3	6	8
To Temple, - - - - -		3	2	o
To Chrift Church, - - - -		3	18	o
To Weftbury, - - - -		6	13	4
To the vicar of Kendal, for a fermon, - -		o	10	o
To the vicar of St. Stephen's, one Sunday in Lent,		o	10	o

S   Robert

* A table of this loan money was fixed up in the Council-houfe in the year 1738.

		l.	s.	d.
Robert Kitchen, to parishes, viz. St. Stephen,	– –	2	0	0
Maryport,	– –	2	0	0
All Saints, –	– –	0	10	0
St. Nicholas,	– –	2	0	0
St. Peter, –	– –	2	0	0
St. Ewen's,	– –	1	0	0
St. Auguftin,	– –	1	10	0
St. Thomas,	– –	1	0	0
St. Philip's,	– –	2	0	0
Temple, –	– –	2	0	0
Redcliff, –	– –	2	0	0
St. James,	– .	2	0	0
St. Michael's,	–	1	10	0
St. John's, –	– –	1	0	0
St. Leonard's,	– –	1	0	0
St. Werburgh's,	– –	0	10	0
Chrift Church,	– –	2	0	0
William Chefter, to the poor of St. John's, –	– –	7	16	0
To the almfhoufe on St. James's-back,	–	0	4	0
Thomas White, to almfhoufes of St. John, St. Thomas, St. Michael, Lewin's-mead, 4 s. each per month, is by the year,		9	12	0
To St. John's conduit, –	– –	1	0	0
All Saints' ditto,	– –	1	0	0
To Newgate prifoners,	– –	1	1	8
George White, to the prifoners in Newgate,	– –	5	0	0
To a fcholar in Oxford,	– –	5	0	0
J. Heydon, to the prifoners in Newgate,	– .	3	6	8
Alderman Aldworth, ditto,	– –	1	0	0
Alderman Haviland, for twelve fermons in Newgate,	–	4	0	0
Mr. Lambert, to the hofpital of Trinity, –	–	0	16	0
Joan Ludlow, to the almfhoufe of St. Michael's,	–	1	0	0
Mrs. Wheatly, to All Saints almfhoufe, Nov. 1.	–	0	10	0
Paid yearly by the corporation for charities and fermons, &c. £		224	6	4

Thefe annual general charities were eftablifhed by the committee, whofe meeting ended 1739, as were all thofe that are marked with an afterifk (*) in the lift of wills and in the enfuing annals to be given below.

In

In 1620, 18th October, it was agreed, that "in lieu of charities which could not now be reftored to their right firft intended ufe, 50l. per annum was ordered to be always given to place out burgeffes' children, and 10l. per annum to buy coals for the poor; and in 1622, a quarter part of the faid 50l. was to be applied for placing out poor girls, and in 1626 a quarter part to Bridewell prifoners." In 1634, 6l. per annum was agreed to be paid yearly to maimed foldiers and other impotent perfons, out of Codrington's lands in Portifhead.

Many of Robert Thorn's gifts do not relate to thefe times, becaufe applied before, according to the donor's will; fo alfo thofe of Nicholas Thorn.

In 1625, the mayor, J. Barker, Alderman Whitfon, and others, were appointed to caufe a table of benefactors to be made, and fet up in fome convenient place or in the council chamber.

In the year 1659, 6th Jan. it was ordered in the Common Council Book, No. K 6. that, " whereas feveral fums of gift money have been applied by the chamber to different ufes, the committee of the faid gift money do appoint what feals of the city or of the chamberlain fhould pafs for fuch monies as did properly belong to each feveral donation and fettlement of the worthy benefactors to pious ufes, to the end the city may be fully engaged to make the fame good again." So confcientioufly exact and fcrupuloufly honeft were they in applying the money and eftates left to the city's ufe, according to the wills of the refpective donors!

In the year 1677, 5th May, order was made, " that 1300l. of gift money Alderman Lawford then acknowledged to be in his hands, and that other monies upon that account in his cuftody, be received by the chamberlain, and be put into a cheft with four locks and keys, and Mr. Mayor with three other of the aldermen be clavigers; other clavigers in fucceffion to be elected on the general day of election of the mayor and other officers, which clavigers are to difpofe of the monies." L. p. 101.

October 13, 1659. The following order appears in the Council Books, I. I. p. 115, " whereas there appeared to be a fudden occafion for the mayor and aldermen to be fatisfied and informed as to the foundations, conftitutions, orders, and ftatutes of the refpective hofpitals, and of the lands rents and revenues belonging to them it is ordered, that a committee, with the mayor and two aldermen clavigers and town clerk, fearch into the refpective charters records and evidences relating thereto, and draw up their fentiments in writing." And in 1680, 31ft Charles 2d. 5th of February, the following entry is made : " Whereas there is an act of parliament of the

39th

39th Elizabeth whereby the mayor and aldermen, or any four of them, the recorder and mayor to be two, are made fpecial governors and vifitors over all monies goods and other things given to charitable ufes within the city by any perfon, and to make orders for the due employing the fame and to compel all perfons to yield obedience thereto, notwithftanding which the fame is not obeyed : but in regard other perfons have taken out commiffions and do act contrary to the faid ftatute; it was therefore enacted that Mr. Recorder, Sir John Knight and Sir Robert Cann take care to preferve the rights and privileges granted by the faid act, and to oppofe all proceedings againft it.

The ground rents referved both of the city and country eftates belonging to the chamber of Briftol given for charitable ufes and the common profit of the city, are upwards of 3000l. per annum, and including the rents of the market-houfes and ftandings, fome eftates in hand not leafed off, with the great additional income arifing from fines and for renewals of leafes upon lives continually dropping in fuch a number of eftates fmall and large as they are poffeffed of, the whole amounts to above 10,000l. per annum: in the year 1778, all their eftates and rents produced 14,000l. per annum, though their produce muft vary greatly at different times.

Enabled with thefe large eftates this opulent corporation have not been wanting, befides the above ftanding annual difburfements and others for the public charities, &c. in expending large fums for the general good of the city and better accommodation of the citizens; particularly, they have purchafed ground and builded thereon a new Exchange and erected a new Market behind it at an expence of more than 50,000l. befides doing other public works occafionally to be recited hereafter to their honour.

Great and numerous are the charities in the difpofal and management of the mayor and aldermen, yet the poor of the city for their weekly fupport are under the immediate rule of the governor deputy governor affiftants and guardians of the poor incorporated by act of parliament, of which fee in St. Peter's parifh below.—But befides the mayor, aldermen and common-council of which the corporation confift, and who form the civil government of the city (a regular lift of whom from the earlieft time will be given below in the annals) there are others, who reflect an honour upon the city by their diftinguifhed office, namely the members of parliament, chofen and fent up by the fuffrages of the freemen to watch over their liberties and to tranfact the national bufinefs and thofe affairs the city may be particularly interefted in.

Briftol was a borough at the Conqueft, before Henry 1ft's time, as appears by a charter of his without date, wherein the inhabitants are ftiled by the

name

The back View of the Exchange

Front View of Change

name of burgeffes, **and** in the records of the city is ftill extant a manufcript kalendar compiled by Mr. Ricaut in Edward 4th's time, wherein it is affirmed to be held of the crown in frank burgage, and to have enjoyed " its fraunchifes lybertyes and auntiaunte free cuftoms time out of mind as the city of London; and confequently to have its faid liberties confirmed by Magna Charta as London and other enfraunchifed places had." On which account Mr. Ricaut at the end of the kalendar has for the ufe of the magiftrates exhibited another valuable manufcript, being a true copy of the cuftoms of London, contained in a book belonging to Henry Dravey who in the time of King Edward 3d. was recorder of that city. It is alfo to be noted, that in the privileges granted to Briftol by many of our kings, it is declared that the city fhould enjoy the fame in as ample manner as London itfelf. But that it was a borough before any of the charters have mentioned, fome words contained in thofe of King Henry and King John prove; who while Earl of Moreton only enlarged the privileges of it: and it was afterwards made one town incorporate by Redcliff and Briftol being united, before which time the two parts of the town were under the rule and direction of the fheriffs and officers of its proper counties Glocefter and Somerfet, and fubject to the juftices of affize and King's minifters there, as other boroughs were. It had alfo its guilds in early times; King John's charter taking notice of them as if very flourifhing then and moft probably before the Norman's arrival; when it was governed by its own lords or thanes, like the German Burgraves: fo that it may be concluded, Briftol in the Saxon and Norman times had its lords, thanes, or earls (comites,) under whofe eftablifhment were appointed prepofitors; and this form of magiftracy continued till the 1ft of Henry 3d. as before mentioned. The great privileges granted by the charters of feveral Kings both with refpect to appointing its own officers for the civil government of the city as well as the liberties and advantages it has enjoyed thereby for repairing and improving the town from time to time will fully appear by confulting the letters patent and charters themfelves, which will be inferted in the fubfequent annals of the city under the year in which the feveral grants were made.

Briftol being thus an ancient borough and town-corporate, it fent very early two burgeffes to the great council or parliament of the kingdom by ancient prefcription, though then called a burgh or borough, (yet, of great note, trade, antiquity, wealth and renown) having liberties and officers within itfelf: thefe two men were chofen formerly by the corporation and freeholders of 40s. per annum refiding in the place and by the principal

merchants

merchants (Com-burgenfes, fellow-burgeffes) inhabiting within its walls, as appears by fome ancient returns that were then made: and in the by-laws of the corporation in the time of John Barker merchant, mayor, 1ft Charles 1ft; it is enacted, " that whenfoever any writ for election of knights, citizens or burgeffes for the parliament, fhall come to the fheriffs of this city, the election fhall be made by the mayor, aldermen and common council for the time being, and by the free-holders refident within the faid city and by none elfe;" and it would certainly prevent much riot confufion and expence, had it taken place and thus continued. Thefe when chofen were to anfwer as knights of the county and burgeffes of the town and borough of Briftol. But fince the reftoration the returns often mention the election to be made by the citizens at large to the number of 2000 and upwards, and the right of election is now and has been (as far as the memory of man can go) in the mayor, aldermen, common-council and all the burgeffes (except fuch as receive public relief from parifhes or almfhoufes) and all the free-holders of the county of Briftol qualified according to law. This was the right univerfally agreed on at the many, too many contefted elections in 1679, 1680, 1689, 1695, 1705, 1710, 1713, 1714, 1721, 1727, 1734, 1739, 1754, 1758, 1774, 1780, &c. and fo continues; and each freeman's vote is regularly fcrutinized by obliging him to produce the copy of his freedom and putting him to his oath as well as every free-holder, if required. Hence a general election of members here produces fuch riot difturbances and trouble and is attended often with fuch rancour and animofity between neighbours, as perhaps will not fometimes quite fubfide before the return of another election. So that party is faid here to have been carried, unhappily carried to as high a pitch as in any place in England, and the long lift above of contefted elections in fo fmall a compafs of years is a lamentable but too convincing proof of it; though at prefent this party zeal begins to abate and a more prudent, and temperate way of thinking to take place.

Briftol being anciently parcel of the county of Glocefter, the fheriff of that county ufed to iffue his precept to the mayor and commonalty to elect two burgeffes, who were returned by the two fheriffs of Glocefter and the return endorfed on the back of the writ by the faid fheriffs thus, " Nomina Burgenfium pro Communitatibus Burgi Briftoliæ electorum effend: ad dictum parliamentum Walterus Derby, Johannes Stoke." Thefe were the laft burgeffes for Briftol, that were returned by the fheriffs of Glocefter 46th Edward 3d. anno 1372.

The

The following is the original form by the sheriff of Glocestershire, 1314, the 8th of Edward 3d. apud Spalding on the dorse of the writ : " Quod venire facias duos burgenses de villâ Bristol, istud breve retornatum fuit custodi libertatis villæ Bristol, qui sic mihi respondebat : Eligere feci Robertum Wildemarshe et Thomam le Espoter essend. ad parliamentum apud Westm. in Octabus St. Hillarii, qui manucaptores essend. ad diem et locum prædictos invenire recufarunt, per quod propter eorum vim, malitiam et resistentiam de executione istius mandati ulterius faciendâ intermittere non potui." These Bristol burgesses, refusing to find manucaptors, put the sheriff of Glocestershire to a nonplus.

The first writ issued to the sheriffs of Bristol for electing burgesses, after it was made a county within itself, is the following, which as it is curious and directs the qualifications of the members to be chosen, and was discovered in the White Tower and formerly unknown, I shall subjoin, translating it into English :

" Edvardus, Dei gratia, &c."

" Edward, by the grace of God, &c. to thē sheriff of Bristol wisbeth health. As by the advice of our council, we have appointed a parlialiament to be held at Westminster, on the morrow of Saint Edward the king's day next to come, to talk and treat with our prelates noblemen and chief men, of some difficult and urgent businesses, as well concerning us and expediting our war and the right of us and our crown beyond sea, as also of the state and defence of our kingdom of England and of the English church : we command you, strictly enjoining it, that you cause to be chosen two burgesses of the foresaid county out of the more discreet and more sufficient men, who have the best knowledge in navigation and exercise of merchandize ; and cause them to come to the place and at the time appointed, so that the said burgesses may have full and sufficient powers for themselves and the community of the said county, to act and consent to those things, which then may happen to be ordained (the Lord favouring us) by the Common Council of this our kingdom in the business aforesaid : so as that our businesses do not remain in any wise undone, through a defect of the power in them, or through an improper choice of the said burgesses. We would not that by you or any other sheriff of our kingdom, any one should be elected of other condition than what is specified above, and let us have there the names of the said burgesses and this brief. Witness myself, at Westminster, the 4th of October, 47th year of our reign over England."

In

On the dorfe thereof return is made thus : " Virtute iftins, &c." " By virtue of this brief I have caufed to be chofen and to come to the prefent parliament of the Lord our King at Weftminfter, on the morrow of St. Edward's
day next, two burgeffes of the more difcreet and more fufficient men, who have
the beft knowledge of navigation and merchandize, viz. Walter Derby and
Thomas Beaupine."

To omit all other returns, which were indorfed on the writs themfelves, till
12th Henry 4th. 1410, when the firft indenture for Briftol was annexed to the
writ thus :

" Hæc indentura faĉta, &c."

" This indenture, made between John Spyne, fheriff of Briftol, on the one
part, and T. Young, mayor of the town of Briftol, T. Droys, T. Blunt,
J. Soly, J. Leiceftre, J. Sutton, W. Bouley, J. Eifber, W. Frome, W. Bar-
ret, &c. &c. of the fame town, on the other part, witneffeth, that by virtue
of the brief of the Lord the King, to one part of thefe indentures annexed,
in a meeting held at Briftol, Monday 26th day of October, 13th year of King
Henry 4th. the more difcreet and more fufficient men being gathered together, Thomas Norton and David Dudbroke, merchants and burgeffes of the
town of Briftol, were elected to be in the parliament to be held by the king at
Weftminfter, on the morrow of All Souls, to anfwer as well knights for the
county of Briftol as burgeffes for the faid borough; which faid Thomas and
David, being prefent at the election aforefaid, were forewarned to appear together in the faid parliament on the morrow aforefaid, with the confent and
affent of the faid mayor, and of the aforefaid honeft men and of the whole
town of Briftol, to do all things that may or fhall happen to be ordained in
the faid parliament, and all other things that the faid brief requires. In witnefs whereof, the aforementioned fheriff and the faid mayor, and all the honeft men above-named, have alternately put their feals to thefe indentures,
the year and date above-written."

The writs and indentures were nearly verbatim the fame till about the 25th
year of Henry 6th. 1447, which were both enlarged ; the former by inferting
in it the new ftatutes, and directing the election to be made by the " majority of
men dwelling in the fame county, who have a freehold of forty fhillings a year at
leaft above reprifals, and refidents there ; and giving the fheriff power to examine upon oath every elector, if he has forty fhillings per annum : and if he
make a return contrary to this ordinance, the judges at the affize were to make
inquifition into the matter, and if the fheriff be convicted, he fhall incur the
penalty of 100 l. and be imprifoned for one year without bail ; and the knights

fo returned fhall lofe their wages. They were to be knights, efquires, or gentlemen, none of low degree; they were to be chofen freely and indiffer_ently by thofe at the election, and their names to be inferted in the indenture between the fheriff and electors: and fuch election being diftinctly and openly made, it was to be fealed with his and their feals, and returned into Chancery, annexed to the brief. The election being finifhed, an indenture was made between the fheriff and the merchants and others of Briftol, refiding and dwelling therein, who had a freehold of forty fhillings value in the faid town; the members being Thomas Young and John Sharpe, junior.

The following is a tranflation of the original indenture made between John Troyt the fheriff and the electors on this occafion: " Hæc indentura facta, &c." i. e. " This indenture, made at Briftol the laft day of January, in the 25th year of the reign of Henry the fixth, after the Conqueft, between John Troyt fheriff of Briftol on one part, Richard Fofter mayor of the fame town, John Burton, John Sharp, Thomas Halleway, Clement Bagot, William Cannings, John Stanley, John Shepward, &c. &c. burgeffes and merchants, dwelling and refiding in the town of Briftol, each of whom hath a free tenement of the value of forty fhillings a year above reprifals in the fame town, on the other part, witneffeth, that by virtue of the brief of our Lord the King, tacked to one part of thefe indentures, in full court held at Briftol, Monday the 31ft day of January laft paft, collecting the more difcreet and more fufficient burgeffes of the town of Briftol, Thomas Youn and John Sharp junior of the fame town, merchants, dwelling and refiding in the faid town, were elected to be in the parliament of our Lord the King, to be held at Cambridge on the feaft of St. Scolaftica, the 10th day of February next en_fuing, to anfwer in parliament as well as knights for the county of Briftol as burgeffes for the borough and town aforefaid, according to the form of the charter of our Lord Edward late King of England, progenitor of our Lord the King who now is, granted to the burgeffes of the town aforefaid, and by our Lord the King now confirmed, and according to the form of a certain other ftatute now lately publifhed and enacted in the 8th year of our faid Lord the King, likewife contained in the faid brief, and alfo publifhed in the ftatutes in the parliament of our Lord the King laft held: which faid Thomas Young and John Sharp have been forewarned to be and appear at the aforefaid parlia-ment, at the day and place aforementioned, with the affent and confent of the faid mayor and honeft men aforefaid, who had the greater number of all thofe who can fpend forty fhillings clear yearly and of the whole commonalty of the town aforefaid, to anfwer, do, and confent to all and fingular thofe things

T   which

which fhall happen to be ordained in the faid parliament, and all and fingular the things which the faid brief in itfelf demands and requires. In witnefs of this, as well the aforefaid fheriff as the mayor aforefaid and all the honeft men aforefaid have fet their feals to thefe prefents: Given at Briftol the day and year afore-mentioned."

They were all returned for years afterwards in the fame form, and the right of election the fame. Though the right of election fince the Reftoration has been different and altered, being fince that time vefted in all the burgeffes or freemen at large (except paupers) and in freeholders of forty fhillings per annum, yet the wifdom and propriety of choofing none but merchants or gentlemen, refiding and dwelling within the city, cannot but be commended as a fit example for our future imitation. In the petition of the corporation for renewal of their charter, 14th Charles 2d. it was firft inferted, that the parliament men might be chofen by the mayor and corporation and freeholders of forty fhillings per annum only, but the claufe was not thought proper by counfel at law, and fo omitted.

In the early times of uncorrupt fimplicity, when venality was not known nor practifed, it appears the parliament men had wages allowed them by their conftituents, for their trouble and independent maintenance. And by act of common council, in the time of William Canynges, mayor, 28th Henry 6th. it was ordained, that the parliament men fhould have two fhillings and no more per day, for their expences. * And in the year 1520, 11th Henry 8th. it was ordered by act of common council, that the burgeffes ferving in parliament fhould have twenty fhillings paid them every feffion. Mayor's Kalendar, p. 139.

In the reigns of Henry 3d. and Edward 1ft. no particular fum of expences to be allowed is mentioned in the writs, only in general that " the community by fuch expences be not burdened too much," *ultra modum haud gravetur;* but the 15th Edward 2d. particular fums began to be allowed, according to the quality of the reprefentatives. Knights, by order, had three fhillings per day each; efquires, though returned for counties, had but twenty pence per day. In the 16th Edward 2d. knights had four fhillings per day, efquires returned for counties, cities, or boroughs, two fhillings; but 19th Edward 2d. a knight for a fhire had four fhillings, an efquire for a fhire three fhillings, and a citizen or burgefs two fhillings; and in the following reign, four fhillings became the fettled allowance for a member for a county, and two fhillings for a citizen or burgefs.

Thefe

Thefe allowances feem to be very mean, but when it is confidered that the value of money then was ten or twelve times what it is now, (wheat being then at 3 d. per bufhel) it will appear quite otherwife.

How are the times now altered fince thofe days, in which the office of member of parliament was thought a great burden; and perfons elected were obliged to find fureties (called manucaptors) for their attendance, and were paid their expences of going to London and attending, which ufed to be the fums above-mentioned! And no more was allowed, money being fo fcarce and provifions fo cheap in confequence, as appears by the Chronic. Pet. p. 75. in the year 1336, when wheat per bufhel was only 3 d. — a fat ox fold for 6 s. 8 d. — a fat fheep, 7 d. — fix pigeons, 1 d. — a fat goofe, 2 d. — a pig, 1 d. This was occafioned, as Knyghton and Fabian obferve, by the great fcarcity of money, owing to the wars with France and Scotland.

But how greater ftill is the alteration brought about by time in this refpect now, when inftead of the members having moderate wages allowed them to defray their expences in attending parliament, they are put to fo much trouble and charge in treating their conftituents to procure a feat for even a little borough; how enormous often the expence has been, let the contefted elections for cities and counties fhew, in which befides the rancour and ill will kindled amongft neighbours by a mifguided zeal and party fpirit, rich and refpectable families have been often injured if not ruined, and their patrimonial eftates incumbered.

How much thefe election expences have increafed in a few years (and they are ftill increafing through the kingdom) the following account of difburfements in the feveral parifhes in Briftol by the members on one fide, at a contefted election in the year 1714, will prove by comparing it with the enormous fums that are now advanced and expended in bringing voters from the moft diftant parts in coaches, and treating and maintaining them all during any long election; and there has been fad experience of too, too many of late, that have been carried on at the fhameful expence of more than ten times the fum difburfed on this occafion. Blufh! ye Britifh electors, who boaft of your liberty and giving a free vote, uninfluenced by any mean confideration of intereft! &c. who yet fo evidently do corruptly put the man of your choice who is to ferve you with fidelity, and his friends to a moft enormous expence!

Account of difburfements in the feveral parifhes &c. in the city of Briftol in the election of Sir William Daines and Jofeph Earle, Efq. for members of parliament for the faid city in 1714:

St.

	l.	s.	d.		l.	s.	d.
St. Auftin's, – –	48	12	1	T. Cary's difburfements,	5	10	0
Chrift Church, –	64	15	2	Woman's note at the Coun-			
Caftle precinfts, –	72	15	1	cil-houfe for cheefe,	0	5	5
St. John's, – . –	35	17	6	Sundry notes for knots,	78	18	10
St. James's, – –	347	12	3	Jn. Trapwell for meat and			
St. Mary Port, –	20	1	8	drink, – –	2	1	3
St. Michael's, – –	23	13	9	E. Garlick's difburfements,	13	7	0
St. Nicholas, – –	68	10	2	Ald. Shuter's ditto, –	10	0	0
St. Peter's, . – –	27	6	0	—— Nafh ditto, –	29	2	8
St. Phillip's, – –	207	11	11	—— Whiting ditto, –	34	7	0
St. Mary Redcliff, –	176	2	8	Tho. Cary ditto, –	132	8	2
St. Stephen, – –	136	3	0	Edw. Mountjoy Efq; ditto,	21	4	6
St. Thomas, – –	84	4	0	Nath. Carelefs ditto, –	30	0	0
Temple, – –	189	4	6	H. Swymmer Efq; ditto,	70	0	0
St. Werburgh's, –	97	2	4	Law charges in defend-			
Bonny's note for printing,	27	0	0	ing againft feventy in-			
Woman's note under the				formations, –	108	0	0
Guildhall for beer,	47	17	0	H. Watts Efq; difb. –	30	0	0
J. Bate's for bread and				J. Belcher, – –	15	0	0
cheefe, – –	2	15	9	Total £	2257	9	7

More than twelve times this fum it is faid was expended on each fide (wafted rather) at a late contefted election for the county of Glocefter; and how much for the city of Briftol the contending parties will eafily call to mind not without fome regret at the fhameful profufion and expences in the late ill-judged groundlefs contefts and unreafonable oppofitions: et cui bono?—

O cives! cives! quæ tanta infania cepit!

A remedy for the evils and enormous expences attending on contefted popular elections will, it is much to be lamented, remain a long while among thofe things, that are devoutly to be wifhed but with difficulty ever to be attained in this age of venality licentioufnefs and want of virtue public and private among the infatuated common people of this land. The remedy fhould be fo calculated as to affect the head, to ftop this influence of corruption in the lower members. *

The

---

* As each member before he takes his feat in parliament is obliged to fwear to his qualification, to a certain real eftate he is truly and bona fide poffeffed of, fo it were to be wifhed, a proper oath might be adminiftered to him at the fame time, that he has not given any money, treat, gratuity whatever, place or penfion or promife of fuch to any freeman or freeholder by himfelf or any agent on his behalf for or towards obtaining his feat in parliament, not unlike the oath againft fimony

The following is a lift of fuch members from the 23d. of Edward the 1ft. 1295, who were returned to the parliament for the borough-town of Briftol, whilft part of Glocefterfhire, the return being then made by the fheriffs of that county: But fince it has been fevered from that county, and made a county within itfelf, the 47th of Edward the 3d. 1373, the writs of fummons have always iffued to, and been returned by our own fheriffs. For this end fundry fpecial returns, fchedules and indentures relating to the election of fuch burgeffes and knights (fo far as any records are extant, either in the Tower of London, the Rolls, Petty-bag, Crown-office or among the archives of the city of Briftol, *) have been confulted and examined.

A. R.	A. D.	Parliaments held at	Regis Edvardi 1.
23	1295	Weftminfter	John de Taverner, alias Tavern. (‡)
26	1298	York	John de Taverner, J. de Cheddre.
28	1300	Lincoln	John de Malmefbury.
30	1302	London	Ballivi Libertatis nullum mihi dederunt refponfum.
33	1305	Weftminfter	J. de Wellifhot, J. Hafard. (‡)
34	1306	Weftminfter	Johanes de Taverner, Rober. de Holherft. (‡)
			A council at Weftminfter.
35	1307	Carlifle	Geffery Comper, Nich. Coke, (‡)
			[King Edward the 1ft. died the 7th July, 1307.]
			Regis Edvardi 2.
2	1309	Weftminfter	Stephanus de Bellfmonte, Robert Martyn.
4	1311	London	Rich. Colpeks, Jobes Fraunceys.
5	1312	London	Jobes Fraunceys, fenr. Adam Wellifhot.
6	1313	Windfor	Jobes de Welleftoten, Jobes Methelan.
6	——	Woodftock	Hugo de Langebrugge, Jobes de Axebrugge.
7	1314	Weftminfter	Johes Finreys, Jobes Tropin.

Robert

that they have impofed upon the clergy mutatis mutandis: and it is hoped, our virtuous Houfe of Commons will one day pafs fuch an act. which would prevent the riots, bloodfhed and murders now not umcommon at fome popular contefted elections, as well as the ruinous expences often incurred on thefe occafions, to the great diftrefs of individuals and injury of families, who for years after do not retrive the lofs fuftained thereby.

* Thofe marked thus (‡) were communicated by the great antiquarian Brown Willis, Efq; and thofe with this mark (*) are from the archives of Briftol, &c.

A. R.	A. D.	Parliaments held at	
8	1315	Weſtminſter	Robert Wildemarſh, Tho. de Eſpoter.
12	1319	York	Tho. de Salop, Robert de Lincoln.
12	——	Weſtminſter	Gilbert Pokerell. Richard de Wodehull. (‡)
15	1322	York	Williel de Cliffe, Johes Frounceys.
16	1323	Rippon	Laurentius Pinchard, Tho. de Chiew.
19	1326	Weſtminſter	Johes de Axebrugg, Johes de Frounceys.
20	1326	Weſtminſter	Ballivi nullum dederunt reſponſum.

[King Fdward the 2d. was dethroned 25th of January 1326-7.]

Regis Edvardi 3.

1	1327	Weſtminſter	Edward 2d's. parliament was ſtill ſitting at Weſt-minſter, aſſiſting in the depoſing K. Edward the 2d. which was done accordingly 25th of January.
1	——	Lincoln, September 15	Jobes de Axebrugg, Jobes de Romeney. [See Rymer's Fæd. tom. iv. p. 301.]
1	——	Weſtminſter Nov. 13	The ſame perſons.
1	——	York	Rich. Paves, Hugo le Hunt.
2	1328	New Sarum	Walterus de Eſpoter, Jobes de Brockworth.
2	——	Northampton	Johes de Axebrugg, Hugo le Hunt. (‡)
4	1330	§ Weſtminſter	Hugo le Hunt, Richard le Paves, (*)
4	——	Winton at Eltham	Hugo le Hunt, Jobes Frounceys.
	——		
6	1332	Weſtminſter	Jobes de Romſey, Johes de Axebrugg.
7	1333	York	Jobes Sterry, Johes de Strete.
8	1334	Weſtminſter	Robertus Gyene. (‡)
8	——	York	Jobes de Ottery, Jobes de Strete. (‡)
9	1335	Weſtminſter	Robert Gyene, Jobes Frounceys. (‡)
9	——	York	Hugo de Langebrugg, Jobes de Strete.
10	1336	Northampton	Jobes Frounceys, junr. Tho. Tropin.
10	——	Weſtminſter	Robert de Gyene, Jobes Frounceys. (‡)
11	1337	Weſtminſter	Everardus de Frounceys, Philipus de Torrrington.

Gilbertus

§ This year it was enacted, that a parliament ſhould be holden once in every year. or oftener if need be.

A. R.	A. D.	Parliaments held at	
11	1337	Weftminfter	Jobes Covely, Hugo Albrighton. (‡)
12	1338	York	Gilbertus Peckerill, Rich. Woodhull. (‡)
12	——	Northampton at Walton	Everardus le Franceys, Philipus de Torington.
12	——	Weftminfter	Everardus le Fraunceys, Johes de Strete. (‡)
13	1339	Weftminfter	Everardus le Fraunceys, Jobes de Strete. (‡)
14	1340	Weftminfter	Jacobus Tilley, Tho. Tropyn. (‡)
14	——	Weftminfter	Johes le Hunt, Johes de Wellifhot.
15	1341	Weftminfter	Rober. Gyene, Philipus Torington.
17	1343	Weftminfter	Jobes de Axebrugg, Johes Fraunceys.
20	1346	Weftminfter	Johes Wicomb, Jobes Neel.
21	1347	Weftminfter	Everardus le Fraunceys, Jobes de Strete.
22	1348	Weftminfter	Evarardus le Fraunceys, Jobes de Strete.
22	——	Weftminfter	Everardus le Fraunceys, Tho. de Lodelow.
24	1350	Weftminfter	Jobes Colyngton, Jobes Seymour. (‡)
26	1352	Weftminfter	Jobes Seymour, (but one elefted.)
27	1353	Weftminfter	Thomas Babbcary, Williel. Coumb.
29	1355	Weftminfter	Rich. le Spicer, Reginaldus le French.
31	1357	Weftminfter	Reginaldus le French, Rich. Brampton.
34	1360	Weftminfter	Tho. Babbcarey, Galfridus Beauflour.
34	——	Weftminfter	Reginaldus le French, Williel. Young.
36	1362	Weftminfter	Walterus Frampton, Edwardus Blanket.
37	1363	Weftminfter	Jobes Serjeant, Jobes Stoke. (‡)
38	1364	Weftminfter	Willielmus Hayl, Williel. Cannings.
39	1365	Weftminfter	Williel. Sommerwell, Tho. Denband.
42	1368	Weftminfter	Johes Bathe, (upon a fummons of one burgefs.)
42	——	Weftminfter	Rich. Chamberleyn, Rich. Sydenham.
43	1369	Weftminfter	Jobes Cheddre, Edmundus Blanket.
45	1371	Winchefter	Jobes Bathe. (A council held there.
46	1372	Weftminfter	Walterus Derby, Johes Stoke.

[All thefe burgeffes for Briftol were returned by the fheriff of Glocefter.]

Returned by the fheriffs of Briftol.

| 47 | 1373 | Weftminfter | Walterus Derby, Tho. Beaupine. |
| 50 | 1376 | Weftminfter | Elias Spelly, Tho. Beaupine. |

[King Edward 3d. died the 21ft of June, 1377.]

Regis

A. R.	A. D.	Parliaments held at	*Regis Richardi* 2.
2	1379	Glocefter	Tho. Beaupine, Walterus de Frampton.
5	1382	Weftminfter	Elias Spelly, Jobes Stokys.
6	1383	Weftminfter	Williel. Cannings, Jobes Candavell. (‡)
7	1384	New Sarum	Williel. Cannings, Williel. Sommerwell.
7	——	Weftminfter	Jobes Cannings, * Williel. Frome.
8	1385	Weftminfter	Elias Spelly, Walterus Dodyftill.
9	1386	Weftminfter	Elias Spelly, Tho. Knapp.
15	1392	Weftminfter	Williel. Frome, Jobes Stephanys.
16	1393	Winchefter	Tho. Beaupine, Jobes Stephanys.
20	1397	Weftminfter	Williel. Frome, Johes Banbury.

[King Richard 2d. depofed by his parliament Sept. 29, 1399.]

Regis Henrici 4.

1	1400	Weftminfter	Tho. Norton, Rich. Fannys.
3	1402	Weftminfter	Tho. Norton, Johes Boys.
8	1407	Weftminfter	Jobes Droys, Jobes Mewton.
12	1411	Weftminfter	Tho. Norton, David Dudbroke.

[King Henry 4th. died the 20th of March, 1412-13.]

Regis Henrici 5.

1	1413	Weftminfter met May 15	Tho. Norton, Jobes Leiceftre.
2	1414	Leicefter met April 30	Tho. Young, Jobes Spine. (‡)
2	——	Weftminfter	Thomas Blount, Johes Clive.
3	1415	Weftminfter	Rober. Ruffell, Rober. Colville.
5	1417	Weftminfter	Tho. Norton, Johes Burton.
8	1420	Weftminfter	Tho. Norton, Jobes Spine.
9	1421	Weftminfter	Marcus Williams, Rich. Trenode.

[King Henry 5th. died the 31ft of Auguft, 1422.]   *Regis*

* Son of William Cannings.

A. R.	A. D.	Parliaments held at	
			Regis Henrici 6.
1	1422	Weftminfter met Nov. 9	John Burton, Rogerus Liveden.
2	1423	Weftminfter	John Burton, Rogerus Liveden.
3	1424	Weftminfter	Rich. Trenode, Walterus Power.
4	1425	Weftminfter	Henricus Gildenay, John Langley. (‡)
5	1426	Weftminfter	John Burton, Henricus Gildenay.
6	1427	Weftminfter	John Burton, Henricus Gildenay. (‡)
7	1428	Weftminfter	Rich. Trenode, John Sharpe.
9	1431	Weftminfter	Tho. Fyfhe, Walterus Power. (‡)
11	1433	Weftminfter	Rober. Ruffel, Walterus Power. (‡)
13	1435	Weftminfter	Tho. Fifhe, Tho. Young. (‡)
15	1437	Cambridge	Tho. Young, Tho. Norton. (‡)
20	1442	Weftminfter	Tho. Young, John Sharp.
25	1447	Canterbury	Tho. Young, John Sharp, junr.
27	1449	Weftminfter	Tho. Young, John Sharp, junr.
28	1450	Weftminfter	Tho. Young, John Sharp, junr.
29	1451	Weftminfter	Tho. Young, Williel. Cannings.
31	1453	Reading	John Shipward, merchant, Jobes Bary, gent. (‡)
33	1455	Weftminfter	Tho. Young, Williel. Cannings.
38	1460	Coventry	John Shipward, Phillipus Meed.
38	——	Weftminfter	Tho. Ruffel, John Sharp, junr.
38	——	Weftminfter	John Shipward, Philippus Meed.

[King Henry 6th was depofed by the following King, the 4th of March 1460-61.]

Regis Edvardi 4.

6	1466	Weftminfter	Williel. Spencer, John Bagod,
7	1467	Weftminfter	Williel. Spencer, John Bagod. (‡)
12	1472	Weftminfter	John Twynyhoe, John Bagod.
17	1477	Weftminfter	John Hawkins, Edmund Weftcot.
22	1482	Weftminfter met Jan. 20	Edmund Weftcot, Williel. Wykam (*)

[King Edward the 4th. died the 9th of April 1483.]

U

A. R.	A. D.	Parliaments held at

Regis Edvardi 5.

There was no parliament during this King's reign, which lasted but two months and thirteen days, when he was murdered with his brother Richard Duke of York in the Tower of London.

Regis Richardi 3.

| 1 | 1484 | Westminster Jan. 23. | John Twynyhoe, Robert Strange. (*) The first was recorder of Bristol, 1st Richard 3d. |

Regis Henrici 7.

1	1485	Westminster Nov. 7.	John Esterfield, Robert Strange. (*)
3	1487	Westminster Nov. 9.	John Esterfield, Hen. Vaughan. (*)
5	1489 90	Westminster Jan. 13.	Williel. Toker, Jobes Foster. (*)
7	1492	Westminster January.	
11	1496	Westminster Oct. 13.	Hen. Vaughan, Phillippus Ringston. (*)
13	1498	Westminster	
21	1504	Westminster	Hen. Dale, Tho. Snygg. (*)

[King Henry the 7th. died the 22d of April 1509.]

Regis Henrici 8.

| 1 | 1509 10 | Westminster Jan. 21. | Rich. Vaughan, Hen. Dale. (*) |
| 3 | 1511 12 | Westminster Jan. 15. | Tho. Smyth, Rich. Hoby. (*) |

Rober.

A.'R.	A. D.	Parliaments held at	
6	1515	Weftminfter Jan. 3.	
14	1523	Black Friars, Lond. Ap. 15.	Rober. Thorn, Rich. Hoby. (*)
20	1529	Weftminfter Nov. 3.	Rich. Abyngdon, John Shipman. (*)
28	1537	Weftminfter June 8.	Nicho. Thorn, Roger. Coke. (*)
33	1542	Weftminfter	David Croke, Rober. Ellyot. (‡)

[King Henry the 8th. died the 28th of Jan. 1546-7.]

Regis Edvardi 6.

| 1 | 1547 | Weftminfter | |
| 6 | 1552 | Weftminfter | John Walfhe, David Harris. (‡) |

[King Edward the 6th. died July 6th, 1553.]

Reginæ Mariæ.

| 1 | | Weftminfter | John Walfhe, Efq; Recorder, David Harris, Cent. (‡) |
| 1 | | Oxford | John Walfhe, Efq; Tho. Lancedon. (‡) |

Regis et Reginæ Philippi et Mariæ.

1 & 2		Weftminfter	John Walfhe, Efq. (‡)
2 & 3		Weftminfter	John Walfhe, Efq; Recorder, Wm. Chefter, Alderman. (‡)
4 & 5		Weftminfter	Williel. Tindal, Robert. Butler. (‡)

[Queen Mary died the 17th of Nov. 1558.]

Reginæ

A. R.	A. D.	Parliaments held at	
			Reginæ Elizabethæ.
1	1559	Weftminfter	John Walfhe, Efq; Williel. Carr, Efq. (‡)
5	1563	Weftminfter	John Walfhe, Efq; Williel. Carr, Efq. (‡)
9	1567		Williel. Carr, Efq; Tho. Cheftre, Efq. (*)
13	1571	Weftminfter	John Popham, Efq; Recorder, Phil. Langley. (*)
14	1572	Weftminfter	John Popham, Efq; Phillip Langley. (‡)
27	1585	Weftminfter	Tho. Hannam, Efq; Recorder, Rich. Cole. (‡)
28	1586	Weftminfter	Tho. Hannam, Efq; Recorder, Tho. Aldworth, Efq. (‡)
31	1589	Weftminfter.	Tho. Hannam, Efq; Recorder, Wm. Salterne, Merchant. (‡)
35	1593	Weftminfter	Tho. Hannam, Efq; Recorder, Richard Cole, Alderman. (‡)
39	1597	Weftminfter	George Snygg, Efq; Recorder, Thomas James, Merchant. (‡)
43	1601	Weftminfter	George Snygg, Efq; Recorder, John Hopkins, Alderman. (‡)
			[Queen Elizabeth died the 24th of March, 1602-3.]
			Regis Jacobi.
1	1603	Weftminfter	Geo. Snygg, Efq; Tho. James, Efq. (‡)
	1605	Weftminfter	John Whitfon, Efq.
12	1614	Weftminfter	John Whitfon, Efq; Tho. James, Efq. (‡)
18	1620	Weftminfter met Jan. 20, 1620-1.	John Whitfon, Efq; John Guy, Alderman. (‡)
21	1623	Weftminfter	John Barker, Efq; John Guy, Efq. (‡)
			[King James the 1ft. died the 27th of March 1625.]
			Regis Caroli 1.
1	1625	Weftminfter met June 8.	Nich. Hide, Efq; John Whitfon, Efq. (‡)
1	1625	Weftminfter met Feb. 6, 1625-26.	John Whitfon, Efq; John Doughty, Efq. (‡)

John

A. R.	A. D.	Parliaments held at	
3	1627	Weftminfter met March 17.	John Doughty, Efq; John Barker, Merchant. (‡)
15	1640	Weftminfter met April 13.	J. Glanvill, Efq; Recorder, Hump. Hook, Efq; (‡)
	1640	Weftminfter met Nov. 3.	Hump. Hook, Efq; Rich. Long, Alderman. (‡)
17	1642	Weftminfter	Richard Aldworth, Efq; counfellor at law, Luke Hodges, Efq; (‡)
			[§ King Charles the 1ft. was murdered by his rebellious fubjeɛts January 30th 1648-9.]
			King Charles 2d. began Jan. 30.
6	1654	Weftminfter	(a) Miles Jackfon, Robt. Aldworth, (*)
8	1656	Weftminfter	(b) Robt. Aldworth, John Dodridge, Recorder, (*) Major General Defborough in the room of Dodridge difplaced.
	1659		

Regis

§ In the year 1653, on the 20th of April the Rump parliament was turned out by the army; it had fat twelve years, fix months and feventeen days, during which time, viz. on the 30th of January 1648-9, by an aɛt of their own authority they caufed his facred Majefty King Charles the 1ft. to be moft barbaroufly murdered, by fevering his head from his body before the gates of his own palace, he having reigned 23 years 10 months and 3 days. King Charles the 2d. his fon began his reign the 30th of January, on which day the regicides had murdered his father, although the regal authority did not take place until the happy reftoration of King Charles the 2d. in the year 1660.

(a) During the ftate of ufurpation in this kingdom were the following proceedings, in what they then called a parliament, viz. on the 12th of December 1653, the Speaker, and moft part of the members left the houfe, and furrendered their power to Oliver Cromwell, who took upon him the ftyle of Proteɛtor.—On the 10th of June 1654, the writs bore date by Oliver Cromwell's authority, for calling a new parliament to meet at Weftminfter by the 3d of September following, the reprefentatives that were chofen for Briftol were Miles Jackfon. and Robert Aldworth, (fee Mr. Baves's manufcript, and many others;) this parliament was diffolved by Oliver the 22d of January 1654-5.

(b) On the 3d of July 1656, new writs were iffued out to call a parliament at Weftminfter the 17th of September following; at Briftol were chofen, the 20th of Auguft, Robert Aldworth, and John Dodridge. But Major General Defborough petitioning the parliament againft Dodridge, Cromwell difplaced him, and Defborough fat with Aldworth. On the 4th of February 1657-8 Oliver diffolved this parliament; and the grand ufurper's death happened upon the day of his birth, being the 3d of September following. The parliament which met at Weftminfter the 7th

Regular Parliaments.

A. R.	A. D.	Parliaments held at	
12	1660	Weftminfter met April 25.	(c) J. Stephens, Efq; Recorder, J. Knight, fenr. Merchant. (‡)
13	1661	Weftminfter met May 8.	(d) Sir Humphrey Hook, and Sir J. Knight, Knts. Tho. Earl, Efq; J. Knight, Efq; (‡) — A double return the two firft members were continued and fat anno 1670.
29	1678	Weftminfter met March 6, 1678-9.	Sir Robert Cann, Knt. and Bart. Sir J. Knight, Knt. (‡)
30	1679	Weftminfter	Sir Robert Cann, Bart. Sir J. Knight, Knt. (‡)
31	1680	Oxford	Sir Richard Hart, Knt. Tho. Earl, Efq; (‡)
32	1680	Weftminfter	Sir Robt. Cann, Bart. Sir Walter Long, Bart. (*)

[King Charles the 2d. died the 6th of Feb. 1684-5.]

Regis

of January 1658-9, was called Dick's Convention-Parliament, being the firft which he called. Richard's party deferting him, he confented to diffolve his parliament April the 2d 1659; after which he had a *quietus eft*, for on the 25th of April following the houfe was fhut up, and entrance denied the members. But however, on the 7th of May following, the Rump fat again, but was afterwards turned out of the houfe by Lambert, the 13th of October following. And the 26th of December 1659, the Rump was re-admitted, and on the 21ft of February 1659-60, the fecluded members were reftored. And the 15th of March following the parliament was diffolved, and another called to be holden at Weftminfter April the 25th, 1660.

(c) This parliament met at Weftminfter the 25th of April 1660. And on the 1ft of May his Majefty's gracious letters and declaration were read in the houfe, &c. On the 13th of September following the parliament was adjourned to the 6th of November, having paffed an act for difbanding the army, and an act of indemnity, (the regicides excepted;) and on the 29th of November 1660, the parliament was diffolved.

Admiral Pen, a Briftol man, was polled for, but the corporation favoured Stephens.— Pen was returned for Weymouth.

(d) The writs for fummoning a parliament in England to convene on May the 8th 1661, were fealed the 9th of March. And on the 8th of May the parliament met at Weftminfter, and the Houfe of Lords were again reftored to their ancient privileges; and the convocation alfo began. On the 30th of July they were adjourned to the 20th of November. This parliament often met to difpatch bufinefs, and was often adjourned or prorogued, until the 25th of January 1678-9, on which day this long parliament was diffolved by proclamation, after they had fat nigh 17 years.

A. R.	A. D.	Parliaments held at	
			Regis Jacobi 2.
1	1685	Weftminfter met May 19, 1685.	Sir J. Churchill, Knt. recorder, died foon.(*) And Sir Rich. Hart, Knt. was chofen in his room the 10th December. (‡) Sir Richard Crump, Knt. '(‡) [King James the 2d. abdicated the throne February 13, 1688-9.]
			Regis et Reginæ Willielmi et Mariæ.
1	1688/89	Weftminfter	Sir Richard Hart, Sir J. Knight, Knts. (*) — Elected to be fent to the convention, who voted againft the Prince and Princefs of Orange being made King and Queen.
2	1690	Weftminfter	Sir Rich. Hart, and Sir John Knight, Knts. (‡)
			Regis Willielmi. 3.
7	1695	Weftminfter	Sir Tho. Day, Knt. Robt. Yate, Efq; (‡)
10	1698	Weftminfter	Sir Tho. Day, Knt. Robt. Yate, Efq; (‡)
12	1700	Weftminfter	Sir Tho. Day, Knt. Robt. Yate, Efq; (*)
13	1701	Weftminfter	Sir Wm. Daines, Knt. Robt. Yate, Efq; (‡) [King William died the 8th of March 1701-2.]
			Reginæ Annæ.
1	1702	Weftminfter Aug. 20.	Sir Wm. Daines, Knt. Robt. Yate, Efq; (‡)
4	1705	Weftminfter	Sir Wm. Daines, Knt. Robt. Yate, Efq; (‡) — This was the firft parliament of Great-Britain conftituted by the Union, which commenced on May-day 1707, where the laft members fat. Seffions the 1ft, October 23d 1707, fat on bufinefs, and was diffolved April 15th 1708. The 2d parliament fummoned for July 8th 1708.
7	1708	Weftminfter Nov. 16.	Sir Wm. Daines, Knt. Robt. Yate, Efq; (‡)

A. R.	A. D.	Parliaments held at
9	1710	Weftminfter Nov. 25.
12	1713	Weftminfter Oct. 1.
1	1714 — 15	Weftminfter

Parliaments fince the Union.

The 3d parliament was fummoned for Nov. 25th 1710.

(a) Edw. Colfton, Efq; Jofeph Earl, Efq; (‡)

The 4th parliament was fummoned for Octo- ber 1ft, 1713.

(b) Tho. Edwards, junr. Efq; Jof. Earl, Efq;(‡)

[Queen Ann died the 1ft of Auguft 1714.]

Regis Georgii 1.

The 5th parliament was fummoned for March 17, 1714-15.

(c) Sir Wm. Daines, Knt. Jof. Earl, Efq; (*)

The 6th parliament was fummoned for May 10th 1722.

Jofeph

(a) The 26th of September 1710, a proclamation was publifhed for calling a new parliament. The elections were carried on with great warmth every where. The election began at Briftol, where the citizens chofe their worthy benefactor Edward Colfton, Efq; and Jofeph Earl, Efq. The feffions began November 25, 1710; during which elections were regulated, every member for a borough was to have 300l. per ann. freehold or copyhold; and every knight of a fhire 600l. per annum: the Houfe did not break up the feffions till the 12th of June 1711, after feveral prorogations they met the 14th of January 1711-12, this feffions the parliament fettled the building fifty new churches in London. The feffions which met the 6th of June 1712, concluded peace with France: on the 21ft of June the houfe was adjourned to the 8th of July, from which time by feveral adjournments and prorogations a pro- clamation was publifhed the 5th of Auguft 1713 for diffolving the parliament and for calling a new one.

(b) The writs were iffued out the 17th of Auguft 1713. The election for Briftol began Mon- day the 7th of September 1713; the candidates were Tho. Edwards and Jofeph Earl, Efq; and Sir William Daines, Knt. the election was carried on with much heat on both fides, in fo much that the poll was clofed the Thurfday following, and the two firft were returned duly elected: and the parliament met the 1ft of October 1713, on the 18th by proclamation they were proro- gued to the 15th of February 1713-14 when they difpatched bufinefs, and the 2d of March the Queen made her fpeech, on the 6th of March they adjourned to the 31ft inft. 1714, on the 9th of July following the Queen made her laft fpeech to them and prorogued them to the 10th of Auguft 1714. But Sunday morning a little after 7 of the clock being the 1ft of Auguft, Queen Ann died in the year 1714.

(c) The candidates at this election were Sir William Daines, Knt. Jofeph Earl, Efq; Thomas Edwards and Phillip Freke, Efqrs; there appeared at the clofe of the poll a majority for the two

A. R.	A. D.	Parliaments held at	
7	1721	Weftminfter May 10.	(d) Jofeph Earl, Efq; Sir Abra. Elton, Bart. (*) The 7th parliament was fummoned for Nov. 28th, 1727. *Regis Georgii* 2.
1	1727	Weftminfter Nov. 28.	(e) John Scroope, Efq; Recorder, Abra. Elton, jun. Efq. (*) *N. B.* King George the 1ft. died the 11th of June 1727. The 8th parliament was fummoned for June 13th, 1734.

W   (a) Sir

latter, who were carried about the crofs according to cuftom, in the mean time the fheriffs returned the two former,—Freke and Edwards petition, it was renewed the 2d and 3d feffions.— This was the 1ft feptennial parliament of King George the 1ft. This parliament fat eight feffions ; and was diffolved March the 10th 1721-22.

(d) The candidates were Jofeph Earl, Efq; Sir Abraham Elton, Bart. and William Hart, fenr. Efq; the two firft were returned. This was the fecond feptennial parliament which fat fix feffions of King George the 1ft, was diffolved Auguft the 5th 1727. William Hart, Efq; petitioned.

(e) This was the third feptennial parliament fince the death of Queen Anne, and the 1ft of George the 2d. Mr. Scrope was a joint-fecretary of the treafury. It fat feven feffions, was diffolved April 18, 1734.

(a) In the firft feptennial parliament of King George the 2d 1727, the reprefentatives for Briftol were John Scroope, Efq; recorder and fecretary to the treafury, and Abraham Elton, junr. Efq; Mr. Scroope in the year 1732 when the excife fcheme on tobacco was brought into the houfe, was found to be a great promoter of and a voter for that bill, alfo he voted againft the repeal of the feptennial act in the year 1734, all which gave a general difguft to the principal electors of Briftol, who were determined to oppofe his election in the year 1734. On Wednefday the 15th of May it began, the candidates were Sir Abraham Elton, Bart. Thomas Cofter and John Scroope, Efqrs. the poll continued nine days to the 24th of May, on clofing of which when caft up the numbers ftood, for Sir Abraham Elton, Bart. 2428, for Mr. Cofter, 2071, for Mr. Scroope, 1866, majority for Mr. Cofter 205, whereupon the fheriffs returned the two former. Notwithftanding a petition from the mayor, &c. was brought into parliament for an undue election againft Mr. Cofter in favour of Mr. Scroope who in the end was obliged to withdraw the petition, not being able to prove one allegation therein. Thefe members voted againft the convocation in the fecond feptennial parliament, which fat feven feffions, of which Mr. Southwell fat two, it was diffolved April 28, 1741.

A. R.	A. D.	Parliaments held at	
7	1734	Weftminfter	(a) Sir Ab. Elton, Bart. Tho. Cofter, Efq. (b) died.
12	1739		Edw. Southwell, Efq. (b)
			The 9th parliament was fummoned for June 25th, 1741.
13	1741	Weftminfter	(c) Sir Ab. Elton, Bart. Edw. Southwell, Efq. (*)
14	1742		(d) Robert Hoblyn, Efq.
			The 10th parliament was fummoned for Aug. 13th, 1747.
20	1747	Weftminfter	(e) Edw. Southwell, Efq; Rob. Hoblyn, Efq. (*)
27	1754	Weftminfter	Robert Nugent, and Rich. Beckford, Efqrs.
29	1755	Weftminfter	(f) Jarrit Smyth, Efq; in the room of Richard Beckford, deceafed.

Regis Georgii 3.

| 1 | 1760 | Weftminfter | Sir Jarrit Smyth, Bart. Robert Nugent, Efq. |

Robert

(b) Thomas Cofter, Efq; on Sunday the 30th of September 1739, died at his houfe in the College Green.

(b) To fill up his vacancy a new writ was ordered for another election which began Wednefday the 28th of November 1739, the candidates were Edward Southwell, principal fecretary of ftate for Ireland, and Henry Combe, Efq; Mr. Southwell's intereft was fupported with Mr. Cofter's friends, and Mr. Combe's by the corporation, &c. The poll was kept open for fourteen days at clofing of which the numbers ftood thus, for Mr. Southwell 2651, for Mr. Combe 2203, majority 448. N. B. There remained upwards of 200 neutral votes.

(c) There was no oppofition this election. This was the third feptennial parliament of King George the 2d. which fat fix feffions and was then diffolved June 18, 1747.

(d) Sir Abraham Elton, Bart dying the 19th of October 1742, a new election to fill his vacancy began Wednefday the 24th of November 1742, date of the writ was November 16, 1742, when Robert Hoblyn, Efq; fon-in-law to the late Thomas Cofter, Efq; was chofen without oppofition.

(e) Writs being iffued out for a general election this year, it began at Briftol Wednefday the 1ft of July 1747, Mr. Samuel Dicker declared as one of the candidates, but before the poll was opened he declined and left the town, therefore there was no oppofition, this being the fourth feptennial parliament in the reign of King George the 2d. which fat feven feffions: in the fixth feffion an act paffed for altering the ftile of the year to the firft of January, and alfo a bill for naturalization of the Jews.

(f) The election came on the 2d of March 1756, Thomas Spencer, Efq; and Jarrit Smyth, Efq; candidates; poll clofed the 17th, J. Smyth declared duly elected and returned the 18th of March, but a petition was prefented againft the return.

A. R.	A. D.	Parliaments held at	
6	1766	Weſtminſter	Robert Nugent, Eſq; vacated his ſeat by accepting the office of Firſt Lord of Trade, and was re-choſen Dec. 16 this year, without oppoſition; he was alſo created Lord Viſcount Clare of the kingdom of Ireland.
7	1768	Weſtminſter	Lord Clare, Matthew Brickdale, Eſq. Lord Clare vacated his ſeat the 27th June, on being choſen Vice-Treaſurer of Ireland, and was re-choſen without oppoſition.
14	1774	Weſtminſter	Henry Cruger, Edmund Burke, Eſqrs.
20	1780	Weſtminſter	Matthew Brickdale, Eſq; Sir Henry Lippincot.—The latter dying, a new writ was ſent down for electing another in his room; which occaſioned as great a conteſt here as was ever known, on G. Daubeny, Eſq; declaring himſelf; who was oppoſed by H. Cruger, Eſq; formerly the popular member; but G. Daubeny, Eſq; was returned. Matthew Brickdale, and Geo. Daubeny, Eſqrs.
24	1784	Weſtminſter	Matthew Brickdale, Eſq; Henry Cruger, Eſq. —The latter was choſen againſt Mr. Daubeny the other candidate, though Mr. Cruger was then abroad in America, and he is there a reſident ſince the year 1785.

C H A P. VI.

On the TRADE *of* BRISTOL, FOREIGN *and* DOMESTIC.

BY the good government of the city, by the knowledge, diligence and integrity of its merchants, the trade foreign and domeſtic has from time immemorial been great and on the increaſe; as have been the number of ſhips belonging to the merchants of this port. It was a place very early addiƐted to trade, as William of Malmſbury, in the year 1139, before quoted, (vid. p. 57,) obſerves of it: it is thus charaƐterifed by all writers. Georgius Braunius in Theatrum Urbium, lib. 3. indice, calls Briſtol " famoſiſſimum Angliæ Emporium, &c. The moſt famous place of commerce in England next to Lon‑don, frequented by merchants of many nations, well provided with rivers for bringing in of ſhips, the manner of its ſituation with the high riſe of the tides performing this; the tide not ſpreading here abroad, but ſwelling up * 60 feet in height:" and in the 4th book, " the city," ſays he, "is well built, full of inhabitants, and merchants of divers countries; they ſail twice a year to Newfoundland a fiſhing."

Mercator in his Atlas placing it in Somerſetſhire, as ſome have done in Gloceſterſhire, though truly belonging to neither, being a city and county of itſelf, deſcribes it thus, — " Urbs præcipua Briſtollia pulcherrimis Ædificiis, gemino fluvio & muro, portu, exterorum commerciis, Incolarum frequentiâ illuſtratur." — Cluverius in his geography, ſays, " Briſtollium vulgo Briſtow Hiſpanicarum mercium nobile Emporium, ut Southampton Gallicarum." — It is recorded in Ricaut's kalendar, to have been very early famous for its trade to Andaluſia. And in the year 1466, the Mary, a goodly ſhip (probably one of Mr. Canynges's) whoſe cargo was valued at above 12,000 marks, was taken at the Land's-End by Vice Admiral Slomp of France. In a manuſcript deed " of the appropriation of the church of Wotton to the monaſtery of St. Auguſtin, Briſtol," dated 1131, this city is thus charaƐterifed, " Briſtollium portus publicus & municipium famoſum pro receptione hominum in multitu‑
diné

---

* The tide riſes ſo high at Chepſtow, but at Briſtol about 25 or 30 feet only; above 32 at Rownham.

diné copiosâ de diversis mundi partibus illuc undique confluentium." By the charter of King John, we may learn somewhat of the customs and commerce of the place in that early period; more so by that of Edw. 3. in which time it was so considerable, that it was then entituled to the reputation of being the second city in the kingdom for trade and populousness; and had so much weight as to obtain a charter for constituting it a county within itself, and for ascertaining the pomerium or bounds of the city. This city fell early into the Newfoundland cod-fishing, says De Wit, (Interest of Holland,) 1669.

In Rymer's Fœdera, v. 1. fol. 134, we find that " several of this ever-industrious city had, in the year 1339, set up looms for weaving woollen cloths, in conformity to an act of parliament, that no English wool should be exported out of this kingdom, but be made into cloth within the realm of England, &c." It was at this time great encouragement was given to the cloth manufacture, which the King seems to have removed out of Flanders, (which was the grand mart or staple of wool then,) and settled it in several towns in this kingdom,* especially at Bristol, which set the example followed after by the neighbouring counties: before this the Flemings used to buy the English wool and manu-facture it themselves, but from this act may be derived the source of this staple manufacture of the kingdom. — One Mr. Blanket, then sheriff of Bristol, and many other inhabitants engaged largely in it, set up looms in their own houses, and carried it soon to great perfection; it produced more good to the state than ever was foreseen by the legislature of that time, who formed and pro-jected that useful act of parliament. This cloth trade was carried on in a flou-rishing manner for a long series of years; especially in the parishes of Temple and St. Thomas, many manufactures at different times were encouraged in Bristol.

It was full of clothiers, weavers and tuckers all Hen. 8th's reign; and in 1610 the magistrates gave great encouragement by lending money to set up the Colchester bays-manufacture; and at the Smiths'-Hall were all beggars and poor people set to work at spinning and stocking-making, under the inspection of the parish officers; which shews how attentive they were to promote indus-try among the inhabitants. — The trading companies of the city were put under

proper

---

* Lel. Collect. v. 2. p. 689. " In 29 Edw. 3. was the staple of wools revoked out of Flanders, and set at divers places in England, at Westminster, Cantorbyry, Chichester and Bristow, Lyncolne and Hulle." As early as the 9th Edw. 2. 1316, there was a duty or custom paid the King for every sack of wool carried out of the port of Bristol half a mark; and for every 300 sheep skins half a mark, and for every last of hides one mark; which the King complained the mayor and bailiff had witheld from him, or his assign, Martin Horncastle, the collector and receiver. Rot. 167. a.

proper regulations. — In the days of Edward 4. this city was famous for the woollen manufacture, as appears by the statute 17 Edw. 4. c. 5. whereby this only city, together with London, was exempted from sealing their cloths, kerseys, &c. with a head, according to stat. 4. of the same king, when all other places were obliged by it, and long before, viz. statute the 12th Rich. 2. 1. 14. it is to be noted, that Bristol had excused itself from pursuing the statute of the 47th Edw. 3. c. 1. relating the measure and aulnage of draps, to which by stat. Rich. 2. they were particularly limited.

The cloth manufacture indeed, once a staple here, (for the government and regulation of which the mayor had the name of Mayor of the Staple of Bristol, and held a court called the Staple-Court,) has now much declined, being removed to other places, and to the North of England, where labour is cheaper and though immense fortunes were formerly gained by it here, the parts of the city where it was principally carried on, have greatly declined with it, and left the roomy houses in Temple-street, where still remains the Weavers'-Hall and Tuckers'-Hall, to be inhabited by labourers of another kind. — In Edw. 4th's time they complained of the decay of the trade owing to the wool being exported into foreign parts ; also on account of the removing of the staple from Bayonne, where was a great sale of Bristol drapery ; and the Thouloufe wool being brought another way into other parts of England.

In the year 1459, 37 Hen. 6. Mr. Robert Strange, a great merchant of Bristol, (afterwards founder of St. John's almshouse,) had a goodly ship spoiled by the Genoefe in the Mediterranean ; this ship had a cargo of spices and other valuable merchandife, which the Genoefe, who could not brook the success of our merchants, seized ; this wrong when King Henry understood, he made reprisal on the effects of the Genoefe merchants in London, whom he also arrested and imprisoned until they gave good security to make good the loss, which amounted to 9000 marks. — The Bristol kalendar calls these merchants strangers, Lombard Janneys, by whom are understood the Genoefe, who followed usury and other methods of gain, which the Lombards at this time did, who were the first bankers in London ; whence Lombard-street in London, where the bankers reside, took its name. Kal. p. 122. 6.

One Thomas Strange, probably the son of the above Robert, had twelve ships at one time, says Wm. of Worcester, p. 224, in 1480. — The Brass Battery began here about 1704 : one Sir Simon Clark was the first inventor of making copper : Mr. Coster and Mr. Wayne acted under him as assayists, who afterwards established it here under Sir Abraham Elton. — The said Sir Simon invented white glass, and casting iron in loam.

The

The manufactory of zinc out of calamine stone and black-jack, was established at Bristol about the year 1743, when Mr. Champion obtained a patent for making it. About 200 tons of zinc were annually made at his copper-works, where the manufactory was set up first; and afterwards zinc began to be made at Hanham, near Bristol, by Mr. James Emerson, who had been many years manager of that branch under Mr. Champion, and his successor in the business. — This operation of procuring zinc from calamine was held at first a great secret, and though it be now better known, it is but lately that there were any works of that kind established in any other part of either England or Europe, except those last-mentioned. In a circular kind of oven, like a glass-house furnace, there are placed pots of about four feet each in heighth, much resembling oil jars; into the bottom of each is inserted an iron tube, which passes through the floor of the furnace into a vessel of water. The pots are filled with a mixture of calamine, or black-jack and charcoal, and the mouth of each is then close stopped with clay. The fire being properly applied, the metallic vapour of the calamine issues through the iron tube, there being no other place through which it can escape, and the air being excluded it does not take fire, but is condensed in small particles in the water, and being remelted is formed into ingots and sent to Birmingham under the name of zinc or spelter.

Cambden, Busching in his Polit. Commercial Geography of Europe in High Dutch, 1762, and Anderson, all agree in giving Bristol the name of " a renowned commercial city." " A considerable part of it," says Busching, " lies on the South side of the river Avon, and a still larger part on the North side; having a communication by three stone bridges, also a draw-bridge for letting ships into the Key, or little river stiled Froom. It is by far the largest city in Britain next after London, containing above thirteen thousand houses, and above one hundred thousand inhabitants, both which are constantly increasing. It is said by some to use two thousand maritime vessels, coasters as well as ships, employed in foreign voyages; and it has many important manufactories. Its glass bottle, drinking glass, and plate glass manufacture alone occupying fifteen large houses. Its brass pan and brass wire manufactures are also very considerable. It has a most extensive quay, with dock-yards, &c. for ship-building, sundry good hospitals, and many almshouses and other charitable foundations; infomuch, that this city for its prudent regulations is perhaps outdone by none, and for its vast commerce, wealth and shipping by very few trading cities in Europe." Dr. Campbel in his Political Survey of Great Britain, v. 1. p. 147. gives the following just account of the trade of Bristol, " That great mart,

from

from which the conjunction of the waters of the Severn, Wye, &c. receives the name of the Briſtol Channel, is as conveniently ſituated as can well be ima_ gined, at the conflux of two beautiful rivers, the Avon and the Froom, having bridges over both; the latter falls into the former a little below the city, and their joint ſtreams into the Severn at about four miles diſtance. On the North ſide of the town runs the Quay along the river Froom, to which ſhips even of great burden come up; though for the conveniency of commerce many remain in Hungeroad, and others at Kingroad, which is ſtill lower. If we conſider domeſtic trade, or inland navigation, Briſtol is without a rival, for by the Avon ſhe draws to herſelf commodities from Warwickſhire; by the help of the Teem, ſhe receives thoſe of Herefordſhire and Shropſhire; the Wye brings her alſo ſome part of the tribute of the former of thoſe countries, and of Radnorſhire; and if there be any thing yet left in Herefordſhire and Shrop_ ſhire, the Lugg drains them both: Monmouthſhire and the adjacent parts of Wales ſend their ſupplies by the Uſke; and a great part of Somerſetſhire com_ municates both goods and manufactures by the Ivel, the Parrot and Tone; and Cornwall ſends hither its tin and copper for the pewter and braſs wire and copper company manufactories. Not ſatisfied with all this, the Briſtol traders deal largely by land, and often interfere with thoſe of Hull in the North, and London in the South. — As to foreign commerce, if we view it in groſs, Briſtol is next to London; but if the value of that commerce be compared with the ſize of the reſpective cities, Briſtol has the ſtart; and except in a very few branches, to the participation of which of late ſhe begins to put in her claim in point of intercourſe with all parts of the world, her correſpon_ dence is as extenſive."

Such are the accounts of it by a foreigner, and by a Briton, and that they have not much exaggerated the deſcription, will appear in the ſequel, by conſidering its early attachment to navigation, and its progreſs in trade. It was grown ſo opulent by its commerce in the year 1377, that the mayor and commonalty lend the King, Rich. 2d. 500 marks, which is the firſt inſtance in the fœdera of a lay community's lending money to the crown, except Lon- don; and in the year 1379, the "probi homines de Briſtow," lend 100 marks to him, when Gloceſter lent only 40, and the greateſt 100, which was Cambridge. Fœd. v. 7. p. 210. And in 1386, when the kingdom was threatened with a French invaſion, they lend 200 l. Fœd. T. 7. 543. as much again as York or any city except London. — Thus the city of Briſtol leads the van in all the loans.

In

In Sir Robert Cotton's Abridgement of the Records, p. 623. Henry 6. directs the fees of liveries of his justices to be paid yearly out of the customs of the ports of London, Briftol and Hull; whence may be inferred thofe ports, efpecially the two firft, carried on the greateft foreign commerce. In the roll of Edw. 3d's fleet, at the fiege of Calais, 1347, in the Cotton Library, and Hackluit's Collect. of Voyages, part 1. p. 118. copied from the King's wardrobe, we find the following proportion between the number of fhips furnifhed by Briftol and the other ports.

		Ships.	Mariners.
Weymouth	-	20	264
		15	263 according to Hackluit.
Lime	- -	4	62
Pool	- -	4	94
Wareham	-	3	59
Briftol	- -	22	608
London	- -	25	662
Seton	- -	2	25

Here we fee how nigh the number of Briftol fhips and mariners approaches to that of London, and how much they exceed every other port befides. By ftatute 4 of Hen. 4. it was ordained that all mariners of fhips and other veffels laden with goods and merchandife, entering the realm, or paffing out of the fame, fhall be charged and difcharged in fome great port, and not in any creek or fmall river, upon pain of forfeiture of the goods; and King Henry 5. by proclamation dated 26 Oct. anno regni 16. commanded all officers to fee this act put ftrictly in execution. — Thefe acts made greatly for the port of Briftol, and much improved its commerce; and we find foon afterwards the magiftrates, aware of this advantage and jealous of their liberties and traffic, complaining of fome breaches of this law to the injury of the King's cuftoms at Briftol, by veffels unloading their cargoes at ports and creeks in the Briftol Channel, and at Chepftow and other places in Wales. — In the letters patent 17 Hen. 7. Plymouth, Dartmouth, Sandwich, and others are ftiled " minores portus quam Briftol."

In 1442, (Rot. Parl. 20 Hen. 6.) when a naval force was deemed neceffary, the Commons point out where fhips were to be had, " at Briftol, the Nicholas of the Tower, and Katherine of Bofton."

In 1449, Wm. Canynges is diftinguifhed as a very great merchant here. — In Rymer's f. 11. p. 226. we find two recommendatory letters from Hen. 6. 1449, one to the Mafter General of Pruffia, the other to the Magiftrates of

X   Dantzick.

Dantzick, both in behalf of two of Canynges factors refiding in Pruffia, re-questing all favour and countenance to the faid two factors of Canynges, whom the King calls " his beloved eminent merchant of Briftol."

In 1450 we find by a treaty with Chriftian King of Denmark (Fœd. T. ii. p. 264.) three places prohibited us from trading to, Iceland, Halgefland and Finmark; but the above treaty and an Englifh act of parliament difpenfed with in favour of Canynges, (P. 277. fœd. v. 11.) the Danifh King allowing Canynges in confideration of the great debt due to Canynges from his fubjects of Iceland and Finmark to lade certain Englifh fhips with merchandize for thofe prohibited places, and there to lade fifb and other goods in return: wherefore during his mayoralty of Briftol, becaufe Canynges had done good fervice-unto the King he allowed the fame to be done for two years to come on two fhips, &c.

It is clear that William Canynges and other merchants about this time had each feveral fhips employed in foreign trade. William of Worcefter fays p. 99, of Canynges " In navibus &c." i. e. In fhips he employed 800 men for eight years, and of his fhips he had le Mary Canynges of 400 tons (doliatis) le Mary Redcliff of the burden of 500 tons, le Mary and John of the burden of 900 tons, which coft him in the whole 4000 marks, le Galyott of 50 tons, le Catherin of 140 tons, le Mary Batt 220 tons, le Margaret of Tylny of 200 tons, le Lyttle Nicholas of 140 tons, le Katheryn of Bofton 220 tons, le —— a fhip loft in Ifelond about 160 tons burden. Alfo befide this King Edward the 4th. had of the faid William three thoufand marcs for making his peace." And in p. 224, he names " fhips belonging to Briftol in the year of Chrift, 1480:"

" The Mary Grace 300 tons, le —— of 360 tons, the George 200 tons, Kateryn 180 tons, Mary Bryd 100 tons, Chriftofer 90 tons, Mary Shernman 54 tons, Leonard 50 tons, the Mary of Briftow, —— le George, —— the John 511 tons, a fhip that is juft fitted for fea, John Godeman hath of fhips, —— Thomas Straunge about 12."

Let not the merchants of our days ridicule and defpife the fhipping of their anceftors, which is too common, as we can produce fo refpectable a lift belonging then to a few. Among thefe fhips of Canynges was one of 900 tons, another of 500, &c, although thefe great fhips had Englifh names, it has been not unjuftly doubted, whether we had any at that time of our own building in England fo large; but as Anderfon well obferves, Canynges might have either purchafed them or taken them from the Hanfeaticks with whom he traded, or from the Venetians, Genoefe, Luccefe, Pifans, all of whom had fhips of even larger burden at that time.

How

How intent they were in Briftol upon promoting navigation, appears from the letters patent of King Henry 7th. A. R. 13, * 1495, granted to John Cabot, a Venetian or Genoefe, then refiding as a merchant in Briftol, and to his three fons, Lewis, Sebaftian † and Sanctius, for the difcovery of new and unknown lands.

The following are the letters patent, " Henricus Dei Gratia" &c. Thus in Englifh — Henry by the grace of God &c. Be it known to all, that we have given and granted and by thefe prefents do give and grant to our well beloved John Cabot citizen of Venice, to Lewis Sebaftian and Sanctius, fons of the faid John and to their heirs and deputies full and free authority, leave and power to fail to all parts countries and feas of the caft, of the weft and of the north under our banners and enfigns, with five fhips of what burthen or quality foever they be, and as many mariners and men as they will take with them in the faid fhips, upon their own proper cofts and charges, to feek out difcover and find whatfoever ifles, countries, regions or provinces of the Heathen and Infidels whatfoever they be and in what part foever of the world, which before this time have been unknown to all Chriftians : we have granted to them and every of them and their deputies, and have given them our licence to fet up our banners and enfigns in every village, town, caftle, ifle, or main-land of them newly found; and that the faid John and his fons and their heirs may fubdue occupy and poffefs all fuch towns, cities, &c. by them found which they can fubdue occupy and poffefs as our vaffals and lieutenants, getting to us the rule title and jurifdiction of the fame villages, towns, &c. yet fo that the faid john and his fons and their heirs of all the fruits, profits and commodities growing from fuch navigation, fhall be held and bound to pay to us in wares or money the fifth part of the capital gain fo gotten for every their voyage as OFTEN AS THEY SHALL ARRIVE AT OUR PORT OF BRISTOL, (AT WHICH PORT THEY SHALL BE OBLIGED ONLY TO ARRIVE,) deducting all manner of neceffary cofts and charges by them made : we giving and granting unto them and their heirs and deputies, that they fhall be free from all payment of cuftoms on all fuch merchandife they fhall bring with them from the places fo newly found. And moreover we have given and granted to them and their heirs and deputies, that all the firm land, iflands, villages, towns, &c. they fhall chance to find, may not with-

X 2   out

* Hacluit's Voyages, vol. 3, p. 5, 6.

† Parmenius Budœius has given Cabot the following verfes on his difcovery of North America :

    Hanc tibi jampridem primi invenere Britanni;
    Tum cum magnanimus noftra in regione Cabotus
    Proximus a magno oftendat fua Vela Columbo.

out licence of the faid John Cabot and his fons be frequented and vifited, under pain of lofing their fhips and all the goods of them, who fhall prefume to fail to the places fo found : willing and commanding ftrictly all and fin_gular our fubjects as well on land as on fea, to give good affiftance to the faid john and his fons and deputies, and that as well in arming and furnifh_ing their fhips and veffels, as in provifion of food and buying victuals for their money, and all other things by them to be provided neceffary for the faid navigation they do give them all their favours and affiftance. Witnefs myfelf at Weftminfter, 5th March in 11th year of our reign."

In the thirteenth year of the fame reign there is a record of the rolls con_cerning the voyage of John Cabot and his fons, — thus, " Rex tertio die Feb. anno 13 regni, licentiam dedit &c." The King on the 3d day of Feb. in the 13th year of his reign gave licence to John Cabot to take fix fhips of England in any haven or havens of the realm of England of the burden of 200 tons or under with all neceffary furniture, and alfo to take into the faid fhips all fuch mafters, mariners and fubjects of the King as will willingly go with him * &c.

In confequence of this the voyage was undertaken, and in the year 1497 John Cabot and his fon Sebaftian (with the Englifh fleet fet out from Briftol) defeovered the 24th June, 5 ante merid. that land, which none had before. This land he called primo vifta or firft feen, becaufe it was that of which they had a firft fight from fea; that land which lieth out before the ifland, he called St. John's upon this occafion, becaufe difcovered on St. John's day.

In the year 1497, 24th June on St. John's day, as it is in a manufcript in my poffeffion, " was Newfoundland found by Briftol men in a fhip called the Matthew." Sebaftian Cabot difcovered in his firft voyage Newfoundland, the ifland of St. john and the continent of America, which he failed by in his return home quite to Florida, where his provifions failing, he then returned to England from thence; and finding great tumults among the people and preparation for wars with Scotland, there was then no more confideration had of this voyage: whereupon he went to Spain, where the King and Queen being advertifed of what he had done, entertained him at their charges, and furnifhed out fhips for the difcovery of the coaft of Brafil and the river of Plate, which he effected and was after conftituted pilot major to Spain; and thus England loft the opportunity of farther difcoveries by this great genius in the art of navigation and cofmography. In the 14th year of Henry 7th. Fabian fays " were brought home and prefented to the King three men taken in Newfoundland, cloathed in beafts fkins, eating raw flefh; they fpake fuch

fpeech.

* There is a good account of this voyage in Lord Verulam's Life of Henry 7th, to which I refer.

fpeech as no man could underftand, and in their demeanour were like to bruit beafts, whom the King kept a time after; afterwards I faw two apparelled like Englifhmen at Weftminfter pallace."

In Fabian's Chronicle,* and in Stowe continued by E. Howes, the voyage is related nearly alike; in the latter thus: " This year (1498) one Sebaftian Cabota, a Genoefe's fon, (others fay a Venetian,) born at Briftow, profeffing himfelf to be expert in knowledge of the circuit of the world and iflands thereof, as by his charts and other reafonable demonftrations he fhewed, caufed the King to man and victual a fhip at Briftow, to fearch for an ifland which he knew to be replenifhed with rich commodities: in the fhip divers merchants of London adventured fmall ftocks, and in companie with this fhip, fayled alfo out of Briftow three or foure fmall fhippes fraughte with flight and other groffe wares, as coarfe cloth, caps, laces, points, and fuch other."

Sir H. Gilbert, in his book intitled, A Difcovery of a New Paffage to Cataia, writeth thus: " Sebaftian Cabota, by his perfonal experience and travell, hath fet forth and defcribed this paffage in his charts, which are yet to be feen in the Queen's Majefties privy gallory at Whitehall, who was fent to make this difcoverie by King Hen. 7. and entred the fret, affirmed that he failed very far weftward, with a quarter of North, on the North fide of Terra Labrador, the 11 June, until he came to the Septentrional, latitude of $67\frac{3}{4}$ degrees, and finding the feas ftill open, faid, that he might and would have gone to Cataia, if the enmity of the mafter and mariners had not been." — However he might have been miftaken in that, it fhews what a genius he had for naval adventures. — Peter Martyr of Angleria, in his third Decade, † chap. 6. thus accurately defcribes this voyage: " Thefe North feas have been fearched by one Sebaftian Cabot, a Venetian born, whomme yet but in manner an ‡ infant, his parents carried with them into England, having occafion to refort thither for trade, as is the manner of the Venetians to leave noe parte of the worlde unfearched to obtayne rycheffe; he therefore furnifhed two fhippes in England at his own charges: and firft with three hundred menne directed his courfe fo farre towarde the North pole, that even at the mouthe of July he founde monftrous heapes of ife fwimming on the fea, and in manner continual day light: yet fawe he the lande in that tracte free from ife, moulten by the heat of

* Thomas Languet in Chron. fays, " Sebaftian Cabot, fon of a Genoefe, born in Briftowe profeffing knowledge in the circuit of the earth, was fente from Briftowe to difcover ftraunge countryes, and he fyrfte founde out Newfoundclande in 1498.

† Tranflated out of Spanifh by Lok, Gent. 1612.

‡ So young that it gave room to fay he was born in Briftol, the place in England they fettled at, — nor is it clear he was not born there: but a Briftol man he was, being bred up there from infancy confeffedly..

of the funne. Thus meeting fuch heapes of ife before him, he was enforced to turn his fayles and follow the Weft, fo coaftinge ftyll by the fhore, that he was thereby brought fo far into the Southe by reafon of the lande bending fo much fouthwarde, that it was there almoft equal in latitude with the fea called " Fretum Herculeum," having the North pole elevate in manner in the fame degree. He fayld likewife in this track fo farre towards the Weft that he had the ifland of Cuba on his left hande, in manner in the fame degree of longitude. As he travayled by the coafts of this great land, (which he named Baccalaos,) he fayth that hee founde the like courfe of waters towards the Weft, but the fame to run more foftly and gentlely, than the fwift waters which the Spanyards founde in their navigations fouthwards. Sebaftian Cabot himfelf called thefe landes Baccalaos, from certaine bygge fifhes called by the inhabitants Baccalaos, fo many that they fometimes ftaid their fhippes. He founde alfo the people of thefe regions covered with beaft fkins, yet not without the ufe of reafon. He alfo fayth, there are plenty of beares, which catch fyfh with their clawes and draw them to land and eate them: he declareth alfo that he faw greate plenty of laton (a kind of metal) among the inhabitants. Cabot is my friend, (adds Peter Martyr,) whom I ufe familiarly and delight to have him fometimes keep me company in my own houfe; for hee being called out of England * by the commandment of the Catholike King of Caftile, after the death of King Henry of England the 7th of that name, he was made one of our counfayle and affiftants touchynge the affayres of the newe Indies, lookyng daylie for fhyppes to be fitted out by him to difcover this hidde fecret of nature. This voyage is appoynted to be begunne in March in the yeere next following, beeinge the yeere of Chrifte 1516."

This is a moft curious account indeed of our townfman Cabot's voyage, and being given by his friend and intimate affociate who might have it from Cabot's own mouth, it is moft likely to be true and genuine. In his feventh Decade, printed a few years poffibly afterwards, P. Martyr again mentions " the Baccalaos, as being firft difcovered 26 years fince from England by Cabotus." There are in Mr. Hackluit, to whom I refer, feveral other teftimonies of Sebaftian Cabot's difcoveries of Newfoundland and North America, to which the merchants of Briftol, who formerly according to Georg. Brunius, before quoted, ufed to go once a year to Newfoundland a fifhing, now drive fo confiderable a trade.

In the fecond year of Edward 6. 1549, the King granted to Sebaftian Cabot a certain annuity or yearly revenue of 166 l. 13 s. 4 d. fterling, to receive and enjoy

---

* i. e. From Briftol where he dwelt, and was bred up — he is called in manufcript *penes me*, " a Geneofe's fon, born in Briftow."

enjoy the fame to the faid Sebaftian Cabot during his natural life, out of the treafury of the Exchequer at Weftminfter, at the hand of his treafurers and paymafters there without account or fee, conftituting him grand pilot of England.

In the life of Columbus by his fon, cap. 4. it is related, that a memorandum of his father contains the following particular, which fhows into how far diftant and fuppofed uninhabitable countries the merchants of Briftol had penetrated: " In February 1467, I failed myfelf an hundred leagues beyond Thule, Iceland, whofe northern point is 73 degrees diftant from the equinoftial, and not 63 as fome will have it, nor does it lie upon the line where Ptolomy's Weft begins, but much more to the weftward; and to this ifland, which is as big as England, the Englifh trade, efpecially from Briftol. (Churchill's Voyages, vol. 2. p. 485. 3d edit.)

In William Botoner, p. 267, there is an account of an early voyage made by Briftol men " in two fhips of 80 tons, of Jay, junr. a merchant, who began their voyage 15 July 1480, at the port of Briftol in Kyngroad, for the ifland of Brafyle, taking their courfe from the Weft part of Ireland, plowing the feas through, and Thlyde is mafter of the fhip, the moft fkilful mariner of all England; — news came to Briftol Monday 18th Sept. that the faid fhips failed over the feas for nine months, and found not the ifland, but through tempefts at fea returned to port in Ireland, for laying up their fhips and mariners."

In the little red book, p. 158. is recorded a Latin charter of Hen. 4. exempting the mayor and commonalty from the power and jurifdiftion of the Admiralty of England, not publifhed in the Briftol charters, only the confirmation of it by Edw. 4. — Henry's charter fays, " that confidering the many and notable fervices which very many merchants, burgeffes of our town of Briftol, have done for us and our famous progenitors in many ways with their fhips and voyages at their own great charges and expence; as alfo for the grateful fenfe which we have lately found in the mayor and commonalty of the faid town in freely giving us 200l. in our neceffities for the more readily expediting certain arduous affairs of our kingdom: and alfo fince many of the faid burgeffes and merchants have been grievoufly vexed and difturbed by the lieutenants and minifters of our Admiralty of England, to their great lofs and burden: we therefore of our fpecial grace, mere motion and certain knowledge, have granted for us and our heirs to the mayor and commonalty and their heirs, that the faid town, &c. fhall for ever be free from the jurifdiftion, &c. of the faid Admiralty, &c."

This charter afforded great relief to the merchants, captains, and citizens.

In

In 1527, Robert Thorn of Briftol informed Dr. Ley, ambaffador from Henry 8th to the Emperor Charles, that " he and his partner in a flote of fhips fitted out and armed by the merchants of Seville had ventured and em- ployed 1400 ducats principally, for that two Englifhmen, friends of his, learned in cofmography fhould go in the faid fhips with Sebaftian Cabot, then intended for the Moluccas by the Streights of Magellan in April 1527, but the voyage was performed only to the river of Plate. They were to bring him certain relation of the fituation of the country, and to get expe- rience of the navigation of thofe feas, and information of many other things that he defired to know and any charts by which thofe of the country fail, &c. for if from the iflands of Moluccas the fea doth extend without interpofition of land to fail from north to north eaft point 1700 or 1800 leagues, they fhould come to the Newfounland iflands that the Englifh difcovered, and fo we fhould be nearer to the fpiceries by almoft 200 leagues than the Emperor or the King of Portugal are."

In the year 1583, Sir Humphrey Gilbert performed a voyage for the co- lonization of America, an account of which was written by one Haies, gent. in Hackluit, 3d vol. p. 144. — in which he fays " the firft difcovery of thefe coafts never heard of before was well begun by John Cabot the father and Sabaftian his fonne an Englifhman borne, who were the firft finders out of all that great tract of land ftretching from cape Florida unto thofe iflands which we now call Newfoundland: all which they brought and annexed to the Crown of England, foon after Chriftopher Columbus had difcovered the iflands and continent of the Weft Indies for Spain. In the year 1578, Mr. Antony Parkhurft gentleman of Briftol, who had been four years at New- foundland and had accurately fearched the ifland, fent Mr. Hackluit a letter dated from Briftow, in which he defcribes the great increafe of the fifhery or the number of veffels reforting thither, and a natural hiftory of the ifland. Sir Francis Walfingham 11th March 1582, wrote to Mr. Robert Aldworth then mayor and a merchant of Briftol, commending his good inclination to the weftern difcovery, and recommending to add the two fhips or barks he was then fitting out to the fleet of Sir Humphry Gilbert, to which the faid Mr. Aldworth replied, that the weftern voyage intended for the difcovery of the coaft of America to the fouth weft of Cape Breton was well liked there, that the merchants of Briftol fubfcribed 1000 marks immediately to it, and that they would furnifh a fhip of 60 and a bark of 40 tons. dated 27th March 1583. In 1594, the Grace of Briftol the 4th April failed from Briftol into the great river of St. Laurence for the fins of wales and train oil, as far up

as

as the ifland Nantifcot, and returned to Hungroad 24th September the fame
year. In the Collections of Public Acts it appears, that a patent was granted
in 1502 by King Henry 7th. 9th December, to " James (or Hugh) Elliot
and Thomas Afhurft merchants of Briftol, and to John Gonfalez and Francis
Fernandez, natives of Portugal, to go with Englifh colours in queft of unknown countries upon certain terms exprefled in the grant," whether it was
in any voyage in company with Cabot or another, I cannot determine. —
For I find Robert Thorn afore-mentioned of Briftol, who was fheriff there in
1503, May 1 1514 to Dr. Leigh writes thus; " this inclination and
defire of this difcovery I inherited from my father, who with another merchant of Briftol, named Hugh Elliot, were the difcoverers of the Newfound-
lands, of which there is no doubt, (as now plainly appeareth) if the mariners
would have been ruled then, and followed the * pilot's mind, but the lands
of the Weft Indies, from whence all the gold cometh, had been ours; for all
is one coaft as by the chart appeareth."

One Thorn (the afore-mentioned Robert) a merchant of Briftol is faid by
Mr. Guthrie † to have " prefented a memorial for leave to find out the
north-weft paffage, fetting forth the vaft advantages which the Emperor and
the King of Portugal drew from their American fettlements. But though
Thorn obtained his requeft, no difcovery of any importance then followed."
Nicholas Thorn in his will left all his geographical and nautical inftruments
to the Grammar fchool of Briftol founded by his father Robert.

Many voyages were made afterwards from Briftol with the like public fpi-
rited views of enriching their country as well as themfelves, though not with
equal fuccefs. One ‡ Mr. Guy in 1609, took out a number of perfons of
both fexes, defigning to form a fettlement all the winter in Newfoundland :
he was a member of the common council of Briftol, and mayor in 1618.
" He procured a charter and licence of the King (James) for his intended
plantation, having fome rich merchants of London as well as Briftol joined
with him for the better and more effectual profecuting of the fcheme. Many
of this city did advance money towards it: and fo Mr. Guy with fome other
young merchants being fitted out with more men and all neceffaries took
fhipping here for Newfoundland to make a trial of the place, by ftaying there
all the winter." §

Y In

* Sebaftian Cabot's I fuppofe.
† Hiftory of England, v. 2, p. 1052, vid. Annals for the year 1502.
‡ In a manufcript penes me.
§ John de Laet takes notice of this voyage from Briftol: anno 1608, Angli Johanne Guyo
Briftolienfi ductore ftatas fedes in hac infula fecerunt ad finum conceptionis, &c.

In Stowe's Chronicle continued by E. Howes p. 943 you have a very particular relation of this voyage, " after the patent was obtained, and feveral
noblemen gentlemen and citizens being thereby made a body corporate by
the name of the treafurer and company of adventures and planters of the
cities of London and Briftol for the colony and plantation of Newfoundland
in the fouthern and eaftern parts lying between the degrees 52 and 46, the
company fent fhips with men, women and all neceffaries thither, and ordained maifter John Guy a citizen of Briftol a man very induftrious and of good
experience to be their General in this plantation, who planted a colony of
men and women in the ifland of Newfoundland, (which was firft difcovered
by Sebaftian Cabot and ever fince yearly frequented by the Englifh in fifhing
time;) with them alfo they for their ufe to increafe there, tranfported hennes,
duckes, pigeons, conies, goats, kine and other live creatures, all which did
very well there; this General Guy, ftayed there with the colony both winter
and fummer, whofe natures and conditions in general agreed very well with
the foil and clyme. In this plantation there were fent none but men of civill
lyfe, and of fome honeft trade or profeffion, by which courfe they lived and
profpered the better: fince the date of their charter, 8th James 1. 2d May
1610, they have fent yearly fupplies thither unto the year 1614, mafter John
Slaney Efq; being their firft treafurer."

In an old leger book in the cuftody of Mr. Hackluit (v. 3, p. 500 of his
voyages) written about 1526 by Mr. N. Thorn the elder a principal merchant of Briftol, it was noted, that before that year one T. Tifon an Englifhman had " found the way to the Weft Indies and refided there, and to him
the faid Mr. N. Thorn then a merchant in Briftol fent armour and other
merchandize there fpecified, whereby it appears, that there was an eftablifhed
trade there very early and from the city of Briftol. In the 1ft Elizabeth,
when all merchandize was ordered to be fhipped in none but Englifh fhips,
an excellent policy of that wife Queen, a claufe was added in favour of the
merchants of Briftol, who had fuftained " great loffes at fea from enemies,
who had taken all their beft fhips and much fubftance fo as not to be able to
provide fhips of their own &c." — If there were no Englifh fhips within
forty miles of Briftol, they were allowed to lade their merchandize in foreign
fhips without being liable to aliens duties."

And from Hackluit (2. vol. p. 3.) it appears that certain merchants of
Briftol did not only now (1526) but for a long time before trade by the fhips
of St. Lucar in Spain to the Canaries, fending cloth, foap &c. and returning
with

with dye ftuff and drugs, fugar, kidfkins, and that they alfo fent thither factors from Spain.

Briftol was equally induftrious in eftablifhing manufactories efpecially of foap in 1523, fupplying London with the beft grey fpeckled foap and with white at 1d. per pound. In 1581 it had a chief manufactory of points or pins, and it was a principal myftery exercifed in the town, as were the making of bays and filk hofe; and the fail cloth and glafs manufacture, and that of hats, cotton and thread hofe, &c. is ftill carried on with great induftry.

It appears by the great Red Book of Briftol p. 30, that the mayor, bailliffs and commonalty had a free guild of merchants in the town and fuburb, from time beyond the memory of man, and all things belonging to a guild, viz: to buy and fell in the faid town freely and quietly from all toll and cuftoms, and had other liberties belonging to them, and for the whole time ufed to take a certain fine or (præftacionem) to their own ufe from all who were admitted into the liberties and fociety of the faid guild, to have the liberty aforefaid according to what could be agreed reafonably between them; — the guild was confirmed in their liberties by John Earl of Moreton afterwards King john and by William Earl of Glocefter.

In 7th year of Edward 4, William Canynges being mayor the following ordinances were made for merchants, according to the cuftom from time immemorial.

1. The maior and council fifteen days after Michaelmas were to call a council and to choofe from them a perfon, that hath been maior or fheriff, to be mafter of the fellowfhip of merchants and to choofe two merchants for wardens, and two beedles to occupy as beedles and brokers to be attendant the faid year upon the faid mafters and wardens &c.

2. The mafter and fellowfhip to have at their will the chapel and the draught chamber at Spicers hall to affemble in, paying 20s. per ann.

3. All merchants to attend (if in town) upon fummons, or to pay one pound of wax to the mafter and fellowfhip.

4. All rules for felling to ftrangers of any of the four merchandifes to be kept on pain of 20s. for every default one half to the fellowfhip, the other to the chamber.

5. Nor upon pain aforefaid to fell to any ftranger under the ruled price.

6. If any merchant be in diftrefs he muft apply to the wardens or beedles declaring the fame, and if they provide not a remedy within three days, then the merchant burgefs to fell any of his four merchandifes at his pleafure.

Befides

Befides the guilds or fraternities for the regulation of trade, there were alfo religious guilds; one was inftituted here 24 Hen. 6. that for the foul's health and good of the King, the mayor and commonalty, and for the profperity of the mariners who were expofed to manifold dangers and diftreffes, there fhould be a fraternity erected to the worfhip of God, our Lady, St. Clement, St. George, and all the faints of heaven, to be founded in fuch place in Briftol which the mayor fhould direct, for a prieft and twelve poor mariners to pray daily, as above; to the fupport of which the mafter of every fhip, barge, &c. after his voyage performed, at his arrival in the port fhould pay 4 d. per ton of goods imported, in two days, to two wardens chofen for the craft of mariners and admitted by the mayor, and all fworn by the articles and orders of the fraternity, on pain of 6 s. 8 d. if a mafter, if feaman 3 s. 4 d. if fervant 1 s. 8 d.

1. One half to the mayor, and the other to the fraternity towards the fupport of the prieft and poor: the like penalty to feamen or fervants who refufe or omit paying the 4 d. per ton, and the mafter to forfeit 40 s. for the fame default.

2. Every mafter and mariner to attend at the proceffion of Corpus Chrifti day, with the reft of his craft, upon the like penalties above.

3. Any mariner convicted of having ftoleu goods on fhipboard, or bringing fuch into his fhip, the mate that receives fuch mariner fhall forfeit 20 s.

4. Every mafter and mariner was in his harnefs to attend the mayor during the watches of St. John's feaft, St. Peter's and St. Paul's on like penalties.

5. None to be chofen into the number of the twelve poor men of the fraternity unlefs he has performed his duties for feven years, to be chofen by vote; and if he has been a mafter feven years to receive 12 d. per week, otherwife 8 d. per week for his finding.

6. A warden omitting to pay the faid allowance fix weeks to any poor perfon to forfeit 20 s. half to the profit of the town, half to the fraternity.

7. Every Briftol mariner arriving in any other port after the voyage made, though not in a fhip of this port, to pay at his coming to the city the fame as if he had failed in a Briftow fhip.

There is now an almfhoufe near the Merchants'-Hall, that has fucceeded to this fraternity; and there was formerly a chapel there adjoining, dedicated to St. Clement. — And there has lately been inftituted a fociety called the Captain's or Seaman's Club, by which the widows of captains failing a certain time out of Briftol have a provifion of 8 or 10 l. or more, per ann. for their widowhood.

A Society

A Society of Merchant-Venturers was incorporated within this city by King Edw. 6. by letters patent 14th December 6th year of his reign; and afterwards confirmed by Queen Elizabeth, and King Charles 1st. They are feized and poffeffed of manors * and lands to the amount of upwards of 3000l. per annum, in truft for the maintenance and fupport of certain almfhoufes in this city, and for other charitable ufes. — They have a comon hall to meet and tranfact their bufinefs in, and an almfhoufe for decayed feamen adjoining: their charter gives them feveral privileges, powers, and immunities; and private perfons becoming members of this honourable fociety, enjoy fome particular advantages in fitting out their fhips with refpect to wharfage, which thofe pay who are not free of the Merchants'-Hall.

By an act of council the 13th Cha. 2d. 1661, it was ordered, in confideration the fociety and fellowfhip of merchants will be at the cofts of enlarging and making new a key, from the lower flip of the Key to a certain place in the Marfh called Aldworth's Dock or Key: and alfo make the way paffable by Rownham convenient for coaches or horfes to the Hot-wells, there fhall be the fum of 100 l. iffued out of the chamber towards the advancement and doing of the faid public works: and alfo upon furrender made by the faid fociety of a leafe they have now in being of the duties of anchorage and plankage and kannage, a new leafe fhould be granted to them by the mayor and commonalty, of the faid duties, for the term of fourfcore years, under the old rent and covenants, provided a covenant binding all parties be inferted, that after the new Key be made and enlarged no building fhall be erected on the fame.   Book of Orders, p. 72.

This leafe has been renewed not long fince, about the year 1780.

The

---

* Part of the manor of Clifton belongs to them, the Hot-well fpring and pump-room, and other buildings there, lately much improved; alfo St. Vincent's Rock above it, where ftone is continually digged for making the beft lime, great quantities of which are exported to the fugar iflands for making fugar. — Befides the plants, &c. mentioned before p. 92, there is lately gath'ered here a plant called Wild or Mountain Sage, in great quantities, and fent to very diftant parts as a remedy for old rheumatifms and fixed pains, and debility thence arifing; it is boiled, and half a pint given at a time in thefe complaints and after gouty fits, and they fay to great adv'antage. — From the high part of St. Vincent's Rock, where they dig the lime ftones, to the oppofite fide, a bridge was once propofed to be thrown by Wm. Vick, Efq; an eminent wine-merchant of Briftol, who left a thoufand pounds and intereft to accumulate for a certain number of years, if any one within that time fhould leave any additional fum for the fame purpofe. Unfortunately no one has left any thing fince towards this grand fcheme, and the money is now forfeited to his executors.

The following are the arms of the Society of Merchant-Venturers of the city of Briftol, incorporated the 14th December the 6th of Edw. 6. granted by Took Clarenceiux.

Barry ondè of 6 pieces arg. and azure, on a bend or. a dragon volant vert. on a chief G. a lion paffant or. between 2 bezants—upon the beaufmen on a wreath or. and az. the top of a fhip or. in the fame a man in mail proper, in his right hand a targe, in his left a dart or. fupported with two fupporters, firft a mermaid, the upper part charnè, her hair and fins with an anchor in her hand or. the nether part in proper colours; the fecond fupporter is the figure of Time, the upper part charnè, his wings and nether part or. in his left hand a fcythe, the fhaft fables, fcythe arg. mantled gules, doubled arg.

The arms with the fupporters may be feen engraved in the print of the Merchants'-Hall, fee chap. on St. Stephen's parifh.

So intent have the natives of Briftol ever been on merchandife and navigation, that they frequently have not only ventured their lives and fortunes in fearch of new countries, and opening new fources of commerce, but their induftry has alfo been crowned with fuch fuccefs as to enable them to affift the government in time of public danger with money and fhips, as they did Henry 8. againft the French King, and Q. Elizabeth againft the Spanifh armada. Their knowledge of trade and commercial affairs has been equal to their induftry, and they have been fent for in times paft to Weftminfter by the government to advife concerning trade, particularly by Hen. 6. a. r. 36. And Mr. J. Guy, the merchant and alderman before-mentioned, was fent for to London to confult about the decay of trade and coin in 1622.

Briftol being the largeft and moft convenient weftern port for trade, and having the benefit of water carriage by the fine river Severn for bringing down the heavy goods and manufactures of the North of England hither for exportation, enjoys very great advantages over many other ports.—This noble river, which our anceftors the Britons called Havren, the Romans Sabrina, and

and the Englifh Sevren, rifes out of a high mountain in Montgomeryfhire, called Plinlimmon or Plynlymon ; from hence running South Eaft it receives two fmall rivulets, and then turning direct North paffes through Llanidios, where receiving the waters of five other ftreams and running North Eaft to Newtown, it continues its courfe more to the northward, till it enters Shrop. fhire, and being joined by feveral brooks by the way, at laft reaches Welch. pool ; having in the fpace of twenty miles become from a flender filver ftream a very deep and copious river, and is navigable from thence to its mouth. From Welchpool the Severn runs North, and then turning Eaft after wafhing the fplendid and populous town of Shrewfbury, (fuperior to fome cities,) runs South Eaft to Bridgenorth ; and from thence declining ftill more to the South enters Worcefterfhire and proceeds to Bewdley. The Severn, fwelled with concurring ftreams, traverfes entirely that country, and having watered amongft other places Worcefter and Upton, it paffes forward into Glocefter-fhire and rolls on to Tewkefbury, from whence having vifited Glocefter, and meeting ftill with frefh acceffion of waters, grows to fuch a fize as to be ftiled the Severn Sea, pouring its tide, after a progrefs of more than a hundred and thirty miles, into the Briftol Channel.*

The Severn flowing up the river Avon to Briftol, formerly not only great and ferviceable fhips of burden belonging to merchants, but alfo to his Majefty had of old time continual recourfe hither, fay the manufcripts ; and feveral King's fhips of war have been built in the docks here.†

As the diftinguifhed privileges and conveniences Briftol has by its fituation and free intercourfe with Wales and the North of England by the Severn, became more generally known and experienced, fo has its trade, fhipping and credit increafed ; and as its merchants have met with fuccefs, the induftrious. naturally refort hither to make a fortune, and the rich to improve one. By trade and navigation many places in every kingdom have rofe out of obfcurity, and became eminent examples of its extenfive utility to a ftate, and happy influence on a nation ; and by its decay places, which once made an illuftrious. figure in a kingdom, have from fuperb cities dwindled down into mean towns and villages and funk into obfcurity. With great truth and honour may it be

---

* See William of Malmfbury de Geftis Pontific. lib. 4. of the Hygre or Bore, or fwelling of the tide fuddenly.—Alfo Camden's Glocefterfhire.

† Ships of war built here for government, the Iflip of 30 guns, in 1655. The St. Patrick of 52 guns, in 1660. The Edgar of 72 guns, 432 men, 1046 tons, in 1668. The Oxford of 54 guns, 274 men, 683 tons, in 1674. The Northumberland of 70 guns, 446 men, 1096 tons, in 1679. The Glocefter of 60 guns, 316 men, 896 tons. The Medea of 32 guns, in 1778. The Trufty of 50 guns, and lately many more.

be faid, that by merchandife fuch opulent fortunes have been acquired here as to enable many of our predeceffors to build churches, and endow hofpitals and almfhoufes, and leave fuch noble and princely benefactions for the public ufe behind them, as are not to be equalled in the kingdom by any city, where private merchants and tradefmen were the donors, as will hereafter be made appear: fo that it may be truly faid, they got their wealth by induftry, managed it with prudence, and above all did not forget to difpofe of much of it to public charities.

The trade of this city is efteemed the moft confiderable of any port in the kingdom, London excepted, efpecially to the Weft Indies and North America, to the latter its merchants have the honour of being the firft adventurers, and are faid to employ about 70 large fhips in the trade to the Weft Indies alone. The Guinea trade has been alfo very flourifhing, and employs a great number of their fhipping; though in this Liverpool may probably exceed them. Before the civil war they had a great foreign trade, efpecially to the Weft Indies, but fince the revolution the trade to North America and Newfoundland, to Guinea, the Mediterranean, to Norway, Hamburgh, and up the Baltic has been greatly improved and extended. They trade here alfo with lefs dependence on the Capital than any of the outports. Whatever exportations they make to any part, they can difpofe of the full returns, without fhipping of any part for London in fhips bound thither, or configning their own veffels to London to difpofe of their cargoes. They have buyers at home for their largeft cargoes; whence the fhopkeepers in Briftol drive a great inland trade, being wholefale dealers throughout the weftern counties, which employs a great many carriers and waggoners paffing and repaffing from Briftol to the principal towns. Add to this the navigation of the two great rivers Severn and Wye, whereby they engrofs in a manner to themfelves the whole trade of South Wales, and great part of North Wales, as well as of the Englifh counties bordering on thofe rivers; and they have all the heavy goods by water from Birmingham and the North of England by trows, a very fingular advantage to the foreign or home trade of the place, not lefs than 100 trows being employed in bringing goods to and from Briftol on the Severn. The trade to Ireland is alfo very great, a number of fhips being conftantly employed in it.

The great demand for glafs bottles for the Briftol and the Bath waters, for the exportation of beer, cider, and perry, &c. occafion many glafs-houfes being erected here to fupply it: befides there is a great export of plate or

window

window glaſs, vials, and drinking glaſſes; braſs and copper pans, and braſs wire from the manufaƈtory here.

The diſtillery is alſo become a very capital branch of trade, many great works being ereƈted at amazing expence in different parts of the city; and though nothing is ſo prejudicial to the health of man as drinking ſpirituous liquors in any form, ſo totally deſtruƈtive of human generation and being, ſo ſubverſive of our very exiſtence, cauſing ſlow but ſure death, yet the quantity of rum imported from abroad, of gin and brandy made at home, indicates and proves what a great conſumption of theſe liquors there is now in compariſon of what was a few years ago; when there were but few diſtil houſes and but little rum imported or brandy made here. The miſchief indeed is not confined to ourſelves; it ſpreads far and wide; for the great export of ſpirits to Quebeck and North America, to Africa and other countries it is, that promotes the diſtillery here, as well as their too general and fatal uſe at home; whilſt the great conſumption of barley and wheat, whence they extraƈt this baneful liquor, leaves us often to lament the ſcarcity of grain for our neceſſary uſes, for our wholeſom food and daily ſupport. Such quantities of ſpirits are made here from grain (the growth of the adjoining corn-counties, Gloceſterſhire, Wiltſhire, Worceſterſhire, Herefordſhire and Wales, from which laſt they have it by water,) that they ſend veſſels loaded with ſpirits to London, and even ſupply that city, where yet ſuch large diſtilleries are carried on to ſuch a degree and extent as exceeds all belief. But all, all is conſumed, to the ſhortning of the period of human life (alas! too ſhort!) and the abſolute extinƈtion of our very being, by drying up and hardning the fine veſſels and nerves, rendering them impervious, producing paralytic ſtrokes, hemiplegies, and apoplexies, never before ſo frequent as of late years, ſince the frequent and ſo general uſe of ſpirituous liquors, in punch, toddy or alone unmixed.

The preſent trade of this city to foreign parts is very great; to Florida, Carolina, Maryland, New-York, Philadelphia, Newfoundland and Quebec, ſhips are employed to export our manufaƈtured goods through the vaſt continent of North America, and return with tobacco, rice, tar, deer ſkins, timber, furrs, indigo, logwood, &c. and from the Weſt India Iſlands with ſugar, rum, pimento, mahogany, &c. the produce of the ſeveral countries, the trade thither having increaſed in proportion as the coloniſts have extended their ſettlements: it refleƈts no ſmall degree of honour on the city of Briſtol that Newfoundland and North America to which they now and ever ſince have had ſo great a trade, were firſt diſcovered by a Briſtol man, and the firſt

voyage

voyage made thither was by ſhips manned victualled and fitted out here by Briſtol merchants. It is yet to be proved whither the trade to America will increaſe or decline, ſince ſome of the colonies grown rich and feeling their own importance, have now ſet up for themſelves and thrown off their allegiance and dependence they owed the mother country by a ſeparation in the year 1783. The trade to Africa for ſlaves, (a trade now much complained of and about to be regulated by law) ivory, gold duſt, &c. has been cultivated here with great ſpirit and ſuccefs; the induſtrious tradefmen alſo frequently ſend their goods abroad to great advantage at their own riſque ; and they freight ſhips here for any voyage with the greateſt diſpatch. They employ alſo ſhips in the Streights trade, and up the Baltic for deals, &c. and not long ſince ſent them to Greenland in the whale fiſhery, which proving more uncertain and not ſo advantageous is dropped entirely for the preſent. In war time they have fitted out fleets of privateers to the great anoyance of the enemy's trade and aſſiſtance to government.

The whole trade of this city may beſt be eſtimated by the duties paid on exports and imports annually and the number of ſhips entered out. By ſome manuſcript papers before me it appears that in 1634 the port of Briſtol paid for cuſtoms and impoſts more then 10,000l. and the following years upwards of 25,000l. and they have every year ſince moſt rapidly increaſed.

In the reign of Queen Elizabeth, the amount of the cuſtoms upon an average of ſeveral years was in the port of London 111,000l. and in all the other ports of the kingdom 17,000l. of which Briſtol paid 5000l. whereas in the year 1770 and for years paſt the cuſtoms of the port of Briſtol alone have amounted to upwards of 200,000l. per ann. clear of all bounties paid on exports, officers ſalaries, &c. the exciſe pays alſo 100,000l. per ann. But the following account of the groſs receipts and neat remittances of the two ſeaports of Briſtol and Liverpool (a diſpute having ariſen which paid moſt to government) may be ſatisfactory to the reader, as it gives the remittances for eight years regularly.

GROSS

GROSS RECEIPTS.

BRISTOL.					LIVERPOOL.			
1750	- -	242,283	4	11	1750	- -	215,463	8	4
1	- -	228,517	16	1	1	- -	163,597	17	$10\frac{3}{4}$
2	- -	302,886	5	2	2	- -	200,409	14	$6\frac{3}{4}$
3	- -	301,483	4	$3\frac{1}{2}$	3	- -	210,218	16	$6\frac{1}{2}$
4	- -	297,202	0	$0\frac{3}{4}$	4	- -	258,456	8	$1\frac{1}{4}$
5	- -	333,778	14	$5\frac{3}{4}$	5	- -	202,367	6	1
6	- -	257,560	1	$9\frac{3}{4}$	6	- -	165,438	4	$3\frac{3}{4}$
7	- -	351,211	9	$6\frac{3}{4}$	7	- -	198,946	17	3

£2,314,922   16 $4\frac{1}{2}$ £1,614,898   13   1

Medium.   Medium.

£289,365   7 $0\frac{1}{2}$ £201,862   6 $7\frac{1}{2}$

NEAT REMITTANCES.

BRISTOL.					LIVERPOOL.			
1750	- -	128,580	17	$10\frac{1}{4}$	1750	- -	58,907	5	$3\frac{1}{2}$
1	- -	140,731	0	$6\frac{3}{4}$	1	- -	40,648	3	0
2	- -	158,765	10	$4\frac{1}{2}$	2	- -	44,387	8	$0\frac{1}{2}$
3	- -	170,361	13	$1\frac{1}{4}$	3	- -	45,479	1	$1\frac{1}{2}$
4	- -	156,717	9	$1\frac{3}{4}$	4	- -	59,766	6	$0\frac{3}{4}$
5	- -	177,894	15	$4\frac{1}{2}$	5	- -	49,661	0	$8\frac{1}{4}$
6	- -	156,951	5	5	6	- -	49,976	11	$1\frac{1}{4}$
7	- -	151,516	1	$1\frac{1}{4}$	7	- -	60,263	15	$10\frac{1}{2}$

£1,241,518   12 $11\frac{1}{4}$ £409,089   11 $2\frac{3}{4}$

Medium.   Medium.

£155,189   16 $7\frac{1}{4}$ £51,136   3 $10\frac{3}{4}$

The neat remittance for the year 1764 from Briftol was 195,000l. and from Liverpool but 70,000l. and 2353 veffels entered inward at the Cuftom-houfe Briftol the fame year.

To fhew the great ihcreafe of the trade of this city as well as of the number of its fhipping the account of the anchorage, wharfage and moorage, paid to the fociety of merchants for a certain number of years, is an indubitable proof and of this the following is a true and exact amount for the fpace of thirty two years.

Z. 2   N. B.

N. B. Every veſſel above ſixty tons pays wharfage.

			l.	*s.*	*d.*
In 1745	- - -		918	18	7½
6	- - -		879	19	6
7	- - -		921	13	9
8	- - -		1064	1	5
9	- - -		1080	7	2
1750	- - -		1247	6	0
1	- - -		1253	1	6
2	- - -		1225	10	10½
3	- - -		1271	1	9½
4	- - -		1212	1	11
5	- - -		1209	16	9½
6	- - -		1208	9	10½
7	- - -		1387	1	5
8	- - -		1308	5	11½
9	- - -		1591	14	6
1760	- - -		1379	1	5
1	- - -		1289	0	6
2	- - -		1253	17	8
3	- - -		1351	13	6
4	- - -		1286	8	1
5	- - -		1483	7	2
6	- - -		1481	6	6
7	- - -		1547	5	1
8	- - -		1657	15	2
9	- - -		1593	8	5
1770	- - -		1578	18	6
1	- - -		1514	7	2
2	- - -		1561	0	9
3	- - -		1482	0	6½
4	- - -		1727	18	6
5	upwards of		2000	0	0

The

The numbers of ſhips and veſſels arriving here, and entered out of the port of Briſtol, muſt ever be varying in different years; and to calculate this with any juſtneſs or propriety, the places to which they are ſent ſhould be ſpecified: it has been computed thus, though exactneſs is not to be expected.

Coaſting veſſels annually employed chiefly on the coaſt of Somerſet, Devon and Cornwall, and Wales down the Briſtol Channel, and on the rive Wye and all South Wales, &c. about	1000
In 1788 Ships employed in the trade to Jamaica,	34
To the Leeward iſlands	38
To Africa	37
To Newfoundland	33
To North America about	50
Between Briſtol and Ireland, France, Spain, and London, &c. about	200
	1392

Beſides 103 trows from 50 to 130 tons employed in carrying goods upon the Severn to and from Briſtol.

In the year 1769 there were entered inward at the Cuſtom-houſe 417 foreign ſhips, as appears by the preſentments of the year, excluſive of Londoners, coaſters, &c.

In the year 1742 the privateers fitted out from Briſtol alone exceeded in tonnage number of guns and men, the whole Royal Navy of Great Britain in the reign of Queen Elizabeth; though trade and navigation have flouriſhed and been annually improving here for many years yet it has been ever fluctuating from the time of King Henry 2d. 1139, when William of Malmſbury makes ſuch honourable mention of it to the preſent time.

The following exact account (which may rectify any errors in the above), of the whole number of ſhips and their tonnage, including their repeated voyages, that have traded to this port to and from any kingdom in the year 1787, is taken from the Cuſtom-houſe entries by order of government, when the ſtate of the African ſlave-trade was the ſubject of parliamentary enquiry, and petitions were preſented for its abolition, and an act was paſſed for its regulation.

COASTERS.

	ASTERS. Outwards.			INWARDS. British		Foreign		OUTWARDS. British		Foreign	
	Men. ;181 Vessels. 1632	Tons. 62,139	Men. 6066	Ships.	Tons.	Ships.	Tons.	Ships.	Tons.	Ships.	Tons.
Africa - - -				15	1762	0	0	30	4171	0	0
British Colonies - -				17	1477	0	0	36	3745	0	0
Honduras - - -				0	0	0	0	3	678	0	0
Musquito Shore - -				5	843	0	0	0	0	0	0
United States - -				11	1662	16	3045	11	1879	14	2454
West Indies - - -				71	16,209	0	0	73	16,913	0	0
Alderney - - -				0	0	0	0	1	39	0	0
British Fishery - -				0	0	0	0	7	340	0	0
Flanders - - -				1	80	0	0	0	0	0	0
France - - -				12	1110	3	135	20	1817	8	152
Germany - - -				1	20	3	330	0	0	0	0
Greece - - -				4	537	0	0	0	0	0	0
Guernsey - - -				4	236	0	0	12	605	0	0
Holland - - -				9	860	2	190	5	561	4	441
Jersey - - -				2	116	0	0	0	0	0	0
Ireland - - -				161	9623	0	0	139	9187	0	0
Isle of Man - -				2	68	0	0	1	40	0	0
Italy - - -				17	1709	0	0	4	372	4	690
Norway - - -				1	189	14	3307	0	0	13	2977
Poland - - -				2	461	3	960	0	0	3	960
Portugal - - -				23	2504	1	40	12	1579	2	380
Prussia - - -				8	2293	1	140	3	613	0	0
Southern Whale Fishery				2	382	0	0	2	387	0	0
Spain - - -				37	3633	17	1480	15	1647	18	1691
Sweden - - -				0	0	9	1485	0	0	0	0
Russia - - -				11	2351	0	0	8	2156	0	0
				416	48,125	69	11,112	382	46,729	60	10,445

 and Vessels belonging to this port, their tonnage and number of men, that have traded and from foreign parts; also coasting vessels, fishing vessels, smacks, &c. for the ar 1787.

Foreign Trade.			Coasters.			Fishing Vessels, &c.		
Ships.	Tons.	Men.	Ships.	Tons.	Men.	Ships.	Tons.	Men.
323	53,491	3971	30	3078	192	7	340	30

Of

Of B R I S T O L in PARTICULAR:

Or, of the C I T Y as divided into

Particular D I S T R I C T S, P A R I S H E S, &c.

C H A P. VII.

Of the C A S T L E.

T H E origin, names, civil government, trade, and defcription of the city in general at different periods being hitherto noticed, its feparate and particular hiftory falls next under confideration; and the Caftle with its precincts for its great antiquity and renown claims our firft regard.

This caftle has been the fcene of many interefting tranfactions and hiftorical events; though it is not mentioned in our chronicles exprefly before 1088, 1ft of Wm. Rufus, when it is called by Roger Hoveden "Caftrum fortiffimum." If it was fo foon after the conqueft, "a caftle of the greateft ftrength," fo great as to be made the infurgents head quarters, and the common repofitory of all the plunder of the country, as will appear below; it muft have been built long before, and we muft look farther back for the æra of its foundation into the Saxon times: for though the Saxon chronicle has not mentioned it, yet it muft have been of that time, and if we give credit to Turgot's account, p. 32, "in the year 915 Edward fenr. havyng made alteratyon of the walles of Eryghtftowe newly ybuylden the caflle, beeyng the goodelyefte offyve ybuylden on Abone bankes, and it was a grete checke to the Danes."

A wall around embattled at the top was the firft out-work of defence the city had, and with this it was fecured and inclofed on every fide, till the caftle on the eaftern part, where it was then not moted with the river, was afterwards erected for its greater fecurity and protection.

Leland

Leland fays, out of a book of the antiquities of the monaftery of Tewkfbury, which he met with in Latin, " That Robert, (conful of Glocefter,) built the caftle of Briftolle ;" and in another place, " he buildid the caftelle of Briftowe, or the moft part of it. Every man fayith that he builded the great fquare ftone dungeon, and that the ftones thereof came ou:e of Cäen in Normandie." J. Rofs makes Robert Haymo, in the time of William Rufus, Earl of Glo-cefter, " a founder of Briftol caftle." Mr. Cambden, without quoting the authority of Leland or any one elfe, roundly fays, " Robert, natural fon of Henry 1ft. (commonly called Robert Rufus, conful of Glocefter,) built a large ftone caftle for the defence of this city. This caftle being fcarce yet finifhed, was in 1138 befieged by King Stephen, but he was forced to draw off his forces without effecting any thing."

Unfortunately for Mr. Cambden, Leland, whom he feems to have copied in afcribing the erection of the caftle folely to Robert Earl of Glocefter, no where fays fo, as his own opinion ; he feems rather to doubt it by faying him-felf in another place, " he buildid the molle parte of it. Every manne fayith that he buildid the great ftone dungeon ;" and where he exprefly writeth on Briftow caftle, v. 7. p. 84, he only mentions " the great dungeon towre made, as it is fayde, of ftone brought out of Normandie by the redde Earl of Glocestre." This furely is far from making him to be the original founder of the caftle, as Mr. Cambden has erroneoufly done : and in page 88 of the fame vol. he calls him only " Robertus Conful Lorde of Brightftowe caftle, and founder of St. James priorie in the North fuburbe of Brightftowe :" here he had the beft occafion of calling him the fole and firft founder of the caftle, but he only makes him Lord or Governor of it, as already built as it really was ; for it was certainly held 1088 againft Wm. Rufus, 1ft W. 2d. by the Bifhop of Conftance, before Henry 1ft. father of Robert Earl of Glocefter was at man's eftate ; and in T. Wicke's Chron. under the year 1138, p. 27, it is faid, " Quod Roberto, &c. i. e. King Henry his father affigned to Robert the Earl, thofe fortified caftles of Briftol and Marlebreg, &c." The truth is, Robert was only a repairer of the caftle and rebuilder of fome part of it. — One of the Saxon Kings or Earls of Glocefter, moft probably according to the manu-fcript Edward fenr. was the firft builder, who, according to the Saxon annals anno 911, fent his army out of Weft Saxony and Mercia, which country the Danes had invaded ; he fought and routed them : Ecwills, Halfden and many of the pagan nobility and foldiers were flain, which being a decifive battle, brought the Danes under the power of the Saxon monarch : for though there were many excurfions and engagements afterwards, yet King Edward went on

taking

taking cities, building towns and caflles; and fecuring the habitations of the natives, left fortifications in fuch opportune places, that his conquefts were in no danger: but efpecially it was his care, " that if a town flood on the North fide of a river, he would place another on the South fide againft it, and *vice verfa*, that fo he might be able every where to put a ftop to the incurfions of the enemy."

In this he judged very well in building the caflle of Briftol on the North fide oppofite Redclift; by which means he provided well for the defence of Mercia and Weft Saxony, feparated as it was by the river Avon at this place. By this fituation it became a metropolis to thofe two potent kingdoms, which when united under one Saxon monarch under Egbert the 18th King of the Weft Saxons, in the year 800, foon induced thefe fucceeding Kings to enlarge the city; and in particular Edward the fon of Alfred the Great, to fortify it with a caflle on the Mercian fide, when before either on this or the Weft Saxon fide, or Redcliff, it was only defended by walls embattled and bul_ warks. — The remains of fuch a kind of fortification are ftill there to be feen: the embattled wall rebuilt on the old large and thick foundation of the old one being preferved to this day in the fame line and fituation: the two gates in it Redcliff and Temple were afterwards rebuilt in a modern ftyle; and the ancient tower Eflewyn, afterwards tower Harratzs being deftroyed, another building was erected there in its ftead.

This caflle was pleafantly fituated on a rifing ground at the Eaft part of the town, which was a great advantage to it as a fortrefs; it was bounded on the North by the river Froom, and on the South by the river Avon, having a deep trench, ftill called Caflle-Ditch on the Eaft fide, where an arm of the Froom embracing it difcharges itfelf into the Avon, moating it with water on that fide: on the Weft part it was defended by a deep trench or ditch, from Newgate acrofs the Avon near St. Peter's church, over the middle of which was a draw-bridge leading to the caflle-gate from the town, where was what I find called the Barbicana Caftri, near the Eaft part of St. Peter's church: it was fortified within with very ftrong walls embattled at the top, and had a fally-port, ftill fo called, leading into the prefent Queen-ftreet, built on an arch, which the river Froom flows through. Its out-works were very large, extending to Lawford's-Gate, which ftill retains its ancient Saxon name, *Hlaford's-Gate*,[*]

or

---

[*] Wm. Corbet of Chadfly, held a tenement at Lawford's-Gate for keeping it, 17 Edw. 2d. — Wm. of Worcefter, p. 210, fays, " Porta Lafford, &c. Lafford's-Gate was rebuilt anew by Walter Barnftaple, in the time of Edward 3d. or Richard 2d. where, at a ftone, end the bounds of the city.

or the Lord's gate, fo called from the Lords or Governors of the caftle. It ftands eaftward of the caftle, between which is a large fpace of ground now built into a wide ftreet, called the Old Market from a market of old being kept there, not only for the ufe of the town as may be fuppofed, but principally for the ufe of the garrifon in the caftle. The great avenue to the city out of Glocefterfhire was through this gate, over which in two nitches were placed two ftone figures reprefenting two of the Lord-Wardens of Briftol caftle; fuppofed to be Anglo-Saxon Kings or Earls of Glocefter; and a vellum maufcript of Rowley, *penes me*, tells whom they reprefent in thefe words: " Allwarde, a Saxon, was a fkyllyd carveller in ftone and woude: hee lyved yn the regne of Eldred, he carvelled the worke of the chappelle in the caftle and the ymageries wych thenne ftoode in fayde chapelle, of Ælle and Coër-nicus wardens of the caftle yn daies of yore: Robert of Glocefter removed them to the walle of the ynwarde towere, from whence the prefent Lorde Warden †hath ta'ne them: Mayftre Canynge fayne woulde have the fame to be in hys cabinette, but mie Lordis intent is to place them at the gate of the caftle or owtfyde of the waulls, as a goodlye fpecktalle for menne to behoulde and yn footh goodly fpecktalles they be, beyng featty'd and couroned in robes of eftate and paramented — Ne are enfayrer carvel than thofe of owre daies of durable ftone, and the depyfture of theyr faces beyng ftyll remaynynge by meanes of theyr beynge keepen from the unwere."

About the year 1130, Robert Earl of Glocefter, bafe fon of Henry 1ft. began to rebuild this ancient and ftrong caftle, which was now become greatly impaired; and it being the head of his barony of Glocefter, by ancient tenure, and a place of ftrength capable of being rendered almoft impregnable by fituation againft any military operations of thofe days, and perhaps forefeeing the ftorm that was likely to arife about the fucceffion to the crown, he, agree-able to a promife made to his father Henry 1ft. to fupport the intereft of his fifter Maud the Emprefs, and love to his nephew Henry 2d. then a child, fet about putting himfelf in a pofture of defence in cafe of exigency, and rebuilt this his caftle of Briftol in a very beautiful, ftrong, and defenfible manner. He firft removed many of the old buildings erefted by the Saxons; on the walls of which were difcovered rude paintings in water colours, which is called in Rowley's manufcripts " a coppie of peynftynges founde onne caftle walles ftondeyng ynne Godefrye's dayes enthoghten Saxonne." — A

Saxon

---

† The gate was taken down in 1776. And thefe ftone figures are removed hence, with two others from Newgate, to a caftle-like building at Briflington, a mile from Briftol, and are there to be now feen.

Saxon King is reprefented with a fcepter in his hand, and feveral men at work fixing large pieces of timber in the ground, others with hammers driving fpike nails, and faftening timber together, forming a kind of ladder-work, &c. in all probability it is a rude fketch of the firft walling the town by Brighthric, or building the caftle by Edw. fenior.

Many other antiquities were doubtlefs deftroyed in removing the ruins of the old caftle, but Earl Robert feems to have preferved as much of the ancient building as it was thought would not interfere with his grand defign : — " The outer walle of the caftle (fays Rowlie's manufcript) ftooden ynne the daies of Williamme Conqueroure ; the fquare caftle wythynne was ybuyldenne bie Robyrte Conneful of Glouceftre, as bee the croffe ynne the area, and the fmall ftronge holde whyche was thenne a watche towre, ecke the two watche towrettes wythynne the walle of the ould caftle. The ftronge holde yftondeth atte dyftaunce from the owtre walle of the oulde caftle onne boncke of Avon, havyng fyrfte a fquare walle of yttes own, and yn the fame twayne of buyld_ ynges of this make [meetynge at thefe [ ]." Vid. plate No. 11. — Hence it appears what Robert Earl of Glocefter did to the old caftle : — he preferved the old wall round it, and erefted the new buildings within, and the crofs; but as Rowlie does not mention the chapel as built by him, No. 3, this was probably part of the old caftle, as alfo the lodge of arrow-men, No. 4, both built in an older ftyle. From the plate alone we can form a juft idea of thefe buildings, it is engraved from drawings on vellum, preferved to this day, to which is added an explanation. The elevations or fronts, No. 1, 2, 3, 4, joined together, formed the infide of the fquare, and in the middle of this inner court ftood the crofs, No. 9. No. 5 was a moft elegantly enriched front to the outer court and the back part of No. 1, as No. 8 was the back part of No. 3, 7 of 2, 6 of 4. But as I have luckily the original explanation, that is the moft authentic as well as only defcription now extant, I fet it down in the very words of the manufcript: " The caftle foundatyonne as ytte ftoden ynne the daies of Rob. Conf. Gloceftre, wythe Geoffries logge as ytte then was:

Fyrfte, the Governours halle fronte.

2. The new-ybulden fronte.

3. The chapelle.

4. The logge of arrow-men.

5. The backe of the Governoures halle wythe toweres.

6, 7. Encrenelled fydes.

8. The backe of the chapelle.

9. The croffe.

10 The

10. The two watche towrettes
11. The fmalle ftronge-holde on the bancke of Avon, with the founda-
    tyonne of the ftronge holde near the old walle of the Myttyer caftle.
12. Geoffries logge.
13. The river Avon.
14. The river Froom.
15. Caftle Ditch.
16. Walle of the olde caftle.
17. Mote next the city, where was a draw-bridge."

The elevations of the buildings No. 1, 2, 5, are fo elegant in their defign,
the fronts fo noble and grand, and the windows fo neat and juftly proportioned, and the ornaments of No. 5 in particular fo very many and rich, that it
gives one fome idea of the good tafle of the rebuilder and founder, who was a
man of rare endowments of mind, and did honour to the age in which he
lived. — The ftatues in the front marked (5) reprefented fome of the great
men who fignalized themfelves in thofe days, or diftinguifhed this city by their
favour prefence and protection; fuppofed to be Henry the 1ft. at the bottom,
father of the founder; Robert Earl of Glocefter himfelf, Henry the 2d.
Robert Fitzhamon, and other Lords of Glocefter before him; Geoffrie Bifhop
of Conftance, and fome of the Anglo-Saxon Earls and Kings, Brightric, fenr.
Alfred and others. The arms at the top are Robert Earl of Glocefter's, and
Milo's Earl of Hereford.

The caftle of Briftol is thus defcribed by a writer in the days of King
Stephen, out of a manufcript in the collection of Archbifhop Laud: " Ex unâ
tamen regione, &c." *i. e.* " On one part of the city, where it is more expofed
and liable to be befieged, a large caftle rifes high with many banks, ftrength-
ened with a wall, bulwarks, towers, and other contrivances to prevent the
approach of befiegers; in which they get together fuch a number of vaffals
both horfe and foot, or rather I might fay of robbers and freebooters, that
they appear not only great and terrible to the lookers on, but truly horrible;
and it is fcarce to be credited: for collecting out of different counties and
regions, there is fo much the more numerous and freer conflux of them, the
more eafier under a rich Lord and the protection of a very ftrong caftle, they
have leave to commit whatever pleafes them beft in this rich country." — This
fhows the reafon of the via defenfiva, or defence ftreet, (vid. Bottener, p. 236,)
being made betwixt the caftle and the city, as a guard againft the depredations
of thefe freebooters, the licentious foldiery of the caftle, upon the peaceable
citizens, as the caftle was exempted from the jurifdiction of the city and its
                                                                    officers,

officers and under its own Governors, who were not always prefent to reftrain them, or might fometimes connive at the irregularity or infults of the military.

William of Worcefter gives the following account of the caftle of Briftol in the year 1480, and the dimenfions of the feveral parts. I fhall give the whole in Englifh, tranflated from the Latin, which is fo defective as to render it difficult to make fenfe of in fome places. He thus defcribes the walls and circuit of it, page 208, via a portâ, &c.

" The road from the gate of the entrance to the caftle of Briftol, (called in another place, p. 217, the gate of the deep ditch to the doors (*valvas*) of the entrance of the caftle,) is near the Eaft part of the church of St. Peter ; and you go on marching by the wall of the ditch of the walls of the caftle through Newgate and along the ftreet called the Weer, and over Weer-bridge, leaving the watering-place on the left hand, and making a circuit by the wall of the caftle-ditch towards the South, near the crofs in the Old Market ; thus continuing to a great ftone about a yard high of freeftone, erected at the extremity of the bounds of the city of Briftol ; fo proceeding on to the gate of the firft or eaftern entrance of the caftle at the Weft part of St. Philip's church, which is at the end of a lane behind the Old Market ; this contains in a circuit of one part of the tower and walls of the caftle 420 fteps." At p. 217, he fays, " the whole circuit contains 2100 fteps." — *N. B.* His fteps vary, but are about 21 inches. —— In another place he mentions it, p. 259, in Englifh thus : " The quantite of the dongeon of the caftell of Briftol afrer the informatione of . . . . . . porter of the caftell, the tour called the dongeon ys in thyknefs at fote 25 pedes, and at the ledyng place under the leede cuveryng 9 feet and dimid ; and yn length Efte and Weft 60 pedes, and North and South 45 pedes, with fowre toures ftandyng uppon the fowre corners : and the hyeft toure called the mayn, *i. e.* myghtyeft * toure above all the fowre toures ys 5 fethym hygh abofe all the fowre toures, and the wallys be yn thyknefs there 6 fote. Item, the length of the caftelle wythynne the wallys Efte and Weft ys 180 virgæ. Item, the brede of the caftelle from the North to the South, wyth the grete gardyn, that is from the water-gate to the mayng rounde of the caftelle to the walle northward toward the Blak-frerys, 100 yerdes. Item, a baftyle lyeth fouthward beyond the water-gate, conteynyth yn length 60 virgæ. Item, the length from the bullwork at the utter gate by Seynt Phelippes chyrch yerde, conteynyth 60 yerdes large. Item, the yerdys called fparres of the halle royalle, conteynyth yn length about 45 fete

of

---

* This term is ufed in the manufcript of Rowlie in the explanation before at fig. 11.

of hole pece. Item, the brede of every fparre at fore conteynyth 12 onch
and 8 onches.''

And in another place, p. 269, he again defcribes in Latin: " Porticus
introitus aulæ, &c." — The porch or entrance into the hall is ten yards long,
with an arched volt over, at the entrance of the great hall.

" The inner entry into the porch of the hall is 140 fteps, meaning the
fpace and length betwixt the gate of the caftle walls and the walls of the area
of the utterward; the length of the hall is 36 yards, or 52 or 54 fteps, the
bredth of the hall is 18 yards or 26 fteps; the heigth of the walls outfide the
hall is 14 feet, as I meafured them; the hall formerly very magnificent in
length bredth and heigth, is all tending to ruin. The windows in the hall
double, the heigth (de 11 days) contains 14 feet. The length of the rafters of
the hall is 32 feet, the Prince's chamber on the left fide of the King's hall is 17
yards, in bredth 9 yards and has two pillars made with great beams but very
old. The length of the front before the hall with . . is 18 yards. The
length of the marble flone table is 15 feet, fituated in another part of the hall
for the King's table there fitting. The length of the tower in the Eaft part of
it is 36 yards, its bredth at the weftern and South part is 30 yards. The length
of the utter-ward of the caftle from the middle gate, and lately feparated from the
inner ward of the chapple, the principal chamber of the hall is 160 fteps. The
length of the firft entrance to the caftle by the gate is 40 fteps, that is from the
ftreet of the caftle by entering at the firft gate of the caftle into the utterward.
The chapple in the utterward or firft ward is dedicated in honor of St. Martin,
but in devotion to St. John the Baptift, a monk of St. James ought to celebrate
the office every day, but does it but Sunday, Wednefday and Friday. There
is another very magnificent chapple for the King and his lords and ladies,
fituate in the principal ward on the North fide of the hall, where beautiful
chambers were built, but are now naked and uncovered, void of planchers or
roofing. The dwelling of the officers of the kitchen belong to the inner ward
near the hall on the left fide, that is on the South part of the hall. The
dwelling of the conftable or keeper is fituate in the firft or utterward on the
South part of the magnificent tower, but is all pulled down and ruinous, which
is great pity.''

According to William of Worcefter's meafurement of the caftle, being 540
feet from Eaft to Weft, or 180 yards; and 300 feet or 100 yards broad from
the North (from the garden to the water of Froom) to the South; it ftood
upon an area containing 3 acres 2 roods and 35 perches exactly, (3 acres
and $\frac{3}{4}$ wanting 5 perches;) whether the great garden within the Baftyle, (an

embattled

embattled wall 60 yards long running towards St. Philip's church-yard,) was part of this ground, is uncertain. In the grant of the caſtle by Cha. 1ſt. to the corporation, who purchaſed it of him in 1626, mention is made of " all that cloſe lying without the ditch of the caſtle, called by the name of the King's Orchard, containing two acres." — If the Governor's or " Gonſtable's hall, with the magnificent tower, was all pulled down and ruinous" in William of Worceſter's time, 1480, it is no wonder his deſcription is ſo very defective and gives ſo poor an account of this grand caſtle.

John Leland, who viſited it about the 26th year of Henry 8th, and ſaw it in its decay, thus deſcribes it : " In the caſtle be two courtes. In the utter courte, as in the northe-weſt part of it, is a great dungeon-tower, made as it is ſaid of ſtone browghte oute of Cane in Normandye, by the redde Erle of Gloceſtar. A praty churche and muche loggyng in two area : on the ſouthe ſyde of it a great gate, a ſtone bridge, and three bullewarks in *lœva ripâ ad oſ-tium frai.* There be manie towres yet ſtandynge in both the courtes, but alle tendith to ruine. The caſtle and moſte parte of the towne by northe ſtandith upon a grownde metely eminent, betwixt the ryvers Avon and Fraw, alias Froom." Itin. vol. vii. p. 84. 2d edit.

If the caſtle, ſo large and beautiful a building, as deſcribed in the manu_ſcript, entituled, Rowleie; of ſuch extent and meaſurement, as noted by William of Worceſter, was ruinous in the time of the latter, 1480, it is no wonder, that Leland, in Henry 8th's. time, almoſt 100 years after, ſhould find it in decay, and ſay of it, " all tendith to ruine."

It is left to the candid reader to compare the deſcriptions above of the caſtle, and its ſtate and condition at different times. That, called Rowleie's, was either a drawing of it in his own time, or taken from one made long be-fore, when in its perfect ſtate; which is moſt probable, as he repreſents himſelf as a great collector of ancient drawings of buildings, churches, chapels, and the like for himſelf or friend Mr. Canynge. Though this caſtle agrees in ſhape and external diſpoſition with ſome other old caſtles, yet it is more deco-rated with images, ornaments, and tracery work, and in a finer ſtile than is commonly ſeen in ſuch buildings; which makes it appear as if ſome other decorations had been added, eſpecially if compared with a part of the old caſtle, of which there is a print extant at the ſide of an old plan of Briſtol, by Millard, of the year 1672, wherever he got it : a copy of which is here alſo pre-ſented to the reader, together with the ground plot of the pentagonal fort on St. Michael's-hill, with a ſcale of yards; both of which are too curious to be omitted in a work of this kind, eſpecially as this preſents us with a view of part of

Briſtol

Briſtol caſtle in the later times, as it ſtood in the time of the grand rebellion in 1641. (See the plate.) But that in its original ſtate it was very beautiful may be collefted from William of Worceſter's defcription and Leland's, and from what Robert, the rhyming monk of Gloceſter, fays of Robert Earl of Gloceſter's improved building of it.

" And Briſtow throw hys wyfe was alfo hys,
    And he brogt to gret ſta the towne as he yut ys,
    And rerde ther an caſtel myd the noble tour,
    That of alle the tours of Engelonde ys yhelde the floure." p. 433.

It is remarkable, befides the figures in the front of the Governor's hall, there are the arms reprefented of Robert Earl of Gloceſter near the top, carved in the ſtone, G. three bow-reſts or. with fingular propriety; alfo G. two bends, one arg. the other or. which were born by Milo Fitzwarren, Earl of Hereford, whofe father is faid by Sir Wm. Dugdale to have been Conſtable of England, and to have been a builder (rather rebuilder or repairer) of the caſtle of Briſtol; and the fon * was in ſtrift league with Robert and of the Emprefs Maud's party at Briſtol, and affiſted him in keeping his caſtles in favour of Maud.

A drawing being found reprefenting Robert the Earl armed cap-a-pee, it is here preferved in the fame plate with the caſtle which he is faid fo elegantly to have repaired.

There was formerly a chapel or church, dedicated to St. Mary Magdalen, poffibly the "praty church," mentioned by Leland above, (or one of thofe two mentioned by William of Worceſter) of which I have the following old account, in a vellum manufcript, by Rowlie:

" Seynſte Marie Magdalenes chapele. — This chapele was ybuylden bie Ælle, wardenne of the caſtle, neere Ælle-gate, fythence cleped New-gate ; yn thys chapele was yfworne a treatye between Goddwynne Erle or Abthane of Kente, Harold eſtfoons Kynge of Englande, Leofinus, hys brodres, and oder nobles of the londe Ælle, the founder theereof, was a manne myckle ſtronge yn vanquyſheynge the Danes: hys ymagerie ynne ſtone whylom ſtooden yn fayde chapele, and ys nowe atte the greete yate. Hee dyd ybuylde the fame in Dccccxviii. Hee dyde of hys woundes, gotten ynne honourable combatte ynne Bryſtowe caſtle. Sayde chapele ys nowe ynne rewyn."

If

---

* Leland, Collcft. vol. i. p. 41. Milo conſtabulorius, anno 1141, apud Briſtoldum pofitus jamque confulatus honorem adeptus; rediens a Briſtoldo obtulit fuper altare lanthony leunculum ,chalcedonicum : teſtes primæ donationis imperatrix Robert. Comes Gloceſtriæ, &c.

If in ruin fo long ago, it is no wonder we can fee fo little trace of it at this day. It is fomewhat extraordinary, that the figures of Ælle and Coer_niens, that ftood in the faid chapel, afterwards at Lawford's-gate, have not only efcaped hitherto uninjured the devouring hand of time, but are now preferved as a curiofity, by a Briftol gentleman, to adorn a very handfome gate at a Gothic, caftle-like building, erected at Briflington his country feat, in the neighbourhood of this city. There were two other figures carved in ftone at Newgate in niches, which feemed to have been removed formerly from the caftle adjoining to that place; probably at the time of its demolition: That of Robert Earl of Glocefter, much abufed, has a fmall model in ftone of a kind of caftle in his hand, which he fo much repaired as to give him the honour of being a founder; and the other of Godfrey Bifhop of Conftance better preferved, has a moft venerable afpect, long beard, with a chalice in one hand, in the act of taking off the cover with the other, a proper emblem in the hand of a bifhop. There are few remains of Briftol caftle now extant: on the fouth fide in many places are to be feen parts of the old wall, bound_ing the dwelling-houfes there, and Gothic windows: and on the eaft fide are two Saxon arches with an arched roof in a room there, or poffibly an en_trance; it has the appearance of a church or chapel, but now makes part of the houfe of a cooper, and is his fhop.

Not far diftant from the caftle without Lawford's-gate is a place called Barton Regis, giving name to the hundred: it was fo called, becaufe a farm or barton in the King's hands to fubfift the caftle, and demefne lands there re_ferved for its ufe; the caftle itfelf after the Conqueft in the year 1200 being a royal demefne, before that it was appendent to the honour and barony of Glocefter, and as the lawyers fpeak, the *caput honoris*.

It appears from Domefday-book, " that this bertune was taxed at fix hydes [*] t. William 1ft. there were forty-two plow tillages whereof three were in demefne, (I fuppofe for the ufe of the caftle) : this manor together with Briftow paid a yearly rent of one hundred and ten marks to the King, and the burgeffes re_turned that Bifhop G. had thirty-three marks [†] and one mark of gold." A Norman mark (fays Rapin) was then valued at 13s. 4d. by which the fum amounts to 73 l. 6 s. 8 d. fterling, and the thirty-three marks to Bifhop

---

[*] A hyde of land, according to the manufcript of Joannes Glaftonienfis, was 160 acres, a fardel 10, a virgate 40, a hyde 160, a fee 640 acres.

[†] This Bifhop G. was Godfrey Bifhop of Conftance, cuftos of the caftle, who had 28 l. an annual fum paid him, and referved in after grants to all the conftables of the caftle.

G. is 28l. within a few fhillings, the annual fum paid to the conftables of the caftle.

The following is copied out of the original Domefday-book. " In Bertune apud Brifton erant vi hid. In d'nio iii car. & xxii vill'i & xv bord. cum xxv car. Ibi x fervi. & xviii colib'ti h'ntes xiiii car. Ibi 11 molini de xxvii folid. Q'do Rogerius recep. hoc m. de Rege inveni ibi ii hid & ii car. in dominio & xvii vil'i & xxiii bord. cum xxi car. Ibi iv fervos & xiii colib'tos cum iii car.

In uno membro ejufdem m. Manefgodesfelle-vi boves in do'nio.

De eadem t'ra ten. Ecc'la de Briflow iii hid. & i car. habet ibi. Unus Rad-chenift. ten. i hid. & h't i car & iv bord. cum i car. Hoc m. & Briflou red-dit regi cx mark. argenti; burgenfes d'nt q'd Ep's G. h't xxxiii mark. argenti & unam mark. auri p'ter firmam regis."

This extenfive manor of Barton Regis (including Kingfwood) is now di-vided among feveral Lords, the Duke of Beaufort, Archer of Barr's-Court, (formerly Newton,) Efq; —— Chefter, —— Bragg, —— Blathwait, —— Crefwic, Efqrs. as will be feen below in the parochial hiftory of St. Philip's.

The three hydes of land and one carucate the church of Briftou is faid in Domefday-book to hold in the manor of Bertun Regis in William the Conqueror's time, are now fcarce to be found, nor to be gueffed at. — The manor of Blackfworth there indeed was part of the endowment of St. Auguftin's monaftery afterwards by Robert Fitzharding.

Having now fhewn the antiquity, foundation, fite and dimenfions of the caftle, and given a general defcription of it, I proceed next to an hiftorical account of its Governors, Conftables or Wardens from time to time, noting the facts and extraordinary occurrences which have rendered it famous in hiftory.

About the year 920 ELLA was Lord of the caftle, and gained many fignal victories againft the Danes with his Briftowans, particularly at Watchet; though our Saxon chronicles yet printed have taken little notice of this heroic champion againft the Danes, nor indeed of the caftle over which he prefided. The following old poëm was made to the memory of this chieftain about the year 1460, and tranfcribed from an old parchment in the hand-writing like that in ufe in Henry the 6th.'s time, and fubfcribed T. Rowleie.

SONGE

SONGE toe ELLA. *

O thou or what remaynes of thee, Ella the Darlynge of futuritie,
Lette this mie fonge bolde as thie Courage bee, as everlaftynge

to pofteritie ; Whenne Daciaes Sonnes, whofe lockes of bloude
Red hue Lyke Kynge-Cuppes burftynge wythe the mornynge dewe,

Arraunged in drear Arraie, upon the letthalle daie, fpread·
far ande wyde on Watchettes fhore, there dydft thou furyoufe

Stande ande bie thie burlie Hande, Befprenged all the
Meeds wythe gore, drawne bie thie anlace felle, downe

to the depthes of Helle, Thoufands of Dacians wente,
Briftowanes Menne of myghte, Ydar'de the bloudye fyghte

And acted deeds full Quente — O thou wher'ere (thie bones
at Refte,) thie fpryte to baunte delyghteth befte, Whetherre

upon the bloude embrewed plaine, or where thou kennft
from farre the Horrid Crie of Warre, or feeft fome

Mountaine made of Corfe of Slayne, or feeft the
hatched Steede, yprauncynge oer the Meede, ande

Neyghe to bee amenge the poynted fpeeres, or ynn
Blacke Armour Stalke arounde ymbattled Bryftowe

once thie Orounde, And glowe ardurous onne the Caftle
Steers, or fierie rounde the Mynftere Glare, Stylle

lette Bryftowe be made thie care, Garde it fromme
foemenne and confumynge fyre, Lyke Avones ftreem

enfyrke ytte rounde, ne lette a flame enharme the
grounde, Tylle inne one flame alle the whole worlde expyre.

* Lord of the Caftle of Brigftowe ynne Daies of yore.

Turgot obferves that Ella died of his wounds in Briftol caftle, and from
hence it appears he was alfo buried in the chapel he had there built: and
of his memorial ftone I have an old drawing with his figure, &c. above
defcribed with the name Æ ΓΓE over the head, as royally defcended crowned, and with two keys in his hands as governor of the caftle, and a chain
round his neck; it was in the ruinous ftate of the chapel faid to be removed

and

and preferved by Mr. Canynge afterwards. There are in manufcript the arms of Ella blazoned thus, in Saxon: Seeld a græfen, a fhield with croffes patee all over the field. Ella was a name of note in the Saxon times, and is mentioned by Lambard, Top. Dict. p. 106, under Ellandon as " one of the firft Saxon capitains," and as giving name to that place and to Ellesfield, and to Ellecroft a place near York.

A bridge near the Caftle of Briftol is in ancient deeds called Elle-bridge, and the ftreet next it Elle-bridge-ftreet, now corruptly Ellbroad-ftreet, and there is a place near Watchet called Ellworthy to this day, not improbably named from the fame chief who diftinguifhed himfelf fo much there.

2. Coernicus fucceeded Ella in the government of Briftol caftle : we know nothing more of him than what is mentioned before by Turgot, p. 32.

3. The following two lord wardens of the caftle we have little account of, except having their names handed down to us as fuch by Turgotus, Harward and Smallaricus, 4. Vincent, 5. Adelwyn, 6. to them fucceeded Egwyn, to him 7. Aylwardus; called Aylward Sneaw (from his fair complexion) * he was defcended from Edward fenr. the founder of the caftle, and not improbably his natural fon, of whom Leland gives the following account out of a Latin record of the Antiquities of Tewkfbury, — " Anno Dom. 930, Sub Ethelftano &c." i. e. " In the year 930 Aylward Meaw (or Sneaw) fo called from his white complexion, of the race of Edward fenior King of the Weft Saxons, was a man valiant in arms under King Ethelftan. This Ailward for himfelf and his wife Algiva in the time of Ethelred and Dunftan the Bifhop erected a fmall monaftery in honor of God, St. Mary and St. Bartholomew on his own ground at Cranbourne about the year 980. He died on the calends of January Anno Dom. .... His fon Algar with his wife Algiva fucceeded to his fortunes by right of inheritance. The 8th governor of the caftle was Adelbryghte. The 9th Amftuarde, and 10th the above mentioned Algarre were fucceffive governors of Briftol caftle : 11th Leofwyn, fon of Earl Godwyn, in the life time of Algar, feems by the great power of his father and family to have got the government of the caftle of Briftol, and Edward the Confeffor by a particular charter granted and confirmed it to him in the 9th year of his reign 1049, which being very curious I have inferted before p. 33, as preferved in the original manufcript of Turgot's account of Briftol and no where elfe.

Upon

---

* A gate called Aylward's Gate, fince Pithay Gate, formerly preferved the name here of this Saxon nobleman, the ftreet alfo called Aylward-ftreet. — Botoner, p. 184.

Upon Earl Godwin and his fon's being obliged to leave the kingdom, and having forfeited the King's favour, Briftol caftle feems to have reverted to its right owner, who was Briftric the brother of Algar, lord of the caftle before Leofwyn. During Leofwyn's holding the caftle was that very memorable tranfaftion of Godwin and his family and many of the nobility entering here into a folemn league againft the King in the year 1050, for fiding fo much with the French, introducing its language and laws, &c.

12. Briftric fucceeded to Algar's poffeffions, he was a Saxon nobleman of large eftates in the county of Glocefter, of which he was Earl, and confequently had the caftle of Briftol of right, being part of that barony.* He was a principal man in his country, and employed in an embaffy to the court of Baldwin Earl of Flanders, where Maud daughter of that Earl fettled her affeftions on him, but not meeting a fuitable return (a crime not to be forgiven by the ladies) fhe meditated revenge, and being afterwards married to William Duke of Normandy, who conquered Harold and got the crown of England, refolved to gratify her vindiftive temper by ftirring up her hufband againft Earl Birtrick, whofe power and large poffeffions fhe might reprefent as dangerous in the hands of a fubjeft: and her artful infinuations met with but too much fuccefs, for the King at that time bent upon degrading even to ruin all the rich and powerful Englifh barons, caufed the unhappy and innocent Birtric to be arrefted at his manor of Hanley by Salifbury, and fent a prifoner to Winchefter, where he died without children many years after, 7th Hen. 1ft. Leland thus reprefents it, (vol. 6. p. 85,) " Inne the later reygne of the Danes and Edwarde the Confeffour was Ælwardus Meaw Erle of Glocefter, and he was countid as foundir of Craneburne: Ailwerdus had a funne callyd Briftrice Erle of Glocefter, aboute the tyme of the cummyng of Duke Wyllyam of Normandie ynto England. Matildis, wife to Wm. the Conqueror, afked Briftrice yn gifte of her hufband, and having hym put hym in the caftle of Hanley befides Sarefbyrie, and there he dyid. Sum fay Matildis would have had hym afore Duke Wylliam to her bufband, but he refufing it had after hard favor at her handes." All his eftates, among which was the caftle of Briftol, the head of his barony, were feized by the crown, and fettled by the King on Maud his wife:—As Leland obferves, " King William gave the preferement of the counte of Glocefter onto his wife Matilde." She had it till her death the 1ft of November 1084.

This

* His name is varioufly wrote, Briftric, Brightric, and Birtric; the laft feems to be right from the Saxon derivation, Birt or Birth and ric, i. r. rich by birth or inheritance, as he was " viro prædiviti," fays Leland.

This Brictric, fon of Aylward Meaw, favoured much the city of Briftol, and Mr. Canynge preferved in his cabinet " a ftonen bed belonging to Erle Brictric, formerly kept in tower Errys." He was defcended from Brictric King of the Weft Saxons; and in Mr. Canynge's collection of antiquities was " an hyftory of Brythricus King of Weft Sexonnes, and annales from hym to Brythrycus the Erle:" but now irrecoverably loft, and faid to be wrote by Turgot a Saxon monk, and continued by Rowlie.

William the Conqueror held the caftle of Briftol fome time in his own hands, and at the time of his death, 1087. 13. Godfrey Bifhop of Conftance appears next to have the cuftody or poffeffion of it, either by grant from the King, or Queen Matilda during her life; being appointed Vice Comes of Glocefter-fhire, and the deputed or Lieutenant-governor of the Lordfhip of Briftol and its caftle; or by feizure on the death of William 1ft. to keep it for Robert his fon the lawful heir to the crown. In the year 1072, when the great caufe about the primacy of Canterbury over York was determined at Windfor in the prefence of the King and his nobles, the inftrument was figned there by all prefent, among whom is, " Ego Gosfrydus Conftantienfis Epifcopus unus ex primatibus Angliæ confenfi."

In Thorp's Regiftrum Roffenfe, fol. p. 28, is the following, which fhews Godfry to have been a great man in thofe days: " Placito inter Lanfrankum Epifcopum & Odonem Epifcopum Baionenfem. Huic placito interfuit Goffridus Epifcopus Conftantienfis, qui in loco Regis fuit & Juftitiam illam tenuit." About 1072, this Godfrey Bifhop of Conftance, or Coutance, was a monk brought over from Normandy with Theodwin, whom King William had promoted to the abby of Ely; and under him having the chief government of the affairs of the monaftery, was upon the death of Theodwin 1075, ordered by the King to take upon himfelf the adminiftration of the abby till the King fhould fix upon a fucceffor, which was in about feven years. Godfrey was prefent in the year 1080 with Odo Bifhop of Baieux, and Haymo the King's fewer, (Dapifer,) and other barons legati regis, at an affembly at Rentford, to enquire into the lands belonging to the church of Ely. The figure of Godfry is ftill preferved in the Ely table, a painting of great antiquity hung up in Ely palace, in which are the figures of the monks of Ely, and the knights fent down to be quartered on them by William the Conqueror, with their arms; in the firft compartment of this picture are Opfalus Miles Baliftarum Dux, cum Godfrido monacho, a fhield between the two heads, f. arg. plain crofs gules. If this painting or Ely table fhould be older than the 14th century, which is the utmoft extent in which oil painting is placed by Mr. Walpole in his anec-

dotes

dotes on painting in England, vol. 1. p. 24, it will fet afide all the received opinions hitherto on that fubject.

The time that thefe knights were withdrawn from Ely fixes this event to the time of Godfrey's adminiſtration, for they were called away and fent from Ely into Normandy on the infurrection of Robert the King's fon, who in 1077 was endeavouring to feize the dukedom of Normandy.—Godfrey after this in 1081 was by the King promoted to be Abbot of Malmfbury.—(Vid. Bentham's Hiſtory of the Church of Ely, p. 106, 1771, and appendix p. 5.)

We find alfo that in the year 1088, the laſt year of William the Conqueror, among the witneſſes of the grants and confirmation to the monaſtery of St. Mary at York, of Stephan the abbot and Wm. Rufus, was Godefridus Biſhop of Conſtance, " qui eo tempore Northumbrorum confulatum regebat," (fays Leland in Collect. v. 1. p. 26.)

What a great man in his time and how much favoured by his King this Biſhop of Conſtance was, appears from the numerous and large grants of lands he held. Orderic vitalis, l. 4, fays, " Galfridus, &c." that Galfrid Biſhop of Conſtance obtained from the gift of King William 280 villages, (villas,) which we commonly call manors, (a manendo,) from remaining or refiding upon them, and that the Weſt Saxons of Dorfet and Somerfet having affaulted Montacute, (Montemacutum,) received a check from this prelate at the head of the men of Monmouthſhire, (Guentani,) London and Salifbury. Under the year 1070 he calls him, magiſter militum. He ferved his fovereign faithfully in feveral battles againſt the Danes and Engliſh, and he affiſted at a council at St. Paul's 1079, and at the Conqueror's funeral : he died himfelf in 1093.

This Godfrey the Biſhop being in the intereſt of Robert William the Conqueror's eldeſt fon, with his nephew Robert de Mowbray, in 1088 haſtened to Briſtol to fecure the caſtle, then a ſtrong and defenfible fortrefs, for the next lawful fucceſſor, and to keep it as a place of arms and an afylum on their declaring in his favour. It is thus related in the Saxon Chronicle, Gib. edit. p. 193, " Godfrith Bifcop and Rodbeard a munbrœg, ferdon to Bricgſtowe and hergodon, and brohton to tham caſtell the Hergunge." That is, " Biſhop Godfrey, and Robert a diſturber of the peace, went to Brigſtowe and committed fpoils and brought their booty into the caſlle." Radulphus de Diceto exprefly calls it the bifhop's own caſtle, " in caſtello suo Briſtoa." Our Engliſh chroniclers in that year, 1088, have not omitted mentioning this tranfaction.

On

On this combination in favour of Robert being defeated, who fold his birth-right, or rather compounded with his younger brother Wm. Rufus, for the trifling penfion of 3000 marks per ann. for the prefent, and affurance of the crown after his deceafe, our Lord Warden of the caftle, the Bifhop of Conftance, retreated into Normandy as fuppofed, being not heard of afterwards, leaving behind him here a lafting memorial of himfelf in a ftone carved figure lately in being in a niche on the left going through Newgate, removed thither out of the caftle, and fince to Briflington. — Duke Robert was through his credulity and eafy difpofition cozened of his right of fucceffion on the death of his brother Wm. Rufus by his other brother Henry 1ft. who not only deprived him of his crown here, but at length of his dukedom of Normandy alfo, which having fought unjuft occafion of invading, the Duke was conquered and taken prifoner, and fent into England; hiftorians fay, he was fhut up in Cardiff caftle, where he remained in prifon till his death; but a vellum manufcript roll (penes me) mentions " his leaving his gauntelette in Brigftowe caftelle," which was preferved afterwards to later times, and at length came into the poffeffion of the great Mr. Canynge, who placed it in his cabinet. He was probably firft fent to Briftol and removed afterwards to Cardiff, to be more out of the way, as the people had an affection for him. — I have a drawing of a ftone figure in a praying pofture once kept in the caftle church, under which is infcribed, " Carne of Roberte Courtehofe mynde yn caftelle chyrche." This figure is ftill extant, being fixed in a wall at the upper end of the North aile of St. Philip's church. And it may be inferred from this, that it is not improbable but that Robert was not only a prifoner in Briftol caftle, but might alfo have loft his eye-fight there by the hot brafs bafon which was ordered to be applied to his eyes to take away his fight by his cruel brother, to prevent his efcape; and then it is likely was fent to die in Cardiff caftle in a remote place. The Saxon Chronicle, p. 230, 17. mentions it clearly, that in 1126, " the King permitted his brother Robert to be taken away from Roger Bifhop of Sarefbury, and committed him to his fon Robert Earl of Glocefter, and fuffered him to be brought to Bricftowe and there to be kept in ward in the caftel," adding that this was all done by advice of his daughter and of David King of Scotland.

14. In 1089, Wm. Rufus, in confideration of the great fervices done him by Robert Fitz Haymon his gentleman of the bedchamber, and an active opponent to the Norman faction flirted up in favour of his brother Robert, gave him the honour and Earldom of Glocefter; which with the caftle of Briftol appendent to it he held till his death in 1107, with all the liberties

formerly

formerly. enjoyed by Birtric: he was a great man of his days, left no male iffue, only four daughters. Mabile the eldeft King Henry 1ft. married to his natural fon Robert, which he had by Nefta, daughter of Rhees Prince of South Wales; and unwilling to divide the honour of Glocefter amongft all the daughters of Robert Fitz Haymon, conferred the whole on the eldeft and his fon Robert, and created him Earl of Glocefter.

15. In 1110 Robert was Lord of Briftol caftle by this marriage and creation, being then about 20 years of age.

This great heirefs Mabile, whom he had efpoufed, was a very lofty dame; the monk of Glocefter expreffeth King Henry's courting this lady his ward for his fon Robert in fome curious old rhymes, and her refufal of him at firft, like a true lady of quality, for want of a firname of honour and diftinction.*

> Sir, fheo faide, ich wote your herte upon mee is
> More for myne heritage, than for myfelfe I wis:
> And fuch heritage as Ich have, hit were to me greet fhame
> To take a Lorde, but hee badde any furname : —
> Damofeill, quoth the Kyng, thou feeft well in this cafe,
> Sir Robert Fitz Hayme thi fader's name was : —
> As fayre a name he fhall have, as you may fee,
> Sir Robert le Fitz Roy fhail his name be : —
> Damofeill, he fay'd, thi Lorde fhall have a name
> For him and for hys beires fayre withoute blame ;
> For Robert Erle of Gloucefter, hys name fhall be and is,
> Hee fhall be Erle of Gloucefter, and his heires I wis :
> Inne this forme, quoth fhee, Ich wole, that all my thyng be his, &c.

The whole may be feen in Sandford's Genealog. Hiftory, p. 46.

Thus was the lady's fcruples removed, and Robert's fortune and greatnefs accomplifhed 1109, of this he fhewed himfelf highly worthy in the future conduct of his life. He was the moft valiant captain of his age, and in requital of his father's bounty was very active in defending the rights of Maud the Emprefs and her fon, afterwards Henry 2d. againft Stephen, who ufurped the crown, to whom he proved a continual terror, and he laid the ground-work of all the fucceffes in that war. He was tutor and guardian to the young Prince, and having fortified his caftle of Briftol againft Stephen, he brought him hither as to a place of fafety, and put him to fchool there with the chief

C c   men's

* This ftory is told in nearly the fame manner at the end of Langtoft's Chronicle, v. 2. by Ileam, p. 664.

men's fons of the town. Lord Littleton * thus mentions the fact, and finely characterifes both the tutor and his ward: " He (the Prince, afterwards Henry 2d.) was carried to Briftol, and continued there four years under the care of his uncle, (Robert Earl of Glocefter,) who trained him to fuch exercifes as were moft proper to form his body for war, and in thofe ftudies which might embellifh and ftrengthen his mind. The Earl of Glocefter himfelf had no inconfiderable tincture of learning, and was the patron of all who excelled in it; † qualities rare at all times in noblemen of his high rank, but particularly in an age when knowledge and valour were thought incompatible, and not to be able to read was a mark of nobility. This truly great man broke through that cloud of barbarous ignorance, and after the example of his father Henry 1ft. enlarged his underftanding and humanized his mind by a commerce with the mufes, which he affiduoufly cultivated even in courts and camps. — The fame love of fcience and literature he infufed into his nephew. — The four years ‡ which he now paffed in England (at Briftol) laid the foundation of all that was afterwards moft excellent in him; for his earlieft impreffions were taken from his uncle (Robert), who not only in learning but in all other perfections, in magnanimity, valour, prudence, and all moral virtues was the beft example that could be propofed to his imitation."

Such is the excellent character of this valiant Governor and Lord of Briftol caftle. — In that memorable battle of Lincoln fought the 25th December 1140, § King Stephen was taken prifoner by Robert Earl of Glocefter, who fent him to the Emprefs Matilda then at Glocefter, from whence fhe ordered the King to Briftol caftle, where he was honorably treated for fome time and kept in a fafe but gentle confinement; but by the private inftigation of the Emprefs or fome of her party, the King, fome fay, was afterwards laid in irons under the pretence of being feen beyond the bounds of his confinement. ‖ ——

Robert

* Hiftory of the life of Henry 2d. v. 2. p. 58. 3d edit.

† Wm. Malmfb. dedicated his work to him.

‡ In Holingfhead it is faid, " he was at Briftol four years, being committed to one Matthews a fchoolmafter, to be inftructed and trained up in civil behaviour," p. 55.

§ Robert's fpeech before the battle is preferved in Speed's hiftory, breathing courage, tempered with great prudence and conduct.

‖ Lel. Coll. ex Rogero Hoveden. Anno 1137, Robertus Conful filius Henrici regis nothus tenuit contra Stephanum Reg. fortifimum caftellum quod dicitur Briftow, & aliud quod vocatur Slede. Anno 1140, Stephanus captus ad imperatricem ducitur & in Turri de Briftow captivus ponitur. —— Lel. Stephanus Oderæ in Vinculis — Robertus captus, in cujus Turri Rex captivus erat, cujus folâ captione rex liberari poterat. Igitur abfolutus eft uterque. Step. obfeffam Matildam intra quoddam caftellum & ad deditionem coactam eâ indifcretâ animi fimplicitate ad Briftouam libere ire permifit. Col. v. 3. p. 31.

Robert the Earl was afterwards taken prifoner himfelf near Winchefter, and was efteemed an equal ranfom for the King, who for his greater dignity was releafed firft, after nine months captivity, on the feaft of All-Saints 1141, the Queen and one of her fons, with two principal lords of that party being kept in the caftle of Briftol as hoftages, from the time of the King's being difmiffed from thence till the Earl was alfo releafed and returned to his friends at Briftol, when he fet free the Queen and other hoftages. — This war was now refumed with various fucceffes and difappointments on both fides; but in the year 1146 the Earl of Anjou earneftly defired the Earl of Glocefter would fend back his fon Henry, who then had been abfent from him at Briftol four years, to which the Earl of Glocefter, though unwillingly, confented; but they parted to meet no more, for Robert the Earl died of a fever the 31ft of Auguft or the beginning of September 1147, to the great lofs of Matilda and injury to her affairs, for he was the moft virtuous man confeffedly of thofe times; and his virtue was fuch that even thofe times could not corrupt it: — It was thought he might have attained the crown himfelf, the nation being equally grown tired of Matilda and of Stephen, but he thought it lefs glorious to be a King, than to preferve his fidelity and honour inviolate.

This Earl added fo many new, ftrong and fine buildings to his caftle of Briftol, and rendered it a fortrefs fo much more defenfible, that he may be efteemed juftly a founder, and was thus complimented in a ftone ftatue " formerly preferved in the inner afforciaments of the caftle," then at its demolition fixed up at Newgate on the right hand oppofite the Bifhop of Conftance, fince removed to a gentleman's feat at Briflington. He was buried in the choir at St. James's priory in Briftol, which he had founded in 1129.

Milo Earl of Hereford was appointed to the cuftody of the caftle of Briftol in the wars with King Stephen 1141, where he made great repairs and improvements, as appears by his arms on the top of the governors hall-front G. two bends, one or, the other argent, along with Robert Earl of Glocefter's. — After it was taken Sir Bartholomew de Currifhall (whence the Cheurchill or Churchill family) held it for King Stephen.

16. The next Lord of Briftol caftle was William, eldeft fon and heir of the above Robert: Leland fays, " Robertus Conful had a funne caullid Wyllam that was Erle after him: — Wyllyam dyed yn Brighteftow caftell, and wyllid to be buryid by hys father at St. james, but he was prively conveyed by night onto Cainfham. He had founded there a finale priory in memory of his fon Robert, who died younge 1166: and after he newly repayred it and endowed it, makyng it an abby of canons regular; he gave it the whole lordfhyp of

Marfchefel

Marfchefel and impropriated the benefice to St. James priory, and the benefice came confequently to Tewkfbury." — This William died here in 1173, and had three daughters, Mabile, Amicia and Ifabel.

In the 35th year of Henry 2d. 1189, Ifabel was married to John Earl of Moreton, the King's youngeft fon; to her William had given the earldom of Glocefter, and Henry engaged to give Mabile 100 pounds in portion in lieu thereof. John continued his marriage with her until the firft year of his coming to the crown, 1199, when having no iffue by her he divorced her, and fhe married Jeoffry de Mandeville Earl of Effex: John gave back great part of her fortune, but retained the honor of Glocefter and the lordfhip of Briftol in his own hands with the caftle, which never after returned to the Earls of Glocefter the right heirs. — Leland fays, v. 6. p. 86, " King John had no iffue by her, and kepte her but a yere, (which muft be a miftake,) and fo repudiating her toke to wyfe the Erle of Herefordes daughter, and reteynid yn his hondes the toun and caftelle of Brightftowe within the hundred of Berton, lying in Gloceftyrfhire hard by Brightftowe, as betwixt the foreft of Kingefwode and it: and fo it hathe fynce ftil remaynid yn the Kinges bandes."

The caftle of Briftol having been thus in the poffeffion of 16 lords doing baronial homage or fervice from its firft erection Anno Dom. 915 till the 1ft year of King John, was with the city now become a royal demefne, and annexed to the crown: and from henceforth the Kings of England referved it to their own ufe, chooling the conftable and other officers, keeping a garrifon there, and appointing them falaries and perquifites. King John in the 8th year of his reign granted the town of Briftol in fee farm to the burgeffes at a yearly rent of 245 l. which rent was paid to the 9th of Henry 3d. (the caftle of Briftol excepted,) referving the prifage of beer, as much as the conftable of the caftle and his people there may have need of, alfo the bailiwick of Berton, the chafe of Brull [ii] of Keynfham, and the wood of Furches, all which the King retained in his own hands.* — And the 17th of Edw. 1ft. the townfmen of Briftol paid 23 l. 9s. 10 d. to the conftable of Briftol caftle in lieu of prife of beer, called tyne, belonging to the caftle, and the conftable accounted to the King for the fame, as part of the profits of the caftle. †

What this prifage or tyne was, may be right to enquire: — It is evident the conftables, knights and ferjeants which were in caftles, as well thofe belonging to the King, as thofe before belonging to the barons, did ufe in former ages to exercife great fuperiority over the towns which were near them, as was
this

* Madox Excheq. p. 228, c. 2. (n.) (s.)
† Magn. Rot. 17 Edw. 1ft. Rot. 1. m. 2. a.

this of Briſtol, and alſo over the adjacent country : no wonder men who were covered with ſtcel ſhould domineer over burgeſſes and peaſants, the armed over the unarmed; the former uſed to make captures upon the latter of hay, corn, beer, and other things under divers denominations, to wit, of priſe, tyne of caſtle, forage, &c. — The priſe of beer, priſa cereviſiœ for the uſe of the caſtle of Briſtol was uſually worth by the year 100s. or 5l. and was anſwered to the King as a yearly due. By cuſtom theſe captures became familiar and even rightful. But the burgeſſes of towns were wont to complain of theſe captures to the King, who in ſome charters made to towns, did ſometimes grant amongſt other franchiſcs, that they ſhould be free from priſe, tyne of caſtle, and ſuch like captures.

In 1289 Peter de la Mare renders an account to the King of 23l. 9s. 10d. in lieu of priſe of beer called tyne, belonging to the caſtle, as part of its profits, ſo that tyna caſtri ſeems to have been various at different times. — In the 15th year of Henry 3d. the ſheriff of Gloceſter, Wm. de Putoſt, would not anſwer for the profits of the county, becauſe the King had granted them for the cuſtody of the caſtles of Briſtol and Gloceſter, and for the maintenance of Eleonor his kinſwoman and of all the ſoldiers dwelling in the caſtles of Briſtol and Gloceſter all the profits of the county of Gloceſter and the rent of Berton Regis there of 60 marks by the year, and the priſe of beer worth 100s.

The caſtle of Briſtol being now veſted in the crown and a part of the royal demeſnes in the King's hand, he uſed to iſſue forth his grant of the conſtable-ſhip of the caſtle to his nobles or favorites; who had 20l. per ann. ſalary with all profits belonging to the ſaid office, and the naming of two watchmen to watch by night and by day, and for the keeper of the gate a fee of 2 d. a day, and 3½d. per day for the two watchmen, as appears from the copy of the grant of the ſaid conſtableſhip the 4th Edw. 6th. to Sir William Herbert, knight, together with the ſtewardſhip of the city, in the following form.

Edwardus Sextus Dei gratiâ, &c. i. e. Edward the ſixth by the grace of God, King of England, France and Ireland, defender of the faith, of the church of England and Ireland the ſupreme head, to all to whom theſe pre-fents ſhall come, health — know ye that we in conſideration of the good, true and faithful ſervice which our beloved and faithful ſervant Wm. Herbert knight hath done us in times paſt, of our own ſpecial favour, certain know-lcdge and meer motion, as alſo with the advice of our council have given and granted, and by theſe preſents confirmed to the ſaid W. Herbert knight, the office of conſtable or keeper of the caſtle of our city or town of Briſtol, and warder or keeper of the gate of the ſaid caſtle, and alſo the nomination and
appointment

appointment of the two watchmen to watch as well by day as by night within the faid caftle : and that he have authority and power from time to time to nominate and appoint under him two watchmen within the faid caftle, and we ordain and appoint him the faid W. Herbert, knight, conftable and keeper of the aforefaid caftle, and warder and keeper of the gate of the faid caftle by thefe prefents, to have, hold and enjoy the offices, nomination, cuftody aforefaid and each of them, to the faid W. Herbert by himfelf or by fome fufficient deputy or deputies for the term of his life, together with all and fingular the profits allowances commodities and emoluments freely and as amply as Edward Duke of Somerfet, or any other on account of the faid offices held the fame ; and we further grant by thefe prefents to the faid W. Herbert for the exercife of the faid office of conftable, twenty pounds payable by the fheriff of Briftol out of the ferm of the faid city, and two pence a day for the office of warder, and for the wages of the two watchmen, three pence farthing, together with all other profits, &c. belonging to the faid offices, &c. And as Edward Duke of Somerfet our uncle lately held the office of fenefchall or fteward of the faid city or town of Briftol, with the fee, profits, &c. belonging to the faid office, of the gift and grant of the mayor and commonalty of the fame, which office with the fee and profits, &c. are lately come into our hands and our difpofal, and fo ought to remain by reafon and virtue of a certain act of parliament held at Weftminfter, 4th November laft paft, among other things publifhed and propofed, know ye that we have given and granted by thefe prefents to the faid W. Herbert, knight, the faid office of fenefchal or fteward of the faid city or town of Briftol, as fully as it is come to our hands by reafon of the faid act of parliament and ought to be and remain, to have and to hold the faid office for the natural life of the faid Duke of Somerfet, without any compofition to us or our heirs, &c.

Witnefs myfelf at Weftminfter 27th Feb. 4th year of our reign.

The cuftodes or conftables of Briftol caftle appointed by the Kings of England that have come to my knowledge are next to be confidered, without omitting any memorable tranfactions that have happened here during their government. King John in the 6th year of his reign, confirmed to john le Warre the grant (which he had formerly made to him before he attained the crown of this realm, at the requeft of Ifabel then his wife, daughter and coheir of William Earl of Glocefter) of the honor of Glocefter and caftle of Briftol, with the manor of Briftleton a part of that honor.

In the reign of King john, Hugo de Haftings was conftable of Briftol caftle : whether it was during his cuftody of it or not, does not appear ; but

in

in this reign the princefs Eleanor, called the damofel of Brittany, after a fuc-cefsful battle fought by King John againft her brother Prince Arthur at Mirable in Normandy, 1ft Anguft 1202, was by the King's order fent to Briftol caftle, and there kept clofe prifoner for forty years by her cruel uncle King John, for no other crime but her title to the crown after her brother, who was fuppofed to have been privately made away with. She at laft died here unmarried in miferable confinement in the 25th of Henry 3d. 1241.

In the 7th year of Richard 1ft. 1196, Briftol caftle was befieged, and one Richard Dorefcuilz was amerced 5l. for having affifted at the fiege.

In the 8th year of his reign, 1224, Henry the 3d. having made Ralph de Wilington (called in old writings Radulphus de Caftello) governor and conftable of this caftle, gave him alfo the wardenfhip of the chace of Kainfham, which fhews the Kings of England had once a chace there for the ranging of deer; and in 1229 Hugo de Burge was governor here: and in 1257 King Henry the 3d. came to Briftol, and fummoned Lord Percy to attend him there upon an expedition into Wales.

In 1244 Henry the 3d. ordains that as often as the burgeffes of Briftol fhall choofe a mayor, (the time of war only excepted,) they fhall bring him before the conftable of the caftle to be fworn and admitted.

Roger de Leeburne a baron, Anno 44th Henry the 3d. 1260 was made conftable of the caftle of Briftol.

" In 1264 Guarine de Baffingburne and Robert Walerande, keepers of Briftow made oute fudenly an hofte to Walingford, but they prevayled lyttle," fays Leland ColleÉt. p. 660. It was defigned for the relief of Prince Edward then a prifoner there, under the Earl of Leicefter one of the rebellious barons. Soon after this Bartholomew de Inovence was made conftable of Briftol caftle.

In the Baron's wars in the reign of Henry the 3d. each party being ready to take what advantages fhould offer during that ftate of uncertainty, Prince Edward fon to King Henry, thought it neceffary to ftore with provifions Briftol caftle, which the King his father had intrufted him with: to that end he came to Briftol and would have obliged the townfmen to find him what provifions he wanted; to fupply which he fined the burgeffes 1000l. As people flood then difpofed, this demand made perhaps a little too haughtily raifed a fedition among the townfmen, which forced the Prince to retire haftily into the caftle; he was no fooner there, but the inhabitants refolved to befiege him; or at leaft to keep him fo clofely blocked up that he fhould not efcape, well knowing that for want of neceffaries he could not long refift.

This

This refolution threw Edward into a very great ftraight: he got out of it however by a device, which indeed freed him from the prefent danger, but foon
brought him into another, from whence he could not fo happily difengage
himfelf: he fent for the Bifhop of Worcefter and intimated to him, that he
intended to adhere to the barons; but defired firft to talk with the King his father to perfuade him to give them entire fatisfaction: but being thus blocked up,
he defired him to be fecurity for him and to accompany him to London to
witnefs his conduct. The Bifhop depending on the Prince's fincerity prevailed
on the townfmen to let Edward go; to which they confented and the blockade
was raifed. The Prince and Bifhop fet out on their journey; but when they
came near Windfor, Edward clapping fpurs to his horfe rode away from the
Bifhop, and fecured himfelf in that caftle; but was foon after forced to accept
of the barons terms, and to furrender that caftle to them. This was in the
year 1263.

William fon of Hugh and brother of Gilbert Lord Talbot had cuftody of
the caftle of Briftol, the 18th of Henry 3d.

In the year 1271, Dominus Johannes de Mufcgres was conftable of the
caftle, and William de Stanhurft fubconftabularius.

In 17th Edward 1ft. 1289, Peter de la Mare was conftable of Briftol caftle, and
renders an account to the King of 23l. 9s. 10d. in lieu of prife of beer called
Tyna Caftri belonging to the caftle, as part of its profits. The Scotch Earl of
Marr was taken and confined in Briftol caftle from the year 1306 to 1314.

In the reign of King Edward the 1ft. upon the beginning of his wars in
Scotland, which happened about the year 1295, Bartholomew Badlefmere was
employed by the King, who for his gallant behaviour there, was fummoned
as a baron to parliament, and became a very great man in his time: he was
alfo made governor of Briftol caftle, and received a grant from the King of
the manor of Chilham in Kent. He was a fecond time made governor of the
caftle, town and berton of Briftol.

Roger Bygod fon of Hugh, nephew and heir to the laft Earl, had a grant
from King Edward of the caflies of Briftol and Nottingham to hold for life, and
the 20th Edward 1ft. he furrendered them to him again.

In the reign of King Edward the 2d. Hugh le Spencer Earl of Winton,
called by hiftorians fenior, for diftinction from his fon Hugh, who were both
chief favorites of the King, by their exceffive pride and covetoufnefs became
extremely odious to the people, as well as to the Queen and Prince, who were
both out of England and durft not return; being banifhed by the King as
traitors. The Queen hearing of the fentiments of the people, made fail for

England,

England, where fhe framed a powerful army of mal-contents, who marching
with her to Briftol, where the King then was, were joyfully received by the
inhabitants ; and in teftimony of her welcome Hugh the father being brought
before Prince Edward and the barons attending him, (though 90 years of
age) was condemned to be hanged, which fentence was put in execution on
the 25th of October 1326, in the fight of the King and his own fon Hugh
(who efcaped not his punifhment.) Leland tells us, Col. 673. vol. ii. that
" Sir Hugh Spenfar the father was drawen hanged and behedded at Briftowe,
and his body hanged up with two ftronge cordes, and after four days it was cut
to peices and dogges did ete it : and becaufe he was Counte of Wynchefter
his hedde was fent thither." Upon the death of Lord Hugh le Defpencer,
the King and Hugh the fon early in the morning entered a little veffel behind
the caftle, with defign to get to the Ifle of Lundy, a place of fecurity, or elfe
into Ireland ; but after being many days at fea were perpetually driven back
by contrary winds : and at length being obliged to land, they came afbore at
Glamorgan, from whence they retired to the abby of Neath, where trufting to
the promifes of the Welch they hoped for fecurity. But Hugh not thinking
it fafe to truft them got privately into the caftle of Kaerfilli, which he ftoutly
defended, and in the end obtained of the forces fent by Queen Ifabel a capi-
tulation, with a promife of fafety as to life and limb. After which he got
again to the King, but foon after, viz. on the 16th of November following,
the King, Spencer, Chancellor Baldock, and Simon de Reading and a few
other domeftics, were taken near the caftle of Lantryffern ; fome fay, at the
abby of Neath. On the 20th following they were removed to Monmouth
caftle, where the great feal was forced from the King. From thence they
were all brought prifoners by Sir Henry Beaumont to Hereford, and were
delivered to the difpofal of the Queen and her fon, who foon after ordered
them all (except Chancellor Baldoc) to be hanged : as for the King he was
depofed and kept clofe prifoner at Kenelworth-caftle, from thence he was
removed in April 1327 to Corf-caftle, and then to Briftol-caftle : there he
remained until it was found out that fome of the town had formed a refolution
to affift him in making his efcape beyond fea. Upon this difcovery he was
removed to Berkeley caftle, which was to be his laft prifon : here he was
under the care of Sir John Maltravers, and Sir Thomas Gurney : — " Thefe
champions (fays Stowe) bring Edward towardes Barkley, being guarded by a
rabble of hellhounds, alonge by the Grange belonging to the caftle of Briftowe,
where that wicked man Gorney making a crowne of haye put it on his head,
and the foldiers that were prefent mocked him, faying, " Tprut avaunt Sir

D n
Kinge,"

Kinge," making a kind of noife with their mouths as if they broke wind backwards: they feared to be met of any that fhould knowe Edwarde: they bente their journey therefore towardes the left hande, riding along over the marifh grounds lying by the river Severn; moreover devifing to disfigure him that he fhould not be known, they determined to fhave his head and beard; wherefore as they travelled by a little water that ran in a ditch, they commaunded hym to lyghte from his horfe to be fhaven with the faid cold water by the barber, who faid, " that water muft ferve for this time." Edwarde anfwered, " would they, nould they, he would have warm water for his beard," fo fbed tears plentifully." On the 22d September 1327, they put their bloody orders into execution by thrufting a red-hot iron through a horn pipe up his fundament, which burnt his bowels, and by this horrible murder the unhappy Prince expired.*—In order to conceal their execrable deed, the two murderers fent for fome of the inhabitants of Briftol and Glocefter to examine the body; and there appearing no marks of violence, they concluded he died a natural death; this examination was carefully attefted by witneffes and immediately difperfed over the whole kingdom.

In the year 1336, the 9th of Edward the 3d. an inquifition was taken the 17th of May in the caftle of Briftol, relating to the right of patronage of the houfe of St. Mark of Billifwick in Briftol, before Hugh le Hunte, who was then deputy conftable there; and in the 13th of the fame King, Richard de Kynghefton was conftable of the caftle.

In the 35th year of Edward the 3d. Queen Phillippa grants Edmund Flambard the conftablefhip of this caftle for life, receiving 20l. per ann. befides fees for the watchmen and the officers of the Foreft of Kingfwood and Filwood; he refigned the fame, and then fhe appoints Robert de Foulehurft in his room, which was confirmed by King Edward.

King Edward the 3d. 1373, in his charter feparated Briftol from the county of Glocefter and made it a town and county of itfelf, and ordered that for the future the mayor when chofen fhould not be prefented [as ufually] to the conftable of the caftle of Briftol to be by him accepted: But that prefently

after

---

* By inquifition in Cotton's Abridgement of the Records, it appeared that Thomas Lord Berkley was not then at Berkley, and had no part in this murder. —— Mr. Gray in his Pindaric Ode called the Bard, finely touches this barbarous murder:

Mark the year, and mark the night,
When Severn fhall re-echo with affright
The fhricks of death, thro' Berkley's roofs that ring,
Shrieks of an agonizing King!

after his election, he should take his oath before his next predecessor mayor, in the Guildhall of Briftol.

In the 43d year of Edward 3d. 20th Auguft, Hugh de Segrave was appointed governor of this caftle for life.

And the 15th July, 47th of Edward 3d. John de Thorp had the conftablefhip of this caftle granted to him.

In the 10th year of Richard the 2d. the parliament accufed many of his domeftics of high treafon, three of whom, viz. Sir John Salifbury, Knight, Sir Thomas Trivet, Knight, and John Lincoln, Efq; (after a long confinement in Briftol caftle,) were at length removed to the Tower of London, after which on the 12th of May 1389, Sir John Salifbury was executed at Tyburn, and the other two were difcharged. — King Richard by following his own vicious inclinations, and the advice of his evil counfellors, was his own deftruction. Four of them (in order to efcape the hand of juftice from the Duke of Lan-cafter, who was now in England with an army as a competitor for the crown,) made their efcape from London to the caftle of Briftol with an intention to have made a ftout refiftance, viz. Wm. Scroop Earl of Wiltfhire, Sir John Bufby Knight, who had been Speaker of the Houfe of Commons the laft parliament, Sir Henry Green, and Sir James Bagot, Knights. They came here in the month of July 1399, but were foon followed by the Duke of Lancafter, at whofe arrival the gates of the town were thrown open to the Duke's forces; he immediately commanded the caftle of Briftol to be ftormed; which in four days time fur-rendered at difcretion, and foon after the three firft were beheaded, but Sir James Bagot made his efcape into Ireland. The 29th of September following King Richard was depofed, and not long after he was by eight affaffins and Sir Pierce of Exton, murdered in Pomfret-caftle. — John de Thorp continued conftable of the caftle the 1ft and 3d year of Richard 2d.

Henry the 4th and his wife Joan, Nov. 14, 1413, conftitute Hugh Lutterel conftable of the caftle of Briftol.

King Henry 6th. in the year 1444, granted the manor and hundred of Briftol (with other things) to Henry de Beauchamp, fon of the late Earl of Warwick, in reverfion, from the death of Humphry Duke of Glocefter; and Leland v. 6. Itin. p. 80, calls him, " Dominus quoque Caftri Briftolliæ cum fuis annexis."

The 16th Jan. 21ft of Henry 6th. Sir John St. Loe was made conftable of the caftle of Briftol for life: he died the 12th of March the 26th of Henry 6th.

In the 24th year of his reign 1445, King Henry 6th grants to the mayor, &c. of Briftol, all the gates, ditches, walls and fuburbs of the faid town, with all fairs, markets and courts there and in the fuburbs, with all fines, iffues,

redemptions,

redemptions, and amerciaments belonging to the fame, (the caftle of Briftol and its ditches excepted:) this grant was for 60 years, the mayor, &c. paying into the exchequer per ann. during that term 102 l. 15 s. 6 d. and to the abbot of Tewkefbury (for the time being) for the tythes of the town 14 l. 10 s. to the prior of St. James of Briftol (for the time being) for the yearly rent of the mill at St. James's-Back 3 l. to the conftable of the caftle of Briftol and his officers for the time being, (that is to fay,) to the porters of the gate and watchmen of the caftle, and to the forrefter of Kingfwood, 39 l. 14 s. 6 d. to the (cuftodi maritimo) the warden of the port or quay-warden 6 s. 8 d.

King Edward the 4th. in his progrefs about feveral parts of the kingdom, came to his caftle of Briftol ; when Sir Humphrey Stafford of Hooke had a grant, dated the 15th of June, from the King of the ftewardfhip of the dutchy of Cornwall for life, likewife the conftablefhip of Briftol caftle, and of feveral of the King's forefts, with that of the conftablewick of the foreft of Kingfwood, which in former times was of great extent and annexed to the caftle. This gentleman was a branch of the family of the Earls of Stafford, he died the 6th of Anguft the fame year, according to Dugdale, v. 1. p. 173.

In the 1ft year of Edward 4th. 1461, Sir Baldwin Fulford after fuffering imprifonment with his two accomplices, Bright and Heffant, Efqrs. in Briftol caftle, were executed here, the former having given bond to Henry 6th. that he would either take away the life of the Earl of Warwick, who was then plot-ting to dethrone the reigning fovereign, or lofe his own head. Our old ebro-niclers in the year 1460 mention this fact; Stowe relates it thus under that year : " Sir Baudewine Fulford undertook under pain of loling his head to deftroy the Earl of Warwick, but when he had fpent the King a thoufand marks in money he returned again :" but an additional authentic evidence of this fact is in an old parchment roll, in which among other curiofities preferved in the cabinet of Mr. Canynge, is mentioned "the real bond given to Henry 6th. by Sir Charles Bawdin à Fulford (commonly cleped Baudin Fulford) to teke the life of the Erl of Warwick or lofe his head, which he did to Edward 4th." See p. 45.

By an entry in the old church books of St. Ewen in this city, " for wafhing and clecning the church when King Edward the 4th. came there in September 1461, 4 d." it appears when this event of Sir Baudwyn Fulford happened, and it confirms the account above given ; King Edward having flood at the great window there when he paffed by to his fate. Mr. Canynge was alfo mayor in 1461 to September 29th of that year, when Phillip Mede was chofen, fo that the execution of Sir Baudwin Fulford mull have been the beginning or middle of September 1461. — Mr. Adams's manufcript penes me fays, " King
Edward

Edward came to Briftol in September 1461, where Sir John Bawdin Fulford, Bright and Heffant were beheaded,"—and in 1474 he lodged at the abbey of St. Auftin's there. This family of Fulford was of great note and antiquity in the county of Devon; there is a place of that name near Exeter now, which feems to have given name to the family (de turpi vado) and was their feat and refidence.—John Fulford a defcendant of Sir Baudwin of Fulford, was fheriff of Devon the 27th of Henry 8th. he bore G. a chevron arg.—One of the family, fon of the above Sir Baldwin, lies buried in Exeter cathedral, with an infcription in Gothic letters on a large black marble ftone in the eaftern aile ftill to be feen: Hic jacet magift. Joannes Fulford filius Baldwini Fulford milit. hui. Eccle'. Refid. pr°· Archid'· Tottn. deinde Cornub' ult°· Exon, q. obiit xix die Januarii A. D. xv.xviii cui aiæ ppitietur Deus.—Here lies Mafter John Fulford, fon of Sir Baldwin Fulford, Knight, refidentiary of this church, firft Archdeacon of Totnefs, then of Cornwall, and laftly of Exeter, who died 19th January A. D. 1518, on whofe foul may God have mercy.

This event has given occafion to a poem called the Briftol Tragedy, lately publifhed among Rowley's poems, in which the name is called Sir Charles Bawdin Fulford. In the manufcript (Adams's penes me) he is called Sir John Bawdin Fulford, which fhews how uncertain they were in the name at the time, and that the mifnomer in that poem derogates little from its authenticity. It is remarkable, that one Sir Cantelow in the fervice of Edward the 4th. is introduced as an active perfon in that tragedy; and it appears (by a manufcript, Rich penes me,) that Henry 6th. was taken in difguifed apparel at the abby of Salley in Yorkfhire by one Cantelow, in 1465, and was thence brought to Elftone, and then to the Tower; this is a proof that King Edward the 4th. had fuch a perfon as Sir Cantelow much in his intereft and at his command, and affords fome additional proof of the authenticity of that poem.

In the reign of King Henry the 7th. Giles Lord D'Aubeney held the caftle of Briftol; as did afterwards Sir John Seymour of Walfhall in the county of Wilts Knight, he was the fon of Sir Roger Seymour of Evenfwindon in the county of Wilts Knight, by Cecilia his wife, daughter of John Lord Beauchamp, of Hatche in the county of Somerfet: the faid Sir John in the 9th year of the reign of King Henry the 8th. 1518, was one of the knights for the body of that King; he obtained a grant at that time of the conftablewick of this caftle for his own life, after which to his fon Edward, to hold in as ample manner as the faid Giles Lord D'Aubeny held the fame.

In the 4th year of Edward the 6th. Sir William Herbert was granted the cuftody of this caftle.

Upon

Upon the alteration of religion in 1549, many rebellious tumults broke out in Cornwall, Devonſhire, Norwich, and at Briſtol. At the laſt place timely care was taken to repair and fortify the caſtle and walls of the city, which were mounted with cannon, alſo the city gates, moſt of which were made new ; proper guards being placed night and day to prevent any attempts which might be made by any tumult within the city, or without in order to ſurpriſe the ſame. By the prudent management of Mr. William Cheſter the diſcontented citizens were ſoon appeaſed, by his procuring a general pardon for them ; after which the ſoldiers within the city (commanded by Lord Cray of Wilton) marched to Honiton in the Weſt, where they beat thoſe rebels.

In 1545 and 1553 a mint was eſtabliſhed in the caſtle, and the church plate ſeized at the diſſolution was coined there, and a printing preſs ſet up.

In the reign of Queen Elizabeth, Sir John Stafford, Knight, was by her Majeſty (as a reward of his valour) granted the conſtableſhip of Briſtol caſtle, in which office he continued a long time ; he was alſo one of the band of gentlemen penſioners during the ſpace of 47 years to the Queen and King James the 1ſt. he died on the 28th of September Anno Dom. 1605, and was buried with his anceſtors on the North ſide of the commmunion table in the church of the Virgin Mary in the town of Thornbury in the county of Gloceſter, where his monument gives the above account, which has this inſcription on it : " Heere lieth the body of Sir John Stafford, Knight, a gentleman penſioner, during the ſpace of 47 years to Queen Elizabeth, and King James, hee had as a reward of his valour and fidelity, conferred upon him by her Matie the conſtableſhip of Briſtol caſtle, where hee continued a long time. Hee lived (as himſelfe on his death bed confeſſed) in the frail and ſlippery courſe of a ſoldier, and a courtier, from the time of his manhood neere unto the time of his death ; notwithſtanding ſenſible of his end and that accompt hee was to give at the laſt day, hee did fully and freely forgive all men fealing the ſame by calling for and receiving the bleſſed ſacrament as a pledge of his forgiving other men and of the forgiveneſs of his own ſins ; for whatſoever the frailty of his life or bitterneſs of the diſeaſe whereof he died might be, his hope of a better life through the mercies and ſufferings of his Redeemer, made him a conquerour over and beyond thoſe humane frailties. Hee dying in the found faith of a penitent ſinner, a loyal ſervant to his Prince, a lover of his country, wherein he did beare the chiefeſt offices of truſt and credit, and a founder of an almſhouſe in the pariſh where he lived, endowing

the

the fame with 10 pounds per annum to be paid for ever, obiit 28° die Septemb A° Dni. 1624.

In cujus memoriam et veritatis hujus teftimonium nepos ejus Sciens videns que hoc monumentum pofuit hac fretus fpe votoque inquiens;

Non aliter cineres mando Jacere meos."

Arms or rather the creft, though it is in a fhield, gules a wolf's head or. and the Stafford knot or.

In the year 1602, 6th of March a petition was prefented to the privy council from the mayor and commonalty of the city of Briftol, complaining that Sir John Stafford, Knight, keeper of his Majefty's caftle of Briftol, being feldom or never refident there, but leaving a mean and unworthy deputy in his ftead hath of late time fuffered many poor and indigent people, to the number of 49 families confifting of about 240 perfons, to inhabit within the faid caftle, who for the moft part are perfons of lewd life and converfation and in no way able · to relieve themfelves but by begging and ftealing to the great annoyance of the citizens, the rather for that the faid caftle being exempted from the liberties of the city though it ftandeth within the body of the fame, doth ferve for a refuge and receptacle of malefactors as well of the city as others that fly thither to efcape juftice : it was thought and ordered to the petitioners humble requeft, that for avoiding the prefent inconvenience · and preventing the like for the future, the Lord High Treafurer of England and Chancellor of the Exchequer calling the faid John Stafford before them, fhould take order for removing the perfons then refiding in the faid caftle unto fuch places where they laft dwelt, and alfo that there be not hereafter any more admitted to inhabit there, but only fuch as Sir John Stafford will undertake for their fufficiency and good behaviour, to the end the city be not further charged or molefted by them, or his Majefty's caftle peftered with any fuch bafe cottagers or fcandalous inmates.

By a charter bearing date the 13th of April the 5th of King Charles the 1ft. 1630, the faid King grants to the mayor, burgeffes and commonalty of the city of Briftol, all that his caftle of Briftol, (as the ancient demefne and parcel of the poffeffions of the crown of England,) with its walls, ditches, banks, houfes, buildings, courts, orchards, gardens, waters, water-courfes, lands, &c. within the circuit or precincts thereof. And in confideration that the fituation thereof was 30 miles from the city of Glocefter, but contiguous to the city of Briftol; and by reafon that no juftice of the peace for the county of Glocefter lived near the faid caftle to inhabit, and that the officers of the city of Briftol having no authority within the fame, as not being a part of the faid

city,

city, whereinto many thieves, malefactors, and other diforderly livers within the precincts of the faid caftle have fled, and from thence have efcaped from the hands of juftice; all which being confidered, the King did ordain and grant that from henceforth the fame fhould be feparated from the county of Glocefter, and made a part of the city and county of Briftol and in all refpects to be fubject to the fame powers as that of the faid city; and that all the inhabitants of the caftle be made free-men of Briftol, and that from henceforth no officer of the county of Glocefter fhould have any power or authority therein; the King referving his right to all his tenants dwelling within the faid caftle as his demefne or parcel of the poffeffions of his crown.

By one other charter bearing date at Weftminfter the 26th of October in the 6th year of the faid King, 1631,* he in confideration of the fum of 959l. by the mayor or burgeffes and commonalty of the city of Briftol paid into the Exchequer at Weftminfter, which was acknowledged in full difcharge for ever of all that grant made by the faid King to the faid mayor, &c. of all his caftle of Briftol with all its rights, members, and appurtenances whatfoever, in reverfion of three lives of John, Gillian, and Nathaniel Brewfter, granted to Francis Brewfter the 23d of Auguft in the 2d year of the reign of King Charles the 1ft. 1626, or for 80 years if the faid three lives fhould fo long live, under the yearly rent of 100l.

In September 1634 the city purchafed of John Brewfter his eftate and one life more to come of the caftle, with the lands, tenements and appurtenances for 520l. which was prefently paid him, all which was granted to the city in fee farm at 40l. per ann. rent for the fame by the King in recompence of charges for billeting foldiers, tranfporting them to Ireland, and fitting out fhips againft the pirates. It was by application to the Queen and her interceffion with the King this grant was obtained. The city had fpent 1100l. in billeting the foldiers.

The premifes particularly fpecified in reverfion in the above charter are, viz. the caftle of Briftol, the manfion-houfe within the fame, and all that clofe lying without the ditch of the caftle called by the name of the King's Orchard, containing two acres, and all that parcel of land called the Inner Green; and thofe tenements (which then amounted to 53) within the precincts, fite, compafs, or circuit of the faid caftle, with all that wood-yard there with its appurtenances, and all and fingular the houfes, buildings, ftructures, barns, ftables, dove-houfes, orchards, gardens, lands, tenements, cottages, halls, chambers,

---

* After this grant in the fame year 1631, a new armoury was built in the caftle of Briftol.

chambers, fhops, cellars, follars, entries, outgoings, ways, paths, void places, eafments, fruits, waters, water-courfes, wharfs, profits, commodities, advan-tages, emoluments and hereditaments whatfoever thereto belonging, excepting out of this grant all advowfons of churches, hofpitals and chapels, and other ecclefiaftical benefits, and all knights fees belonging to the faid premifes, with all mines of lead, tin, or other mines-royal whatfoever, thereto belonging : all which are granted to the faid mayor &c. and their fucceffors for ever to be held from him the King, and his heirs and fucceffors, as of his manor of Eaft Greenwich in the county of Kent, by fealty only, in fee and common foc-cage and not in capite, nor by knights fervice; yielding yearly to the faid King and his heirs and fucceffors a fee-farm rent of 40l. of lawfull money to be paid into the exchequer at Weftminfter &c.

All within the caftle precincts granted by King Charles the 1ft, was con-firmed to the faid mayor &c. in the 16th year of the reign of King Charles the 2d. dated 22d of April 1664, being after the happy reftoration.*

At the beginning of the unnatural rebellion againft King Charles the 1ft. the magiftrates of the city of Briftol thought it neceffary to repair the for-tifications of their caftle and the walls of the city, which was done accor-dingly by the 23d of October 1642, and alfo to build at the citizens expence a fort on Brandon-hill, with a communication to another fortification on St. Michael's-hill, which was afterwards turned into a royal pentagonal fort (commonly called the royal fort;) fee the plate : from this was a communi-cation to another fortification called Colfton's mount, (from his having the command thereof and being alfo deputy governor of the city and caftle.)

Lord Paulet fent Sir Ferdinando Gorges with Mr. Smyth of Afhton to get leave to bring in certain troops of horfe into Briftol, but the mayor Richard Aldworth refufed, having received exprefs orders from the King it was faid to receive no forces on his fide or the parliaments, but to keep and defend the city for his Majefty's ufe. Sir Alexander Popham fent 500 horfe to Bedminfter intending to lodge them in Briftol to make up 1000 on the parliament's behalf, but the corporation then refufed him, and fet the train bands to watch and ward as well without the gates as within to keep out all ftrange forces by night and by day, 100 at leaft armed with pikes and mufquets and ball. The gates and portcullifes were repaired and made ftrong with great chains hanged up within them, and great ftrong rails full of

E e   long

* The office of keeper of King's wood foreft, and of the foreft of Filwood, was granted by the faid King to Colonel Humphry Cook, in 1660.—See Sir Robert Atkyns Hiftory of Gloceſter-fhire, p. 492.

long iron fpikes without every gate, fo that no horfes could pafs by or over them. The caftle was likewife repaired within with many forts on the walls to plant ordnance on them for defence, the great tower was likewife well repaired with the battlements where they were decayed at the top: the old walls of the tower by the approbation of workmen were found very ftrong, which caufed them to mount great ordnance on the top of the tower to fcower the hills far about. Some elms in the marfh were cut down to make carriages for great ordnance and within were two pieces of great ordnance planted, with gunners to attend them at need.

After this came Colonel Effex towards the city with an army, horfe and foot on behalf of the parliament, which the city intended to keep out, and for two days the gates were double warded for refiftance. The magiftrates befides their old ftore of munition of which they were well provided, pro- cured 300 new mufquets made to furnifh the train bands and others that wanted. The third day which was the 5th December 1642, notice came of the approach of Colonel Effex's army from Berkley and Thornbury, the citizens prefently arrayed themfelves for defence, the mayor and all the council were at the Tolfey, ftudying how beft to preferve the city for his Majefty's fervice, but in the midft of their good endeavours came the mayor's wife and many women more with her with petitions to receive in the parliament's army, and fo diflurbed the council with their importunities, that the women prevailed and procured the gates to be opened to the great grief of the commons pre- pared to fight in defence of their liberty. This wicked council our mayor and aldermen payed foundly for afterwards. The 30th of December Sir Alexander Popham went to Exeter with one thoufand men. Lord Paulet being denied entrance into Briftol, marched to Wells and weftward, and having fuftained fome lofs there and at Sherborne embarked at Minehead for Cardiff where his fon-in-law T. Smyth, Efq; of Afhton died, and his corpfe was brought over to be buried where he was born.

The turbulent and the difaffcctcd to the King, began now to be very clamorous, and fome of the magiftrates it is faid, (under hand) had no great objection to the parliament caufe. Thofe that were immediately concerned were the right worfhipful Richard Aldworth then mayor, and Jofeph Jackfon, and Hugh Brown Efqrs. the fheriffs; when in the beginning of December the two regiments of foot were admitted, Colonel Effex their commander imme- diately took upon him the government of the caftle of Briftol. Thofe citi- zens that were loyalifts and would not declare for the rebels, began to feel the weight of their oppreffions; in fo much that at length it became very
                                                                    dangerous

dangerous for them to walk the ſtreets, or if found without the city they were ſent priſoners either to Taunton or Berkley caſtles. With ſuch deſpotick power did the rebels behave ; that Colonel Eſſex, offended at one of his ſoldiers for modeſtly aſking for his pay, inſtantly ſhot him through the head.

From this time the caſtle was governed by various maſters. On the 16th of February 1642-3, five troops of horſe and five companies of foot entered the city, commanded by Col. Nath. Fiennes, Col. Popham, and Clement Walker, &c. And the 27th they were followed by Sir Edward Hungerford's forces, and the caſtle was now made a garriſon for the parliament, and for-tifications added to it. Soon after theſe gentlemen came to the city, Col. Eſſex was made a priſoner ; and Fiennes was appointed governor of the city and caſtle. In conſequence of this, an oppreſſive tax was laid upon the citizens, to pay the rebel forces &c. which amounted to the ſum of 55l. 15s. per week,* aſſeſſed on their lands, goods, money at intereſt, and ſtock in trade ; this levy laid on every man's property, was to laſt for three months, or till the King's troops were diſbanded, which was confirmed by the rebel parliament ; and the firſt payment was to begin on the 1ſt of March following ; this ordinance extended over the kingdom where the rebel army had any power.† The ſtanding committee appointed for this occaſion were Robert Aldworth then mayor, Joſeph Jackſon, and Hugh Brown the ſheriffs, Rich-ard Holworthy, alderman, Luke Hodges, and Henry Gibbs. The power theſe had in conjunction with the officers of the army, viz. Cols. Fiennes, Popham, Walker, &c. was great, and produced many acts of oppreſſion. In March, 1643, an aſſociation of ſome of the principal inhabitants of this city, was entered into, for letting into the city Prince Rupert with ſome of his Majeſty's forces then at Durdham Down ready to their aid : but before it could be put in execution the deſign was diſcovered by ſome tattling females active on the parliament's ſide the night before ; which was on the 7th inſtant, and two of the principals who had his Majeſty's commiſſion for ſo doing, were taken into cuſtody, viz. Robert Yeomans, Eſq; one of the laſt year's ſheriffs, and Mr. George Boucher, a wealthy merchant ; who experienced the greateſt cruelties at the hands of the rebels ; chained by their necks and feet in a diſmal dungeon within the caſtle for twelve weeks, during which time they were deprived of the liberty of ſeeing or ſpeaking with their near-eſt relations, or any other acquaintance ; confined in the dark without the

E e 2 benefit

* See Ruſhworth's Colls. from p. 932 to 938.

† In Fiennes Letters to Mr. John Gunning junr. of Briſtol, his demand was 200l. of him by the bearer, which was his man Ralph Hooker, on pain of military diſcipline.

benefit of fire or candle, with flender diet and pining grief extremely ema-
ciated, at length they were brought to their trials before a court-martial at
the houfe of Mr. Robert Rogers at the bridge end: where they received
fentence to be hanged. * In purfuance of which they were brought from the
caftle on the 30th of May, 1643, to the place of execution, which was in
Wine-ftreet, near the Guard-houfe; many perfons were ftruck down for
praying for them; nay they were denied the Rev. Mr. Towgood and Mr.
Standfaft, two of the Church of England divines, to affift them with their
prayers; inftead of whom were fubftituted three of the moft violent and noto-
rions fchifmatics they could choofe out of Briftol, viz. Cradock, Rofewell,
and Fowler, who inftead of comforting them in their laft moments reviled
them, charging them with hypocrify and apoftacy, to the moment they were
turned off the ladder. † About this time Walter Stephens, a leader amongft
the rebels, demolifhed the Virgin Mary's chapel on Briftol bridge: and on
the 17th of July 1643, Governor Fiennes gave orders to demolifh St. Peter
and St. Philip's churches; but this happily was prevented on the 22d inft. by
Prince Rupert's appearing with 20,000 men to attack the city, which he did
on the 24th in fix different parts; which obliged Fiennes to draw forth his
forces out of the caftle, confifting of 2500 foot and a regiment of horfe and
dragoons: he divided them into fix bodies to defend the walls of the city. ―
However on the 26th Colonel Wafhington found means to force a paffage
through the hollow way betwixt Brandon-hill and Windmill forts (fecure from
the fhot) to Froom-gate, but with the lofs of about 500 of the King's forces,
that were killed by the rebels out of the windows of their houfes. At length
Fiennes ordered a parley to be beat, ‡ when it was agreed on the 27th inftant
that the garrifon with divers citizens fhould march out of the city; on which
Prince Rupert became governor of the city and caftle.

The following is a true relation of the taking of Briftol, in a letter from an
eye witnefs to the governor of Oxford, July 30, 1643. (Britifh Mufeum, pamph.
fol. fheets, No. 3.)

"At

* In May, 1643, Fiennes had of the King's friends then prifoners in the caftle, Sir
Walter Pye, Sir William Crofts, knights, and Colonel Connefby, &c."
† See Mercurius Rufticus, or the Countries Complaint, printed 1648. See alfo a little pam-
phlet publifhed on the occafion, where a very explicit account is given of the moft barbarous
ufage, unjuftly inflicted on thefe fuffering gentlemen, extended even to their young families after
their death. In a pardon granted by Charles 1ft. to the mayor, burgeffes, and commonalty of
Briftol, dated 4th Feb. 19th of his reign, 1643: Nathaniel Fiennes, Richard Cole, Walter
White, Thomas and Richard Hippifley, Robert Baugh, and Herbert, late provoft marfhal at
Briftol, were excepted, being actors or advifers and affiftants in the above deteftable murder.
‡ Vide State Trials, vol. i.

" At the affault of Briftol the outworks were very ftrong, and coft near 500 common men's lives on the King's fide. Colonel Herbert Lunsford was flain, and the Lord Vifcount Grandifon fhot and Mafter Bellafis wounded in the head by his own fword, which was ftruck to his head by a mufket when they rufhed in upon the works : neither of them in any great danger. It was the hotteft fervice that ever was in this kingdom fince the war began. In his Majefty's army there are at leaft 14000 armed men. The city was furrendered on Wednefday upon this condition ;—That the commanders were permitted to ride out with their fwords, and the common men to march out with their fticks in their hands, fo many as were pleafed to go; but at leaft 1000 of the garrifon foldiers very willingly remain in the caftle to ferve his Majefty. Colonel Fiennes marched out without moleftation or hurt, who attempted before to efcape; but was ftopped by the feamen, who are his Majefty's friends. The Royalifts found in the city 1700 barrels of gunpowder, with match and bullets proportionable, 60 brafs pieces of good ordnance, and all the arms, 18 good fhips in the river belonging to merchants, and 4 fhips belonging to the Earl of Warwick, that came lately to relieve it, which have good ftore of am- munition in them. The city gives 1400l. by way of compofition, to fave them from being plundered; upon which his Majefty hath fent a proclamation ftrictly to prevent it, that it fhall be death for any foldier to plunder. Sir Arthur Afhton came poft to Oxford on Friday to inform his Majefty of the ftate of things there. Upon which the council of war and council of ftate agreed to fend away Sir John Pennington fpeedily to Briftol, to have the com- mand of the fhips, and a proclamation to all mariners that are willing to ferve the King to this effect, that they fhall have their pardon who have ferved under the Earl of Warwick, and alfo their pay that is due from him prefently paid at Briftol, and his Majefty's pay and his favour for the future.

Informations of the 31ft July were,

Briftol taking,

Exeter fhaking,

Gloucefter quaking.

The report is that Briftol is to pay but 50,000l. in money for compofition, but that they are alfo to cloath 1500 of the King's foldiers according to their quality : common men 3l. a fuit, and gentlemen and commanders 6l. which amounts to 140,000l. There was found in the caftle of Briftol 100,000l. as is reported."

The day before the city was taken all the family plate of John Harrington, Efq; of Kelfon, was for fecurity removed into Briftol caftle, among which was

a large

a large golden font, in which Sir John Harrington (afterwards a very ingenious poet) was chriftened ; a prefent from Queen Elizabeth, his godmother. His houfe had been plundered feveral times : he is faid to have been the only one of that family ever tinctured with difloyal principles. Prince Rupert with part of the forces, confifting of 900 horfe, 2500 foot, and 1500 auxiliaries, hav_ing now poffeffion of the city, his Majefty Charles 1ft. with Prince Charles and the Duke of York, came hither on the 3d of Auguft, where the King during his ftay lodged at Mr. Colfton's houfe in Small-ftreet ; and he ex-tended his moft gracious pardon to many of his inveterate enemies, for which they afterwards made a moft ungrateful return, joining afterwards the rebels, who under Fairfax and Cromwell, having gained fome advantages in the Weft, determined to lay fiege to and retake Briftol, of which the following is the particular relation given by themfelves.

" After reducing Sherborn, Briftol being confidered as the only confiderable port the King had in the whole kingdom for fhipping, trade, and riches, and alfo a magazine for all forts of ammunition and provifions, it was refolved to march thither for reducing that city. Two thoufand horfe were fent before, under Commiffary-General Ireton, to perferve the towns adjacent to Briftol from plunder and firing, for the better accommodation of our quarters ; and advice was fent to Vice-Admiral Capt. Moulton, riding about Milford-haven, to fend fhips into Kingroad to block up Briftol by fea, as this army intended to do by land. Thurfday, Auguft 21. General Fairfax and Lieu-tenant-General Cromwell went and viewed the town, which was now ap-proached ; appointed guards and quarters on the weft fide of the river, and quartered themfelves at Kainfham that night, where divers lords fent for paffes to come out of the city to go beyond fea, but were all denied. Friday 22. A general rendezvous of horfe ; all this day fpent in fetting guards on Somer-fet fide, where the country men maintained a paffage, the head quarters being this day removed to Hanham. Saturday 23. Fairfax and Cromwell employed the whole day in fettling the quarters and guards on the other fide Briftol. The cannon played this day from the great fort and Prior's-hill fort, but hurt none but one dragoon, who had his thigh fhot off. The Royalifts alfo fallied out with a party of horfe, but were drove back, when Sir Richard Crane was mortally wounded. The head quarters removed to Stapleton. Auguft 24. the Lord's day. A fally out of the fally port near Prior's-hill fort, repulfed by Colonel Rainfborough's brigade and horfe. Tuefday 26. A third fally on Somerfet fide on a poft of Colonel Welden's, at Bedminfter, 10 killed and as many wounded. Sir Bernard Afhley, a royalift, taken and died a few days

after

after of his wounds. Thursday 28. The fort of Portishead point, after four days siege, taken with 6 pieces of ordnance, by which means a communication was laid open with the ships in Kingroad. Friday 29. A fast observed by the army to seek God for a blessing upon the designs against Bristol: Mr. Del and Mr. Peters kept the day at the head quarters, but were disturbed by a sally about noon upon the quarters at Lawford's-gate; 3 or 4 soldiers taken. Sunday, August 31. Captain Moulton from Kingroad held a meeting with the General, and offered to assist storming the city with his seamen. Monday, September 1. Prince Rupert with 1000 horse and 600 foot sallied out about twelve at noon the sixth time in full career upon our horse guards with much fierceness, and were made to retreat very hastily; Captain Guilliams killed and Colonel Okey taken by Prince Rupert. Orders given to view the line and works, and the soldiers to make faggots and all fitting preparations for a storm. September 2. After a council of war held, it was determined to storm Bristol; and the manner was referred to a committee of the colonels to present in writing to the General the next morning, to be debated in a general council of war, which was agreed to be in the following manner: Colonel Welden with his brigade of four regiments were to storm in three places on Somerset side, 200 men in the middle, 200 on each side as forlorn hopes to begin the storm; 20 ladders to each place, two men to carry each a ladder at 5s. apiece, two serjeants to attend each ladder at 20s. each; each of the musquetry that followed the ladder to carry a faggot, a serjeant to command them, and to have the same reward; 12 files of men with fire-arms and pikes to follow the ladders to each place where the storm was to be, those to be commanded each by a captain and lieutenant, the latter to go before with 5 files, the captain to second him with the other 7; the 200 men appointed to second the storm to furnish each party of them 20 pioneers who were to march in their rear, the 200 men commanded each by a field officer, and the pioneers each by a serjeant; (those pioneers were to throw down the line to make way for the horse,) the party that was to make good the line to possess the guns and turn them; a gentleman of the ordnance, gunners and mattrosses to enter with the parties, the drawbridge to be let down, two regiments and a half to storm in after the foot, if way was made: much after this manner was the general brigade under Colonel Montague's command, consisting of the General's, Col. Montague's, Col. Pickering's, and Sir Hardresse Waller's regiments to storm on both sides Lawford's-Gate, both to the river Avon and the lesser river Froom, the bridge over Froom to be made good against horse with pikes or to break it down. Colonel Rainsborough's brigade, consisting of his own, Major

General

General Skippon's, Col. Hammond's, Col. Birche's, and Lieut. Col. Pride's regiments to ſtorm on this ſide the Froom, beginning at the right hand of the ſallyport up to Prior's-hill fort, and to ſtorm the fort itſelf as the main buli-neſs: 200 of this brigade to go up in boats with the ſeamen to ſtorm Waterfort (if it could be attempted:) one regiment of horſe and a regiment of foot to be moving up and down in the cloſes before the royal fort and to ply hard upon it to alarm it, with a field officer to command them: the regiment of dragoons with two regiments of horſe to carry ladders with them and to attempt the line of works by Clifton and Waſhington's breach.

Such was the manner of the ſtorm agreed on, though alterable according to circumſtances; the cannon baſkets were ordered to be filled, ſeamen and boats ſent for, and September 4th being Thurſday, the weather which had been ſo extream wet before, began to alter, and the great guns began to play from the new battery againſt Prior's-fort; ſummons were alſo ſent to Prince Rupert.

To Prince RUPERT.

S i r,

"FOR the ſervice of the Parliament I have brought their own army before the city of Briſtol and do ſummon you in their names to render it, with all the forts belonging to the ſame, into my hands for their uſe. — Having uſed this plain language, as the buſineſs requires, I wiſh it may be as effeƈtual with you as it is ſatisfaƈtory to myſelf, that I do a little expoſtulate with you about the ſurrender of the ſame; which I confeſs is a way not common and which I ſhould not have ſo uſed, but in reſpeƈt to a perſon of ſuch ſort, and in ſuch a place: I take into conſideration your royal birth and relation to the crown of England, your honour, courage, all the virtues of your perſon, and the ſtrength of that place, which you may think yourſelf bound and able to main-tain. Sir, the crown of England is and will be where it ought to be, we fight to maintain it there; but the King miſled by evil counſellors, or through a ſeduced heart has left his parliament and people, (under God the beſt aſſurance of his crown and family:) the maintaining of this ſchiſm is the ground of this unhappy war on your part; and what ſad effeƈt it hath produced in the three kingdoms is viſible to all men. To maintain the rights of the crown and kingdom jointly; the principal part is, that the King in ſupreme aƈts con-cerning the whole ſtate, is not to be adviſed by men of whom the law takes no notice but by the parliament, the great council of the nation, in whom (as much as man is capable of) he hears all his people as it were at once ad-viſing him, and in which multitude of counſellors lies his ſafety and his people's intereſt.

intereſt. To ſet him right in this hath been the conſtant and faithful endeavour of the parliament; and to bring thoſe wicked inſtruments to juſtice that have miſled him is a principal ground of our fighting. Sir, if God makes this clear to you, as he hath to us, I doubt not but he will give you an heart to deliver this place, notwithſtanding all the conſiderations of honor, courage and fidelity, &c. becauſe their conſiſtency and uſe in the preſent buſineſs depends upon the right or wrongfulneſs of what has been ſaid. And if upon ſuch conviction you ſhould ſurrender the city, and ſave the loſs of blood and hazard of ſpoiling ſuch a place, it would be an act glorious in itſelf, and joyful to us, for the reſtoring you to the endeared affections of the parliament and people of England, the trueſt friends to your family it hath in the world. But if this be hid from your eyes, and ſo great, ſo famous, and ſo ancient a city, ſo full of people be expoſed through your wilfulneſs in putting us to force the ſame to the ruin and extremity of war, (which yet we ſhall in that caſe as much as poſſible endeavour to prevent,) then I appeal to the righteous God to judge between you and us, and to requite the wrong; and let all England judge whether to burn its towns, and ruin its cities, and deſtroy its people, be a good requital from a perſon of your family which have had the prayers, tears, money, and blood of this parliament; and, if you look on either as now divided, both ever had the ſame party in parliament, and among the people moſt zealous for their aſſiſtance and reſtitution; which you now oppoſe and ſeek to deſtroy; and whoſe conſtant grief hath been that their deſire to ſerve your family hath been ever hindred, and made fruitleſs by that ſame party about his Majeſty whoſe councils you act and whoſe intereſt you purſue in this unnatural war. I expect your ſpeedy anſwer to this ſummons by the return of the bearer this evening, and am,   Your Highneſs humble ſervant,

Sept. 4, 1645.   THO. FAIRFAX."

A N S W E R.

S i r,

" I Received your's by your trumpet, and deſire to know if you will give me leave to ſend a meſſenger to the King, to know his pleaſure therein. I am,   Your ſervant,

                                        R U P E R T."

R E P L Y.

S i r,

" YOUR overture of ſending to his Majeſty to know his pleaſure, I cannot give way to, nor admit of ſo much delay as that would require; wherefore

F f   thereby

thereby I cannot but underſtand your intention intimated not to ſurrender without his Majeſty's conſent, yet, becauſe it is but implicit, I ſend again to know more clearly if you have any more poſitive anſwer to give from yourſelf, which I deſire to receive ; and which I deſire may be ſuch as may render me capable to approve myſelf,

Your Highneſs humble ſervant,

Sept. 5, 1645.　　　　　　　　　　　　THO. FAIRFAX."

Whereupon his Highneſs after a council of war was held ſent 17 propoſitions, that during a treaty he might ſtrengthen the works within, and hear from the King ; and had he conſented to the demands, a confirmation by parliament would have been required, which protraction of time was deſigned for the advantage of the beſieged. In anſwer to this Sir Thomas Fairfax propoſed three commiſſioners, Colonels Ireton, Fleetwood and Pickering, to conclude a treaty, provided ſuch treaty be ended by nine o'clock that night, dated 7th Sept. 1645. But the Prince ſtill willing to delay deſires him to ſet down his doubts and exceptions to the propoſitions in writing to which he would give a ſpeedy anſwer, dated the ſame day, which occaſioned another letter with 20 propoſitions from Fairfax, aſſerting his tenderneſs of the city and of the effuſion of blood, &c. dated Stapleton 8th Sept. 1645. In this Prince Rupert finding omiſſions in ſeveral clauſes, and ſome wholly left out, ſent a letter the ſame day, inſiſting upon all the forts and lines, except the caſtle, to· be ſleighted and demoliſhed, when he would ſend commiſſioners to regulate and ſettle things between them ; but Fairfax in a letter dated the 9th Sept. 1645, inſiſted on his propoſitions and would admit of no farther delay, to which his Highneſs would not conſent.

The 6th of September every thing prepared for the ſtorm ; the General in the field and the ſoldiers ready with faggots at their backs, but the buſineſs deferred till Monday morning two o'clock. The 9th Sept. trumpet returning with unſatisfactory anſwer, at twelve o'clock at night the General was in the field to give orders about drawing out the men and managing the ſtorm the next morning. The 10th Sept. at two in the morning the ſignal was given to fall on at one inſtant round the city by ſetting fire to ſome ſtraw and faggots at the top of an hill, and the firing four great guns againſt Prior's-hill fort, from the place the General was to reſide at all the time of the ſtorm, being an old ſmall farm-houſe oppoſite the Prior's-hill fort, conveniently lying upon any alarm. — The ſignal being given, the ſtorm immediately began round the city and was terrible to the beholders. Colonel Montague and Col. Pickering

with

with their regiments at Lawford's-gate entered fpeedily, and recovered 22
great guns, and took many prifoners in the works; Major Defborough advancing with the horfe after them, having the command of the General's
regiment, and part of Col. Groves's. Sir Hardreffe Waller's, and the General's regiments, commanded by Lieutenant Colonel Jackfon, entered between
Lawford's-gate and the river Froom; Col. Rainfborough's and Col. Hamond's
regiments entered near Prior's fort; Major General Skippon's and Col.
Birche's entered nearer to the river Froom; and the regiment commanded
by Lieutenant Colonel Pride was divided, part affigned to the fervice of
Prior's fort, and the reft to alarm the great fort, and afterwards they took a
little fort of Welchmen. The feamen that were at firft defigned to ftorm by
water (the tide failing) affifted in ftorming the line and works, the horfe that
entered here, (befides the forlorn hope,) fo valiantly led on by Capt. Ireton,
were in feveral parties commanded by Major Bethel, Major Alford, and
Adjutant General Flemming, being of Colonel Whalye's, Col. Riche's and
part of Col. Graves's regiments. And after the line was broke down by the
pioneers and a gap made in the fame, the horfe with undaunted courage
entered, and within the line met with a party of the enemy's horfe, put them
to a retreat, mortally wounded Col. Taylor (formerly member of the houfe of
commons) of which wounds he died, and took divers prifoners. This fo
difheartened their horfe (perceiving withal our foot to be mafter of the line
and their men beaten off) that they never came on again to give one charge,
but retreated and ftood in a body under the favor of the great fort and
Colfton's fort. In the mean while Prior's-hill fort obftinately held out,
playing fiercely with great and fmall fhot on our men for two hours after the
line was entered; our men all that time in like manner plying them hard with
mufket fhot in at the port-holes, until they brought up ladders to the fort;
but it being an high work many of the ladders proved too fhort, through
which fault fome that got up were beaten down again. Notwithftanding, this
difheartened them not, but up they went again upon the greateft danger and
difadvantage, fome at laft creeping in at the port-holes, and others got on the
top of the works; Capt. Lagoe of Lieutenant Colonel Pride's regiment being
the firft man that laid hold on the colours, and in the end we forced the enemy
within to run below into the inner rooms of the work, hoping to receive
quarter, but our foldiers were fo little prepared to fhew mercy, by the oppofition that they met withal in the ftorm, and the refufal of quarter when
it was offered, that they put to the fword the commander (one Major Price
who was a Welchman) and almoft all the officers, foldiers and others ·in the

fort,

fort, except a few which at the entreaty of our officers were fpared their lives. Moft happy it was that the ftorm began fo early, for otherwife had the enemy had daylight when we firft entered, we could not have attempted Prior's-hill fort, in regard the great fort and Colfton's fort on the one fide and the caftle on the other might have cut off all our men as faft as they had been drawn up, but being in the dark they durft not fire for fear of killing their own men, their horfe during the ftorm being drawn up between the great fort and Colfton's fort: but on Somerfet fide fuccefs was not anfwerable to this on this fide, our forces there being put to a retreat though they went on with much courage; the works on that fide were fo high that the ladders could not near reach them, and the approach unto the line of great difadvantage. Left during the ftorm the Prince (in cafe he faw the town like to be loft) fhould endeavour to efcape with his horfe, to prevent the fame Commiffary General Ireton's, Col. Butler's and Col. Fleetwood's regiments of horfe were appointed to be in a moving body upon Durdham-Down, that place being the moft open way and moft likely for the Prince to efcape by; befides part of thofe horfe did alarm that fide of the line and the great fort towards Durdham-Down and Clifton during the ftorm; as likewife to fecure the foot, Col. Okey's dragoons alarming Brandon-Hill fort and the line towards Clifton. — About four hours after taking Prior's-hill fort a trumpet came from the Prince to defire a parley, which the General embraced on account of the city's being fet on fire in feveral places, and on condition of the fire being immediately ftopt: which was done accordingly, and fo the treaty proceeded, and by feven at night was concluded according to articles.

I. That his Highnefs Prince Rupert, and all noblemen, officers, gentlemen, and foldiers, and all other perfons whatfoever, now refiding in the city of Briftol, and in the caftle and forts thereof, fhall march out of the faid city and caftle and forts with colours, drums, pikes, bag and baggage. The Prince his Highnefs, gentlemen, and officers in commiffion, with their horfe and arms, and their fervants with their horfe and fwords, and common foldiers with their fwords, the Prince's life guard of horfe with their horfe and arms, and 250 horfe befides to be difpofed of by the Prince, and his life guard of firelocks with their arms, with each of them a pound of powder and a proportion of bullet; and that none of the perfons, who are to march out under this article, are to be plundered, fearched, or molefted.

II. That fuch officers and foldiers that fhall be left fick or wounded, in the city, caftle, or forts, fhall have liberty to ftay till their recovery, and then have fafe conduct to go to his Majefty, and in the interim to be protected.

III.

III. That such persons abovementioned, who are to march away, shall have sufficient convoy provided for them to such garrison of the King's as the Prince shall name, not exceeding fifty miles from Bristol, and shall have eight days allowed them to march thither, and shall have free quarter by the way, and shall have two officers to attend them for their accommodation, and twenty waggons for their baggage, if they shall have occasion to use them.

IV. That all the citizens of Bristol, and all noblemen, gentlemen, clergymen, and all other persons, residing in the said city and suburbs, shall be saved from all plunder and violence, and be secured in their persons and estates from the violence of the soldiers, and shall enjoy those rights and privileges, which other subjects enjoy under the protection and obedience to the Parliament.

V. That in consideration thereof, the city of Bristol, with the castle and all other forts and fortifications thereof, and all the ordnance, arms, ammunition, and all other furniture and provisions of war, excepting what is before allowed, shall be delivered up to Sir Thomas Fairfax to-morrow, being Thursday, the 11th of this instant September, by one o'clock in the afternoon, without any diminution or embezzlement, his Highness Prince Rupert then naming to what army or garrison of the King's he will march.

VI. That none of the army, who are to march out on this agreement, shall plunder, hurt, or spoil the town, or any person in it, or carry any thing but what is properly his own.

VII. That upon these articles being signed, Colonel Okey and all persons now in prison in the city of Bristol and the castle and forts of the same shall immediately be set at liberty.

VIII. That sufficient hostages be given to Sir Thomas Fairfax, such as he shall approve this night, who are to remain with him until the city be delivered.

IX. That neither the convoy or officers sent with the Prince shall receive any injury in their going and coming back, and shall have seven days allowance for their return.

X. That upon delivering of the town, sufficient hostages be given for the performance of the articles on both parts.

Signed by us, Commissioners on the behalf of his Highness Prince Rupert,

JOHN MYNNE,
W. TILLYER,
W. VAVASOUR.

Signed by us, Commissioners on the behalf of Sir Thomas Fairfax,

ED. MONTAGUE,
T. RAINSBOROUGH,
JOHN PICKERING.

While

While Sir Thomas Fairfax and the Lieutenant-General Oliver Cromwell were both fitting on the top of Prior's-hill fort, a piece of ordnance was fhot off thither from the caftle, and the bullet grazed upon the fort within two hands breadth of them, but did them no hurt at all; fo narrow was their efcape.

In the ftorm feveral of the Parliament officers both horfe and foot were killed, and many wounded. Major Bethel was fhot entering the line, of which wound he fhortly after died, &c.

Thurfday, September 11, Prince Rupert marched out of the great fort, as alfo many ladies and gentlemen. Oliver Cromwell, Lieutenant-General, fent the Parliament a long account of the taking Briftol, calling it " the work of the Lord, which none but an Atheift could deny," and that " 140 cannon-were taken, 100 barrels of powder, &c. with the lofs of only about 200 men."

This was a very important acquifition to the rebel leaders both in the army and the Parliament, and as great a lofs and injury to the King's affairs.

Prince Rupert incurred a fevere cenfure from the King, and though he was folicited to enter into treaty by his officers and a council of war, who thought the pofts and city not tenable any longer; yet the King's friends were fo diffatisfied with the Prince's behaviour, that it drew from him a public vindication of his conduct; and as the former account is the reprefentation of the rebels, it will be proper to fubjoin Prince Rupert's own account of the matter, extracted from a pamphlet called, a Declaration and Narrative of the State of the Garrifon and of the City of Briftol, publifhed 1645.

" On Prince Rupert's coming to Briftol, the conftitution of the garrifon had by the eftablifhment contributions fettled for 3600 men for that and the fubordinate garrifons, as Nunney, Portfend Point, &c. but on his exacter enquiry, the prefidiary foldiers which went for 8 or 900 men were really in the judgment of honeft and judicious perfons betwixt 5 or 600 effective; the auxiliary and trained bands by interruption of trade and by the peftilence then raging there and by poverty and preffures laid upon them were reduced to 800, and the mariners betook themfelves to other parts or the enemy. The commiffioners intrufted for the contribution and fupport of the garrifon abandoned the town upon the enemy's approach, and many confiderable perfons had leave to quit the town, which difheartened the reft. For feenring the place his Highnefs drew in fo many as to make 2800 men upon fight. But after the enemy approached, he could never draw up on the line 1500, and it was impoffible to keep them from getting over the works, and many of thofe were new levied Welch and unexperienced men. The line to be defended was above four
miles

miles in compafs, the breaft-work low and thin, the graff very narrow and of no depth, and by the opinion of all the colonels not tenable, on a brifk and vigorous affault. The great fort, which had the reputation of ftrength, lay open to Brandon-hill fort, which if taken would from its height with the can‗ non command the whole plain within it, and the want of water was not to be borne many days. For the like confideration of danger to the line from another part, his Highnefs built a reboubt without, which on that fide prevented the enemy from erecting a battery, as likewife three others during the fiege, and drew a line of 500 foot. After the misfortune which happened to Lord Goring's army, the lofs of Bridgwater and Sherborn, and upon his Majefty's fudden recefs out of Wales, the Prince conceiving it would be beft for his Majefty's affairs to remain here, and that the enemy's defigns would be for Briftol after their former fuccefles, he gave orders for all inhabitants to victual themfelves for fix months; and upon ftrict furvey there were 2500 families then remain‗ ing in the city, whereof 1500 through indigence and want could not provide for themfelves. To fupply this defect, 2000 bufbels of corn were imported from Wales; and on the certain approach of the enemy, all the cattle there‗ abouts was ordered to be drove in, by parties commanded out for that pur‗ pofe. The ammunition was fcant, confidering there were in the forts, caftle, line, and ftreets, above 100 cannon mounted; the quantity of powder not ex‗ ceeding 130 barrels, and at his Highnefs's coming there was not mufket balls for three hours fight, wherefore he caufed great quantities of lead to be caft into bullets; and the manufacture of match was quite down, and fet up by his Hignefs during the fiege.

Thefe preparations made the colonels of pofts to be confulted about the te‗ nablenefs of the line; their judgment was, that notwithftanding the works and line were very defective, the circuit large, the foldiers few; yet if a general ftorm could be once repelled, the enemy would be difcouraged from attempt‗ ing a fecond time, and the feafon of the year might incommodate the befieg‗ ers. —On which account they determined upon the beft general defence to be made upon the whole, wherein all might fhare alike.

The line was generally three feet thick; the height five feet where higheft.

The graff commonly fix feet broad, feven at the wideft; the depth in moft parts four feet, five where deepeft.

Between Prior-hill fort, Stoke's-croft-gate, and beyond the little river Froom towards Lawford's-gate, in which places the enemy entered, not five feet high.

The graff five feet broad, and that part of the line much decayed.

The

The ditch of the great fort on the right hand of the gate, before the face of the bulwark, was not four feet deep and eighteen broad ; fo that horfes did go up and down into it.

The higheſt work of the fort was not twelve feet high, the curtains but ten. Within one hundred feet of the fort there was a deep hollow way, where the enemy might lodge what troops he pleafed, and might be in the graff before night ; and that part of the fort was minable.

Brandon-hill fort was about twelve feet above the level of the great fort, and that not being able to make long refiſtance, the enemy gaining it would command the other.

The hedges and ditches without the line were neither cut nor levelled, fo that they lodged their men near our works fecurely at their firſt approach.

A general defence being fixed on, the colonels were all ordered to the feveral poſts and forts upon the line, and his Highneſs being folicitous for feenring the place, the enemy on the 22d of Auguſt appeared on Pile-hill, on the fouth fide of the town, he fent a party of horfe commanded by Sir Richard Crane (who in that action received his death's wound) to encounter them ; a little before that Bedminſter was fired on intelligence that the enemy intended that night to quarter 2000 men in it, and notwithſtanding the fire they drew thither and plied their fmall ſhot all night. Auguſt 23. The Prince caufed a traverfe or blind of earth to be made within the drawbridge at Temple-gate, and a battery raifed in the Marſh for feeuring the river and fcouring the fields beyond it. The enemy began fome breaſt-works and a battery on the hill without Temple-gate, with a traverfe acrofs the way to hinder our fallies. — Inſtructions for delivering the city up to the Parliament, figned Thomas Fairfax and Oliver Cromwell, were privately fent to the citizens, Auguſt 25, 1645. Upon the intercepting thefe papers, his Highneſs caufed feveral active and fufpected perfons to be reſtrained, which prevented the defign, and by his perfonal prefence prevented the great fort from furprifal ; and in the mean time to interrupt the enemy's working made feveral fallies, which all fucceeded according to defign. Auguſt 26. Soon after a ſtorm being expected by the enemy's drawing together great bodies of horfe and foot, his Highneſs double manned the line, but nothing followed. Auguſt 28. Five Parliament ſhips entered Kingroad, and forced Captain Broom who commanded the Tenth Whelpe to run up the Severn for fecurity. Auguſt 29. The enemy was making a bridge over the Avon to conjoin their quarters. September 3. His Highneſs began a work or cutting off within the line by Lawford's-gate, when Sir Thomas Fairfax fent a fummons to furrender.

The

The castle and great fort indeed might have held out some time, but no assistance from the west nor from the King was to be relied on, and the enemy could have blocked up the castle and advanced 12,000 men to have fought a battle if required, or else have secured themselves within the lines against all opposition — besides it appeared they were so absolutely masters of all the passes, and had so barricaded up the ways that a small force might have hindered now a great army. And at that time General Pointz so closely observed his Majesty's motions, that relief was very improbably to be expected, — and Col. Massey was upon the watch to intercept Lord Goring: and as the line was forced, Pryor's-hill fort an important place lost, the officer to whose trust it was committed deserting it, (who never since that time appeared and who was said to have been killed,) the city on resistance must have been exposed to the spoil and fury of the enemy, so many gallant men who had so long and faithfully served his Majesty (whose safeties his Highness conceived himself in honor obliged to preserve as dearly as his own) had been left to the slaughter and rage of a prevailing enemy, and the Scots being on the 8th of September at Glocester, an intermediate place near which his Majesty must have marched to the relief of Bristol, cut off all hopes of succour from him.

At a council of war held at Newark the 18th of October 1645, Prince Rupert desiring to clear himself for the surrender of the city and garrison of Bristol, before Montague Earl of Lindsey lord chamberlain, Richard Earl of Cork, Jacob Lord Astley field marshal general, John Lord Bellasis captain of the horse guards, Charles Lord Gerrard, Sir Richard Willis, John Ashburnham Esq; treasurer at war, produced a narrative of the matter of facts during the siege, and the King was pleased to say, his said nephew was not guilty of the least want of courage or fidelity to him in the doing thereof, but withall believed he might have kept the castle and fort a longer time; the King having absolutely resolved to have drawn together all the forces he possibly could and to have hazarded his person for his relief, the design being then so laid that in all probability it would have succeeded; yet as the Prince did what was done by the advice of a council of war of that garrison, and could not have expected relief and had received no intimation from the King thereof, and had a tender regard for the preservation of so many worthy officers and soldiers that had so long and faithfully served the King, he on these reasons capitulated. — The King hearing a second time the whole matter the 21st of October, was pleased to declare that Prince Rupert was not guilty of any the least want of courage of fidelity to him, and the Lords gave the same

G g   opinion

opinion on the point : Given at the court at Newark, the 21ſt Oƈt. 1645. — The forts, city and caſtle without any defacing thereof, with all arms, ammunition, &c. were delivered up Thurſday the 11th of September 1645, by three o'clock in the afternoon.

The forts, city and caſtle being evacuated by the King's troops, the rebels found a great booty therein ; 140 cannons, 100 barrels of gunpowder, proviſion in the royal fort (where at preſent the elegant ſeat of T. Tyndall, Eſq; is built) ſufficient to ſerve 150 men for 320 days, and the caſtle was victualled for near half ſo long, ſays a manuſcript penes me. To increaſe the misfortunes of the times the plague broke out this year, of which died 3000 perſons.

Philip Skippon who had been appointed governor of Briſtol caſtle, was commiſſioned by the parliament in the year 1646 to carry 200000l. (which was half the price ſet upon the head of his Majeſty Charles the 1ſt. by the Scots) into Scotland to induce them to deliver the King up into his enemies hands, which was accordingly done the 16th of February the ſame year.

This was the laſt keeper but one and governor of Briſtol caſtle before its final demolition ; he had been Major General on this occaſion, of great ſkill and experience in military operations, which he had acquired abroad in foreign wars ; and had it not been for this one man, neither the zeal or conduct of Fairfax, nor the brutal courage of Oliver Cromwell and his troops puſhed on by a ſpirit of enthuſiaſm, would have ſucceeded in carrying the city againſt Prince Rupert, who was acknowledged to be a General of conſummate abilities.

The caſtle and city being now reduced under the power of the parliament and its officers, it is a grievous unpleaſing taſk to recite the ſeveral oppreſſions the citizens underwent ; one would wiſh to throw a veil over ſuch ſcenes of wanton cruelty, but hiſtorical truth obliges us to notice them here agreeable to the maxim, ne quid falſi dicere audeat, ne quid veri non audeat. — Hiſtory records theſe bad effects of party rage, and of falſe religious zeal and love of liberty carried beyond the bounds of law, as a leſſon to poſterity againſt ever committing ſuch outrage againſt the common principles of humanity under the pretence of liberty, in the ſacred name of religion, and under the maſk of greater piety and reformation. — Beſides the heavy contributions laid on the merchants and tradeſmen loyaliſts, informers were encouraged by an act paſſed the 26th of March 1644, and committees appointed in ſeveral counties to enquire after the clergy and ſchoolmaſters not well affected to the parliament government, and to place others of their own learned, able, godly and

fit

fit perfons in their room and in poffeffion of their churches. — Accordingly the ftauding committee for Briftol the 20th of February 1645-6, fequeftered the Rev. Richard Towgood vicar of St. Nicholas, " for his great difaffection to the parliament of England and their proceedings," for which he was committed to Briftol caftle, where foon after the Rev. Mr. Richard Standfaft rector of Chrift Church, being alfo fequeftered was confined. One Evans a preaching taylor was put into his living by the committee. The Rev. Mr. Peirce vicar of St. Philip's was alfo fequeftered, and one Edward Hancock, late a Butler to Sir George Horner knight, was put into his living, where he continued till the reftoration of Charles the 2d. and being then removed he afterwards kept a public-houfe at Horfield, more agreeable to his former employment. The Rev. Mr. Brent vicar of Temple was alfo fequeftered; and many orthodox clergy and others to the number of about 50 perfons, were confined clofe prifoners in a difmal room in the caftle, and there treated with a rigour and cruelty not to be defcribed here — The ufe of the common prayer-book was by an ordinance of parliament in Oct. 1647, under penalty of fine and imprifonment for the third offence prohibited.

Let it with cool reflection be well confidered, that from this polluted fountain of the rebellion 1641 have fprung the feveral divifions in religion among us:

Hâc fonte derivata clades in patriam populumque fluxit. Hor.

The churches themfelves as well as the paftors did not efcape the rage of thefe merciful and meek reformers; the organs were pulled down, furplices torn to pieces, tombs defaced, the church plate ftoleu. By an ordinance of the 8th of Auguft 1643, and May following, made by the Lords and Commons, order was given to demolifh all monuments of idolatry and fuperftition, as altars, crucifixes, images, reprefentations of the Trinity, &c. but images, pictures, coats of arms in glafs or ftone fet up for any monument of King or nobleman, or perfon not reputed a faint to be continued. Cromwell's foldiers were bad judges of this diftinction, they broke moft of the curious painted glafs, tore away the brafs, iron and lead from many monuments and defaced the infcriptions, which is to be lamented now by all lovers of antiquities, the ruin they fpread in all country churches has never been repaired to this day.

The church and ftate being at length in a manner fubverted by the murder of the King, the government of the city and caftle was given by the parliament to Mr. Adrian Scroop the laft keeper, after which the royal arms and motto were every where thrown down and defaced in all public places in this city.

After

After Oliver Cromwell was proclaimed protector orders were given for demolishing the fortifications of the castle of Bristol, which was began the 3d of January 1655 to be dismantled; and in 1656 a new road was made into the county of Glocester through the said castle : a gate was erected 1659 called castle gate, (in 1766 removed,) before this the common road was through Newgate into the county of Glocester.

Since the demolition of the castle two handsome streets have been built on its site, Castle-street and Castle-green ; on the castle orchard without the sally-port have risen other streets, Queen-street, &c. And Cromwell's levelling orders have been so well executed that few traces of this venerable structure are now to be seen, which has made such distinguished figure in history, and been the subject of so much contention.

King Charles the 2d. in his several journies to conceal himself from his pursuers by the assistance of his faithful friends once passed through this city on horseback in disguise, riding before Mrs. Lane towards Leigh-manor house, drest like a country fellow before his mistress; where he lay concealed for some time and used to turn the spit in the kitchen by way of disguise : the block he sat on is preserved there to this day. — In passing through the city he could not resist an inclination of turning a little out of his way to take a view of the castle, the scene of so many interesting transactions.

In the year 1771, General Melvyl coming to Bristol, and having a great curiosity in tracing out the remains of ancient encampments and fortifications, examined the lines and entrenchments made round the city in the year 1643, the better to account for Prince Rupert whom he regarded as a great military genius, giving up the city. The author of this history gave him all the intelligence then in his power ; but could have supplied him with better, had he received before a curious paper containing the several fortified posts on the line, with the number of ordnance at each, communicated to him by Edmund Turnor, Esq; of Panton-house, Lincolnshire, whose ancestor * had a commission

* Sir Edmund Turnor was the youngest son of Christopher Turnor of Milton-Ernis, in the county of Bedford, Esq; and brother of Sir Christopher Turnor of Milton-Ernis, knight, one of the Barons of the Exchequer in the time of Charles the 2d. —— At the breaking out of the civil wars he engaged in the service of the crown, and was the 4th of December 20th of Charles 1st. with a salary of 13s. 4d. a day for himself, and 3s. 4d. each for three keepers of the stores, appointed Treasurer and Paymaster of the garrison there. The 10th of February 1645 he was appointed to the command of a troop of horse. He was taken prisoner at the battle of Worcester 1651. —— Anno Domini 1663 he received the honor of knighthood, and was appointed Surveyor General of the out-ports, and was one of the Farmers General of the customs. —— In 1681 he served the office of High-sheriff for the county of Lincoln, where he had purchased a considerable property. —— An account of his life and charities is published in Wilford's Lives of worthy persons, folio, 1741, pages 81 and 784. Likewise in Bishop Kennet's Case of impropriations.

miffion from Charles the 1ft. in 1644, of Treafurer of the garrifons of Briftol, Bath, the town and caftle of Berkeley, Nunny caftle, Farley caftle, and Portfhead-point:

"At the Water fort were 7 ordnance, with a mafter-gunner, 17s. 6d. a mate, 14s. and 3 gunners, each 10s. per week." This fort was at the point of Brandon-hill, next Limekiln-lane, fronting the Avon, above and oppofite the glafs-houfe.

"At Brandon-hill fort, ordnance 6, with a mafter-gunner, mate, and 2 gunners." On the very fummit.

"At the great fort, ordnance 22, with a mafter-gunner, mate, and 6 gunners, and commiffary of victuals." This was the Royal fort, now the fite of the houfe and gardens of Thomas Tyndale, Efq:

"At the redoubt, ordnance 7, with a mafter-gunner, mate, and 2 gunners." This was fince called Colfton's mount, behind the Montague on Kingfdown.

"At Prior's-hill fort, ordnance 13, with a mafter-gunner, mate, and 3 gunners." This is fince called Ninetree-hill.

"At Lawford's-gate, ordnance 7, with a mafter-gunner, mate, and 6 gunners."

"At Temple-gate, ordnance 14, with a mafter-gunner, mate, and 5 gunners."

"At Redcliff-gate, ordnance 15, with a mafter-gunner, mate, and 4 gunners."

"At the Caftle and Newgate, ordnance 16, with a mafter-gunner, mate, 11 gunners, and commiffary of victuals, at 1l. 10s. per week."

"At Froom-gate and Pithay-gate, ordnance 2, with 2 gunners."

This clearly fhews where the ftrongeft fortifications were; but there are no traces of the line farther than Prior's-hill, by any marks on the furface of the ground; for defcending the hill from Prior's-hill fort you get into low ground, which has been filled up or built upon fince that time, though the line it appears extended acrofs by the city peft-houfe or lodge over the Froom to Lawford's-gate, thence acrofs the Avon to Tower Harratz and to Temple-gate, and to Redcliff-gate after the Borough-wall unto the river fide, where it ended.

C H A P.

C H A P. VIII.

Of the ABBY *of St.* AUGUSTIN, Bristol; *or Monaſtery of Black Regular Canons of the Order of St.* Vietor.

THE Monks, who were the early writers, make little mention of Briſtol ; a place of traffick, a trading town, chiefly intent on maintaining them-ſelves in ſecurity, and defending their habitations from any foreign invader in their well-choſen retreat, was not deemed worthy of being celebrated in their writings. Here were no religious houſes then erected, no ſuperb monaſteries endowed, to entitule it to their notice. This ſtate of the city is well deſcribed in the following little poem, ſaid by Chatterton to be tranſlated by Rowley, " as nie as Englyſhe wyll ſerve, from the original, written by Abbot John, who was ynductyd 20 yeares, and dyd act as abbatt 9 yeares before hys induc-tyon for Phillip then abbatt : he dyed yn M.C.C.XV. beynge buryed in his albe in the mynſter."

With * daitive ſteppe Religyon dyghte in grcie,
  Her face of doleful hue,
Swyfte as a takel † thro'we bryght heav'n tooke her waie,
  And ofte and ere anon dyd ſaie
   " Aiè ! me !'what ſhail I doe ;
  " See Bryſtoe citie, whyche I nowe doe kenne,
   " Aryſynge to mie view,
  " Thycke throng'd wythe foldyers and wythe traffyck-menne ;
   " Butte faynctes I feen few."
Fytz-Hardynge roſe ! — he roſe lyke bryghte foune in the morne,
   " Faire dame adryne thein eyne,
   " Let alle thie greeſe bee myne,
For I wylle rere thee uppe a Mynſter hie ;
  " The toppe whereof ſhail reech ynto the ſkic ;
   " Ande wyll a Monke be ſhorne ;"
   Thenne dyd the dame replie,
   " I ſhall ne be forelourne ;
  " Here wyll I take a cheryſaunied reſte,
  " And ſpend mic dales upon Fytz-Hardynges breſte."

As

---

* Perhaps haitive, or haiſtiff, haſty, from the French haity, haſty.   † Arrow.

As foon as Briftol became the feat of religion and a monaftery was built there and endowed, it makes fome figure in the monaftic hiftories, became the fubject of their pens, and is occafionally celebrated in their writings, as much as other places. This monaftery of St. Auguftin began to be erected in the year 1140; and it appears, that it was fuccefs in trade by which Hardyng accumulated fuch a fortune here as to enable the fon to build and to procure the royal favour to endow this abby.

It was built on a rifing ground, with a delightful profpect of the hills around in the north-weft fuburb of the city and in the manor of Billefwick. The area of the buildings appropriated for the abbot and his monks was very large and extenfive, as by the rule of St. Auguftin, to whom it was dedicated, they were to live here together in common. The walls and part of the large refectory or dining room now converted into a prebendal houfe, the abbot's houfe now partly rebuilt and made a palace for the Bifhop's refidence, two fides of the cloifters with a curious chapter-houfe, and fome old beautiful arches and gate-ways, are ftill to be feen. Thefe with the church evidently demonftrate the whole to have been once a very fpacious and magnificent monaftery. William of Worcefter, p. 188. fays, " Sanctuarium locum Sancti Auguftini, &c." " The fanctuary-place of St. Auguftin from the caft, where is the entrance of the fanctuary, unto the fartheft gate for entering the court of the abbot, from the offices, houfes, and granaries of the bakers, brewers, ftable-keepers, of my lords the abbots, &c. contains 360 fteps, as you go by the church of St. Auguftin. The breadth of the fanctuary from the gate aforementioned to entering the lane called Frog-lane contains 240 fteps. The breadth or diftance of the place from the weft part of the gate of the Gauntes to the gate of the entrance of the church of the abby of St. Auguftin contains acrofs 180 fteps." From this it appears it was of large extent. Leland (Itin. vol. v. p. 60.) mentions, " St. Auguftine's blak chanons, extra mœnia. "

In the reign of King Stephen there lived in Briftol one Harding, a rich merchant, faid in fome manufcripts to have dwelt in Baldwin's-ftreet, and that he was a younger fon or grandfon of a King of Denmark : the infcription over the college gate-houfe calls him, " filius regis Daciæ." Others fay he was the fon of Walburga, fifter of Ednothus the good friend of Harold of an ancient and noble family of the Saxons, eminent in the days of Edward the Confeffor, who married a daughter of the King of Denmark named Livida. Leland fays, " Hardingus ex profapiâ, &c." " Harding was fprung of the royal race of the kingdom of Denmark in the time of William the Conqueror, and inhabited Briftol in the year of our Lord 1069, made afterwards Lord of Berkeley."

Berkeley." Abbot Newland's pedigree in Berkeley caſtle mentions him, " as deſcended of the royal line of the Kings of Denmark and the youngeſt fon ; and accompanying Duke William from Normandy was at the battle of Haſt-ings." And fome fay, that Harding's mother Godiva was fiſter to Robert Duke of Normandy's father. In the Britiſh Muſeum is an ancient pedigree, which gives the following account, vide No. 1196 and 1178, fol. 123, 124. " Hardinge, Dane and inhabitant and mayor of Briſtol (to whom Maud the Empreſs gave the caſtle, town, and barony of Berkeley) bore for arms gules a chevron argent, was of the line of the King of Denmark, and was of great wealth and poſſeſſions in both the counties of Gloceſter and Somerſet ; he mar-ried Lyvida, a noble woman, and had by her iſſue three fons and two daugh-ters, his eldeſt fon was Robert Fitzharding firſt Lord of Berkeley by gift of Henry 2d. This Robert uſed to feal with his father's arms alone, alſo with the figure of a man armed on horſeback, which his fon Maurice alſo fome time uſed. Jordayn, the third brother of the faid Robert and uncle to Mau-rice, fealed his deeds with an impreſſion only of two lions endorſed without any ſhield ; and Helena only ſiſter of Lord Maurice married Robert, fon and heir of Lord Durſley."

The following verſes of the old monkiſh poet, Robert of Glouceſter, gives fome account of Hardyng.

A burgeys of Briſtow tho' Robert Hardynge
For grete treſour and richeſſe fo well was wyth the kyng,
That he yaft him and his heires the noble barony
That fo rych is of Berkely, with all the feignorie ;
And thulk Robert Hardyng arered futh, I wyfs
An abbey at Briſtow of St. Auſtyn that is,
Syr Rychard le Fitzroy of whome we fpake before,
Gentleman he was inough, tho' he were laſt ybore ;
For the Erles daughter of Warren his good moder was,
And her fader King John, that begat a perchas,
Sir Morris of Berkly wedded futh bycas
His daughter, and begat on her the good Knyght Sir Thomas.

All accounts agree of Hardyng's immenſe riches and large poſſeſſions, of his holding Wheatenhurſt in Gloceſterſhire, of Earl Briſtric in mortgage, and of his dying 16th Henry 1ſt. 1116, at Briſtol, where he had been mayor or governor. He is expreſsly called mayor of Briſtol in Dr. Cox Macro's manuſcripts. Cambden fays, " he was of the blood royal of Denmark and an alderman of Briſtol." He had a fon Robert Fitzharding : Leland fays in v. 6. 43,

" Anno

" Anno 1135, Robertus filius Hardyngi &c." i. e. Robert fon of Hardyng begat of Eva his wife four fons, Maurice de Berkly, Robert de Were, Nicolas de Tickenham, Thomas Archdeacon of Worcefler; and that the monaftery was founded the 3d ides of April 1148." And in v. 6. Itin. p. 50. he fays " they bare not fyrfte the name of Barkelye but Fitzharding, whereof one named Robert was a nobleman, and in procefle the Fitzhardynges married with the heirs general of Durfley, and the name was taken of them and continued." And in his Collect. v. 2. p. 912, he fays " Thomas was fon and heyr of Robert Fitzhardynge, which Robert was fonne and heyre to the younger brother of the Kinge of Denmark : which Robert in time of King William the Conqueror, inhabited Brighteflow and there foundid the pryorie of St. Auguftine." This Robert Fitzharding was of great account with Robert Earl of Glocefter, and joined him with all his interefl in behalf of Maud the Emprefs and her fon Henry the 2d. the only heir to the crown from Henry the 1ft. againft King Stephen, who had ufurped it. Briflol and its caftle being in the hands of her brother Robert Earl of Glocefler and efteemed a place of ftrength and refuge for Maud the Emprefs, fhe placed her fon here to fchool among the chief mens fons of the town : and as Baker in his Chronicle records it " he was brought into England by his uncle Robert in 1141, and was put to fchool being then nine years old at Briflol under the tuition of one Mathews, where he remained four years." Here he grew much delighted with Robert Fitzhardyng, which friendfhip and affection begun in their tender years and fchoolboy days left fuch an impreffion on their minds, as was not to be effaced, when both were advanced to a riper age, fo that Henry when he came to the crown knighted this Robert Fitzharding, then mayor or governor of Briflol after his father, and made him heir of the Berkley eftate of Roger Lord of Berkley and Durfley, confifcated for adhering to King Stephen againft his mother Maud, and in recompence of his father Harding's fupplies of money in fupporting her caufe, and in memory of the fon's friendfhip and acquaintance in their younger years, he made him the firft Lord of Berkley, from whom the prefent Lord Berkley is lineally defcended. — He granted him alfo the manor of Bitton with lands in Berkley of 100l. yearly value. Leland in Collect. v. 2. p. 912 fays " for as much as Roger Lord of Berkley and Durfley had but a doughter caullid Eva and was married to the bloude of the Fitzhardynges (at this tyme I am not certain whether Eva was married to Robert Fitzhardynge or Thomas his fon,) but becaufe that Eva was heir of Roger Lord of Berklie and Durfley becaufe of the inheritaunce by his wife Eva, the name of Fitzhardynge was turned into

Berkley

Berkley and fo did continue." Others fay, Alice Lord Durfley's daughter was married to Maurice Robert Fitzharding's fon.

By Abbot John Newland's manufcript relating to the foundation of this monaftery, it appears that Robert Fitzharding firft Lord of Berkeley and prime founder of it deccafed, a canon of the fame, as is evident by his obit in their mortilage, which was yearly in the chapter-houfe in this fort rehearfed, viz. " This day deccafed Robert Fitzharding canon, and our founder;" and the fame is witncffed by the charter of his fon Maurice, fecond Lord Berkeley in thefe words : " Be it known to all Chriftian men, that I Maurice fon and heir of Sir Robert Fitzharding have granted and confirmed for the health of my foul and of all my anceftry, to the church of St. Auftin by Briftol, the which my lord and father hath founded, all fuch things which my faid father hath given and granted to the canons of the faid church, viz. within Berkeley Hernefs, Almondfbury, Horfield, Afhelworth, and Cromhall, the which he gave unto them when he became and was a canon : the which Sir Robert died February 5, 1170, and was buried between the abbot's and prior's ftall, and next to the abbot's ftall entering in the choir, and Eva his wife was buried by him, who died the 12th of March following." He was 75 years old at his death. Maurice died the 16th of June, 1189, and was buried in the parifh church of Brentford, and had iffue Robert and Thomas both Lords of Berke-ley, for that Thomas fucceeded his brother Robert who died without iffue, which faid Robert Lord of Berkeley was firft founder of the hofpital of St. Catherine in Bedminfter, and was brought up in his youth in the court of Henry 2d. his obit was celebrated yearly at the faid hofpital with great folem-nity. (Vide chapter on Redcliff parifh below.)

Sir Robert Fitzharding firft Lord of Berkeley began the foundation of the abbey of St. Auftin's in 1140, and built the church and all the offices in fix years time ; when Simon Bifhop of Worcefter, Robert Bifhop of Exeter, Geoffry Bifhop of Llandaff, and Gilbert Bifhop of St. Afaph, dedicated the church of the faid monaftery, and then afterwards Simon Bifhop of Worcefter induĉted fix canons of the monaftery of Wigmore, gathered and chofen by the faid Sir Robert into his church and monaftery, on Eafter-day, April 11, 1148.

" For which good Lord Sir Robert our founder and dame Eva his wife thefe be the fpecial things due for them, befides the general prayers continu-ally done in divine fervice by day and by night : firft a daily fpecial prayer faid for them and all other fundators and benefaĉtors at the hour of feven in the morning, and alfo daily prayers by name in our chapter-houfe openly. Alfo they have other rites folemnly fung with ringing on the eve of their anniver-

fary

fary and on the morrow commendations; the abbot for the founder, and the prior for the foundrefs, executing the divine fervice. On the morrow of the day of the anniverfary one hundred poor men be refrefhed, every one of them having a canon's loaf of bread called a myche and three herrings therewith, and amongft them all two bufhels of peafe: alfo another dole that day fhall be given of money, cake, and loaves; the abbot having a cake price 4 d. with two caftes of bread and 4 d. for wine; the prior, fub-prior, and almoner, every of them two cakes price 2 d. each, with one caft of bread, and 2 d. for wine; every fecular fervant of the houfehold within the monaftery to have a penny cake and a caft of bread; every frier within every houfe of the four orders of Briftol to have a loaf, and likewife every prifoner within the gaol of Newgate of Briftol a loaf: and all the reft of the bread undealt to be dealt at the gate of the faid monaftery among poor people, and every man taking part of this dole fhall have forty day's pardon. And in the day of the anniverfary of dame Eva his wife fhall be dealt to fifty poor men fifty loaves called myches with three herrings apiece, and amongft them all a bufhel of peafe."

This Robert the founder for whom the monks had reafon to pray by his deeds laid down upon the altar, endowed this monaftery with the manors of Almondfbury, Horfield, Afhelworth, Cromehall, Cerney, Blackensford,* and divers lands in Erlingham in the county of Gloucefter; and the manor of Leigh near Bedminfter, and St. Catherine's near Portbury in the county of Somerfet; Fifehead, in the county of Dorfet; and the manor of Bellifwick juxta Briftol, wherein the monaftery is feated; and with the churches and advowfons of Tickenham and Portbury, in the county of Somerfet, and the churches and advowfons of Berkeley, † Wotton, Bolnhall, Beverfton, Afhelworth, and Almondfbury, and all other his churches and advowfons in the hundred of Berkeley with their chapels, in the county of Glocefter, and with divers houfes in Briftol.

Second Robert, fon of Robert Fitzharding, gave to this monaftery the church of St. Nicholas in Briftol, ‡ divers meffuages in the faid town, and lands in Paulet, in the county of Somerfet.

Firft

* The manor of Blackfworth in 1746 confifted of eighteen meffuages and land in copyhold, fix in leafehold, the whole amounting to 647 l. per annum, befides coal-works. Rownham-ferry, a part of it, then let at 100 l. per annum.

† In the reign of Queen Anne, by act of parliament the Lord of Berkeley gave the rectory of of Sutton Boninton, in the county of Nottingham, to the dean and chapter of Briftol, in exchange for the faid Lord to have the prefentation of Berkeley church.

‡ It is ufual now for the Bifhop to have his vifitation-fermon there, probably from its being the firft church in Briftol given to the monaftery.

First Maurice, eldest brother to the above Robert, gave in dotem or towards the marriage portion of that monastery (as the deed calls it) two hides of land in Hinton, and one in Alkinton, in the parish of Berkeley, and the tithes of all pannage of his chafes of Micklewood, Appleridge, Oakley, and Weak or Wotton parks, and pasture for so many oxen as will till a plow-land to feed with oxen, as pure and perpetual alms. He died the first of Richard 1st. 1189, and is buried at Brentford near London, out of some pique to the abbot of St. Augustine, who had offended him : vide the Dean's manuscript. This lord was the first that took upon him the name of Berkeley and lived there.

Third Robert Lord Berkeley, son of the above Maurice, confirmed all his father's and grandfather's grants to this monastery, and also gave to the said church all his houses, lands, and tenements within the walls of Bristol, which (as the deed expresseth) were many and great. He also gave divers lands in Berkeley, Ham, Cowley, Nibley, and Hulmancot, in the county of Glocester. This lord took up arms against King John, and with other nobles invited Lewis the French King's son into England, for which his estates were seized to the King's use. In the beginning of Henry 3d's. reign he was pardoned for a fine of 966l. He was a pious and good man, and built St. Catherine's hospital at Bedminster, at Brightbow, where now a glafs-house is erected. — Also he gave about the year 1207 his fountain, called Huge Well, to the parishioners, &c. of St. Mary Redcliff in Bristol. He died the fourth of Henry 3d. 1220, and is buried in the north aile of St. Augustine's monastery over against the high altar (in an arch lying) in a monk's coul, a usual fashion for great lords in those times; Julian and Lucy, his two wives, are buried near him : Lucy survived him, and afterward married Hugh de Gourney.

First Thomas Lord Berkeley, brother to the above Robert, also confirmed to the monastery all the donations of his ancestors by particular name, and likewise gave them divers lands in Berkeley, Cowley, and Hinton, in the county of Glocester, also common of pasture for twenty-four oxen in Ham, and discharged all their lands in the hundred of Berkeley and Portbury from all service and earthly demands. He was also a great benefactor to St. Catherine's hospital nigh Bristol. He having offended King Henry 3d. was obliged to enter himself a Knight Templar, and so was honourably banished : he died in the 76th year of his age and in the 27th of Henry 3d's. reign, 1243, and lies buried in the fouth aile of St. Augustin's, under the arch next the rood altar, where his wife was also buried. The Lords of Berkeley did bear in their arms a chevron only, till this Thomas charged his coat with ten crosses, which

which Sir John Preſtwich very ingeniouſly ſuppoſes was given him for his great devotion to the church, and alluding to the ten Ave Mary prayers.

Second Maurice Lord Berkeley, ſon and heir to the above Thomas, confirmed to the abbot and convent all the lands which his anceſtors had given them, and all other freeholds given them within his fee and lordſhip, and alſo gave them lands in Berkeley, Beverſton, Wolgaſton, and Erlingham, and common of paſture of ruther beaſts and ſwine to feed in divers of his manors. By another deed he grants a common of paſture to them for twenty-four oxen, ſeven ſows, and one boar with the breed of an year old, in Walmergaſton, Ham, Lafrid, and Gorſt. Maurice ſecond Lord Berkeley married Iſabel, daughter of Maurice de Creoun, a baron in Lincolnſhire, by Iſabel his wife, daughter of Hugh le Brun Earl of March by Iſabel, widow to King John; ſo as that this elder Iſabel Lady Berkeley was indeed on the mother's ſide neice to King Henry 3d.—Says Kennet in parochial antiquities.

Lord Maurice died in the 9th year of King Edward 1ſt. anno 1281, and lieth buried in the north aile of this monaſtery, next to the altar of Sir Maurice. He died ſeized of the manors of Berkeley, Cam, Hinton, Cowley, and Alkington, and of Redcliff-ſtreet without Briſtol, belonging to the manor of Bedminſter.

Second Thomas Lord Berkeley, ſon of the above Maurice, was thirty years old at his father's death: he confirmed to the abbot and convent all the donations which his father and anceſtors had given them, alſo directed that the lands given by them ſhould be a manor within the hundred of Berkeley, and ſhould be called the manor of Canonbury; and granted them a court leet with ſtocks, pillory, and tumbrel in the ſaid manor, except in the town of Berkeley; alſo he reſtored to them their plate and veſtments, which had been plundered from them in the barons wars, being of great value, as Abbot Newland particularly has ſet them down to the value of 32l. 3s. 4d. In conſideration of his ſervices in the wars, he had grant of the liberty to hunt the hare, fox, &c. in the King's foreſts of Mendip * and Kingſwood. This Lord Thomas was a wife, prudent perſon; he kept two hundred attendants in his family. — The 15th of Edward 1ſt. 1287, a quo warranto was brought againſt him to ſet forth his claim of markets and fairs in the manor and hundred of Berkeley: he pleaded his grant from King Heury 2d. which was allowed. Alſo the abbot of St. Auguſtin was ſerved with the ſame warrant, to ſet forth his title to court leets in Berkeley, which was allowed. This lord was at moſt battles in Edward the 1ſt's. reign. He was conſtable and general of a great army led into France,

and

* Munedup or Moinedoppe in ancient records, many knolls or hillocks, where minerals have been dug. Mendip, in Somerſetſhire.

and was one of the plenipotentiaries to make the peace. Having taken the field twenty-eight times, at laſt he was taken priſoner at the fatal battle of Bannock's-Burrough in Scotland. He married Jane, daughter of William de Ferrers Earl of Derby. He died in the 76th year of his age and 14th of Edward 2d. 1321, and lies buried with Jane his wife in the arch between the veſtry and upper end of the fouth aile in this monaſtery: See the arms on the fouth fide of his tomb in the veſtry. He gave the friers minors and friers preachers of Gloceſter and Briſtol divers quarters of wheat out of his feveral granaries.

Third Maurice Lord Berkeley fon and heir to the laſt Lord Thomas, alfo confirmed the gifts and grants of his anceſtors to this monaſtery. This Lord had a child at 14 years old. He died a priſoner in Wallingford caſtle the 19th of Edward 2d. 1326, he was firſt buried there, but his body was afterwards removed to this monaſtery and is buried in the fouth aile under the arch before the choir door, whereby appears the miſtake of Grafton, who writes that King Edward 2d. was committed to the care of this Lord Maurice in Berkeley caſtle, whereas he died the King's priſoner fix months before the King's impriſonment.

Thomas Lord Berkeley the third of that name, and fon and heir to the laſt Lord Maurice, confirmed to the abbot and convent all the gifts and grants of his anceſtors, by a general recital of all their benefaEtions; alfo he granted to them all eſtrays and comelyrs as by the bailiff of the faid Lord ſhould be found upon any of the faid abbot's lands. This Lord Thomas is faid to have been privy to the murder of King Edward the 2d. at Berkeley caſtle, but he got off on his trial; and Stowe clears him. He married Margaret daughter of Roger Mortimer Earl of March, whoſe arms in painted glaſs is in this church in the choir, (over the Codrington's monument.) He was buried in the church of Berkeley the 35th of Edward the 3d. 1361. It appears in Pryn's Abridgment of the Records of the Tower, that he was not guilty of the murder of King Edward, but that Thomas de Cornay and William de Ogle did it, while he lay fick at Bewdley. He was a great combatant, was at the battle of PoiEtiers and wounded therein, and built Beverſton caſtle by the gains he acquired in the wars.—Wolſtan v. 1..f. 126. The Lord Thomas de Berkelie with licence of King Edward 3d. founded a perpetual chauntry in the abbacy of St. Auguſtin, Briſtol, and gave to William de Underlith chaplain and his fucceſſors chaplains, perpetually to cȩlebrate every day divine offices in the aforcfaid abbacy for his foul and the foul of Margaret formerly his wife, and for the fouls of all the faithful, two meſſuages and 20s. rent, with their appertinances in Briſtol,

dated

dated the 25th April 1348. Witneffes Maurice de Berkly his deareft fon, Tho. de Bradftone.

Maurice Lord Berkeley the 4th of that name, was fon and heir of the laft Lord Thomas, he obtained a papal bull from Pope Urban the 2d. for 40 days pardon and releafe of pennance injoined to every one that fhould in the church and monaftery of St. Anftin (being then ruinous and to be repaired) upon the feftival days in the year hear mafs, or fay kneeling three ave maries, or fhould give any veftment, ornament, gold, filver, books, chalifes, or any aids of charity to the repair of the faid church ; and whoever fhould pray there for the life and good eftate of the noble Lord Maurice de Berkeley and the noble Lady Elizabeth his wife and their children, or for any being in pur-gatory, fhould be releafed 40 days of the pennance injoined them, which for the infallibility thereof is alfo under the feals of four cardinals yet extant. In the 40th of Edward the 3d. 1366, Lord Maurice gave to Wm. Winchcomb chaplain, a houfe before the gate of St. Auguftin's monaftery, with the garden and dove-houfe, (now the dean's houfe,) and feveral houfes in Broad-ftreet in Briftol, to pray in faid monaftery for the foul of Margaret his mother, and lands in Portbury to pray alfo for his father and wife deceafed. This Lord was a great warrior in Spain, he was married at eight years old to Elizabeth daughter of Hugh Lord Spencer, and died the 42d of Edward the 3d. 1368, of his wounds at the battle of Poiéters, and lieth with Margaret his mother who died the 5th of May 1337, (daughter to Roger Mortimer,) at the monaftery of St. Auftin in the great tomb under the arch between the old chapel of our Lady and the north aile, at the foot of the pulpit fteps.

The fourth Maurice was fucceeded by his fon Thomas, the fourth of that name, who held the manors and hundred of Bedminfter, Harecliff and Portbury, and the third part of Portifhead *inter alia* ; the manors of Limeridge-wood, Wefton in Gordan, and Walton : to him fucceeded James his coufin and heir male, who dying 1404 was buried at St. Auguftin's, Briftol; he gave fix marks to find a prieft to pray for his foul in that church.

William Lord Berkeley grand nephew to Thomas Lord Berkeley the fourth of that name, and fon of Lord Maurice the fourth laft-mentioned, gave to this monaftery by deed dated the 4th of Henry the 7th. 1489, feveral houfes in London, and lands in the counties of Worcefter and Buckingham, in recom-pence whereof the abbot and convent accepted this Lord Marquis and the Lady Anne his wife (who was daughter of John Fiencs Lord Dacres) into their fpiritual fociety and fraternity, and admitted them to the participation of all the benefits, works and merits wrought by him, as well in maffes, hours,

prayers,

prayers, watchings, faftings, difcipline and hofpitalities, as in alms or other benefices which hereafter fhall be done or had in their monaftery, with the addition from their fpecial grace and bounty, viz. that when the deaths of this Lord and his wife fhall be made known to them, there fhall be as much faid and done for their fouls, as for the brothers and fifters and other benefactors of the faid place : this William ftood in fuch favour with King Edward the 4th. that he had a grant of 100 marks per annum from the King during his life, to be received out of the cuftoms of the port of Briftol. He was the firft of this family created a Marquis, the 4th of King Henry the 7th. 1489. He was feized at one time in his own right and in the right of his wife, of above 120 manors, but fpent a great part of them to purchafe honours, pardons and protections againft his enemies. He alfo took occafion to except againft his brother Maurice the fifth as his fucceffor, becaufe he had not married with a perfon of honourable parentage, (fhe being Ifabella daughter to Philip Mead Efq; defcended from the Meads of Meads-place in Fayland, in the parifh of Wraxall, Somerfet, then alderman of Briftol,) and gave all his lands from him, alfo he conveyed over the honour of Berkeley to King Henry the 7th. and to the heirs male of his body, by which the baronage was held from his family, it being appendant to the caftle; the crown having kept poffeffion of the honour of Berkeley and many eftates belonging to thefe Lords until the death of Edward the 6th. being 61 years, when they returned to this family again. He died without iffue the 7th of Henry 7th. 1491, and was buried at the Auguftin Friery in London, which he had repaired or new-built.

Fifth Maurice brother to William, being difinherited, bufied himfelf in regaining his inheritance, in which he in part fucceeded, but died the 22d of Henry the 7th.

Maurice Lord Berkeley the fixth of this name was nephew to the laft William, or fon to the laft Maurice, he built a chapel in this monaftery, which is railed in, (where the family of Newtons are buried,) intending therein to be buried, but dying in Calais in the 15th of King Henry the 8th. 1523, was buried in Trinity chapel there. By his will he gave to this monaftery his beft pair of veftments with all the furniture, and 20l. in money, one gilt crofs with all the reliCts enclofed in the fame, with all his beft gilt cofets, alfo one pair of white veftments with all their furniture, and the beft pair of black veftments with his beft miffal, and a good chalice, thefe are the words of his will. He was high-fheriff of Glocefterfhire the 7th of Henry the 8th. 1516; he after was governor of Calais and made a baron by writ the 14th of Henry the 8th. 1523. His wife was Katherine daughter of Sir William Berkeley of Stoke-Giffard;

he

he had no issue, but one bastard son, who is the only unlawful son heard of in this family.

Thomas Lord Berkeley the fifth of that name and brother to the above Lord Maurice, was constable of Berkeley castle which was then in the crown, he died the 24th of Henry the 8th. 1532, and lieth buried in this monastery under a fine tomb with Elenor his first wife: this is said to be the last Lord Berkeley that was buried in this monastery. Sir Robert Atkyns says that this Lord married Elizabeth daughter of Sir Marmaduke Constable of Yorkshire, and his last wife was Cicely widow of Richard Rowden of Glocester Esq. Dugdale says that by his will he ordained that his body should be buried without great pomp or pride in the parish church of Mangotsfield, near to the place where he used to kneel under the partition between the choir and his own chapel; and within a quarter of a year after to be brought to St. Austin's, Bristol, and there buried near unto his first wife.

Thus to this noble family was this monastery beholden for its liberal endowment as well as for its first foundation and erection: each of them distinguished himself as the loving father and patron of this church: they nursed it as it were from its cradle, supported it in its infancy, and still continued to protect and enrich it in the riper years of its maturity; and were doubtless men of as great piety and extensive charity as they were many of them of the greatest abilities both in the cabinet and in the field: they gave such large estates to monasteries from a pious zeal and religious motive, and endowed them with so many benefices, that the family is said to have had but one rectory to which they might present a chaplain, which was Sutton Bonington, and that afterwards was exchanged for the vicarage of Berkeley near their castle.

Besides the benefactions bestowed on this monastery by this noble family at different times as before related, it can also boast of many Kings and Princes that favoured it with their grants and confirmations, and protected it with their power; and many private gentlemen of fortune distinguished it with their bounty.

Amongst the former Henry the 2d. when Duke of Normandy and Earl of Anjou, gave a charter of confirmation of lands and rents belonging to the crown of England to this monastery, " which (says he) I began to assist with my benefaction and cherish with my protection in the beginning of my youth, (*initio juventutis meæ.*)"—King John confirmed all preceding grants, and quit-claimed their land from the view of his foresters, and the rule of the forest (regnardo,) and gave them 44 acres in Eissemore free from all services &c.

He

He alfo granted and confirmed to them Leigh, a member of Bedminſter near Briſtol.—Edward the 2d. alfo by charter confirmed all former grants.

Ralph Earl of Cheſter gave the land of Fifehead in Dorſetſhire and the church of All Saints in Briſtol.

Mabile Counteſs of Gloceſter, mother of Earl William, gave them ſixty acres of land in Romne marſh, between the monaſtery of St. Peter de Mora and the grove towards the north.

William Earl of Gloceſter gave them one hundred acres in Kiburgh between Duneleis and Kenelechi, and Runn and Doneſtone acroſs from ſide to ſide.

Oſbert de Pennard gave the land of Pennard with its appurtenances and liberties, and particularly the paſture between Teach and Clay, and Earl William confirmed it to them.

John de Cogan gave twenty acres of land and two acres of meadow near Pennard. William, ſon of Gregory, gave forty ſolidates of land in Alberton. William de Lond gave the lands of Blackenſword. Gregory de Turry eight ſolidats of rent in Newport. Eudo de Morevil half a virgate of land at Wrokeſhale and the mill of Radeford. Richard de Wrokeſhale, the ſon of Toni, his land of Radeford. William, the ſon of Robert the ſon of Martin, a meſſuage in Blakedone with two crofts, ten acres of land, with common of paſture in the ſame vill. William, the ſon of Aſey, and Galfrid his brother, one rood of land at Weſton.

King John granted and confirmed all the burgages that they had in the town of Briſtol and without, as well in the fair as elſewhere, given to them after the death of William Earl of Gloceſter; alſo the mills they have upon the Trinel, and the lands which they have at Blackenſword.

William de Cliftedon gave the church of Cliftedone. Gilbert de Aldelane gave half a hide of land in Ferenberge. Nicholas, the ſon of Robert (Fitz-harding), the church of Tikeham. Earl William the church of Grantendene, the church of Halbertone, and the church of Ronne and of Flat Holme. William, the ſon of Gregory, the church of Finenere. King John granted and confirmed to them all their liberties and free cuſtoms, and that the canons ſhall be ever free from toll and paſſage for ſhips, men, and boats, and be quit from all exaſtions belonging to him in the ports of the ſea or elſewhere.

By an old deed extant in the biſhop's regiſters of the church of Wells, dated 1257, it appears that the churches of Portbury, Tykenham, Were, and Poulet were then appropriated to the abbot and convent of St. Auguſtin, Briſtol.

This houſe was one of the great abbies, and the whole convent conſiſted of an abbot, prior, ſub-prior, and about fourteen friers or canons regular, profeſſing the

rule

rule of St. Auguftin, of the order of St. Victor; whether they did not increafe the number of their body, according to their income and ability, does not appear; that fuch was the number in 1353 however is clear.

The form obferved in electing the abbot was the following, as I find it in a Latin deed, dated March 7, 1353, when William Coke, the fub-prior, was chofen abbot, about whofe election fome difpute had arifen, which was determined at length by the prior of the church of Worcefter, the fee being then vacant: — " Walter de Shafeftbury, prior of the monaftery of St. Auguftin, Briftol, and the under-written canons regular of the fame, viz. frier Thomas de Bykenore, Robert Dunfterre, Simon de Tormarton, Robert Syde, John de Lammer, Richard Martyn Chamberlain, John Badminton, Walter Cheltenham, Laurence de Cyrencefter, John Snyte, John de Launfton, Walter Raguim, Adam Horfelye, John Goldenye, John Strete, making the convent of the faid monaftery, being met in the chapter-houfe, and having received the licence of Philippa Queen of England their patron to choofe an abbot in room of Ralph Afche the laft abbot, who died the 1ft of March, 1352, the word of God being firft expounded and an hymn de Sancto Spiritu fung, all prefent then in the chapter-houfe being ordered folemnly to depart who had no right in this election of an abbot, the Queen's letter of licence was firft read, and confideration had among themfelves concerning the mode of the election, which was determined to be by fcrutiny; three fcrutators out of the whole were then chofen, who were feparately to receive the vote of each prefent in a fecret manner and write it down, and fo continue the fcrutiny till the major part of the canons of the whole convent fhould confent to the fame fit perfon; which being done, the fcrutators privately retiring to one corner of the chapter-houfe, and having wrote and reckoned the votes, they publifhed their fcrutiny to the reft in common, by which it appeared that nine of them confented to name William Coke, the other eight of them divided their votes to different perfons. The beft and major part of the whole convent having thus given their votes for William Coke, thereto qualified as a religious man, profeffing the rule of St. Auguftin and the order of canons regular inftituted in the faid monaftery, honeft, of a lawful age above thirty, in the order of priefthood, born in lawful wedlock, on all which accounts the election was unanimoufly ordered to be made by Robert Syde thus: " In the name of the high and undivided Trinity, Father, Son, and Holy Spirit, Amen. Whereas the monaftery of St. Auguftin, Briftol, is now vacant by the death of Ralph Afch the laft abbot, who has been ecclefiaftically interred, and all thofe who could be prefent and had right of electing a future abbot at

a day

a day and hour appointed for fuch election came together and agreed, that the faid election fhould be made by fcrutiny, which was accordingly made and publifhed, it was clearly found that the beft and major part of the faid whole convent agreed upon frier William Coke, the fub-prior, a provident and difcrete perfon, competently learned, eminent for his morals and converfation in life, a prieft in orders, exprefsly profeffing the rule of St. Auguftin, and the order of canons regular in the faid monaftery, of ripe age, begot in lawful matrimony, prudent in all temporal and fpiritual matters, whom nothing prevents of canonical inftitution. Therefore I Robert Syde, precentor of the faid monaftery on behalf of myfelf and the whole convent by the power given me by the whole convent, invoking the grace of the Holy Spirit, do elect our faid brother William Coke for abbot of the monaftery aforefaid :" and immediately afterwards we all and every one (the faid elect only excepted, who then neither approved nor difapproved the faid election) with one accord confented to and exprefsly approved of the faid election fo folemnly celebrated ; and lifting up the faid elected brother William Coke with our hands amongft us, and finging folemnly Te Deum Laudamus, we carried him to the high altar of the faid monaftery, and reclined him upon the faid altar according to cuftom, and faying the ufual prayer over him, we commanded the faid election to be publifhed in the Englifh tongue to the clergy and laity then in the faid monaftery in great multitude affifting, by the faid frier Robert Syde there prefent, taking on him that order by our direction. The day following 16th March at three o'clock we caufed to be prefented the procefs of the faid election by our fellow canon and proctor Richard Martyn to the faid elected abbot, defiring that he would vouchfafe to yield confent to the faid election ; he willing to fee the faid procefs and to deliberate concerning it received it, and at nine o'clock the fame day the faid proctor required of him confent to the faid election in this manner : " I frier Richard Martyn, the proctor of the prior and convent of canons regular of St. Auguftin, Briftol, in the diocefe of Worcefter, do prefent to you our elect lord for abbot of the faid monaftery the procefs of election made of you ; I alfo require in my own and the name of the faid prior and convent humbly, that you would vouchfafe to impart your confent to the faid election." After this the faid elect after fhort deliberation anfwered the faid proctor, and confented to it in this manner : " In the name of the Father, Son, and Holy Spirit. Amen. I William Coke, canon regular of the monaftery of St. Auguftin, Briftol, in the diocefe of Worcefter, obferving from the tenor of the procefs of election of an abbot of the faid monaftery made of me, which procefs has been offered to me and examined, that the faid election has been made in canonical form, repofing

hope

hope in God of my ability in the faid matter, and unwilling on this occafion to refift the divine will, in honour of God and the glorious Virgin and of St. Auguftin to whofe honour this monaftery was built, do confent to this election made of me." Thus was the election of an abbot conducted in all its forms; nothing now remained but the convent applying to the Bifhop of Worcefter to confirm their choice and to confer the benediction of the abbot, which finifhed the whole, and the abbot was inducted and inftalled by the prior of St. James, to whom a commiffion from the fee of Worcefter was directed for that pur-pofe. Whether this abbot conducted the affairs of the monaftery with pru-dence and good conduct and reformed abufes does not appear; but it is very certain, fuch abufes often exifted there, and in very early times.

In the year 1234, upon the refignation of David the abbot, William prior of the fame church (called William de Bradftone) fucceeded, and received the benediction of an abbot at Worcefter, and fatisfied the facrift concerning his cup and alb (or gown) and the convent in the procurations of 40s. (ann. Wyg.) and in 1242 Walter de Cantelupe Bifhop of Worcefter vifited the monaftery, and upon the refignation of William the abbot, Wm. the Camerarius de Keynfham fucceeded and made the fame fatisfaction.

In the year 1278, 9th Nov. Godfrey Bifhop of Worcefter, in his vifitation of the abby of St. Auguftin, Briftol, found it as well in temporal as fpiritual matters greatly decayed, (damnabiliter prolapfam) and ordered, " that in future they do not as bees fly out of the choir as foon as fervice is ended, but devoutly wait as become holy and fettled perfons, not as vagrants and vaga-bonds; and returning to God due thanks for their benefactors, and fo receiv-ing at laft the fruits of their religion, to which they have fpecially devoted themfelves. And as the prefent abbot was not fufficiently inftructed to pro-pound the word of God in common, he appointed others in his ftead: and that filence be better obferved than ufual, that no one go out without urgent neceffity, and not then but when two are in company, one the elder the other the younger, licenfed by the abbot, or the prior in his abfence.

In the chapter correction was to be done without refpect of perfons, harder penance to be impofed on the more grofs and frequent offenders. In the re-fectory the friers were to be provided as was requifite and the eftates would allow, and to keep filence there as the regular obfervance requires, and there all were to live in common and eat, unlefs neceffity force them to do other-wife, and no brother was to difpofe of the fragments of the table, but the whole be laid up for alms. In the infirmary food and drink was to be pro-vided for the fick, and other things ufeful for them: antl he forbad under a

curfe

curfe that any feign himfelf fick when he is not fo, to live a diffolute life and fraudulently defpife God's worfhip ; and on the like penalty he forbad any fecular perfons being introduced to them except the phyfician and the fervants of the infirmary, nor fhould the friers that were in health meet there for the fake of drinking and furfeiting. Alfo in their meals all were to abftain from detraction and obfcene fpeech, but ufe words of honefty and good tendency to edify the foul. The abbot was to correct all mifdoers in the chapter-houfe, only not publicly ; and when the abbot eat in the refectory or infirmary, his fervants and clerks were to dine with the ftrangers in fome common room and not in their own chambers, nor have any drinking there as was ufed. And as the temporal revenue was not well managed, he ordered that the abbot fhould have two receivers to write diftinctly and openly from whom, what, and when they received, that none receive but thofe two, and that the abbot fhould provide a brother to keep the granary in the abby, and receive from the manors and churches the corn of every kind by diftinct tallies from the deliverers, and further fhall make tallies againft thofe who have the cuftody of the bread and beer, and others who fell corn from the granary. That the abbot fhould fwear all his fervants for the faithful difcharge of their duty, and for rendering a juft account yearly when required ; and that the bailiffs fhall be examined and their accounts approved by four examiners of the convent chofen every year for that purpofe : that at the end of the year what was received and expended, and on what occafion, and what remains may appear to all.

And as the abbot had a fuperfluous family and ufelefs, he appointed that he fhould have a moderate family as William his predeceffor ufed to have, one or two chaplains, two or three fcutiferos and no more; and that his chaplain receive the expences of the abbot when he goes abroad from the receivers, and receive nothing from the bailiffs or fervants, and account with the receivers on his return : and that when the abbot goes from his principal houfe he fee that it be firft well provided with victuals and other things that may be wanting in his abfence, and not keep fplendid entertainments out of his houfe as he ufed, unlefs neceffity and evident ufe require, and this with the confent of the convent. And that Henry of the granary, Hugh the feller of the corn, and Roger the porter be removed from their offices and others more faithful be appointed in their room. And that all ufelefs fervants be turned out, and only the ufeful and neceffary kept; that in his next vifitation nothing be found offenfive but what fhall be profitable to the monaftery.

And

And in the year 1280 John the abbot being very ill detained by ficknefs, the monaftery was again on the decline, and the monks defpifed the rules of the houfe, for which the bifhop threatened them with ecclefiaftical cenfure.

But in the year 1282 he again vifited the monaftery and ftopped there three days; the firft day he vifited St. Auftin's, and the fecond and third the houfe of St. James and St. Mark, and was at his own expence, and found all well (tam in capite quam membris) only that the old abbot lived out of the monaftery in fome manor of his to the lofs of the convent; and that they were burdened with a debt of 300l. fterling, becaufe Bogo de Clare took from them that year a certain church of 150l. againft all juftice.

In the year 1320 the Bifhop of Worcefter at his vifitation corrected feveral irregularities in this monaftery; he ordered all the hounds they kept to be removed, the almoner frier Henry de Glouceftre to be difplaced, and enquiry to be made concerning frier John de Scheftebury accufed of incontinence with certain women unknown, and concerning William Barry for fowing dif-cord among the brethren; that the fick be better provided for, that the bre-thren have a fufficiency, but in cafh as hath been accuftomed, that the mafs of the Bleffed Virgin be duly and folemnly celebrated, that the 40d. be diftri-buted in the convent and not be detained by the prior or fub-prior; that William Barry under a fentence of excommunication for apoftacy be ab-folved, and that his pennance of drinking water only, which he has done conftantly on a Wednefday, be difpenfed with, and that he may drink beer and eat pulfe, but abftain from eating fifh.

In the year 1322 peace was reftored and the difpute fettled between the monaftery of St. Auguftin and the houfe of St. Mark concerning the area or plain called the Cemitery of St. Auftin's, Briftol, and the ufe of the fame.

In 1371 the King fent a letter to William Bifhop of Worcefter, ordering him to vifit the abby of St. Auguftin, Briftol, as Henry who then prefided over it, it appeared had wafted the rents of the faid abby by incurring excef-five charges and other mifmanagement, whereby the divine fervice there was almoft at an end, all alms-giving ceafed, and the canons difperfed for want of fupport, unlefs remedies were foon ufed.

Silvefter Bifhop of Worcefter obliged the abbot and convent of St. Auguftin to pay in right of their prebend of Berkeley five marks a year to the facrift of the church of Worcefter, to find a lamp to burn before the tomb of John, formerly the illuftrious King of England, buried in that church, (L. Rub.
Wygorn,

Wygorn, p. 195. 6.) which was confirmed by Walter the Bifhop the 15th of the kalends of November 1310.

Abbas Santi Auguftini &c. *i. e.* The abbot of St. Auguftine's, Briftol, paid to the Lord Bifhop 3l. 6s. 8d. at the two feafts that is at Eafter and Michaelmas, out of a penfion of the church of Berkeley, which is the fum of five marks above-mentioned, and probably on the fame account.

In 1374 the prior of the church of Worcefter, the fee being then vacant, by authority of the court of Canterbury, iffued a decree for the regulation of the houfe of St. Auguftin, by Briftol, then in great difputes and diforders ; by which he ordained, 1. That alms fhould be done there as ufed according to cuftom and the eftates of the monaftery. 2. That the prior in the abfence of the abbot fhould grant the licences. 3. That the canons in the Infirmary' fhould be relieved while fick, and be provided with victuals more nice than for the healthy and with medicines their ficknefs may require ; and that the patient have 40s. as a favour as ufed. 4. That feven canons worthy of truft have the cuftody of the common feal, and each have one key of it, and the faid keepers be deputed by the abbot. 5. Alfo that the canons go out honeftly to their labour according to cuftom, and have their leifure after dinner in due places as the time permit. 6. That provifion be made for the fecular clerks ufed to finging in the chapel of the Bleffed Virgin, and that they be fupported as of ancient cuftom. 7. That the facrift at his own expence provide for the wax candles that ufed to burn in the faid chapel, and lamps in the church fix, &c. that the chamberlain (camerarius) provide the fame to burn in the dormitory. 8. That five of the older and healthier canons be chofen, with whofe advice the abbot may treat of the greater matters relating to the houfe, and do for the beft ; without whofe advice the corn of the monaftery above ten pounds value fhall not be fold in anywife, and that thefe advifers be chofen by the abbot and convent ; by whofe advice officers of the monaftery fhall be deputed to render an account of their fervices every year or oftener, at the will of the abbot, who may remove them at his pleafure. 9. That as to the fpiritualities of the convent for their habit and other things, collectors be deputed and two receivers by the abbot and convent, who may faithfully deliver and keep the money due and in this part ufed, and diftribute it among the convent by the fupervifion of the abbot and the faid five advifers. 10. That the bedding in the Infirmary be amended, reftored, and honeftly kept. 11. That as to the fecular fervants in the Infirmary, Refectory, or elfewhere on the part of the convent, they fhall be appointed by the abbot and the faid five advifers, which fervants fhall fwear not to divulge to any one the fecret coun-

fels

fels of the convent but faithfully conceal them; and that they will minifter and maintain no matter of difagreement betwixt the abbot and convent and any others, but cherifh peace and love; whoever is found culpable to be removed from their offices. 12. That the beft bedding of all that die in the convent be removed into the Infirmary for the ufe of the fick. 13. That there be had one (brevigerulus) carrier of the fervice books, to do his office and have his ufual fupport. 14. That the cook have no fecular perfon about him in his office. 15. That as to the receival of the common money of the monaftery two prudent men of the convent fhall be chofen by the abbot and the five advifers, and the abbot to be a third, and they to have three keys of the cheft in which the faid money is to be depofited by them, and each fhould carry one of the faid three keys, and then at the command of the abbot and the council of the faid five advifers the faid money fhould be expended for the ufe of the monaftery and convent as fhould feem needful. 15. Alfo that the bread and beer fhould be made better, and alfo be in more competent quantity than hitherto. 16. That as to the kitchen, the convent fhould be provided with two forts of flefh in fufficient quantity at the difcretion of the abbot and the faid five advifers, and that the like be done concerning fifh on fifh-days; and on the fabbath days they fhould be ferved with frefh fifh when to be got; and the convent fhould then after one year be ferved out of the kitchen as had been accuftomed, unlefs any thing fhould happen to prevent fulfilling it, on which occafion the abbot and five advifers were to determine. 17. That for the five marks claimed by the convent out of the manor of Bageruge the abbot would grant fix marks out of Marsfeld if the profits thereof will arife to that fum, otherwife out of the other proventions of the monaftery. 18. Alfo that as to knives being bought yearly for the convent, let them be provided as had been accuftomed.

These regulations were eftablifhed and done in the chapter-houfe of the monaftery in the year 1374, the 27th of Auguft, and confirmed by the official of the fee of Worcefter fetting his feal with witneffes, as appears by the Latin deed in Regift. Wygor. fed. Vecante, f. 179, which I have tranflated above.

In 1345, ift Jan. Wolftan Bifhop of Worcefter confirmed to the monaftery of St. Auguftin the feveral churches of Afhelworth, Berkeley, Wappely, Almondfbury, alfo St. Nicholas, St. Leonard, All-Saints, and St. Auguftin's the Lefs in Briftol.

In 1480, in the time of William Hunt abbot, the prior and convent granted an obiit and mafs to be called Abbot William's Mafs, to be perpetually celebrated by one Cofrere a prieft at feven o'clock every morning, in a certain new chapel of the Bleffed Mary the Virgin, fituate in the Eaft end of the conventual

church,

church, for the good eſtate of the ſaid William while he ſhall live and for his ſoul after he is departed, &c. for that the ſaid William devoutly diſpoſed had cauſed to be erected at his own expence many great barns houſes and other coſtly edifices, as well in divers manors belonging to the ſaid monaſtery as in the ſaid monaſtery itſelf, and had made anew the covering of the whole conventual church, as well by battlements with ſtones and pinnacles decently placed round the ſaid church as by timber, lead and other neceſſaries, and had given to the monaſtery there for ever to remain certain veſſels ſilver and gilt, and ſome other jewels (jocalia) ſilver and gilt of no ſmall value, and conferred many other gifts and benefits on his monaſtery while he was abbot. The convent enſured to the Biſhop of Worceſter the manor of Gorwell in Somerſet, with a right of common on Menydepe for the prior to pay for ever for this obiit, which was eſtimated at 8l. a year; he died the 14th March 1480.

In 1481 John Newland alias Neilheart, was choſen abbot in his ſtead.

The following is a liſt of the abbots from Brown Willis, and from the regiſters of Worceſter and abbot Newland's manuſcript compared with others.

1. Richard the firſt abbot was inſtituted in 1148 and governed 38 years, (28 according to Newland,) till his death.

2. Phillip ſucceeded and was removed 1196 (according to the Mon. Anglic. v. 1. p. 1034.) to Bellelande in Yorkſhire.

3. John, he governed 29 years, and died the 12th of February 1215, and another of the ſame name ſucceeded. See page 246.

4. John (according to Newland Joſeph) died in ſix weeks, and others ſay 31 weeks after his election.

5. David was choſen 1216, reſigned or died 1234, and was buried under a marble with the figure of a human ſkull and croſs on it, near the Elder Lady's Chapel, ſtill to be ſeen there.

6. William de Bradeſtone, his arms are in the window over the high altar, A. on a canton, G. a roſe or. barbed proper. He was of Winterborne in the county of Gloceſter; he reſigned the 20th of Auguſt 1242, after which he lived ten years.

7. William Long, called Camerarius de Cainſham, ſaid to have been a monk there; he died the 17th of May 1264, and lies buried in the North aile on the left hand of Hugh Dodington.

8. Richard de Malmſbury, he died the 13th of September 1276, after governing 12 years.

9. John

9. John de Marina elected the 10th of October 1276, was long troubled with sickness and died the 26th of February 1286, having governed 10 years, and was buried in the chapter-house.

10. Hugh of Dodington was confirmed abbot 1287, pat. 9th of Edward 1ft. died the 26th of November 1294, after governing 8 years, and was buried in the cross North aile betwixt two other abbots.

11. James Barry, he obtained the royal assent the 16th of December following, pat. 22d of Edward the 1ft. he governed 12 years and died the 12th of November 1306, and was buried under a marble on the South side of the Rood altar. In 1299 going to Almondsbury late in the evening, many armed men entered suddenly and broke in upon him and took away what the abbot had there for his houshold, and killed his steward. Annal. Wygorn.

12. Edmund Knowles, or de Knolle, was elected by virtue of the royal licence dated the 30th of November 1306, (1311 Reg. Wyg.) he governed about 26 years. He is in Newland's account said to have begun rebuilding the church anew the 25th of Edward the 1ft. the 20th of August, that is now standing from the ground, (" Ecclesia jam funditus diruta," Reg. Wygorn,) with the vestry and also the King's-hall and chamber, and the fratry; and procured of the King a confirmation of all the possessions of the monastery. The fourth Maurice Lord Berkeley was a great promoter of this grant, and procured a papal bull to get benefactions towards rebuilding the church, see the patent and clause rolls the 31ft of Edward the 1ft. and the 10th of Edward the 2d. 1317. Abbot Knowles died the 9th of June 1332, and was buried against the North wall before the Rood high altar; his figure is in pontificalibus carved in freestone, lying on his back with a crosier in his hand and mitre on his breast; arms G. or. a chevron arg. three roses of the first.

13. John Snow was the first abbot of this monastery summoned to parliament, and indeed the last; he received the benediction from the Bishop of Worcester at Hartlebury-palace the 4th of July 1332, (the 17th of June according to Newland); having governed 9 years he died July the 12th, 1341.

14. Ralph Ash, or Asch, was confirmed abbot the 2d of August (21ft July Reg. Wyg.) 1341, died the 1ft of March 1353, and was buried in the middle of the choir : he bore for arms a tree in a field all proper; he petitioned to be discharged from attending the parliament, as expensive to his house, and obtained it in 1341.

15. William Cook was installed by mandate from the prior of Worcester in the vacancy of that see the 7th of March 1353, resigned in October 1363, and

K k 2
died

died the 8th of April following, 1364, and was buried before the door entering the Lady's chapel, where the crofs of lead is ftill to be feen. According to Newland he refigned 1365 and died 1366, and that in his time it was found by inquifition what lands the monaftery poffeffed as by efch. the 45th of Edward the 3d. 1330, memb. 72, in the Tower of London.

16. Henry Shellingford, alias Blebery, elected 1366, he died the 2d of December 1388, and was buried in the nether tomb of the prefbytery which he caufed to be made befide the high altar. He is faid to have wafted the poffeffions of the monaftery by injurious leafes and his own exorbitant expences, &c. as appears by a letter of Edward the 3d. the 45th year. Reg. Wygorn. Lynn. fol. 48.

17. John Cerny governed 5 years, he died the 5th of October 1393, and was buried in the over tomb of the prefbytery.

18. John Daubeny governed 35 years, and died the 26th of January 1428.

19. Walter Newbury met with great trouble in his office, being unjuftly expelled for five years, and one Thomas Sutton intruded into his place, till thruft out by the convent for dilapidations and other waftes committed in fuffering quit rents to be loft; hence no account is taken of his death. As to the abbot Newbury he was a great benefactor to his church, and built the offices to the manor-houfe of Leigh, alfo the manor-houfes of Fyfhead in Dorfetfhire, and of Almondfbury and Afhelworth in Glocefterfhire, belonging at prefent to the bifhoprick of Briftol: he governed 35 years, died 1463 the 3d of September, (1473 Reg. Wyg.) and was buried againft the North wall of the chapel, carved in ftone in pontificalia, lying on his back with crofier and mitre.

20. William Hunt elected the 11th of September 1463, (9th Oct. 1473, Reg. Wyg.) and having governed 18 years, (7 years Reg. Wyg.) died the 14th of March 1481; he was a liberal benefactor to his monaftery; rebuilt the roof of the church and ailes, and caufed the lead to be new caft all from the tower eaftward, for which he had a yearly mafs decreed him perpetually to be obferved; his arms were az. a St. Andrew's crofs or.

21. John Newland, alias Naileheart, elected the 6th of April 1481; arms arg. three nails or. peircing an heart vuln'd proper: he was a very learned man, of great abilities, and often employed by King Henry the 7th. in foreign embaffies: he beautified his church and added many buildings to it, and wrote its biftory and account of the family of the Berkeleys, ftill in manufcript: having governed 34 years, he died the 12th of June 1515, and

was

was buried here under a ſtately monument.—In Wood's Athenœ Oxon. v. 1,
p. 639, may be read a long account of him, " that he was called the good
abbot, a perſon ſolely given to religion and alms deeds," &c.

22. Robert Elliot elected the 27th of September 1515, (7th Sept. Reg. Wyg.)
he enjoyed it 10 years before 1. Somerſet, which I take notice of becauſe his
name is omitted in the liſt of abbots in the chapter-houſe, and by Brown
Willis; he had ſome ſhare in building the ſtately gate-houſe with abbot
Newland, at leaſt the upper part of it above the arch, where they made nitches
in which they did not forget to place their own ſtatues with their arms underneath. On the floor of the cathedral are a great many ſquare bricks with the
initials R E for this abbot's name; alſo ſhields of arms with the ſame initials,
which are arg. on a chief G. two mullets of the firſt.

23. John Somerſet elected about 1526, died 1533; he bears the Somerſet
arms.

24. William Burton elected the 9th of September 1534, he with John
Giles and 17 others of the monaſtery ſubſcribed to the King's ſupremacy, and
three years after deceaſed, the 28th of Henry the 8th. 1537.

25. Morgan Guilliam ap Guilliam elected 1537, being the laſt abbot; he
ſurrendered his monaſtery into the King's hands the 9th of December 1539,
and obtained a penſion of 80l. per annum for life, he died before the year
1553.—In Fuller and Speed's biſtory he is charged with keeping ſix lewd
women, but it is thought without very good evidence; theſe and worſe crimes
were imputed to the monks as a ſtrong and plauſible excuſe for diſſolving
their houſes.

As this houſe was one of the great abbies, it came to the crown by the
ſtatute of the 31ſt of Henry the 8th. and was certified to be worth in old rents,
according to Speed 767l. 15s. 3d. per annum, to Г idg. clear 670l. 13s. 11d.
and ſome little proviſion was made for the monks then turned out.

The following account appears entered in the book of penſions on the
date of the King's commiſſion, which has this entry dated December the 9th
31ſt Henry the 8th. 1539.

> Pirſt, " To Morgan Guilliam late abbat there, with the Manſion Place
> of Lee, (that is Abbot's Leigh,) the garden, orchard and dove-houſe
> to the ſame adjoyning and yealding, (and alſo 20 loads of fyer-wood
> yearly to be perceyved and taken out of the wood of the ſaid mannor
> by the aſſignment of the Kings Highneſs's ſurveyor or keeper
> there

there during his life without any thing yielding or paying for the
fame,)   -   -   -   -   £ 80 0 0

				£		
Item, To Humfry Hicman late prior there,			-	8	0	0
John Reftal,	-	-	-	8	0	0
John Carye,	-		-	6	13	4
Nicholas Corbett,	-	-	-	6	13	4
Henry Pavye,	-		-	6	0	0
William Wrington,	-	-	-	6	0	0
William Underwood,	-		-	6	0	0
Richard Hill,	-		-	6	0	0
Richard Orrell,			-	6	0	0
Richard Sterley,			-	6	0	0
Richard Hughes,			-	6	0	0

Sum   £ 151 6 8

It is uncertain what became of thefe religious afterwards. In the year 1553
John Reftal, Richard Orell, Richard Kerfey, Richard Hughes, and William
Underwood, were living and received their penfions.—In 1554 Rich. Hughes
was made a prebendary of this church.

King Henry having got infinite treafure by fuppreffing thefe religious houfes,
the better to palliate that feeming facrilege doubtlefs greatly cried out againft
by the people of thofe days, made a fhew of refunding part by erecting fix
new bifhopricks, of which this diffolved monaftery was one, which in the 34th
year of his reign was erected into a bifhoprick, confifting of a Bifhop, Dean
and fix Prebendaries, &c. though like other things ordered in that confufion
the diocefe was very much diftant from the fee. The church of the monks
was fixed upon for the cathedral; which began to be demolifhed, and was
like to undergo the common fate of other ancient and venerable ftructures
(once the glory and ornament of the Englifh nation:) If my author rightly
informs me, the rapacious difpofition of the men of thofe times was fuch, that
for the fake of the lead with which the weft part of this church was covered,
they were actually fet to work upon the fame, and after they had uncafed the
roof, quickly proceeded to deftroy the ftructure itfelf (which was in part
effected) but a ftop being put to the fame by order from the King, by his being
informed, that there was yet left ftanding of the fabrick fufficient to make it
a cathedral for the bifhop's fee, the further deftruction was prevented, and
it was left in that ruinous condition at the weft fide of the tower ftill to be
feen,

feen, a ftanding monument of the precipitate **and confufed diforder** with which matters were then carried on, and of the rage then ftirred up and violence ufed againft the monks and their fuperb buildings, where great hofpitality was obliged to be kept for the relief of the poor; while the monafteries ftood there was no act for their relief, fo amply did thofe hofpitable houfes fuccour thofe in want, whereas in the next reign 39 Eliz. no lefs than eleven bills were brought into parliament for that fole purpofe, and how real a burden the poor tax has been fince needs not be mentioned. The refection and fupport of the poor was one of the articles often inferted in the grants to thofe houfes. This good cannot then be denied them.

In one of the plays attributed to Shakefpeare, wrote certainly as early, called the Life of Lord Cromwell, in edition of Tonfon, 1728, vol. ix. p. 166. this ufe of the monafteries is thus infifted on by Gardiner.

    Gardiner. Have I not reafon when religion is wrong'd?
             You had no colour for what you have done.
    Cromwell. Yes: the abolifhing of antichrift,
             And of his Popifh order from our realms:
             I am no enemy to religion,
             But this is done; it is for England's good;
             What did they ferve for? But to feed a fort
             Of lazy abbots and of full-fed friers?
             They neither plow nor fow, and yet they reap
             The fat of all the land, and fuck the poor:
             Look what was their's is in King Henry's hands,
             His wealth before lay in the abby lands.
    Gardiner. Indeed thefe things you have alledged, my Lord,
             When, God doth know, the infant yet unborn
             Will curfe the time the abbies were pull'd down;
             I pray you where is hofpitality?
             Where now may poor diftreffed people go
             For to relieve their need or reft their bones,
             When weary travel doth opprefs their limbs:
             And where religious men fhould take them in.
             Shall now be kept back by a maftiff dog,
             And thoufand thoufands, &c.

Though the drones were turned out of the hive, yet the buildings fo fuperb and fo ornamental to the kingdom might have been fpared, and converted to
                                       the

the ufes of charity and hofpitality and be made houfes of induftry to employ the poor, like country work-honfes fo much talked of now, though fo
flowly put in practice on account principally of the expence in erecting them.

To conclude the account of this abby, I here add a copy of the foundation
charter, preferved ftill in Berkeley caftle, with a tranflation, referring the
reader for the reft of the deeds, &c. to the places where they may be
confulted.

Prioratus Sancti Auguftini de Briftol in agro Glouceftrenfi.

Carta Roberti filii Hardingi, de fundatione ejufdem.

* Robertus filius Hardingi, omnibus hominibus et amicis fuis, et univerfis
fanctæ ecclefiæ fidelibus, ad quos hæc carta pervenerit, falutem : Sciatis quod
cum Dominus Rex Henricus manerium de Berchallé, et totam Berchaleiernefſe
mihi in feodum et hæreditatem dediffet, et Cartâ fuâ confirmâffet, cum omnibus
libertatibus et rebus ad Berchaleiernefſe pertinentibus, in ecclefiis, in nemoribus,
in pratis, et pafturis, et in omnibus aliis rebus, fieut fuerunt tempore Henrici
regis avi fui : Ego confenfu et affenfu ipfius domini mei regis, ecclefias de
Berchaleiernefſe; fcilicet, ecclefiam de Berchalé, et ecclefiam de Were,
et ecclefiam de Beverftan, et ecclefiam de Effeleward ; et ecclefiam de Almo-
defburi, fingulis cum capellis, et terris, et libertatibus ad ipfas ecclefias pertinentibus, pro falute animæ meæ, et domini mei regis, et anteceſſorum meorum, et uxoris meæ, et liberorum, dedi et conceffi ecclefiæ Sancti
Auguftini de Briftoll, et canonicis regularibus ibidem domino fervientibus, in perpetuam et liberam elemoffinam, nullo jure retento, mihi vel
hæredibus meis, in prædictis ecclefiis, cum eas vacare contigerit. ——
Similiter et omnes ecclefias de Berchaleiernefſe, ubicunque fuerint, cum
capellis et omnibus corum pertinentiis dedi, et conceffi prædictis canonicis
in perpetuam elemofinam, et hac meâ cartâ confirmavi. Hiis teftibus,
Henrico Decano Moretoniæ, et Mauritio fratre ejus, Giraldo perfona ecclefiæ de cam, W. de Saltmaris, et Adamo fratre ejus, Helia filio Hardingi,
Richardo fcriptore, et Alano de Bedmeniftra.

The priory of St. Anguftin, in Briftol, in the county of Glocefter.

A deed of Robert fon of Harding concerning the foundation thereof.

Robert fon of Harding to all men and his friends, and all the faithful to
to the holy church, to whom this charter fhall come, health: know ye that
whereas our Sovereign Lord King Henry gave to me in fee the manor of
Berchalle, and all Berchallcirenefſe and all that belong to the fame, and by
his deed hath confirmed the fame with all the privileges thereto belonging,
with its appurtenances both in churches, woods, meadows, paftures, and in
                                                                          all

* Ex ipfo autographo in armario cartarum prænobilis Georgii Domini Berkley, apud Berkley
caftrum.

all other things, as they were in the time of his grandfather King Henry. I therefore with the full affent and confent of the faid Lord my King have given and granted to the church of St. Auguftin of Briftol, and to the canons regular there ferving God, for the health of my own foul and the fouls of my King, my anceftors, my wife, and children all thofe churches belonging to Berchaleirneffe, (to wit) the church of Berchallé, Were, Beverftan, Effe-lefward and Almodefbury, with all chapels, lands, and privileges, with the appurtenances to thofe churches belonging, to be held in free and perpetual alms, no right being retained by me or my heirs in or to the faid churches, when they become vacant: I have likewife given and granted all the churches belonging to Berchaleirnefs, wherever they fhall be, with the chapels and all their appurtenances to the faid canons in perpetual alms, confirming the fame by this charter. Thefe being witneffes: Henry Dean of Moreton and Maurice his brother, Girald, the parfon of the church of Cam, W. of Saltmarfh, Adam his brother, Heli the fon of Harding, Richard the fecretary, and Alan of Bedminfter.

    [This deed is of about the year 1148. Bifhop Tanner, in his Notitia Monaftica, p. 480. thinks this is the foundation charter.]

    The other following deeds, public records, books, &c. as quoted by Bifhop Tanner, in the Notitia Monaftica, (edition by J. Nafmith, A. M.) give a full and fatisfactory account of many particulars of the hiftory, endowments, rig..ts, advowfons, &c. of the abby and bifhopric, to which I refer.

    Vide in Monaf. Ang. vol. ii. p. 232, 233, cartam Roberti filii Hardingi de fundatione* prioratus: carmina quædam Anglic. de Roberto Harding. pat. 11, Edw. 2d. p. 2d. m. 29. per infpex. recit. cartas Henrici Ducis Normanniæ confirm. Almodefberiam, Wappeleiam, etc. Roberti filii Hardingi et Johannis com. Moriton.

    See Monafticon Anglicanum, vol. ii. p. 232, the deed of Robert fon of Harding of the foundation of the priory and certain Englifh verfes of Robert Harding, 2d Edw. 2d. p. 2, m. 29, reciting the deeds of Henry Duke of Normandy confirming Almondfbury, Wappling, &c. Of Robert fon of Harding and John Earl of Morton.

    In Willis's Hiftory of Abbies, vol. i. p. 225, &c. an account of this church, with a catalogue of the abbots,

I. L

ibid

    * Thus the title in the Monafticon. But this charter was not made till after King Henry 2d. came to the crown, and this monaftery was certainly founded before his reign, he having whilft only Duke of Normandy made feveral donations to it, and declaring in one of his grants that this monaftery " cepi initio juventutis meæ fovere et juvare." — I rather think the charter of Rob. fil. Harding. Mon. Angl. vol. ii. p. 232, b. lin. 64, is the foundation charter.

ibid p. 324, and App. p. 65, 66.

In his Survey of Cathedrals, vol. i. p. 758, a further account of this church, an account of perfons buried there, of the endowment of the bifhopric and chapter, with a catalogue of the bifhops, deans, archdeacons, and prebendaries, and the names of all the parifhes in the diocefe, &c.

In Le Neve's Fafti, p. 48, the fucceffion of the bifhops, deans, archdeacons, and prebendaries of this cathedral.

In Rileii Plac. Parliam. p. 165, concordiam inter Bogonem de Clare et abbatem St. Auguftini Briftol, 21 ft Edw. 1ft.

In Ryley's Pleas of Parliament, p. 165, between Bogo de Clare and the abbot of St. Auguftine of Briftol, the 21ft of Edward 1ft.

In Dugd. Baron. vol. i. p. 358, 359, of a chantry, &c. herein founded by Thomas Lord Berkeley.

Year Books, 35th Hen. 6th. Mich. § 43. In Stevens's Supplement, vol. ii. p. 140, a catalogue of the abbots.

In Rymeri Conventionum, &c. tom. v. p. 246, pat. 15th Edw. 3d. p. i. m. 13, pro abbate, de non veniendo ad parliamentum quia non tenet per baroniam nec de fundatione regis *

In Ryder's Conventionum, &c. vol. v. p. 246, patent, 15th Edw. 3d. p. 1, m. 13, concerning excufing the abbot for not coming to parliament, becaufe he did not hold the fame, by reafon of the barony nor as the foundation of a king.

Concerning the erection of the bifhopric.

Tom. xiv. p. 748, pat. 34th Hen. 8th. p. 10, m. 26, de erectione epifcopatus.

Tom. xv. p. 77, pat. 37th Hen. 8th. p. 9, m. 25, fuper diftributione 40 l. per ann. eleemofynarum per decanum et capitulum.

Vol. xv. p. 77, patent 37, Henry 8th. p. 9, m. 25, the diftribution of the 40 l. per annum in alms by the dean and chapter.

Ibid,

* Printed alfo in Stevens's Appendix, p. 350.

Ibid, p. 370, commiſſionem ad de-privandum Paulum epiſc. Briſtol, A. D. 1554.

Ibid, p. 459, pat. 3 et 4, Phil. et Mar. p. 10, m. 24, pro exoneratione Johannis epiſc. Briſtol. a primitiis et decimis, ratione epiſcopatus.

Tom. xvi. p. 524, pro Joanne Thornborough epiſc. electo, deca-natum et prebendam in eccl. Ebor. in commendam poſſidentes, eo quod epiſ-copatus Briſtol tam exilis eſt.

Regiſtra, cartas originales, &c. pe-nes R. R. dom. epiſcopum et decanum et capitulum eccle. eath. Briſtol.

Regiſtrum five potius hiſtoriam fun-dationis hujus cœnobii a Joanne New-land abbate contextam, MS. apud caſtrum de Berkeley in com. Gloceſt.

Abbreviaturas quarundam conceſſi-onum huic abbatiæ in MS. Macro, 12, ii. f. 2, a. f. 18, a.

Fin. Buckingh. 5 Joan. n. 125, de terris in Finemere ; fin. in div. com. 11 Joan. n. 55, de advoc. eccl. de Lanvernac, Glamorg.

Cart. 36 Hen. 3. m. 13.

Plac. in com. Somerſet. 8 Edw. 1. aſſiſ. rot. 27, de c. acris terra: in Legh.

Cart. 13 Edw. 1. n. 15, pro mer-cato et feria apud Almundeſbury, Glo-ceſterſhire.

The ſame, p. 370, a commiſſion to deprive Paul Buſh, Biſhop of Briſtol, in the year 1554.

The ſame, p. 459, patent the 3d and 4th of Philip and Mary, page 10, m. 24, concerning the exemption of John Biſhop of Briſtol from firſt fruits and tythes.

Vol. xvi. p. 524, concerning John Thornborough, his being elected Bi-ſhop of Briſtol and his holding the deanery and prebendary of York in commendam, becauſe of the ſmallneſs of the income of the biſhopric of Briſtol.

The Regiſters and original writings &c. in the keeping of R. R. Lord Bi-ſhop and the dean and chapter of the cathedral church of Briſtol.

The Regiſter or rather the biſtory of the foundation of this monaſtery, by John Newland, abbot, to be found in the caſtle of Berkeley, in the county of Gloceſter. (Manuſcript.)

Abridgments of certain grants to this abbot in Dr. Macro's manuſcript, 12. ii. f. 2, f. 18, a.

Certain fines in Buckinghamſhire, the 5th of John, n. 125, of lands in Finemere: fines in div. com. 11 John, n. 55, concerning the church of Lan-vernack, Glamorganſhire.

Pleas in the county of Somerſet, 8th of Edw. 1ſt. in the rote of aſſizes the 27th, concerning 100 acres of land in Legh.

A deed the 13th of Edward 1ſt. n. 15, for holding a fair at Almondſ-bury, in the county of Gloceſter

Ibid,

Ibid, n. 35, pro lib. war. in Al-
mundefbury, Harfold, et Crumhole,
Gloceftr. Leye, Somerfet. Fifhide,
Dorfet.

The fame, n. 35, for a free War-
ren in Almonfbury, Horfield, and
Cromhole, in the county of Glocefter,
Leye, in the county of Somerfet, and
Fifhead, in Dorfetfhire.

Plac. in com. Gloceftr. 15 Edw. 1ft.
quo war. rot. 16, pro libertat. in Berke-
lehernes, &c. pat. 23 Edw. 1. m.

Pleas in the county of Glocefter the
15th of Edward 1ft. by which are war-
ranted certain privileges, roll the 16th
in the hundred of Berkeley, &c.
Patent the 23d of Edw. 1ft. m.

Pat. 5 Edw. 2. p. 1, m. 22, pro
eccl. de Wotton approprianda.

Patent 5th Edward 1ft. p. 1. m. 22,
of the appopriation of the church of
Wotton.

Cart. 11 Edw. 2. n. 17.
Pat. 4 Edw. 3. p. 2. m.
Pat. 8 Edw. 3. p. 2, m. 3, pro eccl.
de Fifhyde.
Pat. 11 Edw. 3. p. 3, m. 32, vel. 33.
Pat. 18 Edw. 3. p. 2, m. 6, vel. 7,
et m. 46, vel. 47, de excambio cum
priore S. John. Jerufalem.
Pat. 26 Edw. 3. p. 1. m. 10.
Pat. 26 Edw. 3. p. 3, m. de Claven-
fwell. efcaet. Somerfet. 27 Edw. 3.
n. 52.
Pat. 32 Edw. 3. p. 2, m. 12.
, Pat. 40 Edw. 3. p. 1. m. 35, vel. 36.
Efcaet. Gloceftr. 45 Edw. 3. n. 72.
Efcaet. Dorfet. 49 Edw. 3. p. 2,
n. 46.
Pat. 20 Rich. 2. p. 2. m. 11, de ter-
ris, pafturis, et hofcis, in Berkeley,
Gloceftr.
Ibid, m. 22, pro eccl. de Fifhide
approprianda.
Pat. 12. Edw. 4. p. 1, m. 15.·
Ibid, p. 2, m. 16 et 24, rec. in
fcacc. 16 Hen. 8. Mich. rot. 10.

For the church of Fifhead.

Of an exchange with the priory of
St. John of Jerufalem.

Of Clavenfwell efchaet, Somerfet.

Of the lands, paftures, and woods, in
Berkeley, Glocefterfhire.

Of appropriating Fifhead,

Pat.

Pat. 34 Hen. 8. p. 10, (10 Jun.) pro dotatione epifcopatus.

Ibid, (Nov. 28.) pro dotatione decani et capituli.

In Atkyns's Glocefterfhire, p. 212, manor and advowfon of Almondfbury, of Afhelworth, p. 222, Arlingham, &c. &c. &c.

In Hutchin's Dorfetfhire, vol. ii. p. 301, advowfon of Fyfehead, and lands in G. Kington.

In Adamo Domerham, p. 197, poffeffiones hujus abbatiæ infra bundas foreftarum in Somerfet.

In Dr. Archer's Account of Religious Houfes, p. 632, advowfons hereto belonging in the diocefe of Bath and Wells.

William of Worceftre Dimenfiones Ecclcfiæ, p. 233, 289.

Leland, Colle&. vol. i. 85. Itin. vol. i. 91, 94, &c.

Pat. 34th Henry 8th. (10th June) endowment of the bifhopric.

Endowment of the dean and chapter, (Nov. 28.)

In Adam Domerham, p. 197, the poffeffions of this abby within the bounds of the forefts in Somerfet.

C H A P.

CHAP. IX.

Of the BISHOPRICK *of* BRISTOL, *its* DIOCESE, CATHEDRAL, &c.

THE Abby of St. Auguſtin ſo liberally endowed, ſo powerfully protected, and ſo ſtrongly ſecured by royal charters and confirmations, was now
to yeild to the common fate of other religious houſes which were ſeized for the
King's uſe, though it was thought their riches were the occaſion of their ruin,
and their gold, jewels and eſtates were wanted to enrich the royal coffers;
yet ſome plauſible excuſes were to be found for the diſſolution; and the commiſſioners ſent upon this buſineſs in many places probably had ſome juſt
warrant for their proceedings, yet they often exceeded their commiſſions.

The low finances of the King and an exhauſted treaſury were the principal
reaſons of their uſing this violent meaſure; they caſt about them in their
neceſſities and here found a ready ſupply to their wants. But there are ſome
cauſes that have been unnoticed, which ſurely contributed in their natural
tendency to haſten and facilitate the diſſolution, and aboliſh the monaſtic
life.—The late great increaſe of trade and navigation, and the diſcovery of
America not long before, and the advantages of a free extended commerce
had begun now to open men's minds and to give a ſpring and activity to them
unknown before, and to take them off from the quiet ſtill life of contempla-
tion and religious retirement. The monks themſelves too grew leſs ſtrict in
their diſcipline, leſs obſervant of their rule, mixing more with the world,
which was often complained of in the viſitations of their houſes by the biſhops;
their number being ſeldom kept up, in many not enough to make a convent,
or ſociety. — A buſy life of commerce and attention to trade eagerly purſued
would probably produce ſimilar effects now, would ſoon ſupplant religion
and baniſh it out of the kingdom, if our conſtitution of government in church
and ſtate were not ſo intimately blended, and our religious eſtabliſhment not
made part of the law of the land, ſo that one cannot long ſubſiſt without the
other, but each now mutually ſupports the other, and will neceſſarily do ſo,
and the Chriſtian religion will thus continue in England ever to flouriſh

in

in its purity amongft us. — Henry the 8th. whofe profufion of expence and ftrong paffions impelled him to take, and undaunted fpirit and refolution ena- bled him to execute this bold undertaking, was a man of underftanding and great abilities, and if we may believe his royal word, had fome good motives in this ruin and defolation of monafteries, intending much the reformation of abufes, increafe of religion, and encouragement of learning : — in erecting fix new bifhopricks out of the fpoils of the abbies he gave fome proof of thefe good intentions. His expreffions in the deed of erection of the bifhoprick of Briftol are very pointed: " Divinâ nos clementiâ infpirante," &c. i. e. " Infpired by the divine clemency, We from our heart affecting nothing more than that the true religion and true worfhip of God may not only not be abolifhed, but that rather it may be wholly reftored and reformed to the pri- mitive rule of its own genuine purity ; and having corrected the enormities into which the life and profeffion of the monks in the long courfe of time had moft deplorably increafed, (exorbitaverat,) we have endeavoured as far as human infirmity can provide againft it, that in future in this fame place inftructions out of the holy oracles and facraments of our faving redemption may be purely adminiftered, the difcipline of good manners be fincerely kept, youth be liberally inftructed in learning, old age failing in ftrength be cherifhed with things neceffary for their fupport, that alms to the poor may abound, and the repairs of highways and bridges may from hence be fupported, &c. We have therefore erected this bifhoprick, &c."

Briftol was judged fit for this purpofe, being a large populous place and convenient for honour and dignity with regard to fituation, though part of the diocefe is very far diftant from the fee.

For the foundation of it is taken chiefly out of Salifbury, by feparating the county and archdeaconry of Dorfet from that diocefe; out of Worcefter, by taking feveral parifhes in Glocefterfhire, (part of which lay in Briftol city, then in that county ;) and out of Wells, which had three churches or chapels alfo in the fame city. — The number of parifhes in this diocefe, which befides Briftol city contains the whole county of Dorfet, are, as D. Heylin tells us 236, of which 64 are impropriated ; though in truth it has 256 churches and chapels, of which 221 are in the county of Dorfet in that archdeaconry, 3 in Briftol city on the Somerfetfhire fide in the archdeaconry of Bath, and the reft in the deanry of Briftol ; which deanry befides 15 parifhes within the liberties of the city comprehends 17 more out-lying churches and chapels in Glocefterfhire, moft of which, though heretofore under the archdeaconry of Glocefter, (befides little St. Auguftine's and St. Philip's in Briftol, which ftill

belong

belong to the fame archdeaconry,) are now fubject to the immediate jurifdiction of the Bifhop of Briftol and his Chancellor, and exempted from arch-
diaconal jurifdiction. The county of Dorfet ftill remains under its proper
archdeacon, who has thefe deanries all in Dorfetfhire under him, viz. Dor-
chefter, Bridport, Pimperne, Shaftefbury, Whitchurch, firft and fecond part;
the two other deanries are Briftol, (all of it heretofore in the archdeaconry of
Glocefter and diocefe of Worcefter,) and Bedminfter cum Redclift in Somerfetfhire, in the archdeaconry of Bath, (formerly in the diocefe of Bath and
Wells.) The clergy tenths according to Heylin's account amount to
353l. 18s. and a farthing.

DIOCESE of BRISTOL.

First Fruits.				Yearly Tenths.		
l.	s.	d.		l.	s.	d.
294	11	0¼	Bifhoprick of Briftol - - -	27	14	4¾

The cathedral—dedicated to the Holy and undivided Trinity—olim the
conventual church of St. Auguftin's monaftery.

N. B. The yearly tenths were altered by judgment of the court of exchequer Hilary term the 8th of Eliz. to 27l. 14s. 4¾d. The patent of erection
of this bifhoprick bears date June the 4th, 1542, the 34th of Henry the 8th.
as in Rymer, v. 14, p. 748. The deanry of this church is in the gift of the
King, and not charged with firft fruits and tenths.

ARCHDEACONRY of BATH, and formerly in the diocefe of Bath and
Wells; DEANRY of REDCLIFT CUM BEDMINSTER in the county
of Somerfet.

CITY of BRISTOL.

Names of Churches and Chapels. Value in King's books. Rated 1534.	Pattons of Livings. Clear value as returned 1711.	Religious Houfe, To which anciently impropriated.	Yearly Tenths.
l. s. d.			
3 4 2 St. Grofs, alias Temple church cur. } l. s. d. 33 2 8	City of Briftol,	Knight Templars,	l. s. d. 0 6 5
12 6 3 St. Mary Redclift vic. St. Thomas. cap. Abbot's Leigh, Holy Trinity. } 40 13 8	{ Prebendary of Bed- minfter in the church of Salif- bury.	Prebendary of Bedminfter. }	1 4 7½

Formerly

Formerly in the ARCHDEACONRY of GLOCESTER and DIOCESE of WORCESTER.

Names of Churches and Chapels. Value in King's books. Rated 1534.			Clear value as returned 1711			Patrons of Livings.	Religious Houſe, To which anciently impropriated.	Yearly Tenths.		
l.	s.	d.	l.	s.	d.			l.	s.	d.
4	3	4	All-Saints vic. 21	11	8	Chapter of Briſtol.	Abby of Briſtol.	0	8	4
6	0	0	St. Auſtin's the leſs vic. 5	10	0	Ditto.	Ditto.	0	12	0
11	0	0	Chriſt-Church, alias Trinity rec.	3 8 0 }		City of Briſtol.				
			St. Ewen's, alias St. Owen's rec.	0 6 8 }		Ditto.				
			St. James's cur.			City of Briſtol.	Priory of St. James, Briſtol. Abby of Tewkeſbury.			
7	4	7	St. John Baptiſt rec. cum St. Laurence now demoliſhed.	5 8 1		Ditto.		0	14	5½
12	0	0	St. Leonard's vic.	4 1 5		Chapter of Briſtol.	Abby of Briſtol.	1	4	0
6	0	0	St. Michael's rec.	5 18 11		City of Briſtol.		0	12	0
			St. Mark's cur.	.		Ditto.	College of the Gaunts in Briſtol.			
7	0	0	St. Maryport rec.	6 6 10		Duke of Chandois.	Abby of Keynſham.	0	14	0
21	1	3	St. Nicholas vic.	7 16 6		Chapter of Briſtol.	Abby of Briſtol.	2	2	1½
6	7	6	St. Peter's rec.	0 12 5		City of Briſtol.		0	12	9
15	0	0	St. Philip and St. Jacob's vic.	43 16 5		Ditto.	Abby of Tewkeſbury.	1	10	0
16	0	0	St. Stephen's rec.	20 13 11		The Crown.	Abby of Glaſtonbury.	1	12	0
10	0	0	St. Werburgh's rec.	33 6 8		Ditto.	Abby of Keynſham.	1	0	0

County of GLOCESTER, DEANRY of BRISTOL, and ARCHDEACONRY of GLOCESTER,

20	0	0	Almondſbury vic. St. Mary.	40 13 10		Biſhop of Briſtol.	Abby of Briſtol.	2	0	0
			Clifton cur. St. Andrew.	10 0 0		Rev. Mr. Taylor.	College of Weſtbury.			
7	0	0	Compton Greenfield rec.	48 1 3		Lady Lippincott.		0	14	0
6	12	6	Elberton, annexed cur. to Olveſton 1770.	46 0 0		Biſhop of Briſtol.	Abby of Briſtol.	0	13	3

Names

Names of Churches and Chapels. Value in King's books. Rated 1534. l. s. d.	Patrons of Livings. Clear value as returned 1711. l. s. d.		Religious House, To which anciently impropriated. Yearly Tenths l. s. d.
7 0 0 Filton St. Peter rec.	36 11 3	M. Brickdale, Esq;	0 14 0
30 0 0 Henbury, St. Mary, vic. cum. Auft and Northwick chapels.	28 4 6	Sir J. H. Smyth and Mr. Gores; Lord Middleton & Mrs. Collton.	See of Worcester. 3 0 0
11 4 9 Littleton rec.	35 17 6	Lady Lippincott.	1 2 5¼
Mangotsfield cur.	20 0 0	Late Mr. Dowle.	Priory of St. James's, Bristol.
Horfield cur.	3 0 0	Bishop of Bristol.	Abby of Bristol.
24 0 0 Olvefton vic. St. Helen cum Cap de Alvefton.		Chapter of Bristol.	Abby of Bath. 2 8 0
Stapleton, HolyTrinity cur.	14 0 0	Tho. Smyth, Efq;	Priory of St. James's, Bristol.
6 0 0 Stoke-Gifford, St. Michael cur. this lies in two parifhes, viz. Winterborne and Almondfbury, but is prefented to by	20 12 5	Dutchefs Dowager of Beaufort.	0 12 0
Weftbury, HolyTrinity cur.	13 16 0	Mr. Fane.	College of Weftbury.
27 7 6 Winterborne, St. Michael rec.		St. John's College, Oxford.	2 14 9

Of thefe churches above-mentioned taken out of Wells and Worcefter diocefe Anno 1542, all thofe of Briftol are fubordinate to the bifhop's chancellor, who inftitutes to them all, except St. Auguftine's and St. Philip's, which with the out-lying parifhes ftill belong to the archdeacon of Glocefter, though the remaining part of the diocefe, which is entirely in Dorfetfhire yet remains to that archdeacon as it did heretofore while it belonged to the fee of Salifbury.

For that part of Briftol diocefe that lies wholly in the county of Dorfet, and the names of the feveral parifhes, I refer to Ecton's Liber Valorum republifhed lately by Mr. Bacon under the name of Liber Regis, and to the Rev. Mr. Hutchins's Hiftory of Dorfet.

Of

Of the CATHEDRAL of BRISTOL.

This church is dedicated to the Holy and undivided TRINITY; the feal of the Dean and Chapter formerly was The Trinity, the Son in the bofom of the Father on a crofs with a dove at his ear; on the reverfe the figure of Henry the 8th.—The grofs impropriety of this reprefentation of the Triune God, three agents in one Jehovah or Divine Effence, of the one God acting in three perfons in the gracious plan and offices of man's redemption, induced them in 1624 to change their feal for three ducal coronets in pale, a faltier crofs charged with three fleures de lis and a portcullis. See the plate of the cathedral.—It has belonging to it a dean, fix prebendaries or major canons, fix minor canons or prieft vicars, (one of which is to be facrift,) one deacon, fix lay-clerks or finging-men, one mafter of the chorifters, one fub-deacon, fix chorifters, two mafters of the grammar-fchool, four alms-men, one fub-facrift or fexton, one proctor who was to be the virger, one butler, two cooks; in all 39 by Henry the 8th's. foundation: though the places of the inferior members being of fmall value are feldom kept entirely filled as provided for in the ftatutes, which are mutatis mutandis the fame with thofe of Glocefter and others of the new foundation.

The firft Bifhop was Paul Bufh, and befides fix major canons or prebendaries, fix minor canons were then appointed at ten pounds per ann. for each minor canon; 6l. 13s. 4d. for the gofpeller and epifteller; the fame for each of the fix finging-men, and 10l. for the organift. In the old liber valorum in firft edit. the deanry was rated at 100l. per ann. and each of the prebendaries at 20l. per ann. but the referved rents alone of the dean and chapter eftates amount now (1788) to 845l. per ann. which however fcarcely pays the prefent expences of the church and officers, the falaries of the minor canons, organift, &c. now advanced; but the renewals of leafes of eftates on lives generally produce near 200l. per ann. to each prebendary and 400l. to the dean, though the amount muft vary every year.

Befides the falaries to the officers of the church, Henry the 8th. has appointed by the ftatutes of foundation 20l. per ann. to be given among poor houfeholders and other poor people, and 20l. per ann. to make and repair the highways; and he made in 1545 the chancellor of the court of augmentations, and dean of the royal chapel, and their fucceffors and others commiffioners to fee this and other like benefactions out of the new-erected cathedral chapters duly paid every year, pat. 37th of Henry the 8th. p. 9 M. 25, (Rymer. Fœd. v. 15. p. 77, 78, 134.) A declaration from time to time of the bellow-

M m 2

ing

ing and employing the faid money in alms and highways was to be delivered yearly into the court of augmentations by order of Edward the 6th. the firſt year of his reign, and the commiſſioners were to receive from the deans and chapters yearly 40 marks for their care and trouble herein.

According to the ſtatutes the above-mentioned is the number of the officers, and it is put out of the power of the dean and chapter (biſhop or archbiſhop) to innovate or alter any thing contained in the body of the ſtatutes, ſub pœnâ perjurii & amotionis perpetuæ ab ecclefiâ noſtrâ, (faith the King,) reſervamus tamen nobis & ſucceſſoribus noſtris poteſtatem mutandi &c.

The dean, " Qui femper domi apud fuam ecclefiam præfideat &c." vid. ſtat. c. 4. et c. 8.

The fix prebendaries, "Domi fe continere & in ecclefiâ noſtra femper refidentes effe volumus." Stat. c. 12.

Six minor canons, " Quorum refidentia fit perpetua, ſtat. c. 22. ad dei landes in ecclefiæ noſtræ Templo affidue decantandas conſtituimus." Stat. 21. c.

One deacon, one fub-deacon, " Qui evangelium & epiſtolam legent."

One præcentor, " Sit ex minoribus canonicis unus, officium ejus eſt in ecclefiâ noſtra pfallentes cum decano moderari et voce alios præcinere ac veluti Dux effe : abfentias omnes notare : libros choro deputatos bene curare." Stat. c. 23.

Six chorifters, " Vocibus fonoris et ad cantandum aptis. c. 25.

One orgainiſt, " Sit honeſtæ famæ, vitæ probæ, cantandi et organa pulfandi peritus, docendis pueris et divinis officiis cantandis ſtudiofè vacabit." c. 25.

It no where appears that the King or his ſucceſſors have ever diſpenſed with or changed this number, or the reſpeƈtive duties of the places; and the benefits reſulting from the ſtriƈt obſervance of the ſtatutes would be many and great in this and every other cathedral church, the open violation of them in fome and negleƈt of them in others have been known to contribute much to the very ill performance of the fervice, leſſening the congregation, ruin of the houfes, decline of religion and piety, negleƈt of hoſpitality and charity,. and many ancient good orders belonging to the churches.

In the endowment of this church the biſhop had a large though not a very convenient houfe appropriated to him, adjoining to the cathedral, which was formerly the abbacy or abbot's lodgings : it opens into the caſt cloiſter and confiſts of feveral fpacious apartments, many of which were well repaired. and neatly fitted up by Biſhop Smalridge ; fince his time it was ſuffered to go toto decay, but a late worthy and generous Bishop, Dr. Butler, in 1744, had great part of it taken down and rebuilt, at the expence of near 5000l.

Many of the apartments are large and ornamented in a grand manner, and the whole house is now exceedingly convenient, by means of the prebendaries receiving certain lands of his lordship, which lay behind the south side of Trinity-street for their's, which lay contiguous to his palace : this enabled him to add to the palace a handsome garden and walks. The chapel which is in the house is also very neatly repaired, and wainscoted with cedar : it is very small, being only fifteen feet long and eleven broad ; in the windows is a great quantity of painted glass, which was lately repaired, and there is more in other parts of the house yet to be seen, with the names and arms of two or three of the last abbots and the first bishop. The whole fabric is a handsome and commodious dwelling, which his lordship and the succeeding bishops have made their place of residence for about five months in the year, during which time once a week they keep an open table for all the clergy and gentry : and Bishop Butler, in expending so large a sum upon the fabric of the palace then going to decay, which he knew himself should not long enjoy, shewed his most noble and generous spirit and proved him worthy of his high office.

In 1744, whilst the palace was rebuilding a parcel of plate fell through the floor in the corner of one of the rooms, which by this accident was found to be decayed, and occasioned the floor's being taken up, when to the surprize of the workmen a room appeared underneath, in which were found a great many human bones, and instruments of iron, it was supposed to punish the refractory and criminals. At the same time was discovered a private passage to this dungeon, originally constructed with the edifice, being an arched way just large enough for one person to pass in at a time made in the thickness of the wall, one end terminated in the dungeon, and the other in an apartment of the house, which by all appearance had been used as a court ; but both entrances of this mural passage were walled up and so concealed that no one could suspect it to be any other than one solid thick wall.

The deanery which stands at the west end of the church appears to be a good house : it was repaired in the time of Dean Creswick, and almost entirely rebuilt by Dean Warburton. The present yearly value of the deanery is estimated to be as good as the reserved rents of the bishopric. The six prebendaries have all houses within the cathedral limits, but not residing, they let them out at good rents. The minor canons and singing men are now destitute of habitations within the church precincts, though the chapter-books

for

for 1529, folio 33, mention the petty canons' chambers in the inner green near the dean's gardens.

The weſt and fouth ſides of the cloiſters are pulled down, the ſite and ex‑tent of them are ſtill to be ſeen. The eaſt and north cloiſter would probably have been likewiſe demoliſhed, but that the firſt leads into the chapter-houſe and biſhop's palace. What remains of the cloiſter is covered with a ſloped roof of ſtone like a ſhed, which was not the original roofing, that being for‑merly of lead. The whole formed an handſome and elegant ſquare, but makes now a very mean appearance ; for in the year 1655, Walter Deyos being mayor of Briſtol, the lead was taken off from the cloiſters as well as from the cathedral, and depoſited in the chamberlain's hands ; but a ſtop be‑ing put to any farther ſpoil, an order was made the 8th of January 1655, that the lead removed from the cathedral and cloiſters adjoining ſhould be ſold, and laid out in the neceſſary repairs of the ſaid cathedral. Tolzey Book, p. 99. This was the ſecond pillage this cathedral has ſuffered ſince the general ſack in Henry 8th's. reign. In the middle of the cloiſters leading out of the church is an entrance into the chapter-houſe, which is a very elegant curious building, and has a very handſome ſtone roof of two arches, the pil‑lars being adorned with curious twiſted carved work in the Saxon ſtile of architecture, and it is in length 46 feet and in breadth 26 in the inſide, and was as much in height till the floor was lately raiſed four feet by laying a deal floor above the pavement, to render it leſs damp and make it more conve‑nient for the chapter's meeting upon buſineſs, which they now tranſact alto‑gether here ; and they have fitted up a preſs for their books and regiſters, and in place of the fine old circular window have put in four large modern faſhes. There is ſet up over the door this inſcription : " Capitularis hæe domus reparata et ornata fuit, A. D. 1713, Honorabili et Reverendo Roberto Booth, S. T. P. decano, Jacobo Harcourt, S. T. B. vice-decano, Hugone Waterman, A. M. theſaurario."

The ſquare of the cloiſters was 103 feet every way, there is a door yet leading out of the weſt part of the church. Adjoining to the deanery is a noble gate-houſe, remarkable for its well-turned arch and curious workman‑ſhip. (See the plate.)

This fine gate is in the ſtile of what Sir Chriſtopher Wren calls the Saxon architecture, before the Gothic or rather Saracenic with pointed arches was introduced in this iſland after the cruſades. The arch is of ſuch curious workmanſhip, that words cannot poſſibly give any idea of it, the engraved plate but an imperfect one. The ſcrolls, twiſts, and other ornaments are ſo

interwoven

interwoven and intricate, that the eye is puzzled in furveying them, and is at lofs where to fix and trace them out. The fweep of the arch is very much admired, though by the ground's being rofe by time its height is lefs, and fo the proportion of it originally is in fome refpeﬅ injured by it. It has been very well preferved, and fuffered very little by time. The rooms over the arch are of much later ereﬅion than the arch itfelf, being repaired and altered by the abbots, particularly by Abbot Newland alias Nailheart, who was a great builder, and in compliment to the founder of the monaﬅery placed his effigy, with a model of the conventual church in one hand and the foundation charter in his other, in one of the niches over this arch, with the ﬅatue of Henry 2d. next him, and underneath them and juﬅ above the crown of the arch the following infcription, in Gothic letters, rifing out of the ﬅone: " Rex Henricus fecundus et Dominus Robertus. filius Hardingi filii Regis Daciæ bujus monaﬅerii primi fundatores extiterunt." There is no date, and had the infcription been placed there at the very time of the ereﬅion of the monaﬅery, 1148, no doubt but the date would have been added. On the fouth fide are the ﬅatues in ﬅone of the Abbots Newland and Elliot, in whofe time, 1515, the rooms over the arch probably underwent fome great alteration, who then fixed up their own figures there, and probably the Latin infcription. Inﬅead of the prefent fafh window there was formerly a projeﬅing bow window with fmall fquares of glafs leaded; this I have preferved in the plate, as it was the original form of the building, and more fuitable than the prefent; and a kind of turret of old was carried up on the back part of it, which was the antient ﬅair cafe leading to the rooms over the gate; this has been deﬅroyed by building a handfome houfe on the eaﬅ fide of it. On the weﬅ fide is a poﬅern, now fhut up and ufed by the dean for a coach-houfe; over it is a room formerly the porter's lodge. There are feveral coats of arms carved in ﬅone on both fides of this fuperb gate-houfe. On the north fide at top is Edward the Confeﬀor's carved, which points out the antiquity of this gate, and is preferved notwithﬅanding the alteration it has undergone; next it the arms of England crowned, and Richard de Clare Earl of Pembroke's, being chevronèe of fix or and gules, below Henry 2d. and Fitz-Harding's.

On the fouth fide, befides the abbots in effigy and their arms under, are two figures above them, one the Virgin Mary and Child and the other I have not yet found the name of, nor of the two upper figures on the north fide: they are abbots or noblemen who had been fignal benefaﬅors to the monaﬅery.

In

In the rebellious time of 1641, among other ravages then committed and lands of the bifhopric then fold was " the gate-houfe in Briftol fold March 6, 1649, to John Birch for the fum of 18l. 13s. 4d." as the palace and park were at the fame time for the fum of 240l. to Thomas and John Clark.

This gate-hoofe was leafed out by the bifhop to the Rev. Dr. Sloper, rector of Spetfbury and chancellor then of this diocefe, who being a very charitable man, among other benefactions, left to the mayor and aldermen of Briftol his houfe in College-green, &c. in truft out of the rents to renew the leafes from the Biftop of Briftol, to Mary Hort his neice 5l. and the remainder to buy minion bibles, to be diftributed to poor families by the alderman of each ward, the number to be in proportion of the fize of each ward. This houfe was fold, the bifhop refufing to renew the lives for the corporation, who then put it into Chancery, and it was bought out of Chancery by Hugh Grove, Efq; whofe nephew has lately renewed with the bifhop. The corporation had the pur-chafe money, and now difpofe of the bibles purchafed by the intereft of the faid money every three years.

The monaftery or conventual church itfelf, though not to be extolled for elegance and but a plain ftructure, yet being fituated on an hilly ground, if now compleat as in the print, would prefent a ftriking front and elevation.

William of Worcefter, who furveyed this church about the year 1480, gives the following meafurements : " The choir of St. Auguftin in Briftol contains in length 64 fteps beyond the chapel of St. Mary. The breadth of the nave of the choir with the two ailes contains 50 fteps. The length and breadth of the fquare on every fide contains 22 fteps. The length of frayter-houfe 26 fteps, its breadth 16. The length of the *old church* 80 fteps, of the belfry 24, its breadth 64 fteps. The length of the chapter-houfe 56 fteps, its breadth 18." In another place he mentions, " The church of the canons of St. Auguftin. The chapel of St. Mary contains in length 13 yards, its breadth $9\frac{1}{2}$ yards. The fpace or way of proceffions behind the principal altar before the chapel of St. Mary is 5 yards. The length of the choir from the reredes of the principal altar to the end of the choir contains 29 yards, begin-ning from the end of the aforefaid fpace. The breadth of the nave of the choir and the two ailes of the choir contains 24 yards. There is a decent chapel built on the north part of the aile of the choir containing in length *** yards."

We can collect but a very imperfect idea from thefe vague meafurements. (Vide the print or ichnography.) The prefent cathedral, deprived as it is of its weftern part home to the tower, confifts of the choir and the two fide ailes,

all

all of equal height and part of the nave, curioufly vaulted and the arched roof well fupported, with a crofs aile, and fo compleating but two parts of a crofs. As it now ftands unfinifhed, it is in length from eaft to weft 175 feet, whereof the choir is 100 feet, but in its compleat ftate muft have extended 100 feet farther weftward. The length of the crofs aile from north to fouth is 128 feet. The height of the tower is 127 feet, which ftands in the midft of this aile (as it would in the middle of the church, if the weftern nave was finifhed) as it formerly ftood. It has one fingular beauty not to be met with in any other cathedral, namely, that the two fide ailes are of equal height with the nave and choir, and finely arched and curioufly fupported, well calculated both for ftrength and beauty. The low fide ailes of other cathedral churches take away much of their grand appearance and lofty look, fo obvious in this at the firft view. The breadth of the body and fide ailes is 73 feet, and it is 43 feet to the height of the vaulting.

How the church prefents to us this imperfect mutilated appearance now is a matter deferving enquiry. There is a tradition that the weft part was demo-lifhed home to the tower in that great confufion in Henry 8th's. time, and the materials fold and difpofed of, before that King had determined to convert it into a cathedral and a bifhop's fee. As there is no record to eftablifh this fact, others have thought it was never finifhed : the builders of churches are faid firft to eftablifh the whole plan of their building, then begin at the altar or caft part, ufing that for the religious fervice till by degrees they could com-pleat the whole. Whether they ftopt this building after finifhing the tower is the queftion. That this is not the firft church erected on this fpot, or the fame that was built by Robert Fitzharding the firft founder, appears from a deed I met with in the Lib. Alb. Wygorn, 6. f. 20. for in the year 1311 the church of Wotton was appropriated by the Bifhop of Worcefter to the monaf-tery of St. Auguftin, which was then much decayed, and their revenue re-duced by the expences in rebuilding their church, fumptuoufly built of old by their pious founders, but then through age for the moft part pulled down and the remainder ruinous : in repairing which and in rebuilding they had fpent much and ought to expend much more in the work newly begun. For the relief of thefe expences and their other great neceffities, the bifhop appro-priated to them the church of Wotton, &c." (Dated at London, 11 kal. July, 1311.) The original fays, " Quod ecclefia ejufdem monafterii a piis ipfius fundatoribus antiquis temporibus ad cultum divinum opere fumptuofo conftructa dudum propter ipfius antiquitatem et debilitatem pro majori parte funditùs diruta, in parte refiduâ gravem minatur ruinam ; ad cujus fabricæ reftaurationem plures fumptus appofuerunt et ampliores apponere oportebit in opere ibidem noviter in choato, &c."

In the year 1363, in the time of Maurice Lord Berkeley, the fourth of that name, a contributor, it was greatly repaired and partly rebuilt, as appears by another deed; by which it is clear, that the whole building and reparations it had undergone were not compleated till about that time, 40th Edward 3d. — William of Worcefter mentioning the length of the old church 80 fteps is another proof that there had been fuch an old church before his time, 1480, and before the prefent was erected.

In the lives of the abbots (p. 267.) it is faid Edmund Knowles (who was abbot 26 years) begun building the prefent church anew from the ground, &c. and that he died 1332, which compared with the deeds above, dated 1311 and 1363, fhews by the length of time the building was carrying on, that it muft have been probably compleated in that time, and the ruins at the weftern part (where tenements with gardens were fuffered to be erected to increafe the dean and chapter's revenue) feem to prove that part to have been pulled down, and a large ftone at the end of one of the garden walls evidently points out the extent of the whole building, and was the weftern boundary ftone of this plain but magnificent abby church; but whether thefe be the ruins of the old or firft built church, or of the later erected one by Abbot Knowles, may be ftill an object of doubt with fome, and not eafily folved by any. It is certain fome remains of Gothic arches beyond the tower ftill fbew the church was once continued to the weftward.

The beft idea of the fabric may be formed from a view of the copper-plate print, which reprefents it as compleat, though from the tower to the weftern end be at prefent wanting. It was at one time in very bad repair, but it appears that in the year 1670 1311 l. were laid out on the fabric and prebendal houfes, and that in the years 1681 and 1685 in the deanries of Towgood and Levett 300 l. or more was laid out in mending the floor and beautifying the church, painting the caft end of the choir and other works, and making a fine timber cafe for the new organ, erected by the contibution of the dean and chapter and many other well difpofed perfons in the time of Bifhop Wright,. about the year 1630, at the expence of 550 l. in the whole to Mr. Renatus Harris, organ-builder. The ftalls of the choir, 34 in number, (17 on each fide) are very regular, and fitted up about 1542, when it was made a cathedral, and have pews under them of a modern make. There is a grand feat for the bifhop, erected by Paul Buih the firft bifhop, (his arms being on it) and another oppofite for the archdeacon of Dorfet. The floor is laid with black and white marble, and you go up to the high altar by fteps of the fame, where the

large

large eaft window is adorned with curious Gothic tracery-work, and glazed with painted glafs, on the top the King's arms (Henry 2d.) the Berkeley's of Berkeley and of Stoke Gifford, alfo chevernois of 6 or and G. f. argent on a canton G. a rofe proper, for Abbot Bradftone, alfo for Hunt and Elliot, alfo f. argent three lozenges in fefs gules, alfo feveral figures of men with propheta wrote on them in a fcroll.

Edward Colfton, Efq; gave 260l. towards beautifying the choir and laying the marble about the communion-table, &c. Above the communion-table, and at the bottom of the eaft window, are a variety of painted arms with the letters W. B. interfperfed, for William Burton the abbot, who is faid to have built the altar piece, which was afterwards gilded and repaired by the Deans Towgood and Levet; on each fide are two large fhields of arms, Henry the 2d. and Lord Berkeley's on the right, King Henry the 2d. and Clare Earl of Pembroke's on the left.

In feveral places of the wainfcot of the choir and on the front of the Bifhop's feat are the letters T. W. twifted together in a cypher, which fome fay have been placed there in compliment to Cardinal Wolfey, but the truth is, they were for Thomas Wright, who in 1541 was appointed Receiver-general of the Chapter at their firft foundation, and had the ordering of their officers and fitting up of this church for a cathedral, and took care to fet up his cypher in all parts, as Abbot Newland and Elliot had done before him and fhewed him the example.

In the North aile is a curious painted glafs window and another in the South, the firft reprefents in different compartments the houfe of prayer, with Domus mea domus orationis, and driving the fellers out of the Temple; Our Saviour anfwering, " reddite Cæfari, reddite deo ;" Jacob's ladder, &c. with coats of arms at the bottom : the fecond reprefents Our Saviour in the garden, his refurrection from the tomb, his afcenfion, Abraham about to offer up Ifaac, Jonah coming forth from the belly of the great fifh prepared for him, Elijah in his fiery chariot ; thefe are faid to be given to this church by Nell Gwyn miftrefs to Charles the 2d.

On the Eaft and South fide of the church is a chapel of the Virgin Mary ; an arch adorned with fhields with a chevron only, (the ancient bearing of Fitz-bardings before they added the ten croffes patee,) is now filled up, but when opened communicated through with the South aile, and was the place of burial for fome of the family ; the very bricks on the floor of this chapel have their arms burnt on them and fome arms of the abbots alfo ; it feems to be appropriated chiefly to the ufe of the Berkeley family ; it is now the veftry.

There

There was given to this cathedral fome plate for the communion fervice the 10th of June 1710 by Lady Loyd, a filver patin gilt and filver chalice gilt, with the arms of the cathedral engraved on them: and the 3d of Auguft 1712 John Rumfey Efq; prefented to this church a pair of large filver can_dlefticks, very high and weighty, they coft him 114l. and were taken in 1709 by the Duke and Dutchefs fhips of war in their expedition to the South Seas at Paita by Capt. Woods Rogers.

The tower is a ftrong fquare building, not very high but well proportioned to the fize and heighth of the church; in it hang five bells, the four leaft were caft by Abbot Newland, who died in the year 1515, as appears by the initial letters of his name upon them *J. N.* three of them bear thefe infcriptions, *Sancte Clemens, fancta Margarita, fancta Catharina ora pro nobis*, on the fourth is this, *Clara vocor & clarior ero;* the biggeft has this date, 1570 upon it, 13th Q. Eliz. Here were defigned to be five more as appears by five more vacant frames, out of which there is a tradition the bells were ftolen, but others fay, they were fold to the church of Redclift.

The following Ichnography prefents to the eye the infide of the prefent cathedral, better than any words can defcribe it, the letters of refer-ence pointing out particulars. A. the great North door leading down fteps into the cathedral out of the College-green, the ground having in time been greatly rofe before it. B. The way into the Elder Lady-chapel and fteps. C. The door leading into the Cloifters, Chapter-houfe and Bifhop's-palace. D. The fub-facrift's veftry built on the imperfect part of the church. E. The great crofs aile, font and ftair-cafe to the confiftory and regifter's office. F. The ftone pulpit, feats of the bifhop, dean, prebendaries, and cor-poration of Briftol. G. The choir with feventeen ftalls on each fide. H. The bifhop's throne and the archdeacon of Dorfet's ftall. I. The veftry and fealing-houfe, formerly St. Mary's chapel for the Berkeley's. K. The high altar and fteps to it. L. The fite of the chapter-houfe, which opens to the Cloifters. M. Tombs of Lords Berkeley. N. Tombs of Sir Richard New-ton, or of Judge Newton, temp. Hen. 6th. of Sir John and Sir Henry New-ton. O. Tombs of abbots &c. P. Bifhop Paul Bufh's tomb. Q. Tomb of Sir John Young and his Lady. R. Monument of Bifhop Searchfield and Dean Chetwynd. S. Codrington's monument. T. Tomb of Sir Charles Vaughan. U. The place of the founder's grave-ftone now removed to letter u. W. Grave-ftones of Bifhops Howel, Weftfield and Ironfide. X. Grave-ftones of Dean Tomfon, Croffman and Towgood. Y. Grave-ftones of pre-bendaries

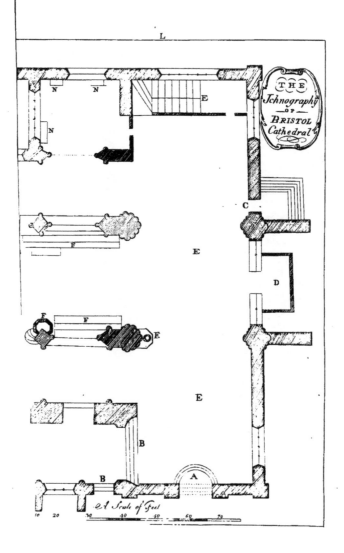

L

N   N

N

E

C

E

D

F

E

F   F

F   E

E

B

B   A

A Scale of Feet

10   20   30   40   50   60   70

THE
Ichnography
OF
BRISTOL
Cathedral

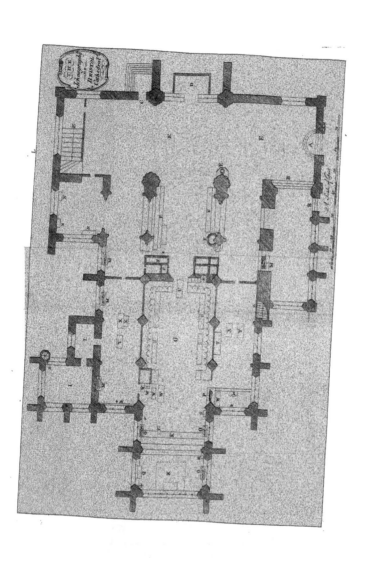

bendaries Saul, Rainſtorp and Towgood. Z. Stair-cafes of the church.
† Mrs. Weeks' monument.

On the North ſide is a ſmall aile called the Elder Lady-chapel, in diſtinction to another Lady-chapel at the Eaſt and South end of the church.—This
on the North ſide appears to have been part of the old church before it was
rebuilt by Abbot Knowles, being much lower than the reſt of the church.—
The ſtyle of the architecture in the pillars, ceiling and windows being quite
different from the remainder of the church ; and the name ſeems to confirm
its antiquity : the chapel alſo where the Newton family are interred and
chapter-houſe ſeem alſo to be of the old foundation ; as do the Cloiſters
though altered, part of the Biſhop's-palace and the building next to it, being
the remains of the common hall, refectory or dining-room of the monks.
From this ſpecimen of the architecture in the Elder Lady-chapel we may form
a good idea of the firſt monaſtery church ; the neatneſs of the black marble
pillars with which it was adorned, and the arched roof ſhews it to have been a
very rich and elegant Gothic building. Though the fine arch itſelf of the
gateway leading into the abby (now the Lower Green) was of the old foundation, yet the upper part over it appears to be of more modern date ; the
ſtatues of the late abbots Elliot and Newland, alias Nailheart, with their arms
being placed in niches over it are a proof, as before obſerved : they retained in
the new-erected church as much as they poſſibly could of the old that would
ſerve their purpoſe, though it was but little, without deſtroying the ſymmetry
and proportion of the whole ; yet there ſtill remains enough to ſhew us that
the preſent is of a new and later erection than the original foundation building,
if records had been wanting to prove it.—In a manuſcript of Biſhop Littleton
in the library of the Society of Antiquarians, is the following account :
" The cathedral appears to be of one and the fame ſtyle of building throughout, and no part older than King Edward the 1ſt.'s time, though fome writers
ſuppoſe the preſent fabrick was begun in King Stephen's time, but not a ſingle
arch, pillar or window agrees with the mode which prevailed at that time.
Indeed the lower part of the chapter-houſe walls, together with the door-way
and columns at the entrance of the chapter-houſe I ſhould pronounce of that
age, or rather prior to King Stephen's reign, being true Saxon architecture.
The inſide walls of the chapter-houſe have round ornamental arches interſecting each other like thoſe in St. Nicholas's chancel, Warwick, which was
part of the old Saxon nunnery church. The great gate-way leading into the
College-green is round, arched with mouldings richly ornamented in the
Saxon taſte.—Query. If this part of the gate-way be not coeval with Fitz-

harding

harding founder of St. Auguftine's, temp. Hen. 1ft. but the infcription and upper part of the gate where the images are placed are far more modern."

The College-green which fronts the cathedral and adds very much to the beauty of the place, is laid out in pleafant walks with rows of lime-trees planted round it, and is the refidence of many genteel families, and reforted to by others for walking on account of its airy and delightful fituation, (propter loci amænitatem, as expreffed in a deed as early as the year 1259.) The Briftol High Crofs, which once graced the center of it, (as appears by the little print annexed,) was removed from High-ftreet hither, for the fake of widening the ftreet and rendering it more commodious for paffengers; and here it remained for years much admired by all, efpecially by ftrangers vifiting this city, till wanting repairs from the injury of the weather, Dean Barton ordered it to be given to Mr. Hoar at Stourton, to adorn his elegant gardens, (where the dean's brother was rector of the place.) It is to be wifhed fuch a curious local piece of antiquity had remained ftill here and been repaired occafionally, as a monument of the piety and gratitude of our anceftors to the feveral Princes who had given charters of liberties to the city: vid. chap. on All-Saints parifh.

This green, however beautiful now and the refort of the gay, the beaux and belles of Briftol to walk in as the Mall is in London, was formerly the common burying-place of the dead, called in old deeds the cemitery of the abbot and convent, by whom a folemn proceffion was ufually made around it on feftival days, and religious rights performed and fermons preached at the great crofs (before the erection of the Briftol High Crofs there) at Eafter yearly and the three following days. There have been found here tomb-ftones, and fkulls and bones dug up when the new houfes were built on the Gaunts fide; and at digging up the old trees the 9th of Henry the 7th. the like bones were thrown up, and more lately in mending the walks and erecting the rails.

I proceed next to the monuments of this cathedral. The piety of our an-ceftors was fuch that they were not content to rely on their daily devotions and other religious acts in their life time for the fafety of their fouls, but they made what they fimply thought a provifion for their fouls after their deceafe, by eftablifhing chantries, obiits, &c. whilft their children have receded fo much from the ways of their fathers, that negligent too often of their religious duties to their God, they feem to pay too, too little attention or care for their fouls even in their life time, much lefs take any thought for their fouls or thofe of their departed relations or friends after their death. But they have been
more

more folicitous about depofiting the dead bodies of their relations and friends, and erecting tombs over them; whether it be from a defire of conveying to pofterity the names of their family, or from a religious perfuafion and hope of meeting them again in another life, fuch monuments or memorials have their ufe and muft not be condemned, as is too much the cafe in this age of levity and affectation of more enlightened underftandings than their anceftors.

The monuments and infcriptions worthy of notice are chiefly the following:

On the north fide in the Elder Lady-chapel, which is 50 feet long, 18 wide, and the fame high, under an arch is an altar tomb with the ftatues in freeftone in full length of Maurice Lord Berkeley and Margaret his mother, or rather of Elizabeth his wife, according to fome manufcripts, with the family arms on his furcoat G. a chevron between ten croffes patee argent. At the head of this monument is the following infcription on a table under the arch, placed the rein 1742,—" To the memory of Robert Fitzharding, who laid the foundation of this church, he lies buried with his lady at the choir entrance, * over whom in the arch of the door-way is a lively reprefentation of the latter judgment. — The monument of Robert Fitzharding Lord of Berkeley, defcended from the Kings of Denmark, and Eva his wife, by whom he had five fons and two daughters: Maurice his eldeft fon was the firft of this family who took the name of Berkeley. This Robert Fitzharding laid the foundation of this church and monaftery of St. Auguftin in the year 1140, the 5th of King Stephen, dedicated and endowed it in 1148, and he died in the year 1170, 17th Henry 2d. From the faid Robert Fitzharding Lord Berkeley Auguftus the prefent Earl is the 22d in defcent."

Near the north door is a very elegant monument againft the weft wall for Mrs. Draper, celebrated by Sterne under the name of Eliza. Genius and Benevolence are reprefented by two beautiful female figures, in which the fculptor has exerted his utmoft fkill. The following is the infcription: — " Sacred to the memory of Mrs. Elizabeth Draper, in whom Genius and Benevolence were united. She died Auguft 8, 1778, aged 35."

Againft the pillar near it is another with an infcription to Mr. Wallis.

In the north aile are grave-ftones with Latin infcriptions, to James Harcourt, prebendary, who died 1739, aged 59, and of his wife, who died 1733, aged 39, and four children.

Another to Richard Towgood, dean, thus: — Hic fitus eft Richardus Towgood, S. T. B. hujus ecclefiæ favente Carolo primo prebendarius nec non parochiæ.

* In the year 1684 Dean Thompfon ordered the two large ftones which once had brafs plates let into them and were then much worn out, to be removed hence under the Dean's feat in the body of the church, where they may be feen in part now.

parochiæ St. Nicolai (dictæ) concionator egregius et frequens, et practicam et fcholafticam theologiam apprime calluit : utrumque nefcias an melius intel-lexerit an candidiùs impertiverit : flagrante bello civili ab exulceratis civibus ecclefia pulfus eft, et quod factioni difplicuerit (cui nefas effet placuiffe) in carcerem detrufus, reftitutâ monarchiâ ad curam revocatus, atq; haud ita poft favente Carolo filio ad Decanatûs dignitatem provectus eft; cui fummâ cum prudentiâ et moderatione præfuit, infulam merviffe contentus. Poftquam per totam vitam, erga Deum, regem, ecclefiam, patriam, fe integerrimè gefferat defideratiffimus fenex (oraculorum facrorum circiter 60 annos in hâc civitate laboriofus idem et fæliciffimus interpres) dierum fatur in cœlum migravit Aprilis 21, anno ætat. s. 89, Sal. n. 1683. Elizabetha uxor in eodem tumulo fepulta jacet quæ obiit Novembris 22, 1685.

Near this are the following : — Here lies Mary Blagdon, daughter of Elizabeth Towgood, wife of Richard Towgood, Dean of this church, who departed this life Sept. 1699.

Richardus Towgood, A. M. hujus ecclefiæ præbendarius Richardi Towgood ejufdem ecclefiæ Decani juxta inhumati meritifque laudibus ornati filius, paternas virtutes, pietatem, fidem, conftantiam, hæreditario quafi jure vindicavit, perantiquæ morum integritatis vir ac per omnia tempora fui fimillimus, defideratus eft 11 Oct. anno ætatis 59, falutis 1713, cum eodem intumulata jacet uxor Elizabetha, quæ mortalitatem exuit 19 Augufti, 1726.

Near the above is placed the following infcription : — In memory of her renowned anceftors, Richard Towgood, S. T. B. Dean of this church the grandfather, and Elizabeth his wife, Richard Towgood, M. A. prebendary, the father and Elizabeth his wife; Mrs. Elizabeth Towgood the daughter, and laft of the family, caufed this monument to be erected, who, having inherited the virtues of her forefathers, and exhibited the fame illuftrious pattern of unaffected piety, undiffembled charity, and unfullied integrity, to the 77th year of her age, followed them to the manfions of eternal reft Jan. 24, 1767.

Next the above is a pyramidal table on which is a bafs-relief head of the deceafed, and the following infcription : — " William Powell, Efq; one of the pantentees of the Theatre-Royal, Covent Garden, died 3d of July, 1769, aged 33 years. His widow caufed this monument to be erected, as well to perpetuate his memory as her own irretrievable lofs of the beft of hufbands:

> Briftol! to worth and genius ever juft,
> To thee our Powell's dear remains we truft :
> Soft as the ftreams thy facred fprings impart,
> The milk of human kindnefs warm'd his heart;

That

That heart, which every tender feeling knew,
The foil, where pity, love, and friendſhip grew:
Oh! let a faithful friend with grief ſincere
Inſcribe his tomb, and drop the heartfelt tear,
Here reſt his praiſe, here found his nobleſt fame,
All elſe a bubble or an empty name.

G. Coleman.

Oppoſite is a neat monument;
"To the memory of Elizabeth Waſtfield, who died at the Hotwells the
26th December 1770, aged 60, wife of Robert Waſtfield, Eſq; of Mile-End
near London, this monument from a juſt ſenſe of her merit and of his
own loſs is erected by her diſconſolate huſband.

Dear ſhade, adieu! the debt of Nature's paid!
Death's threaten'd ſtroke we parry'd but in vain;
The healing ſpring no more could lend its aid,
Med'cine no more could mitigate the pain.

See by her dying form mild Patience ſtand,
Hope, Eaſe, and Comfort, in her train ſhe led:
See! gentle ſpirits, waiting the command,
Huſh her to Silence on the mournful bed.

In vain with heartfelt grief I mourn my friend,
Fair Virtue's meed is bliſs without alloy:
Bleſt change! for pain, true pleaſure without end,
For ſighs and moans, a pure ſeraphic joy!

When Death ſhall that new ſcene to me diſcloſe,
When I ſhall quit on earth this drear abode,
Our freed congenial ſpirits ſhall repoſe
Safe in the boſom of our Saviour-God.

In the ſame aile is an handſome mural monument with the following
inſcription: — " Mary, the daughter of William Shermon, of Kingſton upon
Hull, Eſq; and wife of the Rev. William Maſon, died March 24, 1767,
aged 28.

Take, holy Earth! all that my ſoul holds dear,
Take that beſt gift, which Heaven ſo lately gave;
To Briſtol's fount I bore with trembling care
Her faded form; ſhe bow'd to taſte the wave

O o

And

And dy'd. Does youth, does beauty read the line?
Does fympathetic fear their breafts alarm?
Speak, dead Maria! breath a ftrain divine;
Ev'n from the grave thou fhalt have power to charm:
Bid them be chafte, be innocent like thee;
Bid them in duty's fphere as meekly move;
And if fo fair, from vanity as free,
As firm in friendfhip, and as fond in love:
Tell them, though 'tis an awful thing to die,
('Twas ev'n to thee) yet the dread path once trod,
Heav'n lifts its everlafting portals high,
And bids " the pure in heart behold their God."

Next this is a raifed tomb of alabafter and freeftone gilt, with two marble
pillars fupporting a canopy; between the pillars is the ftatue of a man in
armour: at the top thefe arms: f. a chevron between three children's heads
couped at the fhoulders argent, their peruques or, enwrapped about the neck
with as many fnakes proper, by the name of Vaughan: motto, " Chrifti fer-
vitus vera libertas," with a long Latin infcription to the memory of Sir Charles
Vaughan: —" Sacrum memoriæ prinde ac honori viri prænobilis, cujus hic
exuviæ repulverefcunt, Caroli Vaughani equitis aurati, filii et hæredis Gaul-
teri, ordinis itidem equeftris; ex antiquiffima Vaughanorum Cambro-Britan-
norum profapiâ oriundi, qui quadraginta circiter et feptem annos in terris
agens, poftquam virtute fuis præluxiffet, eruditione doctiffimis quibufque inno-
tuiffet, religione plerifque exemplo fuiffet, amoris conjugalis fpecimen edidif-
fet, munera publica integerrime obiiffet, res privatas fapienter compofuiffet,
ac animæ faluti imprimis confuluiffet; tandem, marcore et phthife confectus,
mori defiit, Februarii die fexto decimo anno fpei fuæ noftrumq; omnium per
Verbum carnem factum adfertæ millefimo fexcentefimo tricefimo MDCXXX.
Expecto donec veniat immutatio mea. Job xiv. Omnia mutantur nihil interit."

On two tables under him are alfo the following Latin infcriptions:

Vxores duxit primo Francifcam filiam Roberti Knolles, equitis aurati quæ
genere formâ et virtute illuftris verum moribunda deferuit mortalitatem; quo
citius et Arctius Chrifto frucretur vitâ vitali, ætatis fuæ anno vicefimo quarto et
redemptionis humanæ 1614:

Deinde Dorotheam filiam Roberti Melleri equitis aurati, quæ marito cha-
riffimo mæfta ac (ni deus voluiffêt) invitê fuperftes monumentum hoc, quale
vides, ad memoriam ejus, quam fieri poteft diutiffime confervandam propriis
fumptibus poni curavit.

At

At the upper end of the north aile is a very handſome monument to Thomas Coſter, Eſq; formerly member of parliament for this city, with the following elegant inſcription. He married Aſtrea, daughter of Sir John Smyth,
of Long Aſhton, Bart. left one daughter by his firſt wife Elizabeth, daughter
of Thomas Rous, Eſq; of Wotton-Underedge ; ſhe married Robert Hoblyn,
Eſq; of Cornwall, member for Briſtol, 1742, and erected this monument to
the memory of her father.

I. S. E.

Thomas Coſter, Armiger

Virtutibus tùm privatis

Tùm publicis præter cæteros inſignis,

Suos ſtudio et amore,

Homines quoſcunque benevolentiâ,

Deum O. M. egregiâ pietate

Proſequebatur :

Ad variam ſcientiam,

In machinamentis præcipue et metallis,

Perſpicaci ingenio,

Ad opes induſtriâ,

Ad honorem probis moribus,

Viam munivit.

A Briſtolienſibus

Ad Senatorii ordinis dignitatem

Sine ambitione, fine invidiâ evectus

Eandem ſummâ fide ſuſtinuit

Suorum civium et totius reipublicæ bono.

Natus Decembris 20, 1684,

Sept. 30, 1739, morte luctuoſâ abreptus ;

Omnibus quibus innotuit,

Sui deſiderium reliquit,

Illi vero longe triſtiſſimum,

Quæ optimi patris memor

Virtutum ejus (quarum exemplar ut

Poſteris quam diutiſſimè prodeſſet)

Memoriam, hoc marmore poſito,

Æternam voluit

I. H.

Under the eaft window and by the fide of Bifhop Paul Bufh is the grave ftone of Thomas Weftfeild, late bifhop of this church, with his and his wives' arms on the fame; the infcription is in the account of that bifhop.

The next under the north wall is : — "Here lieth the body of Mrs. Anne Throckmorton, daughter of Sir Nicholas Throckmorton, late of the foreft of Dean, in the county of Glocefter, Knight. She died the 9th of December, 1698."

In the choir below the altar fteps are grave-ftones with thefe infcriptions, on a black ftone by the door of the chancellor's ftall : — " Quod reliquum eft piiffimæ virginis et chariffimæ filiæ Hermiones, Thomas Goodman, M. D. pater, non fine multis lachrymis, fub hoc marmore depofuit: heu! nimis arƈto carcere pro tanta virtute, cujus fedes eft cœlis. Placidè in Domino obdormivit 11 Aug. anno falutis MDCCXXIV. ætatis 27. Sub eodem marmore fepelitur Thomas Goodman, M. D. pater fenex venerabilis oƈtogenarius

$$\left.\begin{array}{l}\text{Gulielmo III.}\\ \text{Annæ,}\\ \text{Georgio I.}\\ \text{Georgio II.}\end{array}\right\} \text{Medicus regius, obiit Dec. xxiii.}\quad \text{MDCCXXXVIII.}$$

On an old white ftone thus : — " Sub hac petra tumulantur offa . . . . . quondam prior' . . . . . qui obiit vii. Id. Martii, A. D. MCCCCLXXVI. cujus animæ propitietur altiffimus. Amen." Another was, " Hic jacet Margareta Grene, mater Thomæ Grene, quondam canonici hujus monafterii quæ obiit ultimo . . . . ."

On a black ftone by the bifhop's throne is this infcription, with his arms: — " William Bradfhaw, D. D. Bifhop of Briftol, and Dean of Chrift Church in Oxford, died December the 16th, 1732, aged 62."

On the next is an old freeftone with a black ftone let into it, under which lies Bifhop Thomas Howell, of this church, and on the black ftone was engraven only this one word, " Expergifcar."

And the next is an old freeftone, under which lies Bifhop Gilbert Ironfide, without any infcription.

South end of the chancel.

M. S.

Nathanielis Fofter, S. T. P. nuperrimè hujus ecclefiæ preh. et paucis ab hinc annis C. C. C. Oxon Socii.

Dignus fane erat, qui multifariæ laudis exemplar debeat proponi; morum fideiq; integritate, quæ Chriftianum deceat, inculpatus; eruditione, quæ theologum ornet, inftruƈtiffimus; optimarumq; artium cognitione accuratâ præcellens.

lens. Eximiam linguarum peritiam eo unice direxit, ut infitam cuilibet genti indolem penitius infpiceret, proprium fcriptori cuiq. ingenium certiùs erueret puramq; ex ipfo fonte derivaret facri codicis fimplicitatem: hinc naturâ fagax, doctrinâ folers humanæ mentis explorator, philofophorum veterum fectas, primariâ quâdam placitorum communicatione fibi invicem affines, et in diverfa paulatim diductas, fcholarum difcrimina præ ceteris calluit notare, et diftinguere. Hinc porro reconditos Platonis fui fenfus non ut plerumq; fit, leviter tantum perftringit ; fed quod a Platonis olim amico et familiari quodam expectandum fuiffet, fpeciofo verborum involucro exutos coram lectorem fiflit, fidus interpres. Ne talem virum non fatis ob oculos haberint pofteri, hoc amoris luctufq; fui monumentum exftare voluit uxor fuperftes.

Ob. 20mo. Octo. A. D. 1757. Ætat. 39no.

Under the ftained glafs window the eaft end of the fouth aile.

In cemiterio hujus ædis fepultus eft Robertus Booth, S. T. P. Deeanns Briftoliæ, filius Georgii Baronis Delameri frater Henrici Comitis de Warrington. Horum uterque ficuti dubiis admodum temporibus fingularem patriæ fidem ac virtutem præftitit, ita ipfe ecclefiæ majorem, quam ab eo acceperat, dignitatem reddidit.

Verum inter plurimas ejus virtutes eminuit maxime profufa quædam in egenos liberalitas, quæ facerdotem apprimè deceret, verè Chriftianum verèque nobilem. Nat. A. D. 1661, Ob. A. D. 1720, Dec. Briftol, A. D. 1708.

In the South aile.

Sacred to the memory of the Rev. Samuel Love, A. M. Fellow of Baliol College, Oxford, and one of the minor canons of this cathedral, who died October 18th 1773, aged 29.

> When worthlefs grandeur decks the embellifh'd urn,
>   No poignant grief attends the fable bier,
> But when diftinguifh'd excellence we mourn,
>   Deep is the forrow, genuine the tear.

> Stranger! fhouldft thou approach this awful fhrine
>   The merits of the honour'd dead to feck ;
> The Friend, the Son, the Chriftian; the Divine,
>   Let thofe who knew him, thofe who lov'd him, fpeak.

> Oh! let them in fome paufe from anguifh fay,
>   What zeal infpir'd, what faith enlarg'd his breaft,
> How foon th' unfetter'd fpirit wing'd its way,
>   From earth to heav'n, from bleffing to be bleft!

This monument is erected by fome intimate friends of the deceafed, as a teftimony of his worth and their efteem.   Againft.

Againft the communion rails on the North fide, in the wall is an arch wherein is an altar tomb, and thereon the effigies of an abbot lying in full proportion in pontificalia, carved in freeftone, with a mitre on his head feemingly as old as the fabrick of the church. This was in memory of Abbot Edmund Knowles, who died Anno 1332, and built the prefent church (as it is faid) leaving vacant arches in the walls to contain the effigies of his fucceffors, and to hold other monuments in future for perfons to be buried here. See p. 267.

Below and in the fame wall over the bottom of the altar-fteps is another arch, and therein the effigy of an abbot in full proportion in his habit, with a mitre on his head as the former, probably in memory of Abbot Walter Newbery, who died the 3d of September 1463. See p. 268.

Between the above Abbots, a little higher againft the wall is fixed a fmall black marble copartment edged round with freeftone, fet in the wall in memory of Bifhop of Rowland Searchfield, and Dean Chetwynd; the infcription is given in the account of that bifhop.

At the upper end of the North aile, between that and the choir, is a ftone corps of Bifhop Paul Bufh, inclofed with wooden rails, lying on a low tomb raifed from the floor about 18 inches, the tomb is compofed of fix pillars of the Ionick order, which fupport a flat canopy, the whole of freeftone; between the pillars at bottom and round the verge at top is painted an infcription in black letters, to be given in the lift of bifhops.

In the South wall in the Choir, below the altar-fteps, which are all laid with black and white marble, is under an arch the effigy of Abbot John Newland, with his mitre on his head, lying in full proportion as the other abbots; on a fhield at his feet fupported by two angels is his rebus, viz. an heart pierced through with three nails, alluding to his name, he being often times written Newland, alias Nailheart. For the further particulars I refer you to the lift of abbots. p. 268.

A little lower in the place of the confeffionary is a large handfome tomb with two men kneeling in armour, and a woman lying along before them, over them is a canopy fupported by two black marble pillars, at bottom eight children kneeling with a defk between them, on a tablet above their heads this infcription :

Here lie the bodies of Sir John Young knight, and dame Joan his wife; fhe had iffue by him Sir Robert, Jane, and Margaret. She was firft married to Sir Giles Strangewayes knight, by whom fhe had iffue John, Edward, George, Nicholas.

Nicholas, Ann and Elizabeth; fhc was daughter of John Wadham, Efq; and fhe departed this mortal life the 14th of June 1603, aged 70 years.

In the South aile under an arch of the thicknefs of the South wall, opening formerly into the veftry, is an altar-tomb covered with a broad ftone at top, in memory of Maurice Berkeley, who died 1281, (being the fecond of this name,) his arms were formerly painted on the infide of the arch, alfo his arms with thofe of his two wives and that of King Edward the 1ft. were carved in freeftone on the infide next the veftry, now vifible, but no effigies on his tomb now walled up.

On the other fide of the veftry door lower down, in an arch in the South wall is the effigy of a man in armour lying on an altar-tomb, in memory of Maurice Berkeley the third Lord of that name, who died the 19th of Edward the 2d. 1326; his arms on his fhield on his left arm.

At the lower end of the South aile is an arch in the fame wall with a like tomb, and the effigy of Thomas Lord Berkeley the firft of that name in armour, crofs legged, his arms are on his fhield. He having offended King Henry the 3d. was obliged to enter himfelf a Knight Templer. He died in the 76th year of his age, and the 28th of King Henry the 3d. 1243.

In the South aile Gilbert the 14th bifhop of this church, for fo he is called in the infcription, placed the following Latin epitaph to the memory of Alice Gliffon, who died the 24th of June 1662:

In piam memoriam lectiffimæ fœminæ Aliciæ Gliffon, filiæ Gulielmi Gliffon de Marnhill in com. Dorfet generofi in avito hoc tumulo fepultæ Anno Ætatis fuæ 48 pofuit mœftiffimus conjux Gilbertus, hujus ecclefiæ epifcopus decimus quartus, 24 die Junii A. D. 1662.

Samuel Croffman S. T. B.

Hujus ecclefiæ nuper Deeanns Juftorum refurrectionem hinc præftolatur: onus mortale depofuit 4 die Feb. A. D. MDCLXXXII. Militiæ vero fuæ 59.

At the foot of the fecond pillar from the organ is, on an old freeftone, " Elizabetha, filia Samuelis Croffman, hujus ecclefiæ prebendarii, et Gratiæ uxoris ejus; obiit Junii 21, 1668, Ætatis fuæ 13. Spes et deliciæ parentum: præivifti, fequemur."

A little above Bifhop Paul Bufh is a handfome freeftone copartment neatly painted, containing the effigies of a man in armour and a woman kneeling, having books before them under a canopy, being fupported; under them are eight fons and nine daughters, in a table below is the following Latin infcription:

Generofo

Generofo viro domino Roberto Codringtonio, a Codringtonia, in com. Glouceftr. armigero, atauorum imaginibus fplendidiffimo, fidei morumque candore fpeĉtatiffimo Februar. 14 poft incarnatum Deum 1618 Ætatis fuæ 46 ex hoc vitæ ergaftulo emancipato: chariffima conjux domina Anna Codr. ex qua 8 filios, filiafque 9. genuit

Am }
&   } oris { ergò { Monu } Mentum { Mæftiffima   } Robertus Codrintoneus,
Hon }   { Muni }   {   , }   Anagramma:
                                     { pofuit: } ore & Cordejuftus Beon.

Plangite; difceffi; quin plaudite, vita beatà
Eft mihi namque folo, gratior inque polo.
Hic mens, hic foboles, volitatque per æthera vaftum
.   Fama Codringtonei non moritura pii:
Os homini, domino patuit cor, confcia reĉti
Mens mihi, vel nullis contaminata malis;
Ore fui Juftus; merces durabilis annis;
Corde fui Juftus, præmia magna, Beor.

At the top of all, this under the fhield of his arms:

Fides   }   { verbum }
Spes   } Dei { præmium } refpicit.
Charitas }   { fervum }

Codrington, of Codrington in the county of Glocefter. This family was of good note in this county in the time of Henry the 4th. (vide Sir Robert Atkins's State of Glocefterfhire, p. 391.) John Codrington Efq; being ftandard-bearer to King Henry the 5th. in his wars in France; and as it appears by the heralds books, was then armed in a coat with lions in the fervice of the faid King in battle to watch and ward under his banner, and for the good fervices that the faid John Codrington had done, or fhould do, and to the worfhip of knighthood, as it is there expreffed, a farther addition was made to his arms in the 23d of King Henry the 6th. 1445.

Colonel John Codrington Efq; who married Elizabeth daughter of Samuel Gorges of Wraxal in the county of Somerfet, is of this old family, whofe only daughter married Sir Richard Warwick Bamfield of Poltimore in the county of Devon, Bart. Member of Parliament for the city of Exeter, and in the Parliament 1747 for the county of Devon, and his fon Sir Charles Bamfield is Member for the city of Exeter 1788, and refides at Wraxal.— The faid John Codrington Efq; was three times chofen Member of Parliament for the city of Bath, 1721, 1727, 1734. The great grandfather of the late Sir William Codrington of Dodington in the county of Glocefter, Bart. was a youngev younger fon of this family, he was Member of Parliament for Minehead in Somerfetſhire at the time of his death, which happened December the 17th 1738 at Dodington, and was fucceeded by his eldeſt fon Sir William Codrington the prefent Baronet, whofe father Sir William was created Baronet April the 21ſt 1721, in the 8th year of the reign of George the 1ſt.

Anne the fourth daughter of Richard Samwell of Upton in Northampton-ſhire, Efq; by his wife Frances, eldeſt daughter and coheir of Thomas Vifcount Wenman of Tuam in Ireland, married to Robert Codrington of Codrington in Gloceſterſhire, Efq; as may be feen by the arms and infcription on the monument: arms; argent, two fquirrels fejant, addorfed, gules, by the name of Samwell. Creſt, on a ducal coronet, or. a fquirrel fejant, cracking a nut, proper.

Without the choir under the dean and prebendaries feat is an ancient large grave ſtone that had on it braſſes.—N. B. This feems to be the only grave ſtone that had any figure cut on a brafs plate in the whole church, it lay originally at the choir entrance between the abbot's and prior's ſtall, and was in memory of Robert Fitzharding Lord of Berkeley the founder, and his Lady, before it was removed hither.

In the great crofs aile and nave without the choir are many grave ſtones; one clofe under the pulpit in memory of Robert Perry maſter of the Bluecoat-hofpital founded by Queen Elizabeth &c. which bears this infcription, Hic jacet Robertus Perry, orphanotrophii magiſter vigilantiſſimus qui mortem obiit Aprilis 29, 1652.

And this other on a black marble Jying near the ſteps leading to the biſhop's confiſtory, which is kept in a room above ſtairs:

Here lyeth the body of Geo. Smyth, late of North Nibley, in the county of Gloceſter, Efq; who departed this life the 29th day of February 1712-13, aged 48. (with his coat of arms.)

There are alfo many buried in the nave or body of the church with the name and date cut in a white marble ſtone of a lozenge ſhape, fixed in the paving.

In a chapel at the lower end of the South aile, extending itfelf equal with the great crofs aile, is againſt the Eaſt wall an ancient tomb of grey marble, it contained the effigies of two perfons kneeling, and an infcription in brafs underneath them, and their arms behind their heads, but it has been entirely taken away in the civil wars and there's no memorial to whom it belonged; how-ever from William of Worceſter it appears it was in memory of Sir Richard Newton Cradock, who died December the 13th 1444, being one of the

juſtices

juſtices of the common pleas. This with the founder's grave ſtone is the only monument in the whole church that had in braſs inſcriptions or figures belonging to them.

This monument with two others that are in the ſame chapel were in the year 1748 repaired and beautified at the expence of Mrs. Archer of London.

The place where the braſſes were fixed when taken away left impreſſions againſt the tomb, which when repaired was filled up ſmooth and thereon is now put the following inſcription:

In memory of Sir Richard Newton Cradock of Barrs Court in the county of Glouceſter, one of his Majeſties Juſtices of the Common Pleas, who died December the 13th 1444, and with his Lady lies interr'd beneath this monument, which was defaced by the civil wars and repaired by Mrs. Archer ſiſter to the late Sir Michael Newton of Barrs Court 1748.

His arms are argent, on A chevron azure, 3 garbes or.

Againſt the South wall in the ſaid chapel are two handſome tombs, the firſt is compoſed of alabaſter and freeſtone, and has at top three ſhields of arms; on one belonging to a man is 24 coats, and on another belonging to a woman 12 coats, and on a middle ſhield only two coats, viz. of the man and woman impaled.

Underneath lie the effigies of a man in armour and a woman in full proportion, and under them two ſons and four daughters, above them is a tablet with this inſcription:—" Here lies Sir Henry Newton of Barr's-Court in the county of Gloceſter Kt. who married Katherine the daughter of Sir Thomas Paſton, of Norfolk, Kt. by whom he had 2 ſons & 4 daughters; & when he had lived full 70 years religiouſly towards God, loyally towards his Prince, & virtuouſly towards men; ended his life in the year of grace 1599,

In aſſured hope of a glorious reſurrection.

Gourney, Hampton, Cradock, Newton laſt,
Held on the meaſure of that ancient line
Of Barons blood; full 70 years he paſt,
And did in peace his ſacred ſoul reſign:
His church he loved; he lov'd to feed the poor;
Such love aſſures a life, that dies no more.

The other tomb below his is of freeſtone, in memory of Sir John Newton Bart. ſon of Theodore Newton and his Lady, Grace daughter of **** Stone Eſq; who died without iſſue 1661. It is ſupported by two twiſted pillars, having the effigy of the defunct lying in full proportion in armour with a truncheon in his right hand, over him is on two tablets painted againſt the wall the following inſcription:

1ſt Tablet.

1ſt Tablet.

Here lyeth the body of Sir John Newton, Bart. ſon of Sir Theodore Newton, Kt. and his Lady Grace, daughter of . . . . . Stone Eſq; who dy'd without iſſue 1661.

2d Tablet.

He was a man of great courage, & the greateſt loyalty to his Prince, an honour to his country, a credit & noble ornament to his name and family.

At top is on a ſhield theſe arms, argent, on a cheveron azure, three garbes, or. by the name of Cradock, impaled with the arms of Stone, viz. Parte per pale, or. & gules, an eagle diſplayed with two heads azure.

There is a ſhield here with 24 quarterings belonging to this family of Newton of Barr's-Court.

At the lower end of the South aile, extending itſelf equal with the great croſs aile, is againſt the South pillar before the ſaid chapel, fixed in the ſame, a handſome copartment of black and white marble in memory of Jacob Elton Eſq; Captain of the Angleſea man of war of 40 guns, who was killed in an engagement on the high ſeas, his body was thrown overboard and the ſhip taken by the French the 29th of March 1745, the inſcription is,

Jacob Élton

Filius natu fecundus Abrahami Elton Barti.

Rebus nauticis

A tenerâ ætate aſſuetus,

Et in claſſe Britannicâ, etiamnum Adoleſcens

Navarcha ;

Anno triceſſimo fecundo nondùm peraƈto,

Dum contra Gallós

Prælio navali dimicaſſet,

Properatâ quidem,

Sed pulcherrimâ morte

Occubvit,

Die Martii 29no. A: D: 1745.

Qualis erat morum ſuavitas, Amici,

Quæ Humanitas et Benevoleñtia, nautæ,

Quam intrepidè et fortiter ſe geſſit,

Ille Dies

Satis ſuperque teſtatur.

Leve hoc Amoris ſuæ et Deſiderii Monumentum

Vidua mæſtiſſima

Carolina Filia et cohæres Caroli Yate

De Coulthrope in agro Gloceſtriæ

Poni curavit.

Theſe

Thefe are the principal monuments and memorials of the dead whofe remains lie depofited in thefe facred manfions. Our anceftors were very earneft in paying all due honours to good men departed, by erecting monuments and tombs over their bodies, and tranfmitting to lateft pofterity for our imitation the characters of the deceafed, their piety towards God and charity towards their fellow-creatures by infcriptions to their memories, many of which as they are very learned, moft of them inftructive, and all convey fome good leffons of piety, charity, religious devotion, &c. have their ufe in improving the minds of the living : though there may poffibly be a mixture of flattery and human foible in fome of thofe compofitions.—As monuments exprefs our belief of an immortality by fhewing a regard for our departed friends, they fhould not be accufed of vanity and ambition who pay that grateful regard to thofe whom they wifh to meet again in another and better world : though this feems to be one reafon why many worthy men and good families lie now a-days almoft unnoticed in the repofitories of the dead; a tacit confeffion alfo of the flight impreffion death and immortality make now on the minds of their fucceffors.

Having thus finifhed the defcription of this cathedral church and all its parts, I fhall proceed to give an account of its endowment by Henry the 8th. dated the 18th of November the 34th of Henry the 8th. A. D. 1542, out of the ruins of nine monafteries.

Value of the Rents.

General	-	-	£ 739	4 11
Reprifal	-	-	60	1 0
Clear	-		679	3 11

The following fums arife thereout (as appears by the rental) in this manner, viz.

Out of the Monaftery of

	General Value.			Reprifal.			Clear Value.		
	l.	s.	d.	l.	s.	d.	l.	s.	d.
1. St. Auguftin, Briftol, the Abbot	323	18	0½	22	8	3	301	9	9½
2. Michelney, Somerfet, the Abbot and comit. Hertf. - -	122	8	9	13	16	3	108	12	6
3. Bruton, Somerfet, the Abbot	88	11	4	-	-	-	88	11	4
4. Shafton, Dorfet, the Abbot	77	13	1½	0	16	8	76	16	5½
5. Bath, Somerfet, Priory - -	43	16	0	-	-	-	43	16	0
6. St. Ofwald nigh Glocr. Priory Abbot	42	17	8	14	10	8	28	7	0
7. Taunton, Somerfet, Priory -	14	0	0	-	-	-	14	0	0
8. Frithelftoke, Devonfhire, Prior	18	0	0	8	9	1	9	10	11
9. Bradenftock Com. Wilts, Prior	8	0	0	-	-	-	8	0	0
Total -	739	4	11	60	0	11	679	4	0

The

The particulars of each of these, viz. where they lie, and from whence the rents issue, may be seen in the following order:

No. I. The Rents of the Monastery of St. Augustin in six counties.

1. Bristol.

	General Value. l. s. d.	Reprisal. l. s. d.	Clear Value. l. s. d.
Rents in and about the town	101 6 0	13 7 4	87 18 8
Pensions out of rectories	6 8 8		6 8 8—94 7 4

2. Glocester.

	General Value.	Reprisal.	Clear Value.
1. Southerney manor	9 1 0	0 6 8	8 14 4
2. Blackfworth manor	7 0 9	0 10 0	6 10 9
3. Codrington manor -	6 13 4		
4. Rectory of Wapley - -	4 13 4		
5. Erlingham manor	5 17 4		
6. Henton de Everinghill -	0 2 0		
7. Bradley tene. Witton -	3 6 8—20 12 8	3 6 8	17 6 0
8. Berkeley-Hernis rectory	65 6 8		65 6 8
9. Clifton tenement* -	1 0 8		1 0 8—98 18 5

3. Somerfet.

	General Value.	Reprisal.	Clear Value.
1. Wear rectory in pension and compofition -	9 6 8		9 6 8
2. Tenement in Stanton Drew	0 12 0		0 12 0
3. Three fhops in Bath, rent	0 5 0		0 5 0—10 3 8

4. Devon.

	General Value.	Reprisal.	Clear Value.
1. Halberton manor -	15 15 8½	1 6 8	14 9 0½
2. The rectory there -	33 0 0		33 0 0—47 9 0½

5. Glamorgan.

	General Value.	Reprisal.	Clear Value.
1. Penarth manor, with the great tithes - -	19 9 11	0 10 0	18 19 11—18 19 11

6. Wentlock, Monmouth.

	General Value.	Reprisal.	Clear Value.
1. Peterfton manor, with the rectory of Kemney with its appurtenances, alfo St. Melo	34 12 4	3 0 11	31 11 5—31 11 5
Total fum	323 18 0½	22 8 3	301 9 9½ No.

* Clifton one acre of pafture worth 1l. 10s. per annum, encompaffed with several lands of the widow Jane Wilfon, and now in the occupation of Mr. William Hodges. See the furvey in 1649, fol. 30.——Three acres and a half in Clifton were granted by Abbot Burton, fee chapter book. lib. 1. fol. Penultima.

No. II. Out of the monaſtery of Mochelney the rents are in two counties.

1. Buckingham.

	General Value. l. s. d.	Reprisal. l. s. d.	Clear Value. l. s. d.	l. s. d.
1. Seymour Court meſſuage in Marlo – –	7 2 5		7 2 5 —	7 2 5

2. Somerſet.

	General Value. l. s. d.	Reprisal. l. s. d.	Clear Value. l. s. d.	l. s. d.
1. Abbot's Iſle rectory with Stewnly – –	6 0 0	0 9 11½	5 10 0½	
2. Meriot rectory –	12 1 0		12 1 0	
3. Ilmiſter rectory, 20l. cum Horton, 1l. 5s. Ilcombe 2l. 0s. – –	23 5 0		23 5 0	
4. Somerton rectory –	44 13 4	6 16 4	37 17 0	
5. Fifehead rectory –	4 0 0	0 9 11½	3 10 0½	
6. Drayton with the tythes of the lands	12 2 0			
Of the de-mean lands of Weſtover	2 13 4			
7. Morton tythes 1 5 0 —22 0 4		6 0 0	16 0 4	
8. Mildney in the pariſh of Drayton –	3 6 8	.	3 6 8	
			—101 10 1	
Total Sum	122 8 9	13 16 3	108 12 6	

No. III. The rents out of the monaſtery of Brewton are in the county of Somerſet.

	l. s. d.		l. s. d.	l. s. d.
1. Rectory of Banwell with Puxton, Churchill	38 3 4		38 3 4	
2. South Petherton rectory with four chapels annexed and Swell rectory	50 8 0		50 8 0	
			— 88 11 4	
Total Sum	88 11 4		88 11 4	

No. IV.

No. IV. The rents out of the monaſtery of Shafton in the county of Wilts.

	General Value. l. s. d.	Reprifal. l. s. d.	Clear Value. l. s. d.	l. s. d.
1.Tiſbury rec- l. s. d. tory tythes 16 16 8				
The glebe or manor of the fame rectory 3 9 10—20 6 6				
2. Bradford rectory, with the manor and four tenements - -	57 6 7½	0 16 8	76 16 5½	76 16 5½
Total Sum	77 13 1½	0 16 8	76 16 5½	

No. V. The rents out of the monaſtery of Bath are in two counties.

1. Glocefter.

	General Value.		Clear Value.	
1. Olvefton rectory -	17 16 0		17 16 0—17 16 0	

2. Somerfet.

1. Bath-Hampton rectory	10 0 0		10 0 0	
2. Bath-Ford rectory	8 6 8		8 6 8	
3. Bath-Wick prebendary penfion - -	0 6 8·		0 6 8	
4. The vicar of Chew penfion - -	7 0 0		7	
5. Of Newton St. Loe, penfion -	0 6 8		0 6 8	26 0 0
Total Sum	43 16 0		43 16 0·	

No. VI. The rents out of the monaſtery of St. Ofwald near Glocefter. are in the county of Glocefter.

1. Compton Abdale rectory	9 0 0·	6 1 0	2 19 0
2. Norton rectory -	13 6 8	6 14 4	6 12 4
3. Churchdean rectory with Hocalcot - -	11 1 0	0 14 4	10 6 8·
4. St. Ofwald's in four proportions, or St. Ka-therine's rectory -	7 5 4	1 1 0	6 4 4

5. A

	General Value. l. s. d.	Reprisal. l. s. d.	Clear Value. l. s. d.	l. s. d.
5. A pension out of the rectory of Widcombe	0 13 4		0 13 4	
6. A pension out of the rectory of Laffenden	0 8 0		0 8 0	
7. For tythes out of lands of Northcerney -	1 3 4		1 3 4	28 7 0
Total Sum	42 17 8	14 10 8	28 7 0	

No. VII. Out of the monastery of Taunton in the county of Somerset.
| 1. Kingston rectory | 14 0 0 | | 14 0 0 | |

No. VIII. Out of the monastery of Frethil Stoke in the county of Devon.
| 1. Brodwoodwiger with Week - | 18 0 0 | 8 9 1 | 9 10 11 | |

No. IX. Out of the monastery of Braden Stoke in the county of Wilts.
| 1. Marden rectory - | 8 0 0 | | 8 0 0 | |
| General Total Sum £ | 739 4 11 | 60 1 0 | 679 3 11 | |

From these clearly appear the rents granted by King Henry to this church from the said nine monasteries, all lying within eight counties, (reckoning the county of Glocester and the city as one) and in these eight only the rents arise.

1. In the county of Buckingham. l. s. d.
From the monastery of Mechelney - - 7 2 5

2. Glamorgan.
From the monastery of St. Augustin - 18 19 11

3. Wentlock als. Monmouth.
From the monastery of St. Augustin - 31 11 5

4. Devon, from the monastery of
1. St. Augustin - - 47 9 0½
2. Frithelstoke - - 9 10 11 —56 19 11½

5. Wilts, from the monastery of
1. Shafton - - - 76 16 5½
2. Bradenstock - - 8 0 0 —84 16 5½

6. Glocester.

6. Glocefter, from the monaftery of

	l.	*s.*	*d.*	*l.*	*s.*	*d.*	*l.*	*s.*	*d.*
1. St. Auguftin	98	18	5						
2. St. Ofwald — — —	28	7	0						
3. Bath — — —	17	16	0—145	1	5				

7. Somerfet, from the monaftery of

1. Mochelney — —	101	10	1			
2. Bruton — — —	88	11	4			
3. Bath — — —	26	0	0			
4. Taunton — — —	14	0	0			
5. St. Auguftin — — —	10	3	8—240	5	1	

8. Briftol, from the monaftery of

1. St. Auguftin there — — —	94	7	4

——— 679 4 0

And laftly, in this order through every one of thefe counties enquiry may be made into each of the faid rents, to wit, which of them in procefs of time is loft or diminifhed and which encreafed and enlarged, fo that by this means the true value and ftate of the whole may be known, according to which method and diftinction by counties (in the order in which they are above placed) the treafurer's accounts of the yearly rents (hitherto kept in a moft confufed or rather no order) may for the future be made up with great eafe and clearnefs.

Befides thefe rents fo recovered by the royal letters patent to the dean and chapter of this church (or rather intrufted to their fidelity) the advowfons, donations, and rights of patronage of many churches are granted, of which

Some fpecially and namely, viz. from the monaftery of

1. St. Auguftin, Berkeley, Wapley, Halberton, Peterftone alias Kempney.
2. St. Ofwald, Churchden, with Hocalcot, Compton Abdale, Norton, with St. Ofwald.
3. Bath, Olvefton, Hampton, Ford.
4. Bruton, South Petherton with Banwell.
5. Mochelney, Ile Abbots, Ilminfter, Ilcombe, Horton, Somerton, Meriott, Fifehead, Mildney, and Drayton.
6. Shafton, Bradford, Tifbury.
7. Taunton, Kingfton.
8. Bradenftock, Marden.
9. Frithelftoke, Brodwoodwigor.

Q q

In

In general of all the vicarages and other churches whofe rectories are above granted to the fame, but amongft thofe churches intrufted to them fome have perpetual vicars, curates, and ftipendaries.

Some churches or chapels are annexed and adjoin to another parochial church, (as to the mother) the care of providing minifters of which belongs to the vicar thereof.

Others are not thus annexed or only providing minifters for them more properly belongs to them and their farmers.

But they are all fituated in the following fix diocefes :

1. Llandaff.	4. Glocefter.
2. Salifbury.	5. Bath and Wells.
3. Exeter.	6. Briftol.

When the King erected the bifhopric of Briftol, he grants to Paul Bufh, Bifhop of Briftol, all thofe meffuages called the abbots' lodgings within the monaftery of Briftol, to him and his fucceffors.

And grants him the manors of Leigh and Rowborrow, in the county of Somerfet, the rectories of Portbury, Clevedon, and Ticknam, and advowfons of the vicarages :

The manors of Afhleworth, Cromhall, and Horfield, in the county of Glocefter : lands in Slimbridge and Ailberton :

The rectories and advowfons of Afhleworth, Almondfbury, Ailberton, Horfield, Felton, and Kingfwefton, late parcel of the poffeffions of Briftol monaftery :

The rectories and advowfons of St. Hurft and Minfterworth, late parcel of St. Ofwald's monaftery in Glocefter :

Rectory of Tockington, and tythes of Over Compton :

Rectory and advowfon of New Church in the Ifle of Wight, parcel of Battle abby :

Rectory and advowfon of Limington, in the county of Southampton, parcel of Chrift Church priory :

Rectory and advowfon of Buckland, parcel of Hedington monaftery, in the county of Wilts :

Manors and advowfons of Fifhead cum Crockefworth, in the county of Dorfet, parcel of Briftol monaftery, habend. to the bifhop and his fucceffors for ever in puram et perpetuam elymofinam.   Teft, June 10th.

The value of thofe lands, in a furvey taken about that time, I find to be thus rated :

Afhleworth

	l.	s.	d.
Aſhleworth manor, county of Gloceſter - - -	59	6	10
Cromhal manor, county of Gloceſter - - -	17	3	1
Horfield manor and rectory, county of Gloceſter, cum Felton and Kingſweſton, in the ſaid county - - -	49	13	10
Alberton rectory, county of Gloceſter - - -	6	0	0
Almondſbury rectory, county of Gloceſter - -	18	15	0
St. Hurſt rectory, county of Gloceſter - - -	10	19	0
Minſterworth rectory, county of Gloceſter - - -	8	6	8
Leigh manor cum Membris, county of Somerſet - -	56	3	1
Rowborrow manor, county of Somerſet - - -	20	3	5
Portbury rectory, county of Somerſet, cum Tickenham and Clevedon - - - - - -	28	16	6
Fifhead and Crockeford manors, county of Dorſet -	39	3	0
New Church in Inſula Vectæ (in Engliſh) Iſle of Wight, in the county of Southampton - - - -	34	17	6
Limington rectory, county of Southampton - - -	8	0	0
Buckland manor, county of Berks - - -	23	4	11
	£ 380	12	10

The whole of the endowment, according to the firſt valuation,
amounted to . - - - - £ 383 8 4

The lands and biſhop's demeſne at Briſtol not given in, in this particular making up, no doubt, the other 3 l. odd ſhillings.

This was the firſt demand and ſettlement for firſt fruits and tenths, which are now reduced 327 l. 5 s. 7 d. by the following alienations from Briſtol biſhoprick:

Paul Buſh, the firſt biſhop, anno 4th of Edward the 6th. granted to that King the manor of Leigh cum Membris, by deed made May the 25th, 1559. In which the dean and chapter joined Sept. 21 following; and two days after, viz. Sept. 23, the King granted the reverſion of it, after the death of Paul Buſh, to Sir George Norton and his heirs for ever. From Norton's family it came to the Trenchards, ——. I find no other alienations in the patents, though the rents and fines may have been aſcertained, and ſo funk the biſhoprick; in which reſpect Biſhop Fletcher is very much complained of tempore Eliz. This manor of Leigh, rated at 56 l. 3 s. 1 d. reduced the value of the firſt fruits as above-mentioned, from 383 l. to 327 l. which are now paid.

Salt

Sale of the lands of the bifhoprick in the Rebellion, anno 1641.

	l.	*s.*	*d.*
Horfield parcel of the manor, fold March 1, 1647, to Giles Calvert and Adam Haughton, for - - -	410	15	10
Briftol palace and park, fold June 22, 1648, to Thomas and John Clark, for · - - - - -	240	0	0
Mifmore, Prefton, Longford, and Afhleworth manors, parcel of the poffeffion of Glocefter and Briftol fees, fold Sept. 28, 1648, to Alderman Towke, for - - -	3819	1	0⅓

N. B. The three firft belong to Glocefter, and only Afhle-worth to Briftol.

	l.	*s.*	*d.*
Fifhead Magdalen, county of Dorfet, fold June 1, 1649, to john Aclyft, for - - - - -	1333	12	4
Cromhall Abbats manor, county of Glocefter, fold Sept. 28, 1649, to Richard Kirrington and Roger Cook, for -	568	0	2 ·
Horfield and Filton manors, fold Jan. 30, 1649, to Thomas Andrews, for - - - - -	1256	14	0
The Gate-houfe in Briftol, fold March 6, 1649, to John Birch, for - - - - - -	18	13	4
Parcel of Ground near Briftol, fold Auguft 9, 1650, to John Lock, for - - - - - -	21	10	0
Rowborow manor, county of Somerfet, and lands in Marton, in the county of York, parcel of Briftol and York bifhoprics, fold March 21, 1650, to Philip Nye and Theophilus Archer, for - - - - - -	722	1	1

Total £ 8390 7 9⅓ .

The bifhoprick, notwithftanding fome late improvements of the revenue by leafing out the park for building, which now brings in a ground rent of 70l. per annum, is not valued at more than about 500l. per annum ; the Bifhop of Briftol is therefore allowed to hold fomething in commendam with it, as the deanry of Chrift Church, a prebend in St. Paul's church, London, or fome valuable benefice.

The Bifhop of Briftol collates to Dorfet archdeaconry and Fifhead vicar-age, county of Dorfet, Almondfbury, &c, in all 14 benefices, which will appear more clearly with their valuation in the King's books, yearly tenths, lite, dedications, and antient patrons, by the following table.

Diocefe

Diocefe of Briftol, Glocefterfhire.

The following livings are in the gift of the Lord Bifhop of Briftol.

The Bifhoprick of Briftol * was taken out of the diocefe of Salifbury, except Briftol Deanry, which was taken out of Worcefter.

Firft Fruits.				*Yearly Tenths.*	
l.	*s.*	*d.*		*l.*	*s.*	*d.*
291	11	0¾	The cathedral church, (Holy Trinity, olim St. Auguftin.)	27	14	4¼

The deanry of this church is in the gift of the King, and not charged with the payment of firft fruits or tenths, (charter of erection June the 14th 1542.)

Deanry of Briftol.†

Livings difcharged.

Clear yearly Value. Rectories &c. with the patron and proprietor.

40 13 10	Aldmondfbury vic. (St. Mary) penf. abb. Sti. Au-		
No. 1.	guftini 10s. Bifhop of Briftol patron. and impropriator, abb. Sti. Auguftini Briftol, olim impr. — —	2	0	0

Chapels, donations, and curacies.

No. 2. Horfield cur. (Holy Trinity) 3l. certified value, abb. Sti. Auguftini, olim prop. Bifhop of Briftol, now impr. and patr.

46 0 8	Elberton, alias Aylbarton vic. or chap. in the county		
No. 3.	of Glocefter, Bifhop of Briftol propr. and patr.	0	13	3

Diocefe of Briftol.

Deanry of Shafton, Shatefbury.

King's Books. Livings in charge.

7 0 0	Fifhfield, alias Fifehead Magdalen vic. (St. Mary
No. 4.	Magdalen) penf. abb. Sti. Auguftini, Briftol, 60s. fynods and proxies 3s. 4d. ecclef. Sarum 20d.

Mon. fti. Aug. Briftol, propr. Mr. Newman 1677, Sir Richard Newman patr. 1725, Sir Robert Smyth Bart. prefented 1726, the Bifhop of Briftol impr.

I₂

---

* Bifhoprick of Briftol.—The tenths were altered by judgment of the Court of Exchequer, Hilary Term the 8th of Elizabeth, to the fum of 27l. 14s. 4¼d. as above. The patent of erection of this Bifhoprick, dated June 4, 1542, 34th of Henry the 8th. may be feen in Rymer's Fœdera, vol. 14. p. 748.

† Deanry of Briftol.—This Deanry and two churches in the city of Briftol are ftill fubject to the Archdeacon of Glocefter.

In the Diocefe of Glocefter.

Clear yearly Value.	Dean Foreft.	*Yearly Tenths.*

l. s. d. — Living difcharged. — *l. s. d.*

18 0 0 — Minfterworth vic. * (St. George) — 1 1 0

No. 5. Pri. Sti. Ofwaldi, Glocefter impr. the Bifhop of Briftol impr. and patr. but let by leafe to Mr. Pool, and is only a curacy.

Deanry of Glocefter.
Livings difcharged.

37 0 0 — Afhelworth vic. (St. Andrew) — 1 2 11

No. 6. Abb. Sti. Auguftini, Briftol, olim impr. Bifhop of Briftol impr. and patron.

24 0 0 — Santhurft vic. (St. Laurence) — 0 0 0

No. 7. Mon. Sti. Ofwaldi, Glocefter, olim impr. Bifhop of Briftol.

Diocefe of Salifbury, county of Berks.
Deanry of Abingdon.
In the Arch-deaconry of Berks.
Living difcharged.

35 0 0 — Buckland vic. (St. Mary) — 1 16 5½

No. 8. Epifc. Briftol, modernus proprietor. pri. Edington in Wilts, olim propr. Mrs. Mary Millington 1720, by leafe from the Bifhop of Briftol.

Diocefe of Winchefter.
Deanry of the Ifle of Wight.
Living difcharged.

50 0 0 — New-Church vic. (All-Saints) reprif. 21s. 4d. — 1 4 8

No. 9. Mon. de Bello loco impr. Bifhop of Briftol.

Diocefe of Bath and Wells.
Deanry of Redclift and Bedminfter, in the Archdeaconry of Bath, Somerfet.
Livings difcharged.

12 6 11 — Tickenham vic. (St. Quiricus and Julietta) prox. 5d. — 0 17 6½

No. 10. Abb. Sti. Auguftini, Briftol, propr. Bifhop of Briftol.
The King by lapfe 1753.

23 18 7 — Clevedon vic. (St. Andrew) — 1 11 5¼

No. 11. Abb. Sti. Auguftini, Briftol, propr. Bifhop of Briftol.

Clear

* Minfterworth vic.—Sir Robert Atkyns fays, " this is a vicarage turned into a curacy," p. 557.

l.	*s.*	*d.*		*l.*	*s.*	*d.*
27	15	8	Portbury vic. (St. Mary) prox. 6d. - -	1	1	1½

No. 12. Abb. Sti. Auguſtini, Briſtol, propr. Biſhop of Briſtol.

Deanry of Axbridge.
In the Archdeaconry of Wells.
Living diſcharged.

| 19 | 17 | 9 | Rowborrow rec. (St. Michael) ſynods 2s. prox..4d. | 0 | 15 | 0 |

No. 13. Biſhop of Briſtol.

Dioceſe of Gloceſter.
Deanry of Campden.
Livings diſcharged.
Rectories &c. with their patrons and proprietors.

| 29 | 4 | 6 | Eburton vic. * (St. Edburgh) ſynods 2s.   - | 0 | 18 | 11¾ |

No. 14. The King by lapſe 1714. Biſhop of Briſtol 1622, 1638. Abb. Bittleſden in Bucks, olim propr.

Endowments of the Chapter of Briſtol, Anno 1542.

The King grants to the Dean and Chapter of Briſtol and their ſucceſſors, all the ſite and circuit of the late monaſtery of Briſtol, except what was before granted to the Biſhop:

The manors of Codrington, South Cerney and Blackſworth † cum pertinentiis, parcel of Briſtol abby.

A tenement and two cloſes in Weſtborne, lands in Clifton, and meſſuages in Bradley ; lands in Henton in the county of Somerſet, with other hereditaments. in Erlingham; Wapley, Bradley, Goodrington, and Hinton, parcels of ſaid abby.

The rectories of Berkeley, Hinton, and Wapley, and advowſon of the vicarages, parcel of Briſtol abby.

The rectories of St. Ofwald, Gloceſter, Churchdown, Hoculcot, Compton--Abdale, and Norton, parcel of St. Ofwald's in Gloceſter-monaſtery.

Tythes of hay in Wike, Stone, Bovington, Bradſton, Cadbury, Oldminſter;. Hamand Hill in Berkeley pariſh, late belonging.to Briſtol abby.

Tythes of Twigworth and North Cerney, rectories of Widcomb and Laſſinden, and two houſes called the Almories in Briſtol.

A diſtil-houſe

* Eburton, alias Ebrington vic.—Sir Wm. Kite has given 10l. yearly to the vicar. Atkyns's Gloceſterſhire.

† The manor of Blackſworth with other things, was ſold the 21ſt of March 1649 by commiſſioners appointed for aboliſhing deans and chapters &c. to the mayor and commonalty of Briſtol, for the ſum of 3838l. 1s. 2d. paid to Thomas Noel and William Hobſon, two of the treaſurers appointed to receive the ſame.

A diftil-houfe and three mills in Redclift Juxta Briftol, and a meffuage called the Boar's-Head in Briftol.

Three fhops in Walcot-ftreet in Bath, the rectories of Hampton, Olwefton, and Ford, late belonging to Bath monaftery, and patronage of the vicarages.

The rectory and advowfon of Kingfton, parcel of Taunton monaftery.

The rectories of South Petherton, Lopington, Barrington, Chellington, Upton, Sevington, and Banwell in the county of Somerfet.

The rectories of Abbat's Ifle, Ilminfter, Horton, Merriot, Ilcomb, Somerton, Fifehead, Mochelney, Drayton, and Moreton; advowfons of the vicarages, late poffeffions of Mochelney abby.

Penfions payable out of the churches of St. Nicholas 4l. 6s. 8d. St. Auguftine's 2s. All-Saints 2l. St. Leonard's 10s. and St. Michael's in Briftol 2s.

Penfions of Bathwick prebend, rectories of Chew and Newton St. Loo, parcel of Bath monaftery.

The manor and chapel of Peterfton in Wentlog, parcel of Briftol abby.

Advowfons of Kempney and Peterfton in the county of Monmouth, the rectories of Tifbury, Bradford, Winfly, Holt, Atworth, Wraxal, Comberwell, in the county of Wilts, parcel of Shaftefbury abby.

The rectory of Marden in the county of Wilts, parcel of Bradenftock abby.

Advowfons of Tifbury and Bradford manor, rectory and advowfons of Halberton in the county of Devon, parcel of Briftol abby.

Rectory and advowfon of Brodwoodwigor in the county of Devon, parcel of Frithelftock priory, with all their rights, privileges, &c. which belonged to the late monafteries, &c. and were parcels of the faid manors, rectories, &c. here given tenend. to the dean and chapter and their fucceffors for ever. Tefte. Nov. 18th A. D. 1542, and the 34th of King Henry the 8th.

St. Nicholas 4l. 6s. 8. All-Saints 2l. St. Auguftine's 2s. St. Michael 2s. thefe penfions are paid by the minifter of each parifh, St. Leonard 10s. per ann. is paid as a quit-rent by the churchwarden of the parifh for the time being for a houfe in Fifher-lane.

The whole ground rents of the dean and chapter eftates amount to 845l. per ann. which do not pay the expences of the church, fees of office, ftipends to the feveral officers, canons, finging-men, organift, fub-facrift, &c. amounting to about 1111l. per ann. befides the repairs of the church, &c. But the renewals upon fo many eftates upon an average bring in fo much as renders the deanry worth above 300l. per ann. and each prebend above 150l. per ann. though it has fometimes amounted to 400l. per ann. to the dean, and 200l. per ann. to each prebendary, but the fums muft vary. Lord Paulet for

the

the tythes of Hinton and South Petherton, and for the manor of Halberton in Devon, offered 4000l. to put in two lives in 1776, which was under the value; he died 1788, by which those estates fell in to the dean and chapter.

Besides the following churches and chapels, they also formerly presented to Ilminster and Somerton vicarages in the county of Somerset, and to St. Melon's, but by not looking after their right have lost them.

The statutes of the foundation about the chapter, residence of the dean and prebendaries, and other officers, are the fame with those of Glocester collegiate church, printed in Sir Robert Atkyns's ancient and present state of that county in a large folio volume.

The following table gives a particular account of the livings in the gift and patronage of the dean and chapter of Bristol, their value in the King's books, dedication, tenths, &c.

Diocese of Bristol, in Glocester county.

Deanry of Bristol.

King's Books.	Livings remaining in charge.	Yearly Tenths.
l. s. d.	Rectories &c. with their patrons and proprietors.	l. s. d.
24 0 0	No. 1. Olveston vic. St. Mary, cum cap. Alveston, St. Helen, pri. Bath, olim impr. dean and chapter of Bristol, - -	2 8 0
	There was formerly in this parish the free chapel of Tockington, St. John the Baptist, which did belong to the abby of St. Augustin in Bristol, and after the dissolution was given to the bishoprick of Bristol.	

Diocese of Glocester.

| Clear yearly Value. | Livings discharged in the Deanry of Dursley. | |
| 32 0 0 | Hill a donative (St. Michael) abb. Sti. Augustini in Bristol, olim impr. dean and chapter of Bristol, now impro. Sir Edward Fult Bart. | |

City of Bristol.

Livings discharged.

Rectories &c. with their patrons and proprietors.

| 21 11 8 | No. 2. All-Saints vic. dean and chapter of Bristol propr. and patr. - - - | 0 8 4 |
| 5 10 0 | No. 3. St. Augustin's vic. dean and chapter of Bristol propr. and patr. - - - | 0 12 0 |

Clear

Clear yearly Value.				Yearly Tenths.		
l.	s.	d.		l.	s.	d.
4	1	5	No. 4. St. Leonard's vic. dean and chapter of Briftol propr. and patr. - - -	1	4	0
7	16	6	No. 5. St. Nicholas vic. dean and chapter of Briftol	2	12	1½

Diocefe of Salifbury.

Deanry of Pottern, in the Archdeaconry of Sarum.

Livings difcharged.

40	0	0	No. 6. Marden vic. (All-Saints) archidiac. 4s. dean and chapter of Briftol impr. and patr.	0	17	9

Diocefe of Glocefter.

Deanry of Cirencefter not charged.

No. 7. Compton Abdale cur. (St. Ofwald) 7l. certified value pri. Sti. Ofwaldi Glocefter, olim propr. church of Briftol patr.

Deanry of Glocefter, not in charge.

No. 8. Churchdown cur. (St. Bartholomew) 20l. certified value, pri. Sti. Ofwaldi olim propr. dean and chapter of Briftol patr.

No. 9. Norton cur. (St. Mary) 20l. certified value, pri. Sti. Ofwaldi, propr. dean and chapter of Briftol patrons.

St. Catherine, alias St. Ofwald's vic. demolifhed, dean and chapter of Briftol patr.

· Diocefe of Salifbury.

Deanry of Pottern, in the Archdeaconry of Sarum.

Livings difcharged.

42	0	0	No. 10. Bradford vic. (Holy Trinity) with fix chapels,* Archidiac. 7s. 6d. pri. Shaftefbury, olim propr. (vide Leland's Itin. vol. 7. p. 81.) dean and chapter of Briftol propr. and patr.	1	0	1½

Diocefe of Bath and Wells, Somerfet.

Deanry of Axbridge, in the Archdeaconry of Wells.

Livings remaining in charge.

King's Books.   Rectories &c. with their patrons and proprietors.

26	6	0½	No. 11. Banwell vic. (St. Andrew) with Puxton chapel (St. Saviour) abb. Brewton 20s. -	2	12	7¼

Abb. Brewton propr. dean and chapter of Briftol.   'King's

* Bradford vic. hath fix chapels, viz. Weftwood, Stoke (St. Edith), Winfly (St. Mary), W'raxal. (St. James), Aldworth, and Holt (St. Catherine).

12   1 5½ No. 12. Were vic. (St. George) fynods 10s. 8d. ob.
               proxies 2s. abb. Sti. Augustini, Briftol, 9l.
               6s. 8d. dean and chapter of Briftol, abb. St.
               Auftin, Briftol, propr.   -   -   1   4   1¾
               Chapels, donatives, and curacies.
               Churchill (St. John Baptift) chap. to Banwell 16l,
               Puxton (St. Saviour) chapel to Banwell 16l.
           Deanry of Bath, in the Archdeaconry of Bath.
                   Livings difcharged.
13 17 5½ No. 13. Bathampton vic. (St. Nicholas) fynods 2s. 6d.
               pri. Bath, impr. dean and chapter of Briftol. 0 15 8½
25   3   0 No. 14. Ford, alias Bathford vic. (St. Swithin) proxies
               10d. pri. Bath, impr. dean and chapter of
               Briftol.   -   -   -   0 17 9¾
           Deanry of Crewkerne, in the Archdeaconry of Taunton.
                   Livings remaining in charge.
24   0   0 No 15. South Petherton vic. (St. Peter and St. Paul)
               fynods 2s. 3d. proxies 18d. ob.   -   2   8   0
               Abb. of Brewton, impr. dean and chapter of
               Briftol.

Clear yearly Value.   Livings difcharged.
18 15   1 No. 16. Fifehead vic. (St. Martin) abb. of Mochelney,
               imp. dean and chapter of Briftol.   -   0 14 3¼
43   2 11 No. 17. Ifle Abbots vic. alias Abbots Ifle, abb. of
               Mochelney, appr. dean and chapter of
               Briftol.   -   -   -   0 16 (
           Diocefe of Bath and Wells, Somerfet.
40 17 0½ No. 18. Meriot vic. (All-Saints) fynods 12s. 2d. ob.
               proxies 13d. abb. of Mochelney, appr. dean
               and chapter of Briftol.   -   -   1   3   1¾
45   9   3 No. 19. Swell vic. (St. Catherine) fynods 9s. 8d. ob.
               proxies 4d. abb. of Brewton, appr. dean
               and chapter of Briftol.   -   -   0 11 0½

Deanry of Ilchefter, in the Archdeaconry of Wells.

| Clear yearly Value. | Livings remaining in charge. | Yearly Tenths. |
| l. s. d. | | l. s. d. |

10 0 0 No. 20. Mochelney vic. (St. Peter and St. Paul)
[a curacy only] ftipend.* dean and chapter
of Briftol patr. abbey of Mochelney propr.   1 0 0

Deanry of Taunton, in the Archdeaconry of Taunton.

King's Books.   Livings remaining in charge.

18 7 11 No. 21. Kingfton vic.† with Cutfton chapel, fynods
9s. 8d. ob. proxies 8d. priory of Taunton
15s. dean and chapter of Briftol, priory of
Taunton impr.   -   -   -   1 16 9½

Diocefe of York.

Deanry of Bingham, county of Nottingham.
Livings remaining in charge.

15 2 1 No. 22. St. Michael's in Sutton-Bonnington rec. archiepifc. pro. fyn. 6s. pro. prox. 6s. 8d.
dean and chapter of Briftol.   -   -   1 10 2½

Diocefe of Exeter, county of Devon.

Deanry of Tiverton, in the Archdeaconry of Exeter.

Clear yearly Value.   Livings difcharged.

46 0 0 No. 23. Halberton vic. ‡ (St. Andrew) epifc. prox.
2s. 8d. Archidiac. prox. fyn. and cath.
11s. 3d. dean and chapter of Briftol propr.
and patr.   -   -   -   3 2 0

Diocefe of Landaff, Monmouthfhire.

Deanry of Newport.
Livings difcharged.

20 0 0 No. 24. Marisfield, alias Merfhfield vic. (belonged formerly to the abby of Briftol) fyn. and prox.
quolibet tertio anno 20d. dean and chapter
of Briftol patr. and propr.   -   -   0 12 3

35 0 0 No. 25. St. Melon's vic. (belonged formerly to the abby
of Briftol) fyn. and prox. 6s. 11d. chapter
of Briftol, impr. Bifhop of Landaff.   ·   0 1¾
                   Clear

* Mochelney is certified to the Governors of Q. Ann's bounty to be of the clear yearly value of 10l.

† Kingfton vic. is certified to the Governors of Queen Ann's bounty to be of the clear yearly value of 49l. 18s. 8d.

‡ Halberton in the original is called a rectory,—it was in the year 1725 augmented by the Queen's bounty, and the dean and chapter of Briftol and others.

Clear yearly Value.				Yearly Tenths.		
l.	s.	d.		l.	s.	d.
10	0	0	Rumpney vic. (St. Auguſtin's) belonged formerly to the abby of Briſtol, ſyn. & prox. 20d.	0	11	0¾

Chapels, donatives, or curacies.

No. 26. Peterſtone-Wentlog cur. (St. Peter) 12l. certified value, dean and chapter of Briſtol impr.

N. B. The following livings did formerly belong to the abby of St. Auguſtin in Briſtol.

Dioceſe of Bath and Wells.

Deanery of Poulet alias Pawlet.

Livings diſcharged.

47	14	11½	Poulet vic. alias Pawlet (St. John Baptiſt) prox. 20d. ſynods 8s. 5d. ob. The King. Abby St. Auguſtini Briſtol propr. - - -	1	1	9½

Dioceſe of Gloceſter and Deanry of Gloceſter.

Livings diſcharged.

30	0	0	Witcomb magna rec. (St. Mary) Abby St. Auguſtini in Briſtol, olim impr. Sir Michael Hicks.	4	6	8

Deanry of Hawkiſbury.

35	0	0	Wapley vic. (St. Peter) ſynod and prox. 8s. 8d. chapter of Briſtol, (W.) Abby St. Auguſtini Briſtol olim impr. Robert Codrington, Eſq; 1705, tenant to the dean and chapter. - -	0	15	9

Dioceſe of Landaff and Deanry of Landaff.

Livings diſcharged.

8	0	0	Pennarth vic. alias Penmarth (St. Auſtin) epiſc. &c. Archdeacon 7s. 5d. Abby St. Aug. Briſtol propr. Thomas Lewis, Eſq; 1716. - -	0	9	9½

The liberal endowment and revenues of this church, we are told by Heylin, were very much impaired in the time of Queen Elizabeth, when for thirty-two years together it had no biſhop but was all that time held in commendam by the Biſhops of Gloceſter, and it is now eſteemed almoſt the leaſt valuable biſhoprick.

The pious Charles 1ſt. defender of the faith, and of the church of England by law eſtabliſhed therein, the tenth year of his reign, made a very neceſſary proviſional order for the preſervation of the revenues of biſhopricks, inſerted at length in Sir Robert Atkyns's Hiſtory of Gloceſterſhire. p. 12. " by which biſhops

biſhops were enjoined not to let any leaſe belonging to their biſhopricks into lives, which were not in lives already, but that the leaſes ſhould be for years ; for by turning the leaſes of twenty-one years into lives, the preſent biſhop might put a great fine into his own purſe to enrich himſelf, wife, and children, and leave the ſucceeding biſhops, of what deſert ſoever to the church, deſtitute of that growing means which elſe would come in unto them : by which courſe if continued the biſhop would ſcarce be able to live and keep houſe according to his place." This evidences the great care that monarch had for the good of the church and its right government by biſhops. For " prelacy and under it a ſubordination of miniſters in the church," Sir Robert Atkyns obſerves, " is highly becoming the Divine Wiſdom, and therefore belief may eaſily be given to that croud of primitive writers, who tell us epiſcopacy was inſtituted by Chriſt and his apoſtles for the perpetual policy of his church. In human wiſdom indeed it ſeems preferable to parity, and therefore it is natural to imagine, it was inſtituted by the divine. Parity is apt in all ſocieties to breed confuſion, which is the reaſon that many bodies of men have been forced for their own convenience or preſervation to ſet one with more or leſs authority over the reſt. In the very arts, ſciences, and profeſſions, we ſee a preference : the ſchools have their doctors, maſters, and batchelors; the law its ſerjeants, barriſters, and attornies ; the camp its captains, lieutenants, and enſigns ; the Romans their patricians, knights, and plebians ; the country hath its nobility, gentry, and commonalty : and therefore ſince all mankind have, as it were, received theſe three degrees of ſubordination, we can make no difficulty to prefer the epiſcopal (eſpecially if we conſider its firſt original and high deſcent) before any other form of church policy, or to believe that the three orders of biſhops, prieſts, and deacons, were a divine inſtitution for the adminiſtration of the church," which being carefully vigilant over its own members of the eſtabliſhment as to doctrine and diſcipline, and allowing free toleration to all who from tender conſciences diſſent, will thus ever flouriſh, the glory of this nation and the envy of others.

Briſtol being anciently a part of Gloceſterſhire belonged with it to the dioceſe of Worceſter, and the biſhops of that ſee preſided here, till itſelf being erected into a biſhopric by Henry 8th. Paul Buſh was appointed the firſt biſhop, ſome particulars of his life I ſhall here give and ſome account of each of his ſucceſſors in a regular order, as they were promoted to this ſee.

BISHOPS

BISHOPS of BRISTOL.

The arms of the fee are thus blazoned: fable, three ducal coronets in pale or.

1. Paul Bufh, S. T. B. was a native of Somerfetfhire, and entered with the Auguftin friers at Oxford in 1513, was of Wadham College, laft rector or provincial of the order of Bonnes Hommes at Edington in Wilts, canon refidentiary of Salifbury, and chaplain to King Henry 8th. who appointed him by his letters patent, 4th June 1542, the firft bifhop of this new-erected fee, and he received the temporalities of it, 16th June 1542, and was confecrated the 25th of the fame month. He foon after alienated the manor of Leigh, near Briftol, a part of the endowment of the bifhoprick, by which he deprived it of its belt eftate, to its great injury and lofs. On Queen Mary's acceffion, having broken his vow of celibacy, and knowing himfelf obnoxious, he freely gave up his bifhoprick 1553, and had the rectory of Winterborn, near Briftol, conferred upon him, having buried his wife that year. He built the epifcopal feat and made the choir ftalls in the cathedral, and died Oct. 11, 1558, aged 68, and was buried on the north fide of the church, near his wife's grave. — He is faid to have had great fkill in phyfic, and wrote a treatife on falves and curative remedies. There is the ftatue of a fkeleton, the emblem of mortality, lying on his tomb. He had a grant of arms by Chriftopher Barker, Garter king at arms, July 7, 1542, argent a fefs G. between three boars paffant fable, their tufks, hoof, and briftles or. on a fefs, a rofe between two eagles difplayed. Vide Wood's Athen. Oxon. vol. i. p. 89. more of him. He has this infcription on his tomb: " Hic jacet Dominus Paulus Bufh, primus hujus ecclefiæ epifcopus, qui obiit 11 die Octobris Anno Domini 1558, ætatis fuæ 68, cujus animæ propitietur Chriftus.

> Dignus, qui primam circum fua tempora mitram
>   Indueret, jacet hic Briftolienfe Decus :
> A patre Bufh dictus, Paulum baptifma vocavit,
>   Virtute implevit nomen utrumque pari.
> Paulus Edingtoniæ bis meffes preco fecutus
>   Inftituit populum dogmate, Chrifte, tuo :
> Ille animos verbis, impenfis pavit egenos,
>   Hine fructum arbufto protulit ille fuo.
> Ut Madidis arbufta juvant, fic fædere rupto
>   Inter difcordes pacificator erat."

On a ſtone in the choir near to his tomb was this engraved: " Of your charitie pray for the foule of Edyth Buſh otherwiſe Aſhely, who deceaſed 8 Oct. 1553." .

2. John Holyman, S. T. P. a zealous Roman Catholic preacher and wri-ter againſt the Lutherans, bred at Wincheſter ſchool; in 1554, was pro-moted to the ſee of Briſtol upon the deprivation or reſignation of Paul Bulb, and was conſecrated 18th November. See more of him in Wood's Athenæ Oxon. vol. i. 91. Fuller commends him as peaceable and committing no bloodſhed in his dioceſe. He died 20th Dec. 1558. Arms were, argent a chevron gules inter three roſes proper.

3. Richard Cheyney, B. D. after three years vacancy of the ſee ſucceeded, which he held with Gloceſter in commendam ſixteen years. Camden ſays, he was " Luthero addictiſſimus ;" whilſt his ſucceſſor to the ſee of Gloceſter Dr. Goodman ſays, he was a papiſt with all his ſervants, and was once ſuſ-pended for popery. He died 25th April, 1579, and was buried in Gloceſter cathedral. Arms, checky or. and azure a ſeſs G. fretty argent. Vide Wood's Athenæ Oxon. vol. i. p. 592.

4. John Bullingham, S. T. P. retired beyond ſea in Queen Mary's reign, and returning was 1567 made by Queen Elizabeth archdeacon of Huntingdon and rector of Withington and Boxwell in Gloceſterſhire; 1568 was made Doctor of Divinity, prebendary of Lincoln and Worceſter. In 1581, Biſhop of Gloceſter, and had the ſee of Briſtol given in commendam, which he held eight years; and it was then taken from him, and he had Culmington or Kilmington, in the county of Somerſet, in lieu of it. He died 20th May, 1598, Biſhop of Gloceſter, and was buried in that cathedral. Arms, azure an eagle diſplayed argent, in his beak a branch of beech or. on a chief of the laſt, a roſe betwixt two croſſes bottonee gules.

5. Richard Fletcher, S. T. P. bred at Cambridge. In 1583, was Dean of Peterborough and the prebendary of Lincoln: elected Biſhop here 14th Dec. Is ſaid in Sir John Harrington's View of the State of the Church, &c. p. 25. to have taken this ſee on condition of leaſing out its eſtates to courtiers, which he ſo extravagantly did that he left little to his ſucceſſors. In 1593, he was tranſlated to Worceſter, whilſt this lay vacant thirteen years. He attended Mary Queen of Scots on the ſcaffold, February 1586, and diſturbed her much by officiouſly perſuading her then to change her religion. At length marry-ing a ſecond wife, Lady Baker, a very handſome widow, he grew very diſ-contented through the Queen's diſpleaſure, he died ſuddenly by the immo-derate uſe of tobacco, 15th June, 1596, after having ſat Biſhop of London,

where

where he had little enjoyment. He was buried in St. Paul's. Arms, fable, a crofs flenry argent, four efcalops of the fecond.

6. John Thornborough, at King James's acceffion to the throne, after ten year's vacancy of the fee, was tranflated to it from Limerick, 30th May, 1603, with liberty to keep the deanry of York in commendam. He incurred fome cenfure on account of a marriage. He was tranflated to Worcefter, 17th February, 1616. Vide Wood's Athenæ Oxon. vol. ii. p. 1.

7. Nicholas Felton, was bred at Cambridge, a Norfolk man, rector of St. Mary le Bow, Eafton in Effex, and Blagdon in Somerfet, was confecrated Bifhop 18th December, 1617, but tranflated the next year to Ely, and died 5th October, 1626. Arms, G. two lions paffant in pale ermine ducally crowned or.

8. Rowland Searchfield, was of St. John's College, Oxford, confecrated Bifhop 19th May, 1619, died 11th October, 1622, and was buried in Briftol cathedral. Arms, azure, three crofs bows ftringed argent, a chief or. Vide Wood, vol. i. p. 622.

9. Robert Wright, was warden of Wadham college, &c. but marrying he refigned on the 23d of March, 1622, was confecrated Bifhop here, and 1632 he was tranflated to Litchfield and Coventry. In his time the ftone pulpit was made in the body of the cathedral, with the feats for the corporation oppofite to it. Vide Wood, vol. ii. p. 654. Arms, party per pale or. and argent, on a chevron azure, three bezants between as many boars heads couped proper. Motto; Dominus mihi adjutor.

10. George Cook, was bred at Cambridge, confecrated Bifhop 10th February, 1632, and 1636 tranflated to Hereford, where he died 10th December, 1646, and was buried there. Arms, parted per pale, ruby, and fapphire, three eagles pearl.

11. Robert Skinner, was confecrated 15th Jan. 1636, and kept Launton in Oxfordfhire and Greenfnorton in Northamptonfhire in commendam with this fee. In 1641 he was tranflated to Oxford, and during the times of the ufurpation having fuffered much he neverthelefs continued to confer orders, and was the only Bifhop that did it. He was tranflated to the fee of Worcefter, 12th October, 1663, and died in 1670, being buried in that cathedral with the following Latin infcription on a flat marble ftone: — " H. I. E. Rev. in Ch. pater ac Dom. Robertus Skinner, Coll. St. Trinitatis Oxon focius, Carolo primo Britanniarum monarchæ a facris, Doctoratum in Ss. theologiá almæ matris diplomate oblatum fine ambitu cepit. a rectoriá Launton diocæf. Oxon. ad epifcopatum Briftolienfem evocatus, (tantus ecclefiæ lilias meruit

cito

cito fieri parens) mox ad fedem Oxonienfem tranflatus. Turre Londinenfi a perduellibus diu incarceratus tam fine culpa quam examine exivit. A Carolo fecundo ad fedem Vigornienfem promotus poftquam prebyteris fanciendis affuetam dextram fufficiendis præfulibu mutuam dediffet (eorumq; quinque a fuo collegio στγχρονοις) omnibus ante facrilegam ufurpationem epifcopus fuperlles, Junii 14, A. D. 1670, Octogenarius ad fummum animarum epifcopum afcendit prius gratiâ nunc gloria confecratus." Arms, fable, a chevron or. between three griffins heads crazed argent.

12. Thomas Weftfield, S. T. P. was advanced to this bifhopric, 28th January, 1641. He fuffered much from the rebels, and had the profits of his fee unjuftly detained from him ; though afterwards reftored by a committee of the rebel parliament, being of fuch an unexceptionable character that when they reftored to him his rights, the committee gave him a pafs to go to Briftol, adding therein " that he was a perfon of great learning and merit." He was fuch an excellent preacher, that Bifhop King faid he was born an orator. He was fo modeft and diffident, that it is faid he never afcended the pulpit without trembling, and once fainted away when he was to preach before the King. He died 25th June, 1644, and lies buried in the choir of Briftol cathedral with this infcription, which he compofed himfelf before his death: — " Hic jacet Thomas Weftfield, S. T. P. epifcoporum infimus, peccatorum primus. obiit 25 Junii 1644 fenio et mærore confectus : tu lector, quifquis es, vale et refipifce. Epitaphium ipfe dictavit fibi vivus. Monumentum uxor mæftiffima Elizabetha Weftfield marito defideratiffimo pofuit fuperftes." — Arms, f. argent, crofs fable. See Walker's Sufferings of the Clergy, part 2d. p. 3 to 5. Wood, vol. ii. p. 724.

13. Thomas Howell, S. T. P. nominated by the King Bifhop July, 1644, and confecrated by Archbifhop Ufher, and enthronized 12th April, 1645, was barbaroufly treated by the rebels. His palace which was then covered with lead, under pretence of having bought the houfe, they uncovered and fold the lead; which expofed his wife, whom they knew to be then in childbed, to the rain and wind, which with the trouble and grief foon occafioned her death. After many bafe indignities, they dragged him violently out of the palace, of which they after made a malthoufe. He ftruggling awhile for his property, catched hold of the ftaple of the door, not knowing where to fhelter his poor motherlefs family of ten children, but they forced him out ; and there they ground at a mill erected there as well as made their malt for feveral years, — and they had it in defign to put up a furnace for brewing at the caft end of the choir in the place of the altar. The inhuman ufage

usage he received at their hands was such that he could not bear it, but did not long survive their cruelty, and died in less than a fortnight after being thus robbed and pillaged and maltreated. He was esteemed an excellent preacher, and of a mild and meek disposition, a feeling and tender heart, which they broke by this treatment. He died 1646, and was buried in his cathedral at the entrance of the choir out of the south aile, under a plain stone without any other inscription but this one word, " Expergiscar." He found few well affected in his diocese at his coming thither, yet he left few ill affected in it at his death. He left many poor children behind him; but it is said, he was so well loved at Bristol, that after his decease the city took upon them the care of his children's education, in grateful sense of the memory of this their most worthy father. See Wood's Athenæ Oxon. vol. ii. p. 656. Arms, G. a falcon, wings expanded, argent.

14. Gilbert Ironside, S. T. P. was born at Hawkbury near Sodbury, in the county of Glocester, was fellow of Trinity College, Oxon, 1613, rector of Winterborn, Steepleton in Dorsetshire, and Yeovelton in Somersetshire, both of which he kept till the Restoration; had a prebend in the church of of York, and December 1, 1660, was elected to the see of Bristol, after it had been vacant fourteen years. He was looked upon as the fittest person, being wealthy, to enter upon this mean and reduced bishoprick after such long vacancy. He died here 19th September, 1671, aged 83, and was buried close to the steps of the bishop's seat without monument or inscription. Arms, quarterly azure and G. a cross fleury or.

15. Guy Charlton, S. T. P. was a Cumberland man, educated at Queen's College, Oxford, was proctor 1635, vicar of Bucklesbury, Berks, and rector of Havant. He took the side of the Royalists in the rebellion, and suffered accordingly with the rest. After the Restoration he was created Doctor of Divinity, and a chaplain to the King, and dean of Carlisle: and 1660, prebendary of Durham. And the 20th December, 1671, was elected to the see of Bristol, confirmed the 20th January, and consecrated in Henry the seventh's chapel the 11th February following, keeping his prebend in commendam. On the 8th January, 1678, he was translated to the see of Chichester. He died at Westminster, 6th July, 1685, and was buried at Chichester. Arms, or. a lion rampant, G. Motto: " Sans varier."

16. William Goulson, or Gulston, S. T. P. was of Leicestershire, educated at St. John's College, Cambridge, and was chaplain to the Dutchess of Somerset, who presented him to Symondsbury, Dorset. He was chosen Bishop of Bristol 16th January, and consecrated at Lambeth 9th of February,

1678.

1678. He died at Symondſbury 4th April, 1684, and was buried there in the chancel. After his death the Rev. Thomas Long, prebendary of Exeter, was offered this biſhoprick, but he ſcrupling it at firſt was denied it after-wards. The arms of Goulſton are argent over three bars nebule gules, a bend ſable, charged with as many plates. See Wood, vol. ii. p. 684.

17. John Lake, S. T. P. was of Halifax, Yorkſhire, and of St. John's College, Cambridge, biſhop of the Iſle of Man, was tranſlated to Briſtol 12th Anguſt, 1684, and the next year was hence tranſlated to Chicheſter. He was one of the ſeven biſhops committed to the Tower for a ſeditious libel againſt King James 2d. or rather for ſubſcribing a petition to his Majeſty, wherein he and the reſt ſhewed their great averſeneſs to the diſtributing and publiſhing in all their churches the King's late declaration for liberty of con-ſcience, &c. After King William came to the crown he refuſed taking the oaths of allegiance and ſupremacy to him, and was therefore deprived of his biſhoprick. On his death bed the latter end of Auguſt, 1689, he publicly declared againſt them. Arms, A. on a ſaltire engrailed ſ. nine annulets or.

18. Jonathan Trelawney, S. T. P. was of Chriſt Church, Oxon, rector of St. Ives and Southill, county of Cornwall, was conſecrated biſhop 8th No-vember, 1685, and in April, 1689, he was tranſlated to Exeter, and 1707 thence to Wincheſter. He died 19th July, 1721, and was buried at Plint or Plenint in Cornwall, the place of his birth, with his anceſtors. Arms, argent a chevron ſable, betwixt three laurel leaves ſlipt vert, with the arms of Ulſter as a baronet. See Wood, vol. ii. p. 1183.

In Sir John Dalrymple's Memoirs of Great Britain, &c. vol. ii. p. 335. is the following letter from this Biſhop of Briſtol to William Prince of Orange then in the kingdom, 1688.

" May it pleaſe your Highneſs,

" I received the great honour of your Highneſs's letter, and beg leave to return you my moſt humble thanks for thoſe kind opinions you have been pleaſed to conceive of me, which I ſhall endeavour ſtill to preſerve.

" My Lord Shrewſbury (with whoſe conduct we are all extremely pleaſed) will give you a full account of what hath been done here, which if your High-neſs ſhall approve of, it will be great ſatisfaction to me, that I have borne ſome part in the work which your Highneſs has undertaken with the hazard of your life, for the preſervation of the Proteſtant religion, the laws, and the liberties of this kingdom.

" I

" I defire Almighty God to preferve you as the means of continuing to us the exercife of our holy religion and our laws, and humbly befeech your Highnefs to believe me very ready to promote fo good a work, and on all occafions to approve myfelf your Highnefs's

Moft obedient, faithful, humble fervant,

Briftol, Dec. 5, 1688.   J. BRISTOL."

19. Gilbert Ironfide, fon of a former bifhop of the fame name, was confecrated to this fee 13th October, 1689, and July 29, 1691, was tranflated to Hereford. He died 27th Auguft, 1701, aged 69, and was buried in St. Mary Somerfet church, London.

20. John Hall, was mafter of Pembroke College, Oxon, and rector of Aldgate, and was confecrated here 30th Auguft, 1691. He died February 4, 1709-10, at his college, aged 77, and was buried at Bromfgrove, in the county of Worcefter, the place of his birth. Arms, A. on a chevron engrailed, inter three lions heads erafed, fable, an etoile or.

21. John Robinfon, S. T. P. was of Cleafly, in Yorkfhire, and bred at Oriel College, 7th Auguft, 1710, was made dean of Windfor and prebendary of Canterbury, and confecrated bifhop 19th November, 1710, Lord Privy Seal, and one of her Majefty's honourable privy council and firft plenipotentiary at the congrefs at Utrecht, 1712. He was 13th March, 1713, tranflated to London, and dying 11th April, 1723, aged 72, was buried in Fulham churchyard. Arms, vert on a chevron f. between three bucks paffant or. as many etoiles of the laft. See his arms in the weft window of Briftol cathedral in coloured glafs, alfo a runic infcription. See Gent. Mag. for Auguft, 1780, p. 373.

22. George Smalridge, S. T. P. was of Litchfield, and ftudent of Chrift Church, Oxford, from Weftminfter fchool, was prebendary of Litchfield, minifter of St. Dunftan's in the Weft, which he quitted June, 1711, and afterwards was canon of Chrift Church, and 1713 dean, and was coufecrated bifhop 4th April, 1714, and was foon after made Lord Almoner to Queen Ann. Whilft he was bifhop here he repaired many of the rooms in the palace at his own coft. He died at his deanry 27th September, 1719, and was buried at Chrift Church, Oxon. Arms, f. a crofs engrailed or. between four buftards refpecting each other argent.

23. Hugh Boulter, S. T. P. was of Magdalen College, Oxon, M. A. 12th May 1693, B. A. 28th March, 1705, D. D. 1ft July, 1708, confecrated bifhop here 15th November, 1719, being before archdeacon of Surry, rector St. Olave's and dean of Chrift Chrift, and one of George 1ft's. chaplains, who

attended

attended him abroad. On the 3d November, 1724, he was tranflated to the archbifhoprick of Armagh, and was made Lord Primate and Metropolitan of all Ireland in room of Dr. Lindfey, deceafed. His arms are, or. on a chevron G. three men's fkulls of the field.

24. William Bradfhaw, was born at Abergavenny in Monmouthfhire, and bred at Baliol College, Oxon; took his degree of M. A. at Cambridge, was afterwards D. D. and dean of Chrift Church, Oxon, 23d Auguft, 1724, and was elected bifhop here 21ft September, 1724. He was prebendary of Canterbury and Oxon, and rector of Fawleigh in Hampfhire. He died at Bath and was buried in Briftol cathedral 16th December, 1732, aged 62. Arms, argent, two bends fable.

25. Charles Cecil, S. T. P. of Chrift Church, Oxon, D. D. and one of his Majefty's chaplains in ordinary, rector of Hatfield in Hertfordfhire, a defcendant of the Cecils Earl of Salifbury. He was elected Bifhop of Briftol 15th January, 1732-3. In the year 1734 he was tranflated to the bifhoprick of Bangor, and died in 1737. Arms, barry of ten, argent and azure, over all fix efcutcheons fable, 3, 2, 1, each charged with a lion rampant argent.

26. Thomas Seeker, L. L. D. of Exeter College, Oxon, M. A. 4th Feb. 1723, for which he was grand compounder. July 9, 1733, he was prefented to a prebend of Durham and the rectory of St. James, Weftminfter, and then to the bifhoprick of Briftol the 2d January, 1734-5, and confecrated the 19th. In 1737 he was tranflated to the fee of Oxford, and thence to London, and afterwards to the archbifhoprick of Canterbury. Arms, gules, a bend engrailed or. between two bulls head. or.

27. Thomas Gooch, D. D. was mafter of Gonville and Caius college, Cambridge, and elected bifhop here 28th May, 1737, and the year following was tranflated to Norwich, and thence to Ely, and died at Ely houfe, Holborn, 14th February, 1754, and was buried the 21ft in the chapel of Gonville and Caius college, where a monument with an elegant infcription is erected to his memory. Arms, azure, three boars paffant argent.

28. Jofeph Butler, L. L. D. of Oriel college, took his degree of Bathelor of the Civil Law 10th June, 1721. He was elected bifhop here 6th November, 1738, and confecrated 3d December. He held alfo the deanry of St. Paul's, London, with this fee, and was confirmed therein in 1740. He was clerk of the clofet, 1736, to Queen Caroline, and after her deceafe clerk of the clofet to the King. In Auguft, 1738, he was made prebendary of Rochefter and had the valuable rectory of Stanhope in the bifhoprick of Durham, which he refigned on being made dean of St. Paul's. In Auguft, 1750, he

was

was tranflated to Durham. In the year 1744 he rebuilt the bifhop's palace at Briftol then going to decay, which coft him 5000l. where he ufually refided five months in the fummer. Living a fingle life and having no relations dependent on him, he laid out all his income, and generoufly expended more, during the twelve years he was Bifhop of Briftol, than he received from the whole fee. In the year 1750 he propofed to the corporation the feparation of the out-parifh of St. Philip and Jacob, and building of a new church in Kingf-wood for the better inftruction of the colliers and poor inhabitants there in the Chriftian religion. In 1750 an act of Parliament was obtained for that pur-pofe, and his lordfhip opened the fubfcription with 400l. and procured 400l. more out of Queen Ann's bounty, the corporation fubfcribed 100l. &c. It is the more generous act, as he was foon to leave his palace here and quit the diocefe, being about this very time to be tranflated to Durham, which took place the fame year 1750, where he employed 130 workmen to repair that palace alfo, and became an annual fubfcriber of 400l. to the county hof-pital there. He died Tuefday 16th June, 1752, at Bath, in the 63d year of his age, and was buried in a deep brick grave, in which Gilbert Ironfide in 1671 was interred, at the foot of the bifhop's feat in Briftol cathedral, Bifhop Howell lying on the right, and Bifhop Bradfhaw on the left fide, with the following infcription on his ftone :

H. S.

Reverendus admodum in Chrifto Pater
Jofephus Butler, L. L. D.
Hujufce primò diæcefeos,
Deinde Dunelmenfis, Epifcopus,
Qualis quantufq; vir erat,
Sua libentiffime agnovit ætas :
Et, fiquid præfuli aut fcriptori ad famam valent
Mens altiffima, ingenii perfpicacis et fubacti vis,
Animufq; pius, fimplex, candidus, liberalis;
Mortui haud facile evanefcet memoria.
Obiit Bathoniis
16 kal. Jul. A. D. MDCCLII.
Annos natus LX.

His arms are, argent, between two bendlets engrailed, three covered cups fable.

29. John

29. John Conybeare, S. T. P. born in Devonſhire, was educated at Ti-verton ſchool, afterwards fellow of Exeter college, Oxon, where he took his degrees of A. M. and D. D. was-eſteemed learned, and cultivated a fine ge-nius by ſtudious application ; an eminent orthodox divine and powerful prea-cher. In 1742 be was made Dean of Chriſt Church, and 1750, 27th Nov. Biſhop of Briſtol, and 1751, 9th Auguſt, came hither being his firſt viſitation. He died 13th July, 1755, and was buried here After his death four volumes in octavo of his ſermons were publiſhed,· to which moſt of the nobility, clergy and gentry ſubſcribed.

30. John Hume, D. D. of Chriſt Church college, Oxford, rector of Barnes in Surry, and biſhop here 23d July, 1756, and in 1758 he was tranſlated to Oxford, and in 1774 to Saliſbury, where he continued to his death.

31. Philip Young ſucceeded biſhop here 4th Auguſt, 1758 ; had heen maſ-ter of Jeſus college, Cambridge, and canon reſidentiary of St. Paul's, and was tranſlated to Norwich in 1761.

32. Thomas Newton, was born 1ſt December, 1703, O. S. ſon of John Newton, a conſiderable brandy and cider merchant, by a daughter of Rev. Mr. Rhodes, who was conſumptive and died of that diſorder, when her ſon was but a year old, from whom he ſeemed to have inherited a tender conſtitu-tion. He was educated in the free ſchool of Litchfield, under the direction of Mr. Hunter, famous for having produced ſeveral perſons of note and emi-nence. He was ſent at fourteen years of age to Weſtminſter ſchool, by the advice of Dr. Trebeck, whoſe daughter his father had married for a ſecond wife. The ſchool at that time was never in higher eſtimation, having five hundred ſcholars, under the auſpices of Dr. Friend and Dr. Nicholls. In 1719 he loſt his friend and patron, Biſhop Smalridge. He continued ſix years at Weſt-minſter ſchool, in the laſt was captain. In 1723 he was elected to Cambridge through Dr. Bentley, where he reſided eight months every year, till he had taken his Batchelor of Arts degree, when he was choſen fellow, after which he went to ſettle in London, and prepared himſelf according to his inclination from a child for holy orders, and compoſed about twenty ſermons, which he wrote in a large legible character, that he might never have occaſion to copy them. In all his compoſitions at ſchool, at the univerſity, and every where, always his method was to finiſh the whole before he wrote down any part of it; and to ſome of his friends he repeated ſeveral of his ſermons word for word before he committed a tittle to writing, ſo that he ſaved abundance of paper, without blotting or interlining, and could eaſily have preached without notes if he pleaſed. His title for orders was his fellowſhip, and he was ordained

deacon

deacon 21ſt December, 1729, when twenty-ſix years old; and prieſt in February following by that great and worthy prelate Biſhop Gibſon. He became
curate at St. George's church, Hanover-ſquare, and continued for ſeveral
years aſſiſtant preacher to Dr. Trebeck, whoſe ill health diſabled him from
performing his duty. His firſt preferment was that of reader and afternoon
preacher at Groſvenor chapel in South Audley-ſtreet, and by this means became tutor to Lord Carpenter's ſon, being taken into that family, where he
lived ſeveral years much at his caſe, and in great intimacy and friendſhip of·
Lord and Lady Carpenter; and living at no kind of expence, he was tempted
to gratify his taſte in the purchaſe of books and paintings and prints, and
made the beginning of a colleƈtion, which was continually receiving conſiderable additions and improvements.

Here he ſtuck for ſome time without any promotion, ſometimes preached the
turns of ſome of the prebendaries of Weſtminſter Dr. Friend and Dr. Nichol,
and was in the friendſhip of Biſhop Chandler and the Biſhop of Durham; the
latter, though he continued biſhop twenty years, yet he beſtowed no preferment on this young man (Newton), of whoſe company he was ever ſo very de-
ſirons that when he ſtayed away any time from his houſe in viſiting him, he
ſent for him and kindly reproved him. In 1738 he became acquainted with
Dr. Pearce, afterwards Biſhop of Rocheſter, who freely and in a moſt handſome manner offered to appoint him morning preacher at the chapel in Spring
Garden, where was a very full and polite congregation, conſiſting principally
of noble families from Whitehall and of thoſe of the Lords of the Admíralty,
and other good families in that neighbourhood. This piece of preferment
was the beginning of a valuable conneƈtion with a very learned and a very
good man Biſhop Pearce. He was afterwards with Dr. Pearce frequently at
dinner at Lord Bath's, who proved a moſt ſincere, worthy, and valuable
friend to him; and by means of Mrs. Ann Deane Devoniſh, intimate with the
Prince and Princeſs of Wales, he became noticed by their Royal Highneſſes,
and introduced to the acquaintance of the Earl of Bath, two of the moſt fortunate circumſtances of his life. He was now appointed firſt chaplain to the
Earl of Bath, by whoſe intereſt in the ſpring 1744 he was preferred to the
reƈtory of St. Mary le Bow in Cheapſide, ſo that he was forty years old before he obtained any living. He now quitted the chapel in Spring Garden,
his fellowſhip became vacant, and in 1745 he took the degree of Doƈtor in
Divinity. During the Rebellion he publiſhed two ſermons on the occaſion,
and one preached the 18th of December before the Houſe of Commons. In
the ſpring of 1747 Dr. Newton was choſen leƈturer of St. George's, Hanover-

T т   ſquare,

square, in the room of Dr. Savage, deceased; and in the month of August following he married his first wife Jane, eldest daughter of Rev. Dr. Trebeck, an unaffected, modest, decent, young woman, with whom he lived seven years very happy in mutual love and harmony. As they had no children they continued to board in the parsonage house with Dr. Trebeck, free from the trouble of house-keeping. In 1749 was published Dr. Newton's quarto edition of Milton's Paradise Lost, which has gone through eight editions, a sign of its being well received. The Prince and Princess of Wales did him the honour of being two of his subscribers. He next published the Paradise Regain'd and other poems of Milton. In 1751 Dr. Newton preached a funeral sermon on the death of the Prince of Wales at St. George's, which excited the notice of the Princess, who made him one of her chaplains, and was particularly gracious to him ever after. In 1754 he lost his father and wife. It was happy his mind was now much engaged in writing the Dissertations on the the Prophecies, for plunging deep into study was a great relief to him in this affliction. This work was well received and translated into French and German in 1761. In 1757 he at length after many promises and disappointments by the Duke of Newcastle, procured a prebend of Westminster, in the room of Dr. Green, deceased, and was made sub-almoner to Gilbert, Archbishop of York, who gave him also the precentorship of that church, which he held till he succeeded Dr. Young in the bishoprick of Bristol and residentiaryship of St. Paul's. He was consecrated bishop at Christmas, 1761, the King having of his own motion made him bishop, so that he was not indebted to any minister for his promotion. Though in the year 1764 he was offered the primacy of Ireland, yet being then past sixty, and having no family to provide for, and preferring a quiet competency to pomp and greatness, he continued Bishop of Bristol and Dean of St. Paul's to his death. He usually resided at Bristol all the summer season, attending his cathedral church as often as his health very tender and precarious would permit, lamenting the too frequent absence of the dean and non-residence of the prebendaries, and even remonstrating against it. Having frequent returns of spitting of blood and never without a cough, he at last expired without a groan, sinking down in his chair as he attempted to take out his watch to see what it was o'clock, on February 15, 1782, and was buried Thursday 28th in the vaults under the south aile at St. Paul's.

33. Lewis Bagot, a very learned and pious man, was made Dean of Christ Church, Oxford, 21st January, 1773, where he preserved good discipline, and was promoted to this bishoprick, and translated to Norwich the next year.

He

He has publifhed a volume of very ingenious difcourfes, in which he has confuted the fpecious opinions of Deifm and Infidelity by the moft convincing arguments.

33. Chriftopher Wilfon fucceeded, being one of the prebendaries of St. Paul's, London, and is the prefent Bifhop, 1788.

DEANS of BRISTOL, with the time of their inftallation.

William Snow, laft prior of Bra-denftock, 4th June, - 1542	William Levett, 10th January, 1685
William Whiteheare, 26th July, 1551	George Royfe, 10th March, 1693
George Carew, 5th November, 1552	Hon. Robert Booth, 20th June, 1708
Henry Jolliffe, 9th September, 1554	Samuel Crefwick, 8th Sept. 1730
John Sprint, 16th February, 1570	Tho. Chamberlayne, 24th Dec. 1739
Anthony Watfon, 21ft July, 1590	William Warburton,* 25th Oct. 1757
Simon Robfon, 21ft April, 1598	Samuel Squire,† 21ft June, 1760
Edward Chetwyn, 26th July, 1617	Francis Ayfcough, 5th June, 1761
Matthew Nicholas, 22d June, 1639	Cutts Barton, - - - 1768
Henry Glemham, 14th Sept. 1660	John Hallam, 22d February, 1781
Richard Towgood, 1ft May, 1667	
Samuel Croffman, 4th February, 1683	
Richard Thomfon, 25th May, 1684	

The ARCHDEACONS of DORSET.

The endowment of this archdeaconry in the church of Briftol is the impropriation and advowfon of Guffage All Saints in Dorfetfhire. The valuation of it for the firft fruits was 82 l. 12 s. 8 d. in the year 1534.

Thomas

---

* He was a learned man and great writer and polemical divine. His Julian is efteemed much, and his Divine Legation of Mofes is replete with learning, but contains fome paradoxical notions. He was prefented to the bifhoprick of Glocefter, in which he continued to his death.

† He wrote fome tracts on religion, and was made Bifhop of St. David.

Thomas Cranmer, 10th Dec. 1542
John Cottrell, 4th April, 1551
Toby Matthews fucceeded, after-
  wards Archbifhop of York, a
  native of Briftol.
Henry Tuckner, - -   1574
Edward Wickham, - -   1607
Richard Fitzherbert, 27th Aug. 1621
Richard Meredith, 25th July, 1660
Ralph Ironfide, - -   1668
John Fielding, 25th March, 1683

Robert Cooper, 5th March, 1697
Edward Hammond, 10th May, 1733
John Walker, 2:ft May, - 1740
  Died at 82, 8th November,
  1780, after being forty years
  archdeacon
George Hand, 18th November, 1780

PREBENDARIES of BRISTOL, and the time of their being prefented.

It has been ufual, in giving the fucceffion of the prebendaries, to rank them in order according to the ftall they filled when living, placing the fucceffor in the ftall of the deceafed, which for the fake of method fhall be followed here, and it really is the cafe at St. Paul's and moft other cathedral or colle-giate churches; but in Briftol the fucceffor takes the loweft ftall, and there is a general remove, though it is uncertain when that method was adopted. But as there are no particular eftates or livings annexed to each ftall here, and the whole chapter income is thrown together and divided, it is a matter of little confequence, but for the fake of order and the cuftomary method.

FIRST STALL.

John Gough, 4th June, - 1542
John Barlow, - - -   1545
John Rixman, - -   1554
William Dalby, - -   1558
Arthur Sawle, - - -   1559
Richard Hackluyt, - -   1585
Chriftopher Green, - -   1616
Richard Towgood, - -   1660
Samuel Croffman, - -   1667

Richard Thompfon, - -   1684
Walter Hart, 13th September, 1685
  Deprived 1690, for not tak-
  ing the oaths to King William
  and Queen Mary
Nathaniel Lies, - -   1691
John Sutton, 22d July, - 1723
Walter Chapman, 15th Feb. 1740

SECOND STALL.

Roger Edgeworth, 4th June, 1542
Chriftopher Pacy, - -   1560
Thomas Thackam, 11th Sept. 1590
William Buckle, 12th Sept. 1592

Robert Gullyford, rector of
  Wraxal, Somerfet, 16th Sept. 1596
Thomas Biffe, 19th February, 1612
Thomas Tucker, 23d Nov. 1632
Richard.

Richard Standfaſt, 25th Auguſt,	1660	James Harcourt, 24th Nov.		1711
John Rainſtorp, 30th Sept.	1684	Henry Waterland, 16th April,		1739
Thomas Cary, 20th May,	1693			

THIRD STALL.

Henry Morgan, 4th June,	-	1542	William Yeamans, 26th Dec.	1622
Richard Huys,	- - -	1554	John Weeks, 3d March, -	1633
John Bridgewater,	- -	1563	Thomas Horne, - -	1669
Clement Forthe,	- -	1576	Richard Smith, 30th April,	1697
Robert Temple,	- - -	1584	Joſeph Caſberd, 2d June, -	1717
Samuel Davies, 12th Sept.	-	1661	G. Henry Rooke, 23d Nov.	1751

FOURTH STALL.

Roger Hughes, 4th June,	-	1542	George Cuthbert, 20th Oct.	1629
John Cottrel, 31ſt December,		1572	William Kempe, 23d Oct. -	1660
Thomas Withered,	- -	1573	Samuel Wood, 29th June, -	1664
John Saunders,	- -	1577	John Chetwynd, 29th June,	1668
John Dixe, 24th May,	-	1596	Charles Liveſay, 10th March,	1693
John Wilkinſon, 19th Feb.		1613	John Caſtleman, 22d May,	1739

FIFTH STALL.

Richard Broom, 4th June,	-	1542	John Daſhfield, 16th July, -	1660
John Williams, 4th March,		1543	Theophilus St. Quintin, 9th Nov.	1665
Thomas Sylke, 4th June,	-	1546	Stephen Creſpion, 3d Auguſt,	1683
Francis Willis,	- -	1576	Hugh Waterman, 11th Dec.	1711
Charles Langford,	- -	1586	Richard Monins, 30th July,	1746
William Hill, 26th February,		1606	John Aylmer, 15th September,	1750
Robert Marks, 13th Sept.	-	1619		

SIXTH STALL.

George Dogeon, 4th June,	-	1542	John Baron, 24th November,	1713
Thomas Bayley, 23d January,		1552	Henry Head, 2d March, -	1721
Edward Green,	- -	1583	John King, 12th June, -	1728
William Norris, 12th Nov.	-	1627	John Billingſly, 20th Sept.	1738
George Williamſon, 7th Aug.		1643	Nathaniel Forſter,* 1ſt Feb.	1754
Richard Towgood, 30th July,		1685		

The

* He publiſhed a neat and correct edition of the Hebrew Bible in 4to. in elegant types, not deformed with points, an invention of the Rabbies, and was ſkilled in Hebrew learning, ſo neceſſary to a divine.

The Prebendaries that regularly fucceeded after the Rev. Dr. Forfter were,

Horace Hammond, 15th June,	1754	Thomas Powis, 30th March, 1779
Jofiah Tucker,* 10th October,	1756	
Bertie Henley, 7th January,	1758	
John Cocks, 28th Auguft, -	1758	
James Welton, 21ft July, -	1760	
Charles Tarrant, 9th February,	1761	
Edward Dicey, 28th January,	1773	
William Speke, 6th February,	1776	

CHANCELLORS of BRISTOL DIOCESE.

John Cotterel, 4th June, -	1542	Henry Jones, 16th November,	1669
William Dalby, - -	1556	Charles Sloper, 4th June, -	1695
John Sprint, - - -	1572	Carew Reynell, 13th Sept. -	1727
William Jones, - -	1574	William Cary, 28th Jan.	1744-5
Felix Lewis, - - -	1580	James Backhoufe, - -	1759
William Clark, 9th March,	1584		
Francis James, 31ft July, -	1590		
Sir James Huffey, - -	1603		
Gilbert Jones, 26th Auguft,	1625		

* Afterwards Dean of Glocefter, diftinguifhed for his various ingenious writings on trade, politics, &c.

CHAP. X.

Of the COLLEGIATE CHURCH *and* HOSPITAL *of the* VIRGIN MARY
and St. MARK, *called the* GAUNTS *of* BILLESWYCK,
now the MAYOR's CHAPEL.

THIS Church is fometimes called St. Mark's, being dedicated as above,
not to St. Martin as Prynne has it; at other times the Gaunt's of Billefwyck from the original founder and the name of the manor in which it was
built, and with part of which it was endowed. — This name of Billefwyck was
probably given to it from the pleafantnefs of the fite of it, (Bellus vicus.)
It is not a very large or elegant ftructure, but by a generous vote of the corporation of this city, the patrons of this curacy, in 1722 it was repaired at the
expence of the chamber and beautified, and it is now made a chapel for the
mayor and corporation to attend divine fervice and hear a fermon every
Sunday morning and on public days, for which the reader has 25l. per ann.
and the preacher 20s. for every fermon. It was before this time by their
pemiffion made ufe of by the French refugees as a place of worfhip, who have
ejected their chapel fince in Orchard-ftreet.

It is obfervable that this chapel is not built as churches commonly are Eaft
and Weft, but rather nearer to the North and South, for which fome affign
this reafon, that it was to point to the place of refidence of the joint founders
and their anceftors, Berkeley Caftle; others that it fhould point towards the
lands with which it was endowed.

The foundation is by fome fuppofed to be begun by Robert de Berkeley,
alias de Were, the fecond Lord of Berkeley, who married Alicia daughter
and heirefs of Robert de Gaunt Baron of Folkingham, and to be finifhed by
his only fon Maurice de Gaunt, who had affumed the furname of Gaunt from
his mother's family. The exact year when built is a little uncertain, one
manufcript has it in the year 27th of Henry the 3d. Maurice died.* the 14th
of Henry the 3d. 1230. Robert de Gourney his heir and nephew is more
juftly fuppofed to be the founder by order or by the will of his uncle Maurice

de

* Maurice's charter is extant in the church of Wells.—Sir Rob. Atkyns, p. 475.

de Gaunt; and a charter belonging to St. Augustin's monastery dated 1251, seems to point it out that the year of its erection was immediately after the death of Maurice de Gaunt, 1230. William of Worcester says, "Ecclesia religionum &c.—The church of the religious called les Gauntes, the nave of it is 43 steps in length, 26 steps in breadth." p. 188. And in p. 247, " in the sanctuary of St. Augustin on the North part of the town of Bristol is the church of religion dedicated to St. Mark."

The church at present, which was formerly much larger, consists of a body and one side aile; the length from the South door in the Green is about 123 feet, its breadth 24 feet and a half, the height from the floor to the roof, which is neatly wainscotted in the inside, is about 37 feet, the covering is of stone tiles: behind the altar is a lofty window of painted glass, which has been taken away and plain glass fixed in its room. It represented in the most beautiful colours Judas betraying our Saviour and delivering him to the soldiers, the scourging, the bearing of the cross, crucifixion, taking down from the cross and ascension from the tomb; the figures were large and in good drawing; above these in the upper part of the window still remain painted in glass the arms or badge of the house, viz. f. gules three geese argent; also the arms of Robert de Gourney, a founder and benefactor, viz. f. or. three pales azure; and likewise those of the Berkeleys: over this window on the outside is a date run into the freestone with lead, 1823 (1423.) At the entrance of the South door behind the large window there is a gallery with this inscription, " This gallery was erected and the chapel beautified at the charge of the chamber of this city, John Becher, Esq; mayor, and Noblet Ruddock and John Rich, Esqr. sheriffs, in the year 1722;" and in the year 1772 a neat organ was put there and the whole chapel again repaired and beautified.

At the East side this aile is joined by another about 14 feet and a half broad, making the whole church next the Green to be 39 feet broad: here is a large freestone pillar which supports two arches, making the widest part of the church about 36 feet in length, and about 36 feet longer it is walled up, having a door for communication out of the greater into the lesser aile, in all 72 feet long: 36 feet of which is a flat wainscot roof with several carved coats of arms, differing much from the other part of the aile. In this aile are several handsome monuments. The tower at the North end of this aile is in height to the leads 86 feet, having 115 steps; the whole building is of freestone 16 feet by 17 square, with battlements 5 feet high from the leads with pinnacles at each corner; in the tower are six bells: the best idea of it may be formed from the copper-plate   Under the tower at the East front is a small low door to enter the church, and on the North fide another by which you enter into a fmall room, formerly a confeffional with two arches in the wall between this room and the high altar for the prieft and penitent; there are eight curious niches round the room in which images were formerly fixed. The roof is vaulted with freeftone, in the center of which are two curious fhields with feveral coats of arms in freeftone, viz. England and France, the Gourneys, Points of Aƈon in the county of Glocefter, &c.

The floor is covered with fquare glazed bricks having many coats of arms on them, and under the floor is a large vault, the entrance of which in 1730 fell in, and upon examining the corps there depofited, fuppofed to be thofe of the founders of the church, there was found a gold bodkin entangled in fome hair, but it was clofed up again. This room is now ufed by the chaplains of the church to put on their furplices &c. On the Weft fide of the great aile is a large arch anfwering to that under the tower, and probably the church might originally extend further that way; on the fame fide were the cloifters belonging thereto, and alfo the old hofpital of Billefwyck, fcarce any remains of which are now extant; and the orchard belonging to it was ordered the 41ft of Elizabeth the 19th of June, then holden by Mr. Beach, not to be let after to any perfon but to be referved to Queen Elizabeth's Hofpital; but in procefs of time it was built upon and converted into a ftreet, now called Orchard-ftreet.

In this fmall but neat church are many ftately and fuperb monuments and fome ancient ftatues in ftone. The right of fepulture in the ground before this church was formerly difputed, and William Chew perpetual vicar of St. Auguftin's the Lefs was accufed in the year 1426 at a court held in the faid church, and found guilty of with-holding and receiving to his own ufe the oblations and cuftomary dues and offerings for burying the dead that lived and died within the bounds of the hofpital of St. Mark, ufually enjoyed by the mafter and brethren there; particularly that in 1420 on Palm Sunday he carried away the bodies of William Leach and Chriftin the mother of John Hore, and Andrew Hutchins, from the cemitery of the faid hofpital or houfe of St. Mark, though they lived and died there, and feized and kept dues to the value of a 100 fhillings; and that the faid William heaping evil upon evil did alfo draw away and folicit Sybil Hutchings, who lived within the precinƈs of the faid hofpital, from purification after childbirth to be made by her of right in the faid hofpital, and kept the wax tapers and the garment called chryfmar, the offering to the faid hofpital and the other obventions on account of the faid purification belonging to the religious brethren of St. Mark, and

U u   unjuftly

unjuftly refufed giving any fatisfaction; which the faid vicar Chew confeffed, and was therefore condemned in ecclefiaftical excommunication for his obfti_nacy, but on his caufing the bodies which he had rafhly and injurioufly buried in the churchyard of St. Auguftin the Lefs out of their proper burial place to be carried back and interred with all cuftomary forms obferved in the faid hofpital of St. Mark; and on his returning the taper and chryfmar and the 100 fhillings, the mafter and brethren there acknowledged themfelves fatisfied, and at the petition of the faid brethren and William the vicar, he was ab_folved from the fentence of excommunication given againft him, " cum Sancta ecclefia nulli claudat gremium."

The right of fepulture formerly was no fmall thing to contend for, fince many of the beft families and the greateft barons in the land often by their will ordered their bodies to be buried in fuch a particular religious houfe, and it was very beneficial to the friers to enjoy fuch a privilege, fince commonly fome endowment for a chantry, fome annual celebration of the obiit was left them at the fame time with lamps, maffes, &c. for the fouls of the perfons there depofited, many inftances of which will hereafter occur. To fhew farther the difpofition of thofe times; I find alfo in the time of William Long being abbot, a difpute arofe betwixt the monaftery of St. Auguftin and the houfe of St. Mark, concerning the fite of the faid houfe and works carried on there, and their inftituting a college there, and concerning the poffef-feffions given by will of Maurice de Gaunt the founder for fupport of the poor, and fome loffes having been incurred, and concerning the right of fepulture there. It was at length thus fettled: that the faid houfe of St. Mark fhould be free from all exactions and claims of that of St. Auguftin, and have all tenths and oblations that may arife within its bounds; that it fhould have a free monaftery at their own difpofal and management, a free burying ground, ornaments, bells, &c.; that the bodies of any dead might be received and buried, but that the plain of St. Auguftin was the common burial ground belonging to St. Auguftin's monaftery, &c. &c. and to finifh the matter at length Walter Bifhop of Worcefter to prevent any more contention and rancour between them ordered that neither of them fhould have common of pafture in the faid plain, as they both agreed in its being the cemitery of St. Auguftin; but if any animals fhould enter the faid plain or green for pafture, and the owner not remove them, being thrice warned by the vicar of St. Auguftin the Lefs, or fome other clerk of the faid church, he might pound them till freed by difcharge: the delinquents to pay half a mark as a mulct to the bifhop; that the bodies lately buried before the gate of the houfe of St.

Mark

Mark remain there, but that the earth rofe above the level be removed and made plain, on account of the pleafantnefs of the place : neverthelefs it fhould not be the lefs reckoned a cemitery by the removal of the earth. He ordained that on account of the pleafantnefs of the place the dead bodies fhould be buried in that part of the cemitery where they were ufed to be and no where elfe, unlefs the diocefan or his official fhould think, that ufe required it, and that thofe of the houfe of St. Mark might have free ingrefs, egrefs, in and out of the faid plain, for the fake of going, walking, and wandering where they pleafed, of driving carriages, drays, and carts through the roads ufeful and neceffary for them, and accuftomed. He ordered alfo that the abbot of St. Auguftin might mow the faid plain without hindrance of any one and ftrew the grafs in his churches of St. Auguftin the Greater and the Lefs, with this provifo that the abbot make no defence called *Hayinge* in hindrance of the granted privileges to the houfe of St. Mark ; but the mower while there muft not be hindred, referving all accuftomed privileges and rights to the monaf-tery of St. Auguftin and thofe that dwell there, except the right of pafture. This deed is dated 1251.

This right of fepulture being thus acknowledged here, the houfe of St. Mark reaped great advantages from it, and efpecially from the burials in their church, lands being frequently granted them by families buried there, they only finding a prieft to pray for the fouls of the departed. Few fmail churches have fo many handfome monuments, many belonging to noble fami-lies, which I fhall proceed to give fome account of as they occur.

MONUMENTS in the church of St. MARK.

At the entrance on the 22d of Auguft, 1680, was buried Captain William Bedlow, without any memorial or infcription, though he deferved to be chro-nicled for the particulars of his life. He is faid to be concerned in the Rye-houfe plot in Charles 2d's. time, and with Titus Oates pretended to difcover the authors of the death of Sir Edmunfbury Godfrey, 1678; and on the oaths of thefe two many were executed, who all denied the charge with their lateft breath. Bedlow was buried near the great door next the green, and his funeral expences are faid to be difcharged by the chamber of the city, his goods having been feized and carried out of the houfe for the large debts he had contracted.

At the weft end of the eaft aile, next the College-green, is a lofty hand-fome monument with the following infcription thereon.

Near

Near this place lie the remains of William Hilliard, Efq; who was born at Sea Houfe in the parifh of Ilminfter, in the county of Somerfet:

After having by his bright parts foon acquired the knowledge ufually taught in fchool, he entered himfelf a gentleman commoner in Wadham college in Oxford, where he made himfelf mafter of the liberal fciences; then travelled over the greateft part of Europe, and returned to his native land a compleat gentleman, and mafter of the European languages; was put into the commiffion of the peace, for which he was well qualified. He married Mary the widow of William Blome, Efq; one of the daughters and coheireffes of Gabriel Goodman, Efq; who by her laft will left 200l. to erect this monument to his memory. Among other charitable legacies he left 100l. to the poor of the parifh of St. Auguftin in this city.

The following was infcribed on a ftone here to Dr. Patrick Keir: —
" Morte tandem oppreffus qui olim triumphos reportavit H. S. E. Patrick Keir, M. D. Vir egregiâ indole et modeftâ, eâ morum fuavitate ut quot ufus eft familiaribus tot fibi conciliavit amicos, ea morum fuavitate ut conciliatos ufque affervaverit: rei medicœ eximiè peritus, aliorum falutis curator fedulus, prodigus interim fuæ; fimilis vitæ cultus modeftus et luxuriæ animofus boftis, cautus in neceffitudinibus amicitiæ ineundis, in fervandis fidus: fi plura velis ætas præfens, quæ novit, enunciet, pereunte illâ huic marmori nepotes credant. Obiit 17 Decembris. Ætatis 37." He wrote a treatife on the Briftol waters.

In the fame aile are fome neat monuments againft the wall, and in the tables thereof are epitaphs infcribed:

To Henry Walter, Efq; fometime mayor and alderman, &c. who died 11 July 1742, aged 75.

Henrico Blaake de Pinnels Agro Wilton'. obüt 10 Julii 1731, ætat 72.

To John Gookin of Highfield, he died 12 March 1627, aged 11.—A neat ftatue of a boy kneeling on one knee, well executed.

Memoriæ æternæ Georgii Upton Armigeri viri optimi & ornatiffimi qui cum 55 annos bene vixiffet, placide obdormivit Jan[ii]. 25[e]. natali fuo A. D[i]. 1608.

> Quæ lux prima tulit te, te abftulit, ergo fuperftes
>   Cum nequeas vitæ vivere vive neci:
> Integra vita fuit, pia mors, mens dedita Chrifto,
>   Hæc facient tumulo te fupereffe tuo.
> Lugens pofuit Edwardus Biffe.

To

To the never dying memory of Margaret Throgmorton, late wife of Sir Baynam Throgmorton of Clovellwal in the county of Glocefter, Bart. and youngeft daughter of Robert Hopton of Whiteham in the county of Somerfet, Efq; fhe died 18 Aug. 1635, aged 25, with 14 lines of poetry in her praife in Englifh. Arms, G. or. a chevron argent, barry of fix fable, creft on a wreath, a falcon volant proper.

To john Carr, an arched tomb in the wall with no ftatue on it or epitaph, but in the front fome plain fhields, and in a cypher ɪ. C.

To Sir Henry de Gaunt, his ftatue at length on his back in an arch. He was the fecond mafter of the hofpital of Gaunts about 1230.

Gulielmo Swift, publicæ fcholæ hujus civitatis moderatori. Obiit pridie calend. Junii anno falutis 1623, ætat. 52.

To the virtuous Dorothy Popham, late wife of the Hon. Col. Al'. Popham. She died March, 1643. Alfo Sir Francis Popham, Knight, who died 16 March, 1646. Arms, in a fhield 32 coats quartered, the firft is two bucks heads for Popham. This Dorothy was daughter of —— Cole, Efq; of Nail_ fea, Somerfet. Alexander fon and heir of Alexander and Dorothy is buried here, May, 1642.

At the upper end of this eaft aile on a raifed tomb lie the ftatues of two Knights armed in mail fave their faces, their right hands on their fword hilts, on the left their fhield, with their legs acrofs, which fhews them to be knights of the holy war or crufade, which ended with Henry 3d's. reign, 1268. None of thefe crofs-legged monuments are of later date than Edward 2d. or beginning of Edward 3d. nor earlier than King Stephen. It is uncertain whom they reprefent, probably the Berkeleys or Gourneys.

In the weft aile next the pulpit is a curious monument with the ftatue of a lady kneeling, and on each fide two men in clergymen's habits drawing afide a curtain, with the following infcription underneath : — " Memoriæ facrum hic fita funt offa ornatiffimæ fæminæ, Dominæ Mariæ Dom. Edwardi Baynton, nuper de Bromham in comitatu Wiltoniæ reliclæ, fæmina fuit ad antiquum morem compofita, illibatæ vitæ, pietate, forma et omni laude maternali virtute muliebri ornata fuam poft quam vitam nimis eheu brevem nec a moleftiis penitus liberam, piam, fidam, pudicam, caftam, generofam hofpitalitate caritate, aliifq; quam plurimis virtutibus excultam omnibus, etiam egenis, caram egif_ fet; eam cum ingenti omnium utriufq; fexûs, quibus aut fama, aut facie nota fuit, luctu ac dolore reliquit, pro fæliciori commutavit, et Chrifto placide obdormivit ætatis fuæ 44, Anno Domini MDC fecundo. Sordes terra tenet, tenet ingens fpiritus æthrâ æthercofque locos, hic reftant offa fepulta.

Huic

Huic ejus filii gemini dom. Robertus et dom. Nicolaus, quos fuo utero conju_ gali peperit fructifero pofuêre monumentum.　Arms f. a bend lozengè argent.

In the fame aile is an handfome monument with a fhield of the arms of Berkelev of Stoke-Gifford at top, and in the table the following epitaph, over a ftatue in armour at full length — " Domini Richardi Berklæi militis in fuam mortem carmen monitorium :

> Cum genus et nomen cupiant cognofcere cuncti,
> Mentem nemo : fi quis, qui fum, inquirere pergat,
> Nefcio, refponde, hunc verum fe noffe moneto.

Whom youth could not corrupt, nor change of days
Add any thing but years : he full of them
As they of knowledge ; what need this ftone praife
Whofe epitaph is writ in th' hearts of men :
That did this world and her child fame defpife,
His foul with God, lo here his coffin lies.

> Obiit Aprilis 26, A. D. 1604. Ætatis fuæ 71."

In the chancel is a large finely ornamented and carved tomb and on it within an arch the ftone figures of Sir Thomas de Berkeley and Catherine his lady, daughter of John Lord Bottetourte.　Sir Thomas died 35th Edward 3d. 1361.　There are two fhields over them ; one has the Berkeley arms of Stoke quartered with Bottetourte, which are or. a crofs engrailed fable ; the other fhield is paly of fix or. and azure for Gourney.

Next this is another arched tomb for Miles Salley, abbot of Einfham, after_ wards Bifhop of Llandaff : he died in 1516.　His ftone figure with mitre and crofier is on the tomb.

Againft the wall above is the following on a monument : — " Here lieth the body of Elizabeth James, late wife of Francis James, Doctor of the Civil Law ; a woman for her excellent virtues and fingular wifdom to be equalled by few of her fex.　As fhe lived very religioufly and godly, fo fhe died May 1, 1599.　Chariffimæ conjugi pofuit fuperftes maritus."　Dr. James lies buried at Barrow-Minchin church, in the county of Somerfet.　Vide Wood's Athenæ Oxon. vol. i. p. 759.

Under this is a very grand carved freeftone Gothic arched tomb and monu_ ment with the figure of a man in an alderman's gown, with a fon behind him, with the following epitaph on a table : — " Thomas Aldworth obiit Pebruarii 25, anno 1598.

Briftoliæ

Briſtoliæ quondam qui mercatoris in urbe
   Munere funĉtus eras, bis quoque prætor eras,
Hæc cineris· Aldworthi tuos tenet urna, ſed omnis
   Virtutis meritis arĉtior urna tuis, &c."

Under the ſtone figures is the following inſcription : — " Hic jacet Johannes Aldworth, civis, mercator, hujus civitatis vicecomes hujuſque orphanotrophii quondam theſaurarius qui obiit 18 Decembris, 1615, ætatis ſuæ 51, et Fran-ciſcus filius ejus optimæ ſpei juvenis qui 5 Septem. 1623 obiit, ætatis ſuæ 24. Terram cum cælo commutavit, placidè in Domino requiens.

   En pater et natus tumulo conduntur eodem
      Ille rei multæ, ſic fuit ille ſpei :
   Ille probus prudens, pietatis cultor et œqui,
      Qui norit leĉtor, crederet, iſte foret.
   Ille viæ medium cum vicerit, iſte ſed oram,
      Cum Chriſto regnant ſuaviter in patriâ."

Above is a ſtone with an epitaph to Catherine, the⁻ wife of Hopkins Vaughan, of Caldicot, who died 6th May, 1694. Alſo to George Vaughan, Eſq; his ſon : he died 16th Sept. 1701, aged 38.

Another monument is here to Thomas James, mayor, and parliament man for this city, &c. : he died 1615. Alſo Thomas James, Barriſter at Law, his grandſon : died in 1685. Alſo Alexander James, of Tydenham : he died 1713.

In the chancel is a very ſuperb monument for William Birde thus : — " Gulielmus Birde obiit Oĉtobris 8, A. D. 1590.

   Clarus, prædives, ſapiens et pro grege Chriſti
   Sollicitus, ſedem et viĉtum cultumque miniſtrans
   Dormit in hoc tumulo, ſed ſpiritus æthera ſcandit :
   Vix dedit biſee virum Briſtollia noſtra diebus
   Conſimilem, ſeu virtutem, ſeu cætera ſpeĉtes.
   Gratus erat patriæ civis, jucundus amicis
   Progeniemque ſuam multâ cum laude reliquit."

The ſword of magiſtracy lies on his tomb.

On a ſtone here is the following : — " Here lieth the body of Robert Gorges, who departed this tranſitory life March 1, 1619. Alſo Sir Robert Gorges, Knight, and Elena his wife, who died 5th November, 1617." This is of the family of Gorges of Wraxal near Briſtol, where they had a ſeat and park. They bore anciently for arms, a whirlpool, in alluſion to the name,

afterwards

afterwards checky or. and azure. The prefent Lady Dowager Bampfylde is the laft of this family, whofe fon Sir Charles Bampfylde poffeffes the manor of Wraxal, and there refides in 1788. Ralph de Gorges by Edward 1ft. was fummoned to parliament, and was at the fiege of Karlaverock caftle in Scotland, of whom one fays, " There faw I Sir Ralph de Gorges, a new dubbed knight, more than once beaten down to the earth with ftones, but he was of fo great a fpirit as not eafily to defift; all his harnefs and attire was mafcled with gold and azure." Many of the Gorges family lie buried in the church of Wraxal: Sir Thomas Gorges is buried at Salifbury cathedral, with a long infcription on a very large and handfome monument.

On a table againft the wall above Aldworth's monument is the following: " To the pious memory of Thomas Moore and Elizabeth his wife, buried in the fame grave near this place.

> Envying their loves Death them divorc'd in fpight,
> But now in kindnefs doth them reunite :
> She fick'ning ftole from him with ling'ring pace
> He hither came longing her to embrace :
> So croffes, accidents, the felf fame fate
> Rob man of blifs and make him fortunate.
> Their virtues were admir'd, their hearts were one,
> One faith they held, one pure religion :
> Living belov'd by all, fo dead they have
> A general forrow and a fingle grave ;
> Where let them reft in peace, till both fhall rife
> With bodies glorified above the fkies.

She departed this life June 7, A. D. 1673. He September 16, 1675.

As the church (which with the monuments and infcriptions has now been fully defcribed) was formerly called the Gaunts church, fo the old hofpital thereto belonging went by the name of Gaunts of Billefwick according to Dr. Tanner's account, becaufe " Maurice de Gaunt * built this hofpital in Billefwick manar, in the north-weft fuburb of the town of Briftol, near the monaftery of St. Auguftin, before A. D. 1229, † for one chaplain and one hundred poor people to be relieved every day. For which ufe he gave the manor of Paulet and feveral

---

* Leland, Itin. vol. vii. p. 73, afcribes the foundation of this houfe to Sir Henry de Gaunt, and faith it was intended for a college of priefts, &c. But Maurice's charter is extant in the regifters at Wells.

† Anfelm Bifhop elect of St. David's is one of the witneffes to Robert de Gourney's confirmation of his uncle's charter, and A. D. 1229 was the year of his election.

feveral mills, &c. to the canons of St. Auguftin, and feems to have made his hofpital entirely fubjeft to their management and direftion. But after his deceafe Robert de Gourney his nephew and heir made it a diftinft houfe for the maintenance of a mafter * and three chaplains, and the relief of one hun‑ dred poor people every day." It was dedicated to the Virgin Mary and St. Mark,† and valued 26th Henry 8th. at 112l. 9s. 9d. per annum, Dugd. 140l. as Speed. ‡ Leland, Colleft. vol. i. p. 83, fays 140l. and calls it " hofpi‑ tale feu prioratus St. Marci evangeliftæ de Bellifwike alias Gauntes."

Vide in Monf. Angl. tom. ii. p. 455. cartam Roberti de Gourney, pro maner. de Poulet, molendinis de Were et Radewick, &c. ad fuftentationem, &c.

See in Monafticon Anglicanum, vol. ii. p. 455. the deed of Robert de Gourney of the manor of Poulet and the mills of Were and Redwicke, &c. and the provifion for keeping them in repair, &c.

Dr. Archer's Account of Religious Houfes, &c. p. 606.

In Prinn's Records, vol. iii. p. 123. ex bund. certif.

50 Henry 3d. 1266, de ecclefia de Kantokefheved (dioce. Bath.) Ibid, p. 856. prohibitionem archiepifco. Cantuar. quia tenuit placitum de ad advocatione hujus domus, 28 Edw. 1. 1300.

The 50th of Hen. 3d. concerning the church of Kantokfhead (in the diocefe of Bath). The fame, p. 856. the pro‑ hibition of the Archbifhop of Canter‑ bury, becaufe he held pleas concern‑ ing the jurifdiftion of this houfe, the 28th Edward 1ft. 1300.

In Raftall's Entries, p. 463. b. fub titulo, quare impedit de hofpital. plac. dom. Mauritii Berkeley, mil. de ma‑ giftro eligendo. Years book, 7 Edw. 3. Hill S. 17. 12 Henry 4. Micha. 13.

In Raftall's Entries, p. 463. b. un‑ der the title of quare impedit of the hofpital. The pleas of the houfe of Sir Maurice de Berkeley, Knight, con‑ cerning chufing a mafter.

In Willis's Hiftory of Abbies, vol. ii. p. 85. et Append. p. 9.

W w　　　　　　　　In

* The governor of this houfe is fometimes called prior, and the houfe itfelf a priory of the or‑ der of St. Anftin, as Leland, Colleft. vol. i. p. 85.

† Not St. Marwyn, as Prynne, vol. iii. p. 123.

‡ Leland, vol. v. p. 74. faith it had 300 marks by the year. Page 53. he calls the Gaunts of Briftol the Bonnes Hommes (or good men), an order of friers brought into England by Edmund Earl of Cornwall, A. D. 1283, others fay 1290, placed at Afhrugg.

In regiſtro penes rev. W. decan. et capit Wellenſ. Mauritii de Gaunt fun_datoris cartam.

In regiſtro Joannis Drokensford epiſc. Bathon. et Wellenſ. ordinationes Vicariorum de Stokland (A. D. 1317) et Overſtowey, A. D. 1327.

Cart. 31 Hen. 3. m. 4. pro. lib. war. in Paulet et Stokeland. Pat. 4. Edw. i. m. 9. Plac. apud Wilton. 9 Edw. 1. aſſiſ. rot. 3. de maner. de Winterborn Gunnore: Cart. 18 Edw. 1. n. 69. pro cod. maner. a rege conceſſo. Rec. in ſcacc. 20 Edw. 1. rot. 8. de Ancelino de Gurney olim advocato. Cart. 6 Edw. 2. n. 7. pro maner. de Paulet, Stockland, etc. Pat. 8 Edw. 2. p. 1. m. 3. de terris et paſturis in Compton excambiatis cum epiſc. Bathon. et Wellenſ. ibid. m. 4. pro eccl. de Stokland approprianda: Pat. 20 Edw. 2. m. Pat. 16 Rich. 2. p. 1. m. 4. de maner. de Winterborn Gunnore et Winterborn Cherburgh. Pat. 6 Hen. 4. p. 2. m. 23. pro Villis de Paulet et Buro: Clauſ. 7 Hen. 4. p. 1. m. 11. Eſcaet. 7 Hen. 4. n. 23. Pat. 4 Hen. 5. m. 26. de commun. paſtur. in Southamme et Northamme. Rec. in ſcace. 14 Hen. 6. Mich. rot. 9. de maner. de Paulet et clauſo vocat. Gaunteſham.

In Itin. Will. Worc. p. 188. dimenſiones Eccleſiæ. Lel. Coll. v. 1. 85. Itin. v. 5. 64. vol. 7. 88. 92.—In Atkyns Gloe. p. 214 of the manour of Gaunt's Urcot.

The 13th of King John, Maurice de Gaunt on an inquiſition for knight ſervices for each county, was rated for Dorſet 1 milit. & dimid.

Leland, in Itin. v. 6. f. 100. ſays, " Maurice de Gaunte was Lorde of Beverſtane Caſlle by Tetbyrie:" and oppoſite has this note, " Loke wither Mauric wher not firſt caullyd Barkely & then *Gaunte* a loco tantum natalium." And v. 8. f. 67. a, he ſays, " Baronia de Gaunt partita inter Rogerum de Kerdeſton, & Julianam de Gaunt & petrum de Marley hœredes Gilberti de Gaunt—patet recorda de Anno 19 Edw. 1.—Colleɛt. v. 3. p. 32. 1144 Gilbertus de Gaunt monaſterium de Bridlington Caſtrum fecit ſibi.

Gilbert de Gaunt accompanied his uncle William Duke of Normandy into England, who having vanquiſhed Harold divided his enemies lands among his Norman friends and followers of his fortune; amongſt whom he particularly favored his nephew, and gave him ample poſſeſſions and created him Earl of Lincoln, which the poſterity of Gilbert de Gaunt enjoyed for five generations, till the male line failed in 1306. It appears in Doomſday (in iisd: Comit:) what exorbitant grants he made him, for in 10, 11, 12 and 13 year of his reign this Gilbert de Gaunt alone was ſeized of one lordſhip in Berkſhire, two in Oxfordſhire, three in Yorkſhire, ſix in Cambridgeſhire, one in Huntingdonſhire, five in Northamptonſhire, one in Rutlandſhire, one in Warwickſhire,

ſhire, eighteen in Nottinghamſhire, and one hundred and thirteen in Lincolnſhire, being 154, which was a large eſtate indeed for ſo ſhort a time. He
married Alice daughter of Hugh de Montfort, a great baron of thoſe days,
and had two ſons and one daughter by her; Walter the eldeſt ſucceeded his
father in the title and honour of the earldom of Lincoln about the year 1096,
and was buried at Bardney abby. The chief ſeat was at Folkingham in
Lincolnſhire. Robert the ſecond ſon married Alice daughter of William
Paganel who founded the priory of Drax in Yorkſhire, and by her had two
daughters only; Juliana married to Jeoffrey Luttrel, and Alicia married
Robert the ſecond ſon of Robert ſirnamed Fitzharding, becauſe the ſon of
Harding a younger ſon of the King of the Danes. This Robert had by Alice
de Gaunt his wife a ſon named Mauritius, and a daughter named Emma;
Maurice took upon him the ſurname of de Gaunt, looking on that as the moſt
noble; and Emma his ſiſter married Anſelm de Gourney, younger ſon of
Hugh de Gourney, a Norman made Earl of Gourney by William Rufus; he
bore pally of ſix pieces or. and azure, (the arms are in painted glaſs in the
window of St. Mark's church,) he had iſſue Robert de Gourney. Afterwards Maurice de Gaunt dying the 14th of Henry the 3d. without iſſue; the
15th of Henry the 3d. this Robert de Gourney as heir to his uncle Maurice de
Gaunt did his homage and had livery of the manor of Poulet in the county of
Somerſet, and of his uncle's manors of Beverſton, Weſton, Radwick, Over,
and Aylburton; and made a ſolemn declaration in the King's preſence that he
did not lay any claim to the three hundreds of Bedminſter, Harecliffe, and
Portbury in the county of Somerſet, acknowledging that his uncle Maurice de
Gaunt was only tenant for life of thoſe hundreds, and after his deceaſe without
iſſue male they were to go to Thomas de Berkely by virtue of an entail.

It may be obſerved here, that though the family of the Berkelies are
deſcended from the ancient barons of Berkley before the conqueſt, and ſince
the conqueſt by Robert Fitzharding the founder of St. Auguſtin's monaſtery
juxta Briſtol, from the ancient kings of Denmark; and by Alicia one of the
daughters and heirs of Robert de Gaunt, from Baldwin Earl of Flanders; yet
this Robert de Gourney was the right heir at law, and had the inheritable
blood both of Harding and Baldwin preferable to the Berkelies; and entered
and claimed all the inheritable lands of Maurice de Gaunt and had livery of
them.

Robert de Gourney performed his homage in the ſame year for half a knight's
fee deſcended to him by the death of Robert de Harptree his grandfather: he
was deſcended from the famous Hugh de Gorney, ſo called from their caſtle

and feignory in Normandy, who came over with William the Conqueror, and his posterity were the most confiderable barons in the kingdom until the end of the reign of Henry the 3d. and had great poffeffions, efpecially in Gloceſter-ſhire and Somerfetſhire, (befides his royalties of de Gournay and de Pleffey in Normandy,) as alfo in Wilts and Dorfet, which amounted in the whole to twenty-two knights fees and a half; an eftate equal if not fuperior to the firſt peers in the kingdom :* and as his anceſtors took their furnames from a place in Normandy, fo this gave name to feveral places in the county of Somerfet, as Harptree Gourney, Harington Gourney, Gourney Slade, Gourney Were or Nether Were, alfo Barrow Gourney, where he founded a place of nuns. This Robert de Gourney was the founder of the Gaunts Hofpital in his ancient manor of Bellifwyck, (which with others came to him from Maurice de Gaunt his uncle afore-mentioned,) on the North fide of the hilly ground on which St. Auguſtine's monaſtery was built; where Robert Fitzharding formerly had a houfe he lived in while he was building that monaſtery, which defcended to Robert de Berkley his fon, and from him to Maurice de Gaunt his heir, and from him it came to Robert our founder his nephew. — Leland v. 7. f. 70, mentions, "Hardyng and Robert his funne havynge a fayre howfe at Port-cheſter and another yn Bryſtow towne, and that Sir Henry Gawnte was a knight fometyme dwellynge not farre from Brandon Hill by Bryſtow:" and f. 68, that "Gurney us'd to lie muche at Richemonte caſtle: it ſtondith in the roote of Mendipe Eaſte of Briſtowe in the paroche of Eſte Harptree by the

---

* There are many things upon record of the family of *de Gourneys:* — Hugh de Gourney had his lands feized by a precept to the Conſtable of Briſtol Caſtle from the King for hunting in the King's chace (Kingſwood) by Briſtol for three days without licence, 7th of Henry the 3d. M. 9. 26th of Henry the 3d. Robert our founder gave 20 pounds, no fmall fum in thofe days, to be excufed attending the King into Gafcoyne: and the 41ſt of Henry the 3d. he had fummons to be at Briſtol with horfe and arms to march againſt the Welch. — The 41ſt of Henry the 3d. in Dorſo N. 6. and the 42d of Henry the 3d. he had a like fummons to be at Cheſter. —— Vid. Maddox Formul. Anglic Chart. 100. Hathewifia de Gurneio Lady of the fee, confirms a grant of land in . Clive Ware made by Alexander de Badicumb, one of her vaffals in the court of Barow, Somerfet, which Robert de Gurney her father gave him for his fervice; this land is furrendered to the Lady with five fardels of land in Bacwell by a *branch of a tree*, and by the fame feifin is given by her to the purchafer to hold of her in capite, he gives a gold ring for his recognifance, witnefs Thomas de Buritona (Boreton), Matthello de Gurney, Roger de Batvent, and feventeen others. This eſtate of Barrow is now in the poffeffion of John Gore, Efq; whofe family had great eſtates at Gelfdon in Hertfordſhire, and were diſtinguiſhed for their loyalty in Charles the 1ſt's. time: at Gelfdon church there is a handfome monument, with a long infcription of the antiquity of the family as coming out of Wiltſhire, (Whitley near Devizes,) "ex antiquo Gorœorum ſtemmate in agro Wiltonienſi." — Francis James, doctor of the civil law, whofe wife is buried in this church of Gaunts, lies buried at the church of Barrow, which was the oratory of the nuns there.

the paroche chirche of yt; there ſtondith yet a peece of the dongeon of it: — that there is another village by Eſt Harptree caullyd Weſt Harptree Gurney— and there bee varietie of armes that Gurney gave in the glaſs wyndowes and his cote armure: — Gurneys lands came to Newton * of Barres Courte: — Gurney was Lorde of Stoke Hameden, and there lieth buried yn a col‑ legiate chapple by the ruyns of his caſtle: hee was chefe foundar of the howſe of Gauntz, at Briſtow, as ſome ſay — he was foundar of the priorie of nunes call'd Baron Gurnay in Somerſetſhyre — he was Lorde of Whitcombe and Richemonte Caſtle, by Mendepe 3 miles from Welles, — it is now elene downe — it came after to Hampton, then to Cradock, alias Newton: — Gurney had the fourthe parte of the Lordſhipe of Mendype." — At Stoke under Hambden Leland met with many antiquities of the Gurney family; v. 2. Itin. f. 54, " I ſawe at Stoke in a bottom hard by the village very notable ruines of a great manor place or caſtelle, and yn this remaynith a very auncient caſtelle whereyn be divers tumbes of nobil men and wimen. — In the ſouth weſt ſide of the chapelle be 5 images on tumbes, on hard joynid to ano‑ ther; 3 of menne harneſhid and ſhildid and 2 of women: ther hath bene inſcriptions on eche of them, but now ſo fore defacyd that they cannot bee redde: I ſaw a ſhelde or 2, al verry of blew and white — ther be alſo in this part of the chapelle 2 tumbes without images — there is in the north ſide of the body of the chapelle a tumbe in the waulle without image or writeing, and a tumbe wyth a goodly image of a man in armes in the north ſyde of the quiere of the chapelle with a ſheld as I remembre al verrey, and even afore the quier dore, but withoute it lyith a very grete flatte marble ſtone with an image in braſſe flattely graven and this wryting yn French aboute it:

" Ici giſt le noble & vailiant Chiváler Maheu de Gurney jadys ſeneſchal de Landes, & capitain de Chaſtel Daques pours noſtre Seignor le roy en la Duche de Guyene, que en ſa vie fu a la battaile de Bueamarin, & alla apres a la ſiege D'Algezire fur la Sarazines, & auxi a les battailes de la Scluſe, de Creſſy, de Yngeneſſi, de Peyĉters, de Nazara, D'Ozrey, & a pluziers autres batailles, & aſieges, en les ques il gagna noblement graund los, & honour per le ſpace de ${}_{\overset{xx}{iiii}}$ & xvj anns & moruſt le xxvi jour de Septembre l'an notre Seignor Jeſu Chriſt ᴍᴄᴄᴄᴠɪ, que de ſalme dieux eit mercy Amen." — There was beſydes this grave another in the weſtende of the bodye of the chapelle having a grete flate ſtone without inſcription: — I markid in the window 3 fortes of armes, one al verry blew and white, another with 3 ſtripes gules downright in the fielde of gold, the 3 was croſs lettes of gold manie intermixt in one yn a felde as I remembre gules: — There is a provoſt longyng to this collegiate chapelle now

yn

yn decay where fumtyme was gode fervyce and now but a meſſe fayde a 3 times
yn a week."

I make this long quotation from Leland to prove the greatneſs of this family
of Gourney, who founded our hofpital of Billefwyke, his feat and manor,
which he the rather chofe for its fite, either by order of his uncle Maurice de
Gaunt in his will, * and to perpetuate his name, he having died without
iſſue ; or becaufe it ſtood nearly oppofite to that noble monaſtery, dedicated
to St. Auguſtin by Robert Fitzharding, grandfather to Maurice de Gaunt, and
his own great grandfather. Here he laid the foundation, and lived to fee it
completely finiſhed, with the elegant chapel before defcribed, and a cloiſter
within it, though built low after the manner of thofe religious houfes, and endowed it with lands, &c. and appointed by a deed Henry de Gaunt maſter of
the hofpital, who alfo was a benefaѐtor to it, as appears by the following liſt of
benefaѐtors. There is great reafon to believe that he founded it at the defire
and direѐtion of Maurice de Gaunt his uncle, who might be willing to have his
name preferred, and the charter feems to imply as much. It not only fays,
" when I am in full fcifin and poſſeſſion of my lands by defcent from my
uncle," (by an ouſter de main) which fhewed he did not intend to meddle with
the profits of thefe lands, but likewife as if it were by direѐtion from his uncle
revokes all agreements made by him with the canons of St. Auguſtin about
tythes of corn. The family of Gaunt being now extinѐt in the male line, we
find none after Henry de Gaunt as a benefaѐtor to it of that name, though
many others gave large poſſeſſions to it afterwards, as will hereafter appear.

The original deeds relating to this houfe are fo many that they fill a large
book of a folio fize clofe written with abbreviations, a copy of which authentic
curious manufcript I have in my poſſeſſion. I ſhall abſtraѐt from it thofe only
that more immediately concern the endowment of this religious houfe of charity, and give any light into its ancient foundation and original inſtitution. I ſhall
quote this alfo under the title of Gaunt's Book, being a manufcript never feen
by any of our writers of ecclefiaſtical hiſtory and antiquities, neither by
Dugdale, Stevens, Leland, Tanner, nor Mr. Willis. There were feveral
benefaѐtors, who very liberally endowed it after its firſt foundation as appears
by the following abſtraѐts, in which (1.) the founders names, and their orders
and regulations concerning this ancient hofpital will be recited, (2.) its endowment with lands, houfes, manors, &c. by fucceſſive benefaѐtors, (3.) a
liſt

---

* By a deed of compofition, dated 1251, between the houfe of St. Auguſtin near Briſtol and
the houfe of St. Mark, " ratione teſtamenti vel Doni Mauritii de Gaunt et elemofineræ ejufdem,
fuper fitu domus ejufdem et opere novo ibidem inchoato et Collegio ididem habendo."—It appears
it was Maurice's will.

lift given of the masters of this house, their time of succession or resignation, &c. until its final dissolution; also an account of the present new hospital called Queen Elizabeth's which has been erected and endowed in its place.

The following is an abstract of the principal benefactors of the religious house and hospital of St. Mary and St. Mark, &c.

Maurice Berkeley de Gaunt, son of Robert, was the first principal founder of this house or hospital of the Gaunts by direction of his will, or beginning it just before his death. The 14th Henry 3d. 1230,* he died at Portsmouth without issue, leaving Emma his only sister his heirefs. She married Anselm de Gourney, who descended from Hugh de Gourney, who came into England with William the Conqueror, by whom she had one only child, named Robert de Gourney. Maurice at his death gave by deed to the King Beverston Aylbyrton, and Weston, whence it is called Kingsweston at this day.

Robert de Gourney,† the only heir and nephew to Maurice de Gaunt, by his deed ‡ gave or confirmed to the said house his manor of Paulet, &c. the mills of Were and Redwick, with all ponds, waters and water courses, fish and all improvements to the said mills, and four marks rent in Bristol, viz. out of the house of Robert the son of Harding which David la Warr possessed two marks, out of the house of Peter la Warr in Broad-street one mark, out of the house of Richard the cordwainer near the fishery one mark, and his house of Billefwick, for the support of three chaplains and the feeding of twenty-seven poor persons every day § with pottage; each person to have the weight of 45 s. in bread, made of wheat, barley, and bean flour. He reserved in the said deed a power to himself and his heirs of placing in a master of the said house as often as the mastership should become void by death or otherwise, (that is to say) at any time when such vacancy shall happen.

* In the register of Clerkenwell in Biblioth. Cotton. is a charter or grant of Maurice de Gaunt to the nuns of Clerkenwell in Middlesex of all rent he had in the manor of Durfley, to which deed Sacer de Quinci Earl of Winchester was a witness, who was earl in 1207.

In an inquisition, 13th King John, of knights service in each county, in the county of Somerset is " Mauritius de Gaunt 1 milit et dimid."

† Atkyns's History of Glocestershire, p. 475. he is said to give the manor of Gaunts Urcot, in the county of Glocester to this house, which was sold to the city of Bristol for public uses the 33d Henry 8th. 1540. Vide p. 214.

‡ Now extant in Gaunts Book of Deeds manuscript, p. ii. and Dugdale's English Monasticon Anglicanum, p. 166. Ibid, vol. ii. p. 455.

§ His deed as above mentions only twenty-seven persons, though Dugdale says one hundred persons. Vide vol. ii. p. 455. — By one other deed he adds one more chaplain, in all four, and eight clerks; all which was confirmed before the Justices of Eyre at Ivelchester the 2d Feb. 1243. Those deeds are in Gaunts Book. p. 3, 4.

pen. The management of the lands and revenues of the houfe, together with the difpofal of the alms belonging to the fame, fhould remain under the direction of the chaplains for the time being; to whom he the faid Robert granted a power to choofe a mafter out of themfelves or others, and to prefent fuch mafter to him and his heirs; when fo done, the faid Robert fhould prefent him fo chofen, and approved of by him or his heirs, for admittance by the Bifhop of Worcefter, who may inftitute fuch mafter chofen to the almonary of the faid houfe. And if at any time hereafter the faid Robert or his heirs fhall without reafonable caufe oppofe fuch mafter elected, then the Lord Bifhop of Worcefter may notwithftanding admit him on the prefentation of the chaplains. And at any time hereafter upon the mifbehaviour of the mafter, the bifhop for the time being may remove him upon conviction thereof, and may admit another as above appointed. *

Accordingly the faid Robert de Gourney by his deed † duly executed prefents and approves of Henry de Gaunt (who calls himfelf clerk and brother of Maurice in his deed) for the mafterfhip of the faid houfe, which Sir Henry by his deed ‡ confirmed all former grants, and further granted the manors of Poulet, § Stockland, of Erdecote, and lands of Bruham, the mills of Were and of Langford, with all his right in Delyamour and Lynagan in Cornwall, of the donation of William Cannel, the burgage and rents in Briftol and the houfe of Bellifwick, ‖ for the fupport of the mafter of this houfe, and twelve brothers clergymen

* This deed is in the Gaunts Book, p. 3.

‡ Ibid, p. 3. At the death of Robert de Gourney, which happened in the 53d year of King Henry 3d. 1269, he left by Hamifia de Longcamp his wife Anfelm his fon and heir, who alfo died the 14th Edward 1ft. 1286, whofe great eftate defcended to his fon and heir John de Gourney, who alfo died the 19th Edward 1ft. 1291, and left Elizabeth his only daughter and heirefs, who married to John Ap Adam, who had iffue Sir Thomas Ap Adam. He fold the manor of Kingfwefton, which formerly belonged to Maurice de Gaunt, to Sir Maurice Berkeley the 4th Edward 3d. 1330, and at the fame time fold off the manor of Beverfton to Thomas Lord Berkeley, vide Atkyns's Hiftory of Glocefterfhire, p. 273, 274. and 475. The Ap Adam and Berkeleys were alfo benefactors to this houfe of the Gaunts.

‡ Gaunts Book, p. 1.

§ In this manor is a clofe of pafture three hundred acres called Gaunts' Ham, mentioned in an old deed as belonging to this hofpital, and not to the King.

‖ The mayor and corporation of Briftol are feized of another manor at Winterbourne, in the county of Glocefter, for the ufe of Gaunts hofpital in Briftol. Sir Robert Atkyns's Hiftory of Glocefterfhire, p. 843. In a deed in Gaunts Book, p. 12. there the King's writ of enquiry is, whether he has a right to prefent to the mafterfhip of St. Mark's, then vacant, on account of his manor of Wynterbourn Gunnor, which the brothers of St. Mark held of him in Soccage, 29th year of Edward the fon of Henry 5th. But this is by Salifbury, in Wilts, and alfo belonged to this houfe.

gymen and five brothers laymen and twenty-seven poor people, out of which number twelve are to be scholars to serve only in the choir in black caps and surplices, as the same was ordained and confirmed formerly by Walter Lord Bishop of Worcester. This Henry is said in Leland, Itin. vol. 7. to be the brother of Maurice de Gaunt, and that he lies buried in the vesturye under a flat stone.

The following is an abstract of the said bishop's ordinance dated in 1259.

Walter Bishop of Worcester, with consent of Robert de Gourney and Henry de Gaunt, joint founders of the lands, rents, &c. by them given to the said house, viz. that the lands, &c. by them given should for ever remain to that house, for the support of a master and three chaplains, and that the alms to poor Christians agreeable to each of their deeds should every day be observed; and that twelve scholars be admitted or removed at the will of the master, who are to officiate in the choir in black caps and surplices, according to the direction of the chaunter, master, and faculty of the house, out of whom one is to be chosen to direct and instruct the rest, for which his stipend shall be larger than the rest; and it is ordained that three clerks in sacred orders and five lay friers do wear the same habit of those friers of the hospital of Lechlade,* differing only in the badge of the said hospital, which is a cross argent and the shield gules with three geese argent. And if it should happen that either of the said six clerks should by the said master be promoted to the sacerdotal order, nevertheless he may administer in the church according to the direction of the chaunter, provided the number of chaplains, clerks, and friers, so admitted by the said master not having the habit, exceed not thirteen, unless in process of time the revenues of the house increase, at which increase let as many be added to the charity as the master of the said house shall think fit. At the admittance of each person into the brotherhood he shall have the shield only fixed on his habit, which shall be worn during the year of probation, at the end of which time if he is found a fit proficient then the shield with the cross shall be fixed to the same; or within the time of his probation, if he desire or plead for this right, he may have the shield with the cross impressed on his upper habit, by vowing the substantials of the order, viz. continence, obedience, and abdication of property, and other regulations of the said house to be observed.

Any person after admission and within the time of probation, if he should be found not fit, may depart or be removed by the master. In fasting and other things to be observed by the members of this house, let it be accord-

ing

* Lechlade was a priory of black canons, or rather an hospital of a master or prior and certain poor and infirm brethren. Leland's Itin. vol. ii. p. 17.

ing to the cuftom of the friers of the hofpital of Lechlade; but in divine offices according to the cuftom and order of Sarum. In burying the dead, whether prince or prelate be fent for burial, the faid chaplains and clerks, are to wear the habit of the faid hofpital, or in their more folemn apparèl, according to the cuftom of Sarum, may meet the fame, provided the faid habit is not ufed elfewhere, but in the choir, or elfewhere when free from ecclefiaftical office.

As to mafs and its folemnities the faid chaplains and clerks are to obferve the following rules, viz. one mafs fhall be celebrated in the morning for the Bleffed Virgin Mary, the fecond for the dead, and the third for the day, this to be continued every day : the other chaplains may celebrate mafs for the living and the dead, and chiefly for the benefactors of the houfe at the diferetion of the mafter. Divine fervice being ended, two chaplains and the aforefaid fix clerks wearing the badge of the houfe, with two lay-brothers each with a little knife in his hand fhail cut the bread for the impotent and weak, who are to be ferved to their will between one and three, before the chaplains and clerks fhall dine : that receiving their prefcribed portion there, they may neverthelefs get elfewhere what is neceffary for them.

The mafter, chaplain, clerks, and the brethren bearing their habit may fleep in one houfe, and may eat and drink in the dining-room, but no fecular perfon fhall eat there or any where within the bounds of the hofpital unlefs by fpecial leave of the mafter, or detained there by ficknefs, when he muft be refrefhed in the infirmary. If any ftranger fhall make a vifit to the mafter, he may be at liberty to dine in his chamber or elfewhere at his choice; but then he is to have one or two of the aforefaid chaplains at table with him. If the faid mafter fhall dine out of the refectory, or lie out of his bedchamber, or travel abroad whether within or out of the town of Briftol, one or two chap- lains are to be with him, firft appointing one of the chaplains or brethren of the order to officiate in his ftead. No chaplain, clerk, or brother fbali eat or drink out of his houfe in the fame town unlefs in the prefence of his bifhop or patron, or in religious houfes, nor without confent of the mafter or his vice- gerent, and then fome of the brethren in their habit fhall be with him, leaft any of them fhould be feen wandering abroad alone in the town out of the precincts of the faid houfe; and at table the mafter and chaplains fhali ufe only black mantles and black cowls, but elfewhere they fhall have the arms of the houfe outermoft, a f. gules three geefe paffant arg. If on horfeback or afoot within the town they fhail wear black caps with the arms of the houfe worked thereon. The chaplains, clerks, and brethren fhall eat good bread of good
corn,

corn, and be ferved with good beer and good pottage, &c. at the direction of the mafter. They fhall not purchafe any wine for their own ufe, nor make feaftings to the lofs or detriment of the faid poor.

At dinner and fupper time, or at the entertainment of a legate, a lecture fhail be fpoken as ufual at other religious houfes, to be directed by the chaunter.

If any of the chaplains and clerks know how to write or account, at the command of the mafter he ought to write and note down thofe things which turn out for the ufe of the houfe. If any of the lay-brethren have been verfed in any of the mechanick arts, he may follow it for the advantage of the houfe at the will of the mafter, whofe bufinefs fhali be affigned them by the mafter as well within as without the houfe, and the work committed to them be care-fully attended to and not injured by their removal from the work. And in cafe that part of the land of Paulet belonging to the faid houfe which lies near the fea, fhould at any time be flooded by the fea and deftroy the produce of the land, notice thereof being given to the Bifhop of Worcefter and to the patron by the mafter of the houfe, and an inquifition taken of the truth thereof, in this cafe the allowance for the poor with all charges incident thereto fhall be leffened until the lofs be made good.

Finally the Bifhop granted for himfelf and his fucceffors that the houfe of St. Mark be quit and freed from procurations and vifitation of the arch-deacon of the place or his official, and from obedience to the archdeacon to be obferved as far as relates to religious matters for ever. — And the houfe and faid poor to receive vifitation of the Bifhop or his official according to law.

Walter by the grace of God Bifhop of Worcefter having feen this ordinance above, confirmed it by the pontifical authority, fealed with the faid Bifhop's feal, with the feal of the houfe of St. Mark, and that of Robert de Gourney patron, and of Henry de Gaunt mafter, in the year of grace 1259, on the morrow of the exaltation of the crofs.

Leland is of opinion in his Itinerary, vol. 7. p. 73, that " this houfe of the Gaunts was intended for a college of priefts, &c." which is confirmed by a deed dated 1251, de fitu domûs & novo opere & collegio ibidem habendo ; though it is ufually called Elemofynaria : — He alfo obferves that the governor of this houfe was fometimes called prior, and the houfe itfelf a priory of the order of St. Auguftin, vol. 1. p. 85. and it is fo called often in the Gaunts deeds. He alfo affirms the religious belonging to this houfe were called Bonnes-homes, or good-men. Vol. 5. p. 58. Sir Robert Atkyns

ays,

fays, p. 534, that " Edmond Earl of Cornwall, fon of Richard, who was brother to King Henry the 3d. was founder of the firft monaftery or college of the order of Bon-homes in England the 5th of Edw. 1ft. 1277, and were diftinguifhed by wearing a blue coat. (See Atkyns, p. 3. A. D. 1283, Kennet's Paroch. Antiq. p. 300. Leland, vol. 2. p. 332. but Rymer's Fœdera, vol. 1. p. 165, fays, A. D. 1290.) Which was at Afhrug in Hertfordfhire. There were but two other monafteries in England of this order; the Gaunts at Briftol, and Edington in Wiltfhire, the laft of which was founded by William de Edington of Winchefter the 26th of Edw. 3d. 1352.

The following BENEFACTORS have occurred in making abftraĉts from the folio manufcript in Latin, called Gaunt's Book.

The manor of Paulet and its appurtenances were given by the aforefaid Robert de Gourney, as well as Were-Mill, Radwick, and the four marks of rent in Briftol; and of the gift of Andrew Loterel the manor of Stockland and its appurtenances, of the gift of Maurice de Gaunt that part of Stockland next the hundred of Canington, &c. were all confirmed to the mafter and brethren of the hofpital of Billefwick by King Henry by his charter dated the 18th of November the 17th year of his reign 1233.

Edward the 1ft. gave the manor of Winterbourn Gunnore in Wilts, before he was King in the 52d year of his father's reign, and confirmed it after he was King the 13th of May 1290.

Edward the 3d. confirmed all the aforefaid grants, and that which Alexander D'Aundo, or De Anno made to the faid hofpital of all that land and bolk (wood) called Halfbarrow, with its appurtenances, in the manor of Aychton, and that grant which Idonea Gaunfel the wife of Richard the Huntfman made of all that land and tenement which fhe had in Erdicote, and all the right fhe had in La Lee Hancdone, and Hogeftone; and the land called Sturte in Gete and its appurtenances, with the advowfons of the chapels of Lee and Erdicote, and all rents, villenages, cuftodies, liberties, &c. and all right in the' faid land belonging to her or her heirs: he confirmed alfo the grant which Richard Curteis of Briftol made to the mafter and brethren of faid hofpital of his right to a meadow called Wambroke; and the grant which William Gannel made of a tenement which he had of John le Brun in de Lianour, and Linagon : dated the 1ft of May in the 6th year of his reign 1333.

Several houfes and gardens in Frogmere-ftreet (now Frog-lane) were given to this hofpital by Gilbert le Colere 1286, and Henry of Devon; Roger Gyngyure 1252, Reginald Bagge 1252, Roceline Tanner 1267, Ralph

Morell,

Morell, Julian Kepe, Eglentine Bulerin 1252, Eve Kerdyff 1256, Elias of Stoke 1271, John Droys 1418.

Robert Guyen Burgefs of Briftol gave a garden called Billefwyk, and a tenement with two acres of land, in 1290, for which he got licence againft the Mortmain ftatute of King Edward.

In 1326 the Bifhop of Bath and Wells appropriated to this houfe the vicarage of Overftowey, and in 1314 Stockland.

Jordan de Berkeley gave the houfes oppofite St. Anftin's the lefs and garden, which were Henry the Archdeacon's, the fon of Robert Harding, to Henry Gaunt mafter, his heirs and fucceffors to the houfe of St. Mark, paying two fhillings yearly to the abbot of St. Anftin, 1235.

Richard Palmer granted a gout through his garden next the land and curtilage of Henry de Gaunt down into the tide in the Frome, in the year 1235; and 1248 John Carpenter gave the ground next the gout.

Margery Palmer gave a tenement next the Back in the parifh of St. Anftin's the lefs in 1288: Edyth Whyttynge gave another tenement with the ground next Henry de Gaunt's, 1267.

John Balle gave a croft under the hill of St. Brendan, which he held of the hofpital of the brethren and fifters of St. John of Redclive, 1267; and Robert Cordar granted the croft next it on the faid hill.

John, Cecily, and Nicholas Aylwarde granted a penny rent out of a houfe in Steep-ftreet, a penny out of a houfe in Thomas-ftreet, and a pound of cummin out of a houfe in Broadmead in the year 1252. Richard Aylwarde gave a tenement on Bromehill in the fuburbs of Briftol, with a pigeon-houfe and three fhillings rent in 1233.

Vincent Bardftaple gave ten fhillings rent out of a houfe in Lewin's-mead next St. Bartholomew's hofpital the 39th of Edward the 3d.

Alice de Mercer gave a houfe near the church of St. Nicholas without the wall and beneath it, the mafter and chaplains of St. Mark admitting her and her hufband to partake of the benefits of faid college every year on the day of their obiit 1256.

Thomas de Emyngton gave a meffuage on Fromebridge, alias Knifefmyth-ftreet, fix fhillings and eightpence rent affize out of a houfe in Baldwin-ftreet and three fhops in Temple-ftreet, and three fhillings rent out of a houfe there; and twelve fhillings rent affize out of a houfe oppofite the flefh fhambles in Wells, 1248:—John mafter of St. Mark's quit-claimed the houfe in Baldwin-ftreet, which extended backwards to the old wall of the town of Briftol, to John Trefour, he paying 2s. yearly rent for it, 1272.

Robert

Robert Cordar gave his right in a houfe in Redclift-ftreet extending from the ftreet forwards to the Lagdiche backwards, for a lamp to the houfe of St. Mark about the year 1271, Galfrid Long being then prepofitor of Radclive.

Richard Curteys gave a houfe in the market (feria) of Briftol next a lane leading to the church of St. Philip and Jacob, 1267, and oppofite the church-yard.

John Efterfield gave the mafter and brethren of St. Mark's the nomination of 8 poor men and 5 poor women to the alms-houfe on St. Michael's-hill-fteps, and to appoint a prieft there, to fing and pray, the 20th of Henry 7th.

Henry of Mudiford gave Maurice de Gaunt and his fucceffors the land of Willemaris for 10 marks fterling.

Andrew Luttrel gave the manor of Stockland, the executors of faid Maurice paying him 40 marks (the deed being witneffed by Robert de Gourney, Gilbert de Gaunt &c. about the year 1269) with the advowfon of the church of Stockland-Gaunts worth about 10 marks by the year, but decreafing in value and being infufficient for the vicar to live upon it, it was endowed by Thomas Bifhop of Bath and Wells with the confent of William mafter and the brothers of St. Mark's with lands, and tythes of hay, rofes or reeds of the whole parifh — of wool, milk, apples, flax, lambs, calves, chicken, pigs, pigeons, all oblations, tenths &c. belonging to the faid church, except of fwans, which were referved by the houfe of St. Mark's who paid him alfo 28s. in money, 1453.

Margery Somery wife of Maurice de Gaunt granted tenths of the mill of Kantockefend, and pafture there for 6 oxen, 2 cows, and 2 heifers, in 1247.

Anfelm de Gourney gave Thomas de Lechlade mafter and his brothers of St. Mark's 3s. rent out of 3 burgages in the town of Were, and all his right in Hyndmore in Compton and Ceddre, 10 Edw. 2d.

William Cannell gave his poffeffion of Deliameur and Linagan, with all its appurtenances and rights in fifhing, meadows, vineyards, meffuages, mills, &c. &c. for 40s. 1233.

John Bruin gave his land in Brewham till the Gaunts were in full poffeffion of Deliameur and Linagan, which was confirmed by Ric. de Mufcegrofs.

John Bifhop of Bath and Wells by leave of King Edward A. R. 20, gave the advowfon of the church of Stowey apud Stoke-Courfey, worth 10 marks, dedicated to St. Peter and Paul, in exchange for 24 acres of moor, a mill, water-courfe in Compton, Cheddre and Nether Were, 1326.

Henry de Gaunt confirmed the grant of Erdicote, and gave all his rent which he bought of the abbot of Kaynfham next the church of the frier preachers in Briftol.   Richard

Richard Gaurfel confirmed the grant of his mother Idonea of all his claim in Erdicote village and its appurtenances, as well in Docham as Winterborne and Hambrook, and Lee and in Hogefton and Havedon and Sturte, in the village of Yate.

Anfelm de Gourney confirmed all the grants of his father Robert, and gave 15 s. rent, affife, the free chapel of Over, and granted that he would never trouble the mafter and brothers of St. Mark concerning the manor of Paulet and its appurtenances, mill of Were, and the rents in that town, or the rents in Briftol and poffeffions and houfes at Billefwick, or other poffeffions belonging to them granted by his father, or the 15 s. rent out of Lee, or tythes for the chapel of St. Swithin at Over or Lee, 1337.

Thomas Ap Adam quit claimed all his right in Lee, near Over, in the parifh of Amandefbury, 1331.

Robert Scay granted and confirmed his lands in Rugh-Erdicot, 1279; and 1299 all his lands in Erik-ftreet, and his claim in the common pafture of Ock-holt, Thornes, and Stonely.

Robert Bylebofte granted one virgat of land in Iron Afton, which he held of Ofbert de Giffard, for his maintenance in food in the houfe of St. Mark, ferving one of the priors there as a fteward or head clerk of the faid houfe, with allowance of 10 s. yearly as long as he ftays and ferves there ; or at his option to have fix marks for the faid land, inftead of his food and the 10 s.

Ifabel Hildefley gave all her right and claim in a meffuage, croft, and garden, and a virgat of land in Iron Afton. And Thomas the fon of Maurice Lord of Berkeley releafed the yearly rent of 6 s. iffuing out of it to him.

Richard Drayton releafed an annual rent of a mark, which he ufed to receive out of a field called Wambrok, paid him by Richard Curtis, who gave the faid field to the houfe of St. Mark, 1235. Wambrook lay towards the Barton of Briftol caftle, alias King's Berton, near the field of the hofpital of St. Laurence, next the parroche of the faid leprous brothers, oppofite Berehulle on the north fide.

John Brues granted fix acres of land in Coluwyfauri in Ireland, in the county of Waterford

William Lord Botreaux Lord of Clifton allowed the plea of the houfe of St. Mark to common of pafture for one bull, fix cows, and twenty-four fheep, at Clifton.

Ignatius of Clifton granted a meffuage, curtilage, and fountain of water to be brought through his land whither they pleafed, 1235.

Ralph

Ralph of Stourton, rector of Beverfton, granted his land of Wytington, with all appurtenances for thirty-two marks of fiiver.

Peter Burgeis and his wife, on condition of a yearly gift of two marks of filver, and a houfe found them at Briftol as long as they or either of them fhould live, granted their land in Slymburgg, Goffington, Hurft, and Ryngefton; and Maurice de Berkeley granted a virgat of land in Slymbrugg, belonging to the Hamlet of Hurfle, with a meffuage, garden, and all his right in it, except the fupport of a lamp in the church of Slymbrugg.

Walter Allayn granted all the meffuage with the mill at Langford, as did Richard de Portefheued, his heir.

Roger de Turba gave privilege of digging in the moor of Tykeham and mowing there, and gathering lefcas et fcirpos, rufhes and reeds, and in thofe places where it was ufual, 1280.

Thefe were the principal grants of lands, &c. made to the houfe of St. Mark of Bellifwick; and are abftracts of the feveral deeds in the manufcript book in my poffeffion, called Thefaurus Chartarum et Munimentorum Domus St. Marci de Billefwyck, except fome law proceedings in relation to titles, confirmations of the fame grants, appropriations of churches, ordinances of bifhops, and agreements between difputing parties about particular rights and privileges in manors, &c. too prolix to be here inferted at length.

The grants were all made in this or the like form: " Omnibus matris ecclefiæ filiis, &c. fciant prefentes et futuri, &c.; or noverit univerfitas, me H. G. divinæ pietatis intuitu et pro falute animæ meæ, &c. conceffiffe remififfe et quietum clamaffe et hâc prefenti carta meâ confirmaffe, Deo beatæ Mariæ et beato Marco et magiftro eleomofynariæ St. Marci de Billefwyck juxta Briftol, et confratribus vel capellanis et clericis ibidem Deo fervientibus, &c. et eorum fucceffioribus ad corum fuftentationem et ad refectionem ejufdem loci pauperum fingulis diebus in perpetuam liberam, &c." — To all fons of the holy mother church, &c. know all men prefent and future, &c. that may fee or hear this, I, H. G. from a view of piety, and for the health of my foul, my father's, the king's, &c. have granted, releafed, and quit claimed, and by this prefent deed confirmed to God, the bleffed St. Mary and St. Mark, and to the maiter of the hofpital of Billefwyck near Briftol, and to the co-brethren, chaplains, and clerks, there ferving God and celebrating divine fervice for the faithful and their fucceffors, for their own fupport and maintenance of the poor there for ever, in free, pure, and perpetual alms, &c.

In the year 1278 (reg. wyg.) Godfrey Bifhop of Worcefter vifited the houfe of St. Mark, Briftol, and found among other things that this houfe was

founded

founded originally for the fupport of an hundred poor in certain eatables and drinkables for ever every day in the year, and that for four years before it had been, it was to be feared not without God's vengeance, damnably omitted, wherefore he ordered this alms to be given as at firft appointed. He found alfo that it was unknown how the houfe is governed, as there were no receivers in the houfe nor ftewards in the manors, &c. belonging to it, who had rendered any account of what had been received and delivered; wherefore he ordered receivers fhould be appointed to receive by tail all money arifing from the faid manors, corn, and other profits of the faid houfe, and further adminifter by tail to the officers of the houfe for the ufe of the houfe; and the faid receivers abroad and fervants fhail firft before the mafter and three or four others of the faid houfe render a faithful account once at leaft in the year, and the officers at home do the like, that fo it may appear what and how much the faid houfe can expend, and how far its goods, &c. will ferve, and what remains in ftore and the like.

The like complaint of withdrawing the alms from the poor by the houfe was made at the vifitation of the Bifhop in May 1284. In 1312 the mafter, William Beauver, and Friers Robert de Redynge, John Yverney, W. de Cant, and J. Belet, were all at variance, accufing each other of great exceffes and enormities to the bifhop, and the mafter kept W. de Cant confined in prifon for penance till the bifhop ordered his releafe, and his being reftored again to his place in the houfe.

Were it not thefe and fuch like irregularities that gave Henry 8th. pretext for diffolving the religious houfes?

In 1346 John de Stokeland precentor was with great form elected mafter or cuftos of this houfe by compromife and agreement among the nine brothers which then made up the convent, who carried him fo chofen to the conventual church from the chapter-houfe, and laid him down upon the high altar according to the ufual form finging Te Deum aloud, he was then declared mafter and afterwards inftalled.

Notwithftanding the liberal grants and ample endowments of their houfe, I find them complaining to John Bifhop of Bath and Wells of the infufficiency of their revenues and eftates to their fupport, out of which they were obliged by cuftom and right from the firft foundation of their houfe to relieve (reficere) an hundred poor * every day befides other almfgivings, and the re-

Y y   lief

---

* The original grant was for 27 poor, which by a fecond founder feems afterwards to have been changed to 100, when the endowment was encreafed. Dugdale fays, " an hundred poor," tho' the grant quoted by him mentions only 27.

lief of others coming thither for hofpitality; and that they the faid mafter
and brethren without any fault of their's on account of the fmallnefs of their
income, and various expences daily increafing upon them, and alfo from the
floods and overflowings of the fea, by which no fmail part of their lands
there fituated in his diocefe were deftroyed, had been fo burdened with
debts, that unlefs other provifion was made, they fhould be obliged
wretchedly to beg in future " contra religionis honeftatem." On this reprefentation the bifhop, pioufly commiferating the neceffities of their houfe,
conferred on them the impropriation of the church of Stock, with its rights,
poffeffions, and appurtenances, referving only to himfelf and fucceffors the
appointment of a vicar for the faid parifh, to ferve in the church to be
prefented to him by the houfe of St. Mark, and an annual penfion of two fhillings to be paid to the dean and chapter of St. Andrew, Wells, and one mark
and an half to the archdeacon. This was granted in the year 1316, 10th kalends of November, and feventh year of the bifhop's confecration. — But in
the year 1326 they made the fame complaint of poverty, and the bifhop liftening to it beftowed on them the church of Overftowey, with all its rights,
fruits, &c. on their paying a penfion of forty fhillings to the dean and chap-
of Wells, towards the repairing the fabrick of that church, referving the fole
appointment of the vicar to the church of Overftowey. Whether their neceffities were real or feigned, this bifhop feems to have greatly favoured thefe
brethren of St. Mark's houfe; and if we confider how defirous the religious
houfes or regulars were then of appropriating church livings, and what pre-
tences they fet up of greater charity, fanctity, and more religions offices, obferved among them, and urged in their loud complaints to the bifhop, (orig.
" gravis eorum querela auribus noftris infonuit") it is no wonder the bifhops
were often deceived by them, and the fecular labouring parifh clergy thus
deprived of lawful fupport from the rectorial tythes, through the canting mif-
reprefentation and hypocrify of thefe religious. By this we may fee the
means made ufe of by the religious, as they were called of thofe days, to advance themfelves and their houfes. They deceived the people by an outward
ftricter difcipline and fuperftitious difplay of religion, miracles of their faints,
and by pretended claims to infpiration, and by the greater purity of the
lives of their monks, nuns, and friers, which impreffed the minds not only
of the laity, but of fome bifhops in their favour; whilft the fecular clergy
of their refpective parifhes grew hereby into lefs efteem, and had the valuable
part of their livings taken from them without a caufe, through the weaknefs
and lenity of the bifhops liftening to thefe faife claims, who changed the

rectorics

rectories to benefit the monks into vicarages, by appropriations; a lofs felt by the parochial clergy to this day, many thereby being reduced to great ſtraits now for a moderate maintenance by their livings, the lords of manors whoſe anceſtors purchaſed the abby lands and therewith the rectorial tythes, enjoying the clergy's right, and the patrimony of the church. May we not ſee here the bad effects of liſtening to the falſe pretenſions of religious zeal, and the claims of ſuperſtition; how the vulgar are again deceived by this outward ſhew of ſtricter lives and a ſtricter religion; the true religion deformed inſtead of reformed in its doctrines, the clergy treated with diſreſpect if not contempt, their tythes however ſmail diſputed or withheld, and every leader of a new ſect (like the regulars, monks, or friers of the ſeveral orders of old) preferred before them, to the neglect and perverſion of the true eſtabliſhed Chriſtian doc_trine and ſubſtitution of ſome ſtrange, falſe opinions in its ſtoad. But to return from this digreſſion. Theſe churches of Stockland and Overſtowey were very richly endowed, eſpecially by Hugh de Bonville, who granted to God and St. Peter the apoſtle of Overſtowey all its poſſeſſions in oxen, cows, ſheep, ſwine, goats, free from all herbage and pannage and all ſecular ſervice and gave liberty when and where they pleaſed for huſbote, heybote, and vir_bote, and for all other buſineſs they had need of or deſired, which liberty he had for ſome years hindered againſt the health of his ſoul, but returning to his mind and aſking pardon for his fault, he reſtored the honour and privi_lege of the ſaid churches; (we may in vain expect the lords of manors, the preſent poſſeſſors of tythes, to follow his example in this) he gave alſo all his wood, land, and meadow of Stowey-Harpet near the old caſtle, and ſeveral more acres of land on the caſt ſide of the caſtle, and a mea_dow near the fountain of St. Peter, and ſeven acres on the weſt ſide of of the caſtle, and ten in Lamcrofte. He afterwards gave this church of Over_ſtowey * to the church of St. Andrew of Stock, and the monks there ſerving God free from all ſervice, &c. only when God ſhould inſpire him to be wil_ling to take to a ſtricter life, they ſhould receive him as a brother or monk, &c. By letters patent from King Edward, A. R. 20, John Biſhop of Bath and Wells granted theſe churches wholly to the maſter and friers of St. Marks, for their better ſupport.

Such have been the benefactors of this hoſpital, and ſuch the lands with which it has been endowed, which at the diſſolution being purchaſed by the corpo-

ration

---

* In 1625 there was a great diſpute between one Selleck, farmer of this rectory of Overſtowey, and the vicar, Mr. Arundel, a painful and honeſt miniſter, who was denied his right; and Arthur Biſhop of Bath and Wells tried to compromiſe the matter, and wrote to the dean to apply to the corporation of Briſtol in favour of the vicar, that he might have ſome part of the coin ground as well as the leſſer tythes, as of old cuſtom he had beyond the memory of man.

ration has added many fine eſtates to the chamber of Briſtol, in truſt for public uſes and common profit of the citizens. I proceed next to give a liſt of the
maſters of this religious houſe of Gaunts, otherwiſe St. Mark of Belliſwick.

The firſt founders were Maurice de Gaunt and Robert de Gourney his
nephew; the firſt appointed Henry de Gaunt firſt maſter, which was confirmed
by his nephew.

PATRONS.

Robert de Gourney. Henry de Gaunt continued to 1268, and then reſigned
the year before his death through weakneſs of body,
and was ſucceeded by
Gilbert de Watham, who was precentor of the convent.
Thomas de Lechlade ſucceeded about 1274, and go-
verned to 1285.
Almaricus French ſucceeded in the reign of Edw. 1ſt.
Robert de Redynge in 1286, reſigned 1299.
William Belvere, alias Beaover 1312, and reſigned.

Lord Tho. ap Adam. Ralph de Tetbury 1334, 4 Maij to 1344, deprived.

Maurice de Berkeley, Richard de Yate 1344 to 1346.

ad nominationem   John Stockeland 1346.
conventus.

The Convent.   Walter Brunynge Oct. 12,   1360 (Regiſ. Wygorn.)
Thomas de Over 28 July   1370
Wm. Lane canon of St. Auſtin 1391
John St. Paul occurs in   1410
Nicholas Sterne died   1437
John Hall ſucceeded   1437
John Moulton reſigned   1442

The Biſhop by way   William Wyne elected   1442 5 Feb.(Regiſ.Wyg.)
of compromiſe with   William Prowe   -   1467
the convent.   John Mede died   -   1494
Richard Collins ſucceeded   1494
Thomas Tylar died   -   ·1515
Richard Bromfield occurs   1527
J. Coleman ſucceeded & reſign'd 1534

In the 26th year of King Henry the 8th. A. D. 1534, this houſe or college of Gaunts was reſigned by John Coleman the maſter and his brethren to
commiſſioners appointed, for the ſaid King's uſe, in form as followeth: —
" Know all men by theſe preſents &c. that wee John the maſter or prior of
the

the hofpital of the Gaunts, and the brethren of the fame in the diocefe of Worcefter with one confent (uno ore & voce) &c. have fubfcribed our names, dated in our chapter houfe the 11th day of the month of September 1534. ——— John Coleman mafter, John Helice, Richard Fitchett, Robert Benet, Thomas Pynchyn his brethren. Given under our common feal with two labils of parchment fealed with red wax."

Thus was this rich houfe with all its lands and poffeffions, plate and orna- ments refigned into the King's hands; its value was then computed at 112l. 9s. 9d. per ann. as Dugdale reckons; 140l. as Speed, a manufcript penes me, makes it 184l. 9s. and 420 ounces of plate came to the King's hands. Leland fays, * " It hath 300 marks of land by the year."

It was granted the 33d of Henry the 8th. 1540, from the crown to the mayor, burgeffes and commonalty of Briftol for public ufes, who are now in the place of the mafter and cobrethren of this hofpital of St. Mark, and are poffeffed now of the church, the fite of the hofpital, the houfes in Billefwyk belonging to it, the orchard ground now called Orchard-ftreet &c. and other lands and eftates with which the houfe was originally endowed.

At the diffolution the manor of Paulet and vicarage of Over Stowey were granted by the crown to the family of the Volgraves and Dorington in the county of Somerfet; and the fite of the hofpital with the tenements adjoining and houfes thereto belonging in Briftol, and the manor of Stockland-Gaunts, and the advowfon and vicarage of Stockland in the county of Somerfet to the city of Briftol; but for the further evidence of the difpofal of the lands and goods belonging to this houfe here is annexed an abftract of the inquifitions taken of all that belonged to this convent the 31ft of Henry the 8th. as they remain on record in the Exchequer.

" Billifwyke, otherwife called the Gaunts nigh Briftol late a religious houfe furrendered to the ufe of the Kings Majeftie and of his beires for ever by deed thereof made bearyng date under the convent feale of the fame late monaftery the ixth day of December 31 year of the reigne of the moft dreade Sovereigne Lord King Henry the Eighth and the fame day and year clearly diffolved and fuppreffed.

The clere yearly value of all the poffeffions belonging to   *l.*   *s.*   *d.* the faid late religious houfe, as well fpiritual as temporal, over and befides xixl. vi s. viii d. in fees and annuities granted to diverfe perfons by convent feale of the fame late monaftery for term of life,   -   -   -   -   -   -   165   2   4

Whereof

---

* Itinerary v. 7. p. 85. 2d ed.

Whereof pencions affigned to the late religious dyfpatched, viz.

	l.	s.	d.
John Colman clerk, late mafter there by the year, - -	40	0	0
Richard Fletcher late fteward of the houfeholde there, -	6	13	4
John Ellis clerk affigned to be curate of the parifh of St. Marke, fo longe as he fhould ferve, if he refufe the fame cure then to have but 6 l. - - - - - -	8	0	0
Thomas Pynthin clerke - - - - -	6	0	0
	60	13	4

And fo remayneth clere - - 104 9 0

Records and evidences belonging to the faid late houfe remaine in the Treafury under the cuftody of Edward Carne doftor of law, the keys whereof remaine in the cuftody of Richard Powlet Efq; receiver.

Church houfes and buildings appoynted to remaine undefaced, viz.

The church there appointed for the parifh church—as heretofore hath been ufed.

The lodgeings called the maflers lodginge with hall, hottery, pantry and kitchen—committed to the cuftody of the faid Doftor Carne.

Deemed to be fuperfluoufe, devided into honeft tenentaries with convenient rents referved—to the ufe of the King.

Leads remaining to the ufe of the Kings Majeflies, none but onlie upon the faid church, which is the parifh church abovefaid efteemed to vij foders—nil.

, Bells remaining in the fteeple there vi. whereof iij affigned to the parifh and remain to the ufe of the Kings Majeftie iij—poiz by eft. m m lb. weight.

Jewels referved to the ufe of the Kings Majeftie—none.

Plate of filver referved to the fame ufe, viz.

Silver gilt - 77 oz.
Silver parcel gilt 156 oz.
Silver white 180 oz.
——— 413 oz.

Ornaments referved—none.

Summe of all the ornaments, goods and chattells lately belonging to the faid late houfe, fold by the faid commiffioners as particularly appeareth in the booke of fale thereof made ready to be fhewn,

l. s. d.
33 5 5

Whereof payments to the late religious and fervants difpatched, viz.—To iij religious perfons late priefts of the faid late houfe of the Kings Majeflies reward, - - - - - 6 0 0

To xvi men and children fervants and queriftors of the faid late houfe for their wages and liveries, - - - - 10 9 4

Of

Of debts owynge by the faid late houfe,—To diverfe perfons for victuals had of them to the ufe of the faid monaftery with xiij l. payd to the late mafter, therefore the payment and dyfcharge of all the refidue of the debts by the faid late houfe by covenaunte

	l.	s.	d.
	13	0	0

And fo remaynith clere - - 2 16 1

Debts owynge to the faid late houfe by the fame — none.

Patronage of churches belonging to the faid late monaftery.—Com. Somerfet, vicaridge of Stockland-Gaunts by the year—vicaridge of Overftowey com. Somerfet."

Certainly this was a rich hofpital when fo much was found and accounted for to the crown four years after it was diffolved, when they made it their bufinefs to fecure their eftates by gifts and private grants, after flourifhing from about the year 1230 to the fatal time of the diffolution above 300 years; and being furrendered to the King in 1540, three years after being veited in the crown by act of parliament. And though they diffolved the hofpital and divefted it of its revenues, yet the chapel ftili ftands, 1788, as a monument of the unjuft abufe of a noble charity by the religious, and application of its revenues fince to other purpofes, and as a memorial to preferve the memory of the pious founders and benefactors to all pofterity.

The churches of Stockland Gaunts, now called Stockland Briftol and Overftowey, with lands thereto belonging, and other great eftates at Overftowey and Stoke Courfey, and other lands elfewhere, recited in letters patent, 33d Henry 8th. were with lands of other religious houfes then diffolved for 1000l. granted to the mayor and commonalty of Briftol, of which fum 528l. 10s. 8d. was rifen by the contribution of the veftries of each parifh and other private perfons; the veftry of St. Nicholas gave 46l. 15s. 3d. towards it and took bond of the chamberlain to acquit and fave them harmlefs againft the King or any other perfon, and the other parifhes did the fame. The lands bought with the money fo rifen (the city alone being not able of their then public ftock to make this valuable purchafe of Henry 8th.) were all that houfe and fite of the hofpital or houfe of St. Mark de Billefwick, alias the Gaunts, &c. See the particulars, p. 133.

The corporation affifted by the veftries and private perfons were enabled by the acquifition of thefe vaft eftates to employ them, as they had engaged to the citizens, to the public ufes and advantage of the city; and immediately hereupon fet about making the city gates free and quit for ever from all manner of toll or cuftom, demanded by the fheriffs for the time being; and the fheriffs were to receive out of the chamber 44l. per annum in

lieu

lieu thereof: and the Key and the Back were thenceforth to be free for all provifions brought thither, as recorded in the great White Book of Briftol, folio 61, vide alfo annals for that year, 1540, and public proclamation was made concerning it. This was applying part of the income of thefe new acquired eftates to fuch public ufes, that it received the general united voice of public approbation and great rejoicings were made on the occafion, and their pofterity reap the advantage of it to this day.

But nothing could be more piously defigned, and indicate a nobler fpirit of charity and humanity, than erecting and new founding another hofpital on the very fpot where thefe Bonnes Hommes or good men ufed formerly to difpenfe with fuch a bountiful hand relief to the neceffitous and daily food to the hungry poor. This was actually begun by the munificence of John Carr, Efq; a worthy citizen, who by his will, dated April 10, 1586, gave his manor of Congerfbury to the corporation of Briftol (after paying his debts and compounding with his brother and heir Edward Carr to the fum of 5000l.) towards erecting and founding an hofpital for maintaining and educating poor orphans and children in effect according to the hofpital of Chrift Church in London. A royal charter was then obtained March 21, 1590, in the 32d year of Queen Elizabeth for this purpofe, and this new hofpital was eftablifhed on the petition of the mayor, aldermen, and commonalty, by an act of parliament paffed 1597, 39th of Elizabeth. * The great capital meffuage or manfion houfe of the late old hofpital (which with the cloifters was taken down) called St. Marks of Bellifwyck or the Gaunts, then inhabited by Gabriel Bleek, Efq; and granted among other things to the corporation by Henry 8th. was fitly appropriated to this ufe for its healthy fituation. And that " the governors of the faid hofpital might daily increafe the number of the faid poor orphans and children to be relieved and fuftained there" (the very words of the act) the Queen granted them licence to purchafe manors, lands, &c. and feveral other benefactors, whofe names fhould be recorded with honour for promoting fo much the welfare of the city, contributed large fums and annual rents for this laudable undertaking.

The corporation of Briftol gave feveral thoufand pounds, which they might eafily fpare out of the large eftates the chamber had acquired by the purchafe of the old Gaunts hofpital here of Henry 8th. and it muft be ever efteemed a well-judged and truly commendable application of the public money ; but their trouble and long care in procuring the firft eftablifhment of this hofpital, as well as fupporting it afterwards and ftill improving it, muft not be forgot.   William

* A private act, vide Statutes at large, chap. iii.

William Carr, Efq; gave 17 l per annum ; John Carr, Efq; his fon, gave his manor of Congerfbury ; the Society of Merchant Venturers were benefactor ; William Bird, Efq; mayor, gave 530 l. ; Mr. Samuel Hartnell, 33 l. per annum ; Mr. Robert Dowe, 100 l. ; Mr. John Barker, 17 l. 16 s. per annum; Mr. John Gollop, 81 l. per annum ; in 1602, the Lady Mary Ramfey, 1000 l. ; Anthony Standbank, 15 l. per annum ; Mr. Thomas Farmer, 400 l. ; Edward Colfton, Efq; alfo gave 70 l. per annum, and 500 l. in the year 1702 towards rebuilding and enlarging the faid hofpital ; he has always fix boys therein, and has provided 10 l. to put each an apprentice out of an eftate in Congerfbury ; the whole charge to him being about 1500 l. The coats of arms of thefe benefactors are painted in this church, with the fums given. Other benefactions were given by the parifh veftries and private perfons to a great amount to pay off the mortgage on Mr Carr's manor of Congerfbury.

In 1703, the great and truly charitable Mr. Colfton propofed to the magiftrates to increafe the hofpital of Gaunts or Queen Elizabeth, by a farther endowment by himfelf for one hundred boys inftead of forty-four, then maintained and taught there, if they would erect a fabric equal to fo great a foundation and fit for their reception ; but through the private oppofition of fome, a narrow, felfifh, factious fpirit of others, and the envy of not a few, the undertaking was fpoiled ; but his liberality was not withheld notwithftanding from the place, nor did his charity toward this his native city fbine with lefs ardour in being difappointed in this open, generous intention of his to join his charity with that of the city : for reftrained as it was in one place it broke out in another, and he then turned his thoughts towards erecting an houfe for one hundred boys on St. Auguftin's-back — a noble nurfery for youth, equal to a royal foundation ! Of which hereafter in the chapter on St. Auguftin's parifh.

This hofpital of Queen Elizabeth was opened for the reception of poor boys in 1589, and William Bird, then mayor, gave 500 l. in his life time, and a tax on lead and iron was laid for three years towards its fupport. 1596, J. White gave 10 l. 1598, John Aldworth, 50 l. Mrs. Ann Golfion, 200 l. which with 200 l. out of the chamber and the 1000 l. of L. M. Ramfey purchafed an eftate at Winterbourn of 100 l. per annum. William Gibbs gave 10 l. in 1602 for repairs and a fermon in the hofpital. 1685, Andrew Barker gave fix houfes and 100 l. to put out the boys apprentices. In 1702, the hofpital began to be rebuilt in a large and more commodious manner. In the year 1716 the fum of 40 s. ufed to be paid before that time for each

Z z

boy's

boy's admiffion to the governor thereof for the time being was laid afide, and the boys fince admitted gratis.

In 1659 before the hofpital was rebuilt, when only twenty-eight boys were maintained there, the number was increafed by an order of council to forty, and the mafter's (Mr. Sneed's) falary from 7l. 16s. per annum, was augmented to 16l. per annum, during the pleafure of the houfe, and it was ordered he fhould not prefume to be abfent above three days together in a year without leave of the mayor; and the following rules of admiffion were agreed on:

1. That no boy be admitted that hath any loathfome or infeftious difeafe, or any deformity or imperfcftion that may prevent his being placed out as an apprentice.

2. No boy to be admitted unlefs his petition be figned by the mayor and four aldermen and the treafurer, importing his age, name, parifh, and the time of his admittance, to be recorded by the mafter.

3. That a certificate be given of the boy's age under the hands of the minifter and churchwardens of his parifh, that he is ten years old and not under.

4. That no boy be chofen, whofe father hath not been a free burgefs of Briftol, or a poor boy of Congerfbury, of which parifh there fhall be always one, fon of one of the city tenants there.

5. No boy to be continued paft the age of fixteen; if not placed out then to be returned to his parents or friends, or overfeers of the parifh.

6. The mafter is not to teach or entertain any tablers without leave of the mayor, four aldermen, and the treafurer.

7. The boys to be inftrufted in reading, writing, and cafting accounts, and rendered capable of being apprenticed out.

8. That upon the boy's admiffion forty fhillings be paid to the treafurer, and the boy furnifhed with one fuit of apparel, two fhirts, two bands, two pair of ftockings and fhoes.

This laft rule was difpenfed with by order, 1716, and the mafter has now 10l. a year allowed him for maintaining, cloathing, and inftrufting each boy, from the corporation, under their direftion and vifitation.

Thus have we feen this houfe of St. Mark or Gaunts erefted and fo liberally endowed, perpetually to remain diffolved, notwithftanding the care of the founders to fecure it by royal charters, &c. It was next changed into a fchool and orphan-houfe for poor boys, natives of Briftol and of Congerfbury, under the name of Queen Elizabeth's Hofpital, who granted her
charter

charter of foundation, appointing the corporation of the city governors and a body corporate for eſtabliſhing and promoting the ſaid hoſpital, which was farther confirmed by act of parliament the 39th year of her reign, 1597. But ſee the inſtability of human ordinances, notwithſtanding this charter of the Queen and an act of parliament, this houſe has again ſuffered another change, being in (1783) converted into a public Grammar-ſchool for the citizens ſons to reſort to for education, firſt founded in another place leſs convenient in Chriſtmas-ſtreet by Mr. Thorn, formerly the Bartholomew hoſpital or priory, and the orphan or poor city boys were ſent to occupy the ſaid ancient ſchool at St. Bartholomew's, henceforth to remain and be called Queen Eliza-beth's Hoſpital in the place of the other.

The exchange of the houſes thus made, it was afterwards thought proper to get it confirmed by act of parliament, which was accordingly done. But though the places or ſites of theſe reſpective foundations were changed, the endowments of each remain the ſame and diſtinct as at firſt, and are likely ſo to continue, unleſs another revolution or change ſhould be projected and take place.

The corporation have been ſo provident, and the eſtates the Orphan-ſchool was endowed with have been ſo carefully managed and the revenues ſo im-proved, that the boys may now be increaſed and one hundred well and ſuffici-ently ſupported therein, as recommended by Queen Elizabeth's charter; but forty-four alone are maintained here, and the addition not yet made.

C H A P. XI.

Of the CHURCH and PARISH of St. JAMES and PRIORY.

THIS church and the priory to which it belonged were built in the north ſuburb of the city. Leland ſays in his Itinerary concerning the priory, (vol. vii. p. 85. 2d edit.) " it ſtondith by Broadmeade by northe from the " caſtle on a hilly grounde, and the ruines of it ſtondithe harde buttynge to " the eſt ende of the pariſh churche of that name."

It was founded by Robert Rufus, natural ſon of King Henry 1ſt. by Neſta daughter of Rhees ap Tudor after the death of Robert Fitzhamon, who had

enjoyed

enjoyed the whole honour of Glocefterfhire, and died in the year 1107, and is buried on the north fide of the choir at Tewkfbury, in his epitaph cal-led "hujus loci fundator," leaving iffue only four daughters, to the eldeft of whom Mabilia the King married his fon Robert, and with her gave him the entire honour belonging to her father, and in 1109 created him firft conful, Earl of Glocefter, and Lord of Briftol. * He was the moft valiant military genius and warrior of that age. He bore the following arms: G. three refts or. (fee the plate) and they were fo depicted in Tewkfbury abby. He built this priory † and a chapel here on his domains, dedicating it to the honour of God, the bleffed Mary, and St. James the apoftle, and having placed therein black monks of the Benedictine order, he endowed it with lands, liberties, and poffeffions, and enriched it with ornaments, &c. and conftituted it a priory, member, or cell to the monaftery of Tewkfbury, and fubject thereto in all refpects as the priory of Cranbourne. This illuftrious Earl died at Glocefter of a fever the 31ft of October, the 12th of King Stephen, 1147, and was buried in the middle of the choir of the priory chapel, now the parifh church of St. James, in a fepulchre of grey marble, (or green jafper, Dugdale) fet upon fix pillars of a fmall height. In his tomb was found (many years after) a writing of parchment concerning him and the time of his death: Leland fays, vol. vii. p. 85. " a brewer in Brightftowe had this wryting."

His only fon William fucceeded to his father's honours and eftates, and became a great benefactor to this priory and the monaftery of Tewkfbury, as appears by King Henry's deed of confirmation about the year 1181, viz. he gave all his freehold in Effelegia (Afhly) and right to the fair held at Whit-funtide in Briftol, and the tenth penny of his mills in Newport in Wales, Runne, Stapleton, and Leovenath, and his burgage rents ‡ out of Newport-meadow, which he ordered fhould be within this parifh (now Broadmead) fituated between the caftle and the church of St. James in Briftol; and all the churches that were the fee of the faid earl, with a meffuage of oue Allen's in or near the fhambles of Briftol. § He died in the caftle of Briftol in 1183, and was conveyed away and buried in his abby of Keynfham, which he had

founded

* Vide chapter on the caftle, p. 209. Sir Robert Atkyns's Glocefterfhire, p. 714, 728.

† Leland, Collect. vol. i. p. 217. fays, " cella St. Jacobi de Briftow pertinet ad Tewkfbyri: Robertus conful Gloc. primus fundator prioratus St. Jacobi."

‡ To the monaftery of Tewkfbury he gave " decimam de exitibus Briftoliæ, called alfo deci-mam cenfus Briftol," the tythes of the town of Briftol; before the Conqueft as belonging to the honour or lordfhip of Glocefter given to Robert Fitzhamon, who endowed the abby with it, fince purchafed by the corporation. The tythes were reckoned at 14l. 10s. per annum fee farm rent.

§ Monaft. Anglic. vol. i. p. 513.

founded the 11th of Edward 2d. in memory of Robert his only fon deceafed, leaving only three daughters. About the year 1193, Henry Bifhop of Worcefter by deed confirmed all the benefactions of Earl William to the church of Tewkfbury, viz. the churches of St. James at Briftol with the priory and its appurtenances, the churches of St. John, of the Holy Trinity or Chrift Church, of St. Jacob of the Market, (or St. Philip and Jacob) of St. Owen's, of St. Michael, in Briftol, and of St. Brendan without the vill of Briftol, and the church of Edricfton, &c.

The prior had not only the privilege of a fair at St. James's in Ebdomanâ pentecoftes by Earl William's charter, confirmed by King Henry 2d. but the full prifage of wines coming to the port of Briftol from twelve o'clock the Saturday before the feaft of St. James to the fame hour the Saturday following; and by inquifition taken 4th Edward 2d. it was allowed that the prior had fuch prifage and other free cuftoms, and the liberty for taking 4d. for every hogfhead fo imported by virtue of the faid charter, on which the King granted prohibition againft Thomas Chaucer, his capital pincerna, in favour of the prior.+ In 1673, 7 Aug. the mayor and commonalty having purchafed of Sir Charles Gerard this prifage of wine with other rents, the Whitfon court, and its privilege, &c. the Whitfuntide preceding a court was held in behalf of the city, and feveral fhips of wine happening to arrive in this port that week, the officers of the faid court and city feized feveral tons of wine for prifage, which being fold by the truftees and officers of the city to Sir Robert Cann and other perfons, it was engaged to fave harmlefs the merchants againft fuch as claimed under Sir William Walters' patent for prifage, and others who might moleft them on that account. Book of Orders, K, p. 250.

The fite of this priory § was large, and extended from the weft end of the prefent church or Whitfon-court (where the prior held court for his lands without Lawford's-gate and Redlonde) to the barton of St. James, and confifted of a large manor-place or manfion-houfe with a fpacious long hall, a buttery adjoining to the fame, a long gallery extending weftward to the

church

+ Little Red Book of Briftol, p. 96.

‡ Vide charter of Edward 4th. 1461, p. 82, 91, 180.

§ The endowment of it I find thus in a deed: William Earl endowed it with the manor of Keinfham or Chainfham, alfo the village of Chewton-Cainfham, Cherleton, Stokewood, and Stoketon and Felton, with its woods, members of the manor, and feven librates of land in Buthftoke, alfo all the manor of Merfefeld except the advowfon of the church, alfo Ortum de Bertonu de Briftolle cum ortulano et tenemento quod tenuit: et 7 folidatas et 6 nummatas tetræ in-

church, rooms under and about the hall, and chambers at the weſt end of the
long gallery, that adjoined to the church there, a great green court adjoining to the ſame, a great gate-houſe entering by the churchyard into the ſaid
green court, together with a dwelling-houſe adjoining the ſaid gate-houſe,
alſo a great ſtable in the ſaid court, a brew-houſe and bake-houſe near to
the kitchen-door, a little garden adjoining to the ſame brew-houſe, and another garden lying between the weſt end of the church there and the ſaid great
gate-houſe, alſo a little way or lane leading out of the great court to the weſt
part of the gate entering into the way that parts Shooter's cloſe and the Montague's; all which is the weſt part of the ſaid manſion-houſe. On the caſt
part or ſide were galleries and chambers in them, parlour, &c. united with
the weſt part, a little ſquare green court, and incloſed ground with a pigeon-
houſe, a large barton extending from the gate in the Barr's-lane, whereby
was the pound, two great barns, alſo ſeveral buildings lying on both ſides the
ſaid barton. Such is the deſcription met with in a manuſcript deed of
partition between the heirs of H. Brayne, 1579, which ſhews it to be a large
and ſpacious priory.

At the caſt end of the church in the year 1753 part of the ruins of the
priory was ſtill to be ſeen, being a ſquare room with niches in the wall round
it, in length 24 yards, and of breadth in the clear 8 yards; poſſibly the refectory for the monks. It appeared to have been vaulted with freeſtone, of
which the ſide walls were built very ſtrong. Two brick-fronted houſes are
now built on the ſite of it.

Biſhop Tanner, in his Not. Monaſ. deſcribes this priory, and refers to a
great number of deeds* of grants to it by different Kings and others.—
The following are the names of the priors that have occured.

1374.

Berchull extra foffatum feriæ inter gardinum quod fuit avi mei et aquam avenæ, alſo all the rents
of pepper and cummin, which my grandfather had at Briſtol within the town and without, and
that part of the land which was of my fee beyond the bridge of Avon, at the head of the bridge
on the road as you go down to the Avon, alſo the churches of St. Mary and of St. Werburgh,
Briſtol, &c. &c.

* Vide in Monaſ. Angl. tom. i. p. 513. ex pat. 2d. Henry 4th. p. 2. m. 7. cartam R.
Henry 2. confirm. donatorum conceſſiones : cart. antiq. T. n. 24. ſcil. Henry 2. de libertat. apud
Aſſeliam.

Regiſtrum brevium, f. 247. ſub titulo ad quod damnum, de conceſſ. c. marcar. reddit. ad
inveniend. duos capellanos.

Stevens's Supplement, vol. i. p. 516. Leland, Collect. vol. i. p. 85. Itin. vol. vi. p. 79.
vol. vii. 91.

1374. Thomas Norton, prior, 21 Richard 2d. Richard Bycefter, prior, 1 Henry 4th. Richard Winchefter, prior, 6 Henry 6th. 1428. William Newport, prior, 35 Henry 8th. Robert Circefter, prior, who furrendered his priory at the diffolution, Jan. 9, 1540, and had allowed him at his dif-miffion, an annual penfion of 13 l. 6 s. 8 d. for his life.

Leland in Itin. vol. vi. fol. 88. fays, " Robertus Nothus, &c. i. e. Robert the bafe fon of Henry ufed on all folemn days to have with him the abbot of Tewkfbyri with twelve monks of Briftol," and that " this Robert built the caftle of Briftolle, and gave every tenth ftone of the caftle towards building the chapel of St. Mary, near the monaftery of St. James at Briftol."

William of Worcefter mentions (1480) the meafurements of the priory and church. " The length of the church of St. James 54 fteppys, bredth 40 fteppys. The length of the priory of the aforefaid church 40 fteppys. The length of the chapel of the Bleffed Mary there 40 fteppys, its bredth 12 fteppys. The bredth of the churchyard 130 fteppys, length of the churchyard of St. James 150 fteppys." In another place he fays, " The chapel of the Bleffed Mary of St. James contains in length 21 yards, its bredth 7 yards. The bredth of the chapel of St. Ann contains 4 yards, the length of the faid chapel 8 yards. The length of the nave of the church of the priory of St. James contains $15\frac{1}{2}$ yards or 26 fteps. The length of the nave of the parifh church an-nexed to the nave of the church of the faid priory contains 22 yards or 40 fteps.."

This priory being a cell to the abby of Tewkfbury and parcel of that great houfe was diffolved with it, and granted, 35 Henry 8th. to Henry Brayne, Efq; citizen and merchant taylor of London, (together with the lordfhip of Hadnoke in the marches of Wales, belonging to the diffolved pri'ry of Lanthony near Glocefter) for the fum of 667 l. 7 s. 6d. yielding and paying to the King and his heirs, &c. yearly the fum of 3 l. 10 s. $9\frac{1}{2}$ d.

for

Munimenta nonnulla pertinentia ad ecclefiam S. Jacobi prope Briftol, 27 Henry 7. MSS. in-ter. codd. R. P. Johannis Moore, n. 351. in bibl. publ. acad. Cantab. f. In Itin. Will. de Worc. p. 120, 290. Dimenf. Ecclef.

In cartulario archiepifcopatus Cantuar. inter libros MSS. autoris in bibl. Bodl. Oxon. p. 192, profeffionem de fubmiffione vifitationi dom. archipifc. Cantuar. A. D. 1260. Atkyns's Glocc-fterfhire, p. 547, 687, 727.

Cart. Antiq. K. n. 30 fcil. R. Hen. 2. de libertat. pat. 25. Hen. 3. m. i. de amotione corporis alienoræ confanguineæ regis a prioratu S. Jacobi Briftol ad monaft. de Ambrefbury.

Pat. 28. Edward 1. 1300, n. 17. de terra de effelega et feria, &c.

Pat. 13. Edward 3. 1339, p. 2. m. 16. vel. 17.

Pat. 20. Richard 2. 1396, p. 2. m. 22.

Pat. 1. Henry 4. 1399. p. 7. m. 6. vel. 7.

Pat. 7. Edward 4. 1467. p. 1. m.

for the faid priory of St. James and lands belonging thereto, manor-houfe, tenements, and hereditaments, in the county of Glocefter. It appears by a deed of fale penes me the following churches paid H. Brayne and his heirs in right of patronage an annual rent or penfion, formerly referved to the monaf_ tery of Tewkfbury, viz. the rectory of St. Peter, 1 l. rectory of Chrift Church, 10 s. rectory of St. John for the church, 10 s. and the churchyard, 13 s. 4 d. rectory of St. Ewen, 6 d. and 1 lb. of wax, the rectory of St. Michael, 4 s. vicarage of St. Philip and Jacob, 1 l. 6 s. 8 d. By this eafy and cheap pur- chafe Brayne and his heirs enjoyed this large eftate and the above penfions and advowfon of the parfonage or rectory of St. James, as it is in fome deeds called, but it may be rather deemed a donative, as by the deed Brayne was always bound to find a prieft for the church and to allow him a ftipend for the cure of fouls there; alfo the right of patronage to the feveral churches in Briftol above-mentioned that paid him the penfions, with all tythes of corn, hay, wool, lamb, &c. belonging to the church of St. Philip and St. Jacob, and the cuftoms and all profits of the fair and prifage of wine in Whitfon week, which belonged to the priory of St. James; alfo the right of pre- fentation to the vicarages of the parifh churches of Mangotsfield and Staple- ton, the former paying him 1 lb. of wax, the latter 2 lb. yearly. Robert Brayne, Efq; on the death of his father fucceeded to thefe eftates, and from him they defcended to Dame Emma, wife of Sir Charles Somerfet, and to Ann Winter, wife of G. Winter, Efq; fifters and co-heireffes to the faid Robert Brayne, as appears by deed of partition, dated 27th January, 21 ft Elizabeth, 1579, penes me. Sir Charles Somerfet enjoyed the fame with the patronage of the churches until his death, 11th March, 1598. He was buried in his church of St. James, and left an only daughter, who married Sir Charles Redcliff Gerrard, Knight.

By an old deed it appears that this churchyard, &c. was leafed for thirty years to George Harrington, mayor, and others, the parifhioners, by Sir C. Gerrard, 15th October, 1617, for the fum of 26 l. 13 s. 4 d. as a fine, toge- ther with the herbage of the faid churchyard, all privy tythes and oblations, alfo tythe pigs, and all tythes of gardens and orchards lying and being within the parifh of St. James, except tythes of hay, corn, grain, lambs, calves, or wool, belonging to the manor-houfe of St. James, yielding and paying yearly to the faid Sir Charles Gerrard the fum of 3 l. 6 s. 8 d. and providing an able and fufficient paftor or curate for the church, and paying all tenths, procurations, &c. going out of the faid rectory or parfonage, and

keeping

keeping the church and chancel in good reparations when required to the end of the faid term.

About the year 1626 Sir Charles Gerrard granted and conveyed the premifes then in leafe to the churchwardens and inhabitants, to Robert Aldworth and G. Harrington and their heirs in truft for the mayor and corporation, who then received the 3l. 6d. 8d. and 2s. 6d or a couple of capons in lieu of tythes, and for the church-yard as appears by the chamberlain's receipt, who ftill continues to receive the fame; and alfo the feveral penfions out of the churches of St. Peter, Chrift-Church, St. Ewen's, St. Michael, and St. Philip's; to which and to this church of St. James the mayor and corporation of Briftol have now the right of prefentation, the firft time they exercifed this right was in the year 1627, and they gave for all thefe advowfons the fum of 450l. only, as appears by Sir Charles Gerrard's receipt the 18th of May 1627. After this leafe had expired the corporation of the city, the 19th of July 1670, by an aft of common council agreed to grant the parifhioners and feoffees of the parifh another leafe for 30 years, if Mr. Paul the minifter fhould fo long live and continue minifter, and receive the agreed ftipend of 40l. per annum, being a moiety of the profits of the fair,* as appears by an entry in the veftry books, except and referved to the corporation the great tythes and the parfonage-houfe, which Mr. Paul then let out, built lately by fome well difpofed perfon, and which houfe is for the fole ufe of the minifter and his fucceffors for ever, except alfo the yearly rent of 3l. 6s. 8d. and the moiety of the profits of the fair to the faid minifter to be paid half yearly, the parifhioners to pay all fubfidies, tenths &c. and repair the chancel.

The 17th of July the 24th of Cha. 2d. 1672, the corporation of Briftol purchafed of the King the feveral rents referved to the crown payable by H. Brayne and his heirs for the church of St. James and the lands belonging thereto. Vid. p. 132.

This priory and its fuperb buildings being thus fold and parted between different perfons, were foon difpofed of to others, and the old erections converted to various ufes; and the ruin of it is become fo compleat, that no traces of it at prefent (1788) are feen.

The church alone remains to point out its fite, which Robert Earl of Glocefter founded in 1130, and it was called according to Leland, " the chapel of the Bleffed Virgin Mary and St. James," which was made a parifh church (the city increafing towards the then priory) upon petition of the inhabitants to Thomas Chefterton then abbot of Tewkefbury and to the priory

A A A   of

* In the year 1689 the churchwardens received for the ftandings of the fair about 80l.

of St. James, who admitted them to hear mafs and to celebrate all other divine offices for the living and the dead as in other diocefan churches on certain conditions agreed upon by a deed of indenture, penes me, dated at Tewkefbury St. Andrew's day 1374; the prior was to appoint one officiating minifter or clerk, called in the deed Aquæbajulum or carrier of the holy water, or more if neceffary : the provifion and donation of which office was to be referved always to the prior, and he was to be fupported by a moiety of the profits arifing from the fixing of pales or any thing elfe penetrating or occupying the foil of the church-yard at the fair annually held there at the feaft of St. James, together with half the profits arifing from ringing the bells for the dead, and at their anniverfaries, and two proceffionals. The parifhioners on their part were to build one fquare belfry (campanile) of ftone in form of a tower, at their own expence, but the prior to find the ftone and earth for the mortar, as much as was neceffary and could be found within the limits of the priory and its demefnes; that the bells fhould be placed therein at the joint expence of both parties, and not to be removed but by the confent of both, and to be ufed in common by both, and to be repaired at their mutual expence.

Hence it appears that this church was part of it parochial, and part of it conventual, belonging to the priory or convent: and William of Worcefter, p. 290, defcribes the nave of the one as joining and annext to the nave of the other, and meafuring 22 yards in breadth and $15\frac{1}{2}$ yards in length : and p. 247 he mentions, " the parifh church of St. James near the church of the priory in the Eaft part of the town of Briftol." It had a chancel, but that is pulled down, being the monaftery church or chapel aforementioned ; and fo the tower is left ftanding on the Eaft end between the church and chancel, and ferved formerly to the ufe both of the parifh and convent.

The church-yard or fpacious burying ground belonging to this church was confecrated by Simon Bifhop of Worcefter about the year 1129, as appears by his deed of confirmation * of all tythes and churches which this church poffeffed, in which is mentioned that of St. Peter of Briftol, within (infra) or beneath the caftle and without the lordfhip of the borough; and it adds, " moreover in that day in which he dedicated the church-yard of the church of St. James† at Briftol, then in building, (becaufe the burgeffes ufed to be carried to burial where they would out of his diocefe) he commanded by his epifcopal authority, that none of the faid city fhould now be carried elfewhere to be buried except to Tewkefbury; he alfo there appointed and

ordained

---

* Stephens Addit. to Dugd. Monaft. v. 2. p. 191. No. 161. 24.

† " Cemiterium Ecclefiæ Sancti Jacobi apud Briftol ædificandæ dedicavit."

ordained that the church fhould be fubjcct by a perpetual right to the monaftery of St. Mary of Tewkefbury on the petition of mafter Benedict the abbot, and with the confent of Robert the King's fon Earl of Glocefter, and the Countefs Mabilia his wife."

This deed afcertains the time of the foundation of this church to be when Benedict was abbot, who continued fo from 1124 to 1137, when he died, fo that at a medium 1130 may be deemed nearly the time when it was firft built and confecrated, which is 18 years before the great monaftery of St. Auguftin in this city (now the cathedral) was built.

The church of St. James being at firft only a chapel to the adjoining priory, was not a very large or magnificient ftructure, though it is not void of elegance and beauty, the arches of the ailes however are admired as being of the true Saxon architecture, femicircular, with pillars round, plain and maffive, the capitals a very little ornamented — a fpecies of arch Robert Earl of Glocefter the founder feems to have copied from fome in the fine old caftle of Briftol, which he was repairing and enlarging at this very time: it confifts of three ailes of equal length, the middle is 29 feet and a half broad and 47 feet two inches high, and the whole breadth of the church from North to South is 66 feet.

At the Weft end is an organ and gallery, towards the erecting of which Edward Colfton Efq; gave 100l. The tower which is built of freeftone is very ftrong, plain but neat, 29 yards and 2 feet in height, adorned at prefent with a modern baluftrade and an urn at each corner: here is a very mufical peal of 8 bells, with a clock and dial at the South fide: — The veftry-room at the fouth weft end defaces this fouth view of it, the only one that can be taken (vid. plate). — The weft end of the middle aile is in a great meafure hid by the parifh houfes, which buildings bring in a revenue to the church. — There is here a pretty Gothic window, the figure may be feen in the plate, and other embellifhments in that tafte; this weftern end being formerly the entrance ufed by the monks. — This church was repaired at the expence of 600l. by the veftry and parifhoners when the Rev. Mr. Bayley was incumbent, about the year 1698; and it was again repaired about the year 1768, the altar embellifhed with a painting of the transfiguration, new pews and fpacious galleries erected the better to accommodate the numerous parifhioners with room, but ftill it is very infufficient for fo large a parifh. Application therefore has been lately (1787) made to parliament and an act obtained for dividing it into two parifhes, and erecting another church to be called St. Paul's.

So ftrict obfervers of the fabbath were the people of this parifh no longer ago than 1679, that at a veftry then held here four perfons were judged guilty of a moſt heinous crime and were cited into the ſpiritual court for purloining the Lord's day in travelling to Bath on foot, to the great diſhonour of Almighty God and true religion, for which they confeſſed their ſins in the ſaid court and paid 20s. for the uſe of the pariſh. — The preſent patrons of this church are the corporation of Briſtol, and the value of the living above 400l. per annum. In the year 1291, amongſt the valuations of the ſeveral benefices taken from the Lincoln manuſcript, is the following, "the priory of St. James, Briſtol, without the borough, paid to the church of Tewkeſbury 23 marks (15l. 6s. 8d.) per annum, and ſeveral churches paid penſions to the prior of St. James, viz. St. Michael's, St. Ewin's &c.

The following is a LIST of the MINISTERS of this Church.

PATRONS.		
Abby of Tewkeſbury.	1164	Picard, clerk to William Earl of Gloceſter. The monks in turn belonging to the priory performed the divine offices in the church till the diſſolution.
Henry Brayne, Eſq;	1544	Bartholemew Owyne, he died May 10th 1570.
Sir Charles Somerſet.	1571	William Wolff.
	1576	David Williams, diſplaced the next year.
	1577	William Jones, died 1585.
	1586	Thomas Twinborow, died 1594.
	1594	Thomas Newton.
Sir Charles Gerrard.	1601	John Powell.
	1616	John Maſon.
Corporation of Briſtol.	1629	William Batchellor, died the 30th of June 1636.
	1636-7	John Paul, not conforming he reſigned 1663.
	1663	Thomas Horne, died 1697, buried in this church.
	1697	Benjamin Baily, died the 25th of April 1720, aged 49, he publiſhed a volume of Lent ſermons.
	1720	Samuel Creſwick, D. D. 1727 Dean of Briſtol, and afterwards tranſlated to the deanry of Wells, but held this cure till 1753.
	1753	—— Price, removed from Temple, buried here and ſucceeded by
	1771	Carew Reynel, buried here and ſucceeded by
	1783	Dr. Small, the preſent incumbent.

The

The Rev. Mr. Batchellor, Mr. Paul, and Mr. Horne had feveral fums paid them by the parifh veftry (befides the yearly collection from the parifhioners) as wages, fuch as 30l. 40l. and 50l. which as leffees under the corporation bound to find a minifter they were obliged to pay.

The impropriation of the chapel of Stapleton dedicated to the Holy Trinity, as well as Mangotsfield, belonged to this church ; and becaufe they of Stapleton ufed always to bury at St. James's, the abbot of Tewkefbury the 5th of May 1438 granted them licence to bury at Stapleton, fo as they came to hear mafs at St. James's, and they paid two pounds of wax for this privilege for ever. By ancient deeds without date it appears that Poyntz granted to the church of St. James tythe of hay in Tockyng ton manor.

The chauntries in this church were three, one in the 1ft year of Henry 4th. eftablifhed by John Stone by licence from the King; he gave the prior two meffuages and one fhop in Briftol and its fuburbs, for one monk to celebrate mafs daily for his foul at the altar of St. Thomas. — John Spicer fheriff of Briftol, by will the 19th of Henry 6th. 1440, founded a chauntry here for one prieft and feven monks to fing mafs for ever for the repofe of his foul and his wife Avis's, and for all the faithful; the annual rents by the rent roll penes me, amounted to 10l. 1s. diftributed to the prior, monks and finging priefts, to the mayor and fheriffs for attending ; the bedeman and for wax tapers, and for bread for the dole to the poor. — William Ponam by will 1454 gave feveral tenements for a chauntry at the altar of the Virgin Mary to be celebrated for his and his wife Edith's fouls, and for his obiit the 9th of February, the proctors to be paid for attending and diftributing bread to the poor. Thefe two laft chauntries were fequeftered to the King's ufe the 1ft of Edward 6th. for non-payments of fubfidies and tenths. See p. 63, 64.

There are in this church but few monuments : — The firft to be mentioned is the founder of this priory and church, Robert Earl of Glocefter, of whofe character and fame fee before in the chapter of the caftle, pages 194. 209. In the fouth wall once there was a ftone figure preferved of a man habited like a pilgrim, fuppofed to be for him, which is remembered by fome old perfons now living,* which in the feveral repairs this church has received is now deftroyed and loft, or concealed by the high wainfcot feats there.

The Princefs Eleonora (called the Damoifelle of Brittany) was buried+here

after

---

* In the fouth aile near the belfry door in 1710 was a tomb, with a naked figure at full length, fuppofed then to be for the founder Robert Earl of Glocefter, manufcript penes me. — + 1. Cart. Antiq. K. n. 30 Scil. R. Henr. 2d. de libertate. patent 25 H. 3. M. 1. de Amotione coporis Alionoræ confanguineæ Regis a prioratu Sancti Jacobi Briftol ad monafter. de Ambrefbury.

after a cruel confinement of 40 years in Briftol caftle by King John her unnatural uncle, who had ufurped her right to the crown of England : her body was removed hence to the nunnery of Ambrefbury in Wiltfhire, to which fhe had given the manor of Melkfham near Lacock in Wilts, a licence being obtained for its removal of King Henry the 3d. the 25th year of his reign, 1241.

The next perfon to be mentioned is Sir Charles Somerfet, who with his lady Emma lie buried on the fouth fide of the altar; and a very handfome monument is erected there to their memory, with the following infcription : againft the monument is the ftatue of a man in armour kneeling at an altar, and oppofite to him his wife in the fame pofture, and behind her an only daughter alfo kneeling; it is a fpacious lofty monument adorned on each fide with Corinthian pillars, and embellifhed at top with the arms of the family in a large fhield:

Memoriæ & pietati facrum
Carolus hoc parvo tegitur fub marmore MAGNUS,
Corpore procero & præluftri ftemmate MAGNUS,
Sed famâ, virtute, fide (ut fas credere) MAJOR
Per zelum Cælum fcandens fit MAXIMUS ; adde
Principis ut vivens fuerat vexillifer ifte,
Principis ut moriens Chrifti vexillifer ifte.

My body earth, my breath was borrow'd ayre,
My dated leafe expired years of ftrife,
My foul with ftamp of God, temple of prayer,
Diffolv'd by death mounted to glorious life :
Life was but lent conditional to dye,
Death made the period of mortalitye,
And gave me entrance to eternitye.

Above the heads of the figures on the table within a fcroll is the following infcription :

Sir Charles Somerfet Knight 5th fon * to the Right Honourable Henry Earl of Worcefter and ftandard bearer unto her Majefties honourable band of gentlemen penfioners who married Eme widow of Giles Morgan of Newport Efquire, daughter and co-heirefs to Henry Brayne Efq; by whom he had one fole daughter firft married to Ratcliff Gerrard Efq; and after to Edward Fox Efq; he deceafed the 11 day of March Anno Domini 1598, being of
the

* See the pedigree of the Earls of Worcefter, and Dukes of Beaufort in Atkyns's Glocefter-fhire, p. 244.

the age of 64 years who lyeth here intombed with his wife Eme who departed Anno Domini 1590.

On a brafs plate at the entrance of the middle aile was the following infcription to Robert Daws, fon to Samuel Daws of Wotton-under-edge in Glocefterfhire, clothier, who died the 31ft of July 1667, aged 16.

> Matris ego quondam fola & chariffima proles
> Hic jaceo tumulo conditus ecce meo:
> Doctrinæ ftudio fimul ac pietatis amore
> Incubui, fragilis dum mihi vita fuit:
> At deus incurfu properantem femper eodem
> Abftulit, & cælis eft mihi fola quies.

In the north aile againft the wall are the following monuments and infcriptions:

To David Barrett M. B. who died Feb. 28. 1734. aged 40.

To Tho. and Eliz. Hicks grand children of Henry Dighton Efq; Tho. died Sept. the 1ft. 1689. Eliz. 28 Dec. 1694. Alfo

To Tho. Hicks Gent. who died the 10 of Jan. 1716 aged 69 and Martha his wife who died 6 July 1719 aged 68.

To Mr. Henry Dighton who died the 15th of March 1673 aged 64 and Judith his wife who died the 30th of Jan. 1721 aged 87 and George Dighton their eldeft fon who died the 23d of April 1702 aged 68.

Againft the weft wall is a marble monument with an infcription:— To Mary Scandrett daughter of George Dighton wife of Captain Chriftopher Scandrett, who died Dec. the 20th 1737 aged 66 with Chriftopher Mary and George their children.

In the fouth wall is a marble monument:— To Mary the wife of Walter Edwards Efq; daughter to the Right Honourable Richard Freeman of Battford in the county of Glocefter Efq; fometime Lord High Chancellor of Ireland, diftinguifhed by her birth but much more by her virtues, highly exemplary in the characters of wife and parent; conftant in her devotions, unblemifhed in her life. She died the 12 of July 1736 in the 37th year of her age leaving iffue 2 fons Walter and Tho. arms F. erm and S. party per bend a lion rampant or. quartered with F. az. 3 lozenges in feff. or.

On the firft pillar next the fouth window is a handfome monument with the following infcription and arms, F. er. and S. party per bend a lion rampant or. quartered with F. G. a chevron er. between 3 efcallops or.

Juxta hanc parietem in adjacente areâ triumphalem Chrifti fervatoris reditum expectat, Thomas Edwards armiger. vir, in lege municipali exercitatiffimus,

fpectatæ

fpeĉatæ fidei, probitatis eximiæ, et fingularis induftriæ, cui, five clientium numerum, five varia, quæ expedivit negotia, fpeĉemus, pancos admodum in his omnibus reperiemus pares, fuperiorem neminem. illi in laboris folatium (rara vivendi conditione) conceffit deus, ut non imminuto animi vigore, non gravï morbo implicitus, fine tædio, fine vitæ faftidio, fœlix conjuge, liberis, fortunis, ad extremum deveniret feneĉutem: et cum nihil amplius vel in votis reftaret, ut morte facili, et optimo cuique invidenda, inter fuorum lacrimas et fufpiria e vivis excederet: nuptias bis fecit, e primis filium unicum, tres filias fufcepit; e fecundis fex filios, duas filias, ex ambabufquinque filios, duas filias reliquit fuperftites. Ipfe obijt 7 mo. die Julij A. D. 1727°. Ætatis fuæ 83 tio natus 17 die Martii 1644 to.

Jana Edwards filia Johannis Walter Thomæ Edwards uxor dileĉiffima, & vere vidua cum quo conjunĉiffime vixit annos quadraginta quinque matrona omni laude digniffima eodem loco fuos cineres reponi voluit, obiit Februarii oĉavo die A. C. 1733 tio. Ætatis fuæ 81 mo.

On a brafs tablet near the upper door was cut a figure in an alderman's robes, with four fons behind him; oppofite to him his wife with four daughters behind her, all kneeling before an altar, with an infcription to Henry Gibbs mayor, who died the 19th of May 1636, aged 73, and to Ann his wife who died 15th December 1631, aged 70.

In the chancel on a ftone — Wm. Batchelor minifter and preacher of this parifh died 3 Jan. 1636.

On another thus on a brafs plate — Hic jacet Rev. Benj. Bayly A. M. hujus ecclefiæ per annos prope viginti tres Reĉor cum tribus liberis multifque aliis amicis, Quibufcum affurgere & in corpore immortali revivifcere, O! Quantum Gaudium! Quantæ congratulationes! O Deus Bone! O Benigne Pater! Te oramus ut acceleres regnum tuam, nofque quam fubitò tubam iftam cæleftem quâ ex bifce fordibus ad nubes evocemur, exaudiamus: O! fimus ex eorum numero, pro quibus Chrifti fanguis haud incaffim effundebatur, cœlifque recepti Beatificâ vifione fruamur: tibi pater filioque tuo falvatori noftro gratias pro tanto mumere in æternum agentes. Obiit 25 Aprilis A. D. 1720. Ætatis fuæ 49.

On another was a long Latin infcription to Wm. Hobfon, fon of Henry Hobfon; he died 1654, Ætat fuæ 57, with the arms quartered Hobfon and Colfton. — And near this, to Margaret Colfton, who married the faid Wm. Hobfon; fhe was only daughter of William Colfton the elder, fhe died 11 May 1647, aged 41. — John Pears, a worthy benefaĉor to this city, died 18 Aug. 1662.

The Chefter family are buried 'here; on a raifed tomb covering a vault againft the wall of the old priory were infcriptions

To James Chefter, who died the 17th of March, 1560.

To William Chefter, who died the 1ft of January, 1572-3.

To Edward Chefter, who died in 1580.

To Walter the fon of William Chefter, who died the 21ft of September, 1641, aged 88.

Thomas Chefter, fon of the above William Chefter, was mayor of Briftol: he purchafed the manor of Almondfbury, and was high fheriff of the county of Glocefter in 1577, and was buried Sept. 24, 1583.

As this parifh is very large and confequently is burdened with many poor, fo it is very happy to be fo liberally endowed with charitable inftitutions and benefactions, as appears by the following accounts and the tables of benefactors.

BENEFACTORS to the Church and Poor of St. James's Parifh.

		l.	s.	d.
1599, Alderman Coale gave to the almfhoufe on St. James's-back 4l. per annum for ever - - - -		80	0	0
1604, Mrs. Alice Coale gave 12l. per annum, to be paid by 20s. per month, to three almfhoufes in this parifh for ever		240	0	0
Mr. Thomas Brooks gave a tenement to the almfhoufe in Lewin's-mead of 6l. per annum to twelve poor for ever		120	0	0
Alderman Robert Kitchen gave 40s. per annum to four houfe-holders quarterly for ever - -		40	0	0
Alderman Packer gave 10s. per annum to the poor for ever out of the houfe at the Grofs Keys by the Fifh Market		10	0	0
Mr. Cox gave 20s. to the poor for ever - -		20	0	0
1536, Mrs. Harrington gave 2s. in bread weekly.				
Alderman George Harrington gave 40s. per annum to the poor for ever - - - - -		40	0	0
Mr. Thomas Clements gave 20s. per annum to the poor for ever - - - - - -		20	(	
Mr. William Sage gave 3l. per annum to the poor, and 20s. for two fermons yearly, for ever - -		80	0	0
Mr. Pierce gave 20s. for a fermon the 5th of November yearly - - - - - -		20	0	0
Mr. Francis Gleed, fome time fheriff, gave 40s. to be paid 10s, quarterly to four houfekeepers for ever -		40	0	0
Alderman Richard Vickris gave 1s. per week for ever		52	0	0

B b b   Alderman

	l.	s.	d.
Alderman Miles Jackſon gave a garden the rent thereof to the poor in bread for ever.			
William Davis and his wife gave 50l. the profit thereof to the poor for ever - - - - -	50	0	0
1668, John Lewis gave 10l. the profit thereof to the poor	10	(	
Mr. Thomas Walter, woollen-draper, gave 4s. in bread weekly to the poor for ever - - -	10	8	0
Alderman Arthur Farmer gave 40l. the profit thereof to ſix houſekeepers for ever - - - -	40	0	0
Thomas Farmer, gentleman, gave 50l. the profit thereof in bread and coal to the poor for ever - -	50	0	0

Second Table.

	l.	s.	d.
1668, Abraham Birkins gave 40s. yearly to the poor for ever	40	0	0
Mr. William Hobſon the elder, merchant, ſome time ſheriff of this city, gave 40s. per annum to the poor of this pariſh by 10s. a quarter for ever - - -	40	0	0
Mrs. Farmer, reliƐt of Mr. Thomas Farmer, gentleman, gave 40l. the profit whereof to the poor in bread for ever	40	0	0
1670, Mr. Charles Powell, ſome time ſheriff of this city, gave 20l. the profit whereof to the poor in bread for ever -	20	0	0
1671, Thomas Geſt, of Exon, tucker, gave 10l. the profit whereof to the poor in bread for ever - - -	10	0	0
Henry Price, gentleman, gave 100l. the profit whereof to poor houſekeepers on St. Thomas-day yearly for ever	100	0	0
1672, Henry Dighton, of this pariſh, brewer, gave 5l. per annum to buy ten coats for ten poor men of this pariſh for ever	100	0	0
1673, Mr. Robert Markham, of London, gave 5l. the profit thereof to be given to the poor on St. James's-day yearly for ever - - - - - -	5	0	0

Third Table.

	l.	s.	d.
1678, Mrs. Mary Walter, widow, gave 20l. half of the profit to be given to the miniſter for a ſermon on the firſt Lord's-day next after the 9th day of November, in the afternoon ; and the other half of the profit in bread to the poor for ever - - - -	20	(	
1679, Captain Gabriel Deane, of this pariſh, gave 30l. the profit to the poor for ever - - - -	30	0	0

1679,

		l.	*s.*	*d.*
1679, Richard Chriſtmas, of this pariſh, gave 50l. the profit in bread weekly for ever - - - -		50	0	0
1680, Mr. Robert Haines and Mrs. Catherine Large gave 100l. to the poor - . - - -		100	0	0
1681, Ann wife of Mr. Thomas Horne, gave 20l. to the poor		20	0	0
1685, Mr. Jeremiah Holway gave 30l. the profit thereof to the poor in bread for ever - -. - -		30	0	0
Timothy Parker gave 5l. the profit for ever - -		5	0	0

FOURTH TABLE.

1685, Mrs. Catherine Dighton gave 50l. the profit of it to be given to ten poor widows of this pariſh by 5s. apiece yearly for ever - - - -		50	(	
1686, Mr. Samuel Hale, merchant, gave 10l. the profit thereof weekly to the poor in bread; and alfo the intereſt of 230l. towards the apprenticing of poor children in feven parifhes of this city yearly for ever, of which this is one		240	0	0
1687, Sir William Cann, Knight and Baronet, gave 100l. to four parifhes, whereof this hath a quarter part, the profit thereof to be diſtributed to the poor the 8th of January for ever - - - - -		25	0	0
Mr. Godfrey Vanitterne gave 20l. the profit to the poor yearly for ever - - - -		20	0	0
Mr. Anthony Wood, fugar-baker, gave 20l. the profit to eight poor houfekeepers on the 2d of April for ever		20	0	0
1690, Mr. Edward Tilly, merchant, gave 25l. the profit thereof to be given to the poor of this pariſh in bread weekly for ever - - - - -		25	0	0

FIFTH TABLE.

1688, John Lawford, Efq; fome time mayor and alderman of this city, gave 50l. the profit thereof to be given to the poor of this pariſh in bread weekly for ever -		50	0	0
1690, Mr. John Sandford, junr. gave 10l. the intereſt to be diſtributed to the poor of this pariſh the 14th of February for ever		10	0	0
Mr. John England gave 10l. the churchwardens and over-feers being intruſted to diſtribute the profit thereof to fix poor widows, not receiving alms, on St. Thomas'-day for ever - - - -		10	0	0

1690,

1690, Samuel Poſkins, of this pariſh, mariner, left 5l. to be given   *l.*   *s.*   *d.*
in bread to the poor, which was diſtributed.

1703, Mrs. Mary Bickham, widow, gave 100l. the profit thereof
to the poor of this pariſh in bread every Sunday for ever   100   0   0

1705, Iſaac Davis, Eſq; ſome time ſheriff of this city, gave 100l.
the profit thereof to be given to the poor of this pariſh in
bread weekly for ever   -   -   -   -   100   0   0

1713, The gift of Mr. Stephen Chapman, ſenr. 20s. per annum
to the miniſter of this pariſh and his ſucceſſors for ever
to preach a preparatory ſermon to the ſacrament upon
Good Friday, and another 20s. to be diſtributed equally
to eight poor houſekeepers not receiving alms, but frequenting public prayers and the ſacrament, at the will
of the executor, on the 20th of December yearly for
ever   -   -   -   -   -   -   40   0   0

1716, Mr. John Lord, junr. of this city, merchant, gave 10l.
the intereſt thereof to be diſtributed in bread yearly
to ſuch poor inhabitants of this pariſh as the churchwardens ſhall think fit   -   -   -   -   10   0   0

William Whittington, late of Stapleton, in the county of
Gloceſter, Eſq; deceaſed, gave to this pariſh 100l. to be
laid out in purchaſing of lands in fee, which he ſo
ſettled as the yearly rents thereof may be by the miniſter and churchwardens diſpoſed of according to their
diſcretion for the uſe of ſuch decayed and poor inhabitants as ſhall not receive other alms or aſſiſtance   100   0   0

1718, Mrs. Eſther Paul gave to the poor of St. James in Briſtol
5l. the profit thereof to be laid out in bread, and diſtributed on St. Paul's-day yearly   -   -   5   0   0

1722, Thomas Winſtone, Eſq; gave 100l. the intereſt thereof
to be laid out in buying of ſix coats for ſix poor men not
receiving alms, to be delivered to them on the Sunday
next after the 22d day of November yearly for ever   100   0   0

Sixth Table.

1715, The Rev. Mr. Stephen Chapman, deceaſed, gave 40s.
yearly to this pariſh for ever, whereof 20s. to the miniſter for a ſermon on the 30th of January, and 20s. to
ſuch poor of the ſaid pariſh who attend ſuch ſermon   40   0   0

1718,

1718, Mr. Michael Pope, a diffenting minifter of this parifh, gave 50l. the intereft thereof, viz. 20s. for a fermon on the Sunday next after the feaft of St. Michael, and 30s. in bread to the poor the week following yearly for ever   50   0   0

1724, Mr. John Brittain gave 20l. the intereft thereof to the poor in bread on Chriftmas-day yearly for ever   20   (

1727, Mrs. Alice James, widow, gave 40l. the intereft thereof to the poor not receiving alms, whereof 20s. to two poor widows and 20s. in bread on Chriftmas-day yearly for ever   40   0   0

1730, Mr. John Haythorne gave 30l. the profit thereof, viz. 20s. to the minifter for a fermon on Chriftmas-day in the afternoon, 6s. in bread to the poor, and 4s. to the clerk and fexton yearly for ever   -   -   -   30   0   0

1731, Mr. Charles Weekes gave 100l. the intereft thereof to be laid out in fix gowns to be given to fix poor women on the 1ft of November yearly for ever   -   --   100   0   0

Mrs. Martha Stephens left by her will, dated 1726, two meffuages or tenements, the profit thereof (after the deceafe of her hufband William Stephens) to be given to ten poor widows (not receiving alms) yearly for ever.

1720, George Packer, of this city, merchant, left by will 33s. 3d. per annum to this parifh for ever, whereof 21s. to the minifter for a fermon on the 28th of January, 5s. to the organift, 5s. to the clerk, and 2s. 6d. to the fexton   33   10   0

1723, Mrs. Ann Merrick gave 200l. the intereft thereof to be paid the minifter for reading prayers in the church once every day for ever   -   -   -   -   200   0   0

1729, Mr. Ifaac Hollier, of Woolverhampton, left per will 10l. the intereft thereof to the poor of this parifh in bread yearly for ever   -   -   -   -   -   10   0   0

1734, Mrs. Jane Edwards gave 21l. the profit to augment the gift of her mother, Mrs. Mary Walter, viz. 10s. 6d. to the minifter, and 10s. 6d. to the poor in bread on the firft Sunday after the 9th of November for ever   -   21   0   0

1741, Mr. James Jeanes, merchant, left by will 130l. the intereft thereof to be laid out in fix coats for fix poor men, and fix gowns for fix poor women, inhabitants of this parifh at Chriftmas yearly for ever   -   -   -   130   0   0

In

In the middle aile are two brafs branches. That before the pulpit has engraven on it thus: " The gift of Hugh Cornifh, of this parifh, houfe-carpenter, the 21ft of December, 1706." That near the organ-loft thus: " Jofeph Badger, churchwarden, Thomas Jones, William Barwick, Jofeph Hifcox, Jofeph Hook, feur. Jofeph Wood, and William Prior, gave this branch to St. James's church, September 14, 1697.

N. B. The 1s. per week given to the poor of this parifh by Alderman Richard Vickris, and the fame fum per week to Redcliff and Temple, &c. in all 10l. 8s. come out per annum of two tenements in High-ftreet.

It appears from the rent roll, that the annual rents paid for houfes in hand and lands on leafe for lives paying lord's rent belonging to this parifh church amounted in 1743 to 190l. 16s. 6d. per annum, and are probably fince by the good management of the veftry much increafed. There are alfo certain annuities or yearly gift money payable out of eftates fettled to the poor of this parifh, amounting to 84l. 18s.

YEARLY GIFTS.

	l.	s.	d.
The gift of Thomas Walter, woollen-draper, out of Hook's Mills eftate	10	8	0
Of Mr. Packer, out of a houfe on the Quay, near the Fifh Market	3	0	0
Of Mr. Cox, for coal, paid by the chamber of Briftol	1	0	0
Of Mr. Francis Gleed, by Chrift Church veftry	2		
Of Mr. Henry Dighton, in coats	5	0	0
Of Mr. Charles Weeks, in gowns	5	0	0
Of the Chamber of Briftol, fundry gifts	10	4	0
Of Mr. Thomas Clements, by Mr. Simkin, 1630	1	0	(
Of Mrs. Boucher and Langton, by the Merchants'-hall, as feoffees, to poor widows, at 5s. each, about 80l. to all the parifhes, of which this has a part, perhaps about	5	0	0
Of Mr. Birkin, paid by the churchwarden of St. Maryport	2	0	0
Of Alderman Vickris	2	12	0
Of St. Peter's Hofpital, for the poor-houfe in Barr's-lane	10	14	0
Of the treafurer of Queen Elizabeth's Hofpital	4	0	
Of Mr. Stephen Chapman, fenr. by Job Gardener's executors	1	0	0
Of Mr. Stephen Chapman, junr. by Mr. Okey's executors	1	0	0
Of Mr. James Tucker, out of a houfe in the Pithay	0	10	0
Of Mr. Winftone	5	0	0

The

	l.	*s.*	*d.*
The gift of Mrs. Dighton, in shifts - - - -	2	10	0
Of Mr. Whittington, out of a house in the croft	9	0	0
Of Michael Pope, for a sermon, &c. - -	2	10	0
Of Mr. John Haythorn, in bread and a sermon	1	10	0
£	84	18	0

This parish is of great extent, and has been every year increasing in buildings and number of inhabitants, which has occasioned it to be divided, 1788, into two parishes, and another church soon to be erected here to be called St. Paul's: see p. 85. A line drawn through Merchant-street, Barr's-lane, Stoke's-croft, and up through Hillgrove-street, marks the division of the two parishes, all on the right being allotted to St. Paul's. In 1749 it appears the whole parish consisted of 1347 houses rated to the poor at 733l. per annum, and there were that year 398 marriages, 400 christenings, 416 burials; but in 1559 there were only 8 marriages, 10 christenings, 7 burials. In 1709 the poor rate was 207l. 14s. 5d. King's tax 588l. 3s. 4d. burials 100, christenings 100, weddings 50. But now in the year 1788 each of these have been so amazingly increased by the new streets and numerous accession of inhabitants, as almost to exceed belief, and the rates for the poor have risen in proportion. From the 25th March, 1565, to the 13th February following, 188 persons died of the plague in this parish; from the 3d July, 1575, to the 20th Jan. following, 137; from the 20th August, 1603, to the 22d March, 1603-4, 390; from the 11th April, 1645, to the 18th February, 1645-6, 340 persons.

There were in this parish two frieries; one house of Franciscan or grey friers, another of Dominican or black friers. Whilst the order of grey friers flourished the custody of Bristol had nine convents under it, and each friery had a common seal; this of Bristol had St. Anthony of Padua.

It was the head convent of this custody. William of Worcester, 1480, thus describes it:—" Chorus ecclesiæ," i. e. " The choir of the church contains in length 28 yards or 50 paces, the breadth of the choir 9 yards or 18 paces, the length of the nave of the said church with the two great ailes contains 28 yards or 50 paces, the breadth of the nave with the two ailes contains 27 yards or 52 paces, the breadth of the belfry square tower contains 4 yards or 7 spaces; there are 4 arches in the north nave of the church, and as many in the south." Leland says, " The grey friers house was on the right bank of the Frome water, not far from Bartholomew's hospital." And that rightly describes its situation, as on the same side of Lewin's-mead with it, and at no great distance from it; the Presbyterian meeting-house and the large

sugar-house

fugar-houfe next it are built upon its fite, and not a trace of it now is to be feen, though once a large grand and noble building, being one of the capital cuflodies of Francifcans in the kingdom. Bifhop Tanner notes it, and refers to fome old deeds concerning it.

In an old deed penes me Spencer's almfhoufe ftill in being is defcribed as directly oppofite the houfe of the grey friers, which points out the fite of it as above given.

In the year 1334 in the church of the friers minors, Briftol, were ordained by the Bifhop of Worcefter 171 accolites, 150 fub-deacons, 39 deacons, and 73 priefts. Before the diocefe of Glocefter and Briftol were taken out of Worcefter the Bifhop had very numerous ordinations.

1485, Brother John Whitfield was cuftos of the cuftody of grey friers, Briftol.

This friery was founded before the year 1234, and after its diffolution King Henry 8th. granted the fite of it to the mayor and citizens of Briftol for public ufes: fee p. 134.

The black or Dominican friers, called alfo friers preachers from their office, was on the right hand of the Froom river, according to Leland, founded by Maurice de Gaunt, uncle to Robert de Gourney, fo that this houfe muft have been founded as early as 1228 or 1229. I refer to Tanner for the ancient deeds concerning it; though few of the houfes of the friers were ever endowed, yet many of them were large and flately buildings and had noble churches, in which great men often chofe to be buried, which brought great honour and profit by legacies to them: a curious grave ftone was dug up here with a very old date to it by the workmen in making foundations for building here in the year 1748: fee the engraved print. This church by the ruins of it appeared to be of large extent, and muft have been a magnificent pile of building. It extended from the Were on one fide towards Rofemary-lane on the other; one part of the cloifter is turned into a hall for the fmiths company, and ano-part for that of the bakers; and the Quakers meeting-houfe together with the burial ground and other buildings are upon the fite of this friery. The infcription on the engraved plate is as follows:

⋈ R E N N A L D Golde: Gift: Ici
  Dev: [cftu] De Sa Alme. E ------ G ----- MCC j.
In * 1321, Nicholas Saltford was prior of this friery.

                  In

* 14 Richard 2d. 16th June, the mayor, &c. made a compofition with Nicholas Saltford prior of the friers preachers (near the Were), whereby he granted the prior a feather of water, out of the pipe and conveyance that runs by the Barrs, and had its head near the chapel mill;

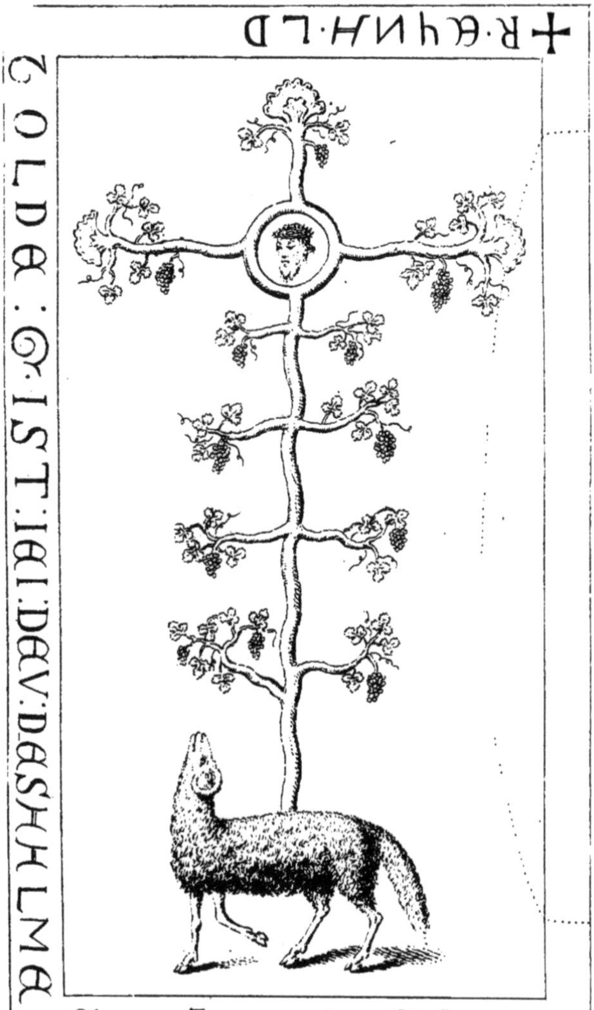

In 1530, John Hilfey, the black frier, of Briftol, was made Bifhop of Rochefter, and was the 66th bifhop: he enjoyed it but three years, Stow. William of Worcefter fays, p. 233. " The length of the choir of the church of friers preachers contains 26 yards or 44 paces, the breadth of the choir 8 yards or 14 paces, the length of the nave of the church 31 yards or 58 paces, its breadth 21 yards or 34 paces, the cloifter 40 paces on all 4 fides.— Maurice de Berkeley, Lord of Beverftone caftle, died 5th May, 1466, and it appears was buried here, as were (by the martyrology calendar of thefe friers) John Viel, Efq; firft fheriff of Briftol, who died 9th March, Walter Frampton, who died 2d January, Richard Spicer, 1ft June, Matthew de Gurnay, one of the founders of this houfe of friers, 28th Auguft, Lady Maud Denys, October, 1422, Sir William Daubeny, Knight, who lies in the choir : the heart of Robert de Gurnay is buried in this church, Anfelm de Gurney lies in the choir, who died 15th November."

The fite of this fpacious friery was granted, 31ft Henry 8th. 1539, to William Chefter, Efq;

Within this parifh are feven almfhoufes and an Infirmary, which have fucceeded the two frieries, the Francifcan and the Dominican here, to the much greater advantage of the public, and more effential good of individuals. In Lewin's-mead an almfhoufe was founded about the year 1493, (dedicated it is faid to the Holy Trinity) for thirteen perfons, by William Spencer, executor to the will of William Canynges, deceafed, out of the refiduary goods and eftate of the faid Canynges, and by his direction. He alfo appointed, 8th Henry 7th. 67l. 6s. 8d. to be lent to the bailiffs of the town for the time being, and 20l. to the mayor, they paying weekly 2s. to the prieft (or chaplain) of St. George's chapel on every Saturday, who fhould immediately diftribute the fame to the poor of this almfhoufe, which Mr. Spencer had built. (Vide Great Red Book penes camerar. Briftol, f. 317. and Book of Wills.) At prefent this almfhoufe is much out of repair and neglected. The rooms are upon the ground floor, low, and damp. Mr. Thomas Brookes, mayor, 1526, gave a tenement in Tucker-ftreet (called the Salmon) of 6l. per ann. for ever to this houfe : it is faid he charged all his lands in Briftol to pay

C c c   the

and the water of the fountain near the faid current by the conduit of the town ufq; ad le Key pipe to be repaired by the mayor, and brought into a barrel covered with an arch for their ufe : and on that condition the prior granted to the mayor his fountain called Pennywell, and the conduit leading from it to the garden of the faid friers, paying yearly to the prior of St. James 12d.—Page 178. Great Red Book. In the deeds referred to by Tanner are, pat. 51. Edward 3. m. 36. de fonte vocat. Pennywell, p. 15. Richard 2. m. 25. pro conductu aquæ faciendo a fonte vocat. Pennywell, 19 Richard 2. pro medietate prifarum pifcium regi.

the annuity of 6l. But their chief fubfiftence now is from weekly pay of the poor from St. Peter's Hofpital. Alice Cole, relict of Alderman Richard Cole, by her will, dated 1604, gave to thefe poor people 6s. 8d. per month for ever; it is paid by the treafurer of Queen Elizabeth's hofpital. The churchwardens of All Saints parifh for the time being pay them 2s. 6d. per quarter, as the gift of Alderman Cole, (fee his will.) Thomas Silk gave them 1l. per annum. The fite of this almfhoufe is defcribed in old deeds (penes me) to be oppofite the houfe of the grey friers, next Point-makers-hall, extending from Lewin's-mead into the water of Froom backwards, and over againft the diffolved houfe of the grey friers. It was granted the 13th of January, 18th Elizabeth, to the mayor and commonalty, at 1s. rent annually.

Another almfhoufe on St. James's-back is faid to be built by William Chefter, Efq; mayor, in his life time for fix perfons. By his will, dated 1558, he gave 6d. per week among them for ever, iffuing out of his lands called the Black Friers, within this parifh. Ann Golfton (1602) gave 4l. per annum to this almfhoufe. In the year 1557 Mr. Philip Griffith gave to thefe poor alms perfons 20s. per annum, as did (in the year 1582) Thomas Chefter, fon of William Chefter, 4s. per annum. In 1599 Alderman Richard Cole by will gave them 4l. per annum, alfo Alice his relict in 1604 gave by will 6s. 8d. per month for ever. William Carr, 1547, gave 1l. 1s. 4d. yearly conditionally.

In a lane called the Barr's is alfo another houfe for twelve poor perfons to inhabit, which was purchafed with the poor's money, in the year 1693, by the feoffees of the parifh, and rebuilt in 1752.

On the weft fide of Merchant-ftreet is an almfhoufe, built A. D. 1701, by the Worfhipful Company of Merchant Taylors of this city, where are nine rooms for the reception of poor men, members of that company, their wives, and widows. Their weekly pay from the Company is 3s. each. On every faint's day, and on every Wednefday and Friday throughout the year, are to be read there the morning prayers of the Church of England.

On the fouth fide of Stoke's-croft was built an almfhoufe in that memorable time of the South Sea bubbles, A. D. 1722, by Mr. Abraham Hook, merchant; his intention was to have endowed it for poor Proteftant Diffenters, but his defign never took place. At prefent there are twelve rooms for the reception of poor decayed women, who are placed in by the truftees of the Prefbyterian congregation in Lewin's-mead, who purchafed this houfe. — They live rent free, but have no weekly pay. Here is alfo an uncertain number of poor boys educated in reading and writing gratis, but their fupport is from their parents. At

At the north-eaſt end of Milk-ſtreet is a ſmall tenement where five poor women, maidens or widows, being Baptiſts, live rent free. Their weekly pay was 1s. 6d. each. This houſe was given and endowed by Mrs. Elizabeth Blanchard, who had never been married. She died about 1722.

In the year 1740 a neat hoſpital was built of freeſtone at the ſouth-weſt corner of Milk-ſtreet, (having over the door theſe words : " In memory of Mr. Thomas Ridley and Sarah Ridley, being brother and ſiſter never married, erected A. D. 1739.) In purſuance of Mrs. Ridley's will, dated 1716, her truſtees with 150l. ariſing from the intereſt of 2200l. which ſhe had given, purchaſed in the year 1735 a piece of ground in fee farm for this building. This hoſpital is for the ſupport of five old batchelors, and the like number of old maids, being Proteſtants, to inhabit there during life or till they ſhall marry. In the year 1742, the men and women were admitted into pay at 3s. each per week. Standfaſt Smith, apothecary, by will, gave theſe alms people all a ſuit of cloathes each at his death, and 10l. per annum for their better ſupport during the life of Hannah Powles, his ſervant-maid.

The Infirmary, the next charitable inſtitution in this pariſh, was firſt thought of in the year 1736, and in November that year a ſubſcription was opened for erecting it ; and in December the firſt general meeting of the ſubſcribers was held, at which ſome general rules were offered for the well governing ſuch a ſociety, which at ſeveral ſucceſſive meetings received alterations and additions. Certain buildings and ground in lower Magdalen-lane in this pariſh being judged a proper place for it were purchaſed on a leafe of 999 years of Mr. A. Sharpe of Dublin, the ground rent being 21l. per annum, and another ground rent of 2l. 16s. per annum. In 1737, 20th June, it was opened for the reception of out-patients, and the 15th December following for inpatients, Perſons of all parties and perſuaſions joined in this public charity, deſigned to be, what the title over the entrance expreſſes, Charity Universal, and calculated for the relief of the human ſpecies without diſtinction. Though it was capable at firſt of holding only 34 beds, yet as the ſcheme by voluntary ſubſcriptions had then never been tried out of London, there would have been great reaſon of doubting its ſucceſs, had not Mr. Elbridge, comptroller of the cuſtoms here, undertaken it almoſt under his ſingle direction and at his own expence. He lived long enough to ſee himſelf its great and general uſe, and having laid out in his life time in the building and furniture, &c. at leaſt 1500l. he left at his death in 1738 the ſum of 5000l. to it. From the year 1738 to the year 1756, 11532 in-patients were admitted and 22343 out-patients. How much it has ſince improved by additional benefactions, the

annual

annual accounts publifhed by the fociety fufficiently fhew, and the table of
benefactors, amongft whom the following fhould be recorded : *l.* *s.* *d.*

		l.	*s.*	*d.*
1742, The Corporation of this city, during pleafure, per ann.		30	0	0
The Society of Merchants, ditto	- - -	20	0	0
1745, The Right Hon. Thomas Earl of Thanet	-	500	0	0
1751, A friend of Paul Fifher	- · -	1000	0	0
Richard Percival, Efq;	- -	3000	0	0
1757, Onef. Tyndall, Efq;	- - - •	500	0	0
1761, Martha Payne	- -	500	0	0
1767, John Heylin, Efq;		500	(	
1771, Mary Iunys	• - - -	1000	0	0
1772, Right Hon. Thomas Earl of Thanet	- -	500	0	0
1774, Right Hon. Lord Berkeley of Stratton, in the 3 per cent.				
confols. annuities	- - - -	1000	0	0
Peter Wilder	- - - -	500	(	
John Scandrett	- - •	500	0	0
1777, Mary Ann Peloquin	- - -	5000	0	0
1781, William Miller, Efq; by his executors	- -	500	0	0
1782, Ann Hort	- - - -	500	0	0
1786, Elizabeth Bridgeman, New South Sea annuities	-	1000	0	0
1788, William Turner, of Wraxal, Efq;	- - -	1000	0	0

From the year 1738 to 1788 (fifty years) the money given to this charity in
particular fums at different times (by benefactors living or at their death by
will, and collected at places of public worfhip occafionally) amounts to the
fum of 45550l. and upwards, befides the yearly contributions and the fupport it receives from the annual fubfcribers, citizens and neighbouring
gentlemen.

In the year 1787 it was refolved to rebuild this Infirmary upon a larger
fcale upon the fame fpot. In 1788 one wing was compleated, the apartments
are more fpacious and lofty for free air, fo neceffary to prevent infection and
diffipate the noxious effluvia from the difeafed crouded together. It will be
a noble well-contrived building when finifhed, though it will be very expenfive
and break in upon the capital fund of fupport.

There are alfo in this parifh at prefent one Roman Catholic chapel on St.
James's-back, feven meeting-houfes of Proteftant Diffenters, one of Ana-
baptifts in Broadmead, one of Independents in Callowhill-ftreet, one Tabernacle of Methodifts under the rule of the late Mr. Whitefield's preachers,
one of Methodifts in the Horfe-fair under the rule of Mr. Wefley, one of

Moravians

Moravians in Magdalen-lane, one of Quakers in Rofemary-lane, and one of Prefbyterians in Lewin's-mead. The two laft occupy the very fpot and fite of the two frieries, the Dominican and Francifcan of old. The Quakers meeting-houfe is a neat, fpacious building, in a quiet, retired fituation ; and the meeting-houfe in Lewin's-mead is now rebuilding.

CHAP. XII.

Of the CHURCH and PARISH of St. AUGUSTINE the LESS, and the CARMELITE FRIERY, its Site, &c.

THIS Church was firft founded by the abbots of St. Auguftin's monaftery near it, as a chapel for the accommodation of the inhabitants, who had erected houfes and lived without the claufum or precincts of the convent. It had therefore a very early origin, probably foon after the erection of the monaftery. It is mentioned in Gaunt's deeds in the year 1240.

But in the year 1480 it was fo far decayed as to require to be rebuilt and much enlarged. Under that year William of Worcefter, p. 229, thus defcribes it, Ecclefia Parochialis, &c. i. e. "The parifh church of St. Auguftin newly built and erected this year 1480, contains in length with the two ailes excepting the choir 24 yards. The breadth of the faid church contains 6 yards or 18 feet, and each aile contains in breadth 4 yards or 12 feet; in the whole the breadth is 42 feet, as told me by a parifhioner. The length of the chancel when built will contain 10 yards."

To enlarge the church the ailes have been lengthened very confiderably at their Eaft end not many years ago, but after all it was found very infufficient for the parifhioners, many new ftreets being built in this healthy and pleafant part of the city. Two large fide galleries were therefore erected of late, and an organ placed in front at the weft end, the gift of Henry Cruger Efq; of this parifh, member for the city. Over the chancel on the knots of the fret are thefe two coats — a heart pierced with 3 nails, with J N — for John Newland, alias Nailheart — the other, in chief two mullets pierced, for the abbot Elliot, — both were great builders and have placed their arms in the

glafs.

glafs windows of this chancel, and the prebendal honfes as well as in the
cathedral — they probably contributed towards the building or repairing of
this church.

It is a plain fabric, has three long ailes with a chancel, and is neatly pewed;
has a tower built by contributions of the parifhioners with four pinnacles at
the weft end with two bells: it is large enough now conveniently to hold the
numerous congregation of this well-inhabited parifh: the church is well
fituated on the fide of the College-Green in the middle of a fpacious churchyard walled in.

The following have been VICARS of this church of St. Auguftin the Lefs.

PATRONS.			
Abbot and convent	1249		William ———, vicar.
of St. Auguftin's.	1291	18 Jan.	Serlo de Steynenton.
	1302		Walter Battayle.
	1311	6 July	Peter Tredington.
	1348	7 Nov.	John Besford.
	1361	29 April	Thomas Janekin or Jackfon.
	1365	8 Feb.	Richard Cobyngton—Rich. Barnefby
	1369	18 Oct.	John Rovyarc.
			John Cook.
	1372	25 Dec.	William Cote.
	1373		John Rovyare.
	1391		John Balle.
	1416	8 March	William Chew—by death of Balle.
	1464	26 Nov.	John Frewen—by death of Chew.
	1469	3 March	Richard Faunt—by death of Frewen.
	1471	22 June	Hugh Lewys, alias Martyn—by death of Faunt.
	1472	31 July	Philip King—by refignation of Lewis.
			Walter Morrys.
	1488	5 Oct.	John Gryffyth.
	1506	4 Dec.	Edm. Smallwood—by death of Gryffyth.
	1514	29 Nov.	William Wyett—by death of Smallwood.
Dean and Chapter	1541		Henry Collins.
of Briftol.	1546		Walter Ivye, vic.
	1594		William Robinfon.
	1604		Clement Lewis.
	1612		Robert Watfon, minifter.

PATRONS.		
Dean and Chapter	1632	Jacob Read—died Sept. 10.
of Briſtol.	1660	James Read.
		Mr. Wootton, vicar and maſter of the grammar-ſchool.
	1728	James Taylor M. A.—died 14 Aug. 1734.
	1734	John Sutton.
	1745	J. Caſberd, D. D.

It is remarkable that this church of St. Auguſtin the Leſs is not valued in the Lincoln manuſcript 1291, but is wholly omitted, perhaps it was included under the cathedral. It was ſequeſtered 1 Edw. 6. ſee p. 63.

In 1394 Joan Seys gave to the proƈtor of this pariſh an eſtate to have a chaplain to celebrate divine offices for the ſoul of herſelf and mother.—In 1405 William Folkynham gave 10l. to the fabric and ſeveral tenements to the mayor &c. to have his obiit celebrated here yearly by two chaplains.

The monuments in this church are few.—On the ſouth wall a monument with this: M. S. Elizabethæ (ſub marmoriolo juxta poſitæ) Johan. Goddard arm. dileƈtiſſimæ uxoris quæ obiit 29 Oƈt. 1705.

At the entrance of the chancel on a white marble ſtone: H. S. E. Maria conjux—Prichard Gen. Chariſſima cum 6 natis, quibus hoc poſuit mærens pater—Maritus obiit 8. mater 4 Maii (92).

On the north wall of the chancel is a monument and inſcription to Robert Cecil ſon of the Hon. Robert Cecil, brother to the late James Earl of Saliſbury; he died 30 Jan. 1707, aged 17. Arms, Barry of ten arg. and azure on 6 ſhields ſable, a lion of the firſt on each.

Near the veſtry door: H. S. E. Robertus Baſkerville M. D. natus 33 anuos.—Obiit 6 Julii A. D. 1700.

Round a ſtone thus: " Nathaniel Pownel Regiſtrar of the Dioceſe of Briſtol and Dorſet, deceaſed 28 March 1611."—He was alſo reƈtor of Wraxal in the county of Somerſet, and built the parſonage houſe there—the following is the inſcription :

In memoriam viri optimi prudentiſſimi
Mariti ſui dileƈtiſſimi Nathanielis Pownell
Dioceſ: Briſtol & Dorſer. Regiſtrarii —
Vix natos luxi, cum mors ingrata mariti
Me jubet in Lachrymas protinus ire novas.
Oh! bis bina mihi ſervet tua pignora Chriſtus,
Parte aliquâ ſinc te ſic fruar ipſe tui.
Priſcilla Pownell uxor lugens poſuit.

On

Arms, a chevron between 3 lions g. quartered, with a crofs fleury between 4 efcalops.

Near this is, " Robert Watfon minifter, deceafed 10 Sept. 1612."—Alfo a handfome monument to Sir William Daines, with a long epitaph, who died 5 Sept. 1724, aged 68; and to Sir Hugh Owen, who died 13 Jan. 1698, aged 53.

BENEFACTORS to the Church and Poor of St. Auguflin's Parifh.

		l.	s.	d.
1594, Mr. Robert Kitchen, fome time mayor and alderman of this city, gave to poor houfe-holders of this parifh for three quarters of a year 10s. per quarter for ever		30	(	
1639, Mr. George Harrington, fome time mayor and alderman of this city, gave the like gift as above - -		30	0	0
1661, Mr. Francis Gleed, fome time fheriff, gave 10s. a quarter to a poor houfe-holder for ever - -		40	0	0
1659, Mr. Daniel Vivers gave 10l. the profit yearly thereof to two poor houfekeepers not receiving alms for ever		10	0	0
1665, Mr. James Read, vicar of this parifh, gave 10l. to remain to raife 10s. per annum, to be given to ten poor people for ever - - - -		10	0	0
1668, Thomas Farmer, gentlemen, gave 50l. the profit thereof to be given unto poor houfekeepers of this parifh at St. Thomas-day yearly for ever in coal or bread -		50	0	0
1672, Henry Price, gentleman, gave 20l. the profit thereof to be given unto poor houfekeepers of this parifh at St. Thomas-day yearly for ever - - -		20	0	0
Mr. John Hayman, of this parifh, merchant, gave 22l. the profit thereof to be diftributed in bread to the poor weekly for ever - - - -		22	0	0
1676, Captain John Martin, of London, born in this parifh, gave 50l. the profit thereof to be diftributed weekly to the poor in bread for ever - - -		50	0	0
Mrs. Mary Boucher, and her daughter, Mrs. Joan Langton, widow, gave lands for the payment of 10s. apiece to fifty-two poor widows of this city yearly for ever, of which this parifh hath a proportion.				
1684, Mr. John Read, linen-draper, of St. Nicholas parifh, gave 20l. the profit thereof to be diftributed to the poor of this parifh weekly for ever - - -		20	0	0

l.   s.   d.

1685, Mr. Jeremiah Hollway, of this city, merchant, gave 15l. the profit thereof weekly in bread to the poor of this parish for ever   -   -   -   -   -   -   15   0   0

1689, Sarah the wife of Thomas Langton, Esq; and daughter of Sir William Hayman, Knight, gave 100l. the profit to be distributed upon Christmas-day to ten poor widows of this parish, not receiving alms, for ever   -   100   0   0

1701, Mary Bickham, widow, gave 100l. the profit thereof to the poor of this parish in bread every Sunday for ever   100   0   0

1702, Sir William Hayman, Knight, gave 4l. yearly for ever, to be distributed equally between eight poor widows of this parish, not receiving weekly alms, on Christmas-day yearly; also 20s. for preaching a sermon yearly for ever on Christmas-day in the morning: these monies together with Mrs. Sarah Langton's gift are payable out of a house in Horse-street   -   -   -   100   0   0

1706, Mr. Thomas Beames, of London, gave the inheritance of lands, in the parish of Shepton, in Somersetshire, which now yield 3l. yearly rent clear of taxes, the profit to be distributed in this church to the poor of this parish in good bread and cheese on the first Sunday in every month for ever   -   -   -   60   0   0

1708, Sir William Clutterbuck, some time mayor and alderman of this city, gave to this church a gilt plate, weighing 28 ounces, to be used at administration of the sacrament of the bread, and also 40l. in money, the profit thereof to be given in the church to the poor of this parish in bread upon every Lord's-day for ever   -   -   -   50   0   0

1710, Mr. George Rogers, of Cork, gave 10l. the profit thereof to the poor of this parish for ever   -   -   10   0   0

1714, William Swymmer, Esq; alderman, gave 100l. the profit thereof to be distributed yearly to the poor of this parish in cloathing on All Saints-day for ever   -   100   0   0

1715, Thomas Cole, Esq; born in this parish, gave 30l. the profit thereof to the poor in bread for ever   -   30   0   0

1716, Mrs. Sarah Colwell, of this parish, gave to the church-wardens 20l. the interest thereof to be paid to the support of the charity-school yearly, and in failure of such school, to such poor widows as they or their successors shall think fit   -   -   -   -   20   0   0

D d n

1718,

	l.	s.	d.

1718, Mr. Samuel Hartnell, of this parifh, gave the inheritance
of lands in the parifh of Henbury, in Glocefterfhire, now
lett at 33l. per annum, to put three poor boys in Queen
Elizabeth's Hofpital for ever, two of which are to be out
of this parifh   -   -   -   -   -   660   0   0

Mrs. Ann Hartnell, his widow, gave 50l. the profit to five
poor widows, not receiving alms, of this parifh, on
Michaelmas-day for ever   -   -   -   -   50   0   0

1722, July 30, John Romfey, Efq; late town clerk of this city,
gave 20l. the yearly profit of which is to be diftributed
to the poor of this parifh   -   -   -   20   0   0

Captain John Williams, of Caldy ifland, in the county of
Pembroke, gave 10l. the profit in bread to the poor on
the 25th of Auguft for ever   -   -   -   10   0   0

1723, Mr. Robert Naylor, of this parifh, gave the fum of 40s.
per annum to be paid unto four poor houfe-holders of
this parifh, not receiving alms, on Chriftmas-day for
ever, as the minifter and churchwardens fhall think fit: 40   0   0

Mr. Charles Ansforde, of St. Stephen's parifh, gave 25l.
the profit thereof to five poor houfekeepers of this
parifh, not receiving alms, on the 10th of June for ever   25   0   0

1722, Anthony Swymmer, Efq; fome time mayor and alderman
of this city, received from the churchwardens and veftry
of this parifh 290l. * (as will appear by the veftry-book)
with an intent to put more to it and build a houfe. He
dying foon after, his brother Mr. William Swymmer and
executor, knowing his promife, gave the fouth corner
houfe in Orchard-ftreet, neareft to the city hofpital
and joining to Alderman Beecher's, to the poor of this
parifh for ever, and the rents thereof to be diftributed
as the minifter and churchwardens for the time being
fhall think fit ; it is let now for 32l. a year on a leafe
for feven years   -   -   -   -   -   310   0   0

                                                            1726

* Viz. Sir William Clutterbuck's gift for   -   -   -   40 l.
    Mrs. Mary Bickham's gift for   -   -   -   100
    William Swymmer, Efq; his gift for   -   -   -   100
    And Mrs. Ann Hartnell's gift for   -   -   -   50
                                                    ‾‾‾
                                                    290

	l.	*s.*	*d.*
1726, April 18, Mr. John Maſkall, of the pariſh of Lye, gave 10l. the profit thereof to be yearly diſtributed to the poor of St. Auguſtine's pariſh, as the miniſter and churchwardens of the ſaid pariſh for the time being ſhall think fit	10	0	0
Mr. William Raymond, ſome time of this pariſh, gave 100l. for the uſe of the poor, the intereſt thereof to be diſtributed as the miniſter and churchwardens for the time being ſhall think fit - - - -	100	0	0
1739, John Price, Eſq; alderman of this city, in his life time gave the ſum of 100l. the intereſt thereof to be diſtributed yearly on the 15th of June for ever equally between ten poor houſekeepers of this pariſh, not receiving alms, by the vicar and churchwardens for the time being, the firſt payment to be made June 15, 1739	100	0	0
1740, Mr. Peter Wilkins, late of this pariſh, left by his will 30l. the intereſt thereof to be diſtributed to four poor houſekeepers of the ſaid pariſh, not receiving alms, on Good Friday yearly for ever - - -	30	0	0
And alſo 20l. to the charity-ſchool in the ſaid pariſh as long as the ſaid ſchool continues, and on failure thereof to be applied as above - - -	20	0	0
1733, Mrs. Ann Winter gave 50l. to the poor of this pariſh, the intereſt thereof to be diſpoſed of at the diſcretion of the churchwardens for the time being -	50		
1777, Captain Prankard gave 100l. to the poor, ſeamen's widows to be preferred.	100		
1735, William Hilliard, Eſq; gave 100l. to the poor of this pariſh, the intereſt thereof to be diſpoſed of as the veſtry ſhall direct.	100		
1745, George Packer gave 50l. to the poor of this pariſh, the intereſt thereof to be diſpoſed of as the miniſter and churchwardens ſhall direct; alſo 50l. the intereſt thereof to the charity-ſchool in this pariſh.	100		
1748, Captain William Chaloner, of this pariſh, gave 50l. the intereſt thereof to be diſpoſed of by the churchwardens to eight poor houſekeepers, not receiving alms, on the 26th day of January for ever.	50		
1757, Mrs. Elizabeth Whitchead gave 100l. the intereſt thereof to the poor as the veſtry ſhall direct - -	100	0	0

1762,

1762, Mr. Walter Laugher, merchant, of this city, gave 100l. to
the minister and churchwardens, the interest thereof to
eight poor widows of this parish, not receiving alms, on
the 7th of December yearly for ever   -   -   100 0 0

1736, Mrs. Ann Aldworth, of this parish, gave three tenements
in Frog-lane, the house called the Boar's Head and Salmon being the corner house is one, with two others
adjoining, to the poor of All Saints and this parish, the
25th of December for ever.

Robert Sandford, of Bristol, Esq; gave 100l. to be placed
out at interest, which was to be paid to four poor housekeepers, not receiving alms, on St. Thomas-day for
ever -   -   -   -   -   - 100 0 0

1758, Mrs. Ann Thurston gave by will 300l. to be placed at
interest, the produce thereof to be given to such poor
sick persons as the churchwardens shall think proper objects at 3s. 6d. per week to each during their illness   300 0 0

1764, Mr. Edward Gwatkin gave 50l. the interest to ten poor
housekeepers, not receiving alms, on the 20th of February for ever -   -   -   -   50 0 0

1765, Mrs. Mary Griffith gave 100l. the interest thereof to eight
poor housekeepers on Good Friday for ever - 100 0 0

In this parish was the house of the Carmelite friers. Leland, vol. v. p. 53. says, " The priory of the Carmelites was the fairest of all the houses of the frieries in Bristol, and stood on the right ripe of Frome over against the Key." According to Speed it was founded in the year 1267 by King Edward 1st. perhaps when Prince of Wales. It was granted after the dissolution by King Henry the 8th. for the use of the city. According to William of Worcester in 1480 the church of the priory was of the following dimensions: " The nave or body contains 45 paces, the breadth thereof 25 paces, the tower and spire or broche is 200 feet, the breadth of the tower is 9 feet each way."

In the 12th of Henry 4th. 1411, Peter Thomas was prior of the frier Carmelites of Bristol; and in the year 1466 John Milverton, who for opposing the bishops was committed prisoner to the castle of St. Angelo, Rome, for three years, wrote many excellent things, at length loaded with grief and age he died at London, 30th of January, 1496. John Stow, a Bristol Car-melite, was an ingenious poet soon after the time of Chaucer. John Spine, a

native

native of Briſtol, and a Carmelite frier there, became Doctor and Profeſſor of of Divinity in Oxford, and a noted preacher, writ ſermons for the clergy and ſolemn diſputations, and died in 1454. Frier John Walton, D. D. and prior here the 26th of December, the 13th of King Henry 6th. 1434. Nicholas Cantilupe was a Carmelite frier here, and D. D. of Cambridge, and died at Northampton, 1441, leaving many monuments of his literature: theſe were in the catalogue of the moſt celebrated learned men of Engliſh birth that were writers of the order of the Carmelites. John Hooper, S. T. P. was a man of great learning, took upon him the habit of the white friers, Briſtol, went abroad after the diſſolution of monaſteries, and getting acquainted with ſome of the reformers, on his return, May 15, 1550, was made Biſhop of Gloceſter, and was burnt the 9th of February, 1559, before the weſt end gate of his cathedral, in the time of Queen Mary.

The ſite of the Carmelite priory was moſt certainly where Mr. Colſton's ſchool now ſtands: ſeveral very ancient arches are now extant, and its being oppoſite the Key ſhews it to be ſo; and though there is a place called White Friers in Lewin's-mead, yet I rather think it to be an error by confounding it with the Grey Friery acknowledged to be there ſituated. In old deeds of Redcliff pariſh I find the hill near Colſton's ſchool called Frier's-hill, and a garden there deſcribed as on one ſide the friery.

The old deeds in the cuſtody of the Merchants-hall indeed prove this to be the ſite of the Carmelite friery. The area and extent of their friery and church on the ſouth-weſt ſide thereto belonging was very ſpacious, and in a deed, October 1, 5th Edward 3d. 1376, mention is made of a ciſtern near the Carmelites, called the ciſtern of the pipe of St. John in Broad-ſtreet, which goes through Pipe-lane next the ſite of this friery, which had a feather from the ſaid pipe allotted for its uſe, which is ſtill continued to Mr. Colſton's ſchool.

This Carmelite friery was of large extent occupying all the ground from the Red Lodge and garden down the hill to St. Auguſtin's-Back, now Mr. Colſton's School, and was bounded by Pipe-lane on the weſt and Steep-ſtreet on the eaſt: and beſides the houſe and lodgings for the friers, which Leland celebrates as the " faireſt of all the houſes of friers;" their church was moſt elegant and ſpacious with many chapels in it, and I find in manuſcripts many very good families lie buried therein.

Upon a view of frank pledge made the 12th of Hen. 4th. by John Fyſher mayor, and John Olyff ſheriff &c. for the town, Peter Thomas prior of the Carmelites renounced to the ſaid town 12½ feet and 11 inches of land near

the

the church of the convent of the Carmelites in the fouth part, which had been granted by Robert Dudbroke late mayor to the prior and his brethren.

The fite of this houfe was granted the 6th of May the 33d of Hen. 8th. by the name and title of " all that houfe or fite of the late diffolved houfe of Friers Carmelite commonly called the White Friers within the faid town of Briftol, and the meffuage and houfe called the Hoopers' Hall with the appur-tenances, within the lite of the faid late houfe of Friers Carmelites, and for all yards, orchards &c. as well within as near adjoining to the faid fite, fept, walk, circuit and precinct of the faid houfe of Friers Carmelites here-tofore in occupation of David Hobbes &c."

It was purchafed at the diffolution together with the Gaunts (vid. p. 134.) by the corporation of the city, who afterwards 10th Eliz. fold the fite of the friery to Thomas Chefter Efq; but the lodge, the gardens, orchards on Stoney-hill &c. belonging to it were fold to Thomas Rowland merchant, who for the fum of 26l. 13s. 4d. conveyed it in fee the 7th of April the 20th of Eliz. to Sir John Young, whofe fon and heir Robert Young of Hafelborough in the county of Wilts, the 28th of March the 41ft of Eliz. fold the Red Lodge and the houfe on St. Auftin's-Back then new-built and called Sir John Young's lower houfe, in occupation of dame Joan Young his widow, to Nicholas Strangeways of Bradly in the county of Glocefter Efq. — Queen Elizabeth on coming to Briftol kept her court and held a council at this houfe of Sir John Young; and it was the ufual refidence of the nobility vifiting Briftol. — In 1642 it was inhabited by Sir Ferdinando Gorges, and was offered by him for entertaining the Marquis of Hertford here at that time. It was afterwards purchafed by Mr. Lane and converted into a fugar-houfe, till the pious and charitable Mr. Golfton in the year 1708 bought it to erect a fchool for a mafter, two ufhers, and 100 boys to be cloathed, maintained and inftructed in reading, writing and arithmetic, and in the church catechifm from feven years old till they are fourteen, when they are to be placed out apprentices, he allowing 10l. to each at their going out : the expence of erecting and endowing this fchool compleatly finifhed by him in his life time was 40,000l. the eftates in lands and ground rents he gave for endowing it produced then 1318l. 15s. 6d. per ann. and the charge of fitting up the fchool and dwelling-houfe &c. amounted to about 11,000l. Out of the eftate a clergyman is to be paid 10l. per ann. for inftructing the boys in the church catechifm. — He alfo gave at his death to continue twelve years after it 100l. per ann. either to thofe who had been apprenticed from the hofpital of St. Auguftin's-Back, or for the apprenticing of boys from Temple School by 10l. each, the charge about 1200l.

John

John Purrier Efq; merchant of London, out of a juft fenfe and grateful acknowledgment of the advantage he received in early life from being educated at this fchool, did in his life time about the year 1782 fettle fo much money in the funds as would make an addition of 5l. to the 10l. each boy's apprentice fee given by Mr. Colfton, making it 15l. and alfo prefented 100 new filver badges worn by the boys, and 100 brafs ones

Befides this fchool or hofpital of Mr. Golfton, and alfo the hofpital of Queen Elizabeth, (of which fee page 376,) this parifh can alfo boaft of a very noble charity by Alderman Whitfon called the Redmaids Hofpital, who by his will dated the 27th of March 1627 left many and great benefactions to the city, (vid. his will hereafter) among the reft an endowment out of his manor of Burnet (formerly belonging to Tewkefbury abby) for the educating and maintaining of 40 maidens, who were fome to learn reading and needle-work, fome houfehold bufinefs and other employment to fit them the better for fervice; and the firft 12 maids chofen out of 12 parifhes were by order of common council placed in a houfe the 4th of October 1634, fituate near the College-Green, on the fite of the Gaunts Hofpital or houfe of St. Mark's. — In the year 1655 the 3d of April it was referred to the city furveyors to confider about erecting an hofpital for maids adjoining to the houfe hitherto ufed for that purpofe according to Alderman's Whitfon's gift, and how the work fhould be fully carried into execution according to the intent of the founder and for the honor of the city: by which order it appears the endowment had hitherto but partially taken place, or had been difcontinued during the rebellion and ufurpation of Cromwel, and was now reftored, the houfe or hofpital being new-built and enlarged, which is now a very commodious houfe for the defign, in a quiet retired fituation, and is managed with great prudence and œconomy to the relief of families, lafting advantage to the poor girls and general good of the community.

The fettlement of this charity was long in agitation betwixt the feoffees of Alderman Whitfon and the corporation; at laft the city agreed to add 30l. per ann. to Mr. Whitfon's endowment of the manor of Burnet near Cainfham then let at 90l. per ann. and in lieu of monies the perfonal eftate of Mr. Whitfon left to the chamber for good ufes within the city and paid into the city ftock, 40l. per ann. more was agreed to be advanced towards the new building and additional endowment of the Red-maids Hofpital.

On the 2d of September 1659 Mrs. Mayorefs and Joan Hobfon widow were appointed vifitors of the maids hofpital, with thefe inftructions, 1. To vifit two days in each month in perfon the faid children. 2. To make due enquiry

into

into their bodily health. 3. To obferve their cleanlinefs and convenient change, fo that they be kept neat and free from vermin. 4. To enquire into the wholefomencfs and proportion of their diet. 5. To take due notice whether they are taught to read Englifh and employed in work that may be for their future preferment. 6. To fee that two of them be every week employed about houfehold affairs. 7. To take care that the vacant places be fupplied by direction and approbation of the mayor and aldermen. 8. On all occafions to reprefent to the mayor and aldermen what is amifs that remedy may be applied. G. Hellier mayor, Tolfcy book II.

C H A P.   XIII.

Of the CHURCH and PARISH of St. MICHAEL.

THIS church is a rectory dedicated to St. Michael the Archangel, fituated on a hill of great height, on the north fide of Briftol. The founder of it was probably Robert Fitzhaymon, who endowed his abby of Tewkfbury with this church. Two large figures in painted glafs in the eaft window over the communion table were fome years paft taken down and deftroyed, with the following infcription without date : " Orate pro animabus Jobis Burlington et Johannæ Uxoris ejus qui Johannes et Johanna iftam feneftram fecerunt et fpcciales erant benefactores hujus ecclefiæ." In the year 1193 it was in the prefentation of the monks of the abby church of Tewkfbury, as appears by the confirmation of Henry Bifhop of Worcefter of all the benefactions which Simon, bifhop of the fame diocefe, had granted to the church of Tewkfbury, the monks thereof having then lately prefented Richard Cumblan to it. In the the year 1291 this benefice was in the archdeaconry of Gloccfter and deanry of Briftol, and its yearly value then taken was fix marks and a half, and it was fubject to an annual payment of four fhillings for the prior of St. James's part or fharc.

At the diffolution of religious houfes the prefentation of this church (with many others in Briftol, appendages and parcel of the abby of Tewkfbury) were for 667l. 7s. 6d. fold off by letters patent the 35th of the faid King to Henry
Braync,

Brayne, Efq; who became patron and proprietor of this and the other churches in Briftol. And as this was then fubject to a yearly rent or penfion of four fhillings, the fame became payable to the faid Brayne and his heirs for ever, and now to the corporation. The rector of St. Michael for the time being now pays an yearly ftipend of 2s. to the dean and chapter of Briftol, which was formerly paid to the monaftery of St. Auguftin.

The church confifted of two ailes and is but fmall, fcarcely fufficient to accommodate the parifhioners. The tower is at the weft end, from which it extends in length to the then altar 73 feet, the aile on the fouth fide including the old veftry room at the eaft end was about 73 feet. The height of the roofs (which were of timber plaftered) was about 26 feet, fupported with 4 freeftone arches and 3 pillars, and was covered with ftone tiles. The breadth of the two ailes 37 feet. Before the north and fouth doors were porches, over the fouth door the veftry room.

William of Worcefter fays, " In length it contains 46 paces or 26 yards, in breadth 10 yards or 20 paces, the fquare tower of the new belfry contains a fquare of four fides each 5 yards without the wall, the fouth porch of the church is 11 feet long and 10 broad." The tower is ftrong, and at top has freeftone battlements with four pinnacles of a moderate height, and is furnifhed with a peal of fix bells, which were caft and put up by a fubfcription and pound rate in the year 1739. On the eaft fide of the tower over the roof is a niche wherein is fixed a figure of an abbot, or as fome imagine that of St. Michael the patron faint.

Some years paft the worthy benefactor Edward Colfton, Efq; gave 50l. for the repair of this church.

It was fequeftered on the 1ft of April in the 1ft year of Edward 6th. 1547. (See page 63.) The clear yearly value in the King's Books was 5l. 18s. 11d. Yearly tenths were 12s.

In the year 1749 this parifh confifted of 380 houfes which were rated to the fupport of the poor that year 227l. at about 11d. in the pound : but the poor rate is fince greatly increafed, as well as the number of inhabitants.

In the year 1774 a furvey was made of the fabrick, and it was found fo decayed in the walls and roof that it would require 985l. 19s. at a moderate computation to put it in good repair. It was therefore judged better to build a new church entirely for the better accommodation of the increafed parifhioners, which was done by fubfcription of the inabitants and others, being 77 feet long and 62 broad, with a vault or croud under it for a place of burial : this was 20 feet broader on the north and 5 on the fouth fide than the

F f f   former

former church: the Corporation gave 300l. and the Merchant's-Hall 150l. which with the fums collected amounted to upwards of 2200l. the foundation was laid with great formality the 4th of July 1775, and the church was opened the 22d of June 1777. The old tower is preferved.

The rector chiefly depends on the voluntary benevolence of the parifhioners.

	l.	s.	d.
The annual rent of his parfonage houfe at the fouth gate of the church-yard - - - - - -	15	0	0
For monthly prayers &c. at Forfter's chapel, paid by the corpora_ tion of Briftol per ann. - - - - -	10	0	0
For a fmall houfe at the north gate of the church-yard per ann.	5	0	0
For Queen Ann's bounty, it being fettled in two chief rents iffuing out of two houfes in St. James's church-yard, Briftol -	7	0	0
For tythe of the two parks - - - - -	1	18	0
For a paddock - - - - - -	0	4	0
For two fermons - - - - - -	2	2	0
Ditto Mr. Peter Davis on the 1ft of March in the evening -	1	10	0

Which with voluntary contributions &c. amount in all to about 200l. per annum.

The prefent patrons are the corporation of Briftol, who purchafed the fame in the year 1627 of Sir Charles Gerrard Knight, who married Elizabeth daughter of Sir Charles Somerfet Knight, and grand daughter of the aforefaid Henry Brayne Efq.

The prefent incumbent is the Rev. George Wilkins A. M.

A LIST of the RECTORS from old deeds and the regifters of Worcefter.

PATRONS.

The abbot and convent of Tewkefbury.	1193 Richard Cumblain was rector.
	1282 Robert de la More prieft.
	1286 13 kalend. June, Wm. de Bleyngel.
	1308 8 kalend. Nov. Wm. de Bath, accolit.
	1309 7 id. May, Ralph de Baketon.
	Helia was chaplain there.
	1313 4 kalend June Johannes de Wygorniâ prieft.
	1334 11 non. Oct. John Wycheforde.
	1360 11 Dec. Peter de Dodmancote clerk by refignation of Thomas Southwel.
	1361 15 Feb. Symon de Collewell prieft.

PATRONS.

1369 4 Dec. Richard de Marchynton prieſt by reſignation of
William Allen.

1376 5 July John Pitwell.

1402 12 Oct. John Hogkere by change with John Chamberlain rector of this church.

1405 9 May, John Hoy.

1411 31 Aug. John Boure.

1420 9 Nov. Philip Briſtow by change with Thomas Faucon-
berg the laſt incumbent.

1460 17 May, Maſter David Cokland by reſignation of John
Harptree.

1464 12 July, John Free by the death of Cokland.

1465 24 Sept. John Berſey by reſignation of John Free.

1470 6 Oct. Thomas Howell rector of St. Maryport, by
change with John Berſey.

1483 1 Aug. Thomas Galcon by reſignation of Leonard
Davy the laſt rector.

1512 6 April, Thomas Hall by reſignation of Alexander
Overton the laſt rector, reſerving a penſion of
10 marks.

1523 3 April, John Morys by reſignation of Thomas Hall,
reſerving 40s.

1524. 4 Feb. Thomas Nichols.

1526 4 Sept. John Fyſhe A. M.

1648 Philip Perry rector, died 17 Feb. 1649 and was
buried here.

Mayor and   1665 Mathias Bradie rector, buried here 22 Dec. 1676.

Corporation of   1677 John Rainſtorp rector, died 1 May 1693.

Briſtol.   1693 Samuel Paine rector, buried here 20 April 1721.

1721 James Taylor rector, buried at St. John's March 1722.

1722 Samuel Jocham rector, buried here May 30, 1743.

1743 Rumney Penroſe rector, died 19 July 1749, buried at
Bedminſter.

1749 John Culliford rector.

1766 Samuel Seyer M. A. rector.

1776 George Wilkins M. A. rector.

MONU-

MONUMENTS.

On the north wall was formerly a brafs plate, fince ftolen away, with the following infcription:

Mors fpernitatra gloriam B . . . .

" Pray for the dead, for thou muft dye Jehu mercy."

At one end of this monument this coat—parted perpale arg. and G. a bend counterchanged—for Chaucer of Woodftock t. Ric. 2.

A monument by the church door with a Latin infcription:—" To Nicolas Hill a lawyer, who died Nov. 1597, and to his wife Dorothy who died Nov. 1599."

In the further north window of the chancel, a table thus infcribed:

Dominus $\begin{cases} \text{dedit.} \\ \text{abftulit.} \end{cases}$

Anna filia Richardi Afh Ætatis fuæ tertio, obiit 24 Maii

With the figure of an afh tree with a fmall branch, and dated 1645.

This Afh $\begin{cases} \text{In May} \\ \text{was then} \end{cases}$ cut down $\begin{cases} \text{Sprouts the fame day} \\ \text{yet lives for aye.} \end{cases}$

On the grave-ftone:

Rak^d. up in afhes here doth $\begin{cases} \\ \end{cases}$ Afh $\begin{cases} \text{remain} \\ \text{again.} \end{cases}$
In hope that afbes fhall be

Afhes to Afh return fhall and arife,

Which Afh in afbes here expecting lies.

On the floor is a ftone infcribed to Mr. Richard Afh merchant, who died 21 Aug. 1666, aged 70, 4 of his children, and Margery his wife, who died 23 Jan. 1693, aged 79.

Under the communion table:—" Samuel Paine hujus ecclefiæ rector obiit 18 Jan. ætat 57. 1721-22."

" Thomas Percivall obiit 1741."

" Thomas Percivall eldeft fon of Jofeph Percival merchant, died 16 June 1741, aged 20."

There is at the fide of the altar a magnificent monument to Jofeph Percivall Efq; with a great but juft character: he died 28 June 1764.

On a brafs plate was:—" Philippus Perrey hujus ecclefiæ paftor obiit 17 calend Feb. 1649.

Philippus, filius Philippi, matris amicæ
Primitias debitas qui rediere Deo."

On a ftone:—" William Stretton fen. departed this life the 28 June 1694, aged 37.

On

On a monument in the fouth aile was the following infcription :

Hic juxta fitus eft Thomas Alvy generofus equeftri familia jurorum in comitatu Wilt: oriunduf; qui cum innumeras fere hujus, nonnullas etiam prioris feculi vicffitudines expertus effet ; Jacobum regem triplici unitum regno vidiffet ; Carolum primum barbare divifum ploraffet ; expirantes leges, femimortuam ecclefiam, dominantem rempublicam, prementem tyrannidem horruiffet: aufpicante tandem Deo, Carolum fecundum primi filium redivivum, leges et ecclefiam repullulantes grate falutaffet : ingruente tandem improborum confilio repetendâ palluiffet ruinâ, aliorum fæpius compofuiffet, lites fuas vero frugaliter confuluiffet, vivendo quafi feffus cælum maturus petiit : perge viator fortefque humanas humanus meditaris, obiit Jan. 24 A. D. 1682 et ætatis 90.

In Englifh thus:

Hard by is placed Thomas Alvy gentleman, fprung from a knightly family of the Jurors in the county of Wilts: who after he had experienced the almoft countlefs changes of this and fome alfo of the former age, bad feen King James joined to a treble kingdom, had bewailed Charles the 1ft. barbaroufly feparated from it ; had dreaded the ftate expiring, the church half dead, a commonwealth ruling, tyranny oppreffing, at length by the favour of God having gratefully faluted King Charles the 2d. the fon of the 1ft. on his return, the church and ftate beginning again to flourifh ; the council of the wicked at length getting into place having grown pale at the return about to be repeated, after he had often fettled the difputes of others, but fparing in council for his own as if tired of living, in a ripe age he went to heaven : Go paffenger and as a man meditate on man's condition. He died the 24th of January 1692, in the 90th year of his age.

In the fouth aile :—" Anno 1743 obiit Samuel Jocham A. M. hujus ecclefiæ rector anno ætatis 50."

Near this:—" Expectat refurrectionem Sara Samuelis Jocham hujus ecclefiæ rector amabilis uxor, mulier omni virtute inftructa, apta vivere, parata mori. obiit 29 Maii 1736 ætatis 45."

Near the veftry a handfome monument with a long Latin infcription :— " To John Ridout Efq; of Dorfetfhire, who died 1670 the 26th of Auguft, in his grand climacteric.—Arms, parted per pale arg. and gules a griffin rampant counter-changed.

Many of thefe monuments and infcriptions have been deftroyed in rebuilding this church.

BENE-

on the third Saturday after Lady-day, 10s. to another on the tenth Saturday after Midfummer, and 10s. to another on the firft Saturday after Chriftmas; the three perfons to be nominated by the mayor and aldermen and churchwardens and overfeers of the poor of St. Michael's parifh.

1639, Mr. George Harrington gave 30s. per annum, to be paid by the chamberlain in the fame manner as that of Mr. Kitchen's.

1634, Mr. George White gave 5l. per annum to the poor of faid parifh. It is charged on a houfe near the Red Lodge, as may appear by the Book of Wills in the chamber of Briftol, which houfe was late. in the poffeffion of Capt. John Hitchens, and fince Henry Woolnough and Mrs. Henvil. This is received and paid by the fenior churchwarden of St. Werburgh.

1639, Mr. Thomas Clement gave 20s. per annum to the poor. It is charged on a houfe in Broadmead, late Mr. Baugh's, payable by Mr. Abraham Pope.

1640, Mr. Thomas Harrington gave 52s. per annum, to be given to the poor in weekly bread, to be paid half yearly by the chamberlain.

1660, Mrs. Joan Langton gave 50s. per annum, to be given to the poor in weekly bread. This is charged upon a garden oppofite the parfonage houfe, late in the tenure of Mr. Anthony Hodges, the leafe of which when expired comes to St. Michael's parifh.

1661, Mr. Francis Gleed gave 10s. a quarter to a poor houfe-holder, not receiving weekly alms. This is payable out of a houfe in High-ftreet, late Slooper's and now Sedon's. The perfons that are to receive the faid charity are to be nominated by the churchwardens of the faid parifh, and no perfon to receive the faid gift more than once in one year. The feoffees are thofe of Chrift Church in Briftol. It is paid by the veftry-clerk.

1661, Mr. Thomas Farmer gave 50l. which purchafed an annuity of 50s. per annum

annum for ever of Edward Smith, currier, charged on and payable out of a houfe in Lewin's-mead, and now received of the widow of John Smith, and the fame to be given in bread or coal.

1671, Mrs. Elizabeth Farmer gave 50l. which purchafed from the chamber of Briftol three fee farm rents, viz. one of 26s. 8d. charged on and payable out of a certain houfe at the head of the Key belonging to Mr. Charles Harford, and 24s. charged on and payable out of a certain houfe called the Tower of the Key, another of 5s. 6d. charged on and payable out of a houfe in Chriftmas-ftreet. This is difpofed of to the poor in weekly bread according to the donor's direction.

Mr. Edward Cox gave 10l. to the feveral parifhes in this city, for coal in the month of December, of which the mayor for the time being ufed to fend 17s. 6d. to this parifh by the fenior ferjeant, but by fome means it is now reduced to 15s. a year.

1685, Mr. Jeremiah Hollwey gave 15l. the profit thereof to be given yearly in bread or coal for ever.

1689, Mrs. Elizabeth Wiggens gave 10l. the profit thereof to be given to the poor in bread every firft Sunday in the feveral months, houfe-holders to be preferred.

1690, Mr. Thomas Stratton, fenior, gave 25l. the profit thereof to be given weekly in bread for ever.

Thefe three laft-mentioned gifts, with 10l. that remained undifpofed of in Mr. Richard Gravet's year of churchwardenfhip, being part of the annual gift of Mr. Carr and Mr. White, were by an order of veftry paid into Mr. George Skufe the 1ft of January, 1704, for one annuity or chief rent of 50s. per annum, charged on and payable out of two houfes in Horfe-ftreet, next above Skinner's Slip.

1693, Mr. James Seward gave 40s. per annum to be paid at Chriftmas to eight poor widows 5s. each, they not receiving alms, to be nominated by the churchwardens, &c. and that no perfon is to have the benefit of the faid gift two years together. This 40s. is charged on and payable out of a houfe over the gate at the lower end of Small-ftreet in Briftol, and is paid by James Seward.

1690, Mr. Eufebius Brooke gave 7l. per annum to the poor, to be difpofed of at the difcretion of the churchwardens, &c. This is charged on

and

and payabie out of the building in a ground near the Royal Fort called Tinkers Clofe, which is now leafed out for lives, or years which when expired an addition of 3l. per annum will be made to the above 7l. It is paid by the tenants or by Robert Holmes, Efq; Mrs. Jane Mixon gave 10l. Alexander James, Efq; 10l. Mr. Benjamin Willoughby, 5l. With this 25l. and the interest of Mr. Mixon's and Mr. James's, which was made up 5l. more, with part of Mr. Carr's gift money, was purchafed of Jacob Knight, Efq; one fee farm rent of 13s. 4d. payable out of a tenement in Baldwin-ftreet, now in the poffeffion of Thomas Cother Smith, paid by Lydia Gregory, and one other tenement fee farm in Back-ftreet of of 20s. 4d. which is to be given to the poor in bread (to be paid by Mary Lawrence) on every Chriftmas-day, as the gifts of Mrs. Jane Mixon and Alexander James, Efq; The other 5s. is to be given every 29th of September in two-penny loaves of bread immediately after the fermon is ended to thirty poor people of this parifh, who have been prefent all the time of divine fervice and the fermon that evening, and behaved themfelves decently all the time, as the gift of Mr. Benjamin Willoughby.

Richard Haynes, Efq; gave 10s. per annum, to be paid to the minister of this parifh for preaching a fermon every 29th of September in the evening. It is chargeable on and payable out of two acres of ground in Charlton Field, in the county of Glocefter, being part of the eftate of him the faid Richard Haynes.

1664, Jofeph Jackfon, Efq; in the year 1664 gave unto the poor of this city 110l. which was put into the chamber on the fecurity of the common feal of the mayor, burgeffes, and commonalty, and continued there until the 21ft of January, 1707, without any diftribution of the interest, it never being demanded, which the common council at that time taking into confideration did then order that the faid feal fhould be taken up and a new one given for 300l. in lieu of the 110l. and the interest of it from the year 1664, and that the chamberlain fhould pay every 22d of January 12l. for the interest thereof; and in the year 1712 it was agreed by the mayor and aldermen that it fhould be paid to the officers of the five parifhes or places following, viz. St. Michael's, 40s. Caftle Precincts, 4l. St. Philip's, 40s. St. Thomas, 40s. St. Mary Redcliff, 40s. to be by them diftributed in the fame manner as Mr. Kitchen's and Mr. Harrington's

Harrington's gifts, according to the directions of the faid bencfac-
to the poor of the faid five places or parifhes, viz. 10s. apiece to a
poor burgefs or widow of fuch.

Mr. Anthony Hodges gave a piece of Ground at Shirehampton, the profit thereof to be diftributed in bread every year on the 11th and 17th
days of June to the poor of this parifh.

Richard Gravett gave 50s. a year (and at the requeft of George Gravett
his fon, deceafed, 50s. a year more) for ever, to be difpofed of and
laid out as followeth, viz. 3l. 6s. thereof for coal and 22s. for
bread; 3s. worth of which coal and one 12d. loaf is to be given to
each to ten poor inhabitants of the parifh of St. Michael, who are or
have been tradefmen, artificers, or mariners, not receiving weekly
alms, or to the widows of fuch; but if no fuch are to be found who
need or defire it, the number is to be made up with labourers or
their widows (thofe who frequent God's holy worfhip and attend his
ordinances in the church to be preferred.) This is to be given on
the 15th of November yearly. The 5l. per annum is charged on
payable out of a houfe in Chriftmas-ftreet, late in the tenure of Mr.
Standing, apothecary.

Mr. Thomas Morgan gave 50l. to the poor which is to be difpofed of
at the difcretion of the parifh officers.

Mr. William Cook gave 10l. to be put out at intereft at 10s. per
annum, which is to be laid out every Chriftmas in fixty two-penny
loaves, and given to the poor of faid parifh as the parifh officers
fhall think fit.

1625, Bartholomew Ruffell, blackfmith, by his will dated the 3d of February
gave his houfe wherein he then dwelt in Horfe-ftreet (after the death
of Agatha his wife) to the feoffees of the parifh of St. Michael, the
rent thereof to be yearly given to the poor, and alfo to repair the
faid parifh church when need fhould require it. This houfe was
lately occupied by Samuel Jones or —— Stephens.

The houfe built on the triangular ground in Steep-ftreet near and adjoining to Trenchard-lane, now in the feveral tenures of John
Roach, —— Sturton, and the widow Teague, belongs to this parifh
church, but not known for what particular ufe given.

Richard Gravett, Efq; paid into the hands of the Reverend Samuel
Jocham, rector, and thofe of the churchwardens of this parifh, 10l.
intereft thereof to defray the expence of thofe who fhall meet agree-

able to his deed of fettlement, wherein twenty-two poor people are by them to be nominated for his gift the 15th of November and the 18th of December for ever. And at the fame time for them to infpeἀ the Green Book to fee if it be diftributed according to the appointment of the donor.

Mrs. Anne Longman, widow, gave 195l. to the poor of this city, of which this parifh hath a part.

Within this parifh were of old two religious houfes; one dedicated to St. Mary, confifted of nuns under a priorefs, the other to St. Bartholomew, called the houfe or hofpital of St. Bartholomew, confifted of friers or brothers and fifters; the nuns alfo it appears had a reἀor and fome friers with them. John is called reἀor hofpitalis Mariæ Magdalenæ in Gaunt's deeds about the year 1300.

The foundrefs of this nunnery to St. Mary Magdalen * was Eva daughter of Godiva, fifter to William the Conqueror. It is not certain whether fhe built it whilſt the wife or widow of Robert Fitzharding.

Hiftory informs us that fhe largely endowed this houfe of nuns with lands and tenements, and became the firſt priorefs thereof, † and fo continued to the time of her death, in the year 1173. She was buried next her Lord, between the abbot's and prior's cell in the monaftery of St. Auguftin. The fite of this houfe was pleafant and it extended from the King David inn on the fouth up the hill northward adjoining to a lane called the Montague's, from thence up the faid lane eaftward to a lane oppofite the Fort-lane leading down into Magdalen-lane fouthward, and then up the faid lane weftward to the King David inn.

The number of inhabitants that refided within its walls, or the regulations of this houfe are uncertain. The 21ſt of Edward the 3d. 1347, Agnes de Gloucefter was priorefs thereof and Brother John was reἀor, and the Bifhop of Worcefter was patron. The following accouut is given by Leland of its fuppreffion in the reign of King Henry 8th. or the next fuccceding reign. He fays, " On the north fide of the town of Briftol flood St. Magdalen's houfe of nuns, which was fuppreffed of late years, when fuch as were under 300 marks of rent by the year were put down, and that it was valued the 26th of Henry 8th. at 21l. 11s. 3d. per annum, and granted the 31ſt of the faid King (1540) to Henry Brayne, Efq; and John Marfh." The fite of it

is

* Leland's Itin. vol. vii. p. 72. Prynne; iii. 714. and vide pat. 4. Edw. 3d. (1330) p. 1. m. 40. vel. 41.

† Dugdale's Baronage, vol. i. p. 351. vide Atkyns's Hiftory of Glocefterfhire, p. 261.

is now in the poffeffion of the family of —— Jones, Efq; at Stowey, in the county of Somerfet. In the 1ft year of King Edward 6th. 1547, this houfe was fequeftered to the King's ufe, p. 134.

We are much obliged to the ingenious John Warburton, Efq; Somerfet herald, for communicating his manufcript of the particular fums arifing from the fale of many religious houfes in all parts of England, amongft which are thefe lands and tenements, viz. in Wefton St. Laurence, Filton, and Henbury, in the conty of Glocefter, which was parcel of the late priory of St. Mary Magdalen, near Briftol, &c. as by the King's letters patent under the great feal of England more plainly appear.

This nunnery and hofpital being endowed with the following lands, &c. was fold off the 37th Henry 8th. 1546, viz. in Weftbury, South Mead, at Iron Acton a tenement, at Berton Regis a meffuage and meadow, at Codrington lands called Magdalen-croft, at Filton a meadow, at Laurence Wefton fix acres.

In the year 1284 Bifhop Giffard of Worcefter vifited the nuns (moniales) of the Magdalen houfe at Briftol, where he found nothing to be amended, except that the vicar of St. Michael's detained from the nuns for three years 2s. and 2lbs. of pepper and cummin yearly rent, to the reftitution of which he was condemned by the bifhop, who preached there : his text was " Filiæ tibi funt, ferva corpus illarum," &c. Eregiftris ecclefiæ Wygorn.

PRIORESSES.

1347, Agnes de Gloucefter. Giff. f. 210. a.

1349, 27 March, Maud de Luttleton, a nun, was fet over this houfe as priorefs. Wolft. v. 1. 146.
> She refigned 21 July, 1356, and the bifhop committed the care of this houfe to Julian, a fifter nun, during its being void. Brian, v. 1. 18. b.

1363, 2 Auguft, Margery Longe, one of the nuns there. Barnet, f. 27.

1369, 29 October, Elizabeth Wodecroft. Lyn. f. 20. b.
> Alice Claybile died priorefs, and was fucceeded by

1421, 4 December, Joan Walys, a nun of the fame houfe. Morgan, v. 1. f. 66.
> Catherine Brown died priorefs, and was fucceeded by

1520, 4 March, Eleanor Graunte, a nun of the fame houfe, moribus undique ornata et virtutibus infignita.

There

There was another religious houfe called the Hofpital of St. Bartholomew the Apoftle for the fupport of men and women. It ftood at the weft end of Lewin's-mead, near the Grey Friers houfe, and the garden of it extended backwards and lay over againft the hofpital of St. Mary Magdalen on the hill of St. Michael.

This like many other fimilar foundations was in ancient times both a priory and an hofpital under the government and direftion of fome regular canons: for in William of Worcefter, p. 208, it is ftiled "quondam prioratus &c." *i. e.* formerly a priory of canons regular founded by the anceftors of Lord de la Ware, and now an hofpital of poor perfons. And p. 252, "an hofpital houfe for the poor with a church formerly of canons of St. Auguftin, and now an hofpital houfe for fupport of poor perfons in the church of St. Bartholomew." The following account from a parchment writing under the name of T. Rowley calls it a priory—and it is fo far confirmed in this by William of Worcefter's manufcript, which was never feen by Chatterton.

The Rolle of Seynɛte Bartholemeweis Priorie.

In the year of our Lorde Chryfte M.CCLV Syre Gawyne * de Rokefhalle & Syre Johnne de Toedmage founded thys pryorie to the honore of Seynɛte Bartholomewe: itte lyeth onne the fyde of Seynɛte Mychaels Hylle, whych parte there lyeynge ys the pryorie for twentie Auftynians ande pryncipall havyng a long courte to Froome Gate ande the arrowe toweres whyche there bee. Atte the ende of the courte ys the Lazarre howfe for thylke who havethe the leprous brennynge. Everich abbotte hydertoe haveth encreafed this houfe ande meynte knights & cytyzens yeven londes & monies thereto, fo that even nowe the place ys full pleafaunte to beholde. The gate is hyghe botte the modde maie ryfe to the annoie thereof. Above itte on. eyther fyde bee imageries, the one of the vyrgyne & chylde & the other of a warrioure and moche enfeemynge to bee for Johnne de Barklie who ybuylden the gate & yeven xx markys ande a tenemente there toe fhryve the leperes wythe 10 markys bie the yeere to a fadre of the blacke frierie to fhrive the lepeirys and 50 markys in lyke tyme to dreffe ande docke theyre forres, fayinge, lette us cure both fpryte & bodye. From the yate we paffe toe the ache chambre where attendeth foure maftre barboure furgeonnes under the behylte of the Auftynian Frere aforefayde—This havethe the ufe of the rolles whyche here bce yeven fome bye Johane de Barkelie & others bie Syrre Walterre Derbie and

---

* One Sir Galfrid de Wrokefhalc was 6 Edw. 1. 1278, at the perambulation of the bounds of Menedip, as appears by a deed in Adam de Domerham, v. 2. p. 685.

and Syr John Vyel * knyghtes & citizens & manie others : the beſte rolles of
the whole bee Gylbertines † rolle of Ypocrates :—The fame fryarres booke
of brennynge, ‡ Johan Stowe of the cure of mormalles § & the waterie leproſie—
the rolle of the blacke mainger : F. Lewis a Wodefordes booke of ailes—the
booke of tymes & Phantaſies & Chryſtmas maumeries bie F. Gualter de
Tockington—further other maumeries & plaies of myracles bie meinie wythe
ſomme of Roberd de Chedder in Frenche & Englyſh, one as plaied at
comitatynge the cyttye the whyche is a quainte peece of wytte & rhyme :
Theſe bee alle the bookes ynne the ache Camberre & of the reſte of the Lazar
houſe bee cellis & beddis for the Lazars, becynge manie in number, the
onlie roome elſe ys the halle where the pryoure ſummoneth councel of
Bredrenne of phyſique blacke whyte grey & odhers : whanne ſome doughtie
worke ys to bee donne on a Lazar, and the maſtre barber ſurgeonne recevyth
theyre order, the fryeres havethe for attendance iij groates fothe ſyttynge
as was lefte bie the wordhie knyghte Syr Johan Somerville—lefte hurte ande
ſcathe bee done to the lepers, the whych mote bee avoyded ; the ſayings &
notiſes of the freeres bee wrote yn a rolle from the whych the barbour ſur-
geones learn muche ande none botte thoſe of Seynte Bartlemews maye loke
thereynne : by whych meanes the barboure ſurgeonis wyll bee ſervytours
there wythoute paye to gayne knowleche of aylimentes & theyr trew curis. ‖

Here

* Theſe are mentioned in the charter of Edw. 3d. as commiſſioned to ſettle the bounds of the
city.

+ This author is mentioned in Chaucer as a ſkilful phyſician : his real name was Rauſe de
Blondeville, called Gilbertine from being of the order of St. Gilbert.

‡ Whether this be the leproſy, ſome burning eruptive ſkin, or the lues venerea has been diſputed.—Becket ſurgeon in a treatiſe on the Brenning of the ancients makes it the latter.

§ Chaucer ſays, " on his ſkin a mormalle had he & a blacke manger."

‖ It is to be admired how few books of phyſic were in the library of this hoſpital—but our
wonder ceaſes when we conſider how few Leland met with in that viſit he made to the religious
houſes before the diſſolution—in ſome houſes were the following phyſic books found :

V. 4. Lel. Coll. p. 46. In Bibliotheca Ramſey Cænob. " Practica Gilberti Anglici."

P 273. Chirurgia Joannis de Baro. de Cænob. Albani Oribaſius.

P. 264. Libellus Galeni—Galenus de Morbo—Liber de febribus ex Arabico tranſlatus Con-
ſtautino Monacho—de Bathe Vulnerarius a ſurgeon—Leproſus Sax. hreoſrig.

P. 17. Tabulæ Ludovici de Garlion Doctoris Medicinæ de eiſdem rebus—Scriptæ Londini
1482—Rogerus Bacon de Erroribus Medicorum—Volumen Magiſtri Ricardi de re Medica—
Compendium torins medicinæ ſeu practica Gilberti Anglici—Gull. Holm. Franciſcanus de ſimpli-
cibus medicinis juſtum volumen—Fuit deflorator medicorum, vixit 1415. . Ægidius de plantis.
Ricardus Medicus de ſignis. Plinius ſecundus de re medica. Oribaſius de ſimplici medicinâ
Antidotarius Nicolai de re medica—Expoſitio ſuper libros aphoriſmorum autore Gilberto Anglico
& Compendium Medicinæ.

Here bee twa wyndows of paynctid glafe : & fortie featis for the Freeres wythe the walles carven & peynctd, beeynge in all fulle faire & of goode handiwurcke. From the Lazar houfe to the pryourie bee a large cloyftered courte wyth windowes thereto. Inne the middeft of thys cloyfter bee the bochorde, wyth fulle mainte bookes thereyn yeven bie dyvers wordie knyghtes whofe armoures bee there to bee feene. The rolles bee fyrfte—a texte Hebraike & Englyfhe wyth ftoddes of goulde, the notes fome bie Bradwardin, fome by pryoure Walter de Lofynge & here bee the pfaulmes in godelie verfe bie Johan Stowe the Bryftoe Carmelyte—alfoe mainte bookes of the Trynitie emprovynge what Maftre Canynge & myfelfe thynkethe, yatte the " hallie fpryte ys yatt whyche gyveth wyfdom & holdethe up † heaven & earthe & lyfe & brethe bie the powers of kynde whych fpryngeth from that allene. The rolle of Symon de Gaunte de principio—patterne of Seyncte Luke—Turgottes rolles. Bede, Afferius, Ingolphe—Meinte rolles of lyttle worthe to Goddis fervyce. Scripture myracles & maumeries—The legende of the Earles of Glouceftre—plaies of the Earles of Glouceftre bie Johan Stowe fulle of wytte & godelie wordes.

Legende of the knyghtes of the Swanne, twa plaies of the fame by Johan Stowe—Legende of the Seynctes. Maumeries of the lyke by the Freeres of the grey ordre wyth other Maumeryes by divers wryters.

Inne the bochorde bee alfo peyncteynges & there bee one onne the walle of Bryftowe ynne the reygn of W. Roufe as walled bie Geoffrie Byfhoppe of Conftance & a drawynge of Geoffreis Logge & walls of the fame, wythe dreeynges of Robert of Gloucefterre his caftle ande eke dreeynges of a fpyre & endeynge botte of a chyrche the whyche I have ne feene butte ytte mote bee made for the pryourie toure whyche havethe no fpyre to be putte onne the famme—the fpyre bee a quaynte wurcke, the botte lyke that of Wefteburie ybuylden by Maftre Roberte Canynge ; others bee alfoe yn this bochorde—a fmall rolle of elf-lockes bye John Stowe emproveynge them not to be the worke of fprytes as meynt do owlyfhlie enthyncke—From the bochorde come wee to the chapele where bee meynte naumeries as depyčted ynne the rolles hereon of Syr Gawyne de Rokefhall & others : inne the wyndowe bee manie hatchmentes in heraldique manner, the whych bee alfoe

here

---

† That is. the natural agents called here the powers of kind, act by and under the direction of the Holy Spirit the infpirer of wifdom, fcriptural wifdom.—It is faid that ɪ. Milverton and others held, that God governed the world &c. without any natural agents : but Rowley fpeaking of them fays, " theie eider meane Godde be the powers of kinde or natural agents or theie know not what themfelves meane."

here dreene.   Here bee toe a quainte peece of cofier wurcke bie a nonne of Tuckefburye of the lyfe of Seynête Barptholomew.   From the chapele to the friourie is a fmall fpace.   The friourie haveth little thereyn that is of worthe, but the cellis bee dernie & well yroughten in wode—but the buyldynge be not compyghte.

Thus endeth the rolle of Seynête Bartholomew & here folleweth a lyfte of the pryoures.

M.C.C.OV. Richard the broder of Syr Gawyn de Rokefhall.

M.C.C.XXII. John the chanter who fyrfte had the fetyve amerheaded crofier, whych crofier bee yn the revetrie havynge depyêted thereonne the 12 apoftles of our Lorde under dyvers ftonis.

M.C.C.X.L.I.X. Walter Bronefcombe afterwardes Byfhoppe of Exonecefter.

M.C.C.L. John de Kynton.

M.CC.L.XXXX.II. Engelram de Courcie.

M.C.CC.X. Wyllyam de Blondeville.

M.CCC.XV. Walter de Lofynge.

M.CCC.XXXVI. Robert de la Corner.

M.CCC.LX. Johannes le White.

M.CCC.LXX. Rogerus de Somerville.

M.CCC.XCIII. Everarde de la Yate.

M.CCCC.XX. Edmonde Holbeck.

M.CCCC.XXXVI. John Warlewafte.

M.CCCC.L. Reginald Mottecombe.

M.CCCC.LVII. Radulph de Beckington, who now doth hold the fame priourie.   Thus dothe ende the rolle of Seynête Bartbolomewis priourie bie Thomas Rowley.

It appears from ancient deeds there was alfo a priorefs appointed for this hofpital; though by inquifition it was proved that it was a very ancient foundation, of which there was no account but by public fame, that the cuftody of it was always in men and not in women: the following occur priorefles whatever their authority might be—1 Aug. 1363 Elizabeth Batte—Joan Joye—1368 Maud Coveley.—In 1382 Robert Cheddre leaves a legacy to the fifters of St. Bartholomew's, book of wills, p. 8.

It is faid in a deed 1386 that Lord de la War was the true patron to prefent, and that the rents and profits of it confifted in lands cultivated and rents to the value of 30 marks &c.

This houfe with all the lands, &c. thereto belonging was by licence from King Henry 8th. anno regni 24, purchafed by the executors of Robert

Thorn,

Thorn, Efq; of Sir Thomas Weft, Knight, and Lord la Warre, patrons and founders, George Croft, mafter, and the brethren and fifters of the faid hofpital, and conveyed to the mayor, burgeffes, and commonalty of Briftol, for erecting a free grammar-fchool, in purfuance of the will of the faid Robert Thorn. This and fome other hofpitals in Briftol were probably in bad condition in Leland's time, he having placed this amongft thofe in ruin. Robert and Nicholas the fons of Robert Thorn were alfo great benefactors to this fchool. The head mafter thereof is at prefent allowed 6ol. the under mafter or ufher 4ol. per annum.

The bailiff who collects the rents for the corporation of Briftol pays at Michaelmas to the head mafter of this fchool 1l. 13s. 4d. and the ufher 16s. 8d. as the gift of Mrs. Netheway to buy each of them a hat.

There are certain lands and tenements called the Bartholomew's, (the rents collected by the bailiff) lying and being in Wickwar, Horfield, Stapleton, Winterbourn, Briflington, Almondfbury, and in Briftol, to the amount in 1740 of 89l. 4s. 6d. in ground or referved rents.

For the greater encouragement of freemen's fons educated at this fchool, feveral well-difpofed perfons have left exhibitions for fuch when fent to the univerfity of Oxford, as appears by enquiry made in the Chamber Book of Orders the 23d of Auguft and 12th of William 3d. 1700.

Mrs. Ann Snigg gave two exhibitions of 6l. each payable yearly for ever towards the maintenance of two youths in the univerfity, fons of free burgeffes, to be chofen out of the Grammar-fchool of Briftol by the mayor and common council.

Mr. White gave an exhibition of 5l. yearly for the fame purpofe for one young man, in the fame manner to be chofen.

Mr. Alderman Whitfon gave two exhibitions of 1ol. per annum to two young men, to be chofen out of the fame fchool.

About the year 1700 it was agreed to fend all thefe fcholars that were exhibitioners to Baliol college, and Dr. Maunder, the prefident, agreed to receive them there, that by their friendfhip and mutual affiftance, after being bred at Briftol Grammar-fchool, they might affift each other in their ftudies, and the corporation be more eafily informed where they were and what progrefs and improvement they made in their learning, and the corporation ordered 1ool. as a prefent from the city towards completing the additional buildings of Baliol on this occafion; but fince that time they are not confined to one college, and the exhibitioners are placed to what college the parents may think beft,

and

and the exhibitions given to freemen's fons of Briftol, to whatever college they may happen to belong.

By a decree upon a commiffion of the High Court of Chancery, 12th July, 8th James 1ft. it was ordered that the mayors for the time being fhould continue to be fpecial governors of this fchool and yearly vifit it, and from time to time with advice of the aldermen and common council for ever hereafter as often as they fee occafion difplace or place the fchool-mafter and ufher, and from time to time make orders and rules for the education of youth there in grammar and other good literature, fo that they be not repugnant to the laws and ordinances fet down by the founders. It was alfo decreed that only 4d. fhould be taken by the fchool-mafter for every fchool-boy's admiffion, and in fuch form freely to be taught as fet down by the founders.

This fchool has long flourifhed under the care and patronage of the corporation, and the diftinguifhed abilities of the mafters who have prefided here, and have greatly fupported its credit. For encouragement of the mafter and better accommodation of boarders (and he is allowed to take fome) the houfe at the Bartholomews's, being old, dark, and in a low inconvenient fituation, was exchanged for the more airy and fpacious hofpital of Queen Elizabeth in Orchard-ftreet; but the endowments of each feparately remain the fame, the place only being charged (fee page 379.) fo that this free grammar-fchool continues to grow in efteem, to the great advantage of the citizens of Briftol, who are inclined to give their fons a learned education at little expence, and prepare them for the univerfity or any of the profeffions of divinity, phyfic, or law, and who have a natural right and gratuitous claim to the privileges of this fchool and the fellowfhip and exhibitions in Oxford belonging to it. There are certain rules and ordinances for the well-governing of this fchool and about the qualifications of fchool-mafter and ufher, which have been agreed on and confirmed by the corporation, the truftees and vifitors of the fchool, who from time to time have advanced the falaries of the mafter and ufher, that the founder's good defigns of a free grammar-fchool be punctually fulfilled, and not fruftrated by deviating from the original foundation calculated for the cafe, relief, and emolument of the citizens.

There is in this parifh a chapel dedicated to the Three Kings of Cologn, and an almfhoufe to it adjoining, having fourteen chambers for the habitation of one prieft, eight poor men, and five poor women. Its fituation is at the top of Queen-ftreet and Steep-ftreet, and it was founded about the 19th year of Henry 7th. 1504, by John Fofter, mayor in 1481. After his death this charity was augmented by John Efterfield, mayor in 1488, 1495, one of his

executors.

executors. The land on which it is built was purchafed by Mr. Fofter only for a term of years of the abbot of Tewkfbury, but was afterwards bought in fee by Mr. Efterfield. No perfon was to be admitted on this charitable foundation but Englifh, and none under the age of fifty years or married. The mayor and aldermen of Briftol for the time being had power to place in feven men, and Mrs. Mayorefs four women ; the other two perfons were to be placed in by the mafter of the houfe of St. Mark of Billefwyck for the time being. The prieft was daily to fay mafs between the hours of eight and nine in the morning for the good eftate of the fouls of John Fofter and Elizabeth his wife, their fathers and mothers ; for James Venables, the faid John Efterfield, merchant, and for Alice and Maud his late wives, &c. for which the prieft was to have 5l. 6s. 8d. per annum. The whole accounts of this charity are to be produced by the bailiff that collects the rents, &c. on the 11th of November yearly, and then audited before the mayor and the town clerk, when if prefent the mayor was to receive 5s. the town clerk 1s. 8d. and the bailiff 20d. for their trouble.

This charity was further augmented by Dr. George Owen, phyfician to King Henry 8th. which in the year 1748 brought in 86l. 19s. 10d. per annum. The rents of the lands given by Fofter, &c. in the fame year produced 77l. 11s. per annum, being chiefly out upon lives. The government of this houfe at prefent is in the magiftrates of Briftol, by whofe care and good menagement the poor there (fourteen) are now paid each of them 2s. 6d. per week. In the Chriftmas they have double pay, and in Eafter and Whitfon weeks they are paid 5s. more than their ufual pay, and at fome time in the year they have fhirts, fhifts, and coal given them.

The rector of this parifh is paid by the chamberlain of Briftol 10l. per annum for prayers and a monthly fermon to be preached in this chapel, to the clerk 26s.

The annual difburfements out of Fofter's lands, Dr. Owen's, and thofe called the Bartholomew's, all blended together for the fupport of Fofter's almfhoufe, Bartholomew's grammar-fchool, and for the fchool in Redcliff churchyard, are,

	l.	s.	d.
To the mafter of the grammar-fchool at Redcliff - -	4	0	0
To the mafter and ufher of the Bartholomew's grammar-fchool, one year - - - - -	102	10	0
To fourteen perfons in Fofter's almfhoufe at 2s. 6d. each, one year	91	0	0
To the rector of St. Michael's parifh for fervice there -	10	0	0
To the clerk of that parifh, his yearly falary - -	1	6	0

To

To other contingencies paid by the bailiff one year, with other   *l.*   *s.*   *d.*
difburfements, amounting to about 40l. per annum   -   40   0   0

                                          £ 248 16 0

On the fide of St. Michael's-hill in this parifh Edward Colfton, Efq; having purchafed of the mayor and commonalty of the city of Briftol two acres and three quarters and thirty-feven perches of pafture ground, known by the name of the Turtles, alias Jonas Leafes, on part of this ground in the year 1691, he built and finifhed an hofpital or almfhoufe of freeftone with a chapel for divine fervice, the charge of which amounted to about 2500l. having three meffuages or tenements erected upon fome other part of the faid ground adjoining to the hofpital. And in the year 1696 he endowed the fame with lands and fee farm rents, &c. in Northumberland. This houfe hath twenty-four apartments for twelve men and twelve women, freemen, or the widows, fons, or daughters of fuch freemen, or born in the city of Briftol, or that have lived in the faid city for twenty years before admittance, which houfe is for ever to be called Colfton's Almfhoufe. The founder during his natural life referved a power to himfelf of placing in the poor when any vacancy fhould happen, and after his deceafe he gave the fame power for ever to be in the mafter, wardens, affiftants, and commonalty of the Merchant Venturers within the city of Briftol, and appointed them vifitors or governors thereof, and invefted them with lands, rents, &c. for its fupport, viz. to each perfon of this houfe 3s. per week ; but upon the death of any perfon there belonging, no fucceffor fhall be intitled to that pay till three months after the death of the predeceffor, which fhall be kept in ftock for keeping the houfe in repair, and that out of the twelve men one fhall be chief brother of the houfe, who fhall weekly or once in a fortnight receive the allowance of 3s. each from the mafter wardens, &c. for every perfon there, and for his care and pains he fhall be allowed full 6s. per week, and at his death another elder brother fhall be chofen by the company of merchants out of thofe men in the houfe And that each perfon in the houfe either before or after Chriftmas fhall receive twenty-four facks of coal and 10s. for foap and candles. And that in the chapel room fhall be read the Common Prayer according to the liturgy of the Church of England by a perfon in holy orders, to be appointed by the founder during his life, and after that by the mafter, wardens, &c. of faid company, who fhall pay him 10l. per annum. And if the ftock of the houfe fhould fall fhort, then to deduct 1s. per week out of every one's pay, but not to continue above one year. And if that is not fufficient then

                                               the

the refidue to be fupplied by not filling up the places of any of the fix decayed failors in the Merchant's almfhoufe, all which endowments came to about 8500l.

The accounts of this houfe are always to be kept feparate, and once a year the houfe to be vifited by the twenty truftees or lefs, and when by death they are reduced to four then to convey to twenty others.

Rules to be obferved in this hofpital.

1. That prayers be read in the chapel every mornin and evening in the year, except Sunday, Wednefday, and Friday mornings, when there are prayers at the parifh church: if the reader neglect, then 1s. to be flopt for each neglect out of his pay.

2. Prayers to begin at eight o'clock in the morning and at three in the afternoon from Lady-day to the 29th of September, and from the 29th of September to the 25th of March at nine o'clock in the morning and three in the afternoon.

3. All perfons belonging to the houfe fhall attend the prayers in the chapel, or in the parifh church, ficknefs only excepted, on the forfeiture of 6d. for each default.

4. All fines fhall be applied to the ftock of the houfe, and that the chief brother do keep a book to note down all the affairs of the houfe, which fhall be produced to the mafter, wardens, &c.

5. The bonfe to be vifited by the governors twice a year.

6. That once a year the accounts fhall be made up relating to the bonfe.

7. That none be chofen into the houfe but thofe of the communion of the Church of England, nor under the age of fifty, unlefs for a chief brother, nor any vicious perfon, &c.

8. That there be in the houfe always four men or women out of Temple parifh, two of Chrift Church, and two out of St. Michael, provided the premifes be not rated to the poor of St. Michael's parifh.

9. No inmate fhall lodge in the houfe, or child or children be kept there by day or night.

10. The chief brother fhall have the care of the houfe and the inhabitants therein, and remark in a book what is done amifs.

11. The gate fhall be locked every night at nine o'clock in the fummer, and in the winter at eight: and that lying out three nights in the year fhall be fufficient for expulfion. The elder brother fhall appoint one of the houfe to lock the doors and to ring the bell for prayers.

12. Thefe rules fhall be read at the time of vifitation.

At

At the north-east entrance into the Royal Fort-lane in this parish is a school erected by John Elbridge, Esq; in his life time. At his death, which happened the 22d of February, 1739, he left by his will 3000l. to endow this charity for the cloathing of twenty-four female children once a year and educating them in reading, writing, cyphering, and sewing: there is no allowance for diet or lodging. In pursuance to his will in the year 1748 his trustees erected a handsome house with two apartments, which cost 287l. for the habitation of the school-master and mistress. The master's salary is 20l. and the mistress's 15l. per annum, she having the benefit of their work, and both allowed coals and candles. The annual income for the support of this charity is about 90l. per annum, which arises from South Sea annuities, settled by the Lord Chancellor, and invested in the hands of feoffees and trustees for the said uses.

A charity-school is established by the parishioners of St. Michael and St. Augustin, for keeping the poor boys belonging to each parish at school and instructing them in reading, writing, cyphering, and the church catechism. It is chiefly supported by the contributions of a few gentlemen of each parish, and has few benefactions as yet bestowed on it.

C H A P. XIV.

Of the CHURCH of ALL SAINTS, and HOUSE and SOCIETY of KALENDARIES.

THIS church is very old, being one of those built in the center of the city supposed to be founded by one of the Anglo-Saxon Earls of Glocester, dedicated to All Saints, a festival kept on the first of November.— It is mentioned by Leland as early appropriated to the monastery of St. Augustin. Robert Fitzharding with Robert Earl of Glocester then Lord of Bristol translated the fraternity of Kalendaries from the church of Holy Trinity or Christ Church to this of All Saints. It is but a small church of three ailes, the north and south being of equal length; at the west end of these a house projects over two large freestone pillars into the church, which hurts

the

the appearance of it and flattens the found of the organ, erected between them in the year 1740 at the expence of 249l. The middle aile is in length 70 feet, and in height about 49; the fide ailes are each about 30 feet high; the roof is all of timber; the outfide covered with Cornifh tile, repaired the 10th of Henry 8th. by Robert Elliot, then abbot of St. Auguftin, as alfo was the chancel by a decree from the Bifhop of Worcefter. On its north-caft fide was a low freeftone tower taken down in the year 1713, and in the year 1716 it was begun to be rebuilt by the voluntary contributions of the citizens at the expence of 589l. 10s. 3d. towards which Edward Colfton, Efq; gave 250l. The church books fay that in 1443 the fteeple was repaired. William of Worcefter mentions the length of it to be in toto 23 yards or 74 fteps, and its breadth 20 yards or 34 fteps. In 1451 Sir John Gyllard, prior of the Kalendaries, built the curious wainfcot ceiling over the north aile called Jefus's aile, on which are carved, gilt, and painted many curious emblems of the fufferings of Chrift, but growing to decay and found dangerous was taken down in the year 1782 and rebuilt: over this aile at the fame time was conftructed a large room for a public library under the government of the prior and mayor. And it appears from deeds that the houfe at the north-weft end of the church, part of which was over the public conduit and at its back part projected into the church, was the houfe of the Kalendaries, out of which by a door they communicated with the library. The houfe at the fouth-weft end refting on the pillars of the church is the vicarage-houfe, built by Thomas Marfhall, vicar and one of the Kalendaries, about the year 1422. There is a deed in the regifters of the church of Worcefter, (Morgan, vol. i. folio 70) entitled, " Fundatio Manfi Vicarii omnium Sanctorum." The founder Marfhall erected the building at his own expence, partly on the ground of the church and partly on the churchyard, for the perpetual refidence of all the future vicars, and he obtained of Philip Bifhop of Worcefter confirmation of it for that ufe, who ordered an annual obiit on the 7th of January and prayers for the foul of the faid Marfhall, to be celebrated in this church by all fucceeding vicars, and that they fhould pay 6s. 8d. in the following manner: fix groffos monetæ (groats) equally between fix chaplains then prefent, at the exequies and mafs 12d. for two wax candles, 10d. to the parifh clerk (clafficum vel campanas pul-fanti) 2d. to the crier for proclaiming the obiit, and 20d. worth (denariatus) of bread to be diftributed among the poor, and 6d. each to the proctors of the church to fuperintend the faid ordinance. This church was new pewed in the year 1757 in a neat and elegant manner, the ground floor then very low much rifen, and the pulpit removed to the oppofite fide; but in the year 1770 was

farther

farther embellished, the feats being taken up and fixed anew and the whole
painted and beautified at a very great expence, and though small it now makes
a very neat appearance: a painting of the falutation of the Virgin Mary is
fet up over the altar. In the year 1728 eight new bells were caft at the
expence of 134l. 10s. 9d. befides the fix old ones, the tenor not to exceed
1700lb. weight, and the reft in proportion. There were feveral altars in this
church, at which obiits were celebrated. In 1241 Alice Hazle left a tenement called the Green Lettice in High-ftreet of 5l. 6s. 8d. per annum, to difcharge the expence of her obiit on the 10th of July annually at the crofs or
rood altar entering the chancel. In 1433 Martin Draper gave 12d. a year to
maintain a lamp to burn there, and John le Gate gave 4s. per annum to find
five tapers to burn before our Lady's altar. The following perfons founded
chauntries here for the good of their fouls and for their friends: John Haddon,
vintner; Sir Thomas Marfhall, vicar, who died the 17th of January, 1434;
Sir William Rodberd, vicar, who died the 6th of June, 1453; Thomas
Holway, who died the 13th of December, 1454; Everard French eftablifhed
a chauntry here, and Henry Chefter, who died the 14th of February, 1470,
for himfelf and his wife Alice, who died the 16th of December, 1485. The
obiit of John Snigg was kept the 18th of September, 1490, and that of Sir
Nicolas Parker, vicar, the 8th of Auguft, 1436, he gave 8s. per annum to
provide 10lb. of wax for two tapers to burn before the high altar. The gifts
to the ufe of this church in rich ornaments and veftments are furprizingly
great, and it appears by the church deeds that on the 14th of Anguft, 1459,
there was upwards of 423 ounces of filver plate belonging to thefe altars. It
would be endlefs to reckon up the number of chalices, patens, croffes both
gold and filver of great weight, fome weighing upwards of ninety ounces, embellifhed with rubies and other precious ftones, tabernacles, fpoons of gold,
ampullas, cenfers, candlefticks, paxes, cruets, fhips, fepulchres, bells, gilt
crowns, angels painted, ftained cloths for the coronation of our Lady, Lent
cloths for the rood altar, curtains, veftments of velvet, filk, gold, filver, &c.
fringes, banners, frontels, corporaffys, &c. mafs books, antiphonerycs, pfaw-
ters, books for the organs, legends, proceffionals, grayles, ordinals, &c.

On the 14th of Auguft, 1549, the following jewels were weighed at All
Saints church by which the riches belonging thereto may be eftimated.

			Ounces.
A great crofs of filver, all gilt, weight	–	–	159
A fmall crofs, all gilt, with a crucifix	–	–	60
One pax of filver, all gilt, with a little cup and fpoon	–	$44\frac{1}{4}$

Two

	Ounces.
Two cenfers, all gilt - - - - -	68
Two candlefticks of filver, part gilt, with a little pax, and a fhip of filver, part gilt - - - -	91¾
	423½

All thefe valuables with many more too tedious to enumerate fell into the hands of Henry 8th. and Edward 6th. at the diffolution, and the plate it appears by the following receipt was all coined for his Majefty's ufe.

" On the 13th of Anguft, 1549, was received by me, Robert Recorde,
" comptroller of his Majefty's mint of Briftol, to his Highnefs's ufe, of Mr.
" William Younge and John Pykes, proctors of All Hallows in Briftol, in gilt
" filver 19lb. 11½oz. and in parcel gilt 15lb. 3oz.

" ROBERT RECORDE."

There was annually performed in this church a general obiit for all good doers about the year 1500, the expence thereof paid by the churchwardens as follows:

	l.	s.	d.
To the vicar 4d. to five priefts for the dirge, 1s. 3d. -	0	1	7
To the clerk for his labour and bell - - -	0	1	2
To three bufhels and a half wheaten meal, at 1s. 6d. per bufhel	0	5	3
To three ounces and a half faffron 4s. 4d. and 2 oz. cloves, 8d.	0	5	0
Bread to poor people, 7d. pottle of oil, 1s. -	0	1	7
To three gallons of claret wine - - -	0	2	0
To three gallons of malfmy wine - - -	0	3	0
To two gallons of fack - - - -	0	1	4
To the fexton for laying the hearfe - -	0	0	2
To baking the cakes, 1s. 4d. finging ale two dozen, 2s. 2d.	0	3	6
	£ 1	4	7

In 1552 much plate ftill remaining, it was on the 6th of Auguft, 6th year of King Edward 6th. delivered to his commiffioners for the ufe of his mint then at Briftol, two chalices and fix bells excepted, which were left till the king's pleafure was further known. The plate in ufe at prefent confifts of two filver flaggons, 92 ounces; one filver cup and cover gilt, 32 ounces; one filver gilt plate, 14½ ounces; one ditto, 14 ounces.

This vicarage is valued in the King's Books at the clear yearly value of 21l. 11s. 8d. the yearly tenths now difcharged were 8s. 4d. An annual crown rent of 4s. is paid out of a houfe in High-ftreet and one in Broad-ftreet.

The patrons are the dean and chapter of Briftol.

The

'The living is eftimated to be worth to the vicar annually,

	l.	s.	d.
In Eafter dues and furplice fees, about - -	60	0	0
By a free gift out of the veftry ftock - - -	30	0	0
By the annual rent of the vicarage-houfe, if let -	26	0	0
£	116	0	0

And to a lecturer annually for fervice every Sunday

afternoon, per annum - - -	20	0	0
A collection for him at Eafter, about • -	15	0	0
£	35	0	0

VICARS of All Saints Church.

PATRONS.

The abbot and
convent of
St. Auguftin.

William Santocke.
1278 Michael Ruffelyn.
1280 Sir William Selke, of the fraternity of Kalendaries.
1286 William Scoche.
1304 Sir William Lenche, a frier of the Kalendaries.
1307 Sir Walter Ifgar, a Kalendary, died 1 Dec. 1321.
1311 Adam de Weftbury.
1326 Richard le White.
Sir William Salle.
Sir William Mooche.
Sir William Colas, a Kalendary.
1407 Sir Thomas Marfhall, a Kalendary, and was a great
benefactor to the church.
William Ryall, chaplain.
1434 Sir Richard Parkhoufe, a Kalendary, died 8 Aug. 1436.
1436 Sir William Rodberd, died 1453.
1453 Sir William Were, died 1482.
Sir John Gyllarde, prior of the Kalendaries, built the
aile of Jefus and library aloof, and expended on the
library 217l. died 1451.
1453 Sir Maurice Hardwyk, gave the great ledger-book to
record all things, ftill in being.
1472 Sir William Howe, a Kalendary.
1479 Sir John Thomas, ceiled the roof of the choir.
1484 Sir Thomas Haxby, a Kalendary, died 19 June, 1484.
1486 Sir John Harlow, prior of the Kalendaries, died
6 Dec. that year.

1488 Sir John Thomas.

Sir Thomas Turber, a Kalendary.

1503 Sir Richard Bromfield.

1518 John Flook.

1533 Thomas Molence.

1536 Thomas Pacy.

Dean and
chapter of
Briſtol.

1541 Humphrey Hyman.

Robert Roolate, died 1567.

1567 Thomas Gleſſon.

1577 William Haſtlen.

1591 John Knight.

1598 Francis Arnold, died 13 July, 1611.

1611 Robert Marks, alfo vicar of South Petherton.

1617 William Gregory.

1620 Richard Towgood.

1626 George Williamſon. Of him ſee Wood's Ath. Oxon

1685 Richard Roberts.

1686 John Rainſtorp, died 1 May, 1693.

1693 Thomas Paradice, died 1701.

1701 Thomas Cary, died 30 Oct. 1711.

1711 James Harcourt, and vicar of South Petherton, died
1739.

1739 Thomas Gardiner, died ſoon of a fever.

1739 Joſiah Tucker, precentor of the cathedral, afterwards
Dean of Gloceſter.

1749-50 William Pritchard, died 1753.

1753 John Berjew, the preſent vicar, 1788, and vicar of
Bathford.

There are ſome very neat and elegant monuments in this church. One
very large was at the upper end of the north aile, ſupported with three fluted
pillars, &c. with the following inſcription, but in the late repairs removed.

" Humfridus Toius, Londinenſis, jacet in hoc tumulo qui obiit 16 Oct.
1577.

    Hunc mors peccati merces ſubtraxit amara
      Qui Deo dives erat, religione pius :
    Qui ſibi purmultum coluit cœleſtes alumnos
      Fortunæ que bonis pavit et ipſe pios :

                        Chriſticola

Chriſticola ut vivus fuit is, tumulatus abibat,
Tum Chriſti poſuit vulneribuſque fidem.
Impenſas egit in hoc tumulum Margeria conjux prediſti Humfridi Toii.''

In the middle aile is a monument creſted by Edward Golſion, Eſq; to the dear memory of his father and mother, four ſons, and two daughters. William the father died 21 November, 1681, aged 73 ; Sarah the mother died 22 December, 1701, aged 93. Edward Colſton, junr. died 5 April, 1719; Sarah his daughter, 28 January, 1721, aged 15; Mary his wife, 29 November, 1733, aged 49.

On an old ſtone under the reading deſk was the following: — " Thomas Colſton, mayor and alderman of this city, died 16 November, 1597, with the following lines:

" Death is no death, now Thomas Colſton lives,
Who fourſcore years hath lived to his praiſe :
A joyful life now Chriſt doth to him give,
Who wrong'd no wight, each man commends his ways.
Death him commands to bid this world adieu ;
Thrice happy thoſe who die to live anew.

At the upper end of the fouth aile is the following inſcription, and a monument: ſee the print.

" To the memory of Edward Colſton, Eſq; who was born in the city of Briſtol, and was one of the repreſentatives in parliament for the ſaid city in the reign of Queen Ann. His extenſive charity is well known to many parts of this kingdom ; but more particularly to this city, where his benefaſtions have exceeded all others. A liſt of which is on his monument as followeth. He lived 84 years, 11 months, and 9 days, and then departed this life the 11th of Oſtober, 1721, at Mortlake in Surry, and lieth buried in a vault by his anceſtors in the firſt croſs alley under the reading deſk of this church.

The PUBLIC CHARITIES and BENEFACTIONS given and founded by EDWARD COLSTON, Eſquire.

In BRISTOL.

On St. Michael's-hill.

1691, An almſhouſe for 12 men and 12 women ; the chief brother to receive 6s. the other 3s. per week beſides coal, &c. To a chaplain 10l. per annum. The whole to be paid by fee farm rents on eſtates in Northumberland, Cumberland, and Durham, and by ſome houſes and lands near the houſe. The charge about - - - - - - 8500

In King-ſtreet.

Six ſailors to be maintained in the Merchants' almſhouſe, by a   *l.*
farm in Congerſbury, Somerſet. The charge about   -   600

In Temple-ſtreet.

1696, A ſchool for 40 boys to be cloathed and taught, endowed with
an annuity out of the manor of Tomarhear, Somerſet. An
houſe and garden for the maſter. The charge about   3000

In the College-green.

1702, To the rebuilding the boys' hoſpital   -   -   -   500
And for 6 boys to be cloathed, maintained, inſtructed, and
apprenticed. A farm of 70l. per annum in Congerſbury.
The charge about -   -   -   - · -   1500

In St. Peter's pariſh.

To the Mint workhouſe   -   -   -   -   200
And for placing out poor children -   -   -   -   200

On St. Auguſtine's-back.

1708, An hoſpital for a maſter, two uſhers, and a catechiſt, and
100 boys to be inſtructed, maintained, and apprenticed.
The charge about -   -   -   -   -   40000
One hundred pounds per annum to be given for twelve years
after his death, either to thoſe who have been apprenticed
from the hoſpital of St. Auguſtine's-back, or from the apprenticing of boys from Temple ſchool, by 10l. each   -   1200
To the ſeveral charity-ſchools each 10l. per annum, given for
many years while he lived, and to be continued for twelve
years after his death.

To the repairing and beautifying of churches.

All Saints	-	- 250	St. Michael	-	- 50	
Cathedral	-	- 260	St. Stephen's	-	- 50	
Clifton	-	- - 50	Temple	-	- 160	
St. James	-	- 100	St. Thomas	-	- 50	
St. Mary Redliff	-	100	St. Werburgh	-	160	——1230

For reading prayers at All Saints every Monday and Tueſday
morning, 7l. per annum   -   -   -   140
For twelve ſermons at Newgate, 6l. per annum   -   -   120
For fourteen ſermons in Lent 20l. per annum, now diſcontinued   400

In LONDON.

To St. Bartholomew's hoſpital   -   -   -   2500
To Chriſt Church   ditto   -   -   -   -   2000

To

					l.
To St. Thomas's hofpital	-	-	-	-	500
To Bethlehem ditto	-	-	-	-	500
To the new workhoufe without Bifhopfgate			-	-	200
To the Society for propagating the Gofpel			-		300
To the Company of Mercers		-	-	-	-	100

In Surry at SHEEN.

An almfhoufe for fix poor men, built and endowed.

At MORTLAKE.

For the education and cloathing of 12 boys and 12 girls, 45l. per annum - - - - - - 900

To 85 poor people at his death - - - - 85

In LANCASHIRE.

Towards building a church at Manchefter - - - 20

To 18 charity-fchools on feveral parts of England for many years after his death, 90l. per annum.

To the augmentation of 60 fmall livings - - 6000

In all £ 70695

This great and pious benefactor was known to have done many other excel-cellent charities, and what he did in fecret is believed to be not inferior to what he did in public.

On the pedeftal under him is : " Edward the fon of William Colfton, Efq; and Sarah his wife was born in this city, November 2, 1636. Died at Mortlake, Surry, October 11, 1721, and lies buried near this monument." He was buried October 27, 1721. See more of him in the chapter of the lives of eminent Briftol men hereafter.

Over the north door is a neat monument " To the memory of Edward Colfton, Efq; eldeft fon of Alexander Colfton, Efq; and Sophia his wife, and great great nephew of Edward Colfton, Efq; He died November 12, 1763, aged 24."

Sir John Duddleftone, Bart. lies buried with dame Sufanna his lady under the firft pew coming into the church, on the right hand, at the north door. — He was created a baronet January 11, 1691. He was the firft baronet of his family, and was an eminent tobacco-merchant in the houfe fronting the fouth fide of St. Werburgh's tower, the back part of which is now called Shannon-court, within the parifh of St. Werburgh, who, on Prince George of Denmark's arrival to fee this city, was the firft perfon that invited him to his houfe, whereupon when that Prince came to London, he got him firft knighted and afterwards a baronet's patent.

In

In the middle aile was a ſtone with this :—" Hic jacet Thomas Marſhall, vir bonæ memoriæ, quondam vicarius hujus ecclefiæ, qui obiit 17 die Junli, A. D. 1434, cujus animæ propitietur Deus, Amen." Out of the month of his figure in braſs on the ſtone proceed three ſcrolls thus inſcribed—Redemptor meus vivit.—De teriâ furrcêturus fum.—In carne meâ videbo fervatorem meum.

Near this—" Hic requiefcunt corpora bonæ memoriæ Johannis Haddon, vynter et chryſtinæ uxoris fuæ et Aliciæ filiæ diêti Johannis qui obiit 11 Martii, 1433, quorum animabus proprietur Deus, Amen."

" Gulielmus Rodbert, quondam vicarius, obiit 6 Jun. 1453."

" Richardus Roberts, A. M. nuper vicarius, obiit 25 Sept. 1686."

" Robert Aldworth, town clerk, 20 March, 1675."

" Chriſtopher Kedgwin, mayor and alderman, died 14 February, 1617, aged 68."

In the chancel is a monument with his ſtatue half length of Mr. John Doughty, mayor and alderman and burgeſs in parliament, with Engliſh verſes underneath. He died 1629, aged 67. Arms, f. or. a croſs fleury gules.

In the chancel a neat monument againſt the wall :—" In a vault near this place lies interred the body of Deborah Freeman, wife of John Freeman, of Clifton, Efq; ſhe departed this life, April 8, 1766, aged 62 years. If the loſs of an endearing wjfe, affeêtionate mother, ſincere friend, and generous benefcêtrefs, diſtreſſes her huſband, children, acquaintance, and neceſſitous poor; yet the confideration that all thefe focial and moral charaêters were fpiritualized and immortalized to the life-giving principles of Chriſtian faith and divine love revives the hearts of all that knew her in the glorious hope of meeting her purified in her eternal ſtate."

On another near this :—" To the memory of John Freeman, Efq, late of Clifton, formerly of this pariſh, who by the bleſſing of Divine Providence on great natural abilities, prudence, integrity, and induſtry, acquired an affluent fortune, which he employed in adminiſtering relief to the diſtreſſed, and inſtruêtion to the ignorant. His charity was not the tranſient impulfe of cafual compaſſion, but the regular effcê of fettled principles. He adorned an honourable old age with the exaê exercife of the focial and religious duties, and by a ſtriê courfe of temperance attained to the age of 84. As he lived in the Chriſtian faith, he died in the full perfuaſion of the Chriſtian hope on the 28th of Anguſt, 1786."

On another :—" To Abigail Freeman, wife of John Freeman, junr. Efq; ſhe died 16th March, 1764, aged 28. Abigail their daughter 13th January, 1784,

1784, aged 2 years 6 months; alfo Elizabeth their daughter 16 April 1787, aged 6 years.

BENEFACTORS to the Church and Poor of All Saints parifh.

	l.	s.	d.
Robert Colfton the fon of William Colfton Efq; deceafed, a native of this city, gave 6l. per ann. for prayers to be read Monday and Tuefday throughout the year, and to the clerk and fexton 10s. per ann. -	130	0	0
1701, John Hicks Efq; fometime mayor and alderman of this city, gave the fum of 12l. 10s. the income yearly to fuch poor of All Saints parifh as do not receive alms, -	12	10	0

1709, Samuel Bayley Efq; fometime fheriff of this city, gave 24l. the intereft thereof to be applied on St. Andrew's day in every year as follows :

For a fermon - - -	0	12	0
To the clerk - - -	0	2	6
To the fexton - - -	0	1	6
To each of the 8 alms-women 1s. -	0	8	0——24 0 0

	l.	s.	d.
1714, Thomas Bayley of this city merchant gàve 10l. the intereft thereof to be given to the poor of the almfhoufe in bread the 16th of April for ever, - - -	10	0	0
1724, John Cook of this city diftiller gave 20l. for the payment of 20s. for preaching a fermon on the 30th of January for ever, - - - - -	20	0	0
1738, Thomas Gibbs late of this parifh gave 50l. for payment of 5l. for cloathing the 8 poor women in the almfhoufe on the 8th day of April every fecond year for ever, by the churchwardens and veftrymen, - -	50	0	0
1594, Robert Kitchen, mayor and alderman of this city, by his will dated the 9th day of June, gave 10s per ann. to a poor houfholder, to be paid by the chamberlain of this city on the 25th day of March, - - -	10	0	0
1639, Alderman George Harrington gave 10s. per ann. for ever to a poor houfekeeper of this parifh, to be paid by the chamberlain the 25th of March yearly, - -	10	0	0

Mr. Roger Hurte by his will gave 10l. to the churchwardens of this parifh as a flock, that the churchwardens for the time being fhall every year give to each of the poor

		l.	s.	d.

women in the parifh almfhoufe 1s. each, viz. at Mi-   *l.* *s.* *d.*
chaelmas and at Chriftmas to buy them wood and coals,   10 0 0
Alfo he gave the faid parifh 5l. more provided the faid
churchwardens fhall procure a fermon to be preached in
the church of All Saints on the firft Sunday in Lent in
the afternoon, the preacher to have 6s. 8d.   -   5 '

1599, June the 20th, Mr. Richard Cole, then deceafed, gave a
tenement in the Barrs called the Greyhound, let at 1l. 8s.
per ann. rented by Richard George brewer, and two gardens in St. Philip's parifh, each let at 8s. in all per ann.   2 4 0

To be given as follows :

	l.	s.	d.
To the prifoners in Newgate in coals -	0	10	0
To ditto for three truffes of rye-ftraw -	0	9	0
To ditto in bread - - -	0	3	0
To the almfhoufe in Lewin's-mead -	0	10	0
To the Taylors almfhoufe - -	0	10	0
To the churchwardens of All Saints for time being	0	2	0

——— 2 4 0

Gift SERMONS to be preached at All Saints Church &c. in a frame in the
veftry-room.

BENEFACTORS NAMES.
                                             l. *s.*

	l.	s.
January 30th, the martyrdom of K. Charles the 1ft. by Mr. John Cook,	1	0
February 2d, the Purification, by Dr. White, - -	2	10
The firft Sunday in Lent, by Mr. Rogert Hurte, - -	0	10
May 1ft, St. Philip and Jacob, by Dr. White, - -	2	10
Sunday after St. James's day, by Alderman Richard Cole, -	0	10
Sunday before September the 15th, by Alderman Richard Cole,	0	10
November 1ft, All Saints day, by Dr. White, - -	2	10
November 17th, Queen Elizabeth's acceffion, by Mr. Peter Millard,	0	10
November 30th, St. Andrews, by Mr. Samuel Bayly, -	0	12
December 28th, Innocents day, by Dr. White, - -	2	10

For reading morning prayers every Monday and Tuefday, by Mr.
  Robert Colfton fon of William Golfton Efq; - -   6 0 0

The ground rents arifing from the lands and tenements leafed out on lives
belonging to the parifh amount to 150l. per ann. what the renewals for lives
yearly produce muft be uncertain and vary.

The almfhoufes and public ftruftures within the precinfts of this parifh come
next to be confidered.—The firft and earlieft to be noticed is the houfe of
                                                       Kalendaries,

Kalendaries, which was fituated at the fouth-weftern part of the church. William Botoñer, (p. 190, 253, 170.) whofe uncle Thomas Botoner was a brother here, defcribes it " a college of priefts founded of old, or fraternity in honour of the feaft of Corpus Chrifti, long before the Conqueft, about the year 700, as I myfelf faw and read in letters certificatory of an old hand in the time of Wolftan the bifhop. The church is fituated on the fouth-weft part of the parifh church of All Saints, and before the time of Edward 3d. was fituated in the parifh church of the Holy Trinity, as was certified to me by a relation of ——, prior of the faid priory." He adds farther, " a pretty houfc or conduit for water is under the houfe of Kalenders."

Thefe Kalendaries were fo antient and fo fingular an inftitution, that no city in this nation can boaft of the like either with refpeft to antiquity or ufe. William Botoner is a good evidence of their early origin, and could not be miftaken in what he faw and read in the certificatory letters or writings of their antiquity before the Conqueft in the year 700. And the confirmation of the rights of this focieiy by Gualo the cardinal and pope's legate after crowning King Henry 3d. at Glocefter, 1216, in thefe words, " Propter antiquitates et bonitates in eâ Gildâ repertas," fhews the antiquity and ufefulnefs of this fraternity, which flourifhed in Briftol from fo early an age, and continued to diffufe knowledge and inftruftion amongft the clergy and laity fo long, and was not diffolved till the time of Henry 8th. at the general diffolution of reli‐gions houfes.

It appears from records that they were a fociety of religious and laity like a college de propagandâ fide, wherein Jews and other Infidels were converted; youth inftrufted and liberally maintained, in the fame manner and under the like direftion as at the Rolls in Chancery-lane, London, and as the cuftody of the rolls was committed to the latter, fo the former preferved the archives of the town of Briftol, whence they were called the Fraternity of the Kalen‐ders, * from keeping a kalendar or monthly regifter of all the public afts, re‐giftering deeds, rolls, &c. as that of London took the Rolls, both implying the fame office of chroniclers or public regifters, of which no great cities were deftitute.

The following copies of original deeds ftill extant in the chamber of Briftol are convincing proofs of fuch an eftablifhment here, and of the fire that hap‐

I i i.   pened

* The law diftionaries call thefe kalendæ rural deans' chapters and conventions of the clergy, fo called becaufe formerly held on the kalends or firft day of every month; but our fociety here confifted of clergy and laity, and were of a peculiar kind and a more extenfive inftitution, as will appear hereafter.

pened in their bochord or library over All Saints church, which deſtroyed the the moſt valuable records of this city.

Friday after the feaſt of St. Peter and Paul, 7 Edw. 3d. 1333. By indenture under the ſeal of John (by divine permiſ. miſſion) then abbot of the monaſtery of St. Auguſtine of Briſtol, in the dioceſe of Worceſter, and the convent of the ſame place, to whom impropriation of the church of All Saints in the dioceſe and city aforeſaid belonged, reciting that the co-brethren of the fraternity of the Kalendaries of Briſtol, out of a devout zeal for the increaſe of divine worſhip, being deſirous of erecting a houſe contiguouſly adjoining to the ſaid church and on the walls thereof, and of the dimenſions after mentioned, to be appropriated for the uſe and habitation of the prieſts and co-brethren of the ſaid fraternity, who then did and thence after for ever in future ſhould celebrate divine ſervice for the ſouls of their co-brethren and of all the faithful deceaſed, agreeable to the rights and rules of the ſaid fraternity, had humbly requeſted his (the abbot's) ſpecial licence and conſent for that purpoſe; he (the abbot) being willing to grant their requeſt as far as may be without prejudice to the ſaid church or his own rights, did out of regard for the ſaid co-brethren and their fraternity as far as he had power grant for him and his ſucceſſors, that it ſhould be lawful for them to build and when built always to poſſeſs a houſe of that ſort for their uſe upon the wall of the north ſide of the ſaid church, that is to ſay, extending downwards from the door on the ſame ſide and the pillar oppoſite it 30 feet in length, and containing towards Corn-ſtreet acroſs the ſaid pillar 23 feet in breadth. To be had and holden to the ſaid co-brethren prieſts or their ſucceſſors co-brethren for ever, ſo that the ſaid co-brethren prieſts or their ſucceſſors prieſts ſhould in future no wiſe be moleſted in the premiſes contrary to the then grant by him the ſaid abbot or his ſucceſſors or any other perſon in their name, which ſaid grant was agreed by them ſo to be reſtrained as that the ſaid church under the ſaid houſe ſhould by no means be made narrower, ſhorter, or more confined, or the foot-ſtanding for the pariſhioners or others of the faithful who ſhould come there be leſſened: and theſe conditions were therefore added to the ſaid grant, ſaving likewiſe always to the ſaid monaſtery and him (the abbot) and his ſucceſſors the right of appointment and preſentation to the vicarage of the ſaid church.

N. B. The impreſſion of the ſeal of this deed is three men's heads, probably deſigned to repreſent the three perſons of the Trinity, ſaid to be the general ſeal of the Kalendars.

This ſeems to be the grant of a place for rebuilding and enlarging their houſe.   Why

Why this gild, called *Gilda aut fratria communitatis cleri & populi villæ Briſtolliæ*, was removed from the church of the Holy Trinity or Chriſt Church does not ſo clearly appear, unleſs we ſuppoſe it to be done at the ſolicitation of Robert Harding, who was a great favourite of Henry 2d. and the founder of the monaſtery of St. Auguſtin, to which he had given the church of All Saints. Theſe particulars are recorded in the little Red Book, p. 83, 84. wrote in good Latin, now in the chamber of Briſtol. I obtained a ſight of the original deed concerning theſe Kalendaries, which I have tranſlated and inſerted at length, as it is a very curious deed and mentions theſe Kalendaries as extant and having their place of meeting at Chriſt Church even before the Conqueſt.

" Venerabili in Chriſto patri Domino Thomæ Dei gratiâ Wygorniæ epiſcopo ſuns humillims et devotis Robertus Hazell, reĉtor eccleſiæ de Derham et deeanns Chriſtianitatis Briſtolliæ ſubjeĉtionem omnimodam tanto patri debet reverentiam et honorem, &c."

" We have received your order containing the following tenor : Thomas, by divine permiſſion, Biſhop of Worceſter, to the beloved in Chriſt Maſter Robert Hazell, and dean of Briſtol, grace and benediĉtion, &c. In the year 1318, June 8, at Chiſſebury, mandate was iſſued for an inquiſition into the rights, charters, and liberties of the fraternity of Kalendaries, to which inquiſition were called the abbot and convent of St. Auguſtin, Briſtol, frier John de Leye, proĉtor, and certain burgeſſes of Briſtol, alſo the mayor and commonalty of the ſaid town, and the other reĉtors and vicars of the ſaid deanery, ſome appearing perſonally and others by their proĉtors, in the church of All Saints, we proceeded in the enquiry ; by which we have found that formerly the ſaid ſociety was called the Gild or fraternity of the community as well clergy as laity of Briſtol, and the place of meeting of the brothers and ſiſters of the fame was uſed to be at the church of the Holy Trinity, Briſtol, in the time of Aylward Meau and Briſtric his ſon, Lords of the ſaid town, before the Conqueſt; the beginning of which gild and fraternity exceeded the memory of man. But after the Conqueſt in the time of William the Baſtard, William Rufus, and Henry, Kings of England, and of Robert Fitzhaman, conſul of Gloceſter and Lord of Briſtol, and founder of the monaſtery of Tewkſbury, and the ſubſequent time of Stephen the King, taking the town of Briſtol by war from Robert Earl of Gloceſter, founder of the priory of St. James and caſtle of Briſtol and its lord, which King Stephen being dead in the time of Henry ſon of Maud the Empreſs King of England, one Robert Harding, burgeſs of Briſtol, by the conſent of the ſaid King Henry and Earl

Robert

Robert and others, whom it concerned, removed the faid gild or fraternity from the church of Holy Trinity and eftablifhed fchools at Briftol for the converfion of Jews and the inftruction of youth, under the difpofal of the faid fraternity, and protection of the mayor of Briftol for the time being and monaftery of St. Auguftin in its fuburbs, and he appropriated the church of All Saints to the faid monaftery, and he caufed a vicar to be chofen out of the chaplains of the faid gild or fraternity, and to be prefented by the abbot and convent of the faid monaftery to the Bifhop of Worcefter, of which vicarage the faid monaftery every year ordered a third part to be appropriated in the name of the rectory. And when the heirs of the faid Robert Harding and the mayors of Briftol for the time being, in the time of Richard and John Kings of England, protected the rights and liberties of the faid gild and fraternity, Gualo, cardinal of the apoftolic fee and general legate, fent to the kingdom of England, came to Briftol, who after he crowned Henry fon of King John at Glocefter King of England, kept a general council at Briftol, in which council the king and cardinal approved and confirmed the faid gild and fraternity on account of its antiquity and goodnefs found therein, which legate commanded and enjoined William de Bleys, Bifhop of Worcefter, and his fucceffors, to protect the faid gild to the praife of God and all faints and amendment of devotion, and union of the clergy and laity of Briftol: he moreover procured a confirmation of all the rights of the faid guild, as the poffeffion of all the goods they then poffeffed or that they fhould get in a juft manner, and efpecially all the houfes, lands, poffeffions, rents, and all other goods, he took under the protection of the apoftolic fee, which the Bifhop of Worcefter approved, and tolerated the faid gild and fraternity. Many other things we made inquifition; of all which for their diffufenefs we cannot now write, and thus we have executed your command diligently. Given at Briftol, &c."

After an inquifition taken by Wolftan Bifhop of Worcefter in Briftol, July 10, 1340, it was by him ordained with confent of the prior and chaplains of the college or fraternity of Kalendaries of All Saints church, " that the antient rules obferved time immemorial fhould be eftablifhed by authority ecclefiaftical, that the faid college fhould have one prieft-prior, to be chofen by the major part of the chaplains and co-brethren without any folemnity of confirmation, confecration, or benediction of any one required, and eight chaplains, fecular brothers, to celebrate for their defunct brethren and benefactors every day; the admiffion of which ever belonged to the founders of fuch their titles or chauntries, whether one, two, or three, &c. during the life of fuch founder, but after their death to the prior and cofreres of the college without

out prefentation or inftitution elfewhere fought, which if they neglect for two months then it devolved to the Bifhop of Worcefter, unlefs any difpute arife, which however if not decided in fix months, it was ftill to devolve to him.

On the firft Monday in every month after the firft bell in the church of All Saints, the brethren, clergy and laity were all to meet, being fummoned before hand, and commendation being faid by the prior and chaplains, mafs was to be celebrated by note by one of the chaplains deputed for that purpofe in his turn, and oblations to be offered by all the co-brethren for the fouls of the brethren and all the faithful departed, and as well for the dead as for the living, efpecially for the infirm brethren prayers were to be faid particularly. And in the middle of the month the prieft was to celebrate mafs for all the brethren then alive, and if any fhould die the brethren were all to attend his funeral, and were to fay every day *placebo et dirige* and one fpecial collect in their mafs for thirty days after his deceafe. The laymen and thofe who were not priefts of the faid fraternity were to fay for thirty days thirteen paternofters and aves for the foul of the defunct, unlefs they had rather celebrate one fpecial mafs for him. If any brother fhould be declining to want or fall into ficknefs, he was to be fupported by the alms of the co-brethren for a whole year, or lodged in fome hofpital by the affiftance of the brethren. — They were ordered to promote peace, avoid contentious difputes, extinguifh fchifms. All the profits of the fraternity and oblations were to be collected by two fit perfons, chofen by the prior and priefts, and to be kept in the common cheft for the neceffary ufes of the college and for pious ufes and almfgivings; they were to render account twice a year of all receipts and expences. And if the brothers were not prefent and the maffes omitted, they fhould be fined or expelled the fraternity. In the year 1464 John Bifhop of Worcefter by deed eftablifhed the ordinance of the houfe of Kalendars to fettle all difpules betwixt the mayor and the brethren or chauntry priefts there, concerning the election of a prior and his duty there; that as often as the prior by death or refignation fhould become void, the mayor of the town holding confultation with the chaplains or chauntry priefts, with the confent of the greater part of them and of the common council of the town, fhould name and prefent under the feal of the town to the bifhop and his fucceffors within two months a chaplain, a batchelor of divinity, or mafter of arts, and a fcholar in theology fufficiently inftructed in holy fcripture and preaching of the word, to be prior of the faid houfe of Kalendars, and nothing fhall prevent his being inftituted and canonically admitted, if he be found fit in all things, &c. And if the mayor defer prefenting beyond two months, then it fhall be

lawful

lawful for the bifhop to confer the priory on one graduate duly inftructed, and he ordered that John Shipward, mayor, and his fucceffors
fhould when chofen into their office take their oath to fupport and defend the
faid prior and his co-freres or chauntry priefts and their tenants in all their
rights; and in cafe of the mayor, &c. not complying, he fhould lofe the prefentation to the faid priory when void, and it might be then lawful for the
chauntry priefts themfelves to prefent one duly inftructed, &c. for prior to be
admitted by the bifhop. The prior thus entituled and inftituted as before fhall
conftantly refide in the faid houfe, and fhall take cuftody of a certain library
newly erected at the bifhop's expence in the faid houfe, fo that every feftival
day at two hours before nine, and for two hours after, free accefs and recefs
may be granted to all willing to enter for the fake of inftruction, and the faid
prior if duly required fhall lay open doubtful and obfcure places of fcripture
to all that afk him according to his beft knowledge, and fhall read a public
lecture every week in the faid library according to the appointment of
the bifhop and his fucceffors: and left through negligence of the faid prior
the books fhould in any wife be alienated or loft, he ordered that three inventories fhould be made of all the books, one to remain with the dean of Briftol,
another with the mayor for the time being, and the other with the faid prior,
fo that as often as any book fhall be given or bequeated to the faid library,
within fifteen days after it is acquired it fhall be by the faid dean or other
honeft perfon appointed hy the mayor placed and chained in the faid library,
and wrote down in fome part of the inventory with its true value. He ordered
alfo that once every year there fhould be a due collation of all the faid
books with the inventories or catalogues by the dean, prior, and another appointed by the faid mayor, on a certain day between the feaft of St. Michael
and All Saints at their own choice; and if it fhould happen that fome book
through neglect of the faid prior fhould be carried out of the faid library
and ftole, the faid prior fhall reftore the faid book to the library under
penalty of 40s. above its true value; and if he cannot reftore it again, then
the value of the book and 40s. befides, 20s. to the mayor and the reft for the
ufe of the library, chaining the books, &c. was to belong, and be appro-
propriated to the faid library. And it was ordered, that as often as the faid
prior or any of the chauntry priefts fhould preach within the town of Briftol,
in the conventual church of St. Auftin, or at the crofs near the faid church, in
their fermons they fhall pray for the good ftate of the bifhop whilft living,
and for his foul when departed, and alfo for the good ftate of the mayor for the
time being and true patron of the faid houfe or priory; and the prior, for his

perfonally

perfonally refiding and for his diligence about the library and the books therein depofited, fhall annually receive out of the fruits and proceeds of the faid houfe of Kalendars at the four ufual terms of the year in equal portions 10l. and the reft of the profits of the faid houfe fhall be converted to the fupport of the reft of the brethren as many as can be fupported at the difcretion of the bifhop and of the prior for the time being, fo as none of them fhall receive more than twelve marks annually, and the furplus of the profits to be depofited in the common treafury fafely for the reparation of the houfe and its tenements. And if the faid prior abfent himfelf for fome honeft caufe, he fhall declare the reafon, to be approved of or not by the bifhop or mayor, fo as he may. by no means be abfent above one month in a year together or at times unlefs upon very urgent occafion to be approved of by the bifhop or mayor, and then in his abfence the fenior brother fhall have the keeping of the faid library. All thefe things more firmly to obferve, the prior was to fwear at his inftitution : and that no prior fhould ever obtain any difpenfation contrary to this ordi_ nance, he was to be bound by an oath, under penalty of privation. — Signed by John Harlowe, prior, and John Shipward, mayor, expreffing their confent.

In the year 1466 one John Chaunceler of Keynfham gave 100 marks for the reparation and rebuilding of the houfe of Kalendars and its ruinous tene_ ments, and to augment and promote the divine worfhip, for which at the inftance of the Bifhop and of William Canynges mayor patron, the prior was to make four fet fermons, two at Keynfham and two at Briftol, (one at the conventual church of St. Auftin or at the crofs near it, and the other at the church of Redclift,) every year ; and in thefe fermons was to exhort the people to pray for John and Edyth Chaunceler and for their fouls after they are departed ; and their fouls were to be fpecially named in the bede rolle or memento ; and a fpecial collect faid every day for their fouls by a chaplain and a paternofter and ave maria, and after their deaths folemn exequies by note were to be done in the church of All Saints for the fouls of the faid John and Edyth.

We may hence conclude, that in the time of W. Canynges mayor a regular library was inftituted in Briftol, and open to all fo early as 1464, and weekly lectures given at it, which fhews literature was not at fo low a ftate here as many would have us imagine ; on the contrary that it was early cultivated by this fociety under the patronage of the Bifhop of Worcefter and the mayor, and at the very time too in which Rowley is faid to have lived and flourifhed, which thofe engaged in the controverfy about him would do well to obferve.— The names of the priors of this houfe fo little known or noticed by our monaf-

tic

tic writers that have come to my knowledge are the following: 1440 John Cyllard—1451 John Hemmynge alias Davy—1464 John Herlow—1526 Roger Eggeworth—1542 Thomas Sylke—12th of Henry the 8th. Wm. Grofs prior.

There were five chauntries belonging to this houfe and five chaplains or chauntry priefts, one of which was chofen prior, though the Bifhop of Worcefter Lynne in 1369 inftituted a chaplain here with this caution, that it fhould remain as of old it had been, a Fraternity of Kalendars; the fociety was fo ancient and of fo long ftanding, they were at a lofs whether to call it a priory or not.

That they preferved the records of the city and regiftered the public tranfactions as well as thofe of their own fociety is proved by fuch a kalendar now extant in the chamber of Briftol, written by Robert Ricaut a Kalendary, who was town-clerk here in the reign of Edward the 4th. To him we owe the many curious notices we have not only in the two red books, the book of wills, orphans &c. but more efpecially in the kalendar or mayor's regifter, which was firft undertaken by him.—He was of this fraternity and feems to have been one of the chaplains above mentioned, and favours Geoffrey of Monmouth as to biftory and matters of antiquity.

In the beginning of the kalendar he fhews his monkifh genius and turn of mind. He firft exhibits the picture of the infant Chrift lying nakĕd, God the Father on one fide in the clouds like an old man, and oppofite to him the Bleffed Virgin on a throne or fella of ftate, over which is a canopy amidft ftars, an angel on the left hand with a trumpet, on the corner of a chequered pavement a matron ftirring a poffet or bafon of broth for the babe, and under the whole thefe words:

" In honorem Dei omnipotentis gloriamq; laudem fuæ benedictæ matris pro tranquillitate pacis ac profperitate villam Briftolliæ inhabitantium nec non pro confuetudinibus, ordinationibus libertatibus et franchefiis dictæ villæ melius in pofterum corfervandis et manutenendis, ad requifitum et mandatum venerabilis viri Willielmi Spencer, majoris de villa et omnium difcretorum virorum dicti majoris confultorum ego Robertus Ricaut extunc ibidem communis clericus electus a fefto Sancti Michaelis Archangeli, anno regni regis Edw. 4. poft conqueftum 18: iftum librum incepi compofui et confcripfi de diverfis croniclis confuedinibufq; legibufq; libertatibus ac aliis memorandis neceffariis diverfis ad perpetuam rei memoriam inviolabiliter obfervandis.

Adfit principio Sancta Maria meo. Amen."

On

On the other fide is written thus :

" Jefus facri ventris fruĉtus — Piæ matris prece duĉtus ;

   Sit mihi viæ dux eduĉtus — Libenter in hoc opere.   Amen.

Thanked be the highe name of our Lord and famous Chriſte Jefu, excellent glorie & eternal reverence to his bleſſed moder Scinte Marie, honour laude & due preiſinge be to all the faintes of hevyn : for as moche as this noble & worſhipful town of Briſtowe," &c.   Page 1. a.

By the foregoing authentic deeds not only the exiſtence of fuch a fociety, but alfo their place of abode is clear beyond a doubt.   Before the Kalendaries were removed to All Saints and had their library in the rood-loft or chamber adjoining to the ſtreet on the north fide of that church, their houfe and fchool were in Wine-ſtreet near Chriſt Church, probably at the corner of High-ſtreet, where was their church, formerly one of the four churches round the High Grofs, the old ribbed arches in the cellar there ſtill pointing it out.   This fociety had great benefaĉtions beſtowed on them, and many grants of land in town and country ; their lands are often mentioned in old deeds, fome in the Old Market, Baldwin-ſtreet, &c. and by an inquifition taken anno 1547, 1ſt Edward 6th. by John Cottrel, Doĉtor of Laws, vicar-general to Paul Buſh, firſt Biſhop of Briſtol, the " Domus Kalendariorum" before its diſſolution, paid to the crown 21s. 10½d. and there were two chauntries there, one by Sir' Thomas Merryfield, whereof he was prieſt, rated at 16s. (fee p. 62.)   In pat. 34, Edward 3d. p. 2. m. 11. the Domus Calendariorum is mentioned, and an original deed in Latin of John Harlow, prior, and his cofreres under their common feal, dated 6th of Edward 4th. 1466, of lands in Marſh-ſtreet was in poſſeſſion of Peter le Neve, Efq; Norroy.   The above does fufficiently evidence the antiquity and reputation of this fociety, which being diſſolved was valued the 26th year of Henry 8th. 1534, at 10l. 18s. 8d. per annum, * and penfions were paid to fome of the fociety after the diſſolution.   Mayſter Leland in his Itinerary thus defcribes this fraternity, as if he had feen here the above deeds.

Itin. vol. vii. p. 87. " A remembraunce of memorable aĉtes done in Bright-ſtow out of a litle boke of the antiquities of the houfe of Calendaries in Brightſtow.

" The antiquities of the Calendaries were for the moſte parte brent by chaunce.   The Calendaries otherwyfe cawl'd the Gilde or Fraternitie of the Clergie and Commonaltie of Brightſtow, and it was firſte kepte in the churche of the Trinitie, fens at All Hallowes.   The original of this fraternitie is out

K к к   of

* Dugd. Monaſt. vol. i. p. 1040.

of mynd. Ailarde Mean and Bitrick his funne, Lords of Brightflow, afore the Conquefte. Hamon Erle of Glocefter afore the Conqueft and Lorde of Brighftow. Roberte, conful, funne to Hamon was Erl of Glocefter and Lorde of Brightflow and founder of Tewkfbury, &c. Robert Earl of Glocefter and Robert Harding tranflated the fraternity of Calendaries from Trinitie to the churche of All Hallows. In it were fchools for converfion of Jews, &c."

The houfe where they inhabited after their removal from Chrift Church or Trinity adjoined the church of All Saints at the weftern end, as by the deed appears, and on the fite of it was built the London Coffee-houfe, now a dwelling-houfe, and the conduit of All Saints; and it poffibly extended farther, as at building the Exchange a vaft quantity of bones were dug up, poffibly out of the burying-ground there of this fociety. I have a drawing of it under the name of Rowleie, about the year 1467, which he calls " the chyrche oratorie of the Calendaries, whereof the weftern fpyre beynge brent, the flandeynge parte was pyghte downe, and the refectorie ybuylden wyth ytts roiens. Inn itte was 8 hundredthe bookes, in the bochorde meinte Sexonne Hyftorie and Lege. Itte was ybuilden by Eva Fytzhardynge and Lewis de Ghente inn 1092."

This account feems to agree with the original deed above mentioned of John Chauncellor of Keynfham, granting 100 marks for rebuilding this houfe in 1466. The lofs fuftained by this fire was irreparable, as the fociety was fo ancient, and as the records of the city-as well as thofe of their own fraternity were in effect deftroyed by it, fo that any uncertainty concerning the firft foundation and early ftate of this city may be eafily accounted for, by deriving it from this deftructive accident by fire; a lofs greatly to be lamented, but never to be repaired.

There was a library room over the north aile of the church of All Saints, not long fince to be feen, to which the Kalendaries had a communication by a door out of their houfe, but by late alterations of the church and houfe adjoining it has been deftroyed.

The old church books mention a fire happening here in 1466 through the careleffnefs of a drunken point-maker, which burnt two houfes next the fteeple, William Rowley and John Compton being churchwardens that year.

About 1350 Stephen Gnowfale gave this parifh a tenement in All Saints-lane, which was made convenient for an almfhoufe, which was fold for 420l. in 1739, and the fouth and eaft part of the Exchange is built on its fite, and the feoffees built a new almfhoufe adjoining to St. John's. In 1400 the

grand

grand prior and proctor of the priory of St. James granted the parishioners a little conduit of water, to which the spring rising in the Prior's Orchard (now Bird's garden) was conveyed, and thence in leaden pipes under ground to a public cistern in Corn-street for the use of the city, to which Thomas White, Esq; gave 20s. per annum for its repair in the year 1541, payable by the chamber out of an estate at Hinton Derham, Glocestershire. This cistern in 1601 was rebuilt at the expence of 125l. 11s. 1d. defrayed by the vestry.

As great part of the Exchange and new market are in this parish, some account of them should find a place here.

In the year 1720 a scheme was set on foot to build an Exchange, but it proved abortive. But in 1721 an act of parliament was obtained to enable the mayor, burgesses, and commonalty of Bristol to build an Exchange, and a committee of fifteen gentlemen were appointed to carry the work into execution and extend their design to a general market, in lieu of those which incumbered the streets of the city, who in the latter end of the year 1738 came to a resolution to purchase the proper lands, and proceed with their intended work. In 1740-1, 30th January, they agreed with Mr. John Wood, a learned and and ingenious architect, to contrive a building round an area, for about 600 people to assemble in, in such a manner as to have the outward appearance of one grand structure to front Corn-street, with two taverns in front, the sides for houses, insurance and other public offices, the back part for an arcade with rooms over it, part of the general market.

The 10th of March, 1740-1, the first stone was laid, the following inscription being first cut on its uppermost bed.

Regnanti Georgio II.*
Pio, Felici, Augusto,
Libertatis et Rei Mercatoriæ
Domi Forifque Vindice
Primarium Lapidem hujus Ædificii
Suffragio Civium et Ære publico extructi
Posuit
Henricus Combe, Prætor.
A. C. M.D.CCXL.

Several pieces of new coin were thrown under the stone, which was now laid with great solemnity, amidst ringing of the bells and joyful acclamations of the citizens. The mayor first and the rest of the gentlemen attending striking the stone with a mallet when fixed in its place three times. They then with-

drew

drew from the foundation to the Council-houfe, where they drank profperity to the work begun. In the afternoon the populace were treated with ale, upon the Exchange ground, at the chamber expence.

After the work was thus begun, it was carried on according to the ftrict rules of œconomy, and with all the expedition and difpatch; fo that the whole fhould, now built, extend 110 feet in front, by 148 feet in depth.

This ftructure is fituated aimoft in the center of the city, and fronts north-ward to Corn-ftreet. The whole building as well infide as outfide is fronted with white freeftone of the Corinthian order, upon a ruftick bafement, or ra-ther a bafement compofed of regular ftones, fome with chamfered edges, fome with plain edges. The central parts break forwards and make a tetraf-tyle of almoft whole columns, fupporting a pediment, in the tympan of which the King's Arms are carved in ftone ; the chamber windows are dreffed with rich tabernacles ; the attic windows are fquare with architraves round them, and they rife no higher than the bottom of the capitals of the order ; fo that the fpaces between the capitals of the columns and pilafters in this front are fil-led with feftoons, which reprefent Great Britain and the four quarters of the world, with the chief products and manufactures of every country.

The feveral parts whereof this front is compofed are fmall, which muft be attributed chiefly to the narrow ftreet wherein they are to be viewed ; all the mouldings proper to be carved are enriched ; the framing of the doors of the front gate is divided in a fort of Mofaic work by large iron nails ; the pannels of the doors are adorned with ornaments in caft metal; and the front of the building on each fide thefe doors are defended from the ftreet by deep areas, with handfome iron pallifadoes upon the back walls of thofe areas.

The fouth front to the general maket is quite regular. The central part of the front breaks forward to fupport a pediment, in the tympan of which the arms of the city are carved in ftone, and over that there is a turret, in the front whereof the dial of a clock is fixed for the ufe of the market people. The ends of this front break forward likewife and are finifhed with a dome at each end, upon which there are ftone pedeftals, wherein fome of the funnels of the chimnies are with fome difficulty brought up. The domes and pedeftals are fix feet more in flank than they are in front, which was owing to the increafe of the arcade.

The fouth front and fo much of the fide fronts as is level with it confifts of two ftories of building, in which the outfide of the arcade appears rufticated, and all the apertures in the remainder of the firft ftory of the fide fronts are dreffed in the fame tafte, that is, with ftones cut out in a regular form. The

windows

windows over the arcade are of the tabernacle kind, as well as the central windows of the fecond flory of the fide fronts.

The roof over the veftibules and over the middle of the arcade is finifhed with domes fupporting ftone turrets, and thofe domes are fo contrived as to appear part of the architeฐure of the infide of the building, in thofe turrets fome of the funnels of the chimnies of the back work are with difficulty brought up. The turret facing the principal entrance of the Exchange has a clock and dial placed therein, for the ufe of fuch as frequent the place of Exchange. The merchants arms adorn the weft front of the turret on the eaft fide of the periftyle, as a compliment for their benefaฐion of 2000l. towards the work, and the moft ancient arms of the city are carved on the caft front of the turret on the weft fide of the place of Exchange. See the prints.

The building was fo far compleated by the beginning of Auguft, 1743, that the 21ft of September was named as the day on which it fhould be opened. The corporation of Briftol having ordered that the market, which was to have been held on Wednefday the 21ft of that month, fhould be kept upon Tuef-day the 20th, and public notice was accordingly given by the crier, upon Friday before the Exchange was opened the chamber refolved to difcharge at the city expence the poor prifoners confined in Newgate for debt, that every citizen might enjoy liberty upon the day of opening the Exchange. They alfo refolved to treat the workmen employed in the building with a handfome din-ner, and direฐed that bread and wine fhould be ready at the Council-houfe, after the Exchange fhould be opened, for all gentlemen without diftinฐion to refrefh themfelves with.

The mayor of Briftol, Sir Abraham Elton, Bart. invited the corporation and fociety of merchants to dine with him at the Merchants-hall upon the day of opening the Exchange, and propofed to the mafters of the feveral trading companies to treat the members of thofe companies with wine at their refpeฐive halls, which was accordingly performed.

As the Exchange is the fole property of the corporation of Briftol, fo it was ordered that the ceremony of opening it fhould confift in the corporation meet-ing the fociety of merchants and other traders of the city at the Guildhall in Broad-ftreet, in walking with them from that hall in proceffion to the Ex-change. Now the dawn of the day appointed for doing all this was proclaimed to town and country, by the difcharge of feveral cannons from Brandon-hill, and then the morning was ufhered in with ringing of bells. The fhips were foon dreffed with their proper colours; flags were difplayed upon fome of the churches, and the ftreets through which the proceffion was to be made were by an order of the magiftrates fwept and cleared from every annoyance.

The.

cheered upon the day of opening this building.

Ten o'clock was the time appointed for the general meeting of fuch as were concerned in the ceremony of opening the Exchange, by which hour the parties began to repair to the Guildhall, and then as the weather was fine the ſtreets and houſes were ſoon lined with an infinite number of people from all parts of the town and country. At eleven the proceſſion began from that hall in the following order, or as near it as it was poſſible for the companies to fall in with the train. — Mr. Colſton's boys under the tuition of their maſ- ter led the way, and they were followed by the city hoſpital boys governed by the mayor and aldermen, then came the exchange-keeper with a noble ſtaff in in his hand, and he was followed by the incorporated companies of the city in their formalities, with their colours borne before them, with each of their ref- peƈtive wardens. The maſons company went 1ſt, tylers 2d. porters 3d. hal- liers 4th. carpenters 5th. tobacco-pipe-makers 6th. turners 7th. hatters 8th. ſadlers 9th. innholders 10th. bakers 11th. butchers 12th. tanners 13th. cord- wainers 14th. wire-drawers 15th. joiners 16th. dyers 17th. whitetawers 18th. hoopers 19th. ſmiths 20th. ſurgeons 21ſt. (with muſic before them) weavers 22d. taylors 23d. The city muſic with the addition of two French horns went next after theſe companies, and they were ſucceeded by the city officers, who walked according to their ranks, with the ſteward of the ſheriff's court in his barriſters habit, and the chamberlain in his gown bearing a mace of gold. The town clerk was ill, and could not attend the proceſſion. Then came the corporation in their ſcarlet robes, with their ſword of ſtate borne before them by the ſword-bearer in his gown and cap of maintenance. The mayor and mayor eleƈt went firſt, the ſenior alderman, and after them the reſt of the cor- poration according to their ſeniority. To theſe ſucceeded the maſter, war- dens, affiſtants, and members of the Merchants-hall, and the whole was cloſed with a long train of coaches and chariots to 48 in number.

This proceſſion paſſed up Broad-ſtreet, down High-ſtreet, and ſo on to the Back, from thence they went into Queen's-ſquare at the north-eaſt corner, and

paſſing

paffed through the ftreets on the eaft and fouth fide of that fpacious area, came out upon the lower end of the Key oppofite the place where the Princefs Augufta, a letter of marque fhip, lay repairing from the damages fhe had received, in the laft of four victorious battles with the Spanifh privateers in the prefent war, one of which privateers her captain blew up in the king's channel, and was particularly rewarded by the Admiralty for his gallantry, good conduct and courage in that brave action. From this glorious object the proceffion was continued up the Key, and then from the north end of it the parties entering Small-ftreet paffed from that ftreet to the Exchange.

This circuit of ground was about 2000 yards in length, the whole train of people and coaches extended about three quarters of a mile, and the proceffion lafted about two hours, during which time the bells kept ringing and the cannons firing.

When the corporation came to the Exchange they entered the building by the gate in the north front, paffed through the hall to the periftyle,* walked along the porticos thereof to the weft, and from thence came towards the center of the piazza, where an haut-pas or rather a fquare plinth † was prepared, which Thomas Stevens, Efq; fteward of the fheriff's court, directly afcended from the eaft fide. Then the mayor commanded filence to be kept, and the doors of the front gate which were fhut to keep out the populace to be opened, after which Mr. Stevens addreffed himfelf to the merchants and tradefmen, by the order of the corporation firft named the building, and then gave them the ufe of the periftyle of it for a place of Exchange in a long fpeech.

When the fpeech was ended the mayor began three huzzas, then Mr. Stevens retired, and Mr. Thomas Fane, clerk of the Merchants-hall, took his place, and addreffing himfelf to the corporation in thefe words:

" Mr. Mayor and Gentlemen of the Corporation,
" The merchants are very fenfible of the obligations they are under to
" you, for the great care you have taken in building this Exchange, and I am
" commanded in this public manner to return you their thanks for the fame."

This being over, Mr. Mayor began three huzzas, after which the corporation and fociety of merchants with the mufic before them, &c. walked to the Council-houfe, where they were refrefhed with wine, and from thence in their coaches went to the Merchants-hall to a dinner which was prepared for them. The refpective companies alfo retired to their refpective halls, to regale themfelves with the wine Mr. Mayor had prefented them with, and the evening of

the

* Periftyle is a place encompaffed with pillars ftanding round about on the infide.
† A plinth is the lowermoft part of the foot of a pillar, being the form of a tile or fquare brick.

this day was concluded with ringing of bells, difcharging guns, and making bonfires in proper places: all which with the whole tranfactions of the day was conducted without any ill accident, or any of thofe diforders too frequently committed at public rejoicings, which may be attributed to this, that the feftival of opening the Exchange was in the nature of it agreeable to all parties, and if pageantry on this occafion had been thought neceffary, the public had certainly been gratified with it. But what pageantry could exceed a folemn proceffion of the magiftrates and whole collective trading body of a city, that pays the government a cuftom for their goods of above 150,000l. a year?

The firft Wednefday after Lady-day, being March 27, 1743, the General Market behind the Exchange was firft opened.

C H A P. XV.

Of the CHURCH *and* PARISH *of the* HOLY TRINITY *or* CHRIST CHURCH, *with* St. EWEN's *confolidated.*

CHRIST Church is a rectory rated in the King's Books at 3l. 8s. clear: its Yearly Tenths, now difcharged, 1l. 2s. It is of very great antiquity, though the exact time when founded is a little uncertain. Rowley's manufcript fays, " it was founded 920 by Ella, lord-warden of the caftle, and that it was fpired by Alricvs Sneaw in 1004," perhaps Aylwardus Sneaw. It is certain in taking down part of the fpire to rebuild it in 1765 a date in lead was found let into the ftone near the top 1003 or 1004, as the workmen affirmed ; and in 1787, when this church was taken down to be rebuilt, a ftatue of a Saxon earl fitting in a niche was difcovered walled in at the front, defigned very probably for the founder of it, either Ella above mentioned or Aylwardus Sneaw, in whofe time the fraternity of Kalendaries flourifhed here. But its antiquity is fully afcertained from its being the refidence of that fociety before the Conqueft. Philip the prieft in 1153 granted a moiety of this

church

church which he poffeffed to the church of Tewkſbury, in the time of Robert Earl of Glocefter, which was confirmed by Earl William and John Biſhop of Worcefter. (See Stephens, vol. ii. No. 161, 31. Add. to Dugd.)

The Earls of Glocefter were patrons to prefent to this benefice, and it is thence moft probable that the Saxon earls were the founders, and Robert Fitzhaymon and Robert Earl of Glocefter his fon-in-law received it from them as part of the honour of Glocefter. It is certain, that the latter founded the priory of St. James, (which fee) and made it a cell to the abby of Tewkſbury, and this church being an appendage to the fame abby, by right of patronage paid a penfion or yearly rent to it of 10s. As that abbot and convent had the patronage, fo not content with that in the year 1469 they procured of John Biſhop of Worcefter the appropriation of it, whereby they got the whole profits of the church, a common artifice with them, which has laid the foundation of fo many poor vicarages now, they finding only a chaplain to do the duty, and paying to the church of Worcefter yearly 3s. 4d. and to the archdeacon of Glocefter 3s. 4d. but this appropriation was after fome time revoked by the biſhop.

" In this church, fays Leland, was fyrfte kepte the Calendaries, otherwife called the Gilde or Fraternitie of the Clergie and Commonaltie of Brightſtowe, but fens removed to All Hallows. The original of it is owt of mynde." He there (Itin. vol. vii. f. 87, 88.) mentions their having been tranſlated thither by Robert Fitzharding, Robert Earl of Glocefter, and William his fon, all out of a book of the antiquities of the Kalendaries. The prior and brethren here are mentioned in pat. 34. Edw. 3. p. 2. m. 11.

This church was no very beautiful ftructure. It ftands upon the north quarter of the center of the town, where four ftreets meet, High-ftreet and Broad-ftreet, Corn-ftreet and Wine-ftreet. It was a low building of the model of a quarter cathedral, the tower being very near in the center ; from the ground to the battlements of the tower about 70 feet high, on the center of which a fpire of freeftone rofe about the fame height, on which was a copper dragon, inftead of a weather-cock. The tower handfome, very high, and had four pinnacles of folid freeftone about 12 feet high, with copper vanes on them. In the tower was a peal of ten bells, which chimed at the hour of one, fix, and eleven, with two dial plates to the clock at the weft end of the fouth aile, one facing Corn-ftreet and the other High-ftreet; on the fides of this dial were two men carved in wood, with a hammer in the hand of each that ftruck a bell every quarter of an hour.

The

The middle aile in length from the high altar to the weſt door was 94 feet, from the ground to the cieling of the ſame aile 41 feet high, the length of the chancel 18 feet. The north and ſouth ailes each 59 feet long. The body of the church was ſupported on the north and ſouth ſide with four arches and five pillars. The width of the church from the north to the ſouth door 54 feet. — William of Worceſter (p. 216) ſays, " The length of the church of the Holy Trinity is 22 yards, its breadth 35 ſteps. The road of High-ſtreet there at the High Grofs is 24 ſteps broad, of Wynch-ſtreet 16 ſteps, of Broad-ſtreet 14 ſteps, of Corn-ſtreet at the High Croſs 14 ſteps."

There was a good organ belonging to this church.

In the year 1751 this church was greatly repaired and beautified and new pewed. A new ſtrong arch was turned under the belfry by the pulpit with inverted arch under ground. The old tower-ſtairs were at the ſame time converted into ſolid wall and filled up, to ſtrengthen and ſupport the tower, which was much cracked, and a new ſtair-caſe was made in the churchyard. Alſo a ſtrong arch was built under the old one at the eaſt end of the ſouth aile. The organ was gilt and repaired. After this church had been two years and ten month repairing, it was opened for divine ſervice on Sunday, November 18, 1753. The expence of the whole was 1500l.

But in the year 1783 the walls of the church and roof were found to be ſo very ruinous and decayed, that the 2d of June application was made to parliament, and leave given to bring in a bill for rebuilding it and widening the ſtreets near it. And 1786 they began pulling it wholly down, and in 1788 it was rebuilt on the ſame ground, only allowing ſome ſpace to widen the ſtreet there, and will ſoon exhibit a beautiful ſtruēture in the center of the city, and afford a good accommodation for the pariſhioners reſorting to it. The new ſpire is beautiful, and the whole building much admired, and is a great ornament to the center of the city, as you go up High-ſtreet.

In the year 1547 were ſequeſtered to the king's uſe all fruits, profits, and emoluments whatſoever, &c. for non-payment of ſubſidies and tenths due 1 May and 25 December laſt. See p. 63.

In 1491 Richard Erle, Eſq; by will gave nineteen tenements and a garden to find a chaplain daily in the chapel of St. Michael in the church of Holy Trinity, to officiate for ever at maſs for the ſoul of himſelf and Thomaſin his wife.

The 24th of Henry 5th. Balle's chauntrie of Bryſtoe was eſtabliſhed, the prieſt to have 8l. per annum. Sir John Chycwe preſented.

Some

Some of the lands with which thefe chauntries were endowed through over-fight were not taken to by the crown fo late as the 15th of Elizabeth, for William Yate, late fheriff, and Thomas Fawcet, of this parifh, proctors, fet forth that they had received the rents of fundry meffuages, &c. fince the dif-folution of chauntries, and had ufually employed the fame among other rents for the wages of the prieft, curates, and clerks of the parifh, the ornaments of the church and the charges of fuch preaching, and the relief of the poor ; but that they were often conftrained to fuits of law for the defence of the title to the premifes : and it appearing that the queen had fome title thereto by the ftatute of 1 Edward 6th. (divers of the tenements having been employed before to fuperftitious ufes) they folicited to purchafe them of the queen, who by letters patent, July 13, in the 30th year of her reign, granted the fame to the church-wardens and parifhioners the 10th of January, 31 Elizabeth, under certain quit rents; and they for a perpetual continuance of the fame to the parifh en-feoffeed the fame to the mayor Aldworth and fourteen others of the parifh, that they might apply the fame tenements to the ufes afore mentioned in future. When the feoffees are reduced to fix or four perfons, a new feoffment was to be made to fourteen others, &c. which was continued to be renewed to the prefent. The rector in 1776 had fome difpute with the feoffees on account of his prevailing on the veftry to grant 100l. if he could get another 100l. as a gift from the corporation the patrons, procuring 400l. Queen Ann's bounty to his church, which he obtained ; but the feoffees judging it a mifapplication of the church ftock in the veftry's granting this 100l. refufed to allow it. This putting the rector upon an enquiry into his right to certain wages paid him out of the church ftock, fometimes 25l. fometimes 30l. per annum, as a gift of the veftry he found that he had a juft right and claim even to more than they al-lowed him as a boon, and therefore as they refufed him to examine the parifh deeds and papers locked up from him, he filed a bill in chancery in October, 1776, which was anfwered by the feoffees and a few of the veftry, and the caufe was heard May 6, 1780, after great trouble and expence to the rector, and the court declared the charity muft be confirmed, and the lands, &c. ap-propriated as in the deeds of 31 Elizabeth, &c. The 18th of June, 1782, the mafter it was referred to made his report, and the rector was now confirmed in having the fum of 80l. per annum for ever from the 25th of March, 1772.

L l l

The

The other appropriations were,	L.	s.	d.
Gifts to the poor and interest of monies whereto they are entitled	43	10	0
A tenement bequeathed to the organist - - -	20	0	0
A gift to the rector, clerk, and sexton, for a sermon -	3	11	0
A gift to the church - - - - -	5	0	0
Sheriff's dues - - . - - -	4	1	4
Ground rent to the chamber of Bristol ' - -	1	12	8½
	£ 77	15	0½

The anxiety the "law's delay" in this suit gave the rector, it was thought, very much impaired his health, as he considered himself very unjustly opprest and persecuted by the feoffees in this matter : it is certain he visibly declined in his health, had several fits of illness, and a paralytic stroke, of which he for sometime recovered, but at last in May, 1785, died suddenly, about three years after the decision of this cause, which will be of such benefit to his successor, having been at a very great expence, which he could ill afford, and not living long enough to receive any advantage from it.

The law expence out of the church stock for this suit amounted to upwards of 1400l. much wanted then to repair or rebuild the church, and to which it had been much better applied.

<h2 style="text-align:center">RECTORS of Christ Church.</h2>

PATRONS.

Abbot and
convent of
Tewksbury.

1147 Philip ——, priest.
1282 William de Lachefferd.
1294 John de Hawkesbure.
1296 John de Bredon.
1298 Ricardus de ——.
1323 William de Bekeford: taxatur ecclesia ad xx libr.
1360 Thomas de Aston.
1369 William de Overyngton.
1406 Johannes Pedewelle.
1415 Thomas Drayton, a Lollard, preached against image
   worship and the proud religious, &c.
1421 John Wright.
1425 William Fydian.
1427 John Dyer.
1450 John Fytswarren, died 1455.
1456 John Stephys.

PATRONS.

1462 John Drover, A. M.
     John Carew.
     Lawrence Cokkys.
1485 William Jonys.
1510 John Godryche, S. T. P.
1538 Johannes Terrel.

Corporation.   1588 Morgan Jones, died 1616.
1616 Nicholas Leigh.
1618 Edward Shaw. Had a rectory-house in the Pithay
       granted him, and taken away 1683.
1621 Morgan Williams.
1630 Richard Standfaft, rector 51 years: being blind, his
       fon John affifted him. See his monument, epitaph, &c.
1682 Charles Brent.
1729 William Smith.
     Daniel Debat, D. D.
1785 Thomas Ireland, D. D.

MONUMENTS.

Amongft the memorials of the dead that deferve our notice is a very fingular little mural monument in the chancel. It is infcribed to the Rev. Dr.
Standfaft, is a plain white marble table, with an hour-glafs in a kind of pediment on the top, and a death's head below it.

" Near this place lieth the body of Richard Standfaft, Mafter of Arts, of
Sidney College in Cambridge, and chaplain in ordinary to his Majefty King
Charles 1ft. who for his loyalty to the king and ftedfaftnefs in the eftablifhed
religion fuffered fourteen years fequeftration. He returned to his place in
Briftol at the reftoration of King Charles 2d. was then made prebendary of
the cathedral church of Briftol, and for twenty years and better (notwithftanding his blindnefs) performed the offices of the church exactly, and difcharged
the duties of an able, diligent, and orthodox preacher. He was rector of
Chrift Church upwards of fifty-one years, and died Auguft 24, in the 78th
year of his age, and in the year of our Lord 1681.

              He fhall live again."

The following verfes were compofed by himfelf to be put upon his monument, and were taken from his own mouth two days before his death:

                                    Jacob

Jacob was at Bethel found,
And fo may we, though under ground.
With Jacob there God did intend
To be with him where'ver he went,
And to bring him back again,
Nor was that promife made in vain.
Upon which words we reft in confidence
That he which found him there will fetch us hence.
Nor without caufe are we perfuaded thus,
For where God fpake with him, he fpake with us.

This worthy divine fuffered greatly in the time of the rebellion, befides be-ing deprived of this his living, which was given to one Evans, a taylor, he was in March, 1645-6, confined in Briftol caftle, " for his difaffeftion to the Parliament of England and their proceedings, which in his printing, praying, and preaching he had expreffed." However during his fequeftration and troubles he was fo well beloved by the veftry of Chrift Church, that they con-tributed to his fupport by an annual falary during his abfence from them, as appears by a letter in the hand of Dean Towgood, a fellow fufferer with him, complaining of his parifhioners of St. Nicholas not afting fo generoufly to him as the others did to Dr. Standfaft.

Dr. Standfaft was fo noted and well-received a preacher in this city, that he was appointed by the mayor and corporation (of which body fome of his an-ceftors had been) to preach the public leftures at feveral churches, gift fermons appointed by benefaftors to the city.

He publifhed a little traft, called, A Handful of Cordial Comfits, which breathes a true Chriftian fpirit, and fhews his true and orthodox principles. — It was reprinted in the year 1767 by his great grandfon, Mr. Standfaft Smith, apothecary. Alfo a Caveat againft Seducers.

He was once purfued by his malicious accufers, but putting on the habit of a thatcher, where he lay concealed near Thornbury, in Glocefterfhire, he was, when they came to look for him, aftually upon the houfe, pretending to be bufy at his work.

There were but few monuments in this church; one with the following infcrip-tion to the Rev. Charles Brent, reftor of this parifh : — " Reverendus Carolus Brent, A. M. antiquâ ftirpe oriundus, hujus ecclefiæ reftor St. Werburgæ vicarius, ac canonicus refidentiarius menevenfis cum duabus uxoribus toti-demque liberis juxta requiefcit ; concionator erat egregius, affiduus, perpoli-tus : vitæ probitate ornavit et fplendore fermonum illuftravit. Magnas Chrif-
tianæ

tianæ religionis veritates, difficillimas theologiæ queſtiones mirâ ſagacitate explicare ac latentem veritatem eruere optimè novit. cum acumine ingenii, ſuavitate morum animi candore, benevolentiâ eruditione, modeſtiâ inter plurimos excelluiſſet, emigravit, Jun. 13, A. D. 1729, ætatis 63."

Another monument near with the following inſcription : — " Hic juxta reconditur Elizabetha Samuelis Pye, chirurgi uxor perdileĉta, obſtetrix fida, prudens, perita remimiſcimini, leĉtores, quarum ope naſcimur; dein vitâ probe funĉtæ haud inviti recordamini obiit 28 Apr. 1725."

Underneath was an inſcription to that eminent ſurgeon Mr. Samuel Pye, who was buried here September 20, 1759.

Juxta etiam requieſcit Samuel Pye,
qui variâ ſcientiâ, experientiâ longâ
et judicio ſagaci in morbis difficilioribus
ſanandis chirurgiam et obſtetriciam
in hac urbe ſumma ad faſtigia
provexit :
probitate morum intaminatâ, conſtanti,
inſeneſcens, honore plenus ac annis
hanc vitam meliori commutavit.
20 Sept. 1759,
Æt. 74.

In the firſt croſs aile was a braſs plate with a device of two hands holding up a heart, out of which proceed three ſcrolls, on which the following words were inſcribed : — " Credo quod redemptor meus vivit, deterrâ ſurreĉturus ſum, in carne mea videbo Dominum ſalvatorem meum." And underneath the following epitaph : — " Orate pro animabus Thomæ Balle, burgenſis villæ Briſtoliæ et Aliciæ uxoris ſuæ et pro illa Margerettæ filiæ eorundem qui quidem Thomas, obiit A. D. 1400, quorum animabus propitietur Deus."

On a freeſtone on the ground : — " Hic jacet Johannis Scynte, obiit 1467."

On a ſtone is an inſcription to Francis Glead, who, having done well for the poor departed this life, June, 1, 1661, ætatis 67.

If ſtewards will be true to their intent,
Their works ſhall be a laſting monument.

In the middle aile on a ſtone : — " To Suſanna the wife of Anſtin Goodwin, linen-draper, and daughter of Cornelius Lyde, of Stanton Wick, Eſq; Somerſet. She died the 13th of June, 1738, ætatis 59."

" To Robert Yate, of this city, merchant, who died the 31ſt of December, 1682, aged 67."

In

In the chancel was a brals figure of a man with three scrolls coming from his heart: — " Credo quod redemptor meus, &c." And underneath the following: — " Hic jacet magister Johannis Fitzwarren quondam rector hujus ecclesiæ, qui obiit 6 Sept. 1455, cujus animæ propitietur Deus."

The following are the particular BENEFACTORS to this parish.

		l.	*s.*	*d.*
1594, Robert Kitchen gave 4l. 12s. per annum, 10s. a quarter to the poor, and 52s. in bread		92	0	0
1636, Henry Yate gave a chief rent of 4l. per annum, 1l. for a sermon and 3l. for the poor.				
1639, George Harrington gave 2l. per annum, 10s. a quarter to poor housekeepers		40	0	0
1640, Abel Kitchen gave 2l. 12l. per annum to the poor in bread		52	0	0
1661, Francis Gleed gave a chief rent of 3l. per annum, 1l. for a sermon and 2l. for the poor.				
1668, Thomas Farmer gave lands of 2l. per annum for bread or coal for the poor.				
Arthur Farmer gave 2l. per annum, to be laid out in lands, the produce to be given to fix poor families		40	0	0
1676, Robert Markham gave 10s. per annum in bread for the poor on St. James's-day		10	0	0
1678, Edward Hearn gave 2l. per annum in bread for the poor on St. James's-day		40	0	0
1684, Elizabeth Hearn gave 10s. per annum in bread for the poor on St. James's-day		10	0	0
Mrs. Boucher and Langton gave lands in Bedminster of 80l. per annum to poor widows of the city, of which this parish has a share, at 10s. each.				
1685, William Colston gave 5l. per annum to fix poor housekeepers		100	0	0
1686, Philip Tiler gave 10s. per annum to one poor housekeeper		10	0	0
1687, Martha Lane gave 10s. per annum to the poor the 22d of December		10	0	0
1688, John Lawford gave 2l. 10s. per annum to the poor in bread to be given every Sunday		50	0	0
Nicholas Shute gave a tenement of 2l. per ann. to the poor.				
1701, Arthur Grant gave 10s. per annum to two poor widows		10	0	0
1708, Sir William Clutterbuck gave 2l. 10s. per annum, 1l. for a sermon, 10s. to the clerk, and the remainder to the poor in bread		50	0	0

1712,

	l.	*s.*	*d.*
1712, Mary Grant gave 10s. per annum to two poor widows	10	0	0
1740, Nicholas Baker gave 2l. 10s. per annum to four poor widows	50	0	0

Alderman Gibbs gave a chief rent of 3l. per ann. to the poor.

George Saltern gave a chief rent of 2s. per ann. to the poor.

1715, Alice Sloper gave 100l. for the ufe of the church.

1767, Robert Bolter gave 3l. 10s. per annum to the poor	-	100	0	0
Avis Brown gave 14s. per annum to the poor	-	-	20	0	0
—— Cox gave 10s. per annum to the poor in coal	-	10	10	0

This parifh is poffeffed of various eftates for charitable ufes, to promote divine fervice, to repair the church, and relieve the indigent, amounting to about 160l. per annum in 1759, befides fines for renewals on fo many leafe-hold tenements: though the expences of repairing the church from time to time and fome ill-judged law fuits have greatly impaired their income, that they were obliged to folicit the benevolence of the public towards rebuilding the church in 1787.

The Briftol High Crofs was firft erected near this church, in the center, where four ftreets meet. See the plate.

The year 1373 may be deemed the æra from which Briftol may date fome of its greateft improvements, and the citizens in commemoration of Edward 3d.'s feparating it from the county of Glocefter and conftituting it a county within itfelf, and fixing its pomerium or boundaries by an ample charter for that pur-pofe, rebuilt the removed Crofs on the very fpot where the old one ftood, embellifhed it in a moft fuperb manner, and placed King Edward 3d. together with three preceding royal benefactors, very well carved for the time, in the vacant niches of the then perhaps defaced faints. Thus gratitude and the loy-alty of the citizens were the laudable motives to this undertaking.

King John was placed northward fronting Broad-ftreet. He gave the city the firft and very extenfive charter of privileges, efpecially all the void ground on the banks of the rivers, thereby " to amend the town by build-ing," &c. vide annals for the year.

King Henry 3d. was fixed fronting Wine-ftreet caftward. He confirmed Henry 2d's. charter, that eftablifhed it a mayor town and that of King John, and joined Redcliff to Briftol, making it one corporate town. Vide annals.

King Edward 3d. was fixed towards Corn-ftreet weftward. He made Briftol a county of itfelf, &c. as above. Annals 1373, the year of re-erecting the Crofs in High-ftreet by voluntary contributions.

King Edward 4th. they added afterwards to the other three figures, placing him to front High-ftreet fouthward. Vide annals, 1461.

M M M

Thus

Thus it ftood greatly admired for its antiquity and for its ornaments in which they had been very lavifh for at leaft 260 years; but in the year 1633 the city having continued to receive frefh and repeated inftances of royal fa-vour, and the Grofs itfelf by this time perhaps wanting fome neceffary repairs, it was this year taken down in part, enlarged, and raifed higher in the fame ftyle of architecture, and four other ftatues of kings were now added.

Henry 6th. was placed in a new niche eaftward. He granted and confirmed all the charters of his predeceffors. Annals.

Queen Elizabeth was placed weftward, who had alfo confirmed the charters.

King Charles 1ft. northward. He granted a new charter, and fold the caf-tle and its dependencies to the city, which to the great annoyance of the inha-bitants was before out of the mayor's jurifdiction.

King James 1ft. who had renewed the charters, was placed fouthward.

By this additional fuperftructure and the new figures, it became an object ftill more admired by ftrangers and more efteemed by the citizens. It was therefore now moft curioufly painted and gilded and inclofed with an iron pallifade, and furrounded with freeftone fteps, where all public proclamations were read to the people, and which ferved the market people to fit round when the market was kept in High-ftreet. Thefe improvements coft the cham-ber 207l. and its height from the ground was 39 feet 6 inches.

In the year 1697 in fuch a public eftimation was this Grofs held that it was thought proper to have it frefh painted and gilded, which was done in fuch a coftly manner, that no crofs in the kingdom is faid then to have exceeded it.

Here it ftood a public ornament to the city and the admiration of ftrangers refort-ing hither, efpecially all lovers of antiquity, until the year 1733 a filverfmith who lived fronting it, out of enmity to this ftructure fo efteemed by others, offered to fwear before the magiftrates that every high wind his houfe and life were endangered by the Crofs fhaking and threatening to fall (though it was not generally then believed) and fo requefted its removal. On this pretence and of its obftructing the road by filling up the ftreet, it was taken down and thrown by in the Guildhall as a thing of no value, though its removal was much regretted by moft of the citizens. Here it lay for a long time totally difregarded, till by the interpofition of Alderman Price and a few gentleman in the neighbourhood of College-green, it was refcued from oblivion by a voluntary contribution for erecting it in the center of the green, with the ap-probation of the dean and chapter. Here it made a moft confpicuous figure (fee p. 294) and was greatly ornamental; it adorned its new ftation, and its ftation reflected an ornament to it, and it was here viewed with pleafure by

all

all as a moſt curious piece of antiquity. But even here in time the Croſs loſt that reverence and regard that had been hitherto paid it throughout all ages, for in the year 1763 it was at length found out that this beautiful ſtructure by interſecting one of the walks interrupted gentlemen and ladies from walking eight or ten abreaſt. One Mr. Champion, a great projector, intereſted him-ſelf much in its removal, and ſolicited ſubſcriptions of money to be laid out in removing the Groſs, and widening and rendering more commodious the walks in College-green. The dean and chapter, on whoſe ground it was erected, gave leave for its removal. But many people who ſubſcribed for widening and improving the walks, ſubſcribed alſo for rebuilding the Groſs in any unexceptionable place, but no ſuch could be found in Briſtol — all the money ſubſcribed for the Groſs was ſpent ſolely in laying out the walks, the Croſs itſelf rudely torn down and much injured by the workmen employed, was thrown by in a corner of the cathedral, where it lay for a long while neglected, till Dean Barton gave it to Mr. Hoar of Stourton, who perceiving its value and out of love for antiquities has erected it in a moſt ſuperb manner at his elegant ſeat of Stourhead at the expence of 300l.

SECT. II. — *Of the* CHURCH *of St.* AUDEN, OWEN, *or* EWEN, *conſolidated in* 1788 *with* CHRIST CHURCH.

THIS church, ſituated in the center of the city at the meeting of four ſtreets, is well deſcribed 1480 by William of Worceſter : " The pariſh church of St. Auden with the chapel of the fraternity of St. John the Baptiſt is ſituated in a direct line betwixt the church of St. Werburgh on the weſt and the ſtreet called Broad-ſtreet on the caſt, and the great eaſt window of the altar of the ſaid church is ſituated in Broad-ſtreet." p. 227. And " The length of the church of St. Ewen, i. e. of St. Auden, contains 22 yards, and the breadth of the ſaid church, whoſe caſtern part or altar is directly oppoſite the church of the Holy Trinity, contains 15 yards meaſured by me or 30 ſteps ; and it has one nave on the north part of the aile, and one aile which is the chapel of the fraternity of St. John the Baptiſt." p. 215, 253. In 1631 a tower was erected at the expence of 196l. in the churchyard.

This church though the ſmalleſt is of greater antiquity than moſt. It ap-pears by deeds that " Robert Earl of Gloceſter gave the church of St. Auden to Thurſtan the prieſt of Briſtol, and William the Earl, his ſon, confirmed it

in

in the time of Simon Bishop of Worcester, and requested the bishop to maintain him therein, as he had admitted him in the time of his father Robert." —
This was about the year 1130 or 1140, as Simon died in 1150. St. Thomas
Archbishop of Canterbury by deed confirmed to Thurstan this church with all
its appurtenances, which Robert Earl of Glocester had given to him in alms,
to hold the same freely as Simon Bishop of Worcester had confirmed it to
him. This Thurstan afterwards gave it to God and the church of St. James,
Bristol, and the abby of Tewksbury, to which it paid yearly a small pension.
This was confirmed by William Earl of Glocester.

The great east window of the altar of this church, situated in Broad-street,
as well described by William of Worcester, p. 227. was the place where
King Edward 4th. stood to see Sir Baudwyn Fullford pass by to his execution,
which is confirmed by an entry in the churchwardens book of account,
1 Edward 4th. " Item, for washynge the church payven against K. Edward 4th.
is comynge to Brystow, iiii ob." Which was in September, 1461.

The fouth aile that joined the nave as part of this church was a chapel
dedicated to St. John the Baptist, belonging to a fraternity, called, the Master, Wardens, or Keepers, and Society of Taylors, consisting of brethren and
sisters, who always kept it in repair till its dissolution. It had two altars, one
to St. Catherine and the other to St. Margaret. This gild was erected and
the chapel founded by John Thorp and John Sherp, burgesses, who obtained
a charter of King Richard 2d. October 16, 1398, and the 22d year of his
reign, to found a chapel for a chaplain to celebrate divine service for the good
estate of the king and queen whilst alive and for their souls when departed,
and for the fraternity here perpetually founded and incorporated, and he gave
them power to choose a custos or warden always to be chosen by the co-brethren, and to hold lands, tenements, &c. for the support of the said chaplain
and his successors to the value of 100s. per annum for ever, the statute of
Mortmain notwithstanding. This was confirmed by Henry 4th. in the 1st
year of his reign, and John Thorp and John Sherp put Robert of Glocester
in possession of the said chapel, who was to celebrate divine service at the altar
of St. John in the church of St. Ewin, and to be displaced by the masters and
proctors of the fraternity in case of wilful neglect upon the third admonition.
In process of time by divers benefactions this fraternity, called afterwards the
Masters, Wardens or Keepers and Company of Merchant Taylors, became
possessed of a very considerable estate to the amount of 97l. 16s. 8d. in rents and
ground rents, besides renewals of lives upon their tenements yearly happening.
They had additional privileges also granted them by Queen Elizabeth in 1571,
which

which coſt them 15l. 16s. 1d. and obtained others of the mayor and common council at the expence of 10l. which the queen confirmed. They had then a book of ordinances containing 35 articles, acts, and rules, which were all confirmed by letters patent of King James, dated Auguſt 28, 1615, the ſame were again ratified by King Charles 1ſt. May 15, 1640. This company in the year 1701 out of their great revenues founded an almſhouſe in Merchant-ſtreet with a chapel in the pariſh of St. James. The old chapel in St. Ewen's church in 1551, 4th of Edward 6th. was granted by the parſon and pariſhioners with all their right and title to the mayor and commonalty of Briſtol, paying 6s. 8d. per annum, giving the parſon and pariſhioners power to diſtrain for the ſaid rent upon any of the city lands, with proviſo that if the church were at any time diſſolved then the rent ſhould ceaſe. Upon this the corporation taking down this chapel being one aile of the church built on the ſame ground a Council Houſe in the year 1552, with a ſhed covered with lead, ſupported with five ſtone pillars before it for the council to walk under in the dry, which muſt have greatly darkened the room below. The council chamber above had four high windows of ſtone tracery work with ſmall glaſs ſquares with the king's, the city's, and merchants' arms on top; between the windows was a niche, wherein a ſtatue of Charles 2d. was afterwards placed, which being ſhewn to one of the court ladies coming to Briſtol as an honour to that auguſt monarch, ſhe ſmartly replied, he looked more like a great clumſy porter placed there to keep the entrance. This old Council Houſe was taken down and another in a more modern ſtyle rebuilt in the year 1704, and the ſtatue was then placed againſt the Guildhall.

The RECTORS of St. Ewen or Owen.

Patrons.	
Abbot and convent of Tewkſbury.	1397 Thomas Lye.
1130 Thurſtan ——, prieſt.	1403 John Laury.
1292 Adam de Moreton.	1407 Thomas Ockley.
1317 John Scrovare.	1421 Richard Collyns.
1330 Jacobus ——.	1448 Richard Hankyn.
1348 Symon Bullocke.	1450 Thomas Gyles.
1370 William Botiller.	1452 Thomas Smyth.
1379 Thomas Botte.	1454 Thomas Jacob.
1381 Stephen Swell.	1459 Sir Thomas Seward.
1390 John Darell.	1501 Thomas Pennant.
1393 John Podwelle.	1515 Edward Waterhouſe.

Mr.

PATRONS.	1643 Timothy Whatley.
Mr. Brayne.	1664 James Pownall.
1519 John Rawlyns.	1670 Henry Jones.
1580 Thomas Long.	1673 Tobias Higgins.
1591 William Welles.	1701 James Pidding.
Sir Charles Gerard.	1730 Thomas Taylor.
1631 Thomas Gawen.	1770 Rumney Penrofe.
Corporation.	
1639 Matthew Hazard.	

There are few monuments in this church. There was on the afcent to the pulpit the following infcribed on a ftone : — " Hic jacet Johannes Coleman, nuper rector iftius ecclefiæ, qui obiit 8 die Maii, A. D. 1502."

Alfo on a ftone : — " Thomas Hobfon and Elizabeth his wife, daughter of Edmund Wynch, Efq; of London. She died March 18, 1642. He June 7, 1660, aged 77.

> Thus doth the glory of this world pafs
> We die and wither like the flower and grafs ;
> But fince on earth we are of life bereaven,
> We flew from earth to Chrift our life in heaven."

It appears by the receipt of Robert Recorde, comptroller of the king's mint, that they received in gilt plate 107 ounces, and in parcel gilt 142 ounces; 249 ounces at one time, which belonged to this church. Befides this, which confifted of chalices, pyxes, croffes, cenfers, fhips for carrying frankincenfe, fpoons, boxes, there was a long lift of ornaments, filk and velvet embroidered, veftments, curtains, copes, &c. belonging to this church and to the chapel of St. John.

This church is a rectory, the corporation being patrons ; but the parifh confifting of not more than 27 houfes and warehoufes, the benefit to the rector would be very fmall if the veftry did not allow him a ftipend out of the church ftock of 19l. per annum, befides the contributions from the parifhioners, and a gift fermon by Mr. Hobfon 6s. 8d. *

In

---

* The coft for a breakfaft on Corpus Chrifti day, 1460, is thus entered in this church book :

Item, for a calve's head and hinge - - -	3 d.
Item, for two rounds of beef - - - -	6
Item, for bread and ale - - - - -	8
Item, for Mafter Parfon for his dinner - -	4
Item, for the clerk - - - - - -	2
Item, for bearing the crofs - - - -	2

In 1787 this church was confolidated with that of Chrift Church, and an act of parliament obtained for taking this down and for rebuilding Chrift Church, which laft was compleated in 1788.

***

C H A P. XVI.

Of the CHURCH and PARISH of St. WERBURGA.

IT is a rectory, dedicated to St. Werburga, fuppofed to be the daughter of Wulferus King of Mercia, who had a nunnery erected and dedicated to her honour at Chefter about the year 670. Others fay, fhe was made abbefs by her uncle Ethelred over an ancient nunnery at Trickingham in Staffordfhire, where fhe died in 683. It is fituated in Corn-ftreet, called in deeds of the year 1200 Old Corn-ftreet, near the center of the city; its caft end joins the upper end of Small-ftreet. It has three ailes, the length of each from eaft to weft is 72 feet, its. breadth is in the clear 58 feet, and the height of the middle aile is 26 feet, having an arched plaiftered cieling, the outfide covering being of Cornifh tile, as are alfo the north and fouth ailes, the height of each being 22 feet, and on each fide the middle ailes are five neat fluted freeftone pillars, on which are turned fix arches of the fame ftone, which fupport the whole roof of the church. William of Worcefter, p. 200. fays, " It contains in breadth 19 yards or 34 fteps, and the fquare tower 5 yards on each of the four fides." It had no tower to it for near 200 years after its foundation, when by indenture dated the 11th of April, 1385, between the feoffees and parifhioners of the one part and John Warwyke then rector on the other, it was agreed that in confideration of their granting and confirming to the rector and his fuccefsors for ever a houfe belonging to the parifh fituated in the churchyard, the faid rector granted to them and their fuccefsors for ever his mefsuage fituated in Corn-ftreet, on which ground the tower is now built, being finifhed with freeftone in an elegant manner, having 160 fteps in afcending to the top at 6 inches each, which make the height 26 yards and 2 feet; it is adorned with four pinnacles one at each corner about 10 feet high with a copper vane on each.

In

In the center of the floor at top is built a curious hollow work pinnacle about 20 feet high with a gilt ball and weather cock, and in the tower is a peal of fix bells. Walter Derby, mayor, by will dated 1385, gave 40l. towards building this church, and Mr. Humphrey Brown, by deed dated the 10th of January, 1624, fettled 7l. per annum for ever, iffuing out of his farm at Elberton, in the county of Glocefter, for reading prayers every Monday morning in the year, at fix o'clock, 5l. per annum to the rector, 20s. to the clerk, and 20s. to provide candles during the winter feafon. Thomas Aldworth, 1598, gave 4l. to repair this church. Mr. Burroughs, in 1622, gave 50l. for the fame ufe. As to the other charitable benefactions I refer to the lift of them in the church tables. The 5th of January, the 11th year of Edward 2d. 1318, the king confirms amongft other things the church of St. Werburge and that of St. Mary le Port in Briftol given to the canons of the priory of Keynfham, in the county of Somerfet, by William Earl of Glocefter, for their better fuf-tentation. The churchwardens for the time being then paid an annual acknowledgment of 6s. 8d. to that priory, which fo continued to the final diffo-lution of that houfe, the fite of which with part of its lands was fold to the Bridges family with the prefentation to the church of St. Maryport in Briftol, to which the Duke of Chandos ftill prefents; but this of St. Werburge was retained in the gift of the crown, whofe receiver ftill continues to receive the annual fum of 6s. 8d. This church being much decayed, and obftructing the entrance into Small-ftreet, was partly taken down and rebuilt, and opened again for divine fervice the 8th of February, 1761; the tower was only repaired at top.

Many benefactions were made to this church by fundry perfons for obiits, chauntries, and to find lamps at the feveral chapels and altars within it. In 1245 Simon Clerk, mayor, granted 12d. annually for a lamp to burn in the choir of the chapel founded and dedicated to the Virgin Mary, as did Peter Martur 3s. for divine fervice at the fame chapel in the year 1261, and Nicolas le Barber, in 1304, gave 2s. annually for the fame purpofe, and alfo many others.

This parifh is of fmall extent, confifting of about 46 houfes, and the rectory is valued in the King's Books at 33l. 6s. 8d. clear yearly value, Yearly Tenths, now difcharged, 1l. But in the Lincoln manufcript it appears that in the year 1241, the 19th of Edward 1ft. this church was taxed at fix marks and a half per annum, and by a manufcript (Annal. Wygorn) it is faid, " 1236 confirmavi-mus canonicis de Keynfham C. folidos de ecclefia Sanctæ Werburgæ, Briftol."

The

The Lord High Chancellor prefents to this living. The rector pays to the crown 3s. 4d. per annum.

In the veftry-room over the door on the infide is the following infcription: " Fabricatum fuit hoc facrarium in menfe Julii Annoque Domini MDCXCIV, quo etiam tempore condecorata fuit hæc integra ecclefia fumptibus parochianorum Carolo Brent, A. M. rectore, Georgio Irifh, Abrahamo Eltono, guardianis."

In the fame room is hung up in a frame a lift of the GIFT SERMONS to be preached in this church. —

January 6, Dr. Thomas White's.	June 24, Mr. Humphrey Brown's.
May 22, Mr. Humphrey Brown's.	June 29, Dr. Thomas White's.
March 25, Dr. Thomas White's.	July 1, Mr. Humphrey Brown's.
May 6, Mr. Humphrey Brown's.	Dec. 27, Dr. Tho. White's, 1729.

By the rent roll of the lands belonging to this church the annual amount of the ground rents thereof in 1750 was 47l. 17s. 4d. which has fince been probably improved.

A Lift of the RECTORS.

PATRON.
Abby of Keynfham.

1245 Roger de Sowey.	1474 Thomas Pyttes, refigned with a penfion of fix marks.
1281 Thomas de Mersfeld.	1491 Richard Woode.
1290 William le Roper, removed becaufe married.	1500 John Pecke.
1292 Adam de Solweye.	The King, Patron.
1317 Thomas de la Greeve.	1545 Chriftopher Pacey.
1333 John de la Leech.	Sir William Carr.
1339 Thomas de Berewycke.	1577 Maurice Durant.
1360 Thomas de la Grone.	1605 Edward Toore.
1364 Hugo de Penbrugge.	1608 Richard Collyns
1367 John Warwycke.	1610 John Farmer.
1401 John Molfham.	1634 John Till Adam.
1404 William Congerfbury.	—— Stephens, afterwards mafter of the Grammar-fchool.
1410 William Hawevylle.	1686 Thomas Palmer.
1416 William Felton.	1694 Charles Brent.
1430 Robert Beaumont.	1729 Rumney Penrofe.
1436 Thomas Tonge.	1743 John Culliford.
1440 William Sutton.	175 Richard Symes.
1472 Thomas Merfhe.	

N N N

MONU-

MONUMENTS.

In the north aile is the following infcription:—" Hic jacet Johannes Punchardon, qui obiit 10 Apr. A. D. 1379, cujus animæ propitietur Deus, Amen." Arms, f. fable, five balls arg.

Near this a monument " To Alderman John Barker," a carved figure leaning on his right arm in the robes of a magiftrate. He was mayor in 1607, and died in his mayoralty. Arms, f. az. five efchallops or, quartered with f. gules, a chevron arg. three goats heads of the fecond. He died 1636. " Terrena fperno, fuprema fpero," with ten Englifh verfes.

Near this on a ftone on the floor an infcription to

" Abeli Rogers, generofo, qui obiit 29 Jan. 1632, æt. 20.

> Filius ad parentes:
> Vivo, fruor tandem veris (ne flete parentes)
> Deliciis, cælo, pofteritate, Deo." .

By the veftry a neat monument to

" Robert Earle, Efq; fome time mayor of this city, who died 25 January, 1736, aged 68 ;—a man of ftrict honour and juftice, and remarkably pune-tual in all his dealings. He difcharged the offices of mayor and alderman to the general fatisfaction of the citizens." Arms, G. three efchalops or.

Near this a table monument to Nathaniel Boucher, merchant, who died the 22d of March, A. D. 1627, aged 40, leaving behind him nine children.

Under a flat ftone by the veftry door are buried Giles Earle, gentleman: he died the 6th of January, 1676, aged 85. Alfo Sir Thomas Earle, Knight, mayor and alderman, who died the 24th of June, 1696, aged 67. Alfo Dame Elizabeth Elianor Earle, widow of Sir Thomas, who died the 7th of June, 1709, aged 74. Alfo Jofeph Earle, Efq; M. P. for Briftol, who died the 13th of March, 1729.

In the corner of this aile was a fmall fquare ftone table to the memory of Mr. George Boucher, merchant, who was hanged in Winc-ftreet, May 30, 1643, by the Rebels, with the following verfes on it:

> Sanguis Martyrum femen ecclefiæ.

> Whoever chanceth this way, pafs not by
> Thefe fainted afhes with a carelefs eye ;
> They are undaunted duft and did outbrave
> Whilft they retain'd a foul Death and the Grave ;
> And ftill bear witnefs in our Martyr's right,
> That they dare murder, who yet ne'er durft fight.

Ne'er

Ne'er was fo bold a lion by fuch hares
Worried to death, fo mercilefs their fnares;
Yet he fo ftout that whether none can tell
His courage or their cruelty did excel.
Mirror of Patience! Loyalty! thy fall
Hath proved yet a fuccefsful funeral:
Since 'twas guilt of thy death, no battery
That ftorm'd thefe forts, that gain'd us victory:
For though our foes were fenced with walls and roof,
Yet there's no wall, no fence is confcience proof:
Thus is thy murdering wreath to us become
A laureate, to thee a crown of martyrdom.

G. B.

At the eaft end is a fuperb monument gilded and painted with feveral coats of arms on brafs to Nicholas Thorne and his family, with the following Latin lines.

Hâc Nicolaus humo Thornus jacet, optime lector,
Olim mercator nobilis atque probus;
Cujus dicta fides conftantia facta regebat,
Et virtute vacans actio nulla fuit,
Briftoliæ natus fato quoque functus ibidem,
Qui magis æternùm vivere dignus erat.
Hanc etenim prætor rexitque fcolâque fuperbâ
Ornavit, fratis fumptibus atque fuis,
Munificumque patrem fenfit refpublica tota
Briftoliæ, cujus jam bonitate viget:
Huncque fenes, juvenes, pueri, innuptæque puellæ
Totaque plebs deflet tam cecidiffe citò,
Conjugo quem geminâ et bifquinâ prole beatum
Sedibus his miferis fuftulit omnipotens:
Cujus in ætherias animus penetravit in auras,
Reliquias tantum corporis arca tenet;
Uxoremque eadem fidam tenet arca priorem
Atque hunc qui primus natus utrique fuit.

Qui obiit 19 Aug. A. D. 1546, ætatis fuæ 50.

At the eaft end of the north aile was a large handfome Gothic tomb with brafs plates, with the engraved figure of a man at his devotions and feven fons be-

hind

hind him ; oppofite him a woman with two daughters behind her ; in the center is fufpended a fhield with the family arms, f. gules on a chevron between three cinquefoils arg. as many leopards faces fable. Underneath on a brafs plate the following verfes.

Johanni Smithe et Johannæ uxori ejus
Hugo et Mattheus eorundum filii pofuerunt.

Par jacet hoc tumulo fociale uxore maritus
Jungitur; ut leĉtns, fic tenet urna duos :
Smithus Johannes conjux, vir dignus amari,
Sumpfit Johannam, par in amore decus :
Pignore multiplici par felix luftra peregit
Plurima : nunc regnat junĉtus uterque Deo.   1556.

The creft of the Smith's arms.   On the helm on a wreath arg. and G. a griffin's head erafed G. with two gemmels or.   The 10th Eliz. a new creft was granted by Garter, a roebuck or. horned and clawed arg.

For rebuilding the church and fhortening it to widen the road into Smallftreet, this monument was taken entirely down, and the ground it ftood on thrown into the ftreet.

This John Smith, Efq; was a commiffioner under Henry 8th. 1544, to take the furrender of the hofpital of St. John without Redcliff-gate.   Part of thefe lands, which he purchafed, belong to the prefent Sir John Hugh Smyth, Bart. of Afhton Court, near Briftol, his defcendant at this day.

Againft a pillar in the north aile is a neat monument to John Day, Efq; with a long Latin infcription.   He died the 20th of June, 1718, ætatis 44.

In the chancel : " Johannes Perke, clericus quondam rector iftius ecclefiæ, obiit 1518."

Near this an infcription to

" Humphrey Brown, merchant, who died March 22, 1630, and Elizabeth his wife, daughter of George White, of this city, merchant.

Here lies a Brown a White, the colours one
Pale drawn by Death, here fhaded by a ftone :
One houfe did hold them both whilft life did laft,
One grave do hold them both now life is paft.

Sir John Seymour, of Bitton, fecond bufband of the above Elizabeth hoc fuum amoris fubjunxit teftimonium.

Novimus excelfo monumento ex marmore dignum
Te, licet es parvo nunc fita, velle tuum eft;

Sic

Sic duplex fpecimen gemini produxit amoris,
 Hic pofito, et vivo complacuiffe viro:
Virtutem et cœlis animam fruitura dicavit
 Et cineri cineres, offibus offa dedit."

At the eaſt end of the fouth aile is a large altar monument to William Carr and his wife. He was father of John Carr, founder of Queen Elizabeth's hoſpital. There were fome Englifh verfes on the back of the monument in the year 1759 concealed by the pew, which began thus:

Lo here the end of mortal man
Compaft in flender room;
The clue of Carr's unfpotted life
Wound up by fatal doom, &c.

In rebuilding the church this monument was alfo deſtroyed.

Under the fouth window is a handfome monument with a half arch for the family of Sir Robert Cann, of Compton Greenfield, Bart. Arms, az. fretty arg. on a fefs gules, three leopards faces or. creſt in a mural crown, gules, a plume of fix feathers arg. and az.

The following are the BENEFACTORS to the Church and Poor
of St. Werburgh's Parifh.

1624, Humphrey Brown gave an eftate at Elberton of 7l. per *l. s. d.*
annum, for reading prayers at fix o'clock, mornings, at
St. Werburgh's, and 2l. for four fermons there.

.1622, Dr. Thomas White gave lands of 10l. per annum for four fermons in this church.

1594, Robert Kitchen gave 10s. per annum to a houfekeeper of
this parifh for ever.

1639, George Harrington gave 10s. per annum to a houfekeeper
of this parifh for ever.

1661, Jofeph Jackfon gave 200l. the intereſt thereof for promoting divine worfhip in this church - - 200 0 0

Samuel Heal gave 230l. the intereſt for apprenticing poor
children in feven parifhes, and 10l. to be laid out in bread 230 0 0

1699, Ann Longman gave 195l. to the poor of the city, of which
this parifh has part.

1711, George Lyfons gave 50l. the intereſt to be laid out in bread
for the poor on Saints days - - - 50 0 0

1712, Richard Long gave 1l. 5s. per annum to poor houfeholders 25 0 0

		l.	*s.*	*d.*
1714,	James Crofts gave 2l. 10s. per annum to poor houfeholders	50	0	0
1727,	Sir Abraham Elton, Bart. gave 2l. 10s. per annum to five			
	poor houfekeepers not receiving alms, paid Sept. 11	50	0	0
1736,	Robert Earle gave 5l. per annum in bread weekly to the poor	100	0	0

Mrs. Boucher and Mrs. Langton gave lands in Bedminfter
to poor widows of the City at 10s. each.

Edward Golfton gave 160l. to erect a new altar-piece.

CHAP. XVII.

Of the CHURCH *and* PARISH *of St.* JOHN *the* BAPTIST,
with that of St. LAURENCE *confolidated.*

THIS church confifts but of one aile; the length of the church 80 feet,
the height is about 15 feet; there is a neat but fmall chancel, with a
handfome altar, behind which is a convenient veftry-room; the breadth of
the church is 24 feet. The tower, topt with a flender fteeple, is built upon a
lofty arch over the ftreet, in which are a peal of fix bells. The founder of
the church was Mr. Walter Frampton, who had been three times mayor. This
rectory is worth about 100l. per annum by voluntary contributions and of the
veftry 15l. per annum. Mr. William Burroughs, in 1622, gave a houfe in
Chriftmas-ftreet for the refidence of the minifter.

The yearly value in the King's Books for St. John and St. Laurence rectories
is 5l. 18s. 1d. The Yearly Tenths, now difcharged, was 14s. 5½d.

William of Worcefter fays, " Dedicatio ecclefiæ St. Johannis, &c. The
church of St. John was dedicated the 17th of July. The length of the vaulted
roof of St. John's confifts of fix arches with fix windows on one fide towards
the fouth, and two windows towards the north *fretle vowted.* It is 16 fteps
high, each ftep 8 inches. It is 29½ yards long befides the chancel, and 7
yards broad. The gate of St. John Baptift, upon which is built a fquare tower
and a fpire above it of freeftone with two battlements upon the tower, contains
in length 17 fteps, and was built anew with the church of St. John by Walter
Frampton, a noble merchant of the town of Briftol." p. 167, 197, 208, 216.

On

On each fide of the arched gateway fouth are the two figures of Bellinus and Brennus, two Britifh kings of uncommon prowefs and fuccefs in war, if we believe the fabulous Geoffrey of Monmouth, with their coat armour, an efcutcheon with a portcullis over one, and a flower de lis or. over the other; but it is clear they were put up fince the church was erected, to give fome fanction to the flory of Geoffrey, quoted by William of Worcefter and others, who have made them the founders of Briftol, of as little credit as the ftory of Brute and his Trojans peopling England.

Mr. Robert Strange, who had been three times mayor of this town, the firft time in the year 1475, the fecond in 1483, the third in 1490, founded an hofpital ora lmfhoufe in this parifh, by the foot of the fteps going into St. James's out of Tower-lane, and endowed the fame with lands by the Caftle mill up to Newgate, alfo the Spur-inn in Winc-ftreet did belong to the fame; but by the wicked proceedings of the people then in truft for this charity they had embezzled the revenues of it. A commiffion to enquire into it was held by Dr. Robert Wright, Bifhop of Briftol, and many others, who found that feveral leaves had been cut out of the parifh books which related to this charity, alfo the infcription on his tomb in St. John's churchyard was entirely defaced, and the commiffion proved of no effect; it was held in the year 1640. The great rebellion foon after fpread over the kingdom, which put a flop to any further proceedings. The almfhoufe became ruinous, and was taken down and rebuilt in the year 1721, where now thirteen poor women do inhabit: they are put in by the veftry of this parifh, but there are no lands at prefent with which it is endowed.. The pay to each perfon is 1s. 6d. per week from St Peter's Hofpital, which is an incorporated body of guardians for the poor of the whole city, eftablifhed by act of parliament paffed in the 7th and 8th year of his Majefty King William the 3d. 1696.

The Rev. Mr. Powell 1664 gave money to the chamber to pay 2l. per ann. to St. John's almfhoufe. Alice Cole 1604 gave 4l. per annum. Thomas Sylk 1l. 1s. per annum, 1565.

The feoffees and veftry of this church are poffeffed of near fifty tenements, leafed out on lives, the referved or ground rents of which amounted in the year 1754 to the fum of 86l. 8s. annually befides renewals.

RECTORS

1286 John de Stowey.

1304 Thomas de Cifton, habuit cufto-
diam ecclef. Sti. Joannis.

1309 Dom. Pagan de Briftol.

1337 William de Bermingham.

1361 John Loveftoke de Afton.
John Bonecocke.

1369 Henry Cammile.

1379 Richard Wodecote.
William Wade.

1385 Richard Maykyn.

1388 Richard Wormbrugg.

1392 Richard Croke.

1406 John Shaw.

1420 John Mybbys.

1427 Richard Clerk.

1433 Thomas Wheton.

1460 Nicholas Ruffel.

1465 Thomas Clent.

1505 Walter Walfhe.

1507 John Tofte, by refignation of
Walfhe.

1531 Tho. Tafker, by death of Tofte.
Sir Charles Somerfet, Patron.

1567 Roger Price.
Mayor and aldermen, Patrons.

1580 Roger Rife, 22 Eliz

1604 Wm. Davells, Si. verbi minifter.

1634 Nicholas Pownall.

1660 Thomas Coleman.

1730 James Taylor.

1746 Carew Reynell, and chancellor
of Briftol,
Thomas Bound.
John Davie, M. A.

1779 Rev. J. Johnes, M. A.

There are few monuments in this church. The firft is the founder's on a a raifed tomb with his figure at length in his alderman's robes enclofed with a a railing, at the top of which is the following infcription : — " Hic jacet corpus Gualteri Frampton, mercatoris, et hujus ecclefiæ fundatoris terque villæ Briftolliæ mayoris 1357."

On the ground near this tomb are the effigies of a man and woman in brafs let into the ftone, with fix fons and fix daughters, and the following infcription : — " Hic jacet Thomas Rowley, quondam mercator et vicecomes hujus villæ Briftolliæ qui quidem Thomas obiit 23 Jan. A. D. 1478, et Margaret uxor quæ obiit A. D. 1470. Quorum animabus propitietur Deus, Amen." Out of the month of the man comes a fcroll and thereon, " Sancta Maria ora pro nobis." Out of the woman's, " Sancta Trinitas unus Deus miferere nobis." In the cript or vault under the church is a large tomb of alabafter, and on its
fide

fide the figures of the fix fons and fix daughters with their father and mother, without epitaph, but fuppofed to be for the above Thomas Rowley.

Againft the fouth wall in the chancel is a marble monument to the memory of Andrew Innis, gentleman, who died the 29th of December, 1733, aged 82, and his wife Joan, who died the 3d of May, 1672, and Elizabeth his fecond wife, who died 1711, by whom he had fourteen children.

Againft the north wall is a handfome monument to William Donning, Efq; alderman, who died the 15th of November, 1695. John his fon died the 15th of April, 1701. James, mayor and alderman, died the 8th of March, 1745.

There were two chauntries here founded by Walter Frampton in St. John's, one called Cantaria St. Mariæ, of which Richard fon of John Coke was chauntry prieft, another of which in 1531 John Poppely was prieft. The faid Frampton inftituted alfo a chauntry in the church of Wraxhal, in the county of Somerfet, a delightful village feven miles from Briftol, and ordered the naming of a chaplain to be always by the mayor of Briftol for the time being. There was another chauntry at St. John's alfo by Thomas Rowley, and a chapel of the Holy Crofs.

It may be remarked here, that Rowley was the name of a family that flou-rifhed in Briftol for many years and at different periods. Whether the fo much celebrated Rowley, of whom we have fuch difputed accounts, was chauntry prieft of this chauntry, founded here by his relation, muft be left to the opinion and judgment of the reader. It is recorded in Chatterton's hand-writing that Rowley was chauntry prieft of St. John's. That it was a Briftol family appears from many deeds, in which they are often mentioned. One Thomas Rowley was chauntry prieft at Redcliff.

And in a Bede-roll of All Saints church Walter Rowley and William Rowley are to be prayed for by name among the benefactors to that church. In the year 1479 William Rowley of this city was buried at St. Mary's church of Dam, in Flanders.

At the weft fide of the tower was an old church formerly, dedicated to St. Lawrence. William of Worcefter defcribes it as having been 28 yards long, and 9 yards wide. When it was built is uncertain, but it is of a very old foundation, and going to decay and having but a fmall parifh belonging to it, it was united and incorporated with St. John's in the 22d of Elizabeth, 1580, having been fold in the time of Henry 8th. to H. Brayne, whofe fucceffor Sir

O o o

Charles

Charles Somerfet fold the fite of it for buildings upon lives. John Hawkys, twice mayor, by will, 4 May, 16 Henry 8th. gave a third part of his eftate to the rector and proctors of the church of St. Lawrence, the whole eftate valued at that time at 900l. Some remains of arched windows do now alone point out its fite next to St. John's-gate.

There was alfo not far diftant from this another church, dedicated to St. Giles, over the gate at the bottom of Small-ftreet. This has alfo undergone the fame fate, and was united to St. Leonard's about the time of Edward 3d. and is noticed by William of Worcefter, p. 248.

The following were the RECTORS of St. Lawrence.

PATRONS.

Robert le Ware.	1303	Robert, dictus Ware, de Briftol fuhd. 13 kal. Feb.
John le Ware.	1321	John de Wedmore cap. kal. Maii, taxat ad v marc as.
	1348	John de Quenyngton, pbr. 26 March.
		John Forfter.
Tho. BrokeMiles.	1406	William Dene, 12 May.
	1414	Nicholas Schaldere, 5 May.
		John Wylle.
		Roger Saunders.
J. Dom. de Lyfle.	1446	William John.
	1457	Thomas Wandre, 7 May.
	1460	Robert Chaloner.
	1467	William Adice.
Thomas Talbot.		John Newton.
Vice C. Lyfle.	1499	Thomas Tappefcote, 9 December.
Arthur Planta-genet and Eliz.	1524	Oliver Browne, 6 October.
Uxor ejus.	1526	John Funtayne.
Corporation.	1548	—— ——.

BENEFACTORS to the Church and Poor of St. John Baptift Parifh.

	l.	s.	d.
Mrs. Mary Boucher and her daughter Mrs. Mary Langton, widows, gave lands for payment of 10s. apiece to 52 poor widows of this city yearly for ever, of which this parifh hath a proportion.			
1683, Mrs. Elizabeth Horn gave 10l. the profit thereof to the poor of this parifh for ever - - -	10	0	0
1685,			

	l.	*s.*	*d.*
1685, Mr. Richard Stubbs, merchant, gave 50l. the profit thereof to the poor of this parifh for ever - -	50	o	o
1701, Mr. John Dunning, of this parifh, merchant, gave to the churchwardens 25l. the profit thereof to the poor in bread on the 1ft day of January yearly for ever	25	‹	
1709, Capt. John Price, late of this city, gave to the churchwardens of this parifh 10l. the intereft thereof to be given to the poor in bread on St. John's-day yearly for ever	10	o	o
Mrs. Hannah Cole gave 30l. the intereft thereof to be paid to fix poor widows of this parifh on St. Thomas's-day yearly for ever - - - -	30	o	o
Mr. Robert Kitchen, alderman of this city, gave 20s. per annum to the poor for ever - - -	20	o	o
Mr. George Harrington, alderman of this city, gave 20s. per annum to the poor for ever - - -	20	o	o
Mr. Thomas White gave to the maintenance of this parifh conduit-pipe 20s. per annum, to be paid hy the chamberlain of this city for ever - - -	20	o	o
Mr. William Griffin gave 10s. for a fermon to be preached upon St. John's-day, and 3s. 4d. in bread to be diftributed the fame day to the poor - - -	13	o	o
Mrs. Elizabeth Colfton, widow, gave 10s. per annum for a fermon to be preached on New Year's day for ever	10	o	o
1669, Mr. Edward Langley, of this parifh, merchant, gave two tenements for 58 years, the profit thereof to be diftributed in bread weekly to poor houfekeepers.			
1678, Mr. Edward Hurn, fome time fheriff of this city, gave 30l. the profit thereof in bread to the poor of this parifh for ever	30	o	o
1687, Thomas Edwards, late of this parifh, Efq; gave 20s. per annum for ever, iffuing out of lands in the parifh of St. Philip and Jacob, in the county of Glocefter, which by his will he directed fhould be applied for preaching two fermons yearly for ever in this church, one on St. Thomas's-day and the other on Good Friday -	20	o	o
1733, Mrs. Jane Edwards, widow of the above-named Thomas Edwards, by her will gave 20 guineas to this parifh, the profit arifing therefrom to be laid out in bread annually on St. Thomas's-day, and diftributed by the churchwardens to the poor of this parifh - -	21	o	o

Mr.

	l.	*s.*	*d.*

Mr. Robert Strange, fome time mayor of this city, was founder of this parifh almfhoufe.

Mr. William Chefter, fome time mayor of this city, gave four tenements, the profit thereof to the poor, and 7l. 10s. per annum quit rents.

Mrs. Margaret Tindal gave a dwelling-houfe and 20s. per annum in money.

Mrs. Cole, the wife of Alderman Cole, gave to the poor of the almfhoufe 6s. 8d. per month   -   -   -   6 10 0

Mr. Thomas Coleman, fome time rector of this church, gave to the poor of the almfhoufe 4s. per month   52 - -

Mr. Andrew Yates gave 16s. per annum to the poor of the almfhoufe.

Mr. William Burrowes gave a dwelling-houfe to the rector of this parifh.

1661, Mr. Francis Gleed gave 40s. per annum to four houfe-keepers quarterly, 10s. each to fuch as receive no alms   40 0 0

1669, The parifhioners have purchafed 5l. 4s. per annum for 2s. a week in bread to the poor of this parifh for ever.

1719, Mr. Samuel Hartnell, of St. Auguftine's parifh, gave the inheritance of lands in the parifh of Henbury, in Gloce-fterfhire, now let at 33l. per annum, to put three poor boys in Queen Elizabeth's Hofpital for ever, one of which is to be of this parifh.

Juft under the tower on the fouth next Broad-ftreet is St. John's ciftern, to which is brought by lead pipes from Park-ftreet the fpring-head a conftant fupply of water. To repair the pipe when out of order Thomas White left 20s. per annum. A large feather from this ufed to fupply the Carmelite friery, afterwards called Sir John Young's Great Houfe, (now Colfton's Hof-pital) and in 1654 this feather, which had been made fo large as to deprive the citizens of the water, was ordered by the mayor and commonalty to be cut off and the pipe laid level in the ftreet, the conduits and pipes of the city being under their care, and the churchwardens of St. John were ordered to fee it duly executed, and to enter into any ground or place to the fountain head to view and amend the defects. As early as October 1, 50 Edward 3d. 1376, Walter Derby being mayor, an agreement was made with Hugh White, plumber, at his own coft during life to bring the water to the Key pipe, All Saints

pipe

pipe and St. John's pipe, at the yearly fum of 10l. Mention is made of a ciftern near the Carmelites called, " the ciftern of the pipe of St. John's, in Broad-ftreet."

In this parifh of St. John is the Guildhall of the city, a very ancient ftructure, thus defcribed by William of Worcefter, in 1480, p. 239, " The breadth of the Gylhalle of Briftol in Broad-ftreet contains 23 yards with the chapel of St. George, founded by Richard Spicer, a famous merchant and burgefs of the town, about the time of King Edward 3d. or Richard 2d. There is a very worthy fraternity of merchants and mariners belonging to the faid chapel. This chapel contains in length 20 fteps befide the fpace of the chancel, its breadth 12 fteps."

The Guildhall is a lofty, long, fpacious, and airy room, arched with wood work, and well adapted for the bufinefs of holding the quarter feffions and yearly affizes. The jury retire into St. George's chapel to agree about the verdict; and there is a very convenient grand jury room and galleries fitted up for the witneffes and fpectators upon trials, feats for the judge, mayor, aldermen, and fheriffs, and a court for the counfellors and a bar for the prifoners.

The Taylors'-hall is alfo in this parifh, built on void ground given to the fraternity of Taylors of St. Ewen's, wherein they meet on feftival days in their gowns to wait on the mayor, and where they tranfact the bufinefs of their fociety.

Bridewell, of old called Monkenbridge or Munkbridge, the common prifon of the city, was once an old tower and fortification, new built in 1577, and rebuilt in 1721 by the chamber at the expence of 1053l. 3s. To this there were many benefactors. Thomas Chefter, 1582, gave 2l. per annum, and Thomas Kelky 20l. And 1507 Peter Matthew 100l. to keep the poor in Bridewell at work. Sir John Young 20l. Sir William Young 50l. and 1597 Margaret Brown 10l. Thomas Aldworth 15l. to the fame ufe and to buy them bedding. In the year 1694 Froom-gate in this parifh was removed.

C H A P.

C H A P. XVIII.

Of the CHURCH *and* PARISH *of St.* NICHOLAS, *with St.*
LEONARD's *confolidated.*

THIS church of St. Nicholas is of great antiquity, being one of thofe
which bounded the old city, and was built on a line with the city wall,
fo that the account in the manufcript under the name of Rowley as it is the
only, fo it may probably be the trueft. " Thys chyrch was founded by Erle
Britrycke in M...XXX, and fythence was yeven to Seynête Auguftynes mynfterre in Bryftowe, as we may fee wyth the ftorie of the mynfterre ynne the
notable worke of the abbate." Now it is very certain that Abbot Newland left
in manufcript the hiftory of his church and the Berkeley family, and mentions
Robert third fon of Robert Fitzharding (about 1172) having given unto that
monaftery the church of St. Nicholas in Briftol. The dean and chapter of the
cathedral are the patrons. In the year 1503 this church was partly rebuilt,
for in the will of Thomas Knapp, an eminent merchant and late mayor, 20l.
is given " towards building St. Nicholas church." The building was fpacions
laid out in the form of two ailes, the one north terminated with a beautiful
chancel, adorned with an altar-piece, being a painting on the wall in per-
fpeêtive, to which there was an afcent by twelve fteps, with a pavement of
black and white marble, which had a noble effeêt as you approached the altar.
It was fituated over the arched gateway called Nicholas-gate, where was a
clock, and over it a ftatue in ftone of Henry 2d. who in his young days was
educated at Briftol, and at a fchool in this parifh. The roof of the church
was covered with lead, and fupported with four arches and five flender pillarst
all of freeftone, which on the fouth fide leaning threatened to give way, and in
1730 being repaired the following infcription was placed near the entrance of
the church there : " Hæc compta Dei domus modo collapfura quatuor novis
columnis fuffulta et ornata ftabilimen et ornamentum recepit. Firmins fta-
biliatur precibus, evangelio, puritate morum, clarius ornetur continuato cætu
congregantium." There was a veftry-room on the fouth fide that projeêted
over the ftreet. Here you entered into an arched place or vault called the

Croud,

Crond, of almoſt the whole length and breadth **of the** church, which had a row of four large pillars, and on the north ſide five arched openings with iron bars for windows, to let in light into this dark repoſitory of the dead. Leland takes notice of this, Itin. p. 85. " where is a church of St. Nicholas *cum cryptis.*" Croud is then an abuſe of the word *crypt*, from the Greek ꭓρυπɩω, to hide, a hiding place for the dead. William of Worceſter deſcribes it thus, p. 201. " The breadth of the whole vault or croud with the two ailes arched with the number of five pillars contains 12 yards, and five great pillars and five arches are in the ſaid croud. Alſo the ſquare belfry tower contains 5 yards, ex omni parte." And p. 284. " The length of the croud of St. Nicholas contains beſides the chapel with 7 yards for the breadth of the chapel of Holy Croſs 31 yards, its breadth contains 12 yards, 1½ foot." The high ſpire or ſteeple was conſtructed of wood, ſtrongly and curiouſly framed together and covered with lead, the pieces jointed and let one into the other, which William of Worceſter calls " magnum pinnaculum ſeu ſpera de mearenno elevata cum plumbo cooperta."

There were ſix bells in the tower, and the great clock bell was fixed in the ſteeple above the reſt, with this inſcription on it : " Georgius Campana Briſtow ad voluntatem maior et communit. removetur tempore Walteri Darby, maioris, A. D. 1369."

When the paſſage over the old bridge and through the arch of St. Nicholasgate up High-ſtreet was become ſo very inconvenient and dangerous, that it was thought neceſſary to take down the bridge and St. Nicholas-gate, upon which the chancel of the church ſtood, it was long debated whether it would not be better to rebuild the church wholly, as it was a very old ſtructure, and removing a part might endanger the whole. Accordingly the bridge commiſſioners having allowed the veſtry 1400l. for the damages the church muſt neceſſarily ſuſtain, and 1000l. more towards building it anew, the plan for rebuilding the church, though it might be at an additional expence, was approved of, and in October, 1762, they began taking down the church. In two old arches in the ſouth wall were found two ſkeletons of perſons, who muſt have been buried there ſoon after or at the erection of the wall of the church ; perhaps when rebuilt in the time of Thomas Knapp before mentioned in 1403. In conſtructing the new church they preſerved the croud without diſturbing the aſhes of the dead ; but found the tower and ſpire too defective to be kept ſtanding, they therefore took them down alſo, and built the preſent noble ſtone tower and ſpire in the ſame place, which was not finiſhed till 1768. The old ſix bells were new caſt into a fine peal of eight bells beſides the clock bell

nion of moft it has not fo ftriking an effect as the old form of building;

> — — — — the high-embowed roof
> With antique pillars maffy proof,
> With ftoried windows richly dight,
> Cafting a dim religious light.   MILTON.

Divine fervice is no where better kept up than in this church. Befides daily prayers here celebrated from time immemorial, there is a lecture-fermon preached every Tuefday afternoon, for which the preacher is paid 25l. per annum by the chamber of the city and a fermon morning and after-noon on Sundays. For the afternoon fermon the vicar is paid 20l. per annum out of the chamber, the gift of Humphrey Brown in the year 1629, who vefts an eftate at Filton in Glocefterfhire in the mayor and commonalty, for them " to provide and maintain for ever a learned lecture-fermon on every Lord's day in the afternoon at St. Nicholas in Briftol, or at St. Werburgh's, or fome other church in the city, by fome able, learned, and godly preacher, a Batche-lor in Divinity at leaft, for the better inftructing the people in the deep myfte-ries of God, and of his faving health, &c."

There was a vicarage-houfe and garden formerly belonging to the vicars of this parifh, but it was taken away by the veftry in 1625, and upon complaint of Mr. Towgood they allowed him 4l. per annum in lieu of it; but upon his re-turn after his fequeftration they promifed to allow him 14l. per annum towards houfe rent, which however it appears they never performed, alledging he had nothing to fhew for it, fo they revoked their promife. The houfe is defcribed in deeds as fituated in Back-ftreet, in the Rackey on the north fide, 22 Feb. 9 Eliz. p. 447. of Book of Wills and Enrolment of Deeds in the chamber of Briftol.

This vicarage is worth to the minifter above 200l. per annum, by collections from the parifhioners, befides the gift fermons and furplice fees.

The

The following is a Lift of the V I C A R S from the year 1240.

PATRONS.

Abbot and convent of St. Auguftin.

1240 Walter Filomena.
1286 Michael Ruffelyn.
1301 Adam le Jeovene.
1311 Walter de Saunford.
1313 Walter de Kemefcote.
1341 Thomas Egifton.
1348 John de Bettoner.
1349 William de Tormerton.
1352 Walter Afch.
1361 Thomas Spette.
1369 John Cromme.
1378 William Brythlampton. ·
1387 Nicolas Adams.
1404 Thomas Yotflete.
1405 John Vaughan.
1430 William Parker.
1446 John Arffos.
1493 John Burton.
1508 Thomas Coke, A. M.
1515 Thomas Hannibal.

Dean and chapter, Patrons.

1551 John Raftal.
1593 George Harris.
1602 William Robinfon.
1620 George Hanis.
1626 Richard Towgood.
      Samuel Croffman.
1700 John Read, vic. to 1713.
      John Gafkarth, by nomination
      of Lord Guilford, in a letter
      to Dean Tompfon.
      William Goldney, died 1747.
1748 John Caftelman.
      John Camplin, D. D. precentor
      of the Cathedral, vicar of
      Olvefton and of Elberton in
      the county of Glocefter, and
      lecturer of the Church of St.
      Mary-Redcliff.

There were formerly the following Chauntries belonging to the Church of St. Nicholas.

	l.	*s.*	*d.*
A chauntry by Richard Spycer - -	12	7	11
Four by Everard Le French - -	26	3	9
Another by William Spencer - -	5	0	0
Two others by Thomas Knappe - -	13	6	8

There was a religious gild or fraternity of the Holy Ghoft within the crowd of St. Nicholas, cum capellâ in honorem Santæ Crucis ibidem; they received rents with the brotherhood and cafualties 18l. 5s. per annum.—The expences of the priefts and clerk for celebrating the Holy Ghoft mafs and anthems, yearly falary was 6l. 13s. 4d. which with wine, ringing the bells and cleaning the croud amounted to about 9l. per annum in toto, and cofts " for the drynk-yng of the brotherhoode on Holy-rood day" amounted to 5l. 6s. where the wheat in 1529 is charged 21d. per bufbel, candles 1d. per pound, 14 gallons of milk 1s. 2d. double ale 2d. per gallon, &c.

The

The following are the principal MONUMENTS to be met with here.

John Whitfon alderman, and a great benefactor to the city, lies buried in the crowd, his figure in ftone well carved and painted in his alderman's gown, on a handfome arch tomb, with fquare pyramidal pillars on the fide, and over him a table with the following infcription:—The particulars of his charitable endowments and gifts will be fhewn in the lift of wills and charitable donations, and are fet down on the monument.

" In memory of that great benefactor to this city John Whitfon, mayor and alderman, and four times member in parliament for the fame, who died in the 72d year of his age, A. D. 1629; a worthy pattern to all who came after him : out of his feveral eftates he bequeathed, viz. *l.   s.   d.*

To 52 poor childbed women	- 52	0	0 per annum.
To the Redmaids Hofpital	- 120	0	0 ditto.
To Redcliff Grammar-fchool	- 8	10	6 ditto.
To the Merchants' Almfhoufe	- 26	0	0 ditto.
To poor fcholars at Oxford	- 20	ı	0
To poor houfekeepers -	- 52	0	0
To poor widows - -	- 26	0	0
To St. Nicholas parifh -	- 3	0	0
To the ufe of merchants and poor tradefmen intereft free -	- 500	0	0

The grave where he and his three wives lie and one daughter is clofe before the monument; he was buried the 9th of March 1629: he was hurt by a fall from his horfe, which was the fuppofed caufe of his death; and being captain of the trained bands of the city, they attended his corps to St. Nicholas church, and the mufqueteers gave him three vollies over the grave at the interment, according to the military cuftom.

In the north wall of the crowd is a monument with a Latin infcription : " To Francis Knight Efq; who died 20th Aug. 1616."

In the caft wall of the chancel was a fmall marble monument to Edward Runcomb Efq; of the ifland of Montferat, born at Goathurft in the county of Somerfet; he died the 11th of Sept. 1712, aged 53.

Near this another to Elizabeth Hart, daughter of —— Wynn of Denbeigh, fhe died Oct. 1734.

Alfo to Sir Richard Hart, who died Jan. 16, 1701.

In the wall was this infcription in a table at the foot of the veftry fteps:

" Dum precaturus afcendis ad domum Dei
Moriturus refpice domum mortuorum :

En

En fub hoc facro fornice criptam vetuflam
Vetuftiorem fordibus collapfoque folo fa&am
Simplex munditiis nitet ;
Ut decet ecclefiam Anglicanam :
Nam in honorem Dei
In ufum fepulturæ
In gratiam fuperftitum
Hoc cœmiterium ad planitiem reda&um
Repurgatumque novis ornabatur cancellis
Impenfis parochianorum
Curâ Ædilium
A. D. 1718."

Near the fteps was the following infcription : — " Hic jacet Johannes
Papinham, quondam mercator et burgenfis villæ Briftolliæ, qui obüt 7 Apr.
1438."

BENEFACTORS to the Church and Poor of St. Nicholas Parifh.

		l.	*s.*	*d.*
1583, Mr. William Tucker, alderman, gave 40s. per annum, at Eafter 20s. and at Chriftmas 20s. and 6s. 8d. for a fermon next Sunday after Trinity Sunday for ever		46	‹	
1595, Mr. John Brown, alderman, gave twelve fhifts, fix for men and fix for women, to the value of 26s. 8d. per annum, one year to the Merchants' almfhoufe in the Marfh, and two years to this parifh, and fo to continue for ever - - - - -		26	‹	
Mr. Matthews gave 40s. per annum, 20s. at Eafter and 20s. at Chriftmas, for ever - - - -		40	0	0
Mrs. Alice Webb gave 20s. per annum upon Good Friday for ever - - - - -		20	0	0
1597, Mr. George Snow gave 20s. per annum, 10s. at Michaelmas and 10s. at Chriftmas, and 6s. 8d. for a fermon the Sunday before the 24th of June for ever -		26	0	0
1620, Mr. William Challoner gave 12d. per week in bread, and 10s. for a fermon the 9th day of January - -		62	0	0
1628, Mr. John Whitfon, alderman, gave 50l. per annum to poor houfe-holders of this parifh, and 20s. for two fermons, viz. upon the 28th day of October and the 7th day of November, for ever - - -		70	0	0

1591,

	l.	*s.*	*d.*
1594, Mr. Robert Kitchen, alderman, gave 40s. per annum to four poor houfe-holders quarterly for ever -	40	0	0
Mr. John Langton, alderman, gave 40s. per annum to four houfe-holders quarterly, and 12s. for a fermon to be preached at Horfield on the firft Sunday in Lent, for ever - - - - - -	52	0	0
1639, Mr. George Harrington, alderman, gave 40s. per annum to four houfe-holders quarterly for ever -	40	0	0
Mr. William Pitt, merchant, gave 50l. the profit thereof to the poor in bread for ever - - -	50	0	0
Mr. Roger Hurt gave 6s. 8d. for a fermon on the 24th of June for ever - - -	6	10	(
Mr. William Burrowes gave 20s. for a fermon on the 3d of May for ever - - - - -	20·	0	0
Mr. John Henry gave 10s. for a fermon upon St. John's-day, the 27th of December, for ever - -	10	0	0
Mr. George Hart gave 20l. the profit thereof to the poor in bread for ever - - - -	20	0	0
Mr. Abraham Birkin gave 40s. per annum to four poor houfe-holders (receiving no alms) quarterly for ever	40	0	0
Mr. Michael Deyos, merchant, gave 12d. per week in groat bread to three poor houfe-holders (not receiving other alms) for ever, and 13s. 4d. to the minifter of this parifh for a fermon to be preached on the 3d day of Auguft in the morning, and 4s. 8d. to the clerk and fexton for ever - - - -	70	0	0
Sir Thomas Langton gave 50l. the profit thereof to the poor in bread weekly for ever, and 20s. for a fermon to be preached upon Good Friday for ever -	70	0	0
Mr. John Dymer, fheriff of this city, gave 10l. the profit thereof to the poor in bread quarterly for ever -	10	0	0
1675, Mr. Edward Baugh, of this parifh, linen-draper, gave 100l. the profit thereof to be given to the poor in bread weekly for ever - - - -	100	0	0
Mr. Thomas Bevan, of this parifh, a member of the common council, gave 20l. the profit thereof to be given to the poor in bread weekly for ever - -	20	0	0

1678,

		l.	*s.*	*d.*
1678, Mr. Richard Holland gave 10l. the profit in bread to the poor of the almfhoufe on Eafter-day for ever, and 10l. towards building it, founded by the parifh 1638 -		20	0	0
1680, Alexander James, Efq; fome time mayor and alderman of this city, gave 20l. the profit thereof to the poor of this parifh for ever - - - - -		20	0	0
1681. Mr. Timothy Parker, fome time fheriff, gave 10l. the profit thereof in bread weekly to the poor for ever		10	0	0

Mrs. Mary Boucher and her daughter Mrs. Joan Langton, widows, gave lands for the payment of 10s. apiece to 52 poor widows of this city yearly for ever, of which this parifh hath a proportion. (N. B. The lands lie in the parifh of Afhton, and let at 80l. per annum.)

1683, Mr. George White, fome time fheriff and alderman of this city, gave 10l. the profit thereof to four poor houfe-holders not receiving alms quarterly - -		10	0	0
1686, Mr. John Hart, merchant, gave 10l. the profit thereof to be given in bread to the poor of this parifh weekly for ever		10	0	0
1687, Mr. George Morris, merchant, and member of the common council, gave 20l. the profit thereof to the poor at Chriftmas and Eafter for ever .. -		20	0	0
Mr. Richard Vaughan, a member of this parifh, gave 10l. the profit thereof to the poor in bread on St. Thomas's-day yearly for ever - - - -		10	0	0
Sir William Cann, Knight and Bart. gave 100l. to four parifhes of this city, whereof this hath a fourth part, the profit thereof to be diftributed to the poor the 8th day of January for ever - - -		25	0	0
Mr. Charles Herbert, grocer, gave 10l. the profit to be given to the poor of this parifh upon the 28th day of June for ever - - - -		10	0	0
Mr. Stephen Watts, merchant, once a member of the common council, gave 10l. the profit to be diftributed to the poor at Chriftmas for ever - -		10	0	0

1688, The 23d of January, the Lady Ann Cann, relict of Sir Robert Cann, of this city, Knight and Bart. born in this parifh, gave 10l. per annum for twenty years to the poor of this parifh, widows chiefly to be relieved.

1690,

	l.	*s.*	*d.*
1690, Mrs. Elizabeth Hall, widow, gave 100l. which according to her will was laid out in the purchafe of a houfe, the rent whereof (all charges deducted) is for the preaching of twelve fermons yearly, viz. on the firft Saturday in each month in the afternoon for ever -	100	0	0
Mrs. Margaret Abbey, widow, gave 50l. the profit thereof for the better relief of the poor, which was accordingly to her will diftributed ˙ - - - -	50	0	0
Mr. John Sandford, junr. gave 10l. the profit thereof to be diftributed to the poor on the 14th of February yearly for ever - - -	10	0	0
Mr. George White, fome time fheriff of this city, gave 10l. the profit thereof in fix-penny bread to the poor (not receiving alms) at Chriftmas for ever -	10	0	0.
1693, Sir William Cann, Knight and Bart. a former benefactor to this parifh, gave 103l. for payment of 40s. per annum for a fermon yearly on St. George's-day againft Atheifm and Prophanenefs, and 13s. 4d. yearly to the clerk, organift, and fexton, and 3l. 10s. per annum to be equally divided to feven poor houfe-holders of this parifh the fame day (fuch as frequent divine fervice to be preferred) for ever - - - -	103	'	
1694, Mr. Jedidiah Pickford, a member of the common council, gave 30l. the profit thereof to the poor in bread at Chriftmas and Eafter for ever - - -	30	0	0
Mr. David Reynon, churchwarden, (born in this parifh) gave 30l. for payment of 36s. to nine poor families on Candlemas-day for ever - - -	30	0	0
1699, Mrs. Ann Longman, widow, gave 195l. to the poor of this city, of which this parifh hath a proportion.			
1706, Mrs. Jane Mitchell gave 10l. the profit in bread to the poor at Chriftmas yearly - - -	10	0	0
1708, Mr. Charles Roynon, of this parifh, gave 20l. the profit in bread on every Lord's-day - - -	20	0	0
1710, Mr. William Higgs, late of this parifh, gave 20l. to poor houfe-holders and others within this parifh, which fum was diftributed to them accordingly the 23d day of December ₃ - - - -	20	0	0

1712, Auguſt the 6th, Mr. William Evans, of this pariſh, in
 memory of his dutiful daughter Martha Evans, gave
 20l. to pay 10s. to the miniſter for a ſermon on the
 ſame day, and 10s. in bread to the poor for ever

1713, The Rev. John Read, D. D. late vicar of St. Nicholas
 church, gave 20l. to the poor of this pariſh, the intereſt
 thereof is to be diſtributed in bread at the diſcretion of
 the churchwardens on the firſt Sunday after the 15th of
 February for ever - - - -

1714, Mr. James Croft, of this pariſh, gentleman, gave 50l. the
 profit thereof to poor houſekeepers of this pariſh yearly,
 at the diſcretion of the overſeers and churchwardens

1716, The 23d of January, William Jackſon, Eſq; ſome time
 mayor and alderman of this city, gave 50l. the intereſt
 thereof to poor houſekeepers of this pariſh (not receiving alms) in coals for ever, as the veſtry ſhall direct

1718, Mr. William Bayly, ſome time ſheriff of this city, gave
 50l. the intereſt thereof to poor houſekeepers of this
 pariſh, not receiving alms, on the 25th of March for
 ever - - - - -

1722, Capt. John Williams, of Caldee iſland, in the county of
 Pembroke, gave 10l. the profit thereof in bread to the
 poor on the 25th of Auguſt for ever - -

1725, Mr. Chriſtopher Wallis, a member of the common council, and churchwarden of this pariſh, gave 30l. the intereſt
 whereof is to be diſtributed to poor houſekeepers on
 the 24th day of October for ever - -

1726, Capt. Joſeph Whitchurch, late of this pariſh, merchant,
 gave 20l. the intereſt thereof to the poor of the almſhouſe on the firſt Sunday in December yearly for ever

1727, Mr. Derrick Popley gave 10s. per annum for a ſermon on
 the firſt Sunday in Lent for ever - -

1728, Mr. John Brittain, tobacconiſt, gave 20l. the profit to the
 poor of this pariſh on St. John's-day yearly for ever

1729, Mrs. Alice James, widow, gave 20l. the profit in twelve-
 penny bread to the poor of this pariſh, not receiving
 alms, on Chriſtmas-day yearly for ever - -

	l.	s.	d.
	20		
	20	0	0
	50	0	0
	50	0	0
	50	0	0
	10	0	0
	30	0	0
	20	0	0
	10		
	20	0	0
	20	0	0

1730,

	l.	*s.*	*d.*
1730, Mr. Richard Bradley, late of Bewdley, gave 10l. to the poor of this parifh, which was accordingly to his will dif-tributed - - - - -	10	0	0
Mr. Richard Leverfedge gave 50l. the interest whereof is yearly on the 18th of Augu to be paid to five poor houfekeepers of this parifh - - -	50	0	0
1731, Mrs. Elizabeth Tudor gave 10s. per annum to be di tributed on the 8th day of June to two poor widows not receiv-ing alms - - - - -	10	0	0
1732, Dr. John Ga karth, late re or of All Hallows Barkin in London, formerly vicar of this parifh, gave 30l. to the poor of this parifh, as the ve ry fhould dire -	30	0	0
1733, Mr. John Haythorne, fenr. formerly of this parifh, whi-tawer, gave 10l. the intere to be di tributed to the poor of this parifh in bread yearly on the 24th of June for ever - - - - - -	10	0	0
1734, Mr. John Stephens, late of this parifh, hooper, gave 20l. the intere to be di tributed to the poor yearly on the 26th of January for ever - - - -	20	0	0
1737, Henry Walter, Efq; alderman, gave 50l. to the poor of this parifh, which was di tributed according to his will	50	0	0
1741, Mr. Thomas Hungerford, fenr. formerly of this parifh, linen-draper, gave 50l. the intere thereof at 4 per cent. to be di tributed to the poor, 20s. in coal and 20s. in bread yearly on St. Thomas's-day for ever	50	0	0
1741, Mr. Paul We ton, late of this parifh, grocer, gave 20l. the intere thereof to the poor on St. Paul's-day for ever	20	0	0
1742, Mr. Richard Willet, late of this parifh, di tiller, gave 24l. the intere thereof to fix poor houfe-holders, not re-ceiving alms, on the 29th of May for ever -	24	0	0
1683, John Read, linen-draper, gave 30l. to the poor in bread weekly for ever - - - -	30	0	0

In a table in St. Nicholas church is the following li of GIFT SERMONS.

	l.	*s.*	*d.*
Fir Sunday in every month, Mrs. Elizabeth Hall's -	6	0	0
January 9, or Sunday after, William Chaloner's - -	0	10	0
Good Friday, Sir Thomas Langton's - - -	1	0	0

April

				l.	s.	d.
April 23, Sir William Cann's, Knight, 1693	-	-	-	2	0	0
May 3, William Burrowes's	-	-	-	1	0	0
Sunday after Trinity, William Tucker's, alderman	-	-	0	6	8	
Sunday before the 24th of June, George Snow's	-	-	0	6	8	
June 24, Roger Hurt's	-	-	-	-	0	6	8
Anguſt 6, Mr. William Evans's, 1712	-	-	-	0	10	0
Auguſt 3, Mr. Michael Deyos's	-	-	-	0	13	4
October 28, November 7, } John Whitſon, Eſq;	-	-	-	-	-	-
December 27, Mr. John Henry's	-	-	-	0	10	0
Firſt Sunday in Lent, to be preached at Horfield, the gift of John Langton, alderman	-	-	-	-	-	0	12	0
Firſt Sunday in Lent, Derrick Popley's	-	-	-	0	10	0

The ground rents and tenements belonging to this pariſh produce annually about 190l. per annum.

In this pariſh was formerly a chapel dedicated to St. John, and another on Briſtol Bridge, erected and founded by King Edward 3d. and his Queen Phi‑lippa, and endowed by the mayor and burgeſſes of Briſtol, to which many left legacies. John Hanker and John Hackſton gave two meſſuages and three ſhops on the Back of Avon to John Gweyn, chaplain there, to pray for their fouls and their wives, &c, 49 Edward 3d. Pope Boniface, the 11th year of his pontificate, by a ſpecial letter denounced the wrath of the Almighty and of the apoſtles Peter and Paul againſt any one who ſhould hinder divine offices being performed in this chapel, ſaving neverthelefs to the church of St. Nicholas its proper rights, dated at Rome the 11th year of his pontificate; which chapel however has long ſince been defecrated.

The Cooper's-hall in King-ſtreet in this pariſh preſents a building with a handfome front, the elevation of which was publiſhed by Halfpenny, the ar‑chitect, in 1744. The weſt front is 65 feet 9 inches broad, and the ſection 65 feet 4 inches. See the plate.

The Cuſtom-Houſe is a large and ſpacious brick building in the center of the north ſide of the ſquare, conveniently ſituated for the merchants to have recourſe to, was built by the corporation and poſſeſſion taken of it in 1711.

There is alfo here an almſhoufe erected on ground next the then city wall, granted to the veſtry of this church for this purpofe. It ferves for the habi‑tation of feveral poor people; but it has no endowment, all here receiving pariſh pay

SECT. II.—*Of the* CHURCH *and* PARISH *of St.* LEONARD.

AT the weſt end of old Corn-ſtreet formerly ſtood three arched gateways forming together a triangle. The ſouth gate led to Baldwin-ſtreet, the north to the Key, and the eaſt which was largeſt led to Corn-ſtreet, over which ſtood a plain freeſtone tower, 65 feet high from the ground, and 18 feet in front from north to ſouth and from eaſt to weſt 10 feet, having four ſmall freeſtone pinnacles at the top, ſurrounded with freeſtone battlements. In the tower were only two bells, one large and the other ſmall. Under the bell-loft within the church was built againſt the eaſt window a beautiful neat altar. The communion table and rails round it were of mahogany, and part of the floor was laid with black and white marble. The body of the church conſiſted but of two ailes, extending over the three gateways; and as part of the floor was of timber covered with paving ſtones and over the arches, it could not admit of any corps being buried there, but on the north ſide was a ſmall crypt where the dead uſually were interred, at the end of which you aſcended by a flight of thirteen ſtone ſteps to the only door of the church, at the weſt end of the north aile, which was in length 35 feet, and the ſouth aile from the altar to the weſt window about 55 feet and 30 feet high to the ceiling: the width of both ailes was 30 feet. Hence it appears the church was but ſmall, plain, and of an antient fabric, being ſuppoſed to be built ſoon after laying out the firſt boundaries of the old town, to the walls of which it joined on each ſide. It is ſaid in the manuſcripts of Rowlie, " Itte was ybuilden bie Algar, a Saxon, in 1010. It has a chauntrie to the honour of St. Baldwynne, whoſe ſhryne was therein keppen." It is mentioned in a deed, 25 Edward 1ſt. 1297, wherein Simon de Burton, about this time founding Redcliff church, grants the tenements he then lived in in Corn-ſtreet, newly built within the gate of St. Leonard, to John Diſto, which afterwards paid 6s. 8d. twice a year for the maintenance of a lamp to burn in this church. It is a vicarage, rated in the King's Books at 4l. 1s. 5d. clear yearly value, the number of dwelling-houſes about ſeventy-four, and nine warehouſes. Mr. William Pennoyer, a native of the pariſh, in the year 1670, gave 16l. per annum for preaching a lecture-ſermon here once a week, and it was endowed with 200l. Queen Ann's bounty, which with the voluntary contributions of the pariſhioners made the living about 55l. a year to the vicar. It was in the preſentation of the dean and chapter. The laſt incumbent was the Rev. Mr. John Davie, who removed to St. John's, to which he was preſented April 1766, in lieu of this church, which was then pulled down to lay open a new ſtreet called Clare-ſtreet, ftreet, and the parifh confolidated with St. Nicholas. In 1319 the chapel of St. Giles which belonged to this church being ruinous was pulled down, the chancel bells, books, and veftments deftroyed, and in 1331 its revenue being impaired it was wholly annexed to St. Leonard, to which it had been of old fubject, and the facraments and religious offices were to be no more continued there without licence from the vicar, to whom all tenths and oblations were to be paid.

In this parifh in St. Leonard's-lane is a free fchool, endowed by Mr. Pennoyer with 10l. per annum to a mafter to teach 20 boys to read, write, and cypher, and the accidence. He gave alfo 10l. per annum to an honeft widow woman to teach twenty girls to read and few, and 5l. per annum to the poor of the faid parifh for ever.

This church was fhut up in June 1766, and January 28, 1771 they began to take it down, and fold the altar piece to Backwell in Somerfetfhire.

A lift of the V I C A R S of St. Leonard's church, fo far as can be found in the church books, and in Regift. Wygorn.

PATRONS.	
Abbot and convent of St. Auguftin.	1492 William Clark.
1274 Richard de St. Auguftino Capell.	1525 Francis Pollard.
1290 John Dumyng, 3 March.	1530 John Hawks.
1323 Robert le Toyt, 3 March.	1534 Thomas Silke.
1326 Philippus de Caftro Goderiċti, died 1328.	1559 Mr. Vaughan.
	1575 Thomas Caverleye, the firft Proteftant minifter.
1328 Hugh de Aċton.	
Philip Sherer.	1600 Mr. Dickley.
1393 William Brytlampton.	1612 Mr. Waltfon.
1409 Thomas Chamberleyn.	1613 Richard Williams.
1410 Nicholas Clerkelap.	1626 John Norton, M. A.
1420 Roger Pert.	1690 Samuel Payne.
1426 Robert Pewfey, 25 March.	1721 Robert Clark.
1447 Thomas Knight.	1732 John Sutton.
1450 John Tornour.	1734 Samuel Jocham, 12 September.
1453 Sir John Lewis.	1743 William Prichard, 9 July.
1479 William Croffe.	1750 John Berjew, 19 July.
	1753 John Davie, 9 May.

In the year 1615, the 20th of March, Robert Redwood by will gave an houfe in King-ftreet adjoining the town wall, there to be converted to a

library

library for the public ufe, and ordained that the vicar of St. Leonard's fhould be librarian, if a graduate in the Univerfity and his religion anfwerable thereto, to be approved of by the mayor and aldermen. This houfe with fome additions was further granted the 12th of April 1636, by Richard Vicaris merchant to the mayor or comonalty to the fame ufe. The 27th of October 1738, it was agreed by a committee of the corporation to rebuild this houfe, now become ruinous, from the ground, of the following dimentions, 38 feet long, 25 feet wide in the clear, with cellars underneath and offices not exceeding ten feet high for the librarian, and the library room over that 16 feet high, and the front above the ground fhould be built with freeftone. This plan was executed in the year 1739, with an handfome elevation. The old books which were given by Tobias Matthews, Archbifhop of York, a native of Briftol, and various people, to the number of 500 were depofited during the building, in the Council-houfe, and then brought back to the library room, and replaced in elegant oak cafes. In the year 1738-9, it appears Wm. Jeffries Efq; mayor, expended in building the library, - - - - - 184 6 7

1739-40, Stephen Clutterbuck Efq; mayor, - - 681 3 0

Henry Combe Efq; mayor, - 435 18 6.

Total £ 1301 8 1

But this library has received great improvement and a new eftablifhment by the Briftol Library Society, having this place granted them with the ufe of the books of the old library by the corporation, and by a new wing being added to the former building in 1786, to hold the number of books now added yearly to the former colleftion, purchafed by the money arifing from the annual fubfcribers and other benefactors, that it now contains a large feleft colleftion of books in various fciences and languages of the beft editions, which each fubfcriber under certain rules and regulations, has the liberty to take home to perufe at his leifure, and the library is opened three times in the week mornings at 11 o'clock, and four times a week at 6 o'clock in the evenings, for the citizens fubfcribing yearly one guinea to refort there to read.

Several lands and tenements were given to this church for obits and chauntries. In 1482 Elias Spelly gave lands yielding yearly 5l. 8s. 8d. and Agnes his wife ditto 1l. 13s. 4d. and 20 marks in money. John Barr, in 1501, gave 40l. to buy veftments, and 60l. for a chauntry for priefts to fing for his foul for ten years after his death. Wm. Cooder, 2l. per ann. and a chalice wt. 23 ounces alfo 20 ounces of filver to make the oil vat, and 40l. to buy the beft fuit of blue velvet with branches of gold. Wm. Wodington gave to the gilding of
the

the figures of our Lady, St. Leonard, and St. Giles, 6l. The plate belonging to this church amounted to 222 ounces and half, which was taken to by King Henry 8, and Edward 6, and 13th Auguſt 1549 was delivered into the king's mint of Briſtol for his highneſs's uſe by virtue of his majeſty's letter, the jewels and plate belonging to this church 13lb. 8 ounces two chalices excepted as appears by Mr. Records receipt. In 1553 a freſh demand was made upon the pariſh, when they left them only one chalice, wt. 9 oz. and three bells. In 1424, ſome remarkable charges occur which ſhew the price of things at that time, paid 2d. for a quart of wine, 8d, for waſhing the ſepulcre, paid for two ſacks of coals, 2d. (by which it appears coalpits were opened near Briſtol as early as that year,) paid for two pounds of candles 2d. In the year 1476 the annual income from ground rents &c. for the ſupport of the church amounted to 9l. 18s. 4d. In 1514, it amounted to 11l. 18s. 4d. In 1751, to 34l. 10s. 4d.

C H A P. XIX.

Of the CHURCH and PARISH of St. STEPHEN.

THIS church is dedicated to St. Stephen the protomartyr, and formerly belonged to the abbots of Glaſtonbury, who were probably the founders, being patrons of it till the diſſolution. It paid yearly two marks to the infirmary of that abby, (ſee Johann. Claſton. v. 2. p. 417.) which was the gift of Henry Biſhop of Worceſter about the year 1378: it paid alſo a pound of cummin to Glaſtonbury, which had five meſſuages in Briſtol ſituated in Marſh-ſtreet, at a place called Glaſtonbury-court to this day. The church ſtands between the outward and inward walls of the city on the banks of the Frome, which ground the tide formerly flowed over, whence the ſtreet adjoining took the name of Marſh-ſtreet alias Skadpull-ſtreet, the river Frome running nearer this church of old and through Baldwin-ſtreet into the Avon: it is frequently mentioned in very old deeds. In 1304 the rector had a legacy left him. William of Worceſter, p. 282. ſays, " The height of the tower of St. Stephen from the erthe table to the gargyle is 21 fathom or 42 yards, and the height from

from the gargyle to the crope which finifhes the ftone work is 31 feet, and its breadth the caft and weft part is 12 feet, and north and fouth 14 feet and from the ground to its very deep foundation is 31 feet; and it has four ftories, and in the fourth ftory are the bells." And p. 235. he fays, " The church is 30 yards long and 19 broad, and 44 high, and has feven arches on each fide and feven windows, and in each fide and each window four dayes; and that the tower is (p. 120.) 125 feet high, befides 31 feet below the ground; and (p. 268.) that the foundation for building is here fo bad that they dig 47 feet to make a foundation, and that they found a boat there and a *togh* of bay cloth and a great tree fquared of 16 feet long found." There was no tower to this church till the reign of Edward 4th. about 1470. Camden fays, (after Leland, vol. vii. f. 61.) it was erefted by John Shipward, a wealthy merchant, with great charge and moft curious workmanfhip. This is confirmed by an old infcription formerly on painted glafs under the effigies of a man and woman in the great weft window, now deftroyed: " Orate pro animabus Johannis Shipward et Catherinæ uxoris ejus, qui Johannes iftam feneftram fecit et fuit fpecialis benefaftor hujus ecclefiæ." This tower is very lofty and finely proportioned, and a fpeftator is ftruck with its beauty. It has from the ground to the top 177 ftone fteps, each 8 inches high, and meafures on the outfide 39 yards and 1 foot, and is adorned on the top with four neat Gothic hollow worked pinnacles, each 15 feet high; in one of them the largeft a bell is fixed on which the clock ftrikes the hour. In 1703 three of thefe pinnacles were blown down in a hurricane on November 27, which by their fall did great damage to the fouth aile. There are eight bells in the tower, lately new caft. The church has three ailes, the middle one 88 feet long, the fouth aile 88 feet, at the end of which is the new veftry room: the north aile 60 feet. The church is 56 feet broad: the middle aile above 50 feet high, the fide ailes 25 feet. The whole church is neatly wainfcoted, and was new pewed with mahogany by a fubfcription of the parifhioners in 1733. There were formerly feven chauntries endowed for finging mafs for the fouls of the founders, (fee p. 63.) According to the Lincoln manufcript, this church was rated at fix marks and a half. The value of the reftory to the incumbent is thus to be computed, viz. in Tucker-ftreet 12l. and Redcliff-pit 5l. at Lawrence Wefton, Glocefterfhire, 4l. voluntary contributions and furplice fees make the whole amount to about 250l. per annum.

In Regift. Wygor. is a Latin deed, confirming to the monks of Glaftonbury an annual penfion out of this church of two marks to their infirmary, dated

the

the 8th of the calends of May, 1315. In 1375 Richard Brandon gave 100 fhillings to the fabric, and 1398 John Vyel " legavit ecclefiæ Stephani," i. e. " gave to the church of St. Stephen one ring in which was fet a ftone, part of the very pillar to which Chrift was bound at the fcourging, to be kept among the relics for ever." In 1473, the 14th of December, John Shipward, fenr. was interred here : he left large eftates to the poor, efpecially to the fraternity of St. Clement, and gave this church two curious miffals, a large gilt chalice, rich veftments for the high altar, the Guillows-inn in High-ftreet with other tenements, fix gardens for two chaplains to celebrate his obiit, the rector with nineteen chaplains, and the mayor, fheriffs, and their officers to attend, who where to choofe the chaplains, and difmifs them if incorrigible. Mrs. Ann· Peloquin left 400l. to this church, and her houfe in Prince's-ftreet for the perpetual habitation of the vicar. The prefent patron is the King, and it is prefented to by the Lord Chancellor. The learned and Rev. Jofiah Tucker, D. D. is the prefent incumbent. The lands and ground rents belonging to this church amount to about 50l. per annum. At the diffolution 154 ounces of filver plate belonging to this church, befides many coftly veftments, were fold for the ufe of the king.

R E C T O R S of St. Stephen's Church.

PATRONS.

Abbot and convent of Glaftonbury.

1304 Walter de Mynte.
1330 William de Beynton.
1337 Hugh de Babynton.
1344 Walter le White.
1348 Thomas le Younge.
1360 Roger le Teflayre.
1387 Thomas Barton.
      William Eftcourte.
1436 Robert Catryke.
1438 John Gomond.
1465 John Harlowe de Stoke, died December 6, 1486.
1480 William Boket.
1494 Sir Thomas Hanfon.
1498 John Eftrefeld, A. M.

1504 Richard Collyns, mafter of St. John's hofpital, Redclive.
      The Crown, Patron.
1554 Hugh Jones.
1562 John Knight
1588 John Tyfon.
1610 Alexander Lawes.
1621 Robert Higgins.
1628 Hugh Hobfon,
1641 Richard Harward.
1642 Henry Jones, chancellor of this diocefe, died 1695.
1671 Nicholas Penwarne.
1691 Charles Livefay.
1708 Thomas Frankland.
1731 Henry Becher.

1743 Alexander Stopford Catcott, a good poet, profound linguift, well fkilled in the Hebrew and the fcripture philofophy, and judicious fchoolmafter.

1749-50 Jofiah Tucker, D. D. the prefent incumbent, 1788.

BENEFACTORS to the Church and Poor of St. Stephen's Parifh.

	l.	s.	d.
1594, Alderman Robert Kitchen gave 10s. a quarter for ever	40	0	0
1674, Mr. John Dymer, fome time fheriff of this city, gave 10l. the profit thereof in bread quarterly for ever -	10	0	0
Mrs. Mary Boucher and her daughter Mrs. Joan Langton, widows, gave lands for the payment of 10s. apiece to 52 poor widows of this city yearly for ever, of which St. Stephen's hath a part			
1678, Mr. John Miner, mariner, gave two tenements and a cellar, the profit to be employed for the binding of apprentices of feamen's fons for ever; alfo the moiety of fix tenements, a ftable, and two gardens, for the maintenance of a fermon to be preached in St. Stephen's church the firft Friday in every month for ever, and 20l. the profit thereof to be given in bread to the poor the beginning of December yearly for ever - - -	20	0	0
1685, Mr. Jeremiah Holloway, merchant, gave 20l. the profit in bread to the poor of St. Stephen's parifh for ever	20	0	0
Mr. Thomas Ware, roap-maker, gave 9d. a week in bread for ever - - - - -	38	5	0
1686, Elizabeth Dickefon gave 5l. the profit in four-penny bread the 2d of February for ever - - -	5	0	0
1687, Mr. George Morris, a member of the common council, gave 20l. the profit to the poor at Chriftmas and Eafter for ever - - - - -	20	0	0
Sir William Cann, Knight and Bart. gave 100l. to four parifhes in this city, whereof this hath a quarter part, the profit thereof to be diftributed to the poor the 8th of January for ever - - - -	10	0	0
1690, Mrs. Margaret Abbey gave 40l. to the poor, which was diftributed according to her will, and given in bread every Lord's-day - - - - -	40	0	0

1594,

1594, Mr. Robert Kitchen, mayor and alderman of this city, *l. s. d.*
gave 1s. per week for ever   -   -   -   52 0 0

1637, Mr. Francis Derrick, merchant of this city, deceased, gave
1s. per week for ever   -   -   -   52 0 0

1638, The parishioners of this parish have purchased 5l. 4s. per
annum for 2s. per week in bread to the poor for ever   104 0 0

Mr. William Eaton and Mary his wife, of this parish, deceased, gave 11d. per week for ever   -   -   47 10 0

1649, Mr. Richard Long, mayor and alderman of this city, deceased, gave 6ol. the profit thereof to the poor weekly,
paid by the chamberlain 3l. per annum   -   -   60 0 0

1659, Humphrey Hooke, Esq; twice mayor and alderman of this
city, gave 4s. in bread and 4s. in coal weekly to the
poor of this parish for ever   -   -   -   416 0 0

1661, Mr. Francis Gleed, some time sheriff of this city, gave 10s.
a quarter to a poor house-holder for ever   -   40 0 0

1701, Arthur Grant gave 20l. the profit to be distributed at
Christmas yearly to four poor house-holders not receiving alms   -   -   -   -   -   20 0 0

1709, Captain John Price, late of this city, gave to the churchwardens of this parish 10l. the interest thereof to be
given to the poor in bread on Twelfth day yearly for
ever   -   -   -   -   -   10 0 0

1713, Mrs. Mary Showell, of this parish, widow, gave 10l. the
interest thereof to the poor in bread on the first Friday
after the 18th of August yearly for ever   -   10 (

1714, Mr. Isaac Elton, of this parish, merchant, and member of
the common council, gave 50l. the profit thereof to be
distributed in bread and coal to the poor of this parish,
not receiving alms, on the 22d day of November
yearly for ever   -   -   -   -   50 0 0

1722, Captain John Williams, of the island of Caldy, in Pem-
brokeshire, gave 10l. the profit thereof to be given to
the poor in bread on the 25th day of August yearly for
ever, by the churchwardens   -   -   10 0 0

Mr. William Prosser, needle-maker, gave 20l. the profit
to a poor family, having more than one child and not
receiving alms, on the 16th of August for ever, by the
churchwardens   -   -   -   -   20 0 0

		l.	*s.*	*d.*
1727, Mr. John Newman, of this parish, plumber, gave 26l. the interest to the poor in bread weekly for ever -		26	0	0
1731, Mr. William Freke, merchant, gave 50l. the interest thereof to the poor of this parish yearly for ever		50	‹	
1732, Mr. Thomas Ereke, merchant, gave 50l. the interest thereof to the poor of this parish yearly for ever -		50	0	0
Mr. James Couch, apothecary, gave 10l. the interest thereof to four poor widows, not receiving alms, on Michaelmas-day yearly for ever - - - -		10	0	0
1738, Mr. James Brown, of this parish, gave 10l. the interest thereof to poor people, not receiving alms, on Good Friday yearly for ever - - -		10	0	0
1744, A dial over the west door, the gift of Mr. Thomas Horwood, of this parish.				
1639, Alderman George Harrington, of this city, gave 40s. per annum to four housekeepers for ever - -		40	0	0
1781, Mrs. Ann Peloquin gave to the poor of this parish 400l. and a house for the rectors - - - -		400	0	0

The following are the principal MONUMENTS of this Church.

In it was buried the 9th of April 1575, Margery wife of George Snigge, Esq; who this year was mayor of Bristol, she died of the plague.

George Snigge, Esq; alderman, was buried the 13th of Feb. 1582.

Sir George Snigge, Knt. Son of the above George Snigge, was buried the 23d of December, 1617. He died the 11th of Nov. and lay in state six weeks, at Merchant Taylor's Hall in Broad-street, from which hall he was conveyed to this church and buried.

At the upper end of the chancel where the communion table, now stands, against the altar, was the tomb of Sir George Snigge, Knt. being inclosed with iron grating, and thereon a statue leaning on his right side, in the habit of a judge. His body was buried in a leaden coffin under the monument, but when the church was new pewed with mahogany in the year 1733, this monument was taken down and removed to the east end of the south aile where it now stands, with a Latin inscription translated into English thus:

" Here lies the body of George Snygge Knt. serjeant at law, one of the Barons of the Exchequer, a most skilful judge, formerly recorder of this famous city, who in his life time zealously applied himself to the worship of God; he impartially administered justice, was a diligent promoter of virtue, and a severe opposer of vice; he was always a charitable reliever of the poor and needy. He died to the great loss and grief of this his honoured city and much

loved

loved country (whofe intereft he had always at heart) the 11th day of Nov. 1617, in the 73d year of his age.

His loving daughter Ann Snigge hath erected and dedicated this monument in perpetual teftimony of her pious gratitude and duty to her moft dear father.

Conditur hoc tumulo juris lequamque peritus,
Jus aliis vitæ dixerat atque necis ;
Jus rigidum fævæ mortis vitare nequivit,
Omnia fub leges quæ vocat atra fuas.
At vero fpolium mors atra reportat opimum,
Exultans victrix, Io triumpe, canat.
Eripuit, fateor, miferam mors improba vitam,
Morbis, ærumnis, anxietate gravem.
Aft invita refert etiam mors improba vitam,
Plenam cælefti lumine luce Dei.
Eripuit veros quos præbet mundus honores,
Cæleftique dedit femper honore frui.

Againft a pillar is a neat monument to " Thomas Freke, Efq; merchant, and Frances his wife and five children, fhe died the 22d of Nov. 1724, aged 31, he died the 12th of July 1732, aged 38. Arms barre or and fable on a chief 3 mullets of the 1ft."

Another handfome monument to " Martin Pring, merchant, fometime general to the Eaft Indies, &c.

Hic terris multum jactatus et undis.

He died 1626, aged 46."

Another to " John Frankland, D. D. dean of Gloucefter, and mafter of Sidney College, Cambridge, 22 years rector of this parifh, he died Sept. the 3d 1730, aged 56."

On a ftone is an infcription to " Sir Humphry Hook, of Kingfwefton in the county of Gloucefter, he died the 16th of October, 1677, and his wife Florence daughter of Sir Hugh Smyth of Long Afhton, Bart. fhe died the 3d of Sept. 1692, aged 60, alfo 2 fons and 4 daughters."

Another to " Samuel Clarke, merchant, who died the 20th of Oct. 1679,

Cælum erat in votis vivi, poft fata potitum,
Affequitur vitam vita beata piam.

In the fouth aile is a monument to " Robert Kitchen and his wife, he died the 5th of Sept. 1594, he was a great benefactor to the poor of this city."

The

The parifh of St. Stephen is large, extending from along Clare-ftreet, the Quay, Marfh-ftreet, King-ftreet, Prince's-ftreet, into the Square, one half of which is in this parifh, in which was a chapel dedicated to St. Clement, now demolifhed : on the fite of it is built a fpacious hall for the Society of Merchant Venturers, incorporated by King Edward 6th's. letters patent, and afterwards confirmed by Queen Elizabeth and King Charles 1ft. It is built of freeftone, and confifts of two noble lofty rooms, forming the fhape of an L, adorned in the infide with the portraits in full length of fome principal mer-chants, benefaftors to the fociety and the commonalty of Briftol. The beft idea of it may be formed by viewing the plate. This fociety are feized of divers manors, lands, and tenements in truft, for the maintenance and fupport of fundry hofpitals, fchools, and almfhoufes, particularly thofe of Edward Colfton, Efq; once a worthy member and great ornament of this fociety, as he was an honour and bleffing to the houman race, of whom fee p. 443. In 1699 they built their left wing of their almfhoufe for poor failors and their widows, contiguous to their hall, rebuilt the old one, and united both angles, for the maintenance of nineteen men and twelve women ; fix of the men have 2s. a week granted them by Edward Colfton, Efq; by fee farm rents for ever.

The merchants and traders of Briftol not free of this company pay certain fees for wharfage on fhipping goods, which freemen of the city and company are exempted from, which produces a confiderable income to this fociety, who hold it as leffees under the corporation for 90 years. The leafe lately expired has been again renewed.

I find in a deed the " Senefchallos Gildæ Mercatorum" mentioned as early as 1240, which proves the exiftence then of a gild of merchants in Briftol, and to have been of great antiquity.

In 1595 the poor in the Merchants almfhoufe were maintained by one penny in the pound on feamen's wages, and three halfpence on every ton of fhipping ; but thefe payments are now difcontinued, and others fubftituted for the relief of feamen in diftrefs, under the title of the Seaman's Hofpital, for which a fund is rifen but no building erefted.

The Quay conduit, fo ufeful not only to the inhabitants of this parifh, but alfo to the merchants whofe fhips are fupplied with water and the water cafks belonging to them are oftentimes filled there, was in the year 1601 built anew, for which work this parifh gave 10l. Mr. J. Barker, merchant, 25l. and the chamber of Briftol was at the remaining expence. The water is brought in lead pipes from Glafs Mill, a mile and a half from the city. This conduit was

removed

removed in 1782, when the tontine warehoufes were built, and the old houfes in the Fifh-market taken down and a new and commodious ftreet built called Stephen's-ftreet in their place.

The act for the relief and fupport of maimed and difabled feamen and the widows and children of fuch as fhall be killed, flain, or drowned in the Mer_chants fervice was made in 1747, the 20th of George 2d.

The corporation of the Merchant Venturers of Briftol are appointed truftees for the duties received there.

The fund arifes from 6d. per month to be paid by feamen in the Merchants fervice from all fhips belonging to Briftol, and the mafters of fhips are im_powered to keep in their hands 6d. per month out of the wages, fhares, or other profits, payable to each feaman.

No hofpital is built, though ground was once laid out for it under Brandon-hill, it being alledged the truftces can relieve many more unfortunate objects.

C H A P. XX.

Of the CHURCH of St. PETER and St. PAUL, and that of St: MARY LE PORT.

IT is a rectory, founded before the Norman Conqueft by one of the Anglo_Saxon Kings or Earls of Glocefter foon after the caftle, to which it feemed at one time to have belonged. And when the earldom of Glocefter was given to Robert Fitzhamon the founder of Tewkfbury monaftery, he gave this rec-tory to it; and in 1130 Simon Bifhop of Worcefter confirmed by deed all the churches to that monaftery which it then poffeffed, among which the church of St. Peter of Bricfton with the tythes of the rents of Bricfton is particularly mentioned with its appurtenances within the caftle of Briftol (which it had anciently enjoyed) as well as out of the domains of the borough of the town.— In 1106 King Henry 1ft. confirmed all things given by Robert Fitzhamon and others to the church of Tewkfbury, among which is the church of St. Peter of Briftol, then written Bricftou, and the tythes of the rents of Briftol. (Atkyns's Glocefterfhire, p. 738.) And in the year 1194 Henry Bifhop of Worcefter

by

by his charter teftifies that, on the prefentation of the monks of Tewkfbury, he had admitted Richard Cumblain to the moiety of the church of St. Peter, which Stephen de Ripum held before him, paying a yearly penfion out of it of 3s. to the church of St. James in Briftol, then a cell to Tewkfbury. In the Lincoln manufcript, 1291, 11s. was paid to the prior of St. James, and in 1553 augmented to 20s. per annum, afterwards received by Henry Brayne, Efq; the purchafer of this and other churches of Henry 8th. at the diffolution.

It was fituated near to the wall of the caftle next the barbicana caftri, de-fcribed to be at the eaft end of the church. It has three ailes, the north and fouth being 96 feet long, the middle is 111 feet long; their height about 36 feet; the width of the whole body of the church is 54 feet. The arched roofs co-vered with Cornifh tiles are fupported with feven neat pillars of freeftone, on which are turned fix arches. The tower is large and plain, not very lofty, 26 yards and 1 foot high, with four pinnacles of folid freeftone, each about 12 feet high, and battlements round it. It has eight bells, with a clock and dial.

This church was decaying and out of repair, and 1749 a faculty was ob-tained out of the Bifhop's Court to repair and beautify the whole, which coft upwards of 800l. out of which 421l. 12s. was raifed by a pound rate on the land holders at 4s. 3d. in the pound, and the reft taken up on the parifh fecu-rity. At the eaft end of the fouth aile was a chapel, dedicated to the honour of the Bleffed Mary of Bellhoufe. It belonged to a fraternity then newly be-gan fo called, to which William Spicer in the year 1500 gave a garden and houfe in Marfhall-ftreet, as did others. John Efterfield in 1504 had a yearly obiit folemnized here for ever on the 18th of February.

R E C T O R S.

Patrons.	
Abbot and convent of Tewkfbury.	1362 Petrus de Woodmancote.
1181 Stephen de Ripum.	1369 Nicholas de Waffebourne.
1184 Richard Cumblain.	1384 Thomas Vefey.
1224 David ——.	1392 Thomas Pine.
1285 Robert de Leche.	1399 John Grey.
1288 Gregory de Wanberge.	1401 James Fitz Hugh.
1332 John de Draycote.	1409 Thomas Lye.
1333 John de Kemefegh.	1425 Thomas Stevens.
1338 Richard de Greneville.	1431 William Edwards.
1347 John de Wolfrington.	1446 Robert Loude.
1352 Philip Maris.	1450 Hugh Pavis.
	1462 Thomas Bever.

1564

1464 Nicholas Smyth.
1488 William Tyſher.
1499 John Thomas.
1510 William Fadur.
1526 John Williams
1533 John White.
1542 John Pill.
1546 Sir John ap Howel.
     Corporation, Patrons.
1561 Sir John ap Alrede.
1565 Robert Commandre.
1574 David Martyn.

1582 Thomas James.
1610 John Burnley.
1618 Robert Pritchard.
1642 John Blagroe.
1664 Robert Forſith.
1667 Joſias Pleydell.
1689 Hugh Waterman.
1746 John Jones.
1760 Dr. Barry
1781 Thomas Broughton.

MONUMENTS.

At the entrance of the church on a large flat ſtone were three braſs figures, now taken away, and the following inſcription: " Sub hoc marmore tumulatum eſt corpus clariſſimi viri Johannis Eſterfield, hujus oppidi mercatoris et ejuſdem bis maioris et aldermanni una cum corporibus Aliciæ, ſcolaſticæ, et Matildis uxorum ejuſdem Johannis, qui obiit 18 Feb. A. D. 1507, quorum animabus propitietur Deus." Underneath on a ſcroll: " Domine mi miſerere mei."

In the middle aile on a large ſtone were three braſs figures for Andrew Norton, Eſq; and his wives Elizabeth and Helen, he died the 1ſt of Sept. 1527.

In the fame aile is a magnificent monument to the memory of Robert Aldworth, merchant and alderman of this city, who died the 6th of Nov. 1634, with a long latin inſcription. He was a great benefactor to this city.

In the north aile a monument to George Harrington, Eſq; mayor and alderman of this city, he died the 2d of Jan. 1689.

Upon a ſtone in the middle aile was this " Sir John Cadaman, Knt. was beheaded in the caſtle, for killing Miles Gallowhill an officer of the garriſon, while Prince Rupert had poſſeſſion of Briſtol, and was buried in this church the 9th of April, 1645.

In the ſouth aile is a very large tomb within a Gothic arch, adorned with a great deal of curious workmanſhip and various arms without any inſcription, there is the figure of a lady carved, lying upon the tomb who was of the family of the Newtons, of Barrs Court, Gloceſterſhire, as appears from the arms.

In the churchyard was buried the poet Savage, who having experienced a variety of good and bad fortune, at length died in Newgate, and was buried here, Newgate being in this pariſh.

Near

Near the churchyard was formerly an almfhoufe, now deſtroyed, erected by Robert Aldworth, who alfo built the parfonage-houfe, oppofite to which is St. Peter's pump or well of St. Edith, remarkable for fine water.

St. Peter's church plate confiſts of one flaggon, $74\frac{1}{2}$ ounces, coſt 20l. 17s. 4d. infcribed, " Ex dono parochianorum in ufum facræ euchariſtiæ, A. D. 1682," one filver chalice, 1570, two filver plates, 1682.

BENEFACTORS to the Church and Poor of St. Peter's Pariſh.

1625, Mr. Richard Wickham gave 42l. 8s. the profit thereof to the poor for ever.

Mr. Chriſtopher Kedgwine gave 10s. a year for a fermon for ever.

Mr. Thomas Clements gave a houfe for two fermons yearly, and the reſt to the poor for ever.

Mr. Robert Aldworth gave 100l. the profit thereof to the poor for ever.

1591, Mr. Robert Kitchen gave 40s. a year to the poor for ever.

1639, Mr. George Harrington gave 40s. a year to the poor for ever.

1658, Mrs. Elizabeth Spurt gave 40s. February 17, 1657, 20s. for a fermon the 29th of June and 20s. to the poor of this pariſh yearly for ever.

1661, Mr. Francis Gleed, fome time fheriff, gave 10s. a quarter to a poor houfe-holder for ever.

1673 Mr. Henry Northall gave a houfe in Broadmead for the ufe of the poor for ever.

1661, Mr. William Balman gave 52s. yearly to the poor alms-folks of this pariſh, being 12d. in bread every Lord's-day for ever.

1677, Mrs. Mary Davis gave 20l. the profit thereof 10s. for a fermon on the 17th of July, the reſt to the poor in bread for ever.

Mrs. Mary Boucher and her daughter Mrs. Joan Langton, widows, gave lands for the payment of 10s. apiece to 52 poor widows of this city yearly for ever, of which this pariſh hath a proportion.

1682 Mr. Vincent Thorn, merchant, gave 10l. the profit thereof to the poor for ever.

1683, William Colſton, merchant, gave 10l. the profit thereof to two poor houfekeepers of this pariſh yearly for ever.

1685, Mr. Nicholas Tilly, of this pariſh, gave 50l. the profit thereof in two-penny bread to poor houfekeepers weekly for ever.

1686, Mr. Samuel Hall, merchant, gave 10l. the profit thereof weekly to the poor in bread for ever, and alfo the intereſt of 230l. towards the placing apprentices of poor children in feven pariſhes of this city yearly for ever, of which this pariſh is one.

1688,

1688, John Lawford, Efq; fome time mayor and alderman of this city, gave 12d. a week in bread to the poor of this parifh for ever.

1690, Mr. Edward Tilly, of this parifh, gave 100l. to four parifhes in this city, whereof this parifh hath a quarter part, the profit thereof to be given weekly to the poor in bread for ever.

1691, Edward Fielding, Efq; and alderman of this city, gave 20l. the profit thereof to be given to two poor houfekeepers of this parifh (receiving no alms) on St. Thomas's-day yearly for ever, and formerly gave 10l. towards fetting up the bells.

1692, Mrs. Elizabeth Fielding, widow, gave 10l. the profit thereof to one poor inhabitant of this parifh (receiving no alms) on St. Thomas's-day yearly for ever.

1695, Mr. William Opie, fome time fheriff of this city, and inhabitant of this parifh, gave 26s. a year, to be given weekly in bread to three poor people of this parifh for ever.

1699, Mrs. Ann Longman gave 195l. to the poor of this city, of which this parifh hath a part.

Samuel Wallis, Efq; fome time mayor and alderman of this city, gave 20s. for preaching a fermon annually in this church on the day of electing a governor, &c. for the better providing for the poor of this city, and 5s. to the clerk and fexton to be divided between them, received from the treafurer of St. Peter's Hofpital.

1698, Mr. Thomas Harris, late of this parifh, apothecary, left 10l. to be diftributed to five poor houfekeepers, 10s. each, for four years.

1699, John Hicks, Efq; fome time mayor and alderman of this city, gave the profit of a houfe in Temple-ftreet, to be diftributed yearly to fix of the pooreft men or women of this parifh (not receiving alms) on the 13th day of February for ever.

1703, Mr. Richard Beauchamp, late of this parifh, now of London, gave 30l. the profit to be diftributed to three poor houfekeepers of this parifh (not receiving alms) on Good Friday for ever.

1706, Mr. Robert Berkeley, late of this parifh, gave the fum of 100l. the profit thereof to be employed for the placing of a poor boy of this parifh apprentice every year for ever, the faid boy not belonging to the Mint.

1707, Mrs. Sufanna Haynes, of this parifh, gave 30l. the profit thereof to be diftributed among fix poor women of this parifh equally on the 13th of April yearly for ever.

1712, Mrs. Hannah Fielding, daughter of Alderman Fielding, gave 20l. the profit thereof for the keeping at fchool a poor child or children of this parifh yearly for ever.

1714, Sir William Clutterbuck, Knight, fome time mayor and alderman of this city, gave 40l. to this parifh, the profit thereof to be given to the poor in bread every Lord's-day for ever.

Thomas Trye, of Hanham, Efq; gave 40l. to this parifh, the profit thereof to the payment of 40s. per annum for ever to the minifter of the faid parifh, for inftructing the youth in the church catechifm during the time of Lent.

1720, Mr. John Short, of the Caftle Precincts, gave 30l. the profit to four poor widows of this parifh (not receiving alms) on the 1ft of Novem-yearly for ever.

1724, Mr. Richard Gravett, Efq; gave 20l. the profit thereof to the poor of this parifh on the firft Sunday in every month for ever.

Mrs. Elizabeth Fitzall, of the Caftle Precincts, gave the fum of 100l. the intereft of it to be diftributed half yearly in bread among poor houfekeepers in this parifh (not receiving alms.)

1728, Thomas Moor, Efq; of St. Michael's parifh in this city, gave 50l. the intereft thereof to be laid out by the churchwardens in cloath-ing poor houfekeepers in this parifh on the 4th of January yearly, and one moiety of 8l. 15s. being the ground rent of two houfes on St. James's-back, to be likewife laid out by the churchwardens in cloathing poor men on St. Thomas's-day yearly for ever.

1733, Mr. James Birch, late of this parifh, gave 60l. the profit thereof for a fermon in this church and a dinner for the veftry on the 10th of December yearly for ever.

1746, The Rev. Mr. Hugh Waterman, fifty-feven years rector of this parifh, gave 100l. viz. 20s. part of the intereft thereof for a fermon the fecond Sunday in Auguft; the remaining intereft to cloath fome poor perfon or perfons of this parifh (frequenting the communion of the church of England) at Chriftmas for ever.

The ground rents and tenements belonging to this church eftate produce about 80l. per annum, befides renewals. - This parifh is of no large extent, confifting only of 203 houfes in 1749, paying 225l. poor rate to St. Peter's Hofpital at 11½d in the pound. This hofpital was erected at the great houfe in St. Peter's church yard, formerly inhabited by Thomas Norton, Efq; M. P. for this city in 1399 &c. afterwards by Robert Aldworth, Efq; and in the

years

years 1696, and 1697, the 7th and 8th of William 3d. the hofpital was eftablifhed by act of parliament, with a governor and deputy governor, treafurer and guardians. The money they were empowered to raife in the year 1696, for the city poor was 2380l. 16s. in 1716, 3500l. in 1736, 3500l. in 1756, 4500l. in 1763 it was 6842l. 7s. 9½d. and in 1783, 16548l. 12s. 2½d. which makes the fum of 9706l. 4s. 5d. increafe of expenditure in 20 years, owing chiefly to the number of poor gaining fettlements by renting houfes of 10l. a year, and being charged and paying in their own name to the poor rates. Befides being erected as an hofpital for the fupport of the poor of the city, fundry benefactions were given at different times to eftablifh an infirmary there for the relief of the fick and difeafed, which amounted in the whole to 4905l. 10s. 0d. as appears by the tables in the committee room. The corporation of the poor have a feal, being a hive of bees flying about, with this infcription, " Sigillum Guber: dep: Gæb: affiftant: et Guardian - pauper: Civitat: Briftol:" with this motto " Hyemis memores æftate laborant."

Newgate in this parifh was built by a tax on the inhabitants of the city, for every 100l. ftock 1s. 6d. for every 20l. per annum 3d. It bears the following infcription on the front.

Ædificatum
Sumptibus Civium et incolatum
Hujus Civitatis.
Anno Domini MDCXCI
Johanne Knight Equite Prætore
Roberto Dowdin }
Johanne Yeamans } Vicecomitibus.

SECT. II.—*Of the* CHURCH *of St.* MARY LE PORT.

IT is dedicated to the Virgin Mary, and moft probably had William Earl of Gloucefter for its founder: for he is exprefly faid about 1170, in the time of Henry the 2d. to have granted and confirmed this church to the priory of Keynfham, for the fuftentation of the canons there, as appears in the recital of King Edward 2d deed dated 5th Jan. 1318, confirming that donation. In the Lincoln manufcript 1291, is the valuation of this rectory thus, " Ecclefia Beatæ Mariæ portus Abbati Keynfham 20s."

It has two ailes and ftands on a rifing ground above the Avon the north fide of it; and there formerly was a gradual afcent to it from the river: where fhips of old time ufually difcharged their cargoes — fee p. 97, note, whence it took the name of Mary of the port. The fouth aile from the great weft door

under

under the tower to the altar is in length 107 feet, the north aile 73 feet, the two ailes are 37 feet in breadth, the fouth aile is 26 feet high: and the roof covered with Cornifh tile, and the whole fupported with fix freeftone arches and feven pillars neatly fluted and painted, the pews are of Dutch oak, and the altar piece neatly embellifhed and painted, infcribed at the top with Johovah Alëinu, in Hebrew characters within a glory; יהוה אלהינו Jehovah our Aleim is one Jehovah. The tower has 108 fteps, and is from the ground to the floor of the leads 72 feet, on it are four pinnacles, in it are eight bells put up in 1749, being then recaft; on the tenor very old was this infcription in Gothic letters, " Maria: filii: tui: auxilio: Guberna: parochiæ: tuæ in Horâ."—There were many chapels in this church.—Phillis Holloway in 1417 gave 20l. by will to found a chapel for a prieft to pray for her foul.—Mr. John Inhyng 1457 by will gave fifteen fhops and a rack in Bear-lane in Temple-ftreet, and a houfe there for mafs to be celebrated for ever on Valentine's day in the chapel of St. Katherine, and that eight priefts fhould attend the celebration, each to have 4d.—John Newman fettled the rent of his tenement in the Shambles for another mafs.—Thefe chauntries were all fuppreffed 37 Henry 8th. 1546, and given to the King.

The following curious account of this church was given by Chatterton, as tranfcribed by him from Rowley, which is fubmitted to the judgment of the reader:

Seynête Maries Chyrche of the Porte.

Thys chyrche was ybuyldenne in M..XVI. by a Saxonne manne cleped Eldred, botte fomme thynkethe he allein dyd itte begynne lcevynge oders to fynyfhe ytte fromme a ftone in the futh walle onne whyche ytte was wrotenne, Eldredrus pofvit primum lapydem in nomine patris filii et fpiritus fancti, M.XVI. butte underftonders of auntyauntrie fynde ytte enured in buyldeynges folclie reared bie the manne emcntioned. Itte was endowed wythe the landes wytheoute the walles of Bryftowe, and exempted for its paryfhe from caftle tyne. Ynne ytte was a manne ynne Chrieftcnmas M.C:X.XX. fleene wythe a Levynbrondc. Ynne M.CCC. ytte was repayred bie Roberte Canynge of the houfe of Wylliam Canynge. Bie the bochorde of the revef-trie ytte appeeres thatte manie dowghtie dyfputes haven beene han of the Flefhe Shammble claymen bie the queene ynne dower ynne caftle garde. Before the daies of Roberte Canynge, greete fyre of Wyllyam Canynge, greete barkes dydde ryde before Corporatyonne ftreete, butte Maftre Roberte have-yuge twoe of large howfen in Radclefte and workehowfes meinte wilieile drewe the trade to the oder fyde of the brugge toe the greete annoïc of

Seynête

Seynﬆe Marie of the Porte the honowre of Seynﬆe Marie of Redclefte, the enlargemente of thatte fyde, and the honowre and dygnenefs of hys owne familie. From him dyd the glorie of the Canynges ryfe ; Mr. Wyllyam Canynge having his pyﬂure, whereyn ys he commandeynge houfes to ryfe from the moddie bankes of ryver. He repaired as aboove yn atone for forwyninge the trade, and was there imburyed undorre a ﬆone full fayre of whomme dydde I thus wryte, whyche ys graven onne brafs and wylle eftfoones bee putte on hys ﬆone :

Thys Morneynge Starre of Radcleves ryfynge raie,
A true man, goode of minde, and Canynge hyghte
Benethe thys ﬆone lies moltrynge yuto claie,
Untylle the darke tombe ﬁheen an aeterne lyghte.
Thyrde from hys loyns the prefente Canynge came ;
Houten are anie wordes to telle his doe,
For aie, ﬁhall lyve hys heaven recorded name,
Ne ﬁhalle ytte die whanne tyme ﬁhall be ne moe.
When Mychaels trompe ﬁhall founde to rize the foulle
He'lle wynge toe heaven with kynne and happie be their dole.

RECTORS of St. Maryport.

PATRONS.	
Keynﬁham abby.	1501 Richard Boyce.
1272 Robert ——, reﬂor.	1534 Lodowick Johns.
1288 John Homme.	1543 Bartholomew Leweck.
1314 Simon de Welles.	Sir Thomas Bridges, Patron.
1327 John le Leche.	1544 Thomas Creede.
1335 William de Pendleford.	1547 John Pitt.
1342 William Horfeley.	1560 Richard Arthur.
1348 William de Taverner.	1605 Alexander Lawes.
1388 John Wefton.	1620 Edward Alman.
1396 William Ryel.	1663 Robert Forfith.
1400 Richard Roche.	1664 George Willington.
1411 Walter Ellyott.	1671 Jofias Pleydell.
1417 Thomas Stephens.	1689 Hugh Waterman.
1436 David Brenny.	Duke of Chandois, Patron.
1448 John Kemeys.	1716 William Saunders, D. D.
1453 Roger Rygelyne.	1750 John Collinfon.
1465 John Talbot.	1779 John Neal.
1470 John Berfey.	
1482 John Hawley.	

The

The Monuments and Epitaphs in this church worthy notice are the following:

At the eaft end of the north aile is an old arched monument with two pillars at the fides, at the top of each are the letters j. E. but what names they defignate it does not appear from any infcription.

In this aile are three neat marble monuments againft the north wall,

" To the memory of Thomas Smith, apothecary, fon of Bernard Smith, apothecary, mayor of Taunton, and Catherine, daughter of Nicholas Standfaft, apothecary, grand daughter of Richard Standfaft, M. A. chaplain in ordinary to his facred Majefty King Charles 1ft. who on account of his inviolable loyalty to the king and firm attachment to the church, was for fourteen years deprived of the rectory of Chrift Church in this city, whereof he was incumbent upwards of fifty-one years; but on the reftoration of the king reftored to his benefice, and promoted to the dignity of a prebendary of the cathedral church of this city, wherein notwithftanding a total privation of fight he continued to difcharge the refpective duties of each province, as an able, diligent, and orthodox divine   Thomas Smith died October 8, 1730: Catherine, his wife, April 15, 1743."

Within the north door under this monument about three feet on the eaft fide of the door was to be feen in the ground an old mooring poft, preferved till lately, to which fhips were formerly moored, when they were difcharged on the beach, where the Shambles lately were, now Bridge-ftreet, fee William of Worcefter, p. 170. 189. before the building of the ftone bridge over the Avon in 1247.

Another near the former, " To the memory of Standfaft Smith, apothecary, a native of this parifh, this ftone is infcribed by Thomas Smith, his elder and furviving brother.   Inheriting the found principles of his family, he was ever a ftrenuous advocate for our moft excellent conftitution in church and ftate, and having lived in great efteem for his free and public fpirit and liberality on all occafions, he died much lamented the 18th of October, 1774."

Another thus: " Beneath this monument are depofited the remains of Thomas Smith, gentleman, late of the parifh of St. James, apothecary, but a a native of this. He died the 28th of October, 1779. Being folicitous of giving fome teftimony of his veneration and regard for the religious offices of the church of England, which when living from principle he admired and loved, he left by will 400l. the intereft thereof for celebrating divine fervice every Wednefday and Friday morning in this church of St. Maryport for ever."

Another,

Another, " To the memory of Thomas Kington, of Notton, Wilts, Efq; who changed this fhort life for a bleffed immortality, October 15, 1786, aged 48 years. He married Sufanna, youngeft daughter of Auftin Goodwin, Efq; formerly one of the fheriffs of this city : by her he had nine children, four of whom lie buried with him in the fame vault. Under the deepeft fenfe of her own and of her children's lofs, his afflicted widow infcribes this ftone to the beft of hufbands, and the beft of fathers."

At the entrance of the weft door was : " Hic jacet corpus Johannis Borus hujus villæ... et Agnetis quondam uxoris ejus. Obiit 10 Feb. 1476, quorum animabus propitietur Deus."

BENEFACTORS to the Church and Poor of this Parifh.

1594, Robert Kitchen gave 10s. a quarter to the poor for ever.

1639, George Harrington, alderman, gave 10s. to the poor for ever.

1661, Francis Gleed gave 10s. a quarter to the poor for ever.

1668, Abraham Birkin gave 10s. a quarter in bread, and 20s. for a fermon.

1685, Mrs. Boucher and Langton gave 10s. apiece to feveral poor widows.

1690, Mr. Edward Tilly gave 25l. the intereft to the poor in bread for ever.

1695, Mrs. Elizabeth Pitt gave 10l. the intereft yearly to the poor.

1736, A private donation of ten guineas, the intereft in bread yearly.

1774, Standfaft Smith, apothecary, gave this church the branch and crimfon velvet furniture for the defk and pulpit, &c.

1782, Thomas Smith gave 400l. 40s. to the clerk and fexton and the remainder of the intereft to the rector for reading prayers twice a week. The money was laid out in the funds.

There is a fmall churchyard adjoining walled round.

In the year 1749 this parifh confifted of about 96 houfes, then rated to the poor 128l. at 10½d. in the pound ; but is fince much enlarged and improved by the new buildings in Bridge-ftreet. The churchwardens ufed to receive a fum for the penns for fheep and fwine, which ufed to be placed every market day in front of the church and the houfes there, before the new prefent market was laid out.

This parifh eftate in the rents of tenements and ground rents produces about 78l. per annum, and the church has in plate one filver flaggon 57 ounces 10 pennyweights, one filver cup and cover gilt 57 ounces 5 pennyweights, and two filver plates 28 ounces 15 pennyweights.

CHAP.

C H A P. XXI.

Of the C H U R C H *and* P A R I S H *of St.* P H I L I P *and* J A C O B.

THIS Church was founded early, being firſt a chapel to a religious houſe or priory (probably Tewkeſbury) of the order of St. Benedict, ſituated at the caſt part of the preſent church; which was afterwards enlarged as the inhabitants increaſed, and the old market held here for the uſe of the caſtle and the town brought a great conflux of people.—The exact time when it became parochial is not known, but it was very early, being mentioned in Gaunt's deeds before the year 1200, and like St. James became a pariſh church through the acceſſion of inhabitants.—The preſent church is large and ſpacious, conſiſting of a body and ſide ailes, and a handſome embattled tower (with eight bells and a clock) on the ſouth ſide between the church and the chancel. It appears to have been built at different times, and was repaired not long ſince at a very large expence.

It was a rectory, but afterwards made a vicarage and appropriated to the abby of Tewkeſbury, and purchaſed by H. Brayne of Henry 8th. in 1578: Sir Charles Somerſet and G. Winter Eſq; who married the coheireſſes of Brayne, had the right of patronage, and fold it to the mayor and commonalty of Briſtol, the preſent patrons.

It is rated in the King's books at the clear yearly value of 43l. 16s. the yearly tenths were 1l. 10s.

It is worth to the incumbent in tythes in the out-pariſh, collections and fees about 200l. per annum.

There were two chauntries here, one founded by J. Kemys 12s. another by Robert Forthey 12s. which were ſequeſtered 1 Edw. 6th. 1547.

William of Worceſter, p. 247, ſays, " there was a pariſh church here near the church of the priory in the caſt ſide of the city."

The length of the body of the church from the end of the chancel, compoſed of the middle, north and ſouth ailes, is 26 yards; the length of Kemys's aile is 16 yards, and 4 yards and 1 foot wide, and 8 yards high.

In

In the year 1388, the 2d of April, Henry Wakefield Bifhop of Worcefter, by deed in the White Book at Worcefter, f. 337, 338. appropriated and an- nexed the then rectory of St. Philips to the monaftery of the Bleffed Mary of Tewkfbury, they having complained to him of their poverty and inability of maintaining hofpitality to all comers at their houfe, fituated as it was next to the public road, and of their loffes and ruinous ftate of their buildings and other burdens they were fubject to, a grant therefore alfo being obtained of the King, referving only out of the fruits and profits of the faid church a fit and fufficient portion for the fupport of the vicar, to be prefented by them and admitted by the bifhop, which portion was to be comprehended under the grant and appropriation of it to them, exprefsly to be deducted out of the pro- fits of the faid church. They were to take poffeffion upon the death or refig- nation of the then rector, and to difpofe of the rents and profits of it, &c. at their will, paying annually to the cathedral church of Worcefter half of a mark or 10s. an annual penfion every Michaelmas-day, under the penalty of 5l.

And by a deed, dated 1394, entituled, " Dotatio Vicariæ Sti. Jacobi," (Reg. Wyg. Clyfford, f. 75.) Richard Bifhop of Worcefter ordains, that Hugh Hope, the firft vicar, fhall have a manfe or dwelling-houfe built for him, at the expence of the abbot and convent, to be maintained and fup- ported afterwards by the faid vicar and his fucceffors, and fhould receive out of the profits of the faid church yearly by the hands of the prior of the priory of St. James twelve marks of filver : all other profits arifing out of the faid church received by the vicar to be paid to the religious of Tewkfbury or their prior of St. James, the vicar to do all the duty, and have the cure of fouls in the faid parifh ; and as by a ftatute of the 4th of Richard 2d. the diocefan upon all appropriations of churches fhould order a convenient fum of filver to be diftributed amongft the poor of the parifh out of the profits of the church, Richard Bifhop, 1403, ordered 6s. 8d. only to be given at Chriftmas yearly to the poor by the religious of Tewkfbury, on account of the fmallnefs of the church and its revenues.

In 1279, 12th Sept. procefs was iffued out of the office of the Bifhop of Worcefter againft Peter de la Mare, conftable of the caftle of Briftol, and others his accomplices, for infringing the privileges of the church, in taking out William de Lay fled for refuge to the churchyard of St. Philip and Jacob, for carrying him into the caftle and imprifoning him, and laftly cutting off his head. Nine or ten being involved in this crime, their fentence was to go from the church of the Friers Minor in Lewin's-mead to the church of St.

Philip

Philip and Jacob through the ftreets naked, except their breeches and in their fhirts, for four market days for four weeks, each receiving difcipline all the way: and Peter de la Mare was enjoined to build a ftone crofs at the expence of 100s. at leaft, that one hundred poor be fed round it on a certain day every year, and that he fhould find a prieft to celebrate mafs during his life where the bifhop fhall appoint.

The ftone crofs above is mentioned by William of Worcefter: " Altæ crucis prope foffam caftri Briftoll."

A lift of the RECTORS and VICARS of the church of St. Philip and Jacob.

PATRONS.

Abbot and convent of Tewkfbury.
1275 Rich. Hammond de Newynton.
1290 Robert Anketul.
1328 Ralph de Wymborne.
1331 Walter de Kaerwent.
1340 Walter Freeman.
1346 Richard le Small.
1348 John de Wydcombe.
Nicholas de Ufk.
1349 Nicholas de Fifherton.
1351 William Sandevere.
1394 Hugh Hope, firft vicar.
1400 John White.
1420 Philip Fulgare.
1421 Stephen Graunger.
1422 John Heaneman.
John Faurthermore.
1435 John Laurence.
1471 Richard Chylde.
1475 Lodowic Williams.
1481 Mile Terre.
1493 Robert Browne.

1504 Thomas Strange.
1505 James Botiller.
1511 William Burgill.
1513 John Gardiner.
1526 John Collis, A. M.
1545 Nicholas Corbet.
David Conden.
Mayor and common council, Patrons.
1562 Thomas Colman.
1604 William Yeman.
1633 John Pierce.
1661 Edward Hancock.
1663 Thomas Godwyn.
1675 Thomas Cary.
1712 Jofeph Taylor.
1723 William Cary, fon of Tho. Cary.
1758 Carew Reynell, fon of the Chancellor Carew Reynel, Bifhop of Down and Connor.
1770 James New.

MONUMENTS.

In Kemys's aile by the chancel is a handfome monument with his figure in robes of magiftracy to H. Merrit, Efq; fheriff of this city, and a benefactor to the parifh, he died the 11th of Sept. 1692, in the 71ft year of his age.

In

In the north aile on a ſtone is an inſcription to H. Merrit, the younger, goldſmith : he died the 10th of June, 1698, aged 40.

A neat monument to the memory of three children of Thomas and Mary Chamberlain.

Another to Thomas Warren, who died January 23, 1722, aged 68.

On a ſtone an inſcription to Gabriel Wayne : he died the 15th of January, 1722, aged 75.

On a raiſed tomb an inſcription to Edward Cox, merchant, who died Auguſt 3, 1627, aged 57.

Another inſcription to Thomas the ſon of H. Whitehead, who died the 15th of Auguſt, 1700. Alſo William Whitehead, ſome time ſheriff, who died the 25th of February, 1720, aged 40.

In the chancel are ſeveral hatchments of the Elton family, and on a ſtone an inſcription to Iſaac Elton, merchant, who died the 23d of October, 1714, aged 34, and his two daughters both baptized Mary ; and on another to Elizabeth the wife of Peter Day, Eſq; daughter of Sir Abraham Elton, Bart. who died the 6th of November, 1718, aged 26. Alſo on a ſtone the following inſcription : — " Hic ſita ſunt offa Johannis Price interioris templi Londinenſis juris conſulti, qui poſtquam per 40 amplius annos pace ſummâq; rerum affluentiâ fruitus vir reipublicæ ſtudioſus vixerat, et revulſas dein ab effrenatâ turbâ ſacratas heu! olim feliciſſimi regni leges, violaram majeſtatem et jus omne divinum humanumque viderat, reducta demum per ſereniſſimum regem urbe hâc avitâ prædia ſuburbana reverſus pertæſus fragilitatis humanæ fatis conceſſit quintâ die idus Octobris anno ſalutis 1643, ætatis ſuæ 61."

On a ſtone is the figure of a croſs bow and a dog and round the verge of it, " Thomas Putley, ſome time keeper of the Queen's foreſt, departed the laſt day of October, A. D. 1596." — This was when Kingſwood was a demeſne, and in poſſeſſion of the crown.

Here is alſo a monument to William Vigor, gentleman, who died the 20th of February, 1719 ; alſo his ſon William, who died the 19th of June, 1730, aged 33.

An inſcription to Thomas Cary, vicar of this church : he died the 30th of October, 1711, aged 61.

BENEFACTORS to the Church and Poor of St. Philip's Pariſh.

1705, Mr. Samuel Davis, ſome time ſheriff of this city, gave 50l.   *l.   s.   p.*
     the profit thereof to the poor of the in-pariſh weekly in
     bread for ever   -   -   -   -   50   0   0

1708,

	l.	s.	d.

1708, Mr. John Edwards, of this parish, wheelwright, gave 50l. the profit thereof to be diftributed to ten poor houfe-keepers of the in-parifh, not receiving alms, on the 27th of January yearly for ever - - -   50 0 0

1709, Mr. Nicholas Whiting, of this parifh, gave 10l. the profit thereof to the poor of the out-parifh for ever -   10 0 0

1712, Mrs. Eleanor Bayly, widow, of the out-parifh, gave 20l. for the ufe and benefit of this church, to be difpofed of at the difcretion of the prefent churchwardens   20 (

1715, Jofeph Jackfon, Efq; fome time mayor and alderman of this city, gave 40s. yearly to the in-parifh for the bene-fit of their poor, and 4l. yearly to the poor of the Caftle Precincts for ever - - -   120 0 0

1712, Mr. Samuel Perry gave 5l. to the out-parifh for binding out an apprentice (not upon the alms) to a free tradef-man in this city yearly for ever - - -   100 0 0

Henry Whitehead, formerly mayor and alderman of this city, gave 40l. the intereft thereof to be difpofed of by the churchwardens to poor houfekeepers of the in-parifh not receiving alms on Candlemas-day yearly for ever   40 0 0

1730, Mr. John Jaines, of this city, mariner, gave in his life time two tenements in Cheefe-lane, the profit thereof for the cloathing of as many poor men's widows of this parifh, as the clear rent fhall amount to on. Sept. 29, for ever.

Mr. Edward Cox, of this city, gave 8l. per annum to the poor, and 4l. for eight fermons yearly for ever.

1694, Mr. Alderman Kitchen gave 40s. per annum to houfe-hol-ders who are poor for ever.

1639, Mr. Alderman Harrington gave 40s. per annum to the poor for ever.

Mr. Abraham Clements gave 30s. per annum to the poor of the out-parifh, and 10s. for a fermon the 1ft of January for ever.

Mr. Francis Gleed, of this city, gave 40s. to the poor to be paid quarterly for ever.

Mr. William Burroughs gave 20s. per annum to the poor for ever.

Mr..

	l.	*s.*	*d.*
Mr. Thomas Farmer gave 50l. the profit thereof to the poor for ever - - - -	50	0	0
Mr. William Curtice gave 50l. the profit thereof to the poor for ever - - - -	50	0	0
Mr. Abraham Birkins gave 5s. per annum to the poor in bread for ever - - - -	5	(	
Mr. John Harford gave 5l. 15s. 4d. per annum to the poor for ever.			
Mr. Timothy Parker gave 5l. the profit thereof to the poor in bread yearly for ever - - -	5	0	0
Mrs. Mary Boucher and her daughter Mrs. Joan Langton, widows, gave lands for the payment of 10s. apiece to 52 poor widows of this city yearly for ever, of which this in-parifh hath a proportion.			
1734, Capt. John Roure, of this parifh, merchant, gave 20l. to to the churchwardens, the profit thereof to be given in bread to the poor of the out-parifh on the 27th of Auguft yearly for ever - - - -	20	0	0.
Mr. Anthony Whitehead, of this parifh, gave 20l. the profit thereof to the poor houfe-holders of the out-parifh, not receiving alms, on the 1ft of May yearly for ever	20	0	0
1685, Mr. Jeremiah Hollway, of this city, merchant, gave 30l. the profit thereof to the poor of the in parifh yearly for ever - - - -	30	0	0.
1686, Mr. Samuel Hale, merchant, gave 10l. the profit thereof weekly to the poor in bread for ever: and alfo the intereft of 230l. towards the placing apprentices of poor children in feven parifhes of this city yearly for ever, of which this parifh is one.			
1687, Sir William Cann, Knight and Bart. gave 100l. to four parifhes in this city, whereof this hath a quarter part, the profits thereof to be diftributed to the poor the 8th of January for ever.			
1688, John Lawford, Efq; fome time mayor and alderman of this city, gave 50l. the profit thereof to the poor of the in-parifh yearly in bread for ever - -	50	0	0
1689, Mr. William Scott gave 10l. the profit thereof to the poor of the in-parifh yearly for ever - -	10	0	0
	1689,		

	l.	s.	d.

1689, Mrs. Elizabeth Pitts, widow, of this parish, gave 20l. the profit thereof to the poor of the in-parish yearly for ever   20   0   0

1690, Mr. Edward Tilly, of this city, gave 100l. to four parishes, whereof this in-parish hath a quarter part, the profit to be given to the poor in bread weekly for ever.

1692, Mr. Henry Merritt, some time sheriff of this city, gave 50l. the profit thereof weekly in bread to the poor of the out-parish for ever   -   -   -   -   50   0   0

     Mr. Edward Terrill gave 50l. the profit to the poor of the in-parish for ever   -   -   -   -   50   0   0

     Dr. Sherman gave 9l. 10s. the profit to the poor of this parish for ever   -   -   -   9   10

     John Brown, labourer, gave 10l. the profit to the poor of this parish for ever   -   -   -   10   0   0

1695, Mr. Walter Stevens, of this parish, gave 3l. 13s. 4d. per annum, to be distributed in bread to the poor of the in-parish weekly for ever.

1701, Mrs. Barbara Merritt, widow, gave 30l. the profit thereof yearly to the poor of the out-parish for ever   -   30   0   0

     Herbert Vaughan, Esq; gave 10l. the use thereof to the poor of the in-parish for ever   -   -   10   0   0

1720, Mrs. Christian Blackbourn, widow, gave to the minister for two sermons on Ash Wednesday and Good Friday in the afternoon yearly for ever 10s. each, to the clerk 1s. 6d. each, and to the sexton 1s. each.

     Mr. Joseph Colebrook, of the out-parish, gave 10l. the profit thereof to the poor of the out-parish in bread on the 16th of October yearly for ever   -   -   10   0   0

     Mr. William Vigor, of this parish, gave 20l. the profit thereof to be given to the poor of the in-parish in bread on the 2d of February yearly for ever, by the church-wardens of said parish   -   -   -   20   0   0

     Capt. James Smith gave 3l. 6s. 4d. yearly for ever, for preaching two sermons, one on the 4th of January and the other on the 9th of May, and for bread to the poor of the out-parish, and 12l. 10s. to the in-parish, the interest thereof to be given yearly in bread to poor housekeepers, not receiving alms, at the discretion of the churchwardens respectively.

1720,

	l.	*s.*	*d.*
1720, Mr. Henry Gibbes, of this city, gave 10l. the intereſt thereof to the poor of this pariſh for ever -	10	0	0
1727, Sir Abraham Elton, Bart. gave 50l. the intereſt thereof to to be paid on the 1ſt day of May yearly for ever to the miniſter for preaching a ſermon, if it falls on a Sunday then it is to be preached the day following 20s. and the reſidue thereof to be equally divided between ten poor houſe-holders within the out-pariſh not receiving alms for ever - - - - -	50	0	0
Mrs. Alice James, widow, gave 20l. the intereſt thereof to be given in twelve-penny bread to the poor of this pariſh, not receiving alms, on Chriſtmas-day yearly for ever - - - - -	20	0	0
1728, Mr. William Welſh, Mr. Daniel Shewring, and Mr. John Pittman, gave 20l. the profit thereof to poor houſe-keepers of the out-pariſh on the 8th of March, not receiving alms - - - -	20	0	0
1733, Mrs. Dionis Gibbes, in memory of her brother Mr. Harrington Gibbes, merchant, of this city, gave 50l. the profit thereof to be diſtributed as followeth: 20s. for the miniſter to preach a ſermon on the 28th of September in the afternoon if not on a Sunday, but if ſo on the day following; and the remainder to be diſtributed by the churchwardens in bread to the poor of the out-pariſh yearly for ever - - - -	50	ı	
Edward Colſton, Eſq; gave 10l. per annum for twelve years after his death to the charity-ſchool of St. Philip's	10	0	0

A liſt of GIFT-SERMONS to the pariſh of St. Philip's, Briſtol.

January 1, Thomas Clement's, Eſq;   May 1, Sir Abraham Elton's, Bart.
January 4, Mrs. Elizabeth Smith's.   May 9, Mr. James Smith's.
Eight Sundays in the year, Mr. Cox's.   September 28, Mrs. Dionis Gibbes's.
Aſh Wedneſday and Good Friday,
Mr. Chriſtopher Blackbourne.

In St. Philip's pariſh is the hoſpital dedicated to the holy and undivided Trinity, and St. George, on the ſouth ſide within Lawford's gate. It was founded by John Barſtaple merchant and burgeſs of Briſtol, who had ſerved the office of mayor three times, Iſabella his wife is ſaid to have founded an
hoſpital

hofpital on the north fide of the gate. This John Barftaple provided for fix poor men and fix poor women, and a prieft to officiate to them, in the hofpital, with chambers and gardens to each, he endowed the fame with certain tenements to the yearly value of 30l. 10s. 4d. for ever, I cannot find any valuation of this hofpital the 26th Henry 8th. But it was happily preferved at the reformation, and granted by Queen Elizabeth anno regni 20th 1578, 14th Feb. to Peter Gray, Efq; of Segenfee, Bedfordfhire, at 20s. per annum, and then purchafed for 100 marks by the corporation to apply it to charitable ufes, who have fo carefully improved the revenues, that there are now ten poor men, and twelve poor women, maintained at 3s. per week each; the yearly income of the faid eftate was increafed in 1749, to 298l. 18s. 4d. This charity has been further augmented by the benevolence of Mr. John Matthews a burgefs of Briftol, with 18l. per annum, given in the year 1521, fo that the whole amounts to 316l. 18s. 4d. per annum, and the vicar of St. Philip's, in which parifh this hofpital is, hath 8l. per annum, to read prayers to them every Thurfday and Saturday in the week for ever, and for one fermon and facrament on Holy Thurfday. The clerk of the parifh has for his trouble 40s. per annum.

As the yearly income is increafed, the corporation did in the year 1739 make an additional building to that hofpital on the north fide of the gate of the fame foundation, placing therein twenty-four women only, twelve of which have 3s. per week as being upon the old foundation, and in the new additional building are placed twelve men, fix of which have 2s. per week and the other fix at prefent have only houfe rent free. Bifhop Tanner, in his Notitia Monaftica, p. 483. fays, that this hofpital was founded anno 4 Henry 5th. 1416, and fays there was certainly fome foundation before that of John Barftaple's time, though probably not fully fettled. * But he was mifinformed, for Ifabel his wife, who is faid to be a joint founder with him, died in the year 1400, and his death followed in October 1411, which is feveral years before the time mentioned by the Bifhop to be founded, and their grave ftones with each infcription on them are now to be feen in the year 1788.

The following infcriptions are under his and his wife's figures, being brafs let into freeftone with his cypher and a coat of arms under his wife; they lie on the right and left fide of the high altar. She died the 1ft year of King Henry 4th. and her bufband the 13th of the faid king. Under his, " Hic
jacet

* Vide the Licence of King Henry 5th. to John Barftaple in the city chamber.
Pat. 3. Hen. 4. p. 1. m. 16. Par. 9. Hen. 4. p. 1. m. 4. pro gilda ibidem facienda.
Pat. 13. Hen. 4. p. 4. p. 1. m. 3. pro ten. in Rugeway.
Pat. 4. Hen. 5. p. 1. m. 2. vol. iii.

jacet Johannes Barſtaple, burgenſis villæ Briſtol, fundator iſtius loci, qui obiit 15 kalen Octob. litera Dominicalis D. A. D. MCCCCXI. cujus animæ propitietur Deus, Amen." Under her's, " Hic jacet Iſabella, quond. uxor Johannis Barſtaple, quæ obiit A. D. MCCCC. cujus animæ propitietur Deus, Amen."

The religious gilds were founded chiefly for devotion and alms deeds, the ſecular for trade and alms deeds. Thus King Henry 5th. by patent letter of his great ſeal gave licence to found this religious gild or fraternity to the honour of the Holy Trinity and St. George in the ſuburb of Briſtol, and made it perpetual thus : — " Rex omnibus ad quos, &c. ſalutem. Sciatis quod cariſſimus pater noſter Dominus H. nuper Rex Angliæ per literas ſuas patentes (he doth not ſay of what date) de gratia ſua ſpeciali conceſſerit et licentiam dederit, pro ſe et hæredibus ſuis quantum in ipſo fuit, Johanni Barſtaple, to found an hoſpital or almery and a gild, in ſuburbio Briſtolliæ — et quod utraq; domus hoſpitalitatis ſive elemoſinariæ ac fraternitatis ſive gildæ prædictarum, per ſe perpetua et incorporata exiſteret imperpetuum, et quod unus capellanorum prædictorum eſſet cuſtos domus hoſpitalitatis ſive elemoſinariæ prædict (œ) ac cuſtos domus hoſpitalitatis ſive elemoſinariæ Sanctæ Trinitatis juxta Laffordeſyate in ſuburbio Briſtolliæ nuncuparetur, et alter eorum capellanorum eſſet magiſter ſive cuſtos fraternitatis ſive gildæ prædictæ, et magiſter ſive cuſtos fraternitatis ſive gildæ Sanctæ Trinitatis juxta Laffordeſyate in ſuburbio Briſtolliæ nuncuparetur imperpetuum, et quod uterq; cuſtodum prædictorum per ſe eſſet habilis ad perquirend (um) et recipien (dum) terras tenementa et alias poſſeſſiones quecumq; habenda ſibi et ſucceſſoribus ſuis imperpetuum ita quod neuter illorum de poſſeſſionibus alterius in aliquo nullatenus ſe intromitteret, et quod uterq; cuſtodum prædictorum nomine ſuo præ notato, et ſucceſſores fui, in quibuſcumq; curiis noſtris et alibi placitare et implacitari poſſet, ac commune ſigillum haberet imperpetuum, quodq; uterq; cuſtodum prædictorum ac fratres et ſorores"—might make ordinances and conſtitutions for the government of their houſe, as by the ſaid letter patent might appear. The preſent king, viz. Henry 5th. granteth leave to transfer the ſaid almery and gild, and to found a gild or fraternity in honour of the Holy Trinity and St. George. — " Et quod fraternitas ſive gilda prædicta per ſe perpetua et incorporata exiſtat in perpetuum, et quod ipſi annuatim quendam magiſtrum de ſeipſis eligere poſſint, who magiſter gildæ ſive fraternitatis Sanctæ Trinitatis et Sancti Georgii Briſtolli (æ) nuncupetur imperpetuum. Et quod prædictus magiſter gildæ ſive fraternitatis predictæ ſimulcum gilda ſive fraternitate prædicta ſint perſonæ habiles et capaces ad perquirend (um) et recipiend (um) terras tenementa et alias poſſeſſiones quæcumq; habend (a) et tenend (a) fibi et fucceſſioribus fuis imperpetuum, and that nomine prænotato they may plead and be impleaded. In cujus, &c. tefte rege apud Weſtmonaſterium 15 die Februarii." Pat. 4. Hen. 5. m. 1.

In the out-pariſh of St. Philip and Jacob, without Lawford's-gate, upon the north ſide of the road to Bath, in the hundred of King's Barton, at the eaſt end of the city, in the county of Gloceſter, was an hoſpital for leprous perſons, dedicated to St. Laurence, before the 8th Henry 3d.* The patronage of the maſterſhip was in the crown, but was granted 3d Henry 5th. to Humphrey Duke of Gloceſter. Sir Robert Atkyns ſeems to confound this laſt account, for he aſſerts that the hundred and manor of Barton with the advowſons of the hoſpital of St. Laurence did belong to Edward Duke of York, grandſon to King Edward 3d. p. 421. Biſhop Tanner ſays in his Notitia, p. 481. that it ſeemed afterward that this hoſpital did belong to the college of Weſtbury. Sir Robert Atkyns, p. 802. confirms the ſame, and that King Edward 3d. granted the hoſpital of St. Laurence near Briſtol † towards their maintenance, and that this and all other eſtates belonging to that college, at the diſſolution of religious foundations, were granted to Sir Ralph Sadleyr, the 35th Henry 8th. (Vide p. 850.) The original grant from Henry 8th. to Sir Ralph is in the poſſeſſion of Sir John Hugh Smyth, of Long Aſhton, Bart.

Vide in Mon. Angl. tom. xi. p. 438. cartam regis Henrici 3. (anno regni 32,) de quadam felda conceſſa iſti hoſpitali.

Pat. 8. Hen. 3. m. 10. quod leproſi de S. Laurentio fit quieti de hundredis, &c.

Pat. 32. Hen. 3. m. 3. Pat. 14. Edw. 2. p. 2. m. 3. de cuſtodi conceſſ. per regem. Pat. 3. Hen. 5. p. 1. m. 8.

By the original grant, dated 24th March, 25th Henry 8th. among other things belonging to the late diſſolved collegiate church of Weſtbury, as houſes and meſſuages in Briſtol and large poſſeſſions in Henbury, Auſt, Penpark, &c. was granted the ſite of the hoſpital of St. Laurence near Briſtol, and all manors, lands, tenements, to the late hoſpital belonging, ſituate, lying, or being in Netherwyk, Overwyk, and Hennewyk, paying the king for the ſite of the ſaid hoſpital 1l. 4s. 10d. for the lands in Netherwyk, &c. 4s. 8½d. for Weſtbury college 19s. 10d. and for the manor of Clifton 1l. per annum.

By

* King John, in the year 1208, and alſo King Edward 2d. the 10th of his reign, confirmed divers lands to the maſter and brethren of this hoſpital of lepers of St. Laurence.

† This confirmation was of the ſite of the hoſpital of St. Laurence near Briſtol, with all its lands and tenements in Redwick, which lately belonged to the college of Weſtbury, was alſo granted the 35th of Henry 8th. 1542, to Sir Ralph Sadleyr, Knight. Vide Sir Robert Atkyns, p. 475.

By a furvey of the manor of St. Laurence, taken in April 1629 by H. Lely penes me, then part of the poffeffions of Sir Ralph Sadleir, of Stondon, in the county of Hertford, Efq; it appears that the manor-houfe, &c. was then in poffeffion of Robert Hooke, of Briftol, Efq; and its fite, together with the chapel-houfe, &c. abutted fouth on London highway and Chapel-lane on the Eaft, St. Laurence lecze on the north and weft parts; and that the fum total of acres of the demefnes of this manor was 205 acres 1 rood; fum total of the yearly value was 96l. 13s. 4d. and the fum total of the then yearly rent being out on lives was 16l. 8s.

This was but a fmall part of the poffeffions belonging to the college of Weftbury, which was granted at the diffolution, 36th Henry 8th. to Sir Ralph Sadleyr. They had lands in Henbury, &c. which then yielded from the leffees yearly, as from valuation and furvey then taken (according to the original rental penes me) appears as under:

	l.	s.	d.
At Henbury, Compton, Redwyck, Northwyke, Weftbury, Cote, Laurence-Wefton, Shirehampton, Charleton, tythes of Weftbury, Rydeland, Cote, and Stocke - - -	116	13	1
Befides woods, Gooddown-grove full of oaks 9 acres, Hygwood 50 acres, Goddy-grove 29 acres, Comb-wood under Blaze-hill 18 acres, Afh-grove 17 acres.			
From the demefne lands of the bifhop of Worcefter -	26	12	6
Other eftates granted out at the court then held - -	108	0	0
The manor of Clyfton, leafe-rents - - -	10	0	0
The manor of St. Laurence, without Lawford's-gate, and land in Syfton belonging thereto - - - -	9	5	8
Tenements and lands in the city of Bryftowe - -	23	9	8
Befides heriots, &c.			
Total £	294	0	11

St. Philip's out-parifh being large and populous, in the parliament held 1751 an act was paffed for dividing the parifh of St. Philip and Jacob, and for erecting a church in the new intended parifh; the preamble to which recites, " that the church was not large enough to contain the inhabitants." In order to promote that good intention, Thomas Chelter, Efq; lord of the manor, gave a piece of ground in Kingfwood, the fite of the church dedicated to St. George, churchyard, parfonage-houfe, and a field near it. Dr. Butler, Bifhop of Briftol, gave 400l. towards the maintenance of the new vicar, befides which he obtained 400l. more from the Governors of Queen

Ann's

Ann's Bounty. The corporation of Briftol gave towards building the church 250l. provided they fhould have the prefentation of the living, which they now enjoy ; the Merchants Society gave 150l. Mr. Onefi. Tyndal 100l.

The act was after fome delays carried into execution, and on Tuefday March 3, 1752, David Peloquin, Efq; mayor, attended by the aldermen, and the other commiffioners appointed for building the new church, went in their coaches in proceffion to the fpot marked out for the purpofe, and laid the firft ftone of the ftructure, putting under it feveral pieces of the coin of George 2d. the upper part of it had the following infcription :

Templum hoc
Dei Opt. Max. Gloriæ
Et Hominum indies peccantium Saluti
Sacrum
Erigi voluit pietas publica ;
Abfit Tamen,
Quod inter ignota nomina
Reverendi admodum in Chrifto patris
Jofephi Butler,
Nuper Briftollienfis Epifcopi
Lateat Nomen.
D. D. D. 400l.
Jam tum ad Dunelmenfes migraturus.

On the lower part of the ftone was this :

Regnante Georgio fecundo
Jufto, Clementi, Forti,
Angularem hunc Lapidem
5 Non. Mart. 1752.
Pofuit
David Peloquin, Civitatis Briftoll. Prætor.

Thus at the expence of 2853l. 17s. 7½d. was the church and vicarage-houfe compleated, and a place of worfhip erected for the refort of the numerous inhabitants of Kingfwood, which from being a wild foreft for deer is now become a well-inhabited place, with feveral thoufand induftrious and civilized people, living happily in their neat cottages. This chace of Kingfwood was a demefne of the crown belonging to Briftol caftle, but was in procefs of time divided, by a mutual confent and combination among the feveral lords, who had eftates confining upon it, and not by any grant from the crown, as was made appear by furvey and inquifition taken May 26, 1652, by Endimion
Porter

Porter and others in the Exchequer, when it was proved the total improved value of the whole chace was per annum 1241l. os. 4d. Total of acres 3432 and 2 roods. Total of grofs value for cottages, timber, coal-mines, &c. 2082l. 10s. For deer about 30, formerly 1500 or 2000, 30l. But the *Nullum Tempus* bill that has fince been paffed has now fixed the right in the prefent lords, however dubious their title was before.

One Mr. Dyer of Briftol was the reputed ranger of Kingfwood chace, and a duty called chiminage was ufually paid at Lawford's-gate for ever pack-faddle paffing through the faid chace during the fairs of St. James and St. Paul.

Leland, vol. vi. p. 67. has, " Antiquæ limites foreftæ de Kingefwode." — " The forefte of Kingefwode cummythe onte Barres Courte, Mayftre New-ton's howfe," vol. vii. p. 12.

C H A P. XXII.

Of the CHURCH *and* PARISH *of* TEMPLE, *otherwife* HOLY CROSS.

IT derives its name from the religious fociety of Knight Templars, its founders, an order inftituted about the year 1118, wearing an habit white with a red crofs upon the left fhoulder ; their fuperior was called Mafter of the Temple. In Mouaft. vol. ii. p. 530. is an account of the eftates granted to them, among which are " apud Briftol ex dono Comitis Roberti, &c. lands at Briftol of the gift of Earl Robert, part of which was built on by the brethren themfelves, part by other men, &c." This points out clearly the time when this church and parifh were founded, in the reign of King Stephen, when Robert Earl of Gloceffer flourifhed. By its proximity to Briftol, being fepa-rated from it only by the river Avon, it foon increafed in inhabitants, efpe-cially after the erection of the bridge : a great market was held at Stallage-crofs, and a free and frequent intercourfe betwixt thofe on both fides of the river foon took place. The church feems to have been built at feveral times.

The following curious account of this church tranfcribed from an original old vellum manufcript, faid to be written about the year 1460 by Rowlie, is the moft ancient :

" Tys

" Tys uncouthe whanne thys chyrche was fyrſt ybuilden, natheleſs I reede yn the bochorde of the reveſtrie, that in 1271 ſyx women in Eaſter wake dyd doe penaunce for ewbrice, goeynge from St. Paulle's croſſe to the new chyrche of Templarres : certis is the evente knowen, howgates ytt became crouched. Gremondei, a Lumbard, dyd make grete boaſte that hee woulde ybulden a chyrche moe freme thanne anie yn Bryſtowe. The Knyghtes Templarres eftſoons dyd hem emploie, Gnoffenglie deſpyſeinge the argues of Johannes a Brixter, a Bryſtoe manne borne, who the ſame woulde have ybuylden on the hylle cleped Celnile-hylle, and ſythence Pyll-hylle, alleageynge therefore that the river han formerlic ranne thorowe St. Paules ſtrete, and a lane aneare whylome was cleped Rhiſtreete, in Saxonne tongue the ſtrete of the ryver : bie reaſon wherofe the bottome m'ote be moddie, and ne able to beare a chyrche. Natheleſs the halle worke was begonne in the veric lane of Rhi-ſtrete ; but tyme eftſoons ſhewed the trouthe, for the towre ne hie nor heavie ſouke awaie to the ſouthe, tareynge a large gappe fromme the chyrche's bod-die : a maconne was kyllen and three of more aneuthe ſleÿne. To the ob-ſervynge eyne the whole order of the chyrch is wronge, and ſeemethe as tho' ſhaken bie an erthequake. The Knyghtes Templarres let itte lie unconſe-crate untylle ſyxtene yeeres, whanne for Gremondie agayne deſpyſinge John a Brixter, ytte was crenelled atoppe goynge ne hier than beefore, glayzeinge the wyndowes and ſyngeynge thereynne. Botte the pryncypalle dyeynge, another dyd hym ſucceed, whoe dyd ſende for Johnne a Bryxter and em-ploied hym. He than began tó ſtaie the ſame bie pyles and rayſed the ſame as hie againe ynn the towere makeynge ytte ſtronge and laſtable, leave-ynge the fyrſte battlementes to ſhew howe farre hee dyd rayſed ytte. Hee dyed, and eyn 1296 Thomæ Ruggilie added the three ſmalle chapelles for dailie chauntries, one of whych was graunted to the weavers bie Kynge Edward of that name the fyrſte."

The leaning poſition and crookedneſs of Temple tower is generally noted, and Brunius or Braun in his Theatrum Urbium, (Coln: 1576) mentions it in the following terms — " Præcelſam habet & elegantem &c." i. e. " The church of Holy Croſs has a very high and elegant tower which I may venture to compare in thickneſs and heighth with that of St. Martin's the Leſs at Cologn. When the bells that are in it found, it is ſo moved this and that way that at length by the too great and frequent ſhaking, it has ſeparated from the body of the church ; and has made a chink from the very top of the roof to the foundation, gaping ſo wide as to admit four fingers bredth. Abraham Ortelius wrote me word, that himſelf put a ſtone of the ſize of a gooſe egg

into

into this chink, which he faw himfelf give down wards as the place was nar-row or wide, and at length by the frequent colifion was fqeezed to pieces; and that when he put his back againft the tower, he was afraid he fhould be oppreffed by its fall; that the mayor and others of authority there told him, the whole fabrick of this church formerly fhook and was like to fall before this chink was made there, and with fuch force, that the lamps were put out and the oil wafted: of this there were many living witneffes in that parifh. But the church now, becaufe it is not affected by the found of the bells, ftands without motion."

It appears by the will of Bernard Obelly, 1390, and of Reginald Taylor Tucker, dated 1397, that Temple Tower was building anew to which he gives 5l. and a miffal to the altar of the Holy Trinity, near which was the image of St. John the Baptift. But William Botoner, p. 228 fays " The height of the fquare tower was built anew by the parifhioners in the year 1460, for the ringing of large bells," and p. 203, that " the new belfry tower is five yards fquare on every fide," (ex omni parte) or in the whole.

What this new building in 1460 was, is uncertain; but the above will of Reginald Taylor feems to point out the certain time, when the tower was new built; that the firft work was ill executed and wanted to be repaired, appears not improbable, confidering how much it funk at the foundation.

In 1772, it was examined and found by meafurement to lean at the South Weft corner three feet nine inches from the perpendicular.

It appeared from opening the ground in the year 1774, to put in new gate pofts at the entrance of the church, that thick foundation walls extended from the tower into the ftreet fifty or fixty feet, laid there doubtlefs for an addi-tional fupport to that inclining fide of the tower; upon forcing through them the water gufhed out and prevented their being further traced or the piles being difcovered that probably fupport them. This however fhews the great care that had been taken at times to fupport the tower, built as it is on fuch marfhy and foft ground.

William of Worcefter in 1480 fays, " The moft beautiful church of the Temple is founded in honour of the Holy Grofs in the manor and ftreet called Temple-ftreet, and has great liberties and franchifes." p. 261, " it contains in length 53 yards, being twice meafured by me." p. 239, " the breadth of the church-yard is 570 fteps in the whole."—The church is from caft to weft 156 feet long, the chancel is 74 feet, and the body of the church 82; it is 50 feet high, the chancel is 19 feet wide, and the north and fouth ailes 59 feet wide. It was ceiled and beautified in 1701 at the expence of 300l. out of the parifh.

ftock,.

flock, and 100l. was given by Mr. Colfton, who alfo gave 10l. more towards the handfome portal. It was now pewed, and a ftately organ built over the weft door; and now the long ailes, large windows, lofty ceiling, flender pillars, and its fpacious area ftrike you -with awful furprife at firft entering this facred building. There is a beautiful altar of curious workmanfhip, and on each fide a painting of Mofes and Aaron well executed; and the floor is neatly paved with diamond-cut ftones. On entering the weft door in the middle aile in the floor is laid in white marble, a crofs about 5 feet long, to preferve the remembrance of the two croffes of old inlaid with freeftone among bricks, with which the church was before paved. In 1724 a new marble font was erected here.

The ancient arms of the church was the fame as thofe of the Knight Templars, and of the Temple in London, the Holy Lamb and crofs—the lion and the crofs at the entrance feems to be a miftake of the artift.

It was made a vicarage in 1342 by Ralph Bifhop of Bath and Wells, the endowment of which is ftill extant in the regifters of Wells, a copy of it (penes me) I compared with the original there the 15th of April 1772, by which it appears that the prior and brethren of the hofpital of St. John of Jerufalem, to whom the lands of the Knight Templars had been given, were to receive of the vicar 100 fhillings out of the fruits and proceeds of the faid church, and the vicar was to receive the whole refidue of all oblations, fruits and proceeds of the faid church befides; together with a houfe for his habitation: and the prior and brethren were to repair the chancel alway; and the vicars were to bear all other charges &c. and the prior &c. were to prefent to the vicarage upon every vacancy.

A chauntry was founded here by John Fraunces, 5th of Edw. the 3d. and another by William Ponam.—This living is rated at the clear yearly value of 33l. 2s. 8d. the tenths now difcharged were 6s. 5d. It is rated in the King's books at 3l. 4s. per ann.

The corporation purchafed the patronage of this church with part of the lands, once the property of thefe religious, as appears by the following deed:

" Memorandum. That we the meare the burgeffes and communaltie of the citye or towne of Bryftowe in the countie of Bryftowe do defyre to bye and perchafe of the Kyng's Hyghneffe the manor of Temple Fee and all the howfes, byldinges, land, tenths, mede, pafture, rent, fervyce, libertys, franchyfes, and all other profytts and commodityes to the fame manor belongyng, wyth the appertynances fett lying and beyng withyn Bryftowe aforefaid, and withyn the libertyes of the fame, and in Portbury and Welt Wefton, and alfo a certain

vacant

vacant peece of ground lyinge upon the Burge of Bryſtowe: and alſoe all ſuch howſes, buyldinges, edyfices, londys, miede, paſture, rents, profetts, &c. the whych were late, and belonged to Sir John Dudley Knight, of the honorable order of the garter, Vyſcount Lyſley, which ſayd manor and all other londe, tenths, hereditaments mentioned and comprized in the particulars to theſe preſents annexed, the ſeid maer, burgeſſes and communaltie do affirme and declare to the Kynges Hyghneſs to be of the cleer yeerly value to his Hyghneſs in yeerly rents and fermes of 71l. 16s. 2d. over and above all yeerly outcharges and repryſes, and not above. In wytneſs whereof Sir Edward Beynton Knight, and Gyles Dodyngton, deputes and attorneys to the ſeyd maer and burgeſſes and communaltie, ſufficiently authoriſed, deputed and conſtituted by the wryting of the ſaid maer &c. of Bryſtow under their common ſeale, to theſe preſent have ſet theyr ſeveral ſeales and ſubſcribed theyr names. Yoven the laſt daie of June the 36 yere of the reygne of the ſeyd ſovereygne Lorde Kynge Henry the Eigth.

EDWARD BEYNTON.
GYLES DODYNGTON.

To this is annexed a ſchedule entitled,
Pacell. Terr: et poſſeſſionum nuper prioratus,

Sive hoſpitalis ſancti Johannis Jeruſalem in Angliâ, among which are the yearly quit rents of many houſes in Temple-ſtreet, rents of lands by copy of court roll in Weſt Weſton, Portbury and in Briſtol: Temple Mead was let by indenture under the ſeal of the ſaid late priory to John Campton on paying yearly 3l. 6s. 8d. the clear rent of all theſe lands was then 14l. 7s. 10d. and the rental of all the other lands of Temple manor, called Lord Lyſle's, which was very large, and conſiſted not only of tenements in Temple-ſtreet, but in every part of the city, and in Barton Regis hundred, amounted to

	l.	s.	d.
the clear annual rent of 57l. 8s. 3d. - - -	57	8	3
	14	7	11
	71	16	2

A ſum, which ſince the purchaſe made by the corporation of Briſtol, amounts now to a clear yearly ground rent, beſides renewals of lives, as follows:

	l.	s.	d.
Fee farm rents only of the knights of St. John of Jeruſalem for one year, are - - - - -	22	14	1½
Fee farm rents and rack rents of Lord Liſle's lands, are, for one year	116	6	4
	139	0	5½
	71	16	2
Increaſe in ground rents alone ſince the 36th year of Hen. 8th. £	67	4	3½

Temple meads, part of the lands belonging to the houſe of the Knight Tem-plars, were therefore exempt from tythes, and are ſo to this day, the corporation holding thoſe lands in the ſame manner as the religious did.

The ſite of the houſe of Knight Templars, and afterwards of the prior and brethren of St. John of Jeruſalem, is at preſent not very eaſily to be traced—I ſuppoſe it was near to the church of their erection, and as I find Beer-lane and Temple-Comb mentioned in deeds to be in ſuburbio; the preſent ſite of Dr. White's hoſpital and the houſes adjoining ſeem to be the ſpot, where old arches ſtill appear to point it out, though ſome have placed it at Temple-Gate, where the Auguſtine friers afterwards had their houſe and church, of which below.

The vicar chiefly depends on the free gift and contributions of his pariſhioners, amounting in the whole to about 150l. per annum, ſurplice fees included, beſides two little dwellings. The preſent incumbent is the Rev. Mr. Eaſterbrook.

VICARS of Temple.

PATRONS.	
Prior of St. John of Jeruſalem.	1614 Richard Knight.
	1639 Abel Lovering.
1342 John Jurdan.	1642 Jacob Brent.
William de Hetherington.	1660 John Chetwin.
1370 Walter Berforde.	1672 Arthur Bedford.
1447 William Bonavy.	1700 William Cary.
1452 John Veſſe.	1723 Samuel Curtis.
1473 Nicholas Whithel.	1738 Henry Becher.
1475 John Maſou, alſo rector of	1743 Thomas Jones.
Wraxal.	1756 John Price.
1476 John Thomas.	1767 Alexander Stopford Catcott,
1512 Robert Feſtham.	author of an ingenious trea-
Corporation.	tiſe on the Deluge.
1563 Edward Togood.	1779 Joſeph Eaſterbrook.
1575 Richard Barwick.	
1600 Richard Martin.	

The following are the principal Monuments and Inſcriptions in this church.

In the chancel: " Samuel Curtis vicar died 14 Jan. 1738, aged 44."

A monument with inſcription to, " John Stone, thrice mayor, who had 4 wives; he died 24 June 1575; with his effigy and his 4 wives," with the brewers arms.

" To Jacob Brent vicar, who died 22 Oct. 1666, aged 60; with ſome acroſtic verſes."

" To

" To John Thomas vicar, who died 1 Jan. 1476."

" To John Chetwin vicar, who died 4 Dec. 1672, aged 50."

" To Walter Berforde vic."

In the north wall a handfome monument with a long Latin infcription :
" To George Knight Efq; maior, who died 13 Dec. 1659, aged 89.—Alfo Sir John Knight his fon, alderman, who died 16 Dec. 1683, aged 71.—Alfo his fon John, who died 29 May 1684, aged 38.—Alfo Thomas Knight Efq; fon of Sir John, who died 26 April 1699.—Alfo Ann the wife of George Knight Efq; who died 19 Aug. 1645.—Martha the widow of Sir John Knight, who died 20 Jan. 1696.—Alfo Mary wife of John Knight Efq; who died 17 Oct. 1673.—And Ann Knight daughter of Thomas Knight, who died 22 Sept. 1725.—Arms paly of 6 arg. & G. quartered, with parted per bend ermine and fable counterchanged, a lion rampant or.

In the fouth wall of the chancel a monument, " To Alderman Crabb, who died 14 Oct. 1702, aged 87."

On a black ftone an infcription : " To John Hawkins Efq; eldeft fon of Sir John Hawkins Knight, alderman, he died 27 March 1738, aged 57.—Alfo Sir John Hawkins, who died 6 July 1723, aged 74."—Arms f. arg. a St. Andrew's crofs fable, charged with 5 fleurs de lis or.

Under a brafs figure an infcription : " To Richard Loyd, with fix fons and feven daughters, he died 13 May 1621."—Arms f. ermine, a St. Andrew's crofs fable.

At the entrance into the chancel lie the family of Hinde, with infcriptions : " To John Hinde Efq; mayor, who died 28 April 1699, aged 68.—Elizabeth daughter of Richard Brickdale, and grand daughter of John Hinde Efq; fhe died 1 Aug. 1723."

John Brickdale Efq; one of his Majefty's Juftices of the Peace for the county of Somerfet, and father of Matthew Brickdale Efq; prefent Member of Parliament for Briftol (1788) was buried at Temple, being their family burying place. He died 2 November 1765.

In the Weavers Chapel is the brafs figure of a man in the pofture of devotion, with the following lines :

> Es téftis, Chrifte, quod non jacet hic lapis ifte,
> Corpus ut ornetur, fed fpiritus ut memoretur :
> Huc tu quo tranfis, magnus, medius, puer, an fis,
> Pro me funde preces, dabitur mihi fic Veniæ fpes.

The date was 1396.

Hic

Hic jacet Dus Richardus Goldekeme quondam Capellanus ſtæ Catherinæ, obiit die menſis Maii A. D. 1443, cujus animæ propitietur Deus amen.—There is a croſs on the ſtone with ʝ. H. S.

At the eaſt end of this chapel was the Holy Lamb in painted glaſs, alſo quarterly G. a lion rampant or. with checky or. and az.—The Gorges arms.— And in the north window were formerly thoſe of Hungerford, Punchardon, Bradeſton, Ferrers, Morgan, Arthur, Fitzwarren alias Blunt, Brook, England, Valance, and of Eleanor of Caſtile Queen of Edward 1ſt. all in-painted glaſs, now ſtolen away.

There is a curious ancient braſs ſconce with twelve branches, on the top the Virgin and child in her arms in full proportion, and under them St. Michael killing the dragon, of very neat workmanſhip, probably uſed in the time of the Knight Templars.

BENEFACTORS to the Church and Poor of Temple Pariſh.

1634, Mr. George White, merchant, gave by will to the churchwardens and pariſhioners of Temple in Briſtol for the time being 25l. in money, to be paid into the hands of the overſeers of the poor, to be by them and the churchwardens ſo laid out and ſettled that by the profit thereof ariſing a ſermon may be yearly preached in Temple Groſs in Briſtol upon St. Georg's-day (being the 23d of April) for ever.— The preacher to be nominated by the mayor and aldermen of the city of Briſtol.

1639, Mr. George Harrington, alderman, hath given 40s. yearly to four houſekeepers by 10s. a quarter for ever.

Mr. William Pitt hath given the uſe of 25l. to the poor for ever.

1594, Robert Kitchen, alderman, gave 10s. for a ſermon and 12d. weekly in bread, and 40s. yearly to four houſekeepers by 10s. quarterly.

1622, Thomas White, D. D. for two ſermons yearly, and founder of an almſhouſe for ten perſons.

Mr. Edward Batten and Mary his wife gave 40l. the benefit thereof to be diſtributed in bread weekly to the poor of this pariſh for ever.

Mary Stile gave 10l. the benefit thereof to be diſtributed in bread weekly to the poor of this pariſh for ever.

Mr. Richard Ditty gave 10l. the benefit thereof to be diſtributed in bread weekly to the poor of this pariſh for ever.

1656, John Barker, alderman, gave one annuity to the churchwardens of Temple pariſh of 4l. 6s. 8d. per annum for ever out of a houſe in Temple-ſtreet, to have thirteen ſermons preached in the year, viz.

one

one every Sunday in the month in the parifh church of Temple, but if in cafe it is omitted for the fpace of three months then the annuity to ceafe.

1659, George Knight, Efq; late mayor and alderman of this city, gave 8d. weekly in bread to the poor, and 12s. 6d. for a fermon yearly for ever.

1661, Mr. Francis Gleed, fome time fheriff of this city, gave 10s. a quarter to a poor houfekeeper for ever.

1668, Arthur Farmer, Efq: alderman, gave 40l. the profit thereof to be diftributed upon All Saints-day to fix poor families of this parifh for ever.

Mr. Abraham Birkin gave 40s. per annum for ever to four houfe-holders, receiving no alms, quarterly for ever.

Mrs. Mary Beekham gave a houfe in Frog-lane, the profit thereof in bread to the poor.

Mrs. Mary Gray gave 50l. the profit thereof, viz. 6s. 8d. for a fermon on the Sunday after St. Andrew's-day, and the reft for putting poor fatherlefs children to fchool.

1683, Mr. Thomas Goldfmith gave 10l. per annum for ever; 4l. per annum in bread to the poor of this parifh, 40s. a year to the cloth workers almfhoufe, and 40s. a year to the poor of the weavers almfhoufe, each to have it given quarterly; and 40s. a year to be given to Martha Hyatt for her life, and after to fix poor widows of the faid parifh on St. Thomas's-day for ever.

1683, Sir John Knight the elder, alderman of this city, gave 20l. the profit thereof to be given in bread weekly for ever, befides 22l. given to the poor immediately.

1685, Mr. Jeremiah Holway, fenr. merchant, gave 20l. the profit thereof to be given weekly in bread to the poor of this parifh for ever.

1686, Mr. Robert Amberfon, merchant, gave 25l. the profit thereof to be given in bread to the poor of this parifh weekly for ever.

Mr. Samuel Hale, merchant, gave 10l. the profit thereof in bread to the poor of this parifh for ever. And the profit of 230l. to feven parifhes to place a boy or girl apprentice, whereof this parifh hath a proportion.

1688, Mr. John Lawford, alderman, gave 52s. in bread yearly for ever.

1689, Mr. William Middlemore, dyer, gave 10l. yearly for five years to the poor of this parifh, beginning March 25

1690,

1690, Mrs. Alice Weft gave three houfes, the profit thereof to the poor of this parifh for ever.

Mrs. Margaret Abbey, widow, gave 30l. to the poor of this parifh, which was diftributed according to her will.

1699, Mrs. Ann Longman, widow, gave 195l. to the poor of this city, of of which this parifh hath a part.

1702, Mr. John Hudfon, of this parifh, clothier, gave 13s. 4d. to the minif- ter, 4s. to the clerk, and 2s. 8d. to the fexton, for a fermon on St. John's-day for ever ; and 20s. for four widows or houfekeepers of this parifh, not receiving alms.

1706, Sarah Smith, widow, daughter of Mr. Thomas Smith, gave 6s. 8d. apiece to three poor widows of this parifh on St. Thomas's-day for ever.

1701, Edward Golfion, Efq; gave 100l. towards the ceiling and beautifying of this church, and 60l. more for a portal and altar-piece.

1703, Mrs. Sarah Golfton, widow, gave 50l. the profit thereof to be yearly and equally given to fix poor houfekeepers of this parifh, not receiving alms, at Chriftmas for ever.

1709, Mr. George Hudfon, the only fon of Mr. John Hudfon, gave 20l. to 80 families of Temple parifh, which was diftributed as by will. the intereft of 50l. to fix houfekeepers not receiving alms, viz. 8s. 4d. to each, to be diftributed by the churchwardens of the faid parifh on Afh Wednefday, and 10s. for a fermon on the fame day for ever.

1712, Mr. Abraham Spirring gave 30l. the profit thereof to the poor of this parifh in bread weekly for ever.

1713, Mr. John Gray, cloth-worker, born in this parifh, gave 40s. a year for ever, viz. 10s. for a fermon to the minifter, 2s. 6d. to the clerk, 1s. 6d. to the fexton, and 26s. paid for the relief of four fick fa- milies on the 17th day of November, at the difcretion of the church- wardens.

The fame Mr. Gray gave the refiduary part of his eftate, which amounted to 110l. to be diftributed by his executors to fuch poor perfons as they think fit. Ordered, that it fhall be applied towards the main- tenance of the charity-fchool girls of this parifh for ever.

1716, Mrs. Jane Shute, daughter of Sir John Knight, of this parifh, deceafed, gave 10l. to the poor of this parifh, the intereft thereof to be given in bread on Chriftmas-day yearly for ever.

1721,

1721, Mr. John Brittain gave 20l. the intereſt thereof to the poor in bread on Chriſtmas-day for ever.

1722, Capt. Matthew Nicholas gave 20l. the intereſt thereof to be paid yearly to four poor ſailors widows, and for want of ſuch to four poor houſe-holders of this pariſh for ever, to be diſtributed on the 9th of November, being his birth-day.

1724, May 11, Mr. John Newman, plumber, gave 26l. the profit in bread, made into two-penny loaves, to the poor of this pariſh on the Lord's-day for ever.

Mrs. Grace Brown, gave 15l. the intereſt to five poor widows, not re-civing alms, on the 5th day of March for ever.

1729, Mr. Iſaac Hollier, of Wolverhampton, left 10l. by will, the intereſt thereof to the poor of this pariſh in bread yearly for ever.

1731, Mrs. Elizabeth Nicholas, widow, gave 30l. the intereſt thereof to be diſtributed to ſix poor ſailors widows, or (if none) to ſix other houſe-keepers, not receiving alms, yearly, on the 1ſt day of February, being the day of her birth.

1725, Mrs. Ann Knight, daughter of Thomas Knight, Eſq; third ſon of Sir John Knight, late of this pariſh, gave 100l. the intereſt thereof to be given in bread, to ſuch poor of this pariſh as are moſt in need of it: one half of it on the 9th of May, and the other half of it on the 22d of September for ever. She alſo gave two large ſilver candle-ſticks for the uſe of the church.

1740, June 24, Mr. John Jayne, mariner, of Temple pariſh, gave 140l. the intereſt thereof for the education and cloathing of the poor charity girls of the ſaid pariſh for ever.

1681, Mr. Abraham Short, of Hambrough, and ſervant to Mr. John Hine, of this pariſh, fugar-baker, gave 10l. the uſe thereof weekly in bread to the poor for ever.

Mrs. Mary Boucher and her daughter Mrs. Jane Langton, widows, gave lands for the payment of 10s. apiece to 52 poor widows of this city yearly for ever, of which this pariſh hath a proportion.

1682, William Colſton, Eſq; merchant, and ſome time ſheriff of this city, gave 50l. to this pariſh, the profit thereof weekly in bread to the poor for ever.

1670, Mr. Richard Vickris, alderman, gave 52s. yearly for ever in bread.

Mrs. Lucy Peſter, widow, gave unto the poor of this pariſh 50l. the profit thereof yearly for ever.

1678,

1678, Mr. William Goldfmith gave 10l. the profit thereof to be diftributed in bread, on the 20th of January, to the poor of this parifh yearly for ever.

1672, Mr. Thomas Gueft, of Exon, gave 10l. to the poor of this parifh, the profits thereof for ever.

1676, Mr. Robert Markham, of London, gave 10l. the profit thereof to be given to the poor of this parifh in bread on St. Paul's-day yearly for ever.

The following are the GIFT-SERMONS preached in this church.

Sunday after St. Paul's-day in the morning, Alderman Kitchen's.

Afh Wednefday, Mr. Geo. Hudfon's.

April 23, Mr. George White's.

Afcenfion-day and Tuefday in Whit-fun week, Mr. T. Warren's, fenr.

Midfummer-day, Dr. White's.

November 17, Mr. John Gray's.

Sunday morning after St. Andrew's-day, Mrs. Mary Gray's.

St. Thomas's-day in the forenoon, Dr. White's.

Chriftmas-day in the morning, Mr. George Knight's.

St. John's-day, Mr. John Hudfon's.

Thirteen fermons in the year, on the firft Sunday in the month, in the afternoon, Mr. John Barker's, alderman.

The lands and tenements belonging to this parifh produce in ground rents about 170l. per annum, befides renewals of lives.

The 26th year of Henry the 8th. a great controverfy arofe betwixt the Lord prior of St. John of Jerufalem in England, and the mayor and commonalty of Briftol, relating to the privilege of fanctuary in Temple-ftreet, and of having a law day to hold court with the ufual privileges, and return a brevium and execution of the fame in the faid ftreet; claiming alfo that his tenants and inhabitants within the faid ftreet being not burgeffes, might vend their merchandifes therein in open fhops; all which articles were denied by the mayor, and after much variance the matter was referred to Sir J. Fitz-James chief juftice, and Richard Broke chief baron, who ordered that the liberty of fanctuary fhould be void, and that proceffes fhould be ferved in the faid ftreet by the city officers without difturbance of the Lord prior.—The reft of the matters in difpute were referred to another time; but Henry the 8th. fettled them moft effectually at the reformation, by the fuppreffion of religious houfes.

There were fome peculiar privileges belonging to Temple Fee, of which —— Arthur Efq; is named as lord, alfo mentioned by William of Worcefter; which

which in time were loft: and in the year 1490 it is faid, " there was no court, bayly or conftable of Temple Fee for ten weeks," and afterwards that ' Temple Fee was broken."

In this parifh and in Temple-ftreet on the north fide within the gate was a friery of brothers Eremites of St. Auguftin.—Of this houfe Bifhop Tanner in his Notitia Monaftica, in folio, p. 483, fays, " The Auguftine friers houfe was hard by the Temple-gate, within it on the north weft." It was founded by Sir Simon and Sir William Montacute, about the beginning of the reign of King Edward the 2d. and was granted the 35th of Henry the 8th. 1543, to Maurice Dennis.

Vide in Mr. Willis's hiftory of abbies, vol. 2. p. 325, the dimenfions of the church and chapter houfe.

Pat. 6 Edw. 2. p. 2. m. 2. vel. 3. Pat. 11 Edw 2. p. 1. m. 10. ibid. p. 2. m. 22. de cccc. ped in longit. et cc. ped in latit. conceff. Will. de Monteacuto pro manfo elargando: pat. 17 Ed. 2. p. 2. m. 6.

William of Worcefter in 1480 gives the dimenfions of the Briftol frieries; and of this, " The length of the body of the Auguftynian brethren's church contains 30 yards or 54 paces, the breadth thereof contains 9 yards or 16 paces; the length of the chapter-houfe 24 yards, the breadth thereof 8 yards; the length of the cloifters contains 30 yards, the breadth thereof 3 yards; the breadth of the belfry 5 yards." He adds, " In 1320, the day before the ides of July, the place of the brother Eremites of the order of St. Auguftin was confecrated; there is in the church one fmall nave and only one aile."

In the year 1366 Sir John de Gourney Lord of Knowle granted the ground for an aqueduct from Pile-hill to Temple-gate near this houfe, for the ufe of the friers here, from a fountain called Ravenefwelle at a place called Hales.

The 11th of Edward 3d. licence was granted to William de Montacute for a certain piece of land in the fuburbs of Briftol, containing 200 feet in length and 40 in breadth, contiguous to the manfion of the beloved the prior and brethren of the order of St. Auftin to enlarge their manfion, faving to the lords of the fee all due fervices, by letters patent dated at Wyndefore. This was a grant of the land in the Great Garden.

Thomas Lyons, Efq; 5th Henry 4th. granted the friers leave to bring their aqueduct direct through his land called Brandiron-clofe otherwife Long Croft with power to dig the ground, &c.

Thefe original deeds are in Temple veftry.

Temple conduit was built 1561, and 1587 J. Griffen gave two tenements to keep it in repair. This water courfe is kept in very good order, and the

fountain

fountain head is yearly vifited by the parifh officers, and they have expended great fums to preferve it at different times and to prevent the fprings from being ftopped. You enter the cavern by a door at the fide of the hill, on the very bank of the Avon on the left hand of the Bath road at Totterdown, and paffing through a narrow cut in the folid rock for 125 yards exactly in length, you come to the refervoir or large trough of freeftone, into which three or four fprings rifing with force through crevices in the bottom of the rock are conti_ nually flowing in bubbling ftreams, from hence the water is conveyed in large leaden pipes laid at the bottom of the channel cut in the rock, which pipes you walk upon in going to the ciftern, the roof above in the rock being from 10 to 20 feet high in fome places; the water is conveyed from the pipe head through the fields next it quite to Temple-gate, where is a ciftern arched over for public ufe : a feather conveyed it to the religious houfe adjoining, now be_ longing to Mr. Warren. From the gate it is now led through Temple-ftreet to the Neptune, and to a large ciftern the fouth fide of the church and from thence with a fmall feather to the vicarage-houfe, which ferves the ftreet with great conveniency as well as the neighbourhood.

In the year of our Lord 1613 Thomas White, D. D. being a native of this parifh and then living, erected an hofpital in Temple-ftreet called the Temple Hofpital, for eight men and two women, and one man and one woman were afterwards added by himfelf. He endowed the fame with lands and tenements of the yearly value of 52l. or thereabouts.

In the year 1622 he enfeoffed and confirmed to the mayor, burgeffes, and commonalty of the city of Briftol, and their fucceffors for ever in truft, four meffuages and tenements, fituate in Grays Inn-lane, in the county of Middle_ fex, near the city of London, then in the occupation of Sir Ralph Haufby, Knight, of the yearly value of 40l. to be applied to divers charities. And after his death, a rent charge of 140l. per annum was directed to be iffuing out of the manor of Bradwell, in the county of Effex, and licence of Mort_ main obtained in 1626 from King Charles 1ft. to purchafe the faid annuity.__ By his will alfo he directed that one man and one woman fhould be added upon the foundation of the faid hofpital to thofe ten before appointed, now twelve in number.

Firft fettlement was   -   -   -   £ 52
Second ditto for increafe of alms   -   6
Third ditto by his will   -   -   -   40
Total   £ 98   per annum.

In

In Temple-ſtreet at the corner of the way leading to Great Garden is an hoſpital erected, and endowed with lands and tenements in Breach Yate and Wyck and Abſton to the value of 200l. or 300l. per annum. This gift is by the directions and appointment of Mr. Thomas Stephens, alderman of this city, the ſame being enfeoffed to divers gentlemen of the ſaid city, for the maintenance of twelve women there with a weekly allowance to each of them of 2s. 6d. One other hoſpital in the Old Market was founded by the ſame perſon, and endowed with the ſame lands as above. His will bears date the 6th of April, 1679.

The next charitable foundation in Temple-ſtreet, but nearer Temple-gate on the ſame ſide of the way is the ſchool of Edward Golſton, Eſq. It was erected and endowed by him in the year 1711, for the educating in reading, writing, and cyphering, and perfecting in the underſtanding of the church catechiſm as it is now eſtabliſhed by law, and alſo for cloathing forty poor boys of this pariſh yearly for ever. The ſaid Edward Colſton, Eſq; was a native of this pariſh. See p. 443. The eſtate with which he endowed his charity-ſchool in Temple-ſtreet is an annual fee farm of 80l. per annum. The charge was about 3000l.

In a deed dated 1393 I find mention is made of an hoſpital or almſhouſe within Temple-gate, oppoſite the houſe of the Auguſtinian brethren, and in another dated 1471 it is called Domus Elemoſynaria Johannis Spycer juxta portam Templi, of this there are no remains at preſent.

There is a ſchool for girls, firſt founded by the benefaction of Mr. John Gray, and improved and ſupported at preſent by voluntary contributions.

Under the Tuckers'-hall is an ancient hoſpital, ſuppoſed to have been founded by the Tuckers' company, wherein ſix poor people have their dwellings, and 20s. per annum from the ſaid company; but they received an additional benefaction from Mrs. Sarah Smith of 40s. per annum in the whole.

The following are the particular benefactors to the company of Cloth Workers and to the ſix poor of the ſame company under their hall:

Mr. Thomas Goldſmith gave one ſilver caudle cup, weight $11\frac{1}{2}$ ounces, to the uſe of the company, in memory of his ſon Thomas Goldſmith.

	l.	s.	d.
John Sprint gave 6s. 8d. yearly for ever, paid them on Candlemas-day	0	6	8
Henry Davis gave 6s. 8d. yearly for ever, on Good Friday	0	6	8
Richard Floyd gave 6s. yearly for ever, on New Year's-day	0	6	0
Mr. Thomas Goldſmith gave 2l. yearly for ever, paid them quarterly	2	0	0
Mrs. Sarah Smith gave 2l. yearly for ever, paid to them quarterly	2	0	0
Paid them out of the rent of the hall at St. Paul's fair　－	0	15	0
The whole yearly income to the ſix poor　£	5	14	4

In

In Temple-ftreet is alfo a large hall called the Weavers'-hall, where the mafters and company meet to choofe officers and accompany them before the mayor to be fworn according to their charter; where they ufed to audit their accounts and keep their leafes and records. They have feveral lands given them, which they hold under feoffees for the ufe of the poor of the hofpital under the Weavers'-hall for four poor women, who have about 1s. per week each from the Weavers' company. Alfo by a grant dated the 22d of December, 1673, (now in the cuftody of the mafter of the Weavers) from the mafter and company of Tuckers, the faid poor are intitled to fome perquifites by them granted at St. Paul's fair, to be paid the mafter and wardens of the Weavers' company on every 2d day of February, for the benefit of the poor for ever. The poor here had at firft only 2s. 6d. per quarter, the gift of Mr. Thomas Goldfmith; but they afterwards alfo received an addition of 40s. per annum, the gift of Mrs. Sarah Smith, payable out of an eftate at Max Mills, in the county of Somerfet.

Round the bell at the Weavers'-hall was this infcription in Gothic letters: "Elizabeth de Burco: libera de ira Dei nos Jefu Chrifte."

In 1786 this Weavers'-hall, ufed as a chapel for the Methodifts, was let on a leafe for 100 years at an advanced rent of eight guineas per annum to the Jews for a fynagogue, who have decorated it in a neat expenfive manner. It was opened for their ufe the 15th of September, 1786, with great ceremony, mufic, &c.

Under this is a fmall chapel with a large ftone table, where divine fervice was antiently performed, but for many years hath been totally omitted. To this company belong feveral pieces of plate, and a horn like that at Queen's college in Oxford. The Weavers' chapel in Temple church alfo belongs to them, and they keep it in repair and receive for breaking the ground there. Prayers are read in it by the vicar yearly the 29th of May and the 5th of November in the morning, for which they pay 5s.

This company has declined greatly with the trade of clothing in this city.

The money collected for the ftandings, &c. at the winter Briftol fair, kept in Temple-ftreet at St. Paul's tide, but the day is changed fince to the 1ft of September, is applied to charitable ufes, being firft applied to repair the water pipes and conduit of this parifh, and the remainder is diftributed to the poor.

Edward 6th. granted the charter the 24th of May 1550, for holding this fair for eight days to the mayor and commonalty, who " out of charitable compaffion to the poor of the parifh and their better relief and fupport," did by indenture the 28th of September, 2d Charles 2d. give and grant to the

church-

churchwardens and parifhioners and their fucceffors full power and authority for and in the name of faid mayor and commonalty, to gather and levy and receive all tolls, ftallage, profits, and revenues of the fair, to be employed for the relief of the poor and reparations of the faid parifh and the water courfes thereunto belonging, the churchwardens paying to the corporation at Lady_day for ever the fum of 20s. The fair is accordingly proclaimed the day be_fore it is held by the city crier, charging all to fell no wares till the following morning at feven o'clock.

CHAP. XXIII.

Of the CHURCH and PARISH of St. THOMAS.

THIS was from the earlieft times a chapel to Bedminfter, and is called in old deeds by the name of the Chapel of St. Thomas the Martyr, and feems to have arifen upon the increafe of buildings and inhabitants on Red_cliff fide of the city ; for Redcliff-ftreet itfelf was part of the manor of Bedmin_fter of old, and belonged to Thomas de Berkly as fuch. In a manufcript (penes me) the church is faid " to have been very old, and being foullie rent " and crafed was rebuilden by Segawen or Segovian, a Lumbard gouler or " ufurer ;" but in what year is not mentioned. It is very apparent, that it was built at different times. The prefent ftructure is lofty and fpacious, after the Gothic order, with a lofty nave and long fide ailes, and the tower at the weft end with bells without any fpire ftrong and plain. It is in length from the weft door to the high altar 46 yards, the porch is 3 yards and 2 feet, and the breath of the whole church 19 yards 1 foot.

William Botoner, p. 214. fays, " The length of the church of St. Thomas contains 73 fteps or 48 virgæ or yards, its breadth 21 yards." But in p. 204. " The church of St. Thomas with the choir contains in length 80 fteps, its breadth 55 fteps ;" and in p. 239. he fays, " It is 43 yards in length," which fhews the uncertainty of his meafurement."

This church is often mentioned in old deeds as early as the year 1200. It is next to Redcliff the largeft as well as moft elegant building, though only a

chapel

chapel like it to another (Bedminſter) church. This pariſh formerly being well inhabited and full of clothiers, and their dependents required ſuch a ſpacious church to aſſemble in for divine ſervice. where every individual thought it his duty or was obliged to attend, eſpecially every ſabbath-day. Edward Colſton, Eſq; gave 50l. towards the repairs of this church. Near the middle is a cupola raiſed or glazed lanthorn, alſo an organ which coſt 360l. is at the weſt end.

John Stoke eſtabliſhed a chauntry the 15th of March, 6th Richard 2d. for two chaplains to celebrate every day before the altar of the Virgin Mary in this church, where the ſaid John Stoke was buried, for the ſouls of his Majeſty and of the commonalty of Briſtol, of himſelf and Joan his wife, &c. and he left to the proctors 5l. 5s. per annum for them to have his obit held annually and that of his three wives on the 27th of May.

John Burton, burgeſs of Briſtol and merchant, by will dated March 1, 1454, 3d of Henry 6th. gave lands and tenements to Nicholas Pittes, vicar of Red-cliff and St. Thomas, Philip Mede and others, to find a chaplain for a per-petual chauntry in this church at the altar of St. John the Baptiſt, near which he was buried, to pray for the King and Queen, himſelf, and Iſabel his wife.

Robert Chepe left meſſuages and tenements in Redcliff-ſtreet, Temple-ſtreet, and Defence-ſtreet, 11th Henry 4th. for a chauntry prieſt to pray for his ſoul and that of Agnes his wife, at the altar of St. Nicholas in the church of St. Thomas.

Richard de Welles having obtained licence of Mortmain of King Edward 3d. did by will bequeath tenements in Fuller's-ſtreet for a chauntry in the chapel of St. Thomas, at the altar of the Holy Trinity and the Virgin Mary, which was confirmed by Ralph Biſhop of Bath and Wells, at Banwell March 9, 1333.

The principal Monuments and Inſcriptions are the following:

A monument to Edward Bovey, with braſs figures with four ſons behind him, and two daughters behind his wife, with an acroſtic of ten lines. He died the 20th of April, 1662. Arms, or. 3 croſs bows G. impaling Giffard G. three lions or. paſſant.

Another, large, " To Edward Morgan, Eſq; alderman, who died 13 Sept. 1669, aged 61." Arms, or. a griffin rampant ſ. quartered with G. two bars or.

" To Richard Crump, alderman and member of parliament, who died 14 January, 1699, aged 72." Arms, chevernois of ſix, or. and G.

" To Charles Greſley, apothecary, of an antient family in Derbyſhire," with a long Latin inſcription. Arms, vaire, arg. and G.

" To

" To Humphrey Brent, A. M. minifter of this church," with a long Latin infcription in his praife. He was buried under the communion table 1677, aged 40.

" To Maurice Ceely Trevillian, Efq; who died 2 April, 1781, aged 74."

" To John Haythorn, who died 14 January, 1732, aged 74; and to Nicholas-Haythorn his fon, who died 6 March, 1733, aged 38; Anna his mother, who died 27 July, 1710, aged 44; alfo Henry Haythorn, who died 11 July, 1737, aged 27."

" To Ezekiel Longman, Efq; fheriff, who died 9 Auguft, 1738; and Sufanna his wife, who died 6 March, 1733, aged 58."

" To John Berrow, Efq; mayor, who died 29 November, 1745, aged 60; and Mary his wife, who died 1 July, 1745, aged 60." Arms, arg. a fefs f. betwixt three goats heads couped erafed of the fecond.

" To George Hellier, alderman, who died 21 April, 1656; and Eleanor his wife, who had fix fons and eight daughters: fhe died 28 Anguft, 1643."—Arms, G. chevron or. betwixt three fpur-rowels of the fecond, quartered with chevernois of fix or. and G.

On a high tomb near the font was this: " Robertus Rogers, aldermannus, obiit 11 Apr. 1633, ætat. 80. Alionora uxor, obiit 15 Jañ. 1624.—Richardus Rogers, miles filius Roberti, obiit 18 Aug. 1635, æt. 39. Rebecca uxor, obiit 3 Jan. ...., ætat. 20. Sine prole.—Richardus filius Richardi ex Maria conjuge, obiit 18 Julii 1634. Ævo primo."

In the churchyard a tomb with infcription " To Matthew Warren, 1639." Arms, az. within three mullets or. a lion rampant of the fecond.—Alfo Judith Warren, daughter of William Gibbs, fheriff, with feveral children, nine fons and five daughters. Date obliterated.—Pofuit Matthew Warren non fine lachrymis 7 May, 1627." c

In the fame wall, " To William Gibbs, fome time of the common council of this city: he died 3 April, 1603. Alfo Ann Loyd, daughter of William Gibbs: fhe died 4 December, 1625." Arms, arg. three battle axes in fefs f. a crefcent in chief.

Sir Philip Gibbes, Bart. of Hilton park, near Wolverhampton, is defcended from this William Gibbs of Briftol. One George Gibbes, brewer, bought an eftate at Bedminfter in the year 1625 for the lives of his three fons, George, William, and Matthew.

There are feveral tenements and lands belonging to this church, which together produce about 140l. per annum, befides renewals of lives.

The church plate is one large filver chalice 24 ounces 2 pennyweights, one ditto gilt, 1695, 13 ounces 5 pennyweights, one filver in ufum facræ enchariftiæ,

riftiæ, 1685, two flaggons large, the gift of Thomas Woodward, 1635, 37 ounces 15 pennyweights, one fmall, donum Thomæ Heathcote, 16 May, 1630, 36 ounces 15 pennyweights, two candlefticks, the gift of Mr. John Gibbs, fenr. 1717.

The vicars of St. Thomas are the fame as thofe of Redcliff, to which it is a chapel.

The collection for the vicar annually amounts to about 90l.

BENEFACTORS to the Church and Poor of St. Thomas's Parifh.

Benefactors to St. Thomas's almfhoufe in the Long-row.

1292, Mr. Simon Burton, five times mayor of this city, founded this almfhoufe for fixteen perfons. (He is buried therein.)

1530, Thomas White, Efq; fome time mayor, gave 4s. per month for ever to the poor therein.

1547, Mr. John Sprint gave 3s. 4d. on Good Friday for ever.

1566, Mr. Thomas Silk gave 3s. at Eafter and 3s. at Chriftmas for ever.

1550, William Pyckes, Efq; fome time mayor, gave 6l. 13s. 4d. per annum for ever, to be diftributed to the poor of the almfhoufe.

1634, Matthew Warren, Efq; fome time mayor, gave 10s. on the fecond Sunday in Lent for ever.

1647, Mr. John Cox gave 10s. on St. John's-day for ever.

Mr. Robert Wory, of London, a native of this parifh, gave 5l. per annum, to be paid on the 1ft day of May, Auguft, November, and the 2d of February by equal proportions yearly for ever.

1669, Edward Morgan, Efq; fome time mayor and alderman of this city, gave 12d. per week to the poor in bread for ever, out of his lands at Pitnell at Tockington, in the county of Glocefter.

1670, Sir William Penn, Knight, gave 30l. the profit thereof for ever to the poor of this parifh.

1672, Mr. James Brathwayte, fon-in-law of Mr. Richard Crumpe, gave 10l. to the ufe of the poor on the 22d of October for ever.

1673, Mr. Chriftopher Brinfden gave 30l. the profit thereof to the minifter for a fermon 10s. to the clerk 2s. 6d. to the fexton 1s. 6d. and the reft to the poor, on St. Bartholomew's-day or the 24th of Auguft for ever.

1674, Mr. Edward Grant gave 30l. the profit thereof to the poor houfekeepers of this parifh at Chriftmas for ever.

1677,

1677, Mr. James Friend gave 20l. the profit thereof in equal diſtributions to four ſick families yearly for ever.

1680, Mr. Samuel Wharton, ſome time ſheriff of this city, gave 20s. to be equally diſtributed to four poor houſe-holders or widows, not re_ceiving weekly alms, on St. Thomas's-day yearly for ever.

1683, Mr. Nathaniel Webb, grocer, and member of the common council, gave 20l. the profit thereof to the poor at Michaelmas yearly for ever.

1684, Mr. Michael Hunt, ſoap-maker, a member of the common council, gave 20l. theprofit thereof to the poor at Michaelmas yearly for ever.

Mr. Richard Brayfield, grocer, gave 10l. the profit thereof to four houſe-holders at Chriſtmas yearly for ever.

1685, Mr. Robert Amberſon, gentleman, gave 100l. the profit thereof to ſix poor houſe-holders, not receiving alms, yearly for ever.

1686, Mr. Samuel Hale, merchant, gave 10l. the profit thereof to the poor in bread weekly for ever; and alſo the intereſt of 230l. towards the placing apprentices of poor children in ſeven pariſhes of this city yearly for ever, of which this pariſh is one.

1687, Mr. Charles Herbert, of this city, grocer, gave 10l. the profit thereof to the poor of this pariſh yearly for ever.

1691, Mr. Robert Wory, citizen of London, born in this pariſh, gave 100l. the profit thereof to the poor in the almſhouſe yearly for ever.

1693, Mr. James Seward gave 10l. the profit to be diſpoſed of to the poor on Sunday for ever.

1695, Mr. Edmund Laggat, of Chew Stoke, gave 20l. the profit to the poor of this pariſh for ever.

1699, Mr. John Gore, gent. gave 20l. the profit thereof, viz. during his life 12s. to four of the moſt aged perſons in the almſhouſe two men and two women, and 12s. to four houſekeepers (poor and not receiving alms) and after his deceaſe to eight like poor houſekeepers on St. John's-day yearly for ever.

1701, Mr. John Worgan, wine-cooper, gave 50l. the profit thereof to the poor, of which this pariſh hath 32s. per annum for eight houſe-keepers, viz. 4s. each on the 29th of September for ever.

1706, Mr. John Hipſley, of this pariſh, gave 40l. the profit, viz. 20s. per annum to the miniſter for catechiſing the children and reading prayers on week days, and 20s. per annum to four poor ſick families of this pariſh for ever.

1709, December 20, Sir Thomas Day, Knight, born in this pariſh, ſome time member of parliament and twice mayor and elder alderman of this

city, gave 10l. to the poor in bread at his funeral, and 30l. the profit thereof to the poor in bread weekly for ever; and 50l. more towards rebuilding the almfhoufe in the Long-row.

1714, Mr. Charles Jones, of this parifh, foap-maker, gave 20l. the profit
thereof to the poor of this parifh for ever.

1716, Jofeph Jackfon, Efq; fome time alderman of this city, gave 40s. a year
for ever, 10s. of it to be paid every quarter to a poor burgefs or burgefs's widow of this parifh.

1737, Mr. Edward Dowell, late of this city, gave 100l. the profit thereof to
forty poor houfe-holders of this parifh on St. Thomas's-day yearly
for ever.

Mrs. Lydia Williams, late of this city, widow, gave 100l. the profit
thereof to eight poor widows of this parifh, not receiving alms, on
the 18th of October yearly for ever.

Mr. George Bridges, late of this parifh, diftiller, gave 10l. the profit
thereof to the poor yearly for ever.

Mr. Samuel Nelmes, late of this parifh, diftiller, gave 10l. the profit
thereof to the poor in the almfhoufe in coal on St. Thomas's-day
yearly for ever.

1724, Mr. John Newman, plumber, gave 20l. the profit thereof in bread to
the poor of this parifh on Sundays for ever.

1726, Mrs. Althea Hopkins gave 20l. the profit thereof to four fick families
of this parifh, not receiving alms, quarterly for ever, at the diferetion of the churchwardens.

1727, Mr. Matthew Worgan gave 40l. the profit thereof to eight poor families of this parifh, not receiving alms on the 28th of October for
ever.

1730, Mr. Morris Thomas gave 20l. the intereft to the poor in bread on the
1ft of March for ever.

1785, Mr. T. Lewis gave 20l. the intereft thereof in coals yearly for ever.

1651, Mrs. Julian Stibbins gave 20s. to the poor yearly for ever.

1656, Mr. Chriftopher Tovey gave 20l. the profit thereof weekly to the poor
for ever.

Mr. George Hellier, alderman, gave 40l. the profit thereof 10s. yearly
for a fermon, the reft for ever to the poor in bread.

1658, Mr. Samuel Hellier gave 10l. the profit thereof weekly to the poor in
bread for ever.

Mr. Thomas Longman gave 30s. upon St. Thomas's-day to fix houfekeepers yearly for ever.

1659,

1659, Edmund Denton, in the county of Buckingham, Efq; and Elizabeth his wife, daughter of Sir Richard Rogers, Knight, gave 45l. to the poor of this parifh for ever, the profit of which is to be diftributed to them in bread weekly.

Mr. George Longman, of London, fon of Mr. Thomas Longman, of this parifh, gave 50l. the profit thereof to be difpofed of as followeth: 20s. for a fermon, the clerk 5s. the fexton 2s. 6d. and the reft of the intereft to be given in bread to the poor on the 14th of February yearly for ever.

1679, Mrs. Mary Boucher and Mrs. Jane Langton, widows, gave lands for the payment of 10s. apiece to 52 widows of this city yearly for ever, of which this parifh hath a part. N. B. The lands were purchafed in 1679.

1567, Mr. Walter Weft gave 20s. yearly to the poor for ever.

1620, Thomas Hobbin gave 4l. 10s. to be diftributed yearly for ever to the poor at Chriftmas, and 10s. for a fermon.

1626, Chriftopher Woodward gave 10s. yearly for ever to the poor, and 10s. for a fermon.

1630, Mr. Ralph Farmer gave 1s. per week in bread for twenty years.

Mr. Robert Kitchen gave 20s. to two houfekeepers yearly for ever. Paid by the chamberlain of Briftol.

1632, 1635, Sir Richard Rogers and Mr. Robert Rogers gave 2s. 8d. per week in bread to the poor for ever.

1634, Mrs. Eleanor Woodward gave 10s. yearly for ever.

Mr. Matthew Warren the elder gave 10l. for a ftock to the ufe of the poor for ever, and 10s. yearly to the almfhoufe.

1639, Mr. William Pitt, of this parifh, merchant, gave 30l. in land to the poor for ever.

Mr. George Harrington gave 20s. to two poor houfe-holders yearly for ever. Paid by the chamberlain of Briftol.

1642, Mrs. Mary Stile, widow, gave 10l. the profit yearly to the poor for ever.

1661, Mr. Francis Gleed, fome time fheriff, gave 10s. a quarter to a poor houfe-holder.

1667, Mr. John Pope, aldermen, gave 10s. for a fermon, and 20s. per annum to the poor of this parifh on the 5th of November yearly for ever.

1668, Mr. Michael Deyos, merchant, gave 40s. per annum in bread and coals to four poor widows for ever.

1668, Mr. Anthony Farmer, alderman, gave 40l. the profit thereof to be diſtributed on All Saints-day to fix poor families of this pariſh for ever, the heads thereof to be freemen of this city.

GIFT-SERMONS to be preached in St. Thomas's church.

New Year's-day, Mr. C. Woodward's.
St. George's-day, Mr. Geo. Benſon's.
Eaſter Monday, Sir R. Rogers, Knt.
Tueſday in Rogation week, Mrs. Eleanor Woodward's.
Whit Tueſday, Mrs. Julian Shuter's.
St. Thomas's-day, Mr. Tho. Holbin's.
Chriſtmas-day, Mr. George Hellier's, alderman.

Innocents-day, Mr. Robert Rogers's, alderman.
Firſt Sunday after All Saints-day, Mr. John Pope's, alderman.
The ſecond Sunday in Lent, Mr. Matthew Warren's.
February 14, Mr. George Longman's.
Bartholomew's-day, Mr. Chriſtopher Brimſden's.

In this pariſh was an almſhouſe, erected by Simon de Burton about the year 1292. Leland, vol. vii. p. 89. mentions it: " The almeſehowſe by Seynt Thomas churche is called Burtons Almſhowſe. Burton maior of the towne and founder is buried in it." It was rebuilt at the expence of the pariſh.

Thomas Silk 1566 gave yearly 1l. 1s. Walter Weſt 1567 gave 15s. yearly. William Picks or Pikes, mercer, by will 1551 gave 6l. 13s. 4d. to ariſe out of land purchaſed by his executors, and veſted in the corporation that the chamberlain ſhould pay that ſum yearly to the ſixteen poor of this houſe. Thomas White gave them 2l. 8s. per annum by the chamberlain. Robert Wory gave 5l. per annum by the churchwardens. The reſt of their maintenance they receive from St. Peter's Hoſpital, the general poor houſe of the city.

The ſaid William Picks gave this pariſh alfo 20l. " towards fetching home of the water to St. Thomas's pipe." To this others had been contributors, particularly John Stokes 1381, who by will ordered to be buried in this church in St. Mary's chapel, and " bequeathed money towards the new work of bringing water from Redcliff and Temple-gate to the church of St. Thomas in a leaden conduit." But afterwards by an agreement with the veſtry of Redcliff, and a ſmall yearly gratuity, and being at the joint expence of repairing the Redcliff pipes when out of order, this work was placed on a permanent footing ; and the inhabitants are ſupplied with water here whenever it flows at Redcliff, being brought thence in leaden pipes.

In

In 1570 William Tucker, draper, then mayor, did at his own great charges purchafe a market to be kept in St. Thomas-ftreet on Thurfday throughout the year.

In the grant of Queen Elizabeth of St. Thomas-ftreet market, 11 December, the 13th year of her reign, the poverty of the inhabitants and ruinous ftate of the houfes there are mentioned as reafons for granting the inhabitants the privileges of a market: " Cum nobis detur intelligi, &c. i. e. Since it is made known to us by the mayor and commonalty that not only the ftreet cal-led St. Thomas-ftreet, but alfo the houfes, ftructures, and edifices in it are reduced to ruin and decay, to the great nuifance of that part of the city; and that the late inhabitants being forced by want, through the decay of their trade of making woollen cloths have fuffered their houfes to go to ruin; and that a certain almfhoufe fituated near the faid ftreet for the fupport of many poor, and alfo a certain canal or pipe of water fituated there which be-yond the memory of man has been fupported and maintained chiefly by the faid inhabitants, are now in fuch a flate on account of their poverty, that in a fhort time they will come to extreme ruin, if a remedy be not provided, &c. We therefore confidering the premifes, as alfo that the faid mayor and com-monalty and inhabitants of the faid ftreet may be the better able to fupport and maintain as well the faid houfes and buildings in the faid ftreet, as the aforefaid almfhoufe and pipe of water, have granted of our free grace, &c. to the faid mayor and commonalty and their fucceffors, that they may have one market every Thurfday (die jovis) in each week in the faid ftreet of St. Thomas for yarn, wool, (averiis) cattle, and all other things: and we grant to the afore-faid mayor and commonalty and their fucceffors all flallage, picage, toll, and cuftoms of the faid market with their appurtenances, alfo the toll and weighing of yarn, wool, and other things, &c. and all other ufual profits of a market." Page 80 of the Great White Book of Briftol.

This grant being obtained, Michael Soudley, apothecary, with the reft of the veftry, builded the market place and a kind of tolfey the whole breadth of the church in front, with a flat covering of lead fupported by pillars of free-ftone, and round it were afterwards pofts with brafs caps for telling money or writing upon, on which were the dates and names of the donors, Thomas Day, Efq; 1691, Nathaniel Day his fon 1691, John Gore, of Knowle, gent. 1691, Robert Stevens, of Knowle, gent. 1691, Nicholas Baly, foap-maker, 1691; but thefe with the erection were all removed in the year 1781.

The Wool-hall there feems to have been built at the fame time, having the arms of Queen Elizabeth upon it. That the parifh might have the benefit of of this market, the feoffees of this church purchafed the fame with all its

profits

profits from the corporation, and paffed away certain houfes in Wine-ftreet, being St. Thomas church land, to the ufe of the chamber, where were afterwards erected a meal or corn market and two new houfes in their room; but the churchwardens of St. Thomas were obliged by covenant to pay the corporation 20s. a year rent for the royalties of the market, and 2s. 6d. for fuit to Temple Fee out of feveral tenements, alfo 5s. per annum for the fheep market. The market was then proclaimed in form to be holden the firft time the Thurfday after Lady-day, the 13th of Elizabeth, and fo for ever to continue.

CHAP. XXIV.

Of the CHURCH and PARISH of St. MARY-REDCLIFF.

REDCLIFF (Radcclivia, Ruber Clivus) with St. Thomas and Temple parifhes, like Southwark in London, lie on the fouth fide of the city and of the river. All ancient deeds agree in proving its antiquity, then part of the manor of Bedminfter. But Leland mentions it (in Cygrn. Cant.) " as being added to the city after the bridge was built, and being furrounded with a ftrong wall, when William Earl of Glocefter governed this province and city." And Camden very erroneoufly calls Redcliff, " fome little houfes belonging to the fuburbs, joined to the reft of the city by a ftone bridge."

In the year 789 the Saxon King Brightricus, or Bithrick, is faid to have erected a church of " durable ftone, goodlye to beholde," alfo a pallace, of both which at prefent not the leaft traces are to be feen to afcertain their fite. But in an old vellum roll (penes me) is the following fhort account of it: " Ynne dolvynge wythynne the walle was foundo in the howfe of Johannes Cofhe in Radcleve-ftreet a parchmente in whych was wroten the accounte of Brythrycus pallace called Rudhalle wyth the walles of Radcleve :"

Alfo of " the auntyaunte gate of Saynte Marye ybuylden by Kyuge Bythrycus in the year DCCXXXXXXXXIX; as itte flooden in daies of Edwarde Confeffoure;" it was preferved in a rude drawing, being embattled at top, and adorned with two fhields with a crofs patee on each fide of the window, and the

the fame on each fide of the top of the arch, where was to be feen the foot of a portcullis to let down.

The fame Weft Saxon King Britrick is faid alfo to have built "the afforcia-ments crafen afterwards by the Danes."—Of all thefe buildings of antiquity there are however at prefent no remains.—The old gate of Redcliff has been taken down, and rebuilt in an elegant manner in 1730; and this laft alfo to render the ftreet more commodious was taken down in the year 1772.

The old chronicles of Briftol (in the city chamber and others) mention a church built to our Lady at Redcliff by Sir Simon de Burton, under the year 1294. An old church there before tending to ruin had feveral grants of land by will made towards repairing it, fome of which are dated fo early as the year 1207, 1229, 1230, a proof of the old church afore-mentioned being erected before Sir Simon de Burton's:—there are alfo feveral original indulgences (penes me) granted by feveral bifhops with relaxation of penance on certain conditions, viz. that "they would devoutly vifit the church of the Bleffed Mary of Redcliff in Briftol, and there charitably contribute towards the repair of the fame, and pray for the fouls of thofe there interred;" the foul of Helen de Wedmore is in one particularly to be prayed for, whofe body is there buried as mentioned in the indulgence, one of which bears date Briftol 1232, being granted by John Bifhop of Ardfert; another by Peter Quivil Bifhop of Exeter, dated at Radeclyve 1287; another by David Archbifhop of Gaffel, dated at Briftol in the firft year of his confecration 1246;* another by Chriftian Epifcopus Hymelacenfis, dated at Briftol 1246, in the year of his pontificate; and another by Robert Bifhop of Bath and Wells, dated 4 kalend. of November 1278, in the fourth year of his confecration. Thefe were all found in Canynge's cheft over the north porch of the prefent church of Red-cliff: as they were granted towards promoting the repairs of the fabrick of a church here then in ruins, they undeniably prove that there was a church here dedicated to the Bleffed Mary of Redcliff long before the time of that mentioned to be built by Sir Simon de Burton, fuppofed to be the firft founder of a church here.

The

* Omnibus ad quos prefens fcriptum pervenerit : Chriftianus Dei gratiâ Hymelacenfis Epifcopus falutem æternam in domino : de mifericordia Dei Omnipotentis et Gloriofæ Virginis genetricis ejus & omnium fanctorum meritis plenius confidentes omnibus confeffis & vere penitentibus qui caufa venerationis & orationis ecclefiam beatæ Mariæ de Redclive pie & devote vifitaverint nec non de bonis fibi a deo conceffis ad reparationem ejufdem ecclefiæ alequid caritative contulerint atque pro animabus quorum corpora ibidem requiefcunt oraverint de injuncta fibi pænitentiâ decem dies relaxamus—datum apud Briftolliam Anno Gratiæ MCCXLVI, pontificatus noftri Anno.

The following account of Sir Symon de Byrtonne, and of his being a founder of a church at Redcliff, is tranfcribed from a parchment manufcript of Rowley's, communicated by Chatterton :

" Symonne de Byrtonne eldeft foune of Syrre Baldwynus de Byrtonne was borne on the eve of the annunciation M.C.C.XXXXXXXV. hee was defyrabelle of afpeft and in hys yowthe much yeven to Tourneyeynge, and M.C.C.XXXXXXXX at Wyncheftre yule games won mycklé honnoure, he abftaynyd from marryage, he was myckle learned & ybuylded a houfe in the Yle of Wyghte after fafhyon of a pallayfe royaul goodlye to behoulde wyth carvelly'd pyllars on whych was thys ryme wroten : Fulle nobille is thys Kyngelie howfe and eke fulle nobille thee, echone is for the other fytte as faynftes for heaven bee. Hee ever was fullen of almefdeeds and was of the poore beloved : in M.C.C.LXXXV Kynge Edwarde * kepte hys Chryftmaffe at Bryghtftowe and proceeded agaynfte the Welchmenne ebroughtenne manye ftronge and dowgh-tee knyghts, amongft whom were Syrre Ferrars Nevylle, Geoffroie Freeman, Clymar Percie, Heldebrand Gournie, Ralph Mohun, Syr Lyfter Percie, and Edgare Knyvet, knyghtes of renowne, who eftablifhed a three days joufte on Saynfte Maryes Hylle : Syrre Ferrars Nevylle appeared dyghte in ruddy armoure bearyng a rampaunte lyon Gutte de Sangue, agaynfte hym came Syr Gervayfe Teyfdylle who bearyd a launce iffuynge proper but was quycklie overthrowen : then appeared Leonarde Ramfey who had a honde iffuante holdeynge a bloudie fwerde peercynge a couronne wyth a fheelde peafcnue wyth fylver ; hee ranne twayne tyltes but Neville thrown hym on the thyrde rencountre : then dyd the aforefayd Syrre Symonne de Byrtonne avow that if he overthrowen Syrre Ferrars Nevylle, he woulde there crefte & buylde a chyrche to owre Ladye : allgate there ftoode anigh Lamyngtonnes Ladies chamber : hee then encountred vygoroufly and bore Syrre Ferrars horfe and man to the grounde remaynynge konynge, viftore knyght of the Joufte, ande fettynge atte the ryghte honde of K. Edwarde. Inne M.CCLXXXXI hee per-formed hys vowen ybuylden a godelye chyrch from a patterne of St. Ofwaldes Abbyes Chyrche and the day of our Lordes natyvyty M.C.CCI, Gylbert de Sante Leonfardoe Byfhope of Chycheftre dyd dedicate it to the Holic Vyrgynne Marye moder of Godde."†

Though

* This circumftance is proved by our old chronicles under the year 1285, " Rex Edw. 1. per Walliam progrediens occidentalem intravit Glamorganciam, quæ ad Comitem Gloveruiæ nofcitur pertinere : Rex dein Briftolliam veniens feftum Dominicæ nativitatis co Anno ibi tenuit."

† The poem of the Tournament in the printed collection of Rowley's poems feems to bear fome relation to this account of Sir Symon de Bourton, which if genuine muft tend to confirm the authenticity of that poem.

. Though other proofs cannot be produced at prefent concerning thefe particular anecdotes of the life of Sir Symon de Burton, yet it is moft certain from
indubitable records, that he was a citizen of Briftol of the greateft eminence
and rank in it, had been chofen mayor fix times (vid. annals below for the
years 1291, 1292, 1294, 1296, 1303, 1304,) of great wealth and renown,
and a very bountiful benefa&or there, having ere&ed an almfhoufe about 1292
in the Long-Row, in the parifh of St. Thomas, where Leland fays he was
buried, and the almfhoufe rebuilt ftill retains his name. I find his arms
blazoned thus: f. azure, a crefcent within a bordure or. by the name of
Burton: by others thus, azure a fefs between three talbots heads erafed or.

This church of de Burton's feems not to have been completed, or to have
obtained very large endowments, for a manufcript (Hobfon's) fays, " Simon
de Burton, mayor in 1294, had two years before began to build Redcliff
church, but he lived not to finifh it, which afterwards William Cannynges did,
and gave lands to repair it for ever."

Whether the church was dedicated for religious offices before it was finifhed,
and was left to be completed afterwards is worthy of enquiry, for it can be
proved that in the year 1376 (fee the mayor's calendar) " William Cannynges
built the body of Redcliff church from the crofs aile downwards, and fo the
church was finifhed as it is now." This was but 75 years after the dedication
of Burton's church, fo that it may be prefumed to be the completing that which
was begun and partly built by him; efpecially as it was their cuftom in all large
works of this kind " to lay out the plan, build part, and leave it to be completed by their fucceffors in future times.* They ufually began at the eaft
end or choir part, which when finifhed was confecrated, and the remainder
carried on as far as they were able." Such large buildings required great
expences as well as long time, and great labour to finifh them, at an æra too
when money was fcarce and many good workmen not eafily procured. As a
confirmation of this, in feveral wills dated about the year 1380 &c. (for the
church muft have taken many years to be completed) money is often given to
the fabrick and repairing of Redcliff church.† This William Canynges was
for the fixth time mayor of Briftol in the year 1389, a merchant of great
fortune, weight and refpe& among his fellow-citizens; in a ftation of life fitted
to be a leading man, and to have the chara&er of a founder of fuch a work,
promoted no doubt by donations by will and voluntary contributions of other

Z z z   devout

* Vid. Bentham's Hiftory of the Church of Ely.

† One will dated 1388, of John Muleward, mentions a gift in money, " ad opus beatæ Mariæ
de Redeclyve:" which fhews the work was then going on.

devout and well-difpofed people, as well as by grants and indulgences from the bifhops of thofe days. He lived to the year 1396, when the church was probably finifhed.

But this church erected at fo much coft, and that had been fo long time in building, was at St. Paul's tide 1445-6 fo much damaged in a ftorm of thunder and lightning, that the lofty fpire or fteeple was thrown down, and falling upon the body of the church injured it fo much, that it was almoft ruinous. The manufcript accounts of·this are related nearly in the fame manner, in two very ancient ones it is recorded, " 1445, at St. Paul's tide was very tempftuous weather, by which Redcliff fteeple was overthrown in a thunder clap, doing great harme to the churche by the fall thereof, but by the good devotion of Mr. William Canynges it was reedified to his everlafting prayfe."—Another, though differing in the year, fays in 1442, (the year Mr. William Canynges was mayor,) " This William Cannynges wyth the helpe of others of the worfhipfulle towne of Briftol kepte mafons and workmenne to edifie, repayre, cover and glaze the church of Redcliff, which his grandfather had founded in the days of Edward the 3d."—In another thus : " William Canynges reedified and enlarged the church of Redcliff almoft deftroyed by lightning in 1445, in fo exquifite a manner, that he has ever fince paffed for the founder thereof, and he afterwards gave 500l. to keep it in repair."—Here we have a fecond William Canynge, fon of John and the grandfon of William, for a founder, which will fettle the doubts that have arifen about *his* being the fole original founder of this church.—There was one here before Burton had began, and Canynge's grandfather had completed this.—Leland fays of St. Sprite's chapel, " this ons a paroche before the buildyng of Redcliff greate new chyrche." Whether this or another, may be a little uncertain : one there certainly was, long before the year 1200, as is proved by old deeds. That the laft William Canynges was affifted by his fellow-citizens contributing towards this great work is very probable; that he kept a great number of carpenters and mafons at work as above-mentioned is proved by William Botoner, p. 99, where he fays, " habuit operarios, carpentarios, mafones &c. omni Dei C. homines:" and p. 191, he mentions " the houfes of the workmen in freeftone for the foundation of Redcliff church," " as fituated near the chambers of Cannynges priefts."—All this tends to prove what part the laft William Canynges had in building or rebuilding Redcliff church to entitle him to the name of a founder, as he has been generally and defervedly efteemed.—The fame plan was ob-ferved by him in rebuilding and reftoring it to its original beauty after being thrown down by the lightning; the fouth aile, where the mifchief fell heavieft,

feems

feems to have been rebuilt with a fomewhat more elevated arch and in a lighter ftyle than the north ; a difference alfo is between the windows of the north and fouth aile.—The fall of fuch a large and very high fteeple upon the church muft have done great injury, and deftroyed every thing wherever it fell.

That Mr. Canynges was a great builder farther appears from his erections afterwards at the college of Weftbury, of which he is called Renovator & quafi alter fundator ; famofus & egregius vir, magnæ induftriæ & circum-fpectionis, & inter æteros fpecialiffimus benefactor ecclefiæ de Redcliff: (in a deed dated 1474 he is fo called.)—He was the chief promoter of the work, the principal and "moſt fpecial" benefactor to it; he was then the wealthieft and wifeft (ditiffimus & fapientiffimus, as William Botoner, p. 83, calls him,) for fuch an undertaking: his piety and devotion excited him to profecute, and his great riches enabled him to complete it: and whatever others might have con-tributed towards it, the whole feems to have been under his moft judicious conduct and management, as he was confeffedly the chief man of the city and moft capable of fo grand a work.—Regard to his anceftors muft alfo have been a powerful motive with him, as it was renewing and reinftating a work his grandfather had fignalized himfelf in completing ; which feems to be implied in one of his deeds, wherein he fays concerning his benefactions to this church, "ut piæ voluntas antecefforum meorum &c." "that the pious will of my anceftors &c. might be obferved &c." and as to his piety and devout turn of mind, it cannot fo well be feen as in his own words, in a deed dated the 6th of Edward the 4th. for eftablifhing the chauntry of St. Catherine in this church.*

The following deed concerning a grant of money to the friers minor of this city for their better fupport fhews his pious and charitable difpofition: " Be it known unto all men, that the 29th of November in the year 1465, we the guardian and friers minor all of the convent of Briftol there dwelling, confi-dering the affection of pure devotion of the worfhipful man William Canynges which he daily fhews to the order of our feraphick father St. Francis and efpecially to our convent aforefaid in exhibiting his alms and manifold benefits long fince conferred upon us, and in future to be beftowed—for out of his pious

Z z z 2   charity

* Cum ego Willielmus Canynges mercator villæ Briftolliæ, per quam plurimos annorum curriculos fecularibus negotiis multiformiter explicatus honefto cum labore mercatorio rem augere domefticam induftriofe curaverim, imminente mihi tandem debilitate fæculi animadvertens tam mundiales profperos orbis quam gloriam & fplendorem inftabiles & fictitios quali ictu oculi multoties evanefcere, fummamque felicitatem in rebus cæleftibus Dei complacentiâ in fui divini cultús augmento aliifque operibus Caritatum ad animorum fidelium medelam perfiftere concernens, &c. fundandi cantariam perpetuam litteras patentes regias impetravi &c.

charity for the relief of the faid convent he has faithfully given and paid to the fame convent twenty pounds on the year and day aforementioned.—By tenor of thefe prefents with licence of Frier Thomas Radnor then minifter of England we have promifed and granted to the faid William Canynges and Joanna his wife that their names be infcribed in the gift-book (datario) of our convent among the chief benefactors of the faid convent, and that they be recommended as the cuftom is; and we have further promifed and granted to the faid William Canynges and Joanna his wife, that' their obit the fecond feftival next after St. Peter every year in the church of our faid convent fhall be folemnly celebrated with exequiis mortuorum and mafs of requiem by note for the foul of the faid William Canynges and Joanna his wife, of John Canynges and Joanna his wife father and mother of the faid William Canynges, of John Milton and Joanna his wife and for the fouls for whom it is bound to pray and of all the faithful departed, and fince from the teftimony of Chrift in the gofpel, the workman is worthy of his hire the aforefaid William loving his own foul and mindful of the words of Chrift hath ordained and appointed by himfelf, his heirs and executors to the brothers of the faid convent every year for ever on the day aforefaid as well in his life time as after his death in recompence of their labours One quarter of an ox of the value of forty pence four quarters of a good fheep of the price and value of fixteen pence Englifh money and forty pence in pure money to be given for bread and ale; that therefore the faid promife and grant may be fo confirmed as not to be broken, I Frier Thomas minifter of England in virtue of that holy obedience to all the guardians and friers of the aforementioned convent prefent and future do command that they folemnly celebrate as well in their life time as after their death when it comes the exequies for the dead with mafs of requiem every year on the faid day for the fouls of the faid William and Joanna his wife and of all the abovementioned and moreover that they caufe this to be read in the chapterhoufe by the friers there gathered together once in the year namely on the vigil or day of nativity of the bleffed St. Francis.: In witnefs of this grant and promife the feal of my office together with the feal of the keeper of the cuftody of Briftol and convent of Briftol is openly appendant—Done, read and fealed at Briftol before the friers of the aforementioned convent in their chapterhoufe met the day and year abovewritten."—The feal is very curious, exhibiting feveral figures well engraved ftanding, one kneeling about to be killed with a fword held up, the original deed in latin penes me.

Mr. Canynge's family had long flourifhed here as the wealthieft merchants and principal men of the city; his grandfather William had been fix times, his

his father John bayliff and mayor, and himself five times mayor.—But the principal thing for which William Canynges the son of John is celebrated, is the part he had in re-edifying and repairing the church of Redcliff thrown down in a storm of thunder and lightning.

This church has received the general approbation, and attracted the applause and admiration of all good judges ; though large and spacious, it has a light and airy appearance ; the pillars neat and slender, not over large and massy. It is sufficiently ornamented, yet not crowded with little parts and mean decorations, broke every where and divided into small pieces, scarce perceivable by the eye. The high embowed roof, being a solid arch of freestone, is lofty and grand, and adorned at the meeting of the ribs of the several little arches with curious twists and knots, scarce one alike. Over this is a wooden roof for the leaden covering 6 feet betwixt the two in height.

This church is built on a red sandy rock or cliff, from which it derives its name. The ascent to this stately structure (on the north-west side) is by steps most of them being 18 feet long, sufficient to admit twelve men abreast, which were new laid with Purbeck stone in 1753, and ornamented with a rail and a handsome balustrade of freestone, as is also the western side of the churchyard. In length the whole church with the Lady chapel is 239 feet, and from north to south of the great cross ailes is 117 feet ; the breadth of the three cross ailes is 44 feet, the breadth of the body and two side ailes is 59 feet ; the height of the two north and south ailes from east to west is 25 feet, which is also the height of the two side cross ailes ; the height of the middle cross aile is 54 feet, equal to which is the height of the middle aile from the west door to the high altar. The length of the middle aile together with those of the north and south are all equal 197 feet from the west end to the high altar, behind which is the Lady chapel, being in length 42 feet and in breadth 24, in height 26 feet. The whole roof of the church throughout is artificially vaulted with good stone, supported with twelve curious freestone pillars on each side the body of the church, and eight on each side supporting the great cross aile. The whole workmanship is so exquisite, as also its arched foundation on the north prospect, which adds to its height, strength, and largeness, with the adjoining chapel of our Lady at the east end, that it may justly be esteemed one of the most elegant parish churches in England. The whole building makes the form of a cross, and is all covered with lead. The tower which is at the west end of the north aile is in height 148 feet, (which most loftily sheweth itself as an eminent and noble land mark to all the adjacent parts.) In it hang a curious peal of eight bells, which were new cast in the year 1762. In the year 1445-6, about

St.

St. Paul's tide, the fteeple was thrown down in a violent ftorm of thunder and lightning, and though not yet rebuilt, it is hoped will one day be reftored to its former height and beauty by fome well-difpofed perfons or at the veftry's expence.

The entrance into the church is at the great weft door, to which you afcend by fteps. The door is 8 feet in breadth and 12 high, within which is built a great ftone gallery, on which is a grand magnificent organ being in all 53 feet high from the ground to the top of the crown pannel; the great cafe about 20 feet fquare contains one great and leffer organ; the mufical part was executed by Meffrs. Harris and Pyfield, and the whole coft 846l. 7s. Entering at this weftern door you are ftruck with a view of the whole length of the middle aile at once, terminated by the chancel and altar, the height of the curioufly arched roof, the rows of flender lofty pillars on each fide, and the great length makes this a moft advantageous view. There are alfo two leffer doors, one on the north and the other on the fouth fide of the church, over each is a large porch with a room over. The north door was defigned to be the grand entrance, being full of Gothic work nitches for figures of faints and kings, wherein formerly in the days of Popery was the poor's charity-box and an " image of our Lady decorated with a fyne clothe with frynge to cover her," whence this was called, " Capella Beatæ Mariæ in portico ecclefiæ de Redclive," to which Maud Efterfield in 1491 gave a ring. This north porch is a moft fingular Gothic ftruĉture, and feems in proportion and fhape different from the reft of the church; and is probably older and part of the ancient fabric, which being deftroyed by the fall of the fpire in the year 1445, this curious porch efcaped the general ruin and was left ftanding, and now makes a part of the prefent ftruĉture. It appears not to be built at the fame time by the walls not uniting above and fitly agreeing with the reft.

In the year 1754, January 30, were difcovered, upon digging a grave in this porch, two freeftone fepulchres with the fkeletons of two perfons compleat, the bones lying in their natural order.

In the year 1709 in Queen Ann's reign the church was new pewed and beautified by a brief, which rofe 1482l. expences 697l. 7s. neat 784l. 13s. of which Mr. Gollton gave 100l. at which time the altar-piece was taken down, and a moft magnificent one erected at the breadth of one arch farther to the eaftward, which was formerly the paffage behind the altar which opened a communication between the north and fouth ailes, in the middle of which paffage was the entrance at two folding doors into the Lady's chapel. But at this time the entrance into it is at the eaft corner of the fouth aile taken out of the churchyard.

churchyard. The high altar had curious paintings of Mofes with his rod, Aaron in his robes, St. Peter and Paul, with other decorations.

But the altar and chancel were repaired in the year 1757, and three fine paintings put up againft the fronting Gothic eaft window and the two fides of the chancel, done by the fkilful hand of the late ingenious Mr. Hogarth, who had five hundred guineas for them out of the church ftock, but the whole with the frames, alterations, putting up, &c. coft 761l. os. 1d. The middle piece which is much the largeft reprefents the Afcenfion of our Saviour, who is feen high in the air. The emanation of rays from the afcending Deity, beaming through the interftices of the furrounding clouds, is managed with tendernefs and delicacy. The point of time, which the painter has chofen, is immediately after he has difappeared from the fpectators below. In the fore ground on the right fide at the bottom, St. Thomas is reprefented on one knee, and with hands lifted up and clafped together, is ftill eagerly looking upwards with an expreffion of wonder and adoration. On the othe fide is St. Peter in a reelining pofture. Towards the middle is St. John, who, with a group of figures fuppofed to be the other difciples more remote from the eye, is liftening attentively to the two men in white, who appeared upon that great occafion. The back ground is fhut up with rocks and the bottom of the cloudy mafs, except on one fide, where under the fkirts of the low-hanging clouds part of a magnificent city (fuppofed to be Jerufalem) appears to advantage, a long flafh of forked lightning under a darkened fky cafting a livid gloom over it, as a city devoted to deftruction. The fide piece on the right hand of this large picture reprefents the rolling of the ftone to clofe the fepulchre, and the fealing of it in the prefence of the high-prieft. The labour and exertion naturally expreffed in the ftrong mufcular men is happily contrafted by the tendernefs and elegant foftnefs confpicuous in the other fide piece, where the three Marys are come to vifit the empty fepulchre. The angel who is fpeaking to them, and pointing up to heaven with an expreffion that explains itfelf, is a figure of fingular beauty, and, with an afpect of great fweetnefs and benevolence, ftill retains in his look the native dignity of a fuperior being.

Under the picture on each fide the altar is a large Bible difplayed in painting, as opened at thofe places of fcripture which defcribe the biftory exhibited in the paintings, and the whole altar-piece is neatly embellifhed, and the colours fo kept down that they do not take off the eye from the principal pictures.

The floor of the chancel is laid with black and white marble, and you approach the altar by fteps of the fame marble. At the entrance of the chancel

are

are iron gates gilt and painted and finely ornamented ; the fame are alfo at the entrance of each aile of the church.

In the center of the middle and crofs ailes is fixed a pillar and an eagle on the top all of brafs, about 5 feet high, being the gift of Mr. James Walker, feur. of this parifh, pin-maker. — The propriety of which may be thus explain-ed: that " the eagle, the facred bird, carrying the book of infpiration, is employed to a purpofe more honourable and falutary, than when it was fup-pofed to be carrying thunder through the air for the ufe of the heathen Jupiter."

Facing the pulpit is a noble large feat for the magiftrates of the city, over which is a canopy of wood fupported with four carved pillars. In this place in the year 1466 Mr. William Canynges founded a chapel and chauntry, which was dedicated to the honour of God and St. George. He alfo founded ano-' other to the honour of God and St. Catherine, which is faid in a deed to be at the eaft end of the church, others fay at the north porch : but the altar of St. Catherine was at the fouth end of the crofs aile, where Mr. Canynges by will ordered to be buried. * In the old church of Redcliff were formerly keepers of the porches; the prefent porches have feveral apartments with fire places over them, probably for the habitation of the porter, with many of the chaplains and other religious perfons belonging to the fame.

Over the north porch is a large fexagon room, called formerly the Trea-fury-houfe, in which were kept all the archives belonging to the church, † the afcent to which is by a ftone ftair-cafe ; at half way thereof is an apart-ment for a lodging-room, having a fire-place therein, which I prefume might be the apartment affigned for the keeper of the porch. Over the fouth porch is a handfome room wainfcoted, having a chimney in it, on each fide of which are cupboards for keeping the church writings, this being the place where the churchwardens and veftry-men of the parifh now meet to tranfaĉt bufinefs.

Under the north end of the great crofs aile is a large room, at the eaft end of which is a fire-place. There was formerly a communication to this
place

* " In loco quem conftrui feci in parte auftrali ejufdem ecclefiæ juxta altare Sanĉtæ Cathe-rinæ, ubi corpus Johannæ nuper uxoris meæ eft fepultum."—There is a large vault under the monument.

† The trunks are ftill remaining there, particularly one large one, called in a deed of Mr. Canynge's, " Gyfta ferrata cum fex clavibus vocata Cyfta Willielmi Canynges in domo thefauraria ecclefiæ Beatæ Mariæ de Redclive." This cheft furnifhed Mr. Morgan with many curious parch-ments relative to Mr. Canynges and the church of Redclive ; and many very valuable there is reafon to believe were taken away before, and fince difperfed into private hands.—This is faid by Chatterton to have been the repofitory of the manufcripts under the name of Rowley.

place out of the north aile of the church, where a door and ftone ftair-cafe are ftopped up by which they defcended into the room. It might probably be the common dining-room for the officers which belonged to the church, but it is now turned into a burying-place. By the will of Belinus Nanfmoen, 20th March, 1416, it appears there were many poor fcholars choriflers here and feveral chaplains, to which he was a benefactor, and he gave alfo certain canon law books to the ufe of them and the vicar.

At the eaft end of the north aile are two rooms on the firft floor, the firft has a chimney in it, over which is a lodging-room with another chimney in that. Thefe apartments might be affigned for the vicar, chauntry priefts, or chaplains of the church. This place at prefent is made ufe of for keeping the veftments of the vicar, the plate, and other things belonging to the church.

William of Wyrcefter, p. 244. 221. 228. 196. 82. gives feveral particulars relative to Redcliff church and fpire as in the year 1480, when he wrote his account.

P. 221. " The tower of the church of Redcliff in length contain 23½ feet, and in breadth 24 feet. The height of the tower contains 120 feet, and the height of the fpire as it is now broken off contains 200 feet; and the diameter in the upper part of the fracture contains 16 feet. And it has eight panes (pannels), and every ftone in the beginning of the fpire contains in thicknefs 2 feet, and at the top where the crofs is placed it contains in thicknefs 4 inches; and every ftone in the working is 8 feet broad, and the breadth of the garland contains 11 feet. The thicknefs of the walls of the tower at the foundation are 7 feet, and at the height of 120 feet the wall is 5 feet."

P. 196. " The length of the belfry tower in the arch (volta) newly made contains 24 feet from eaft to weft, and 22 feet from north to fouth. And the bafe of the fquare framing of the fpire of Redcliff is of eight pannels. The firft courfe above the place of the fquaring of the fpire confifts in thicknefs of ftones of 2 feet made of two ftones joined together, for it would be hard to reduce one ftone of that thicknefs, and fo it continues diminifhing to a certain height; and there are four coins (fconci) of ftones from one corner of the angle to the next to bind the fpire, which fpire now ftands 100 feet above."

P. 244. " The height of the fpire as it ftands at this day, although broke off by a mifchance from a ftorm and lightning, is 200 feet, by relation of Norton, mafter of the church of Redcliff, and the (feveree) feparation of two windows, one oppofite to the other betwixt two pillars, contains 22 feet and in length 16 feet."

P. 140.

P. 120. " The height of the tower of Redcliff contains 300 feet, of which 100 feet have been thrown down by lightning."

On the 1ſt of April in the 1ſt year of King Edward 6th. 1547, John Cottrell, Doctor of Laws, vicar-general to Paul Buſh, firſt Biſhop of Briſtol, ſequeſtered the tenths of this church and certain ſtipends from ſeveral chauntries there to the king's uſe. See p. 64.

Beſides thoſe chauntries there were two of Everard le French, and one of John Burton and two of Robert Cheepe, and one yearly obiit for Nicholas Pyttes, vicar, and John Blamick, vicar, the expence of each being 13s. 4d. on the octaves of Eaſter.

The following catalogue of ſome of the ancient furniture of this church in the days of Popiſh ſuperſtition, taken from an original record there, is inſerted here as a curioſity.

" A new ſepulchre, well gilt with gold, and a cover thereto, delivered 4 July, 1470, by Maſter William Canynges to the proctors."

" An image of God Almighty ryſing out of the ſame ſepulchre with all the ordinance that longeth thereto," (that is to ſay) " a lath made of tymbre and iron-work that longeth thereto."

Item, thereto longeth heven made of timbre and ſtained clothes.

Item, helle made of timbre and iron work with devills the number of 13.

Item, 4 knyghtes armed keeping the ſepulcre wyth their wepons in their hands (that is to ſay) two ſpeers, two axes, with two paves.

Item, 4 pair of angels wings for 4 angels made of timbre and well paynted.

Item, the Padre, the crown and vyſage, the ball wyth a croſſe upon it well gilt with fyne gold.

Item, the Holy Ghoſt coming out of heven into the ſepulchre.

Item, longing to the 4 angels 4 * chevelers.

Amongſt theſe things there were others as curious, viz. the 6th of Edward the 4th. " four handards of St. George and trappyngs for hys horſe &c."

Leland calls Redcliff church, " Eccleſiarum omnium longe pulcherrima ;"— and Camden, " Eccleſiarum omnium parochialiam (quas unquam vidi) elegantiſſima."—" So large is it and the workmanſhip ſo exquiſite, and the roof ſo artificially vaulted with ſtone, and the tower ſo high, that in my opinion (ſays he) it goes much beyond all the pariſh churches in England I have yet ſeen."

Divine ſervice is performed in this church twice every Sunday and weekly prayers are celebrated every afternoon throughout the year.—Sunday's lecture once in the day is paid for out of the pariſh ſtock, and the veſtry have the

nomination

* It is doubted what theſe were.

nomination of the lecturer and allow him a falary of 26l. per ann. the prefent is the Rev. Dr. Camplin. Before the inflitution of this Sunday's lecture the church ufed to be fhut up one part of the day; and the parifhioners attended the fervice at St. Thomas, which was very inconvenient; and to fhut up fuch a fpacious church as Redcliff one part of the day, was no mark of piety or good management, when the church revenues could fo well afford to have fervice performed twice a day: and were fome pious benefactor to found an evening's lecture to be delivered by candle-light after prayers in this beautiful and fpacious church, fuch an inflitution might have a very happy effect upon the minds of an audience; good order being preferved and regulations properly enforced by the fexton and his affiftants during fervice. Evening is the feafon for medi-tation: the time, the place, the fervice itfelf would command attention, and the divine truths then recommended would be received with the greater ear-neftnefs and acquire an additional force from the circumftances of time and place. Who can without a religious awe and veneration enter this folemn temple, thefe manfions of the Deity even in the day time,

> Where awful arches make a noonday night,
> And the dim windows fhed a folemn light?

With how much greater devotion and pleafing dread muft the religious man approach the Deity in prayer when every thing around by night would naturally tend to infpire it—the twinkling tapers diffufing their religious light through the gloomy arches, the long founding ailes and lofty roofs, and fhewing to advantage the neat ornaments of fuch a fpacious church cannot but incline the foul to a heavenly meditation and make the heart-affecting fervice of our church ftill more affecting—fuch a fcene of things is finely defcribed by Milton in his Penferofo, who was no friend to fhew in religious fervices.

> " Let my due feet never fail
> To walk the ftudious cloyfters pale,
> And love the high embowed roof
> With antique pillars maffy proof;
> And ftoried windows richly dight
> Cafting a dim *religious* light:
> There let the pealing organ blow
> To the full-vole'd quire below,
> In fervice high and anthems clear
> As may with fweetnefs thro' my ear
> Diffolve me into extafies,
> And bring all heaven before my eyes.

Some,

Some, enemies to true religion, with a sneer may call it an imitation of popery, which enjoined the burning of lamps before the shrines of saints in this very church in the time of ignorance and superstition,—but as from this we have happily emerged, the church of England confessedly sitting as Queen among the reformed churches; and there are no shrines and altars to saints here now to tempt the vulgar eye, nor any prayers to be offered to them; nothing to be heard but a pure reasonable service; therefore the objection falls to the ground: reason and common sense may be appealed to, whether service by candle-light sometimes might not tend to prevent nocturnal revels and meetings and keep alive the sense of religion in the mind; so attentive to the usual business of the day, that were not Sunday set apart for other employ, religion would scarce be found among us, I believe in the opinion of most.

But to return from this digression—This church is adorned with a great number of elegant monuments; and some though old have a profusion of carving and Gothic work bestowed upon them.

To begin with the founder's:—At the south end of the great cross aile is a stately monument erected in memory of Mr. William Cannynges and Joan his wife, whose effigies are lying on an altar tomb in full proportion under a canopy handsomely carved in freestone. On the inside of the statues under the arch of his tomb are the following English inscriptions in a table, and on the front a Latin inscription.

" Master Wm. Canynges the richest merchant of the town of Bristow, afterwards chosen five times mayor of the said town for the good of the commonwealth of the same: he was in orders of priesthood seven years and afterwards Dean of Westbury, and dyed the 7th Nov. 1474.* The said William built a college within the said town of Westbury (with his canons) and the said William did maintain by the space of 8 years 800 handycraft men besides carpenters and masons, ev'ry day 100 men. Besides the said William gave King Edward the 4th. 3000 marks for his peace to be had in 2470 tons of shipping.†

Thefe

* His will is dated the 12th of November 1474, he died the 17th of that month. Wm. Bottoner.——His obiit I find was kept on Lammas-Day, the 1st of August 1475, the next year.

† This part of the inscription has given occasion for some weak people to propagate a report much to the prejudice of Mr. Cannyngs' memory; whereas the case was this: Edward the 4th. having his necessities amply supplied by Mr. Cannyngs, he granted him in lieu thereof 2470 tons of shipping free of all impost, as appears by the original instrument in being in the Exchequer.—This explanation was made by one of the Judges, who reprimanded the sexton for abusing the memory of so worthy a citizen in the vulgar story.

Thefe are the names of his fhips and their burthens.

	Tons.			Tons.
The Mary Canyngs	- - 400	The Mary Redcliff	-	500
The Mary and John	- - 900	The Galliot	- - -	50
The Katherine	- - 140	The Mary Bat	- -	200
The Little Nicholas	- - 140	The Margaret	- -	200
The Kathrine of Bofton	- 223	A fhip of Ireland	- -	100

N. B. This account is from William of Worcefter.

No age, no time can wear out well-won fame,
The ftones themfelves a ftately work doth fhow,
From fenfelefs graves ground may we good mens name
And noble minds by ventring deeds we know :
A lanthorn clear fets forth a candle light,
A worthey aft declares a worthey wight ;
The buildings rare, that here you may behold
To fhrine his bones deferves a tomb of gould :
This famous fabrick, that he here hath done,
Shines in his fphere, as glorious as the fun :
What need more words, the future world he fought
And fet the pompe and pride of this at nought :
Heaven was his aim, let it be ftill his ftation
That leaves fuch worke for others imitation.

The Latin infcription is this :

Hic inferius tumulatur corpus nobilis, circumfpefti, magnæque induftriæ,
viri, Willi: Canyngs, dudum mercatoris, et quinquies majoris iftius villæ;
& poftea in ordine facerdotali per feptennium inftituti, ac Decani de
Weftbury; qui in ifta ecclefia conftituit duas Cantarias perpetuas duorum
capellanorum, viz. unum in honorem Santæ Catharinæ; ac etiam unum
clericum ftabiliri fecit, & Mariæ Virgini facravit: & juxta eum, requiefcit
uxor fua Johanna, quorum animabus propitiatur Deus Amen.

There is alfo another monument of Mr. Canynge's with his ftatue well
carved in alabafter, lying along in his prieft robes as dean of Weftbury, with
hands lifted up as in the aft of devotion, and a large book under his head.

Over Mr. Canynge's tomb are the family arms in proper colours, viz. arg,
three moors heads couped fable wreathed azure and argent, no creft. His
obiit was yearly celebrated, for which in the year 1475 there is charged in
the annual account :

For

For our Mafter William Canynge's obüt at Lammas-day as the *l. s. d.*
  compofition fpecyfyeth -   -   -   -   -   2 17 0

Paid for our Mafter William Cannynge's years mynde   -   2 11 8

At his days requiem -   -   -   -   -   0 17 0

For the holy cake for 52 Sundays, wax 5d. per Sunday - 2 7 8

To Sir Thomas Hawkyfoke for his year's wages -   - 6 13 4

To Sir Perfc Welles for his year's wages - , -   - 6 13 4

Not far from the monument of Mr. Canynge's is the following infcription in old charaƈters on a flat ftone, on which is engraved a large knife and a fkimmer:—" Hic jacet Gulielmus Coke in fervitiis Willielmi Canynge cujus animæ propitietur Deus.".

The device cut on the ftone and his being mentioned as in the fervice of Mr. Canynges feems to point him out to be William the cook.

In an old bede-roll among the names of perfons to be prayed for are, " Joanna Canynges, uxor Williclmi Canynges, et Willielmus filius fuus ; Willielmus Colas, the fervant of Myftre Canynge that gave ii autours of woode to the church of Redclyffe.

There were feveral altars here, the altar of St. Stephen, St. Blaze, St. Nicholas, St. Catherine, St. George.

William Colas, the other fervant of William Canynges, 7 Edward 4th. was buried next St. George's chapel, " who hath yeven and delyvred to All Sowles autour, wythynne the chyrche of owre Ladye of Redclyve yn Briftow, by the bandes of Mayftre William Canynges, a chalys wyth a paten of fylvre, wayinge xiii ounces and halfe, fylvre parcel guylte, and the name of the faid William Colas is wrote upon yt, and hys fygure is portryed upon the foot, befydes the crucyfyxe of the fayde chalyce, and fo hys fowle to be praid forre."

Not far from William Coke's ftone is another, nearer Canynge's monument : " Hic jacet Joannes Blecker, pandoxator, cujus animæ propitietur Deus."

This brewer (pandocator) might probably be another fervant of Mr. Canynges, for he orders by deed penes me that his obiit fhould be kept in the chapel of St. Catherine.

Near this is alfo another, " Hic jacet Richardus Coke et Tibota uxor ejus, quorum animabus propitietur Deus."

On a ftone near Canynge's tomb was the following: " Here lies Thomas Chamber, of this parifh, merchant, and his wife Ann. She died 1620, he Oƈtober, 1647.

When

> When I was young in wars I fhed my blood,
> Both for my queen and for my country's good :
> In elder years my care was chief to be
> Soldier to him who fhed his blood for me."

Philip Baunt, merchant, buried at Redcliff in 1404. In his will he gives to John Caunterbury, chaplain here, " quendam librum meum de Evangeliis Anglicè, qui eft in cuftodiâ Joannis Stourton," — a proof they had the Gofpels in Englifh fo early as 1404, though perhaps not in common.

Under the north window of the great crofs aile is a Knight Templar, lying on a plain altar tomb in a coat of mail, with a fhield on his left fide, and a fword in his right hand, all carved in freeftone, probably defigned for Robert de Berkeley Lord of Bedminfter and Redcliff, a benefactor to this church.

About the middle of the crofs aile was buried Everard le Fraunces. Over him is a plain altar tomb, with his figure in the robes of a magiftrate, and formerly the following infcription : " Hic jacet Everardus le French, qui in hâc ecclefiâ duas fundavit cantarias et duas alias in ecclefiâ St. Nicolai, et fuit ter maior hujus villæ cujus animæ propitietur Deus, Amen. M.CCCL."

In the fame aile : " Hic inferius fub lapide marmoreo fepelitur corpus Thomæ Young, armigeri nuper de villa Briftol, ac filii ac hæredis Thomæ Young unius jufticiorum in communi Banco, et Jocofæ uxoris ejus qui quidem Thomas obiit 15 Maii, A. D. 1506, quorum animabus propitietur Deus, Amen." With his coat, lozengè vert and or. on a bend G. three ebecks or griffins heads erafed or. three G.

Sir G. Young of the county of Devon is defcended from this family in Briftol.—Eng. Baronet. vol. iii. p. 334, 339. vol. iv. p. 620.

In the windows were formerly in painted glafs the arms of England, of Harrington, Hungerford, Canynges, Cradock, Berkeley, Mede, Sturton, Dyrick, Says, Graunt, Montague, Cheyney, Fulk Fitzwarren, Sir J. Inyn, Rivers, &c.

Againft the pillar near Mr. Canynge's tomb is fixed a neat marble monument with the following infcription to the memory of one, who juftly deferved the character here given her by her hufband : fhe was taken from him in early life : — " Eheu ! dies atro carbone notanda ! Filius et quatuor filiæ in folamen patris (favente Deo) adhuc vivunt valentque 1789. Filius Highamæ in comitatu Somerfetenfi eft rector.

M. S.

Mariæ, chariffimæ conjugis
Gulielmi Barrett, chirurgi :
Quæ morum fuavitate,

Vitæ

Vitæ fimplicitate,

Benignitate animi,

Pietate in Deum eximiâ

Omnes, quibus innotuit, fibi devinxit :

Conjugali quaque virtute inornata

Maritum dulci amoris copulâ

Conftri&um tenuit, fupremo

Haud citiùs die diffolutâ :

Tabe pulmonari penitus confe&a,

Quam fortitudine Chriftianâ fuftinùit,

In Domino tandem fine gemitu

Placidè obdormivit die 8 Maii 1763,

Ætat. 32.

Filiolum unum cum quatuor filiabus

Sola nunc fælicitatis pignora,

Futuræ fpes, marito reliquît,

Qui hoc monumentum amoris ergo

Bene merenti pofuit.''

At the north end of the fame aile is a monument with the following in_
fcription : — " Near this pillar are depofited the remains of Mrs. Fortune
Little, widow of Mr. John Little, late of this parifh. She died June 28,
1777, aged 57.

Oh ! could this verfe her bright example fpread,

And teach the living while it prais'd the dead :

Then, reader, fhould it fpeak her hope divine,

Not to record her faith, but ftrengthen thine ;

Then fhould her ev'ry virtue ftand confefs'd,

Till every virtue kindled in thy breaft :

But if thou flight the monitory ftrain

And fhe has liv'd to thee at leaft in vain,

Yet let her death an awful leffon give,

The dying Chriftian fpeaks to all that live ;

Enough for her, that here her afhes reft

Till God's own plaudit fhall her worth atteft.

HANNAH MORE.''

At the eaft end of the north aile is ere&ed a large magnificent altar tomb,
curioufly carved all over with work in the Gothic ftyle, to the memory of
Thomas Mede, Efq; and his wife, whofe ftatues in freeftone are lying at length
with

with their coat of arms, S. a chevron ermine between three trefoils flipt argent. He was fheriff of Briftol 1452. His country feat was at Fayland, in the parifh of Wraxal, in the county of Somerfet, then called Mede's Place. — On the outfide of his tomb was fixed a plate of brafs with an infcription on it, part of which is ftolen away and this only remains : " ------ predicti Thomæ Mede ac ter majoris iftius villæ Briftolliæ, qui obiit 20 die menfis Decembris, Anno Dom. 1475, quorum animabus propitietur Deus, Amen." Under the fame tomb lies Philip Mede, Efq; his brother, whofe will bears date 11 Janury, 1471, in which he orders his body to be buried at the altar of St. Stephen, in the church of Redcliff, to which he was a benefactor. His wife Ifabel and John their fon alfo lie here, their figures being engraved on a brafs plate 22½ inches long and 19 broad, which is fixed to the back of the tomb : the infcription on the fide is now deftroyed. He had been thrice mayor and member of parliament for Briftol 36th Henry 6th. 1460. His daughter Ifabella married the fifth Maurice Lord of Berkeley, fee p. 256. by whom fhe had iffue three fons, Maurice, Thomas, and James, and one daughter, Ann.

On the ground under this monument was once the following infcription, now obliterated : " Hic jacet Johannes Mede, burgenfis villæ Briftoliæ, qui obiit 17 die menfis Aprilis, A. D. 1496, et juxta eum requiefcit Alicia, uxor ejus, quorum animabus propitietur Deus, Amen." Out of the mouths of the two figures in the brafs plate above mentioned proceed the following words in a fcroll from the man's, " Sancta Trinitas unus Deus miferere nobis," from the woman's, " Pater de cœlis Deus miferere nobis."

In the fame aile are monuments to the memory of " The Rev. Richard Sandford, A. M. who died 6 Auguft, 1724, and of Elizabeth his fifter, who died 22 September, 1728."

" Of John Tilly, who died 22 February, 1658, and Elizabeth his wife, who died 7 September, 1660."

" Of Sir William Penn, Knight, born at Briftol 1621, of the Penns of Penns Lodge, in the county of Wilts. He was made captain at 21, rear-admiral of Ireland at 23, vice-admiral of England at 31, and general in the firft Dutch wars at 32, whence returning in 1655 he was chofen a parliament-man for Weymouth 1660, was made commiffioner of the admiralty and navy, governor of the forts and town of Kingfale, vice-admiral of Munfter and a member of that provincial council, and in 1664 was chofen great captain commander under his Royal Highnefs in that fignal and moft evidently fuccefsful fight againft the Dutch fleet. Thus he took leave of the fea, his old element, but continued his other employs till 1669, when through bodily

infirmities

infirmities (contracted through the care and fatigue of public affairs) he withdrew, prepared and made for his end, and with a gentle and even gale in much peace arrived and anchored in his laſt and beſt port, at Wanſtead, in the county of Eſſex, 16 September, 1670, being then but 49 years of age and 4 months. To whoſe name and merit his ſurviving lady erected this remembrance." — Over his monument were 3 long old ſtreamers and ſome old armour, and on his ſtone this motto: Dum Clavum teneam, with the arms f. arg. on a bar v. 3 balls of the firſt."

"Of Eliz. Batchelor wife of John Batchelor alderman of this city;—ſhe was daughter of Giles Combes Eſq; of Fifehead in Somerſetſhire, and died 21 Aug. 1683."

In the chancel was a ſtone with a braſs margin let into it, thus inſcribed: "Hic jacet Lodovicus Morris, quondam ballivus villæ Briſtolliæ, burgenſis et mercator, qui obiit quarto decimo die menſis Februarii, A. D. 1464, cujus animæ propitietur Deus, Amen."

Near this, " Orate pro animâ Joannis Willy, qui obiit 27 menſis Junii, A. D. 1454, et Agnetis uxoris ejus, quæ obiit 1450." On the ſtone is a ſhuttle.

Here are alſo ſtones with inſcriptions, " To Sir William Lewis, Knight, and alderman, and four virgin daughters: the former died 23 May, 1712, the latter Bridget died 28 February, 1703, aged 18; Mary, the 8 September, 1710, aged 21; Sarah, 10 January, 1710, aged 28; Elizabeth, 26 March, 1712, aged 20 years and 3 months."

" To Martha, wife of Nathaniel Day, Eſq; daughter of Mr. Robert Hawkeſworth. She died 23 January, 1729."

A monument with inſcription " To Edward Durbin, chemiſt, who died 3 January, 1763, aged 75."

On the floor of the chancel is a large black marble ſtone with braſs curi ouſly laid in and engraved with the figures of a man and woman, with ſix ſons underneath the man and eight daughters under the woman, with the following inſcription: " Hic jacet Johannes Jay quondam vicecomes iſtius villæ, et Joanna uxor ejus; qui quidem Johannes, obiit die 15 menſis Maii, A. D. 1480, quorum animabus propitietur Deus, Amen." This John Jay was a merchant of great eminence, as appears by William of Wyrceſter, p. 267. and Johanna was ſiſter to William of Wyrceſter.

On the right hand as you aſcend the altar is a large flat ſtone with braſs plates curiouſly inlaid, engraved with the figures of a man and woman with a ſhield of arms over and under each, G. on a chevron wavy argent, charged with fleurs de lis f. The inſcription is this: " Hic jacet corpus venerabilis viri

viri Johannis Brook quondam fervientis ad legem illuftriffimi principis fælicis memoriæ regis Henrici octavi et jufticiarii ejufdem regis ad affifas in partibus occidentalibus Angliæ et capitalis fenefchali illius honorabilis domûs et monafterii Beatæ Mariæ de Glafconiâ in comitatu Somerfet, qui quidem Johannes obiit 25 die menfis Decembris Anno Domini milleffimo quingenteffimo 25°, et juxta eam requiefcit Johanna uxor ejus una filiarum et hæredum Richardi Amenæ, quorum animabus propitietur Deus, Amen."

On the floor a black ftone with an infcription in Latin to Sufanna the wife of Sir Robert Yeomans, Bart. and member for the city. She died 20 September, 1680. Refurgam.—Alfo her fifter Elizabeth, wife of William Stafford, of Bradfield, Berks, Efq. She died 20 April, 1671. Per mortem ad vitam. Arms, quarterly, f. a chevron arg. between three fpears heads of the fecond for Yeomans. Azure on a bend or. three mullets G. for Stafford.

In St. Mary's chapel a monument of marble with a Latin infcription to Elizabeth the wife of John Gibb, A. M. prebendary of Bedminfter and vicar of this church, daughter of Nathaniel Ingelo, S. T. P. and of Mary the daughter of Richard Vickris, merchant, and mayor of this city. She died 7 October, 1710, aged 43, after a marriage of 6 years, 1 month, and 7 days.

In the fame on a very large ftone with a figure of the deceafed in his judge's robes engraved in a brafs plate inlaid is an infcription round the margin on a ftrip of brafs: " Hic jacet Johannes Inyn Miles, capitalis jufticiarius domini regis ad placita coram ipfo rege tenenda, qui obiit 24 die Marcii, Anno Domini Milleffimo C.C.C.CXXXIX. cujus animæ propitietur Deus, Amen." — Under the figure are the following verfes:

> Jufte Deus, patiens Judex, mifercre Johannis
> Inyn, jus faciens Miles fuit ejus in annis:
> Urbe recordator fuit hâc Baro Scacarii.
> Summus, et in banco judex capitalis utroque
> Juftitiam voluit connexam cum pietate,
> Militiam coluit fubnixam nobilitate:
> Jufte Johan. fortis Miles jam propitiatus
> Efto, fores mortis fibi claude, remitte reatus.

Underneath his arms, f. or. a fefs az. inter three unicorns heads couped arg. within a bordure of the fame, quartered with a lion rampant, alfo two other fhields. His country feat was of Bifhopfworth, near Filwood, now a farm-houfe in which are ftill to be feen the arms in coloured glafs in the windows. His fon William had Alice, a daughter, married to John Kekewyck 5 September, 1515, who died at Bifhopfworth without iffue 20 May, 1529. His daughter

Ifabel

Ifabel married John Kenn. His fon Chriftopher 1519 had a daughter Eliza-zabeth, who was married to Lord Paulet, of Hinton St. George, whereby this family's eftate at Bifhopfworth came to Lord Paulet, who ftill poffeffes it.

Thefe are the chief monuments and infcriptions in this church, but the churchyard muft. not be paffed by unnoticed, being fpacious, planted with trees, and the walks through it kept very neat: fee the plate. There was an elegant crofs in the center of it, taken notice of by William of Worcefter, p. 211. " Cemiterium ecclefiæ de Radclyff continet 500 greffus; crux pulcher-rima antificiofe operata in medio." It is now deftroyed. Sermons ufed to be preached from it formerly. Here are fome good tombs and infcriptions worthy of notice.

The following is a Lift of the V I C A R S.

1207 William ———, chaplain of Redcliff.

    Richard de Newbery, vicar.

1276 John le Rung, clericus.

1290 Gerard le Tyllet.

1327 Robert de Merfhton, chaplain.

1338 William de Jatton.

1342 Ralph de Clive.

1356 William of Wykeham had the prebend of Bedminfter cum Redcliff.

1374 John French.

1381 William Draper.

1389 Henry de Nethenene.

1391 Nicholas Geill.

1393 John Lamynton, chaplain.

    Thomas Godefellow, chaplain.

1399 John Bufh, chaplain.

1410 William Dudlefburg.

1429 Joannes Phreas or Freas. Vide Lel. de Script. Brit. p. 466.

1434 John Bath.

1496 Roger Saundcy.

1438 Willliam Peircy or Perry.

1446 Nicholas Pittes.

1460 William Sey.

1464 —— Chedworth.

1473 William Chock, younger bro-ther of Sir Richard Chock, of Afhton.

1508 Edward Powell, D. D. V. See Wood's Ath. Oxon. vol. i. p. 46.

1534 Henry Williams, prefented to it by Cardinal Campeius, 2d Edw. 6. See Wood, vol. ii. p. 681.

1550 Thomas Norman.

1555 John Blackfton, deprived 1 Eliz.

1559 Arthur Saule.

1579 Meredith Hamner.

1585 Samuel Davis.

1623 Thomas Palmer. He publifhed a fermon, entituled, Briftol's Military Garden, preached before the Trained Bands.

1636 Giles Thornborough.

1637 John Garfe.

1639 William Noble, ejeﬆed.

1639 Matthew Hazard, intruded.

1660

1660 Francis Horton.
1670 Humphrey Brent.
1678 Richard Thompfon.
1685 William Manning.
1701 John Gibb. He built the large
vicarage-houfe at a great expence.

1744 Thomas Broughton, the learned
publifher of the Dictionary of
all Religions, folio, and the
Profpect of Futurity in 8vo.
and other tracts.
1772 Edmund Spry, A. M. the prefent vicar in 1788.

This vicarage * is valued in the King's Books at the clear yearly value of 40l. 13s. 8½d. and its tenths are difcharged. It is worth to the vicar in voluntary contributions about 100l. per annum, befides furplice fees and gift-fermons, but with St. Thomas and Abbots Leigh all chapels to Bedminfter, the whole affords a decent income to the incumbent.

This church had been at different times liberally endowed with large eftates for fupport of the fabric and of divine offices celebrated therein, as well as for charity to the poor, the aged, and infirm of this parifh ; and by an inftrument out of chancery in the beginning of Charles 2d's. reign it appears a little before that time it had lands to the full amount of 400l. per annum, but during the Commonwealth, with fo little honefty was the church affairs adminiftered, the feoffees and parifh officers granted long leafes and fold lands by collufion to each other for little or no confideration, by which the revenue of the church was wafted. One Cecil was an active perfon in this matter, and is mentioned as highly culpable and ordered to reftore feveral tenements again to the church. The great ravage then committed, and lofs of deeds embezzled during that anarchy, rendered it impoffible to repair at the Reftoration wholly the mifchief done by the levelling republicans of thofe days. Not only the church eftates but the ftructure itfelf did not efcape the ravage; they tore down many of its ornaments and all the lofty pinnacles round the church, which were curioufly carved and added much to its external beauty and have not fince been rebuilt; while on the infide they ftole the brafs plates from the monuments; they broke down the fine organ, and getting together the prayer books and the homilies, and even the bibles, with cufhions, caffocks. &c. they made a bonfire of them, as the funeral pile of the church: and parading the ftreets with ftreamers made of the furplices cut into flags, and tooting upon the organ pipes they marched in triumph through the ftreets.

It

* According to the Lincoln manufcript Bedminfter and its chapels produced 70 marks or 46l· 13s. 4d. the vicar of Bedminfter 8 marks, in all 72 marks or 52l. The temporalitics of Bedminfter paid to the abbot of Whytland 20s. and to the abbot of St..Auftin 8l. 15s. in. all 9l. 15s.

It is not without great œconomy and good management, the church officers have recovered and preferved what eftates now remain, and improved fince its revenue.—By the rental the annual ground or referved rents of the whole, confifting of about 80 feveral meffuages and tenements, amount to about 80l. per ann. and the other charitable benefactions in money &c. to about 39l. 15s. total 119l. 15s. per annum, befides the money arifing from the renewal of leafes of fo many tenements for lives—which have enabled the parifh to lay out large fums to repair the church and embellifh it with paintings and keep it in conftant repair, to pay for additional duty in the fervice, a lecturer, organift &c.

BENEFACTORS to the Church and Poor of St. Mary Redcliff Parifh.

		l.	s.	d.
1594,	Mr. Robert Kitchen alderman, 10s. a quarter for ever,	40	0	0
1632,	Mr. Robert Rogers alderman, 1s. a week for ever,	52	c	
1635,	Sir Richard Rogers, Knight, 6d. a week for ever,	26	ı	
1639,	Mr. George Harrington alderman, 10s. a quarter for ever,	40		
1639,	Mr. William Pitt merchant, 25l. the profit thereof for ever,	25		
1641,	Mrs. Thomafine Harrington, 1s. a week for ever,	52		
1642,	Mrs. Mary Stile 10l. the profit thereof for ever,	10		
1647,	Mrs. Blanch Yeamans 20l. the profit thereof for ever,	20		
1649,	Mrs. Ann Edfon 20l. the profit thereof for ever,	20		
1650,	Mr. George Gibbs brewer, 1s. per week for ever,	52		
1652,	Mr. Robert Edfou dyer, 20l. the profits thereof for ever,	20		
1653,	Mr. Hugh Brown alderman, 54s. yearly for ever,	54		
1654,	Mr. John Haytor milliner, 6d. a week for ever,	26	8	8
1661,	Mr. Francis Gleed, fometime fheriff, 10s. a quarter to a poor houfholder for ever,	40	0	0
1662,	Mrs. Mary Gibbs gave 30l. the profits thereof to the poor for ever,	30	0	0
1667,	Mr. Arther Farmer, fometime mayor and alderman of this city, gave unto this parifh the intereft of 40l. yearly to 6 poor families on All-Saints day,	40	0	0
1668,	Mr. Thomas Farmer, Gentleman, gave unto the poor of this parifh 50l. the profit for ever,	50	0	0
1668,	Mr. Richard Vickris alderman, 52l. yearly for ever in bread,	52	0	0
1670,	William Curtis of London, Efq; born in this parifh, gave 50l. the profit thereof to be diftributed to the poor on Chriftmas-day yearly for ever,	50	0	0

Sir

		l.	*s.*	*d.*
—— Sir William Penn, Knight, gave 50l. the profit thereof to be given to the poor yearly for ever, - -		50	0	0
—— Mrs. Elizabeth Caro gave 5l. the interest to the widow or widows of one husband, yearly for ever at Christmas-day,		5	0	0
1675, Mr. Joseph Bullock in memory of his father Mr. William Bullock of this parish, merchant, gave 70l. the profit thereof to be distributed as followeth, 3l. 4s. to the poor, 15s. to the minister for a sermon upon the 4th of October, and 3s. 4d. to the clerk, and 1s. 8d. to the sexton yearly for ever, - - - -		70	0	0
1675, Mrs. Ann Prewett, late of this parish, widow, gave 20l. the profit thereof to the widow or widows of one husband only, but if there be no such widow in this parish then to some widow in Temple parish, at Christmas yearly for ever, - - - -		20	0	0
—— Mrs. Mary Boucher and her daughter Mrs. Joan Langton, widows, gave lands for the payment of 10s. a piece to 52 poor widows of this city yearly for ever, of which this parish hath a proportion.				
1678, Mrs. Sarah Birks of this parish, widow, gave 20l. the profit thereof to be distributed to the widows of one husband only, on Christmas-day yearly for ever, -		20	0	0
1683, Mrs. Elizabeth Yeamans, widow, gave 10l. the profit thereof to the poor for ever, - -		10	0	0
1685, Mr. Jeremiah Holloway, merchant, gave 20l. the profit thereof in bread to the poor of St. Mary upon Redcliff parish for ever, - - - -		20	0	0
1686, Mr. Samuel Hale, merchant, gave 10l. the profit thereof to the poor weekly in bread for ever: and also the interest of 230l. towards the placing apprentices of poor children in 7 parishes of this city yearly for ever, of which this parish is one, - - - -		240	0	0
1686, Sir Robert Yeamans, Knight and Bart. and born in this parish in the year 1617, gave 50l. the profit thereof to the poor of this parish in bread on every Lord's day for ever, - - - -		50	0	0
1689, John Lawford, Esq; sometime mayor and alderman of this city, gave 50l. the profit thereof to the poor of this parish in bread on every Lord's day for ever, -		50	0	0

		l.	s.	d.

1690, Mrs. Margret Stokes, widow, gave 10l. the profit thereof to the poor widows of this parifh at Chriftmas yearly for ever, - - - -   10 0 0

1691, Mrs. Sufanna Compton, widow, gave 10l. the profit thereof to the poor in bread on Midfummer-day for ever,   10 0 0

1693, Mr. Dennis Pitt's widow, gave 30l. for the fettling of 6 poor boys of this parifh apprentice, - -   30 0 0

1709, William Whitehead, Efq; of this parifh, and alderman of this city, gave 50l. the profit thereof to 10 poor houfe-keepers of this parifh not receiving alms, 5s. to each at Chriftmas yearly for ever, - - -   50 0 0

1719, William James of this parifh, Gentleman, gave 30l. for the payment of 10s. to the minifter for a fermon in the afternoon on the 5th of November in this church, againft pride, atheifm, popery and profanenefs: 17s. more to be diftributed in two-penny bread to the poor of this parifh after fuch fermon, 1s. 8d. to the clerk and 1s. 4d. to the fexton for ever, - - - -   30 0 0

—— Mrs. Mary Carifbrook of this parifh, the fole and virgin daughter of John Carifbrook, Gentleman, gave to feveral diftreffed families (not receiving alms) 40s. a year, being confirmed by her father, and Mr. Theophilos Carifbrook her only brother, to be diftributed on the 27th of May, being the day of her interment, and on the 24th day of December for ever, - - -   40 0 0

1721, Mrs. Ann Tilly of Keynfham in the county of Somerfet, fpinfter, gave 20l. the profit thereof to be diftributed in bread to the poor of this parifh on Chriftmas Eve yearly for ever, - - - -   20 0 0

1724, Mr. John Newman plumber, gave 26l. the profit in bread to the poor of this parifh on Sundays for ever.   26 '

1724, By the voluntery contributions of fome of this parifh was raifed the fum of 20l. and paid into the veftry, the profit thereof to be paid for ringing the bells in memory of the late worthy Edward Colfton, Efq; on the fecond day of November yearly for ever, - -   20 0 0

1733, Mr. William Prewett of this parifh left 10l. a year to the poor of the Spittle-houfe out of the feveral tenements at Cathay for ever, - - - -   10 0 0

				l.	s.	d.
1734,	Mrs. Mary Smith, widow, of this parish, gave to the poor of this and St. Thomas parishes 30l. per ann. for 86 years, and afterwards the rent of several messuages &c.			600	0	0
1737,	Mr. Edward Dowell, late of this city, gave 100l. the profit thereof to 40 poor housekeepers of this parish on St. Thomas-day yearly for ever,			100	0	0
1738,	Mr. John Jaine of this parish gave 150l. the interest thereof to be given to the poor of this parish in cloathing yearly for ever,			150	0	0
1742,	Mr. John Fisher of this parish, distiller, gave 50l. to buy plate for the use of the altar, and also 100l. the profit thereof to apprentice a poor boy of this parish from the charity-school in Pile-street yearly,			150	0	0
1759,	Robert Sandford, Esq; by will gave 1000l. the interest to 30 poor housekeepers yearly not receiving alms,			1000		
1776,	Mr. James Gully left 50l. the interest towards cloathing the poor boys in Pile-street school,			50	0	0
1777,	Mr. G. Watson gave 20l. the interest to Pile-street school,			20	0	0
——	Mr. —— of this parish gave 100l. the interest to Pile-street school,			100	0	0

A LIST of GIFT SERMONS found in the Vestry-room at St. Mary-Redcliff Church.

	l.	s.	d.
January 1st. Mrs. Ann Edfou to the minister	0	10	0
To the clerk and sexton	0	3	0
March 13th. Sir Robert Yeamans to the minister	0	5	6
To the clerk and sexton	0	1	10
Palm-Sunday. Mr. George Gibbs to the minister	0	13	4
To the clerk	0	1	4
Good-Friday to the minister	0	10	0
To the clerk	0	2	0
Three Sermons at Whitsuntide, to the minister	1	10	0
To the clerk	0	3	4
Trinity-Sunday to the minister by agreement, the gift of Tho. Cissill,	0	10	0
October 4th. Mr. Joseph Bullock to the minister	0	15	0
To the clerk	0	3	4
To the sexton	0	1	8

		l.	*s.*	*d.*
November 5th. Mr. William James to the minifter	-	0	10	0
To the clerk - - - -		0	1	8
To the fexton - - - -		0	1	4
Chriftmas-day and Eafter-Sunday the veftry to the minifter	-	2	10	0

About the year 1207 Lord Robert de Berkely granted to this church at the requeft of William the chaplain, all that his fountain of water from a place called Hugewell (beyond Lower Knowle), to have a perpetual conveyance in pipes through his lands to a convenient place for its reception, where it was ever to remain for the ufe of the church and parifh and the minifters thereof, from which refervoir the faid lord granted a pipe an inch wide to convey part of the water to the hofpital of St. John the Baptift for the ufe of the mafter and friers there. The brethren of this hofpital had an ancient chapel contiguous to the weft end of the church dedicated to the Holy Spirit.

This hofpital of St. John confifted of brothers and fifters of the order of St. Auguftin, and in the little red book in the chamber of Briftol, p. 199, Johannes " Farceyn alias Farcey is faid to be the founder of this hofpital or houfe of St. John the Baptift in Redcliffe-putte."—It became in time very well endowed, and had many tenements in Briftol as well as eftates in the country belonging to it.—It was firft under the government and patronage of the Bifhop of Bath and Wells; but for fometime before the diffolution the mayor and commonalty of Briftol are called the true patrons of it.—It was fituated at the bottom of Redcliff-Hill, and extended from Redcliff-Pitt forwards to the Avon backwards—no traces of it at prefent remain except a lane called St. Joänn's-lane there may feem to point it out—houfes are now built on the fite of it. The following is the engagement each member made on his admiffion into this hofpital.

Ego N. P. promitto continenter vivere, et fine proprio juxta regulam & obfervantiam in Domo five Hofpitale Sancti Johannis Baptiftæ Briftolliæ antiquitus obfervatam, & confuetam; profiteorq; ordinem regularem Sancti Auguftini juxta inftituta ejufdem Domûs five hofpitalis—necnon me premiffa fideliter obfervaturum aftringo per prefentes. In cujus rei teftimonium manu meâ propriâ hic me fubfcribo.

Frienborough manor now called Barrow Hill Farm, in the parifh of Farmborough, Somerfet, belonged to this hofpital of St. John, and was granted by Henry the 8th. to Dr. George Owen, the 29th of April the 36th of Henry the 8th. who fold it to J. Bufh of Dulton, Wilts, Efq; the 3d of June the 38th of Henry the 8th.—In 1664 it was fold by Sir Hugh Smyth of Long-Afhton,

together

together with Compton-Dando, to —— Popham, Efq; in which family it now remains.

By a deed, the original in Bifhop Ralph's regifter in the church of Wells, f. 324, it appears that frier John de Monington prior of St. John's hofpital, wifhing to be releafed from the care of faid hofpital, having refigned it into the Bifhop's hands, the Bifhop allotted to him one chamber therein, and the manor of Bifhopfworth and its appurtenances for his fupport, with 9 oxen, with plow and wain and the reft of the apparatus of the faid manor for his life. Dated at Chew 1348, 19th year of the Bifhop's confecration.

This hofpital was well endowed with lands which are mentioned in old deeds, particularly in thofe belonging to the Gaunts.—The following is a lift of fome of the principals (or mafters) of the hofpital of St. John the Baptift without Redcliff-Gate, who were chofen at firft by the Bifhop of Bath and Wells, afterwards by themfelves and recommended by the mayor and commonalty of Briftol the patrons, who prefented them to the Bifhop for inftitution and induction before their admiffion—they took the oath aforementioned in the prefence of the patron.

1261, Brother Thomas.

1292, Edmund dicto le Thyelare.

1343, John de Monigton mafter the 29th of July the 17th of Edward the 3d. he refigned 1348.
       Brother Lawrence mentioned in Gaunts deed p. 62.

1383, William Topefleye mafter.

1430, Nicholas Sterr.

1442, John Hall, inftituted at the prefentation of Clement Bagot, mayor of Briftol, and the commonalty ; this hofpital was by its foundation collegiate, but there being now but one brother in the faid college not 22 years old, therefore for want of brethren it ceafed to be a college.

1467, William Prowe, at the prefentation of William Canynges mayor; he left the rectory of Wraxal for this.

1504, Richard Collins S. T. P. having a difpenfation from the apoftolic fee to hold any benefice, was inftituted and inducted to the rectory of St. Stephen the 16th of March 1504.

1542, Richard Bromefield furrendered this houfe &c. to King Henry the 8th's. commiffioners the 7th of March in the 35th of that King's reign, after above 364 years poffeffion by the friers,—it was granted to Dr. G. Owen.

                        In

In 1306 the Bifhop of Bath and Wells appropriated the rectory of Backwell magiftro et fratribus hofpitalis St. Johannis Brifloliæ (ex lamentabili querelâ) that they were ftarving, &c.

In the year 1383 a grant was made by the mafter and friers to the proctors of the fraternity of the Holy Ghoft there of the ufe of their chapel, dedicated to the Holy Ghoft, in the churchyard of St. Mary de Redeclyve, for the term of fifty years. This grant was made at the very time Redcliff church was finifh_ing by William Canynges the elder, and probably this fraternity ufed to refort to the church of Redcliff, and had a chapel there to their ufe, but were now obliged to apply to the houfe of St. John for the ufe of their chapel in the churchyard.

This chapel of the Holy Ghoft in the churchyard of St. Mary Redcliff, having belonged to the mafter and friers of the houfe or hofpital of St. John the Baptift without Redcliff-gate for many ages was alfo at the furrender of the faid hofpital, &c. taken into the king's hands. Leland fays, " It was a paroche before the building of Redcliff great new church," which feems to be mere conjecture.

In the year 1571 Queen Elizabeth gave the faid chapel by her royal grant to the parifhioners of St. Mary Redcliff, for a free grammar and writing-fchool, as appears by her deed.

This chapel was in length from eaft to weft 56 feet, and in breadth from north to fouth 26 feet. Being converted to the ufe of a public fchool, it has had fome benefactors, and at prefent it has the following endowments:

Doctor George Owen, phyfician to King Henry 8th. by indenture dated the 2d of May, 1552, obliged the mayor, burgeffes, and commonalty of Briftol annually to pay for ever 4l. to the mafter of this fchool.

John Whitfon, Efq; by his laft will dated the 27th of March, 1627, appointed the mayor, burgeffes, and commonalty of Briftol and their fucceffors for ever in truft, that they pay a chief rent of 8l. 10s. 6d. and three bufhels and a half of wheat and three bufhels of rye yearly for ever, out of his manor of Chew Magna, to the mafter of the free grammar fchool at or near Redcliff church in Briftol.

This chapel as it ftood fo near the church of Redcliff as to hide in fome meafure the weftern view of it, was in the year 1766 entirely taken down, and in the wall under the weft window of the chapel was found a ftone coffin with a figure carved on the lid, and under it, " Johannes Lamyngton." * On open-

ing

* John Lamyngton is mentioned among the chaplains of Redcliff church for the year 1393, fo that Lamyngton's Lady's chamber might be the name of this building before the fraternity of the Holy Ghoft gave it the name of St. Sprite's chapel. See p. 568.

ing it the fhape of the whole human body, or rather of its folid parts, was to be feen preferved in the natural pofition, but on being touched fell all into duft. The fchool is ftill continued in St. Mary's chapel at the eaft end of Redcliff church, without any additional endowment.

Beyond St. Mary's or Redcliff-hill near Bright-Bow † was of old the hofpital of St. Catherine, in the parifh of Bedminfter, which now joins to Briftol and is a parifh of large extent. The church of Bedminfter is very ancient, and a vicarage formerly belonging to the abby of Whytland, dedicated to St. John the Baptift, and is mother church to Redcliff and St. Thomas, which with Abbots Leigh are chapels of eafe to it. The hofpital of St. Catherine was in Bedminfter where now a glafs-houfe is built : fome arch windows there ftili point out its fite, and the fields behind it are called Catherine Meads to this day. It was endowed with them and other lands in Afhton. Tanner's Notitia Monaftica by Nafmith refers to deeds concerning it. The following is William of Worcefter's account, p. 294. — " Longitudo navis ecclefiæ, &c. The length of the nave of the church of St. Catherine, called elfewhere the Free Chapel, near Briftol, contains 16 yards, its breadth contains $7\frac{1}{2}$ yards ; the length of the chancel 9 yards, its breadth $5\frac{1}{2}$ yards. 1290, Lord Robert Barkle, the founder and patron of the hofpital of St. Catherine, who died May 3. Lord Thomas de Barkle, Knight, brother of the faid Robert, who gave lands and tenements in Byfhopfworth and confirmed the faid foundation made by the fame Robert. Sir Adam de Heyron, Knight, lord of the village of Afhton, Thomas Heyron his predeceffor, who gave lands to it ; Alexander de Aineto, his anceftors and fucceffors; William Lyons, his anceftors and fucceffors; William Comyn, of Briftol; Richard Dyer ; Julian Sufe ; John the fon of the goldfmith ; Chriftian Roo ; John Stryglyng ; Sir John Thorp, prieft."—Thefe were benefactors to this hofpital. He mentions this hofpital alfo under the following name : " Hofpitalis domus in ecclefia Sanctæ Catherinæ ubi magifter Henricus Abyngdon muficus de capella regis eft magifter." The faid Abyngdon was mafter of St. Catherine's hofpital in the year 1465.

In fome old court rolls, dated the 1ft of Richard 2d. at Ayfchton Merryotts, in poffeffion of Sir John Hugh Smyth, Bart. it appears that the hofpital of St. Catherine was exempted from fuit and fervice at that court, by a charter of Alexander de Alneto then produced, by which lands in Afhton near the church and oppofite Clevedon were granted by him to Robert the mafter and the brethren

---

† Alfo called Brightene-bridge from Brightric, who probably firft made a bridge there, for the better communication between Bedminfter and Briftol.

thren and fifters of that hofpital in free alms," &c. This Alexander de Aineto (of the Alder Grove) was lord of the manor of Afhton and a great man in his time ; and at the end of a manufcript entituled, Liber Ruber Bathoniæ, in the poffeffion of Lord Weymouth at Longleat, written in 1428, is the following epitaph in a hand-writing different from the manufcript in the year 1582.

" Hic jacet Alexander de Alneto et Erneb'orea uxor ejus, et Julius de Alneto filius eorum et Lucia de Marifcis filia corum et Jordanus de Marifcis filius ejufdem Luciæ, et Willielmus de Marifcis filius ejufdem Jordani.—N. B. Dedit Alexander ecclefiæ petri et monachis Bathoniæ Manerium de Chamely anno 1153, reg. Steph. ulti.

To this is fubjoined the following note by the writer: " Eft iftud epitaphium, &c.—This epitaph was carved at the right of the entrance of the ruinous church formerly dedicated to Minerva, to be feen in that place by the curious, December 7, 1582, in the city of Bath."

In 1349 Ralph Bifhop of Bath and Wells admitted Walter de Eftham prieft to the honfe or hofpital of St. Catherine near Briftol, at the prefentation of Lord Thomas de Berkeley, patron.

1343, John de Kynenton, 29th October, prefented.

1357, 4th December, John de Eggefworth. The bifhop received his profeffion following: " Ego Johannes Eggefworth, &c. i. e. I John Eggefworth promife perpetual obfervance of good morals, chaftity, all denial of property, which I will keep from my foul from this time according to the rule of the hofpital of St. Catherine near Briftol, in the diocefe of Bath and Wells, which I henceforth profefs as ordained by the holy fathers, as much as is confiftent with the faid rule, or hereafter fhall be confiftent for me to obferve, and I will lead my life according to regular difcipline." At the fame time he fwore obedience to his diocefan Ralph Bifhop of Bath and Wells. Regift. Radulph. f. 328.

In 1375, Richard Bromdon by will gave 20s. to maintain the caufey at Brightenee-Bonghe and the houfe or convent of St. Catherine near Briftol, called alfo in Dugd. Baron. p. 358. " St. Catherine Pulle near Briftol," to which Lord Berkeley gave lands in Afhton, Portbury, and Bedminfter.

Richard Waldgrave being mafter or cuftos of this hofpital, 1553, an agreement was made that the image of the holy St. Catherine, fixed up in the front houfe between the caufey and the barton of the faid hofpital, fhould be kept clean and in repair. There is a long poem of the Life of St. Catherine, and fome good verfes in it, in the Lib. Rub. Bathon. penes Lord Weymouth.

The

The chapel of St. Catherine was valued at the diſſolution at 2 1l. 15s. 4d. whereof rents reſolute yearly were 5s. 4d. de claro 2 1l. 10s. At its being fold, 2 Edward 6th. it was certified to have a chalice of ſilver, 8 ounces et dimid. ornaments appraiſed at 4s. 6d. bell metal 101 lb. that William Clark was then maſter of St. Catherine's hoſpital, who aſſigned only three cottages for the poor to live in, but no maintenance. The prieſt before him was bound to ſay maſs thrice a week. It hence appears this houſe went gradually to decay, the friers by degrees deſerting it, probably the caſe of many other religious houſes.

Beſides theſe hoſpitals in the pariſh of Redcliff, there is one juſt without Temple-gate called " Rogers's Magdalens of Nunney." Falling to decay, it was rebuilt. It affords a dwelling for eight women and as many men. November 17, 1613, Mr. Rice Thomas, parſon of Norton Malreward, in the county of Somerſet, left them 20s. per annum.

There is alſo an almſhouſe on the ſouth ſide of Redcliff-hill, founded by Mr. Canynges, for fourteen perſons to inhabit.

On the north ſide of Pile-ſtreet in 1739 was founded a free-ſchool for boys, by the joint contributions of many well-diſpoſed inhabitants of this pariſh, which has received the following endowments, and thoſe p. 393, before :

1734, Edward Colſton, Eſq; - - -	£ 20	0	0 per ann.
Matthew Worgan gave in money - -	21	0	0
1742, John Fiſher, gentleman, ditto, the intereſt to apprentice out a poor boy - - -	100	0	0
1749, Giles Malpas built the ſchool-houſe -	120	0	0
John Macie, Eſq; gave - -	50	0	0
Mrs. Gratian Kington - - -	50	0	0

On Redcliff-hill is, 1787, a houſe built for a ſchool for girls, ſupported by voluntary contributions.

In Redcliff churchyard is an almſhouſe for twelve widows, called the Houſe of Mercy, built and endowed 1784 by the late Mr. William Fry, who has appointed feoffees for the management of this charity, where the widows have each a neat room, lodging, and maintenance.

The

The following Interlude is among the moſt early communications of Chatterton to Mr. Barrett, and as it has an immediate relation to the church of Redcliff, is here printed verbatim et literatim from Chatterton's own writing, and ſubmitted to the judgment of the reader :

An ENTYRLUDE, plaied bie the Carmelyte Freeres at Maſtre Canynges hys greete howſe, before Maſtre Canynges and Byſhoppe [1] Carpenterre, on dedicatynge the chyrche of *Oure Ladie of Redclefte,* hight

THE PARLYAMENTE OF SPRYTES.

Wroten bie T. Rowleie and J. [2] Iſcam.

Entroduſtyon bie Queene Mabbe. ——— (*Bie Iſcamme.*)

WHAN from the erthe the ſonnes [3] hulſtred,
Than from the flouretts [4] ſtraughté with dewe ;
Mie leege menne makes yee [5] awhaped,
And wytches theyre [6] wytchencref doe.
Then ryſe the ſprytes [7] ugſome and [8] rou,
And take theyre walke the [9] letten throwe.
Than do the ſprytes of valourous menne,
Agleeme along the [10] barbed halle ;
Pleaſaunte the [11] moltrynge banners kenne,
Or fytte arounde yn honourde ſlalle —
Oure ſprytes [12] atourne theyr [13] eyne to nyghté,
And looke on Canynge his chyrche brygbte.

In

1 john Carpenter, biſhop of Worceſter, who, in conjunſtion with Mr. Canynge, founded the abbey at Weſtbury. 2 John Iſcam, according to Rowley, was a canon of the monaſtery of Saint Auguſtine in Briſtol. He wrote a dramatic piece called " The Pleaſaunt Dyſcorſes of Lamyngeton ;" alſo at the deſire of Mr. Canynge (Rowley being then colleſting of drawings for Mr. Canynge) he tranſlated a Latin piece called Miles Bryſtolli into Engliſh metre. The place of his birth is not known. 3 Hidden. 4 Stretched. I think this line is borrowed from a much better one of Rowley's, viz. " Like kynge cuppes braſteynge wyth the mornynge dew." The reaſon why I think Iſcam guilty of the plagiary is, that the Songe to Ella, from whence the above line is taken, was wrote when Rowley was in London colleſting of drawings for Mr. Canynge to build the church, and Iſcam wrote the above little before the finiſhing of the churchi 5 Aſtoniſhed. 6 Witchcraft. 7 Terrible. 8 Ugly. 9 This is a word peculiar to the Weſt, and ſignifies a churchyard. 10 Hung with banners or trophies. 11 Mouldering. 12 Turn. 13 Eyes.

In fothe yn alle mie [14]bifmarde rounde,
Troolie the thynge mufte be [15]bewryen :
Inne ftone or woden worke ne founde,
Nete fo [16]bielecoyle to myne eyne,
As ys goode Canynge hys chyrche of ftone —
Whych [17] blatauntlie wylle fhewe his prayfe alone.

To Johannes Carpenterre Byfhoppe of Worcefterre. ——— (*Bie Rowleie.*)

To you goode Byfhoppe, I addrefs mie faie,
To you who honoureth the clothe you weare ;
Lyke pretious [18]bighes ynne golde of befte allaie
Eehone dothe make the other feeme more fayre :
[19] Other than you where coulde a manne be founde
So fytte to make a place bee holie grounde.

The fainctes ynne ftone fo netelie [20]carvelled,
Theie [21] fcantlie are whatte theie enfeeme to bee ;
Bie fervente praier of yours myghte rear theyre heade,
Ande chaunte owte maffes to oure Vyrgyne —

D D D D   Was

14 Curious.   15 Bewryen, declared or made known.   16 Well pleafing or welcome.
17 Loudly.   18 Jewels.   19 Carpenter dedicated the church as appears by the following poem, wrote by Rowley :

Soone as bryght fonne alonge the fkyne, han fente hys ruddie lyghte ;
And fayryes hyd ynne Oflyppe cuppes, tylle wyfh'd approche of nyghte —
The mattyn belle wyth fhryllie founde, reeckode throwe the ayre ;
A troop of holie freeres dyd, for Jefus maffe prepare —
Arounde the highe unfaynted chyrche, wythe holie relyques wente ;
And every door and pofte aboute wythe godlie thynges befprente.
Then Carpenter yn fcarlette drefte, and mytred holylie ;
From Maftre Canynge hys greate howfe, wyth rofarie dyd hie —
Before hym wente a throng of freeres who dyd the maffe fonge fynge,
Behynde hym Maftre Canynge came, tryckd lyke a barbed kynge,
And then a rowe of holie freeres, who dyd the mafs fonge found.
The procurators and chyrche reeves next preft upon the ground,
And when unto the chyrche theye came a holie maffe was fange,
So lowdlie was theyr fwotie voyce, the heven fo hie it range.
Then Carpenter dyd puryfie the chyrche to Godde for aie,
Wythe holie maffes and good pfalmes whyche hee dyd thereyn faie.
Then was a fermon preeched foon bie Carpynterre holie,
And after that another one ypreechen was bie mee :
Then alle dyd goe to Canynges houfe an Enterlude to playe,
And drynk hys wyne and ale fo goode, and praie for him for aie.

20 Carved.   21 Scarcely.

Was everic prelate lyke a Carpenterre,
The chyrche woulde ne blufhe at a Wynchefterre.

Learned as Beauclerke, as the confeffour
Holie ynne lyfe, lyke Canynge charitable,
Bufie in holie chyrche as Vavafour ;
Slacke yn thynges evylle, yn alle goode thynges ftable,
Honeft as Saxonnes was, from whence thou'rt fprunge ;
Tho boddie weak thie foule for ever younge.

Thou knoweft welle thie confciene free from fteyne,
[22] Thie foule her rode no fable batements have ;
[23] Yclenchde oer wythe vyrtues befte adaygne,
A daie [24] aeterne thie mynde does aie [25] adave.
Ne fpoyled widdowes, orphyans dyftrefte,
Ne ftarvvynge preeftes [26] ycrafe thie nyghtlie refte.

Here then to thee let me for one and alle
Give lawde to Carpenterre and commendatyon,
For hys grerte vyrtues but alas ! too fmalle
Is mie poore fkylle to fhewe you hys jufte [1] blatyon,
Or to blaze forthe hys publicke goode alone,
And alle hys pryvate goode to Godde and hym ys knowne.

Spryte of Nymrodde fpeaketh. ——— (*Bie Ifcamme.*)

Soon as the morne but newlie wake,
Spyed Nyghte [2] yftorven lye ;
On herre corfe dyd dew droppes fhake,
Then fore the fonne upgotten was I.
The rampynge lyon, felle tygere,
The bocke that fkyppes from place to place,
The [3] olyphaunt and [4] rhynocere,
Before mee throughe the greene woode I dyd chace.

Nymrodde

[22] Rode, complection. I take the meaning of this line to be, " The complection of thy foul is free from the black marks of fin." [23] Covered. [24] Eternal. [25] Enjoy. [26] To break. [1] Blation, praife. [2] Dead. [3] Elephant. So an ancient anonymous author :

The olyphaunt of beaftes is
The wifeft I wis,
For hee alwaie dothe eat
Lyttle ftore of meat.

[4] Rhinoceros.

Nymrodde as fcryptures hyght mie name,
Baalle as ⁵ jetted ftories faie ;
For rearynge Babelle of greete fame,
Mie name and ⁶ renome fhalle lyven for aie :
But here I fpie a fyner rearynge,
Genft whych the clowdes dothe not fyghte,
Onne whyche the ftarres doe fytte to appearynge ;
Weeke menne thynke ytte reache the kyngdom of lyghte.
O where ys the manne that buylded the fame,
⁷ Dyfpendynge worldlie ftore fo welle ;
Fayn woulde I chaunge wyth hym mie name,
And ftande ynne hys chaunce ne to goe to helle.

Sprytes of Aſſyrians ſyngeth.

Whan toe theyre caves aeterne ⁸ abefte,
The waters ne moe ⁹ han dyftrefte,
The worlde fo large ;
Butte dyde dyfcharge
Themfelves ynto theyre bedde of refte.

Then menne ¹⁰ befprenged alle abroade,
Ne moe dyde worfhyppe the true Godde ;
But dyd create
Hie temples grèat
Unto the ymage of Nymrodde.

But nowe the Worde of Godde is come,
Borne of maide Marie toe brynge home
Mankynde hys fhepe,
Theme for to keepe
In the folde of hys heavenlie kyngdome.

Thys chyrche whyche Canynge he dyd reer,
To bee ¹¹ difpente in prayfe and prayer,
Mennes foules to fave,
From ¹² vowrynge grave,
Ande puryfye them ¹³ heaven were.

D n D n 2 *Sprytes*

⁵ .Devifed or faigned.   6 Renown.   7 Expending.   8 Abefte. according to Rowley,
humbled or brought down.   " And Rowleie faies " fhie pryde wylle be abefte."
Entroduⁿⁱⁿn to the Entyrlude of the Apoftate.

9 Preterite of have.   10 Scattered.   11 Difpente, ufed.   12 Devouring.
13 Heaven-ward, fo Rowley.

Sprytes of ª *Elle,* ᵇ *Bythrycke, Fytz-hardynge, Frampton, Gauntes, Segowen, Lanyngeton, Knyghtes Templars, and Byrtonne.* ———— *(Bie Rowleie.)*

Spryte of Bythrycke speaketh.

Elle, thie Bryſtowe is thie onlie care,
Thou arte lyke dragonne ᶜ vyllant of yts gode ;
Ne lovynge dames toe kynde moe love can bear,
Ne Lombardes over golde moe vyllaunt broode.

Spryte of Elle speeketh.

ᵈ Swythyn, yee ſprytes forſake the ᵉ bollen floude,
And ᶠ browke a ſygthe wyth mee, a ſyghte enfyne ;
Welle have I vended myne for Danyſhe bloude,
Syth thys greete ſtruĉture greete mie ᵍ whaped eyne.
Yee that have buylden on the Radcleſte ſyde,
Tourne there youre eyne and ſee your workes outvyde.

Spryte of Bythrycke speeketh.

What wondrous monumente ! what pyle ys thys !
That hyndes in wonders chayne ʰ entendemente !
That doth aloof the ayrie ſkyen kyſs,
And ſeemeth mountaynes joyned·bie cemente,
From Godde hys greete and wondrous ſtorehouſe ſente.
Fulle welle myne eyne ⁱ arede ytte canne ne bee,
That manne coulde reare of thylke agreete extente,
A chyrche ſo ʲ bauſyn fetyve as wee ſee :
The flemed cloudes diſparted from it flie,
Twylle bee, I wis, to alle eternytye.

Elle's spryte speeketh.

Were I once moe caſte yn a mortalle frame,
To heare the chauntrie ſonge ſounde ynne myne eare,
To heare the maſſes to owre holie dame,
To viewe the croſs yles and the arches fayre.

Throughe

" Not goulde or bighes wylle brynge thee heaven were
Ne kyne or mylkie flockes upon the playne,
Ne mannours rych nor banners brave rnd fayre,
Ne wiſe the ſweeteſt of the erthlie trayne.
Entroduĉtyon to the Enterlude of the Apoſtate."

ª Keeper of Briſtol caſtle in the time of the Saxons. ᵇ An Angle-Saxon, who in William the Conqueror's time had Briſtol. ᶜ Vigilant. ᵈ Swythyn, quickly. ᵉ Swelled. ᶠ Enjoy. ᵍ Whaped, amazed. ʰ Underſtanding. ⁱ Conceive. ʲ Elegantly large. ᵏ Frighted.

Throughe the halfe hulſtred fylver twynklynge glare
Of yon bryghte moone in foggie mantles dreſte,
I muſt contente the buyldyng to ¹ aſpere,
Whylſte ᵐ iſhad cloudes the ⁿ hallie ſyghte arreſte.
Tyll as the nyghtes growe ° wayle I flie the lyghte,
O were I manne agen to fee the ſyghte.

There fytte the canons; clothe of fable hue
Adorne the boddies of them everie one;
The chaunters whyte with fcarfes of woden blewe,
And crymfon ᵖ chappeaus for them toe put onne,
Wythe golden taſſyls glyttrynge ynne the funne;
The dames ynne kyrtles alle of Lyncolne greene,
And knotted ſhoone pykes of brave coloures done:
A fyner fyghte yn fothe was never feen.

Byrtonnes ſpryte ſpeaketh.

Inne tyltes and turnies was mie dear delyghte,
For manne and Godde hys warfare han renome;
At everyche tyltynge yarde mie name was hyghte,
I beare the belle awaie whereer I come.
Of Redclfte chyrche the buyldynge newe I done,
And dyd fulle manie bolie place endowe,
Of Maries houfe made the foundacyon,
And gave a threefcore markes to Johnes hys toe.
Then clos'd myne eyne on erthe to ope no moe,
Whylſt fyx moneths mynde upon mie grave was doe.
Full gladde am I mie chyrche was ᑫ pyghten down,
Syth thys brave ſtruƈturc doth agreete myne eye.
Thys ʳ geaſon buyldynge ˢ limedſt of the towne,
Like to the donours foule, ſhalle never die;
But if percafe Tyme, of hys dyre envie,
Shalle beate yttc to rude walles and ᵗ throckes of ſtone;
The ᵛ faytour traveller that paſſes bie
Wylle fee yttes ʷ royend auntyaunte ſplendoure ſhewne
Inne the ˣ crafd arches and the carvellynge,
And pyllars theyre greene heades to heaven rearyngc.

¹ To view.   ᵐ Broken.   ⁿ Well-pleaſing, alſo holy.   ° Old.   ᵖ Chappeaus, hats
or caps of eſtates.   ᑫ Pyghten, pulled down.   ʳ Rare.   ˢ Moſt noble.   ᵗ Heaps.
ᵛ Wandering.   ʷ Ruin'd.   ˣ Broken, old.

Spryte of Y Segowen speeketh.

a Beftoykynge golde was once myne onlie toie,
Wyth ytte mie foule wythynne the coffer laie ;
Itte dyd the maftrie of mie lyfe emploie,
Bie nyghte mie a leman, and mie b jubbe bie daye.
Once as I dofynge yn the wytch howre laie,
Thynkynge howe to c benym the orphyans breádde,
And from the d redelefs take theyre goodes awaie,
I from the fkien heard a voyce, which faid,
Thou fleepeft, but loe Sathan is awake ;
Some deede thats holie doe, or hee thie foule wylle take.
I fwythyn was e upryft wyth feere f aftounde ;
Methoughte yn g merke was plaien devylles felle :
Strayte dyd I nomber twentie aves rounde,
Thoughten full foone for to go to helle.
In the morne mie cafe to a goode preefte dyd telle,
Who dyd h areede mee to ybuild that daie
The chyrche of Thomas, thenne to pieces felle.
Mic heart i difpanded into heaven laie :
Soon was the fylver to the workmenne given, —
Twas befte k aftowde a l karynte gave to Heavne.
But welle, I wote, thie caufalles were not foe,
Twas love of Godde that fette thee on the rearynge
Of this fayre chyrche, O Canynge, for to doe
Thys m lymed buyldynge of fo fyne appearynge :
Thys chyrch owre leffer buyldyngs all owt-daryinge,
Lyke to the moone wythe ftarres of lyttle lyghte ;
And after tymes the n feetyve pyle reverynge,
The prynce of chyrches buylders thee fhall hyghte ;
Greet was the caufe, but greeter was the effecte —
So alle wyll faie who doe thys place profpect.

Spryte of Fytz Hardynge speeketh.

From royal parentes dyd I have retaynynge,
The redde hayrde Dane confefte to be mie fyre ;

The

---

y Aullfurer, a native of Lombardy. z Deceiving. a Leman, whore. b Bottle.
c To take away. d Redelefs, helplefs. e Rifen up. f Aftonifhed. g Darknefs.
h Counfel. i expanded. k Beftow'd. l A loan. m Noble. n Handfome or elegant.

The Dane who often throwe thys kyngdom draynynge,
Would mark theyre waie athrowgh wythe blonde and fyre.
As ſtopped ryvers alwaies ryſe moe hygher,
And rammed ſtones bie oppoſures ſtronger bee
So thie whan vanquyſhed dyd prove moe dyre,
And for one [o] peyſan thele dyd threeſcore ſlee.
From them of Denmarques royalle bloude came I,
Welle myghte I boaſte of mie gentylytie;
The pypes maie ſounde and bubble forthe mie name,
And tellen what on Radclefte ſyde I dyd:
Trinytie Colledge ne agrutche mie fame,
The fayreſt place in Bryſtowe ybuylded.
The royalle bloude that thorow mie vaynes ſlydde
Dyd tynƈte mie harte wythe manie a noble thoughte;
Lyke to mie mynde the mynſter yreared,
Wythe noble carvel workmanſhyppe was wroughte.
Hie at the [p] deys, lyke to a kynge on's throne,
Dyd I take place and was myſelf alone.
But thou, the buylder of this [q] ſwotie place,
Where alle the ſaynƈtes in ſweete ajunƈtyon ſtande,
A verie heaven for yttes fetyve grace,
The glorie and the wonder of the lande,
That ſhewes the buylders mynde and fourmers hande,
To bee the beſte thatte on erthe remaynes;
At once for wonder and delyghte commaunde,
Shewynge howe muche hee of the godde reteynes.
Canynge the great, the charytable, and good,
Noble as kynges if not of kyngelie bloude.

Spryte of Framptone ſpeeketh.

Bryſtowe ſhall ſpeeke mie name, and Radclefte toe,
For here mie deedes were goddelye everychone;
As Owdens [r] mynſter bie the gate wylle ſhewe,
And Johnes at Bryſtowe what mie workes han done.
Beſydes [s] ancre howſe that I han begunne;
Butte myne comparde to thyſſen ys a [t] groffe:

Nete

[o] A countryman, alſo a foot ſoldier. [p] Firſt table in a monaſtery, where the ſuperior ſat. [q] Sweet, or delighting. [r] monaſtery. [s] Another. [t] A laughing-ſtock.

Nete to bee mencioned or looked upon,
A verie ᵛ punelſtre or verie ſcoffe ;
Canynge, thie name ſhall lyven be for aie,
Thie name ne wyth the chyrche ſhalle waſte awaie.

Spryte of Gaunts ſpeeketh.

I dyd fulle manie reparatyons give,
And the Bonne Hommes dyd fulle ryche endowe ;
As tourynge to mie Godde on erthe dyd lyve,
So alle the Bryſtowe chronycles wylle ſhewe.
Butte alle mie deedes wylle bee as nothynge nowe,
Sythe Canynge have thys buyldynge fynyſhed,
Whych ſeemeth to be the pryde of Bryſtowe,
And bie ne buyldeyng to bee overmatched :
Whyche aie ſhalle laſte and bee the prayſe of alle,
And onlie in the wrecke of nature falle.

A Knyghte Templars ſpryte ſpeeketh.

In hallie lande where Saraſins defyle
The grounde whereon oure Savyour dyd goe,
And Chryſte hys temple make to ʷ moſchyes vyle,
Wordies of deſpyte genſt oure Savyour throwe.
There twas that we dyd owre warfarage doe,
Guardynge the pylgryms of the Chryſtyan ˣ faie ;
And dyd owre holie armes in bloude embrue,
Movynge lyke thonder boultes yn drear arraië.
Owre ſtrokes lyke ʸ levyn tareynge the tall tree
Owre Godde owre arme wyth lethalle force dyd ᶻ dree.
ᵃ Maint tenures fayre, ande mannoures of greete welthe,
Greene woodes, and brook lettes runnynge throughe the lee,
Dyd menne us ġyve for theyre deare foule her helthe,
Gave erthlie ryches for goodes heavenlie.
Nee dyd we lette oure ryches ᵇ untyle bee,
But dyd ybuylde the Temple chyrche foe fyne,
The whyche ys wroughte abowte ſo ᶜ biſmarelic ;

Itte

ᵛ An empty boaſt;   ʷ Moſques,   ˣ Faith,   ʸ Lightning.   ᶻ Drive.   ᵃ Many.
ᵇ Uſeleſs;   ᶜ Curiouſly;

Itte feemeth ᵈ camoys to the wondrynge eyne;
And ever and anon when belles rynged,
From place to place ytte moveth yttes hie heade:
Butte Canynge from the fweate of hys owne browes,
Dyd gette hys golde and rayfe thys fetyve howfe.

Lanyngetonnes Spryte fpeeketh.

Lette alle mie faultes bee buried ynne the grave;
Alle obloquyes be rotted mythe mie dufte;
Lette him fyrft carpen that no ᵉ wemmes have:
'Tys pafte. mannes nature for to bee aie jufte.
But yette in fothen to rejoyce I mufte,
That I dyd not immeddle for to buylde;
Sythe thys ᶠ quaintiffed place fo gloryous,
Seemeynge alle chyrches joyned yn one ᵍ guylde,
Has nowe fupplied for what I had done,
Whych toe mie ʰ cierge is a gloryous fonne.

Elle's Spryte fpeeketh.

Then lette us alle do jyntelie reveraunce here,
The befte of menne and Byfhoppes here doe ftande:
Who are Coddes ⁱ fhepfterres and do take good care,
Of the goode fhepe hee putteth yn theyre hand;
Ne one is lofte butte alle in well ᵏ likande
Awayte to heare the Generalle Byfhoppes calle,
When Mychaels trompe fhall found to ynmofte lande,
Affryghte the wycked and awaken alle:
Then Canynge ryfes to eternal refte,
And fyndes hee chofe on erthe a lyfe the befte.

E e e e   CHAP.

ᵈ Crooked upwards, Lat. fimus.   ᵉ Faults.   ᶠ Curioufly devifed.   ᵍ Company.   ʰ Candle.
ⁱ Shepherds.   ᵏ Liking.

C H A P. XXV.

Of the GREAT BENEFACTORS *to the* CITY, *their* CHARITABLE
FOUNDATIONS, ENDOWMENTS, &c.

THERE is not perhaps a nation upon earth, who have made fuch ample
provifion for the poor as this, as well by charitable donations as by
erecting almfhoufes, hofpitals, infirmaries &c. for their relief. By the returns
made by the minifters and churchwardens of the parifhes of England and
Wales to the Houfe of Commons, of private donations invefted in the hands
of truftees and feoffees only in the year 1788, it appears the whole annual produce of the money given was 48,243l. 10s. 5d. of land 210,467l. 8s. 10d.
total 258,710l. 19s. 3d. an immenfe fum annually diftributed, which would be
ftill greater if the enquiries had been extended to corporations companies &c.
It reflects deferved applaufe on the worthy benefactors, who acting upon
motives of true religion and upon chriftian principles have imitated the gracious example of that divine perfon who went about doing good, and left us
an example that we fhould follow his fteps in relieving the fatherlefs, the
widow, the poor, the imprifoned, the ftranger, the difeafed, the hungry and
thirfty ;—yet is it to be lamented, that notwithftanding all thefe liberal benefactions and a conftant and regular levy befides upon all the eftates in the
kingdom by the poor-rates fo burthenfome in each parifh, yet through fome
neglect or mifmanagement, the want of keeping them in regular employ or
fome other caufe, the poor ftill complain in our ftreets, and every where
diftreffed objects prefent themfelves to our view. It is at prefent under the
confideration of Parliament to find a remedy for this great evil.—The worthy
benefactors of old naturally thought they fhould greatly relieve, if not remove
the diftreffes of their fellow-creatures, and ought to be ever efteemed and held
in veneration for the noble charities they beftowed and princely foundations
they eftablifhed. None have more diftinguifhed themfelves than the merchants of Briftol on this occafion : they can boaft of their Canynges and Colfton, two moft refpectable names and characters for charity of the early and

later

later times; befides a long lift of worthies, who have fignalized themfelves for their charitable donations at different periods, founded fchools, hofpitals, and houfes for religious inftruction, attentive to the fupport of bodily wants, and folicitous at the fame time to reclaim the vicious and inftruct the young and the ignorant in the great and important truths of the chriftian religion, pro_viding in the moft liberal manner for the body and foul, humanizing the heart, and giving it good impreffions, feldom afterwards to be crafed.

The following is the long lift of Benefactors this city hath to boaft of, who many in their life time, more at their death, left large fums of money or eftates in land to charitable ufes, impelled thereto by a generous philanthropy or love of their fellow-creatures, and the more noble principle, the religious confideration of fulfilling the exprefs command of their Saviour and their God; and their works do follow them.—Some of them duly fenfible how neceffary both to health and morals, labour and employment in fome bufinefs are, have very judicioufly left fums of money towards a ftock or fund to keep the poor at work, the beft of charities; even the confined prifoner, many in hofpitals, almfhoufes and infirmaries might employ their hands in fome flight bufinefs, as knitting, making toys, fpinning wool, hemp, or cotton &c. to their own emolument and advantage to their health, as well as the good of the commonwealth: whilft living there wholly idle and their hands unemployed, it induces a habit of lazinefs ever after, renders the mind torpid, and the body morbid, and the difeafe inveterate, often protracting the cure.

It will be found at length, nothing but employing the poor will do to alle_viate the burden of the poor-rates this nation now labours under beyond all bounds. Till feveral parifhes that lie contiguous join in erecting a work_houfe to keep their poor at work, no human means will ever be devifed to remedy the evil; the poor without employment will become more wretched and idle, more wicked and more difeafed, relying upon the parifh pay they lofe all good habits of induftry, become indolent and difeafed, notwithftanding the infirmaries and hofpitals erected for their relief.

It is very certain, when charities were invefted in religious houfes formerly, they were often much abufed and perverted to other purpofes than the donor or founder intended, but in a public corporation there is lefs danger of foch abufe; and greater care and better management where fo many fuperintend may juftly be expected, to prevent the charities by length of time deviating from the donors intentions, and ceafing to anfwer the good ends for which they were inftituted. The Corporation of Briftol have to their honour recorded them all in a book, open to the infpection of the whole body, where the wills are all inferted, the lands defcribed which are allotted for their fupport, and their ends afcertained, that nothing but wilful inattention and negleft can ever occafion their being mifapplied or loft.

CITY BENEFACTORS.

		l.	s.	d.
1292, Simon Burton gave land by will, producing 4s. per week, vefted in the corporation of Briftol, to the relief of 16 poor people in an almfhoufe erefted by him in the Long-Row, orphan book C. B. about	- -	220	o	o
1385, Walter Darby by will gave 40l. towards building the tower of St. Werburgh's church, - - -		40	o	
And 17 tenements to be fold and the money to be diftri-buted to the poor.				
And 205l. to religious houfes, - • -		205	o	o
All vefted in the corporation O. B. fol. 15.				
1377, Richard Spicer by will gave 17 tenements to the city's ufe, now the Back-Hall, formerly Spicer's-Hall, corpora-tion O. B.				
1388, Walter Frampton by will gave tenements towards marrying poor maidens and other good ufes, corporation O. B. f. 21.				
1400, *John Barftable by will gave lands and tenements to found an almhoufe in the Old Market, vefted in the corporation, recorded in O. B.				
1403, *Thomas Knapp gave by will to the common profit of the city		133	6	8
And towards repairing St. Nicholas church -		20	o	o
Corporation O. B.				
1434, Mark Williams gave by will to buy corn to ferve the poor at an eafy rate, (corporation little red book f. 71,)		66	13	4
1466, William Canynges gave by deed for divine offices in Red-cliff church - - - -		340	o	o
And in plate to the faid church - -		160	o	o
Vefted in the vicar and proftors of Redcliff.				
1474, He alfo gave by will five tenements and other lands to be fold, the money half to the city's ufe and half to the chauntries, and to the poor, blind and lame, -		60	o	o
He alfo erefted an almfhoufe, corporation great red book f. 247, 291, and O. B. f. 200.				

1489,

		l.	*s.*	*d.*
1489,	Robert Strange gave by deed lands to found St. John's almſhouſe. Veſtry of St. John's.			
1493,	*William Spencer gave 2ol. to be lent to the mayor during his office, and 66l. 8s. 8d. to the ſheriffs, paying 2s. weekly to the poor of the almſhouſe in Lewin's-mead, Corporation	86	8	8
1494,	He gave alſo by will a tenement of 4l. per annum for ſermons &c. Redcliff.			
	John Bagod gave tenements for the uſe of the city, they paying yearly to the priſoners in Newgate 3s. 4d.			
1503,	*John Foſter gave by will lands and tenements for building and endowing Foſter's almſhouſe.			
1521,	John Matthew by will gave lands and tenements to the corporation for Trinity almſhouſe.			
1532,	*Robert Thorne gave by will 3ool. to buy corn and wood when cheap, and ſell to the poor at the ſame price when dear, - - - - -	300	0	0
	And 5ool. to lend intereſt free to young clothiers, -	500	0	0
	And 3ool. towards founding his father's grammar-ſchool,	300	0	0
	And 1235l. in divers charities to be paid by his executors,	1235	0	0
	Cor. G. R. B. f. 233.			
1541,	Thomas Hart by will to the corporation 1ool. to public uſes,	100	0	0
	And tenements the income to free the city gates from toll, G. R. B. of Orphans f. 259, 292.			
1541,	*Thomas White by deed Jan. 14, gave lands in the manor of Hinton Derham, Gloceſterſhire, to feoffees and the chamberlain 11l. per annum, to exempt the Severn trows from paying toll, cuſtom, murage, or keyage for goods carried from the key of Briſtol, payable to the ſheriff or other perſon: and 2l. 8s. to Foſter's almſhouſe, ditto to St. John's ditto, ditto to Spencer's dito, ditto to St. Thomas ditto; 1l. to All-Saints pipe, ditto to St. John's ditto, in all 22l. 12s. per ann. G. R. B. f. 33.			
1542,	He alſo gave by will 1l. 1os. 8d. per ann. to the priſoners in Newgate, G. R. B. f. 235.			
1542,	King Henry the 8th. gave by charter lands to the dean and chapter, they paying thereout 2ol. per ann. to poor houſekeepers, and 2ol. to repair highways.			

1546,

1546, Nicholas Thorne gave by will to the corporation 100l. for   *l.*   *s.*   *d.*
     repairing bridges, 25l. for repairing the banks and a gra-
     nary, 63l. 13s. 4d. to maids on their marriage, 300l. to the
     library at Bartholemew's, 36l. 13s. 4d. for repairing the
     fchool, and 400l. to lend young clothiers,   -   928 6 8

1550, William Pickos by will gave the chamberlain 50l. for re-
     pairing highways, and 20l. for St. Thomas pipe,   70 ‹
     And land 6l. 13s. 4d. per ann. for the poor in Burton's
     almfhoufe, G. O. B. f. 518.

1552, Dr. George Owen gave by deed to the corporation
     tenements value 53l. 16s. 6d. per ann. to pay thereout
     30l. 6s. 8d. to 20 poor in Fofter's almfhoufe at 7d. each
     every Friday, 1l. to other poor on feftival days, 12l. to
     a preacher yearly, 4l. to the mafter of the grammar-
     fchool on Redcliff-Hill, in all 47l. 6s. 8d.

1555, *Richard Whatley gave by will a tenement value 10s. per
     ann. to All-Saints almfhoufe, G. O. B. f. 291.

1558, William Chefter gave out of a tenement called Black Friers
     per ann. 1l. 6s. to the almfhoufe on St. James's-Back, to
     be paid 6d. weekly.

1559, Humphry Hook by will gave the corporation 680l. to pay
     4s. per week to the poor of St. Stephen's in bread, and
     4s. per week in coal, the remainder of the intereft to
     Queen Elizabeth's Hofpital, -   -   -   680 0 0

1560, James Chefter gave to the corporation 6l. 13s. 4d. to the
     ufe of the poor, and 5l. per ann. to the fame ufe,   6 13 4

1564, James Dowle by will gave 10l. to the hofpital in the Marfh,
     and 10l. to repair the caufeway towards Auft, O. B. f. 293, 20 0 0

1565, John Such gave the corporation by will 4l. for the poor of
     the city, and 2l. for the fchool in the Marfh, O. B. f. 295, 6 0 0

1566, *Sir Thomas White by deed gave the corporation and St.
     John's college in Oxford 2000l. to purchafe land of
     120l. per ann. and thereon to raife 1000l. 800l. to be
     lent 50l. each to 16 young clothiers 10 years intereft free,
     and 200l. to buy corn to be fold to the poor without gain,
     and after the expiration of the 10 years to pay yearly to
     22 other cities 104l. a year in rotation for the ufe of 4

                                          young

young clothiers of the faid towns for 10 years in like *l. s. d.*
manner, - - - - 2000 0 0

1566, *Thomas Silk by deed gave the corporation 40l. the intereft
to be paid between 4 almfhoufes, - - 40 0 0

1567, Walter Weft gave a tenement to the poor of St. Thomas
and the prifoners in Newgate equally.

1569, *John Dodrige gave two gilt flaggons, weight 152 ounces 8
penyweights, for the ufe of the mayor.

 *—— Lambert gave the corporation 16s. per annum for
Trinity almfhoufe.

1572, *Francis Codrington by will gave the corporation lands in
Portifhead to find bedding for the poor of Trinity
hofpital.

1574, William Carr by will gave the corporation land value per
ann. 10l. to the poor of the city in the feveral almfhoufes.
And 26l. 13s. 4d. towards the marriage of poor maids, and
25l. to the highways, O. B. f. 312. - - 51 13 4

1575, Ann Carr by will gave the corporation 60l. to cloath poor
people, and 50l. to buy wood and coal to be fold to the
poor without gain, O. B. f. 51. - - 110 0 0

1575, Richard Wickham by will gave 68l. for a library in the
grammar-fchool, - - - - 68 0 0

1575, John Hollifter by will gave the corporation 10l. to buy
wood to fell to the poor without gain, - - 10 0 0

1579, John Hayden gave by will to the corporation 100l. to be
lent to a young tradefman at 3l. 6s. 8d. intereft - 100 0 0

1582, *Thomas Chefter by deed gave the corporation in land 10l.
per ann. to St. John's almfhoufe 7l. 16s. to that on St.
James's Back 4l. and to the people in Bridewell 2l.

1583, Thomas Kelke gave by will to the corporation in land 10l.
per ann. for the ufe of the poor, and 7ol. for different
ufes, O. B. f. 343. - - - 70 0 0

1583, William Tucker gave by will to the feoffees of St. Nicholas
a tenement, 2l. 6s. 8d. per ann. to the poor of that
parifh 2l. and for a fermon there 6s. 8d.

1586, Ralph Dole by will gave out of a tenement in Maryport-
ftreet, 1l. per ann. to repair St. Peter's pump.

1586,

1586, *John Carr by will gave the corporation the manor of Con-   *l.   s.   d.*
gerſbury, to found Queen Elizabeth's hoſpital.

1587, *John Griffen by will gave 100l. to buy corn to ſell to the
poor without gain, and 5l. to repair Bedminſter cauſey;
and to the feoffees of Temple 2 tenements to relieve the
poor and repair the conduit.   -   -   105   10   0

1587, *Anthony Standbank by will gave the corporation tenements
on the Key, the income to Queen Elizabeth's hoſpital,
O. B. f. 378.

1587, Peter Matthew gave by will 100l. to buy wool and flax to
keep people at work in Bridewell, f. 373,   -   100   0   0

1587, Sir John Young gave 20l. to keep the priſoners at work in
Bridewell, Thorn's Audit Book,   -   -   -   20   0   0

1587, John Wilſon by will gave 2 tenements in St. James's, 26l.
per ann. for the Taylors almſhouſe.

1587, William Young gave by will 50l. to keep the priſoners at
work in Bridewell,   -   -   -   -   50   0   0

1589, *William Bird gave 500l. to Queen Elizabeth's hoſpital,   500   0   0

1592, *Richard Coal gave by will, proved in Doctors Commons
1599, lands and tenements to Queen Elizabeth's hoſpital; alſo to the corporation reverſion of lands for the uſe
of the poor of the city, and 85l. for the poor, 30l. for
repairing the roads, and 20l. to marry poor maids, and
1l. for 2 ſermons at All Saints,   -   -   135   0   0

1594, *Robert Kitchen by will gave the corporation 400l. to be   400   0   0
lent young tradeſmen, at 25l. 10l. and 5l. each, intereſt
free; and 7l. 16s. per ann. in bread to the poor of Chriſt
Church, St. Stephen and Temple; 12l. per ann. for
placing out 6 poor children; 2l. 13s. 4d. per ann. towards maintaining a ſcholar at Oxford or Cambridge;
26l. per ann. to poor houſholders of the ſeveral pariſhes
in Briſtol.   -   -   -   -

1595, John Brown gave by will out of 2 tenements on the Were
2l. 6s. 8d. for ſhirts and ſhifts to the poor of St. Nicholas, the remainder of the rent to the poor of the ſaid
pariſh, &c. Book of Wills, f. 7.

1596, George Snow by will gave the feoffees of St. Nicholas a tenement in Tucker-ſtreet, they paying 1l. per ann. to the

poor

		l.	*s.*	*d.*
	poor, and 6s. 8d. for a fermon. He alfo gave 10l. to be diftributed to the poor of Briftol, N. B. of W. f. 14,	10	0	0
1596,	John White gave by will 43l. 6s. 8d. to the poor,	43	6	8
1597,	Margaret Brown gave 10l. to employ prifoners in Bridewell,	10	0	0
1598,	Thomas Aldworth by will gave 108l. to fundry charities,	108	0	0
1602,*	Lady Mary Ramfey gave 1450l. to Queen Elizabeth's hofpital and the poor of the city, - - -	1450	0	0
1602,*	Ann Colfton gave 200l. to the corporation, they to pay 12l. per ann. to the poor of three almfhoufes -	200	0	0
1602,	William Gibbs gave by will 10l. to Queen Elizabeth's hofpital, - - - - - -	10	0	0
1604,*	Alice Cole gave by will 20l. per ann. to feoffees, arifing out of certain lands, for 4 almfhoufes 4l. each and for 4 fermons; alfo 20l. per ann. more, iffuing from the fame, to cloath poor boys; fhe gave alfo 6ol. to poor decayed houfeholders, and 35l. to be divided between certain minifters, N. B. of W. f. 88, - -	95	0	0
1605,*	John Barker by will gave the corporation 20l. as guardians of orphans, - - - -	20	0	0
1605,	Margaret Tindall by will gave a houfe in Broad-ftreet and lands in Worcefterfhire 17l. per ann. to the feoffees of St. John's.			
1609,	John Fownes gave the corporation 66l. 13s. 4d. to pay annually 4l. to rake and clean the walks in the Marfh,	66	13	4
1610,	John Hopkins gave by deed to the Society of Merchants 10l. they paying 13s. 4d. per ann. to the Merchants almfhoufe, - - - - -	10	0	0
1613,*	Catherine Boucher by will gave a covered cup and fkimmer double gilt for the ufe of the mayor, he paying 10s. for a fermon on the eleftion day at Chrift Church.			
1613,*	Thomas White gave lands and tenements, 52l. per ann. to endow a hofpital in Temple-ftreet.			
1614,*	Francis James gave 50l. to lend poor tradefmen 10l. each intereft free for 2 years, - - -	50	0	0
1614,*	John Dunfter gave 100l. to lend to handicaft men at 10l. each intereft free for 5 years - - -	100	0	0
	Tobias Matthews gave books to the library in King-ftreet.			
1615,	Robert Redwood by deed gave a tenement for a library and 200l. to lend poor tradefmen 10l. each intereft free,	10	0	0

	l.	*s.*	*d.*
1617, Joan Murcott by will gave 200l. to the poor,	200	0	0
1618, Elizabeth Hopkins by will gave to the Society of Merchants 5l. for the Merchants almfhoufe, and 5l. for the Taylors almfhoufe,	10	0	0

1619, *Matthew Haviland gave 4l. per ann. out of certain lands to the corporation for 12 fermons in Newgate.

1619, Thomas Holbin gave by will 100l. to the corporation, they paying to the poor of St. Thomas and for a fermon there 5l. per ann. N. B. of W.   100

1620, William Chaloner by will gave the churchwardens of St. Nicholas 3l. 5s. per ann. iffuing out of certain lands, for them to lay out in bread for 6 poor perfons, a two-penny loaf each every Sunday and for a fermon there.

1622, *George Nethway by will gave 50l. to the corporation to raife 3l. per ann. to increafe the falary of the mafter of the grammar-fchool,   50   0   0

1622, *Dr. Thomas White by deed gave the corporation lands, to erect and endow an almfhoufe in Temple-ftreet, and tenements in Grays Inn, 40l. per ann. for the following ufes: to give the prifoners in Newgate 2l. a fermon at Temple crofs on St. John's-day 1l. 4 fermons at St. Werburgh's 10l. 4 fermons at All Saints 10l. one fermon at Temple 5l. to the poor of Temple hofpital in addition 6l. a dinner for the governor of Temple hofpital on St. Thomas's-day 2l. to charges about the hofpital 4l.

1623-4, He alfo by will gave 100l. to the highways,   100   0   0

1621, Samuel Davis gave by will 50l. to raife 2l. 10s. per ann. 1l. thereof to buy coal for the poor of St. Thomas, 1l. for coal for the poor of Bedminfter, and 10s. for a fermon at St. Thomas,   50   0   0

1622, *Jane Ludlow gave 60l. to raife 3l. per ann. 1l. thereof to the poor of St. Michael's, 1l. to Fofter's almfhoufe, and 1l. to the poor of St. Auguftin the Lefs,   60   0   0

1622, Thomas Jones by will gave the corporation 380l. to lend to poor freemen at 20l. each with intereft, the intereft to charitable ufes,   380   0   0

1624 or 1634, William Burrows gave a tenement in Chriftmas-ftreet, for a parfonage-houfe for the minifter of St.

John's,

s.   d.

John's, and 50l. to repair St. Werburgh's church ; and land 16l. per annum to 8 poor old men and women,   -   -   -   -   -   50   0   0

1625, William Griffith gave 1l. per ann. out of land for 2 fermons at St. John's.

1625, Bartholomew Ruffel by will gave a tenement 8l. per ann. to the poor of St. Michael's and to repair that church.

1626, Thomas Towns gave the corporation 100l. for a ſtock to keep poor people at work,   -   -   -   100   0   0

1627, *Edward Cox gave by will the following fums annually : 4l. for 8 fermons at St. Philip's, 10l. for apprenticing poor boys, and 10l. to buy coal for the different parifhes in Briſtol.

1627, *John Whitfon by will gave the corporation tenements 20l. per ann. for 20 lying-in women ; alfo his manor of Barnett, to erect and endow a fchool for 40 poor girls ; alfo quit rents of Chew Magna 8l. 10s. 6d. per ann. and 3 bufhels of wheat and 3 bufhels of rye to the mafter of Redcliff free fchool ; alfo 500l. to lend to young tradef-   500   0   0 men 50l. each for 7 years intereft 10s. for each 50l. ; alfo out of a tenement on the Back 3l. per ann. 2l. thereof to repair St. Nicholas church and 1l. for 2 fermons ; alfo 20l. per annum for 2 exhibitions in Oxford. The refiduary eftate alfo, amounting to about 3000l. was left to the corporation,   -   -   -   3000   0   0

1629, John Doughty by will gave the corporation 100l. to be lent intereft free for 5 years to handicraft men,   100   (

1629, Humphrey Brown by will gave lands in Felton to the corporation, on condition they had 4 fermons in the year preached at St. Werburgh on days therein mentioned, and a lecture every Sunday afternoon at St. Nicholas ; alfo lands in Elberton, for morning prayers at St. Werburgh's.

1630, Robert Redwood by will gave the corporation 200l. to lend 100l. each to poor burgeffes intereft free for 5 years ; and 20l. to the poor of Briftol,   -   -   220   0   0

1630, William Pitt by will gave 10l. to Briftol library, and 8ol. to the poor of St. Thomas, Redcliff, and Temple,   90   0   0

	l.	*s.*	*d.*
1634, Matthew Warren by will gave 20l. to the poor of Temple,	20	0	0
1634, Robert Rogers gave by will 100l. to the corporation; to be lent to 10 burgeffes intereft free, - -	100	0	0
1634, Robert Aldworth gave the corporation by will 1000l. to be lent poor clothiers 50l. each intereft free; and 100l. to the poor of St. Peter's almfhoufe, - -	1100	0	0
1634, *George White by will gave the feoffees of Temple 25l. they to pay for a fermon at Temple crofs yearly; and to the corporation 200l. to lend to 10 poor clothiers intereft free; 100l. to raife 5l. per ann; for relief of prifoners in Newgate; 100l. to buy materials to keep poor people at work; 100l. to raife 5l. per ann. for an exhibition in Oxford; 150l. for a chain of gold for the mayor, if refufed for charitable ufes; alfo a tenement 5l. per ann. for the poor of St. Michael's. - - -	650	0	0
1636, Richard Vickris gave the corporation 2l. per ann. by deed for the keeper of Briftol library.			
1636, *Ann Snigg gave the corporation by will 200l. with which they purchafed an annuity of 12l. per ann. towards maintaining 2 poor fcholars burgeffes of Briftol in Oxford.	200	0	0
1639, *George Harrington gave the corporation 240l. for them to diftribute 26l. at 10s. weekly to poor houfeholders in the parifhes of Briftol, and to pay the clerk 20s. a year for keeping the accounts, - - - -	240	0	0
1640, Robert Strange gave lands to erect and endow St. John's almfhoufe for 15 poor people.			
1641, Thomas Harrington gave the corporation by deed 5l. 4s. per ann. for the poor of St. James's in bread.			
1653, Hugh Brown gave the corporation lands in Mangotsfield for charitable ufes; he alfo gave out of lands in Hambrook 2l. 14s. per ann. to the poor of Redcliff and 2l. 14s. per ann. to the poor of St. John's in bread; he alfo gave to the poor of Temple 3l. to the poor of St. John's 3l. of Redcliff 3l. of St. Philip's 2l. and of St. Auguftin 2l. he gave alfo to the Society of Merchants a tenement and 100l. to maintain 3 poor people in their almfhoufe,	100	0	0

1656,

	l.	*s.*	*d.*
1656, *Richard Long by will gave lands in Sifton, for cloathing poor men in the Merchants almſhouſe, and 100l. to raiſe 5l. per ann. for the poor of St. Stephen's in bread,	100	0	0
1659, *Humphry Hook by will gave the corporation 680l. to give the poor of St. Stephen's pariſh 8s. weekly in bread and coal, the remainder to Queen Elizabeth's hoſpital,	680	0	0
1661, Francis Gleed by will gave 28l. per ann. iſſuing out of tenements to a poor houſholder of 13 pariſhes in Briſtol, 2l. each, 1l. to the accountant, and 1l. for a learned ſermon to be preached at Chriſt-Church on St. Matthew's day.			
1663, *John Pears gave the corporation by will 20l. to pay 1l. per ann. for a ſermon at St. James's the 31ſt of March.			
1664, *Rev. Mr. Powel gave 2l. per ann. to 4 almſhouſes.			
1668, Abraham Birkins gave the feoffees of St. Maryport-lands 10l. per ann. 2l. thereof to 4 poor people of Maryport, 2l. to ditto of St. Nicholas, 2l. to ditto of James's, 2l. to ditto of Temple, and 1l. for a ſermon, 10s. to the collector, and 10s. to the poor in bread.			
1668, Thomas Farmer by will gave the corporation 700l. to raiſe 35l. per ann. 20l. thereof to apprentice out two boys of Queen Elizabeth's hoſpital, and the remaining 15l. to the poor of 6 pariſhes, 2l. 10s. each, - -	700	0	0
1659, George Knight by will gave the feoffees of Temple 36l. the intereſt to pay for a ſermon and bread to the poor annually in Temple pariſh, and out of a tenement 10s. per ann. to the poor of St. Nicholas, - -	36	0	0
1696, Mary Bickham gave the feoffees of Temple a tenement and 100l. the income and intereſt to be given in bread every Sunday to the poor of Temple, alſo 100l. to the pariſh of St. Auguſtin, the intereſt for the ſame purpoſe, -	100	0	0
1670, William Pennoyer by will gave out of lands 41l. per ann. 10l. thereof for the maintenance of a ſchool-maſter in St. Leonard's, 10l. for a ſchool-miſtreſs there, 16l. for a lecture in that church once a week, and 5l. for bread to the poor.			
1670, Michael Day gave 2l. 13s. per ann. to 3 poor houſholders of St. Nicholas, and 13s. 4d. for a ſermon, and 4s. 8d. for the clerk and ſexton.			

1678, John Miner gave lands for a monthly fermon at St. Ste- *l. s. d.*
     phen's, 2 tenements to apprentice feamens fons, and 20l.
     the intereſt to buy bread for the poor of St. Nicholas,   20 0 0

1679, Thomas Stephens gave lands at Wyke and Abſton to
     feoffees to erect and endow 2 almſhoufes, in the Old
     Market and Temple-ſtreet.

1683, Mary Boucher and Joan Langton gave the Society of
     Merchants lands in Bedminſter 8ol. per ann. for poor
     widows, 10s. each.

1685, *Andrew Barker gave the corporation by deed 6 tenements
     and 100l. to apprentice poor boys of Queen Elizabeth's
     hoſpital,   -   -   -   - 100 0 0

1686, John Lawford gave 2l. 12s. per ann. to the poor of St. Peter,
     and 2l. 12s. to the poor of Temple, iſſuing out of tene-
     ments, to be given weekly in bread; he alfo gave 5ol.
     each to St. Philip's, St. James, Redcliff, and Chriſt-
     Church, the intereſt for the fame purpofe,   - 200 0 0
     Mary Gray gave 5ol. 6s. 8d. of the intereſt for a fermon,
     and the remainder to keep poor children at fchool.

1686, Samuel Hale by will gave 23ol. the intereſt to apprentice 230 0 0
     one poor boy or girl out of each of feven pariſhes, and
     7ol. the intereſt to buy bread for the poor of the fame
     pariſhes,   -   -   -   - 70 0 0

1696, Edward Colſton Efq; by deed gave the Society of Mer-
     chants lands to erect and endow an almſhoufe on St.
     Michael's-Hill, and to maintain 6 poor men in the
     Merchants almſhoufe.

1708, He alfo gave them by deed other lands to endow an hoſpital
     for 100 boys on St. Auſtin's-Back, and to endow alfo a
     fchool in Temple-ſtreet, p. 444.

     *Dr. Sloper by will gave the corporation a tenement in
     College-Green of 15l. per ann. to buy bibles for the
     poor in each ward.

1716, Sarah Ridley gave feoffees by will 2200l. to purchafe land
     to endow an hoſpital for old maids and batchelors,   2200 0 0

1725, John Gray gave 12ol. to Temple charity-fchool for girls,   120 0 0

1726, Thomas Warren gave a tenement in Temple-ſtreet, the
     income for a fermon and bread for the poor of Temple.

1729, Ann Aldworth gave tenements, 2l. 10s. of the rent for a   *l.*   *s.*   *d.*
      fermon &c. at All-Saints and St. Anſtin's, the remainder
      to All-Saints almſhoufe.

1749, Peter Davis gave 50l. to the charity-fchool of St. Michael
      and St. Auſtin, and 150l. the intereſt for a fermon and
      bread for the poor of the pariſh of St. Michael's,   200   0   0

1727, Sir Abraham Elton by will gave 50l. each to the pariſhes
      of St. John and St. Werburgh, the intereſt for the ufe
      of the poor, and 50l. the intereſt for a fermon and for
      the poor of St. Werburgh's, and 50l. the intereſt to
      maintain a decayed failor in the Merchants almſhoufe,
      and 100l. to Trinity hofpital,   -   -   300   0   0

1779, Mary Ann Peloquin gave the corporation 300l. the intereſt
      5l. to the rector and 2l. to the curate of St. Stephen's
      for fervice and a fermon on the 25th of December, the
      remainder to the clerk and fexton; and 15,200l. the
      intereſt to 38 poor men and 38 poor women houfe-
      keepers of Briſtol ; 2500l. the intereſt to poor lying-in
      women 1l. 10s. each ; 1000l. to 20 poor fingle women or
      widows and 10 poor men of St. Stephen's upon St. Ste-
      phen's day yearly : ſhe alfo left her houfe in Prince's-
      ſtreet for the perpetual refidence of the rector of St. Ste-
      phen's,   -   -   -   -   19000   0   0

Note, Thofe Benefactions marked thus * were eſtabliſhed by the committee of
the corporation in the year 1739, fee p. 138.

CHAP.

CHAP. XXVI.

A BIOGRAPHICAL ACCOUNT *of* EMINENT BRISTOL MEN.

BIBERT was a native of Briſtol, a monk of St. Benediƈt, and a very famous divine according to Leland, a great hiſtorian and philoſopher, (Stevens Monaſtic, v. 1. 190,) he flouriſhed very early but the time is not well known; he left behind him many works which are now loſt, except ſome ſermons and the biſtory of his own time.

Ralph of Briſtol, being there born was bred in the neighbouring convent of Glaſtonbury. ·Going over into Ireland, he firſt became a treaſurer of St. Patrick's in Dublin, then 1223 Biſhop of Kildare, he wrote the life of St. Laurence Archbiſhop of Dublin, and granted (faith Sir James Ware) certain indulgences to the abby of Glaſtonbury, probably in gratitude for his education therein: he died 1232.

Richard Lavingham, prior of the Carmelite friery in Briſtol, was a great writer in divinity about the latter end of the 14th century, and is reported by Pit, p. 534, to have epitomized Bede's biſtory, beginning his work with " Britannia, cui quondam Albion &c."

John Milverton is mentioned by Sir R. Baker in his chronicle as a man of note in Edward the 4th's. reign, he calls him " a Carmelite friar of Briſtow, and provincial of his order, who becauſe he defended ſuch of his order as preaƈhed againſt endowments of the church with temporal poſſeſſions, was committed to priſon in the caſtle of St. Angelo in Rome, where he continued three years:" he is mentioned by Bale in an epiſtle dedicated to Queen Elizabeth 1548, prefixed to her tranſlation of the godly meditation of Margaret Queen of Auſtria, out of French, who fays, " he was a provyncyall of the Carmelytes and was full 3 years a pryſoner in the caſtle Angelo at Rome at the fute of the Biſhoppes of England for preferring the order of monks and friers above the offyce of Byſhoppes, and loſt fo the Byſhoprick of St. David's to which he had been a little before eleƈted. Thys matter (fays he) have I hearde under the title of Evangelick Perfeƈtyon, moſt depely reaſoned in theyr ordynary dyſ-

putatyons

putatyons at theyr convocatyons and chapters as they then called them, yet by thofe whome I kuewe moft corrupt lyvers,"—Milverton died in London 30th January, 1486, and was buried in the choii of the monaftery church of the Carmelites there, fee Weaver, p. 438. with a Latin infcription in curious monkifh rhymes.

John Stowe, "the Briftol Carmelite," was a poet of fome reputation in Henry 6th's. time. He is mentioned by Rowley in his poem to John Lydgate on Ella, lord of Briftol caftle, together with John Clarkyn, "one of mickle lore." Stowe is noted by Sir Richard Baker, in his Chronicle, as flourifhing in that reign; but he calls him a monk of Norwich, and Doftor of Divinity in Oxford. Dr. Wharton, in his Effay on Poetry in England, vol. ii. fuppofes his name to be Stone, who was a Carmelite at Briftol and died at Cambridge.

Sebaftian Cabot, born at Briftol of Genoefe parents. His father John Cabot and wife then refided there, which moft of the writers agree in. And T. Lanquet, in Chronicle, fays, "Sebaftian Cabote in 1499, the fon of a Ge_noefe and born in Briftol, profeffing himfelf excellent in knowledge of the circuit of the world, was fent from Briftol to difcover ftrange countries, and he at firft difcovered Newfoundland." Vide before p. 173, 174.

John Spine is faid by Pits, p. 673. to be born in this city, and was a Car_melite and Doftor of Divinity in Oxford, leaving fome books of his writing to pofterity. He was buried in Oxford 1484.

Thomas Norton, born at Briftow, is celebrated among the men of note in Edward 4th's. time. As an alchemift, he wrote fome books in that art, and in chemiftry; alfo a poem, mentioned by Wharton, in which he celebrates Mr. Canning. Fuller, in his Worthies, fays of Thomas Norton, that "He boafted himfelf to be fo great a proficient in chemiftry, that he learned it to perfeftion in 40 days, when he was 28 years old, and complaineth that a merchant's wife in Briftol ftole from him the elixir of health, fufpefted to be the wife of William Cannings of Briftol, (cotemporary with Norton) who ftarted up into fuch great wealth and fo fuddenly, the cleareft evidence of their conjefture." He quotes Theat. Chymic. of Elias Afhmole for this, p. 441. but the abfurdity of this conjefture is too apparent. Of this T. Norton, fee more annals 1477. Some fay he ruined himfelf and friends who trufted him with their money, (not un-ufual with thefe enthufiaftic alchymifts) and died very poor in 1477.

William of Worcefter, firnamed Botoner from his mother's family, a native of Briftol, was born on St. James's-back of parents, not ex equeftri ordine as Tanner faith, but tradefmen, whitawers, fkinners, and glovers. In 1431 he firft was fent to Hart-hall in Oxford, where 1434 he ftudied and improved

himfelf

himfelf greatly by the munificence of Sir John Faſtolff, a Knight of Norfolk, in learning of various kinds. He is faid to be the firſt who tranſlated any of Cicero's works into Engliſh. He fays, p. 368 Itin. " 1473 die 10 Anguſti preſentavi W. (de Wainſleet) epiſcopo wintonienſi apud aſher librum Tullii de Seneɛtute per me tranſlatum in Anglicis, fed nullum regardum recepi de epiſcopo." It is not uncommon for authors, eſpecially trànſlators, to go unrewarded. But the work that feemed moſt to engage his attention was an Itinerary, of which he has the honour of having been the firſt projeɛtor; though equal in induſtry yet not in abilities to his follower Leland. Like him he feems to have had an extenſive fcheme in his head, which he had neither abilities nor lived long enough to finiſh, though in óur Briſtol traveller you meet with many things you can find no where elfe. His manuſcript lay long hid in Bennet college library, Cambridge: it was his common-place pocket-book, the companion of his travels; but written in fo vile a charaɛter, that it required an Œdipus to decypher it, which tedious talk was executed by the ingenious Mr. Naſmith, who publiſhed the book with Simeon Simeonis in 1778. He is particular in defcription of the churches, ſtreets, religious houſes, &c. of his native city, though little taſte in architeɛture is difplayed, and often nothing but their meaſurements by ſteps (greſſus) given, without any order obſerved, but things are noted down as they occurred. We ſhould not however eſtimate the ſkill of this writer from the fpecimen herein exhibited, which was only a note-book never finiſhed; he might probably have given us a compleat account of the places he viſited, but lived not to reduce it into form. He died about the year 1484.

William Canynges, of diſtinguiſhed eminence as a principal merchant and foreign trader, as the friend and patron of learning and religion, the able magiſtrate, and charitable benefaɛtor of this city, the wealthy and the wiſe (fapientiſſimus et ditiſſimus, William of Worceſter) was the fecond fon of John Canynges, fometimes written Canynge in deeds, mayor of Briſtol in 1392, 1398, the fon of William Canynges, fix times mayor, buried in capella St. Mariæ in ecclef. St. Thomæ. John Canynges, inheriting a large eſtate from his father and purfuing a mercantile life, increaſed his patrimonial cſtate, and marrying Joan Wotton, daughter of John and Margaret Wotton, had by her three fons and three daughters, and died in 1405 and was buried with his father at St. Thomas's church. He gave by will a third part of his goods to his wife, a third to his children, and a third pro animâ fuâ in religious offices; had very large eſtates and lands in Briſtol and its neighbourhood, which he gave to his wife for her life, the reverſion to his fon William, and alfo giving great
chattels

chattels to his children appointed for them truftees, Joan his wife, Sir Henry Darleton and John Frerer, Efq; who entered into recognizances at the Guild-hall before the mayor for fulfilling their truft, agreeable to the power of prov-ing wills, with which the corporation was invefted by charter, now by difufe loft. He left his children in money 72l. 12s. 6d. to each, which was a good fum then, when wheat was 4d. a bufhel, a fat ox fold for 5s. 4d. a fheep for 16d.

William was five years old at his father's death, and was of age the 5th of Henry 6th. His elder brother Thomas was ten years old at his father's death, was fent to London, became a grocer there, and ferved the office of Lord Mayor in 1456, whilft William refided in Briftol, was bred up to merchandize, in which he was very fuccefsful, and was chofen mayor of Briftol ; fo that the firft and fecond city in the kingdom had two brothers for mayors in the fame year. His mother having married again to Thomas Young, an eminent merchant, 9 Henry 6th, William Canynges, then a minor, feems to have been bred up a merchant under his care, and to have fucceeded his father-in-law Young in bufinefs, who died 1426 about the time of William Canynges coming of age. He then profecuted bufinefs with great diligence. He fays in one of his deeds, " bonefto cum labore mercatorio rem augere domefticam induftriofè curaverim ;" whereby he acquired an affluent fortune, which was increafed by the eftates fettled on his mother falling to him upon her death. How much he was efteemed as a merchant, and to what extent he traded, may be feen in chap. vi. on trade, p. 169, 170. and the names of his fhips in p. 581. and William of Worcefter; but for his private virtues, piety, and charity, his benefactions to the city to promote religious offices, to Red-cliff church, almfhoufes, &c. fee p. 612. are fufficient proofs, were no pri-vate documents wanting, to give us light into his character. — But as every thing relating to the great Mr. Canynges has excited the curiofity of the public fince the publication of Rowley's Poems, I fhall here communicate what has further occurred, that public expectation may be gratified as far as lies in my power, beginning with the pedigree of the family, taken chiefly from original and authentic deeds.

PEDIGREE of the CANYNGES FAMILY.

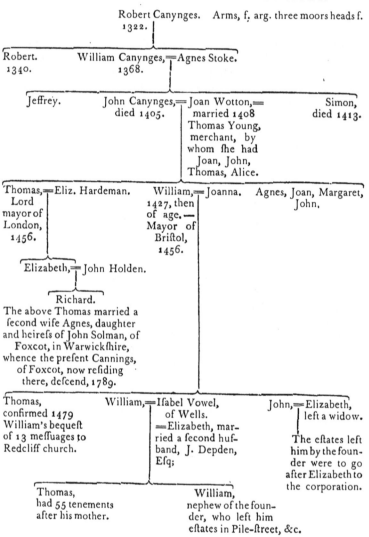

Robert Canynges.   Arms, f. arg. three moors heads f.
1322.

Robert.   William Canynges,=Agnes Stoke.
1340.   1368.

Jeffrey.   John Canynges,=Joan Wotton,=   Simon,
            died 1405.   married 1408   died 1413.
                          Thomas Young,
                          merchant, by
                          whom fhe had
                          Joan, John,
                          Thomas, Alice.

Thomas,=Eliz. Hardeman.   William,=Joanna.   Agnes, Joan, Margaret,
Lord   1427, then   John,
mayor of   of age.—
London,   Mayor of
1456.   Briftol,
                            1456.

Elizabeth,=John Holden.

Richard.
The above Thomas married a
fecond wife Agnes, daughter
and heirefs of John Solman, of
Foxcot, in Warwickfhire,
whence the prefent Cannings,
of Foxcot, now refiding
there, defcend, 1789.

Thomas,   William,=Ifabel Vowel,   John,=Elizabeth,
confirmed 1479   of Wells.   left a widow.
William's bequeft   =Elizabeth, mar-
of 13 meffuages to   ried a fecond huf-   The eftates left
Redcliff church.   band, J. Depden,   him by the foun-
                        Efq;   der were to go
                                              after Elizabeth to
Thomas,   William,   the corporation.
had 55 tenements   nephew of the foun-
after his mother. der, who left him
                   eftates in Pile-ftreet, &c.

In

It muſt be obſerved of this pedigree, that no original deeds hitherto found mention the family names beyond William in the year 1368 bailiff of Briſtol, ſo that there is no name of ROBERT 1322, called " the morning ſtar of Redcliff's riſing ray &c." in the poems aſcribed to Rowley.—But there is no reaſon for diſbelieving the exiſtence of ſuch a man, who through a defeᵭt of records is taken little notice of; but the particulars ſo many and various of his life given us in the manuſcript of Rowley leave little room of doubt.— There might have been a Robert as well as a Symon and Jeffery, both which names occur but once.—Robert is ſaid to have a great mercantile genius, eagerly intent upon commerce and purſuit of riches, which laid the foundation of the greatneſs of the family here afterwards. But whether Robert be a miſnomer, and not a family name, it ſeems clear there was one of ſuch a genius in the family from the following little poem, called an Enterlude, which as it ſhews the diſpoſition of an anceſtor of this as well as many a family, and has not been publiſhed among the poems attributed to Rowley, I here inſert;

The WORLDE.

Fadre, Sonne, and Mynſtrelles.

Fadre. — To the worlde newe and ytts beſtoykenynge waie
　　　Thys coiſtrelle ſonne of myne ys all mie care,
　　　Yee mynſtrelles warne hymme how wyth rede he ſtraie
　　　Where guylded vyce dothe ſpredde hys maſcill'd ſnare,
　　　To gettyng wealth I woulde hee ſhoulde bee bredde,
　　And couronnes of rudde goulde ne glorie rounde hys bedde.

1ſt Mynſtrel. — Mie name is Intereſte, tis I
　　　　Dothe yntoe alle boſoms flie,
　　　　Eche one hylten ſecret's myne,
　　　　None ſo wordie goode, and dygne,
　　　　Butte wylle fynde ytte to theyr coſte,
　　　　Intereſte wyll rule the roaſte.
　　　　I to everichone gyve lawes,
　　　　Selfe ys fyrſt yn everich cauſe.

2d. Mynſtrel. — I amme a faytour flame
　　　　Of lemmies melancholi,
　　　　Love ſomme behyghte mie name,
　　　　Some doe anemp me follie;

Inne fprytes of meltynge molde
I fette mie burneynge fele,
To mee a goulers goulde
Doeth nete a pyne avele,
I pre upon the helthe ;
And from Code redeynge flee,
The manne who woulde gette wealthe
Mufte never thynke of mee.

3d Mynftrel. — I bee the Queede of Pryde, mie fpyrynge heade
Mote reche the cloudes and ftylle be ryfynge hie,
Too lyttle is the earthe to bee mie bedde,
Too bannow for mie breetheynge place the fkie ;
Daynous I fee the worlde bineth me lie
Botte to mie betterres, I foe lyttle gree,
Aneuthe a fhadow of a fhade I bee,
Tys to the fmalle alleyn that I canne multyplie.

4th Mynftrel. — I am the Queed of goulers, look arounde
The ayrs aboute mee thieves doe reprefente,
Bloudfteyned robbers fprynge from oute the grounde,
And airie vyfyons fwarme around mie ente ;
O fave mie monies, ytte ys theyre entente
To nymme the redde Godde of mie fremded fprighte,
Whatte joie canne goulers have or daie or nyghte.

5th Mynftrel. — Vice bee I hyghte onne golde fulle ofte I ryde,
Fulle fayre unto the fyghte for aie I feeme ;
Mie ugfomnefs wythe goldenne veyles I hyde,
Laieynge mie lovers ynne a fylkenne dreme ;
Botte whan mie untrue pleafaunce have byn tryde,
Thanne doe I fhowe alle horrownefse and row,
And thofe I have ynne nette woulde feyne mie grype efchew.

6th Mynftrel. — I bee greete Dethe, alle ken mee bie the name,
Botte none can faie howe I doe loofe the fpryghte,
Goode menne mie tardyinge delaie doethe blame,
Botte mofte ryche goulerres from me take a flyghte ;
Myckle of wealthe I fee whereere I came,
Doethe mie ghaftnefs mockle multyplye
Ande maketh hem afrayde to lyve or die.

Fadre.

Fadre. — Howe villeyn Mynſtrelles, and is this your rede,
　　　Awaie: Awaie: I wyll ne geve a curſe,
　　　Mie ſonne, mie foune, of this mie ſpeeche take hede,
　　　Nothynge ys goode thatte bryngeth not to purſe.

Whether it was a Robert or William Canynges that profited by theſe uſeful and intereſting inſtruƈtions of his father is uncertain, but it is very clear that William and his ſon John were poſſeſſed very early of large eſtates and much wealth, carried on great buſineſs and an extenſive commerce, which was not leſſened by William the laſt founder, of whom we can ſpeak with more certainty. As early as before 1380 there was a trading guild or fraternity, called "The Fraternity of Canynges;" and John Vyel in his will dated the 25th of May 1398, gives "Fraternitati de Canynges" 40s. fraternitati quâ ſum, and there was of old time a houſe called Canynges Lodge, mentioned in deeds in the chamber of Briſtol, where they met, adjoining to Redcliff Church-yard. This proves that the firſt William Canynges the founder was in rank and ability very capable of compleating the work of Redcliff church. The ſecond Wm. Canynges having his father John's great eſtates entailed upon him after his mother, and having proſecuted the mercantile buſineſs to a much greater extent than had been ever known in this city,* (as appears by William Botoner, p. 83. and the account of his ſhipping there,) was very capable of rebuilding the church when ruined by the ſtorm of thunder and lightning in the year 1445-6, intereſting himſelf doubtleſs the more upon the occaſion as his grandfather William had been partly the founder and the finiſher of it, as well as from the pious motive of religion and charity, of which he was all his life a moſt diſtinguiſhed example: and if we give credit to what is ſaid of him in the manuſcript aſcribed to Rowley,† his ability as a man of letters and lover of architeƈture and the fine arts,‡ rendered him ſtill more fit and likely to undertake ſuch a work. He ſeems to have enlarged his mind and cultivated a good underſtanding by learning, which he did not think incompatible with merchandiſe, and which placed him in a higher ſphere, and rendered him a fit companion for the great, and in high eſteem with Henry the 6th. and Edward the 4th. He had been a loyaliſt to Henry the 6th. and ſupported the royal cauſe in the houſe of
　　　　　　　　　　　　　　　　　　　　　　　　　　Lancaſter,

---

* Vid. on Trade of the City, p. 170 he ſays in his deed, " honeſto cum labore rem augere domeſticam induſtrioſe curaverim &c."

† Vid. poems of Rowley 4to. p. 165. 170. 328. 430. 447.

‡ See Rowley's poems " Anent a Brooklet &c." where his life and taſte for learning is particularly noted, alſo the poem called Canynge's Feaſt.

Lancaster, by which however he incurred the difpleafure of the fucceeding King Edward the 4th. of whom he purchafed his peace at the great fum of 3000 marks, as mentioned in William Botoner, p. 99. The weaknefs and pufillanimity of Henry the 6th. and the infamous behaviour of his Queen Margaret, loft him the good-will and intereft at length of this rich and able man.

The following letters from Canynge to his friend Rowley, as tranfcribed and communicated by Chatterton, will fet this matter in a proper light, which are fubmitted to the judgment and candour of the reader.

Canynge to Rowley, Briftol.

I be fulle forrowefulle that you are notte ynne Briftowe, and the more fo as mie Lorde Earle of Warwyke havethe fente me a letter to poclayme Edwarde of Yorke Kynge. Certis ytte will ne be to profitte of the Yorkeyfts if ytte be foe; butte to me the iffue maie be death. Mie bredcren of the councille doe notte bethynke me a manne to advife them, becaufe I wulde not have them doe mean thynges for gayne, therefore mie wordes wylle not availe, for where reveraunce is wanteinge advyce is nought: come as foon as the tymes will fpare you. **WM. CANYNGE.**

Rowley to Canynge, Cirencefter.

Mie Lorde of Warwyke waulkethe fafte to the crowne, lette him beware hee ftrayne not hymfelfe yn takeyng fyke large ftrydes. Was you of power and in poffeffion of caftles I woulde arede you to maintain unto the deathe the caufe of Henrie. Anoder lettere maie reche mee before I can goe hence.

T. ROWLEIE.

Canynge to Rowleie, Briftowe.

Ye would have me declare for Kynge Henrie, I woulde remayne neutre, botte I mufte perforce be for one of the twayne: fucceffyon ys ne the quere, botte who will rule befte: when ones countrie is abentynge to rewin itte ys a foule thynge even to be neutre. A Kynge fhulde bee one who rületh hys peo-ple hymfelfe, and ne troufteth to untrouftie fervants. Mie actions fhewe me no ennemie to goode: but methynketh a holie feyncte maketh notte a goode Kynge. From the daies of Saxon governmente to thys prefente Englande havethe been undone by prieft-kynges. Edgar, Edwarde Confeffour, and Henrie 6th. havethe mette with Danes, Normans, and Warwykes. True Eng-lyfhmen are lyke untoe mafties never pleafed but whan fet a fyghteing. Ho-nours to the mynfter are not allwaie honoures to the throne. Queen Marga-rette

rette havith feen the letter; twas aryghte fhe fhulde. Whatever fhe bee oderwife fhe ys an unfit dame for oure Rynge, ruleinge him lyke a bearn, ande toieynge with her paramoures, of whom I faie not whom. Mie fadre goeynge to courte onne the marriage of Kynge Henrie, the chamberlayne requierynge hys cuftomarie prefente, he wente oute yn greete dole, but kenneynge he mote ne goe there wydoute a guift, he tooke a braffe chaine, and giltynge the fame lyke unto goulde, gave ytte to the Queene, from whence ytte came to Harrie 6th. who dyd yeve ytte to hys Queene, and I have feene ytte rounde the necke of Souffoulke withe the unwordie braffe peepeynge oute to viewe the gould chafeynge. Thys longe goulde brafs chaine beeynge in fothe whilome the necke chaine of an hounde, exccedeynge to fighte mofte of the guiftes, gotten mie fadre a charter for trade; to renewe whych I have givenne 2000 markes and the loane of mie fhyppes to brynge mie countriemenne from Fraunce, haveynge the befte parte of mie hanfe Virgine Marie of tons 1000 burden brente. I bethynke therefore I maie be accounted a common fubjeĉte of the Kynge, and not bounde to hym by gratytude. I wys hym well ynne a pryours coate ynne a mynfterre, and hys Queene and her paramour yn repentance. Under Henrie we mote have peace, but never renome. But doe not thynke I ame a Yorkeyft. Adieu. WILLIAM CANYNGE.

WILLIAM CANYNGE to the EARL of WARWYCK,

Sendeth greetynge. Mie good Lorde, your letterre I haveth confydered; but be not of power to renderre you fervice. Mofte of the cityzens ftande welle affeĉted toe you, but it be not poffitable for hem to availe youe anie waies, excepte bie pryvate conveiaunce of fylver and monies, whyche God wote theie love too welle. I fende you bie Syrre Pierce Aleighe twa hundreth markes. I confulted wythe fome councylmenne of your commande, who telled the fame to Gervaife Clifforde, foe was I enforced to fhewe the fame to Margaret. Take care of your perfon, mie goode Lorde, as I heare Syr Charles Baudyn and his broder John a Fulforde threat your lyfe wyth privie affafynatynge. I bee ne thyrftie for bloude, botte whanne the lymbes be unfounde ungentle meanes muft be ufed bie brennynge, to keepe the heart whole. Kynge Henrie Godde fpare hys lyfe, but the defpoyleynge of three fcore Margarets and Suffoulkes will ne atone for the deathe of the good Duke of Gloucefter, wid whome felle Englyfhe glorie and Englandes peace. Was the caftelle to be gotten yuto the bandes of the cytyzens, ytte fhoulde renderre you fervitude. Botte Syrre Charles Baudyn kepethe it fo ftoutelie, haveynge the bruges adented, that ytte maie not bee. Algate I will engage me to cai-

H h h h   tene

tene hym up the caftleis utter cloftere by fheryve ve areft : gif you wylle behete me, he fhall be yn no danger of deathe. Ytte woulde bee fulle joyfulle to mee yffe yoe would conferre the honoure of knyghthoode on Ralph Morris mie coufenne, whoe ys fulle wordie thereof. Mie greteyngs to mie goode Lorde Edwarde of Yorke, who ys chevycynge the kingdome from the oppreffyon of a leman and her paramoures. I wylle fende to hym whenne the Hanfe fleete ys come three thoufandth markes, wy fhynge mie poore fervices maie bee accepted. Margarette fhalle bee fhutte oute from Bryftowe, and ftakes are placed ynne the grange to lette her if fhe agayne flee to the caftle. Shee departed laft night aftere evenfonge from the caftle, ne one cytyzenne yn her trayne ; butte wheder fhe ys gone I wote notte. Adieu, my good Lorde. Jefus attend you.   WILLIAM CANYNGE.

Upon thefe letters I would only remark, that undoubted records in the city chamber fay that in 1456-7 Queen Margaret came to Briftol, and that John Cline left by will a large fum for the repair of the town walls and forts of Briftol, 40l. of which was fpent thereon, 28th Henry 6th. Great Red Book, p. 77. and another 40l. was ordered by act of the mayor W. Canings and coun_ cil in 1456 for purchafing war ftores, all the faltpetre in the town, and twelve brafs guns, with four chambers each, p. 17. A. B. And about 2 Edward 4th. they fent the King 40 men defenfibly arrayed for the fpace of two months at their own cofts 130l. to attend his fervice ; and in fending men into the north for his fervice, and in navies and fhips twice into Wales; and a third time finding a navy to convey his ambaffadors into Caftile the fum of 1000l. and moreover lent to him 200l. Great Red Book, p. 205. In Ricaut's Kalendar, p. 20. B. in 1460 there was fent to Briftol a parcel of gundowder, faltpetre, and brimftone by John Judde, mafter of the ordnance to Henry 6th. affigned to H. May, merchant. William Cannings, then mayor, knowing this Judde and May to be enemies to the Duke of York, and affiftant to James Earl of Wiltfhire, by affent of the council feized the faid materials. After which the Duke of York fent two commiffions to the faid mayor and common council to take upon them the government and defence of the caftle againft the defigns of the Duke of Somerfet, who purpofed to enter and retain the fame. An army and navy was afterwards fent forth by the mayor and council by order of King Edward 4th. againft the Welch under Jafper Earl of Pembroke, at the cofts of five hundred marks. Whether this coincidence of circumftances at this time does not tend to confirm the facts in the above letters is left to the judgment and candor of the reader.

What

What Mr. Canynges fuffered in this diftracted ftate of the kingdom may be eafily fuppofed, being a very rich man each party had recourfe to him; but the lofs of money he feems not fo much to have regarded, having learnt that dif- fieult point — the true and juft value of money. But when King Edward 4th. in the 7th year of his reign, was on the death of his wife for impofing upon him a marriage, he took the only way he could with fafety to avoid it (and which coincided with his turn of mind) and became a prieft. It appears by the regifter of the Bifhop of Worcefter (John Carpenter) Sept. 19, 1467, he received the firft order of accolyte, 12th of March that of fubdeacon, 2d of April, 1468 that of deacon, and 16th of April, 1468 that of prieft. He fung his firft mafs at the chnrch of our Lady of Redcliff. 3d of June, 1469 he was made Dean of Weftbury. A private manufcript (Friend) wrote in the year 1669 thus relates it: " 1466-7, this mayor (William Cannings) having buried his wyfe, whom he dearly loved, was moved by King Edward to marry ano- ther wyfe, whom he had ordained ; but Mr. Cannings as foon as he had dif- charged his year of mayoralty, to prevent it, tooke on hym the order of priefthood, and fung his firft mafs on Whitfunday at the Lady chapple at Red- cliff, and was afterwards Dean of Weftbury,* which college by Richard Duke of York and Edward Earl of Rutland was founded, and a dean and cannons placed therein. King Edward gave them the hofpital of St. Laurence in the hundred of Barton Regis near Briftol. To this college Mr. Cannings became a great benefactor, and was dean." The Mayor's Kalendar, p. 125. gives a fimilar account, which may be more relied on as it was written about the time of the tranfaction by Ricaut, town clerk, 18th of Edward 4th. Mr. Cannings was a great repairer of this college, and with Bifhop Carpenter (who lies buried in the church of Weftbury) rebuilt great part of it, (fee Leland, Col. vol. i. p. 102) " enlarged it, and furrounded it with a wall, towers, and gates, and endowed it with rents." † Bifhop Carpenter founded an almfhoufe there for fix poor men and fix women, to which Mr. Cannings was a benefactor. A piece of brafs fixed to the cover of a mafs book here had this infcription, Rowley's manufcripts:

H н н н 2

Thys

---

* The Bifhop Carpenter and Dean Cannings are faid to be the founders of this college, but it fubfifted more than an hundred years before ; they much endowed and improved it. Bifhop Carpenter appropriated the rectory of Kemfey near Worcefter to it in 1473, at the requeft of Mr. Canynges. See Dr. Nafh's Hiftory of Worcefterfhire, vol. ii. p. 21, 24.

† Vide Tanner's Notitia, p. 142. alfo Sir Robert Atkyns's Hiftory of Glocefterfhire. — Bifhop Carpenter calls it " Noftrorum fundationis patronatus et diocefeos." His arms are, Paly of fix azure and G. creft on a wreath argent and G. a coney fejant argent.

Thys booken was yeven
To fynge fowles to hev'n,
And when the fyrfte belle doth tolle
Synge maffe for the partyng fowle,
And eke at the abbye
Of Canynges of Weftburie,
Thereynn to ftaie
Untyll the lafte daie.

JOANNES CARPENTER.

On the treble bell, taken down to be recaft in 1774, was infcribed in the Gothic charafter, each letter being inclofed in a fquare by lines, " Sanfta Trinitas nos benedicat." Weftbury college was dedicated to the Holy Trinity and the apoftles St. Peter and St. Paul.

Of Mr. Canynge's becoming a prieft at Weftbury to avoid a marriage propofed by the King, the following letters faid by Chatterton to be tranfcribed from the originals of Mr. Canynge to Rowleie will give a farther account:

1466. To ROWLEIE.

Lyfe ys a fheelde where ne tynfture of joie or tene haveth preheminence. Kynge Edwarde yefterdaie dyd feefte at mie rudde houfe, goeynge ynne the boate uponne the tyde. Canynge, quod hee, I haveth a wyfe for thee of noble howfe. Mie goode Liege, quod I, I am oulde and neede not a wyfe; Bie oure Ladie, quod he, you mofte have one. I faide ne moe, bethynkynge ytte a jefte, butte I now unkeven ytte ys a trouthe: come to mee and arede mee, for I wyll ne be wedded for anie Kynge.   W. C.

1467. To ROWLEIE.

Now, broder, yn the chyrche I amme fafe, an hallie priefte unmarriageable. The Kynges fervitoure attended me to telle, giff I would dyfcharge the 3000 markes I fbonde ne bee enforced on a wyfe, and alfo have mie fhyppeynge allowed. I made anfwere, I was now yfhorne a preefte, and motte notte be wedded. I have made a free guifte of the markes, and wanted but a contynuaunce of mie trade. Alle ys welle; the Kynge ys gone, and I am baillie.   W. CANYNGES.

1468. To ROWLEIE.

I bee now fhutte uppe yune mie college of Weftburie; come mie Rowleie and lette us dyfpende our remaynynge yeeres togyder. Hailineffe ys no where founde: focietye havethe pleafures, eremitage havethe pleafures, butte contente alleyne canne dyfperple payne.   W. CANYNGES.

The

The following little poem on felinefs or happinefs, faid to be written by him, is quite confonant with this laft letter.

Maie Selyneffe on erthe's boundes bee hadde?
Maie ytte adyghte yn human fhape bee founde?
Wotte yee, ytt was wyth Eden's bower beftadde
Or quite erafed from the fcaunce-layd grownde,
Whan from the fecret fontes the waterres dyd abownd!
Does yt agrofed fhun the body'd waulke
Lyve to ytfelfe and to yttes ecchoe taulke?

All hayle, Contente, thou mayde of turtle-eyne,
As thie behoulders thynke thou arte yreene,
To ope the doore to felyneffe ys thyne,
And Chryfte's glorie doth uponne thee fheene.
Doer of the foule thynge ne hath thee feene;
In caves, ynn woodes, yn woe and dole dyftreffe
Whoere hath thee, hath gotten felyneffe.

But Rowley's poem " Anent a Brooklet," publifhed by Dean Milles, p. 439, as it gives a curious account of Mr. Canynge's life family &c. deferves particular notice; and the following lines, part of that poem, are carefully copied by a very ingenious gentleman with the greateft exaftnefs and fidelity, from the original hand-writing on parchment, commuicated by T. Chatterton. — The curiofity of the public has lately been excited by printing the poems of Rowley, and the public expeftation fhould be gratified, and nothing concealed that may tend to a difcovery of the truth—the following is therefore fubmitted to the judgment of the candid reader.

Anent^a a Brooklette as I laie reclynd,
Lifteynge to heare the water glyde alonge,
Myndeynge how thorowe the grene mees^b yt twynd,
Awilft the cavys refpons'd^c its mottring fonge,
At diftaunt ryfyng Avonne toe be fped,^d
Amenged^e with ryfyng hilles dyd fhewe yts heade;

                                        Engarlanded

^a Near.   ^b Meadows.   ^c Anfwered to.   ^d To be fped, or haftened.   ^e Mingled.

Engarlanded wyth crownes of ofyer weeds
And wraytes^f of alders of a bercie fcent,
And flickeynge out wyth clowde agefted^g reedes,
The boarie Avonne fhow'd dyre femblamente,^h
Whyleft blataunteⁱ Severne, from Sabrina clepde,^k
Rores flemie^l o'er the fandes that fhe hepde.

Thefe eynegears^m fwythynⁿ bringethe to mie thowghte
Of hardie champyons knowen to the floude,
How onne the bankes thereof brave Ælle foughte,
Ælle defcended from Merce kynglie bloude,
Warden of Briftol towne and caftel ftede,
Who ever and anon made Danes to blede.

Methoughte fuch doughtie^o men muft have a fprighte
Dote^p yn the armour brace^q that Michael bore,
Whan he wyth Satan kynge of helle dyd fyghte,
And earthe was drented^r yn a mere of gore;
Orr foone as theie dyd fee the worldis lyghte,
Fate had wrott downe, thys man ys borne to fyghte.

Ælle, I fayd, or elfe my mynde dyd faie,
Whie ys thy actyons lefte fo fpare yn ftorie?
Were I toe difpone,^s there fhould lyven aie
In erthe and hevenis rolles thie tale of glorie;
Thie actes foe doughtie fhould for aie abyde,
And bie theyre tefte all after actes be tryde.

Next bolie Wareburgus fylld mie mynde,
As faire a faynƈte as anie towne can boafte,
Or be the erthe with lygthe or merket pywrynde,^u
I fee hys ymage wa'ulkeyng throwe the coafte:
Fitz Hardynge, Bithricus, and twentie moe
Ynne vifyonne fore mie phantafie dyd goe.   &c. &c.

At the conclufion of this poem Mr. Canynges is celebrated by Rowley as
the builder of the church of Redcliff, a work greater than that of any other
founder here named:

Next

^f Wreaths.   ^g Lying on the earth or clods.   ^h Appearance.   ⁱ Noifed.   ^k Named.
^l Frighted.   ^m Objeƈt of the eyes.   ⁿ Quickly.   ^o Valiant.   ^p Dreffed.   ^q Suit of
armour or accoutrements for the arms.   ^r Drenched.   ^s Difpofe.   ^t Darknefs.   ^u Cover'd.

Next Radcleve chyrche, oh worke of hand of heaven,
Where Canynge sheweth as an instrument
Was to my bismarde eynsyghte newlie given,
'Tis past to blazon ytt to good contente:
Ye that woulde fayne the fetyve buyldynge see
Repayre to Radcleve and contented bee.

But it appears from the little essays said to be collected and written by Rowley for Mayster Canynges, that their friendship was founded on their mutual
love of learning and polite literature, and the cultivation of tne useful arts.
The following are printed from the very originals in Chatterton's hand-writing,
sent in two letters to Horace Walpole Esq.

S I R,

Being versed a little in antiquities, I have met with several curious manuscripts, among which the following may be of service to you, in any future
edition of your truly entertaining anecdotes of painting—in correcting the
mistakes (if any) in the notes, you will greatly oblige,

Your most humble servant,

THOMAS CHATTERTON.

Bristol, March 25th, Corn-street.

The Ryse of Peyncteynge, in Englande, wroten bie [1] *T. Rowleie,* 1469, *for*
Maistre [2] *Canynge.*

Peyncteynge ynn Englande, haveth of ould tyme bin yn ure; for saieth
the Roman wryters, the Brytonnes dyd depycte themselves, yn sondrie wyse,
of the fourmes of the sonne and moone wythe the hearbe woade: albeytte I
doubte theie were no skylled carvellers. The Romans be accounted of all
men of cunnynge wytte yn peyncteynge and carvellynge; aunter theie mote
inhylde theyre rare devyces ynto the mynds of the Brytonnes; albeytte atte
the commeynge of Hengeyst, nete appeares to wyttenefs yt, the Kystes are
rudelie ycorven, and for the moste parte beyge hepes of stones. Hengeste
dyd

---

1 T. Rowleie was a secular priest of St. John's, in this city; his merit as a biographer, histo-
riographer is great, as a poet still greater: some of his pieces would do honor to Pope; and the
person under whose patronage they may appear to the world, will lay the Englishman, the antiquary, and the poet, under an eternal obligation. 2 The founder of that noble Gothic pile,
Saint Mary Redclift Church in this city: the Mecenas of his time: one who could happily blend
the poet, the painter, the priest, and the christian perfect in each: a friend to all in distress; an
honor to Bristol, and a glory to the church.

dyd brynge ynto thys reaulme herehaughtrie, whyche dydde brynge peynêteynge. Hengeſte bare an [3] aſce ahrered bie an afgod. Horſa, anne horſe ſauleaunte, whyche eftſoones hys broder eke bore. Cerdyke, a ſheld [4] adryſene; Cuthwar a ſhelde [5] aſægrod: whoſe enſamples, were followed bie the hyndlettes of hys troupe, thys emproved the gentle art of peynêteynge. Herehaughtrie was yn eſteem amongſte them, take yee theſe Saxon acheuementes. [6] Heoſnas un æcced-ſet was ybore of Leof -- an abthane of Somertonne — [7] Ocyre aaded — ybore bie Elawolf of Mercia. [8] Blac border adronet an ſtorve adellice -- the auntiaunte armourie of Briſtowe -- a [9] ſcelde agreſen was the armourie of Ælle Lord of Bryſtowe caſtle -- croſſes in maynte nombere was ybore, albeyt chieſes and oder partytiones was unknowen, untill the nynthe centurie. Nor was peynêteynge of ſheeldes theire onlie emploie, walles maie beē ſeene, whereyn ys auntyaunte Saxonne peynteynge; and the carvellynge maie be ſeene yn imageies atte Keyneſhame; Puckilchyrche; and the caſtle albeyt largerre thane life, theie be of feetyve hondiewarke. Aſſleredus was a peynêter of the eighth centurie, hys dreſſe bee ynne menne, a longe alban, braced wythe twayne of azure gyrdles; labelles of redde clothe onne his arme and flatted beaver uponne the heade. Nexte Aylward in tenthe centurie ycorven longe paramentes; wythoute, of redde uponne pourple, wyth goulde beltes and dukalle couronnes beinge rems of floreated goulde — Aſſlem a peynêter lived ynne the reygne of Edmonde; whane, as ſtorie ſaiethe was fyrſt broughte ynto Englande, the couneynge myſterie of ſteineynge glaſſe of which he was a notable perſourmer; of his worke maie bee ſeene atte Aſhebyrne, as eke at the mynſter chauncele of Seynête Bede, whych doethe repreſente Seynête Warburghe to whoes honoure the mynſterre whylome han bin dedycated. Of his lyſe be fulle maint accountes. Goeynge to partes of the londe hee was taken bie the Danes, and carryed to Denmarque, there to bee forſlagen bie ſhotte of arrowe. Inkarde a ſoldyer of the Danes was to ſlea hym; onne the nete before the feeſte of deathe hee founde Aſſlem to bee hys broder. Aſſrighte chaynede uppe hys foule. Ghaſtneſſe dwelled yn his breaſte. Ofcarre the greate Dane gave heſt hee ſhulde bee forſlagene, with the commeynge ſunne; no teares colde availe, the morne cladde yn roabes of ghaſtneſs was come; whan the Danique Kynge beheſted Ofcarre, to araie hys knyghtes eftſoones, for warre: Aſſlem was put yn theyre ſlyeynge battailes,

fawe

---

3 A ſhip ſupported by a idol.　　4 An imboſſed ſhield; being rudely carved with flowers, leaves, ſerpentes, and whatever ſuited the imagination of the caver.　　5 A ſhield painted in the ſame taſte as the carving of the laſt.　　6 Azure a plate; which is the ſignification of æcced-ſet.　　7 Or Pomeiſè—aad in Saxon was little green cakes, offered to the afgods or idols.　　8 Sable within a border undee, a town walled and crenelled proper.　　9 A ſhield carved with croſſes.

fawe his countrie enfconced wythe foemen, badde hys wyfe ande chyldrene broghten capteeves to hys fhyppe, ande was deieynge wythe forrowe, whanne the loude blantaunte wynde hurled the battayle agaynfte an heck. For fraughte wythe embolleynge waves, he fawe hys broder, wyfe, and chyl. drenne fynke to deathe : himfelfe was throwen onne a banke ynne the Ifle of Wyghte, to lyve hys lyfe forgard to alle emmoife : thus moche for Afflem. ¹⁰ Johne, feconde abbatte of Seynfte Auftyns mynftere, was the fyrfte Eng- lyfhe paynftere yn oyles ; of hym have I fayde yn oder places relateynge to his poefies. He dyd wryte a boke of the Proportione of Ymageries, where- ynne he faieth the Saxonnes dydde throwe a mengleture over theye coloures to chevie them from the weder. Nowe methynkethe fteinede glaffe mote need no fyke a cafinge, butte oile alleyne ; botte albeytte ne peynfteynge of the Saxonnes bee in oyle botte water, or as whylome called eau. Chatelion, a Frenchmane, learned oyle paynfteynge of abbat Johne. Carvellynge ynne hys daies gedered new beauties, botte moftelie was wafted in fmalle and dri- blelet pieces, the ymageries beeynge alle cladde ynne longe paramentes, whan the glorie of a carveller fhulde bee in ungarmented ymagerie, therebie fhewinge the femblamente to kynde. Roberte of Glowfter liffed notte his fpryghte toe warre ne learnynge, butte was the fonne, under whofe raies the flowrettes of the fielde fhotte yuto lyfe : Gille a Brogtonne was kyndelie nor- riced bie himme, whoe depyfted notable yn eau. Henrie a Thonton was a geafon depyftor of countenances ; he paynfted the walles of Mafter Canynge hys howfe, where bee the councelmenne atte dynnere ; a mofte daintie ande feetyve performaunce nowe ycrafed, beeynge done ynne M.CC.I. Henrie a Londre was a curyous broderer of fcarfes ynne fylver ande golde and felkes diverfe of hue. Childeberte Wefte was a depyftour of countenances. Botte

I i i i   above

---

10 This John was the greateft poet of the age in which he lived ; he underftood the learned languages. Take a fpecimen of his poetry on King Richard 1ft.

Harte of lyone ! fhake thie fworde,
Bare thie mortheynge fteinede honde :
Quace whole armies to the queede,
Worke thie wylle yn burlie bronde.
Barons here on bankers-browded,
Fyghte yn furres gaynfte the cale ;
Whileft thou ynne thonderynge armes.
Warriketh whole cyttyes bale.
Harte of lyon ! Sound the beme !
Sounde ytte ynto inner londes,
Feare flies fportine ynne the cleeme,
Inne thie banner terror floudes.

above alle was the peynēter John de Bobunn, whoſe worke maie be ſeene yn Weſtmynſter halle. ¹¹ Of carvellers and oder peynēters I ſballe ſaie hereafter, fyrſt Englyſchynge from the Latyne cis to wytte. Peynēteynge improveth the mynde and ſmotheth the roughe face of our ſpryghtes.

S i r,

I offer you ſome further anecdotes and ſpecimens ,of poetry and painters,
and am   Your very humble and obedient ſervant,

THOMAS CHATTERTON.

March 30, 69, Corn-ſtreet, Briſtol.

Hiſtorie of Peynēters yn Englande. Bie T. Rowley.

Haveynge ſayde yn oder places of peynēteynge and the ryſe thereof, eke of ſomme peynēteres; nowe bee ytte toe be ſayde of oders wordie of note. Afwolde was a ſkylled wyghte yn laieynge onne of coloures; hee lyved yn Merciæ, ynne the daies of Kynge Offa, ande depyēted the countenaunce of Eadburga hys dawter, whyche depyēture beeynge borne to Brightrycke he toke her to wyfe, as maie be ſeene at large in ª Alfridus. Edilwald Kynge of the Northumbers underſtode peynēteynge, botte I cannot fynde anie piece of hys ᵇ nemped. Inne a manſion at Cepenhamme I have ſeene a peynēteynge of moche antiquitie, where is ſytteynge Egbrychte in a royaul manner, wythe kynges yn chaynes at hys fote, withe meinēte ᶜ ſemblable fygures, whyche were ſymboles of hys lyfe; and I haveth noted the Saxons to be more notable ynne lore and peynēteynge thann the Normannes, nor ys the monies ſythence the daies of Willyame le Baſtarde ſo fayrelie ſtroken as aforetyme. I eke haveth ſeen the armorie of Eaſt Sexe moſt ᵈ fetyvelie depyēted, ynne the medſt of an auntyaunte wall. Botte nowe wee bee upon peynēteynge, ſommewhatte maie be ſaide of the poemes of thoſe daies, whyche bee toe the mynde what peynēteynge bee toe the eyne, the coloures of the fyrſte beeynge mo dureynge. Ecca Byſhoppe of Hereforde yn D.LVII. was a goode poete, whome I thus Englyſhe:

> Whan azure ſkie ys veylde yn robes of nyghte,
> Whanne glemmrynge dewedropes ᵉ ſtounde the ᶠ faytours eyne,
> Whanne flying cloudes, betinged wyth roddie lyghte,
> Doth on the brindlynge wolfe and wood bore ſhine,

Whanne

¹¹ I have the lives of ſeveral eminent carvers, painters, &c. of antiquity, but as they all relate to Briſtol may not be of ſervice in a general hiſtorie. If they may be acceptable to you, they are at your ſervice.

ª This is a writer, whoſe works I have never been happy enough to meet with. —
ᵇ Mentioned. ᶜ Metaphorical. ᵈ Elegantly, handſomely. ᵉ Aſtoniſh. ᶠ Travellers.

Whann even ftar fayre herehaughte of nyght,
Spreds the darke doufkie fheene alonge the [1] mees,
The wreethynge [2] neders fends a [3] glumie lyghte,
And boulets wynge from [4] levyn blafted trees.
Arife mie fpryghte and feke the diftant delle,
And there to ecchoyng tonges thie raptured joies ytele.

Gif thys manne han no hande for a peynćter, he han a head : a pyćture ap-
pearethe ynne cache lyne, and I wys fo fyne an even fighte mote be drawn, as
ys ynne the above.   In anoder of hys vearfes he faithe,

Whanne fprynge came dauncynge onne a flourette bedde,
Dighte ynne greene raimente of a chaungynge kynde ;
The leaves of hawthorne boddeynge on hys bedde,
And whyte prymrofen coureynge to the wynde ;
Thanne dyd the [5] fhepfter hys longe [6] albanne fpredde
Uponne the greenie bancke and daunced arounde,
Whileft the foeft flowretts nodded onne his bedde,
And hys fayre lambes [7] befprenged onne the ground ;
Anethe hys fote the brooklette ranne alonge,
Whyche ftrolled rounde the vale to here hys joyous fonge.

Methynckethe thefe bee thoughtes notte oft to be metten wyth, and ne to
bee excellede yn theyre kynde.   Ellmar Byfhoppe of Selfeie was fetyve yn
workes of [8] ghaftlienefs, for the whyche take yee thys fpeeche :

Nowe maie alle helle open to golpe thee downe,
Whylfte azure [9] merke [10] immenged wythe the daie,
Shewe lyghte on darkened peynes to be moe [11] roune,
O maieft thou die lyving deathes for aie ;
Maie floodes of Solfirre bear thie fprighte [12] anoune,
Synkeynge to depths of woe, maie [13] levnnebrondes
Tremble upon thie peyne devoted crowne,
And fenge thie alle yn vayne emploreynge bondes ;
Maie alle the woes that Godis wrathe canne fende
Uponne thie heade alyghte, and there theyre furie fpende.

Gorweth of Wales be fayde to be a wryter goode, botte I underftande not
that tonge.   Thus moche for poetes, whofe poefies do beere refemblance to
pyćtures in mie unwordie opynion.   Afferius was a wryter of hyftories ; he ys
buried atte Seynte Keynas College ynne Keynfham wythe Torgotte, anoder
                              I ı ı ı 2   writer

1 Meads.   2 Adders, perhaps ufed for glow-worms.   3 Gloomy.   4 Lightning.
5 Shepherd.   6 A large loofe white robe.   7 Scattered.   8 Terror.   9 Darknefs.
10 Mingled.   11 Terrific.   12 Ever and anon, often.   13 Thunderbolts.

writer of hyſtories. Inne the walle of thys college is the tombe of [1] Seynĉte Keyna, whych was ydoulven anie, ande placed ynne the walle, albeit done yn the daies of Cerdycke, as appeared bie a croſſe of leade upon the [2] kyſte; ytte bee moe notablie perfourmed than [3] meynte of [4] ymageries of theſe daies. Inne the chyrche wyndowe ys a [5] geaſon peynĉteynge of Seynĉte Keyna fytte-yuge in a trefoliated chayre, ynne a longe alban braced wythe golden gyrdles from the waſte upwarde to the breaſte, over the whyche ys a ſmaule azure [6] coape; benethe ys depyĉted Galfridus, M.LV. whyche maie bee that Geof-froie who ybuylded the geaſon [7] gate to Seynĉte Auguſtynes chapele once leadeynge. Harrie Piercie of Northomberlande was a [8] quaynte peynĉter; he lyvedeyn M.C. and depyĉted feveralle of the wyndowes ynne Thong abbie, the greate wyndowe atte Battaile abbeie; hee depyĉted the face verie welle wyth-alle, botte was lackeynge yn the moſte-to-bee loked-to accounte, proportione. Johne a Roane paynĉted the ſhape to an hayre; he carved the caſte for the ſheelde of Gilberte Clare of [9] thek fetyve perfourmaunce. Ellwarde [10] ycorne the caſte for the feale of Kynge Harolde of moſt geaſon worke; nor has anie feal ſythence hynne ſo rare, excepte the feale of Kynge Henrie the fyfthe, corven bie Joſephe Wheĵgyſte. Thomas a Baker, from corveynge croſſe loafes, toke to corveyng of ymageryes, whyche he dyd moſt fetyvelie; hee lyved ynne the cittie of Bathe, beeynge the fyrſte yn Englande thatte uſed hayre ynne the bowe of the [11] fyddle, beeynge beefore uſed wythe peetched hempe or flax. Thys carveller dyd deceſe ynn M.LXXI. Thus moche for carvellers and peynĉters.

John was induĉted abbot in the year 1186, and ſat in the dies 29 years. As you approve of the ſmall ſpecimen of his poetry, I have ſent you a larger, which though admirable is ſtill (in my opinion) inferior to [1] Rowley, whoſe works when I have leiſure I will fairly copy and ſend you.

The WARRE.

Of warres [2] glumm pleaſaunce doe I chanute mie laie,
Trouthe tips the [3] poynĉtelle wyſdomme [4] ſkemps the lyne,
Whylſte hoare experiaunce telleth what toe ſaic,
And [5] forwyned hoſbandrie wyth blearie eyne,

Stondeth

1 This, I believe, is there now. 2 Coffin. 3 Many. 4 Statues, &c. 5 Curious.
6 Cloak or mantle. 7 This gate is now ſtanding in this city, though the chapel is not to be ſeen. 8 Curious. 9 Very. 10 A contraĉtion of ycorven, carved. 11 Nothing is ſo much wanted as a hiſtory of the violin, nor is any antiquary more able to do it than yourſelf. Such a piece would redound to the honour of England, as Rowley proves the uſe of the bow to be known to the Saxons, and even introduced by them. 1 None of Rowley's pieces were ever made public, being till the year 1631 ſhut up in an iron cheſt in Redcliff church. 2 Gloomy.
3 Pen. 4 Marks. 5 Blaſted, burnt.

Stondeth and [6] woe bements; the trecklynge bryne
Rounnynge adone hys cheekes which doethe fhewe,
Lyke hys unfrutefulle fieldes, longe ftraungers to the ploughe.
Saie, * Glowfter, whanne [7] befprenged on evrich fyde,
The gentle hyndlette and the vylleyn felle;
Whanne [8] fmetheynge [9] fange dyd flowe lyke to a tyde,
And fprytes were damned for the lacke of knelle,
Diddeft thou kenne ne lykenefs to an helle,
Where all were mifdeedes doeynge lyche unwife,
Where hope unbarred and deathe eftfoones dyd fhote theyre eies.
Ye [10] fhepfter fwaynes who the [11] ribibble kenne,
Ende the [12] thyghte daunce, ne loke uponne the fpere:
In [13] ugfommneffe ware mofte bee dyghte toe menne,
[14] Unfelinefs attendethe [15] hounourewere;
Quaffe your [16] fwote [17] vernage and [18] atreeted beere.

The following obfervations muft occur to every reader of thefe letters to
Mr. Walpole on the poetry and paintings of antiquity:

1. Is not Chatterton's offering to produce the whole collection to him to be
inferted in the next edition of the Anecdotes on Painting, a ftrong proof of
himfelf fuppofing them originals or copied from fuch and authentic, or his
own good fenfe would never have rifqued the difcovery of their being otherwife to fo able a judge in fuch things as Mr. Walpole, fo converfant in thefe
very fubjects. However he might impofe upon others, he never would have
chofen fuch a one for the firft trial of his impofition.

2. He fent Mr. Walpole a fecond letter, and offered to continue this correfpondence, and tranfcribe for him every thing of Rowley's he had in his poffeffion for publication.

3. Thefe related to fubjects fo various, would any man with the leaft fenfe
ever attempt a deception in fuch numerous inftances of poetry, painting, carving, heraldry, divinity, antient manners, biftory of Briftol, and other places,
&c.? In each of which he muft neceffarily lay himfelf open to detection.

4. Let the coincidence of feveral circumftances related by Chatterton, and
agreement with the fame recorded in old deeds and in the city books in the
chamber, be weighed and compared, and with other facts, of which he could
not poffibly come at the knowledge.

5. Let

---

6 Laments.   * Earl or conful of Glocefter.   7 Scattered.   8 Smoking.   9 Blood.
10 Shepherds.   11 A fiddle.   12 Compact, orderly, tight.   13 Terror.   14 Unhappinefs.
15 The place or refidence of honour.   16 Sweet.   17 Vintage, wine, cyder.   18 Extracted from corn.

5. Let all the external evidence already advanced on this occasion be well weighed, the difficulty of forging not a few lines but whole pages on parchment be considered, and what ends could be answered by it, &c. and then the impartial will be able to form a just opinion of this matter in dispute.

The critics may contend about the originality of all or any of the manuscripts, about alterations or additions made, about the usage of old and obsolete words and the language of the time, suffice it for the author of this history that he has faithfully and honestly transcribed and printed them. If it offends, and what will not offend, the " genus irritabile vatum," he shall leave them to amuse themselves at their leisure in the way they like best, but wishes nothing but an enquiry after the truth would direct their pens.

Whether they are or are not authentic, whatever alterations in the form or words have been made, and additions and interpolations inserted by Chatterton, they are here faithfully presented to the reader to form his own judgment upon them ; whilst the author cannot but lament the unhappy fate of this misguided youth, who leaving the good principles in which he was educated, and led astray by the false glare of a strong imagination and flattering pride of superior understanding, reasoned himself out of all thoughts of a futurity, and forgetting he was a being accountable for his actions to his Maker and his Judge, put a period to his existence, and committing a murder upon himself rushed out of life into the presence of his Maker, without a desire of atonement or forgiveness, without any belief in or reliance on a Redeemer. In his last letter to a friend, dated August 12, 1770, he says, " Heaven send you the comforts of Christianity; I request them not, for I am no Christian." The following letter, printed from his own hand-writing, shews the prevailing temper of this unhappy youth. His master, Mr. Lambert, the attorney, found a letter upon the writing-desk of Chatterton, addressed to a worthy, generous man, Mr. Clayfield, stating " his distresses, and that on Mr. Clayfield's receiving that letter, he (Chatterton) should be no more." At this letter Mr. Lambert being alarmed sent it to Mr. Barrett, thinking he might dissuade him from this impious attempt on himself, who sending immediately for Chatterton questioned him closely upon the occasion in a tender and friendly manner, but forcibly urged to him the horrible crime of self-murder, however glossed over by our present libertines, blaming the bad company and principles he had adopted ; this betrayed him into some compunction, and by his tears he seemed to feel it — at the same time he acknowledged he wanted for nothing, and denied any distress upon that account. He next day sent the following letter:

To

To Mr. BARRETT.

SIR,

Upon recollection I don't know how Mr. Clayfield could come by his letter, as I intended to have given him a letter but did not. In regard to my motives for the fuppofed rafhnefs, I fhall obferve, that I keep no worfe company than *myfelf;* I never drink to excefs, and have without vanity too much fenfe to be attached to the mercenary retailers of iniquity. — No! It is my PRIDE, my damn'd, native, unconquerable PRIDE that plunges me into diftraction. You muft know that 19-20th of my compofition is pride : I muft either live a flave, a fervant, have no will of my own, no fentiments of my own which I may freely declare as fuch, or DIE! —— Perplexing alternative! But it diftracts me to think of it. I will endeavour to learn humility, but it cannot be here. What it will coft me on the trial Heaven knows!

I am,

Your much obliged, unhappy, humble fervant,

Thurfday evening.   T. C.

Some few weeks after this he planned the fcheme of going to London, and there writing for the bookfellers, &c. Moft of his friends and acquaintance contributed a guinea apiece towards his journey, and he there fettled, but carried his libertine principles with him, cœlum non animum mutans, till the fame pride, the fame principles impelled him to become his own executioner. He took a large dofe of opium, fome of which was picked out from between his teeth after death, and he was found the next morning a moft horrid fpectacle, with limbs and features diftorted as after convulfions, a frightful and ghaftly corpfe. Such was the horrible cataftrophe of T. Chatterton, the producer of Rowley and his poems to the world.

But to return from Rowley to his friend and patron Mr. Canynges. It is remarkable, nothing has been found after the latter's becoming Dean of Weftbury relating to Rowley, nor is he mentioned in the will of Mr. Canynges, in the prerogative office in a book called Wattic, p. 125. dated 12 November, 1474, which has given occafion for many furmifes; but might he not have died before that date, before his patron?

It is now left to the judicious and candid reader to form his own opinion concerning Rowley and Chatterton, whilft the life of Mr. Canynges muft be confidered that of a wife and worthy man, a diligent, rich and honeft merchant, who with the greateft honour and integrity filled the office of chief magiftrate of this city five times, and of reprefentative in Parliament in 1451, and 1455;

and

and leaving the world and its vanities ended. his charitable and pious life in religious retirement.

William Yonge, member for Briſtol the 34th of Edward the 3d 1361, had a ſon Thomas mayor 1411, and member in Parliament 1414, by his will dated the 14th of March·1426, he ſtiles himſelf burgeſs of Briſtol, and orders his body to be buried before the altar of St. Nicholas in the church·of St. Thomas; and leaves legacies to the friers mendicant of Briſtol, and for finding a chaplain to pray for his ſoul in that church for a whole year, and he leaves his wife his manſion in Temple-ſtreet, and other meſſuages there and in the ſuburbs of Briſtol. Thomas Yonge was a great merchant in 1408, and married Joanna the widow of John Canynges, and mother of William Canynges the founder, and there is reaſon to believe had the care of the education of William Canynges then a minor of only ſix years old at his father's death. —This Thomas had two ſons, Thomas and John; Thomas the elder being an eminent lawyer was returned member for Briſtol* in the 15th, 20th, 25th, 27th, 28th, 29th and 33d of Henry the 6th. was appointed King's ſerjeant the 3d of Edward the 4th. and chief juſtice of the common pleas with a grant of ten marks per ann. the 7th of Edward the 4th. and 1463 was recorder of Briſtol: dying 1476 was buried in Chriſt-Church, London: he died ſeized of the manor of North Wraxal, Wilts, with the advowſon of the church and of the manor of Eaſton in Gordano, Somerſet, near Briſtol. Mr. Canynges in his deeds calls this Thomas Yonge brother.

The preſent Right Hon. Sir George Young of Devonſhire is lineally deſcended from this family in Briſtol, arms ermine on a bend between two cotizes ſable, three Griffins' heads eraſed or. creſt on a wreath arg. and ſable a boar's head eraſed vert briſted or. mantled g. double arg.—Motto, Fortitudine & prudentia.

William Grocyne, native of Briſtol, 1467 bred at·Wincheſter ſchool, where when a youth he was a moſt excellent poet. The following tetraſtick is ſaid to be made by him extempore on his miſtreſs pelting him with a ſnow ball.

> Me nive candenti petiit mea Julia; rebar
> Igne carere nivem, nix tamen ignis erat
> Sola potes noſtras extinguere Julia flammas
> Non nive, non glacie, at tu potes igne pari.

He

* 1453 he moved in the Houſe of Commons, that as King Henry had no iſſue, the Duke of York might be declared heir-apparent of the crown; but he was committed to the Tower for this motion.—Smollett's hiſt. v. 5. p. 27.

He afterwards went over to Italy, where he had Demetrius Chalcondilus and Politian for his masters, and returning to England was the first public professor of the Greek tongue in Oxford. There is no more to be added to his honour, except that Erasmus in his epistles often owns him pro patrono suo et praeceptore. He died in 1520, aged 80. Vide Wood, Ath. vol. i. p. 13. Biograph. Brit. p. 201. Foster on Accent and Quant. 1763, p. 210.

John Brook, serjeant at law to King Henry the 8th. and one of the justices of assize in the western parts, was a very eminent lawyer, and chief steward to the abbey of Glastonbury; he lies buried in Redcliff church, with an inscription see p. 587. His son David was chief baron of the exchequer the 1st of Queen Mary. He married Catherine daughter of John Lord Chandois, and died without issue.

Sir George Snygg was one of the barons of the exchequer, a most upright judge and skilful lawyer, and recorder of Bristol. See p. 514.

Dr. George Owen is said in a manuscript penes me to be a native of this city, to which he became a distinguished benefactor: see p. 396. 434. He is celebrated by J. Leland, among the encomia illustrium virorum, p. 96. vol. v. 2d edit. in a copy of Latin verses, both as a philosopher and physician. He was for his abilities highly favoured at court, and appointed by the discerning Henry the 8th. physician to himself, Queen Catherine, and Edward the 6th.— He attended Cardinal Wolsey in his last illness by express order of the King. (Stow.) He was fellow of Merton college, Oxford, lived at Godstow in Oxfordshire in close friendship with J. Smith, Esq; mayor of Bristol, and was a great purchaser of abby lands of Henry 8th. who favoured him much. He died October 19, 1558.

Hugh or Robert Elliot, sheriff of Bristol, principal pilot of this nation, with Mr. Thorn 1527 made a voyage for discoveries, and first peopled Newfoundland, though he met not with public encouragement. Hackluit, Voyag. vol. iii. p. 10. See before p. 177.

John Fowler, a printer here, a second Henry Stephens, a good poet and orator, well skilled in Latin and Greek, abridged Thomas Aquinas, and translated Osorius into English; but not liking the Reformation of Edward 6th. and Queen Elizabeth, went to Antwerp, and died at Namur 1579, and lies there intererd in the church of St. John.

Robert Thorn, born in Bristol, and bred a merchant taylor in London.— He was blessed with a plentiful fortune, and what is more with a liberal mind and charitable and benevolent heart. He is said to have bestowed more than 4440l. to pious uses, and amongst other things founded and endowed the free grammar-school in this city; amidst all not forgetting his poor kindred in the

K k k k   distribution

diftribution of his fortune or enriching the public to the neglect of them, he gave them 5140l. befides large fums he forgave that they owed him. He died a batchelor in the 40th year of his age in 1532, and was buried in the church of St. Chriftopher, London, with the following monumental infcription:

> Robertus cubat hic Thornus, mercator honeftus,
>> Qui fibi legitimas arte paravit opes:
> Huic vitam dederat puero Briftollia quondam,
>> Londinum hoc tumulo clauferat atque diem,
> Ornavit ftudiis patriam, virtutibus auxit,
>> Gymnafium erexit fumptibus ipfe fuis.
> Lector quifquis ades requiem cineri precor optes,
>> Supplex et precibus numina flecte tuis.
>>> Obiit 1532, ætatis vero fuæ anno 40.

Of Nicholas Thorn, brother of the above Robert, fee p. 483.

Robert Thorn the elder, father of the above Robert and Nicholas, was bred a merchant, and was mayor of Briftol 1514, and knighted in Seville. He had all the rule of white foap. — In the Temple church, London, is the following infcription to him:

> Robertus jacet hic Thorne, quem Briftollia quondam
>> Pretoris merito legit ad officium.
> Huic etenim femper magnæ refpublica curæ,
>> Charior et cunctis patria divitiis,
> Ferre inopi auxilium, triftes componere lites,
>> Dulce huic confilio quofq; juvare fuit.
> Qui pius exaudis miferorum vota precefque
>> Chrifte, huic in cœli des regione locum.

In the Briftol grammar-fchool are two paintings of Robert and Nicholas Thorn. Arg. three lozenges G. a lion paffant, or, chief fable, with his cypher T. R. and the following verfes:

> Spina vocor, fupereft tribuatur gloria danti
> Quæ bona pauperibus fpina dat effe Deo.

And over Nicholas Thorn's picture is, "Ex fpinis uvas collegimus."

William Child, Doctor of Mufic, born in this city, was chanter of the king's chapel, obtained licence to proceed Doctor of Mufie at Oxford, which degree he completed in an act celebrated in St. Mary's church, July 13, 1663. He was educated in mufical praxis under one Elway Bevan, the famous compofer and organift of the cathedral of Briftol. He fucceeded Dr. John Mundy as organift at the chapel royal at Windfor, and then was one of the organifts of his

Majefty's

chapel at Whitehall and of the private mufic to King Charles 2d. There are divers compofures by him of tunes to pfalms, catches, rounds, canons, and divine hymns.

William Gibbes, Doctor of Phyfic, was a native of Briftol, his family refid. ing in the parifh of St. Mary Redcliff and having great property there without Temple-gate. He was phyfician to Queen Henrietta Maria and Mrs. Mary Stoner of the antient family of that name in Oxfordfhire.

James Alban Gibbes, of Briftol, fon of William Gibbes of that city, educated a papift at St. Omer's, travelled through Germany, Spain, Italy, &c. and became a compleat fcholar, and was made lecturer of rhetoric at Rome by Pope Alexander 7th. in the fchool of Sapienza and had a canonry of St. Celfus given him by the faid Pope, who having publifhed a book of verfes, our Gibbes had a copy of verfes fet before them. This difcovered Gibbes's poetical genius, which caufed him to be fo much admired that Leopold the Emperor in 1667 did create him poet laureate, giving him at the fame time a gold chain with a medal hanging thereto, to be always worn by him efpecially at folemn times and in public places, which being made known to Clement 9th. he was admitted to his prefence, kiffed his foot, and was congratulated by him; on which account he dedicated his firft volume of poems to that Pope. He fent his gold chain and medal to Oxford in 1670 to be kept there in their archives, as a teftimony of refpect to that fountain of learning. He died 1677, aged 66, and was buried at Rome in the church of St. Maria Rotunda. He was a moft voluminous writer of poems, not without great vanity. There is a head engraved of him before his Latin poems, printed at Rome 1668 in 8vo. and under it the following diftich:

> Tot pro Gibbefio certabunt regna, quot urbes
> Civem Mæonidem affernere fuum.

Dr. Bathurft wrote a folemn piece of irony upon him: " Carmen in honorem viri celeberimi et principis poetarum Domini Doctoris Gibbefii, cum diploma a Cæfareâ Majeftate fibi a merito conceffum æternitati in mufarum templo confecraffet.

> Oxonium gratare tibi, nunc læta theatri
> Limina, Sheldoniafq; arces Gibbefius intrat:
> Cerne et apollinea redimitus tempora lauro
> Effundat jubar et phæhi patris æmulus ardet, &c."

Dr. Gliffon, a phyfician and great anatomift, defcended from Walter Cliffon of this city, was educated in Caius college, Cambridge, and became very eminent. He was made King's Profeffor of Medicine and Fellow of the

College

College of Phyficians, and anatomical reader in that college in 1639. He practifed phyfic in the time of the rebellion at Colchefter in Effex, and was prefent at the fiege. He was chofen prefident of the college, and wrote feve. ral books in his art, and is famous for his difcovery of the capfula communis, vena cava, porta et fellea, and for difcharging the liver of fanguification. He died in St. Bridget's parifh, London, 1677. He and Dr. Wharton difcovered the internal falivary duct in the maxillary gland. His account of fanguifica. tion was efteemed very rational. His Tractatus de Ventriculo et Inteftinis et de Hepate, Amft. 1677, 4to. are among his principal works. He vifited patients in the time of the plague, and kept off the infection by keeping bits of fpunge dipped in vinegar in his noftrils.

Dr. Thomas White was the fon of John White, born in Temple-ftreet, Briftol, became a ftudent at Magdalen college, Oxford, 1566, whence he went to London, and was a noted preacher and much efteemed, was rector of St. Dunftan's in the Weft. In 1584 he was made Doctor of Divinity, had a prebend of St. Paul's given him, and was canon of Chrift Church, Oxon, 1591, and in 1593 canon of St. George's church, Windfor. Being a generous man and very charitable, he expended the eftates he got from the church in charitable ufes to Sion college, erecting almfhoufes, &c. fee p. 554. He died 1 March, 1623. In the chamber of Briftol is his picture with fome verfes under it, which end " Quique ALBOS cœli portamque invenit apertam."

Tobias Matthews was born in St. Thomas parifh on Briftol bridge, bred at Chrift Church, Oxford, was Bifhop of Durham, then Archbifhop of York, and died there 1628. There is a print of Tobias Matthæus, Archiepifc. Eborac. by Renold Elftracke fc. 4to. and a portrait of him in the hall at Chrift Church, Oxford, of which he was dean. He was tranflated from Durham in 1606, and was an ornament to the univerfity as well as to the high fta- tion he filled in the church. He had an admirable talent for preaching, which he never fuffered to lie idle; but he ufed from town to town to preach to crowded audiences. He kept an exact account of the fermons he preached after he was preferred, by which it appears that he preached when Dean of Durham 721, when Bifhop of that diocefe 550, and when Archbifhop 721, in all 1992. He left nothing in print but a Latin fermon againft Campian and a letter to James 1ft. Obiit 29 March, 1628, æt. 82. He had a fon called Sir Tobie Matthews, of whom his father had conceived great hopes from his forward and lively parts; but being fent abroad to complete his education, he was fe- duced by Parfons the Jefuit to the church of Rome, and perfuaded to enter into that fociety. He was afterwards much immerfed in politics in the reign of

Charles

Charles 1ft. and James 1ft. Obiit 13 Oct. 1655. This eminent divine was a benefactor to his native city ; and wishing to excite a love of literature amongst the citizens, he presented them with sundry books towards forming a library of sound divinity and other learning, " for the use of the aldermen and shop-keepers there." See p. 508.

William Haywood, an excellent preacher of his time, was born (being a cooper's son in Baldwin-street) in the city of Bristol, elected scholar at St. John's college, Oxon, by the endeavours of John Whitfon, alderman of this city, (an encourager of his studies) anno 1616, aged 16 years. He was soon made fellow of that house. Dr. Laud had a respect for him and his learning, made him one of the domestic chaplains in ordinary to King Charles 1ft. In 1636 he was actually created Doctor of Divinity. About that time he became vicar of St. Giles in the Fields near London. In 1638 was made canon of the eleventh stall in the collegiate church of Westminster. This person by the Puritans was looked upon as a favourer of Popery and as a creature of Archbishop Laud, for which in the beginning of that rebellion he was thrown out of his vicarage by the long parliament, and was imprisoned in the compter, Ely house, and in the ships, at length he was forced to fly, and his wife and children were turned out of doors and reduced to great want. After which he kept a private school in Wiltshire, under and in the name of his son John. He was restored to his vicarage and other preferments at the Restoration, and died 17 July, 1663, and was buried at Westminster.

William Penn was born at Bristol 1621, see p. 585. where is an account of him as admiral and general in his epitaph. He was vice-admiral at the attack of St. Domingo 1654, and afterwards at the taking of the valuable island of Jamaica, which we have possessed ever since. He was admiral of the white 1655 and knighted. He was father of William Penn, the founder of Pennsylvania, who had turned Quaker by the preaching of one Thomas Low, to the great trouble and regret of his father, who was however reconciled to his son before his death, and left him an estate in England and Ireland of 1500l. per ann. which enabled him to obtain of the king the grant of land in America, and erect Pennsylvania into a province. Sir William Penn the admiral died 16 September, 1670, and was buried at Redcliff church.

Dr. William Thomas, Bishop of Worcester, was son of Mr. John Thomas, a linen-draper of Bristol, who lived in a house of his own on Bristol bridge, where his son was born on the 2d of February, 1613, and baptized at St. Nicholas church the Friday following. He was bred at the public school at Carmarthen, went to St. John's college, Oxford, in his 16th year 1629, from whence

whence he went to Jefus college, where he took 1632 his Batchelor of Arts degree, and was chofen the principal fellow and tutor of his college. In 1638 he was ordained prieft, and appointed vicar of Penbryn in Cardiganfhire, and afterwards to Laugharne. He was deprived of his living by the parliament committee in 1644, from which time to the Reftoration he endured great hardfhips, being a fufferer to the amount of above 1500l. and obliged to keep a little private fchool for the fupport of his family. At the Reftoration he had his living again, and was promoted to the deanry of Worcefter November 25, 1665, and in 1667 was promoted to the fee of St. David, which he held with the deanry of Worcefter. After being Bifhop of St. David's fix years greatly loved and refpeƈted by all, he was tranflated to the fee of Worcefter in the room of Bifhop Fleetwood, and came thither in Auguft, 1683, where he endeavoured to amend the morals of the people, reftore the duties of his church by obliging the prebendaries fome to be always refident, and by great hofpitality and charity recommended himfelf to his funƈion. He refufed to difperfe the king's declaration, and fignified to all his clergy his diflike of it; yet he refufed taking the oaths to King William, and was preparing to leave his palace, when on the 25th of June he pioufly refigned his fpirit into the hands of God, in the 76th year of his age; the whole eftate he left behind him amounting to not more than 800l. which he left to charity.

Edward Colfton, the eldeft fon of William Golfton, mayor and alderman of Briftol, by Sarah daughter of Counfellor Bettins was born 2d November, 1636, in the parifh of Temple. The family of Golfton had long flourifhed in this city. The 31ft of Edward 3d. Hugo Golfton married Edith the widow of John Newland, and Thomas Colfton before that time, 19 Edward 3d. had eftates bequeathed to him in Temple-ftreet by John Wodewrowe. In Guillim's Heraldry mention is made of one Colfton in Effex, having a coat armour of two barbels or fifh refpeƈting each other, p. 69. 1 Edward 3d. from thence the family might probably firft have rifen. Thomas Golfton, 19 Eliz. 1577, was mayor of Briftol, and died alderman 16 November, 1597. William Colfton, the grandfon of this Thomas and father of Edward, ferved the office of fheriff in 1645, and was made deputy lieutenant of Briftol under the Duke of Beaufort, and a fortified redoubt at Kingfdown was called Colfton's Mount from him. He died, aged 73, 1681, and being deaf and infirm in his old age was excufed attending the council as alderman on that account.

Edward Colfton his fon being well inftruƈted not only in learning fit for bufinefs, but in the principles of the chriftian religion according to the purity of the church of England; was at years of maturity fent as a faƈtor to Spain,

where

where he behaved with great diligence and prudence. He cultivated the Spanifh trade of oil and fruit with fuch induftry, that befides the fortune defcending to him from his parents, and fome fay by the death of his brothers, (one of whom is faid to be conful at Venice,) he acquired great riches, fo great that the family fince have never yet given any account how his fortune accumulated fo faft.—It has been faid he was alfo concerned early in the trade to the Eaft Indies;—all agree that he was a moft fuccefsful merchant, and never infured a fhip and never loft one. He firft lived in Small-ftreet, Briftol, and having fo much bufinefs in London, and being chofen to reprefent the city in Parliament, he removed thither and afterwards lived as he advanced in years a very retired life at Mortlake in Surry, conftant in his daily devotional duties and in his attendance on the public offices of the church, and exemplified the fincerity of his chriftian profeffion by the nobleft acts of chriftian benevolence, of which fee p. 622. 444. But his private donations were not lefs than his public, he fent at one time 3000l. to relieve and free debtors in Ludgate by a private hand; and freed yearly thofe confined for fmall debts in Whitechapel prifon and the Marfhalfea; and fent 1000l. to relieve the poor of Whitechapel; and twice a week had a quantity of beef and broth dreft to diftribute to all the poor around him. Any failor fuffering or caft away in his employ, his family afterwards found a fure afylum in him: how folicitous he was of doing good and having his charities anfwer the defign of their inftitution, appears from a letter of his dated Mortlake 8th Dec. 1711, to Mr. Mafon the mafter of the Society of Merchants in Briftol, the truftees of his charity.—" Your letter was received by me with great fatisfaction, becaufe it informs me that the Merchants-Hall have made choice of fo deferving a gentleman for their mafter, by whom I cannot in the leaft think there will be any neglect of their affairs, fo neither of want of care, in feeing my truft repofed in them religioufly performed, becaufe thereon depends the welfare or ruin of fo many poor boys, who may in time be made ufeful as well to your city as the nation by their future honeft endeavours, the which that they may be is what I principally defire and recommend unto you, Sir, and the whole Society. Your humble fervant,

EDWARD COLSTON."

When fome friends urged him to marry, his ufual reply was with a fort of pleafantnefs, " every helplefs widow is my wife and her diftreffed orphans my children."—What adds greatly to his character as a charitable man, he performed all thefe works of charity, however great and extenfive, in his life time; invefted revenues for their fupport in truftees hands, lived to fee the trufts juftly executed, as they are to this day; and perceived with his own eyes the

good

good effects of all his establishments.—That his great fortune might the less embarrass him with worldly cares, he placed it out chiefly in government securities, and the estates he bought to endow his hospital were chiefly ground rents.—And notwithstanding all these public largesses he provided amply for all his relations and dependents, leaving more than 100,000l. amongst them.

Rev. Charles Godwyn, B. D. fellow of Baliol College, Oxford, grandson of Dr. Francis Godwyn, Bishop of Hereford, and great grandson of Dr. Francis Godwyn, Bishop of Bath and Wells; was educated the greatest part of his life in Bristol. His humanity, modesty, candour, probity and inoffensive and un_blameable life, as well as his learning and knowledge of antiquities, justly endeared him to his friends, to whom he was very communicative.—He died the 23d of April 1770, and left a well chosen and valuable library, and a large collection of coins ancient and modern, and the bulk of his fortune to the university of Oxford. He was interred at his own request in the chapel of Wolvercott near Oxford. He drew up and translated the charters of Bristol at the request of the corporation, which were published in the year 1736.

Sir William Draper was a native of this city, his father being a custom-house officer of this port, who placed his son under the Rev. Mr. Bryant, master of the cathedral grammar-school there, where he received the first rudiments of his learning. He went early into the army, and abroad to the East Indies; and had his first regiment given him in 1757 by the King for his services at Madras.—He planned and executed with great conduct and resolution the reduction of the Manilla and the Phillippine Islands the 6 of October 1762, for which bold and spirited enterprise he had the 16th regiment of foot, and had the first vacant red ribbon given him and was created Knight of the Bath.—The Spaniards protested the ransom bills for Manilla, by which the brave troops on that occasion, with their General, suffered a great loss, which could not be recovered without involving the nation in a fresh war with Spain.—Sir William purchased a house at Clifton, in the neighbourhood of his native city; where he levelled the ground opposite the Roman camp and planted a vista of yew_trees, and dug up many Roman coins in levelling the ground.—Here he lived retired for some years, and improved this spot and erected in the front of his house a freestone obelisk, with this inscription on the base:

Gulielmo Pitt, comiti de Chatham,
   Hoc Amicitiæ privatæ testimonium,
Simul et honoris publici monumentum,
   Posuit Gulielmus Draper.

On

On the left to anfwer the obelifk is a Cenotaph, confifting of a raifed tomb fupporting a large vafe, with an urn at top, well executed in freeftone; engraven upon the fide of the vafe are thefe lines:

Sifte gradum, fi quæ eft Britonum tibi cura, Viator,
Sifte gradum; vacuo recolas infcripta fepulcro
Triftia fata virûm, quos Bellicus ardor Eoum
Proh dolor! haud unquam redituros mifit ad orbem
Nec tibi fit lugere Pudor, fi forte tuorum
Nomina nota legas, fed cum terrâque marique
Invictos heroum animos et facta revolvas,
Si patriæ te tangat amor, fi fama Britannum,
Parce triumphales lacrymis afpergere lauros.
Quin fi Afiæ penetrare finus atque ultima Cangis
Pandere clauftra pares, Indofque lacepfere Bello
Ex his virtutem difcas, verumque laborem.
    Fortunam ex aliis.

A table beneath is infcribed with and contains the names of the places taken and of thofe officers of the 39th regiment who perifhed in the Indian war, in taking Arcot, Pondicherry, Manilla, and the Phillippine Iflands.

Sir William engaged in a literary controverfy with the celebrated Junius in defence of the Marquis of Granby, and fhewed himfelf able at the pen as well as the fword, tan marte quam Mercurio.—He afterwards left Clifton and lived at Bath and London, where he died.

ANNALES BRISTOLLIÆ;

OR,

ANNALS OF THE CITY.

A. D.
50
51
52

THE Roman armies having about this time made incurfions into the remoteft parts of Britain, their proprætors took poffeffion of the moft advantageous pofts on the heights and on the great rivers and fortified them with ftrong camps, fee p. 7 to 30; which from ftations became in time to be inhabited, and were like cities, taking the name often of the rivers, on the banks of which they were conftructed; hence the camps at Clifton and Rownham Hill near Briftol, on the river Avon, in the Itinerary had the name ABONE, and from them the Britifh city Caër Brito or Brightftow, rofe up and flourifhed under the immediate care and protection of OSTORIUS SCAPULA, p. 21, who according to Tacitus at this time " cinctis Caftris Sabrinam et Antonam fluvios cohibere parat.

53
54
55
56
57
58
59
60
&c.
&c.

The Roman ftation Abone being 12 or 14 miles from their colony or city Aquæ Solis, Bath, and the next ftation to it on the road from thence to the city Caër Went acrofs the Severn, foon increafed, and in a few years became a moft important fortrefs, confifting of three ftrong camps placed on both fides of the river Avon, and conftantly occupied with troops; and had other entrenched pofts on Leigh-Down, and at Sea-Mills, Henbury and Almondfbury attendant upon it; the ruins of all which are ftill to be feen.—As this received a continual fupply of Roman inhabitants, it became a place of fettlement and a fixed ftation to them, and the city Caër Brito or Priftow near it,

foon

A. D.

foon enlarged itfelf by a conflux of Britons living in fecurity under the Roman government, civilized by free and mutual intercourfe, adopting their manners and habits, and leaving their wandering life in woods built houfes and erected towns for their cohabitation, and by inter-marriages and trafficking with them in fupplying the garrifons with provifions &c. the Britons foon became romanized, the people being united by the ftrongeft ties of intereft, friendfhip, and good neigh-bourhood.

446   This continued till the Roman armies were called away from Britain, and the regular communication betwixt the colonies at Aquæ Solis (Bath) and Caerwent, and Caerlegion acrofs the Severn ceafed. The romanized Britons left in thofe ftations repaffing the Severn, and the camps in the neighbourhood, being now deferted as no longer wanted, they flocked hither to the city of Briftol as a fecure place and well known to them by the frequent intercourfe and refort to it in their journies betwixt thefe feveral ftations, and better calculated to receive the numerous colonies that were attendant on thofe camps than any other place, and to fupply them with all the neceffaries of life by its efta-blifhed trade, and convenient fituation for extending it.—But the civil diffentions of the Britons themfelves amongft each other, gave a check to the flourifhing ftate of this and other cities; till the Saxons impoli-ticly called in, a warlike people, foon fixed themfelves in thofe ftrong
584 camps before occupied by the Romans and drove the poor Britons again into Wales, and poffeffed themfelves of this city; and perceiving the advantages of its fituation for trade &c. they foon improved it with a fortified wall, and at length with a ftrong caftle, which is well expreft by john Leland, " Aucta eft a Saxonibus." After the heptarchy was eftablifhed, the city of Briftol with Glocefterfhire was part of Mercia; and the Anglo Saxon Comites Earls or Lords of Glocefterfhire go-verned the city, of the names of thefe many have come down to us, fee p. 32, 33, till the time of Aylward Sneaw, a defcendant of Edward the
900 fon of Alfred, p. 35, who about the year 900 was a man of valour under King Athelftan, held the barony of Glocefterfhire and lordfhip of Briftol caftle, afterwards inherited by his fon Algar and wife Algiva, from whom it defcended to Birtrick or Britrick, who was Lord High
990 Steward, and a very confiderable man in his country as well as on account of his parentage as poffeffions. Befides the earldom of Glo-ceiter and the feveral manors appendant thereto, he was Lord of
Tewkefbury,

A. D.

Tewkefbury, Avening, Fairford, Temple Guiting, Lea, Wheatenhurſt, Woodcheſter &c. &c. held lands in Emſton, Harfield, Leckampton, and the hundred of Cirenceſter, as appears by doomſday.—He lived in the time of the Confeſſor Edward, who being devoted to the French intereſt in prejudice to this Saxon nobleman, and to pleafe his courtiers

1050 gave the lordſhip of Briſtol and its caſtle to Leofwyn, p. 204. 33. though he held it but a ſhort ſpace through a quarrel betwixt Earl Godwyn and the King.

1067 Hardyng, the anceſtor of the Berkeley family, is ſaid to have accompanied the Norman William into England, and after the battle of Haſtings fettled in Briſtol, and became a rich merchant: he held Wheatenhurſt (now Whitminſter) in mortgage of Earl Birtrick.— Leland fays, " he had a howfe at Portcheſter and another in Brigh-ſtowe towne :" fome manufcripts fay, in Baldwin-ſtreet, where was the chapel of St. Baldwyn, afterwards converted to lay ufe, now the Back-Hall.—He is the firſt magiſtrate of Briſtol we have any account of, though it may be fuppofed he aĉted under the authority of the Cover-nor of the caſtle, before whom the city officers were to be allowed and ſworn. He died the 6th of November 1116.

1068 Earl Birtrick by his great eſtates having attracked the envy of the Norman invaders, and by his gallant and ſplendid appearance at court gained the love of Matilda daughter of Baldwin Earl of Flanders, afterwards married to William the Conqueror, now felt at once the ill effeĉt of the infatiable avarice and enmity of the Norman nobi-lity, and the fury of an highly affronted lady exafperated at a former ſlight ſhewn her, which all concurred to deprive him not only of his eſtate but his liberty, being at the Queen Maud's inſtigation confined at Wincheſter, and his earldom of Gloceſter and lordſhip of Briſtol being fettled by the King on the Queen, (Leland v. 6. f. 82.) who feems to have deputed Haymon a Norman as Governor of Briſtol, and after-wards Godfrey Biſhop of Conſtance, to her death 1084, and this

1086 ·Biſhop Godfrey is mentioned in Doomſday-Book as having in Briſlow thirty marks and one mark of gold. Vide p. 201. 206. To him fuc-ceeded in the year 1090 Robert Fithaymon, who died 1107.

1090 Briſtol from its fituation was early famous for voyages and trade to Ireland. But the following trade one ſhould have fcarce thought had fo early an origin and place here, which ſhews the barbariſm of thofe times recoded in the life of Wulſtan in Anglia Sacra, 2. 258. " There

is

A. D.

is a town called Brickflou oppofite to Ireland, and extremely convenient for trading with that country. Wulfftan induced them to drop a
barbarous cuftom, which neither the love of God nor the king could
prevail on them to lay afide. This was the mart for flaves collected
from all parts of England, and particularly young women, whom they
took care to provide with a pregnancy, in order to enhance their value.
It was a moft moving fight to fee in the public markets rows of young
people of both fexes tied together with ropes, of great beauty and in
the flower of their youth, daily proftituted, daily fold. Execrable
fact! Wretched difgrace! Men unmindful even of the affection of the
brute creation! Delivering into flavery their relations, and even their
very offspring."

1110   Robert Earl of Glocefter, by favour of Henry 1ft. and marriage with
Matilda heirefs of Robert Fitzhaymon, p. 209. was Lord of Briftol,
and in part rebuilt its caftle and fortified it againft King Stephen,
whom he took and confined therein a prifoner. Indeed fuch was the
anarchy of thofe times, that Lord Lyttelton, vol. i. p. 320. obferves,
that " Earl Robert's head quarters at Briftol became during thefe
inteftine diforders a meer ftrong hold of banditti, which the Earl could
by no means reftrain: they made excurfions hence to plunder the neighbouring counties, and returning into the caftle with numbers of miferable captives ; many who could not redeem themfelves they murdered
in torturing to make them confefs what money they could raife, &c."
Thus the power being now vefted in the people and the regal authority
difputed, its natural confequences anarchy and confufion, fire and
fword, murder and devaftation fpread terror through the kingdom, and
the nation in general groaned under the fevereft calamities; the barons
even coined their own money, though the coins are now very fcarce.
Robert's are ftill extant. He died 1147, 30th of October.

1118   Robert Fitzharding founded the monaftery of St. Auguftin, Briftol,
p. 246. and died 1170.

     Dermot King of Lemfter in Ireland, with only 60 men in his com-
pany, fled over to Briftol, where he was entertained by Robert Fitzharding, a nobleman of Briftol of the royal blood of the Danes, and
underftanding there that Henry King of England was then in Aquitain,
he haftened over thither, and with all fubmiffion offered to fubject himfelf and his kingdom to the crown of England, if by his affiftance he
could recover it. Dermot with letters returned to Briftol, where

com-

A. D.

communicating the matter with Richard furnamed Strongbow, Earl of Strigule, it was agreed that the next fpring the Earl fhould fend auxil. liary forces into Ireland to reflore him. Ware's Hiftory of Ireland in Henry 2d.

1149   William Earl of Glocefter and Lord of Briftol, fays Leland, vol. vii. p. 74. " died in Briftol caftle, wyllyd to be buried by his father Robert at St. James's, but he was prively conveyed by night to Cainfham."

1173   Henry the 2d. now detained the honour of Glocefter in his own hands eight years, and then gave Ifabel third daughter of William to John Earl of Moreton his youngeft fon, with the whole honour of Gloucefter and caf_ tle of Briftol and Berton hundred, which Leland, vol. vi. p. 86. well defcribes, adding " fo it hath ftill remayned yn the kynges hands." Henry the 2d. about this time granted a charter to the men of Redcliff under the title of " Homines mei, qui manent in feodo meo in marifco juxta pontem de Briftow," omitted in the publifhed Briftol charters : Henricus Rex Angliæ, Dux Normanniæ, &c. " Henry King of England, Duke of Normandy and Aquitain, Earl of Anjou, to all barons, jufti_ ces, fheriffs, and other his fervants, Englifh or Welfh, wifbeth health. I grant that my men that dwell in my fee in the Marfh near the bridge of Briftow have their certain cuftoms and liberties and quittances through all England and Wales, as my burgeffes, and namely thofe in Briftow and through my land of the county of Glocefter as my charter teftifies; and I forbid that any one do them any injury or reproach upon this account." By this it appears there was a bridge over the Avon in Henry 2d's. time. And foon after he granted a charter to his burgeffes of Briftol, by which he gave them the city of Dublin, extant in Dr. Leland's Hiftory of Ireland. Henry 2d. about this time granted the firft charter to his burgeffes of Briftol without date, though the editor of the Briftol charters in Englifh has through miftake afcribed the date of Henry 3d's. charter of confirmation to this original charter of Henry 2d. which is therein only recited. " Henry King of England, Duke of Normandy and Aquitain, and Earl of Anjou, to all archbifhops, bifhops, abbots, priors, earls, barons, juftices, fheriffs, and to all the men of his land, greeting. Know ye, that I have granted to my bur- geffes of Briftol that they be free of toll and paffage, and all other cuf_ toms throughout my land of England, Normandy, or Wales, wherefo- ever they or their goods fhall come. Wherefore I will and ftrictly

command

command that they have all their liberties, privileges, and free cuftoms freely, fully, and honourably, as my free and faithful men, and that they may be free from toll and paffage and all other cuftoms. And I forbid that any one difturb them hereupon contrary to this my charter, on ten pounds forfeiture. Witnefs, Thomas Kant, William the king's brother, Reginald Earl of Cornwall, Roger Earl of Hereford, Patrick Earl of Salifbury, Richard de Hum conftable, Warren the fon of Gerard chamberlain, Walter de Hereford, John Marfhall, at Salifbury.

1177   The town of Briftow was fined for Sturmis the ufurer.

1184   The burgeffes of Briftol paid a fine of 50l. to have refpite that they might not plead without the walls of their town till the return of the king into England, who was then gone into Normandy.

1189   Henry 2d. confirmed the charter or grant of lands given to the priory of St. James in Briftol by William Earl of Glocefter.

1190   John Earl of Moreton, in the reign of Richard 1ft. now inheriting by the bounty of his father and marriage of Ifabel, the rich earldom of Glocefter and lordfhip of the fee of Briftol, granted to his burgeffes the following charter. The original in Latin is now in the chamber of Briftol, which I have examined; and the officer mentioned therein as provoft is in the original " prepofito," fo that prepofitor feems to be the earlieft chief officer of the city; in Doomfday-Book this officer is mentioned, " Sheruvinus prepofitus de Briftou," who held a manor in Swinefhead hundred in the county of Glocefter.—The " probi homines de Redcliff" before it was united to Briftol were governed in like manner by a prepofitor, as appears in the "hiis teftibus" of fome very old deeds as early as 1200 penes me. The " prepofito de Redcliff" being always the firft witnefs, as in all old deeds of Briftol after mayors were appointed the mayor's name is always put down as the firft witnefs.

The charter of John Earl of Moreton to his burgeffes of Briftow. " John Earl of Moreton to all his men and friends, Frenchmen and Englifhmen, Welchmen and Irifhmen, now prefent and in time to come, greeting. Know ye, that I have granted and by this my prefent charter confirmed to my burgeffes of Briftow, dwelling within the walls and without, unto the bounds of the town, that is to fay, Sandbrook, Bewell, and Brightnee-bridge, and the well in the way near Addlebury

Addlebury of Knoll,* all their liberties and free cuſtoms, as well, and
in as free and full manner as in the time of my predeceſſors. The liberties which are granted to them are theſe: that is to ſay, that no burgeſs of Briſtow may ſue or be ſued out of the walls of the ſaid town in
any plea, except for any pleas of foreign tenements that do not belong
to the hundred of the town; and that they ſhall be free of murder within
the bounds of the town; and that no burgeſs ſhall wage duel, unleſs
he were appealed of the death of any foreigner that was killed in the
town and who was not of the town. And that no man ſhall take an inn
within the walls, by the aſſent or order of the marſhal, againſt the will
of the burgeſſes. And that they ſhall be free from toll, laſtage, and
pontage, † and of all other cuſtoms, through all my lands and terri-
tories. And that none ſhall be judged and amerced in money but according to the law of the hundred, that is to ſay, by the forfeiture of
forty ſhillings. And that the hundred court of Briſtow be kept only once in
ſeven days; and that in no plea any one be charged in meſkeyningham. ‡
And they may lawfully have their lands and tenures, § days of appearance, and duty, through all my lands, whatſoever ſhall be due unto
them. And that for the lands and tenures within the town right be
done according to the cuſtom of the town. And that for the debts
which were made in Briſtow, and for the pledges there made pleas may
be there holden in the town. And that if any one, any where, of any
land ſhall take toll of the men of Briſtow, if he doth not deliver

M M M M   it

* This is the deſcription of the antient boundaries of the town, which were not enlarged at
the perambulation in the 47th of Edward 3d. 1373, when inquiſition was then made of its antient
liberties, upon the oaths of thirty-ſix jurors before juſtices aſſigned for that purpoſe. If you
will obſerve by this charter the bounds here deſcribed correſpond with thoſe agreed upon
when that inquiſition was taken, which was ratified by a record thereof in the court of Chancery,
and exemplified under the great ſeal and confirmed by act of parliament. See Briſtol Charters,
printed 1736, p. 29 to 47, and 51 to 54.

· N. B. Brightnee-bridge then called is now called Bright-bow (from the arch bridge) at the
end of Bedminſter cauſey. Bewell or Bewell's Groſs then called is that where the criminals
now uſually pray before their execution at St. Michael's-hill gallows. The Well then called
in the way near Addlebury of Knoll is that now called Holy Brook Well, going to Lower
Knowl, or rather one at Totterdown, now ſtopped up.

+ Laſtage is a cuſtom in ſome markets and fairs for carrying things; alſo a duty paid for wares
ſold by the laſt, that is, by certain weights, meaſures, or tale. — Pontage is a contribution for
the repairing and re-edifying of bridges; alſo a bridge toll.

‡ That is, if either party on his allegation, vary and change his ſpeech in court, no advantage
ſhall be taken of him to his detriment.

§ Tenure is the manner whereby tenants hold lands and tenements of their lords.

it again after it fhall be demanded to be reftored to the provoft, * he may take and diftrain a fhip for the fame. And that no foreign merchant fhall buy within the town of any ftranger hides, corn, or wool, but of the burgeffes. And that no foreigner fhall have any tavern but in his fhip, nor fell cloth to be cut but in the fair. And that no ftranger fhall tarry in the town with his merchandizes to fell the fame, but only forty days. And that no burgefs any where elfe within my land or jurifdiction fhall be attached or diftrained for any debt, unlefs he be debtor or furety. And that they may marry themfelves and fons and daughters and widows, without licence of their lords. And that none of their lords, by reafon of their foreign lands, may have the cuftody or gift of their fons and daughters or widows; but only of their tenements, which be of their fee, until they be of age. And that no recognizance be made in the town. And that none fhall take tynam † in the town, but to the ufe of the lord of the country, and that according to the cuftom of the town. And that they may grind their corn wherefoever they will. And they may have all their reafonable gilds ‡ in as full manner as they held them in the time of Robert and William his fon, Earls of Glocefter. And no burgefs fhall be compelled to take fureties of any man, except himfelf be willing thereunto, although he be remaining upon his ground. And I have alfo granted to them all their holds, within the walls and without, unto the aforefaid mounds of the town, in houfes and woods in buildings, by the water and elfewhere, wherefoever it fhall be, to be holden in free burgage; that is to fay, by landgable fervice, § which they fhall do within the walls. And I have alfo granted, that every one of them may amend as much as he can, in making buildings, every where upon the bank and elfewhere, without the damage of the borough and town. And that they may have and poffefs all lands and void places, which are contained in the faid mounds, at their wills to build. ‖ Wherefore I will and ftrictly command, that my faid burgeffes of Briftow and

their

---

* The chief magiftrate of any town, in the original " prepofito."

† That is to fay, that a tyne may contain twenty-four gallons; and where it is not taken, there fhall be paid unto us two pence for the fame tyne.

‡ Gild is a fociety of men incorporated by the king's authority.

§ Burgage is a law term, and fignifies a tenure proper to towns and cities, whereby they hold their lands and tenements for a certain yearly rent. It is the fame with landgable fervice.

‖ The mayor and corporation of Briftol claim this right to this day, as lords of the wafte, from this charter, and have thereby annexed great eftates to the city's ufe; all Queen's-fquare, King-ftreet, &c. was city wafte, and part of St. Auguftine's-back, all Prince's-ftreet, and the Key, Grove, and Back.

A. D.

their heirs fhall have and hold all their aforefaid liberties and free cuftoms as aforefaid of me and my heirs, as amply, wholly, peaceably, and honourably, as ever they had the fame, when, well, and in time of peace, without the hindrance or moleftation of any perfon whatfoever. Witnefs, Stephen Rid, my chancellor, William de Wennen, Roger de Dlan, Roger de Newborough, Maurice de Berkly, Robert his brother, Hamar Deval, Simon de Marifco, Gilbert Ralph, William de la Feleyfe, Mafter Benedict, Mafter Peter, and many others at Briftow."

The nature, effect, and extent of this grant may be collected from the grant itfelf. It muft have been highly advantageous to the burgeffes, who muft have behaved in a manner very agreeable to their lord to merit fuch favour from his hands.

1200   After King John came to the crown he granted the town of Briftow in fee farm with a refervation of the caftle to the burgeffes, at the yearly rent of 245l. *

1202   In the third year of his reign I find the following record enrolled that year: " Glouceft. Anno tertio reg. Joannis termino Michaelis tria meffuagia cum pertinentiis in Briftoliâ funt infra libertates Roberti de Berkley, qui nullam vult facere fummonitionem fine breve originali, &c. Rot. xvi."

1209   King John iffued a proclamation at Briftol, forbidding the taking all forts of feathered game throughout England : the firft edict of this kind ever made by any king.

1210   The King compelled the Jews to pay great part of his charge into Ireland. The burgeffes of Glocefter paid 500 marks towards it, whilft the burgeffes of Briftol paid 1000, others their refpective quotas, which were paid into the royal treafury at Briftow ; and one Engelard Cygoine, the fheriff of Glocefter and the king's jufticiary, was King John's treafurer here.

He feized the goods of the Jews; and one inftance of cruelty and oppreffion we have of a Jew at Briftol, who though cruelly tormented refufed to ranfom himfelf. The king ordered that they fhould every day pull out one of his cheek teeth till he would pay down ten thoufand marks, accordingly they pulled out feven in as many days, but on the eighth he relented, and fo with the lofs of feven teeth parted with the money at laft.

M m m m 2   1212

* Madox, Excheq. 228. c. 2. (II.) (S.)

A. D.

1212   Anno 13, Briſtol. Inquiſitio, &c. ubi jurati preſentant quot piſces de quolibet genere piſcium quilibet batellus debet reddere conſtabu_ lario caſtri Briſtolliæ. By this it appears the town was obliged to ſupply the conſtable of the caſtle with a certain quantity of fiſh, and of different kinds, out of every battel or ſmall boat that came in.

King John, after a ſeries of troubles with his barons, left his ſon Henry involved in the ſame, who by the conduct of the brave and wiſe Earl of Pembroke was proclaimed at Gloceſter and there crowned.

1215   Guallo, Pope Innocent 3d's. legate, immediately on this held a ſynod at Briſtol, where King Henry 3d. then young, the regent Earl of Pembroke, and other nobles were convened. It is mentioned by Leland out of a little boke of the Calendaries of Brightſtowe : — " Swalo Cardinale a Romaine legate after the coronation of Henry 3d. at Gloceſter cam to Brighteſtow, and kept a ſynode there tempore Henrici Bleſenſis epiſcopi Wigornienſis." But this memorable tran_ ſaction is more particularly related in Wilkin's Concilia, vol. i. p. 546. " Poſt coronationem Henrici regis terti, &c." i. e. " After crowning King Henry 3d. Guallo the legate held a council at Briſtol on the feaſt of St. Martin, in which he compelled eleven biſhops of England and Wales that were preſent, and other prelates of a lower claſs, and the earls, barons, and knights that were convened, to ſwear fealty to King Henry. He put all Wales under an interdict, becauſe it held with the barons, and excommunicated the barons with all their accomplices, in which Lewis was put at the head." This excommunication of Lewis the French King's ſon, who had been invited over by the barons, gave ſome of them a pretence to refuſe him homage, and ſtrengthened the intereſt of the new crowned king.

1216   At this time the king with his counſellors and tutor came to Briſtol as to a ſafe place, at which time he permitted the town to chooſe a mayor after the manner of London, and with him were choſen two " grave, ſad, worſhipful men," who were called prepoſitors.

Mayors.	Prepositors.
1216 Adam le Page.	Stephen Hankin, Reginald Hazard.

The charter of Henry 3d. confirms that of King John, and farther grants that nonuſage of privileges or freedoms ſhall be of no prejudice, but they ſhall all be enjoyed without diſturbance of any of the king's officers; and that the goods, &c. of orphans and children under age ſhall be committed by the mayor to certain keepers and ſureties, who

ſhall

fhall anfwer at due time for the fame according to the form of the ftatute of fuch recognifances at Weftminfter fet forth. And moreover the burgeffes fhall have view of frank pledge in the town and fuburbs thereof for the good fervice done by them to the King and his progenitors, and for a fine paid, with all things to fuch view belonging, and that they fhould not be queftioned for what has been done before. Witnefs the King at Weftminfter the 28th of February in the ft year of his reign, and confirmed the 5th.

A. D.	MAYORS.	PREPOSITORS.
1217	Martin Underyate.	Richard Martyn, Hugh Upwell.
1218	John Athalle.	Richard Palmer, John Snowe.
1219	Robert Holbraft.	John Oldham, Henry Vynpenny.
1220	Roger de Staines.	Peter le Goldfmith, Robert de Monmouth.
1221	Walter Mombray.	John de Rumney, Philip le Coke.
1222	John de Berdwycke.	Robert de Wefton, William Dexe.
1223	James de Rowborowe.	Thomas le Spycer, Walter Ubbely.
1224	Walter de Wynton.	Richard Martyn, John Metheham.
1225	Hugh de Fairford.	Richard de Bury, John de Broadways.
1226	John de Marfefielde.	William Colepeke, Nicholas Coker.
1227	Henry Long.	Alexander Rope, Henry de Tame.
1228	Nicholas Higham.	William Chard, Richard Bryan.
1229	John Brufelaunce.	Nicholas de Portbury, Wm. de Hayles.
1230	Henry de Berdwycke.	Ralph Atfhip, Walter le Rede.
1231	Elias Spryngham.	John de Kerdyff, John Atwall.
1232	Walter le Praunces.	Henry le Walleys, Thomas de Pedefton.
1233	Richard Aylward.	Gilbert le Plomer, Thomas le Chaloner.
1234	Jordan Brown.	Thomas Updyke, John Ergleys,
1235	James le Warre.	William Clarke, John de Belliter.
1236	Richard de Horton.	William Golde, Richard de Bury.
1237	Phillip de Pawlet.	Thomas Aylward, Roger Cantocke.
1238	Thomas de Wefton.	Richard Ofmonde, John de Gallande.
1239	Robert le Bell.	William le Chilton, Henry le Challoner.
1240	Richard Aylward.	Wm. de Bellemonte, Rob. de Kilmainam.

The ground in the Marfh of St. Auguftine was now purchafed of Abbot Bradfton for making the trench called the Quay, fee p. 68.

1241	William Spackftone.	William de Leigh, Robert Parment.
1242	John Vells.	Thomas Rice, Richard Hackall.
1243	Ralph Moiny.	Paul Cut, Roger Snake.

A. D.	MAYORS.	PREPOSITORS.
1244	Walter Nefham.	Ralph Nupton, John Walker.

This year King Henry granted the following charter: — " Henry King of England Lord of Ireland Duke of Normandy and Acquitain and Earl of Anjou. Know ye, that we do grant and by this our charter confirm, for us and our heirs, to the burgeffes of Briftol, that they may out of themfelves, chofe a coroner. And the burgeffes through the trefpafs of fervants fhall not forfeit their goods. And if any of the burgeffes fhould die within our land or jurifdiction, their goods fhall not be forfeited by death with or without a will. And they fhall have their liberties as free as the city of London. And the neglect of ufage of privileges fhall be no prejudice. And all their liberties fhall be by them freely enjoyed. The difturbers thereof fhall forfeit 20l. And we do grant and confirm the faid charter, as it doth reafonably teftify. And moreover we do grant to the burgeffes, for us and our heirs, that they and their fucceffors, burgeffes of the faid town for ever, fhall be free of murage, ftallage, and pannage through all England and the dominion thereof. And whenever they fhall choofe their mayor in the town aforefaid (time of war excepted) they fhall prefent him to the conftable of the caftle of Briftol as he was wont to be at the Exchequer, and thereof fhall certify to the treafurer. Thefe being witneffes; our beft beloved brother, Edmund Earl of Kent &c." Dated the 28th year of his reign, and confirmed the 40th.

1245	Elias de Axbridge.	John de St. Barbara, Richard de Tilley.
1246	Richard Froftall.	David le Wright, Richard de Lemfter.
1247	Richard Aylward.	William Tonnard, John Norfolk.

The following charter was granted by Henry the 3d. — " Henricus Dei Gratia &c. Sciatis &c. Know ye, that we have granted for us and our heirs to our burgeffes of Redclive in the fuburbs of Briftol, that they for ever fhall anfwer with our burgeffes of Briftol before our juftices, as our faid burgeffes of Briftol do anfwer, and where they anfwer and not elfewhere: wherefore we will and firmly command for us and our heirs, that our faid burgeffes of Redclive in the fuburb of Briftol do anfwer with our burgeffes of Briftol before our juftices as our faid burgeffes of Briftol do anfwer and where they anfwer and not elfewhere as aforefaid. Thefe being witneffes, Richard Earl of Cornwal our brother, Richard de Clare 'Earl of Glocefter and Hertford, John Maunfel provoft &c. Given under our hand at Wodeftoke the 28th of July in the 31ft year of our reign, 1247."

About

About the fame time Maurice Fitzharding confirmed to his men of Redcliff, which was in his lordfhip or fee, all their liberties and cuftoms which Robert his father had granted them in Henry the 2d's. time, which fee before p. 73. " Mauritius filius Roberti omnibus hominibus fuis & amicis falutem. Sciatis me conceffiffe & hac carta meâ confirmaffe hominibus meis de Redclive omnes confuetudines libertates & quietancias quas habuerunt in tempore patris mei & quas pater meus iis carta fua confirmavit: hi funt teftes Elias Capellanus, magifter Mauritius, Adam Dapifer & alii.

After obtaining this charter of the King, the mayor, burgeffes and com- monalty of Briftol, with the confent and joint charges of the men of Redclive, and the governors alfo of Temple fee, (the trench for forming the New Key or Quay begun in 1240, being now completed,) begun building a large ftone bridge over the Avon, p. 75.

Henry the 3d. alfo confirmed the charter of King John, and granted to the burgeffes an additional liberty, that none of them for the future fhould be molefted by any of his juftices of the foreft or any of his bailiffs for venifon found within the walls of the fame town. Dated at Wodeftoke the 36th year of his reign.

A. D.	MAYORS.	PREPOSITORS.
1248	Reginald de Panes.	John Wefton, Walter de Berkham.

The charter of the town being now enlarged the fhire ftones were fet up, both on Somerfet and Glocefterfhire fides, how far the city bounds fhould go; which were again more particularly afcertained afterwards by perambulation, and the charter of Edward the 3d.

1249	Galfridus le Wright.	Walter Tropp, William Snake.
1250	John Adrian.	Walter Dalmage, Henry Farnham.
1251	Roger de Bury.	Thomas de Norwood, John Cornhill.
1252	Elias Long.	Rob. de Bellemont, Gilbert de Malbrege.
1253	Thomas Rowfe.	John Attwood, John Atknowle.
1254	Raynold White.	Ralph Ouldham, William Hafeldene.
1255	Henry Adrian.	Hugh Mitchel, William Sevar.

The King beftowed on his fon Prince Edward the town of Briftol and other revenues.

1256	Adam de Berkham.	Robert Shirley, William Freebody.

A great famine in Briftol, provifions were fo fcarce that people often fought for the carcafes of dogs and other carrion; wheat fold here for 16s. the bufhel. Prince Edward was taken by the Barons, who by the King's connivance had enriched himfelf by the fpoils of

the

the country, the firſt cauſe of the barons wars. The army being diſcharged came and abode at Briſtol, until the Prince made his
eſcape, and they then went to the battle of Eveſham.

MAYORS.	PREPOSITORS.
1257 Roger de Stokes.	Thomas Eldiſham, Robert Pickeridge.
1258 Clement Romney.	Roger Piper, Thomas Winfield.
1259 William de Glouceſter.	John Hartſhorn, Robert Hornebey.
1260 John de Lyne.	Ralph de Bird, Roger de Cantock.

Robert de Peretone, Abbot of Glaſtonbury, diſcharged the many
debts of his abbey; Roger de Cantocke, citizen and prepoſitor of Briſtol,
demanded 82lb. of ſilver, owing ſince the laſt abbot's time; but it was
compromiſed by the interpoſition of friends, and the abbot paid him
15 pounds.

1261 Robert Kilmanam.	Thomas Tremworth, Richard Ruſtheton.
1262 Adam de Berkham.	Thomas Hemmingfield, Geoffry Uſher.
1263 Thomas Rowſe.	Harry de Puxton, Robert Tremworth.

Prince Edward a priſoner in the caſtle of Briſtol.

1264 Henry Adrian.	Joſeph Caparon, William Chadbourn.
1265 Stephen Ormſtone.	Ralph Bardwin, John Exhall.

Prince Edward took Briſtol caſtle from the barons, and the town was
fined 1000l.

1266 Thomas Selby.	Raynold Richards, John Puxton.
1267 Simon Clarke.	William de Belmonte, Roger de Berckam.

This year the prepoſitors were called Seneſchals or Stewards.

MAYORS.	SENESCHALS.
1268 Robert Manſell.	John Legatt, Peter Marten.
1269 Robert Fiſher.	Simon Adrian, Roger Draper.
1270 Ralph Palden.	Richard de Clifton, Thomas Haſelden.
1271 John Wiſſey.	Roger de Cantock, William Bradwick.
1272 Richard de Welles.	Robert Snowand, Simon de Wedmore.
1273 Peter de Keinſham.	John Salkin, Ralph de Ax.
1274 Thomas de Haſelden.	Simon Adrian, William de Marina.
1275 Gerrard le Francis.	John de Portſhead, Robert Lancaſter.
1276 Simon de Bardney.	Rob. de Kingſwood, Raynald de Capener.
1277 John de Lydeyard.	Robert Truelove, William de Scriven.
1278 Roger le Tavernor.	John Bryan, Nicholas Atokes.

Wars were now between King Edward and Lewellin Prince of
Wales, in the midſt of which four ſhips of Briſtol took a prize near the
iſland

island of Scilly, in which was the intended spouse of Lewellin and daughter of Simon Montford, which was well accepted by the King. See Langtoft's chronicle.

A. D.	MAYORS.	SENESCHALS.
1279	Peter de Rumney.	John Hoddy, Thomas Coston.
1280	John Beauflour.	John de Cardiff, Robert de Whetmarsh.
1281	William Horncastle.	William Wedmore, Robert Golding.
1282	Roger Piper, (some Thomas Coker.)	Richard Atokes, William Boyle.
1283	Peter de Rumney.	Richard Tunbrill, William Whitchwell.

King Edward 1st. came from Wales to Bristol about the middle of December, and kept his Christmas here with much content and satisfaction, and held a parliament.

1284	Richard de Mangotsfield.	Henry Horncastle, Galfrid Snell.
1285	Richard de Mangotsfield.	Thomas de Weston, John Tonney.
1286	John de la Ware.	William Howden, Thomas Prestley.
1287	Roger de Grafton.	Thomas Royston, John Bennington.
1288	Roger le Draper.	John de Cheddre, John le Long.
1289	Roger Turtle.	Hugh de Langbridge, John Francis.
1290	Richard Mangotsfield.	Simon de Burton, William Randolph.
1291	Simon de Burton.	John de Cheddre, John de Snow.
1292	Thomas de Tilly.	Walter Glen, Simon Ricroft.
1293	Walter Francis.	Walter Godshalf, Thomas de Weston.
1294	Simon de Bourton.	Robert de Ottery, William Rowbrough.

This year the mayor founded the church of St. Mary Redcliff, and also the almshouse in the Long-Row in St. Thomas parish, see p. 567.

1295	William Randolph.	Thomas Updish, Robert Holdbush.
1296	Simon de Bourton.	Robert de Ottery, William Rowbrough.
1297	John Snow.	John de Long, Adam Welshot.
1298	Richard Mangotsfield.	Jeffery Godshalf, William Marina.
1299	Roger Turtle.	John Francis, Hugh de Langbridge.
1300	Thomas de Tilly.	Richard de Colepitt, Wm. de Glassonbury.
1301	Walter de Adrian.	Robert Bostock, John Horshalt.
1302	Simon de Bourton.	Robert Ottery, Nicholas Rowbrough.
1303	Thomas le Grave.	John Tike, Roger Beauflour.
1304	Simon de Bourton.	William Updish, Robert Hornhurst.
1305	Simon de Bourton.	Robert Ottery, Nicholas Rowbrough.

The

The town of Briſtol gave the King 400l. and it was paid into the treaſury, to be freed from certain payments required of all cities and towns.

A. D.	MAYORS.	SENESCHALS.
1306	William Randolph.	John de Chedder, John de Long.
1307	John Snow.	Nicholas Brerton, Thomas de Barwick.
1308	John Taverner.	William Le Olive, Gilbert Pickering.

King Edward came to Briſtol with Gaveſton in his way to Ireland, to bring him on his way thither.

1309	John Taverner.	Robert de Ottery, Adam Welſcott.
1310	William Randolph.	John Ramney, Walter Trapin.
1311	J. Danſeller.	Thomas Spicer, Robert Randolph.
1312	William Hore.	John Beauflower, Thomas le Spicer.
1313	John le Taverner.	Lawrence de Cary, Richard de Whitt.

This year ſeneſchals were left out and bailiffs choſen in their place.

BAILIFFS.

1314	Raynald de Paines.	Richard Winſman, John le Honte.
1315	William Randolph.	Robert Holburt, John Welliſhotte.
1316	Robert Paſſons.	Richard Colepeck, Henry Winpenny.
1317	Richard Tilly.	Thomas Fraunces, Hugh de Langbridge.
1318	Roger Terrill.	Richard de Paines, Richard le White.
1319	William de Axe.	Roger de Littlebury, Jeffery de Wraxall.
1320	Richard de Tilly.	William Hangfield, Hugh de Prowt.
1321	Richard de Tilly.	Gilbert Pickeril, Clement Turtle.
1322	Roger Terrill.	Thomas le Spicer, Hugh de Langbridge.
1323	John de Keinſham.	Everard le Fraunces, Stephen le Spicer.
1324	John de Romney.	Stephen le Spicer, Gilbert Pickerill.
1325	John de Romney.	John Praunces, Walter Prentis.
1326	Roger Turtle.	Robert Guyen, Robert de Wrynton.
1327	Hugh de Langbridge.	John de Romney, Nicholas Free.
1328	John Francis.	John Atwell, Henry de Francis.
1329	John de Axbridge.	Roger Plewett, Henry Babcary.
1330	Roger Turtle.	Stephen de Spicer, Henry Babcary.
1331	Everard le Frances.	Joſias de Ramy, Thomas Terpin.
1332	Roger Turtle.	Stephen le Spicer, Henry Babcary.
1333	Roger Turtle.	Joſias de Ramy, Peter Teſtin.
1334	Hugh Lanbridge.	Stephen le Spicer, Thomas Terpin.
1335	Roger Turtle,	Richard de Calne, Walter de Pelevell.

7 times mayor.

1336

A. D.	MAYORS.	BAILIFFS.
1336	Everard le Frances.	Thomas Tilly, John de Laxham.
1337	Stephen le Spicer.	Robert de Wrington, John le Spicer.
1338	Stephen le Spicer.	Peter Teftin, William Hanny.
1339	Everard le Frances.	Thomas Turpine, John de Cobbinton.
1340	Roger Turtle.	James Tilly, Thomas Blanket.
1341	Roger Turtle.	Thomas Turpine, Thomas Blanket.
1342	Robert Wrington.	William Hains, Thomas Albon.
1343	Stephen le Spicer.	John Curtis, William Hanny.
1344	Stephen le Spicer.	William Hains, Thomas Albon.
1345	Robert Gwyen.	John Neal, James Tilly.

William de Colford, then recorder of Briftol, at the requeft of the commonalty drew up the ordinances, cuftoms, and liberties of the town and recorded them in writing, together with the by-laws and other memorable things for a perpetual remembrance; and the mayor calling to his affiftance 48 of the more powerful and principal citizens, as Roger Turtle, Robert Gyen, &c. they agreed on many ufeful laws and ordinances, which were confirmed by the charter obtained of Edward the 3d. dated the 16th of October in the 5th year of his reign, including thofe of Henry the 3d. Edward the 2d. John Earl of Moreton.

Amongft many regulations then made it was ordered that no leprous man ftay within the precincts of the town, nor any common woman remain within its walls; and if fnch women be found refiding there, then the doors and windows of the houfes fhall be unhung and carried by the ferjeants of the mayor to the houfe of the conftable of the ward, and there to be kept till the women be removed.—That no whore fhould ever appear in the ftrects, or even within the bars in St. James's without their head covered (capite ftragulato) &c. &c.

1346	Robert Gwyen.	Robert Codner, William Hanny
1347	Robert Wrington.	Roger Banner, Walter Wenlake.
1348	John le Spicer.	John Cobbington, Roger Prentis.

In January this year the plague raged far and near, Regift. Radulp. Epifc. Wellens.

1349	Robert Gwyen.	Edmund Blanket, Raynald French.
1350	John Wickham.	John de Caftlecary, Walter Darby.
1351	John Spicer.	Robert Chedre, Walter Derby.
1352	John de Cobbinton.	Thomas de Coventry, John de Caftlecary.

A. D.	MAYORS.	BAILIFFS.
1353	Richard le Spycer.	Robert Attwall, John Stoke.
1354	Richard le Spycer.	John Stoke, Richard de Dean.
1355	Thomas Babcary.	Richard Hemming, John Cobbinton.
1356	Reynald le French.	Walter Derby, Thomas Inhing,
1357	Walter Frampton.	Richard Bromdon, Jeffery Beauflower.
1358	Reynald le French.	John Stoar or Sore, Henry Vyell.
1359	Thomas Babcary.	Walter Derby, John Stoke.
1360	Robert Chedre.	Elias Spelly, Henry Somerwell.
1361	Richard Brandon.	Walter Derby, William Canynges.
1362	Robert Chedre.	Elias Spelly, Henry Willifton.
1363	Walter Derby.	Henry Willifton, William Woodrover.
1364	John Stokes.	William Hayle, John Bate.
1365	Walter Frampton.	John de Stowe, Henry Willifton.
1366	John Stokes.	William Somervell, John Keene.
1367	Walter Derby.	William Dagon, John Blunt.
1368	John Bath.	John Blunt, John Vyell.
1369	Elias Spelly.	William Canynges, John Vyell.
1370	John Bathe.	Thomas Beaupenny, Henry Vyell.
1371	Richard Spycer.	John Inhynge, John Prefton.

	MAYORS.	SHERIFFS.	BAILIFFS.
1372	Wm. Canynges.	John Vyell.	Tho. Sampfon, Walter Hudly.
1373	Wm. Canynges.	John Vyell.	Tho. Sampfon, Nich. Studley.

This year a new charter was granted by Edward the 3d. fee Briftol charters p. 6. by which the King willing to help the town, and on account of the good behaviour of the burgeffes towards him, and of their good fervice by their fhips and otherwife done in times paft, and for a fine of 600 marks by them paid, granted the town to be feparated from Glocefterfhire and Somerfetfhire and to be henceforth a county of itfelf, to have one fheriff out of three returned into chancery to be chofen by the King, who is to be efcheator, the fheriff to hold his court the firft Monday in every month; and the mayor to hold his court as hath been accuftomed.—The mayor after his election fhall take his oath before his next predeceffor mayor in the Guildhall, and not be prefented to the conftable of the caftle to be by him accepted; that the mayor and fheriff are to hear and determine the feveral offences, and no other juftice to intermeddle; and that the mayor have power to enroll deeds of lands, tenements &c. within the faid town in like manner as in chancery, with

power

power to prove wills of lands &c. within the faid town, and to put the legacies in execution: that they fhall be burdened to fend but two knights and bur-geffes to parliament; and in cafe any thing new and of difficulty fhall happen, the mayor and fheriff fhall choofe 40 honeft men, who together fhall have power to make bye-laws and to raife taxes for the neceffity and profit of the town.—All difturbers to be punifhed by the mayor and fheriff, and all former liberties and charters are alfo confirmed.—Witneffes William Archbifhop of Canterbury primate of all England, and others, dated at Wodeftock the 8th of Auguft, the 47th of Edward the 3d.

At the fame time the King granted a commiffion to 12 men of Briftol, 12 of Gloceftefhire, and 12 of Somerfetfhire, by perambulation to fix by verdict the meets and bounds of the town, as in page 105, which fee.—This charter was confirmed by parliament.

A. D.	MAYORS.	SHERIFFS.	BAILIFFS.
1374	Walter Frampton.	Tho. Beaupeny.	Tho. Sutton, Reginald Towker.
1375	Wm. Canynges.	Henry Vyell.	No bailiffs this year.
1376	Walter Derby.	Wm. Somervell.	Wm. Coombe, Tho. Knappe.
1377	Tho. Beaupeny.	Walter Studly.	Tho. Sampfon, Wal. Tyddeley.
1378	Elias Spelly.	Wm. Coombe.	Wm. Elingham, John Stanes.
1379	John Stokes.	Tho. Knappe.	John Stanes, John Barftable.
1380	Walter Derby.	Wm. Somervell.	Rob. Candever, John Canynges.
1381	Wm. Canynges.	John Candever.	Walter Seymor, John Prifton.
1382	Elias Spelly.	John Canynges.	John Stanes, Wm. Warmifter.
1383	Tho. Beaupenny.	Rob. Candever.	John Somervell, Peter Barogh.
1384	Walter Derby.	Tho. Sampfon.	John Young, Wm. Draper.
1385	Wm. Canynges.	John Somervell.	Roger Tucker, John Bright.
1386	Thomas Knappe.	Peter Barogh.	Wm. Froome, Thomas Athay.
1387	Wm. Somervell.	Wm. Froome.	Thomas Colfton, John Snell.
1388	John Vyell.	Wm. Wodrowe.	Tho. Athay, John Stephens.
1389	Wm. Canynges.	John Barftable.	John Banbury, John Havering.
1390	Elias Spelly.	Tho. Athay.	Rob. Dudbrook, John Selwodde.
1391	Thomas Knappe.	John de Banbury.	John Burtone, Ric. Hanteford.
1392	John Canynges.	Walter Seymour.	Tho. Norton, Ric. Brookworth.
1393	John Somervell.	John Havering.	Wm. Solers, Thomas Blunt.
1394	Wm. Froome.	John Stephens.	John Pryfton, John Caftle.
1395	John Barftable.	Roger Toker.	Rt. Dudbrook, John de Sodbury.
1396	Thomas Knappe.	Wm. Warmifter.	Rt. Brookworth, John Hardwick.
1397	John Banbury.	John Pryfton.	Wm. Draper, Henry Rokerill.

1398

A. D.	MAYORS.	SHERIFFS.	BAILIFFS.
1398	John Canynges.	Robert Baxter.	John le Manner, John Sodbury.
1399	Thomas Knappe.	Thomas Blunt.	Tho. Glocefter, Jeffry Barber.
1400	Wm. Froome.	Robert Dudbrook.	Mark Williams, John Seely.
1401	John Barftable.	Thomas Norton.	Rich. Paines, Simon Algod.
1402	John Stephens.	John Seely.	Thomas Young, Nich. Exetor.
1403	Thomas Knappe.	Thomas Gloufter.	John Droyes, Adam Inhyng.
1404	Rob. Dudbrook.	John Droyes.	Robert Ruffell, Gilbert Joyce.
1405	John Barftable.	Mark Williams.	John Cleve, John Newton.
1406	John Droyfe.	John Eifber.	Jam. Crokys, David Dudbrook.
1407	Thomas Blunt.	Thomas Young.	John Spyne, Robert Barftable.
1408	John Fifher.	John Olyffe.	John Shipward, John Leycefter.
1409	John Droyfe.	James Cokys.	John Sutton, Wm. Bendey.

In the parliament of the 10th of Henry the 4th. the commons of the counties of Somerfet, Briftol and Wilts, exhibited their petition to the King to remove all wears and obftruɛtions of the river Avon, which hindered the free paffage of boats and other veffels to the public prejudice, and much enhanced the price of carriage by water betwixt Bath and Briftol. Before the time of Richard the 1ft. the Avon to Bath was navigable, and wine, wax, falt, wool, fkins and cloth ufed to be carried in veffels between Bath and Briftol; and there is a long deed (Clauf. 4. Edw. 1. Pat. ii. M. 4.) being a writ direɛted to the mayor of Briftol, and Richard de Tikehull fheriff of Somerfet, to fee all wears and obftruɛtions in the river Avon betwixt Briftol and Bath removed; that the faid navigation be free and uninterrupted; which however in the fucceeding reign was again obftruɛted and again ordered to be cleared.

1410	John Seely.	Nicholas Exeter.	Robert Clovelde, Walter Parle.
1411	Thomas Young.	John Spine.	Wm. Stephens, David Ruddeck.
1412	John Cleve.	John Sharpe.	Thomas Hendy, Wm. Barret.
1413	Thomas Norton.	John Newton.	Wm. Wefterly, Walter Milton.
1414	John Droyes.	Robert Ruffell.	John Draper, John Milton.
1415	John Sharpe.	Wm. Bendy.	Nich Baggod, John Shipward.
1416	Thomas Blount.	David Dudbrook.	John Burtone, Nicholas Dennis.
1417	Robert Ruffell.	John Leycefter.	Roger Levedon, Walter Milton.
1418	John Newton.	John Burtone.	Thomas Hollway, John Langley.
1419	James Cokis.	David Ruddock.	Henry Gildency, Thomas Fifh.
1420	Thomas Young.	Roger Lavindon.	Rich. Trenolde, John Cotton.
1421	John Spyne.	Nicholas Baggod.	Richard Arves, Edmund Brown.

1422

A. D.	MAYORS.	SHERIFFS.	BAILIFFS.
1422	Mark Williams.	Richard Trenolde.	Thomas Erle, John Peers.

A mint eſtabliſhed at Briſtol for coining.

A. D.	MAYORS.	SHERIFFS.	BAILIFFS.
1423	John Burtone.	Thomas Holway.	John Hethe, Richard Alexander.
1424	John Leyceſter.	Thomas Earle.	Thomas Hook, Walter Powell.
1425	John Cleve.	Robert Cloveld.	Walter Powel, John Snethe.
1426	Robert Ruſſell.	Nicholas Dennis.	Clem. Baggod, Hugh Whitford.
1427	John Newton.	John Sharpe.	Andrew Parle, John Erle.
1428	Roger Levedon.	Henry Gildney	John Talbot, John Triott.
1429	John Burtone.	John Shipwarde.	Richard Foſter, John Albinton.
1430	John Leyceſter.	Hugh Whitford.	Wm. Dunſter, John Papinham.
1431	Rich. Tranode.	Clement Baggod.	John Spicer, Nicholas Frome.
1432	John Sharpe.	Richard Arſoiſe.	Tho. Noreys, Wm. Canynges.
1433	John Fiſher.	Richard Foſter.	John Engliſh, Thomas Markes.
1434	Tho. Holeway.	Thomas Fiſher.	Richard Roper, John. Stanley.
1435	John Milton.	John Spycer.	Nicholas Hill, William Clynche.
1436	Richard Foſter	Walter Powel.	William Coder, John Forde.
1437	Clement Baggod.	Nicholas Frome.	Thomas Hore, Thomas Balle.
1438	Hugh Whitford.	Wm. Canynges.	Thomas Mede, John Coſling.
1439	John Sharpe.	Richard Roper.	William Pavy, John Shipward.
1440	Nicholas Freme.	John Stanley.	John Whiteford, Wm. Howell.
1441	Wm. Canynges.	John Shipward.	Nicholas Stone, Robert Sturing.
1442	Clement Baggod.	Nicholas Hill.	Richard Hatter, Rich. Haddon.
1443	John Stanley.	William Coder.	Wm. Skermott, Wm. Powney.
1444	John Shipward.	John Foord.	Philip Mead, Thomas Rodgers.

1445-6 This year about St. Paul's tide Redcliff ſteeple was thrown down by a great tempeſt of thunder and lightning, and great damage was received by the ſaid church, which was re-edified by the good devotion of Mr. William Canynges, merchant.

A. D.	MAYORS.	SHERIFFS.	BAILIFFS.
1445	Nicholas Hill.	John Bolton.	Richard Marſhall, Rich. Bayly.

This year a charter was granted the town by Henry 6th. who came to Briſtol at this time. He granted to hold and occupy the town to their ſucceſſors unto the end and during the term of 60 years in reverſion of 20 years to be ended. And moreover he granted to the mayor, &c. during the ſaid term of 60 years certain liberties, franchiſes, &c. under a certain form, yielding and paying yearly to King Henry 6th. and his heirs at the end of the ſaid 20 years, during the ſaid term of 60 years, 102l. 15s. 6d. at the feaſt of Eaſter and St. Michael the archangel, by equal portions

portions to the abbot of Tewkefbury 14l. 10s. to the prior of St. James of Briftol, and to his fucceffors for the time being, for the annual rent of the mill of the faid town, 3l. to the conftable of the caftle of Briftol, and his officers for the time being, that is to fay, to the porter of the gate and watchmen of the caftle, and to the forefter of Kingfwood, 39l. 14s. 6d. to be paid during the term of fixty years as aforefaid. He alfo granted all fines, forfeitures, &c. in as full manner as if he had retained the town in his own hands: fo that the mayor and commonalty may levy, gather, and receive and retain all goods forfeited to the ufe and profit of the fame mayor and commonalty and their fucceffors for ever, and alfo have the court of view of frank-pledge, &c. (the efcheat of lands and tenements in times to come happening being always excepted) all the before-mentioned privileges, liberties, &c. within the faid town and precincts thereof happening or to happen he granted fully, and wholly to the mayor, &c. yielding and paying 102l. 15s. 6d. in manner as aforefaid.

A. D.	MAYORS.	SHERIFFS.	BAILIFFS.
1446	Richard Fofter.	John Troyte.	William Deane, William Talbot.
1447	Richard Fofter.	Thomas Balle.	William Rolph, John Wickham.
1448	John Burtone.	William Pavie.	John Eaftmande, John Bennet.
1449	Wm. Canynges.	Thomas Hore.	Rich. Abberton, Wm. Spencer.
1450	John Burtone.	Robert Sturmy.	John Sharpe, junr. Wm. Dillyng.
1451	John Stanley,	Richard Hatter.	Robert Jakes, John Hofier.
1452	William Coder.	Thomas Mead.	Thomas Afh, William Raines.
1453	Robert Sturmy.	William Howell.	Nicholas Long, Tho. Keynfham.
1454	Richard Hatter.	Philip Mead.	William Hatton, John Cogon.
1455	John Shipward.	Thomas Rodgers.	John Baggott, Robert Bolton.
1456	Wm. Canynges.	William Daine.	Henry Chefter, John Jay, fenr.

This year Queen Margaret came to Briftol with her nobility.

1457	William Coder.	John Wickham.	John Clerke, Robert Ball.
1458	Philip Mead.	John Baggott.	John Hawks, John Jay, junr.
1459	Thomas Rodgers.	Robert Jakis.	John Gaywood, John Saint.
1460	Wm. Canynges.	Tho. Kenyffon.	Wm. Woddington, Lewis Morris.
1461	Philip Mead.	William Spencer.	Robert Strange, Henry Balle.

Edward 4th. in September came to Briftol, and had Sir Baudwin Fulford, Bright, and Heffant, Efqrs. beheaded. See p. 220.

1462	John Wickham.	Rich. Alberton.	John Fofter, Jeffry Griffith.
1463	John Shipward.	John Hawkins.	William Bird, Walter Cofton.
1464	William Coder.	John Cogan.	William Rokye, John Gyton.

A. D.	MAYORS,	SHERIFFS.	BAILIFFS.
1465	William Spencer.	John George.	J. Shipward, junr. E. Weftcot.
1466	Wm. Canynges.	John Gaywood.	Walter Grimfteed, Tho. Rowley.
1467	Robert Jakys.	John Hooper.	Wm. Wickham, John Skevyn.
1468	Philip Mead.	Robert Strange.	John Lancorton, John Goodard.
1469	John Shipward.	William Bird.	Henry Vaughan, John Powke.
1470	Tho. Kainfham.	Henry Chefter.	John Stevens, William Dokett.
1471	John Hawkes.	Wm. Weddington.	John Powke, John Eafterfield.
1472	John Cogan.	John Jay.	John Gurney, John Gregory.
1473	William Spencer.	Edmund Weftcott.	John Swayne, Thomus Flexall.
1474	Robert Strange.	John Fofter.	Thomas Hexton, Wm. Rowley.
1475	William Bird.	Thomas Rowley.	John Sing, Richard Sherman.
1476	John Baggott.	Wm. Wickham.	John Chefter, Philip Caple.
1477	John Shipward.	Henry Vaughan.	John Batkok, Clement Wiltfhire.
1478	William Spencer.	John Shyven.	John Drewes, Richard Bond.
1479	Edmund Weftcott.	John Powke.	John Griffith, John Wofwall.
1480	Wm. Wodington.	William Duket.	Rob. Bonnok, John Houndeflow.
1481	John Fofter.	John Pynke.	Wm. Regent, John Langforde.
1482	Robert Strange.	John Eafterfield.	Thomas Spicer, Henry Dale.
1483	Henry Vaughan.	John Stephens.	John Vaughan, Wm. Gawnfell.
1484	Wm. Wickham.	John Swaine.	John Hemming, William Spycer.
1485	Edmund Weftcott.	Richard Sherman.	Philip Kingfton, Hugh Jones.
1486	Wm. Wickham.	John Snigg.	John Jay, Thomas ap Howell.
1487	John Eafterfield.	John Cheftre.	Nicholas Brown, John Walfh.
1488	John Pinke.	Clement Wiltfhire.	John Howell, John Hurler.
1489	Robert Strange.	Thomas Spicer.	John Taylor, Robert Fourtie.
1490	John Stevens.	William Regent.	Rich. Vaughan, Geo. Mononx.

The ftone bridge on the Were now made, and the ftreets new paved. The city gave the King 500l. as a benevolence.

A. D.	MAYORS,	SHERIFFS.	BAILIFFS.
1491	William Toker.	Henry Dale.	David Cogan, John Eifber.
1492	Clement Wiltfhire.	John Drewes.	John Popley, Roger Dawes.
1493	Henry Vaughan.	Philip Kingfton.	John Keynes, Philip Green.
1494	John Eafterfield.	Matthew Jubbes.	William Ealtby, John Rowland.
1495	William Regent.	Nicholas Brown.	David Lyfton, John Jones.
1496	John Drewes.	Hugh Jones.	Thomas Vaughan, John Elliott.
1497	Henry Dale.	Richard Vaughan.	William Lane, John Spicer.
1498	Philip Kingfton.	John Jay.	John Vaughan, Tho. Weftcott.
1499	Nicholas Brown.	Philip Green.	Richard Hobby, Walter Rice.
1500	Rich. Vaughan.	Hugh Elliot and John Batten, fheriffs this year.	

A new charter granted this year from Henry 7th. to the corporation, that they fhall have fix aldermen, the recorder to be one, with like powers as the aldermen of London, to be chofen for the firft time by the mayor and common council, and always after by the aldermen. And that the two bailiffs to be chofen as of old hath been ufed, fhall likewife be fheriffs of the county, and be fworn into and execute both offices. And the mayor and two of the aldermen, inftead of the fheriffs as before, are (with the affent of the commonalty) to choofe the forty common council-men, with the fame powers as were granted to them by the charter of the 47th of Edward the 3d. And that for the future there fhall be one chamberlain, who fhall be elected by the mayor and common council in the Guildhall: the perfon fo elected fhall be a burgefs, and continue in that office fo long as the mayor and common council fhall pleafe: he fhall alfo take his oath to perform the office of chamberlain before the mayor, &c. and alfo fhall have a feal affixed to his office, with the like powers as the chamberlain of the city of London. That if any of the town of Briftol, &c. for the future fhall be difobedient to the ordinances of the mayor, aldermen, and common council, or fhall be any ways abetting or caufe difturbance on the election of the mayor, or any other officer whatfoever, the offender fhall be punifhed according to the law of the kingdom of England, by the mayor and two of the aldermen. And alfo the faid mayor fhall have power to take the probates of wills of lands, tenements, rents, and tenures, within the faid town, fuburbs, and precincts of the fame, bequeathed within two years after the death of the teftator: fo that fuch tenements and legacies be proclaimed in full court of the Guildhall of Briftol, and enrolled in the rolls of the fame court, the enrolment fhall be of record; and from thence the faid mayor and his fucceffors may have power to put the legacies aforefaid in execution by his officers in form of law, or by due procefs to be made before them by writ ex gravi querela, at the profecution and election of any man who will profecute the fame. And that the mayor and one alderman may hold their courts, and fuch pleas and plaints as at any time before have been ufed and accuftomed, for the time being for ever. And that all fines and amerciaments fhall come to the mayor and commonalty of the town, without accounting to the King, his heirs, or fucceffors.

Alfo Henry the 7th. in the firft year of his reign, dated at Weftminfter, September 24, did give and grant to Thomas Hofkins the office of bailiff of the water of the town of Briftol for term of his life, and at his deceafe it is granted to the mayor and commonalty to chufe one of the burgeffes of the faid town to that office, and he fo to continue fo long as it fhall pleafe the mayor

and

and aldermen of the faid town for the time being, and he fhall be named Bailiff of the Water, alias Water-Bailiff of the faid town; and the mayor, &c.
fhall have power to nominate and conftitute the wages, fees, &c. to the faid
office due and anciently accuftomed, yielding to the King and his heirs a
rent of four marks of lawful money of England yearly, at the feaft of St. Michael the Archangel, and to be accountable for no more than the four marks
as aforefaid to be paid for the fame office. And we grant that any three of the
faid aldermen, whereof two of them fhall be the mayor and recorder of the
faid town, may be juftices of goal delivery within the town, and may have for
the future for ever the like power with other juftices of gaol delivery, faving
always to the King and his heirs all amerciaments at gaol delivery. Thefe being witneffes, our moft dear firft-born fon Arthur, Prince of Wales, Duke of
Cornwall, and others. Dated at Knoll, the 17th of December, in the 15th
year of our reign, 1500. See p. 134.

A. D.	MAYORS.	SHERIFFS.
1501	George Mollins.	Thomas Snyg, Thomas Paruaunt.
1502	Hugh Jones, alias Brewer.	John Collor, John Capell.

In the colle&ion of public a&s, upon the 9th of December this year,
1502, King Henry gave a patent to James Elliot and Thomas Afhurft,
merchants of Briftol, and to John Gonfalez and Francis Fernandez,
natives of Portugal, to go with Englifh colours in queft of unknown
countries, upon certain terms expreffed in the patent.

1503	Henry Dale.	Richard ap Merrick, William Bedford.
1504	David Cogan.	William Jefferis, Edward Penfon.
1505	Roger Dawes.	Thomas Elliott, John Harris.
1506	Philip Ringfton.	William Edwards, John Attwillis.
1507	John Vaughan.	John Edwards, Simon Jarvis.
1508	Richard Hoby.	John Matthews, William Neal.
1509	John Capell.	John Williams, John Wilkins.
1510	John Poplay.	Robert Hutton, Ralph Aprys.
1511	John Rowland.	John Hutton, Humphrey Brown.
1512	John Ellyott.	Thomas Dale, Thomas Broke.
1513	William Bedford.	William Woflcy, John Shipman.
1514	Robert Thorn	John Ware, Richard Tonnell.
1515	Roger Dawes.	Richard Abyngdon, William Vaughan.
1516	John Vaughan.	Thomas Pacy, Edward Prynne.
1517	Richard Hoby.	John Drewes, John Pepe.
1518	John Edwards.	John Hall, William Dale.

A. D.	MAYORS.	SHERIFFS.
1519	John Williams.	Clement Bays, Robert Sailbrige.
1520	Roger Dawes.	William Shipman, Robert Aventry.
1521	John Shipman.	Robert Ellyott, Roger Coke.
1522	John Rowland.	Gilbert Cogan, William Chester.
1523	John Williams.	Robert Chapman, John Davis.
1524	John Hutton.	Thomas Jefferis, John Spring
1525	Richard Abingdon.	Henry White, John Jervis.
1526	Thomas Broke.	George Bathram, David Lawrence.
1527	John Ware.	Thomas Nash, David Hutton.
1528	Richard Tonnell.	Nicholas Thorn, John Thorn.
1529	John Shipman.	William Kelke, Thomas Silke.
1530	Thomas White.	George Hall, Robert Adams.
1531	Thomas Pacy.	William Carey, John Mancell.
1532	Clement Bays.	John Smith, William Pykes.
1533	William Shipman.	William Howell, Anthony Pain.
1534	Roger Cook.	John Brampton, Nicholas Woodhoufe.

The King and his train went to Thornbury and the mayor sent him ten fat oxen and forty sheep for his hospitality, and to Queen Ann a silver cup and cover with 100 marks of gold.

One manuscript says, King Henry 8th. went to Thornbury in his progress, and thence came disguised to Bristol with certain gentlemen to Mr. Thorn's house and secretly viewed the city, which Mr. Thorn shewed him, and he said to Mr. Thorn, " this is now but the towne of Bristol, but I will make it the city of Bristol," which he afterwards did by erecting it into a bishop's fee. See p. 80, 279.

Great disputes about laymen's preaching in Bristol favoured by the mayor, and priests sent to Newgate.

1535	John Hutton.	Thomas Hart, John Northall.
1536	Richard Abingdon.	Richard Prinn, Thomas Moore.
1537	William Chester.	Thomas Winsmore, Rowland Cowper.
1538	Thomas Jeffreys.	David Harris, William Jay.

George Wisard, an heretic, preached in St. Nicholas church, and was ordered to bear a faggot for his erroneous doctrine.

1539	Roger Cook.	William Rowley, William Young.
1540	John Springe. See p. 379.	William Spratt, Richard Morse.
1541	Robert Elliot.	Richard Watley, Robert Saxse.
1542	Henry White.	William Ballard, William Pepwall.

1543

A. D.	MAYORS.	SHERIFFS.
1543	Thomas Pacy, fenr.	Francis Codrington, Thomas Landfdown.

The litany was firft fung in Englifh in a general proceffion from Chrift Church unto St. Mary Redcliff.

1544	Nicholas Thorn.	John Gurney, Roger Jones.
1545	Robert Adams.	William Carr, Robert Davis.
1546	William Cary.	John A Wellis, Thomas Joackym.
1547	John Smyth.	Thomas Harris, William Tindall.
1548	William Pyckes.	Edward Tynte, John Mathews.
1549	William Jay.	Edward Prynne, John Stone.
1550	David Harris.	Roger Milward, Thomas Sheward.
1551	Roger Cook.	William Jones, Nicholas Williams.
1552	William Chefter.	Thomas Tyfon, Anthony Standback.
1553	John Northall.	John Pikes fen. Thomas Pikes jun.
1554	John Smyth.	Giles White, John Cutt.

He died in his mayoralty and was buried in St. Werburgh's church, he was anceftor of the Smyths of Long-Afhton, fee p. 484.

1555	William Young.	Thomas Shipman, John Griffiths.
1556	Robert Saxfe.	George Snigg, William Butler.

In this year Queen Mary incorporated the Merchant Adventurers to Ruffia into a company, confifting of 4 confuls and 24 affiftants; and Sebaftian Cabot born in Briftol of Geneofe parents was conftituted the firft governor, being the chief encourager of this branch of trade.

1557	William Pepwall.	William Tucker, Arthur Richards.
1558	Robert Adams.	John Brown, John Prewett.
1559	Roger Jones.	Thomas Chefter, Thomas Kelke.
1560	William Carr.	Michael Sowdelay, George Higgins.
1561	John Reekes.	John Wade, Thomas Golfton.

This year the citizens of Briftol by the induftry and coft of this mayor, were clearly exempted and freed for ever from the marches of Wales, which had been very burdenfome to them.

1562	John Stone.	John Roberts, William Belfher.
1563	Nicholas Williams.	Thomas Young, Richard Davis.
1564	Anthony Standback.	Edmund Jones, Thomas Slocomb.
1565	John Northall.	William Young, John Jones.

A wind-mill was erected on Brandon-Hill by Mr. Read the town's attorney, where before the chapel of St. Brandon ftood.

1566	John Cutt.	Phillip Langley, Thomas Aldworth.

A. D.	Mayors.	Sheriffs.
1567	William Pepwall.	Dominick Chester, Walter Pykes.
1568	John Stone.	Thomas Kyrkland, Robert Smith.
1569	Thomas Chester.	Thomas Rowland, Richard Cole.
1570	William Tucker.	William Hicks, John Barnes.
1571	John Stone.	Thomas Warren, Randolph Haffell.
1572	John Brown.	William Gibbons, Robert Kitchen.
1573	Thomas Kelke.	Edward Porter, William Bird.
1574	George Snigg.	William Salterne, Robert Halton.
1575	John Prewett.	Michael Pepwall, Nicholas Blake.
1576	John Wade.	John Ash, Richard Ashurst.
1577	Thomas Golston.	William Hopkins, Walter Standfast.
1578	John Roberts.	William Prewett, Ralph Dole.
1579	Thomas Young.	George Bathram, Francis Knight.
1580	Thomas Slocombe.	William Parfey, William Yate.
1581	Philip Langley.	Bartholomew Cook, Humpry Andrews.

By charter this year Queen Elizabeth granted the town 6 more aldermen added to the former 6, with the like powers according to the directions of this and other charters; agreeable to this charter 6 aldermen were sworn this year, and the city was divided into 12 wards, over which were set 11 aldermen, the recorder always made the 12th.

| 1582 | Thomas Aldworth. | Thomas Pollington, John Webb. |

A letter wrote by this mayor to Sir F. Walsingham, extant in Hackluit's Voy. v. 3. p. 182. dated March 27, 1583, concerning the Bristol merchants furnishing 1000 marks and two ships, one of 60, the other a bark of 40 tons, for the discovery of the coast of America S. W. of Cape Breton, and their zeal for the western discovery was greatly commended in a letter from that her Majesty's principal secretary.

1583	Walter Pykes.	Walter Davis, William Ellis.
1584	Thomas Rowland.	Rice Jones, Richard Kelke.
1585	Richard Cole.	Henry Gough, John Hart.

The 17th of March the Earl of Pembroke came from Wales to Bristol to review the trained bands, and he taking the upper hand of the mayor, notice thereof being given to the Queen, she sent for him by post to court and he was committed to the Tower for a time, he paid a fine for the offence.

| 1586 | William Hicks. | Edward Long, John Hopkins. |

1587

A. D.	MAYORS.	SHERIFFS.
1587	John Barnes.	William Vawer, Ralph Hurt.
1588	Robert Kitchen.	Nicholas Hobbs, John Oliver.

Four ſhips were this year fitted out from Briſtol to join the Queen's fleet at Plymouth againſt the Spaniards, their names were the Unicorn, the Minion, the Handmaid, and the Ayde. — The 23d of July the Spaniſh Armada was deſtroyed by our fleet, we took 15 great ſhips and 4791 men, in our Channel. — All the canvas that was brought to the Back-Hall was bought up and ſent to London to make field tents, particularly for the camp at Tilbury. — We took upon the coaſt of Ireland in September 17 more ſhips and 5394 men, in all 32 ſhips and 10,185 men.

1589	William Bird.	John Whitſon, Chriſtopher Kedgwin.
1590	John Hopkins.	George Snow, Hugh Griffith.
1591	Walter Standfaſt.	Thomas James, Walter Williams.
1592	Thomas Aldworth.	Richard May, John Young.
1593	Michael Pepwall.	John Barker, Richard Smith.
1594	Francis Knight.	Matthew Haviland, Thomas Pitcher.
1595	William Parſey.	Richard Rogers, John Sly.
1596	William Yate.	John Boucher, Robert Aldworth.
1597	John Webb.	John Englesfield, Richard George.

This year was a ſcarcity of proviſion in Briſtol, every perſon of ability was obliged to keep as many poor perſons in their houſes as their income would permit, for fear of an inſurrection, wheat being then fold for 20 s. a buſhel, malt at 8 s. Rye at 10 s. Dantzic Rye at 5 s. The parliament in the year 1601 appointed a weekly relief for the poor in every pariſh, and the manner how it ſhould be raiſed.

1598	William Ellis.	William Cary, Abel Kitchen.
1599	John Hart.	William Golſton, John Harriſon.
1600	John Hopkins.	John Boulton, Thomas Hopkins.
1601	William Vawer.	William Hopkins, John Fownes.
1602	Ralph Hurt.	Thomas Farmer, John Aldworth.
1603	John Whitſon.	William Barnes, George Richards.
1604	Chriſtopher Kedgwin.	William Cole, George Harrington.
1605	Thomas James.	John Rowbrough, John Guy.
1606	John Barker.	Thomas Packer, John Doughty.

This year upon the 20th of January, being Tueſday morning, at high-water there aroſe ſo great a flood that the ſea broke down the banks and drowned all the marſh country.   1607

A. D.	MAYORS.	SHERIFFS.
1607	Matthew Haviland.	Robert Rogers, Arthur Neads.
1608	John Boucher.	Thomas Moor, William Young.
1609	Robert Aldworth	Thomas Aldworth, William Challoner.

This mayor was a great adventurer in trade and fuccefsful in merchandize. John Guy returned from Newfoundland from fettling a colony, leaving his fon there. The great fcarcity of corn the preceding year was now fucceeded with a moft plentiful harveft.

| 1610 | John Eglesfield. | Thomas Whitehead, William Pitt. |
| 1611 | William Cary. | William Burroughs, Henry Gibbs. |

Mr. John Guy, with a preacher and feveral men and women, returned to Newfoundland to his fon.

| 1612 | Abel Kitchen. | Chriftopher Cary, John Barker. |
| 1613 | Francis Knight. | Chriftopher Whitfon, John Gunning.[1] |

Queen Ann came to Briftol, and was prefented by the mayor with a rich embroidered purfe of gold, and attended in a grand proceffion of the trained bands and others to her lodgings at Sir John Young's, St. Auguftine's-back, when fhe was faiuted with 42 great guns. Sunday fhe went to the college, and Monday a fham fight at high tide was exhibited for her entertainment, and Tuefday fhe went to Bath. She was fo pleafed with her reception here, that fhe gave the mayor a gold ring fet with diamonds worth 60l. faying, " fhe never knew fhe was a Queen till fhe came to Briftol."

1614	Thomas James.	John Langton, Humphrey Hook.
1615	John Whitfon.	William Baldwin, John Tomlinfon.
1616	Thomas Farmer.	Henry Yate, Henry Hobfon.
1617	George Harrington.	Matthew Warren, William Turner.
1618	John Guy.	Thomas Cecil, Thomas Wright.
1619	Thomas Packer.	William Liffet, Humphrey Brown.
1620	John Doughty.	Andrew Charlton, Peter Millard.
1621	Robert Rogers.	Richard Holworthy, Richard Long.
1622	William Young.	Edward Cox, William Jones.
1623	William Pitt.	Oliver Snell, Ezekiel Wallis.
1624	Henry Gibbes.	William Pitt, junr. Nathaniel Boucher.
1625	John Barker.	George Knight, John Taylor.

By aft of common council Brandon-hill was adjudged to the mayor and fheriffs, but the citizens were allowed to dry clothes there.

| 1626 | Chriftopher Whitfon. | John Lock, Walter Ellis. |

1627

A. D.	MAYORS.	SHERIFFS.
1627	John Gunning.	Richard Aldworth, Richard Plea.

This mayor gave 10s. per week whilst he lived to good uses, as did Alderman Kitchen at his death.

1628	John Langton.	Alexander James, Francis Crefwick.
1629	Humphrey Hook.	Thomas Colfton, Giles Elbridge.
1630	John Tomlinfoa.	Derrick Poppely, Gabriel Sherman.

Charles 1st. by a charter granted that the caftle, with the walls, banks, ditches, houfes, gardens, &c. within the precincts of the caftle be hence_ forth for ever feparated from the county of Glocefter, and made part of the city and county of Briftol, and to be within the bounds, jurif_ diction, and authority of the mayor, fheriffs, coroners, and juftices, &c. and that no officer of the county of Glocefter intermeddle, and that all the inhabitants of the caftle fhall be made freemen of Briftol, and that the mayor fhall anfwer alike for the caftle, although it be parcel of the crown lands, &c. Dated at Weftminfter, 13 April, 5th year of his reign. See p. 224.

| 1631 | Henry Yate. | John Gunning, junr. Miles Jackfon. |

The caftle was purchafed of Charles 1st. who granted it to the cor_ poration for the fum of 959l. in reverfion after three lives, which they alfo bought off afterwards. See p. 225. They paid the King 40l. per annum rent, which was purchafed of the crown in Charles 2d's. time. See p. 134.

1632	Henry Hobfon.	Thomas Jackfon, William Fitzherbert.
1633	Matthew Warren.	Robert Elliott, Thomas Floyd.
1634	Andrew Charlton.	John Langton, junr. Thomas Hook.
1635	Richard Holworthy.	William Cann, William Hobfon.

It appeared by the Cuftom-houfe books the city paid yearly above 25000l. for cuftoms; and towards fitting out a fleet againft France and Holland in league, meditating fome ftroke againft this nation, Briftol gave 2163l. 13s. 4d.

1636	Richard Long.	Richard Vickris, Thomas Woodward.
1637	William Jones.	Edward Peters, William Wyatt.
1638	Ezekiel Wallis.	George Hellier, Luke Hodges.

From September to December the city was never free from commif_ fioners and purfuivants, who examined on oath merchants what com_ modities they had fent to fea, what entries were made at the Cullom_ houfe, what foreign goods imported, &c. for years paft? Agreeable to thefe informations they examined, whereby fome were compelled to accufe one another, and were fent for up to London. Shopkeepers alfo were examined, and had great impofts laid on them. Soap-makers paid 4l. cuftom per ton for foap, the brewers forty marks per annum for a commiffion, which were fuch grievances that it foured the nation much againft the king and government, &c. Four aldermen and fome merchants went to complain to the King concerning the above fevere ufage, on the city's behalf. His Majefty embraced them moft gracioufly, and was forry that by wrong information he had granted fuch oppreffive commiffions, which then however he could not recall ; but gave them liberty to prefer a bill againft them in the Star Chamber, and retain counfellors to plead for them before the privy council ; for before thefe commiffioners, were lords and judges over them. They ftaid at great expence for trial, but it could not be determined; his Majefty wifhed them to follow their fuit, and when it came to the higheft his grace would mediate between them. To add to thefe troubles, corn was fcarce this year and fold for 9s. a bufhel, and would foon have been 20s. if a great quantity of French wheat and other grain had not been imported into Briftol and other ports.

The 28th of July this year, a fhip was launched at the end of the Quay, in which eleven boys were drowned, and fhe was called thence the Drown Boy.

A. D.	MAYORS.	SHERIFFS.
1639	George Knight.	Matthew Warren, Walter Deyos.
1640	John Taylor.	Henry Gibbs, Edward Pitt.
1641	John Lock.	Richard Balman, Robert Yeamans.

The latter part of this year, war was begun by the Parliament againft the King. Denzil Hollis was nominated as fit to command the militia at Briftol. He fubfcribed 1000l. againft the King.

| 1642 | Richard Aldworth. | Jofeph Jackfon, Hugh Brown. |

October 23, the caftle of Briftol was repaired and the walls round the city, a fort made at Brandon-hill, and another on St. Michael's-hill near the windmill afterwards turned to a royal pentagonal fort. Two regiments under Col. Effex were, by the management of the mayor's wife, Mrs. Rogers, and Mrs. Vickris, let into the city. A weekly affeffment was made by the Parliament on all cities and counties. Briftol paid 55l. 15s. per week, levied upon all lands, goods, money, ftock, &c. in the manner of a land tax, (which was a precedent whence the land tax was afterwards taken.) Befides, many were obliged to a heavy compofition to fave the remainder of their eftates. The mob having now the rule, the better fort of inhabitants dared not appear

in.

in the ftreets without being grofly infulted by the rebellious rabble, and if they went out of town they were taken up and fent to prifon. See p. 227.

See p. 227.

A. D.	MAYORS.	SHERIFFS.
1643	Humphrey Hook.	Henry Crefwick, William Golfton.

Auguft 2, the King, Charles 1ft. came to Briftol, and Sunday went to college.

1644	Alexander James.	Nathaniel Cale, William Bevan.
1645	John Gunning.	John Young, Walter Stephens.

The peftilence raged in the city, about 3000 died.

1646	Richard Vickris,	Walter Sandby, Edward Tyfon.
1647	Gabriel Sherman.	Arthur Farmer, George White.
1648	William Cann.	Robert Challoner, Robert Yate.

This mayor did in his year proclaim no King to be in England, and the fucceffors of Charles 1ft. to be traitors to the ftate. He was the firft that did it, after it was refufed by the Lord Mayor of London.

1649	Miles Jackfon.	William Dale, William Yeamans.
1650	Hugh Brown.	James Crofts, George Hort.

The walls about the Royal fort made by order of Parliament, who gave 1000l. towards it.

1651	Jofeph Jackfon.	George Lane, Robert Cann.
1652	Henry Gibbs.	Thomas Amory, Jonathan Blackwell.
1653	George Hellier.	John Pope, Thomas Bubb.

Quakers came firft to Briftol.

1654	John Gunning.	John Lawford, Chriftopher Griffith.
1655	Walter Deyos.	Thomas Harris, John Bowing.
1656	Richard Balman.	Robert Vickris, John Harper.

Oliver Cromwell, November 10, fent for James Nailor, Dorcas Erbury, and other Quaker preachers, to London. The Parliament paffed fentence on Nailor to ftand in the pillory two hours, and then to be whipped by the common hangman, his tongue to be bored through with a hot iron, and his forehead to be ftigmatized with the letter B, and then to be fent to Briftol to be there publicly whipped:—a fevere fentence!

1657	Arthur Farmer.	John Willoughby, Henry Appleton.

December 8, 1657. This day was received a letter from the Lord Protector as follows:

Oliver, P.

Trufty and well beloved, we greet you well: remembering well the late expreffions of love that I have had from you, I cannot omit any opportunity to

exprefs

exprefs my care of you. I do hear on all hands, that the cavalier party are defigning to put us into blood. We are, I hope, taking the beft care we can by the blefling of God to obviate this danger; but our intelligence on all hands being that they have a defign upon your city, we could not but warn you thereof, and give you authority as we do hereby to put yourfelves into the beft pofture you can for your own defence, by raifing your militia by virtue of the commiffion formerly fent you, and putting them in a readinefs for the purpofe aforefaid; letting you alfo know that for your better encouragement herein, you fhall have a troop of horfe fent you to quarter in or near your town. We defire you to let us hear, from time to time, what occurs touching the malignant party, and fo we bid you farewell. Given at Whitehall, this 2d December, 1657.

> To our trufty and well beloved the mayor, aldermen, and common
> council of the city of Briftol.

In purfuance of this command, the city was put into a pofture of defence, by raifing the militia.

A. D.	MAYORS.	SHERIFFS.
1658	Walter Sandy.	Edward Morgan, Nathaniel Collins.
1659	Edward Tyfon.	Francis Gleed, Timothy Parker.
1660	Henry Crefwick.	Richard Grigfon, Thomas Langton.
1661	Nathaniel Cale.	Thomas Stephens, John Hicks.
1662	Sir Robert Cann.	John Wright, Sir Robert Yeamans.
1663	Sir John Knight.	John Broadway, Richard Stremer.

The 5th of September, the King and Queen, with James Duke of York and his Dutchefs, and Prince Rupert, &c. came to Briftol, and were fplendidly received and entertained by the mayor, at a dinner provided on the occafion. They returned to Bath at four o'clock, 150 pieces of ordnance were difcharged in the Marfh at three diftinct times.

1664	John Lawford.	John Knight, Ralph Oliffe.

Charles 2d. confirmed the charters of Charles 1ft. of 1630, 1631.

1665	John Willoughby.	William Crabb, Richard Crump.
1666	Sir Thomas Langton.	John Floyd, Jofeph Crefwick.
1667	Edward Morgan.	Henry Gough, John Aldworth.
1668	Thomas Stephens.	Humphrey Little, Richard Hart.
1669	Sir Robert Yeamans.	Charles Powel, Edward Hurn.
1670	John Knight.	Thomas Day, Thomas Eafton.
1671	John Hickes.	Richard Stubbs, Thomas Earle.

1662.

A. D.	MAYORS.	SHERIFFS.
1672	Chriftopher Griffith.	Edward Young, John Cook.
1673	Richard Stremer.	John Cicil, John Dymer.
1674	Ralph Oliffe.	Samuel Wharton, Edward Fielding.
1675	Sir Robert Cann.	Charles Williams, George Lane.
1676	William Crabb.	Henry Gliffon, Henry Merrett.
1677	Richard Crump.	William Donning, John Moore.
1678	Sir John Lloyd.	William Jackfon, William Clutterbuck.
1679	Jofeph Crefwick.	William Hayman, William Swimmer.
1680	Richard Hart.	Abraham Saunders, Arthur Hart.
1681	Sir Thomas Earle.	Sir John Kight, Richard Lane.
1682	Thomas Eafton.	John Coombes, George Hart.
1683	Sir William Clutterbuck.	Nathaniel Driver, Edmund Arundel.

A quo warranto being brought againft the old charter, it was refigned into the King's hands.

| 1684 | Sir William Hayman. | Giles Merrick, James Twyford. |

Charles 2d. granted a new charter, by which he confirms it as a city incorporate and county within itfelf with the fame bounds ufually enjoyed, and grants the fame powers to the mayor and two fheriffs, &c. that they may have a common feal, and take the oaths of allegiance and the oaths appointed by act of parliament for corporations; that the common council men may not exceed forty-three, to continue for their natural lives, who are to have power to make laws, &c. but not contrary to the ftatutes of the realm, and to be in force but one year if the Lord Chancellor approves thereof. The mayor and fheriffs to be always chofen the 15th of September, and all the oaths adminiftered the 29th. If the mayor or fheriff die, another to be elected by the common council. A recorder to be chofen a barrifter of five years ftauding, to be approved under the royal hand. That there be twelve aldermen, the recorder to be the fenior alderman. That they be refident in the city, and no one elected for mayor, fheriff, or alderman that fhall voluntarily abfent himfelf when to be fworn, and a fine not exceeding 500l. be impofed on thofe refufing to be chofen, unlefs they fwear they are not worth 2000l. The mayor and aldermen to be juftices of the peace, and to punifh offenders at the feffions four times a year. That a town clerk be chofen by them, a barrifter of three years; and a fteward of the fheriffs' court, alfo two coroners. The mayor, &c. to have the regulation of the markets, and may have three fairs for wool, &c. the 18th of April, the 10th of June, and the firft Thurfday after Michaelmas, to be kept in King's-ftreet; and five other fairs for horfes, &c. the

25th.

A. D.

25th of January in Temple-ftreet, on the 25th and 26th of March at Redcliff-Hill, on the 25th and 26th of May in Broadmead, on the 25th, 26th and 27th of September in Temple-ftreet, and on the 25th, 26th and 27th of November on Redcliff-Hill; alfo that they may keep the piedpowder-court there at the faid fairs, with the liberties and cuftoms thereof. 1683, witnefs myfelf at Weftminfter the 2d of June, the 36th year of our reign. PIGOT.

Mayors.	Sheriffs.
1685 Abraham Saunders.	William Merrick, Robert Yate.

On the 25th of June a great alarm in Briftol of the Duke of Monmouth's coming hither from Taunton and Wells: which caufed a great ftir.—The Duke of Beaufort, Lord Lieutenant of the city, drew up 21 companies of foot in Redcliff-Mead.

The Duke of Monmouth certainly was on his March towards the city of Briftol, abounding in money, arms, ftores, and in his own friends, intending to make an attempt upon it, becaufe he was affured of affif_tance from within: but the Duke of Beaufort having declared to the citizens that he would fet fire to the town if they made an infurrection ; Monmouth is reported to have faid, " God forbid that I fhould bring the two calamities of fire and fword together on fo noble a city !" and marched towards Bath : from whence he retired to Frome, and thence to Bridgwater, where from the top of a high tower he took the laft view of a country he forefaw he muft foon quit: whence perceiving Lord Feverfham's horfe and foot lying at a diftance on King's Sedgmore, from each other and carelefly encamped, he refolved inftantly to attack them in the night, but was defeated, and taken afterwards near Ringwood in Dorfetfhire, lying in a ditch covered with fern in the habit of a peafant; he had fome green peafe in his pocket on which he had fub_fifted, with his George of diamonds, having not flept for three nights; from exhauftion of fpirits he fainted and wept.—He was tried and condemned the 15th of July this year to be beheaded, then 30 years old.

Judge Jefferies came to Briftol and opened his commiffion with a long fpeech full of afperity againft the citizens of Briftol, accufing the mayor &c. of pride, and of kidnapping away and felling abroad to his advantage fellows that had been brought before him for fmall crimes, and making them compound to go abroad &c. recorded in the life of Lord Keeper North.—He condemned fix men here for high treafon, three were reprieved.

1686 William Swymmer.	George Morgan, Edward Tocknell.

1687

A. D.	MAYORS.	SHEAIFFS.
1687	Thomas Day.	Thomas Saunders, Thomas Hine.

The 13th of January there came a letter and order of council from King James for difplacing the prefent members of the corporation, and placing others therein named in their room, which was accordingly done.

The 9th of April this year the declaration was brought hither for indulging all perfons in their religion of what kind foever, and in building meeting-houfes, acquainting the next juftice of peace therewith: for which the diffenters prefented an addrefs of thanks from all parts of the kingdom.—The panick that now had pervaded all ranks of people left popery fhould be introduced under this mafk, and the dread of many lofing their lands that once belonged to fome abby, operated fo powerfully, that neither this declaration nor his immediate order for reftoring corporations difplaced, would avail: many great men and bifhops, fee page 332, fided with the Prince of Orange, and many military officers deferted to him.

| 1688 | Wm. Jackfon. | John Lyfton, Jofeph Jackfon. |

The old corporation was reftored by the King's proclamation, which concluded with " his gracious intention of calling a parliament as foon as the general difturbance of his kingdom by the intended invafion will admit thereof." But the 5th of November the Prince of Orange landed in England; and the 13th of Feb. 1688-9 he and his Princefs were proclaimed King and Queen, and on the 15th fo proclaimed here ; whereby our civil and religious liberties were fecured on the firmeft bafis, the bill of rights obtained, and magna charta and our glorious. conftitution in church and ftate invariably eftablifhed,—now admired and envied by all the world.

1689	Arthur Hart.	John Bubb, John Blackwell.
1690	Sir John Knight.	Robert Dowting, John Yeamans.
1691	Richard Lane.	Thomas Bradway, Thomas Opie.

Bifhop Hall occafioned the eftablifhing of the clergy fociety's feaft.

1692	Edmund Arundel.	James Pope, Henry Coombes.
1693	Robert Yate.	Marmaduke Bowdler, John Batchelor.
1694	Sir Thomas Day.	John Hawkins, Sir Wm. Dailies.

Froom-Gate taken down with the houfe over it.

| 1695 | Samuel Wallis. | Wm. Lewis, Wm. French. |
| 1696 | John Hine. | Peter Saunders, Francis Whitchurch. |

A. D.	MAYORS.	SHERIFFS.
1697	John Bubb.	Nathaniel Day, John Day.
1698	John Blackwell.	George Stevens, John Swymmer.
1699	John Batchelor.	Wm. Whitehead, James Holledge.
1700	Sir Wm. Daines.	Robert Bound, Isaac Davis.
1701	John Hawkins.	Samuel Bayly, Richard Bayly.

The coronation day of Queen Ann was celebrated here with great solemnity, and much pageantry displayed by the young men and maidens drest with ribbons and wearing coronets of laurel leaves gilded, attended with musie, and the procession was very noble and grand, the ships were drest out, as well as the churches, gates and houses, cannons firing and bells ringing, windows all illuminated, the whole concluded with burning the figure of the Pope with a triple crown.

| 1702 | Sir Wm. Lewis. | Abraham Elton, Christopher Shuter. |
| 1703 | Peter Saunders. | Thomas Hort, Henry Whitehead. |

A great storm of wind and rain that drowned all the marsh country, and all the cellars and warehouses in Bristol were filled, to the very great damage and loss of the merchants; the boats sent hence saved the lives of many found upon trees &c.

| 1704 | Francis Whitchurch. | Anthony Swymmer, Henry Walter. |

The number of alehouses here were limited to 220, stage plays forbid within the jurisdiction of the city.

1705	Nathaniel Day.	Morgan Smith, Nathaniel Webb.
1706	George Stevens.	Abraham Hook, Nicholas Hicks.
1707	Wm. Whitehead.	Onesiphorus Tindall, Thomas Tyler.
1708	James Hollidge.	Philip Ereke, John Day.

A scarcity of corn, and it being bought up by the merchants to send abroad, occasioned an insurrection of the colliers, which was appeased by reducing the price of wheat to 6s. 8d. per bushel.

| 1709 | Robert Bound. | James Haynes, Thomas Clements. |

The new custom-house in Queen-Square was built by the corporation, at the expence of 2777l. 7s. 5d.

| 1710 | Abraham Elton. | Edmund Mountjoy, Abraham Elton, jun. |

Queen Ann renewed the charter of Bristol, (see Bristol charters, p. 273,) confirming all former charters and liberties, and granting pardon to the mayor and other officers for having executed their offices without approbation under the royal signet, contrary to the charter of the 36th of Charles the 2d. and releasing all such powers in said charter reserved

ſerved of approbation of ſuch offices to which they ſhall be choſen; and releaſing all power in the crown of removing any mayor or other officer, &c. Dated 24 July, 1710.

Twenty marks ſterling to be paid as a fine into the Queen's hanniper.

Cowper, chancellor.

The annual dinner of the Loyal Society was held the 2d of November, Mr. Colſton's birth-day, who could not come being aged, and was repreſented by the Moſt Noble Henry Duke of Beaufort.

A. D.	MAYORS.	SHERIFFS.
1711	Chriſtopher Shuter.	William Bayly, Poole Stokes.

An act of parliament was procured, at the expence of the Duke of Beaufort, to compleat the navigation betwixt Briſtol and Bath; though thirteen years elapſed before any thing was done, when by dividing the expence into thirty-two ſhares, it was ſet about by ſubſcription, and completed December 27, 1727, when the firſt barge was brought to Bath from Briſtol, laden with deals, lead, and meal.

1712	Thomas Hort.	Richard Gravet, Henry Watts.
1713	Anthony Swymmer.	John Becher, Henry Swymmer.
1714	Henry Whitehead.	William Whitehead, Richard Taylor.
1715	Henry Walter.	James Donning, Joſeph Jefferies.

Lord Berkeley was made Lord Lieutenant of this city.

1717	John Day.	Henry Naſh, John Price.
1718	Edmund Mountjoy.	Samuel Stokes, Edward Foy.
1719	Abraham Elton.	Arthur Taylor, John King.
1720	Henry Watts.	Robert Addiſon, Jacob Elton.

The new wharf on the Back, oppoſite King-ſtreet, built by the city, at the expence of 1053l. 3s.

1721	John Becher.	John Rich, Noblet Ruddock.
1722	Henry Swymmer.	Robert Smyth, Lionel Lyde.

A new gunpowder repoſitory built at Tower Harris, which coſt the corporation 143l. 18s. 5d.

1723	James Donning.	John Blackwell, Nathaniel Wraxhall.
1724	Joſeph Jefferies.	Nathaniel Day, William Jefferies.
1725	Robert Earle.	Michael Puxton, Stephen Clutterbuck.
1726	Peter Day.	Ezekiel Longman, Henry Coombe.

An act obtained for erecting turnpikes round the city; but the colliers, not being exempted from paying and under-hand encouraged, cut down and entirely deſtroyed them.

The

The wharf continued to be built on the Back behind the Square for 180 feet forward. It coſt the chamber 488l. 12s. 7d.

A. D.	MAYORS.	SHERIFFS.
1727	Henry Naſh.	Richard Bayly, John Bartlet.
1728	John Price.	Henry Lloyd, Abraham Eton.
1729	Samuel Stokes.	John Barrow, John Day.
1730	Edward Foy.	Edward Buckler, William Barnſdale.

The firſt incendiary letters ever known in the kingdom were ſent to divers perſons here, threatening to fire their houſes if they did not leave ten guineas in certain places. Mr. Packer, ſhip-builder, had his houſe burnt down in conſequence, which ſo alarmed the city that it cauſed a double watch till ſix in the morning. A reward of 400l. was offered. One Power, an Iriſh attorney, was taken up on ſtrong proof and circumſtances; but he got ſome to ſwear ſo, that he was cleared.

1731	Arthur Taylor.	Edward Cooper, William Barnes.
1732	John King.	John Foy, Buckler Weeks.
1733	Jacob Elton.	Michael Pope, Benjamin Gliſſon.

The great crane at the Gibb built by the ingenious Mr. Padmore, and the dock compleated at the expence of the Merchants' Society.— See the print, p. 87. The Prince of Orange viſited this city.

| 1734 | John Rich. | Thomas Curtis, James Laroche. |

Two petitions were preſented to the parliament againſt the return of Mr. Coſter for member, which being thought afterwards unjuſt and ill-grounded were withdrawn. This however occaſioned much ill will among the citizens, ſee p. 161. as Mr. Coſter was a very unexceptionable candidate, a ſenſible and worthy man, and reſident in Briſtol. He lies buried in the cathedral, ſee p. 209. with a handſome monument and elegant Latin inſcription.

1735	Lionel Lyde.	David Peloquin, John Clements.
1736	John Blackwell.	Morgan Smith, Abraham Elton.
1737	Nathaniel Day.	Joſeph Eyles, Henry Dampier.

This mayor fixed up the table of the loan money and benefactors for public inſpection in the Council-houſe, ſee p. 136. and made many improvements in the city.

| 1738 | William Jefferies. | John Combe, Giles Bayly. |

His Royal Highneſs Frederick Prince of Wales and Auguſta his Princeſs came hither from Bath, and were met by the mayor, &c. at Temple-gate, where a platform was erected for the corporation dreſſed

in

in their fcarlet gowns to falute them on their coming, and the recorder delivered a fpeech to them. All the trading companies, with their flags, &c.
walked in proceffion before their coach up High-ftreet and along the Quay to
Queen-fquare to Mr. Combes's. After he had received the compliments of
the clergy, gentlemen, &c. he was conducted to the Merchants'-hall, where
an elegant dinner was provided, and a ball at night. They lay at Mr. Combes's
that night, and returned the next morning at ten o'clock to Bath, highly
pleafed with their entertainment here.

The library, built at the expence of the chamber, amounting to 1600l.
in the whole, was finifhed this year. See p. 508.

A. D.	MAYORS.	SHERIFFS.
1739	Stephen Clutterbuck.	Michael Becher, David Debany.
1740	Henry Combe.	Walter Jenkins, William Martin.

The 10th of March the firft ftone was laid for the foundation of the
new Exchange. See p. 459.

1741	John Bartlett.	John Chamberlain, Henry Muggleworth.
1742	Abraham Elton.	William Cofsley, Jeremiah Ames.
1743	John Berrow.	Ifaac Elton, John Durbin.
1744	John Day.	John Foy, Buckler Weeks.
1745	William Barnes.	Thomas Marfh, John Noble.

The Pretender's Son, having now formed a large body of highlanders, was
advanced into England as far as Derby, and threw the kingdom into the utmoft
confternation. Confultations were every where held, for putting themfelves
into the beft pofture of defence. Numbers of the citizens here met at the Merchants'-hall, and there figned a parchment, containing their refolution to ftand by
King George and the Royal Family; and on another they fubfcribed their
names to fuch fums as they intended to contribute for raifing men for the
King's ufe, which at leugh amounted to 36,450l. They gave about 5l. a man
to inlift, and above 60 were fent to be incorporated in the King's guards, London.

Monday the 7th of October the Trial privateer, and her prize which fhe had
taken, bound to Scotland with firelocks and other warlike ftores, having on
board 6000l. in money and a number of men, came into Kingroad. Two
Irifhmen taken on board the prize were fent to London in a coach and fix
horfes the Thurfday following.

Alfo two London privateers, the 12th of July, landed here the money taken
in two Spanifh fhips, which was depofited in the Cuftom-houfe, where it was
weighed. Its weight and value was as follows:

	Cwt.	qrs.	lb.
1093 Chefts of filver, weight, grofs - - - -	1573	2	10
Tare, at 10 per cent. - - - - - -	97	2	10
Neat -	1476	0	0

1476 Cwt. weight neat is 2,644,992 ounces, at 5s. 6d. per ounce, comes in fterling money to 727,372l. 16s.

Befides five chefts of wrought plate, feveral tons of cocoa, a gold church in miniature, and feveral other valuable things. It was conveyed to London in twenty-two waggons, guarded by foldiers.

A. D.	MAYORS.	SHERIFFS.
1746	Edward Cooper.	Henry Swymmer, Richard Farr, junr.

It is remarkable, that at this time William Cann, Efq; town clerk, John Mitchell his clerk, and James Britton the under clerk, officers under the corporation, were all mad. The former cut his throat with a pruning knife, but not mortally ; the two latter were fent to the mad houfe at the Fifhponds.

| 1747 | John Fry. | John Berrow, Giles Bayly. |
| 1748 | Buckler Weeks. | Jofeph Daltera, Ifaac Baugh. |

The market fheds on the Back to fecure the corn were finifhed.

| 1749 | Thomas Curtis. | William Barnes, John Curtis. |
| 1750 | James Laroche. | George Wear, Jofeph Love. |

A great ftorm of wind in January, and on the 8th of February an earthquake in London, and felt alfo here.

Two fhips, fitted out here for the whale fifhery at Greenland, arrived with two whales; the blubber was boiled at Seamills. This lucrative trade is not revived fince. The naturalization bill of foreign Proteftants was oppofed by the citizens of Briftol.

| 1751 | David Peloquin. | Henry Dampier, Ifaac Baugh. |
| 1752 | John Clement. | Daniel Woodward, Edward Whatley. |

A riot by the colliers from Kingfwood, on account of the fcarcity of corn, kept up for a whole week. The citizens were fworn as conftables, and armed in defence of the city. The colliers refifted; many were wounded, fome fhot and killed, before the riot was quelled, and three were indicted and tried, fome fuffered by fine and long imprifonment.

| 1753 | Abraham Elton. | Henry Bright, Thomas Harris. |

The intended bill to naturalize Jews was ftrongly oppofed in this city by addreffes fent to the members of parliament, from the citizens at large and from the Merchants'-hall.

A. D.   Mayors.   Sheriffs.

1754 Morgan Smith.   Thomas Knox, Thomas Dean.

This year the new ſtone bridge was built and finiſhed at the head of the Key, which coſt the chamber upwards of 2500l.

The bill was alſo paſſed for regulating a nightly watch in this city.

1755 Henry Dampier.   Henry Weare, James Hillhouſe.

The Draw-bridge was rebuilt on a new plan, and much more commodious than the former. It coſt the chamber 1066l. 6s. See p. 88.

1756 Giles Bayly.   Nathaniel Foy, Auſtin Goodwin.

1757 William Martin.   Robert Gordon, Iſaac Piguenit.

Fifty-one privateers fitted out at Briſtol to cruize againſt the French to the public good in taking the ſtores going to the French in America, but many private perſons who hoped to make their fortunes by theſe adventures were great loſers.

1758 Henry Muggleworth.   John Berrow, Samuel Webb.

Friday, November 3, was taken without reſiſtance by the Antelope, of 50 guns, a 64 gun French man of war, called the Belliqueux, 415 men, blown up our channel near Lundy, and could not get back.

1759 Jeremy Ames.   Charles Hotchkin, John Noble.

1760 John Durbin.   Iſaac Piguenit, Samuel Sedgeley.

In January the corporation reſolved to preſent the freedom of this city to the Honourable William Pitt and the Duke of Newcaſtle in two gold boxes. — The act for taking down the old bridge paſſed.

1761 Iſaac Elton.   Joſeph Daltera, William Barnes.

In September, 1761, the day of the Royal nuptials was celebrated in this city with great ſolemnity and eclat, and on December 27 the Duke of York honoured this city with his preſence, by invitation of the mayor and aldermen.

A temporary bridge built above the old one, which was begun to be taken down. See p. 96.

1762 John Noble.   George Were, Thomas Farr.

In October a great flood, ſo that the low lands were all ſeven feet under water.

1763 Richard Farr.   Andrew Pope, John Durbin.

1764 Henry Swymmer.   James Laroche, John Bull.

On the 27th of September, 1764, Mrs. Ruſcomb and Mary Sweet her ſervant murdered at her houſe in College-green, at eleven o'clock in the morning. The wicked author has never been diſcovered.

This year the great New Dock was begun by Mr. Champion.

1765

A. D.	MAYORS.	SHERIFFS.
1765	Ifaac Baugh.	Ifaac Elton, junr. Michael Miller, junr.

The ftone bridge was built at Bridewell, which had hitherto been of wood, now decayed.

The new Theatre built in King-ftreet and opened with the play of the Confcious Lovers with the Miller of Mansfield, for the benefit of the Infirmary.

An aƈt paffed to take down all the fign-pofts and fpouts, and to carry the water down the fides of the houfes into gouts.

Rioting here about the fcarcity of corn, which occafioned an order of Council to ftop all veffels laden with corn till the parliament fat.

1766 William Barnes. William Miles, Henry Cruger.

Caftle-gate taken down, and removed by Mr. William Reeve, merchant, to his feat at Briflington.

Key-lane was widened by taking down the houfes on one fide.

1767 George Weare. Edward Brice, Alexander Edgar.

A new commodious dock made at the Grove, and the Key wall continned round to the market-houfe on the Back.

Brunfwick-fquare in St. James's laid out for building.

1768 Edward Whatley. John Crofts, Henry Lippincott.

September 17, Briftol bridge was finifhed by the contraƈtors.

December 15, William Hillhoufe chofen fword-bearer, in the room John Wraxal, deceafed.

The Bridge rebuilt was now open for paffengers. See p. 96.

1769 Thomas Harris. John Merlott, George Daubeny.

The time of holding the two yearly Briftol fairs was changed from the 25th of January to the 1ft of March, and from the 25th of July to the 1ft of September.

1770 Thomas Deane. Henry Lippincott, Ifaac Elton, junr.

St. Leonard's church and Blind-gate were taken down and the old buildings behind it, by which St. Stephen's church was more opened to view.

1771 Henry Bright. Levi Ames, Jeremy Baker.

The new road opened from Corn-ftreet to the Quay, and Clare-ftreet began to be built.

A ftage coach for paffengers betwixt Briftol and the Hotwells, at a fixpenny fare, began to run regularly; five or fix more were foon added, for the convenience of the inhabitants of Briftol and the Hotwells.

1772

A. D.	MAYORS.	SHERIFFS.
1772	Nathaniel Foy.	John Noble, John Anderson.
1773	Robert Gordon.	Andrew Pope, Thomas Pierce.
1774	Charles Hodgekin.	John Durbin, James Hill.
1775	Thomas Farr.	Edward Brice, John Noble.
1776	Andrew Pope.	John Farr, John Harris.

An act passed for the regulation of lighters, &c. and other purposes.

| 1777 | Sir John Durbin, Knight. | John Fisher Weare, Philip Prothero. |

The American Colonies proclaimed themselves independent of England. And several attempts to fire the city, the shipping at the Key, &c. in his enthusiasm for the Americans, were made by John Aitkin, the painter; a warehouse was burnt down in Bell-lane. The citizens were so alarmed, that gentlemen kept nightly watches; but Divine Justice overtook the villain, and he was hanged at Portsmouth.

1778	Sir John Durbin, Knight.	Benjamin Loscombe, James Morgan.
1779	Michael Miller, junr.	Edward Brice, Joseph Harford.
——	John Bull, (in the room of M. Miller, junr. who died in his mayoralty.)	
1780	William Miles.	Samuel Span, Joseph Smith.
1781	Henry Cruger.	Robert Coleman, John Collard.
1782	Edward Brice.	Rowland Williams, William Blake.

Next to All Saints church the house rebuilt at the south end, and the Tolzey made there 1615 taken down. The Quay conduit erected anew 1703 taken down and removed, and the Fish-Market there in future appointed to be held in St. James's New Market in Union-street.

| 1783 | John Anderson. | John Garnet, Andrew Henderson. |
| 1784 | John Farr. | John Fisher Weare, James Harvey. |

The foundation of the new Infirmary erected on a larger plan was laid June 2. A mansion-house for the mayor's residence fitted up in Queen-square, and a new banqueting-room in Charlotte-street adjoining opened the 5th of April following for company.

| 1785 | John Crofts. | Joseph Harford, Sir Stephen Nash, Knt. |

A Marine Society established here for educating poor boys for the sea service.

| 1786 | George Daubeny. | Evan Baillie, Thomas Daniel. |

A stand of three hackney coaches first set up at the Exchange for the use of the citizens, soon increased to twenty.

November 4, the foundation stone for rebuilding Christ Church was laid.

The

The library in King-ftreet was enlarged with an additional wing built by the Library Society, fo that it now holds conveniently a very large collection of books ancient and modern, of the beft editions, and in all fciences. The Rev. Mr. Alexander Catcott left by will a great many books to it, and a cabinet of very curious, valuable, and fcarce foffils, fhells, ores, &c. for the ufe of the public. See p. 508.

A. D.	MAYORS.	SHERIFFS.
1787	Alexander Edgar.	John Morgan, Robert Claxton.

The three Briftol police or regulation bills were paffed in parliament this year.

| 1788 | Levi Ames. | James Hill, John Harris. |

In this mayoralty, March 5, 1789, a general joy was diffufed through the city on account of the King's happy recovery, and being able to refume the reins of government. Bell ringing, firing cannons all day from Brandon-hill, a general brilliant illumination at night, with tranfparent emblematical devices, and every demonftration of joy that could be difplayed, proved the true affection and loyalty of our citizens for their amiable and auguft Sovereign, who thus reigns in the hearts of his fubjects.

ᴸ [☞ *The Annals may be continued as events occur, and the Hiftory thus proceed.*]

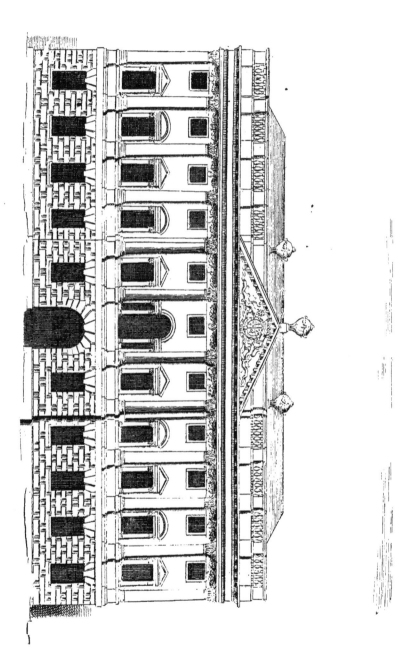

Book :